Adobe® InDesign® CC

The Professional Portfolio

Managing Editor: Ellenn Behoriam
Cover & Interior Design: Erika Kendra
Editor: Angelina Kendra
Copy Editor: Liz Bleau
Printer: Prestige Printers

10 9 8 7 6 5 4 3 2 1

Print ISBN: 978-1-936201-25-9
Ebook ISBN: 978-1-936201-26-6

4710 28th Street North, Saint Petersburg, FL 33714
800-256-4ATC • www.againsttheclock.com

Acknowledgements

About Against The Clock

Against The Clock, long recognized as one of the nation's leaders in courseware development, has been publishing high-quality educational materials for the graphic and computer arts industries since 1990. The company has developed a solid and widely-respected approach to teaching people how to effectively utilize graphics applications, while maintaining a disciplined approach to real-world problems.

Having developed the *Against The Clock* and the *Essentials for Design* series with Prentice Hall/Pearson Education, ATC drew from years of professional experience and instructor feedback to develop *The Professional Portfolio Series*, focusing on the Adobe Creative Suite. These books feature step-by-step explanations, detailed foundational information, and advice and tips from industry professionals that offer practical solutions to technical issues.

Against The Clock works closely with all major software developers to create learning solutions that fulfill both the requirements of instructors and the needs of students. Thousands of graphic arts professionals — designers, illustrators, imaging specialists, prepress experts, and production managers — began their educations with Against The Clock training books. These professionals studied at Baker College, Nossi College of Art, Virginia Tech, Appalachian State University, Keiser College, University of South Carolina, Gress Graphic Arts Institute, Hagerstown Community College, Kean University, Southern Polytechnic State University, Brenau University, and many other educational institutions.

About the Author

Erika Kendra holds a BA in History and a BA in English Literature from the University of Pittsburgh. She began her career in the graphic communications industry as an editor at Graphic Arts Technical Foundation before moving to Los Angeles in 2000. Erika is the author or co-author of more than thirty books about Adobe graphic design software. She has also written several books about graphic design concepts such as color reproduction and preflighting, and dozens of articles for online and print journals in the graphics industry. Working with Against The Clock for more than ten years, Erika was a key partner in developing *The Professional Portfolio Series* of software training books.

Contributing Authors, Artists, and Editors

A big thank you to the people whose artwork, comments, and expertise contributed to the success of these books:

- **Olwen Bruce,** Creative Backup LLC
- **Beth Rogers,** Nossi College Of Art
- **Matthew Guanciale,** Fanboy Photo
- **Debbie Davidson,** Against The Clock, Inc.
- **Charlie Essers,** photographer

Finally, thanks to **Angelina Kendra**, editor, and **Liz Bleau**, copy editor, for making sure that we all said what we meant to say.

Walk-Through

National Parks Info Pieces

Your client is the marketing manager for the National Parks Service (NPS). She wants to create a series of collateral pieces that will be used at tourism centers to lure potential visitors. She hired you to produce a one-sheet flyer that will be distributed in print and online, a rack card that can be placed in area hotels, a postcard that will be given away to park visitors, and a folio file that will work on digital tablet devices.

This project incorporates the following skills:

- ❑ Creating an XML file using tagged frames and content
- ❑ Building a layout from imported XML content
- ❑ Controlling the structure of a layout to merge XML content into tagged frames
- ❑ Placing linked content into alternate layouts
- ❑ Creating interactive overlays for digital folio files
- ❑ Creating alternate layouts for horizontal and vertical tablet orientations
- ❑ Creating a digital folio file for tablet devices

Project Goals

Each project begins with a clear description of the overall concepts that are explained in the project; these goals closely match the different "stages" of the project workflow.

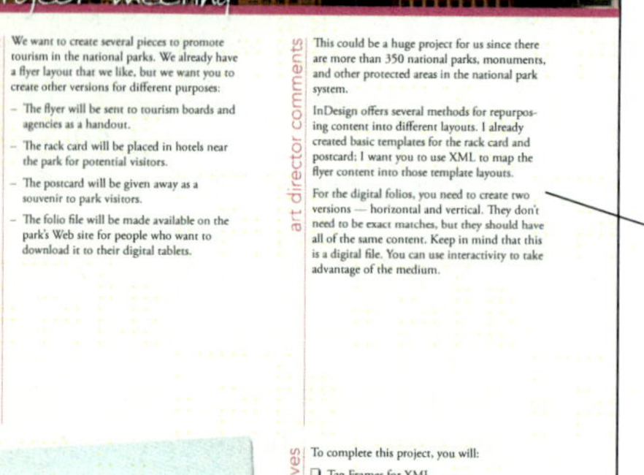

Project Meeting

client comments

We want to create several pieces to promote tourism in the national parks. We already have a flyer layout that we like, but we want you to create other versions for different purposes:

- The flyer will be sent to tourism boards and agencies as a handout.
- The rack card will be placed in hotels near the park for potential visitors.
- The postcard will be given away as a souvenir to park visitors.
- The folio file will be made available on the park's Web site for people who want to download it to their digital tablets.

art director comments

This could be a huge project for us since there are more than 350 national parks, monuments, and other protected areas in the national park system.

InDesign offers several methods for repurposing content into different layouts. I already created basic templates for the rack card and postcard; I want you to use XML to map the flyer content into those template layouts.

For the digital folios, you need to create two versions — horizontal and vertical. They don't need to be exact matches, but they should have all of the same content. Keep in mind that this is a digital file. You can use interactivity to take advantage of the medium.

The Project Meeting

Each project includes the client's initial comments, which provide valuable information about the job. The Project Art Director, a vital part of any design workflow, also provides fundamental advice and production requirements.

project objectives

To complete this project, you will:

- ❑ Tag Frames for XML
- ❑ Review Document Structure
- ❑ Review XML Structure and Attributes
- ❑ Place Unstructured XML Content
- ❑ Update Linked XML Data
- ❑ Import Structured XML
- ❑ Create a File for Digital Publishing
- ❑ Use the Content Collector
- ❑ Manage Linked Object Options
- ❑ Create an Interactive Overlay
- ❑ Define Liquid Page Rules
- ❑ Create an Alternate Layout
- ❑ Create a Digital Folio

Project Objectives

Each Project Meeting includes a summary of the specific skills required to complete the project.

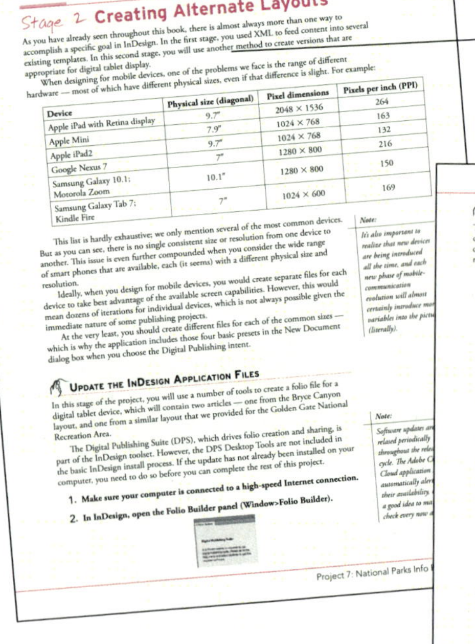

Stage 2 Creating Alternate Layouts

As you have already seen throughout this book, there is almost always more than one way to accomplish a specific goal in InDesign. In the first stage, you used XML to feed content into several existing templates. In this second stage, you will use another method to create versions that are appropriate for digital tablet display.

When designing for mobile devices, one of the problems we face is the range of different hardware — most of which have different physical sizes, even if that difference is slight. For example:

Device	Physical size (diagonal)	Pixel dimensions	Pixels per inch (PPI)
Apple iPad with Retina display	9.7"	2048 × 1536	264
Apple Mini	7.9"	1024 × 768	163
Apple iPad2	9.7"	1024 × 768	132
Google Nexus 7	7"	1280 × 800	216
Samsung Galaxy 10.1; Motorola Zoom	10.1"	1280 × 800	150
Samsung Galaxy Tab 7; Kindle Fire	7"	1024 × 600	169

This list is hardly exhaustive; we only mention several of the most common devices. But as you can see, there is no single consistent size or resolution from one device to another. This issue is even further compounded when you consider the wide range of smart phones that are available, each (it seems) with a different physical size and resolution.

Ideally, when you design for mobile devices, you would create separate files for each device to take best advantage of the available screen capabilities. However, this would mean dozens of iterations for individual devices, which is not always possible given the immediate nature of some publishing projects.

At the very least, you should create different files for each of the common sizes — which is why the application includes those four basic presets in the New Document dialog box when you choose the Digital Publishing intent.

Update the InDesign Application Files

In this stage of the project, you will use a number of tools to create a folio file for a digital tablet device, which will contain two articles — one from the Bryce Canyon layout, and one from a similar layout that we provided for the Golden Gate National Recreation Area.

The Digital Publishing Suite (DPS), which drives folio creation and sharing, is part of the InDesign toolset. However, the DPS Desktop Tools are not included in the basic InDesign install process. If the update has not already been installed on your computer, you need to do so before you can complete the rest of this project.

1. **Make sure your computer is connected to a high-speed Internet connection.**
2. **In InDesign, open the Folio Builder panel (Window>Folio Builder).**

Project 7: National Parks Info

Real-World Workflow

Projects are broken into logical lessons or "stages" of the workflow. Brief introductions at the beginning of each stage provide vital foundational material required to complete the task.

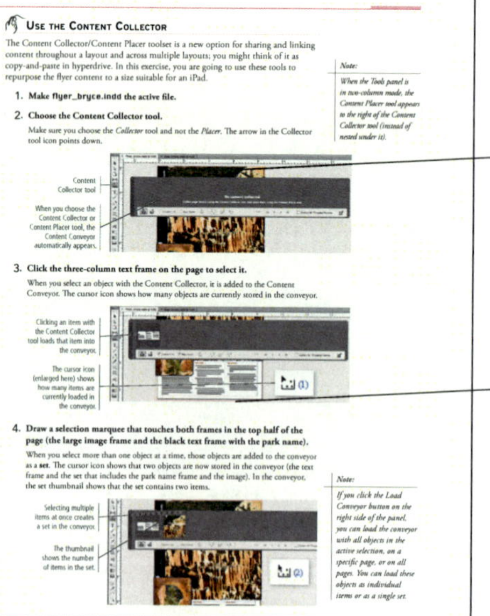

Use the Content Collector

The Content Collector/Content Placer toolset is a new option for sharing and linking content throughout a layout and across multiple layouts; you might think of it as copy-and-paste in hyperdrive. In this exercise, you are going to use these tools to repurpose the flyer content to a size suitable for an iPad.

1. **Make flyer_bryce.indd the active file.**
2. **Choose the Content Collector tool.**

Make sure you choose the Collector tool and not the Placer. The arrow in the Collector tool icon points down.

Note: When the Tools panel is in one-column mode, the Content Placer tool appears to the right of the Content Collector tool (instead of nested under it).

3. **Click the three-column text frame on the page to select it.**

When you select an object with the Content Collector, it is added to the Content Conveyor. The cursor icon shows how many objects are currently stored in the conveyor.

4. **Draw a selection marquee that touches both frames in the top half of the page (the large image frame and the black text frame with the park name).**

When you select more than one object at a time, those objects are added to the conveyor as a set. The cursor icon shows that two objects are now stored in the conveyor (the text frame and the set that includes the park name frame and the image). In the conveyor, the set thumbnail shows that the set contains two items.

Note: If you click the Load Conveyor button on the right side of the panel, you can load the conveyor with all objects in the active selection, on a specific page, or on all pages. You can load these objects as individual items or as a single set.

438 Project 7: National Parks Info Pieces

Step-By-Step Exercises

Every stage of the workflow is broken into multiple hands-on, step-by-step exercises.

Visual Explanations

Wherever possible, screen shots are annotated so that you can quickly identify important information.

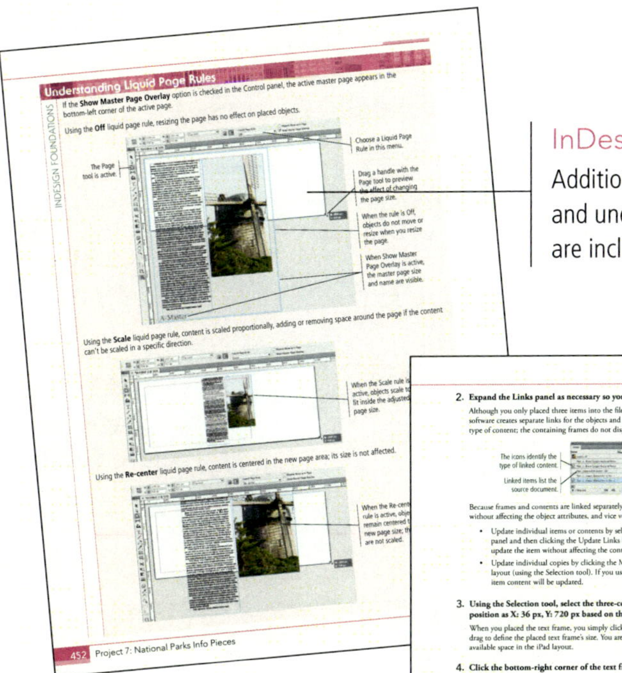

Understanding Liquid Page Rules

If the **Show Master Page Overlay** option is checked in the Control panel, the active master page appears in the bottom-left corner of the active page.

Using the **Off** liquid page rule, resizing the page has no effect on placed objects.

Using the **Scale** liquid page rule, content is scaled proportionally, adding or removing space around the page if the content can't be scaled in a specific direction.

Using the **Re-center** liquid page rule, content is centered in the new page area; its size is not affected.

452 Project 7: National Parks Info Pieces

InDesign Foundations

Additional functionality, related tools, and underlying graphic design concepts are included throughout the book.

2. Expand the Links panel as necessary so you can see most of the items' names.

Although you only placed three items into the file, the Links panel lists six items. The software creates separate links for the objects and the objects' content. Icons identify the type of content; the containing frames do not display icons.

Because frames and contents are linked separately, you can update the linked content without affecting the object attributes, and vice versa:

- Update individual items or contents by selecting a specific listing in the Links panel and then clicking the Update Links button. This method allows you to update the item without affecting the content (and vice versa).
- Update individual copies by clicking the Modified icon on individual items in the layout (using the Selection tool). If you use this method, both the item and the item content will be updated.

3. Using the Selection tool, select the three-column text frame. Define its position as X: 36 px, Y: 720 px based on the top-left reference point.

When you placed the text frame, you simply clicked to place it. You did not click and drag to define the placed text frame's size. You are making this change to better fit the available space in the iPad layout.

4. Click the bottom-right corner of the text frame and drag to the bottom-right margin.

Note: *Choosing the Edit>Place and Link command has the same general effect as selecting an item with the Content Collector tool.*

Note: *There is no dynamic link from the linked copies back to the original, or to other copies of the same object. If you want changes to reflect in all linked copies, you have to edit the original object. This is easily accomplished by Control/right-clicking any of the copies — in the layout or in the Links panel — and choosing **Go to Source** in the contextual menu.*

Advice and Warnings

Where appropriate, sidebars provide shortcuts, warnings, or tips about the topic at hand.

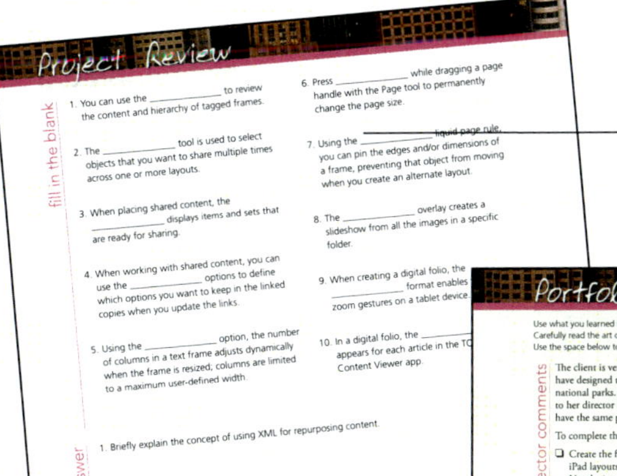

Project Review

fill in the blank

1. You can use the __________ to review the content and hierarchy of tagged frames.
2. The __________ tool is used to select objects that you want to share multiple times across one or more layouts.
3. When placing shared content, the __________ displays items and sets that are ready for sharing.
4. When working with shared content, you can use the __________ options to define which options you want to keep in the linked copies when you update the links.
5. Using the __________ option, the number of columns in a text frame adjusts dynamically when the frame is resized; columns are limited to a maximum user-defined width.
6. Press __________ while dragging a page handle with the Page tool to permanently change the page size.
7. Using the __________ liquid page rule, you can pin the edges and/or dimensions of a frame, preventing that object from moving when you create an alternate layout.
8. The __________ overlay creates a slideshow from all the images in a specific folder.
9. When creating a digital folio, the __________ format enables zoom gestures on a tablet device.
10. In a digital folio, the __________ appears for each article in the TOC Content Viewer app.

short answer

1. Briefly explain the concept of using XML for repurposing content.
2. Briefly explain the differences between using XML and using the Content Collector/Placer to repurpose content.
3. Briefly explain the concept of an interactive overlay.

470 Project 7: National Parks Info Pieces

Project Review

After completing each project, you can complete these fill-in-the-blank and short-answer questions to test your understanding of the concepts in the project.

Portfolio Builder Project

Use what you learned in this project to complete the following freeform exercise. Carefully read the art director and client comments, then create your own design to meet the needs of the project. Use the space below to sketch ideas; when finished, write a brief explanation of your reasoning behind your final design.

art director comments

The client is very pleased with the pieces you have designed to promote tourism in the national parks. Before she presents the project to her director for approval, she would like to have the same pieces for at least one other park.

To complete this project, you should:

- Create the flyer, rack card, postcard, and iPad layouts for Yosemite National Park. Use the images and text that are provided in the **IDCC_PB_Project7.zip** archive on the Student Files Web page.
- Create one additional layout for a letterfold brochure that will include the same content as the other pieces. The inside of the brochure should have only the park name and space for a map of the park. (If you completed Project 5: Ireland Travel Brochure, you can use the same basic 4×9" template that you created in that project.)

client comments

These pieces are exactly what I had in mind. When I pitch the project to my superiors, I want to be able to show them all the same pieces for at least two different parks. That way the committee will see how different colors and pictures will affect the individual pieces but still have a consistent look and feel. I've sent you the text and images for Yosemite for this second set of files.

I'd also like to see one additional layout — redesigning our park map brochure to include this same content but also with a large ... specific park. We already have the map... have to find the files for you; for now j... space on the inside of the brochure.

project justification

Portfolio Builder Projects

Each step-by-step project is accompanied by a freeform project, allowing you to practice skills and creativity, resulting in an extensive and diverse portfolio of work.

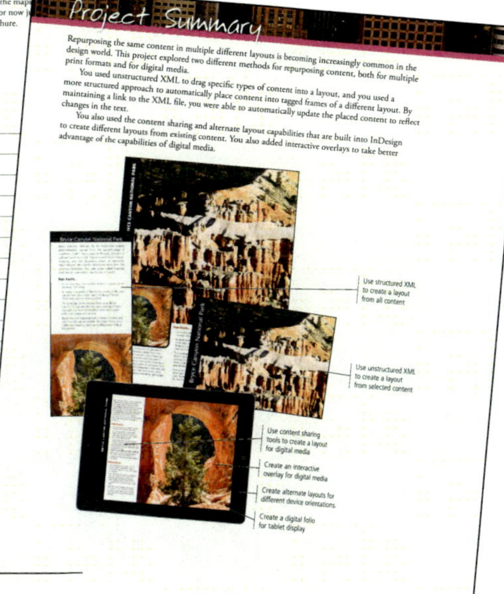

Project Summary

Repurposing the same content in multiple different layouts is becoming increasingly common in the design world. This project explored two different methods for repurposing content, both for multiple print formats and for digital media.

You used unstructured XML to drag specific types of content into a layout, and you used a more structured approach to automatically place content into tagged frames of a different layout. By maintaining a link to the XML file, you were able to automatically update the placed content to reflect changes in the text.

You also used the content sharing and alternate layout capabilities that are built into InDesign to create different layouts from existing content. You also added interactive overlays to take better advantage of the capabilities of digital media.

472 Project 7: National Parks Info Pieces

Visual Summary

Using an annotated version of the finished project, you can quickly identify the skills used to complete different aspects of the job.

Projects at a Glance

The Against The Clock *Portfolio Series* teaches graphic design software tools and techniques entirely within the framework of real-world projects; we introduce and explain skills where they would naturally fall into a real project workflow.

The project-based approach in *The Professional Portfolio Series* allows you to get in depth with the software beginning in Project 1 — you don't have to read several chapters of introductory material before you can start creating finished artwork.

Our approach also prevents "topic tedium" — in other words, we don't require you to read pages and pages of information about text (for example); instead, we explain text tools and options as part of larger projects (in this case, beginning with placing text on a letterhead).

Clear, easy-to-read, step-by-step instructions walk you through every phase of each job, from creating a new file to saving the finished piece. Wherever logical, we also offer practical advice and tips about underlying concepts and graphic design practices that will benefit you as you enter the job market.

The projects in this book reflect a range of different types of InDesign jobs, from creating a client letterhead to implementing a newsletter template to compiling a multi-chapter book. When you finish the eight projects in this book (and the accompanying Portfolio Builder exercises), you will have a substantial body of work that should impress any potential employer.

The eight InDesign projects are described briefly here; more detail is provided in the full table of contents (beginning on Page viii).

project 1

Letterhead Design

- ❑ Setting up the Workspace
- ❑ Creating Basic Page Elements
- ❑ Placing External Images
- ❑ Creating and Formatting Basic Text
- ❑ Printing InDesign Files

project 2

Festival Poster

- ❑ Building Graphic Interest
- ❑ Importing and Formatting Text
- ❑ Graphics as Text and Text as Graphics
- ❑ Outputting the File

project 3

HeartSmart Newsletter

- ❑ Working with Templates
- ❑ Working with Styles
- ❑ Working with Tables
- ❑ Preflighting and Packaging the Job

project 4

Realtor Collateral Booklet

- ❑ Working with Master Pages
- ❑ Controlling the Flow of Text
- ❑ Outputting Variations of Files

project 7

National Parks Info Pieces

- ❑ Working with XML
- ❑ Creating Alternate Layouts

project 5

Ireland Travel Brochure

- ❑ Building a Folding Template
- ❑ Advanced Frame Options
- ❑ Advanced Text Formatting

project 8

Multi-Chapter Booklet

- ❑ Combining Documents into Books
- ❑ Building a Table of Contents
- ❑ Building an Index
- ❑ Exporting Book Files
- ❑ Merging Data into an InDesign Layout

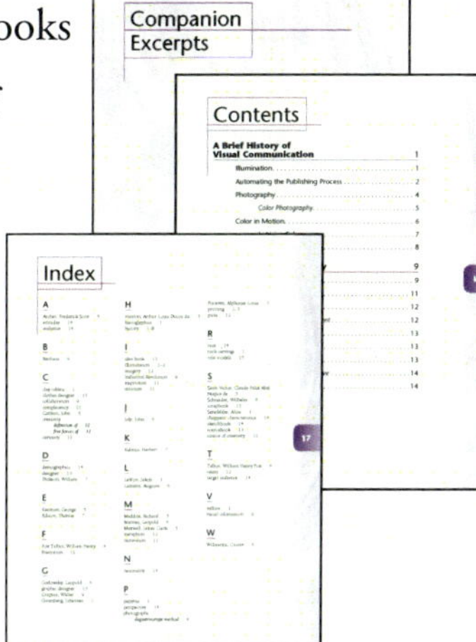

project 6

Digital Layout Variations

- ❑ Controlling Color for Output
- ❑ Creating Interactive Elements
- ❑ Creating EPUB and HTML Files

Our goal in this book is to familiarize you with the majority of the InDesign tool set, so you can be more productive and more marketable in your career as a graphic designer.

It is important to keep in mind that InDesign is an extremely versatile and powerful application. The sheer volume of available tools, panels, and features can seem intimidating when you first look at the software interface. Most of these tools, however, are fairly simple to use with a bit of background information and a little practice.

Wherever necessary, we explain the underlying concepts and terms that are required for understanding the software. We're confident that these projects provide the practice you need to be able to create sophisticated artwork by the end of the very first project.

Contents

Contents

Contents

Contents

Prerequisites

To use *The Professional Portfolio Series,* you should know how to use your mouse to point and click, as well as how to drag items around the screen. You should be able to resize and arrange windows on your desktop to maximize your available space. You should know how to access drop-down menus, and understand how check boxes and radio buttons work. It also doesn't hurt to have a good understanding of how your operating system organizes files and folders, and how to navigate your way around them. If you're familiar with these fundamental skills, then you know all that's necessary to use the Portfolio Series.

Resource Files

All of the files you need to complete the projects in this book — except, of course, the application files — are on the Student Files Web page at againsttheclock.com. See the inside back cover of this book for access information.

Each archive (ZIP) file is named according to the related project (e.g., **IDCC_RF_Project1.zip**). At the beginning of each project, you must download the archive file for that project and expand it to access the resource files that you need to complete the exercises. Detailed instructions for this process are included in the Interface chapter.

Files required for the related Portfolio Builder exercises at the end of each project are also available on the Student Files page; these archives are also named by project (e.g., **IDCC_PB_Project1.zip**).

ATC Fonts

You must download and install the ATC fonts from the Student Files Web page to ensure that your exercises and projects will work as described in the book. You should replace older (pre-2013) ATC fonts with the ones on the Student Files Web page.

Software Versions

This book was written and tested using the initial version of Adobe InDesign CC (v 9.0) software, as released in May 2013. (You can find the specific version number in the Splash Screen that appears while your application is launching.)

Because Adobe has announced periodic upgrades rather than releasing new full versions, some features and functionality might have changed since publication. Please check the Errata section of the Against The Clock Web site for any significant issues that might have arisen from these periodic upgrades.

System Requirements

The Professional Portfolio Series was designed to work on both Macintosh or Windows computers; where differences exist from one platform to another, we include specific instructions relative to each platform. One issue that remains different from Macintosh to Windows is the use of different modifier keys (Control, Shift, etc.) to accomplish the same task. When we present key commands, we always follow the same Macintosh/Windows format — Macintosh keys are listed first, then a slash, followed by the Windows key commands.

Minimum System Requirements for Adobe InDesign CC:

Windows

- Intel Pentium 4 or AMD Athlon 64 processor
- Microsoft Windows 7 with Service Pack 1 or Windows 8
- 2 GB of RAM (8 GB recommended)
- 2.6 GB of available hard-disk space for installation; additional free space required during installation
- 1024×768 display (1280×800 recommended) with 32-bit video card
- Adobe Flash Player 10 required to export SWF files
- Internet connection and registration are necessary for required software activation, membership validation, and access to online services.*

Mac OS

- Multicore Intel processor
- Mac OS X v10.6.8, v10.7, or v10.8
- 2 GB of RAM (8 GB recommended)
- 2.6 GB of available hard-disk space for installation; additional free space required during installation
- 1024×768 display (1280×800 recommended) with 32-bit video card. Supports Retina display.
- Adobe Flash Player 10 required to export SWF files
- Internet connection and registration are necessary for required software activation, membership validation, and access to online services.*

** This product may integrate with or allow access to certain Adobe or third-party hosted online services. Adobe online services, including the Adobe Creative Cloud™ service, are available only to users 13 and older and require agreement to additional terms and Adobe's online privacy policy. The applications and online services are not available in all countries or languages, may require user registration, and may be subject to change or discontinuation without notice. Additional fees or membership charges may apply.*

The InDesign User Interface

Adobe InDesign is a robust publishing application that allows you to integrate text and graphics, either prepared in the program or imported from other sources, to produce files that can be printed to a local or networked printer, taken to a commercial printer, or published digitally. This book is designed to teach you how InDesign can be used to complete virtually any type of project, from a 1-page flyer to a 500-page book.

The sheer volume of available options in InDesign means there are numerous tools and utilities that you need to learn to make the most of the application. The simple exercises in this introduction are designed to let you explore the InDesign user interface. Whether you are new to the application or upgrading from a previous version, we strongly encourage you to follow these steps to click around and become familiar with the basic workspace.

Explore the InDesign Interface

The user interface (UI) is what you see when you launch the application. The specific elements that you see — including which panels are open and where they appear on the screen — depend on what was done the last time the application was open. The first time you launch InDesign, you see the default workspace settings defined by Adobe. When you relaunch the application after you or another user has quit, the workspace defaults to the last-used settings.

1. **Create a new empty folder named WIP (Work In Progress) on any writable disk (where you plan to save your work in progress).**

2. **Download the IDCC_RF_Interface.zip archive from the Student Files Web page.**

3. **Macintosh users: Place the ZIP archive in your WIP folder, then double-click the file icon to expand it.**

   This **Interface** folder contains all the files you need to complete this introduction.

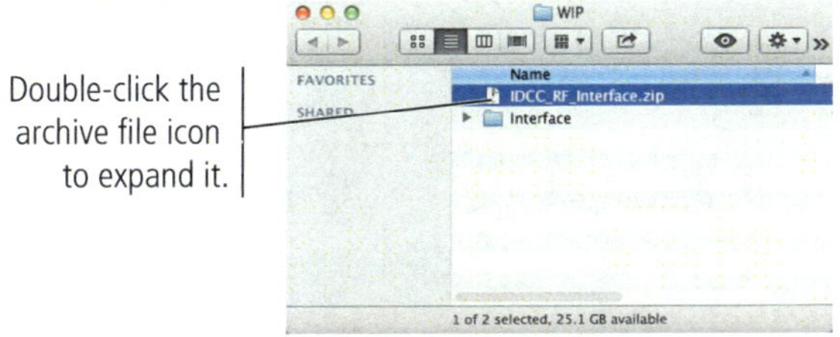

Windows users: Double-click the ZIP archive file to open it. Click the folder inside the archive and drag it into your primary WIP folder.

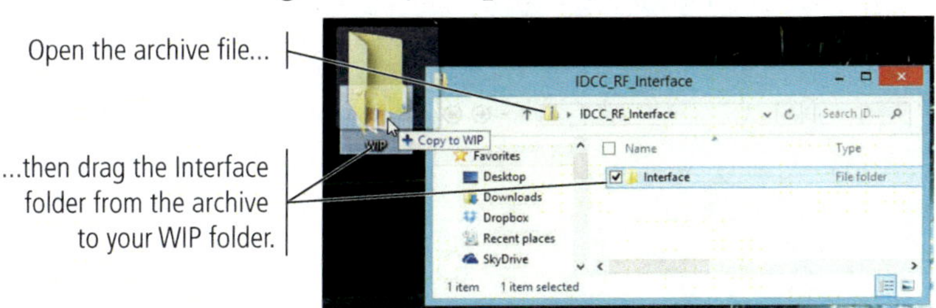

4. **Macintosh users: While pressing Command-Option-Control-Shift, start InDesign. Click Yes when asked if you want to delete preference files.**

   Windows users: Launch InDesign, and then press Control-Alt-Shift. Click Yes when asked if you want to delete preference files.

   This step resets InDesign to the preference settings that are defined by Adobe as the application defaults. This helps to ensure that your application functions in the same way as what we show in our screen shots.

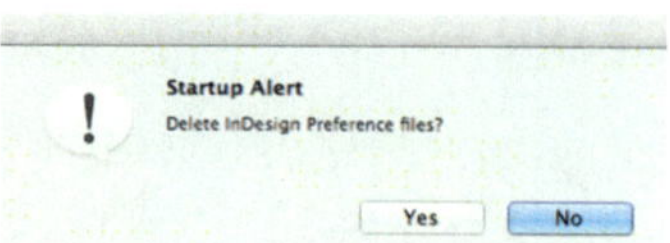

5. **Macintosh users: Open the Window menu and choose Application Frame to toggle that option on.**

   Many menu commands and options in InDesign are **toggles**, which means they are either on or off; when an option is already checked, that option is toggled on (visible or active). You can toggle an active option off by choosing the checked menu command, or toggle an inactive option on by choosing the unchecked menu command.

Note:

On Windows, the Application Frame menu command is not available; you can't turn off the Application Frame on the Windows OS.

   The default workspace includes the Tools panel on the left side of the screen, the Control panel at the top of the screen, and a set of panels attached to the right side of the screen. (The area where the panels are stored is called the **panel dock**.)

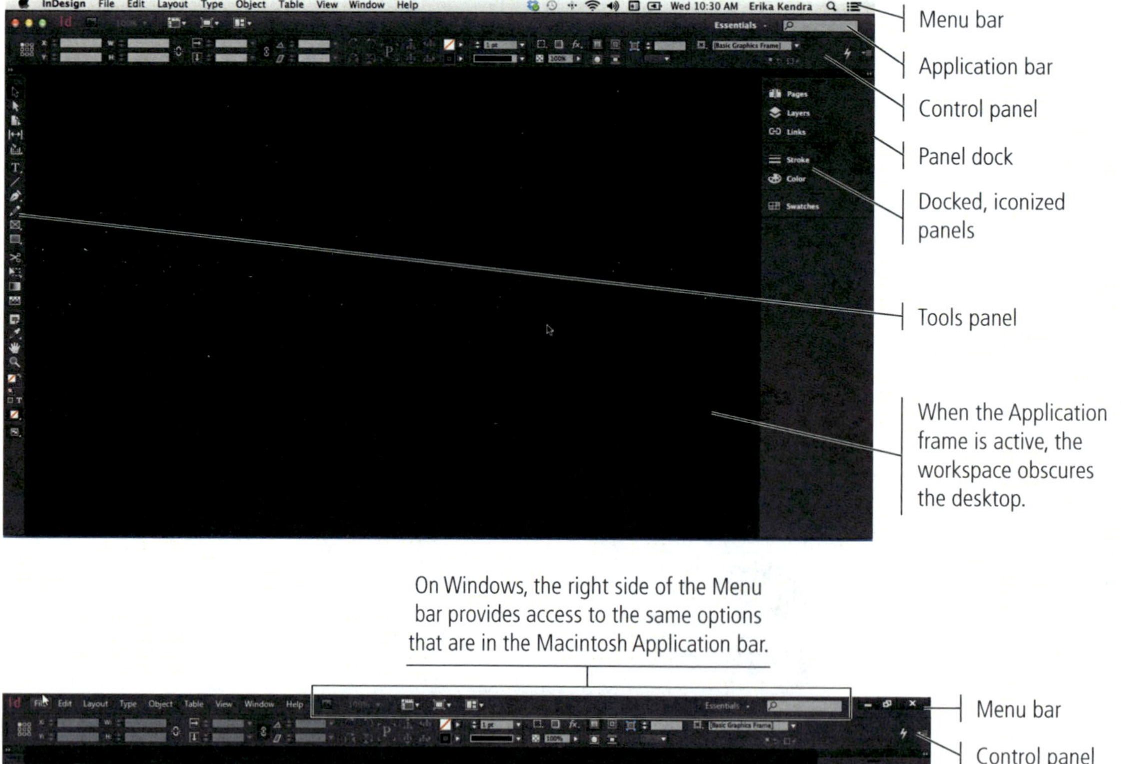

The general Macintosh and Windows workspaces are virtually identical, with a few primary exceptions.

- On Macintosh, the application's title bar appears below the Menu bar; the Close, Minimize, and Restore buttons appear on the left side of the title bar, and the menu bar is not part of the Application frame.
- On Windows, the Close, Minimize, and Restore buttons appear at the right end of the Menu bar, which is part of the overall Application frame.

On Macintosh systems, the Application bar at the top of the workspace includes a number of buttons for accessing different view options. On Windows systems, those same options are available on the right side of the Menu bar.

Macintosh users also have two extra menus (consistent with the Macintosh operating system structure). The Apple menu provides access to system-specific commands. The InDesign menu follows the Macintosh system-standard format for all applications; this menu controls basic application operations such as About, Hide, Preferences, and Quit.

6. **Macintosh users: Choose InDesign>Preferences>Interface.**
   Windows users: Choose Edit>Preferences>Interface.

   Remember that on Macintosh systems, the Preferences dialog box is accessed in the InDesign menu; Windows users access the Preferences dialog box in the Edit menu.

   Preferences customize the way many of the program's tools and options function. When you open the Preferences dialog box, the active pane is the one you chose in the Preferences submenu. Once open, however, you can access any of the Preference categories by clicking a different option in the left pane; the right side of the dialog box displays options related to the active category.

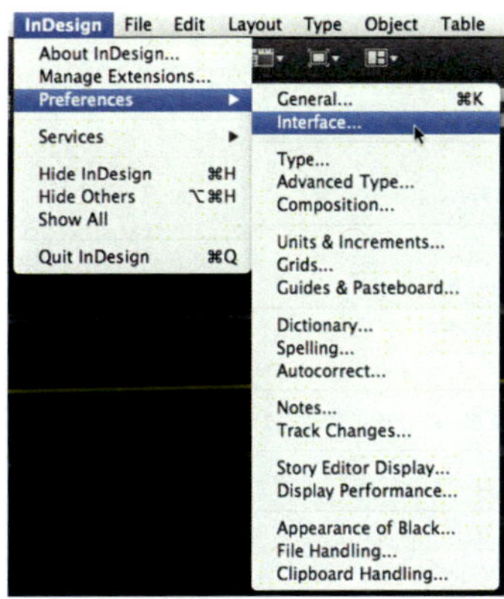

INDESIGN FOUNDATIONS

Understanding the Application Frame

On Windows, each running application is contained within its own frame; all elements of the application — including the Menu bar, panels, tools, and open documents — are contained within the Application frame.

Adobe also offers the Application frame to Macintosh users as an option for controlling your workspace. When the Application frame is active, the entire workspace exists in a self-contained area that can be moved around the screen. All elements of the workspace (excluding the Menu bar) move when you move the Application frame.

The Application frame is inactive by default; you can toggle it on by choosing Window>Application Frame. If the menu option is checked, the Application frame is active; if the menu option is not checked, it is inactive.

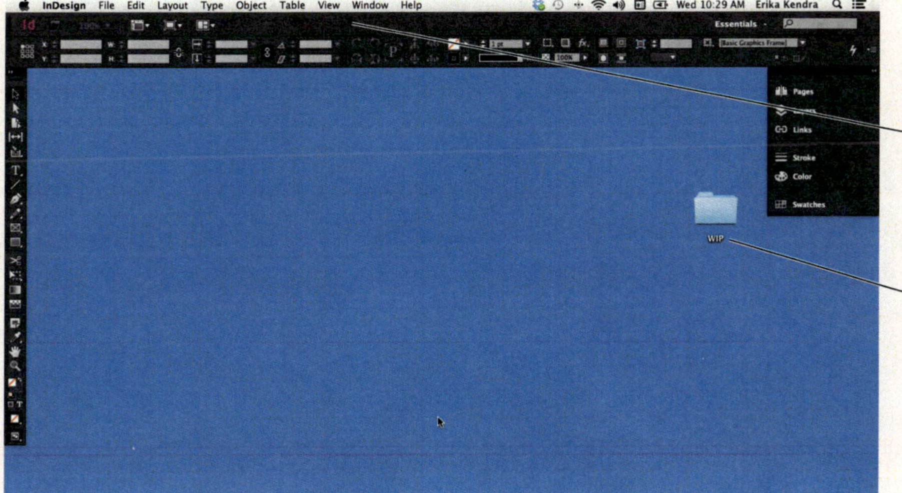

When the Application frame is not active, the Application bar appears below the Menu bar; in this case, the Application bar can be moved or turned off.

When the Application frame is not active, the desktop is visible behind the workspace elements.

7. In the Appearance section, choose any option that you prefer.

You might have already noticed the rather dark appearance of the panels and interface background. InDesign uses the medium-dark "theme" as the default. (We used the Light option throughout this book because text in the interface elements is easier to read in printed screen captures.)

8. In the Panels section, check the option to Auto-Collapse Icon Panels.

Use this option to lighten or darken the user interface.

Check this option.

> *Note:*
>
> *As you work your way through the projects in this book, you'll learn not only what you can do with these different collections of preferences, but also why and when you might want to use them.*

> *Note:*
>
> *You can also activate the Auto-Collapse Icon Panels option in the panel dock title bar's contextual menu.*

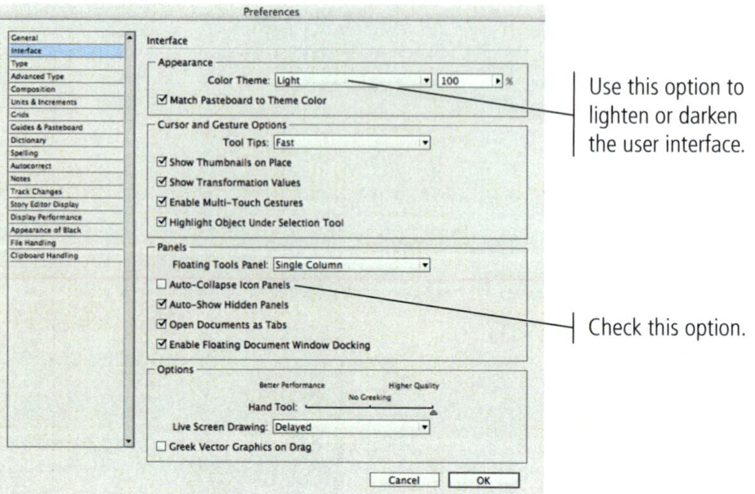

9. Click OK to close the Preferences dialog box, then continue to the next exercise.

Customizing Keyboard Shortcuts and Menus

INDESIGN FOUNDATIONS

People use InDesign for many different reasons, sometimes using only a specific, limited set of tools to complete a certain project. InDesign has built in several sophisticated options for customizing the user interface, including the ability to define the available menu options and the keyboard shortcuts associated with menu commands, panel menus, and tools.

At the bottom of the Edit menu, you can open the Keyboard Shortcuts and Menus dialog boxes to define custom sets. (If you don't see the Keyboard Shortcuts or Menus options in the Edit menu, choose Show All Menu Items to reveal the hidden commands.) Once you have defined custom shortcuts or menus, you can save your choices as a set so you can access the same choices again without having to redo the work.

Click here to access existing saved sets.

Use this menu to access different sets of commands.

Click in this column to hide or show a specific menu command.

Click in this column to add a highlight color to the menu command.

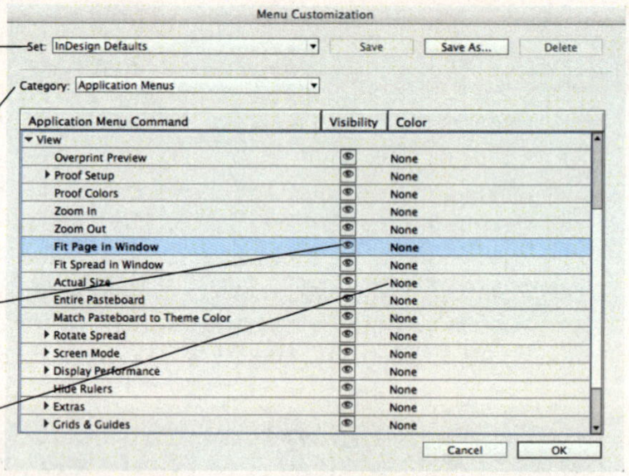

Click here to access existing saved sets.

Use this menu to access different sets of commands.

Select a specific command here...

...view the associated keyboard shortcut here...

...and assign a new shortcut here.

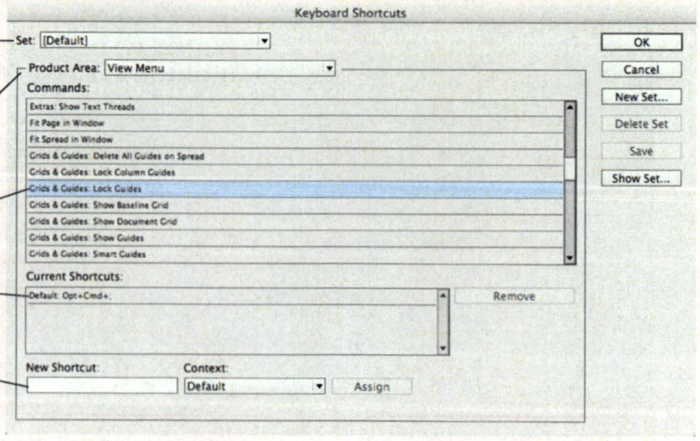

Explore the Arrangement of InDesign Panels

As you gain experience and familiarity with InDesign, you will develop personal artistic and working styles. You will also find that different types of jobs often require different but specific sets of tools. Adobe recognizes this wide range of needs and preferences among users; InDesign includes a number of options for arranging and managing the numerous panels, so you can customize and personalize the workspace to suit your specific needs.

We designed the following exercise to give you an opportunity to explore different ways of controlling InDesign panels. Because workspace preferences are largely a matter of personal taste, the projects in this book instruct you to use certain tools and panels, but where you place those elements within the interface is up to you.

1. **Click the Color button in the panel dock to expand the panel.**

   By default, expanded panels remain open until you manually close them or expand another panel in the same dock column. When Auto-Collapse Iconic Panels is toggled on, the expanded panel collapses as soon as you click away from it.

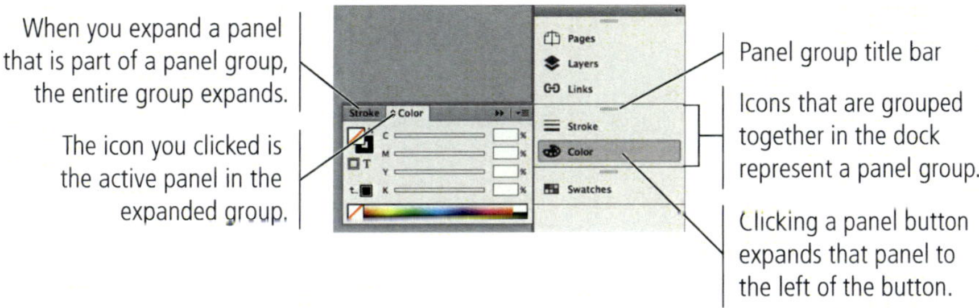

> ***Note:***
>
> *Collapsed panels are referred to as **iconized** or **iconic**.*

> ***Note:***
>
> *All panels can be toggled on and off from the Window menu.*
>
> - *If you choose a panel that's already open but iconized, the panel expands to the left of its icon.*
> - *If you choose a panel that's already open in an expanded group, but is not the active panel, that panel comes to the front of the group.*
> - *If you choose a panel that's already open and active in an expanded group, that panel group is closed.*
> - *If you choose a panel that isn't currently open, it opens in the same place as it was when it was last closed.*

2. **Click away from the expanded panel to collapse it.**

3. **Click the left edge of the docked panels and drag right.**

   When panels are iconized, you can reduce the button size to show icons only. Doing so can be particularly useful once you are more familiar with the application and the icons used to symbolize the different panels.

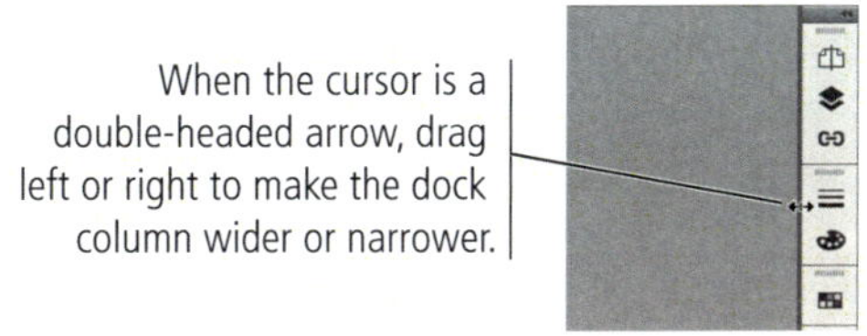

4. **Double-click the title bar above the column of docked panels.**

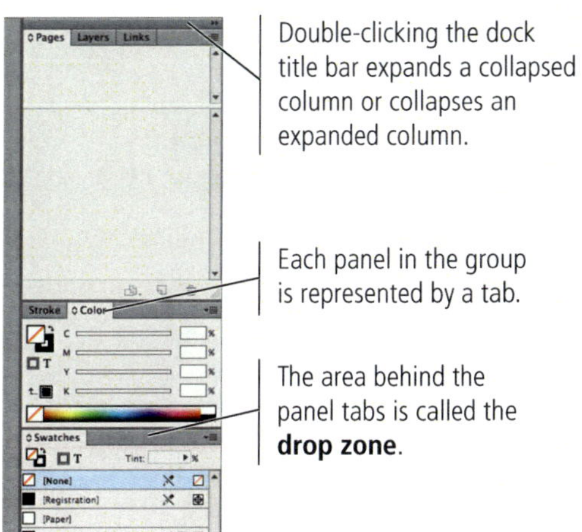

Identifying and Accessing Tools in InDesign

InDesign includes 34 tools — a large number that indicates the real power of the application. In addition to the basic tool set, the bottom of the Tools panel includes options that control the foreground and background colors, as well as the preview mode you're using. You will learn how to use these tools as you complete the projects in this book. For now, you should simply take the opportunity to identify the tools.

Nested Tools and Keyboard Shortcuts

Any tool with an arrow in the bottom-right corner includes related tools below it. When you click a tool and hold down the mouse button (or Control/right-click a tool), the **nested tools** appear in a pop-up menu. When you choose one of the nested tools, that variation becomes the default choice in the Tools panel.

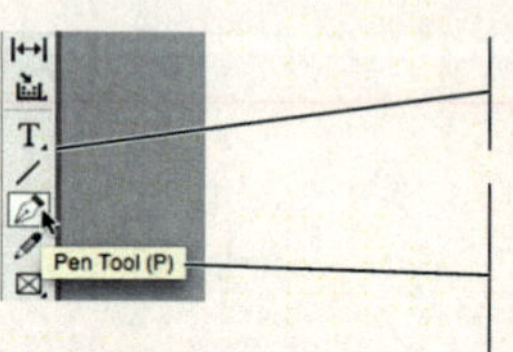

This arrow means the tool has other nested tools.

When you hover the mouse cursor over the tool, a tool tip shows the name of the tool.

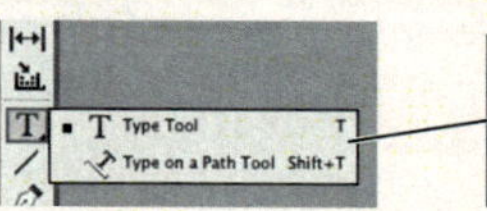

Click and hold down the mouse button (or Control/right-click a tool) to show the nested tools.

Most of the default InDesign tools can be accessed with a keyboard shortcut. When you hover the mouse cursor over a tool, the pop-up **tool tip** shows the name of the tool and a letter in parentheses. Pressing that letter on the keyboard activates the associated tool (unless you're working with type, in which case pressing a key adds that letter to your text). If you don't see tool tips, check the Interface pane of the Preferences dialog box; the Show Tool Tips check box should be active.

Finally, if you press and hold a tool's keyboard shortcut, you can temporarily call the appropriate tool (called **spring-loaded keys**); after releasing the shortcut key, you return to the tool you were using previously. For example, you might use this technique to switch temporarily from the Pen tool to the Direct Selection tool while drawing a custom frame.

Tools Panel Options

In addition to the basic tool set, the bottom of the Tools panel includes options that control the fill and stroke colors (as well as options for what attribute is being affected by color changes) and which screen preview mode to use.

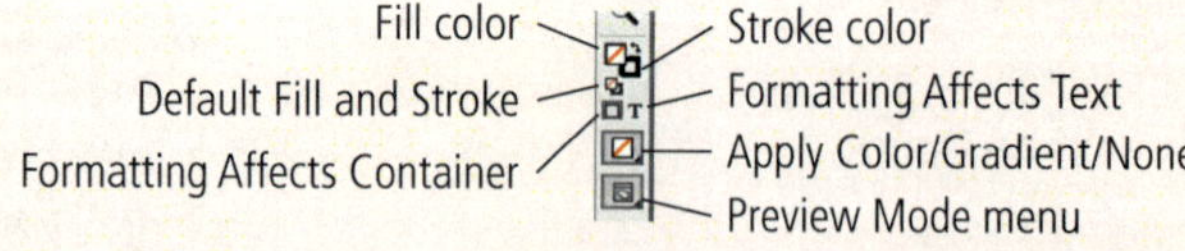

Tool Hints

The Tool Hints panel (Window>Utilities>Tool Hints) provides useful tips about the active tool, including a brief description of the tool and an explanation of the tool's behavior if you press one or more modifier keys and the tool's keyboard shortcut.

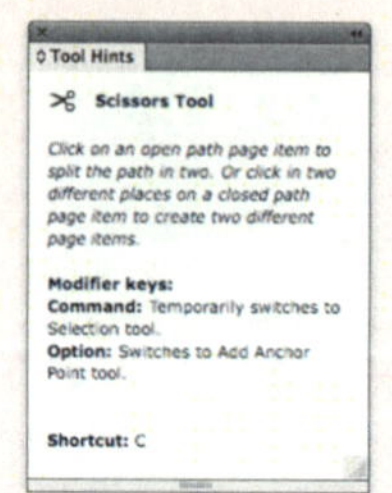

The following image offers a quick reference of nested tools, as well as the keyboard shortcut for each tool (if any). Nested tools are shown indented and in italics.

- Selection tool (V)
- Direct Selection tool (A)
- Page tool (Shift-P)
- Gap tool (U)
- Content Collector tool
    - *Content Placer tool*
- Type tool (T)
    - *Type on a Path tool (Shift-T)*
- Line tool (\)
- Pen tool (P)
    - *Add Anchor Point tool (=)*
    - *Delete Anchor Point tool (-)*
    - *Convert Direction Point tool (Shift-C)*
- Pencil tool (N)
    - *Smooth tool*
    - *Erase tool*
- Rectangle Frame tool (F)
    - *Ellipse Frame tool*
    - *Polygon Frame tool*
- Rectangle tool (M)
    - *Ellipse tool (L)*
    - *Polygon tool*
- Scissors tool (C)
- Free Transform tool (E)
    - *Rotate tool (R)*
    - *Scale tool (S)*
    - *Shear tool (O)*
- Gradient Swatch tool (G)
- Gradient Feather tool (Shift-G)
- Note tool
- Eyedropper tool (I)
    - *Measure tool (K)*
- Hand tool (H)
- Zoom tool (Z)

5. **On the left side of the workspace, review the Tools panel. If you don't see all of the panel options, double-click the Tools panel title bar.**

   The Tools panel can be displayed as either one or two columns; double-clicking the Tools panel title bar toggles between these two modes.

   Some monitors — especially laptops — are too small to display the number of tools that are available in InDesign's Tools panel. If this is the case, you should use the two-column mode.

   The Tools panel can also be floated (moved out of the dock) by clicking its title bar and dragging away from the edge of the screen. To re-dock the floating Tools panel, simply click the panel's title bar and drag back to the left edge of the screen; when a blue line highlights the edge of the workspace, releasing the mouse button places the Tools panel back in the dock. If the Tools panel is floating, you can toggle through three different modes — one-column vertical, two-column vertical, and one-row horizontal.

   Double-click the Tools panel title bar to toggle between the one-column and two-column layouts.

6. **Control/right-click the Color panel group drop zone (behind the panel tabs) and choose Close Tab Group from the contextual menu.**

   As we explained in the Getting Started section, when commands are different for the Macintosh and Windows operating systems, we include the different commands in the Macintosh/Windows format. In this case, Macintosh users who do not have right-click mouse capability can press the Control key and click to access the contextual menu. You do not have to press Control *and* right-click to access the menus.

   Control/right-clicking a dock title bar opens the dock contextual menu, where you can change the default panel behavior. Many elements in InDesign have contextual menus, which make it easy to access item-specific options.

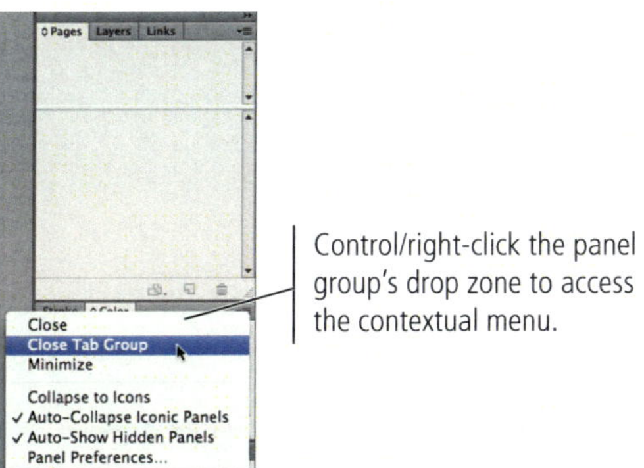

Control/right-click the panel group's drop zone to access the contextual menu.

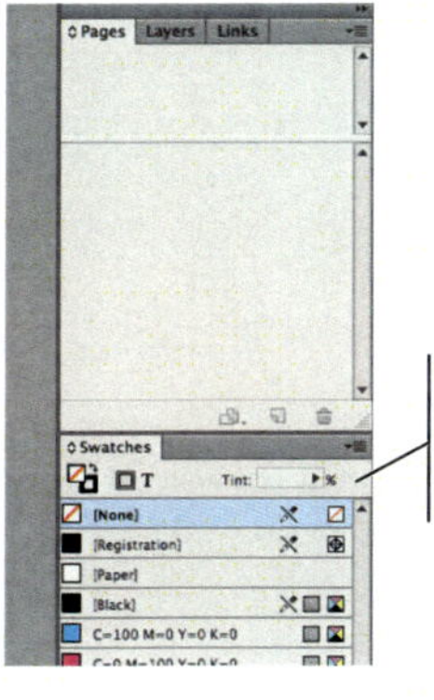

The closed panel group is removed from the panel dock.

Note:

You can choose Close to close only one panel in a group.

7. **Click the Links panel tab in the top panel group and drag away from the panel dock.**

   Panels can be **floated** by clicking a panel tab and dragging away from the dock.

Click the panel's tab and drag to move the panel out of the docked panel group.

When you release the mouse button, the panel floats freely in the workspace.

Floating panel title bar

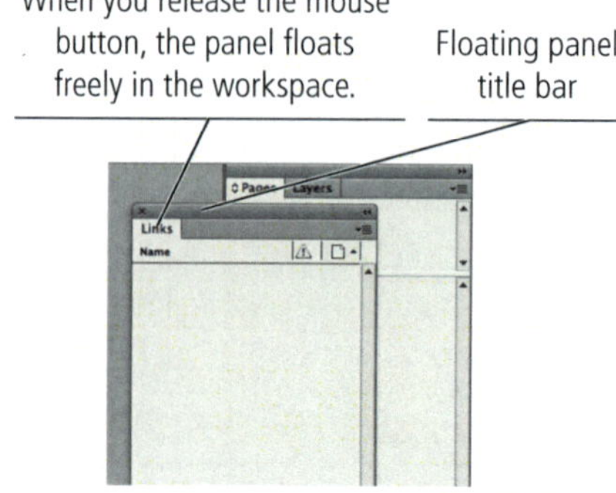

> *Note:*
>
> *Most screen shots in this book show floating panels, so we can focus on the most important issue in a particular image. In our production workflow, however, we make heavy use of docked and iconized panels and take full advantage of saved custom workspaces.*

8. **Click the Links panel tab and drag to the dock, between the Pages and Swatches panels. When you see a blue line between the existing docked panels, release the mouse button.**

   Panels and panel groups can be dragged to different locations (including into different groups) by dragging the panel's tab; the target location — where the panel will reside when you release the mouse button — is identified by the blue highlight.

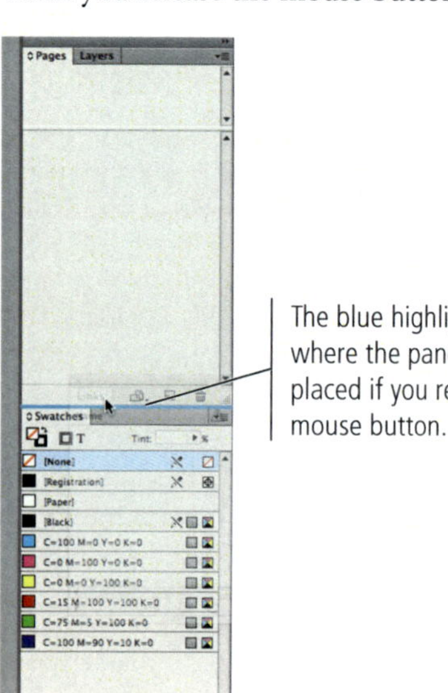

The blue highlight shows where the panel will be placed if you release the mouse button.

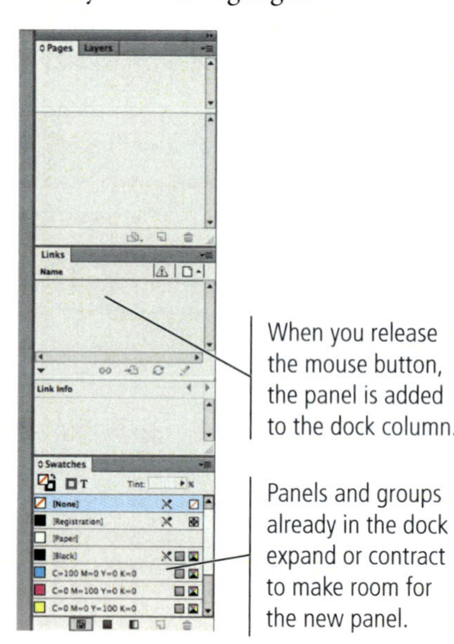

When you release the mouse button, the panel is added to the dock column.

Panels and groups already in the dock expand or contract to make room for the new panel.

> *Note:*
>
> *You can click and drag a panel group's drop zone to float or move the entire group.*

9. **Click the Pages panel tab and drag left until the blue highlight shows a second column added to the dock.**

   As we mentioned earlier, you can create multiple columns of panels in the dock. This can be very useful if you need easy access to a large number of panels and have a monitor with enough available screen space.

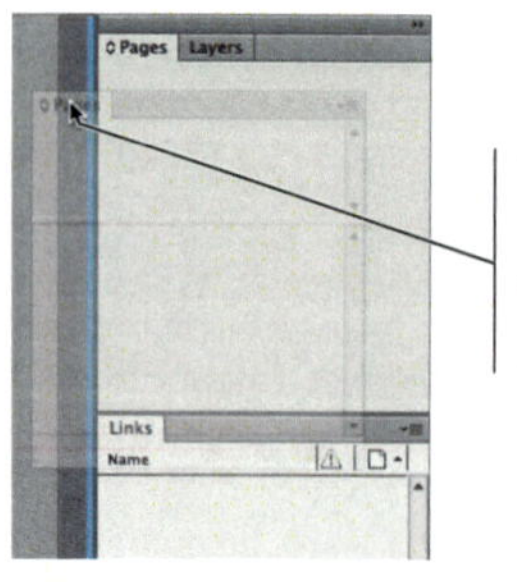

This pop-out "drawer" indicates that releasing the mouse button...

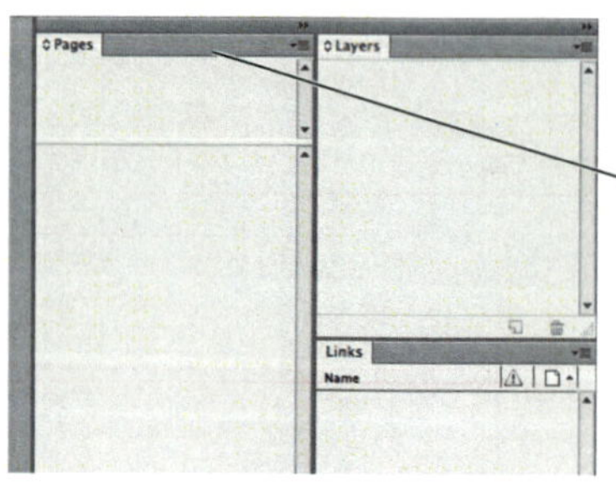

...creates a second column in the panel dock.

10. Double-click the title bar of the left dock column to iconize that column.

You can independently iconize or expand each column of docked panels and each floating panel (group).

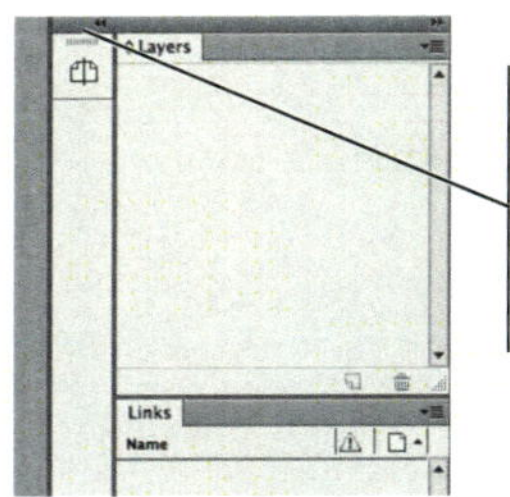

Double-click the title bar at the top of the dock column to collapse or expand it independently of other dock columns.

Note:

Each dock column, technically considered a separate dock, can be expanded or collapsed independently of other columns.

Note:

Each column of the dock can be made wider or narrower by dragging the left edge of the column.

Dragging the left edge of a dock column changes the width of all panels in that column.

11. Control/right-click the Swathes panel tab and choose Minimize from the contextual menu.

You can also double-click the panel tab two times to minimize a panel (group). The first time you double-click the Swatches panel tab, you reduce the panel to a minimum size; the second time you double-click, you collapse the panel to show only the panel tabs.

Clicking a tab in a collapsed panel group expands the group and makes the selected panel active.

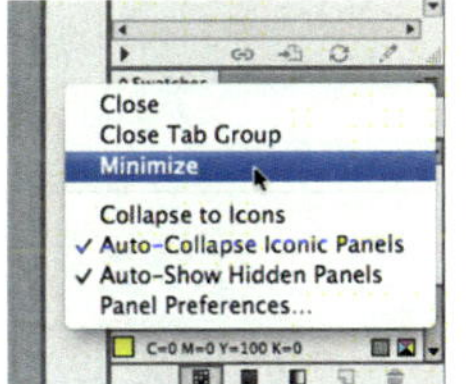

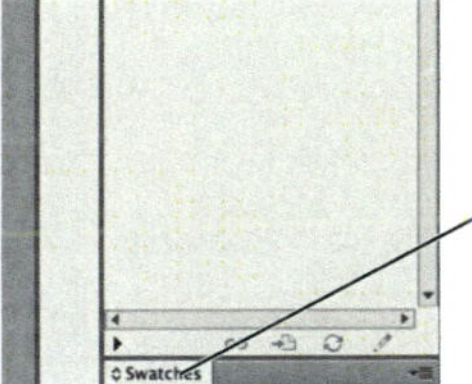

Minimizd panel groups show only the panel tabs.

Note:

On Macintosh, you can also double-click a panel group drop zone to collapse that panel group.

On Windows, double-clicking the drop zone has no effect.

12. In the right dock column, click the bottom edge of the Layers panel group and drag down until the Layers panel occupies approximately half of the vertical dock space.

When you drag the bottom edge of a docked group, other panels in the same column expand or contract to fit the available space.

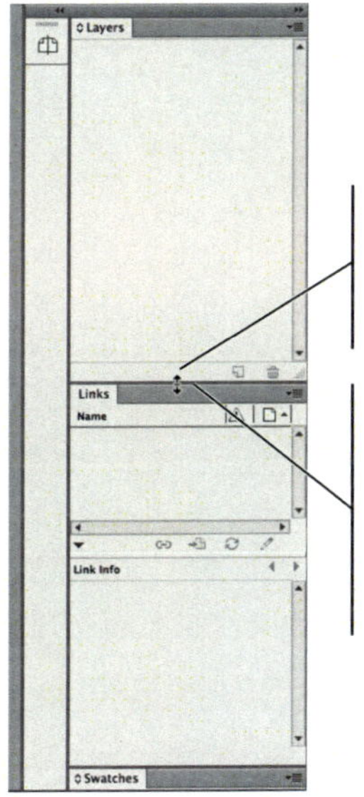

When the cursor is a double-headed arrow, you can click and drag to resize the panels.

Dragging the bottom edge of a docked panel (or group) changes the height of that panel (or group). Other panels in the same column expand or shrink as necessary to fit the column.

13. Continue to the next exercise.

Create a Saved Workspace

By now you should understand that you have extensive control over the appearance of your InDesign workspace — what panels are visible, where and how they appear, and even the size of individual panels or panel groups.

Over time you will develop personal preferences — for example, the Colors panel always appears at the top — based on your work habits and project needs. Rather than re-establishing every workspace element each time you return to InDesign, you can save your custom workspace settings so you can recall them with a single click.

1. **Click the Workspace switcher in the Application/Menu bar and choose New Workspace.**

   Again, keep in mind that we list differing commands in the Macintosh/Windows format. On Macintosh, the Workspace switcher is in the Application bar; on Windows, it's in the Menu bar.

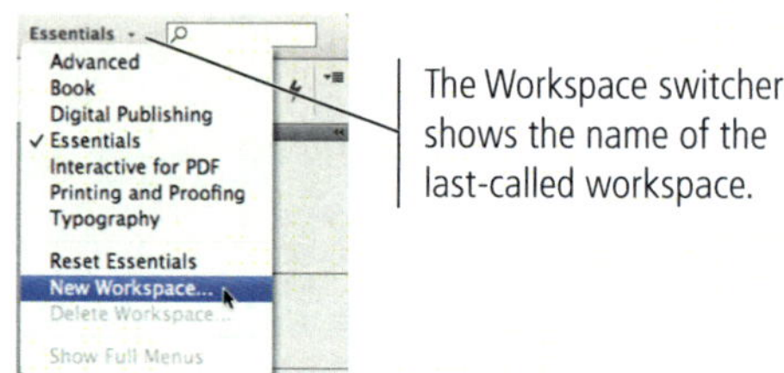

The Workspace switcher shows the name of the last-called workspace.

> *Note:*
>
> *The Delete Workspace option opens a dialog box where you can choose a specific user-defined workspace to delete. You can't delete the default workspaces that come with the application.*

2. **In the New Workspace dialog box, type Portfolio. Make sure the Panel Locations option is checked and click OK.**

   You didn't define custom menus, so that option is not relevant in this exercise.

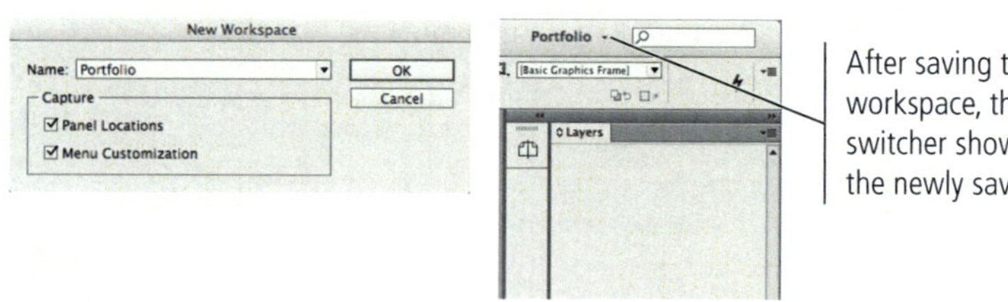

After saving the current workspace, the Workspace switcher shows the name of the newly saved workspace.

> *Note:*
>
> *If you are using a shared computer, you might want to also include your own name in the workspace name.*

3. **Open the Window menu and choose Workspace>Essentials.**

   Saved workspaces can be accessed in the Window>Workspace submenu as well as the Workspace switcher on the Application/Menu bar.

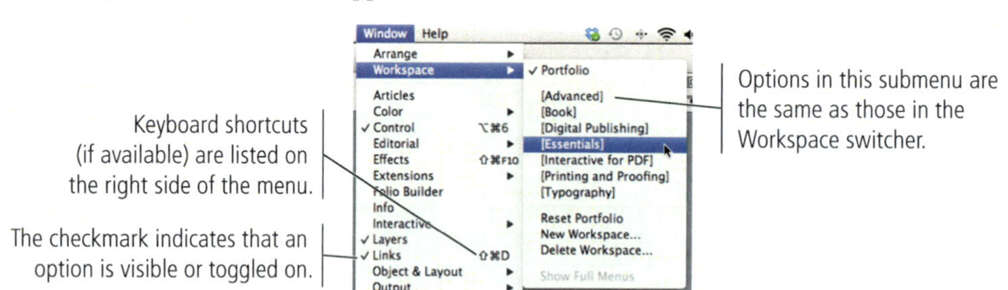

Keyboard shortcuts (if available) are listed on the right side of the menu.

The checkmark indicates that an option is visible or toggled on.

Options in this submenu are the same as those in the Workspace switcher.

> *Note:*
>
> *If a menu option is grayed out, it is not available for the active selection.*

Calling a saved workspace restores the last-used state of the workspace. You made a number of changes since you launched InDesign with the default Essentials workspace, so calling the Essentials workspace restores the last state of that workspace — in essence, nothing changes from the saved Portfolio workspace.

The only apparent difference is the active workspace name.

4. **Choose Window>Workspace>Reset Essentials (or click the Workspace switcher and choose Reset Essentials).**

   Remember: calling a workspace again restores the panels exactly as they were the last time you used that workspace. For example, if you close a panel that is part of a saved workspace, the closed panel will not be reopened the next time you call the same workspace. To restore the saved state of the workspace, including opening closed panels or repositioning moved ones, you have to use the Reset option.

5. **Continue to the next exercise.**

Explore the InDesign Document Views

There is far more to using InDesign than arranging panels around the workspace. What you do with those panels — and even which panels you need — depends on the type of work you are doing in a particular file. In this exercise, you open an InDesign file and explore the interface elements you'll use to create documents.

1. **In InDesign, choose File>Open. Navigate to your WIP>Interface folder and select `sfaa1.indd` in the list of available files.**

   The Open dialog box is a system-standard navigation dialog box. This dialog box is one area of significant difference between Macintosh and Windows users.

Note:

Press Command/Control-O to access the Open dialog box.

2. **Press Shift, and then click `sfaa5.indd` in the list of files.**

   Pressing Shift allows you to select multiple contiguous (consecutive) files in the list.

   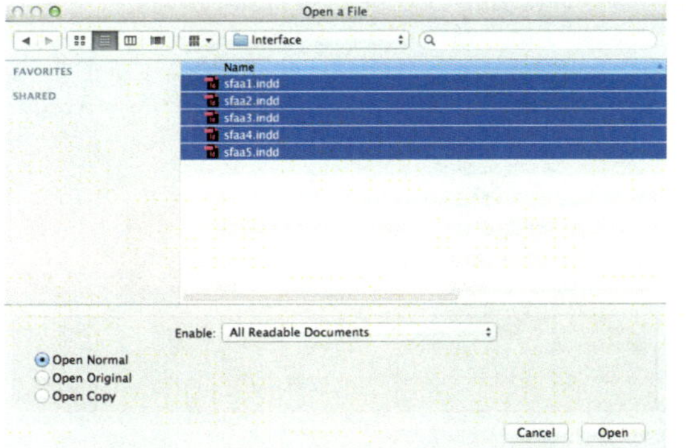

   On Windows, the file extensions are not included in the file names in the Open dialog box.

   You can also press Command/Control to select and open non-contiguous files. (Depending on how files are sorted in your operating system, folders might be listed before other files. If that's the case on your system, you can press Shift or Control to select all five files.)

   One final reminder: we list differing commands in the Macintosh/Windows format. On Macintosh, you need to press the Command key; on Windows, press the Control key. (We will not repeat this explanation every time different commands are required for the different operating systems.)

3. **Click Open to open all five selected files.**

4. **Click the sfaa3.indd tab to make that document active.**

5. **Click the Zoom Level field in the Application/Menu bar and change the view percentage to `200`.**

   Different people prefer larger or smaller view percentages, depending on a number of factors (eyesight, monitor size, and so on). As you complete the projects in this book, you'll see our screen shots zoom in or out as necessary to show you the most relevant part of a particular file. In most cases we do not tell you what specific view percentage to use for a particular exercise unless it is specifically required for the work being done.

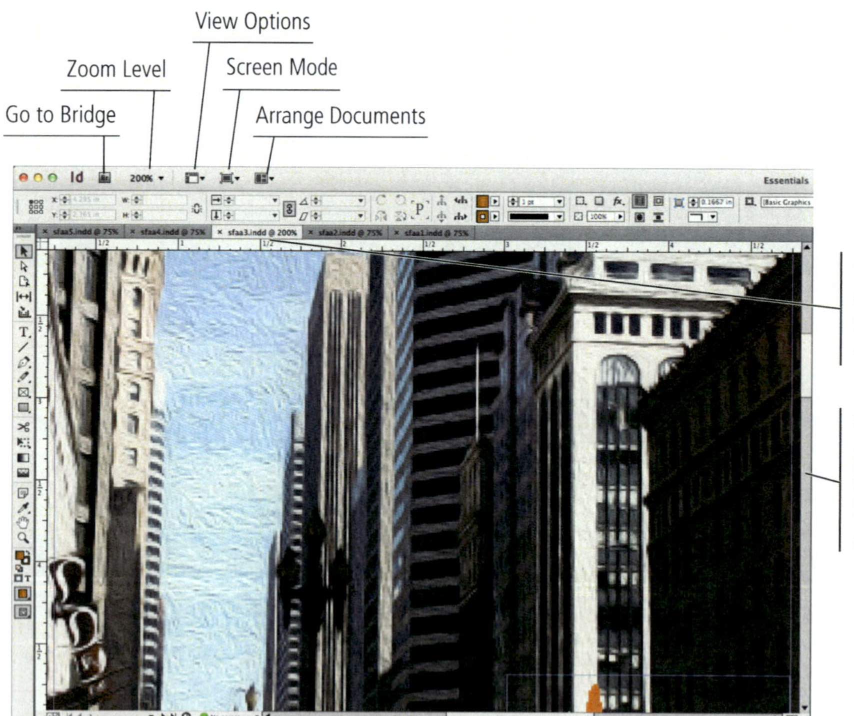

Note:

All open files are listed at the bottom of the Window menu.

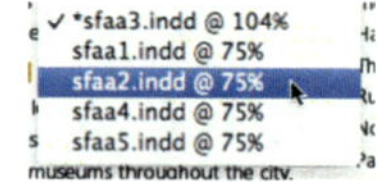

Note:

You can set the viewing percentage of an InDesign document to any value from 5% to 4000%.

6. **Choose View>Fit Page in Window.**

Fit Page in Window automatically calculates view percentage based on the size of the document window.

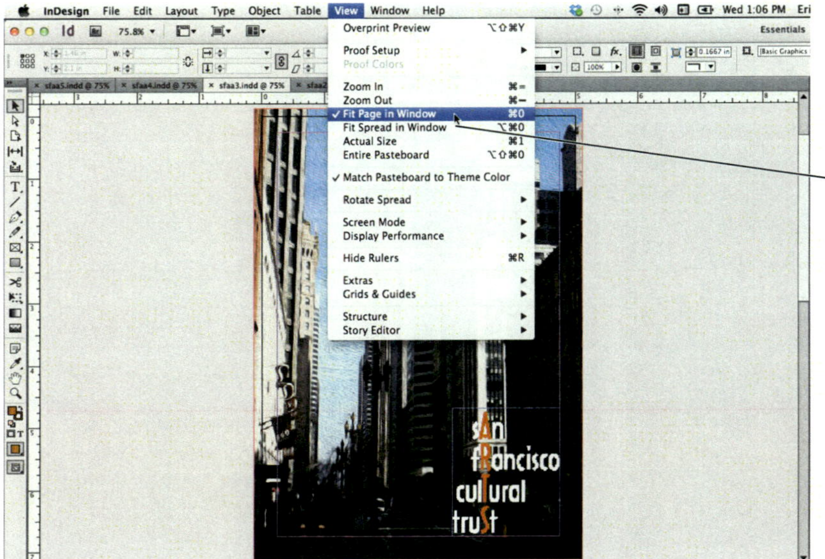

These six options affect the view percentage of a file.

Note:

Fit Spread in Window relates to documents that have left- and right-facing pages, such as a book. You build this kind of document in Project 4: Realtor Collateral Booklet.

7. **Click the Zoom tool in the Tools panel. Click in the document window and drag a marquee around the logo in the bottom-right corner.**

Dragging a marquee with the Zoom tool enlarges the selected area to fill the document window.

Zoom tool cursor

The area of the marquee enlarges to fill the document window.

8. **With the Zoom tool selected, Option/Alt-click in the document window.**

   Clicking with the Zoom tool enlarges the view percentage in specific, predefined steps. Pressing Option/Alt while clicking with the Zoom tool reduces the view percentage in the reverse sequence of the same percentages.

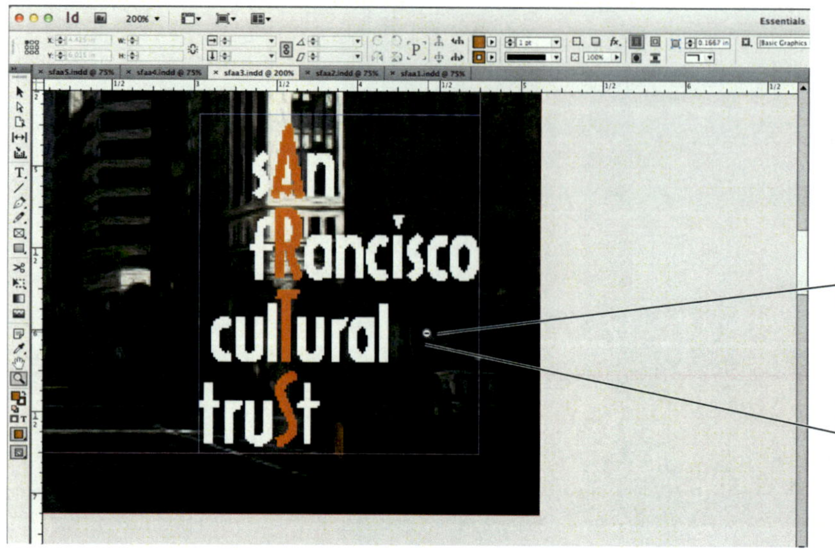

With the Zoom tool active, pressing Option/Alt changes the cursor to the Zoom Out icon.

Option/Alt-clicking with the Zoom tool reduces the view percentage in the predefined sequence of percentages.

9. **Click the Hand tool near the bottom of the Tools panel.**

10. **Click in the document, hold down the mouse button, and drag around.**

    The Hand tool is a very easy and convenient option for changing the visible area of an image in the document window.

Hand tool cursor

Note:

Press the Z key to access the Zoom tool.

Press the H key to access the Hand tool.

Note:

If you click and hold down the mouse button when the Hand tool is active, the page zooms out and a red "view box" appears. You can drag the view box and release the mouse button to recenter the view on the area inside the view box.

11. **Choose View>Display Performance>High Quality Display.**

You might have noticed that the images in this file look very bad (they are badly bitmapped). This is even more evident when you zoom in to a high view percentage. By default, InDesign displays a low-resolution preview of placed images to save time when the screen redraws (i.e., every time you change something). Fortunately, however, you have the option to preview the full-resolution images placed in a file.

Note:

The Fast Display option replaces all placed images with a solid medium gray (in other words, no preview image displays).

Using the High Quality Display, images do not show the bitmapping of the default low-resolution previews.

Controlling Display Performance

INDESIGN FOUNDATIONS

By default, files display in the document window using the Typical display performance settings. In the Display Performance pane of the Preferences dialog box, you can change the default view settings (Fast, Typical, or High Quality), as well as change the definition of these settings. In the Adjust View Settings section, individual sliders control the display of raster images, vector graphics, and objects with transparency.

Choose Fast, Typical, or High Quality view as the default.

Use this menu to review and change the settings for Fast, Typical, and High Quality display.

In the layout, you can change the document display performance using the View>Display Performance menu. If **Allow Object-Level Display Settings** is checked in the View>Display Performance submenu, you can also change the preview for a specific image (in the Object>Display Performance submenu or using the object's contextual menu).

You can turn object-level display settings on and off using the Allow Object-Level Display Settings toggle. To remove object-level settings, choose **Clear Object-Level Display Settings**. (Object-level display settings are maintained only while the file remains open; if you want to save the file with specific object-level display settings, check the **Preserve Object-Level Display Settings** option in the Preferences dialog box.)

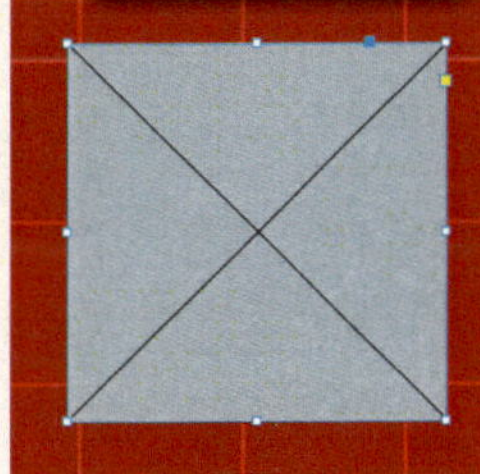

Fast displays gray boxes in place of images and graphics.

Typical shows the low-resolution proxy images.

High Quality shows the full resolution of placed files.

12. **Using the Selection tool, click the background image to select it. Control/ right-click the selected image and choose Display Performance>Typical Display from the contextual menu.**

    In the View menu, the Allow Object-Level Display Settings option is active by default (see the image in the previous step); this means you can change the display of individual objects on the page.

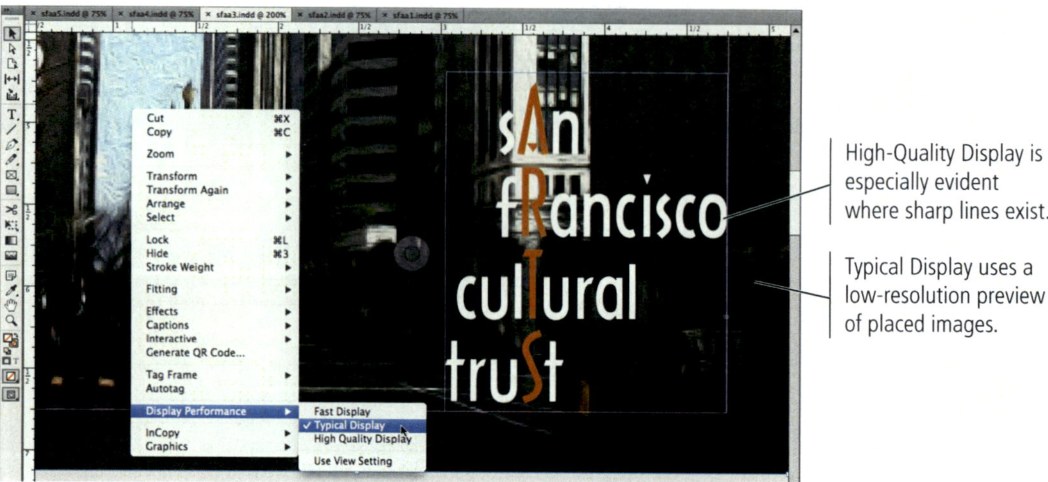

High-Quality Display is especially evident where sharp lines exist.

Typical Display uses a low-resolution preview of placed images.

13. **Choose View>Fit Page in Window to see the entire page.**

14. **Double-click the title bar above the docked panels to expand the panels.**

15. **In the Pages panel, double-click the Page 2 icon to show that page in the document window.**

    The Pages panel is the easiest way to move from one page to another in a multi-page document. You will use this panel extensively as you complete the projects in this book.

Double-click a page icon to display that page in the document window.

16. **Control/right-click the Page 2 icon in the Pages panel and choose Page Attributes>Rotate Spread View>90° CW from the contextual menu.**

Rotating the view only changes the display of the page; the actual page remains unchanged in the file. This option allows you to work more easily on objects or pages that are oriented differently than the overall document. In this example, the front side of the postcard has portrait orientation, but the mailer side has landscape orientation.

> *Note:*
>
> *You can also rotate page views using the options in the View>Rotate Spread menu.*

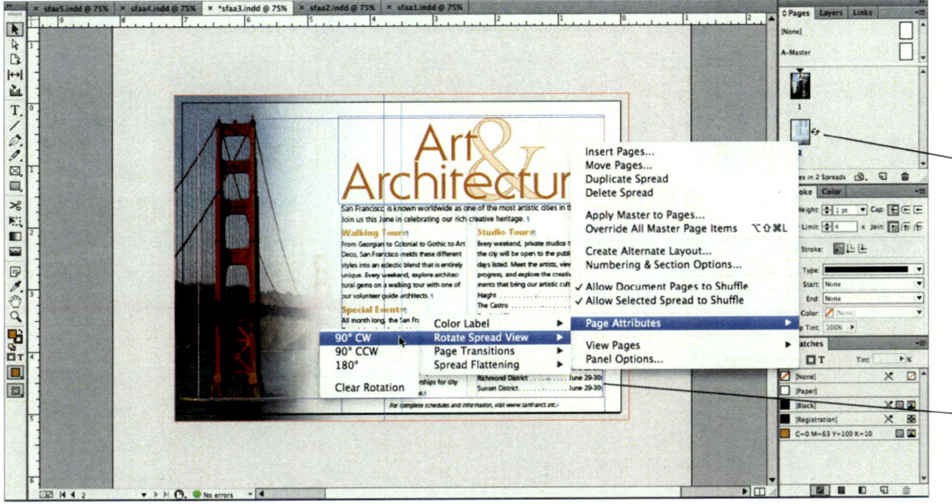

Pages with a rotated view are identified in the Pages panel.

The rotated display makes it easier to work on pages with orientations different from the document definition.

17. **Continue to the next exercise.**

Summing up the InDesign View Options

INDESIGN FOUNDATIONS

Most InDesign projects require some amount of zooming in and out to various view percentages, as well as navigating around the document within its window. As we show you how to complete various stages of the workflow, we usually won't tell you when to change your view percentage because that's largely a matter of personal preference. But you should understand the different options for navigating an InDesign file so you can easily and efficiently get to what you want.

View Menu

The View menu provides options for changing the view percentage. You should also become familiar with the keyboard shortcuts for these commands:

Zoom In	Command/Control-equals (=)
Zoom Out	Command/Control-minus (-)
Fit Page in Window	Command/Control-0 (zero)
Fit Spread in Window	Command-Option-0/Control-Alt-0
Actual Size (100%)	Command/Control-1
Entire Pasteboard	Command-Option-Shift-0/ Control-Alt-Shift-0

Zoom Level Field/Menu

You can use the Zoom Level field in the Application/Menu bar to type a specific view percentage, or you can use the attached menu to choose from the predefined view percentage steps.

Zoom Tool

You can click with the **Zoom tool** to increase the view percentage in specific, predefined intervals (the same intervals you see in the View Percentage menu in the bottom-left corner of the document window). Pressing Option/Alt with the Zoom tool allows you to zoom out in the same predefined percentages. If you drag a marquee with the Zoom tool, you can zoom into a specific location; the area surrounded by the marquee fills the available space in the document window.

Hand Tool

Whatever your view percentage, you can use the **Hand tool** to drag the file around in the document window, including scrolling from one page to another. The Hand tool only changes what is visible in the window; it has no effect on the actual content of the file.

Explore the Arrangement of Multiple Documents

In many cases, you will need to work with more than one layout at the same time. InDesign incorporates a number of options for arranging multiple documents. We designed the following simple exercise so you can explore these options.

1. **With sfaa3.indd active, choose Window>Arrange>Float in Window.**

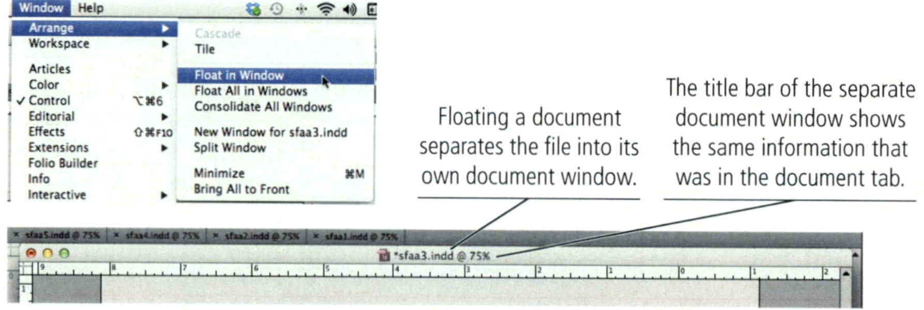

Floating a document separates the file into its own document window.

The title bar of the separate document window shows the same information that was in the document tab.

> *Note:*
>
> *When multiple document windows are open, two options in the Window>Arrange menu allow you to cascade or tile the document windows. You can separate all open files by choosing Window>Arrange>Float All in Windows.*

2. **In the Application/Menu bar, click the Arrange Documents button to open the panel of defined arrangements.**

3. **Click the 2 Up button in the Arrange Documents panel.**

   The defined arrangements provide a number of options for tiling multiple open files within the available workspace; these arrangements manage all open files, including those in floating windows.

   The Consolidate All button (top left) restores all floating documents into a single tabbed document window. The remaining buttons in the top row separate all open files into separate document windows and then arrange the different windows as indicated.

   The lower options use a specific number of floating documents (2-Up, 3-Up, etc.); if more files are open than an option indicates, the extra files are consolidated as tabs in the first document window.

> *Note:*
>
> *If the Application Frame is not active on a Macintosh, the Application bar must be visible to access the Arrange Documents button.*

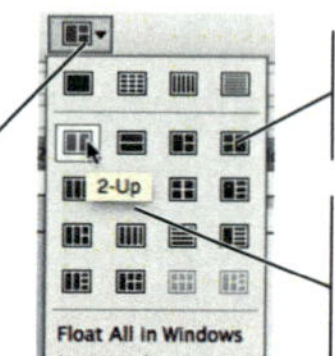

The Arrange Documents panel includes a number of tiling options for arranging multiple open files in the workspace.

The appearance of each icon suggests the result of that option.

Rolling your mouse cursor over an icon shows the arrangement name in a tool tip.

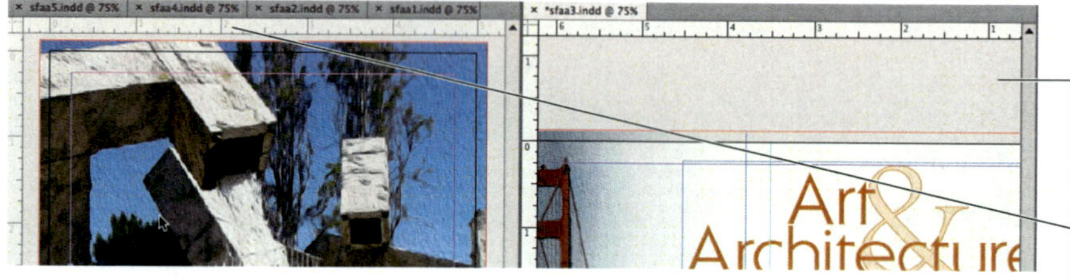

The 2-Up arrangement divides the document window in half, as indicated by the button icon.

Extra documents remain as tabs in the left document window.

4. **Click the sfaa3.indd document tab and drag left until a blue highlight appears around the document tabs in the other panel.**

When you release the mouse button, all of the open files are again part of the same document window.

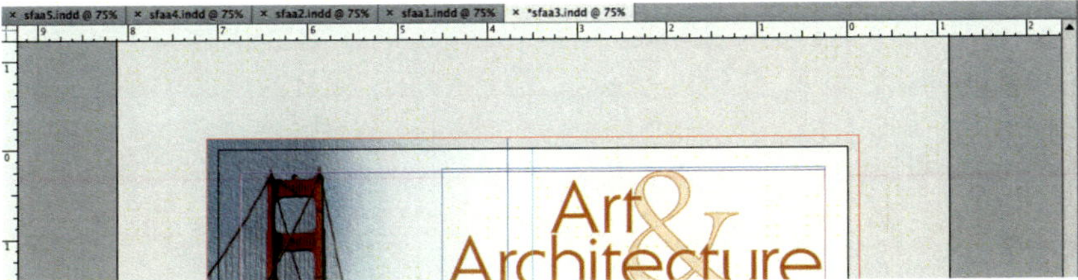

5. **Click the Screen Mode button in the Application/Menu bar and choose Preview.**

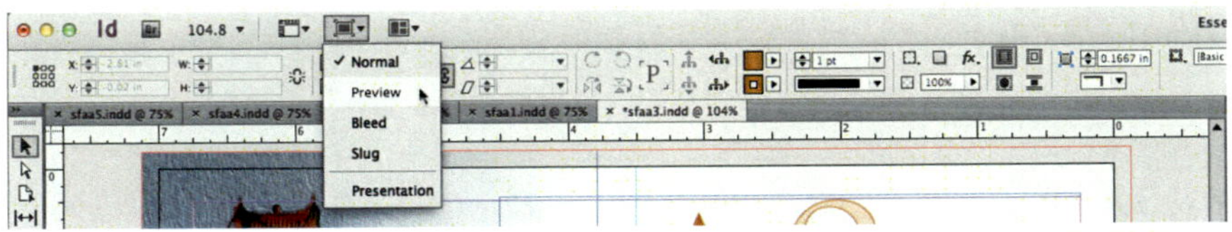

The files you explored in this project were saved in Normal screen mode. In Normal mode, you can see all non-printing elements including guides and frame edges (if those are toggled on). You can now also see the pasteboard surrounding the defined page area; your development work is not limited by the defined page size.

Preview screen mode surrounds the page with a neutral gray background. Page guides, frame edges, and other non-printing areas are not visible in the Preview mode.

Note:

By default, the pasteboard matches the color of that you defined for the user interface in the Interface pane of the Preferences dialog box. If you uncheck the Match Pasteboard to Theme Color option, the pasteboard is white.

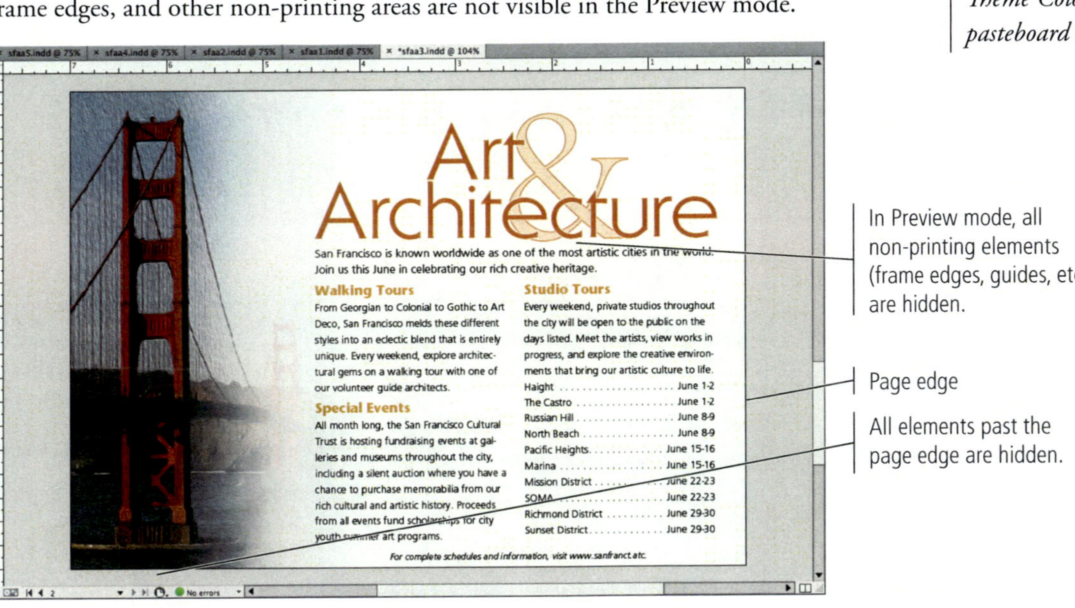

In Preview mode, all non-printing elements (frame edges, guides, etc.), are hidden.

Page edge

All elements past the page edge are hidden.

6. **Click the Screen Mode button at the bottom of the Tools panel and choose Bleed from the pop-up menu.**

   This menu has the same options as the button in the Application/Menu bar. As you will learn throughout this book, there is almost always more than one way to accomplish a particular goal in InDesign.

   The Bleed screen mode is an extension of the Preview mode; it shows an extra area (which was defined when the document was originally set up) around the page edge. This bleed area is a required part of print document design — objects that are supposed to print right up to the edge of the page must extend past the page edge, usually 1/8" or more. (Bleed requirements and setup are explained in Project 1: Letterhead Design.)

7. **Using either Screen Mode button, choose the Presentation mode.**

   Presentation mode fills the entire screen with the active spread. By default, the area around the page is solid black; you can press W to change the surround to white or press G to change it to neutral gray. In Presentation mode, clicking anywhere on the screen shows the next spread; Shift-clicking shows the previous spread.

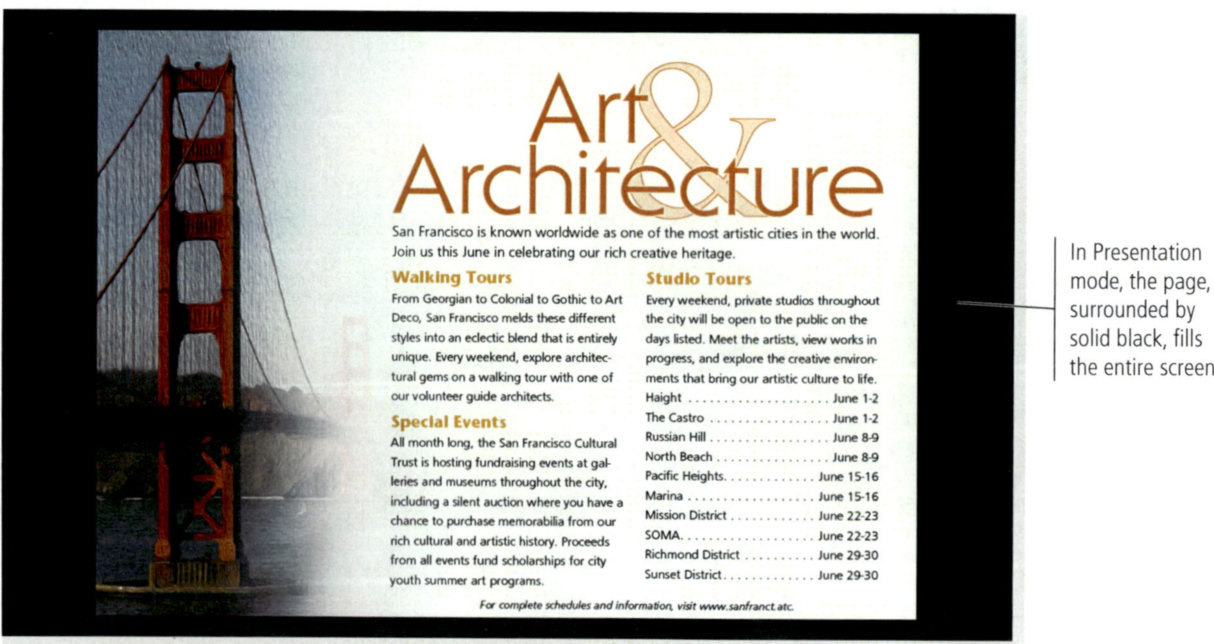

8. **Press ESC to exit Presentation mode.**

9. **Click the Close button on the active document tab.**

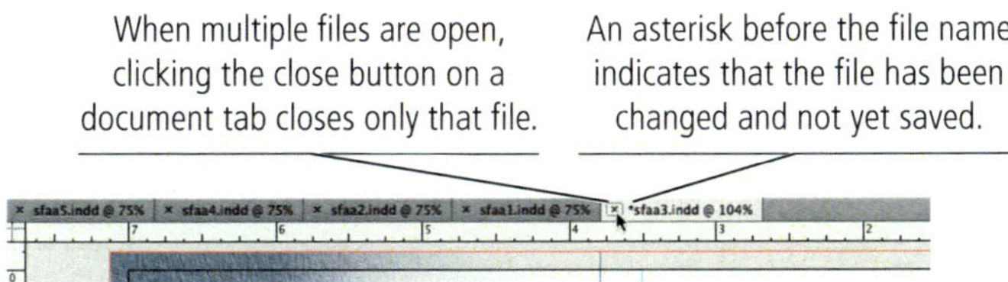

10. **Click Don't Save when asked if you want to save changes to sfaa3.indd.**

    By rotating the spread view on Page 2, the file has technically been changed. InDesign automatically asks if you want to save any file that has been changed before closing it.

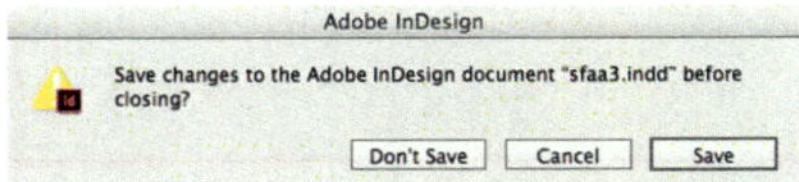

11. **Macintosh users: Click the Close button in the top-left corner of the Application frame.**

    Closing the Macintosh Application frame does not quit the application.

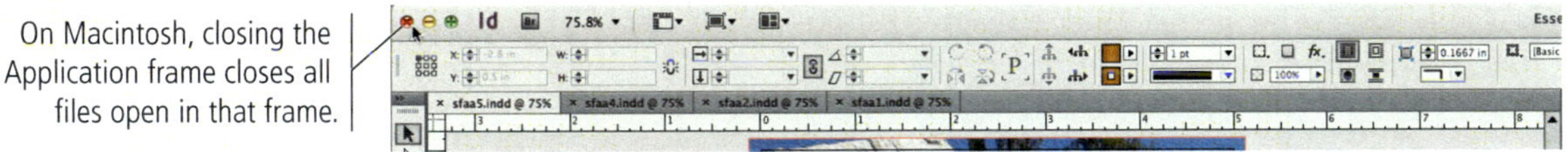

Windows users: Click the Close button on each open document tab to close the remaining files.

Clicking the Close button on the Windows Application frame (Menu bar) closes all open files *and* quits the application. To close open files *without* quitting, you have to manually close each open file, or Control/right-click any of the document tabs and choose Close All.

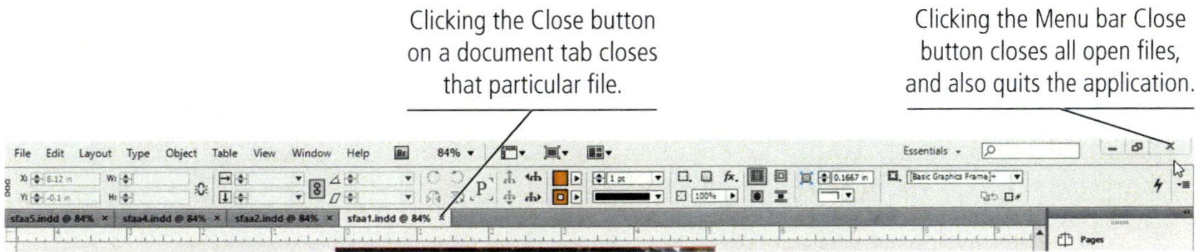

project 1

Letterhead Design

Your client, Amelia Crowe, is a local photographer. She hired you to create a letterhead design that incorporates her personal logo and a set of images representing the kind of work she does. She is going to have the letterhead printed commercially so she can use it to print letters, invoices, and other business correspondence.

This project incorporates the following skills:

- ❑ Creating a new file to meet defined project requirements
- ❑ Using the basic InDesign drawing tools to develop visual interest
- ❑ Selecting objects and object contents
- ❑ Creating and formatting basic text attributes
- ❑ Placing and manipulating external graphics files
- ❑ Printing a desktop proof sample

Project Meeting

client comments

Until now, I've just added my logo and address at the top of a Word document whenever I sent out correspondence. My business has been growing lately, and I want something more professional and more indicative of my work in photographing urban architecture and natural landscapes.

I sent you my logo, which was created in Adobe Illustrator. I also selected a bunch of images that I really like; I want to include at least a few of those on the letterhead to give people an idea of my work.

Can you get my contact information from my email sig file, or do I need to send that to you as a separate document?

art director comments

I've looked over the client's images, and I think we should use all of them. Since she's a photographer, a filmstrip across the bottom of the page will make a nice container; InDesign has everything you need to create the necessary graphics directly on the page layout. I already sized the photos down to thumbnails that should be close to the right size, so you won't have to manipulate the actual image files.

I also copied the client's contact info into a file for you. Since she specifically mentioned two areas of photographic specialty, I want you to include the words "urban architecture & natural landscapes" as a tag line.

It might feel like there's a lot involved in creating this piece, but it's not too complicated. The client liked the initial sketch, so putting in the effort at this point will be worth it.

project objectives

To complete this project, you will:

- ❑ Create a new document based on the requirements of a commercial printer.
- ❑ Place ruler guides to define "safe" areas on the page.
- ❑ Draw basic shapes using native InDesign tools
- ❑ Edit shapes using the Pathfinder and Align panels
- ❑ Work with anchor points and handles to create a complex shape
- ❑ Apply color to fills and strokes
- ❑ Create and format basic text elements
- ❑ Import external text and graphics files
- ❑ Print a desktop proof

Stage 1 Setting up the Workspace

The best way to start any new project is to prepare your workspace. As you learned in the Interface chapter, InDesign gives you extensive control over your workspace — you can choose where to place panels, whether to collapse or expand open panels, and even to save workspaces with sets of panels in specific locations. Because workspace issues are largely a matter of personal preference, we tell you what tools to use, but we don't tell you where to keep the various panels. Many of our screen captures show floating panels so that we can maximize the available space and clearly focus on a specific issue. Likewise, we typically don't tell you what view percentage to use; you should use whatever you are comfortable with to accomplish the specific goal of an exercise.

Define a New Layout File

Some production-related concerns will dictate how you design a letterhead. In general, there are two ways to print letterhead: one-offs on a desktop laser or inkjet printer, or commercially in large quantities. (The first method typically involves creating a letterhead template, which you then use to write and print letters from directly within InDesign — a fairly common practice among graphic designers.)

If letterhead is being printed commercially, it's probably being printed with multiple copies on a large press sheet, from which the individual letterhead sheets will be cut. Most commercial printing happens this way. This type of printing typically means that design elements can run right off the edge of the sheet, called **bleeding**.

If you're designing for a printer that can only run letter-size paper, you have to allow enough of a margin area for your printer to hold the paper as it moves through the device (called the **gripper margin**); in this case, you can't design with bleeds.

The most basic process in designing a layout is creating a new InDesign file. The New Document dialog box has a large number of options, and the following exercise explains all of those. Don't be overwhelmed by the length of this process; in later projects, we simply tell you what settings to define without re-explaining every field.

Note:

Some desktop printers have a minimum margin at the page edges; you're usually safe with 3/8". Many newer inkjet printers have the capability to print 8.5 × 11" with full bleed. Consult your printer documentation to be sure.

1. **Download IDCC_RF_Project1.zip from the Student Files web page.**

2. **Expand the ZIP archive in your WIP folder (Macintosh) or copy the archive contents into your WIP folder (Windows).**

   This results in a folder named **Crowe**, which contains all of the files you need for this project. You should also use this folder to save the files you create in this project.

   If necessary, refer to Page 1 of the Interface chapter for specific information on expanding or accessing the required resource files.

3. **In InDesign, choose File>New>Document.**

   The New Document dialog box opens with the last-used document preset; if no user-defined preset exists, the dialog box opens with the settings that are stored in the Default preset.

   Some of the options we define in the following steps might already be reflected in the New Document dialog box, but we can't be sure because someone might have modified the default settings on your computer. If something is already set to the value we define, simply leave that value as is.

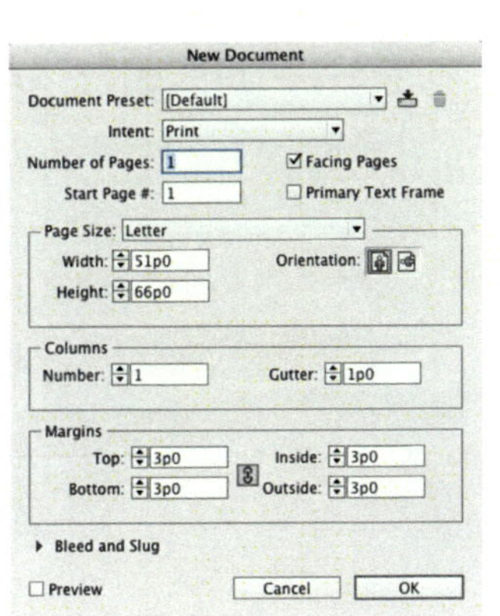

Note:

You can create a new file by pressing Command/Control-N.

4. **Choose Print in the Intent menu.**

InDesign uses picas as the default unit of measurement for print documents; measurements in this dialog box are shown in picas and points, using the "ApB" notation (for A picas and B points). Colors in a print-intent document default to the CMYK color model (see Page 55 in this project).

If you choose Web or Digital Publishing, InDesign changes the default unit of measurement to pixels, which is more appropriate for Web design. Colors in a Web-intent document default to the RGB color model.

> *Note:*
>
> *Picas are the measuring units traditionally used in typography; they are still used by many people in the graphic communications industry.*
>
> *1 point = 1/72 inch*
>
> *12 points = 1 pica*
>
> *1 pica = 1/6 inch*
>
> *6 picas = 1 inch*

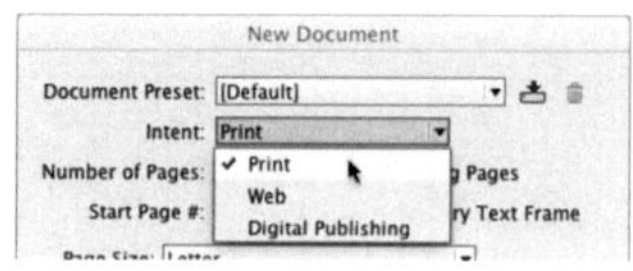

5. **Set the Number of Pages field to 1.**

A letterhead is a single page, usually printed on only one side. A one-sided, one-page document needs only a single layout page in the InDesign file.

6. **Set the Start Page # field to 1.**

This option is useful when you work with multi-page files. Odd-numbered pages always appear on the right, as you see in any book or magazine; you can define an even-numbered starting page number to force the first page of a layout to the left. (This will make more sense when you begin working with longer documents in Project 4: Realtor Collateral Booklet.)

> *Note:*
>
> *You work extensively with facing pages starting in Project 4.*

7. **Uncheck the Facing Pages check box.**

Facing pages are used when a printed job will be read left to right like a book — with Page 1 starting on the right, then Page 2 facing Page 3, and so on. Facing-page layouts are based on **spreads**, which are pairs of left-right pages as you flip through a book (e.g., Page 6 facing Page 7).

8. **Uncheck the Primary Text Frame option.**

When this option is checked, InDesign creates a text frame that automatically fills the area created by the defined page margins. A letterhead design primarily focuses on the area outside of the margins, so you don't need to add a primary text frame to this file.

9. **Choose Letter in the Page Size menu.**

This menu includes a number of common sizes based on the selected intent. Choosing any of these options automatically changes the width and height fields to match the selected size.

> *Note:*
>
> *Choosing Custom in the Page Size menu has no real effect. This setting is automatically reflected as soon as you change the Width or Height field from the standard measurements.*

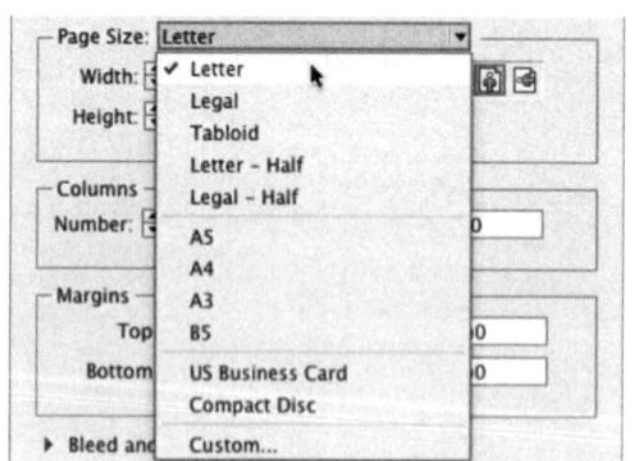

10. **Choose the Portrait Orientation option.**

Portrait documents are higher than they are wide; **landscape** documents are wider than they are high. If you click the orientation option that is not currently selected, the Width and Height values are automatically reversed.

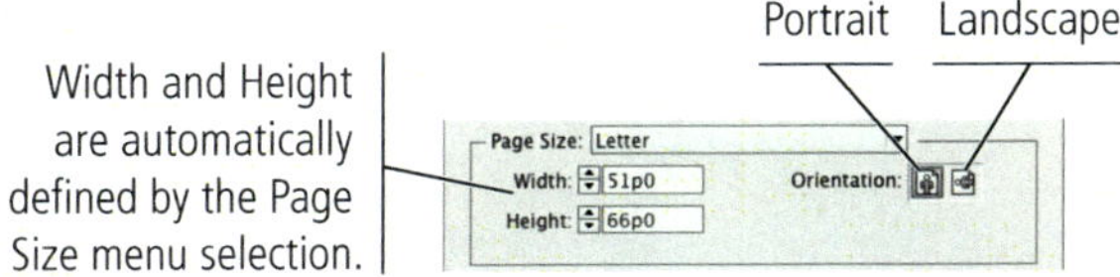

11. **At the bottom of the dialog box, check the Preview option.**

When this option is active, you can see the result of your choices (behind the dialog box) before you click OK to create the new file.

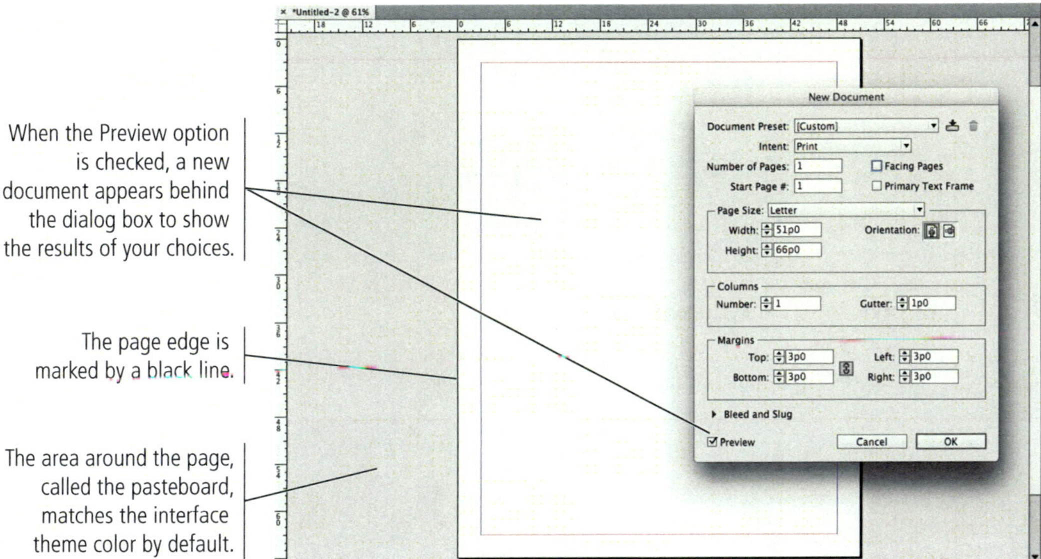

12. **If the chain icon between the Margin fields shows two connected links, click the icon to break the link between the fields.**

When the chain icon is active (connected links or highlighted dark gray), all four margin fields will be the same; changing one field changes all margin values to the same value. For this project, you need to define different values for the top and bottom than for the left and right, so you need to unlink (unconstrain) the fields if they are currently linked.

13. **Highlight the first Margins field (Top) and type 1.25".**

Even though the default measurement is picas, you can type values in any unit as long as you type the appropriate unit along with the value; InDesign makes the necessary conversion for you, so the values will still be displayed in the default units.

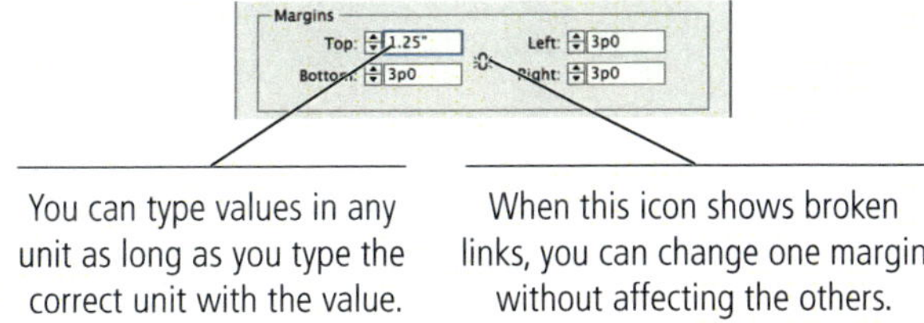

If you enter a value in a unit other than the default, you have to include the alternate unit. This technique works in dialog boxes and panels — anywhere that you can enter a measurement.

Note:

When you work with non-facing pages, the Inside and Outside margin fields change to Left and Right respectively. Technically, non-facing pages do not have an inside (spine edge) or outside (face or trim edge), so there are only left and right sides.

14. Press Tab to move to the Bottom field.

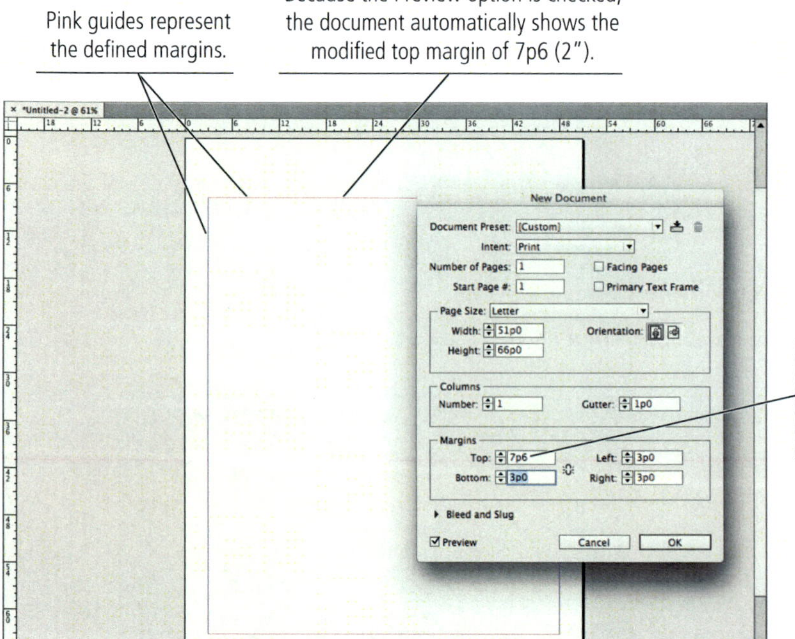

Note:

You can tab through the fields of most dialog boxes and panels in InDesign. Press Shift-Tab to move the highlight to the previous field in the tab order.

15. Change the Bottom field to 2″, then press Tab two times.

The first time you press Tab from the Bottom field highlights the chain icon. You have to press Tab a second time to highlight the Left field.

16. Change the Left field to 1″, press Tab, and then change the Right field to 1″.

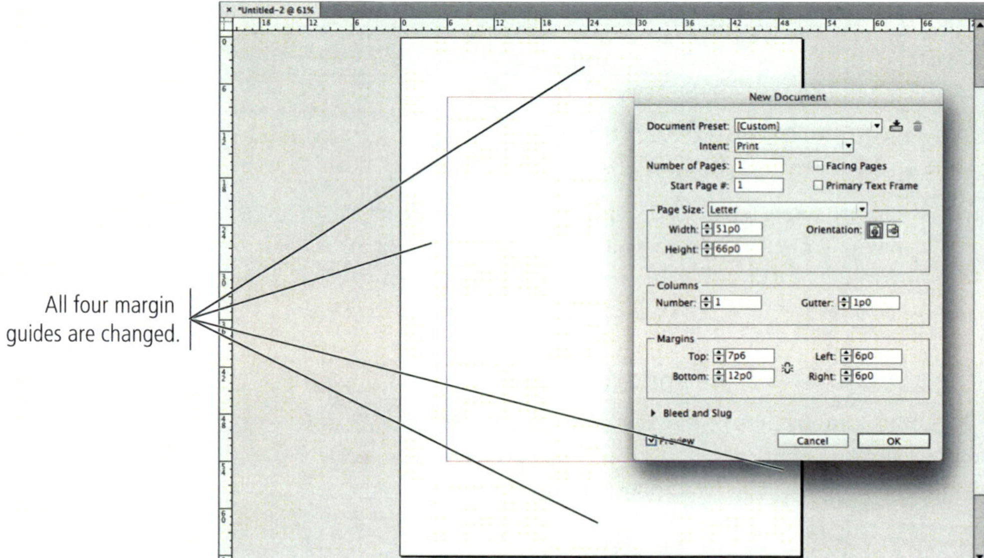

17. **Click the arrow button to the left of the Bleed and Slug heading.**

18. **Make sure the chain icon to the right of the Bleed fields is active (unbroken links), then change the first Bleed field to `0.125"` (the decimal equivalent of 1/8). Press Tab to apply the new Bleed value to all four sides.**

    The letterhead for this project will be printed commercially; the printer said the design can safely bleed on all four sides, and its equipment requires a 1/8″ bleed allowance. In this case, you want all four edges to have the same bleed, so the chain icon should be active to constrain all four Bleed fields to the same value.

19. **Make sure all four Slug fields are set to `0`.**

    A **slug** is an area outside of the bleed, where designers typically add job information that will not appear in the final printed piece. (You'll use this slug area in Project 5: Ireland Travel Brochure.)

    You don't need to type the full "0p0" notation when you change measurements using the default units. Zero pica is still zero, so you don't need to worry about converting units.

Note:

*A **slug** is an element entirely outside the page area, but included in the final output. The slug area can be used for file/plate information, special registration marks, color bars, and/or other elements that need to be printed on the press sheet, but do not appear within the job area.*

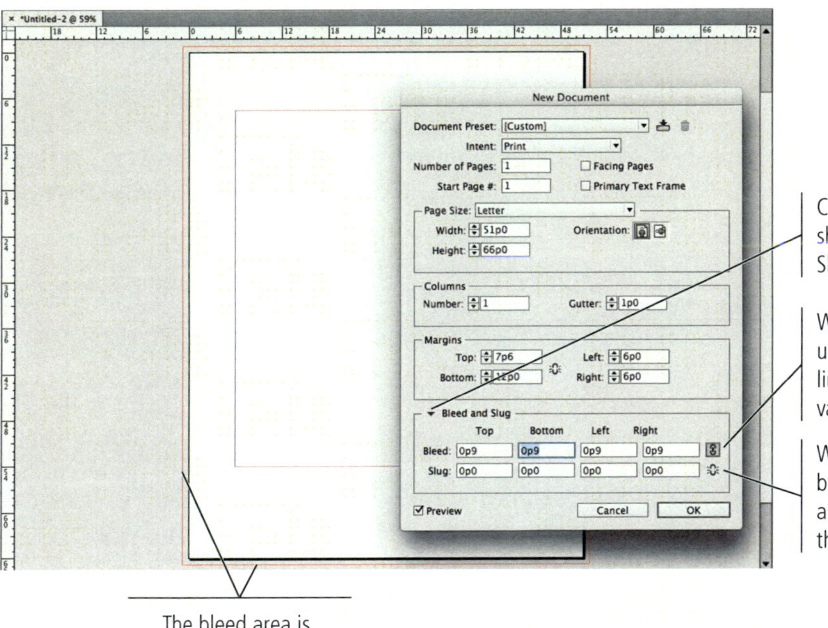

Click this button to show the Bleed and Slug options.

When this icon shows two unbroken links, changing any linked field will apply the same value to the other three fields.

When a chain icon shows two broken links, you can change any one field without affecting the other related fields.

The bleed area is represented by a red line.

20. **Click OK to create the new document.**

    The document appears, filling the available space in the document window. Your view percentage might appear different than what you see in our images.

21. **Choose File>Save As. In the Save As dialog box, navigate to your `WIP>Crowe` folder as the target location for saving the file.**

    The Save As dialog box follows a system-standard format. Macintosh and Windows users see slightly different options, but the basic InDesign functionality is the same.

22. Change the file name (in the Save As field) to identity.indd and click Save.

If the Hide Extension option is checked at the bottom of the dialog box, the ".indd" will not appear in the file name.

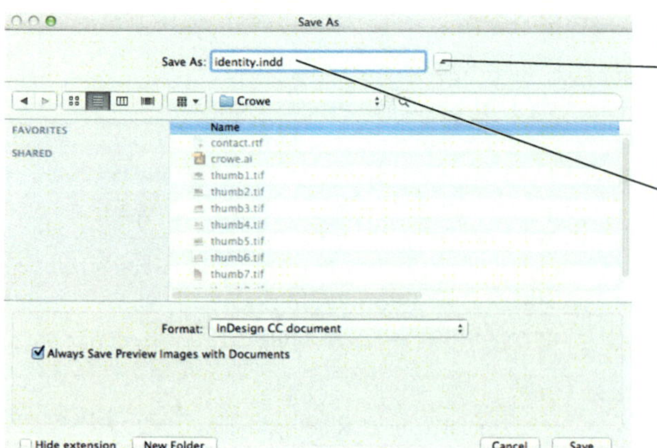

Click here if you don't see the full navigation options on Macintosh.

The extension ".indd" is automatically added to the file name.

> *Note:*
>
> *The first time you save a file, the Save command opens the same dialog box as the File>Save As command. After saving the file once, you can use Save to save changes to the existing file, or use Save As to create an additional file under a new file name.*

23. Continue to the next exercise.

Understanding Document Presets

INDESIGN FOUNDATIONS

A **preset** stores groups of common settings; you define a preset once, and then you can access the same group of settings later with a single click. You'll often use this concept while building InDesign documents — when you use text styles, table styles, object styles, and output documents for printing.

If you frequently define the same document settings, you can save those choices as a preset so that you can create the same document settings with minimal repetition. Clicking the Save Document Preset button in the New Document dialog box opens a secondary dialog box where you can name the preset. When you return to the New Document dialog box, your new preset appears as the selection in the Document Preset menu. Any time you need to create a file with the same settings, you can choose the saved preset from this menu.

Click here to save a new preset.

You can access and manage document presets in the File menu. If you choose one of the existing presets in the menu, the New Document dialog box opens, defaulting to the values in the preset that you called (instead of defaulting to the application-default letter-size page). All the settings you saved in the preset automatically reflect in the dialog box. You can also create, edit, and manage presets by choosing Define in the Document Presets submenu; this opens a dialog box that lists the existing presets.

- Click New to open the New Document Preset dialog box, which is basically the same as the New Document dialog box, except the Preset menu is replaced with a field where you can type the preset name instead of clicking the Save Preset button.
- Select a preset and click Edit to change the preset's associated options.
- Select a preset and click Delete to remove the preset from the application.
- Click Load to import presets created on another computer.
- Click Save to save a preset (with the extension ".dcst") so that it can be sent to and used on another computer.

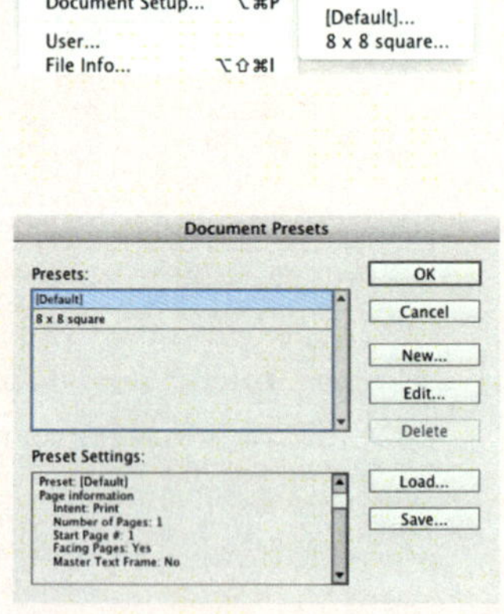

Create Ruler Guides

In addition to the margin and bleed guides that you defined when you created the document, you can also place ruler guides to mark whatever other positions you need to identify in your layout.

The **live area** is the "safe" area inside the page edge where important design elements should reside. Because printing and trimming are mechanical processes, there will always be some variation — however slight. Elements placed too close to the page edge run the risk of being accidentally trimmed off. The printer for this job recommended a 1/8″ live-area margin. You defined the margins for this file to describe the area that would typically occupy the content of a letter; in this exercise you will create ruler guides to mark the live area.

> ***Note:***
>
> *You should become familiar with the common fraction-to-decimal equivalents:*
>
> *1/8 = 0.125*
>
> *1/4 = 0.25*
>
> *3/8 = 0.375*
>
> *1/2 = 0.5*
>
> *5/8 = 0.625*
>
> *3/4 = 0.75*
>
> *7/8 = 0.875*

1. **With identity.indd open, choose View>Show Rulers if you don't see rulers at the top and left edges of the document window.**

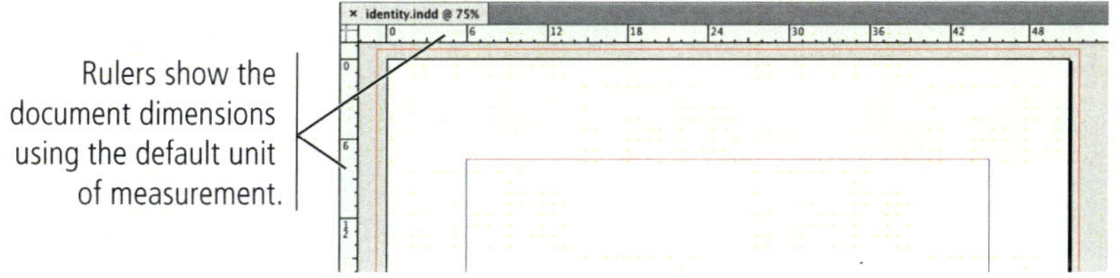

2. **Open the Units & Increments pane of the Preferences dialog box (from the InDesign menu on Macintosh or the Edit menu on Windows).**

   Since most people (in the United States, at least) think in terms of inches, we use inches throughout the projects in this book.

3. **In the Ruler Units area, choose Inches in both the Horizontal and Vertical menus, and then click OK.**

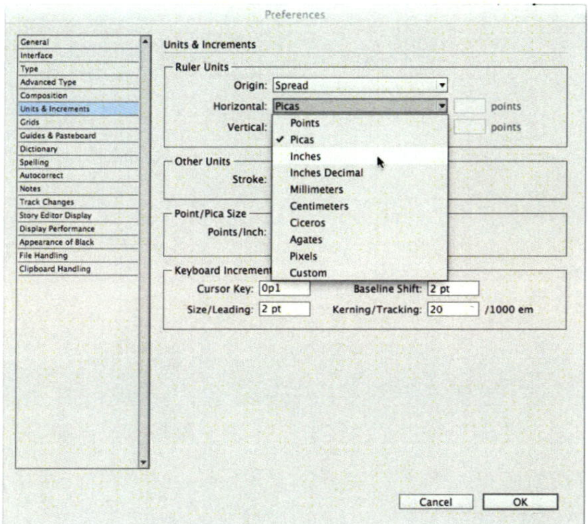

   When you return to the document window, the rulers now display in inches.

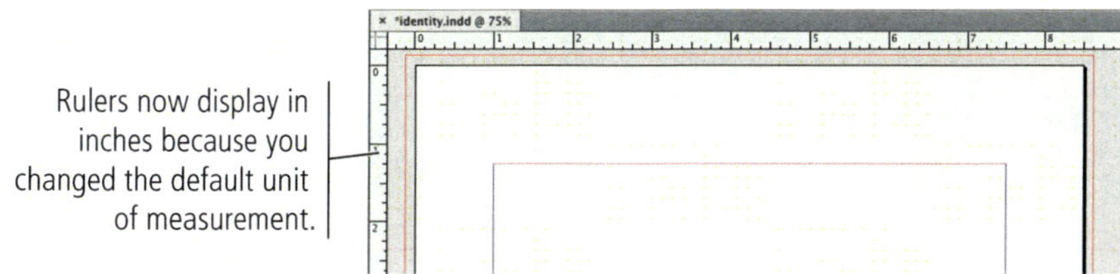

4. **Click the horizontal page ruler (at the top of the document window) and drag down until the cursor feedback indicates that the guide is positioned at Y: 0.125″. With the cursor inside the page area, release the mouse button.**

   As you drag, cursor feedback shows the current position of the guide you are placing; this makes it very easy to precisely position guides.

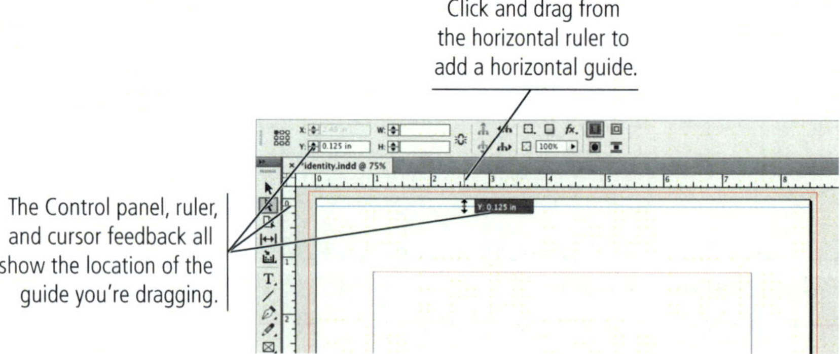

5. **Click the horizontal page ruler again and drag a guide to Y: 10.875″.**

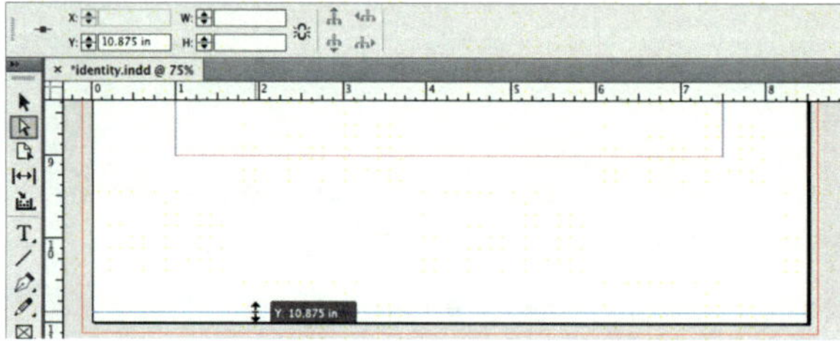

6. **Click the vertical ruler and drag a guide to X: 0.125″.**

   Watch the marker on the horizontal ruler to judge the guide's position.

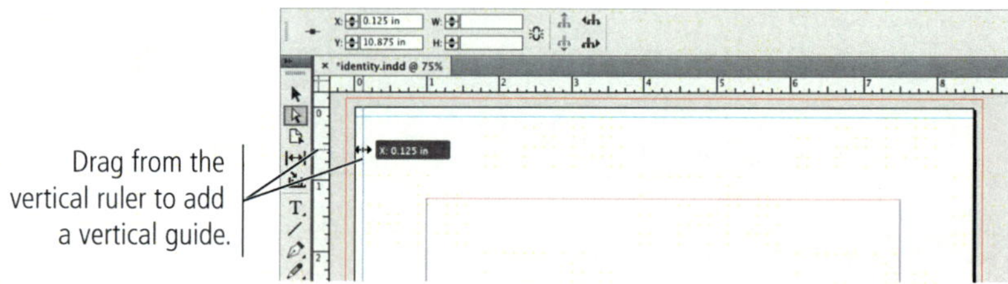

7. **Click the vertical ruler again and drag a second vertical guide to X: 8.375″.**

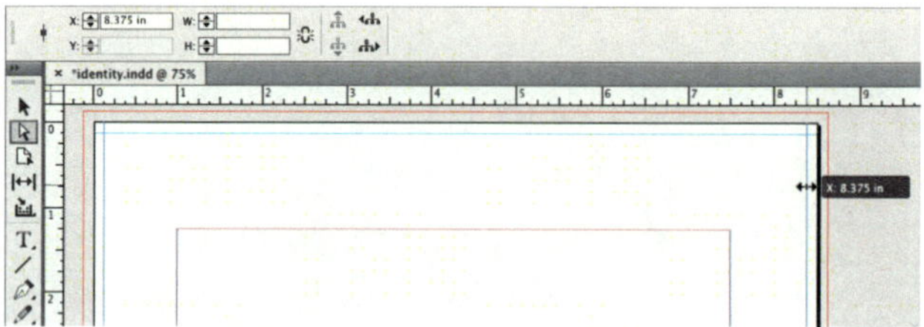

8. **Using the Selection tool, click anywhere in the document space to deselect the guide you just created.**

9. **Save the file and continue to the next stage of the project.**

Note:

Y values define vertical (top-to-bottom) position; X values define horizontal (left-to-right) position.

Note:

If you drag a guide outside of the page edge, the guide will extend across the entire pasteboard. You can also press Command/Control while dragging a guide onto the page to extend the guide the entire width of the pasteboard.

Note:

If the Control panel is not visible, you can show it by choosing Window>Control.

Note:

You can click the intersection of the rulers and drag to reposition the zero point away from the top-left corner of the page. If you do reposition the zero point, you can double-click the ruler intersection to reset the original zero point.

Stage 2 Creating Basic Page Elements

Based on the approved sketch, the client's letterhead includes several elements:

- A "filmstrip" graphic to frame a number of thumbnails of the client's work
- A logo that was created in Adobe Illustrator
- A tag line, separated from the logo with a curved line
- Contact information, which was provided to you as a rich-text file
- Actual thumbnails of the client's photographs, which were supplied to you as ready-to-print TIFF files.

Other than the logo and the supplied photos, you need to create these elements directly in the InDesign file. Fortunately, the software includes sophisticated drawing tools that can create everything you need. Before you begin, however, you should understand the different types of elements that you will encounter when you design files in InDesign.

Vector graphics are composed of mathematical descriptions of a series of lines and shapes. Vector graphics are resolution independent; they can be freely scaled, and they are automatically output at the resolution of the output device. The shapes that you create in Adobe InDesign, or in drawing applications such as Adobe Illustrator, are vector graphics.

Raster images, such as photographs or files created in Adobe Photoshop, are made up of a grid of independent pixels (rasters or bits) in rows and columns (called a bitmap). Raster files are resolution dependent — their resolution is determined when you scan, photograph, or otherwise create the file. You can typically reduce raster images, but you cannot enlarge them without losing image quality.

Line art is a type of raster image that is made up entirely of 100% solid areas; the pixels in a line-art image have only two options: they can be all black or all white. Examples of line art are UPC bar codes or pen-and-ink drawings.

Create Basic Frames

Although much drawing and illustration work is done in a dedicated illustration program such as Adobe Illustrator, you can use the drawing tools in InDesign to create vector artwork. In fact, the drawing tools in InDesign are actually a limited subset of the more comprehensive Illustrator toolset, which means you can create fairly sophisticated artwork entirely within the layout application. In this exercise, you are going to use the basic InDesign drawing tools to create a filmstrip graphic, which will serve as the background for the client's image samples.

1. **With identity.indd open, choose View>Grids & Guides>Smart Guides to make sure this option is toggled on. If the option is already checked, move the cursor away from the menu and click to dismiss it.**

   Smart guides are a useful function of the application, making it easy to create and precisely align objects. Smart guides show the dimensions of an object when you create it; the position of an object when you drag it; the edge and center position of nearby objects; and the distance between nearby similar objects.

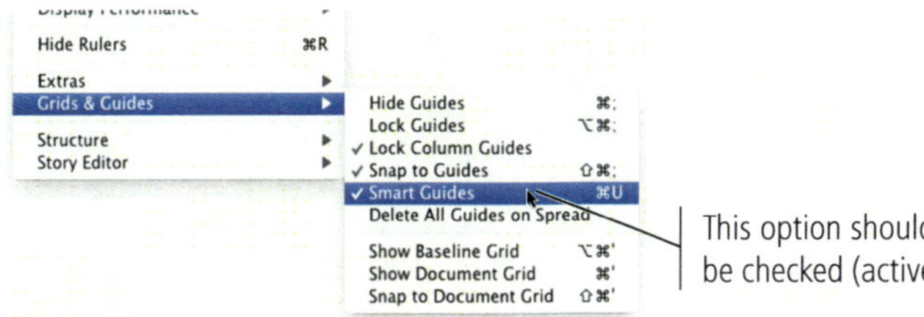

Note:

You can turn off specific Smart Guide functions in the Guides & Pasteboard pane of the Preferences dialog box.

2. **Click the button at the right end of the Control panel to open the panel Options menu.**

3. **If the Dimensions Include Stroke Weight option is checked, choose that item to toggle the option off.**

   When this option is active, the size of an object's stroke is factored as part of the overall object size. Consider, for example, a frame that is 72 points wide by 72 points high with a 1-point stroke. If you remove the stroke from the frame, the frame would then be only 70 points by 70 points.

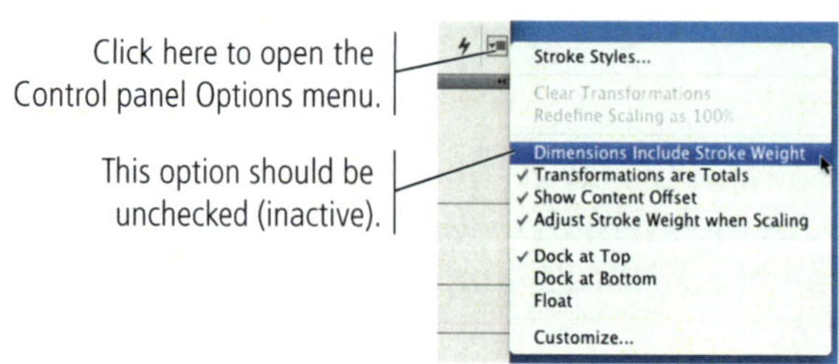

> ***Note:***
>
> *These options remember the last-used settings.*

4. **Choose the Rectangle tool in the Tools panel.**

   If you don't see the Rectangle tool, click and hold the default shape tool until the nested tools appear; slide over and down to select the Rectangle tool.

> ***Note:***
>
> *Tools with nested options default to show the last-used variation in the main Tools panel.*

5. **Click the Default Fill and Stroke button at the bottom of the Tools panel.**

   In InDesign, the default fill is None, and the default stroke is 1-pt black.

6. **Click anywhere on the page, and drag down and right to draw a rectangle that is about 1″ high and 2″ wide.**

   As you draw, cursor feedback shows the size of the shape you are creating.

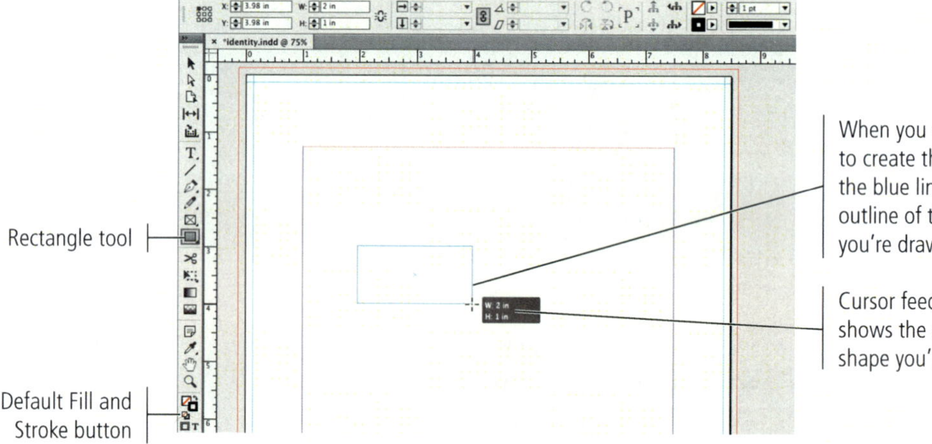

7. **Release the mouse button to create the rectangle.**

Every shape you create in an InDesign document has a **bounding box**, which is a non-printing rectangle that marks the outer dimensions of the shape. (Even a circle has a square bounding box, marking the largest height and width of the object.) The bounding box has eight handles, which you can drag to change the size of the rectangle. If you can see an object's bounding box handles, that object is selected.

> *Note:*
>
> *Press Shift while drawing a shape to constrain the horizontal and vertical dimensions of the shape (in other words, to create a perfect square or circle).*

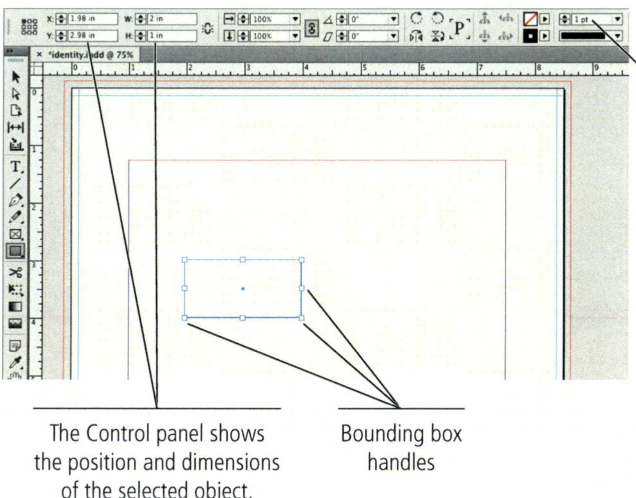

8. **At the bottom of the Tools panel, click the Swap Fill and Stroke button.**

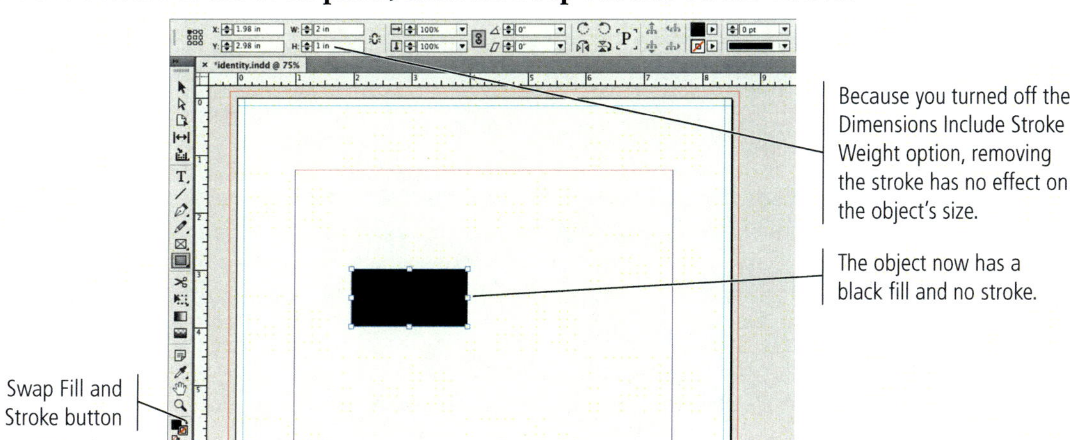

9. **At the left end of the Control panel, select the top-left reference point.**

The Control panel is context-sensitive, which means different options are available depending on what is selected in the document. This panel consolidates the most common options from multiple InDesign panels.

The **reference point** determines how transformations will occur (in other words, which point of the object will remain in place if you change one of the position or dimension values). These points correspond to the object's bounding box handles, as well as to the object's exact center point.

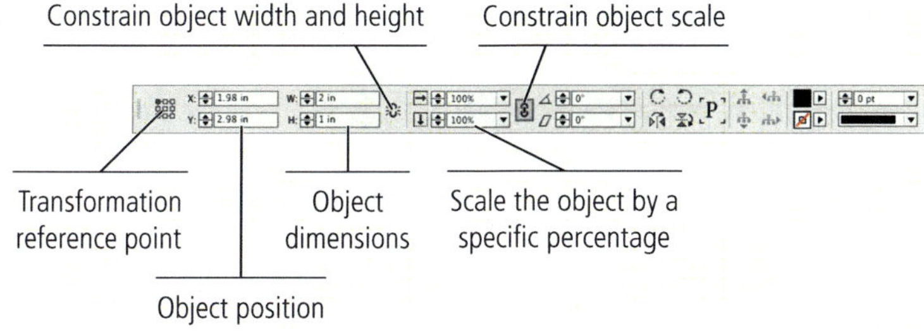

The Control Panel in Depth

The Control panel is one of the most versatile, productive tools in the InDesign workspace, combining all of the most common formatting options into a single, compact format across the top of the workspace. It is context sensitive, which means different options are available depending on what is selected in the layout. Finally, it is customizable, which means you can change the options that are available in the panel.

It is also important to note that the options available in the Control panel might be limited by the active workspace, as well as by the width of your monitor or Application frame.

Essentials Control panel when a graphics frame is selected:

Essentials Control panel when a text frame is selected:

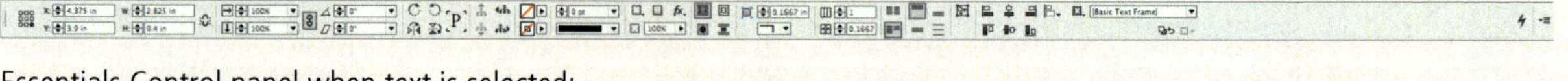

Essentials Control panel when text is selected:

Essentials Control panel when text is selected, using a 13-inch laptop monitor:

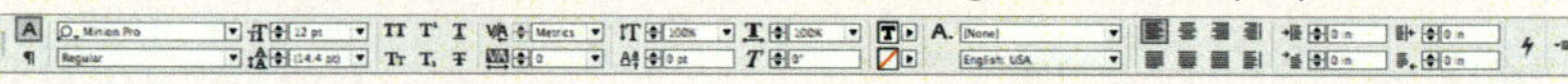

When anything other than text is selected (or nothing is selected), the panel Options menu includes options for controlling the position of the panel (top, bottom, or floating), as well as how transformations affect selected objects:

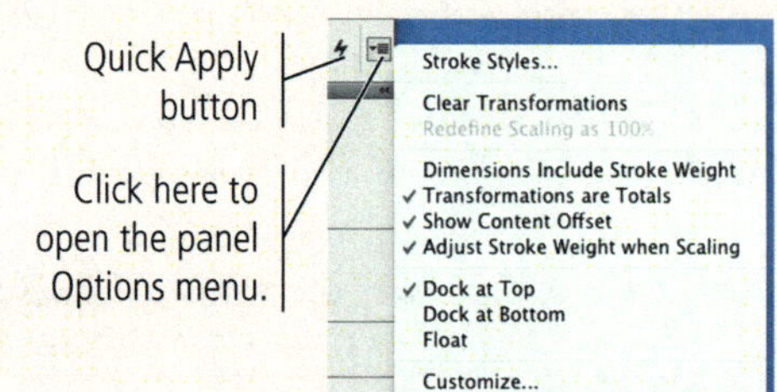

- **Stroke Styles.** This opens a dialog box where you can edit or define custom styles for lines and object strokes.
- **Clear Transformations.** Choosing this option resets an object to its original position (including rotation).
- **Dimensions Include Stroke Weight.** When checked, width and height values include the object width as well as the defined stroke width. For example, if this option is checked, a square that is 72 points wide with a 1-pt stroke would be 73 points wide (using the default stroke position that aligns the stroke on the center of the object edge).
- **Transformations are Totals.** When checked, transformations such as rotation are cumulative for the frame and the frame contents. For example, an image frame is rotated 10°...
  - When Transformations are Totals is checked, the image in the frame also shows 10° rotation; you can change the content rotation to 0° to return the image (but not the frame) to horizontal.
  - When not checked, the image in the frame shows 0° because the content is not rotated relative to its container. You have to rotate the content –10° to return it to horizontal without affecting the frame's rotation.
- **Show Content Offset.** When checked, the Control panel shows X+ and Y+ values for a graphic placed within a frame when the actual graphic (not the frame) is selected.
- **Adjust Stroke Weight when Scaling.** When checked, resizing an object changes the stroke weight proportionally. For example, resizing an object with a 1-pt stroke to 50% results in a 0.5-pt stroke.

Choosing **Customize** in the panel Options menu opens a dialog box where you can define the available options in the panel; anything with a checkmark will be available when it's relevant to the selection in the document.

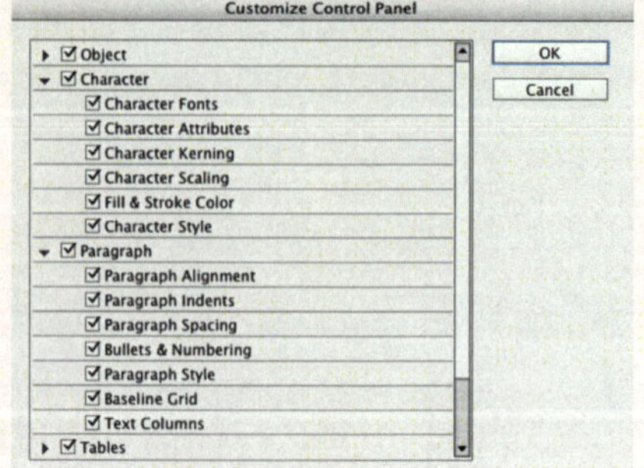

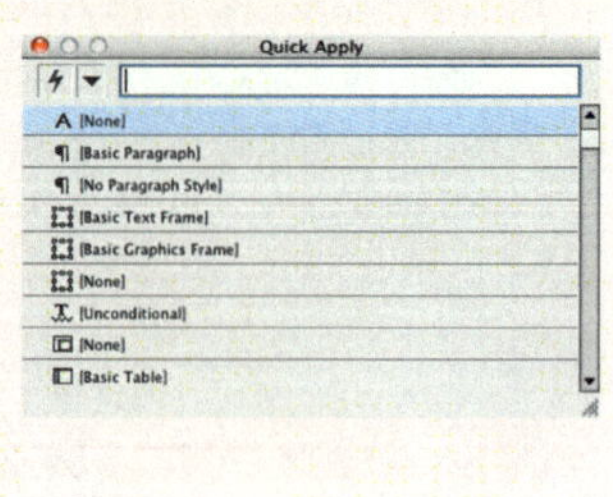

Clicking the Quick Apply button (to the left of the panel Options button) opens a special navigation dialog box. This feature enables you to easily find and apply what you want (menu commands, user-defined styles, and so on) by typing a few characters in the text entry field and then clicking the related item in the list.

10. Highlight the X field in the Control panel and type −0.25, then press Tab to move the highlight to the Y field.

As in dialog boxes, you can use the Tab key to move through the fields in the Control panel. The X and Y fields determine the position of the selected object. X defines the horizontal (left-to-right) position, and Y defines the vertical (top-to-bottom) position.

11. With the Y field highlighted, type 9.5 and then press Return/Enter.

Pressing Return/Enter applies your changes in the Control panel. You can also simply click away from the object to apply the changes, but then you would have to reselect the object to make further changes.

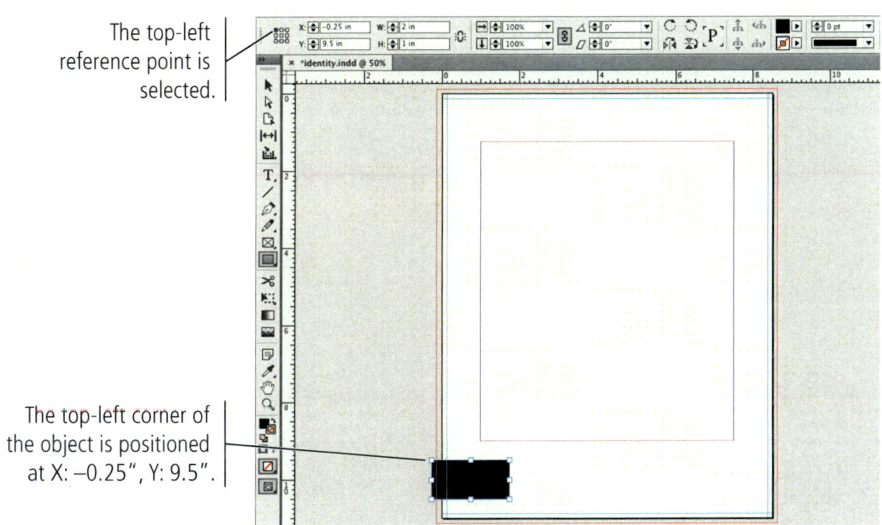

12. In the Control panel, make sure the chain icon for the W and H fields is inactive (not linked). Change the W (width) field to 9″, change the H (height) field to 1.2″, and then press Return/Enter to apply the change.

Remember, you don't need to type the units if you are working with the default units.

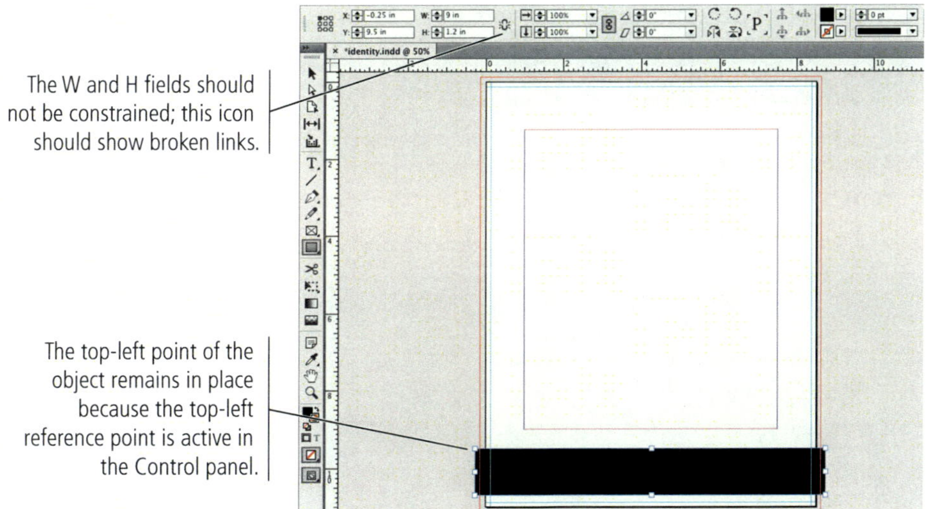

13. Save the file and continue to the next exercise.

Note:

Because inches are now the default unit of measurement for this file, you don't need to type the unit in the field.

Note:

You can use math operators to add (+), subtract (-), divide (/), or multiply (*) existing values in the Control panel. This is useful when you want to move or change a value by a specific amount.

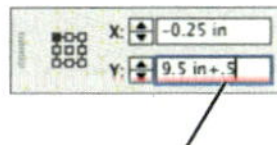

Type +.5 after the value to move the object down half an inch.

Note:

The Transform panel (Window>Object & Layout>Transform) includes the same options that are available in the Control panel when an object is selected with the Selection tool. You can change an object's position or dimensions, scale an object to a specific percentage, and apply rotation or shear to the selected object. The Transform panel Options menu includes the same options that are available in the Control panel Options menu, as well as commands to rotate and flip the selected object.

Create a Rounded Rectangle

In addition to basic rectangles, you can create frames with a number of special corner treatments. The Rounded Rectangle tool automatically creates frames with special corners, but you can also easily modify the corners of an existing frame to create the effect you want.

1. **With identity.indd open, make sure the Rectangle tool is active, then zoom into the left end of the black rectangle.**

2. **Press Command/Control, then click away from the existing shape to deselect it.**

   If you don't deselect the existing shape, the changes you make in the next step would affect the selected object.

   Pressing Command/Control temporarily switches to the last-used Selection tool (Selection or Direct Selection). This allows you to easily make selections — or, in this case, deselect an object — without changing the active tool.

   When you click to deselect the active object, be careful that you don't accidentally click a white-filled object instead of the empty page or pasteboard area.

3. **In the Control panel, click the arrow button to the right of the Fill swatch to open the attached Swatches panel. Choose Paper from the pop-up panel.**

   There is a difference between no fill and 0% of a color. Using 0% of a color — or using the Paper color — effectively creates a solid "white" fill. (In printing, solid white areas **knock out** or hide underlying shapes.)

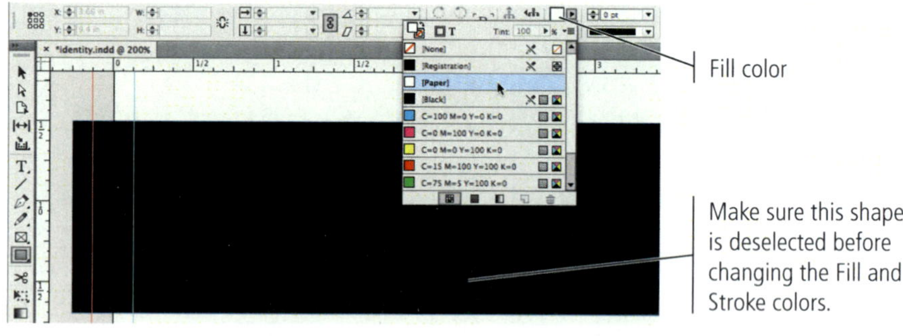

4. **In the Control panel, click the arrow button to the right of the Stroke swatch and choose None from the pop-up panel.**

   The "None" color option essentially removes color from that attribute. Underlying objects will be visible in areas where None is applied.

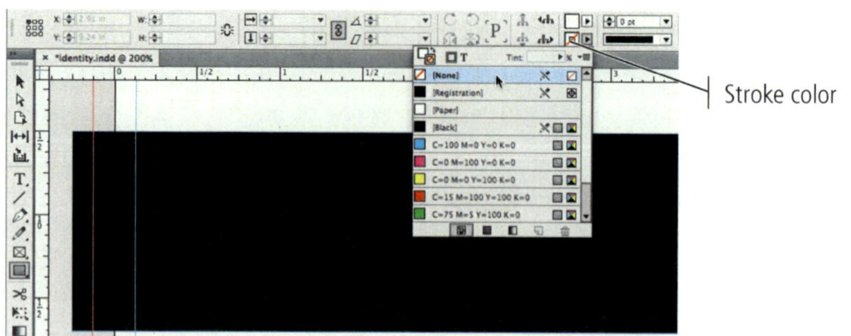

Note:

To deselect objects, you can also choose Edit>Deselect All.

Note:

When an object is selected, changing the fill and stroke values changes those attributes for the selected object. If you change the fill or stroke color value with no object selected, you define the values for the next object you create.

Note:

Paper is basically white, but more accurately named because the paper for a specific job might not be white.

Note:

Changing a fill or stroke attribute when a group is selected affects all objects in the selected group.

5. **Click once on the page to open the Rectangle dialog box.**

   Single-clicking with a shape tool opens a dialog box where you can define specific measurements for the new shape.

6. **In the Rectangle dialog box, set the Width to 0.125″ and the Height to 0.08″, and then click OK.**

   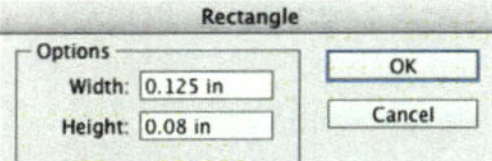

   The new rectangle is placed with the selected reference point where you clicked.

7. **Zoom in so you can more clearly see the small rectangle you just created.**

   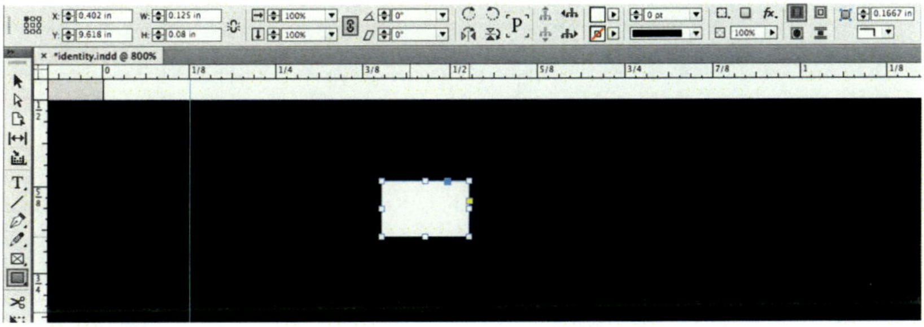

Note:

If you don't see the Corner Shape menu in the Control panel, choose Object>Corner Options to modify the shape of an object's corners. (See Editing Corner Options on Page 40.)

8. **With the new rectangle selected, open the Corner Shape menu in the Control panel and choose the rounded option.**

   Leave the Corner Radius field at its defaut value of 0.1667″ (the equivalent of 1 pica).

   Even though the object now has rounded corners, the **bounding box** still marks the outermost corners of the shape. (You might need to zoom in to see the effect of the new corner shape.)

   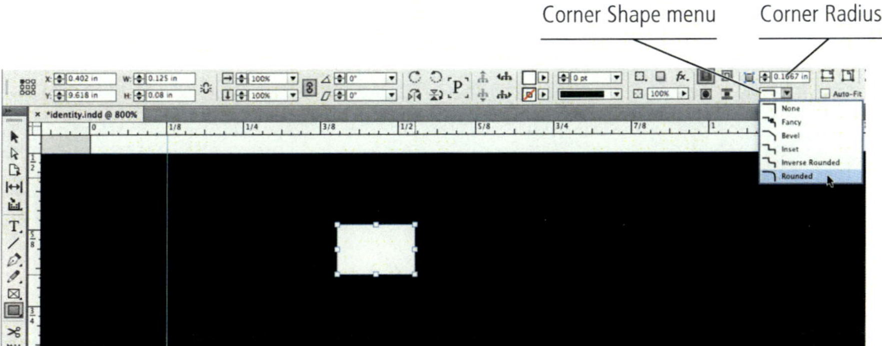

   A rounded-corner rectangle is simply a rectangle with the corners cut at a specific distance from the end (the corner radius). The two sides are connected with one-fourth of a circle, which has a radius equal to the amount of the rounding.

   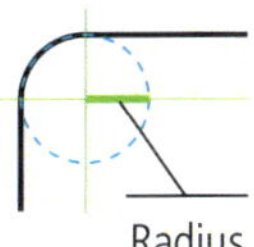

   In this case, the rectangle is so small that the corner radius field is not relevant. The application applied the largest possible radius, which is just large enough to see the effect on the corners of the shape.

9. **Save the file and continue to the next exercise.**

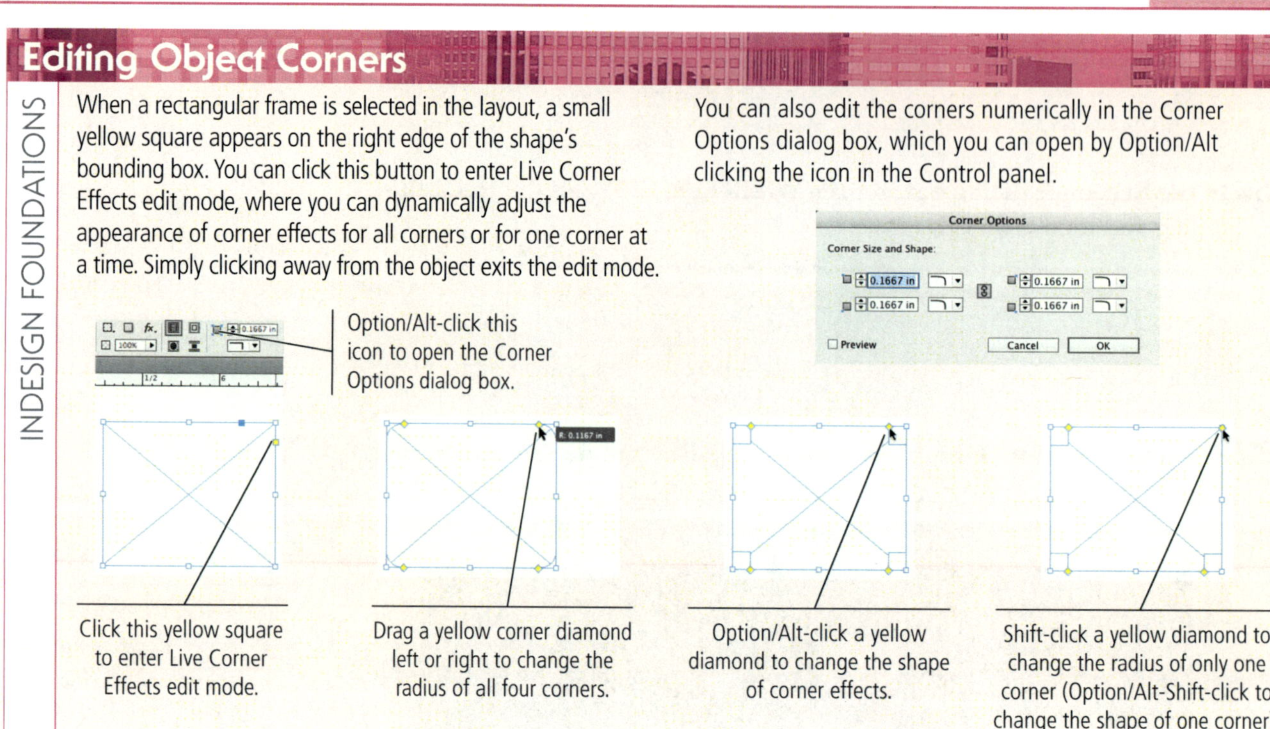

Editing Object Corners

When a rectangular frame is selected in the layout, a small yellow square appears on the right edge of the shape's bounding box. You can click this button to enter Live Corner Effects edit mode, where you can dynamically adjust the appearance of corner effects for all corners or for one corner at a time. Simply clicking away from the object exits the edit mode.

Option/Alt-click this icon to open the Corner Options dialog box.

You can also edit the corners numerically in the Corner Options dialog box, which you can open by Option/Alt clicking the icon in the Control panel.

Click this yellow square to enter Live Corner Effects edit mode.

Drag a yellow corner diamond left or right to change the radius of all four corners.

Option/Alt-click a yellow diamond to change the shape of corner effects.

Shift-click a yellow diamond to change the radius of only one corner (Option/Alt-Shift-click to change the shape of one corner).

Clone, Align, and Distribute Multiple Objects

As you should have already noticed, there is often more than one way to accomplish the same task in InDesign. Aligning multiple objects on a page is no exception. In fact, InDesign offers a number of methods for aligning objects, both to the page and to each other. In this exercise you will explore a number of those options as you create sprocket-hole shapes that will turn the black rectangle into a strip of film.

1. **With identity.indd open, choose the Selection tool in the Tools panel.**

   The Selection tool is used to select entire objects; the Direct Selection tool is used to select parts of objects or the contents of a frame.

2. **Click inside the area of the rounded rectangle, press the Option/Alt key, and drag right. Release the mouse button when the preview shows a small space between the two objects.**

   Pressing Option/Alt as you drag moves a copy of the selected object (called **cloning**). As you drag, a series of green lines mark the top, center, and bottom of the original object. These green lines are a function of InDesign's Smart Guides, which make it easy to align objects to each other by simply dragging.

> ***Note:***
>
> *You can also press Shift to constrain the cloning movement to 45° angles.*

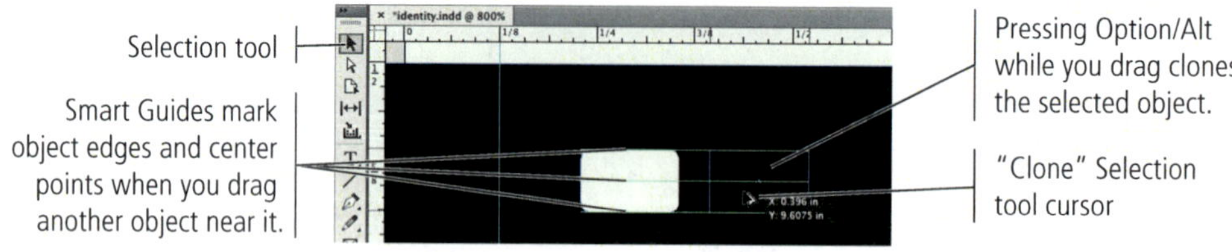

3. **Click the second shape, press Option/Alt, and drag right. Release the mouse button when you see opposing arrows below/between the first and second pair, and the second and third pair of shapes.**

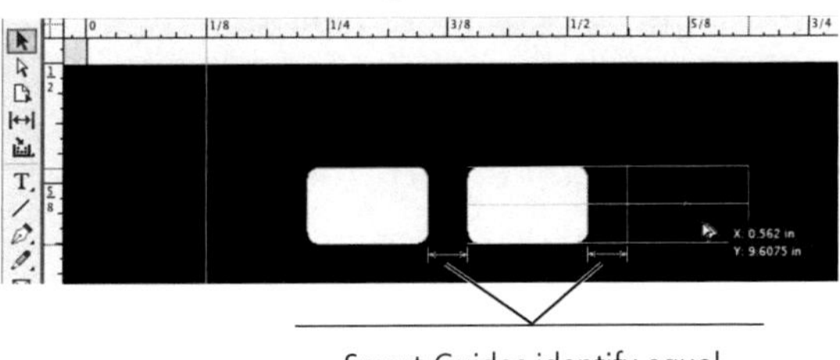

Smart Guides identify equal spacing between multiple objects.

> *Note:*
>
> *Smart Guides also identify equal dimensions when you create a new object near an existing one.*

4. **Press Shift and then click the first and second shapes to add them to the current selection.**

   You can Shift-click an object to select it in addition to the previously selected object(s), or Shift-click an already selected object to deselect it without deselecting other objects.

5. **Click inside the area of any of the selected shapes. Drag the selected objects (the three rounded rectangles) so that a small amount of the black background rectangle is visible above the rounded rectangles, and the left rounded rectangle is centered on the bleed guide.**

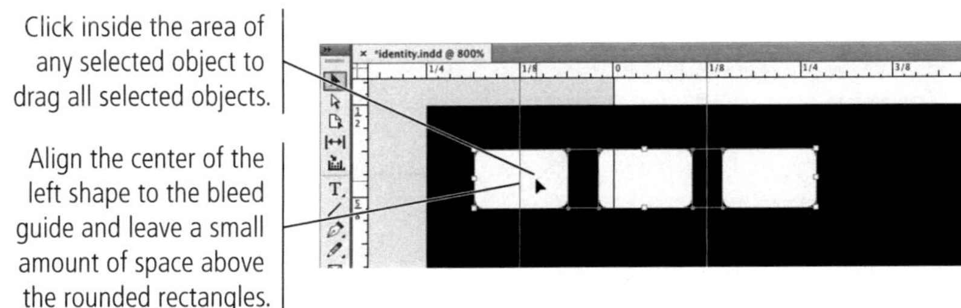

6. **Click away from the active objects to deselect them, then click only the third rounded rectangle. Option/Alt-click and drag right; release the mouse button when the fourth object is evenly spaced with the first three.**

   This step re-establishes the cloning movement as the last-applied transformation.

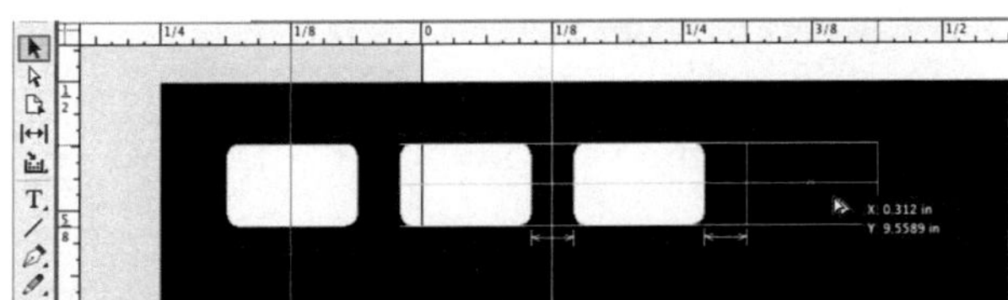

7. **With the fourth object still selected, choose Object>Transform Again>Transform Again.**

   This command applies the last-used transformation to the selected object. Because you used the cloning movement in the previous step, the result is a fifth copy that is spaced at the same distance you moved the copy in Step 6. (The Transform Again command can be used to re-apply rotation, scaling, sizing, and other transformations.)

> *Note:*
>
> *You could also choose Edit>Duplicate, which makes a copy of the selected object using the last-applied movement distance.*

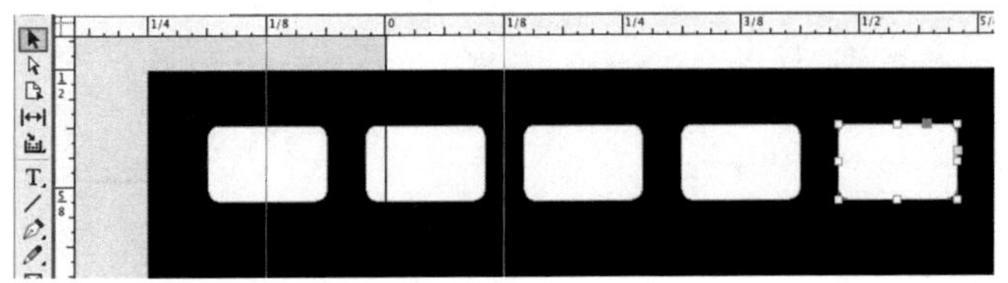

8. **Zoom out so you can see the entire width of the document.**

9. **With the new fifth object selected, choose Edit>Step and Repeat. Activate the Preview option in the resulting dialog box, and type 45 in the Count field.**

   The Step and Repeat dialog box makes a defined number of copies, spaced according to the defined Offset values. By default, these values are set to the last-used movement that you applied in the layout. As you can see, the 50 copies (the original 5 and the 45 that will result from the Step and Repeat process) are all equally spaced, but not enough to fill the filmstrip.

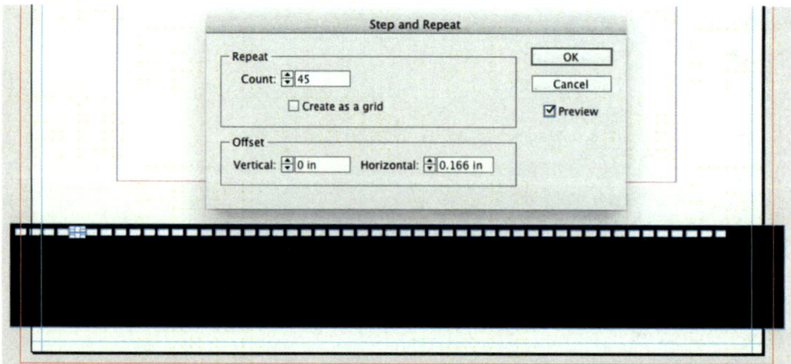

10. **Click OK to make the copies, then click away from the resulting shapes to deselect them.**

11. **Zoom in to the right end of the black rectangle, and select only the right-most rounded rectangle.**

12. **Press Shift, then drag horizontally until the center of the object snaps to the bleed guide.**

    Because this object ends up entirely outside the page edge, the Smart Guides no longer appear to mark exact horizontal movement. Pressing Shift while dragging constrains the movement to 45° angles.

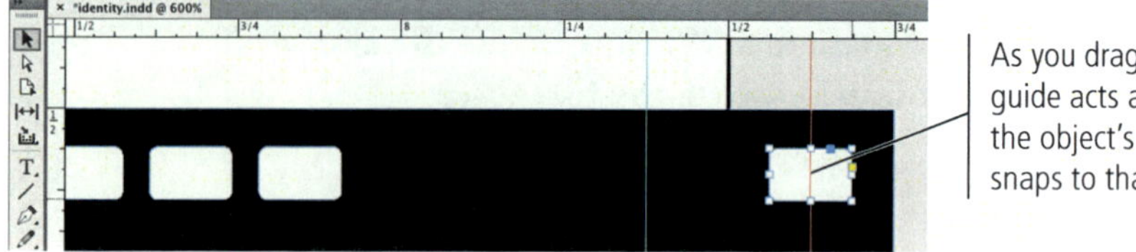

As you drag, the bleed guide acts as a magnet; the object's center point snaps to that guide.

13. **Zoom out so you can see the entire page width, then choose Edit>Select All.**

14. **Press Shift and click the black rectangle to deselect only that object.**

    When you are working with a large number of objects, it is often easier to deselect what you don't want than to select the ones you do want. Steps 13 and 14 show a very easy way to select most, but not all, of the objects on a page.

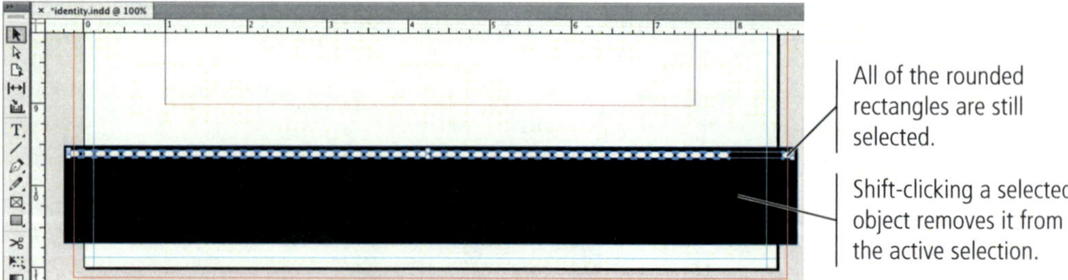

All of the rounded rectangles are still selected.

Shift-clicking a selected object removes it from the active selection.

Aligning and Distributing Objects

You can also use the Align panel to align multiple objects relative to one another, to the page margins, to the page, or to the spread.

The Align Objects options are fairly self explanatory; when multiple objects are selected, the objects align based on the edge(s) or center(s) you click.

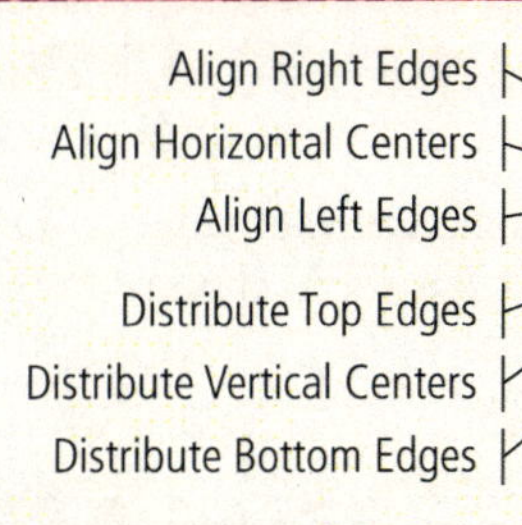
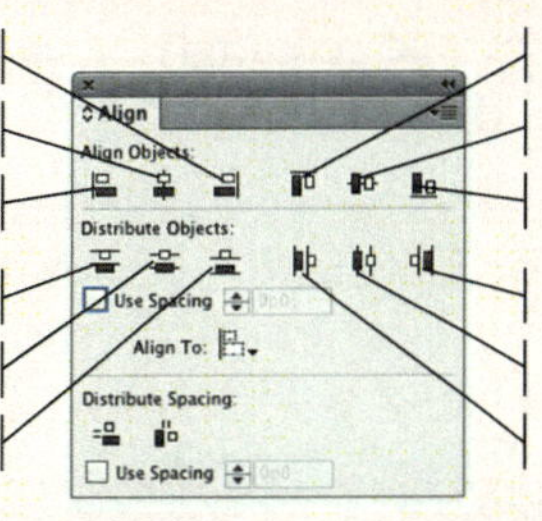

Align To Options

You can use the Align To menu to determine how objects will align.

Using the (default) Align To Selection option, selected objects align to one another based on the outermost edge of the entire selection. In other words, aligning the top edges moves all objects to the same Y position as the highest object in the selection.

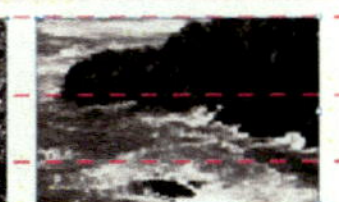

By default, the Align Objects options apply based on the outermost edge of the active selection. (Dashed lines indicate the original top edges of the three selected objects.)

If you use the Key Object option, you can click any object in the selection to designate it as the key. (The key object shows a heavier border than other objects in the selection.)

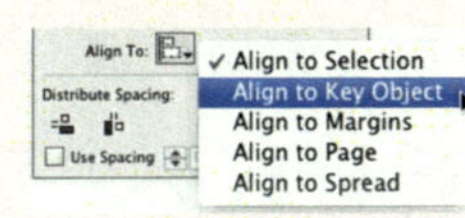

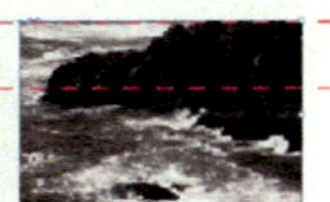

Using the Align To Key Object option, the Align options apply to the edges of the defined key object.

Because you can align objects relative to the document, the align buttons are also available when only one object is selected, allowing you to align any single object to a precise location on the page or spread.

Distribution Options

The Distribute Objects options enable you to control the positions of multiple objects relative to each other. By default, objects are equally distributed within the dimensions of the overall selection; you can check the Use Spacing option to space edges or centers by a specific amount.

By default, the Distribute Objects options equally space the selected objects within the outermost dimensions of the selection.

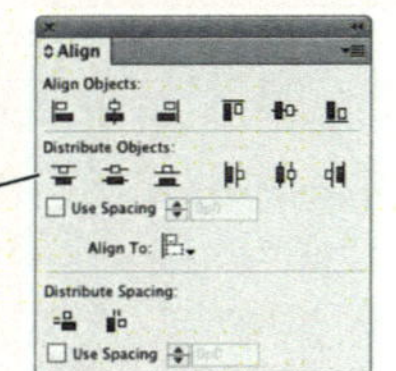

Use Spacing places a specific amount of space between the edges (or centers) of selected objects.

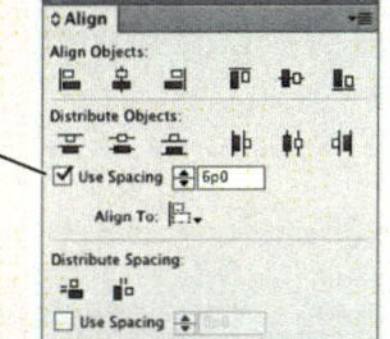

The Distribute Spacing options place equal space between the overall selected objects. You can also check the Use Spacing option to add a specific amount of space between the selected objects.

The Distribute Spacing options place a specific amount of space between selected objects.

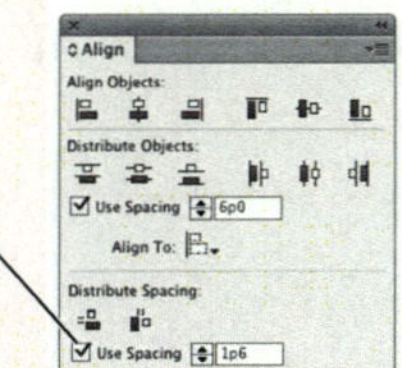

Many of the options from the Align panel are also available in the Control panel; the Align options are also available in all of the built-in workspaces. If you are using the Essentials workspace, the Distribute options are not available in the Control panel; you can turn them on by customizing the panel or by choosing the Advanced workspace option.

15. **Open the Align panel (Window>Object & Layout>Align).**

16. **With all of the rounded rectangles selected, click the Distribute Horizontal Centers button in the Align panel.**

    This button places an equal amount of space between the center points of each selected object. The two outer shapes in the selection act as the anchors; all other objects between the outer objects are repositioned.

17. **Click any of the selected shapes, press Option/Alt-Shift, and drag down. Position the cloned row near the bottom of the black rectangle, leaving the same amount of space as above the rounded rectangles.**

    By pressing Shift, you constrain the drag/cloning action to 45° angles. In this case, you clone the row of shapes to be automatically aligned below the top row.

18. **Save the file and continue to the next exercise.**

Create a Compound Path

Many shapes are composed of more than one path. The letter "O," for example, requires two separate paths — the outside shape and an inner shape to remove the area inside of the letter; without either path, the shape would be incomplete — just a circle instead of a recognizable letter. In this project, you will combine all of the existing shapes so the filmstrip is treated as a single object rather than 101 separate shapes.

1. **With identity.indd open, deselect all objects on the page and then click to select only the black rectangle.**

2. **In the Control panel, click the Drop Shadow button.**

    This button applies a drop shadow to the selected object using the default effect settings. As you can see, the shadow is not visible through the sprocket holes because you filled them with the Paper color — which knocks out all underlying color (including the applied shadow). To make the graphic work properly, you have to remove the areas of the rounded rectangles from the black rectangle.

> *Note:*
>
> *You will learn how to change these effect settings in Project 2: Festival Poster.*

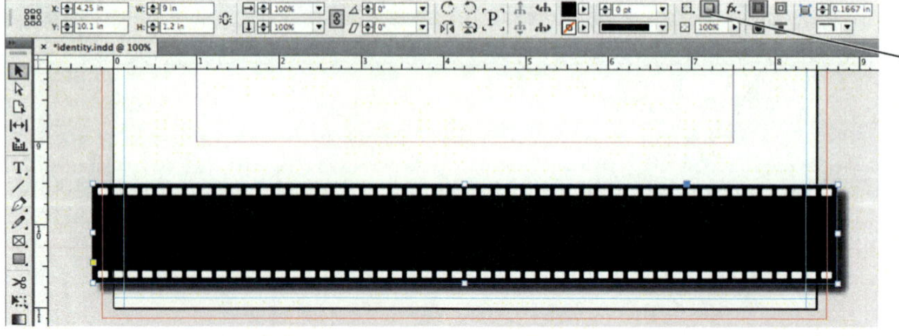

3. **Using the Selection tool, click and drag a marquee that touches all objects that make up the filmstrip graphic.**

Using the Selection tool, any object that is at least partially surrounded by the selection marquee will be included in the resulting selection.

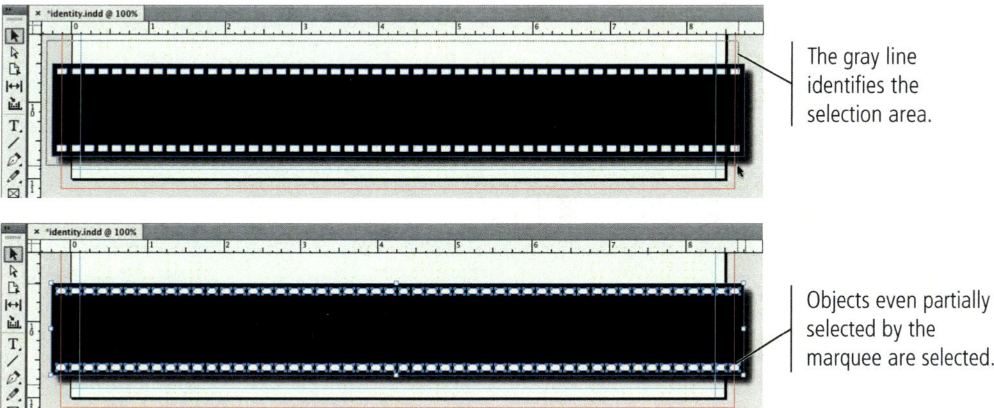

4. **Open the Pathfinder panel (Window>Object & Layout>Pathfinder).**

The Pathfinder Panel in Depth

INDESIGN FOUNDATIONS

You can apply a number of transformations to objects using the Pathfinder panel. (The options in the Pathfinder panel are the same as those in the Object>Paths, Object>Pathfinder, Object>Convert Shape, and Object>Convert Point submenus.)

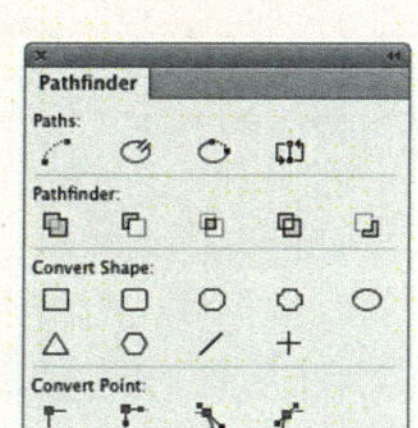

Join Path	Add	Rectangle	Plain Point
Open Path	Subtract	Rounded Rectangle	Corner Point
Close Path	Intersect	Beveled Rectangle	Smooth Point
Reverse Path	Exclude Overlap	Inverse Rounded Rectangle	Symmetrical Point
	Minus Back	Ellipse	
		Triangle	
		Polygon	
		Line	
		Horizontal/Vertical Line	

Path options break (open) a closed path, connect (close) the endpoints of an open path, or reverse a path's direction (start becomes end and vice versa, which is relevant if you use stylized end treatments).

Pathfinder options create complex objects by combining multiple existing objects. When you use the Pathfinder options (other than Subtract), the attributes of the front object are applied to the resulting shape; the Subtract function maintains the attributes of the back object.

- **Add** results in the combined shapes of all selected objects.
- **Subtract** returns the shape of the back object minus any overlapping area of the front object.
- **Intersect** results in the shape of only the overlapping areas of selected objects.
- **Exclude Overlap** results in the shape of all selected objects minus any overlapping areas.
- **Minus Back** results in the shape of the front object minus any area where it overlaps other selected objects.

Convert Shape options change the overall appearance of an object using one of the six defined basic shapes, or using the default polygon settings; you can also convert any existing shape to a basic line or an orthogonal (horizontal or vertical) line.

Convert Point options affect the position of direction handles when a specific anchor point is selected.

- **Plain** creates a point with no direction handles.
- **Corner** creates a point that produces a sharp corner; changing the direction handle on one side of the point does not affect the position or length of the handle on the other side of the point.
- **Smooth** creates a point with opposing direction handles that are exactly 180° from one another; the two handles can have different lengths.
- **Symmetrical** creates a smooth point with equal-length opposing direction handles; changing the length or position of one handle applies the same change to the opposing handle.

5. **Click the Subtract button in the Pathfinder panel.**

   This button removes the area of front objects from the area of the backmost object. The result is a **compound path**, which is a single shape that is made up of multiple paths; interior paths are removed from the background shape, allowing underlying elements to show through.

> *Note:*
>
> *It might take a while for the process to complete because InDesign has a lot of information to process to create the compound shape.*

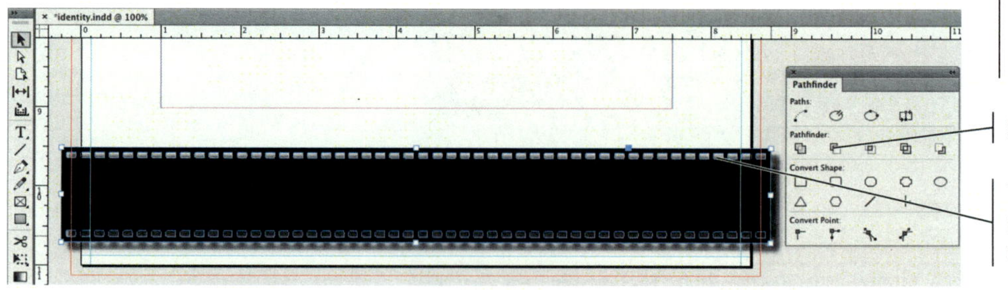

Subtract

The drop shadow is now visible through the holes.

6. **Click away from the active shape to deselect everything.**

7. **Save the file and continue to the next exercise.**

Create and Transform Multiple Frames

Many layouts have defined space requirements for various elements. This letterhead layout, for example, requires eight thumbnail images across the filmstrip graphic, evenly spaced and equally sized — just as you would see on a traditional piece of photographic film. Rather than simply placing the images and resizing the resulting frames for all eight images, you can speed up the process by first creating empty graphics frames that will contain the images when you place them.

1. **With identity.indd open, arrange your document window and view percentage so you can see the entire filmstrip at the bottom of the page.**

2. **Choose the Rectangle Frame tool in the Tools panel.**

   The frame tools work the same as the basic shape tools; the only difference is that the resulting shape automatically becomes a container for imported graphics or images.

3. **Click the left edge of the filmstrip graphic just below the top row of holes, then drag down and right until cursor feedback shows W: 9″, H: 0.8″. Do not release the mouse button.**

Click here to start.

Rectangle Frame tool

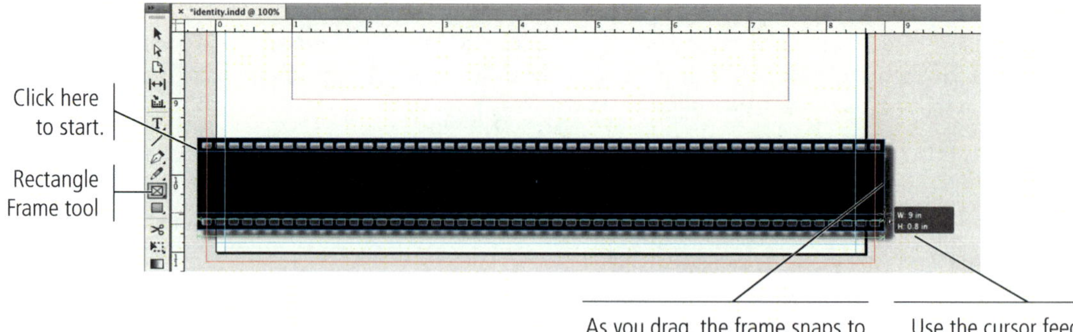

As you drag, the frame snaps to the edges of the existing object.

Use the cursor feedback to monitor the frame dimensions.

4. **While still holding down the mouse button, press the Right Arrow key.**

If you press the arrow keys while creating a frame, you can create a grid of frames within the area that you drag.

- Press the Right Arrow key to add columns.
- Press the Left Arrow key to remove columns.
- Press the Up Arrow key to add rows.
- Press the Down Arrow key to remove rows.

Note:

This method of creating multiple frames, called ***gridified tools****, works with any of the frame or basic shape tools.*

Pressing the Right Arrow key splits the area you draw into two equal-sized frames.

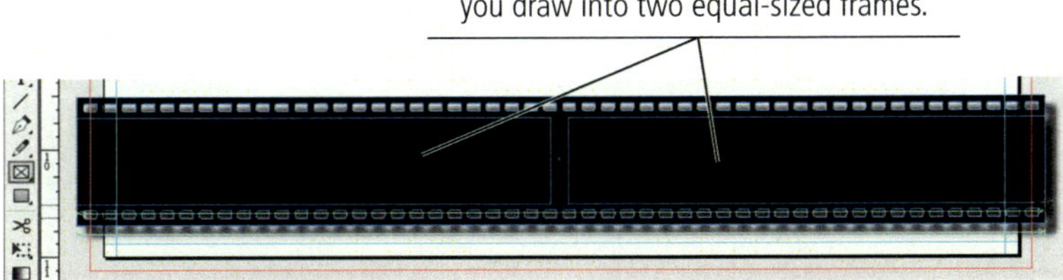

5. **Press the Right Arrow key six more times to create a total of eight frames, then release the mouse button.**

The resulting frames are equal in size, and have the same amount of space between each.

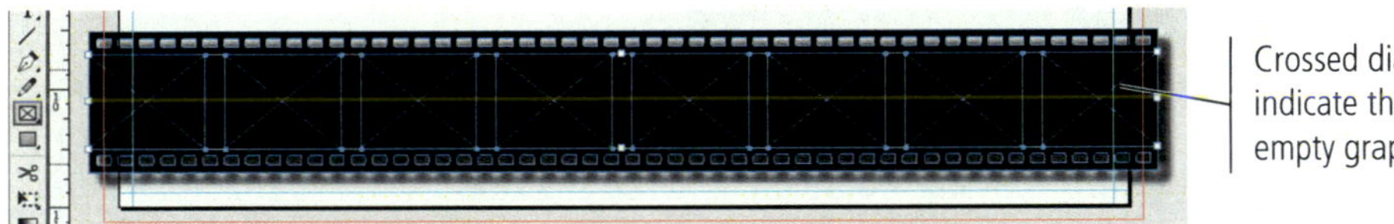

Crossed diagonal lines indicate that these are empty graphics frames.

6. **With the eight resulting frames selected, choose the Selection tool.**

As we stated previously, the Selection tool is used to access and manipulate entire objects. Using the Selection tool, you can:

- Click and drag a handle to resize selected objects.
- Shift-click and drag to resize objects proportionally.
- Command/Control-click and drag to scale selected objects.
- Command/Control-Shift-click and drag to scale selected objects proportionally.
- Press Option/Alt with any of these to apply the transformation around the selection's center point.

Note:

In InDesign CC, you can resize, rotate, or scale multiple objects at once without first grouping them.

7. **Click the right-center bounding box handle of the active selection. Press and hold the Spacebar, then drag left. When the cursor feedback shows W: 8.625", release the mouse button.**

As you drag, the space between the selected objects changes; the size of the actual objects is not affected. This method is called **live distribution**; to work properly, you must click the handle before pressing the Spacebar.

Note:

You might need to zoom in to get an accurate three-decimal value in the cursor feedback.

The Selection tool is active.

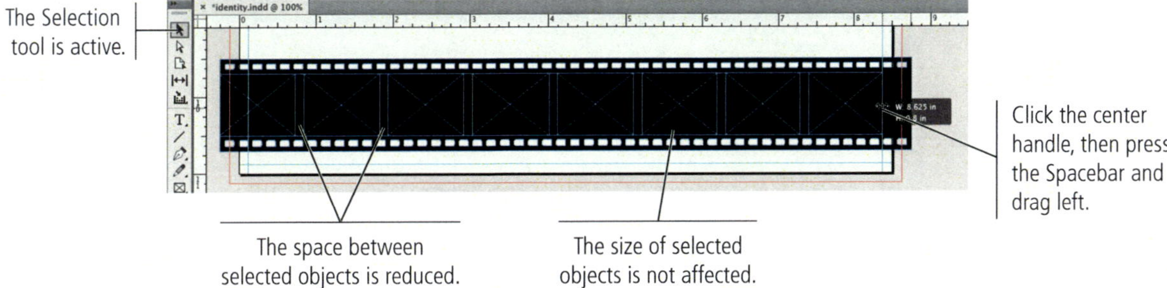

Click the center handle, then press the Spacebar and drag left.

The space between selected objects is reduced.

The size of selected objects is not affected.

8. **Click the right-center handle again. Without pressing the Spacebar, drag right until the handle snaps to the right edge of the filmstrip.**

   Simply dragging the handle resizes the entire selection; the spacing and position of various selected objects relative to one another is not affected.

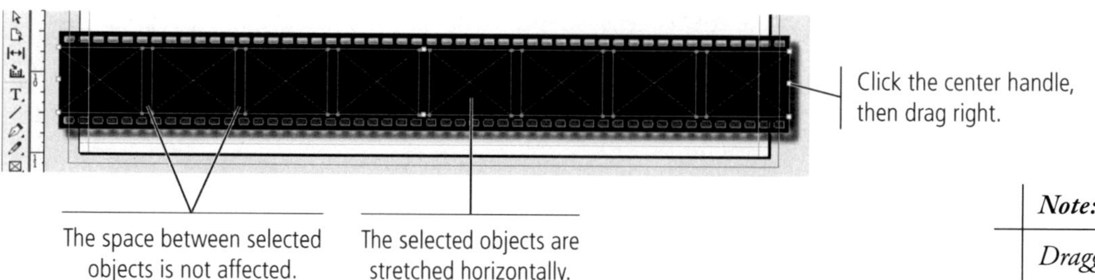

> *Note:*
>
> *Dragging a center handle changes the object size in only one direction.*

9. **With the eight empty frames selected, choose Object>Group.**

   Grouping multiple objects means you can treat them as a single unit. This is necessary when you want to use the align options to position the group of frames relative to other objects without affecting the positioning of the placeholder frames relative to one another.

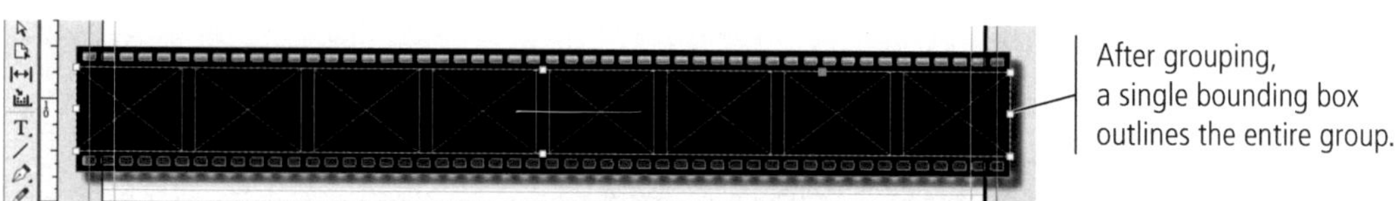

10. **Press Shift, and click the filmstrip graphic to add it to the active selection.**

11. **Using the Align panel or the Control panel, click the Align Horizontal Centers and Align Vertical Centers buttons.**

    Depending on how precisely you created and transformed the frames, this might have a very noticeable effect; it ensures that the frames are centered to the filmstrip graphic.

> *Note:*
>
> *Group objects by pressing Command/Control-G.*
>
> *Ungroup objects by pressing Command/Control-Shift-G.*

12. **In the Control panel, choose the center reference point.**

13. **Place the Selection tool cursor just outside the top-right handle of the selection. When you see the Rotate cursor, click and drag up until the cursor feedback shows 3°.**

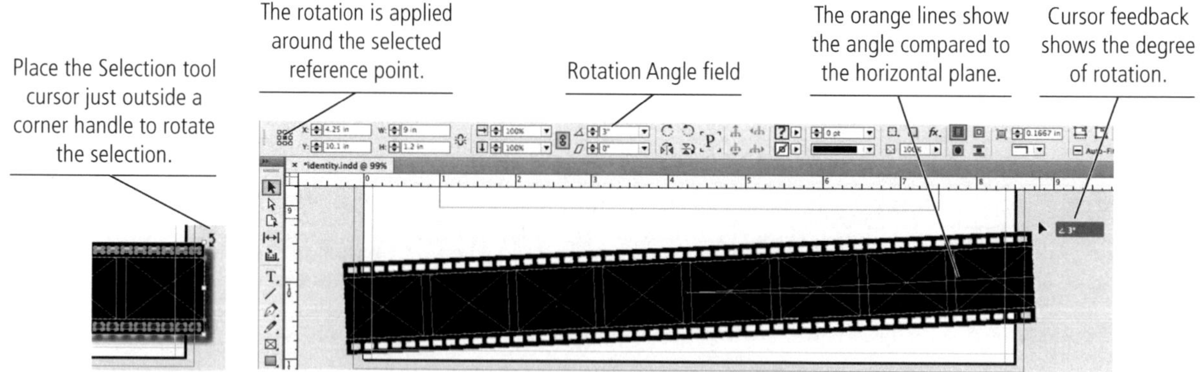

14. **Using the Selection tool, click away from the shapes that make up the filmstrip graphic to deselect the objects.**

15. **Save the file and continue to the next exercise.**

Create a Simple Line

InDesign includes two tools for creating lines: the Line tool for creating straight lines and the Pen tool for creating curved lines called **Bézier curves** (although you can also create straight lines with the Pen tool). In this exercise, you create the most basic element possible: a straight line. You then add anchor points to the line to create a multi-segment path.

Every line is composed of anchor points and line segments that connect those points. Even a simple straight line has two points, one at each end. More sophisticated shapes can be created by adding anchor points, and manipulating the direction handles of those points to control the shape of segments that connect the different points.

This concept is the heart of Bézier curves and vector-based drawing, and can be one of the most challenging skills for new designers to master. The Pen tool (and its variations) is extremely powerful, but also very confusing for new users. The best way to understand this tool is simply to practice. As you gain experience, you will become more comfortable with manipulating anchor points, handles, and line segments.

> ***Note:***
>
> *Bézier curves can be difficult to master without a relatively deep understanding of geometry or trigonometry. The best training is to practice until you can recognize and predict how moving a point or handle will affect the connected segments.*

1. **With identity.indd open, choose the Line tool in the Tools panel.**

2. **Click the Default Fill and Stroke button at the bottom of the Tools panel.**

   The default options for the Line tool are a 1-pt black stroke with no fill.

3. **At the top of the page, click at the left bleed guide and drag to the right bleed guide. Press Shift, and then release the mouse button.**

   As you drag, the cursor feedback shows the length of the line you are drawing. The blue line previews what will appear when you release the mouse button. Pressing Shift as you draw forces or constrains the line to exact 45° angles — including exactly horizontal.

> ***Note:***
>
> *When drawing lines, cursor feedback shows the length of the segment you are drawing.*

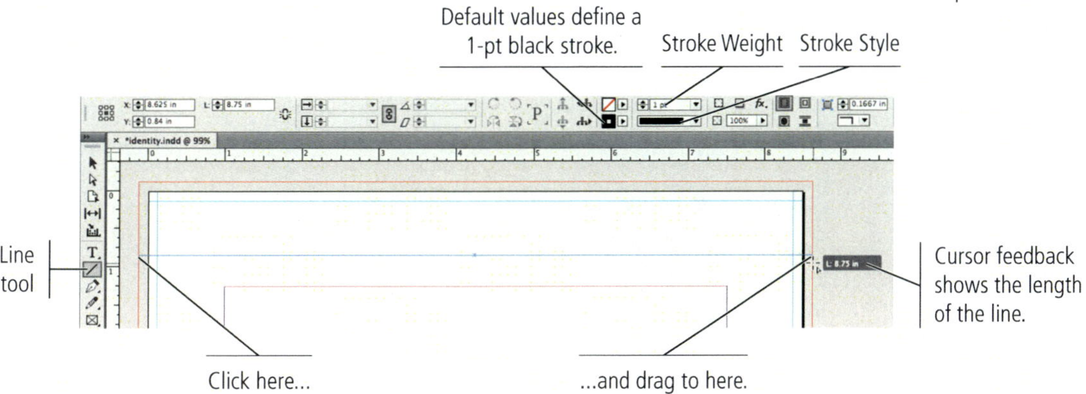

4. **In the Control panel, open the Stroke Weight menu and choose 2 pt.**

   You can choose one of the stroke weight presets from this menu, or simply type any value in the field.

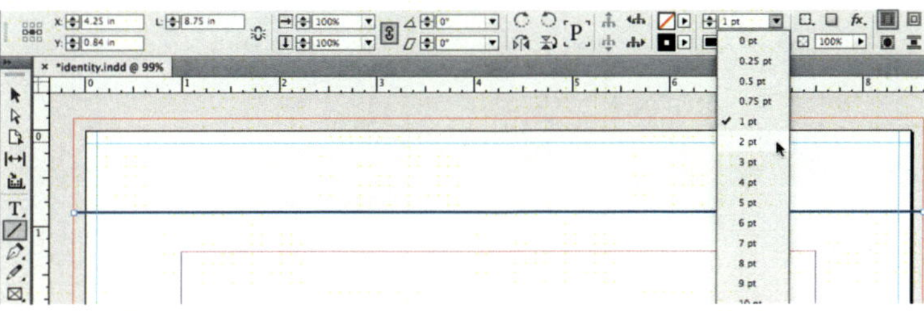

5. **At the left end of the Control panel, change the Y field to 1″ and press Return/Enter to apply the change.**

Because you constrained this line, changing the Y field moves the entire line.

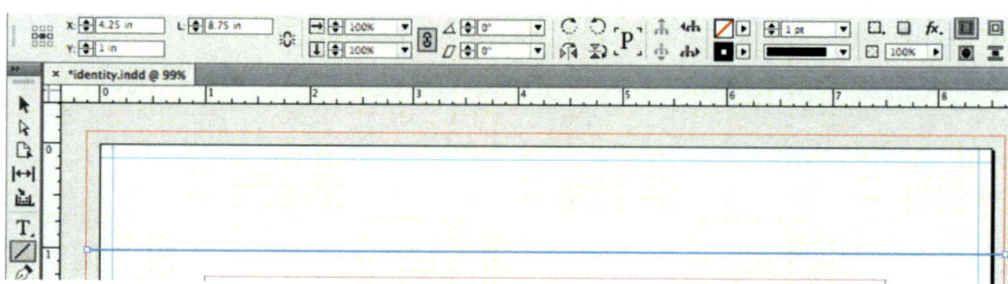

Note:

Remember, you do not need to type the units if you are entering a measurement in the default unit of measurement. We include the units in our steps for the sake of clarity.

6. **Choose the Pen tool in the Tools panel.**

7. **Move the cursor over the line you just created.**

When the Pen tool is over an existing selected line, it automatically switches to the Add Anchor Point tool cursor; clicking adds a new point to the selected line.

If the Pen tool is over a specific point on a selected line, it automatically switches to the Delete Anchor Point tool cursor; clicking removes that point from the line.

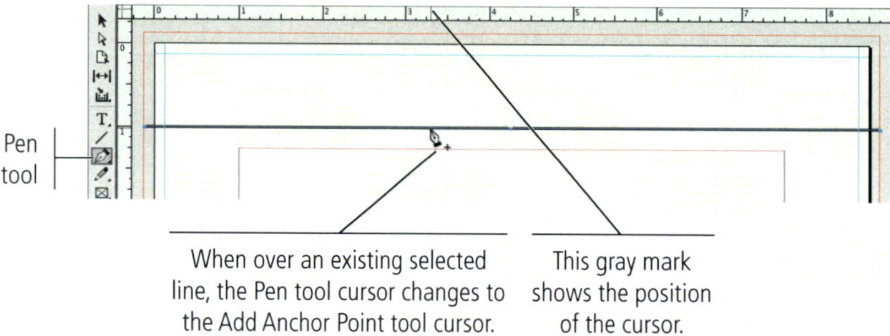

8. **When the cursor is at the 3.625″ mark of the horizontal page ruler, click to add a point to the line.**

The visible center point of the selected line is a bit deceptive. This simply marks the center of the shape (a line, in this case); it is not an actual point on the line.

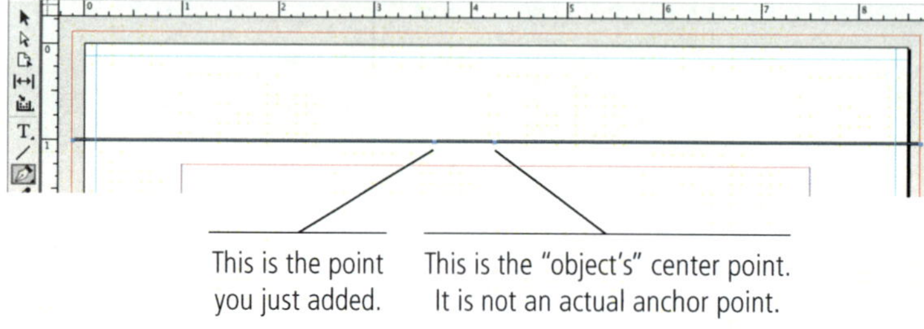

9. **Move the cursor right to the 4.375″ mark and click to add another point.**

All vector objects are composed of anchor points and connecting line segments, even if you don't create each point manually. The original line had two regular points, one at each end, and a straight connecting segment. You added two new points, for a total of four points and three connecting segments.

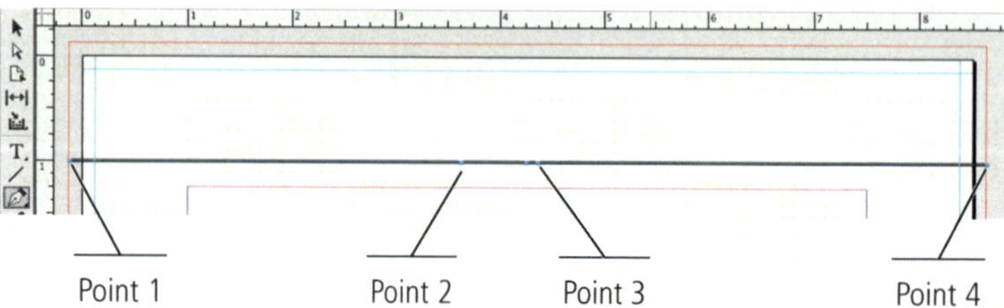

10. Choose the Direct Selection tool in the Tools panel, and click away from the line to deselect it.

The Direct Selection tool is used to select individual pieces of objects, such as a specific point on a line, or a specific line segment between two points. However, you have to first deselect the entire line before you can select only part of it.

11. Move the cursor over the left part of the line.

When the Direct Selection tool cursor shows a small line in the icon, clicking will select the specific segment under the cursor.

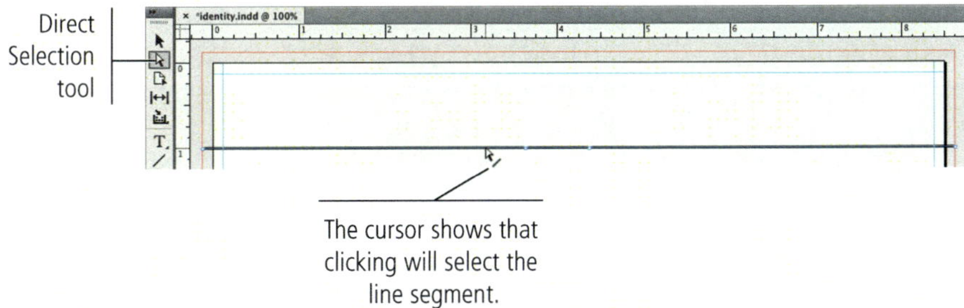

12. Click anywhere between the first and second points on the line. Press Shift, and drag up until the cursor feedback shows the Y position of 0.2".

The segment you selected moves, and the segment between points 2 and 3 adjusts as necessary to remain connected. The segment between points 3 and 4 is not affected.

Note:

You might need to zoom in to achieve the correct position for the segment you are dragging.

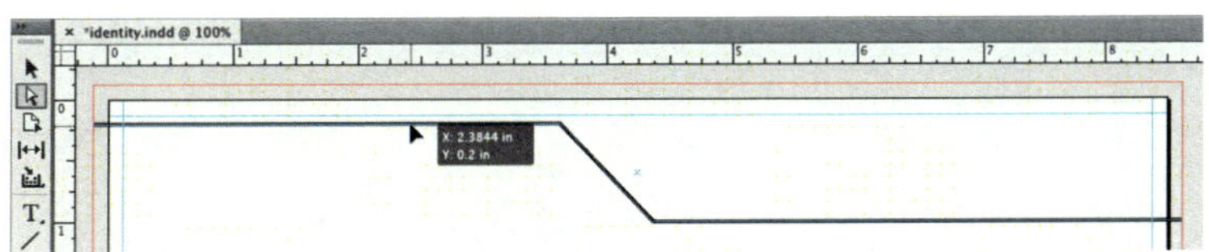

13. Using the Direct Selection tool, click the second point from the left (Point 2).

When the Direct Selection tool cursor shows a small circle in the icon, clicking will select the specific point under the cursor.

14. In the Control panel, change the X position of the selected point to 3.625".

As you can see, you can control the precise position of every point in a shape.

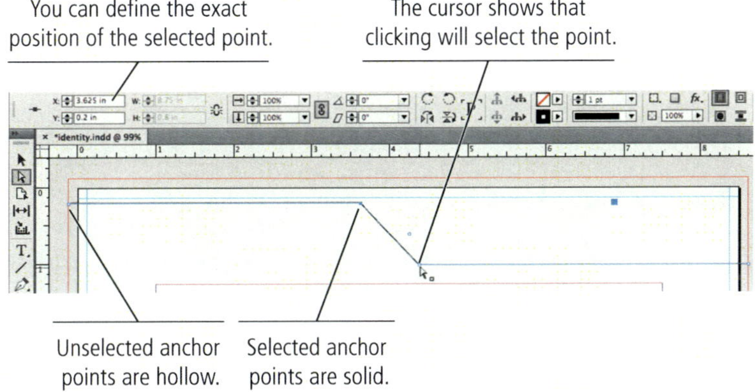

15. Save the file and continue to the next exercise.

Create Bézier Curves

In this exercise you will make very simple manipulations to the straight line you just created. In Project 2: Festival Poster, you will use the Pen tool to create a new curved line. We also encourage you to practice as much as possible using the Pen tool until you are more proficient; for example, try copying the outlines of various shapes in photographs.

1. **With identity.indd open, make sure the line at the top of the page is selected.**

2. **Choose the Convert Direction Point tool nested under the Pen tool.**

   The Convert Direction Point tool changes a corner point to a smooth point. **Smooth points** have handles that control the size and shape of curves connected to that point. You can use the Direct Selection tool to drag handles for a selected anchor point.

   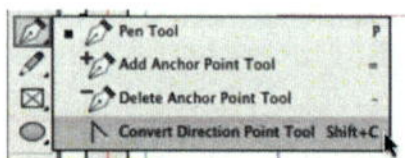

3. **Click the second point on the line, press Shift, and drag right until the ruler shows that the cursor is at 4.125″.**

   When you click a point with the Convert Direction Point tool and immediately drag, you add direction handles to the point. Those direction handles define the shape of the line segments that are connected to the point. As you drag farther away from the point, the affected segment's curve increases.

   Pressing Shift constrains the new direction handles to 45° angles — in this case, exactly horizontal. If you look closely, you can see that the direction handle on the left side of the point is exactly on top of the line.

   By default, clicking and dragging creates a smooth, symmetrical point in which equal-length handles are added to each side of the point directly opposite each other. As long as a point is symmetrical, changing the angle of one handle also affects the handle on the other side of the point.

   Click the point and drag right to add handles.

   Press Shift while you drag to constrain the handle to the horizontal.

   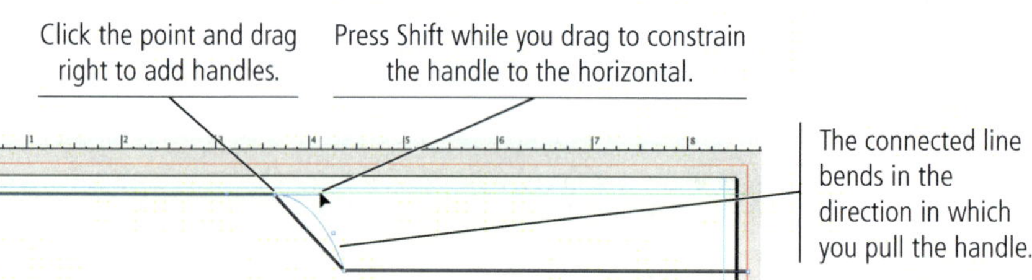

   The connected line bends in the direction in which you pull the handle.

4. **Click the third point, press Shift, and drag right until the ruler shows that the cursor is at 4.875″.**

   As we just explained, the affected curve gets larger as you drag farther away from the point. Because you're dragging exactly horizontally, the horizontal segment on the right is not curving.

   On the left side of the point, however, you can see the effect of converting Point 3 to a symmetrical point. Dragging to the right side of the point adds direction handles on *both sides* of the point; the length and position of the left handle defines the shape of the curve on the left side of the point — which is the one you want to affect in this step.

   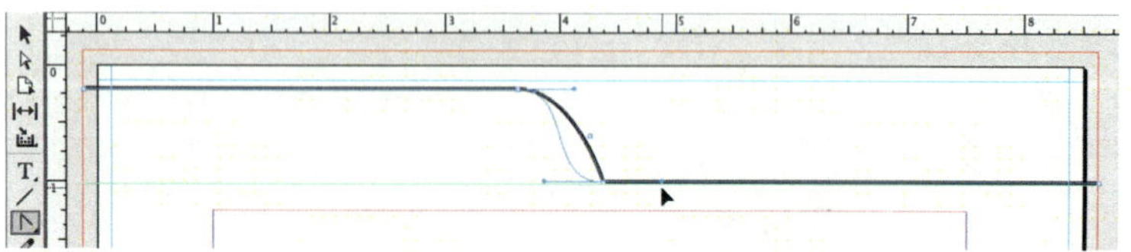

Note:

Using the Convert Direction Point tool, you can click an existing point and drag to add handles to the point, converting the point to a smooth point.

Note:

If you add points to a curved line segment, the new points automatically adopt the necessary direction handles to maintain the original curve shapes.

Note:

The lines that connect anchor points based on the angle and length of the control handles are called Bézier curves.

Note:

When you drag direction handles, the blue lines preview the effects of your changes.

5. **Choose the Pen tool in the Tools panel. (It is now nested under the Convert Direction Point tool.)**

   When you choose a nested tool variation, the nested tool becomes the default option in that position on the Tools panel.

> *Note:*
>
> *If you move an anchor point that has direction handles, the handles don't change angle or length. The related curves change shape based on the new position of the point.*

6. **Move the cursor over the left endpoint of the line. When you see a diagonal line in the cursor icon, click to connect to the existing endpoint.**

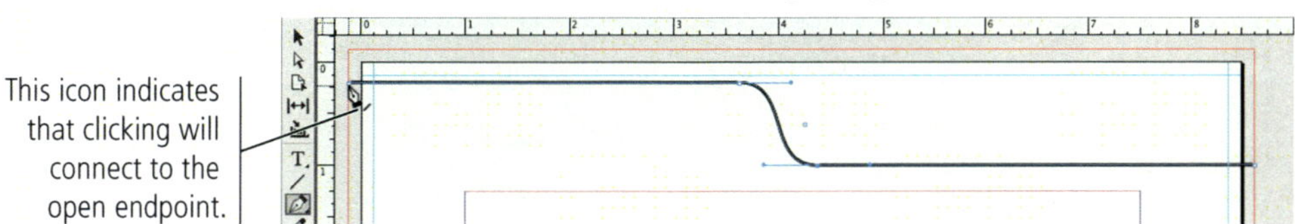

7. **Press Shift, then click at the top-left bleed guide.**

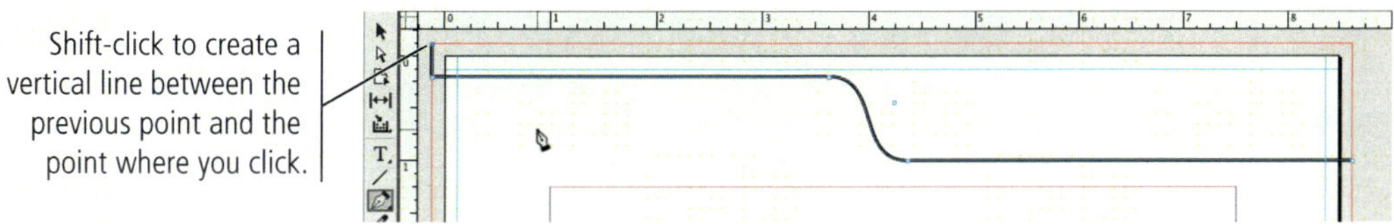

8. **Press Shift, then click the top-right bleed guide.**

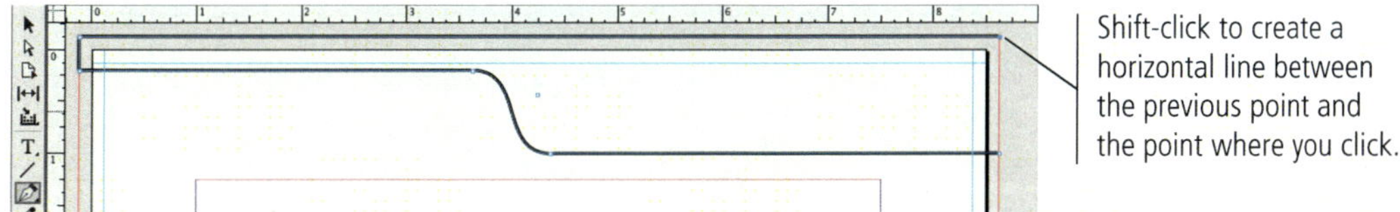

9. **Move the cursor over the open endpoint at the right end of the original line. When you see a small circle in the cursor icon, click to close the shape.**

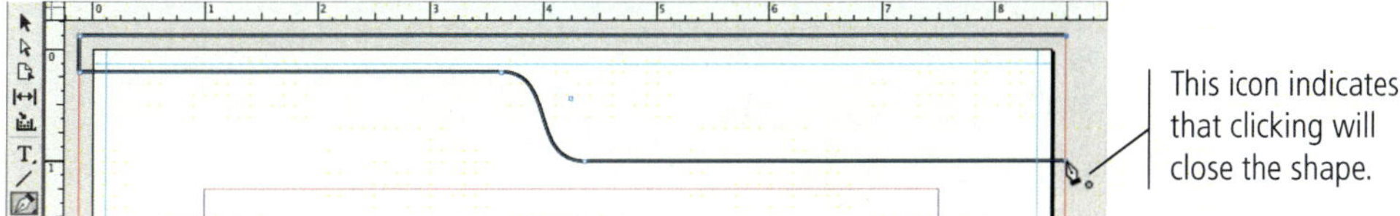

   You could have created this shape as a regular rectangle and then modified the bottom line with the Pen tool. However, our goal was to teach you how to create a basic line, and then how to perform some basic tasks with the Pen tool and its nested variations.

   It's important to realize that there is almost always more than one way to accomplish a specific goal in InDesign. As you gain experience, you will develop personal preferences for the most effective and efficient methods of doing what you need to do.

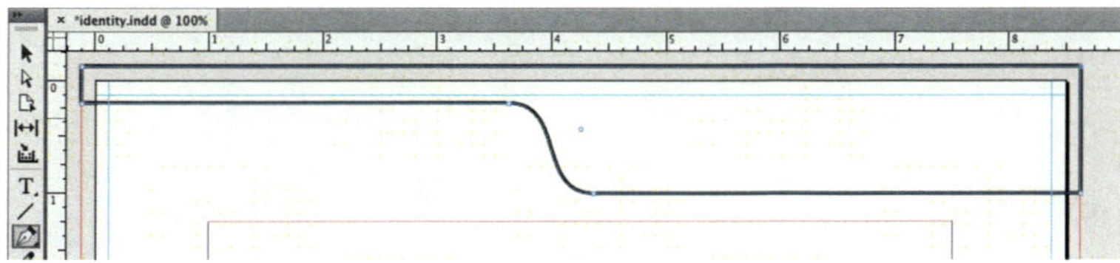

10. **Save the file and continue to the next exercise.**

Understanding Anchor Points and Handles

An anchor point marks the end of a line segment, and the point handles determine the shape of that segment. That's the basic definition of a vector, but there is a bit more to it than that. You can draw Bézier shapes from scratch using the Pen tool, or you can edit the curves that are created as part of another shape (such as a circle).

Each segment in a path has two anchor points and two associated handles. We first clicked to create Point A and dragged (without releasing the mouse button) to create Handle A1. We then clicked and dragged to create Point B and Handle B1; Handle B2 was automatically created as a reflection of B1 (Point B is a **symmetrical point**).

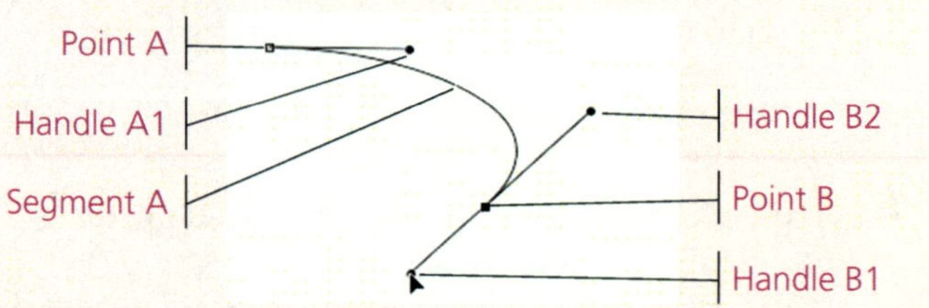

This image shows the result of dragging Handle B1 to the left instead of to the right when creating the initial curve. Notice the difference in the curve here, compared to the curve above. When you drag the handle, the connecting segment arcs away from the direction of the handle you drag.

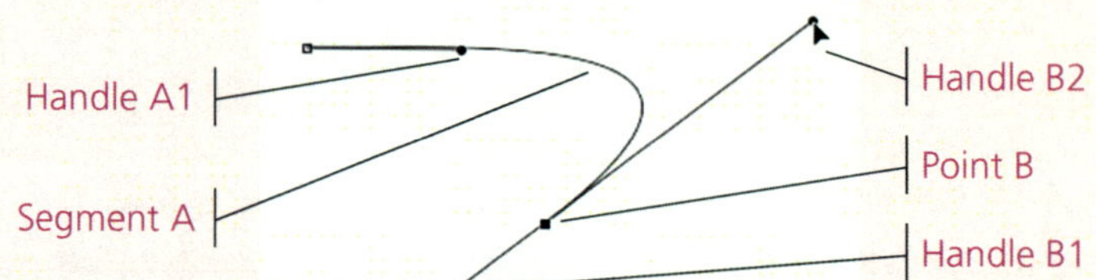

It's important to understand that every line segment is connected to two handles. In this example, Handle A1 and Handle B2 determine the shape of Segment A. Dragging either handle affects the shape of the connected segment.

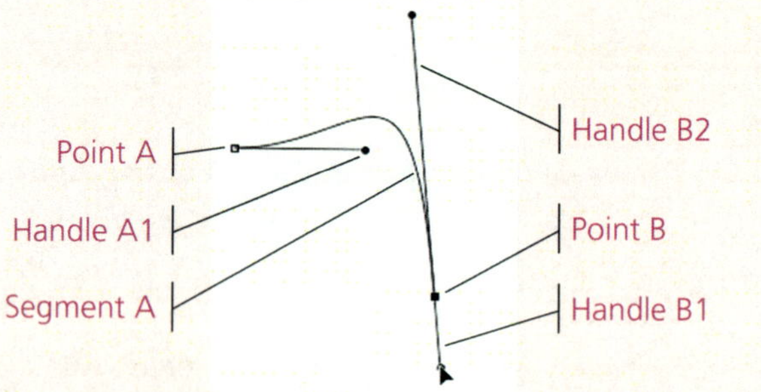

Clicking and dragging a point creates a symmetrical (smooth) point; both handles start out at equal length, directly opposite one another. Changing the angle of one handle of a symmetrical point also changes the opposing handle of that point. In the example here, repositioning Handle B1 also moves Handle B2, which affects the shape of Segment A. (You can, however, change the length of one handle without affecting the length of the other handle.)

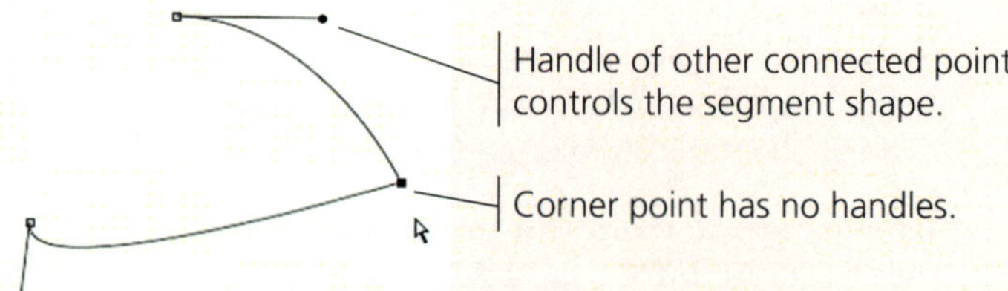

You can create corner points by simply clicking with the Pen tool instead of clicking and dragging. Corner points do not have their own handles; the connected segments are controlled by the handles of the other associated points.

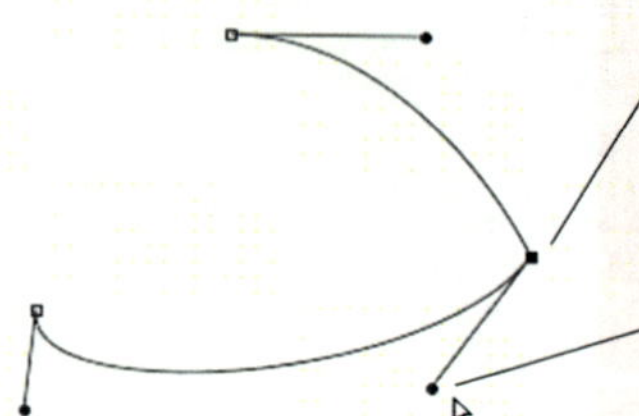

You can convert a smooth point into a corner point by clicking the point with the Convert Direction Point tool [ ] (nested under the Pen tool). You can also add a handle to only one side of an anchor point by Option/Alt-clicking a point with the Convert Direction Point tool and dragging.

Option/Alt-click this point with the Convert Direction Point tool and drag to create only one handle.

This handle controls the connected segment; the handle is not reflected on the other side of the point.

Creating Irregular Shapes with the Polygon Tool

INDESIGN FOUNDATIONS

The Polygon Frame and Polygon tools can be used to create odd shapes with a defined number of straight edges (including triangles).

Clicking once with either Polygon tool opens the Polygon dialog box, where you can define the size of the new object, as well as the number of points on the new shape. To create a starburst, every other anchor point in the shape needs to be closer to the object's center; the Star Inset field determines how much closer those inside points will be to the center (an inset of 0% creates all points at the same distance from the object's center).

If you simply click and drag with the Polygon tool, you create a new shape with the tool's default settings.

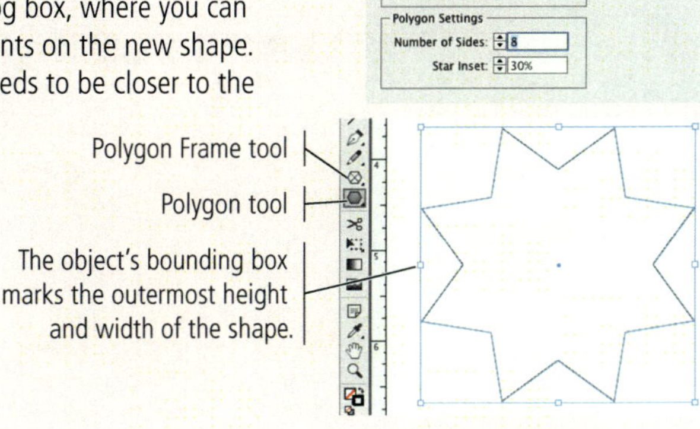

Change Color Values

Although there are several default color choices built into the Swatches panel of every InDesign file, you are not limited to these few options. You can define virtually any color based on specific values of component colors.

When you are building a page to be printed, you should use CMYK colors. The CMYK color model, also called **process color**, uses subtractive color theory to reproduce the range of printable colors by overlapping semi-transparent layers of cyan, magenta, yellow, and black inks in varying percentages from 0–100.

In process-color printing, these four colors of ink are imaged (or separated) onto individual printing plates. Each color separation is printed with a separate unit of a printing press. When printed on top of each other in varying percentages, the semi-transparent inks produce the CMYK **gamut**, or the range of possible colors. Special (spot) colors can also be included in a job by using specifically formulated inks as additional color separations.

Using theoretically pure pigments, a mixture of equal parts of cyan, magenta, and yellow should produce black. Real pigments, however, are not pure; the actual result of mixing these three colors usually appears as a muddy brown. In the image to the right, the left block is printed with 100% black ink. The right block is a combination of 100% cyan, 100% magenta, and 100% yellow inks.

The fourth color, black (K), is added to the three subtractive primaries to extend the range of printable colors and to allow much purer blacks to be printed than is possible with only the three primaries. Black is abbreviated as "K" because it is the "key" color to which others are aligned on the printing press. Using K for black also avoids confusion with blue in the RGB color model, which is used for jobs that will be distributed digitally (Web sites, some PDF files, etc.).

1. **With identity.indd open, use the Selection tool to make sure the shape at the top of the page is selected.**

2. **At the bottom of the Tools panel, click the Swap Fill and Stroke button.**

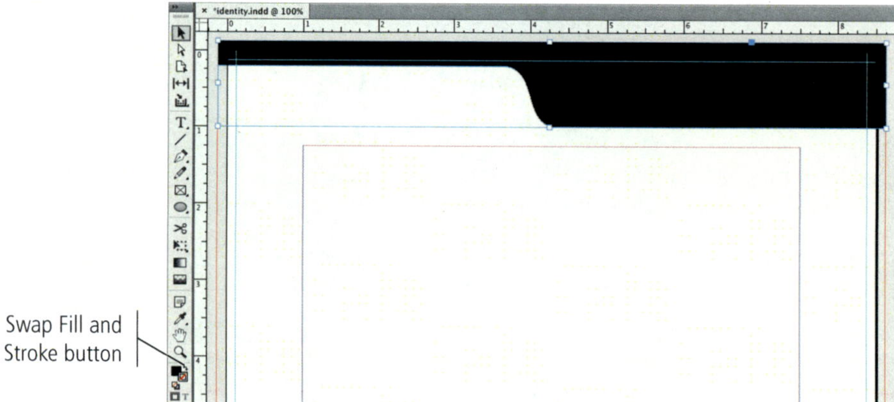

3. **Open the Color panel (Window>Color>Color).**

4. **Click the Fill swatch to bring it to the front (if it isn't already).**

   When you apply color from any of the Swatches panels (including the ones in the Control panel), the Color panel shows a swatch of that color as a single slider. You can use this slider to easily apply a percentage of the selected swatch. (You'll work more with color swatches in Project 2: Festival Poster.)

5. **Click the Options button in the top-right corner of the panel and choose CMYK from the Options menu.**

   This option converts the single swatch slider to the four process-color sliders. You can change any ink percentage to change the object's fill color.

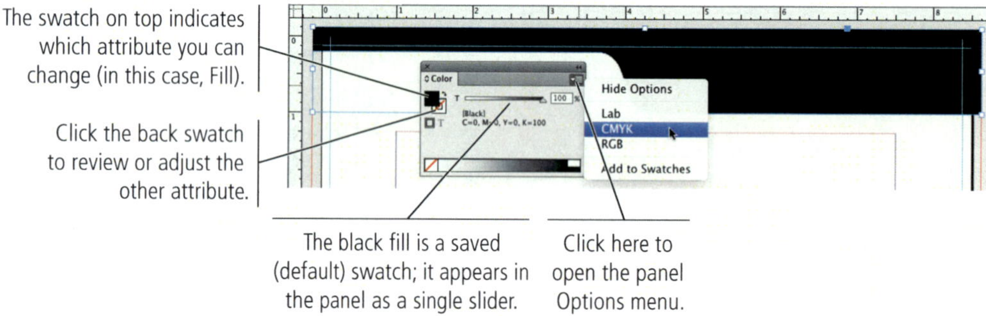

6. **Click the M slider and drag until the field shows 40%.**

   This color, 100% black with some percentage of another ink, is called a **rich black** or **super black**. By itself, plain black ink often lacks density. Rich blacks are commonly used to add density or "temperature" to flat black; adding magenta results in "warmer" blacks, and adding cyan results in "cooler" blacks.

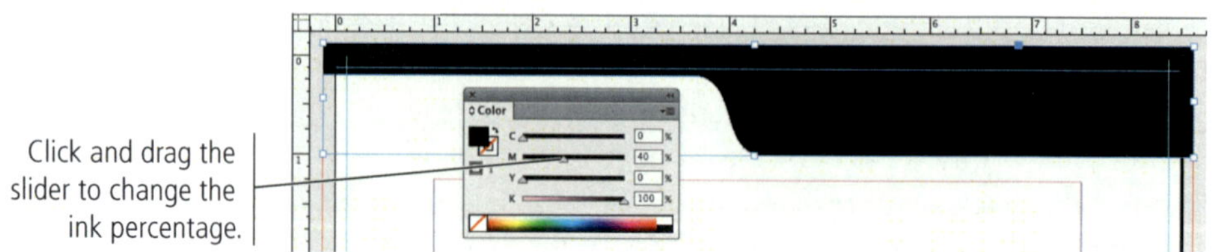

7. **Save the file and continue to the next stage of the project.**

Note:

Remember, all panels can be accessed in the Window menu. Because workspace arrangement is a matter of personal preference, we won't tell you where to place or keep panels.

Note:

You can change the color by typing a specific value or by dragging the slider below the color gradient.

Understanding Resolution

Raster image quality depends directly on the file's resolution; when you work with raster image files, you need to understand the resolution requirements from the very beginning of the process:

- **Pixels per inch (ppi)** is the number of pixels in one horizontal or vertical inch of a digital raster file.
- **Lines per inch (lpi)** is the number of halftone dots produced in a horizontal or vertical linear inch by a high-resolution imagesetter in order to simulate the appearance of continuous-tone color.
- **Dots per inch (dpi)** or **spots per inch (spi)** is the number of dots produced by an output device in a single line of output. Dpi is sometimes used interchangeably (although incorrectly) with pixels per inch.

When reproducing a photograph on a printing press, the image must be converted into a set of different-size dots that fool the eye into believing it sees continuous tones. The result of this conversion process is a halftone image; the dots used to simulate continuous tone are called **halftone dots**. Light tones in a photograph are represented as small halftone dots; dark tones are represented as large halftone dots. Prior to image-editing software, photos were converted to halftones with a large graphic-arts camera and screens. The picture was photographed through the screen to create halftone dots, and different screens produced different numbers of dots in an inch (hence the term "dots per inch").

Image Resolution

When a printer creates halftone dots, it calculates the average value of a group of pixels and generates a spot of appropriate size. An image's resolution controls the quantity of pixel data that the printer can read. Regardless of the source — camera, scanner, or files created from scratch in a program such as Photoshop — images need to have sufficient resolution for the output device to generate enough halftone dots to create the appearance of continuous tone.

Ideally, the printer has four pixels for each halftone dot created. The relationship between pixels and halftone dots defines the rule of resolution for all raster-based images — the resolution of an image should be two times the screen ruling (lpi) that will be used for printing.

Screen Ruling

The screens used with old graphic-arts cameras had a finite number of available dots in a horizontal or vertical inch. That number was the **screen ruling**, or lines per inch of the halftone. A screen ruling of 133 lpi means that in a square inch there are 133 × 133 (17,689) possible locations for a halftone dot. If the screen ruling is decreased, there are fewer total halftone dots, producing a grainier image; if the screen ruling is increased, there are more halftone dots, producing a clearer image.

Line screen is a finite number based on a combination of the intended output device and paper. You can't randomly select a line screen. Ask your printer what line screen will be used before you begin creating your images. If you can't find out ahead of time or are unsure, follow these general guidelines:

- Newspaper or newsprint: 85–100 lpi
- Magazine or general commercial printing: 133–150 lpi
- Premium-quality-paper jobs (such as art books): 150–175 lpi (some specialty jobs use 200 lpi or more)

If you find this information a bit confusing, don't worry. As a general rule for preparing commercial print layouts, most raster images should have twice the pixel resolution (at 100% size) as the line screen that will be used.

72 ppi

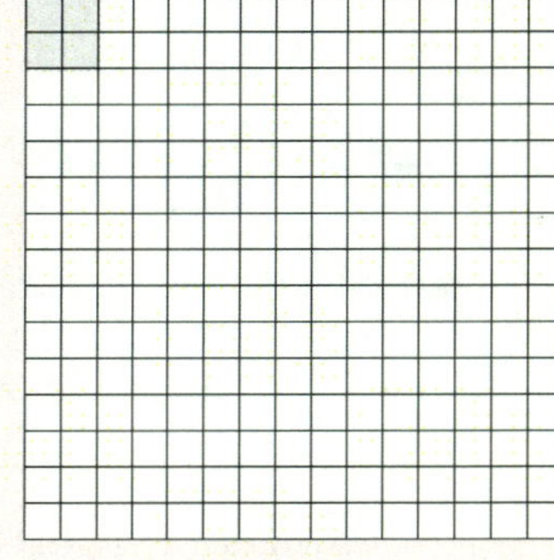

300 ppi

Each white square represents a pixel. The highlighted area shows the pixel information used to generate a halftone dot. If an image only has 72 pixels per inch, the output device has to generate four halftone dots per pixel, resulting in poor printed quality.

The same raster image is reproduced here at 300 ppi (left) and 72 ppi (right). Notice the obvious degradation in quality when the resolution is set to 72 ppi.

Stage 3 Placing External Images

As you saw in the first stage of this project, InDesign incorporates a number of tools for building graphics directly in a layout. Of course, most page-layout projects will include files from other sources — logos created in Adobe Illustrator, raster-based images created in Adobe Photoshop, digital photographs, stock images, and many other types of files can be incorporated into a larger project.

Place an Adobe Illustrator File

Every image in a layout exists in a frame. You can either create the frame first and place a file into it, or you can simply place an image and create the containing frame at the same time. In this exercise, you are going to place the client's logo and transform the file to fit into the space to the left of the curved line at the top of the layout.

1. **With identity.indd open, make sure nothing is selected in the layout.**
2. **Choose File>Place. Navigate to the WIP>Crowe folder and select crowe.ai. At the bottom of the dialog box, check the box to Show Import Options.**

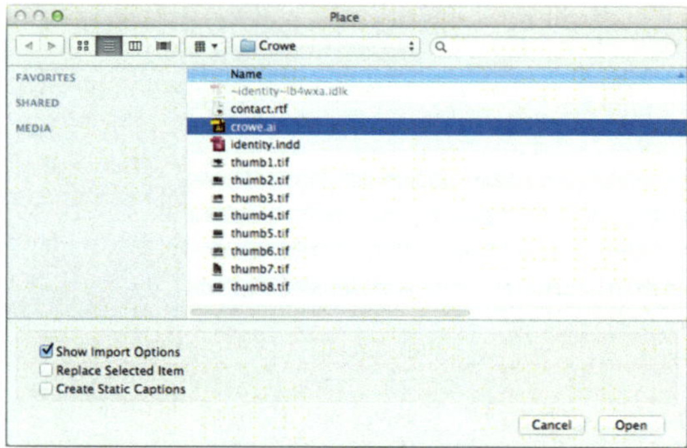

3. **Click Open.**

   When Show Import Options is checked, the Place [Format] dialog box opens with the options for the relevant file format. Every file format has different available options.

4. **In the General tab, choose Art in the Crop To menu.**

   The Crop To menu determines what part of the file will import:

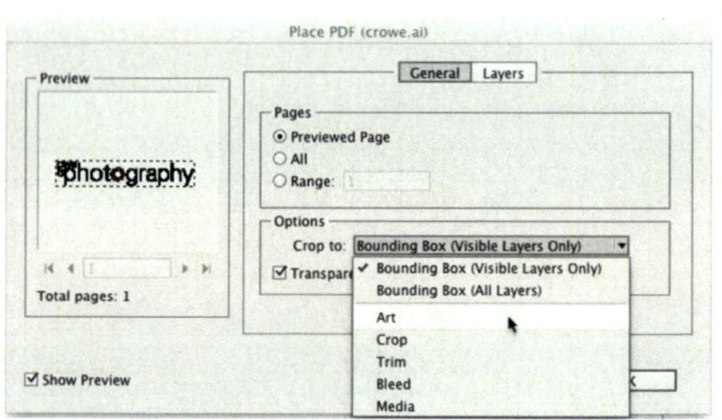

   - **Bounding Box** places the file based on the minimum area that encloses the objects on the page. (You can also choose whether to include all layers or only visible layers in the bounding box calculation.)
   - **Art** places the file based on the outermost dimensions of artwork in the file.
   - **Crop** places the file based on the crop area defined in the file. If no crop area is defined, the file is placed based on the defined artboard dimensions.
   - **Trim** places the file based on trim marks defined in the placed file. If no trim marks are defined, the file is placed based on the defined artboard size.
   - **Bleed** places the file based on the defined bleed area. If no bleed area is defined, the file is placed based on the defined artboard size.
   - **Media** places the file based on the physical paper size on which the PDF file was created. This option is not relevant for native Illustrator files.

   When the Transparent Background option is checked, background objects in the layout show through empty areas of the placed file. If this option is not checked, empty areas of the placed file knock out underlying objects.

Note:

Artwork in an Illustrator file must be entirely within the bounds of the artboard (page) edge. Anything outside the artboard edge will not be included when you place the file into InDesign.

Note:

When you place a native Illustrator file, the dialog box shows Place PDF options because the PDF format is the basis of Illustrator files that can be placed into InDesign.

Note:

In the General tab, you can also define the specific PDF page or Illustrator artboard of the file to place.

5. **Click the Layers tab to display those options.**

   PDF and native Illustrator files can include multiple layers. You can determine which layers to display in the placed file by toggling the eye icons on or off in the Show Layers list. In the Update Link Options menu, you can determine what happens when/if you update the link to the placed file.

   - **Keep Layer Visibility Overrides** maintains your choices regarding which layers are visible in the InDesign layout.
   - **Use PDF's Layer Visibility** restores the layer status as saved in the placed file.

6. **Click OK to load the cursor with the placed file.**

   By default, the loaded Place cursor shows a small thumbnail of the file you're placing. You can turn off the thumbnail preview feature by unchecking the Show Thumbnails on Place option in the Interface pane of the Preferences dialog box.

7. **Click near the top-left corner of the page to place the image.**

   Every image in an InDesign layout exists in a frame. When you click an empty area of the page to place an image, the containing frame is automatically created for you.

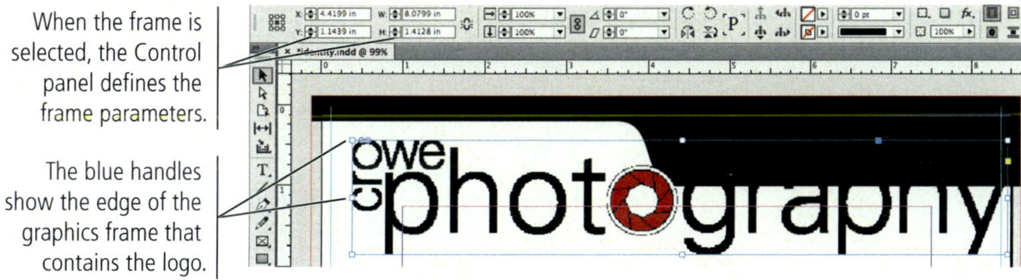

8. **Open the Interface pane of the Preferences dialog box. Choose Immediate in the Live Screen Drawing menu, then click OK.**

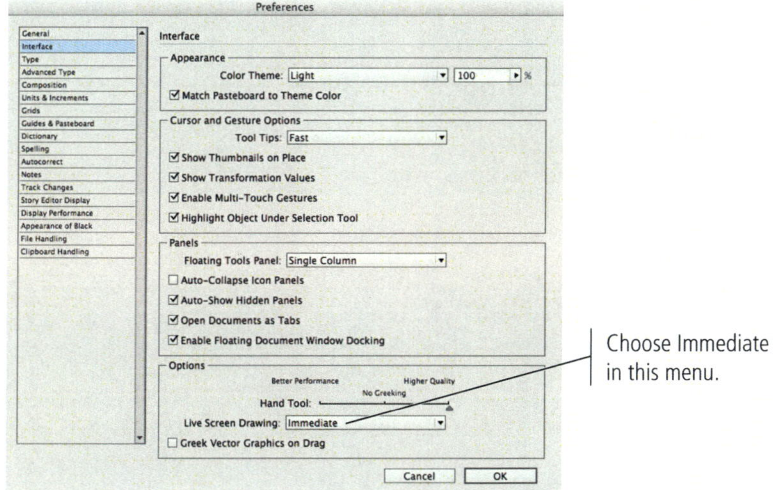

Note:

Remember, preferences are accessed in the InDesign menu on Macintosh and in the Edit menu on Windows.

Live Screen Drawing controls the appearance of an image when you move or resize it. The default behavior, Delayed, means the image does not appear inside the frame while you change the frame parameters (position, etc.).

Using the Immediate live-screen drawing option, the image inside the frame always appears inside the frame when you move or resize the frame. If Delayed is selected, you can click and hold down the mouse button for a couple of seconds to temporarily access the Immediate preview behavior.

9. **With the placed image selected, check the Auto-Fit option in the Control panel.**

10. **Click the bottom-right corner of the frame, then drag up and left to make the frame smaller. When cursor feedback shows the frame is 3.6″ wide, release the mouse button.**

By default, the image contained within the frame remains unaffected when you edit the dimensions of a graphics frame. When the Auto-Fit option is checked, however, resizing the frame automatically resizes the contained image to fit the new frame size; the image remains centered inside the frame. Areas of the resized image outside the resized frame remain visible while you hold down the mouse button.

Because the Immediate live-screen drawing option is active, you can immediately see the result of resizing the frame.

When Auto-Fit is checked, resizing the frame also affects the graphic inside the frame.

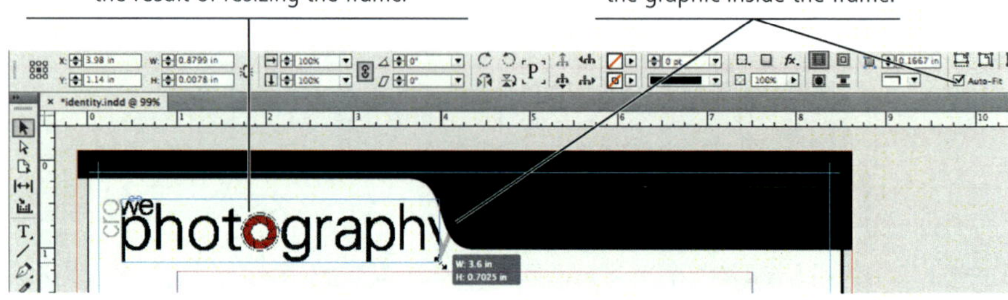

11. **Uncheck the Auto-Fit option in the Control panel.**

If you don't turn off this option, you will not be able to manually apply other frame fitting commands in the next steps.

12. **Control/right-click the selected image and choose Fitting>Fit Content Proportionally from the contextual menu.**

The fitting options can resize the image relative to its frame, or resize the frame relative to its content.

Note:

Unlike raster images, vector graphics can be resized without losing quality.

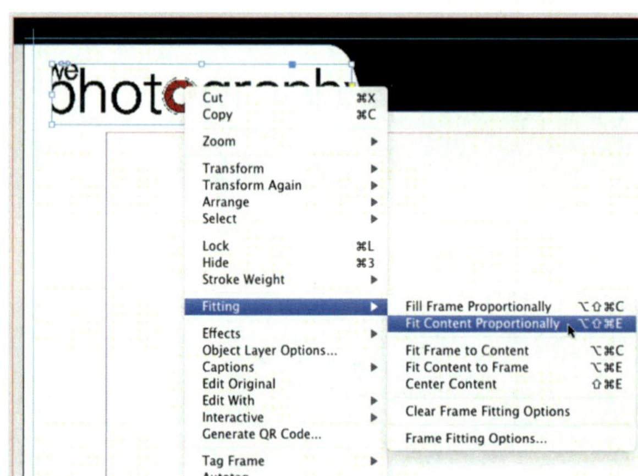

In this case, you defined the available frame width; you are using the fitting options to force the content proportionally into that available space.

Note:

When the Auto-Fit option is not selected, you can press the Command key while resizing a frame to scale the content at the same time.

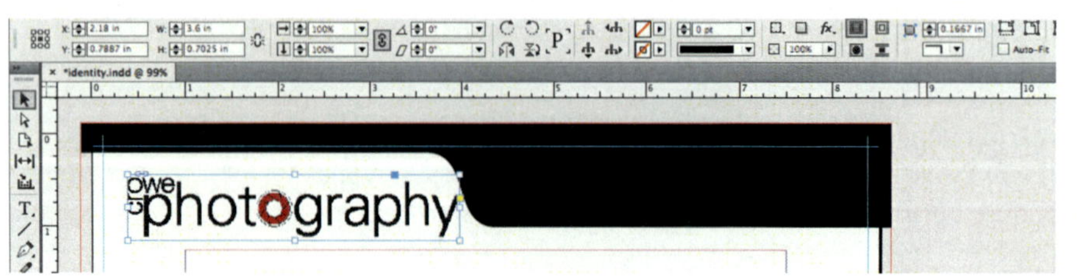

Note:

Press Shift while dragging a corner to maintain the original height-to-width aspect ratio in the resized frame.

13. With the Selection tool active, move the cursor inside the resized frame.

This reveals the Content Grabber, which you can use to access and manipulate the frame's content without the need to switch tools.

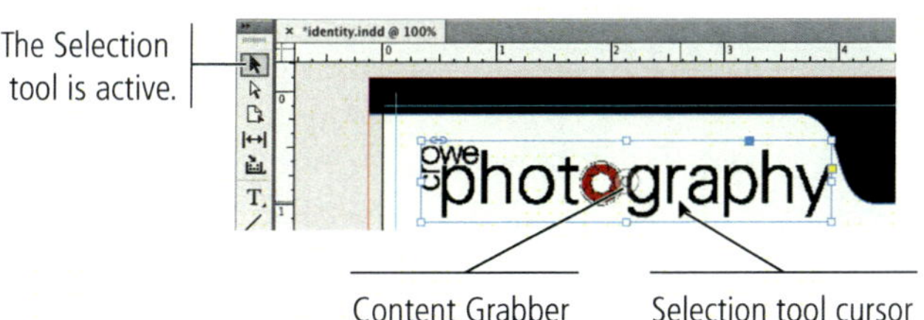

Note:

Depending on the width of your monitor, fitting options might be available in the Control panel.

14. Click the Content Grabber in the logo frame.

When the frame's content is selected, options in the Control panel relate to the placed object and not the containing frame. The X+ and Y+ fields define the position of the image *within the frame*. The Scale X and Scale Y fields show the file's current size as a percentage of the original.

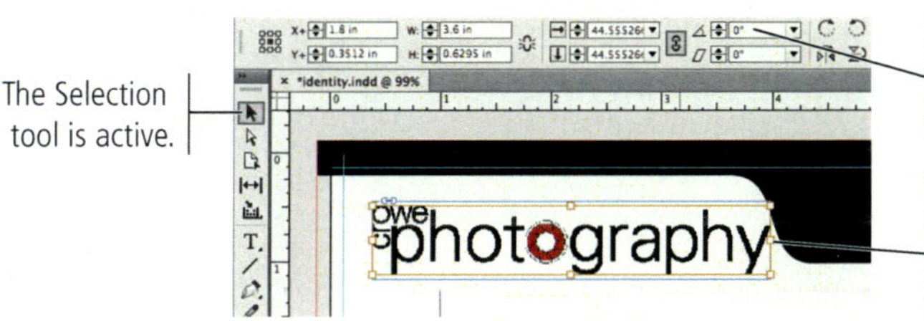

Note:

You can also use the Direct Selection tool to access and edit the content inside a graphics frame.

Content Fitting Options

INDESIGN FOUNDATIONS

The Fitting options resize content relative to the containing frame, or resize the containing frame to match the placed content.

- **Fill Frame Proportionally** resizes content to fill the entire frame while preserving the content's proportions. Some of the image area might be cropped.
- **Fit Content Proportionally** resizes content to fit entirely within its containing frame, maintaining the current aspect ratio of the image. Some empty space might result along one dimension of the frame.
- **Fit Frame to Content** resizes the frame to the dimensions of the placed content.
- **Fit Content to Frame** resizes content to fit the dimensions of the container, even if that means scaling the content out of proportion (stretched in one direction or another).
- **Center Content** centers content within its containing frame, but neither the frame nor the content is resized.

Fitting proportionally places the entire image into the frame; some areas of the frame might be empty.

Filling proportionally fills the frame; some areas of the image might be cropped.

15. **With the frame content selected, select the top-left reference point in the Control panel and change the Y+ field to 0.**

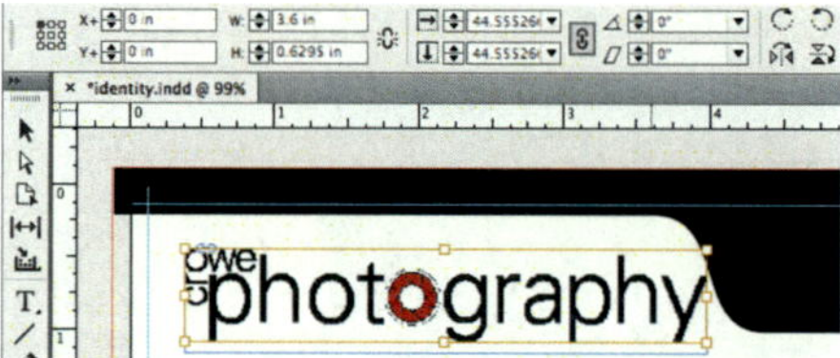

16. **Control/right-click the frame and choose Fitting>Fit Frame to Content in the contextual menu.**

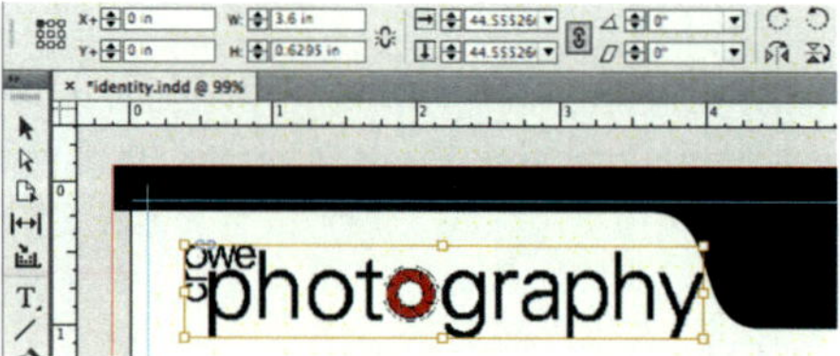

17. **Press Esc to return to the frame of the selected object.**

    The graphics frame is again selected, and the Selection tool is still active.

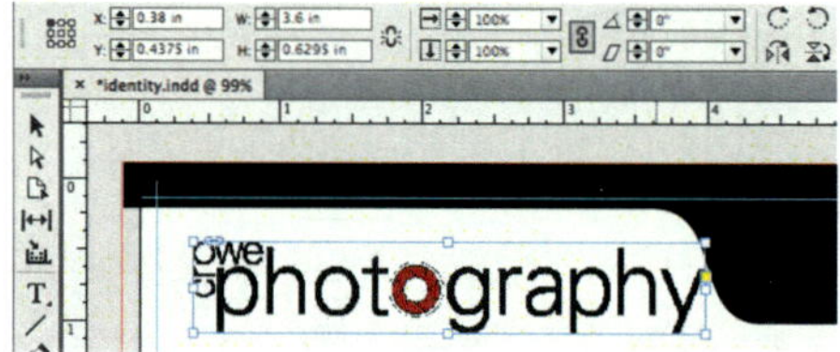

18. **Save the file and continue to the next exercise.**

Place Images into Existing Frames

In many cases, you will need to place an image or graphic into an existing frame and then manipulate the placed file to suit the available space. In the previous stage of this project, you created eight empty graphics frames across the filmstrip graphic; in this exercise, you will place the client's thumbnail photos into those frames.

1. **With identity.indd open, make the filmstrip graphic at the bottom of the page visible in your document window.**

2. **Using the Selection tool, click one of the empty graphics frames.**

    When objects are grouped, the Selection tool selects the entire group.

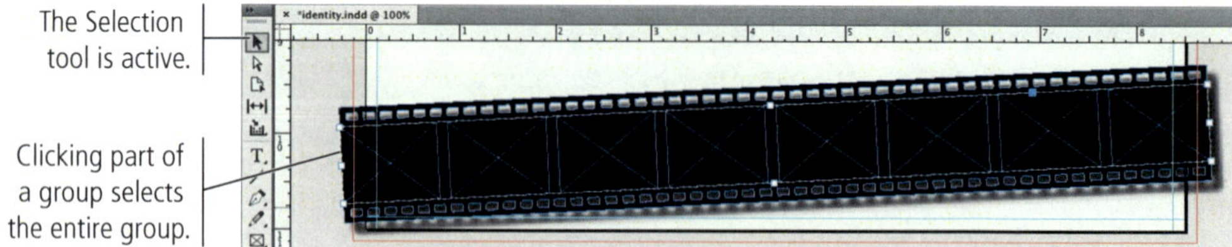

3. **Open the Layers panel (Window>Layers), then click the arrow to the left of Layer 1 to expand the layer.**

   Every file has a default layer named "Layer 1," where any objects that you create exist automatically. (You will use multiple layers in a later project to create multiple versions of a document.)

   The Layers panel also serves another purpose. Every object on a layer is listed in the panel, nested under the appropriate layer name. Groups, which you created in an earlier exercise, can be expanded so you can access and manage the individual components of the group.

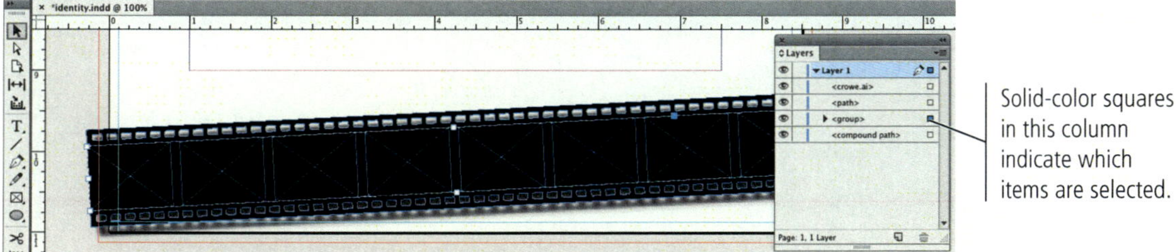

4. **Click the arrow to the left of the <group> item to expand the group.**

5. **Click the Select Item button for the first <rectangle> item in the group.**

   This method makes it easy to work with individual items in a group without first breaking apart the group.

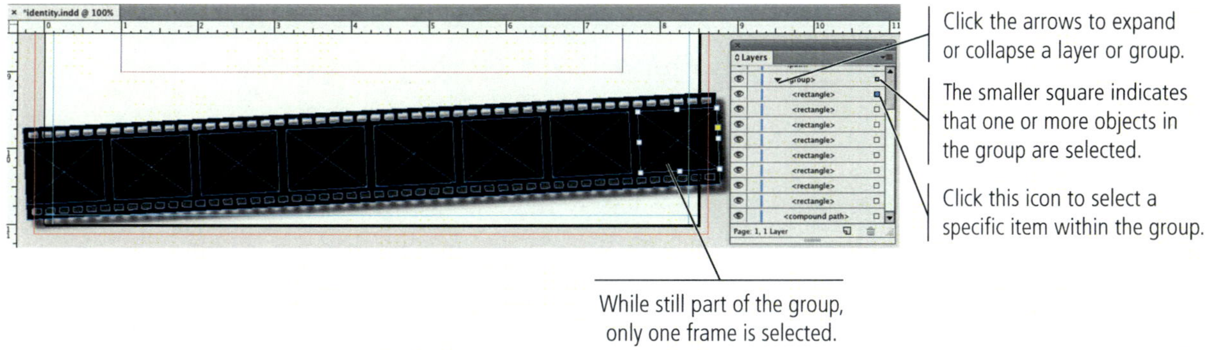

6. **Using the Selection tool, Control/right-click the selected graphics frame and choose Fitting>Frame Fitting Options in the contextual menu.**

   In this case, you know how much space is available, but you don't yet know the size of the images that are intended to fill the space. You can use the Frame Fitting options to determine what will happen when you place any image into the existing frames.

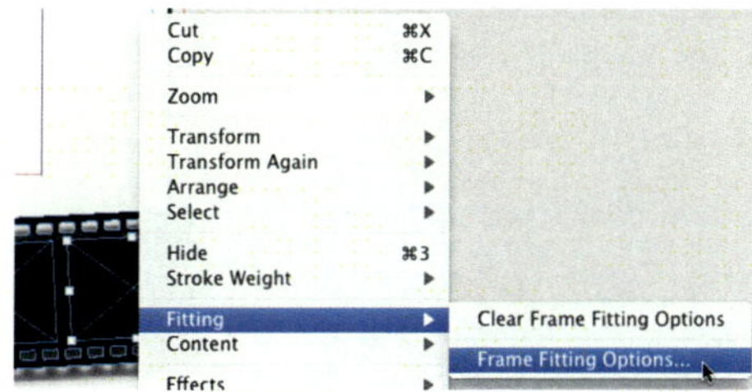

7. **In the Frame Fitting Options dialog box, activate the Auto-Fit option. Choose Fill Frame Proportionally in the Fitting menu, choose the center point in the Align From proxy, and click OK.**

   When an image is placed into this frame, it will fill the entire frame and the aspect ratio of the image will be maintained.

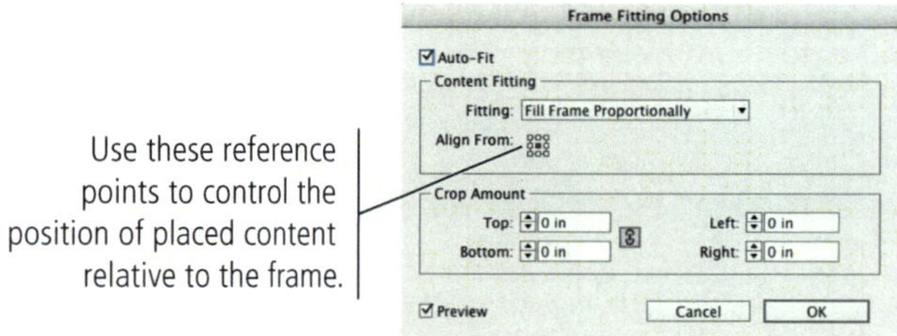

8. **With the Selection tool still active, click the seventh frame to select it.**

   When you are already "inside" a group, you can use the Selection tool to select another individual object within the same group.

Note:

You can also use the Direct Selection tool to select individual objects within a group.

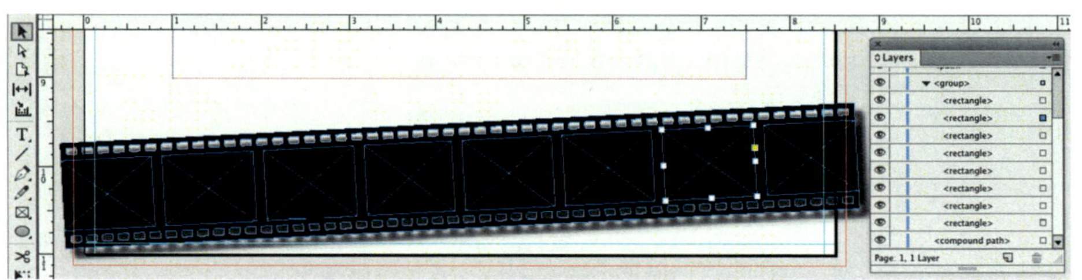

9. **Click the Auto-Fit option in the Control panel.**

   Because the center registration point is the default Content Fitting option, you do not need to open the Frame Fitting Options dialog box for each frame in this filmstrip.

10. **Repeat Steps 8–9 for the remaining six placeholder frames.**

11. **Choose File>Place. If necessary, navigate to the WIP>Crowe folder. Uncheck all options at the bottom of the Place dialog box.**

    If you leave Show Import Options checked, you would see the TIFF Options dialog box for each of the selected images. In this case you simply want to place the images, so you don't need to review the file options.

12. **Click `thumb1.tif` to select it. Press Shift and click `thumb8.tif` to select it and all in-between files.**

    In many cases, you will need to place more than one image from the same location into an InDesign layout. You can streamline the process by loading multiple images into the cursor at once and then clicking to place each image in the correct location.

Note:

Press Shift to select multiple contiguous files in a dialog box.

Press Command/Control to select multiple non-contiguous files.

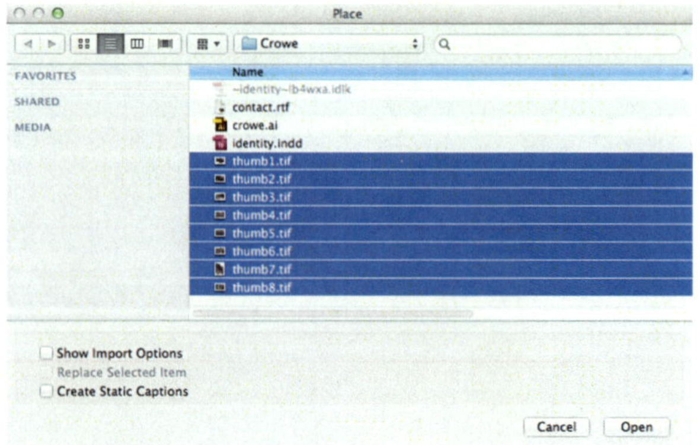

13. Click Open to load the selected files into the Place cursor.

When you select multiple files in the Place dialog box, the cursor is loaded with all of the selected pictures; a number in the cursor shows the number of files that are loaded.

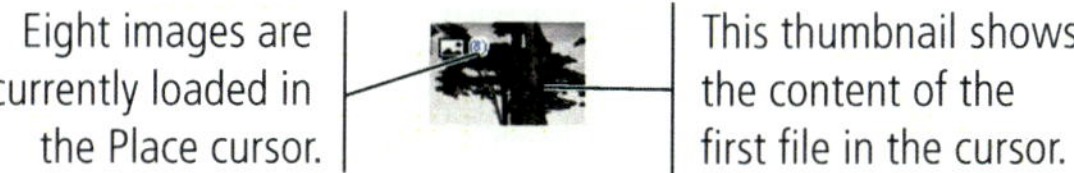

You can use the Left Arrow and Right Arrow keys to navigate through the loaded images, watching the cursor thumbnails to find the one you want to place.

14. Click inside the left placeholder frame to place the first image.

As soon as you place the first file, the next loaded image appears as the cursor thumbnail.

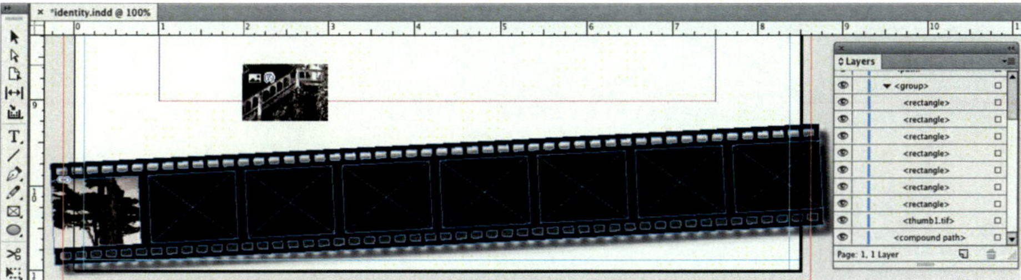

15. Click inside each empty frame to place the remaining loaded images.

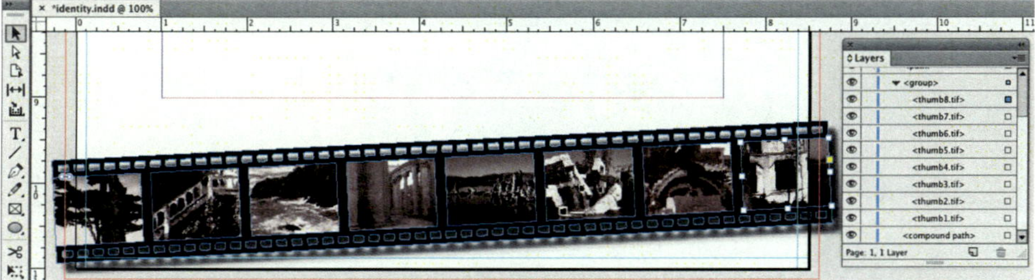

16. Choose the Direct Selection tool, and then click the fifth image thumbnail.

As already mentioned, the Direct Selection tool can be used to access and manipulate the contents inside a frame. This tool does not require ungrouping. (You could also double-click a grouped item with the Selection tool to access only one item in a group, and then use the Content Indicator icon to access the frame content.)

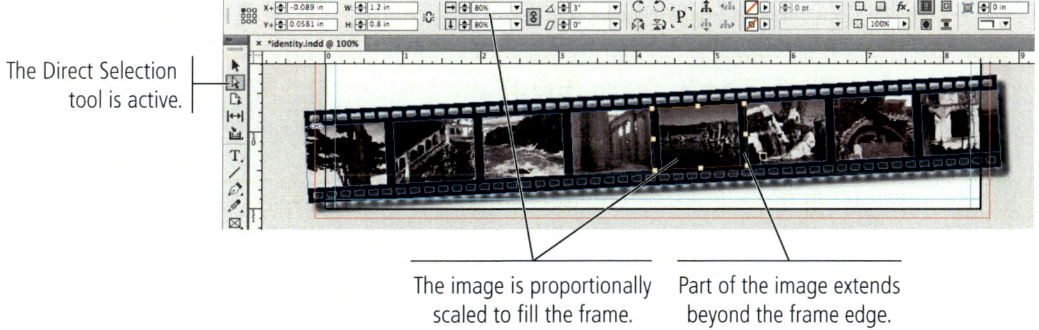

17. **In the Control panel, make sure the link icon for the scaling fields is active (unbroken links). Type 100 in the Scale X field and press Return/Enter to apply the change.**

    Because you used the Auto-Fit option, these thumbnail images have all been placed at (approximately) 80% proportionally. The images are already small, and reducing the percentage makes the detail in the fifth image *too* small. You can always change the image scaling after it has been scaled by the Auto-Fit option.

18. **Click inside the frame area and drag until the right edge of the image is approximately aligned to the right edge of the frame.**

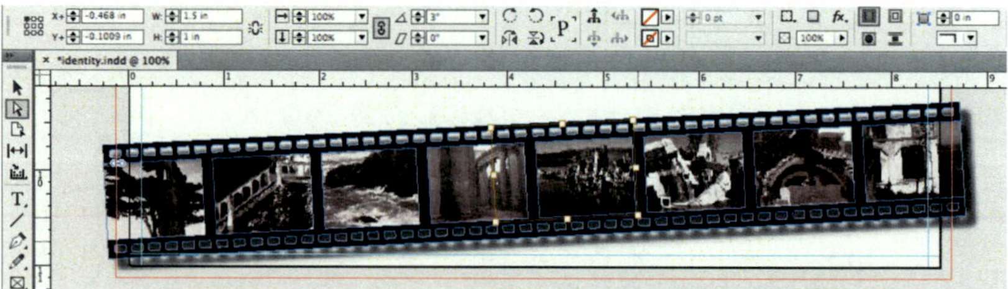

19. **Using the Direct Selection tool, select the seventh image in the filmstrip.**

    Remember, the default reference point for the Auto-Fit option centers the image inside the frame. In this image, the horse's head is cut off.

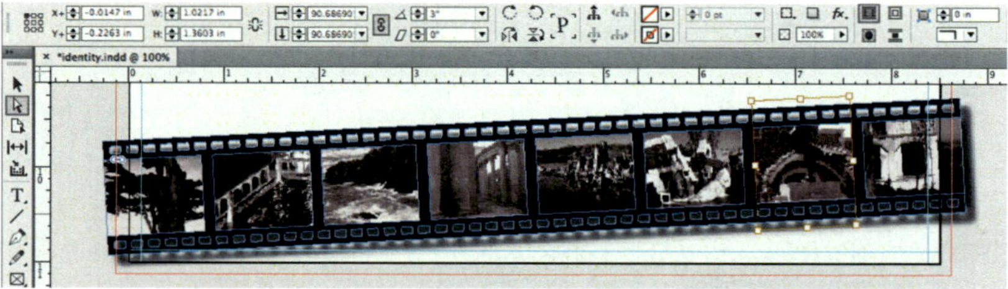

20. **Drag the image down inside the frame until the horse's head is visible.**

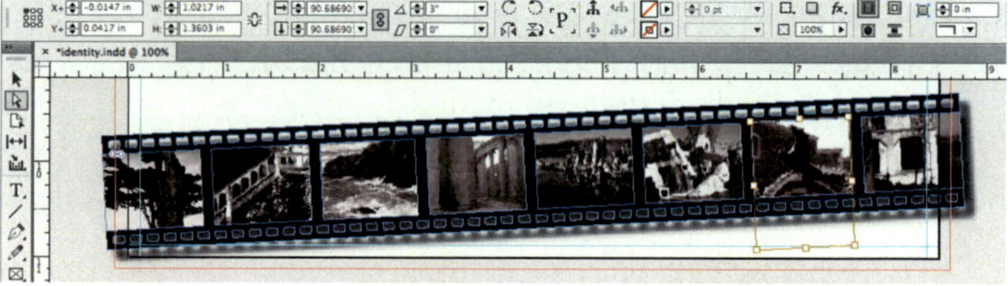

21. **Save the file and continue to the next stage of the project.**

Stage 4 Creating and Formatting Basic Text

InDesign is ultimately a page-layout application, not an illustration program. **Page layout** means combining text and graphic elements in a meaningful way to convey a message. Text can be a single word (as in the logo used in this project) or thousands of pages of consecutive copy (as in a dictionary). Virtually every project you build in InDesign will involve text in one way or another; this letterhead is no exception.

Create a Simple Text Frame

Adding text to a page is a relatively simple process: draw a frame, and then type. In this exercise, you'll create a new text frame and add the client's tag line, then apply some basic formatting options to style the text.

Keep in mind that this project is an introduction to creating elements on a layout page; there is far more to professional typesetting than the few options you use here. InDesign provides extremely precise control over virtually every aspect of every letter and word on the page. In the following projects, you will learn about the vast number of options that are available for setting and controlling type, from formatting a single paragraph to an entire multi-page booklet.

1. **With identity.indd open, select the Type tool in the Tools panel.**

2. **Click in the empty space below the placed logo and drag to create a frame.**

   To type text into a layout, you must first create a frame with the Type tool; when you release the mouse button, you see a flashing bar (called the **insertion point**) where you first clicked to create the text frame.

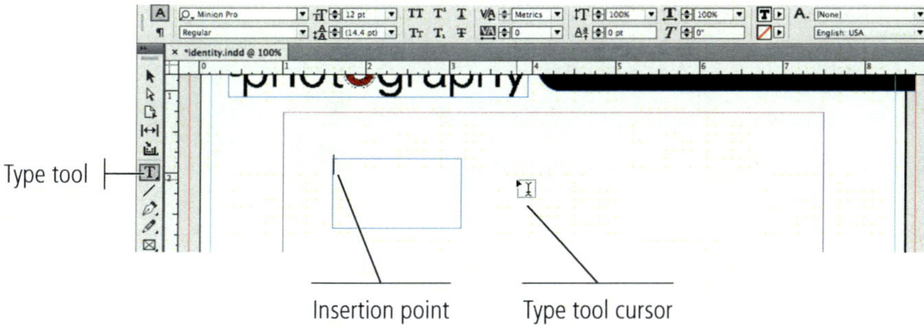

   The tag line for the letterhead is supposed to appear in the black area to the right of the logo. However, if you click inside that area with the Type tool, it will convert the existing shape to a type area. In this case you want a simple rectangular text frame, so you are creating it in an empty area, and then moving it into place.

3. **Review the character formatting options in the Control panel.**

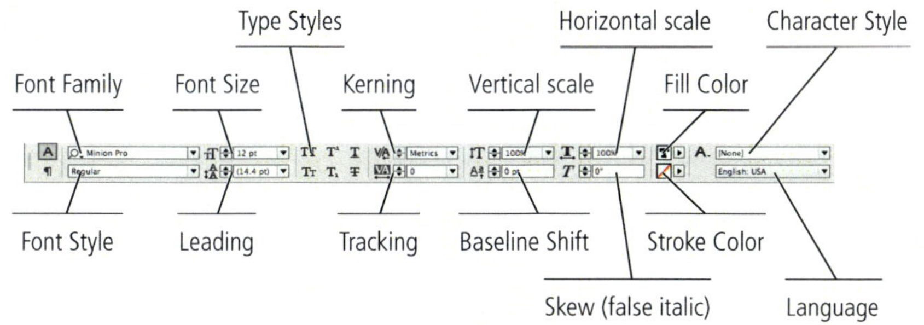

Note:

Remember from the Getting Started section at the beginning of this book: to complete the projects in this book, you should install and activate the ATC fonts that are provided with the book resource files.

4. **Type urban architecture & natural landscapes.**

The text appears, beginning at the flashing insertion point. Depending on the size of your frame, the text might automatically wrap to a second line within the frame.

New text in InDesign is automatically set in black 12-pt Minion Pro. This font is installed along with the application, so it should be available on your computer unless someone has modified your system fonts. Don't worry if your type appears in some other font; you will change it shortly.

> ***Note:***
>
> *Type defaults to a 100% black fill with no stroke. (You can apply a stroke to type, but you should be very careful when you do to avoid destroying the letter shapes.)*

5. **Choose the Selection tool in the Tools panel.**

You must use the Selection tool to change the position and size of a text frame. You can either drag the handles to manually change the frame, or use the Control panel options to define specific parameters.

6. **In the Control panel, choose the bottom-right reference point and then change the frame's dimensions to:**

X: 8.25″	**W: 4.1″**
Y: 0.8″	**H: 0.25″**

Some attributes of a type frame are no different than a graphics frame. You can change the position and size (based on the selected reference point) using the fields on the left end of the Control panel.

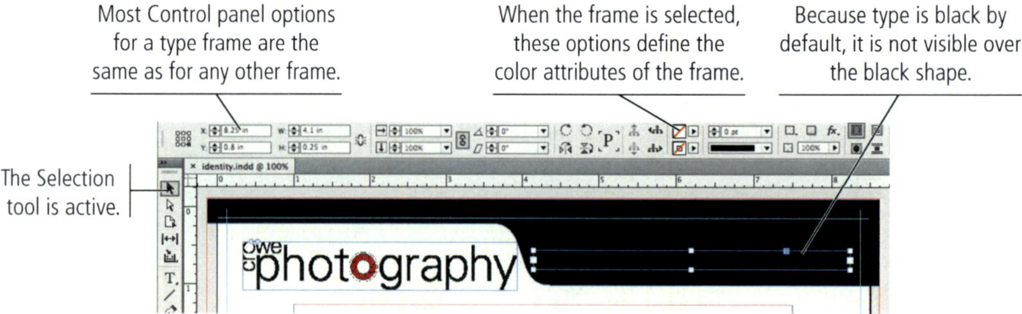

7. **Choose the Type tool, and click inside the repositioned text frame to place the insertion point.**

Because the default type format is black, you can't see the characters on the black background. Because you know they are there, you can still select them.

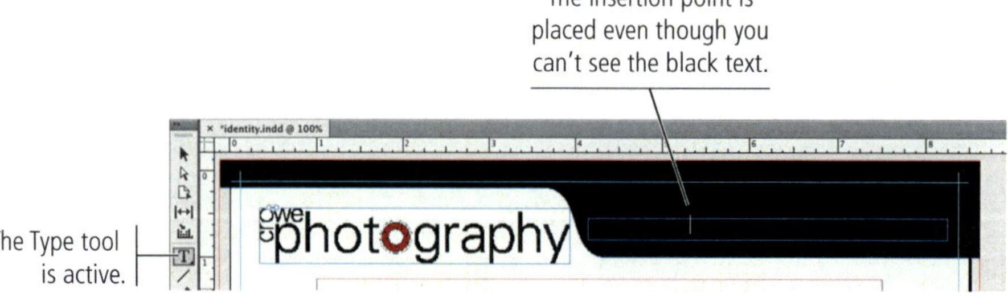

Selecting Text

INDESIGN FOUNDATIONS

You have a number of options for selecting type characters in a frame.

- Select specific characters by clicking with the Type tool and dragging.
- Double-click a word to select the entire word.
- Triple-click a word to select the entire line that contains the word.
- Quadruple-click a word to select the entire paragraph that contains the word.
- Place the insertion point and press Shift-Right Arrow or Shift-Left Arrow to select the character to the immediate right or left of the insertion point, respectively.
- Place the insertion point and press Shift-Up Arrow or Shift-Down Arrow to select all characters up to the same position as the insertion point in the previous or next line, respectively.
- Place the insertion point and press Command/Control-Shift-Right Arrow or Command/Control-Shift-Left Arrow to select the entire word immediately to the right or left of the insertion point, respectively.
- Place the insertion point and press Command/Control-Shift-Up Arrow or Command/Control-Shift-Down Arrow to select the rest of paragraph immediately before or after the insertion point, respectively.

8. **Choose Edit>Select All to select all of the text in the frame.**

Character formatting such as the font, style, and size apply only to selected characters. You will learn about all of the available character formatting options in Project 2: Festival Poster.

9. **In the Control panel, open the Fill swatch panel and click the Paper color.**

The white-filled text now appears over the black background. (It is still highlighted, so it currently appears in reverse.)

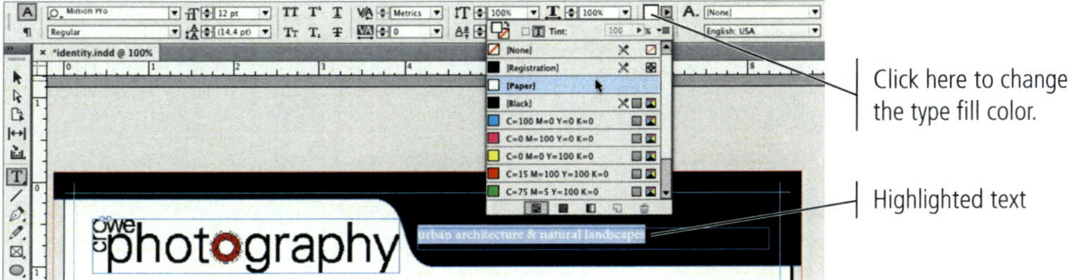

10. **With the text still selected, click in the Font Family field to highlight the current font name.**

11. **With the font name highlighted, type ATC.**

When you type in the Font Family field, the application automatically presents a menu of all fonts that include the letters you type.

By default, the application presents any font that includes the search characters *anywhere in the font name*; a search for "gar" would find both Garamond and Devangari. This kind of search returns all matching fonts in the pop-up menu.

If you click the magnifying glass icon, you can also choose to Search First Word Only. In this case, typing "gar" would automatically change the Font Family field to the first font that begins with those characters; no menu is presented.

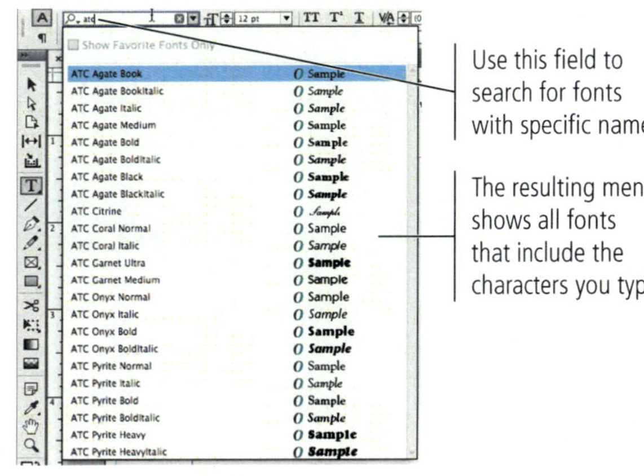

More About Working with Fonts

If you click the arrow to the right of the Font Family menu, you will see a menu that lists every font that is available to InDesign.

The top section of the menu lists the ten most **recent fonts**. By default, these appear in the order they were used (the most recently used appears at the top of the menu). In the Type pane of the Preferences dialog box, you can change the number of displayed fonts; you can also choose to list them alphabetically instead of in the order they were used.

The second section of the menu lists **document fonts** (if any). These are fonts that exist in a "Document Fonts" folder that resides in the same folder as the active InDesign file. Document Fonts are available for the active file even if they are not installed on your operating system. (See Project 3: HeartSmart Newsletter for more about creating a job package).

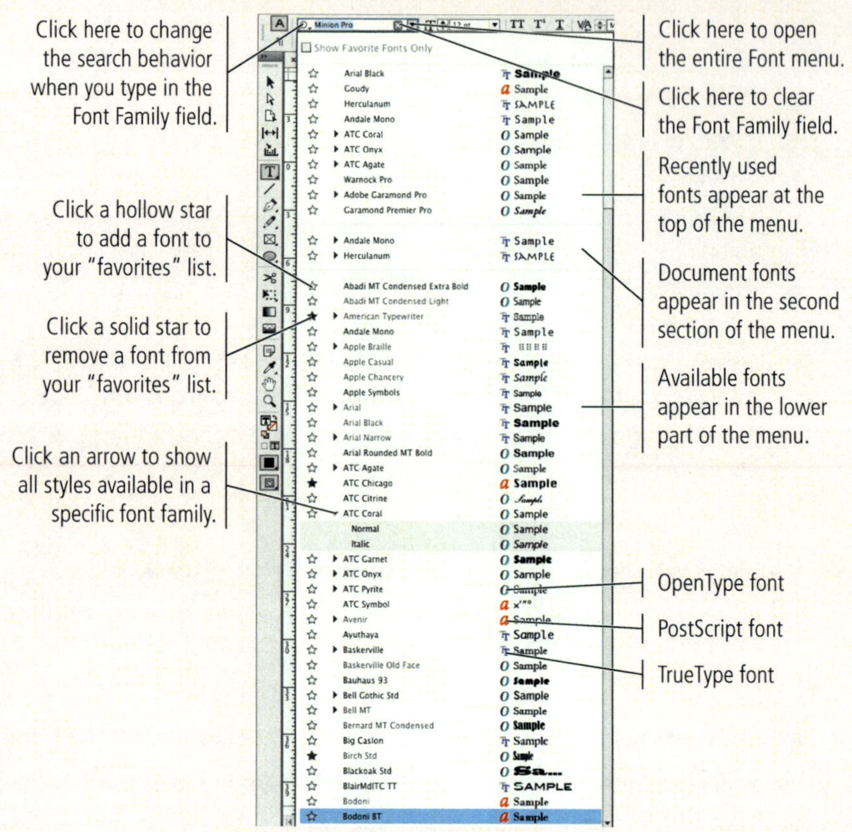

The lower portion of the font menu includes all fonts that are available on your computer. Each listed font includes a number of elements:

- You can use the star icons on the left side of the font menu to define "favorite" fonts. You can then check the box at the top of the menu to show only those fonts that you have marked as favorites.

  Check this box to show only fonts that are marked as favorites.

- The font family names appear in alphabetical order.

  An arrow to the left of a font name indicates that a specific font family includes more than one style. You can click the arrow to show all possible styles.

  If you apply a font that includes more than one style, the style you choose appears in the Font Style menu below the Font Family field. You can open the Font Style menu to change the style without changing the font family.

  Use the Font Style menu to choose a specific style that is available in the selected font family.

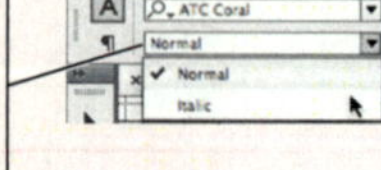

- An icon identifies the type of each font.

  PostScript (Type 1) fonts have two file components (outline and printer) that must both be available for output.

  TrueType fonts have a single file, but (until recently) were primarily used on the Windows platform.

  OpenType fonts are contained in a single file that can include more than 60,000 glyphs (characters) in a single font. OpenType fonts are cross-platform; the same font file can be used on both Macintosh and Windows systems.

  There are other types of fonts, including PostScript Type 3 and Multiple Master, but these should generally be avoided.

- A WYSIWYG sample of each font appears at the right side of the menu. You can change the size of the sample in the Type pane of the Preferences dialog box.

12. **Choose ATC Onyx Italic in the font-search menu.**

After choosing the font you want, you should notice that the Control panel shows ATC Onyx in the Font Family menu and Italic in the Font Style menu.

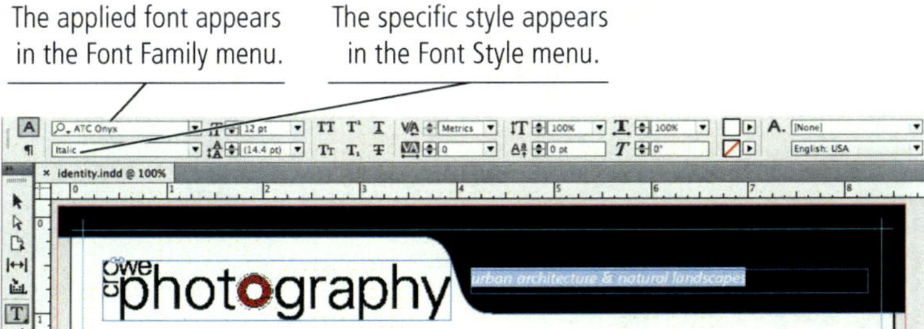

13. **Click the Up-Arrow button for the Font Size field until you see a red icon on the right edge of the frame.**

Each time you click, you increase the type size by one point. The red X is the **overset text icon**; it indicates that more text exists than will fit into the frame.

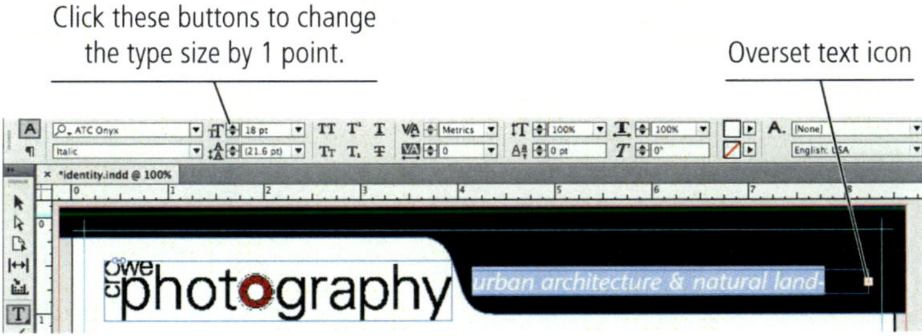

When you see an overset text icon, you can:

- Edit the text to fit the space, which is usually not allowable for a graphic designer.
- Make the frame larger to fit the text, which is not always possible.
- Add more frames to the story and thread the text into the extra frames, which is also not always possible.
- Reduce the type size or adjust other formatting options to make the type fit into the available space, which can make text unreadable (depending on how small you have to make it).

Note:

You can also choose from the common preset type sizes in the menu, or type a specific size in the field.

If you type in the Font Size field, you don't need to type the unit "pt" for the type size; InDesign automatically applies the measurement for you.

Note:

Press Command/Control-Shift-> to increase the type size by 2 points, or Command/Control-Shift-< to decrease the type size by 2 points.

14. **Click the Down-Arrow button once to reduce the type size by 1 point.**

This allows all the type to fit in the frame.

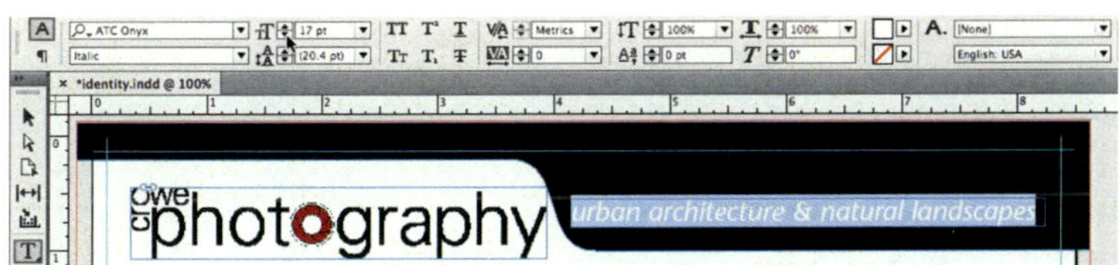

15. **Click anywhere in the selected text to place the insertion point.**

This removes the highlight, indicating that the characters are now deselected.

16. **In the Control panel, click the [Paragraph] Align Right option.**

Paragraph formatting — including alignment — applies to the entire paragraph where the insertion point is placed. You don't have to first select the entire paragraph. (You will learn about the available paragraph formatting options in Project 2: Festival Poster.)

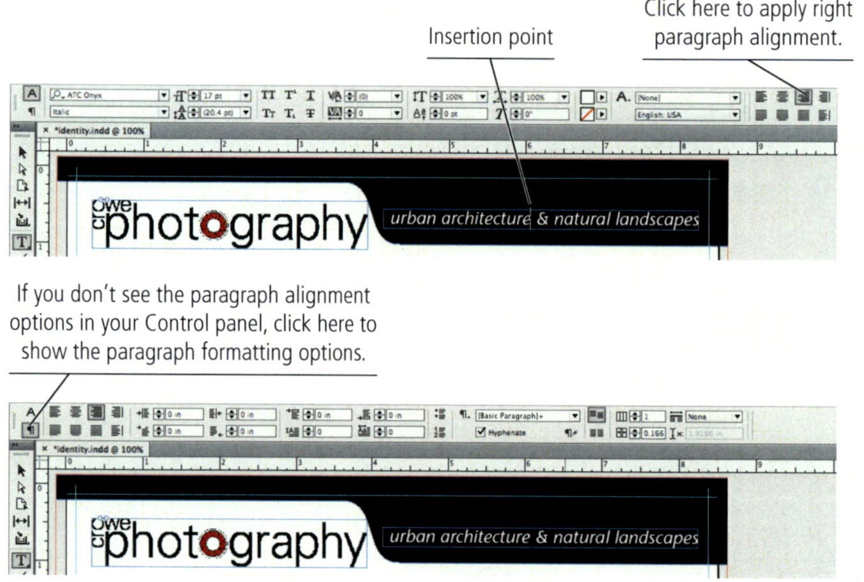

Note:

When a type frame is selected with the Selection tool, you can double-click inside the frame to place the insertion point inside that frame. In this case, the type tool is automatically selected.

17. **Save the file and continue to the next exercise.**

Place an External Text File

You just learned how to create a text frame and create new text. You can also import text that was created in an external word-processing application, which is a common situation when creating page-layout jobs (more common, perhaps, than manually typing text in a frame). In this exercise, you import text that was saved in a rich-text format (RTF) file, which can store type-formatting options as well as the actual text.

1. **With identity.indd open, make sure nothing is selected in the layout and then choose File>Place.**

   Remember, you can choose Edit>Deselect All, or simply click in an empty area of the workspace to deselect any selected objects.

2. **Navigate to contact.rtf in the WIP>Crowe folder. Make sure none of the options are checked at the bottom of the dialog box and click Open.**

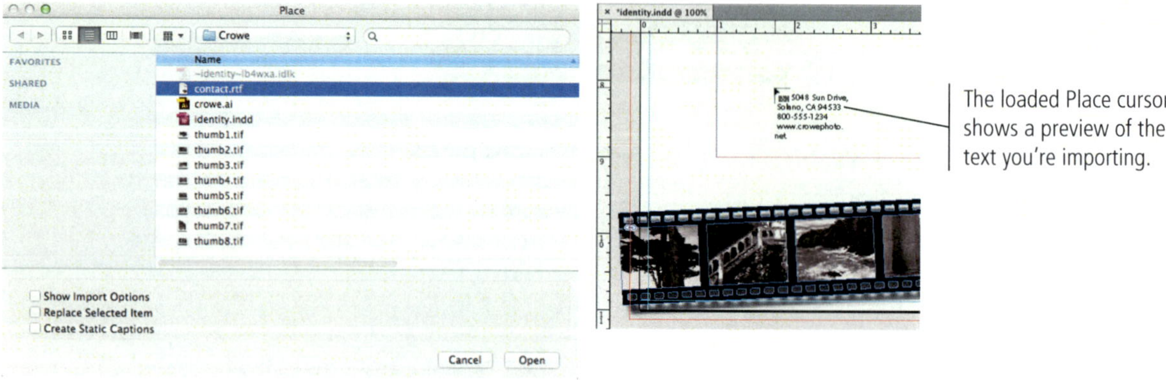

The loaded Place cursor shows a preview of the text you're importing.

3. **Click the loaded Place cursor near the bottom of the page, above the filmstrip graphic but within the margin guides.**

   The resulting text frame is automatically created as wide as the defined margin guides, and extending down to the bottom margin guide on the page.

Placing text from a file automatically creates a text frame to contain the text.

4. **Choose the Selection tool. With the text frame selected, click the Fit Frame to Content button in the Control panel.**

   If you don't see this button, you can Control/right-click the text frame and choose Fitting>Fit Frame to Content.

   When working with a text frame, this option reduces the frame to the smallest possible size that can contain the existing text.

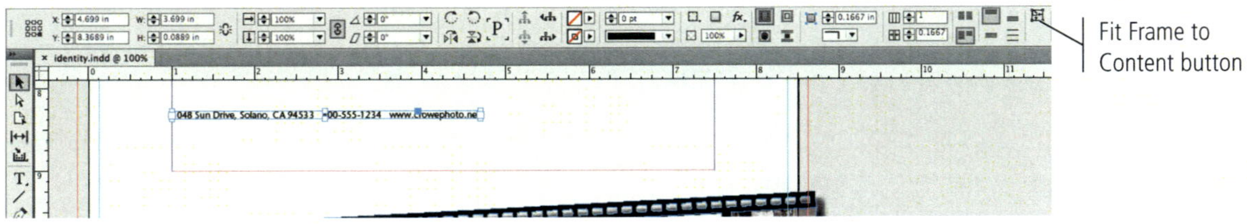

Fit Frame to Content button

5. **Click the bottom-right bounding box handle of the frame. While still holding down the mouse button, press Command/Control-Shift, and then drag to the right. When the Scale X and Scale Y fields in the Control panel show approximately 125%, release the mouse button.**

   As you drag the frame handle, pressing Command/Control allows you to resize the type along with the frame. Pressing Shift constrains the scaling to maintain the original height-to-width ratio.

The Scale X and Scale Y fields in the Control panel shows the percentage to which the frame and its content are being scaled.

6. **Move the cursor outside the top-right corner handle until you see the rotation cursor. Click and drag up until you have rotated the frame by 3°.**

   This is the same angle that you used for the filmstrip graphic.

Note:

You can also use the Free Transform tool to rotate an object, but changing tools is not necessary since the same rotation functionality can be accessed with the Selection tool.

7. **Using the Selection tool, move the rotated text frame into place just above the filmstrip, with the right edge at 8.25″.**

   Use the following image as a guide for placing the frame.

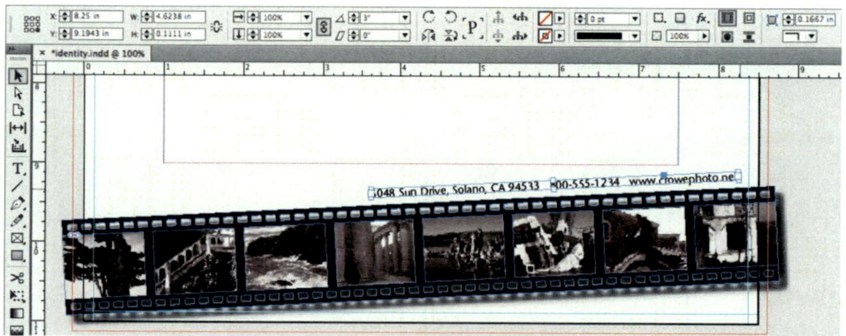

8. **Click away from the text frame to deselect all objects, then choose View>Extras>Hide Frame Edges.**

   This command turns off the blue borders that surround every frame. Frame edges can be very valuable when you're working with some objects, but they can be distracting in other cases. Always remember that you can toggle the frame edges on and off in the View>Extras submenu.

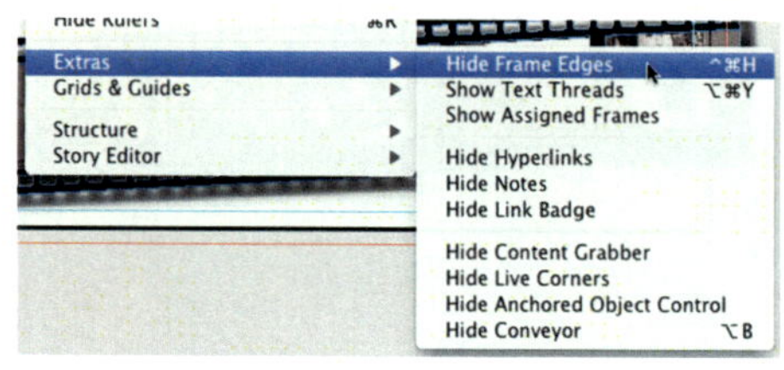

   When frame edges are hidden, moving the Selection tool cursor over a frame reveals its edges. This frame highlighting can make it easier to find exactly the object you want, especially when working in an area with a number of overlapping or nearby objects.

9. **Save the file and continue to the final stage of the project.**

> *Note:*
>
> *If a menu command is not visible, choose Show All Menu Items at the bottom of the menu.*

Tips and Tricks for Working with Layout Elements

Copying and Pasting

The standard Cut, Copy, and Paste options are available in InDesign, just as they are in most applications. Whatever you have selected will be copied or cut to the Clipboard, and whatever is in the Clipboard will be pasted. InDesign has a number of special pasting options in the Edit menu:

Paste. If you are pasting an object (frame, etc.), the object will be pasted in the center of the document window. If you are pasting text, it will be pasted at the location of the current insertion point; if the insertion point is not currently placed, the text is placed in a new basic text frame in the middle of the document window.

Paste without Formatting. This command is available when text is in the Clipboard; the text is pasted using the default type formatting options (12-pt black Minion Pro, if it hasn't been changed on your system).

Paste Into. This command is available when an object is in the Clipboard and another object is selected. The pasted object becomes the contents of the object that is selected when you choose this command.

Paste in Place. This command pastes an object at the exact position as the original. If you paste on the same page as the original, you create a second object exactly on top of the first. You can also use this command to place a copy in the exact position as the original, but on a different page in the layout.

Managing Stacking Order

The top-to-bottom order of objects is called **stacking order**; each object you create is stacked on top of existing objects. When you have multiple stacked objects — especially ones that are closely spaced — it can be difficult to select exactly what you want. Fortunately, the application provides a number of options to make it easier.

When you move the Selection tool cursor over an object, the edges of the object are highlighted. This lets you know what will be selected if you click.

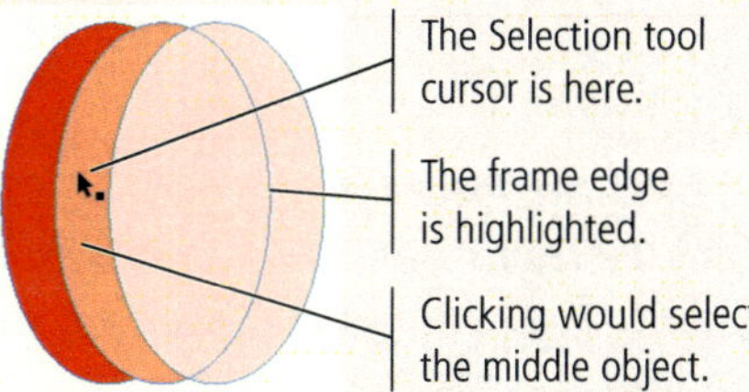

When an object is already selected, InDesign favors the already selected object. This prevents you from accidentally selecting an object higher in the stacking order (for example, if you want to drag only the middle object), but this also means you have to be careful if you do want to select a different object.

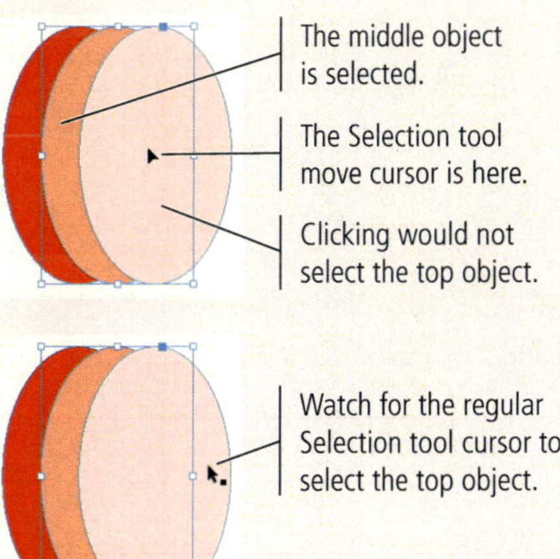

You can use the Object>Select submenu commands (or their related keyboard shortcuts) to access objects relative to their order in the stack.

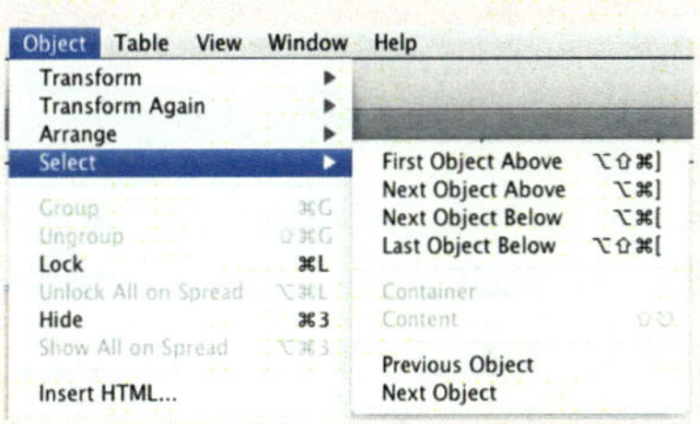

You can use the Object>Arrange submenu commands (or their related keyboard shortcuts) to change the stacking-order position of objects.

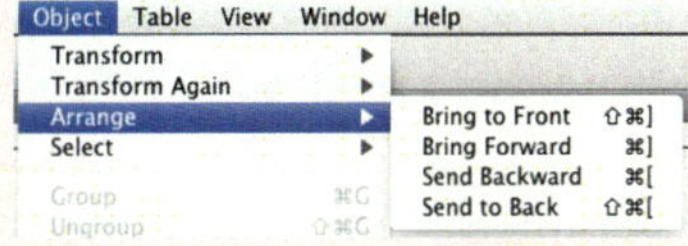

Finally, you can use the individual item listings in the Layers panel to select exactly the object you want, or to rearrange objects in the layer stack.

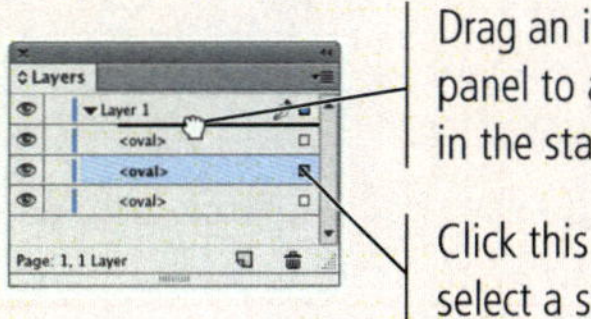

Stage 5 Printing InDesign Files

Although the PDF format is the *de facto* standard for submitting files to a commercial printer, you will still need to output printed proofs at some point in your career — whether to show hard copy to a client or to simply review a document's content away from a monitor. Creating those proofs requires a basic understanding of how the software and hardware translate what you see on the screen to ink on paper.

For a printer to output high-quality pages from Adobe InDesign, some method of defining the page and its elements is required. These definitions are provided by Page Description Languages (PDLs), the most widely used of which is Adobe PostScript 3.

When a file is output to a PostScript-enabled device, the raster image processor (RIP) creates a file that includes mathematical descriptions detailing the construction and placement of the various page elements; the print file precisely maps the location of each pixel on the page. In the printer, the RIP then interprets the description of each element into a matrix of ones (black) and zeros (white). The output device uses this matrix to reconstruct the element as a series of individual dots or spots that form a high-resolution bitmap image on film or paper.

Not every printer on the market is capable of interpreting PostScript information. Low-cost, consumer-level inkjet printers, common in the modern graphic design market, are generally not PostScript compatible. (Some desktop printers can handle PostScript, at least with an additional purchase; consult the technical documentation that came with your printer to make certain it can print PostScript information.) If your printer is non-PostScript compatible, some features in the InDesign Print dialog box will be unavailable and some page elements (particularly EPS files) might not output as expected.

If you do not have a PostScript output device, you can work around the problem by first exporting your InDesign files to PDF (see Project 2: Festival Poster) and then opening the PDFs in Acrobat to print a proof. This is a common workflow solution in the current graphic design industry.

Print a Sample Proof

Not too long ago, every job sent to a commercial printer required a hardcopy proof to accompany the disk as an example of the layout content. As digital file submission continues to gain ground, however, physical printer proofs are becoming less common.

In general, every job you create will be printed at some point in the workflow — whether for your own review, as a client comp, or as a final proof that accompanies a file to the commercial printer. So, whether you need a basic proof or a final job proof, you should still understand what is possible in the InDesign Print dialog box.

Composite proofs print all colors on the same sheet, which allows you to judge page geometry and the overall positioning of elements. Final composite proofs that are provided to the printer should include **registration marks** (special printer's marks used to check the alignment of individual inks when the job is printed), and they should always be output at 100% size.

> ***Note:***
>
> *It is also important to realize that desktop inkjet and laser printers typically do not accurately represent color.*

1. **With identity.indd open, choose File>Print.**

   The Print dialog box includes dozens of options in eight different categories.

   The most important options you'll select are the Printer and PPD (PostScript printer description) at the top of the dialog box. InDesign reads the information in the PPD to determine which of the specific print options are available for the current output.

2. **Choose the printer you want to use in the Printer menu, and choose the PPD for that printer in the PPD menu (if possible).**

3. **Review the options in the General pane.**

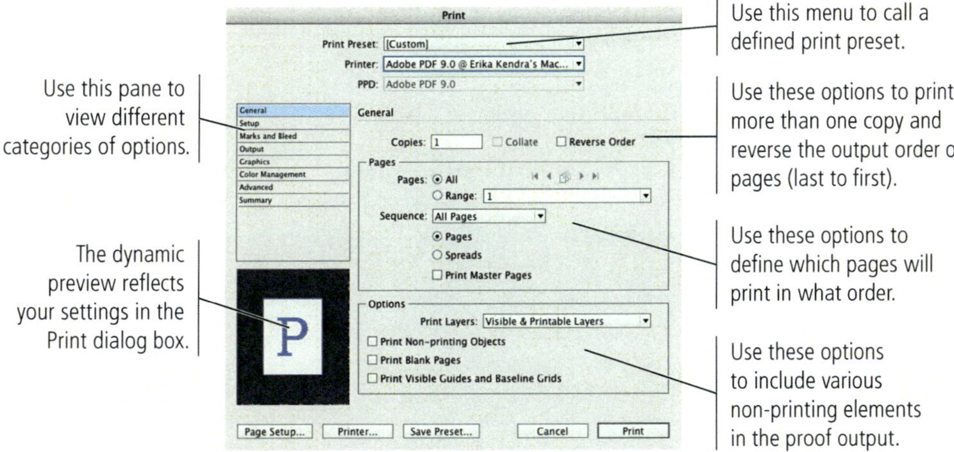

If you frequently use the same options for printing proofs, simply click the Save Preset button at the bottom of the dialog box after defining those settings. You can then call all of those same settings by choosing the saved preset in the Print Preset menu.

4. **Click the Setup option in the list of categories.**

These options determine the paper size that will be used for the output (not to be confused with the page size), the paper orientation, and page scaling and positioning options relative to the paper size.

5. **If your printer can print to tabloid-size paper, choose Tabloid in the Paper Size menu.**

If you can only print to letter-size paper, choose the landscape paper orientation option, and then activate the Tile check box.

To output a letter-size page at 100% on letter-size paper, you have to tile to multiple sheets of paper; using the landscape paper orientation allows you to tile to two sheets instead of four (as shown in the preview area).

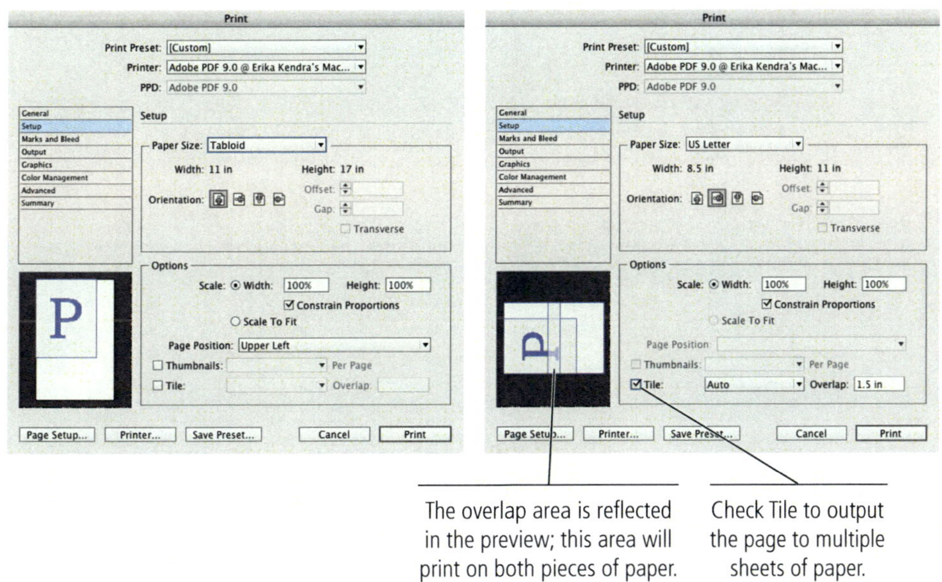

The Offset and Gap fields should only be used when a job is output to an imagesetter or high-end proofing device. They define page placement on a piece of oversized film or on a printing plate.

6. Click the Marks and Bleed option in the list of categories. Activate the All Printer's Marks option and change the Offset field to 0.125". Make sure the Use Document Bleed Settings option is checked.

You can specify individual printer's marks, or simply print them all. For proofing purposes, the crop and bleed marks are the most important options to include.

The Offset value determines how far from the page edge printer's marks will be placed; some printers require printer's marks to stay outside the bleed area, which means the offset should be at least the same as the defined bleed area.

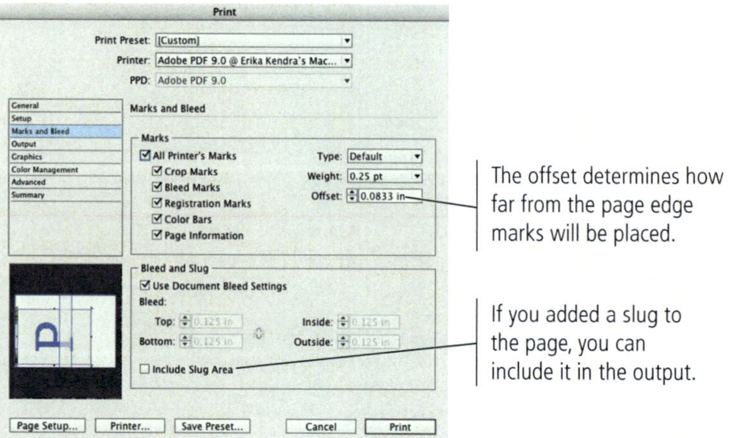

7. Click the Output option in the list of categories. If you can print color, choose Composite CMYK or Composite RGB in the Color menu; otherwise, choose Composite Gray.

In the Color menu, you can choose the color model you want to use. (If you only have a black-and-white printer, this menu will default to Composite Gray.) The composite options output all colors to a single page, which is appropriate for a desktop proof. If you choose either Separations option in the menu, the Inks list shows which inks (separations) will be included in the output.

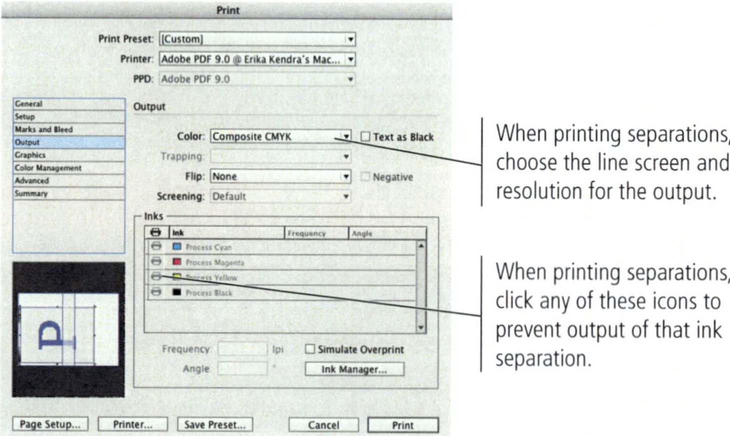

The Trapping, Flip, Negative, Screening, Frequency, and Angle options should only be used by the output service provider; these options relate to the way separations are imaged on a printing plate for commercial print output.

8. **Click Graphics in the list of categories.**

9. **Choose Optimized Subsampling in the Images Send Data menu.**

   This menu determines how much data is sent to the output device for placed images.

   - All, the default option, sends full-resolution image data.
   - Optimized Subsampling sends only the necessary data to output the best possible resolution on the printer you are using.
   - Proxy outputs low-resolution screen previews, which reduces the time required for output.
   - None outputs all placed images as gray frames with crossed diagonal lines. This is useful for reviewing overall placement when developing an initial layout comp.

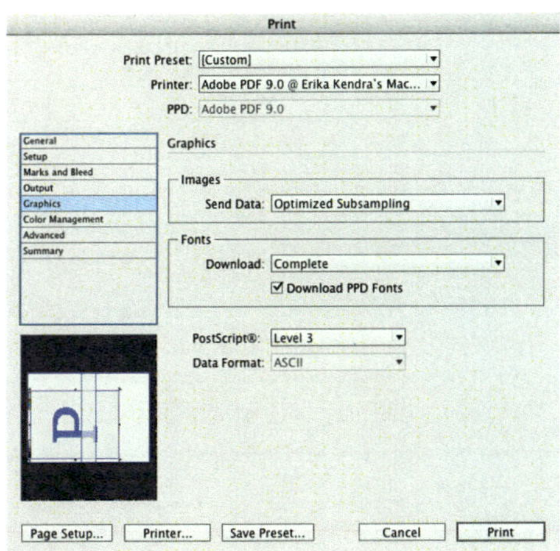

10. **Choose Subset in the Fonts Download menu.**

    This menu determines how much font data is downloaded to the printer. (Font data is required by the output device to print the job correctly.)

    - None sends no font information to the printer. (This can cause output problems, especially if you use TrueType fonts.)
    - Complete sends the entire font file for every font that is used in the document.
    - Subset sends font information only for the characters that are used in the document.

11. **Check the Download PPD Fonts option.**

    Professional-quality output devices include a number of resident fonts, from just a few to the entire Adobe type library. If this option is checked, InDesign sends data for all fonts in the document, even if those fonts are installed on the output device. (This can be important because different fonts of the same name might have different font metrics, which can cause text to reflow and appear different in the print than in the file that you created.)

12. **Leave the PostScript and Data Format menus at their default values.**

    The PostScript menu defines which level of PostScript to use. Some older devices cannot process PostScript 3. You should generally leave this menu at the default value.

    The Data Format menu defines how image data is transferred. ASCII is compatible with older devices, and is useful for cross-platform applications. Binary is smaller than ASCII, but might not work on all platforms.

13. **Click Print to output the page.**

14. **When the document comes back into focus, save and close it.**

Note:

We're intentionally skipping the Color Management and Advanced panes in the Print dialog box. We explain them in later projects when they are relevant to the project content.

Project Review

fill in the blank

1. _______________ is the area of an object that extends past the edge of a page to compensate for variations in the output process.

2. _______________ is a special kind of raster image that has only two possible color values, black or white.

3. The _______________ defines the outermost dimensions of an object; it is always a rectangle, regardless of the object's specific shape.

4. _______________ are based on the concept of anchor points and their defining control handles.

5. ____________________________________ are the four primary colors used in process-color printing.

6. The _______________ tool is used to select entire frames or other objects.

7. The _______________ tool can be used to select the image contained within a specific frame when the frame is part of a group.

8. The _______________ panel can be used to create complex shapes by combining multiple objects.

9. The _______________ can be used to access a frame's content when the Selection tool is active.

10. The _______________ is context sensitive, reflecting different options depending on what is selected in the document.

short answer

1. Briefly explain the difference between a vector graphic and a raster image.

2. Briefly explain how resolution affects a page laid out in InDesign.

3. Briefly explain the concept of process color.

Portfolio Builder Project

Use what you learned in this project to complete the following freeform exercise.
Carefully read the art director and client comments, then create your own design to meet the needs of the project.
Use the space below to sketch ideas; when finished, write a brief explanation of your reasoning behind your final design.

art director comments

The owner of your agency is pleased with your work on behalf of your client. She has decided to create more formal branding for your design agency and wants you to create a new logo and the accompanying collateral pieces with the new logo.

To complete this project, you should:

- ❑ Develop a compelling logo that suggests the agency's purpose (graphic design). Incorporate the agency's name — Creative Concepts — in the logo.
- ❑ Build a letterhead using the same specifications that you used to design the Crowe letterhead.
- ❑ Build a business card that is 3.5″ wide by 2″ high, with 1/8″ bleeds.
- ❑ Build an envelope layout for #10 business-size envelopes (9.5″ × 4.125″).

client comments

For the logo, I want something that really says 'graphic design' — how can we convince clients that we can design their logos if we don't have a good design for our own? Find or create some kind of imagery that people will immediately recognize as graphics- or art-related.

The letterhead should have the company's mailing address, phone number, and Web site. The business card needs to include a name, title, mailing address, email, and phone number. The envelope should only have the mailing address and the Web site. Use your own contact information as placeholder text for everything.

For the envelope, we're going to print pre-folded envelopes so you can't use bleeds. In fact, you need to keep objects at least 0.25″ from the edges.

Keep in mind that you're building a complete identity package, so all pieces should have a consistent look. Whatever you do on the letterhead, you should use similar visual elements on all three pieces.

project justification

Project Summary

We designed this project to introduce you to the basics of page layout with InDesign; you will expand on these skills throughout this book. Creating a new document to meet specific project needs — including page size, margins, and the printer's stated bleed requirements — is one of the most important tasks you will complete in InDesign.

After the page structure is created, InDesign has many tools for creating objects — basic shapes, lines and Bézier curves, placeholder frames, and text frames. The built-in drawing tools can create sophisticated artwork directly on the page, such as the filmstrip in this letterhead layout (although InDesign should not be considered an alternative to Adobe Illustrator for creating all vector artwork). You can also place external image and text files, and then transform those files to meet the specific needs of a given project.

There are many different methods for managing objects and their content. The Selection and Direct Selection tools, the Content Indicator icon, frame edge highlighting, and the Layers panel all provide ways to access only — and exactly — what you want to edit.

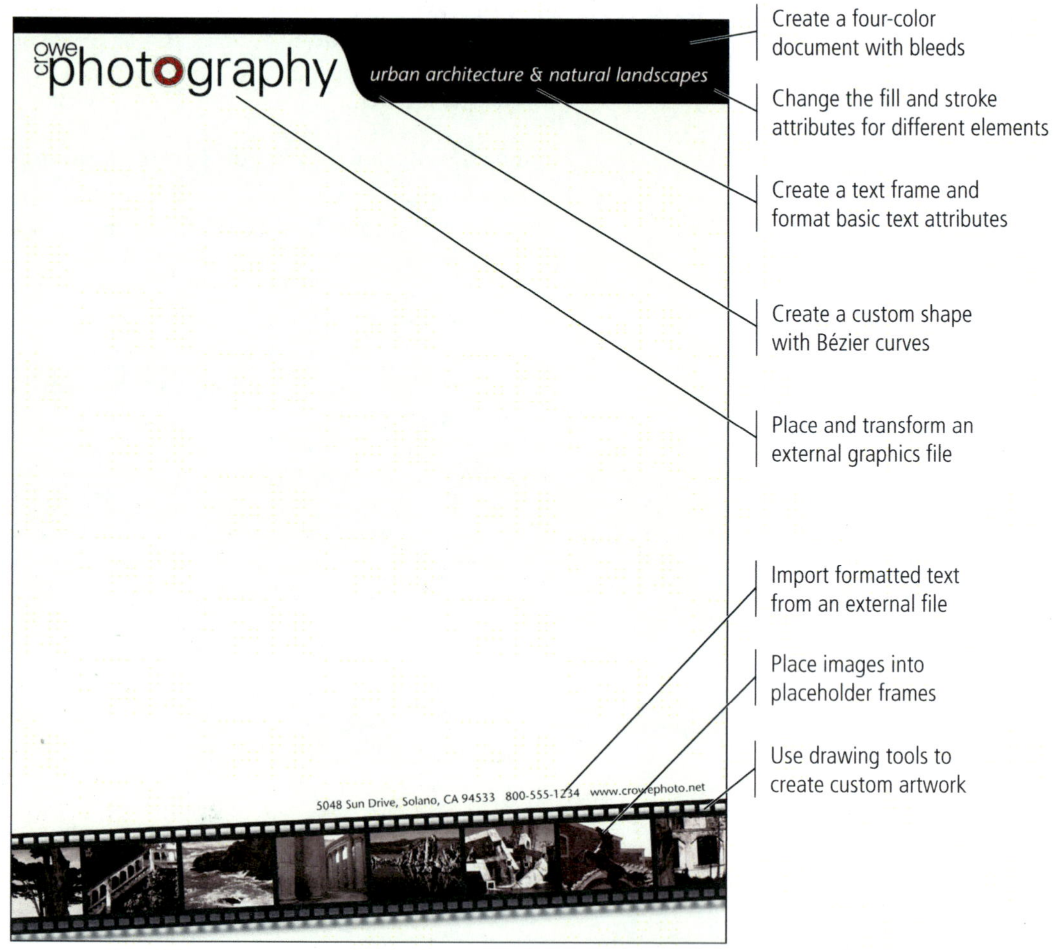

project 2

Festival Poster

Your client is the marketing director for the city of Santa Barbara. She wants to create a poster to advertise the annual Surfrider Festival. She wants to create posters that will be plastered all over the city, from local restaurants and clubs to bus stops and construction sites that don't say "Post No Bills." This type of poster should use very little text set in a large, easy-to-read font, and it needs to be eye-catching from a distance, with large, vivid graphics.

This project incorporates the following skills:

- ❑ Creating a file with the appropriate settings for a five-color, commercially printed poster
- ❑ Using gradients, graphics, and image effects to attract the viewer's attention
- ❑ Adding text elements and applying formatting as appropriate for a poster
- ❑ Threading a single text story across multiple text frames
- ❑ Understanding the various options for formatting characters and paragraphs
- ❑ Using inline graphics to highlight important text elements
- ❑ Creating a PDF file that meets the printer's requirements

Project Meeting

client comments

The poster to promote this festival is basically the "play bill," and we will plaster it all over the city. We want the poster to be very attractive, colorful, and vivid, so the main focus — and most of the poster real estate — should be on the graphics. But the text also has to be readable; I emailed the text I want you to place at the bottom of the poster this morning. Our posters for past years' festivals have always been 11 × 17″, and we want to stick with that size.

art director comments

The client has provided all the pieces you need, so you can get started composing the layout. Most of this job is going to involve compositing multiple images and formatting text, but I want you to go beyond basic image placement. InDesign includes many tools for manipulating images; use some of those to make sure this poster consists of more than just plain pictures.

Finally, I want you to use a special metallic ink for the date and location. That should give the poster just a bit more visual impact than regular flat colors. I think the gold 8005 in Pantone's metallic collection will work well with the other visual elements.

You already know the page size, and according to the printer the poster needs a 1/4″ bleed allowance just to be safe. The final posters should be saved as PDF using the printer's specs, which I'll email to you.

project objectives

To complete this project, you will:

- ❑ Convert the content type of frames
- ❑ Create a custom gradient to add visual impact
- ❑ Create a custom frame using an image clipping path
- ❑ Apply visual effects to unify various graphic elements
- ❑ Create a QR code
- ❑ Thread the flow of text through multiple text frames
- ❑ Format text characters and paragraphs to effectively convey a message
- ❑ Place inline graphics to highlight important textual elements
- ❑ Place text on a path
- ❑ Apply a spot color
- ❑ Create PDF files for commercial output

Stage 1 Building Graphic Interest

In Project 1: Letterhead Design, you learned the basics of placing graphics into a layout and drawing shapes using the built-in InDesign tools. You know that graphics and text are contained in frames, and that objects (including graphics frames) can have stroke and fill attributes. You can use those foundational skills to build virtually any InDesign layout.

InDesign also includes a number of options for extending your artistic options beyond simply compositing text and graphics that were finalized in other applications. The first stage of this project incorporates a number of these creative tools to accomplish your client's stated goal of grabbing the viewer's attention with vivid, attractive graphics.

Set up the Workspace

1. **Download `IDCC_RF_Project2.zip` from the Student Files Web page.**

2. **Expand the ZIP archive in your WIP folder (Macintosh) or copy the archive contents into your WIP folder (Windows).**

   This results in a folder named **Surfing**, which contains the files you need for this project. You should also use this folder to save the files you create in this project.

3. **With no file open in InDesign, open the Units & Increments pane of the Preferences dialog box (in the InDesign menu on Macintosh or the Edit menu on Windows).**

4. **Change both Ruler Units menus to Inches and click OK.**

   In Project 1: Letterhead Design, you changed the default units of measurement for an open file. By changing the preferences with no file open, you're changing the application default preferences; the settings that you define will be applied in any new file you create, but not to already-existing files.

> ***Note:***
>
> *Unless otherwise stated, the remaining projects in this book use inches as the default unit of measurement.*

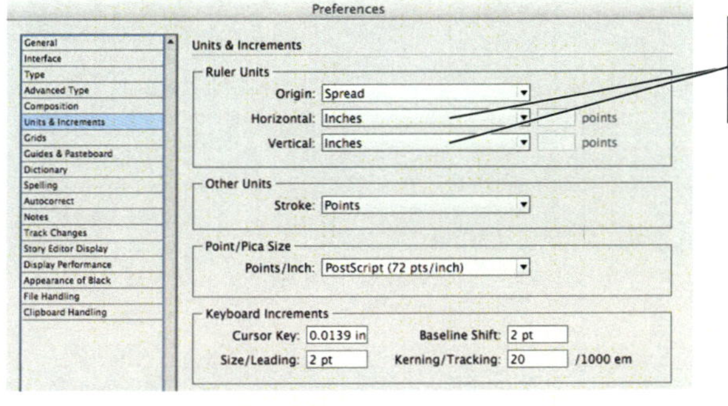

With no file open, change both of these menus to Inches.

5. **Choose File>New>Document.**

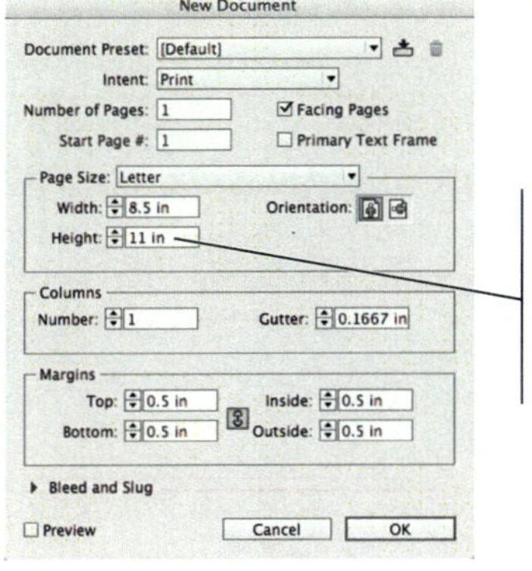

By changing the default units to inches, the measurements in all dialog boxes (including this one) are now shown in inches.

6. **Create a new one-page print document that is 11″ wide by 17″ high (Tabloid-size) with 1″ margins and 0.25″ bleeds on all four sides. Create the file with no primary text frame and without facing pages.**

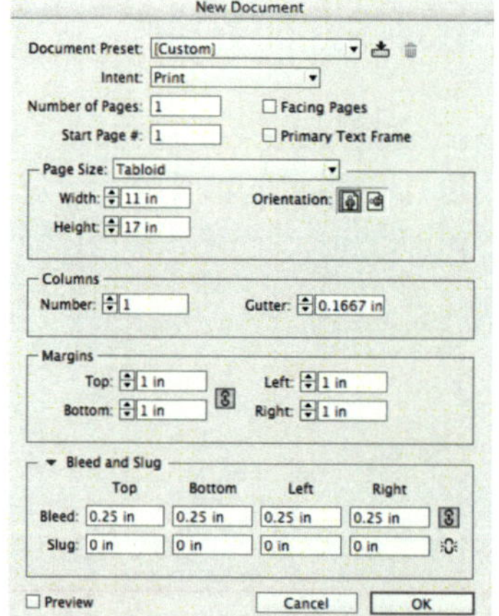

Note:

Industry standards typically call for a 0.125″ bleed, but in this case the printer specifically requested 0.25″ bleed allowance.

7. **Save the file as poster.indd in your WIP>Surfing folder and then continue to the next exercise.**

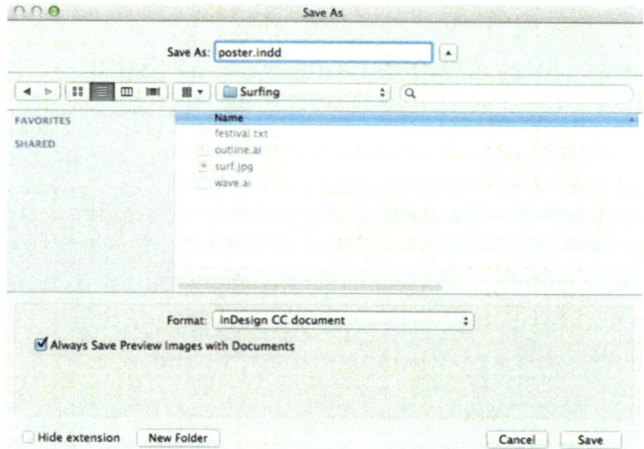

Define Color Swatches

The Swatches panel is used to apply predefined colors to any element in a layout. Six CMYK color swatches are included in the default set for print documents, as well as three special colors (Paper, Black, and Registration) and a None swatch that removes color from the selected attribute.

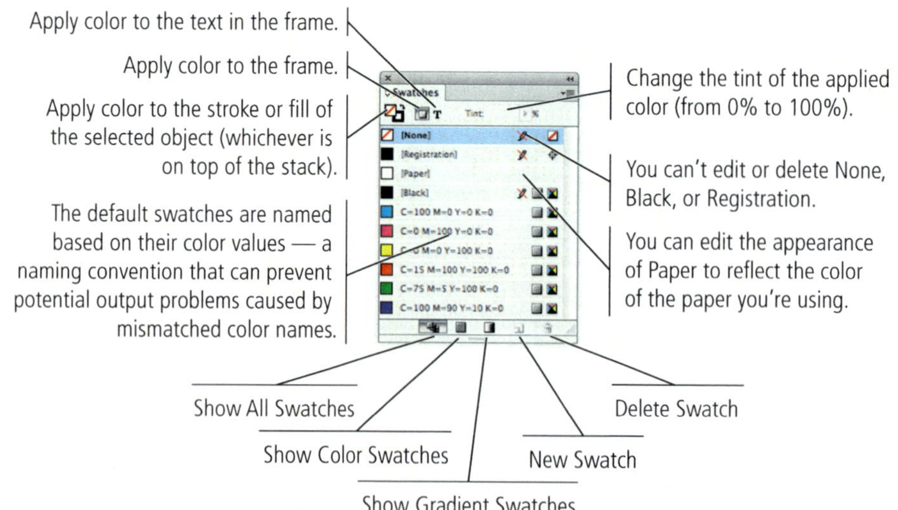

Note:

Using the Fill and Stroke swatches at the top of the Swatches panel, you can apply different colors to the fill and stroke of selected text.

Note:

Editing the appearance of the Paper swatch only affects the on-screen preview. It does not appear in the print output.

You can define colors based on one of three color models (CMYK, RGB, or LAB), or you can call spot colors from built-in libraries of special inks. Each different mode and type of color has an identifying icon in the Swatches panel.

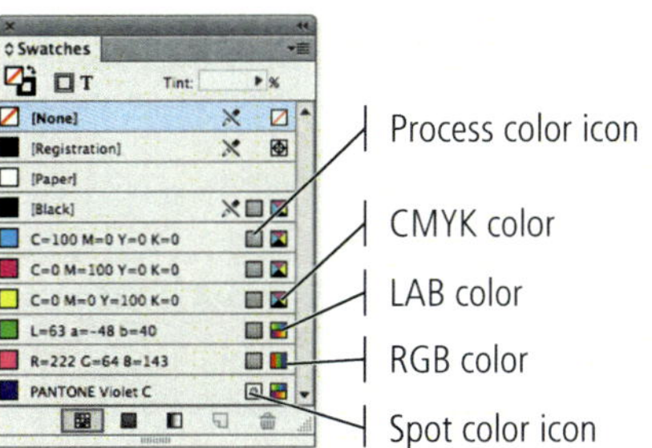

Note:

Anything colored with the Registration swatch will appear on every separation in a job. This color should only be used for special marks or other information placed outside the trim area.

1. **With poster.indd open, open the Swatches panel (Window>Color>Swatches).**

2. **Open the Swatches panel Options menu.**

This menu has options for creating four types of color swatches: Color, Tint, Gradient, and Mixed Ink.

- **Color** swatches store specific colors based on defined percentages of each component ink.
- **Gradient** swatches store specific transitions from one color to another.
- A **Tint** swatch is a specific stored percentage of another swatch, which is useful if you frequently use (for example) a 30% tint of C=100 M=42 Y=0 K=73. You can apply that tint with a single click instead of applying the color and then changing the tint of the applied color. Every click you save is a boost in productivity, especially if you're building layouts with multiple elements.
- **Mixed Ink** swatches allow you to combine percentages of spot and process colors, or of multiple spot colors; this option is only available when at least one spot color exists in the file. The **Mixed Ink Group** option allows you to build multiple swatches at once, based on specific incremental percentages of inks. Be very careful if you use mixed ink swatches; they can be a source of unpredictable color reproduction and potential output problems.

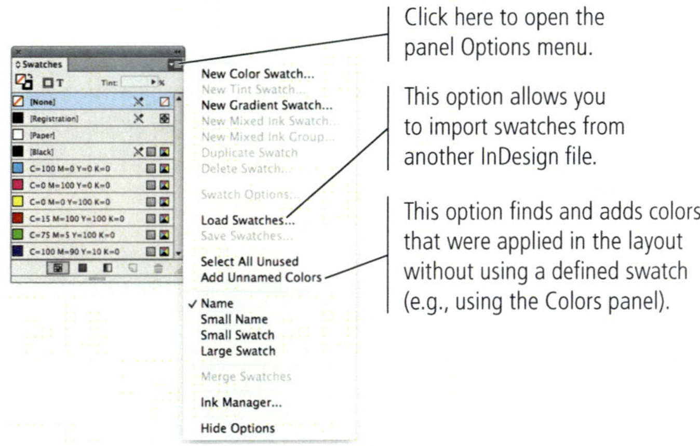

3. **Choose New Color Swatch in the panel Options menu.**

4. **Leave the Name with Color Value option checked. Make sure the Color Type is set to Process and the Color Mode is set to CMYK.**

There is no industry standard for naming colors, but InDesign comes close with the Name with Color Value option. This type of naming convention — basing names on the color components — serves several purposes:

- You know exactly what components the color contains, so you can easily see if you are duplicating colors.
- You can immediately tell that the color should be a process build rather than a special ink or spot color.
- You avoid mismatched color names and duplicated spot colors, which are potential disasters in the commercial printing production process.

Mismatched color names occur when a defined color name has two different values — one defined in the page layout and one defined in an image file that you placed into your layout. When the files are output, the output device might be confused by different definitions for the same color name; the imported value might replace the project's value for that particular color name (or vice versa). The change could be subtle, or it could be drastic.

A similar problem occurs when the same spot color is assigned different names in different applications. For example, you might define a spot color in InDesign as "Border Color"; another designer might define the same spot color in Illustrator as "Spec Blue." When the illustration is placed into the InDesign layout, two different spot-color separations exist even though the different color names have the same values.

Color by Numbers

INDESIGN FOUNDATIONS

If you base your color choices solely on what you see on your monitor, what appears to be a perfect blue sky will probably not look quite right when it's printed with process-color inks. Even if you have calibrated your monitor, no monitor is 100% effective at simulating printed color. As long as monitors display color in RGB, there will always be some discrepancies.

Every designer should have some sort of process-color chart, available from commercial publishers (some printers might provide the charts produced by the exact press on which your job will be printed). These charts contain small squares of process ink builds so you can see, for example, what a process build of C=10 M=70 Y=30 K=20 will look like when printed. These guides usually show samples in steps of 5% or 10%, printed on both coated and uncoated paper (because the type of paper or substrate can dramatically affect the final result).

When you define process colors in an InDesign project, you should enter specific numbers in the CMYK fields to designate your color choices rather than relying on your screen preview. As you gain experience defining colors, you will become better able to predict the outcome for a given process-ink build. Rely on what you know to be true rather than what you hope will be true.

The same concept also applies when using special ink libraries. You should have — and use — swatch books that show printed samples of the special inks. You cannot rely on the monitor preview to choose a special ink color. Rather, you should find the color in a printed swatch book, and then enter the appropriate number in the Pantone field (for example) below the color swatches.

Total Area Coverage

When defining the ink values of a process-color build, you must usually limit your **total area coverage** (TAC, also called **total ink coverage** or **total ink density**), or the amount of ink used in a given color.

This might sound complex, but it can be easily calculated by adding the percentages of each ink used to create the color. If a color is defined as C=45 M=60 Y=90 K=0, the total area coverage is 195% (45 + 60 + 90 + 0).

Maximum TAC limits are between 240% and 320% for offset lithography, depending on the paper being used. If you exceed the TAC limits for a given paper-ink-press combination, your printed job might end up with excess ink bleed, smearing, smudging, show-through, or a number of other printing errors because the paper cannot absorb all of the ink.

5. **Define the swatch with 100% Cyan, 0% Magenta, 100% Yellow, and 25% Black, and then click Add.**

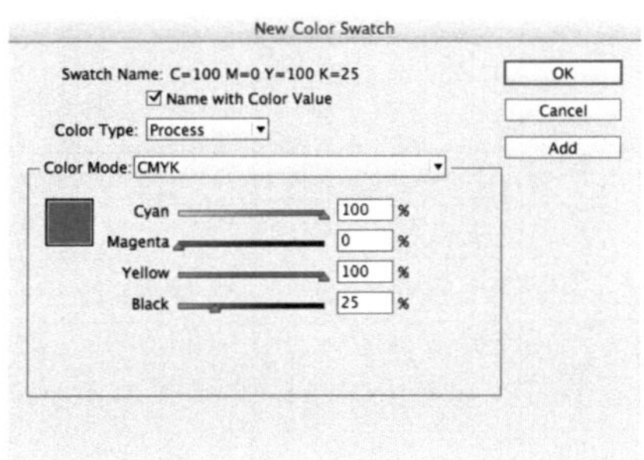

> *Note:*
>
> *By clicking the Add button, you can add more color swatches without having to reopen the New Color Swatch dialog box.*

> *Note:*
>
> *Don't confuse color swatches with ink colors. Because you are using the Process color type, each of these swatches will be printed with the four process inks (CMYK).*

6. **Create two more process-color swatches using the following ink values.**

   Color 1: C=100 M=100 Y=25 K=0

   Color 2: C=40 M=0 Y=0 K=100

   The third swatch — 100% black and some percent of another color — is called **rich black** or **super black**. Remember, when the inks are printed, adding another ink to solid black enhances the richness of the solid black. Adding cyan typically creates a cooler black, while adding magenta typically creates a warmer black.

7. **In the New Color Swatch dialog box, choose Spot in the Color Type menu.**

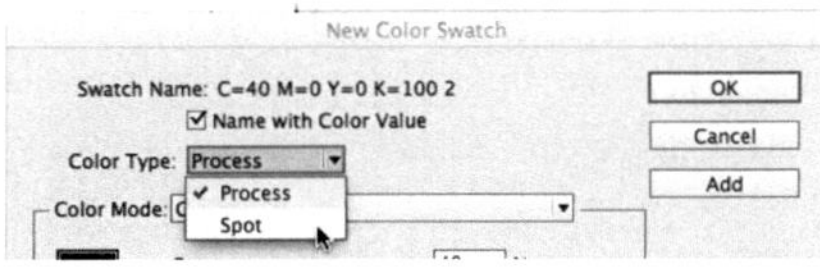

8. **Choose Pantone+ Metallic Coated in the Color Mode menu.**

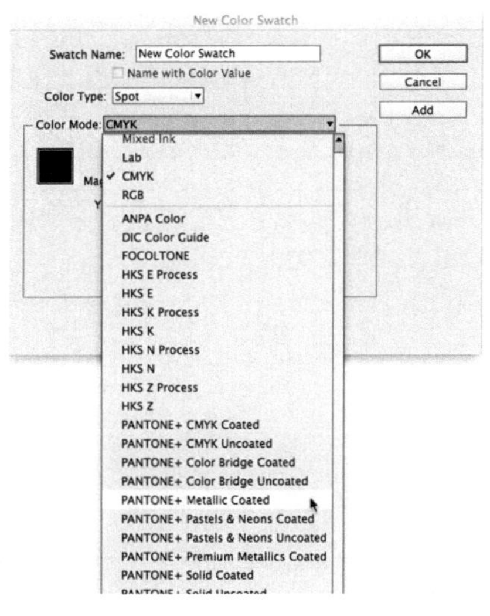

   Spot colors are created with special premixed inks to produce a certain color with one ink layer; they are not built from the standard process inks used in CMYK printing. When you output a job with spot colors, each spot color appears on its own separation.

   Spot-color inks are commonly used when a special color, such as a corporate color, is required. InDesign includes a number of built-in color libraries, including spot-color systems such as Pantone, Toyo, and DIC. In the United States, the most popular collections of spot colors are the Pantone Matching System (PMS) libraries. TruMatch and Focoltone are also used in the United States; Toyo and DICColor (Dainippon Ink & Chemicals) are used primarily in Japan.

   Even though you can choose a color directly from the library on your screen, you should look at a swatch book to verify that you're using the color you intend. Special inks exist because many of the colors cannot be reproduced with process inks, nor can they be accurately represented on a computer monitor. If you specify special colors and then convert them to process colors later, your job probably won't look exactly as you expect.

9. **Place the insertion point in the Pantone field and type `8005`.**

   You can also scroll through the list and simply click a color to select it.

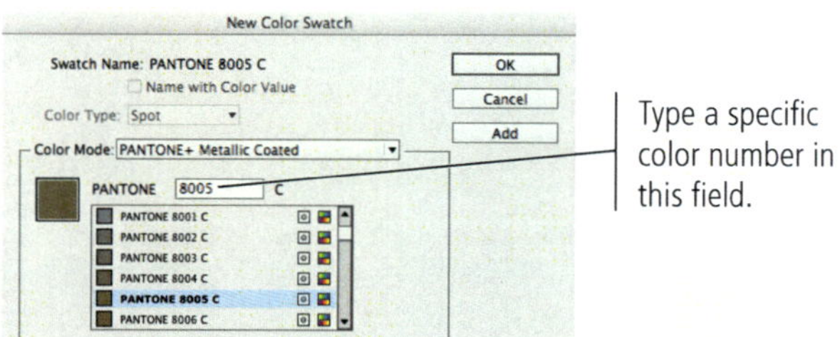

10. **Click Add, then click Done to return to the document window.**

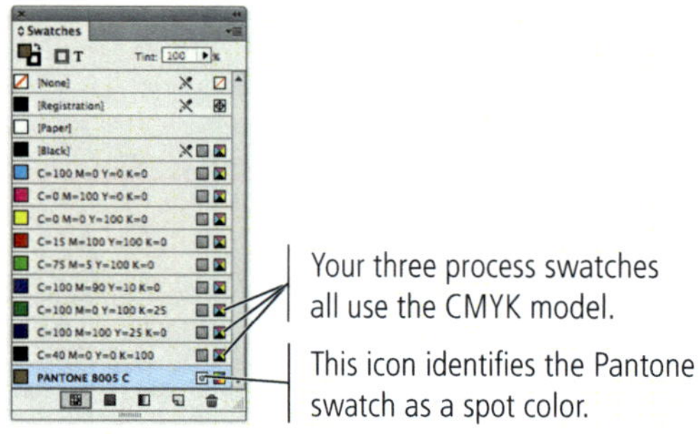

11. **Save the file and continue to the next exercise.**

Note:

Spot colors are safely chosen from a swatch book — a book of colors printed with different inks, similar to the paint chip cards used in home decorating.

When choosing spot colors, ask your printer which ink system it supports. If you designate TruMatch, but they use Pantone inks, you won't get the colors you expect.

Create the Poster Background

The background of this poster is going to be a solid fill of the rich black swatch you defined in the previous exercise. However, an object filling the entire page can cause certain problems. For example, if you try to create a text frame inside the area, you end up converting the frame to a text frame. In this exercise, you use the Layers panel to prevent problems that could be caused by the background shape.

1. **With `poster.indd` open, choose the Rectangle tool in the Tools panel.**

2. **In the Swatches panel, make sure the Fill swatch is on top and click the C=40 M=0 Y=0 K=100 swatch.**

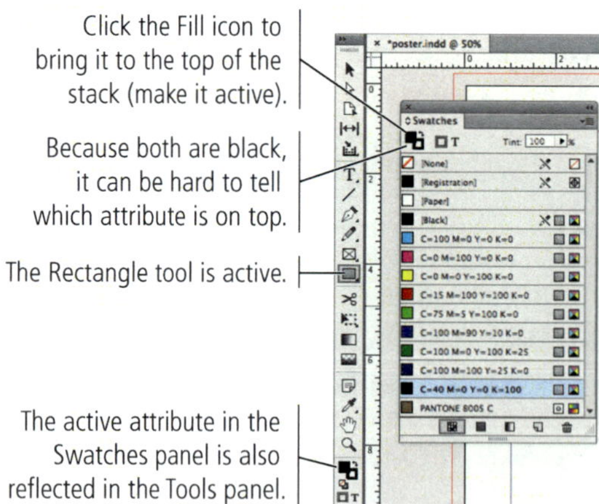

3. **Click the Stroke icon at the top of the panel to activate that attribute, then click the None swatch.**

   By changing the fill and stroke attributes when no object is selected, you define those attributes for the next object you create.

Note:

Remember, all panels (whether docked or not) can be accessed from the Window menu. If you don't see a specific menu command, choose Edit>Show All Menu Items.

4. **Using the Rectangle tool, create a rectangle that covers the entire page and extends to the defined bleed guides.**

   You can single-click to define the rectangle size, and then drag it into position with the Selection tool. Alternatively, you can simply click and drag with the Rectangle tool, using the Bleed guides to snap the edges of the shape.

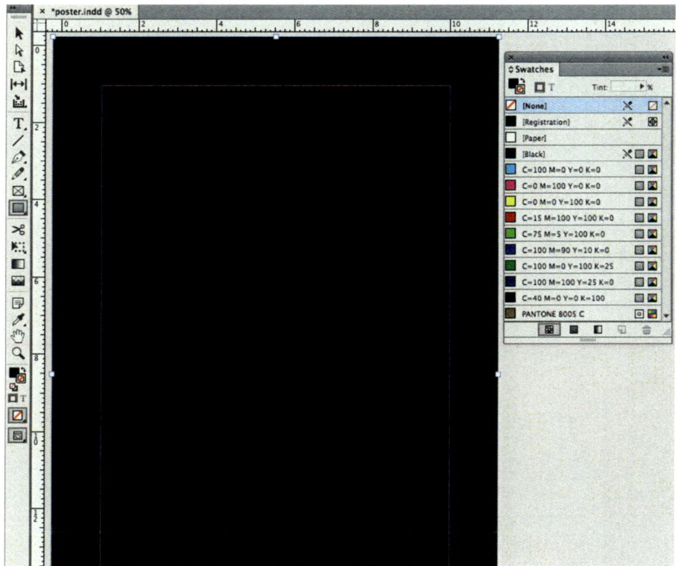

5. **In the Layers panel (Window>Layers), click the arrow to expand Layer 1.**

6. **Click the empty space to the right of the eye icon for the <rectangle> item.**

   The second column in the Layers panel can be used to lock individual items or entire layers. (If you lock a whole layer, all items on that layer are automatically locked.)

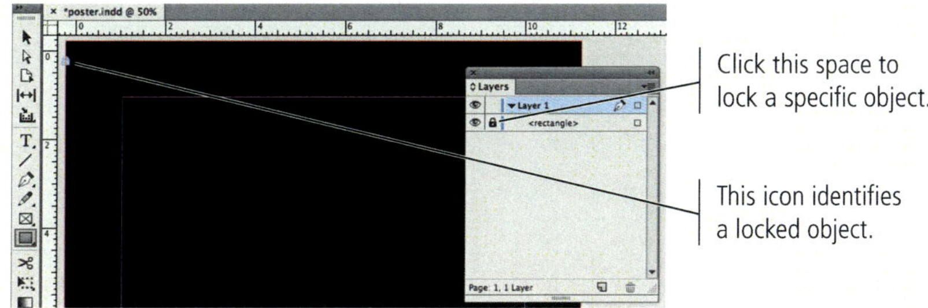

Note:

You can click an existing lock icon in the Layers panel to unlock an object or layer.

You can also click a lock icon on the page to unlock a specific object.

7. **With the Rectangle tool still selected, change the stroke color to the custom green swatch. Using the Control panel, change the stroke weight to 6 pt.**

   When you locked the rectangle in Step 6, it was automatically deselected. This means that changing the stroke and fill attributes does not affect the existing object.

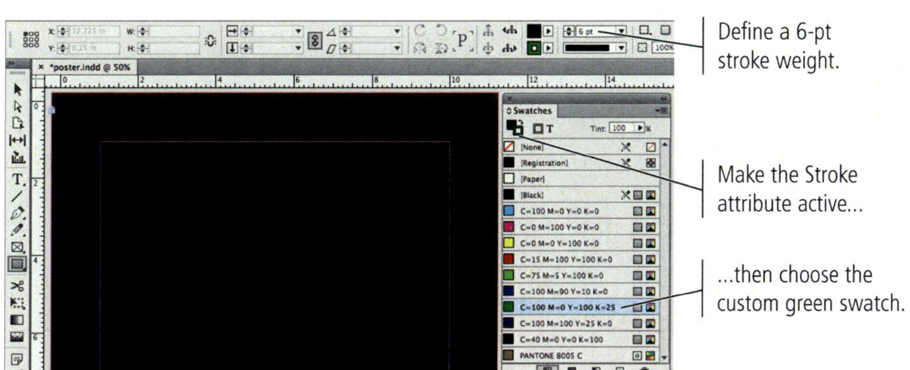

8. **Click and drag to draw a rectangle that fills the area within the defined margin guides.**

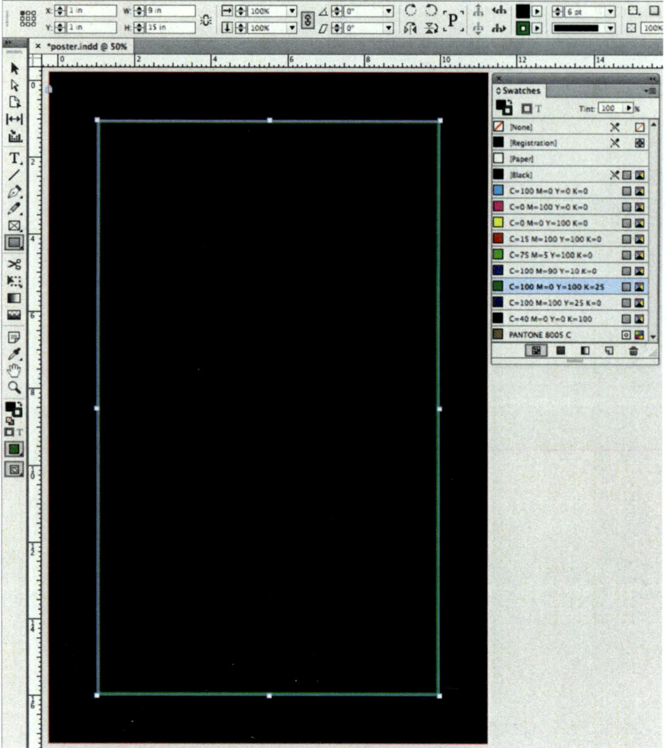

9. **In the Layers panel, click the eye icon to the left of the locked <rectangle>.**

   The visible rectangle has the same fill color as the background shape (which is now hidden). To make it easier to see and work with only specific objects, you can use the Layers panel to toggle the visibility of individual objects or entire layers. (If you hide an entire layer, all objects on that layer are hidden.)

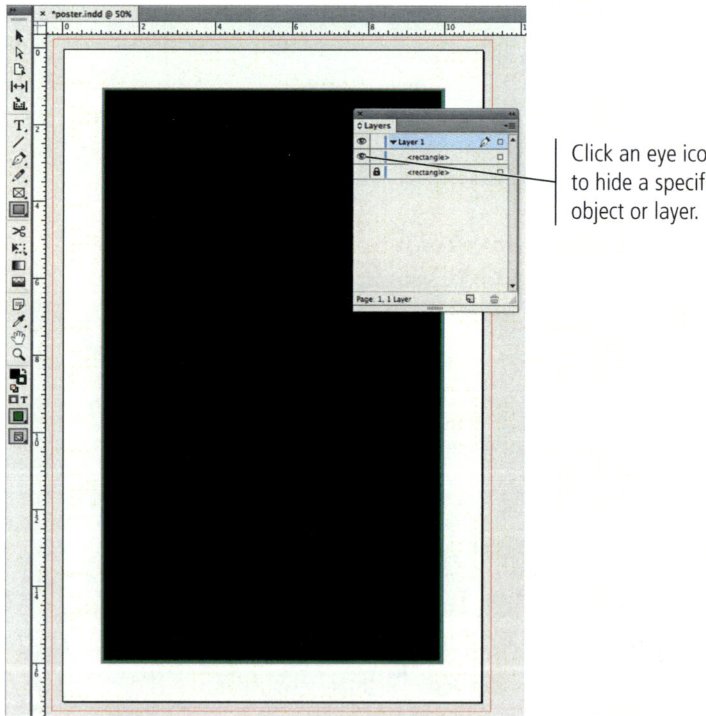

10. **Save the file and continue to the next exercise.**

Define and Apply a Gradient

A **gradient**, also called a **blend**, can be used to create a smooth transition from one color to another. You can apply a gradient to any object using the Gradient panel, or you can save a gradient swatch if you plan to use it more than once.

The Gradient panel controls the type and position of applied gradients. You can apply either linear or radial gradients, change the angle of linear gradients, and change the color and location for individual stops along the gradient ramp.

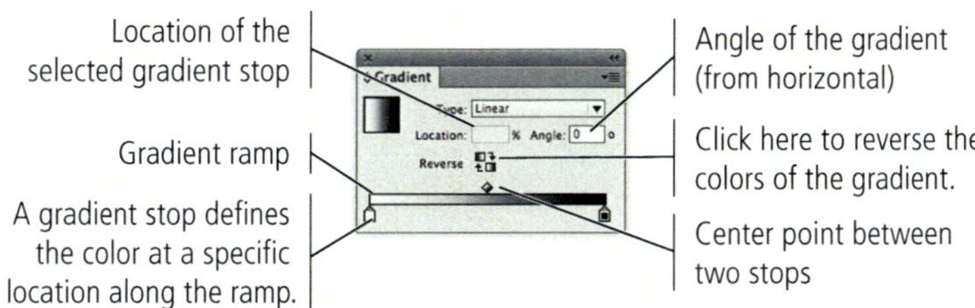

1. **With poster.indd open, choose the Selection tool. Click outside the area of the visible rectangle to deselect it.**

2. **Choose New Gradient Swatch from the Swatches panel Options menu.**

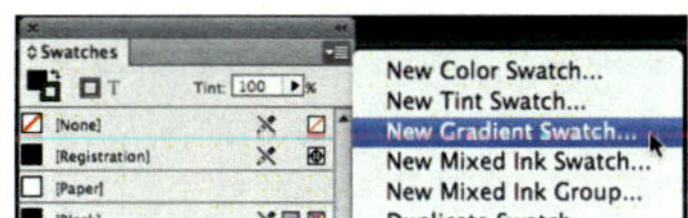

3. **Click the gradient stop on the left end of the gradient ramp to select it.**

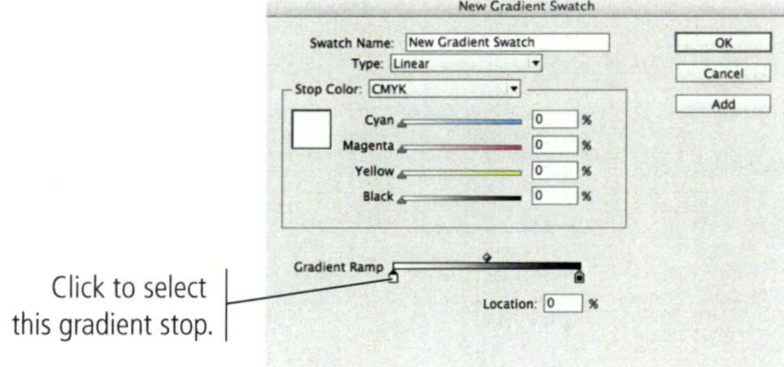

4. **Make sure Linear is selected in the Type menu, and then choose Swatches in the Stop Color menu.**

   You can define gradients using LAB values, CMYK percentages, RGB values, or existing color swatches.

5. **With the first stop selected, click the custom green CMYK swatch.**

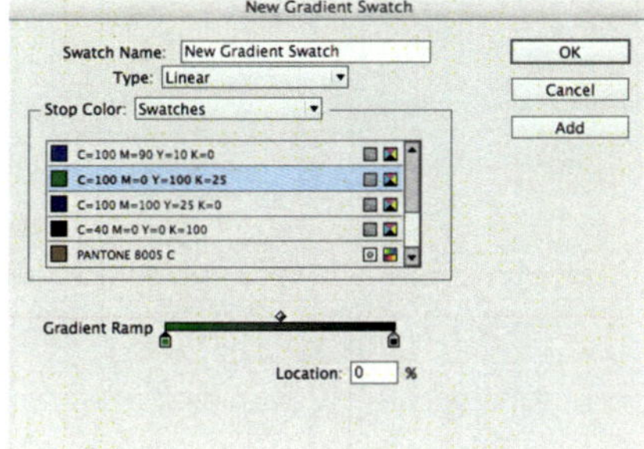

6. **Select the second gradient stop (on the right end of the ramp), and then click the custom blue swatch.**

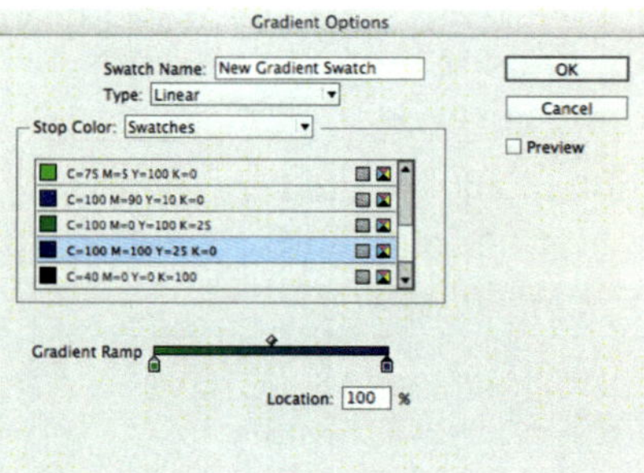

7. **Type Green to Blue in the Swatch Name field and then click OK.**

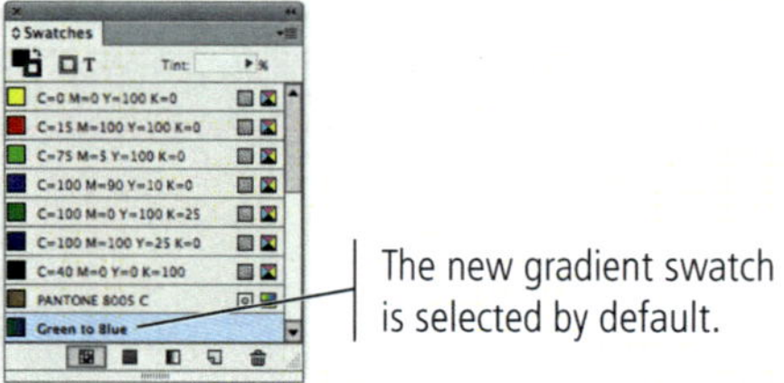

8. **Using the Selection tool, click the visible rectangle on the page to select it.**

9. **Make the Fill icon active in the Swatches panel, and then click the Green to Blue gradient swatch.**

   It is important to remember but easy to forget: make sure the correct attribute (fill or stroke) is active when you change a color.

> ***Note:***
>
> *Press Shift-X to reverse the fill and stroke colors of the selected object.*

10. **Make the Stroke icon active in the Swatches panel, and then click the Green to Blue gradient swatch.**

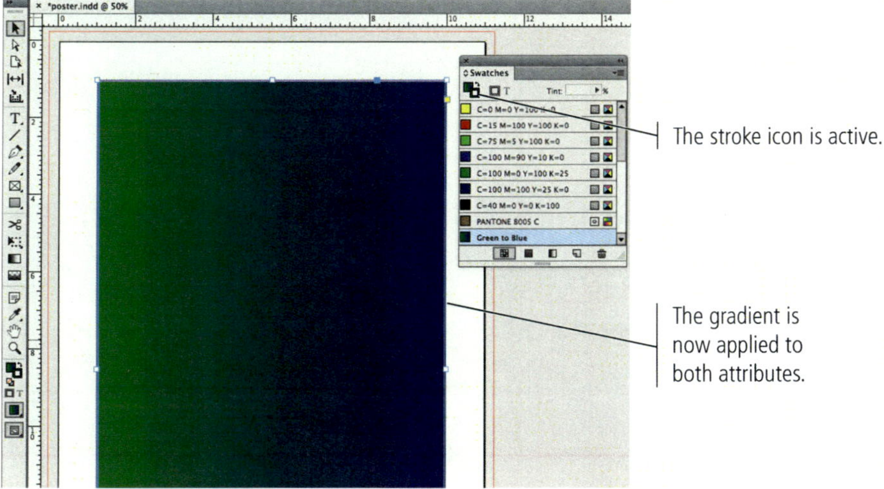

11. **Save the file and continue to the next exercise.**

Modify Gradient Attributes

As you just saw, it is fairly easy to create and apply a gradient. Once the gradient is in place, you can also modify the specific attributes of a gradient, including its angle and the positioning of specific color stops along its length.

1. **With poster.indd open, make sure the gradient-filled rectangle is selected.**

2. **Using either the Tools or Swatches panel, click to activate the Fill icon.**

3. **Using the Gradient panel (Window>Color>Gradient), change the Angle field to 90° to rotate the gradient.**

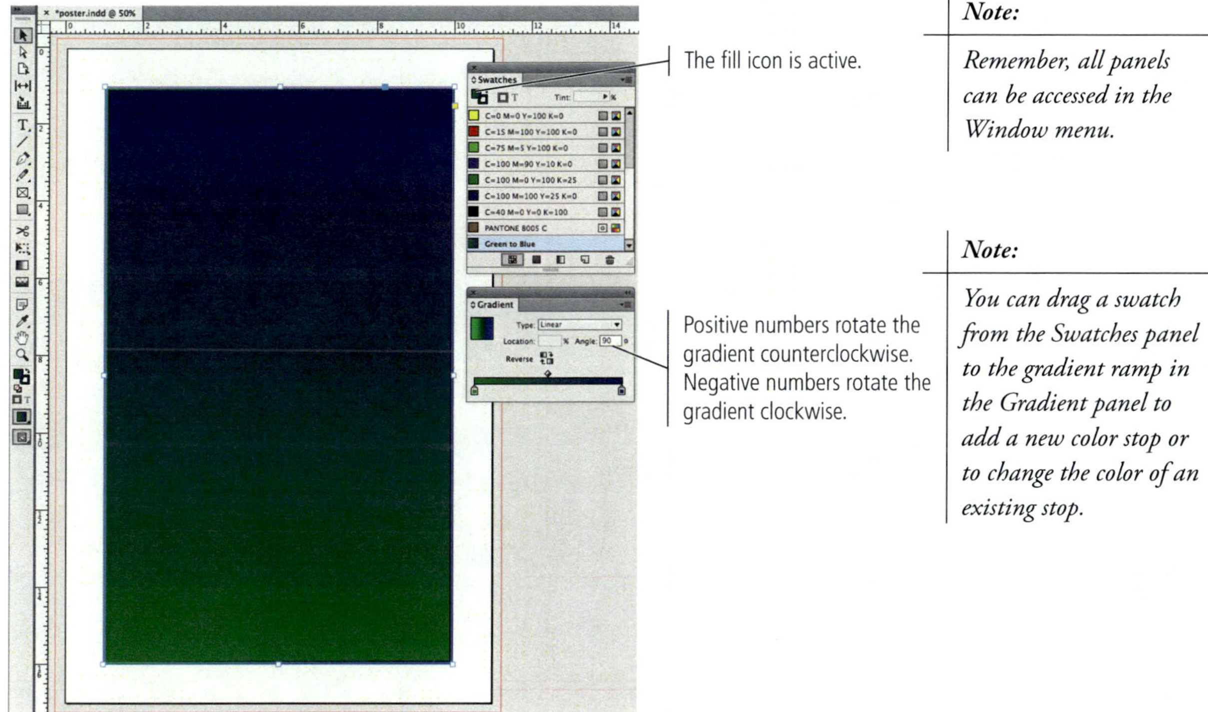

Note:

Remember, all panels can be accessed in the Window menu.

Note:

You can drag a swatch from the Swatches panel to the gradient ramp in the Gradient panel to add a new color stop or to change the color of an existing stop.

4. **Using the Control panel, change the object height to 10″ based on the top-center reference point.**

When you change the shape dimensions, the applied gradients are adjusted so the end stops still align to the edges of the object.

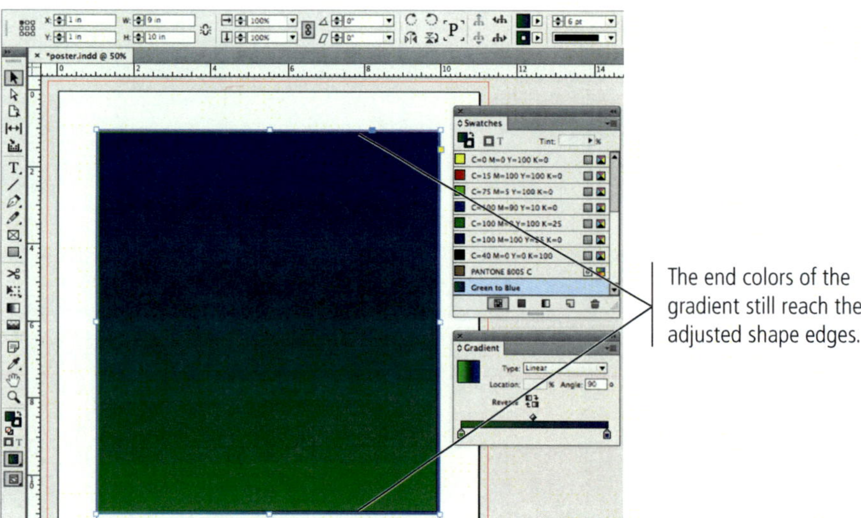

The end colors of the gradient still reach the adjusted shape edges.

The Gradient Tools

Clicking a gradient swatch adds a gradient to the selected object, beginning at the left edge and ending at the right edge (for linear gradients), or beginning at the object's center and ending at the object's outermost edge (for radial gradients). When you drag with the Gradient tool, you define the length of the gradient without regard to the object you're filling.

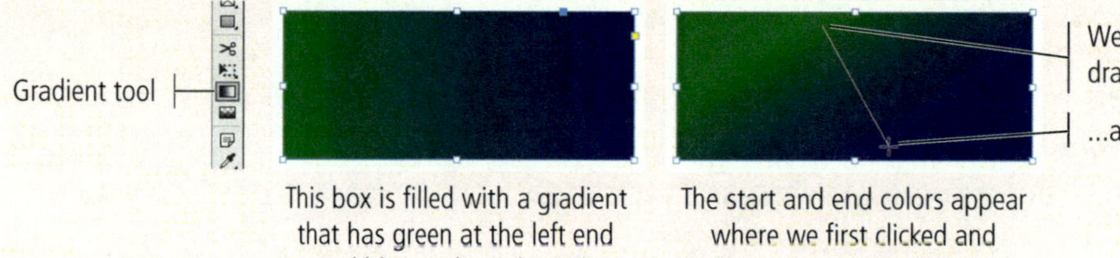

Gradient tool

This box is filled with a gradient that has green at the left end and blue at the right end.

The start and end colors appear where we first clicked and where we stopped dragging.

We started dragging here...

...and ended here.

The Gradient Feather tool has a similar function but produces different results. Rather than creating a specific-colored gradient, the Gradient Feather tool applies a transparency gradient, blending the object from solid to transparent.

Gradient Feather tool

We placed this image over a red-filled shape.

The resulting effect blends the image from solid to transparent, allowing the background object to show.

Dragging to here defines the end point of the gradient feather (the area that will be entirely transparent).

We clicked and dragged from here to define the starting point of the feather effect (the area that will be entirely solid).

5. **With the object still selected, make the Stroke icon active in the Swatches panel.**

   Remember that the attribute on top of the stack is the one you are currently changing. If the wrong attribute is on top of the stack, you will not get the results you are hoping for.

6. **In the Gradient panel, change the gradient angle to –90° so the stroke goes from green at the top to blue at the bottom (the reverse of the fill).**

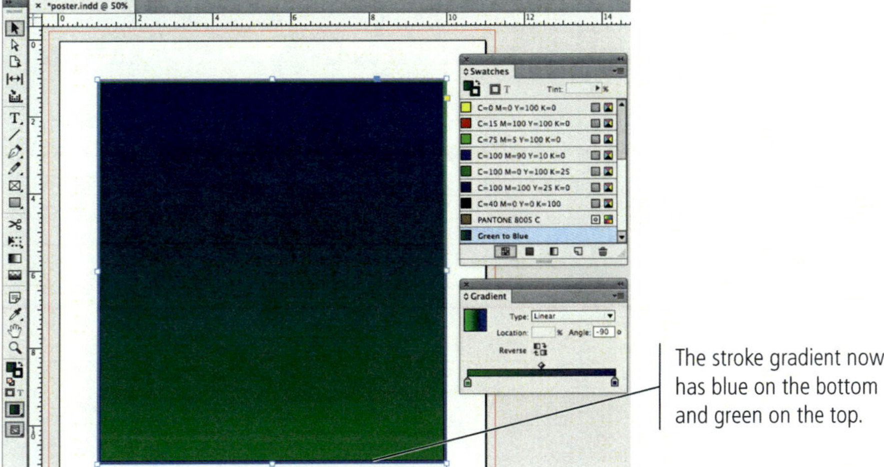

7. **Click away from the rectangle to deselect it.**

8. **Use the Screen Mode button on the Tools panel or the Application/Menu bar to display the layout in Preview mode.**

   This option hides all guides and frame edges, which makes it easier to see the subtle effect created by the opposing gradients. (We also zoomed in to better show the result.)

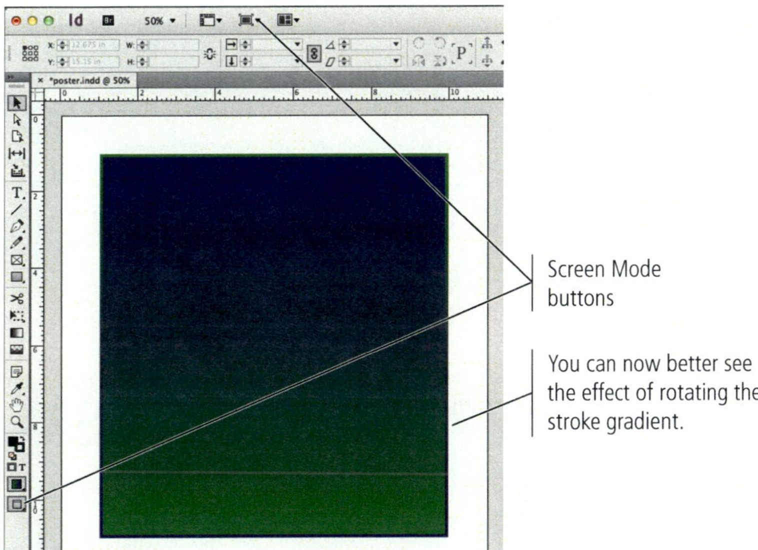

9. **Choose Normal in the Screen Mode menu to restore the guides and frame edges on screen.**

10. **Save the file and continue to the next exercise.**

Create an Irregular Graphics Frame

You can create basic graphics frames using the Rectangle, Ellipse, and Polygon Frame tools. You can also create a Bézier shape with the Pen tool, and then convert the shape to a graphics frame — which means you can create a frame in virtually any shape. However, it requires a lot of work to trace complex graphics with the Pen tool; fortunately, you can use other options to create complex frames from objects in placed graphics.

1. **In the open `poster.indd` file, select the existing gradient-filled rectangle in the layout.**

2. **Choose File>Place. Navigate to `outline.ai` in the WIP>Surfing folder. Check the Show Import Options and Replace Selected Item options, then click Open.**

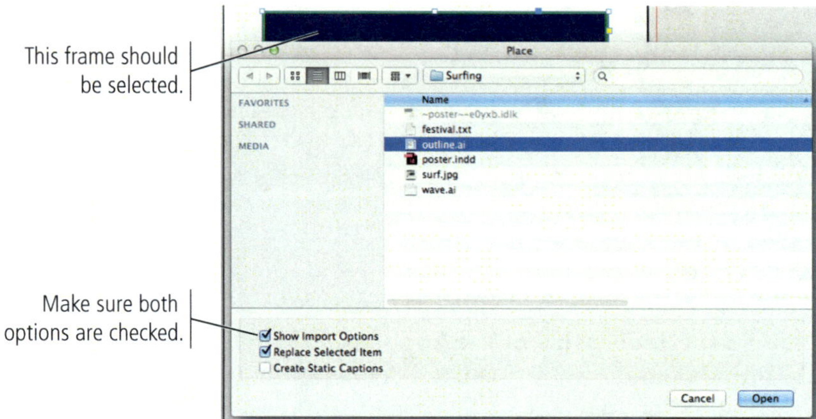

3. **In the resulting dialog box, choose Art in the Crop To menu, then click OK.**

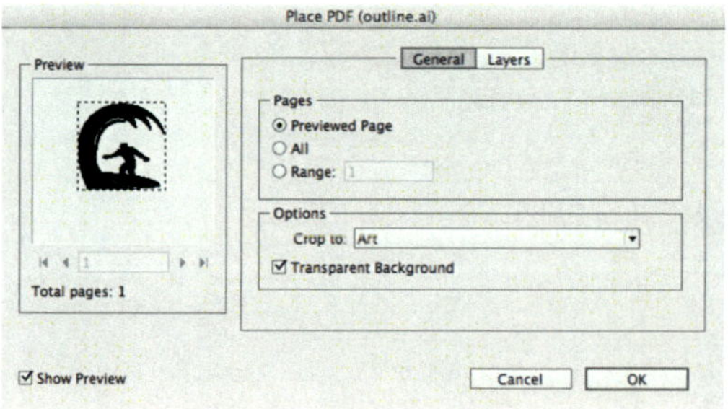

> ***Note:***
>
> *Refer back to Project 1: Letterhead Design for an explanation of the Crop To options.*

Because the existing rectangle was selected and the Replace Selected Item option was checked, the new image automatically appears in the selected frame. If another image had already been placed in the frame, the surfing image would replace the existing image (hence the name of the command).

> ***Note:***
>
> *If Replace Selected Item was not checked in the Place dialog box, the image would be loaded into the cursor.*

4. **Choose Edit>Undo Replace.**

If you accidentally replace a selected item, undoing the placement loads the last-placed image into the cursor.

This is an easy fix if you accidentally replace an image — simply choose Edit>Undo Replace, and then click to place the loaded image in the correct location.

> ***Note:***
>
> *The Undo command undoes the single last action. In this case, placing the image into the frame — even though it happened automatically — was the last single action.*

5. **Click in the white area near the top-right corner to place the loaded image.**

Do not click inside the gradient-filled rectangle; if you do, the loaded image would be placed back into that frame instead of in a new frame.

6. **Using the Control panel, select the top-left reference point and then change the new image frame's position to X: 0.5″, Y: 2″.**

Use the top-left reference point to position the graphics frame.

7. **With the same frame selected, choose Object>Clipping Path>Options.**

A **clipping path** is a hard-edged outline that masks an image. Areas inside the path are visible; areas outside the path are hidden.

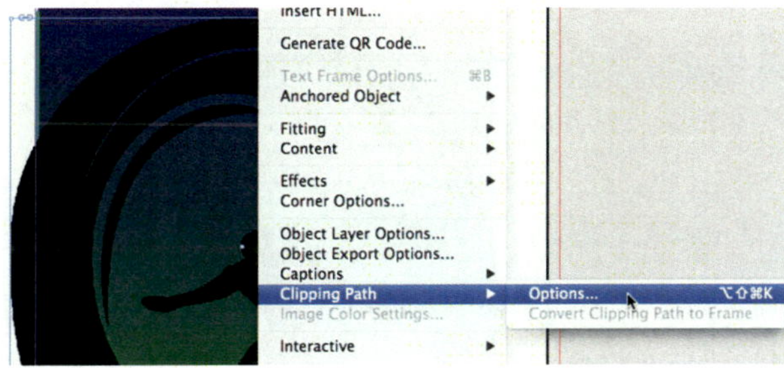

8. **In the resulting dialog box, choose Detect Edges in the Type menu.**

   InDesign can access Alpha channels and clipping paths that are saved in an image, or you can create a clipping path based on the image content. Because this graphic is a vector graphic with well-defined edges filled with a solid color, InDesign can create a very precise clipping path based on the information in the file.

9. **Check the Include Inside Edges option.**

   When this option is not checked, InDesign generates a clipping path based only on the outside edges of the image. The Include Inside Edges option generates a compound clipping path that removes holes in the middle of the outside path.

10. **Click OK to close the dialog box and create the clipping path.**

11. **Choose Object>Clipping Path>Convert Clipping Path to Frame.**

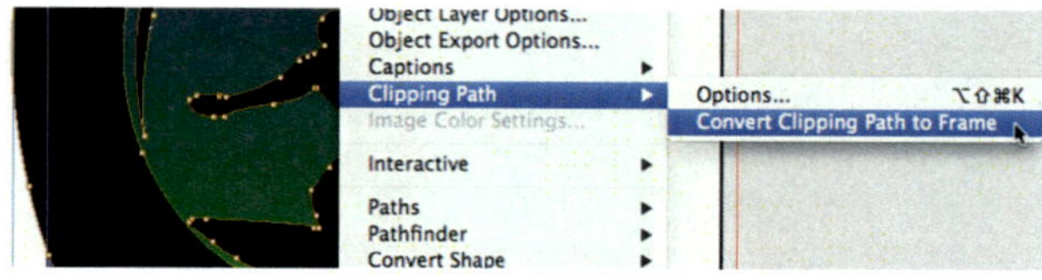

Clipping Path Options

Threshold specifies the darkest pixel value that will define the resulting clipping path. In this exercise, the placed image is filled with solid black, so you can set a very high Threshold value to define the clipping path. In images with greater tone variation (such as a photograph), increasing the Threshold value removes lighter areas from the clipped area.

Tolerance specifies how similar a pixel must be to the Threshold value before it is hidden by the clipping path. Increasing the Tolerance value results in fewer points along the clipping path, generating a smoother path. Lowering the Tolerance value results in more anchor points and a potentially rougher path.

Inset Frame shrinks the clipping path by a specific number of pixels. You can also enter a negative value to enlarge the clipping path.

Invert reverses the clipping path, making hidden areas visible and vice versa.

Include Inside Edges creates a compound clipping path, removing inner areas of the object if they are within the Threshold and Tolerance ranges.

Restrict to Frame creates a clipping path that stops at the visible edge of the graphic. You can include the entire object — including areas beyond the frame edges — by unchecking this option.

Use High Resolution Image generates the clipping path based on the actual file data instead of the preview image.

12. **Using the Direct Selection tool, select the image inside the irregular frame.**

13. **With the frame content selected, press Delete/Backspace to delete the placed file but leave the frame you created.**

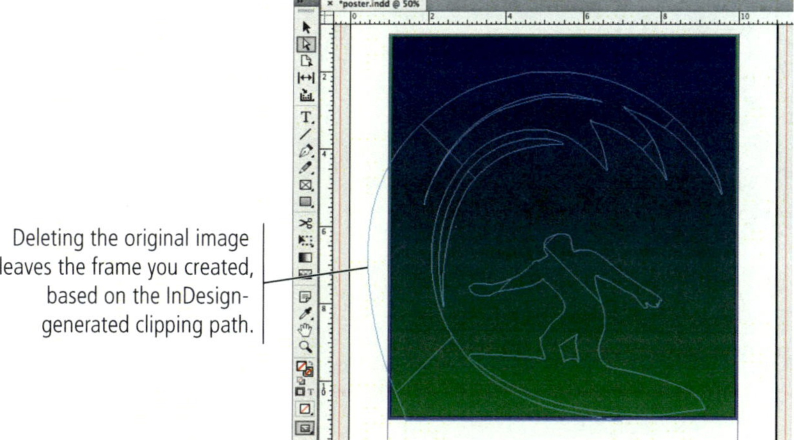

14. **Using the Selection tool, click the irregular graphics frame to select it.**

15. **Choose File>Place and navigate to `surf.jpg` in the WIP>Surfing folder. Uncheck all options at the bottom of the dialog box and click Open.**

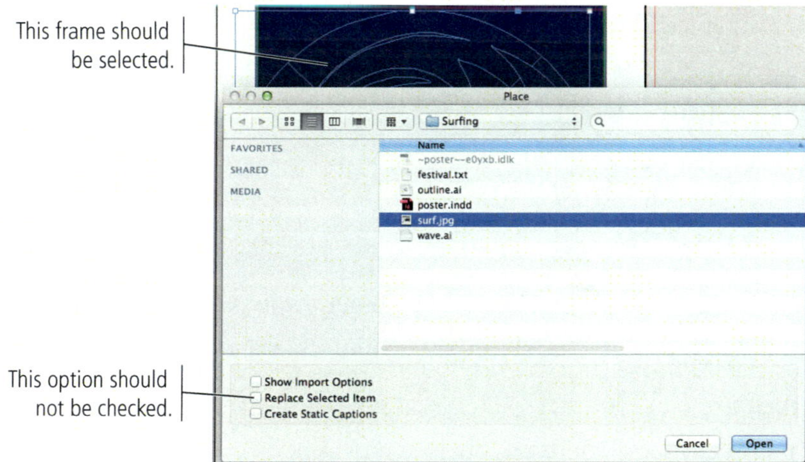

Although the existing frame was selected when you opened the Place dialog box, the new image is loaded into the cursor because you unchecked the Replace Selected Item option.

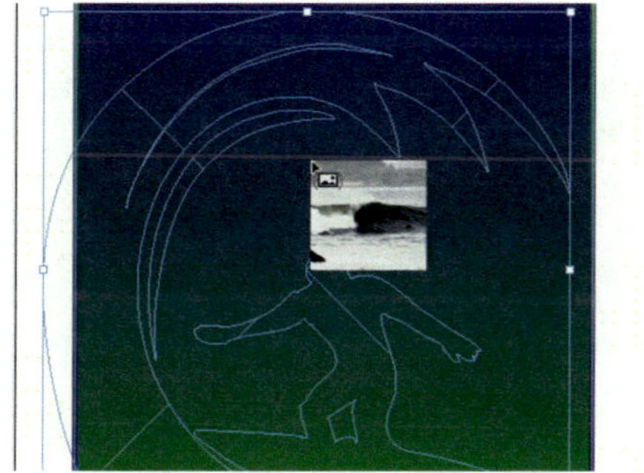

16. **Click inside the empty frame with the loaded cursor to place the image inside the frame.**

17. **Save the file and continue to the next exercise.**

Create Visual Impact with Transparency

The image effects and transparency controls in InDesign provide options for adding dimension and depth, allowing unprecedented creative control directly in the page layout. You can change the transparency of any object (or individual object attributes), apply different blending modes so objects blend smoothly into underlying objects, and apply creative effects such as drop shadows and beveling.

Transparency and effects are controlled in the Effects panel. You can change these options for an entire object (fill and stroke), only the stroke, only the fill, the text (if you're working with a text frame), the graphic (if you're working with a graphics frame), or all objects in a group.

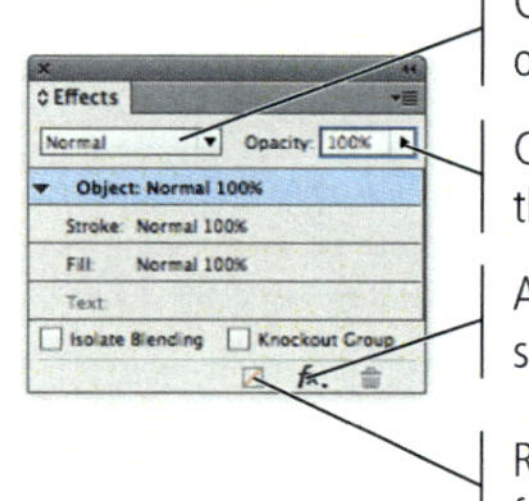

Change the blending mode of the selected attribute.

Change the transparency of the selected attribute.

Apply an effect to the selected attribute.

Remove transparency and effects from the selected attribute.

Note:

The Graphic option is only available when a placed graphic (within a frame) is selected. Group replaces Object in the list only when a group is selected with the Selection tool.

Technical Issues of Transparency

Because all of these features and options are related in some way to transparency, you should understand what transparency is and how it affects your output. **Transparency** is the degree to which light passes through an object so that objects in the background are visible. In terms of page layout, transparency means being able to "see through" objects in the front of the stacking order to objects lower in the stacking order.

Note:

Effects applied to text apply to all text in the frame; you can't apply effects to individual characters.

Because of the way printing works, applying transparency in print graphic design is a bit of a contradiction. Commercial printing is, by definition, accomplished by overlapping a mixture of (usually) four semi-transparent inks in different percentages to reproduce a range of colors (the printable gamut). In that sense, all print graphic design requires transparency.

But *design* transparency refers to the objects on the page. The trouble is, when a halftone dot is printed, it's either there or it's not. There is no "50% opaque" setting on a printing press. This means that a transformation needs to take place behind the scenes, translating what we create on screen into what a printing press produces.

Note:

Transparency is essentially the inverse of opacity. If an object is 20% transparent, it is also 80% opaque.

When transparent objects are output, overlapping areas of transparent elements are actually broken into individual elements (where necessary) to produce the best possible results. Ink values in the overlap areas are calculated by the application, based on the capabilities of the mechanical printing process; the software converts what we create on screen into the elements that are necessary to print.

When you get to the final stage of this project, you'll learn how to preview and control the output process for transparent objects.

1. **In the open poster.indd file, use the Selection tool to select the gradient-filled rectangle.**

2. **Choose Object>Content>Graphic.**

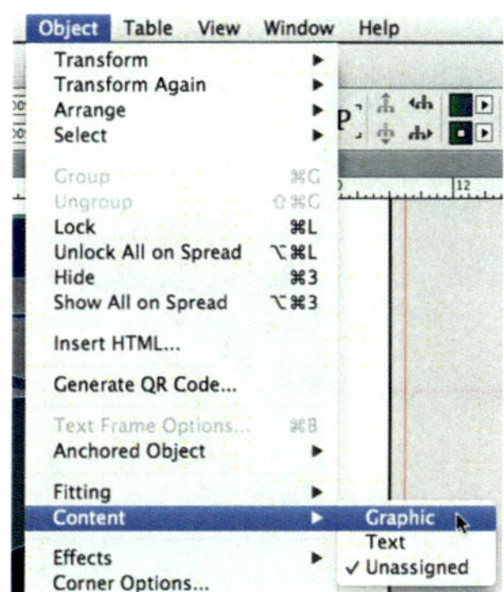

Note:

You can also Control/right-click an object and change its content type in the contextual menu.

When you create a frame with one of the basic shape tools, it is considered "unassigned" because it is neither a text frame nor a graphics frame. You can convert any type of frame (graphics, text, or unassigned) to another type using this menu.

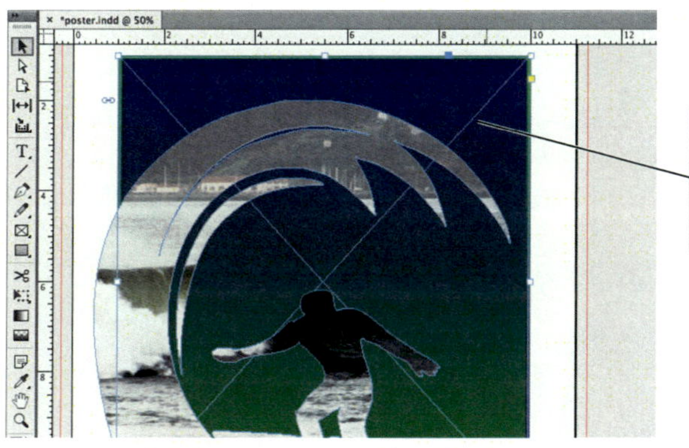

When frame edges are showing, an empty graphics frame shows crossed diagonal lines.

3. **With the gradient-filled rectangle still selected on the page, choose File>Place. Navigate to the WIP>Surfing folder and choose surf.jpg. With the Replace Selected Item option checked, click Open.**

This is the same file you placed into the irregular graphics frame. You are going to use transparency and effects to differentiate the two images.

Because Replace Selected Item was checked, the image is placed directly into the frame.

4. **Move the Selection tool cursor over the image frame to reveal the Content Grabber.**

> *Note:*
>
> *You can turn off the Content Grabber by choosing View>Extras> Hide Content Grabber.*

5. **Click the Content Grabber to access the image in the frame.**

   Remember: When you select an image within a frame (using either the Content Grabber or the Direct Selection tool), the Control panel fields define the position of the graphic *relative to* its containing frame. Negative numbers move the graphic up and to the left from the frame edge; positive numbers move the graphic down and to the right.

6. **Using the Control panel, change the image's position inside the frame to X: –0.5″, Y: 1″ (based on the top-left reference point).**

   This position aligns the image with the irregular-frame image, giving the impression of a single image in both frames (the background rectangle and the irregular surfer-shaped frame).

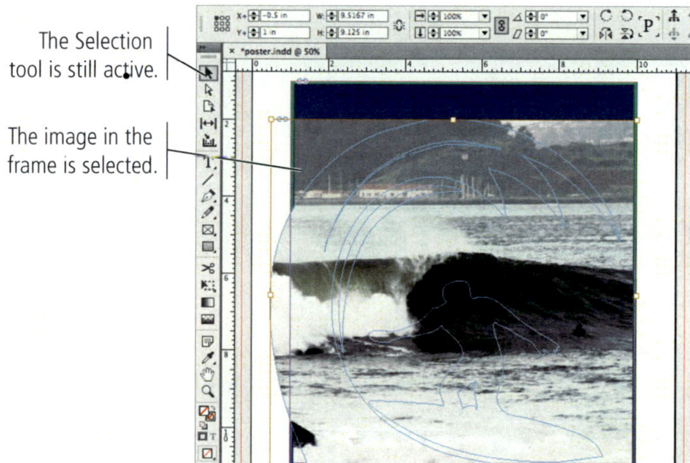

7. **Press ESC to restore the frame (not the frame content) as the active selection.**

8. **Open the Effects panel (Window>Effects).**

When a frame is selected, you can apply various effects to the entire object, or to the object fill only, the object stroke only, or any text within the object.

9. **Using the Direct Selection tool or Content Grabber, select the image inside the frame.**

When the content inside a graphics frame is selected, you can apply effects to the image itself, independent of the frame.

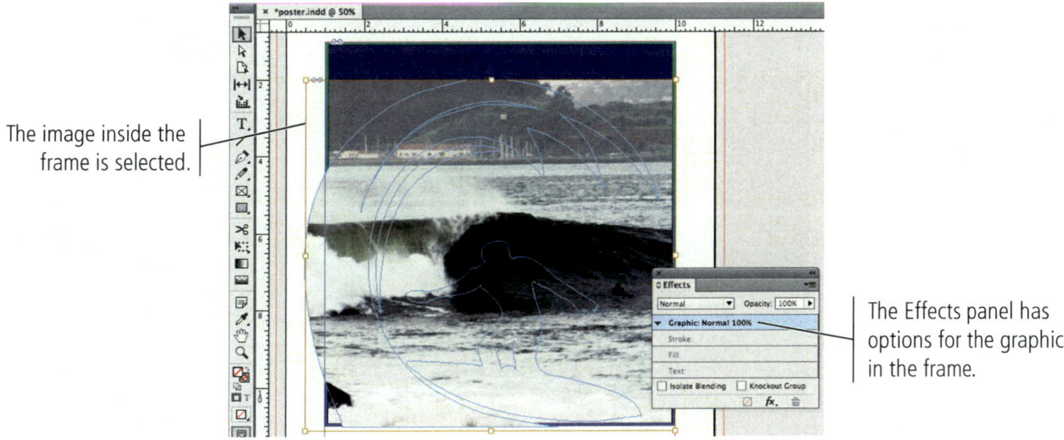

10. **With the Graphic option selected in the Effects panel, choose the Screen option in the Blending Mode menu.**

The image now blends into the gradient background, but there is still a hard line marking the bottom edge of the placed image.

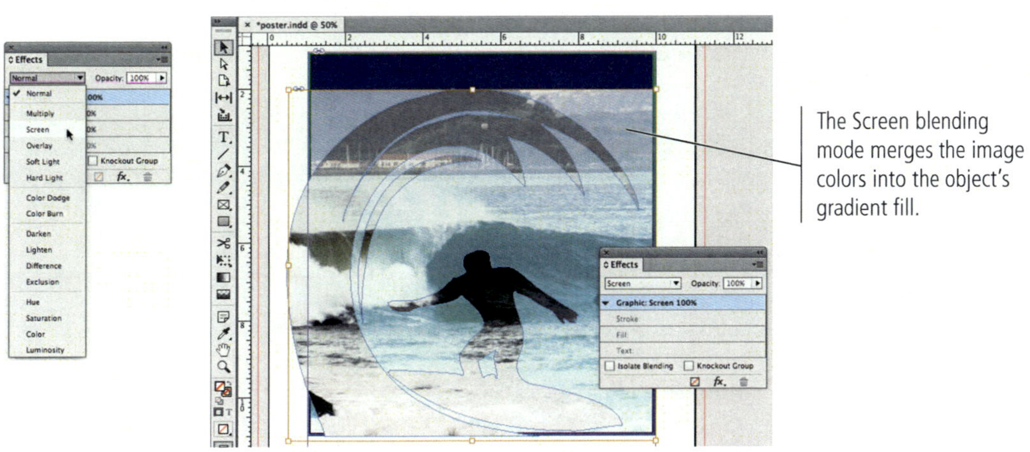

Blending Modes

Blending modes control how colors in an object interact with colors in underlying objects. Objects are set to Normal by default, which simply overlays the top object's color onto underlying objects. (If the top object is entirely opaque, there is no effect on underlying objects.)

- **Multiply** multiplies (hence the name) the base color by the blend color, resulting in a darker color. Multiplying any color with black produces black; multiplying any color with white leaves the color unchanged.
- **Screen** is basically the inverse of Multiply, always returning a lighter color. Screening with black has no effect; screening with white produces white.
- **Overlay** multiplies or screens the blend color to preserve the original lightness or darkness of the base.
- **Soft Light** darkens or lightens base colors depending on the blend color. Blend colors lighter than 50% lighten the base color (as if dodged); blend colors darker than 50% darken the base color (as if burned).
- **Hard Light** combines the Multiply and Screen modes. Blend colors darker than 50% are multiplied, and blend colors lighter than 50% are screened.
- **Color Dodge** brightens the base color. Blend colors lighter than 50% significantly increase brightness; blending with black has no effect.
- **Color Burn** darkens the base color by increasing the contrast. Blend colors darker than 50% significantly darken the base color by increasing saturation and reducing brightness; blending with white has no effect.
- **Darken** returns the darker of the blend or base color. Base pixels that are lighter than the blend color are replaced; base pixels that are darker than the blend color do not change.
- **Lighten** returns whichever is the lighter color (base or blend). Base pixels that are darker than the blend color are replaced; base pixels that are lighter than the blend color do not change.
- **Difference*** inverts base color values according to the brightness value in the blend layer. Lower brightness values in the blend layer have less of an effect on the result; blending with black has no effect.
- **Exclusion*** is similar to Difference, except that midtone values in the base color are completely desaturated.
- **Hue*** results in a color with the luminance and saturation of the base color and the hue of the blend color.
- **Saturation*** results in a color with the luminance and hue of the base and the saturation of the blend color.
- **Color*** results in a color with the luminance of the base color and the hue and saturation of the blend color.
- **Luminosity*** results in a color with the hue and saturation of the base color and the luminance of the blend color (basically the opposite of the Color mode).

**Avoid applying the Difference, Exclusion, Hue, Saturation, Color, and Luminosity modes to objects with spot colors. It could create unpredictable results (at best) when the file is separated for commercial print requirements.*

11. Click the *fx* button at the bottom of the Effects panel, and choose Gradient Feather.

The Effects dialog box opens to show the Gradient Feather options.

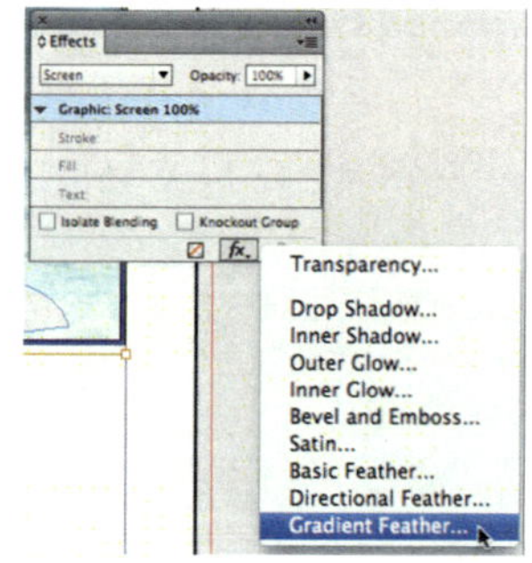

> *Note:*
>
> *If you use the Gradient Feather tool, the Gradient Feather effect is automatically applied.*

12. In the Effects dialog box, click the Preview check box so you can preview your results before accepting/applying them.

The Gradient Feather effect creates a transparency gradient so an object blends into underlying objects instead of leaving a hard edge. The effect is created using a gradient that shifts from 100% opacity to 0% opacity. The levels of opacity in the gradient determine the opacity of the object to which the feather effect is applied.

13. **To the right of the gradient ramp sample, click the button to reverse the gradient.**

14. **Click in the Angle circle and drag until the field shows –90° (the line should point straight down).**

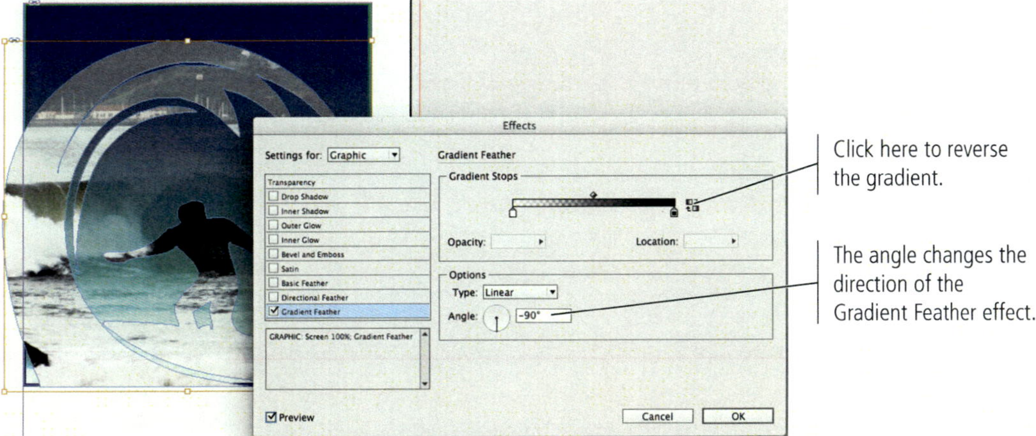

Click here to reverse the gradient.

The angle changes the direction of the Gradient Feather effect.

15. **Drag the left gradient stop until the Location field shows 20%.**

By extending the solid black part of the gradient to the 75% location, the top three-quarters of the affected image remain entirely visible; only the bottom quarter of the image blends into the background.

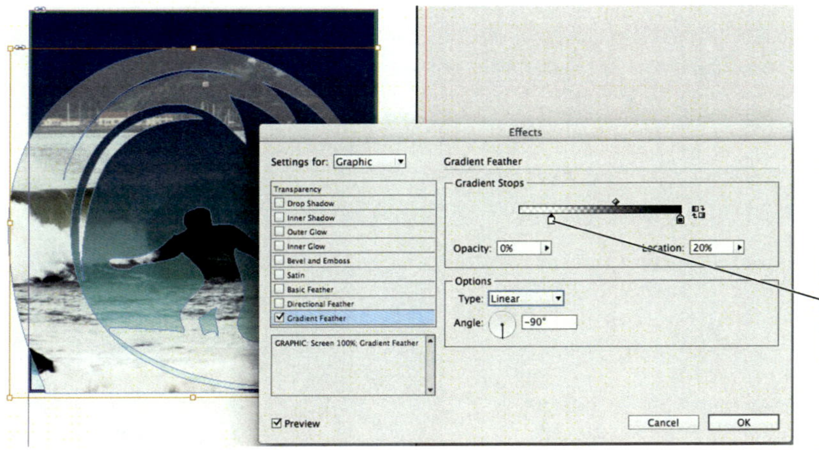

Moving the first stop extends the transparent area of the gradient, which shortens the part of the image that is entirely opaque.

16. **Click OK to close the Effects dialog box and apply your choices.**

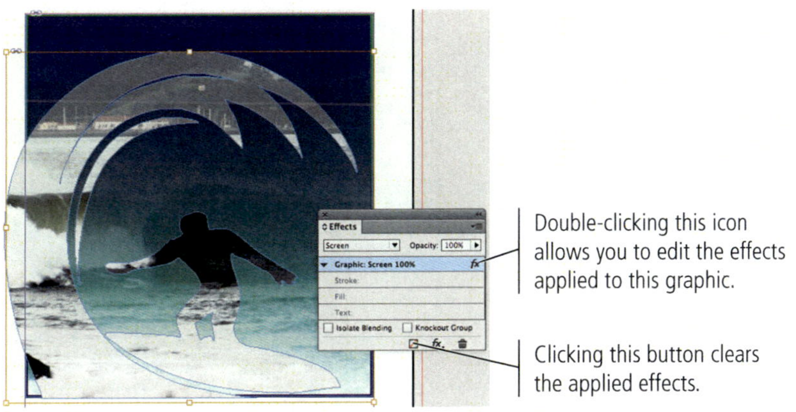

Double-clicking this icon allows you to edit the effects applied to this graphic.

Clicking this button clears the applied effects.

> ***Note:***
>
> *Effects in InDesign are non-destructive, which means they have no effect on the physical file data.*

Applying Effects

InDesign offers nine different effects options, which you can apply individually or in combinations to create unique flat and dimensional effects for any object. The effects can be applied by clicking the *fx* button at the bottom of the Effects panel, by clicking the *fx* button in the Control panel, or by choosing from the Object>Effects menu.

Drop Shadow and Inner Shadow

Drop Shadow adds a shadow behind the object. **Inner Shadow** adds a shadow inside the edges of the object. For both types, you can define the blending mode, color, opacity, angle, distance, offset, and size of the shadow.

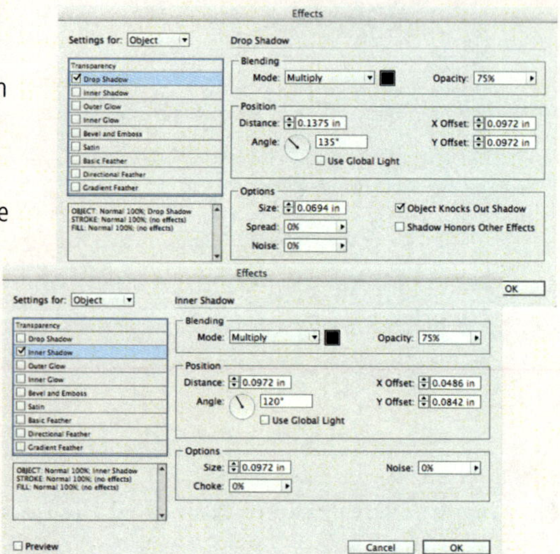

- **Distance** is the overall offset of the shadow, or how far away the shadow will be from the original object. The Offset fields allow you to define different horizontal and vertical distances.
- **Size** is the blur amount applied to the shadow.
- **Spread** (for Drop Shadows) is the percentage that the shadow expands beyond the original object.
- **Choke** (for Inner Shadows) is the percentage that the shadow shrinks into the original object.
- **Noise** controls the amount of random pixels added to the effect.

The **Object Knocks Out Shadow** option for drop shadows allows you to knock out (remove) or maintain the shadow underneath the object area. This option is particularly important if the original object is semi-transparent above its shadow.

The **Use Global Light** check box is available for the Drop Shadow, Inner Shadow, and Bevel and Emboss effects. When this option is checked, the style is linked to the "master" light source angle for the entire file. Changing the global light setting affects any linked shadow or bevel effect applied to any object in the entire file. (If Use Global Light is checked for an effect, changing the angle for that effect also changes the Global Light angle. You can also change the Global Light settings by choosing Object>Effects>Global Light.)

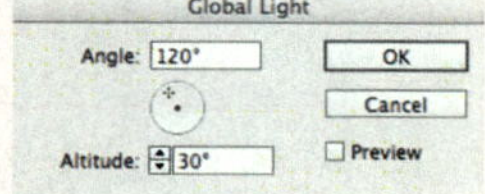

Outer Glow and Inner Glow

Outer Glow and **Inner Glow** add glow effects to the outside and inside edges (respectively) of the original object. For either kind of glow, you can define the blending mode, opacity, noise, and size values.

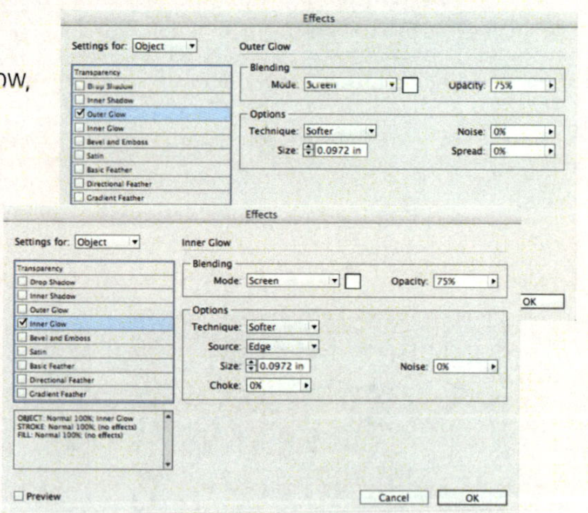

- For either Outer or Inner glows, you can define the **Technique** as Precise or Softer. **Precise** creates a glow at a specific distance; **Softer** creates a blurred glow and does not preserve detail as well as Precise.
- For Inner Glows, you can also define the **Source** of the glow (Center or Edge). **Center** applies a glow starting from the center of the object; **Edge** applies the glow starting from the inside edges of the object.
- The **Spread** and **Choke** sliders affect the percentages of the glow effects.

Applying Effects (continued)

Bevel and Emboss

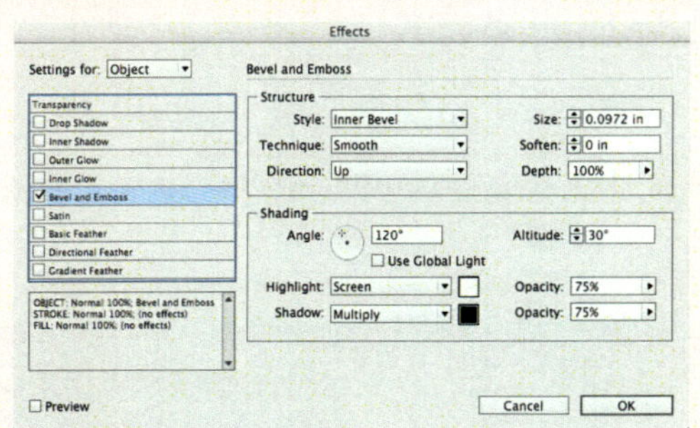

This effect has five variations or styles:

- **Inner Bevel** creates a bevel on the inside edges of the object.
- **Outer Bevel** creates a bevel on the outside edges of the object.
- **Emboss** creates the effect of embossing the object against the underlying layers.
- **Pillow Emboss** creates the effect of stamping the edges of the object into the underlying layers.

Any of these styles can be applied as **Smooth** (blurs the edges of the effect), **Chisel Hard** (creates a distinct edge to the effect), or **Chisel Soft** (creates a distinct, but slightly blurred edge to the effect).

You can change the **Direction** of the bevel effect. **Up** creates the appearance of the layer coming out of the image; **Down** creates the appearance of something stamped into the image. The **Size** field makes the effect smaller or larger, and the **Soften** option blurs the edges of the effect. **Depth** increases or decreases the three-dimensional effect of the bevel.

In the **Shading** area, you can control the light source's **Angle** and **Altitude** (think of how shadows differ as the sun moves across the sky). Finally, you can change the blending mode, opacity, and color of both highlights and shadows created with the Bevel or Emboss effect.

Satin

Satin applies interior shading to create a satiny appearance. You can change the blending mode, color, and opacity of the effect, as well as the angle, distance, and size.

Basic Feather, Directional Feather, and Gradient Feather

These three effects soften the edges of an object:

- **Basic Feather** equally fades all edges of the selected object (or attribute) by a specific width. The **Choke** option determines how much of the softened edge is opaque (high settings increase opacity and low settings decrease opacity). **Corners** can be **Sharp** (following the outer edge of the shape), **Rounded** (corners are rounded according to the Feather Width), or **Diffused** (fades from opaque to transparent). **Noise** adds random pixels to the softened area.
- **Directional Feather** allows you to apply different feather widths to individual edges of an object. The **Shape** option defines the object's original shape (First Edge Only, Leading Edges, or All Edges). The **Angle** field allows you to rotate the feathering effect; if you use any angle other than a 90° increment (i.e., 90, 180, 270, 360), the feathering will be skewed.
- **Gradient Feather** creates a transparency gradient that blends from solid to transparent. This effect underlies the Gradient Feather tool. You can move the start and end stops to different locations along the ramp, or add stops to define specific transparencies at specific locations. You can also choose from a Linear or Radial Gradient Feather effect, and change the angle of a Linear Gradient Feather effect.

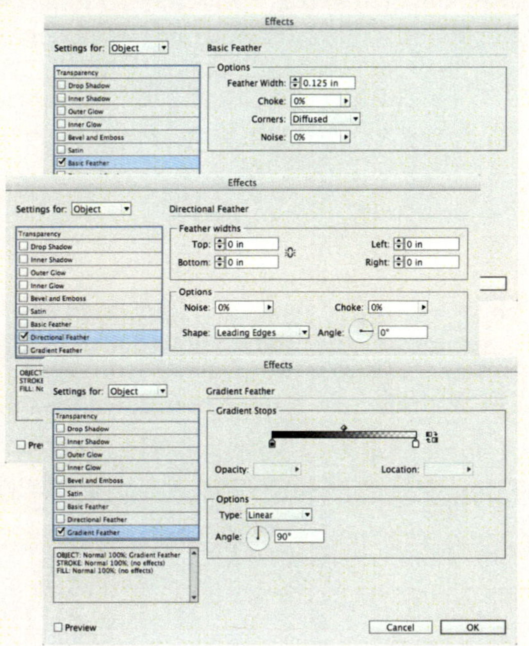

17. **Click away from the active image to deselect it (and its containing frame).**

18. **Using the Selection tool, select the irregular image frame.**

19. **In the Control panel, click the Drop Shadow button.**

    Clicking this button automatically applies the Drop Shadow effect using the default settings.

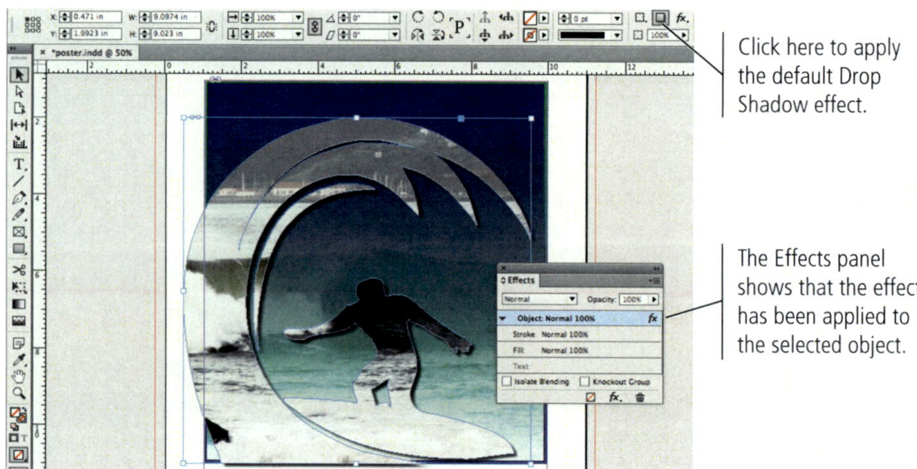

20. **Save the file and continue to the next exercise.**

Create a QR Code

A **QR code** (short for quick response code) is a type of bar code that provides easy access — using a special QR code reader app on a smartphone or tablet — to additional information that is programmed into the code. InDesign CC includes a built-in option for creating QR codes directly in a layout, which makes it simple to incorporate this kind of marketing tool into any layout.

1. **With poster.indd open, create a new rectangle frame in the bottom-right corner of the image area. Define the frame parameters (based on the top-left reference point) as:**

   X: 8″ W: 1.75″
   Y: 9″ H: 1.75″

2. **If necessary, change the frame's stroke weight to 6 pt. Change the frame's fill color to Paper and stroke color to C=100 M=0 Y=100 K=25.**

3. **With the new frame selected, choose Object>Generate QR Code.**

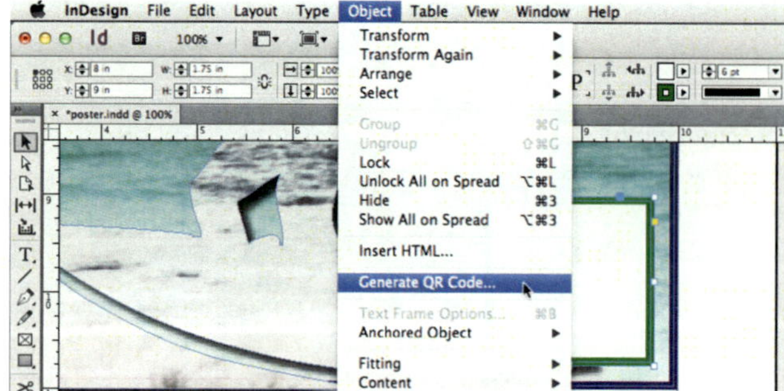

4. **In the resulting dialog box, choose Web Hyperlink in the Type menu and type www.surfriderfestival.com in the URL field.**

You can use the Type menu to define what the QR code does:

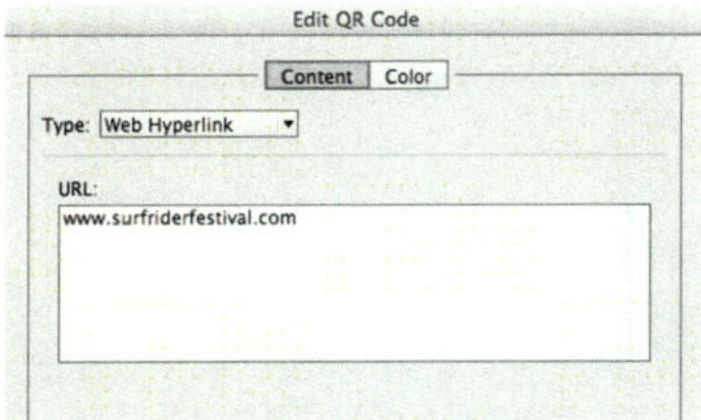

- **Web Hyperlink.** If you choose this option, you can define the specific URL that appears when a user scans the code.
- **Plain Text.** If you choose this option, you can define a plain-text message that appears when a user scans the code.
- **Text Message.** If you choose this option, you can define the phone number and message content that will be sent.
- **Email.** If you choose this option, you can define the email address, subject, and email body that will be included in the resulting email.
- **Business Card.** If you choose this option, you can define the specific fields that are common in digital contact applications (name, company, address, etc.).

Note:

The actual behavior of QR codes depends on the specific device and app being used to scan them.

5. **Click the Color tab at the top of the dialog box. Choose C=100 M=100 Y=25 K=0, then click OK.**

The color you define here determines the color of the actual QR code object. Keep in mind that high contrast between the QR code object and the frame background color helps to make sure the code will work on all devices and apps.

Note:

You can edit the properties of a QR code by choosing Object>Edit QR code (or by Control/right-clicking a QR code in the layout and choosing Edit QR Code in the object's contextual menu.)

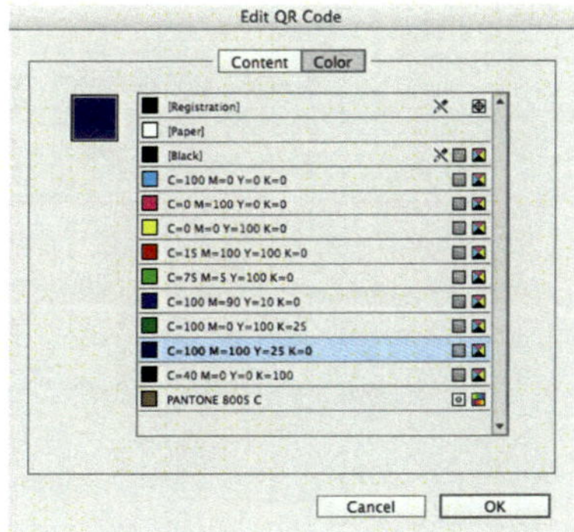

InDesign automatically generates the QR code inside the frame. The resulting graphic is centered in the frame, and scaled to leave a 10-pixel inset from the nearest frame edges.

The QR code is actually created as an embedded EPS graphic (although it does not appear in the file's Links panel). If you select the graphic inside the frame, you can scale it as you would any other placed graphic. Keep in mind, however, that distorting the code graphic might cause it to not work.

The frame containing the QR code is still a graphics frame; the frame's fill color appears behind the QR code.

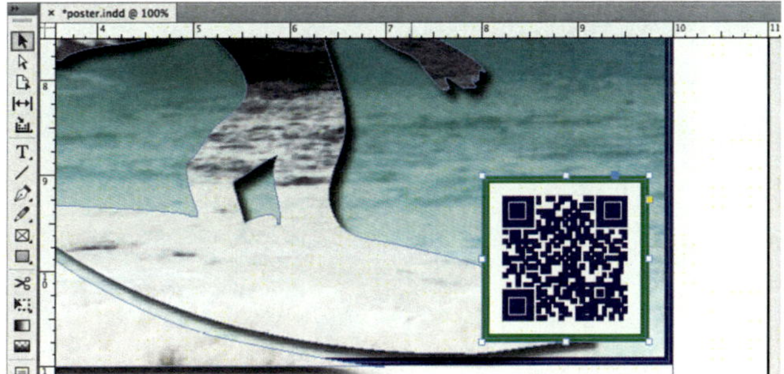

6. **Save the file and continue to the next stage of the project.**

Stage 2 Importing and Formatting Text

Placing text is one of the most critical functions of page-layout software, whether you create the text directly within InDesign or import it from an external file. InDesign provides all the tools you need to format text, from choosing a font to automatically creating hanging punctuation.

Control Text Threading

Some layouts require only a few bits of text, while others include numerous pages. Depending on how much text you have to work with, you might place all the layout text in a single frame, or you might cut and paste different pieces of a single story into separate text frames. In other cases, you might thread text across multiple frames — maintaining the text as a single story but allowing flexibility in frame size and position.

1. **With poster.indd open, zoom into the empty area below the placed images.**
2. **Use the Type tool to create a text frame that is 9″ wide and 1″ high (filling the width between the margin guides).**
3. **Select the frame with the Selection tool, and then use the Control panel to make sure the top edge of the text frame is positioned at Y: 11.25″.**

When the Selection tool is active, you can use the Control panel to change the position and dimensions of a text frame.

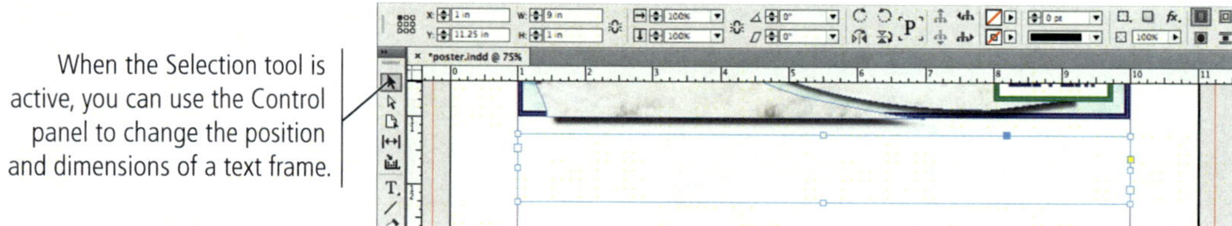

4. **Create three more text frames using the following parameters:**

Frame 2	**X: 1″**	**W: 3.2″**
	Y: 12.45″	**H: 3.55″**
Frame 3	**X: 5″**	**W: 5″**
	Y: 12.45″	**H: 3.55″**
Frame 4	**X: 1″**	**W: 9″**
	Y: 16.1″	**H: 0.5″**

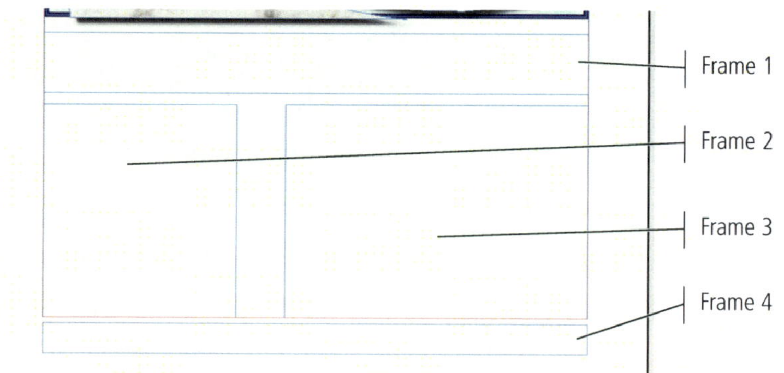

5. **Choose the Type tool, and click inside the first text frame to place the insertion point.**

   When you click in a text frame with the Type tool, you see a flashing insertion point where you click (or in the top-left corner if there is no text in the frame). This insertion point marks the location where text will appear when you type, paste, or import it into the document.

6. **Choose File>Place. Navigate to the file named festival.txt in the WIP>Surfing folder.**

7. **Make sure the Replace Selected Item option is checked and then click Open.**

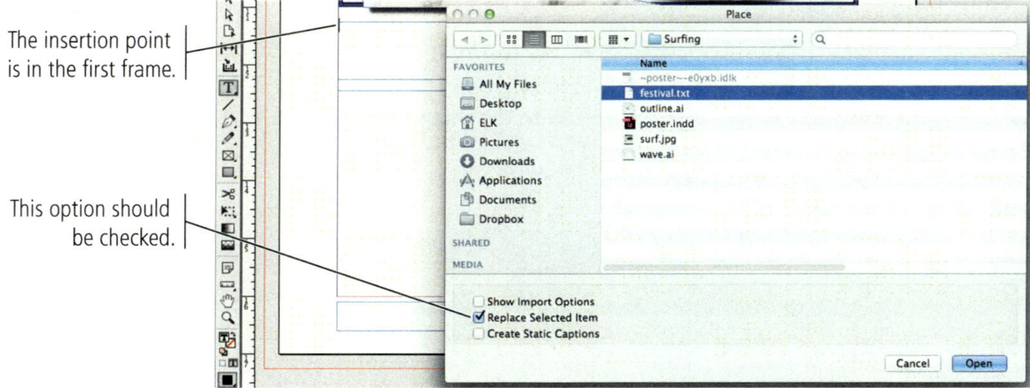

When Replace Selected Item is checked, the text file is automatically imported at the location of the insertion point. (If this option is not checked, the text is imported into the cursor.)

Note:

The overset text icon is visible even when the In and Out ports are not.

8. **Choose the Selection tool in the Tools panel.**

When a text frame is selected, you can see the In and Out ports that allow you to link one text frame to another. In this case, the Out port shows the **overset text icon**, indicating that the placed file has more text than can fit within the frame.

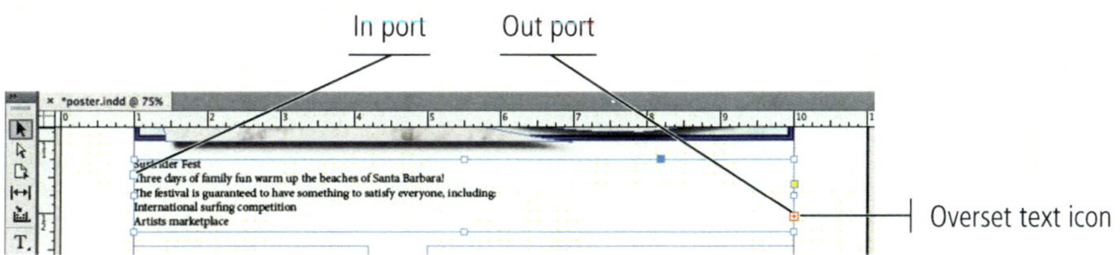

Note:

If you see the overset text icon (the red plus sign), the story does not fit in the current frame (or series of frames). You should always correct overset text.

9. **Click the Out port of the first text frame.**

Clicking the Out port loads the cursor with the rest of the text in the story. When the loaded cursor is over an existing frame, you can click to place the next part of the story in that frame. When the cursor is not over a frame, you can click and drag to create a frame that will contain the next part of the story. You can do this with the Selection tool (as you just did) or the Direct Selection tool.

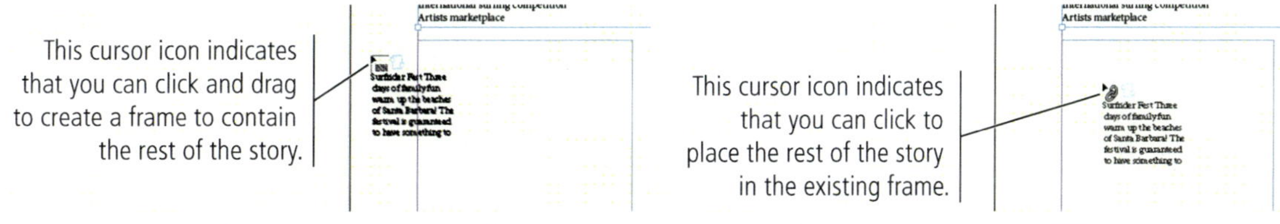

10. **Click inside the second frame to link it to the first frame.**

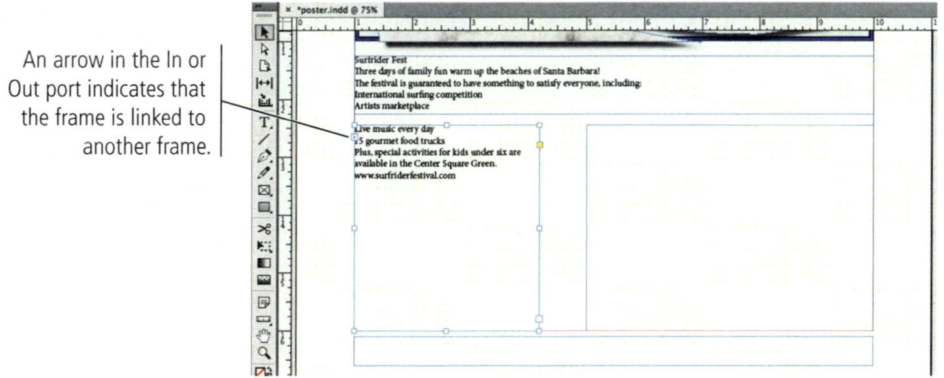

11. **Repeat this process to link from the second frame to the third, and then from the third frame to the fourth.**

    You can define the thread of text frames even when there is no text to fill those frames. Simply use the Selection or Direct Selection tool to click the Out port of one frame, and then click anywhere within the next frame you want to add to the thread.

12. **Choose View>Extras>Show Text Threads.**

    When this option is toggled on (and you are in Normal viewing mode), you can see all of the threading arrows whenever any of the text frames in the thread is selected.

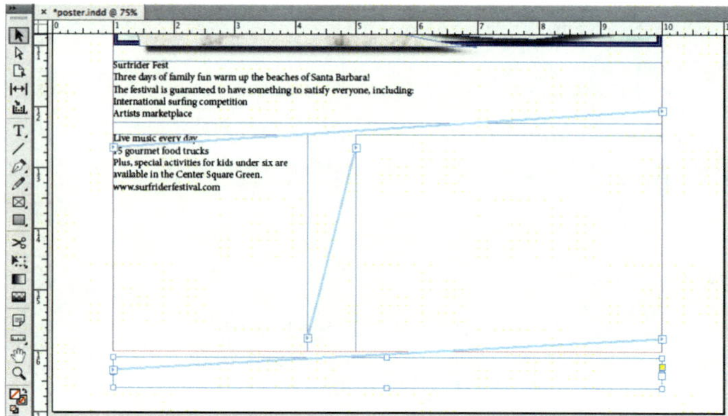

13. **Save the file and continue to the next exercise.**

> *Note:*
>
> *You can also press Command/Control while the Type tool is active to click a text frame Out port and thread the frames.*

> *Note:*
>
> *When you load the cursor with overset text, the loaded cursor shows the text from the beginning of the story — even though the beginning is already placed. This is a quirk of the software; when you click with the loaded cursor, the text will flow into the new frame at the proper place in the story.*

Define Manual Frame Breaks

When you thread text from one frame to another (or to multiple columns in the same frame), you often need to control exactly where a story breaks from frame to frame. InDesign includes a number of commands for breaking text in precise locations.

1. **In the open `poster.indd` file, use the Type tool to click at the end of the first line (after "Surfrider Fest") to place the insertion point.**

    As you complete the following exercises, feel free to zoom in as you think necessary to work with specific areas of your layout.

2. **Choose Type>Insert Break Character>Frame Break.**

    InDesign provides several special break characters that allow you to control the flow of text from line to line, from column to column, and from frame to frame. The Frame Break character forces all following text into the next frame in the thread.

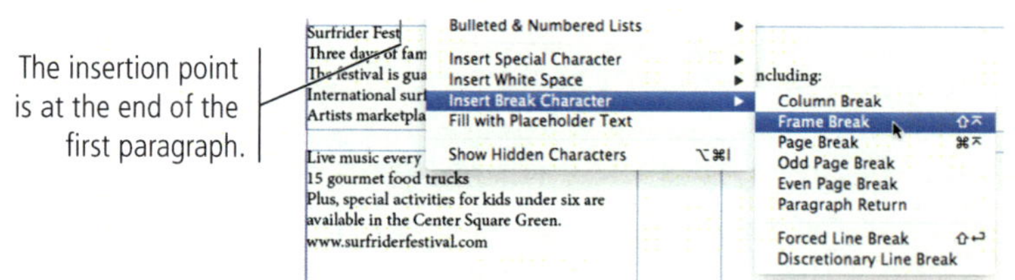

The insertion point is at the end of the first paragraph.

> *Note:*
>
> *Text that appears as a series of gray bars is called **greeked text**. By default, text smaller than 7 pt (at 100%) is greeked to improve screen redraw time. You can change the greeking threshold in the Display Performance pane of the Preferences dialog box.*
>
> *View percentage is part of the determination for greeking text; in other words, if your view percentage is 50%, 12-pt text appears as 6-pt text on screen, so it would be greeked using the default preferences.*

3. **Choose Type>Show Hidden Characters.**

   Each paragraph is separated by a paragraph return character (¶). A paragraph can consist of only one or two words or multiple lines. The important thing is to realize that a paragraph is technically any copy between two paragraph returns (or other break characters).

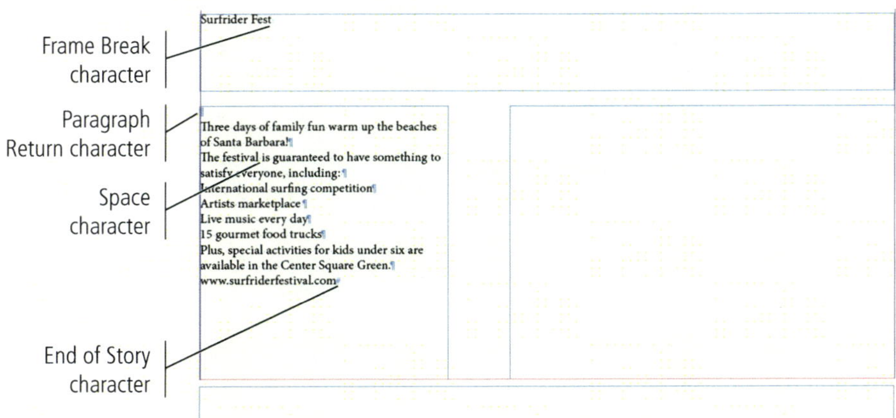

> ***Note:***
>
> *You can also toggle the visibility of hidden characters using the View Options button in the Application/Menu bar.*
>
> 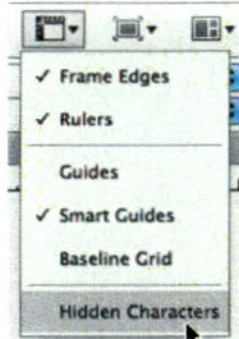
>

When you placed the Frame Break character in Step 2, everything following the insertion point was pushed to the next frame — including the paragraph return character that had been at the end of the first line. This created an "empty" paragraph that should be deleted.

> ***Note:***
>
> *The Forward Delete key is the one directly below the Help key on most standard keyboards. If you are using a laptop, place the insertion point at the beginning of the first sentence in the second frame ("Three sultry days…") and press Delete/Backspace.*

4. **With the insertion point flashing at the beginning of the second frame, press Forward Delete to remove the extra paragraph return.**

   If you don't have a Forward Delete key (if, for example, you're working on a laptop), move the insertion point to the beginning of the next line and press Delete/Backspace.

5. **With hidden characters visible, highlight the paragraph return character at the end of the first sentence in the second frame.**

6. **Choose Type>Insert Break Character>Frame Break to replace the highlighted paragraph return with a frame break character.**

   When text is highlighted — including hidden formatting characters — anything you type, paste, or enter using a menu command replaces the highlighted text.

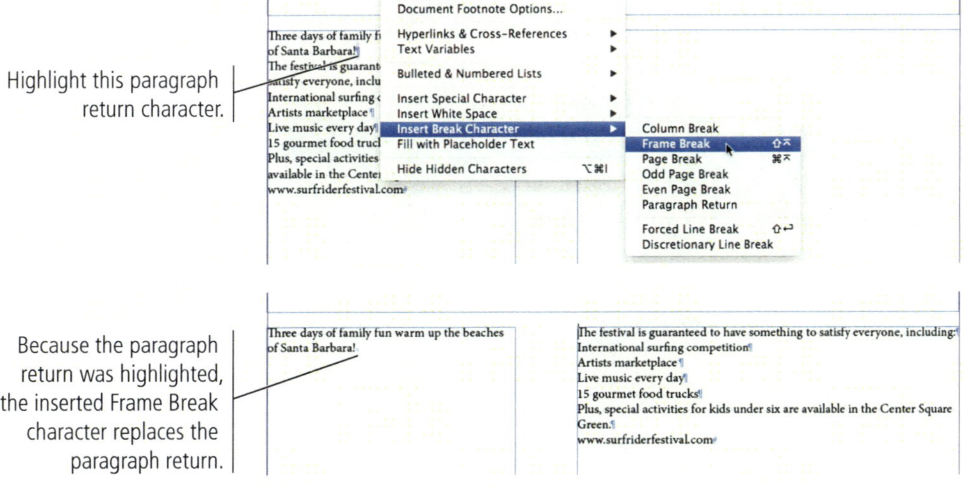

7. **Use the same technique to move only the last paragraph (the Web address) into the fourth text frame.**

Surfrider Fest

Three days of family fun warm up the beaches of Santa Barbara!

The festival is guaranteed to have something to satisfy everyone, including:
International surfing competition
Artists marketplace
Live music every day
15 gourmet food trucks
Plus, special activities for kids under six are available in the Center Square Green.

www.surfriderfestival.com

8. **Save the file and continue to the next exercise.**

> *Note:*
>
> *Press Enter (numeric keypad) to add a Column Break.*
>
> *Press Shift-Enter (numeric keypad) to add a Frame Break.*
>
> *Press Command/Control-Enter (numeric keypad) to add a Page Break, which pushes all text to the first threaded frame on the next page.*

Apply Character Formatting

Once text is in a frame, you can use character formatting attributes to determine the appearance of individual letters, such as the font and type size. These attributes can be controlled in the Character panel (Window>Type & Tables>Character) or the Control panel (depending on which options are visible in the Control panel).

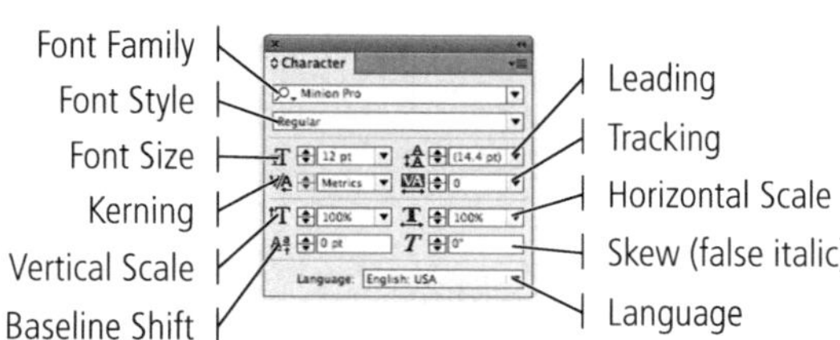

- A **font** contains all of the characters (**glyphs**) that make up a typeface, including upper- and lowercase letters, numbers, special characters, etc. (Fonts must be installed and activated on your computer to be accessible in InDesign.) The **font style** is a specific variation of the selected font, such as bold or condensed.
- **Size** is the height of a typeface measured in points.
- **Leading** is the distance from one baseline to the next. InDesign treats leading as a character attribute, even though leading controls the space between lines of an individual paragraph. (Space between paragraphs is controlled using the Space Before/After options in the Paragraph panel.) To change leading for an entire paragraph, you must first select the entire paragraph. This approach means you can change the leading for a single line of a paragraph by selecting any character(s) in that line; however, changing the leading for any character in a line applies the same change to the entire line that contains those characters.

> *Note:*
>
> *You can change this behavior by checking the Apply Leading to Entire Paragraph option in the Type pane of the Preferences dialog box.*

- **Vertical Scale** and **Horizontal Scale** artificially stretch or contract the selected characters. This type of scaling is a quick way of achieving condensed or expanded type if those variations of a font don't exist. Type that has been artificially scaled in this fashion tends to look bad because the scaling destroys the type's metrics; if possible, you should always use a condensed or expanded version of a typeface before resorting to horizontal or vertical scaling.
- **Kerning** increases or decreases the space between pairs of letters. Kerning is used in cases where particular letters in specific fonts need to be manually adjusted to eliminate a too-tight or too-spread-out appearance; manual kerning is usually necessary in headlines or other large type. (Many commercial fonts have built-in kerning pairs, so you won't need to apply too much hands-on intervention with kerning.)

- **Tracking**, also known as "range kerning," refers to the overall space between a range of characters.
- **Baseline Shift** moves the selected type above or below the baseline by a specific number of points. Positive numbers move the characters up; negative values move the text down.
- **Skew** artificially slants the selected text, creating a false italic appearance. This option distorts the look of the type and should be used sparingly (if ever).

Note:

Tracking and kerning are applied in thousandths of an ***em*** *(an em is technically defined as width that equals the type size).*

In addition to the options in the basic Character panel, several styling options are also available in the panel Options menu.

- **All Caps** changes all the characters to capital letters. This option only changes the appearance of the characters; they are not permanently converted to capital letters. To change the case of selected characters to all capital letters — the same as typing with Caps Lock turned on — use the Type>Change Case menu options.
- **Small Caps** changes lowercase letters to smaller versions of the uppercase letters. If the font is an Open Type font that contains true small caps, InDesign uses the true small caps.
- **Superscript** and **Subscript** artificially reduce the selected character(s) to a specific percentage of the point size; these options raise (for superscript) or lower (for subscript) the character from the baseline to a position that is a certain percentage of the leading. (The size and position of Superscript, Subscript, and Small Caps are controlled in the Advanced Type Preferences dialog box.)
- **Underline** places a line below the selected characters.
- **Strikethrough** places a line through the middle of selected characters.
- **Ligatures** are substitutes for certain pairs of letters, most commonly fi, fl, ff, ffi, and ffl. (Other pairs such as ct and st are common for historical typesetting, and ae and oe are used in some non-English-language typesetting.)

Note:

Choosing Underline Options or Strikethrough Options in the Character panel Options menu allows you to change the weight, offset, style, and color of the line for those styles.

1. **With `poster.indd` open, choose the Type tool in the Tools panel. Triple-click the first line of text in the story to select it.**

   Character formatting options apply only to selected characters.

2. **In the Character panel (Window>Type & Tables>Character), highlight the existing font name and type `ATC G`. Click ATC Garnet Ultra in the resulting menu to apply the new font.**

   As you learned in Project 1: Letterhead Design, the characters you type in the Font Family field result in a menu with all fonts that include the letters you type. After you select the font in the menu, ATC Garnet appears in the Font Family menu and Ultra appears in the Font Style menu.

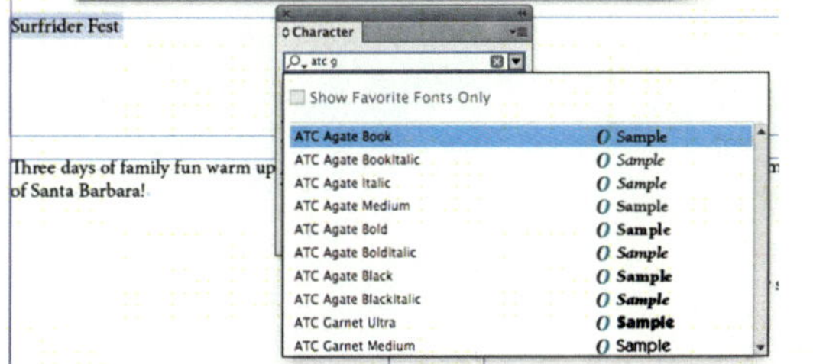

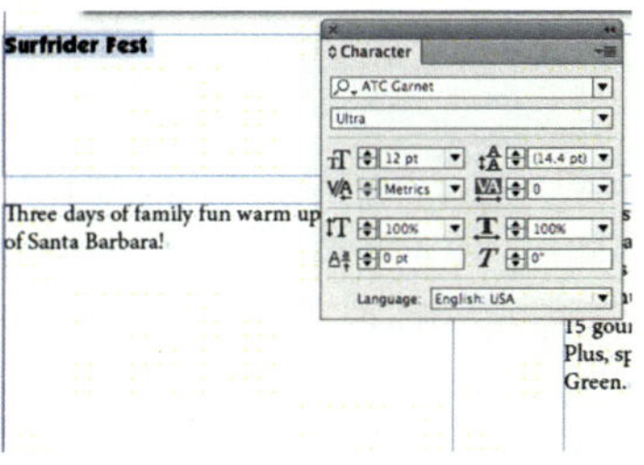

3. **Open the Font Size menu and choose 72.**

   You can choose one of the built-in font sizes, type a specific value in the field, or click the arrow buttons to change the font size by 1 point.

> **Note:**
>
> *You can use the Up and Down Arrow keys to nudge paragraph and character style values when the insertion point is in a panel field.*

4. **Open the Character panel Options menu and choose the All Caps option.**

5. **In the Character panel, type 130 in the Tracking field and press Return/Enter.**

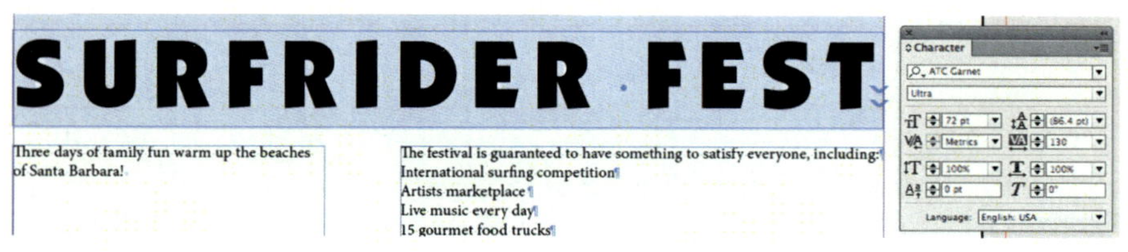

> **Note:**
>
> *Most of these character formatting options are also available in the Control panel.*

6. **Click four times on the text in the second frame to select the entire paragraph.**

   Clicking twice selects an entire *word*, clicking three times selects an entire *line*, and clicking four times selects the entire *paragraph*.

7. **Change the selected text to 35-pt ATC Pyrite Bold Italic and change the Horizontal Scale field to 90%.**

   Horizontal and vertical scaling are useful for artificially stretching or contracting fonts that do not have a condensed or extended version. Be careful using these options, though, because the artificial scaling alters the character shapes and can make some fonts very difficult to read (especially at smaller sizes).

> **Note:**
>
> *Leave the Leading value at the automatic setting. By default, InDesign automatically applies leading as 120% of the type size.*

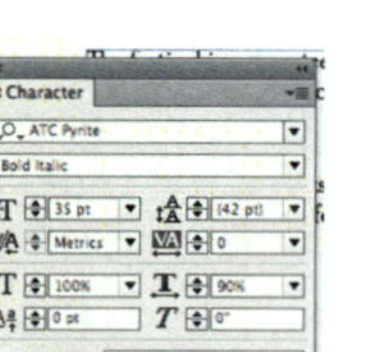

8. **Click three times to select the first line in the third frame, hold down the mouse button, and then drag down to select the other lines in the same frame.**

   When you triple-click to select an entire line, dragging up or down selects entire lines above or below the one you first clicked.

Designing with Placeholder Text

It's always a good idea to begin a project as soon as possible after getting the assignment. When working with clients, however, you will often find that the idea for a project comes before the actual content — sometimes long before the client has finalized the text.

Rather than waiting until the client's content is ready — which is sometimes the day before a project is due — you can design a layout using placeholders to mark the location of pictures and text frames, and even experiment with the appearance of different elements of the text.

With the insertion point placed in a text frame, choosing Type>Fill with Placeholder Text fills the active text frame with **lorem text** (supposedly from a Latin treatise on ethics written by Cicero more than 2000 years ago) using the default text-format settings. If a text frame is linked to other text frames, the placeholder text fills the entire series of linked text frames.

Lorem placeholder text is valuable for experimenting with the appearance of paragraph text, giving you a better idea of what blocks of copy will look like when real content is placed in the layout.

All four threaded text frames are filled with Roman placeholder text.

If you press Command/Control while choosing the Fill with Placeholder Text command, you can define a different language to use for the placeholder text. These options are useful if you want to experiment with a design for a layout in which the text does not use the Roman alphabet — again, the placeholder more accurately represents what the final copy will look like..

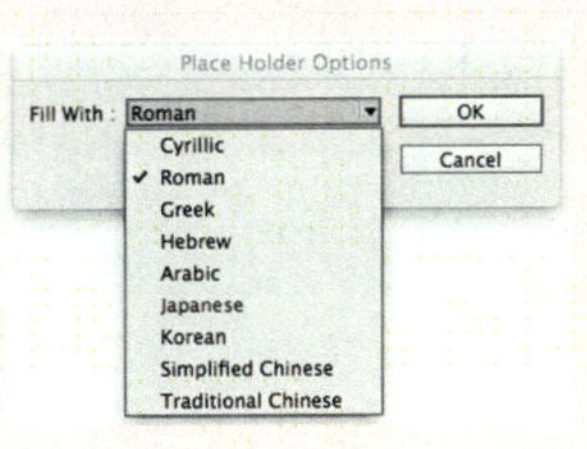

All four threaded text frames are filled with Cyrillic placeholder text.

All four threaded text frames are filled with Japanese placeholder text.

9. **With all of the text in the third frame selected, apply 22-pt ATC Pyrite Bold with 90% horizontal scaling.**

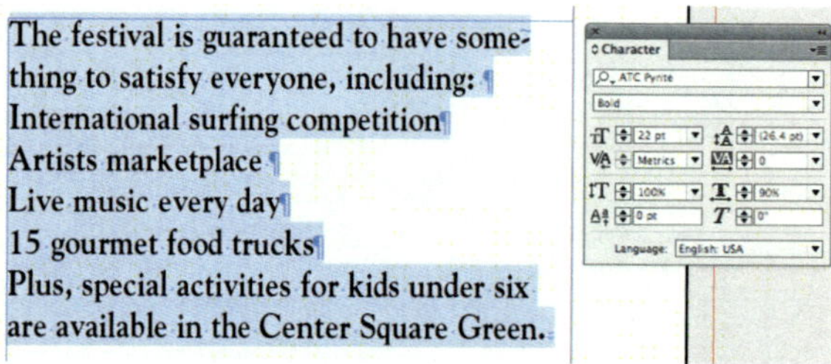

10. **Change the Web address in the fourth text frame to 26-pt ATC Garnet Medium.**

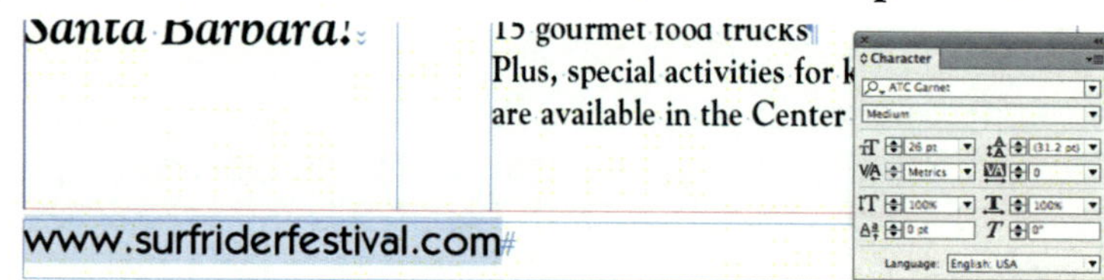

13. **Save the file and continue to the next exercise.**

Apply Paragraph Formatting

Character formatting includes any option that affects the appearance of selected characters, such as font, size, horizontal scale, and a host of others. Paragraph formatting options, on the other hand, affect an entire paragraph (everything between two paragraph return characters). Paragraph formatting can control everything from indents to the space between paragraphs to lines above and below paragraphs.

Paragraph formatting can be controlled in the Paragraph panel (Window>Type & Tables>Paragraph) or the Control panel (depending on which options are available).

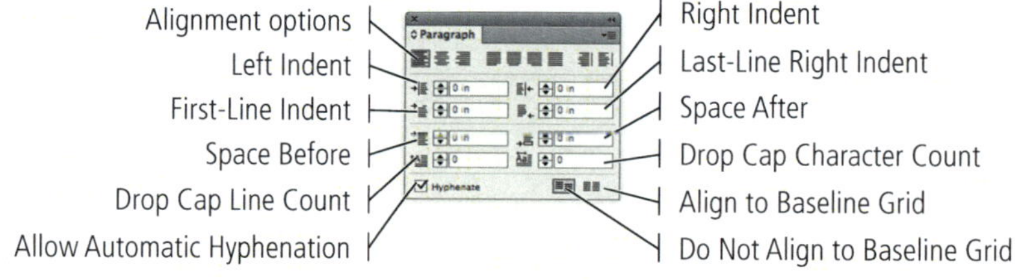

Note:

In InDesign, a paragraph is defined as all text between two paragraph return characters (¶), even if the paragraph exists on a single line.

1. **In the open `poster.indd` file, place the cursor anywhere in the paragraph in the first frame.**

2. **In the Paragraph panel, click the Justify All Lines button.**

   Paragraph formatting applies to the entire paragraph where the insertion point is placed, or to any paragraph that is entirely or partially selected. A paragraph does not have to be entirely selected to change its paragraph formatting attributes.

3. **Place the cursor anywhere in the paragraph in the second frame, then apply right paragraph alignment.**

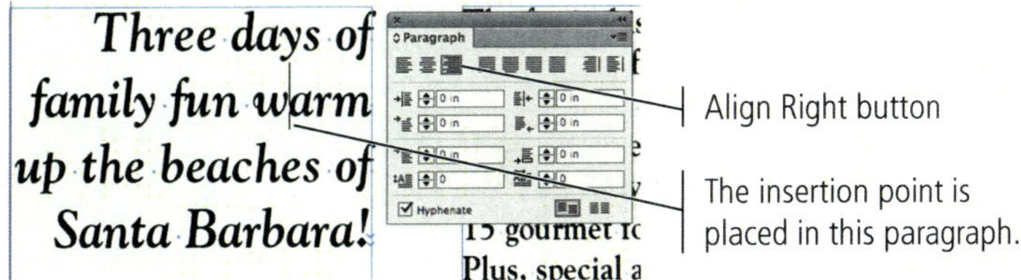

4. **Place the insertion point anywhere in the fourth frame (with the Web address) and apply centered paragraph alignment.**

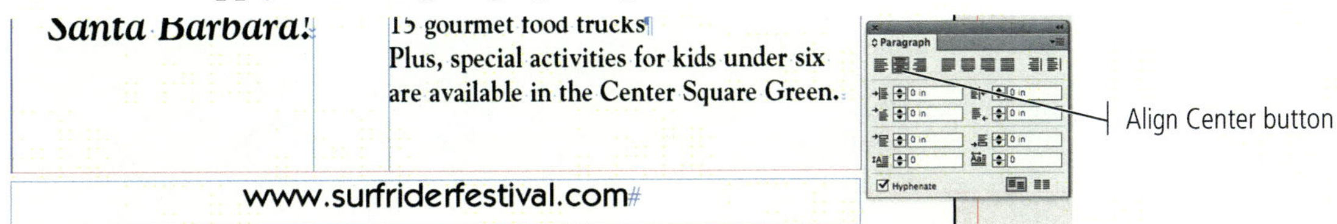

5. **In the third frame, select any part of the first through fifth paragraphs.**

6. **In the Paragraph panel, change the Space Before field to 0.09″.**

Note:

If you want to apply the same formatting to more than one consecutive paragraph, you can drag to select any part of the target paragraphs. Any paragraph that's even partially selected will be affected.

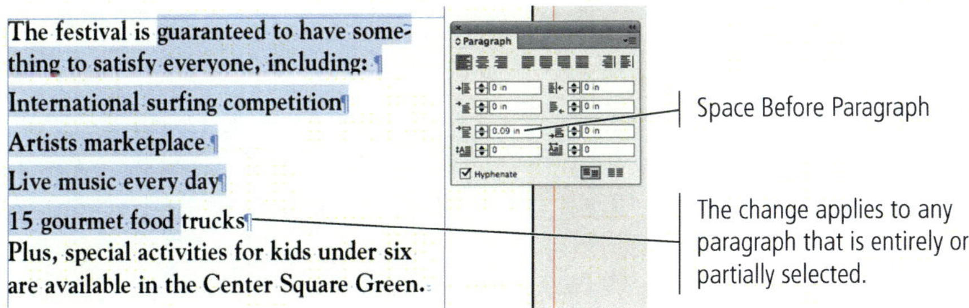

7. **Select any part of the second through fifth paragraphs in the same frame and change the Left Indent field to 0.25″.**

Note:

Remember: A paragraph is all text between two ¶ symbols — even if it occupies a single line.

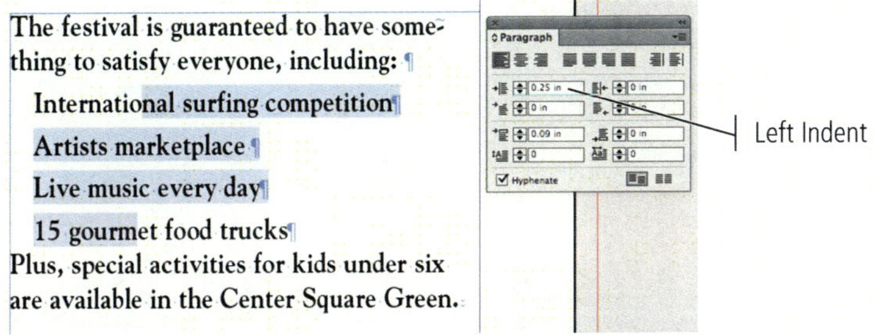

8. **Place the insertion point at the beginning of the sixth paragraph (before the word "Plus") and press Delete/Backspace.**

Note:

The arrow buttons for paragraph formatting options step through values in increments of 0.0625″.

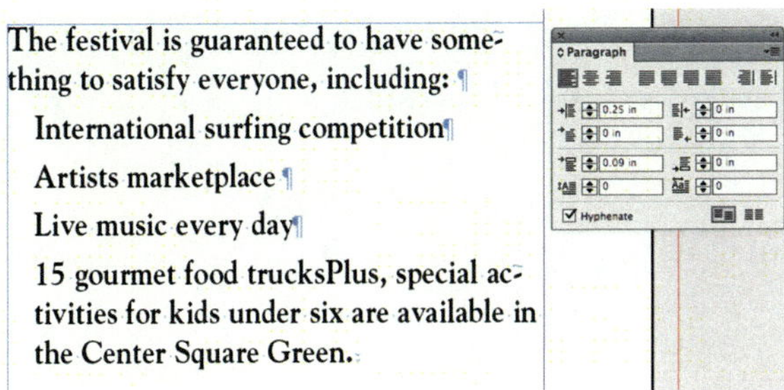

9. **Press Return/Enter to separate the two paragraphs again.**

This is an easy way to copy paragraph formatting from one paragraph to the next. When you re-separate the two paragraphs, the "Plus" paragraph adopts the paragraph formatting attributes of the "15 gourmet food trucks" paragraph.

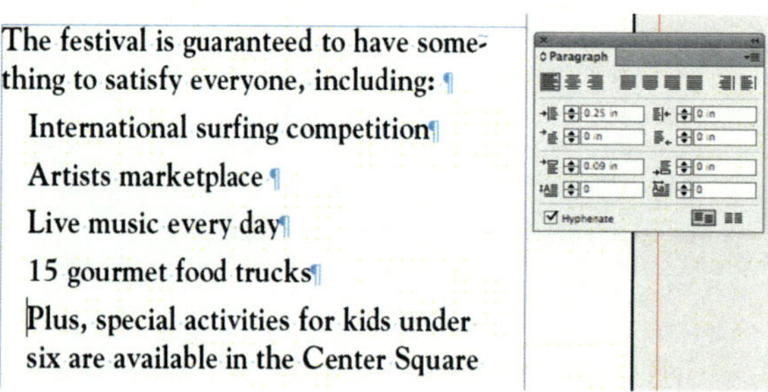

> ***Note:***
>
> *When you break an existing paragraph into a new paragraph, the attributes of the original paragraph are applied to the new paragraph.*

10. **With the insertion point at the beginning of the sixth paragraph, change the Left Indent back to 0.**

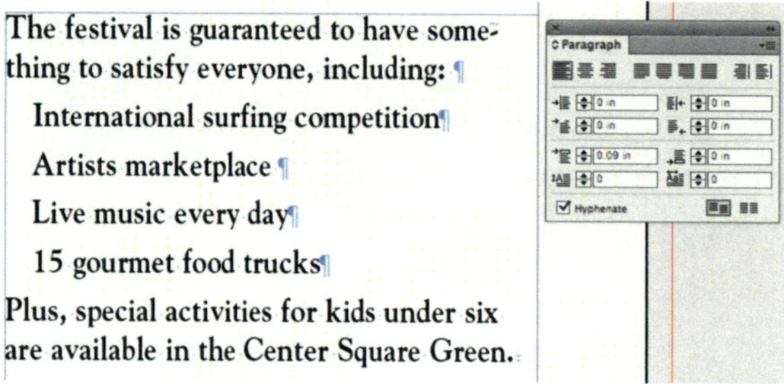

11. **Press Command-Option-I/Control-Alt-I to toggle off the hidden characters.**

Many designers frequently toggle the visibility of hidden characters while working on any given layout. You should become familiar with the keyboard shortcut for this command.

12. **In the Layers panel, click the empty space to the left of the <rectangle> item to make that object visible again.**

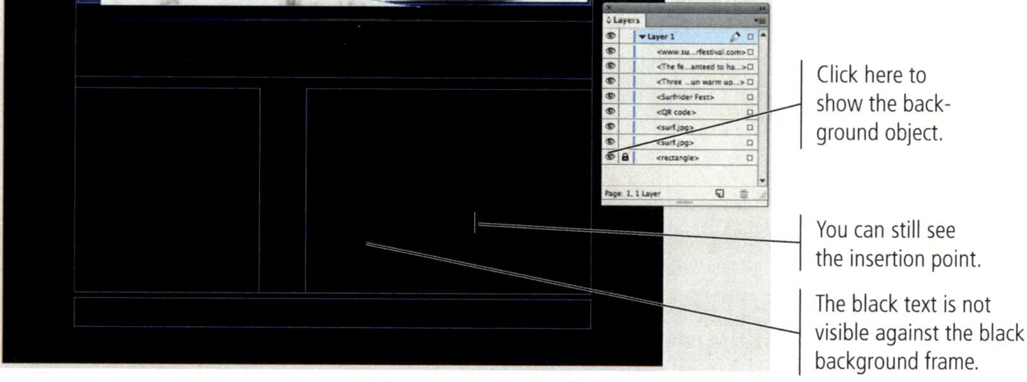

13. **With the insertion point still flashing in the now-obscured text, choose Edit>Select All to select all text in the series of linked frames.**

The Select All command selects all text in the story, whether that story exists in a single frame or threads across multiple frames. This command also selects overset text that doesn't fit into the current frame (or thread of frames).

14. **In the Swatches panel, make sure the Text icon is selected at the top of the panel, and then click the Paper swatch.**

In four-color (process) printing, there is no white ink. To achieve white, you have to remove the colors where you want white areas, which is called a **knockout**. By removing or knocking out underlying colors, the paper shows through — regardless of whether it is white or some other color (e.g., if you print on yellow paper, knockout areas will show the yellow color; this is why InDesign refers to this swatch as "Paper" instead of "White").

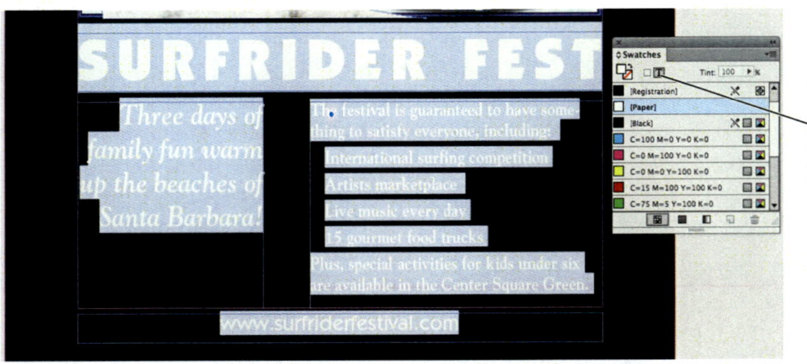

This "T" icon means you are changing the text color instead of the object color.

15. **Click away from the text to deselect it and review the results.**

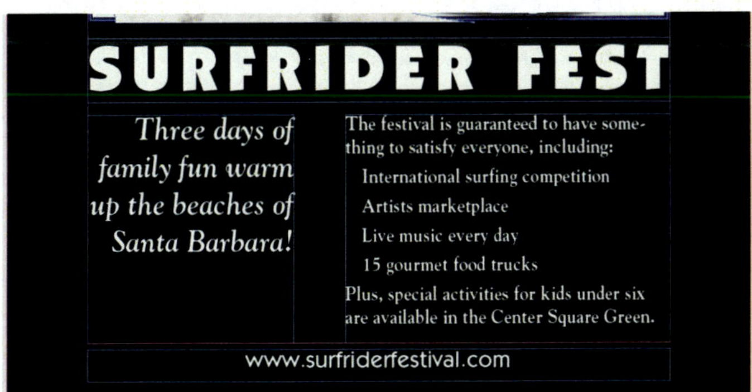

16. **Save the file and continue to the next stage of the project.**

Copying Type Attributes with the Eyedropper Tool

INDESIGN FOUNDATIONS

You can use the Eyedropper tool to copy character and paragraph attributes (including text color), and then apply those attributes to other sections of text.

To copy formatting from one piece of text to another, click with the Eyedropper tool on the formatting you want to copy. If any text is selected when you click the Eyedropper tool, the selected text is automatically re-formatted. If nothing is selected, the Eyedropper tool "loads" with the formatting attributes — the tool icon reverses directions and shows a small i-beam icon in the cursor.

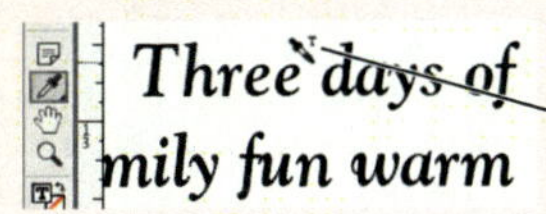

The Eyedropper tool cursor when it is "loaded" with text formatting attributes

You can click the loaded Eyedropper tool on any text to change its formatting, or you can click and drag to format multiple paragraphs at once. As long as the Eyedropper tool remains selected, you can continue to select text to apply the same formatting. You can also change the formatting in the Eyedropper tool by pressing Option/Alt and clicking text with the new formatting attributes you want to copy.

By default, the Eyedropper tool copies all formatting attributes. You can change that behavior by double-clicking the tool in the Tools panel to access the Eyedropper Options dialog box. Simply uncheck the options you don't want to copy (including individual options in each category), and then click OK.

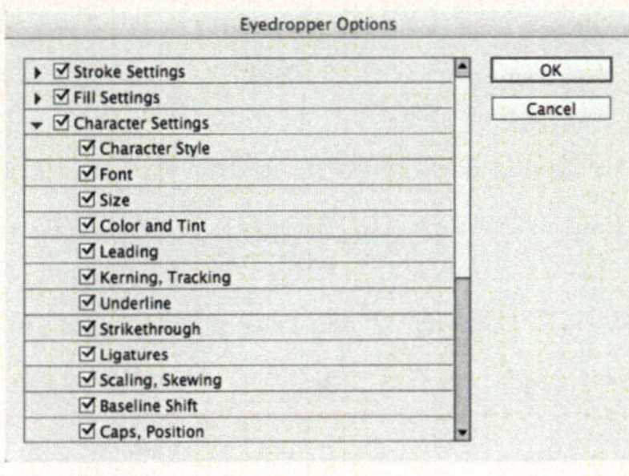

Applying Optical Margin Alignment

INDESIGN FOUNDATIONS

At times, specific arrangements of text can cause a paragraph to appear out of alignment, even though it's technically aligned properly. Punctuation at the beginning or end of a line — such as quotation marks at the beginning of a line or commas at the end of a line — often cause this kind of optical problem. InDesign includes a feature called **optical margin alignment** to fix this type of problem.

Optical margin alignment is applied in the Story panel (Window>Type and Tables>Story).

When this option is turned on, punctuation marks move outside the text margins — either to the left for left-aligned text or right for right-aligned text. (Moving punctuation outside the margins is often referred to as **hanging punctuation**.)

The field in the Story panel tells InDesign what size type needs to be adjusted. The best effect is usually created by defining the size of the type that needs adjustment.

Optical margin alignment option applies to an entire story (including all text frames in the same thread), not just the selected paragraph. If necessary, you can toggle the Ignore Optical Margin option (in the Paragraph panel Options menu) on for individual paragraphs so that the selected paragraph is not affected by optical margin alignment that is applied to the overall story.

The commas on the right side of the frame create the impression of the text being misaligned.

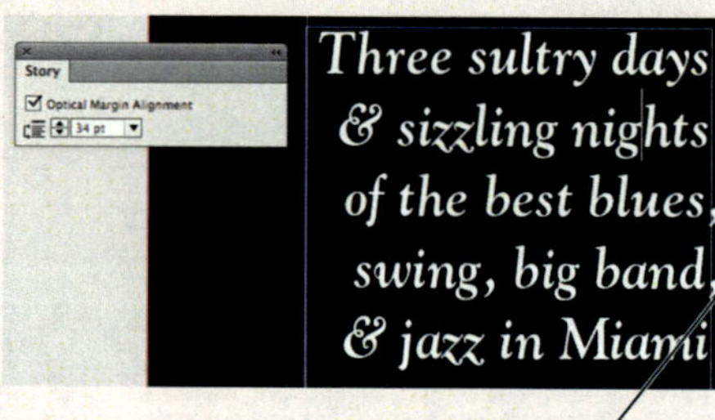

When Optical Margin Alignment is active, the commas move outside the frame edge.

Stage 3 Graphics as Text and Text as Graphics

Now that you're familiar with the basic options for formatting characters and paragraphs, you can begin to add style to a layout using two techniques — flowing text along a path, and placing graphics inline with text. (You will, of course, learn much more about working with text as you complete the rest of the projects in this book.)

Place Inline Graphics

Any graphics frame that you create on a page floats over the other elements in the layout. You can position graphics frames over other objects to hide underlying elements, or you can apply a **runaround** so that text will wrap around a picture box.

You can also place images as inline graphics, which means they will be anchored to the text in the position in which they are placed. If text reflows, inline objects reflow with the text and maintain their correct positioning.

There are two methods for creating inline objects. For simple applications, such as a graphic bullet, you can simply place the graphic and format it as a text character. (An inline graphic is treated as a single text character in the story; it is affected by many of the paragraph-formatting commands, such as space before and after, tab settings, leading, and baseline position.) For more complex applications, you can use the options in the Object>Anchored Object menu.

1. **With `poster.indd` open, place the insertion point at the beginning of the second line in the third frame (before the word "International").**

2. **Choose File>Place and navigate to `wave.ai` in the WIP>Surfing folder.**

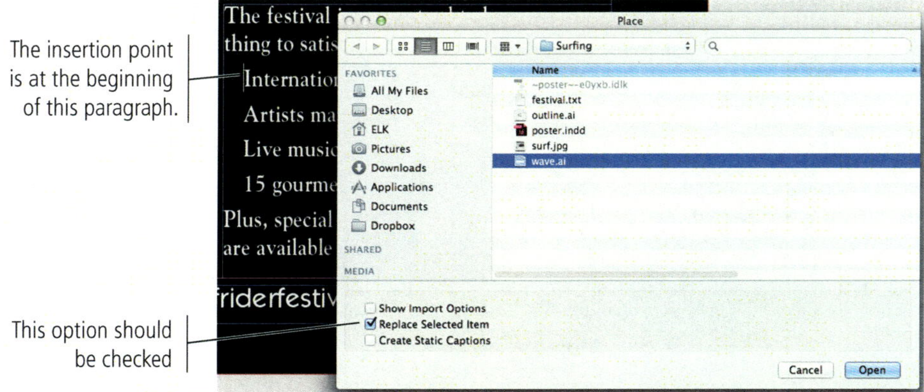

3. **Make sure the Replace Selected Item option is checked, and then click Open.**

If the insertion point is flashing in a story when you place a graphic using the Replace Selected Item option, the graphic is automatically placed as an inline object.

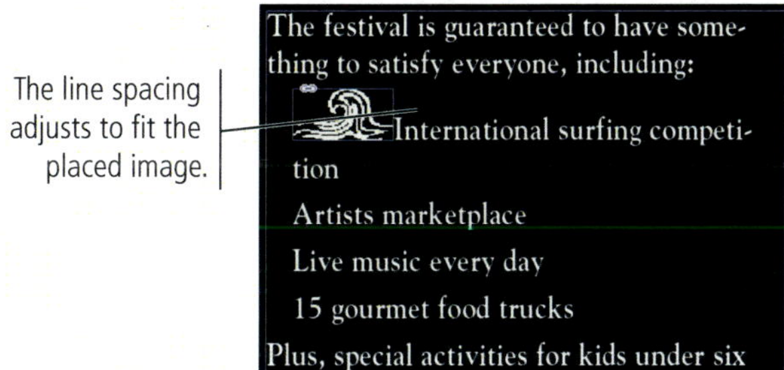

Note:

You can also select an existing object, cut or copy it, place the insertion point, and then paste the object inline where the insertion point flashes.

4. **Select the inline graphic with the Selection tool, and then scale the graphic and frame to 60% horizontally and vertically.**

Although inline graphics are anchored to the text, they are still graphics contained in graphics frames. You can apply the same transformations to inline graphics that you could apply to any other placed graphics.

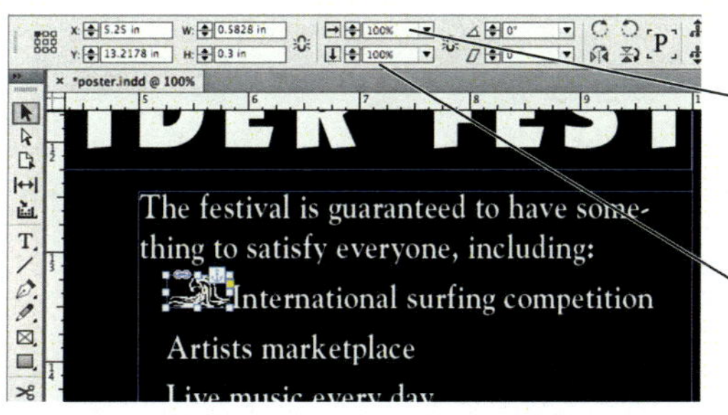

Note:

When you select the frame with the Selection tool, resizing the frame also resizes the frame content.

5. **Choose Object>Anchored Object>Options. Check the Preview option at the bottom of the dialog box.**

6. **Make sure the Inline option is selected, and change the Y Offset to `-0.05"`.**

A negative number moves the anchored object down; a positive number moves it up.

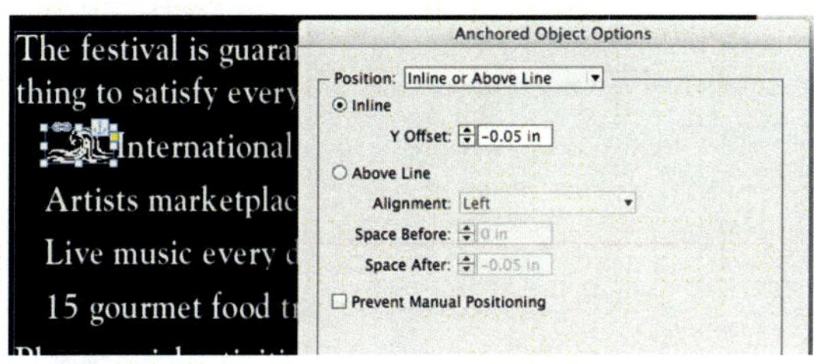

7. **Click OK, and then place the insertion point between the anchored object and the letter "I." Using the Character or Control panel, change the Kerning field to 200.**

Because an anchored graphic is treated like a single character, you can use kerning to add space between the anchored graphic and the following character.

The insertion point is here.

Change the kerning to 200.

8. **Press Shift-Left Arrow to select the anchored object, and then copy the highlighted object/character.**

You can select an inline graphic just as you would any other text character. Copying text in InDesign is the same as copying text in other applications: choose Edit>Copy, or press Command/Control-C.

An anchored graphic can be selected just as you would select any other text character.

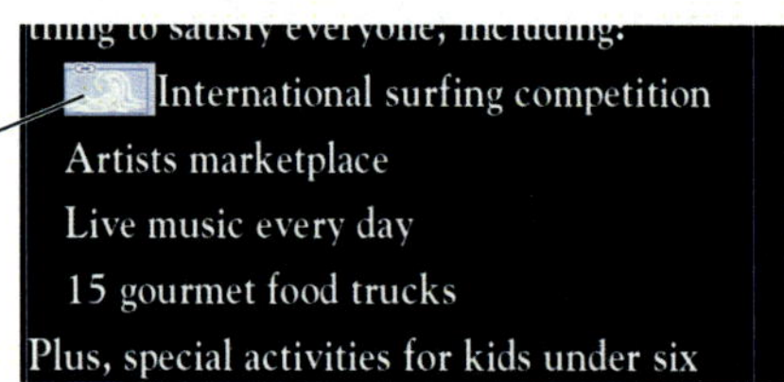

Understanding the Baseline Grid

INDESIGN FOUNDATIONS

The **baseline grid**, a series of light blue non-printing guides that extend down the page at specific regular intervals, is used for controlling and aligning type. You can show the baseline grid by choosing View>Grids & Guides>Show Baseline Grid.

You can force paragraphs to align to the baseline grid, which overrides the defined leading.

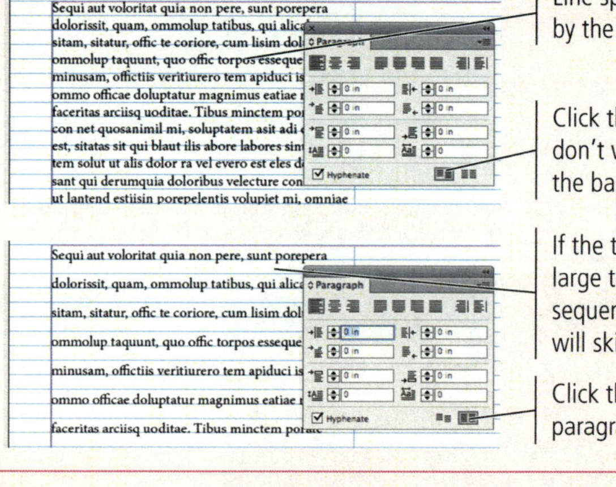

Line spacing is determined by the defined leading.

Click this button when you don't want to align text to the baseline grid.

If the type size or leading is too large to fit each line of text on sequential baselines, the text will skip every other baseline.

Click this button to align a paragraph to the baseline grid.

You can change the overall baseline grid in the Grids pane of the Preferences dialog box. The Start position can be relative to the top of the page (default) or to the top margin. You can also change the increment between lines. The View Threshold value determines the smallest view percentage at which the baseline grid will be visible.

You can also change the baseline grid for a specific frame in the Baseline Options tab of the Text Frame Options dialog box (Object>Text Frame Options).

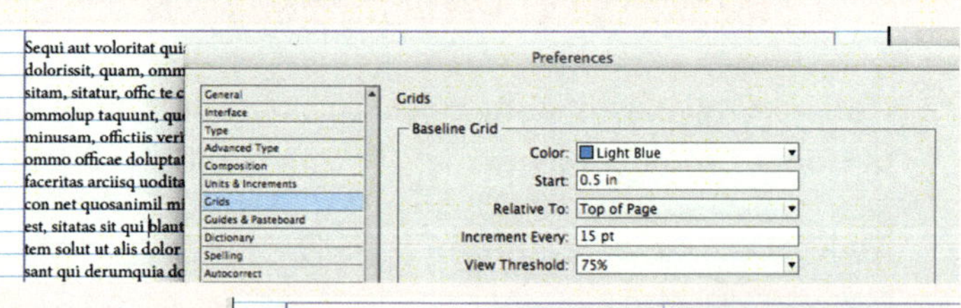

Working with Anchored Objects

The Anchored Object Options dialog box controls the position of an anchored object relative to the frame in which it is placed. Anchored objects can be aligned inline (such as the wave bullets you created in this project) or above the line.

When an object is anchored using the Above Line option, the object can be anchored to the left, right, or center of the frame. If you're using facing pages, you can also choose Toward Spine or Away from Spine so the anchored object will be placed in the appropriate position relative to the spread center (for example, you might specify that all sidebars have to be on the inside edge, close to the spine).

The Inline option aligns the object with the text baseline, adjusted by the Y Offset value.

The Above Line option moves the object above the line where the object is anchored.

When you use the Above Line option, you can also define the space before and after the anchored object. Space Before defines the position of the object relative to the bottom of the previous line of text. Space After defines the position of the object relative to the first character in the line below the object.

When you work with anchored objects, you can use the Selection tool to drag the object up or down (in other words, change its position relative to the text to which it is anchored). If the Prevent Manual Positioning option is checked, you can't drag the anchored object in the layout.

Custom Anchor Options

For complex applications — such as moving an anchored object outside a text frame — you can choose Custom in the Anchored Object Options Position menu.

The anchored object is outside the text frame; it is positioned with custom values.

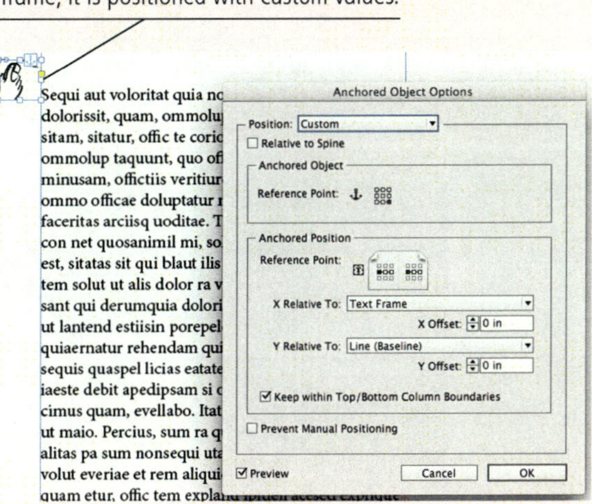

The **Relative to Spine** option, which aligns objects based on the center spread line, is only available if your layout has facing pages. When selected, objects on one side of a spread (such as a sidebar in the outside margin) remain on the outside margin even if the text reflows to a facing page.

The **Anchored Object Reference Point** defines the location on the object that you want to align to the location on the page.

The **Anchored Position Reference Point** defines the page location where you want to anchor an object.

The **X Relative To** field defines what you want to use as the basis for horizontal alignment — Anchor Marker, Column Edge, Text Frame, Page Margin, or Page Edge. The **X Offset** setting moves the object left or right.

The **Y Relative To** field specifies how the object aligns vertically — Line (Baseline), Line (Cap Height), Line (Top of Leading), Column Edge, Text Frame, Page Margin, or Page Edge. The **Y Offset** setting moves the object up or down.

When **Keep Within Top/Bottom Column Boundaries** is checked, the anchored object stays inside the text column if reflowing the text would otherwise cause the object to move outside the boundaries (for example, outside the top edge of the frame if the anchoring text is the first line in a column). This option is only available when you select a line option such as Line (Baseline) in the Y Relative To menu.

You can manually reposition a custom-anchored object by simply dragging the anchored object with the Selection tool. You can also review the anchored position by choosing View>Show Text Threads.

When text threads are showing, a dashed blue line indicates the position of anchored objects.

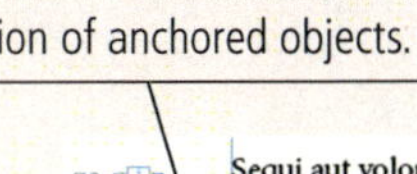

9. **Place the insertion point at the beginning of the next paragraph and paste the copied object.**

   As with copying, pasting text — including inline graphics — in InDesign is the same as in other applications: choose Edit>Paste, or press Command/Control-V.

10. **Paste the anchored graphic again at the beginning of the next two paragraphs.**

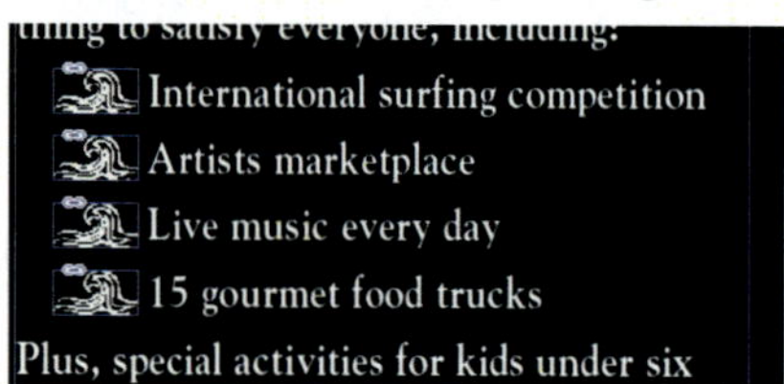

11. **Save the file and continue to the next exercise.**

Working with Anchored Objects (continued)

INDESIGN FOUNDATIONS

Anchored Object Size and Text Position

When an anchored object is larger than the defined leading for the text in which it is placed, it might appear that changing the Y Offset value moves the text instead of the anchored object. In a way, this is true, because the text will move until it reaches the defined leading value; after that, greater changes will move the object and not the text.

Default text position without the anchored object

Text position after placing the anchored object

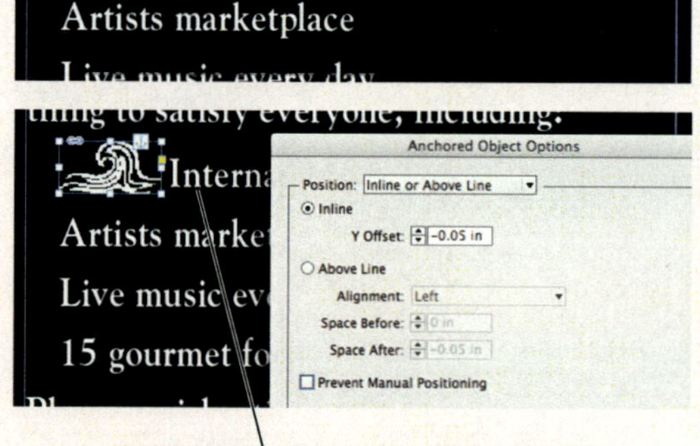

Adjusting the object position allows text to move back to its original place based on defined paragraph formatting.

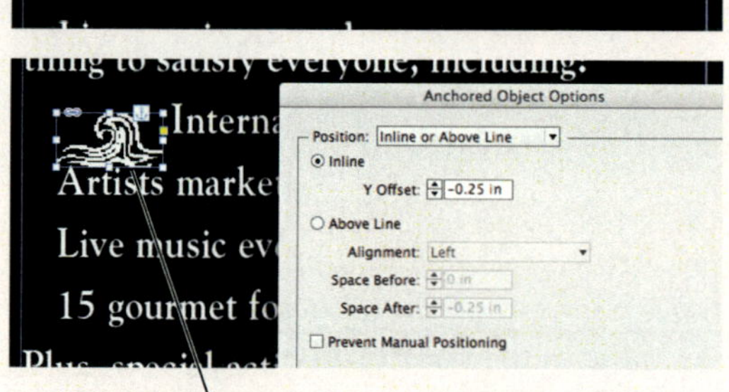

Further adjustments to the anchored object move the actual object by the specified amount.

Creating Anchored Placeholders

If you want to create an anchored object but don't yet have the content, you can use the Object>Anchored Object>Insert option to define the placeholder object. This dialog box allows you to create a frame (unassigned, graphics, or text) of a specific size and even apply object and paragraph styles (if those exist). The Position options are the same as those in the Anchored Object Options dialog box. (You can always resize and reposition the anchored object later.)

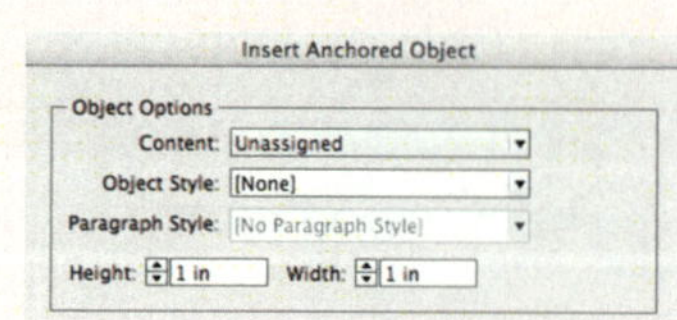

Create Type on a Path

Instead of simply flowing text into a frame, you can also create unique typographic effects by flowing text onto a path. A text path can be any shape that you can create in InDesign, whether using one of the basic shape tools, a complex graphic drawn with the Pen tool, or a path created by converting a clipping path to a frame.

1. **With poster.indd open, deselect all objects in the layout.**

   As we explained previously, you can choose Edit>Deselect All, or use the Selection tool to click an empty area of the workspace. If you use the click method, make sure you don't click a white-filled object instead of an empty area.

2. **Choose File>Place. Select text_path.tif in the WIP>Surfing folder and click Open. Position the top-left corner of the placed graphic at X: 0″, Y: 0″.**

   When this image is loaded into the cursor, click outside the defined bleed area to place the image and not replace the content in one of the existing frames. Then use the Control panel to position the image correctly. (The image that you are placing is simply a guide that you will use to create the shape of the text path for this exercise.)

3. **Click away from the placed graphic to deselect it.**

4. **Choose the Pen tool. Change the stroke value to 2-pt Magenta (C=0 M=100 Y=0 K=0) and change the fill value to None.**

   Because the line in the placed image is black, you're using magenta so you can differentiate your line from the one in the image. The solid white background in the TIF file makes it easy to focus on the line instead of the elements you have already created on the poster.

5. **Using the Pen tool, click once on the left end of the line in the placed image.**

   This first click establishes the first point of the path you're drawing.

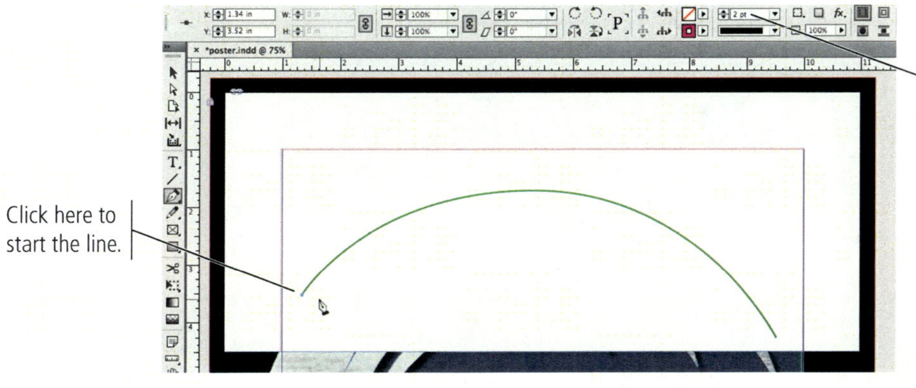

6. **Click near the top of the arc and drag right to create handles for the second anchor point.**

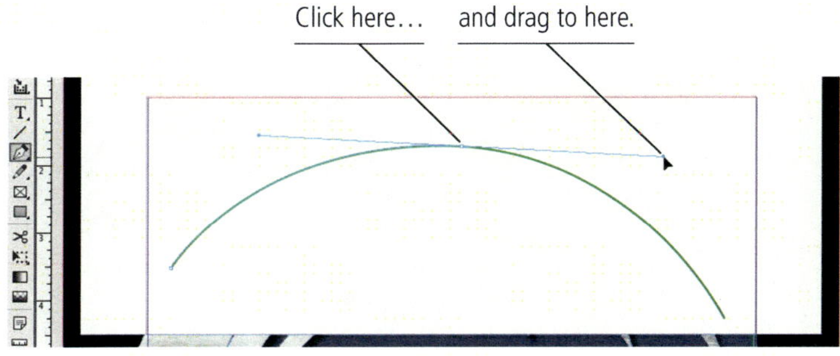

7. **Click again at the right end of the line to create the final anchor point.**

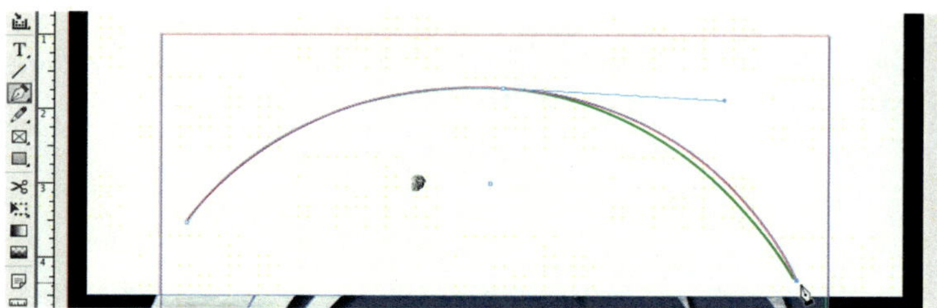

8. **Using the Direct Selection tool, adjust the points and handles until your line closely resembles the one in the placed image.**

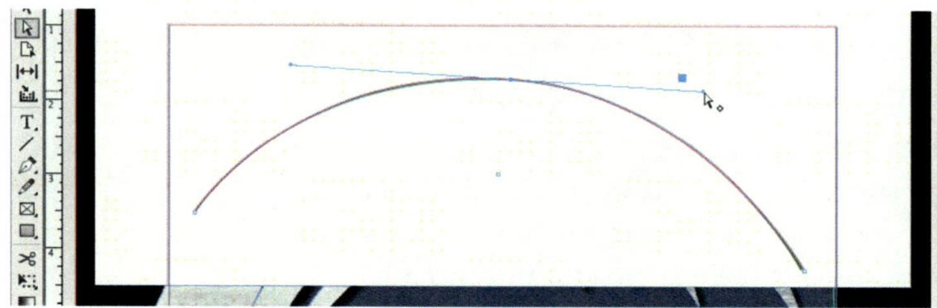

9. **Choose the Type on a Path tool. Move the cursor near the path until the cursor shows a small plus sign in the icon, and then click the path.**

   This action converts the line from a regular path to a type path.

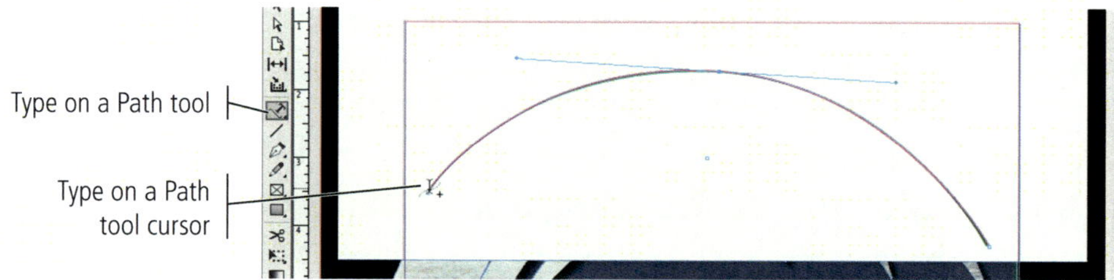

10. **Type April 13-15 ~ South Pier, then format the type as 60-pt ATC Garnet Ultra.**

11. **Using the Selection tool, click the text_path.tif image that you used as a guide. Press Delete/Backspace to remove it from the layout.**

12. Click the text path with the Selection tool to select the actual line. In the Swatches panel, change the object's stroke color to None.

A text path can have a fill and stroke value just like any other path.

When the actual path is selected, the Swatches panel defaults to show attributes of the path (not the type).

13. Click the Text Color button at the top of the Swatches panel, and then click the Pantone 8005 C swatch to change the text color.

You don't have to select the actual text on a path to change its color. You can use the buttons in the Swatches panel to change the color attributes of either the path or the text.

> ***Note:***
>
> *When a text path has no stroke color, you can still view the path by choosing View>Extras>Show Frame Edges.*

Click here to change the type fill and stroke colors.

14. Click the bar at the left edge of the text path and drag to the right about 1/4".

When you release the mouse button, the left edge of the text moves to the point where you dragged the line. This marks the orientation point of the text on the path.

> ***Note:***
>
> *The screen preview of the metallic ink is not especially pleasing; in this case, you simply have to rely on the printed ink swatch to know what the text will look like when printed.*

Drag this line to move the starting point of the text along the path.

15. Choose Edit>Undo (Command/Control-Z) to return the orientation point to the left end of the line.

16. Place the insertion point in the text path and apply centered paragraph alignment.

You can control paragraph formatting on a path just as you can for text in a frame.

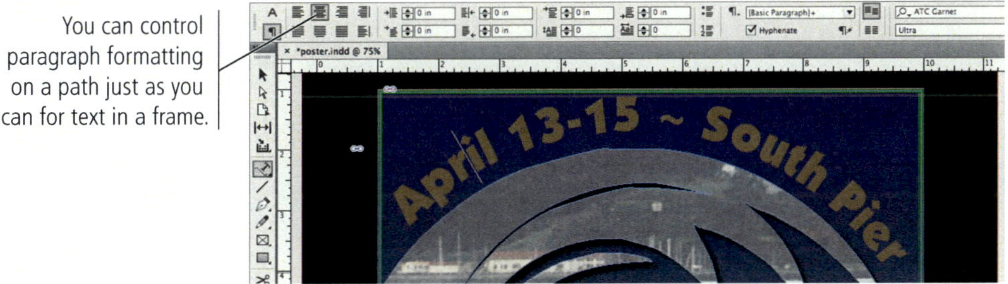

17. Save the file and continue to the next stage of the project.

Type on a Path Options

You can control the appearance of type on a path by choosing Type>Type on a Path>Options. You can apply one of five effects, change the alignment of the text to the path, flip the text to the other side of the path, and adjust the character spacing around curves (higher Spacing values remove more space around sharp curves).

- The **Rainbow** (default) effect keeps each character's baseline parallel to the path.

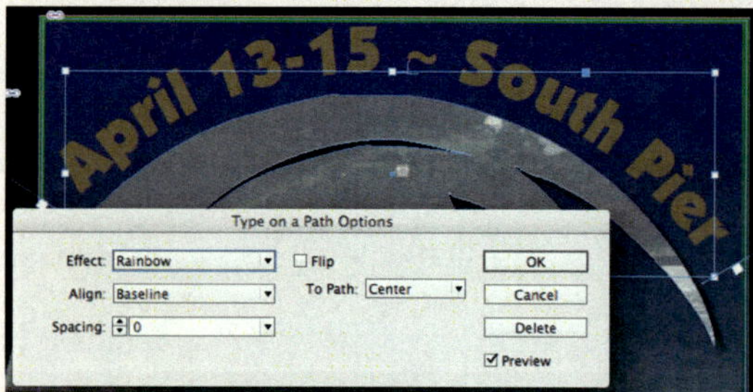

- The **Skew** effect maintains the vertical edges of type while skewing horizontal edges around the path.

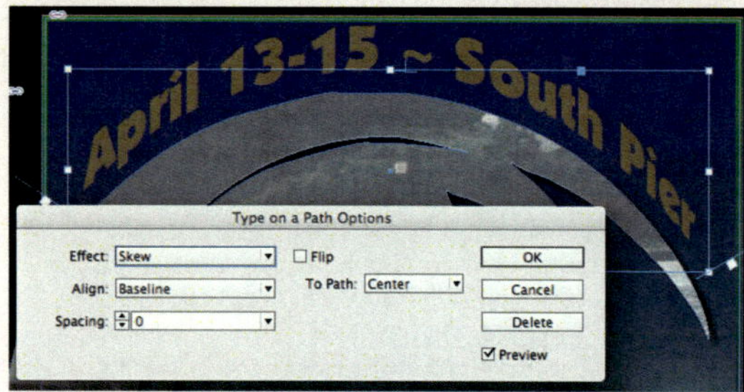

- The **3D Ribbon** effect maintains the horizontal edges of type while rotating the vertical edges to be perpendicular to the path.

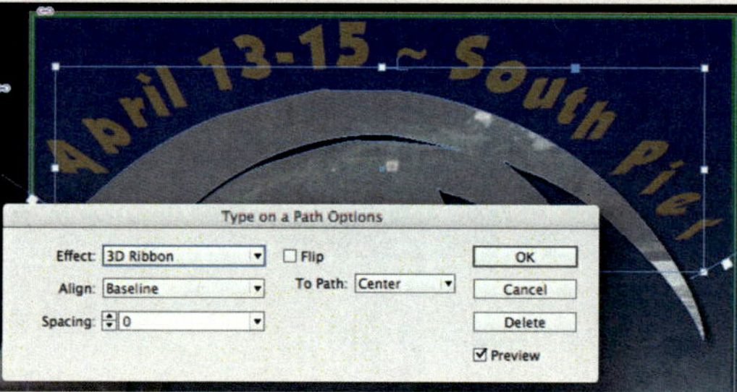

- The **Stair Step** effect aligns the left edge of each character's baseline to the path.

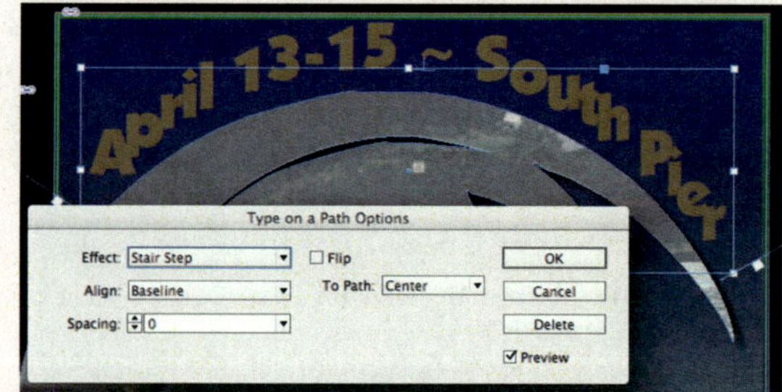

- The **Gravity** effect aligns the center of each character's baseline to the path, keeping vertical edges in line with the path's center.

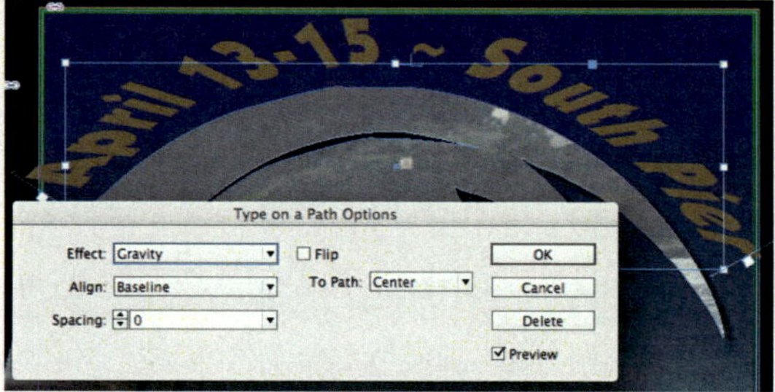

The **Align options** determine which part of the text (Baseline, Ascender, Descender, or Center) aligns to which part of the path (Top, Bottom, or Center).

Stage 4 Outputting the File

If your layout contains transparency or effects, those transparent areas will typically need to be flattened for output. **Flattening** divides transparent artwork into the necessary vector and raster objects. Transparent objects are flattened according to the settings in the selected flattener preset, which you choose in the Advanced options of the Print dialog box (or in the dialog box that appears when you export as PDF, EPS, or another format).

When you work with transparency, InDesign converts affected objects to a common color space (either CMYK or RGB) so transparent objects of different color spaces can blend properly. To avoid color mismatches between different areas of the objects on screen and in print, the blending space is applied for on-screen display and in the flattener. You can define which space to use in the Edit>Transparency Blend Space menu; for print jobs, make sure the CMYK option is selected.

Using the Flattener Preview Panel

INDESIGN FOUNDATIONS

You can use the Flattener Preview panel (Window>Output>Flattener Preview) to highlight areas that will be affected by flattening. If you are working on a layout with multiple pages or spreads, you can apply different flattener settings to individual spreads by choosing Spread Flattening in the Pages panel Options menu.

You can highlight different areas and determine which flattener preset to use for each. Clicking Refresh displays a new preview based on your settings. You can also choose Auto Refresh Highlight.

- **None** displays the normal layout.
- **Rasterized Complex Regions** highlights areas that will be rasterized based on the Raster/Vector Balance defined in the applied preset.
- **Transparent Objects** highlights objects with opacity of less than 100%, objects with blending modes, objects with transparent effects (such as drop shadows), and objects with feathering.
- **All Affected Objects** highlights all objects affected by transparency, including the transparent objects and the objects overlapped by transparent objects. All of these objects will be affected by flattening.
- **Affected Graphics** highlights all placed image files affected by transparency.
- **Outlined Strokes** highlights all strokes that will be converted to filled objects when flattened.
- **Outlined Text** highlights all text that will be converted to outlines when flattened.
- **Raster-Fill Text and Strokes** highlights text and strokes that will have rasterized fills as a result of flattening.
- **All Rasterized Regions** highlights objects (and parts of objects) that will be rasterized when flattened.

Flattener Presets

InDesign includes three default flattener presets:

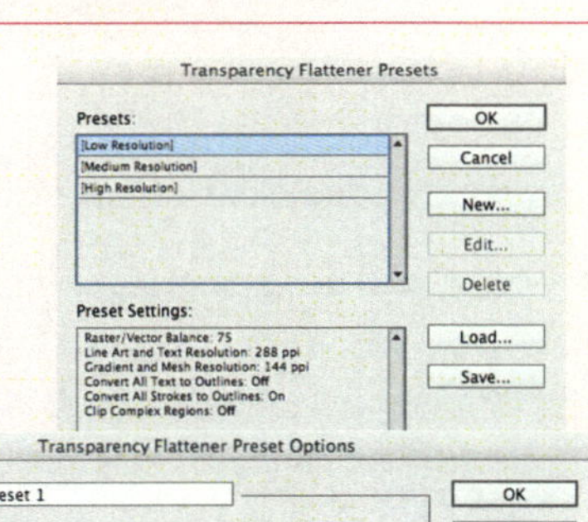

- **Low Resolution** works for desktop proofs that will be printed on low-end black-and-white printers and for documents that will be published on the Web.
- **Medium Resolution** works for desktop proofs and print-on-demand documents that will be printed on PostScript-compatible color printers.
- **High Resolution** works for commercial output on a printing press and for high-quality color proofs.

You can create your own flattener presets by choosing Edit>Transparency Flattener Presets and clicking New in the dialog box. You can also use the Transparency Flattener Presets dialog box to load flattener presets created on another machine — such as one your service provider created for their specific output device and/or workflow.

Export a PDF File for Print

1. **With poster.indd open, choose File>Export.**
2. **Navigate to your WIP>Surfing folder as the target destination and choose Adobe PDF (Print) in the Format/Save As Type menu.**

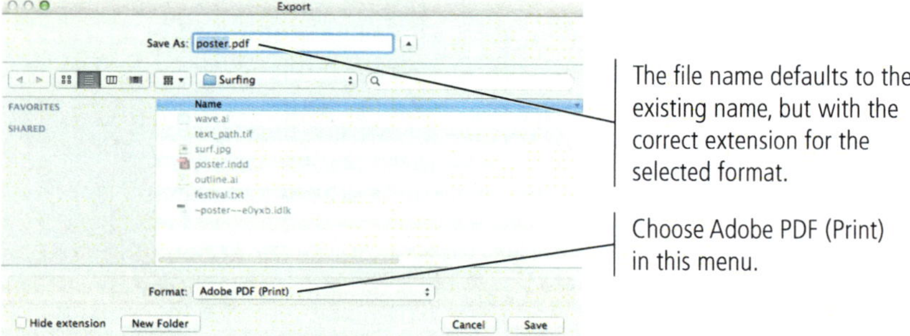

3. **Click Save.**

   Before the PDF is saved, you have to define the settings that will be used to generate the PDF file.

4. **Choose [High Quality Print] in the Adobe PDF Preset menu.**

   The Adobe PDF Preset menu includes six PDF presets that meet common industry output requirements.

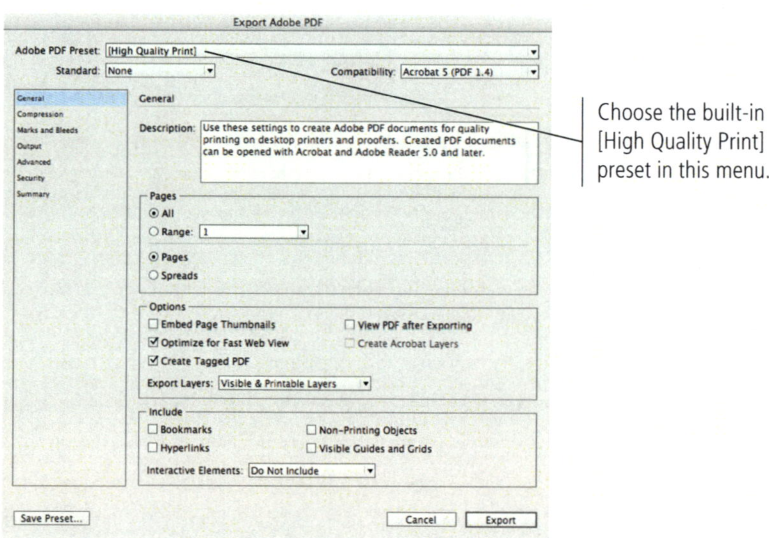

> *Note:*
>
> *The Export Adobe PDF dialog box defaults to the last-used settings.*

Because there are so many ways to create a PDF — and not all of those ways are optimized for the needs of commercial printing — the potential benefits of the file format are often undermined. The PDF/X specification was created to help solve some of the problems associated with bad PDF files entering the prepress workflow. PDF/X is a subset of PDF that is specifically designed to ensure that files have the information necessary for the digital prepress output process. Ask your output provider whether you should apply a PDF/X standard to your files, and if so, which version to use.

5. **Review the options in the General pane, and make sure Visible & Printable Layers is selected in the Export Layers menu.**

   - **Pages** options determine which pages to output, and whether to output facing pages on a single page.
   - **Embed Page Thumbnails** creates a thumbnail for each page being exported, or one thumbnail for each spread if the Spreads option is selected.
   - **Optimize for Fast Web View** optimizes the PDF file for faster viewing in a Web browser by allowing the file to download one page at a time.
   - **Create Tagged PDF** automatically tags elements based on a subset of Acrobat tags (including basic formatting, lists, and more).
   - **View PDF after Exporting** opens the PDF file after it has been created.
   - **Create Acrobat Layers** saves each InDesign layer as an Acrobat layer within the PDF. Printer's marks are exported to a separate "marks and bleeds" layer. Create Acrobat Layers is available only when Compatibility is set to Acrobat 6 (PDF 1.5) or later.
   - **Export Layers** determines whether you are outputting All Layers (including hidden and non-printing layers), Visible Layers (including non-printing layers), or Visible & Printable Layers.
   - **Include** options can be used to include specific non-printing elements.

6. **Review the Compression options.**

   The compression options determine what and how much data will be included in the PDF file. This set of options is one of the most important when creating PDFs, since too-low resolution results in bad-quality printing, and too-high resolution results in extremely long download times.

   Before you choose compression settings, you need to consider your final goal. If you're creating a file for commercial printing, resolution is more important than file size. If your goal is a PDF that will be posted on the Web, file size is at least equally important as pristine image quality.

   You can define a specific compression scheme for color, grayscale, and monochrome images. Different options are available depending on the image type:

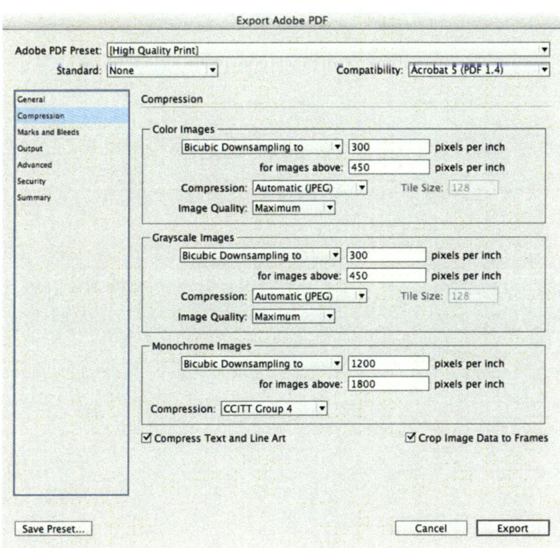

   - **JPEG compression** options are lossy, which means data is thrown away to create a smaller file. When you use one of the JPEG options, you can also define an Image Quality option (from Low to Maximum).
   - **ZIP compression** is lossless, which means all file data is maintained in the compressed file.
   - **CCITT compression** was initially developed for fax transmission. Group 3 supports two specific resolution settings (203 × 98 dpi and 203 × 196 dpi). Group 4 supports resolution up to 400 dpi.
   - **Run Length Encoding** (RLE) is a lossless compression scheme that abbreviates sequences of adjacent pixels. If four pixels in a row are black, RLE saves that segment as "four black" instead of "black-black-black-black."

> ***Note:***
>
> *Since you chose the High Quality Print preset, these options default to settings that will produce the best results for most commercial printing applications.*

Resolution Options for PDF

When you resize an image in the layout, you are changing its effective resolution. The **effective resolution** of an image is the resolution calculated after any scaling has been taken into account. This number is actually more important than the original image resolution. The effective resolution can be calculated with a fairly simple equation:

$$\text{original resolution} \div \frac{\%\ \text{magnification}}{100} = \text{effective resolution}$$

If a 300-ppi image is magnified 150%, the effective resolution is:

300 ppi / 1.5 = 200 ppi

If you reduce the same 300-ppi image to 50%, the effective resolution is:

300 ppi / 0.5 = 600 ppi

In other words, the more you enlarge a raster image, the lower its effective resolution becomes. Reducing an image results in higher effective resolution, which can result in unnecessarily large PDF files.

When you create a PDF file, you also specify the resolution that will be maintained in the resulting PDF file. The Resolution option is useful if you want to throw away excess resolution for print files, or if you want to create low-resolution files for proofing or Web distribution.

- **Do Not Downsample** maintains all the image data from the linked files in the PDF file.
- **Average Downsampling To** reduces the number of pixels in an area by averaging areas of adjacent pixels. Apply this method to achieve user-defined resolution (72 or 96 dpi for Web-based files or 300 dpi for print).
- **Subsampling To** applies the center pixel value to surrounding pixels. If you think of a 3 × 3-block grid, subsampling enlarges the center pixel — and thus, its value — in place of the surrounding eight blocks.
- **Bicubic Downsampling To** creates the most accurate pixel information for continuous-tone images. This option also takes the longest to process, and it produces a softer image. To understand how this option works, think of a 2 × 2-block grid — bicubic downsampling averages the value of all four of those blocks (pixels) to interpolate the new information.

7. In the Marks and Bleeds options, check the Crop Marks option and change the Offset field to 0.25". Check the Use Document Bleed Settings option.

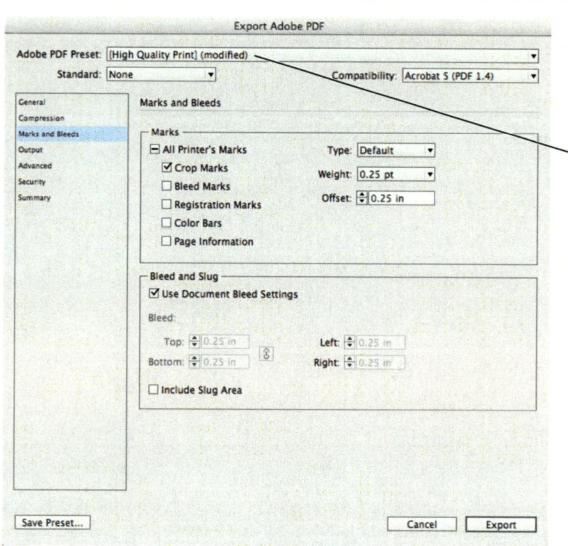

As soon as you choose a setting that is not part of the preset, the preset name shows "(modified)".

8. In the Compatibility menu, choose Acrobat 4 (PDF 1.3).

The Compatibility menu determines which version of the PDF format you will create. This is particularly important if your layout uses transparency (as does the one you created in this project). PDF 1.3 does not support transparency, so the file will require flattening. If you save the file to be compatible with PDF 1.4 or later, transparency information will be maintained in the PDF file.

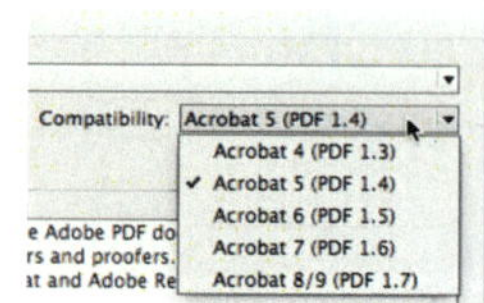

9. **In the Advanced options, choose High Resolution in the Transparency Flattener Preset menu.**

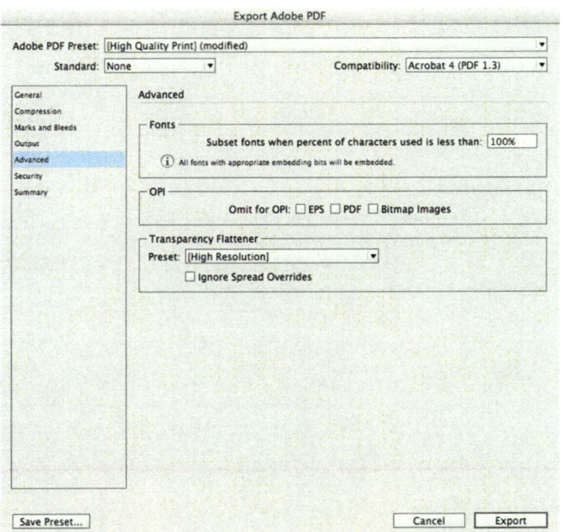

Note:

The Output options relate to color management, which you will use in Project 6: Digital Layout Variations. The Security options allow you to add password protection to a PDF file.

10. **Click Export to create your PDF file. If you see a warning message, click OK.**

Your PDF file will be flattened, so some features (hyperlinks, bookmarks, etc.) will be unavailable. You didn't use those features in this project, however, so you don't have to worry about this warning.

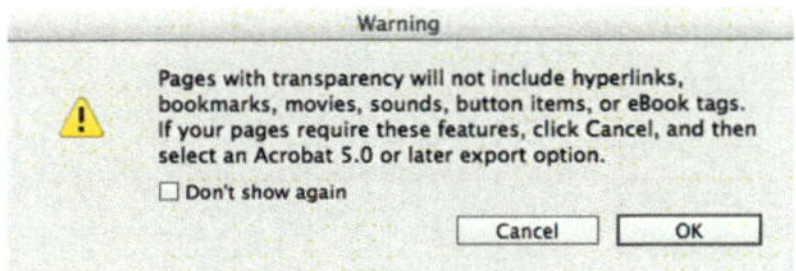

11. **Choose Window>Utilities>Background Tasks.**

The PDF export process happens in the background, which means you can work on other tasks while the PDF is being created. This panel shows how much of the process has been completed (as a percentage), and will list any errors that occur. When the PDF file is finished, the export process is no longer listed in the panel.

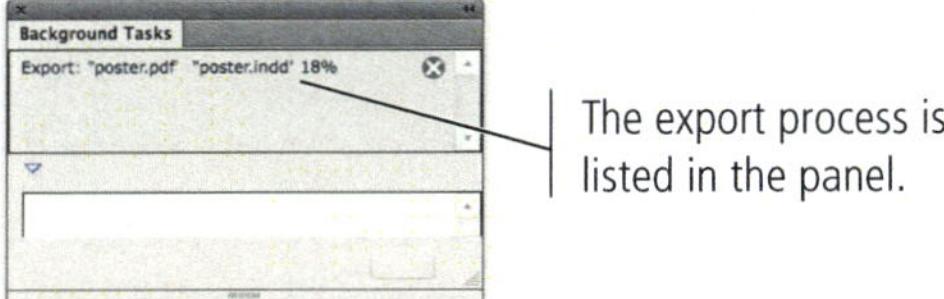

The export process is listed in the panel.

12. **Save the InDesign file and close it.**

Project Review

fill in the blank

1. The _______________ tool can be used to draw the direction and position of a gradient within a frame.

2. The _______________ menu command reveals characters such as paragraph returns and tabs.

3. _______________ is the space between specific pairs of letters. To change this value, you have to place the insertion point between two characters.

4. The _______________ is the theoretical line on which the bottoms of letters rest.

5. The _______________ indicates that more text exists in the story than will fit into the available frame (or series of linked frames).

6. The _______________ can be used to copy type formatting from one type element to another.

7. The _______________ panel is used to apply optical margin alignment.

8. _______________ are objects that are attached to specific areas of text.

9. _______________ is the resolution of an image after its scaling in the layout has been taken into account.

10. _______________ compression for raster images is lossy, which means data is thrown away to reduce the file size.

short answer

1. Briefly explain how transparency is applied to objects in an InDesign page layout.

2. Briefly define a clipping path; provide at least two examples of how they might be useful.

3. Briefly explain the difference between character formatting and paragraph formatting.

Portfolio Builder Project

Use what you learned in this project to complete the following freeform exercise.
Carefully read the art director and client comments, then create your own design to meet the needs of the project.
Use the space below to sketch ideas; when finished, write a brief explanation of your reasoning behind your final design.

art director comments

Your local community theater is planning a summer production of "Down the Yellow Brick Rabbit Hole," a satirical mash-up of "The Wizard of Oz" meets "Alice in Wonderland." You have been hired to create several pieces to advertise the play in local media and in the community.

To complete this project, you should:

- ❑ Design a half-page advertisement for the local newspaper (11.5″ × 10.5″ trim size).
- ❑ Design a full-page advertisement for the community arts and entertainment magazine (8.5″ × 11″ trim size).
- ❑ Design a poster that can be placed in local storefronts and other public venues (11″ × 17″ trim size).
- ❑ Find or create artwork that appropriately illustrates the concept of the play.

client comments

As the director and playwright, I was inspired by Gregory Maguire's unique rewrites of classic fairy tales. But then I started to think about what would happen if the characters from different books met somehow… and this play is the result.

I don't want to spoil anything, but some real sparks fly when the Queen of Hearts and the Wizard of Oz get together! And the wicked witch, well, she's got her hands full trying to escape the clutches of an army of talking caterpillars.

This play is one-third mystery, one-third dramedy, and one-third just plain silly! It's got star-crossed lovers, an evil villain, an inept magician, a rather foolish prince, and even a mad flying monkey that wears some very strange hats.

The only text in the ad should be:

Down the Yellow Brick Rabbit Hole
by Stacey Wrightwood
at the Preston Theater this August
800-555-PLAY for ticket information

project justification

This project combined form and function — presenting the client's information in a clear, easy-to-read manner, while using large graphic elements to grab the viewer's attention and reinforce the message of the piece. As the client requested, the main focus is on the graphics in the top two-thirds of the piece while the relevant text is large enough to be visible but isn't the primary visual element.

Completing this poster involved adjusting a number of different text formatting options, including paragraph settings and the flow of text across multiple frames. You should now understand the difference between character and paragraph formatting, and know where to find the different options when you need them.

The graphics options in InDesign give you significant creative control over virtually every element of your layouts. Custom colors and gradients add visual interest to any piece, while more sophisticated tools like non-destructive transparency and other effects allow you to experiment entirely within your page layout until you find exactly the look you want to communicate your intended message.

HeartSmart Newsletter

Your client is a non-profit foundation that focuses on health education and public awareness. It publishes a monthly newsletter for people on various mailing lists, which are purchased from a list-management vendor. The editor wants to change the existing newsletter template, and wants you to take over the layout once the template has been revised.

This project incorporates the following skills:

- ❑ Opening and modifying an existing layout template
- ❑ Managing missing font and link requests
- ❑ Replacing graphics files to meet specific color output needs
- ❑ Formatting text with template styles
- ❑ Controlling text-frame inset, alignment, and wrap attributes
- ❑ Creating a table with data from a Microsoft Excel worksheet
- ❑ Preflighting the final layout and creating a job package

Project Meeting

client comments

In the past our newsletter was printed as a two-color job on a duplicator. However, the printer just told us that we can go to four-color printing and pay virtually the same per piece as we used to pay.

We need some other changes too. We want to go from four columns to three on the front, and from three columns to two on the back. The checkerboard area on the front usually has four random pictures, and the bar at the top of the back has a single image. Those all used to be grayscale photos, but now you can use color.

We'd like you to make modifications to the template, and then use the template to create the current issue. We sent you the pictures we want to use for this issue, as well as the three text pieces (the main article, a sidebar for the front, and the story for the back). There's also a table in Microsoft Excel format that we want to include on the back.

art director comments

Whenever you work with a file that someone else created, there is always the potential for problems. When you first open the template, you'll have to check the fonts and images and make whatever adjustments are necessary. Make sure you save the file as a template again before you build the new issue.

Moving from two-color to four-color isn't too big a deal — it's actually easier than going from color to grayscale since color adds possibilities instead of limiting them. You have the opportunity to add color to common design elements (including styles), and you should also use the color version of the nameplate instead of the grayscale one.

The printer said they prefer to work with native application files instead of PDF, so when you're finished implementing the layout, you'll need to check the various elements, and then create a final job package.

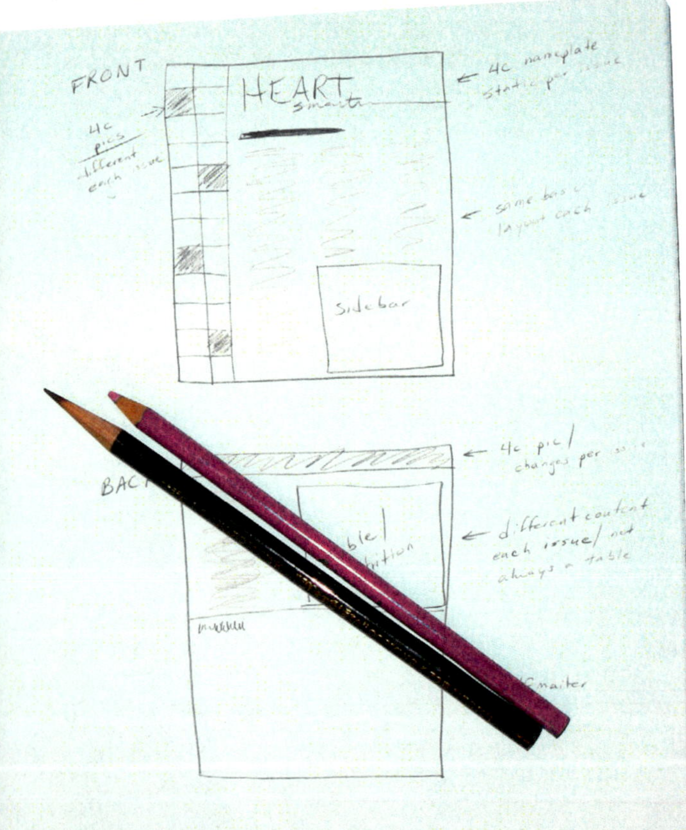

project objectives

To complete this project, you will:

- ❑ Handle requests for missing fonts and images
- ❑ Edit master page elements to meet new requirements
- ❑ Save a layout file as a template
- ❑ Access master page elements on the layout pages
- ❑ Format imported text using template styles
- ❑ Build and format a table using data from a Microsoft Excel spreadsheet
- ❑ Create a final job package for the output provider

Stage 1 Working with Templates

Templates are commonly used whenever you have a basic layout that will be implemented more than once — for example, the structure of a newsletter remains the same, but the content for each issue changes. InDesign templates are special types of files that store the basic structure of a project. Well-planned templates can store layout elements such as nonprinting guides that mark various areas of the job; placeholder frames that will contain different stories or images in each revision; elements that remain the same in every revision, such as the nameplate; and even formatting information that will be applied to different elements so the elements can be consistent from one issue to the next.

Manage Missing Fonts

When you work with digital page layouts — whether in a template or in a regular layout file — it's important to understand that fonts are external files of data that describe the font for on-screen display and for the output device. The fonts you use in a layout need to be available on any computer that will be used to open the file. InDesign stores a reference to used fonts, but it does not store the actual font data.

Note:

Missing fonts are one of the most common problems in the digital graphics output process. This is one of the primary advantages of using PDF files for output — PDF can store actual font data so you don't need to include the separate font files in your job package. (However, PDF can't solve the problem of missing fonts used in a layout template.)

1. **Download IDCC_RF_Project3.zip from the Student Files Web page.**

2. **Expand the ZIP archive in your WIP folder (Macintosh) or copy the archive contents into your WIP folder (Windows).**

   This creates a folder named **HeartSmart**, which contains the files you need for this project. You should also use this folder to save the files you create in this project.

3. **Choose File>Open. Select heartsmart.indt in the WIP>HeartSmart folder, and choose the Open [As] Original option at the bottom of the dialog box.**

   You have several options when you open an existing template file:

   - If you choose **Open [As] Normal** to open a regular InDesign file (INDD), the selected file appears in a new document window or tab. When you use this option to open a template file (INDT), InDesign creates and opens a new untitled file that is based on the template.
   - When you choose the **Open [As] Original** option, you open the actual InDesign template file so that you can make and save changes to the template.
   - You can use the **Open [As] Copy** option to open a regular InDesign file as if it were a template; the result is a new untitled document based on the file you selected.

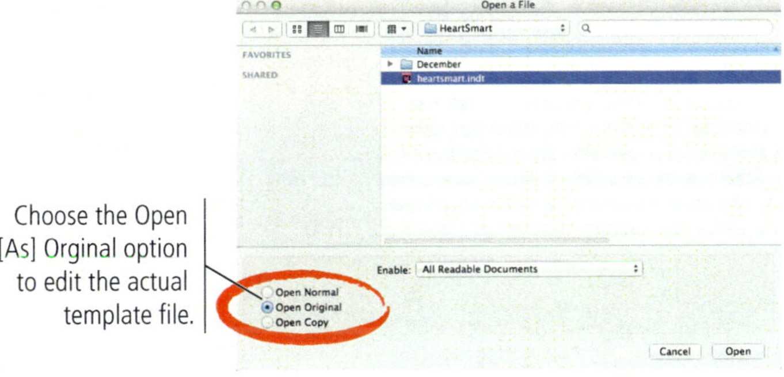

Macintosh

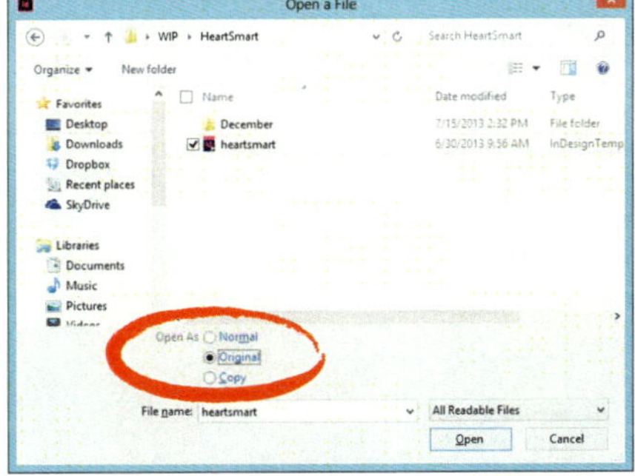

Windows

4. **Click Open, then review the warning message.**

   InDesign stores links to images placed in a layout; the actual placed-file data is not stored in the InDesign file. If placed files are not available in the same location as when they were originally placed, or if they have been resaved since you placed them, you'll see a warning message when you open the file. You'll correct these problems in the next exercise.

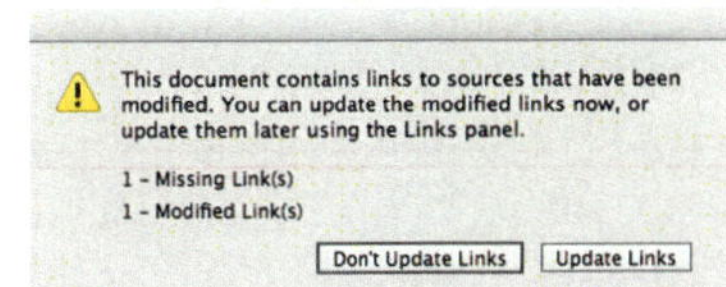

5. **Click Don't Update Links, and then review the information in the resulting Missing Fonts dialog box.**

   Any time you open a file that calls for fonts that are not installed on your computer system, you see this warning. You could blindly fix the problem now (without knowing what will be affected), but we prefer to review problem areas before making changes.

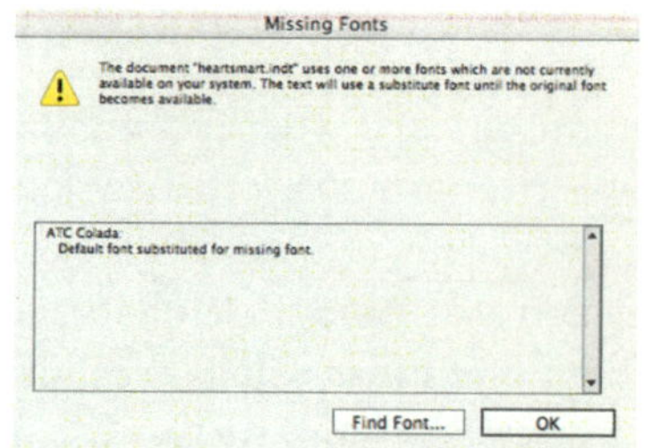

6. **Click OK to dismiss the Missing Fonts dialog box.**

7. **Open the Pages panel (Window>Pages).**

   The Pages panel makes it very easy to navigate through the pages in a layout, including master pages. You can navigate to any page by simply double-clicking the page's icon, or navigate to a spread by double-clicking the spread page numbers (below the page icons).

Note:

If you have the ATC fonts from previous editions installed, you will not see the missing-font warning.

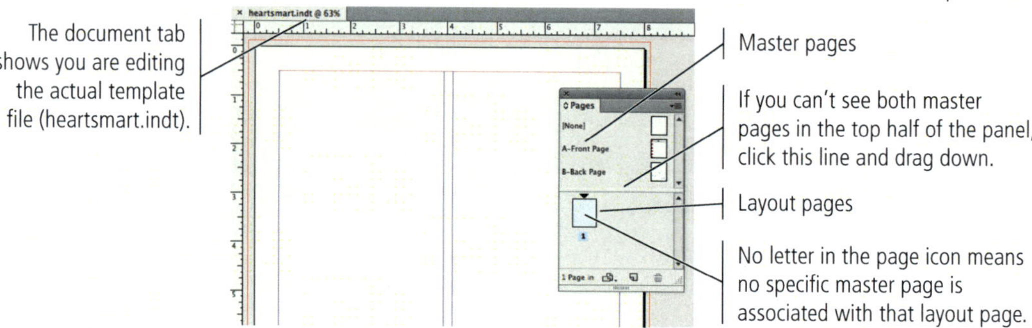

Think of master pages as templates for different pages in the layout. This file, for example, has two master pages: Front Page and Back Page. The letters preceding each master page name are automatically added and used to identify which layout pages are associated with which master page. (This will become clear as you continue through this project.)

8. **Double-click the A-Front Page icon to display that layout.**

   The top area of the newsletter (the **nameplate** area) includes the newsletter logotype, as well as the "Published by..." line and the issue date. A pink highlight around the type shows that the font used in this area is not available.

9. **Using the Type tool, click the frame with the missing font to place the insertion point.**

   The Control panel shows the missing font name in brackets. Any time you see a font name in brackets, you know you have a potential problem.

Note:

If the nameplate information is not highlighted, open the Composition pane of the Preferences dialog box and make sure the Highlight Substituted Fonts option is checked.

The highlighting only appears if you are in the Normal viewing mode.

10. **Choose Type>Find Font.**

    The Find Font dialog box lists every font used in the layout — including missing ones (with a warning icon). You can use this dialog box to replace any font — including missing ones — with another font that is available on your system.

11. **Highlight ATC Colada in the Fonts in Document list. In the Replace With area, choose ATC Onyx in the Font Family menu and choose Normal in the Font Style menu.**

12. **Check the option to Redefine Style When Changing All.**

When this is checked, the font replacement will be applied in paragraph and character style definitions, even if those styles are not currently applied in the layout.

If you don't check the Redefine Style option, you might later introduce another missing-font problem when you apply a style that calls for a missing font.

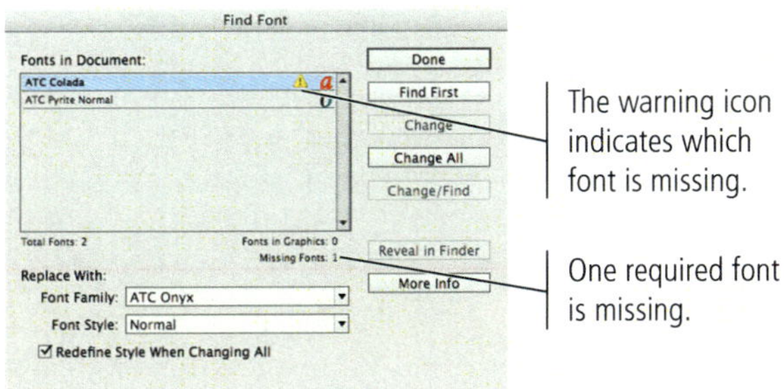

13. **Click Change All to replace all instances of ATC Colada.**

When the Redefine Style option is checked, InDesign provides a warning when overrides have been applied to existing styles.

14. **Click OK to dismiss the warning message.**

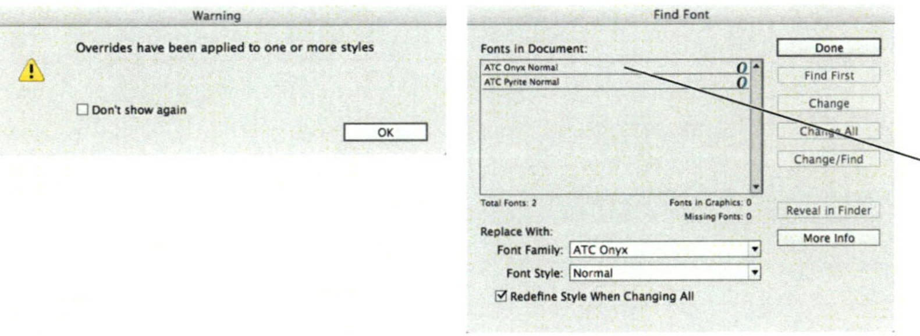

After all instances have been changed, ATC Colada and its warning icon are gone.

15. **Click Done to close the Find Font dialog box.**

Once you have replaced the missing font, the pink highlighting disappears.

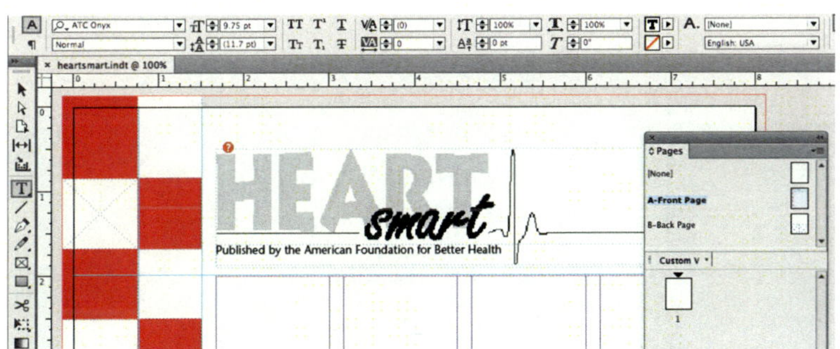

16. **Choose File>Save to save your changes to the template file, and then continue to the next exercise.**

Because you used the Open Original option, you are editing the actual template file; this means you can simply use the regular Save command to save your changes to the template. If you used the Open Normal option to open and edit a template file, you would have to use the Save As command and save the edited file with the same name and extension as the original template to overwrite the original.

Note:

The Missing Font highlighting is only a visual indicator on your screen. It is not included when the job is output.

Note:

You can click the Find Next button to review individual instances of a missing font, or you can click the Change or Change/Find button to replace and review individual instances of the selected font.

Note:

If you click the More Info button, you can see specific details about the selected font, such as the type of font and where it is used.

Replace Missing and Modified Graphics

Placed graphics can cause problems if those files aren't where InDesign thinks they should be. Placed graphics files can be either **missing** (they were moved from the location from which they were originally placed in the layout, or the name of the file was changed) or **modified** (they were resaved after being placed into the layout, changing the linked file's "time stamp" but not its location or file name). In either case, you need to correct these problems before the file can be successfully output.

> *Note:*
>
> *The issue of missing and modified images is a common problem if you zip a job folder into an archive. When you unzip a job folder and open the InDesign file, you will often see a warning about missing/modified images (especially on Windows).*
>
> *To avoid this problem in the resource files for this book, we embedded most of the placed images into the layout files.*

1. **With heartsmart.indt open, display the Links panel (Window>Links).**

   The Links panel lists every file that is placed in your layout. Missing images show a red stop-sign icon; modified images show a yellow yield sign.

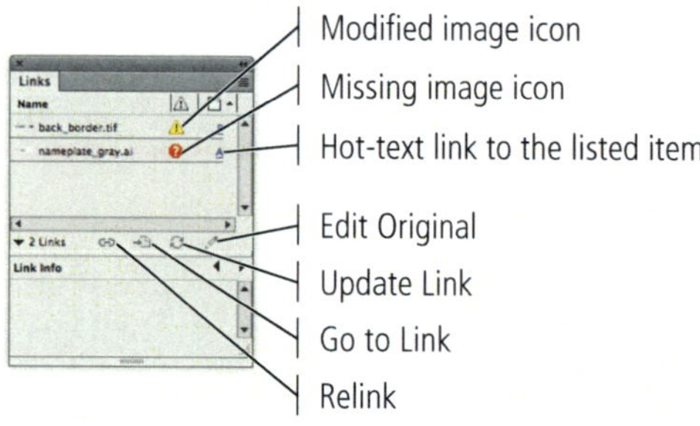

2. **Click the modified back_border.tif file in the panel, then click the Go to Link button in the middle of the panel.**

   You can also use the hot-text link to the right of an image name to navigate to a specific placed image. The Pages panel shows that the B-Back Page master layout is now active because that is where the selected instance exists.

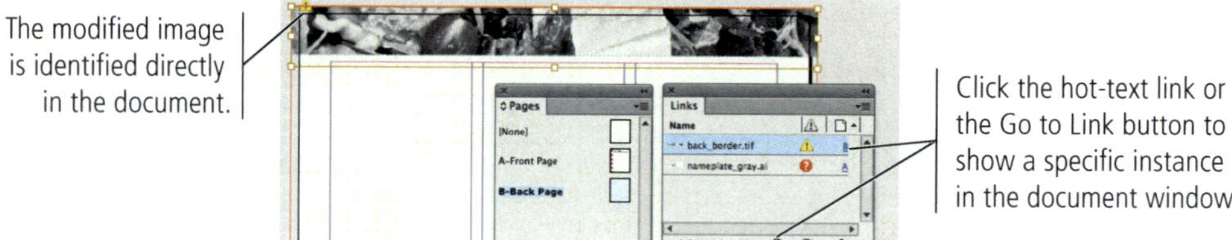

You can easily use the Links panel to navigate to selected images.

- The **Relink** button opens a navigation dialog box where you can locate a missing file or link to a different file.
- The **Go to Link** button selects and centers the file in the document window.
- The **Update Link** button updates modified links. If the selected image is missing, this button opens a navigation dialog box so you can locate the missing file.
- The **Edit Original** button opens the selected file in its native application. When you save the file and return to InDesign, the placed file is automatically updated.

3. **With the file still selected in the panel, click the Update Link button.**

   The person who provided these images used the same file name for the color version of the border image — a common occurrence. After the link is updated, the color version appears in the layout and the link icon no longer shows the modified warning.

> *Note:*
>
> *You can also click the Modified icon in the top-left corner of the image to update the link.*

4. In the Links panel, click the page number hot-text link for the missing nameplate_gray.ai file.

The Pages panel shows that the A-Front Page master layout is now active because that is where the selected instance exists.

The missing image is identified directly in the document.

The Links Panel in Depth

The Links panel lists all files that have been placed into a layout. By default, the panel shows the item name, the status (missing or modified), and the location of that item in the layout. The lower half of the panel shows important information for the selected link, such as color space and resolution. If you open the Panel Options dialog box (from the Links panel Options menu), you can change which information appears in each section of the panel.

Multiple instances of the same image are grouped together.

Click this bar and drag to expand or contract the Link info area without resizing the panel.

Click the column headings to sort based on specific criteria (e.g., filename, status, or page).

Click the hot-text page number to navigate to an item in the layout.

Click here and drag to resize the panel.

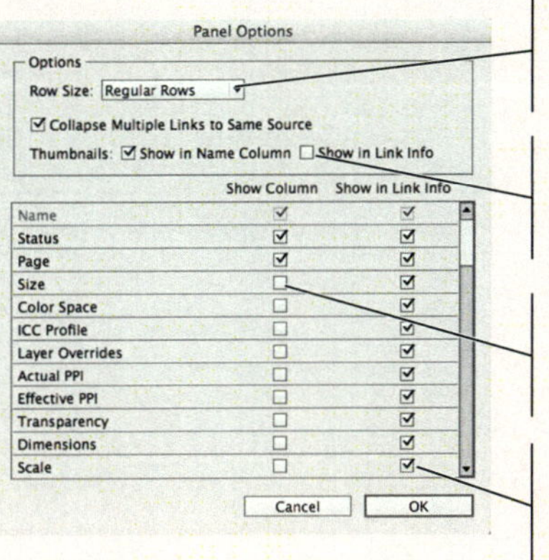

Use this menu to change the size of item thumbnails in the panel.

Check to include item thumbnails in the lower half of the panel.

Use these boxes to change what appears in the top half of the panel.

Use these boxes to change what appears in the lower half of the panel.

Embedding Links

To avoid the problem of missing links, you can embed placed images directly into the layout file by Control/right-clicking an image in the Links panel and choosing Embed Link from the contextual menu.

When links are embedded, there is no longer any relation to the original source file. This means the source files do not need to be included in the job package, and you will not see a missing-link error if the original source file is moved. It also means, however, that any changes in a source file will not result in a modified link warning. To edit an image, you have to manually open the original source file in its native application, save it, then manually replace the embedded image with the edited file.

This icon identifies an embedded link.

5. **Using the Direct Selection tool, click the logo on the page.**

   As part of the Adobe Creative Suite, InDesign supports native Adobe Illustrator files (with the ".ai" extension) that have been saved to be compatible with the PDF format. Illustrator files can include both raster and vector information, type and embedded fonts, and objects on multiple layers in a variety of color models (including spot colors, which are added to the InDesign Swatches panel when the AI file is imported).

6. **Open the Transform panel (Window>Object & Layout>Transform).**

   The options in the Transform panel are the same as those on the left side of the Control panel. As you can see, the selected graphic is placed at 100% (not scaled).

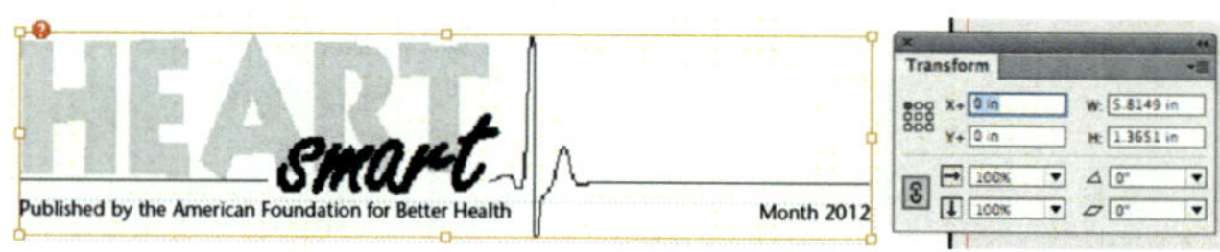

Note:

Make sure you use the Direct Selection tool, or the Content Grabber, to select the actual placed logo. If you select the frame instead, the Transform panel shows the values for the frame instead of the graphic placed in the frame.

7. **Click the Missing icon in the top-left corner of the image.**

   The Missing and Modified icons provide an easy, on-screen method for identifiying and correcting image-link problems.

Note:

You can hide these icons by choosing View> Extras>Hide Link Badge.

8. **In the resulting Locate dialog box, navigate to nameplate_color.ai in the WIP>HeartSmart>December folder.**

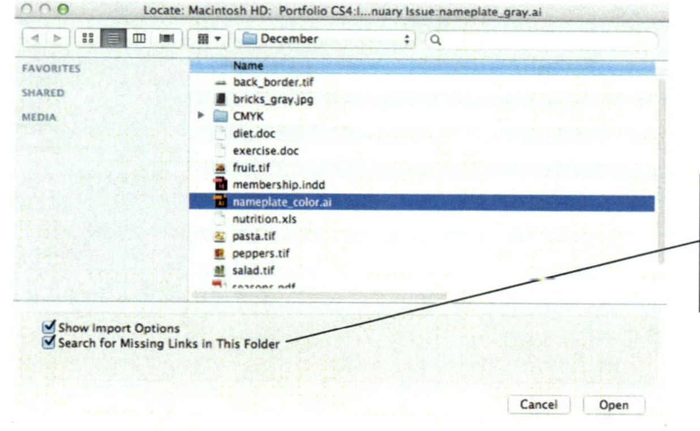

If multiple files are missing, check this box to update all missing links found in the selected folder.

Note:

If the Search for Missing Links option is checked, InDesign will scan the selected folder to find other missing image files.

9. **Check the box to Show Import Options, then click Open.**

10. **In the Place PDF dialog box, choose Art in the Crop To menu and click OK.**

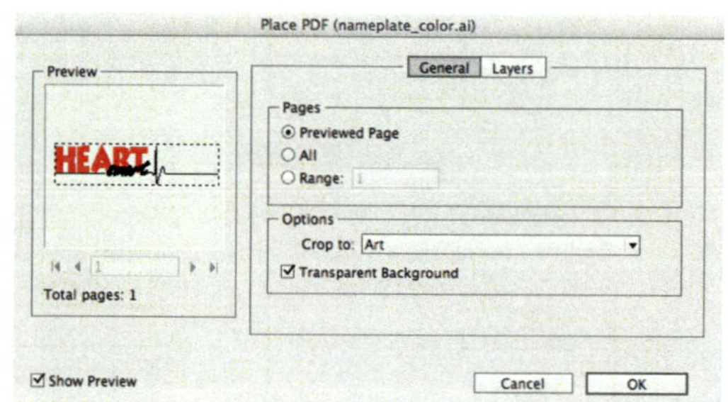

Note:

Refer to Project 1: Letterhead Design for an explanation of the Crop To options.

11. **Click the new image with the Direct Selection tool.**

When you replace a selected file, the new file adopts the necessary scaling percentage to fit into the same space as the original. In this case, the new file is scaled to approximately 93.3% — the size that is necessary to fit the same dimensions as the original.

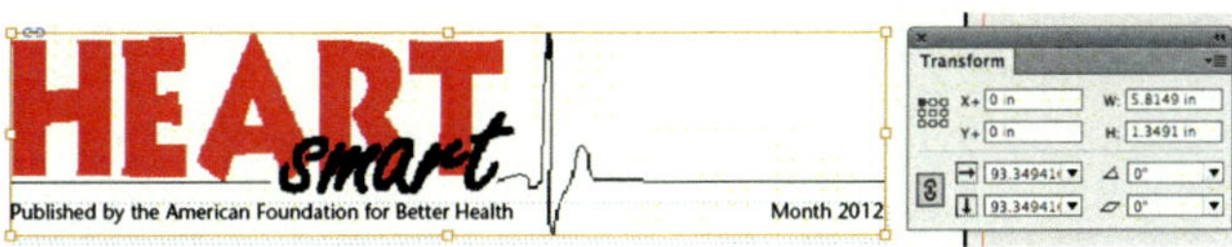

12. **Save the file and continue to the next exercise.**

Edit Margin and Column Guides

Your client wants to make several changes to the layout, including fewer columns and incorporating color into various elements. These changes will recur from one issue to the next, so you should change the template instead of simply changing the elements in each individual issue.

1. **With heartsmart.indt open, double-click the A-Front Page icon to show that layout in the document window.**

2. **Choose Layout>Margins and Columns. In the resulting dialog box, change the Columns field to 3 and the Gutter field to 0.2", and then click OK.**

   Every layout has a default setup, which you define when you create the file. Master pages have their own margin and column settings that can be different than the default document settings.

   Changing the column guides has no effect on the text frame; you have to change the text frame independently.

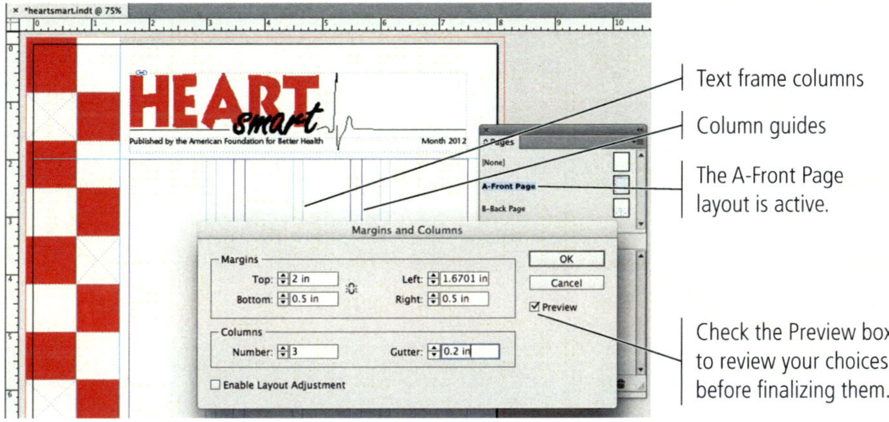

> *Note:*
>
> *You can change the default margins and columns for a layout by choosing File>Document Setup.*

3. **Using the Selection tool, click to select the 4-column text frame, and then Control/right-click the frame and choose Text Frame Options from the contextual menu.**

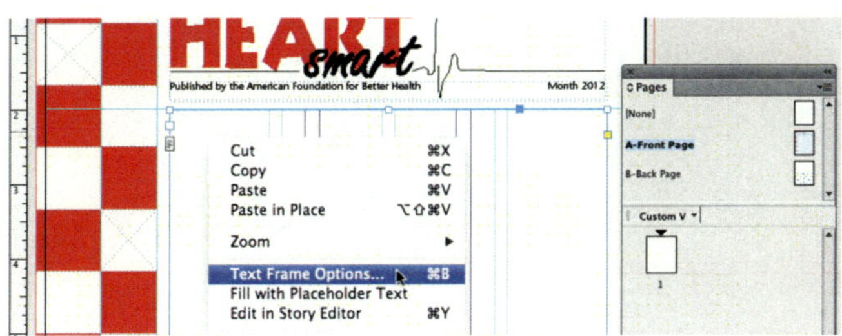

> *Note:*
>
> *You can also access the Text Frame Options dialog box from the Object menu.*

4. **Change the Number of Columns field to 3 and the Gutter field to 0.2″ to match the changes you made to the column guides. Click OK to close the dialog box.**

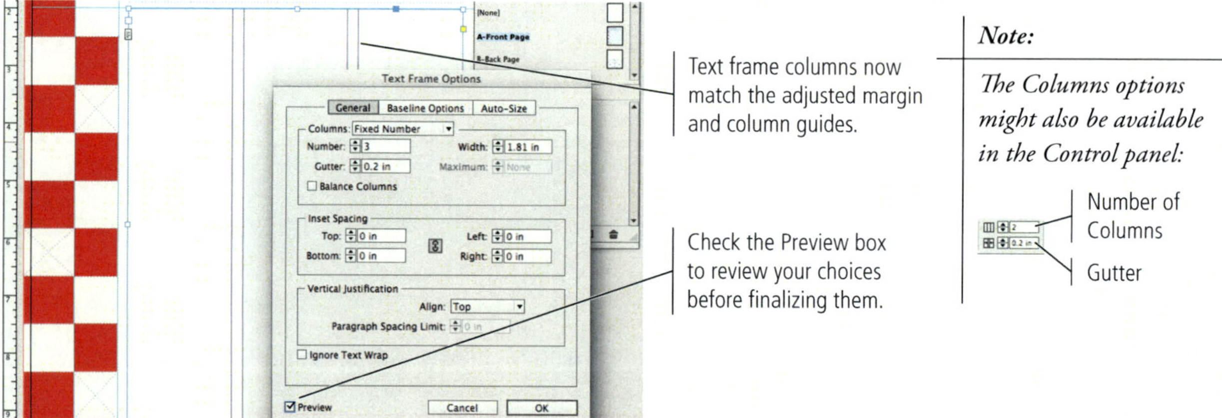

Note:

The Columns options might also be available in the Control panel:

5. **In the Pages panel, double-click the B-Back Page icon to display that layout in the document window.**

6. **Choose Layout>Margins and Columns. Change the Bottom Margin setting to 5.25″, change the Columns field to 2, change the Gutter to 0.2″, and then click OK.**

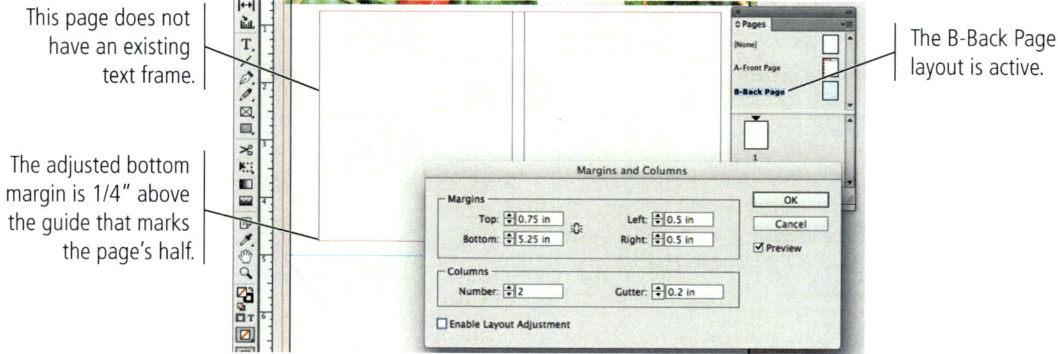

7. **Using the Type tool, create a text frame that fills the adjusted margins on the B-Back Page layout.**

8. **Using the Selection tool, Control/right-click the text frame and choose Text Frame Options from the contextual menu. Change the frame to 2 columns with a 0.2″ gutter, and then click OK.**

   One of the advantages to using a template is eliminating repetitive tasks. Since every issue of the newsletter has a story in this area of the back, it makes sense to create the text frame as part of the master page (and template).

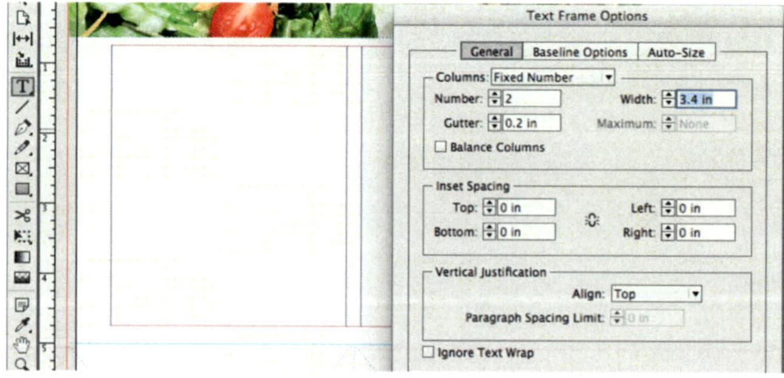

9. **Save the file and close it.**

Understanding Master Pages

There are two kinds of pages in InDesign:

- **Layout pages**, which appear in the bottom of the Pages panel, are the pages on which you place content.
- **Master pages**, which appear in the top of the Pages panel, are the pages on which you place recurring information, such as running heads and footers (information at the top and bottom of the page, respectively).

Master pages are one of the most powerful features in page layout software. Think of a master page as a template for individual pages; anything on the master appears on the related layout page(s). Changing something on a master layout applies the same changes to the object on related layout pages (unless you already changed the object on the layout page, or detached the object from the master).

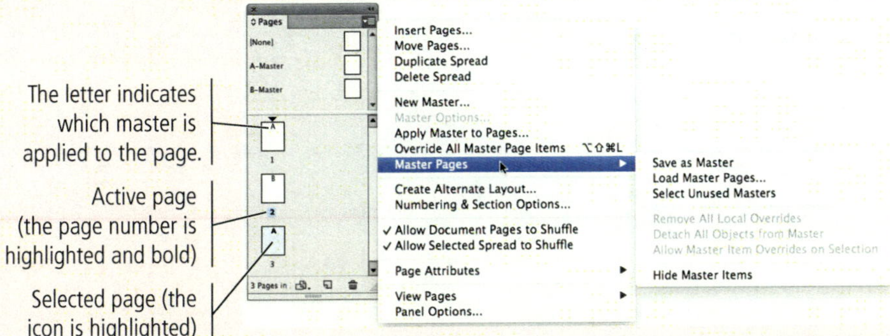

The Pages panel Options menu has a number of indispensable options for working with master pages:

- **New Master** opens a dialog box where you can assign a custom prefix, a meaningful name, whether the master will be based on another master page, and the number of pages (from 1 to 10) to include in the master layout. Because InDesign supports multiple page sizes within a single document, you can also change the size of the master page.

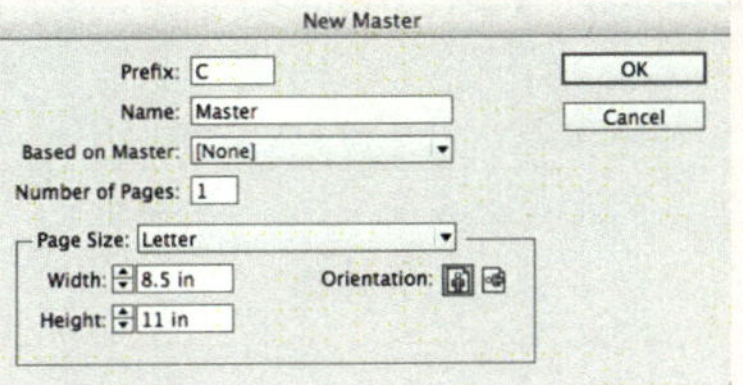

- **Master Options** opens a dialog box with the same options you defined when you created a new master.

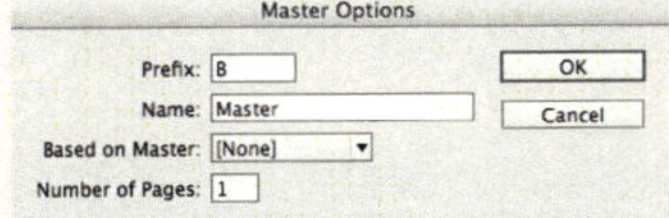

- **Apply Master to Pages** allows you to apply a specific master to selected pages. You can also apply a specific master to a layout by dragging the master icon onto the layout page icon in the lower half of the panel.
- **Override All Master Page Items** allows you to access and change master items on a specific layout page. (It's important to realize that this command functions on a page-by-page basis.) You can also override individual objects by pressing Command/Control-Shift and clicking the object you want to override.

In the Master Pages submenu:

- **Save as Master** is useful if you've built a layout on a layout page and want to convert that layout to a master. Instead of copying and pasting the page contents, you can simply activate the page and choose Save as Master.
- **Load Master Pages** allows you to import entire master pages from one InDesign file to another. Assets such as colors and styles used on the imported masters will also be imported into the current InDesign file.
- **Select Unused Masters** highlights all master pages not associated with at least one layout page (and not used as the basis of another master page). This option can be useful if you want to clean up your layout and remove extraneous elements.
- **Remove All Local Overrides** reapplies the settings from the master items to related items on the layout page. (This option toggles to **Remove Selected Local Overrides** if you have a specific object selected on the layout page.)
- **Detach All Objects from Master** breaks the link between objects on a layout page and objects on the related master; in this case, changing items on the master has no effect on related layout page items. (This selection toggles to **Detach Selection from Master** if you have a specific object selected on the layout page.)
- **Allow Master Item Overrides on Selection**, active by default, allows objects to be overridden on layout pages. You can protect specific objects by selecting them on the master layout and toggling this option off.
- **Hide/Show Master Items** toggles the visibility of master page items on layout pages.

Create a New File Based on the Template

Once you have made the client's requested changes in the template, you can easily begin each new issue by simply opening the template. Only a few more things need to be addressed before you're ready to work on the current issue of the newsletter.

Every issue of the newsletter has one front page and one back page. These layouts are already prepared as master pages, but you have to apply those master pages to the layout pages for individual issues. Since this occurs for every issue, it will remove a few more clicks from the process if you set up the layout pages as part of the template.

1. **Choose File>Open and navigate to your WIP>HeartSmart folder. Select the heartsmart.indt template file and choose the Open [As] Normal option at the bottom of the dialog box.**

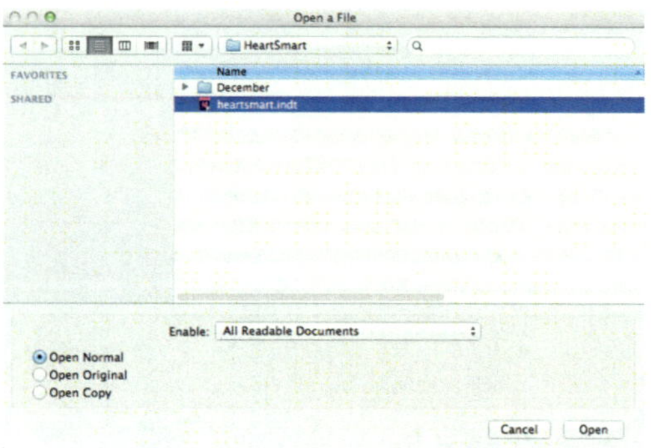

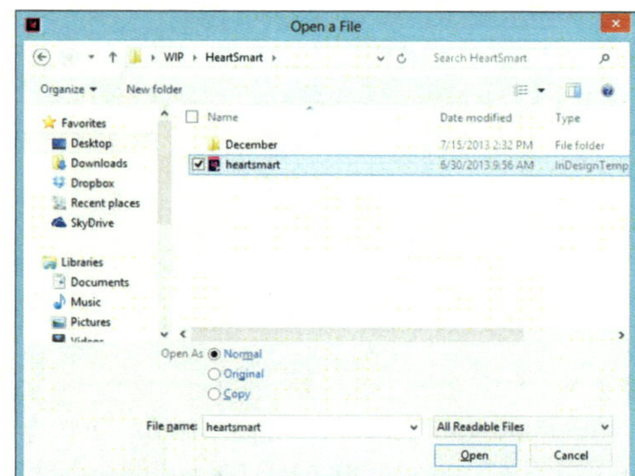

2. **Click Open to create a new file based on the template.**

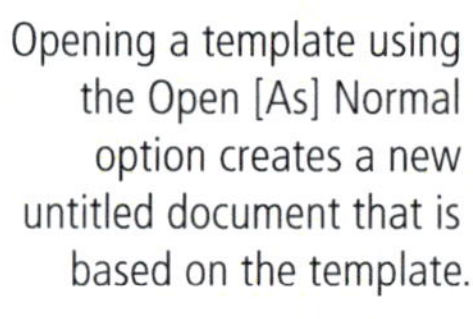

Opening a template using the Open [As] Normal option creates a new untitled document that is based on the template.

3. **Double-click the Page 1 icon in the Pages panel.**

4. **In the Pages panel, drag the A-Front Page master icon onto the Page 1 icon in the lower half of the Pages panel.**

When a master page is applied to a layout page, everything on the master page is placed on the layout page.

Assign a master layout to a specific page by dragging the master icon onto the page icon.

Alternatively, you can choose Apply Master Pages in the Pages panel Options menu. In the resulting dialog box, you can determine which master page to apply to specific layout pages. Some find this easier than dragging master page icons onto individual layout page icons in the panel; it is also useful if you want to apply a specific master layout to more than one page at a time.

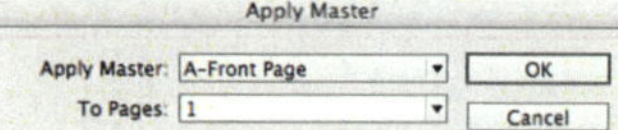

Note:

If you double-click a template file on your desktop, the template opens as if you chose the Open Normal option. To use the Open Original or Open Copy feature, you must choose File>Open from InDesign.

5. **Click the B-Back Page icon and drag it into the bottom half of the Pages panel (below the Page 1 icon).**

   You can add new pages to your layout by dragging any of the master page icons into the lower half of the panel.

Add pages to a layout by dragging any master page icon to the lower half of the Pages panel.

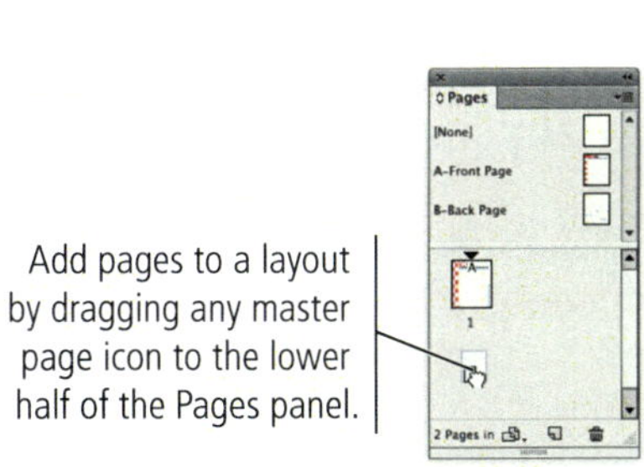

   You can also choose Insert Pages in the Pages panel Options menu. In the resulting dialog box, you can determine how many pages to add, exactly where to add the new pages, and which master page to apply to the new pages. This method makes it easier to add only one page from a master page that includes spreads (see Project 4: Realtor Collateral Booklet), or add multiple pages at one time based on the same master.

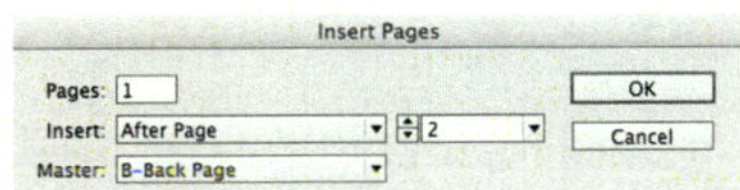

> ***Note:***
>
> *You can change the size of page icons in the Pages panel by choosing Panel Options at the bottom of the panel's Options menu.*

6. **Choose File>Save As. Navigate to your WIP>HeartSmart folder as the location for saving the template.**

   Because you opened the template to create a normal layout file, you have to use the Save As command to overwrite the edited template file.

7. **Change the file name to heartsmart. In the Format/Save As Type menu, choose InDesign CC Template.**

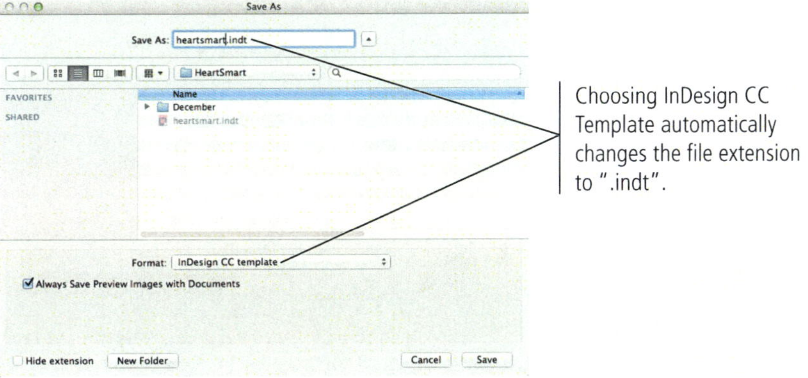

Choosing InDesign CC Template automatically changes the file extension to ".indt".

8. **Click Save, then read the resulting message.**

   Because you defined the same name as the original template, you have to confirm that you want to overwrite the template file with the new version.

9. **Click Replace/Yes. When the save is complete, close the template file.**

Implement the Newsletter Template

By saving your work as a template, you have eliminated a significant amount of repetitive work that would otherwise need to be redone for every issue. There are still some tasks that will need to be done for each issue, such as changing the issue date and adding images to the front and back pages. These elements will change in each issue, so they can't be entirely "templated." But if you review the layout as it is now, you'll see that the template includes placeholders for these elements, so adding these elements is greatly simplified.

1. **Choose File>Open and navigate to your WIP>HeartSmart folder. Select the heartsmart.indt template file, choose the Open Normal option at the bottom of the dialog box, and click Open.**

   As in the previous exercise, opening the template file creates a new untitled document that is based on the template.

2. **Immediately choose File>Save As and navigate to your WIP>HeartSmart folder. Change the file name to newsletter_dec.indd and click Save.**

   The Format menu defaults to the InDesign CC Document option, so you do not have to change this menu to save the new file as a regular InDesign document.

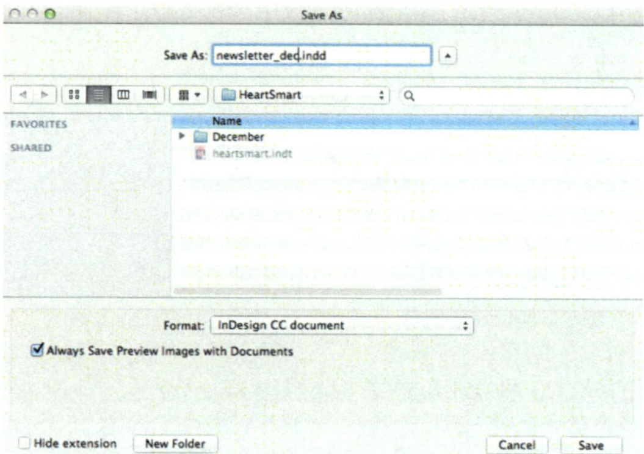

3. **Navigate to Page 1 of the file.**

4. **Using the Selection tool, try to select the text frame that includes the date.**

   This step will have no effect, and nothing will be selected. By default, you can't select master page items on a layout page; changes have to be made on the master page.

   When you change an object on a master page, the same changes reflect on associated layout pages. For example, if you change the red box to blue on A-Front Page, the red box will turn blue on Page 1 as well. Because of this parent-child relationship, it's a good idea to leave objects attached to the master whenever possible.

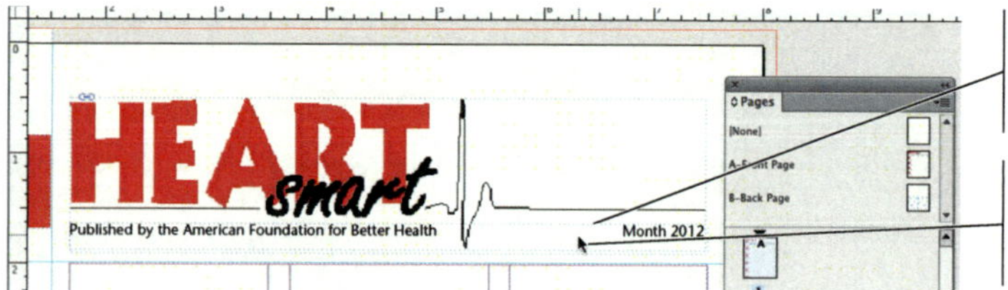

Dotted lines indicate that a frame is attached to the related master page.

You can't select a frame that hasn't been detached from the master.

5. **Command/Control-Shift-click the text frame that contains the issue date.**

   This method detaches an individual object from the master page. It is no longer linked to the master page, so changes to the same item on the master will not be reflected on the associated layout page.

6. **Using the Type tool, highlight "Month 2012" in the nameplate area and type** `December 2013`**.**

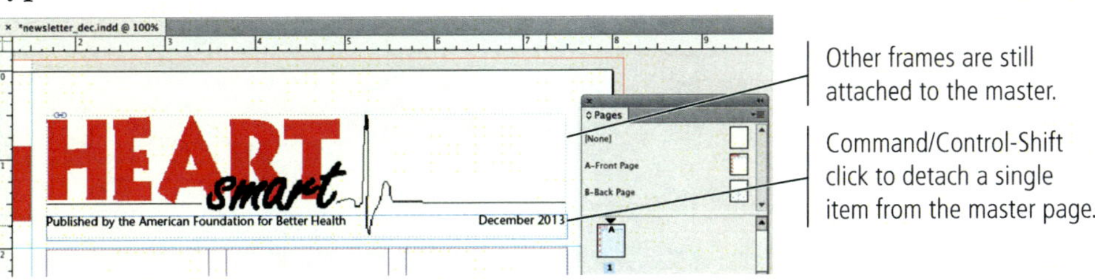

You could have accomplished the same basic result by editing the text on the master page. However, we created these steps so you can understand the concept of detaching master page objects.

7. **Save the file and continue to the next exercise.**

Note:

You can detach all items from the master page layout by Control/right-clicking a page icon in the Pages panel and choosing Override All Master Page Items from the contextual menu.

Place Multiple TIFF Files

TIFF, a common format in graphic design and layout work, is used for raster images such as those from a scanner, digital camera, and many files created in Adobe Photoshop. TIFF files can be one-color (bitmap or monochrome), grayscale, or continuous-tone images. The current version of the format can store clipping paths and alpha channels to define areas of transparency, as well as color profiles to describe the colors in the file.

Note:

TIFF files can also contain multiple layers, but you cannot access those individual layers in InDesign. If you need to control image layers within the context of the page layout, you should save those files in the native Photoshop (.psd) format.

1. **With** `newsletter_dec.indd` **open, deselect everything in the layout.**

2. **Choose File>Place. In the Place dialog box, select the file** `fruit.tif` **(in the WIP>HeartSmart>December folder) and make sure the Show Import Options box is checked.**

   Because nothing is selected in the layout, it doesn't matter if Replace Selected Item is checked or not.

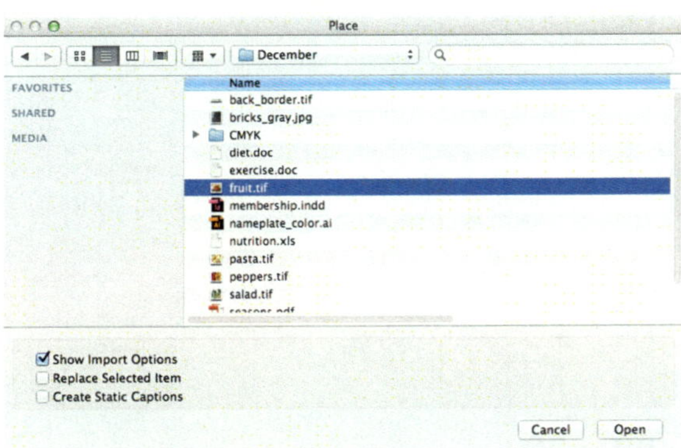

3. **Click Open. In the resulting Image Import Options dialog box, click the Image tab and review the options.**

   If the TIFF file includes clipping path or Alpha channel information, you can activate those options when you place the file. InDesign does not allow access to the layers in a TIFF file; all layers are flattened in the placed file.

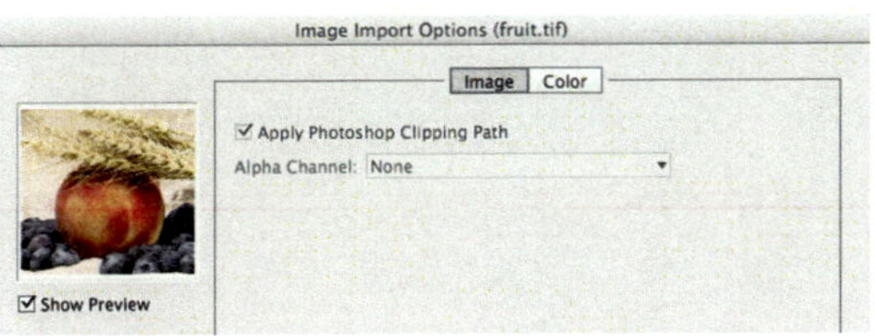

4. **Click the Color tab and review the options.**

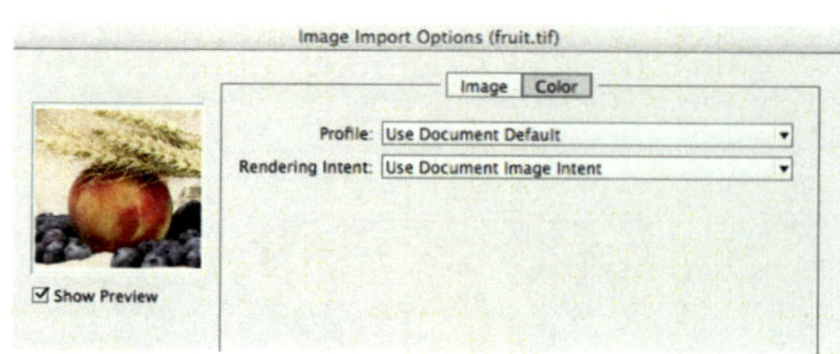

The Profile menu defaults to the profile embedded in the file. If the file was saved without an embedded profile, the menu defaults to Use Document Default. You can use the Profile menu to change the embedded profile (not recommended) or assign a specific profile if one was not embedded.

The Rendering Intent menu defaults to Use Document Image Intent; you can also choose one of the four built-in options for this specific image.

5. **Click OK.**

6. **Click the loaded cursor in the first empty frame in the checkerboard pattern on the left side of the page to place the loaded image.**

When you place the image into the frame, the frame is automatically detached from the master layout.

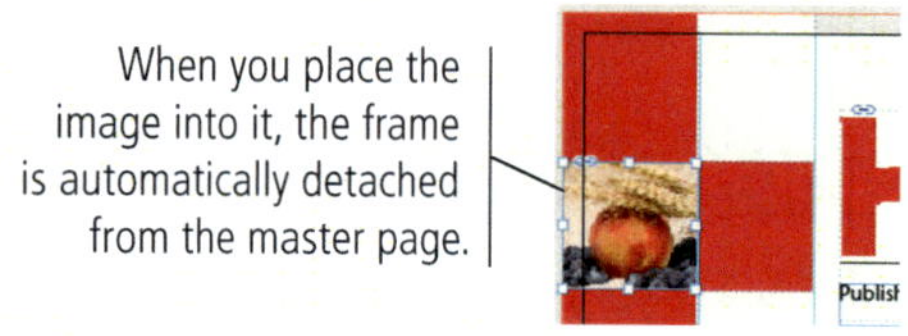

7. **Click away from the placed image to deselect it.**

8. **Make sure the Links panel is visible, then choose File>Place again.**

9. **In the Place dialog box, select `pasta.tif`, `peppers.tif`, and `salad.tif`. With the Show Import Options box checked, click Open.**

Remember, press Shift to select multiple consecutive files. Press Command/Control to select multiple non-consecutive files.

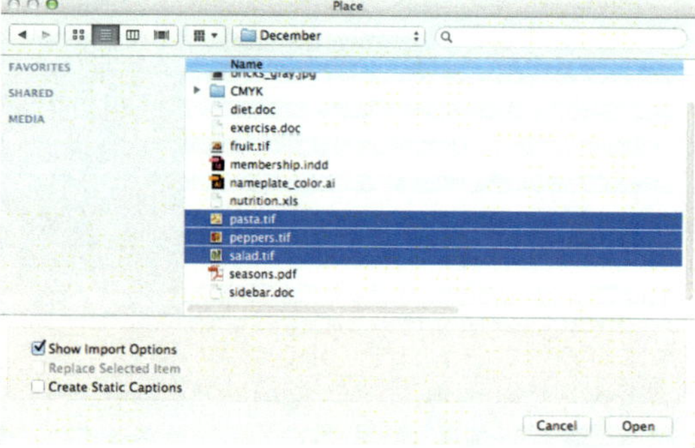

10. **Review the resulting dialog boxes, and click OK in each.**

Because the Show Import Option box was checked when you selected the three files in Step 9, the Image Import Options dialog box opens for each of the three selected files.

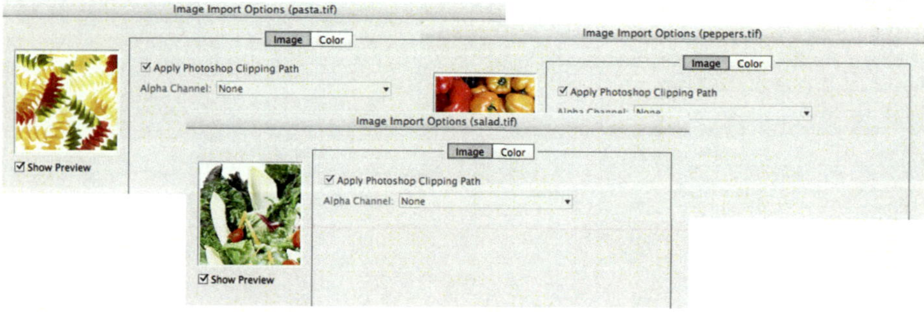

11. **When the images are loaded into the Place cursor, review the Links panel.**

The Links panel can be helpful when you load multiple images into the Place cursor. The active file in the cursor is identified with "LP" in the Page column.

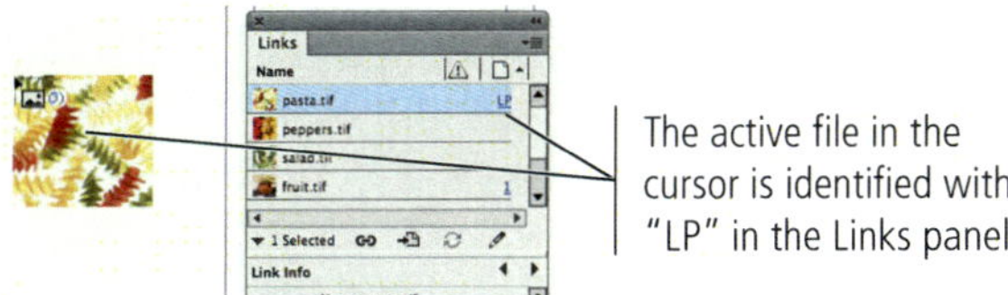

12. **Press the Right Arrow key to change the active file in the Place cursor.**

When multiple files are loaded in the cursor, you can use the Arrow keys to change the active file in the cursor.

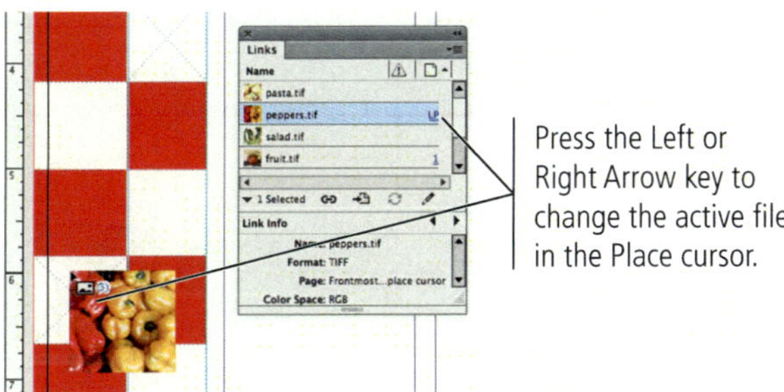

13. **With peppers.tif active in the Place cursor, click the third image frame on the left side of Page 1 to place the image.**

14. **Click to place pasta.tif in the second graphics frame and place salad.tif in the fourth graphics frame.**

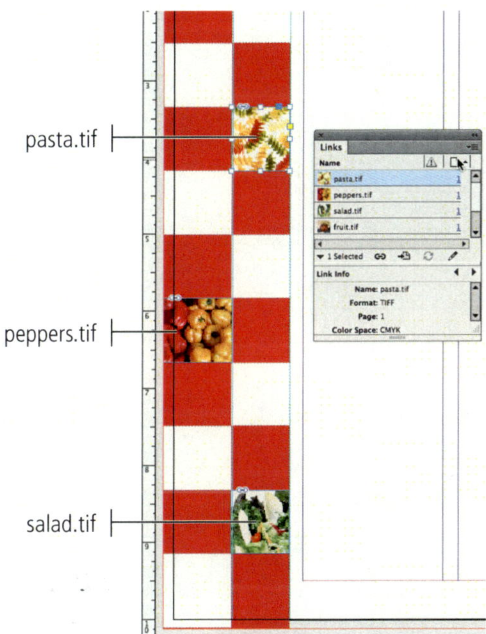

15. **Save the file and continue to the next exercise.**

Place a PDF File

PDF (Portable Document Format) files save layout, graphics, and font information in a single file. The format was created to facilitate cross-platform file-sharing so one file could be transferred to any other computer, and the final layout would print as intended. While originally meant for Internet use, PDF is now the standard in the graphics industry, used for submitting advertisements, artwork, and completed jobs to a service provider.

You can place a PDF file into an InDesign layout, just as you would place any other image. You can determine which page to place (if the file contains more than one page), which layers are visible (if the file has more than one layer), and the specific file dimensions (bounding box) to use when placing the file.

1. **With newsletter_dec.indd open, navigate to Page 2 of the newsletter.**

2. **Choose File>Place. In the Place dialog box, select seasons.pdf (in the WIP>HeartSmart>December folder).**

3. **Make sure Show Import Options is checked and Replace Selected Item is not checked, and then click Open.**

   The options in the Place PDF dialog box are exactly the same as the options you saw when you placed the native Illustrator file. However, the options in the General tab are typically more important for PDF files than for Illustrator files.

   PDF files can contain multiple pages; you can review the various pages using the buttons below the preview image. You can place multiple pages at once by choosing the All option, or you can select specific pages using the Range option.

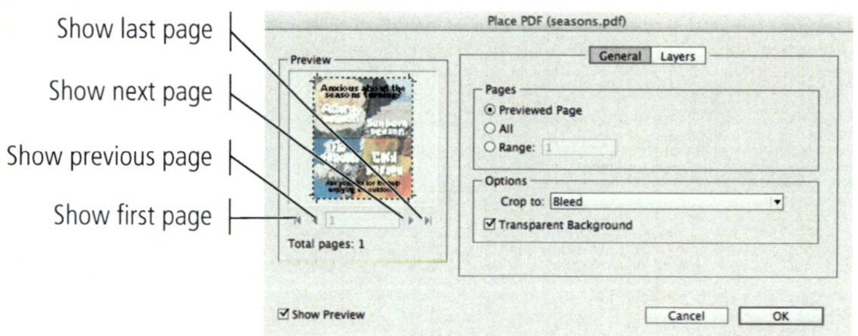

   The Crop To options are also significant when placing PDF files. If the file was created properly, it should include a defined bleed of at least 1/8 inch and trim marks to identify the intended trim size.

4. **Choose Bleed in the Crop To menu and click OK.**

5. **Click the loaded cursor in the left graphics frame at the bottom of Page 2 to place the loaded file.**

Note:

Before placing a PDF file in an InDesign job, make absolutely sure it was created and optimized for commercial printing. Internet-optimized PDF files do not have sufficient resolution to print cleanly on a high-resolution output device; if these are used, they could ruin an otherwise perfect InDesign job.

Note:

Import continuous pages by defining a page range, using a hyphen to separate the first page and last pages in the range. Import non-continuous pages by typing each page number, separated by commas.

Note:

If you place multiple pages of a PDF file, each page is loaded into the cursor as a separate object.

Note:

If you place an Illustrator file that contains multiple artboards, you have the same options for choosing which artboard (page) to place.

6. **Access the placed content by clicking the image with the Direct Selection tool or by clicking the Content Grabber with the Selection tool.**

   This file was created with 1/8″ bleeds on all four sides. In this layout, however, the top bleed allowance is not necessary. When you place the image into the frame, the bleed area on the top causes the image to appear farther down than it should.

7. **With the placed file still selected, make sure the top-left reference point is selected and then change the picture position (within the frame) to Y+: –0.125″.**

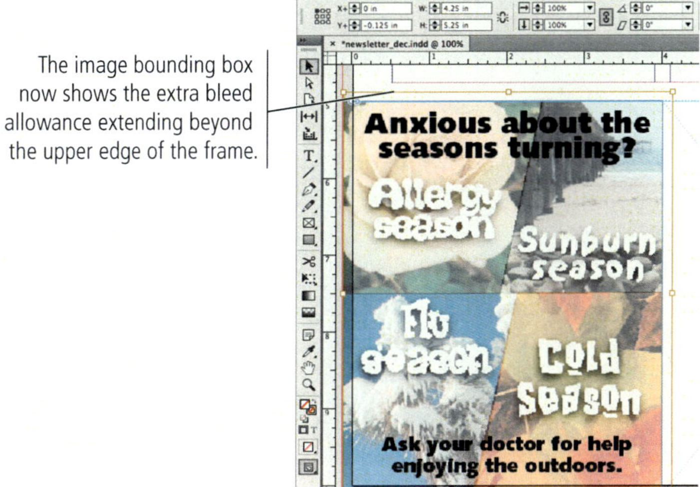

8. **Save the file and continue to the next exercise.**

Place an InDesign File

In addition to the different types of images, you can also place one InDesign layout directly into another. As with PDF files, you can determine which page is placed (if the file contains more than one page), which layers are visible (if the file has more than one layer), and the specific file dimensions (bounding box) to use when the file is placed.

1. **With newsletter_dec.indd open, make sure nothing is selected.**

2. **Choose File>Place. In the Place dialog box, select membership.indd (in the WIP>HeartSmart>December folder). With the Show Import Options box checked, click Open.**

3. **In the General tab of the Place InDesign Document dialog box, choose Bleed Bounding Box in the Crop To menu.**

   The options for placing an InDesign file are mostly the same as for placing PDF files; the only exception is the Crop To menu. When you place an InDesign file into another InDesign file, you can place the page(s) based on the defined page, bleed, or slug, as described in the Document Setup dialog box.

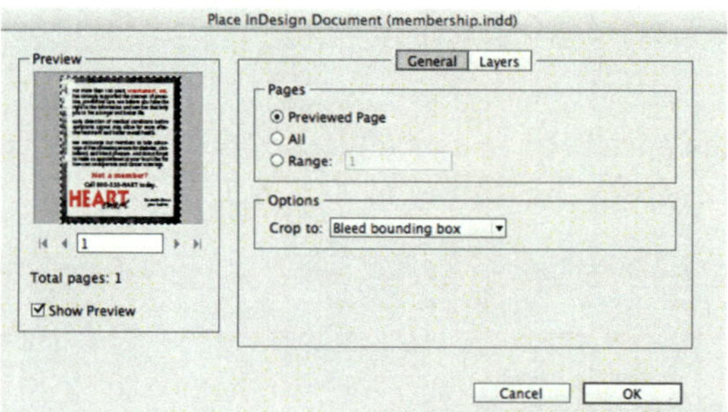

4. **Click OK. Read the resulting warning message and click OK.**

   To output properly, image links need to be present and up to date. Images placed in nested InDesign layouts are still links, so the link requirements apply in those files.

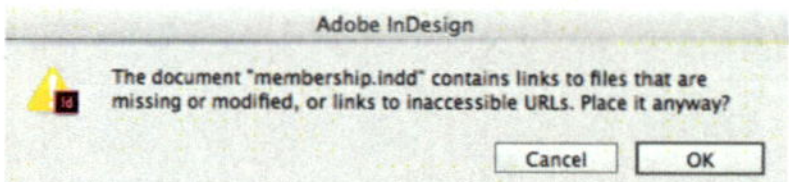

5. **Click the loaded cursor in the empty graphics frame on the right side of Page 2 to place the file.**

   As with PDF files, the bleed areas in an InDesign file might not exactly match the needs of the file where it is placed.

6. **Select the placed image content with the Direct Selection tool and change the content's position to X+ = –0.125″, Y+ = –0.125″.**

7. **Open the Links panel and click the arrow to the left of membership.indd to show the nested images.**

   When you place one InDesign file into another, the Links panel also lists images in the placed InDesign file, indented immediately below the placed InDesign file.

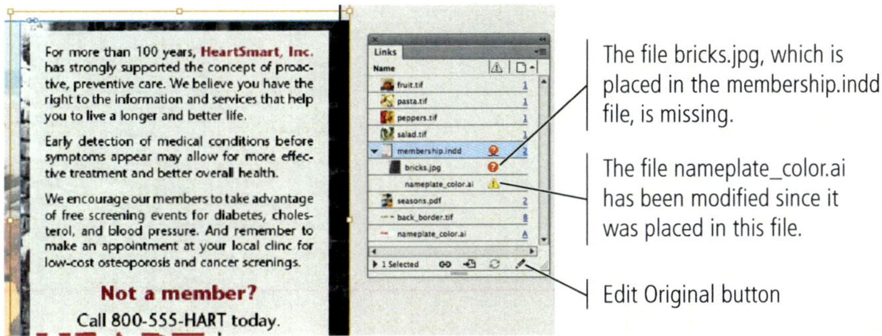

> *Note:*
>
> *The Edit Original option works for any type of placed file (as long as your computer recognizes the file type), including native Illustrator and Photoshop files, TIFF files, JPEG files, EPS files, and so on.*

8. **Click membership.indd in the Links panel, and then click the Edit Original button.**

   When you open any InDesign file, of course, you are warned if a necessary source file is missing or modified (which you already knew from the Links panel of the newsletter_dec.indd file).

> *Note:*
>
> *You can also Control/right-click a specific image in the layout and choose Edit Original from the contextual menu.*

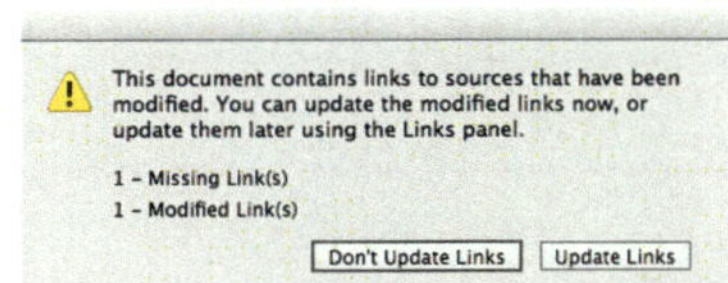

9. **Click Don't Update Links to dismiss the warning message.**

   The Edit Original option opens the file selected in the Links panel. Because membership.indd is a placed InDesign file, that document opens in a new document window in front of newsletter_dec.indd. When the file opens, you see the missing image icon — the reason you are editing the file — in the document and in the Links panel.

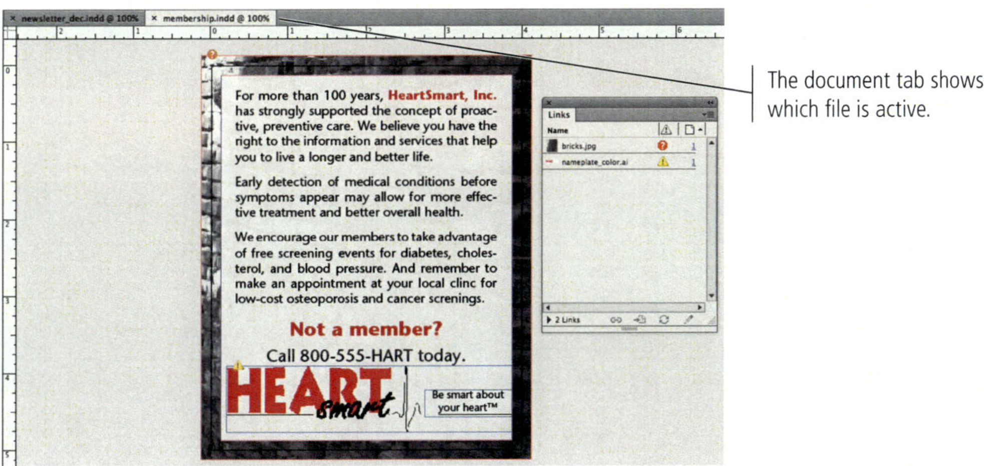

10. **In the Links panel for membership.indd, click the modified file to select it, then click the Update Link button at the bottom of the panel.**

    The Modified icon is removed from the panel and from the graphics frame in the layout.

11. **Click the missing file in the Links panel to select it, and then click the Relink button at the bottom of the panel.**

11. **Navigate to `bricks_gray.jpg` in the WIP>HeartSmart>December folder and click Open.**

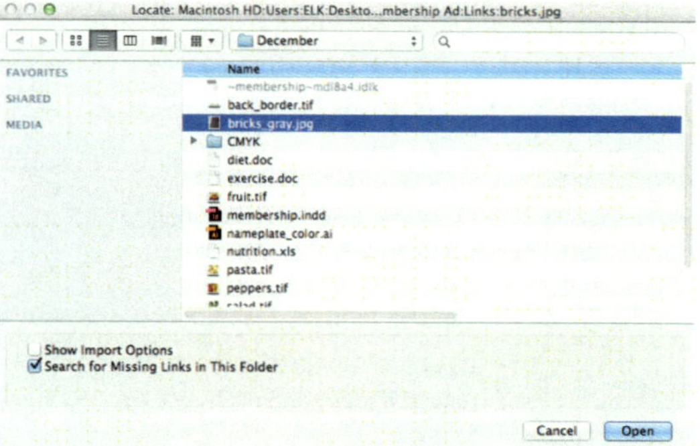

12. **If the Image Import Options dialog box opens, click OK.**

The options for JPEG images are basically the same as for TIFF files. However, most of those options are disabled because the JPEG format does not support clipping paths, alpha channels, or embedded color profiles.

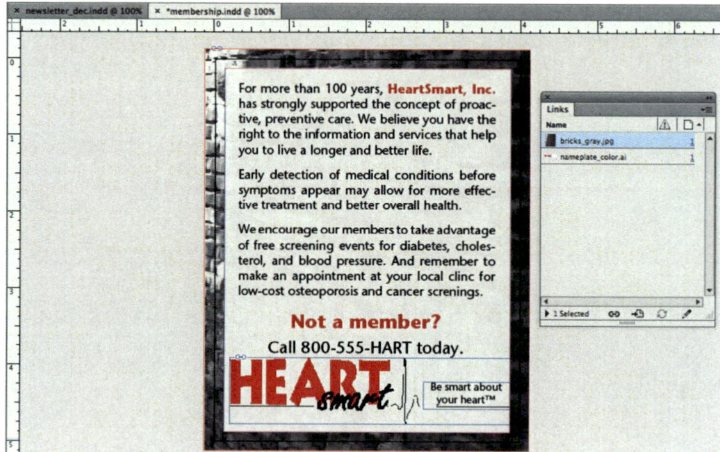

13. **Save the `membership.indd` file and close it.**

When you save and close the membership.indd file, the Links panel for the newsletter file automatically reflects the new placed file.

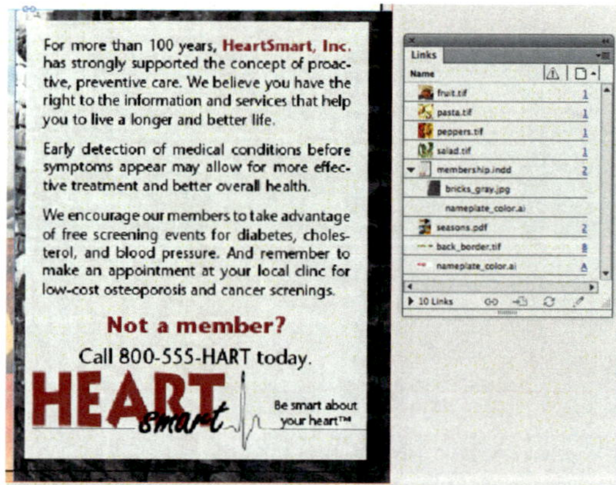

14. **Save `newsletter_dec.indd` and continue to the next stage of the project.**

Stage 2 Working with Styles

The principles of good design state that headings, subheadings, body copy, and other editorial elements should generally look the same throughout a single job — in other words, editorial elements should be consistent from one page to another, whether the job is two pages or two hundred.

In Project 2: Festival Poster, you learned about the various text formatting options that can be applied in an InDesign layout. For any bit of text, there are dozens of character- and paragraph-formatting options, from the font and type size to the space above and below paragraphs. Whenever you work with longer blocks of copy, you'll apply the same group of formatting options to multiple pieces of text.

If you were to change each element manually, you would have to make hundreds of clicks to create a two-page newsletter. Fortunately, InDesign makes it easy to store groups of formatting options as **styles**, which can be applied with a single click.

The major advantages of using styles are ease of use and enhanced efficiency. Changes can be made instantly to all text defined as a particular style. For example, you might easily modify leading in the Body Copy style or change the font in the Subhead style from Helvetica to ATC Onyx Bold. When a style definition changes, any text that uses that style automatically changes too.

InDesign supports both character styles and paragraph styles. **Character styles** apply only to selected words; this type of style is useful for setting off a few words in a paragraph without affecting the entire paragraph. **Paragraph styles** apply to the entire body of text between two ¶ symbols; this type of style defines the appearance of the paragraph, combining the character style used in the paragraph with line spacing, indents, tabs, and other paragraph attributes.

In this project, the client's original template included a number of styles for formatting the text in each issue. Because the text frames already exist in the template layout, you only need to import the client's text and apply the existing styles.

> ***Note:***
>
> *Styles ensure consistency in text and paragraph formatting throughout a publication. Rather than trying to remember how you formatted a sidebar 45 pages ago, you can simply apply a predefined Sidebar style.*

> ***Note:***
>
> *Paragraph styles define character attributes and paragraph attributes; character styles define only the character attributes. In other words, a paragraph style can be used to format text entirely — including font information, line spacing, tabs, and so on.*

Apply Template Styles

Most InDesign jobs incorporate some amount of client-supplied text, which might be sent to you in the body of an email or saved in any number of text file formats. Many text files will be supplied from Microsoft Word, the most popular word-processing application in the United States market.

Microsoft Word includes fairly extensive options for formatting text (although not quite as robust or sophisticated as InDesign). Many Microsoft Word users apply **local formatting** (selecting specific text and applying character and/or paragraph attributes); more sophisticated Microsoft Word users build text formatting styles similar to those used in InDesign.

Styles are most advantageous when working with text-intensive documents that have recurring editorial elements, such as headlines, subheads, and captions; when working with several people concurrently on the same project; and when creating projects with specific style requirements, such as catalogs or magazines.

1. **With Page 1 of newsletter_dec.indd active in the document window, choose File>Place and navigate to the file exercise.doc.**

   All text files for this project are in the WIP>HeartSmart>December folder.

2. **Check the Show Import Options box at the bottom of the dialog box and make sure Replace Selected Item is not checked.**

3. **Click Open. In the resulting dialog box, review the options in the Formatting section.**

When you import a Microsoft Word file into InDesign, you can either preserve or remove formatting saved in the Microsoft Word file (including styles defined in Microsoft Word).

4. **Make sure the Preserve Styles and Formatting option is selected and the Import Styles Automatically radio button is selected. Choose Auto Rename in both conflict menus and then click OK.**

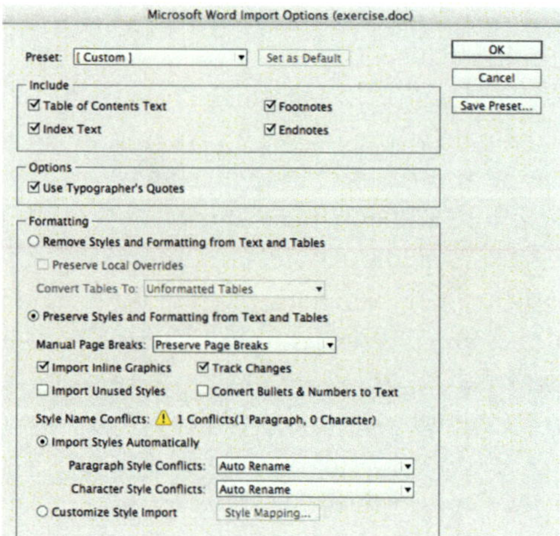

5. **If you get a Missing Font warning, click OK.**

You're going to replace the Microsoft Word formatting with InDesign styles, which will correct this problem.

6. **Click the loaded cursor in the empty three-column text frame.**

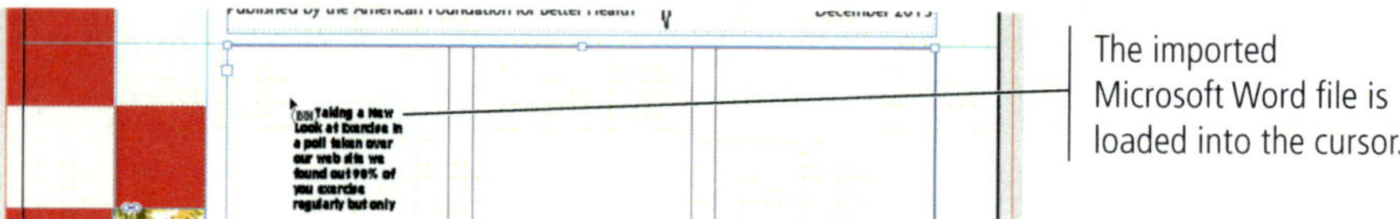

At this point, the story does not fit into the frame because you haven't yet applied the appropriate styles to the imported text.

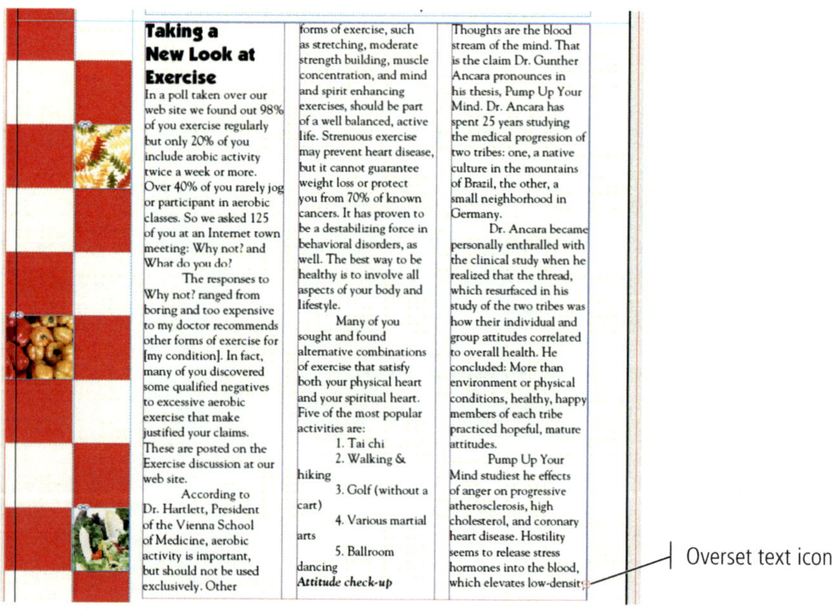

Working with Microsoft Word Files

Microsoft Word files can include a fairly sophisticated level of formatting attributes, from basic text formatting to defined paragraph and character styles to automatically generated tables of contents. When you import a Word file into InDesign, you can determine whether to include these elements in the imported text, as well as how to handle conflicts between imported elements and elements that already exist in your InDesign layout.

If these elements exist in the Microsoft Word file, checking the associated boxes imports those elements into your InDesign file.

Choose this option to convert straight quote marks to typographer's or "curly" quotes.

Choose this option to strip out all formatting applied in the file and import the file as plain text.

Choose this option to import the Microsoft Word file, including formatting.

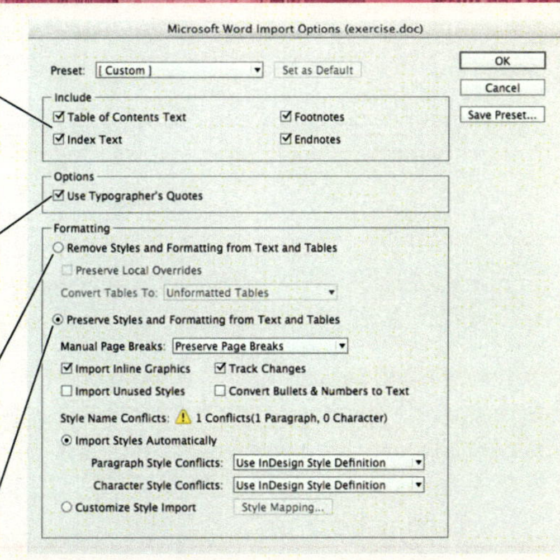

The **Manual Page Breaks** menu determines how page breaks in Word translate to InDesign. You can preserve manual breaks, convert them to column breaks, or ignore them. This option is important because Word users tend to force breaks where appropriate in the file — which rarely translates to a properly formatted InDesign layout. More often than not, you'll end up removing these page breaks, but it might be a good idea to include them in the import and remove them after you've reviewed the imported text.

If graphics have been placed into a Word file, the **Import Inline Graphics** option allows you to include those graphics as anchored objects in the InDesign story. If you choose to include graphics, it is extremely important to understand that the graphics might be embedded into the story instead of linked to the original data file (depending on how the graphic was placed into the Word file).

If you choose **Import Unused Styles**, all styles in the Word file will be imported into the InDesign layout. The most significant issue here is that styles might require fonts that you have not installed.

Word includes a powerful collaboration tool called Track Changes, which allows one person to review another person's changes to a file. (As publishers, we use this feature every day, so editors and authors can review each other's changes before permanently changing the text.) If you check the **Track Changes** option, any tracked changes from the Word file will be included in your InDesign layout. This might cause a lot of items to show up in your text that aren't supposed to be there (typos, errors, or, for example, something the general counsel office removed from the original text for a specific legal reason).

Convert Bullets & Numbers to Text allows you to convert automatically generated numbering and bullet characters into actual text characters. This option is extremely useful if the text includes lists; if you don't check this option, you'll have to manually re-enter the bullets or line numbers into the imported text.

The **Style Name Conflicts** area warns you if styles in the Word file conflict with styles in the InDesign file. (In other words, they have the same style names but different definitions in the two locations). If you are importing styles from the Word file, you have to determine how to resolve these conflicts.

Import Styles Automatically allows you to choose how to handle conflicts in paragraph and character styles. **Use InDesign Style Definition** preserves the style as you defined it; text in the Word file that uses that style will be reformatted with the InDesign definition of the style. **Redefine InDesign Style** replaces the layout definition with the definition from the Word file. **Auto Rename** adds the Word file to the InDesign file with "_wrd_1" at the end of the style name.

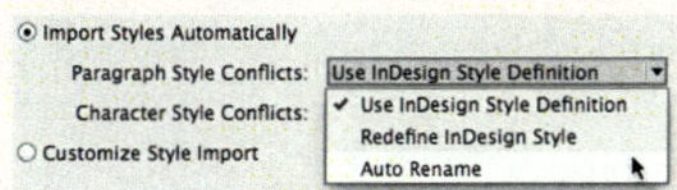

If you choose **Customize Style Import**, the Style Mapping button opens a dialog box where you can review and control specific style conflicts. Click an option in the InDesign Style column to access a menu, where you can choose which InDesign style to use in place of a specific Word style.

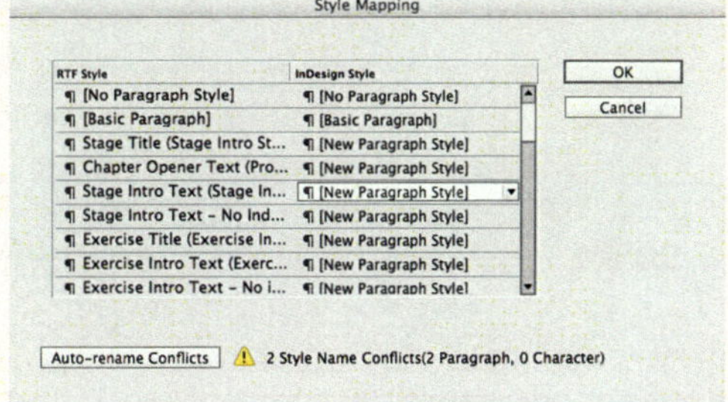

If you always receive Microsoft Word files from the same source, you can save your choices (including Style Mapping options) as a preset, or even click the Set as Default button in the Import Options dialog box.

7. **Open the Paragraph Styles panel (Window>Styles>Paragraph Styles).**

8. **Place the insertion point in the first paragraph of the imported story (the main heading) and look at the Paragraph Styles panel.**

   The imported text appears to be preformatted, but the Paragraph Styles panel tells a different story. This paragraph is formatted as "Normal+."

   When you imported the Microsoft Word file, you preserved the formatting in the file; this is usually a good idea so you can see what the writer intended. Now that the text is imported into your layout, however, you want to apply the template styles to make the text in this issue consistent with other issues.

   When you import text into InDesign, any number of new styles might appear in the Styles panels; the most common imported style is Normal. Text in a Microsoft Word file is typically formatted with the Normal style — even if you don't realize it; user-applied formatting is commonly local (meaning it is applied directly to selected text instead of with a defined style).

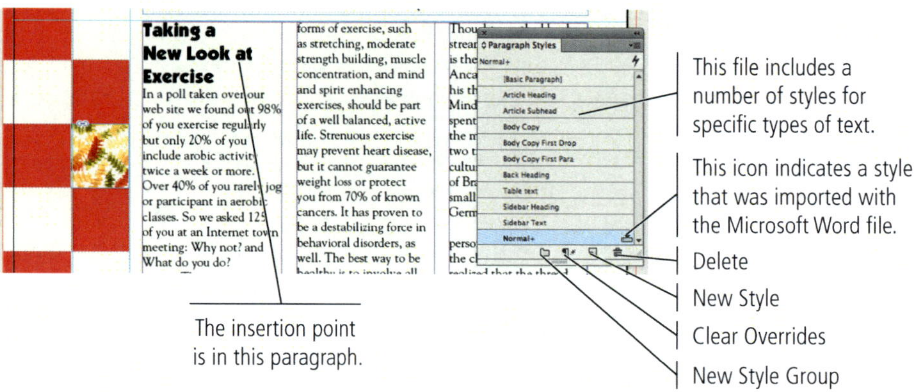

9. **With the insertion point still in place, click the Article Heading style in the Paragraph Styles panel.**

   A number of styles existed in the original newsletter template, so they also exist in any files that are based on that template. You should be able to guess the purpose of these styles from their names; it's always a good idea to use indicative names when you create styles or other user-defined assets.

   Using styles, you can change all formatting attributes of selected text with a single click. Because you are working with paragraph styles, the style definition applies to the entire paragraph where the insertion point is placed.

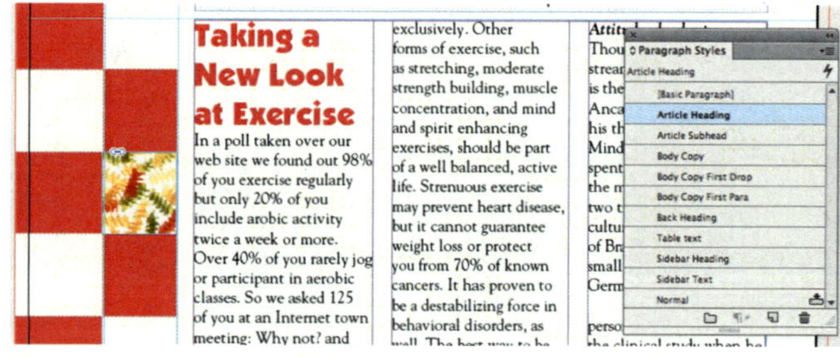

10. **Click and drag to select any part of the remaining paragraphs in the story, and then click the Body Copy style in the Paragraph Styles panel.**

Paragraph styles apply to any paragraph that is partially or entirely selected. You don't have to select an entire paragraph before applying a paragraph style.

Note:

Paragraph styles can include character attributes as well as paragraph attributes; character styles can only define character-formatting attributes.

Any paragraph that is at least partially selected will be formatted with the Body Copy paragraph style.

After applying the style, you might notice that the Body Copy style shows a plus sign in the Paragraph Styles panel. This indicates that formatting other than what is defined in the style has been applied to the selected text (called a **local formatting override**).

If you look carefully at the text, you will see a paragraph ("Attitude check-up") that is bold and italic. The content and context of the styled text indicates that this should be a heading — an important reason for maintaining the styling that was applied in the original text file when you place it into the layout.

11. **With the same text selected, Control/right-click the Body Copy style in the Paragraph Styles panel and choose Apply 'Body Copy', Clear Overrides.**

After clearing overrides, the selected paragraphs have only the formatting that is defined in the applied style.

Note:

You can also clear formatting overrides in selected paragraphs by Option/Alt clicking the applied style name.

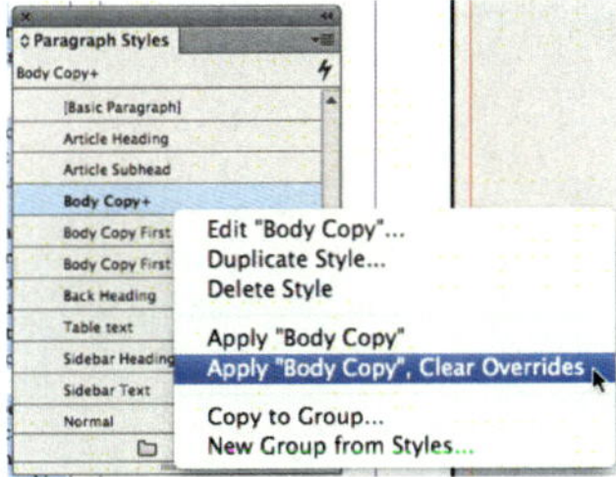

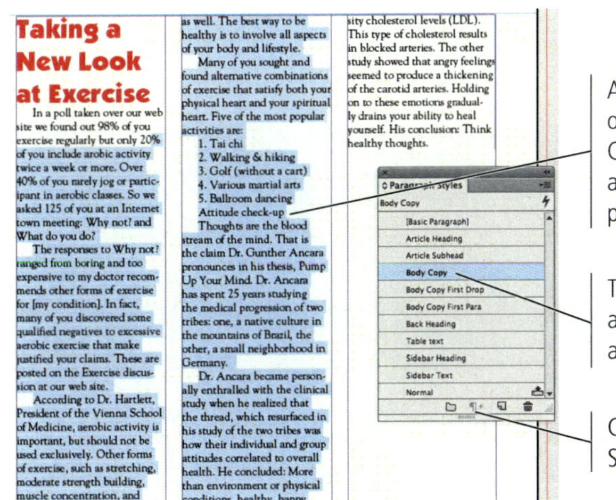

After clearing overrides, only the defined Body Copy formatting is applied to the selected paragraphs.

The plus sign no longer appears next to the applied style name.

Clear Overrides in Selection button

The **Clear Overrides in Selection** button at the bottom of the Paragraph Styles panel basically accomplishes the same goal, but, as the name suggests, it only applies to selected text. Because the first and last paragraphs are not entirely selected, this button would not clear formatting overrides from unselected text in those paragraphs.

12. **In the second column, format the subheading ("Attitude check-up") with the Article Subhead style.**

13. **Format the first paragraph after the main heading (in the first column) with the Body Copy First Drop style.**

14. **Format the paragraph after the subhead (in the second column) with the Body Copy First Para style.**

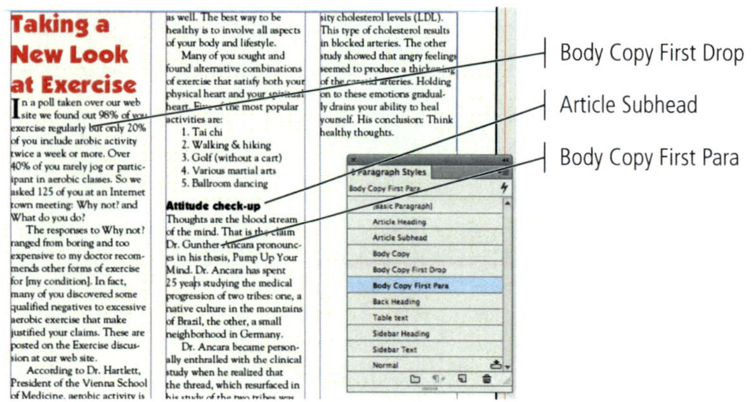

15. **Navigate to Page 2 of the layout, then choose File>Place.**

16. **Navigate to the WIP>HeartSmart>December folder if necessary, then select `diet.doc`. With the Show Import Options box checked, click Open.**

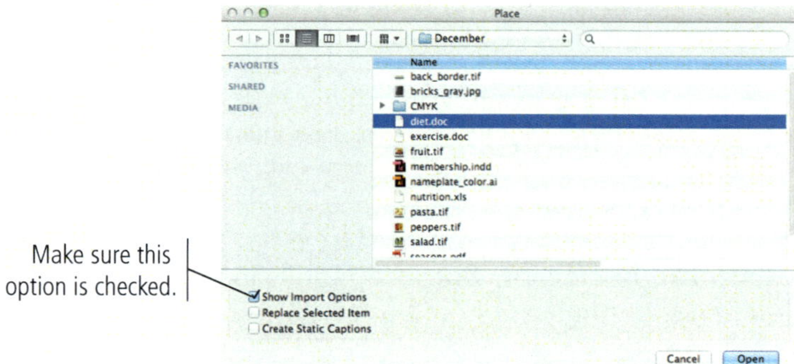

17. **Review the resulting import options, then click OK.**

This dialog box, as with most in InDesign, remembers the last-used options. The impoted styles will be automatically renamed if they conflict with existing InDesign files.

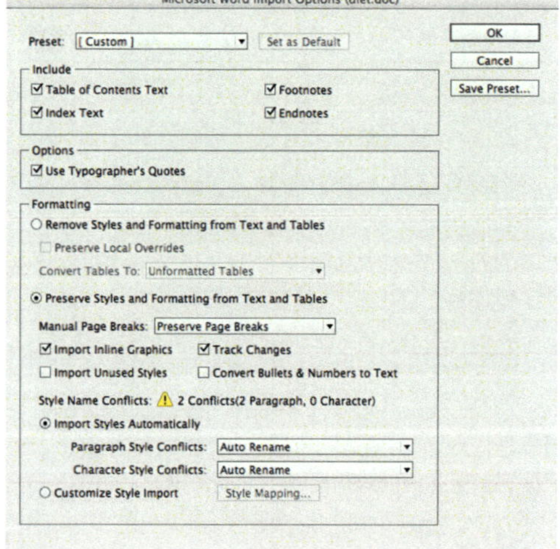

Note:

If a paragraph includes local formatting, simply clicking a new style name might not work perfectly.

Sometimes there is no apparent reason why text imported from Microsoft Word is not properly formatted when you apply a style in InDesign. This is usually caused by formatting options in Microsoft that are not supported in InDesign. You should simply be aware that you often need to clear overrides in the imported text before the InDesign style is properly applied.

18. **Click OK if you get a Missing Font warning.**

    Again, you are going to apply the styles that are built into the template, so you don't need to worry about missing fonts in the imported styles.

19. **Click the loaded cursor between the margin guides in the top half of Page 2.**

    Because you turned off the Show Import Options box in the Place dialog box, the file is imported with the last-used import options. In this case, the formatting is maintained, styles are imported, and conflicting styles are automatically renamed — resulting in the new Normal_wrd_1 style, which conflicted with the previously imported Normal style.

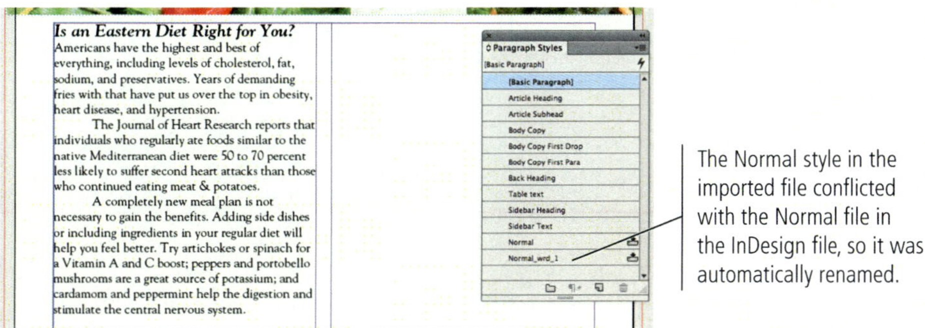

The Normal style in the imported file conflicted with the Normal file in the InDesign file, so it was automatically renamed.

20. **Format the first paragraph with the Back Heading style.**
    Format the second paragraph with the Body Copy First Para style.
    Format the rest of the story with the Body Copy style.

21. **Save the file and continue to the next exercise.**

Edit a Paragraph to Span Columns

As a general rule, headlines in newsletters and newspapers extend across the top of the entire related story. In previous versions of the software, this required a separate frame that spanned the width of the multi-column body frame. InDesign includes a paragraph formatting option that makes it easy to span a paragraph across multiple columns *without* the need for a separate frame. This can be applied to individual paragraphs, or defined as part of a paragraph style.

1. **With newsletter_dec.indd open, navigate to Page 1.**

2. **Place the insertion point in the first paragraph of the story (the heading) and then open the Paragraph panel (Window>Type & Tables>Paragraph).**

3. **With the insertion point still in the same paragraph, open the Paragraph panel Options menu and choose Span Columns.**

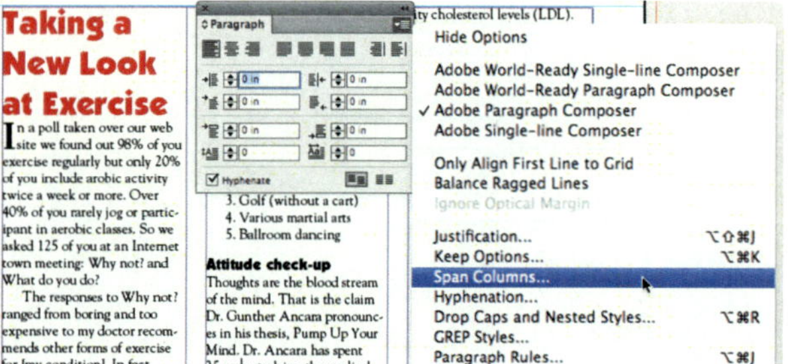

4. **Click the Preview option in the bottom-right corner of the dialog box, then choose Span Columns in the Paragraph Layout menu.**

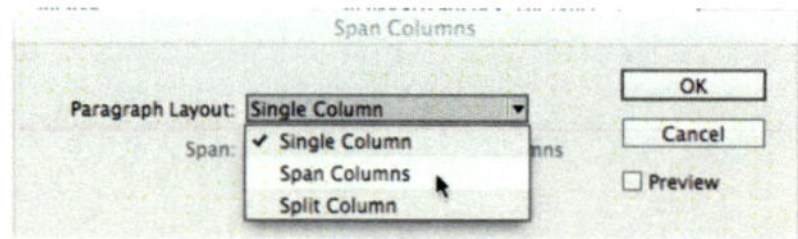

When the Preview option is active, you can see the result of your choices before you finalize them.

Note:

The Split Column option can be used to divide a specific paragraph into multiple columns within a frame's defined column.

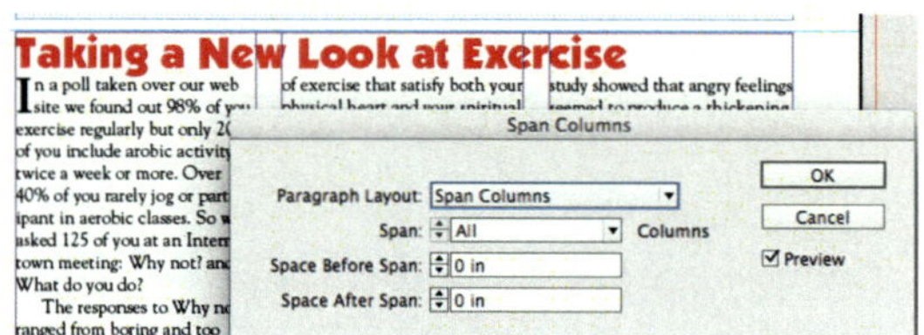

5. **Make sure the Span field is set to All.**

You can use the Span field to extend a paragraph over only a certain number of columns.

6. **Click the Up Arrow button once for the Space After Span field.**

The arrow buttons increase or decrease the related values by 0.0625″.

The Space Before and Space After fields determine how much space is placed between the span paragraph and the paragraphs above or below. (This is the same concept used in the Space Above and Space Below options for regular paragraph formatting.)

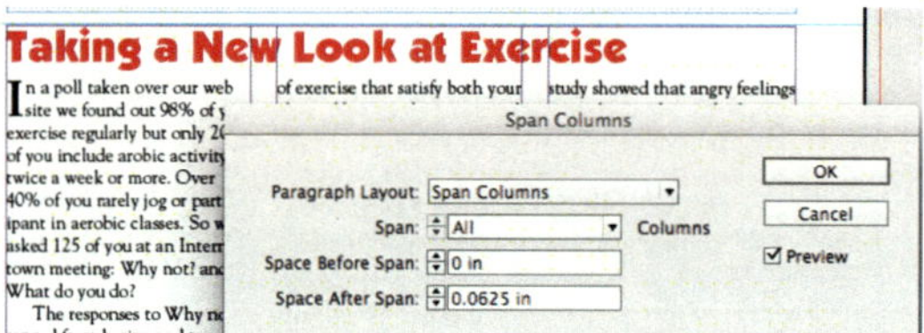

7. **Click OK to finalize your changes, then look at the Paragraph Styles panel.**

The Article Heading style, which you applied to the active paragraph, now shows a + next to the style name. Remember, this indicates a local formatting override, which is intentional in this case.

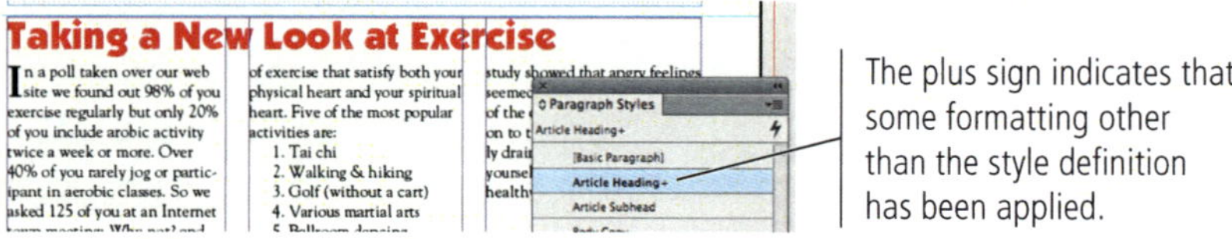

The plus sign indicates that some formatting other than the style definition has been applied.

8. **Save the file and continue to the next exercise.**

Create a Sidebar Box

Many page layouts have a primary story (which might flow across multiple pages), as well as related-but-not-connected stories called **sidebars**. These elements are usually not linked to the main story, and they are often placed in their own boxes with some unique formatting to draw attention to the box. Amateur designers often create three separate elements to achieve this effect — an unnecessary degree of complexity when you can change multiple text frame options to create the effect with a single object.

1. **On Page 1 of `newsletter_dec.indd`, create a new text frame with the following dimensions (based on the top-left reference point):**

   X: 3.67″ W: 3.95″
   Y: 7.6″ H: 2″

2. **Fill the text frame with a 20% tint of Pantone 1945 C.**

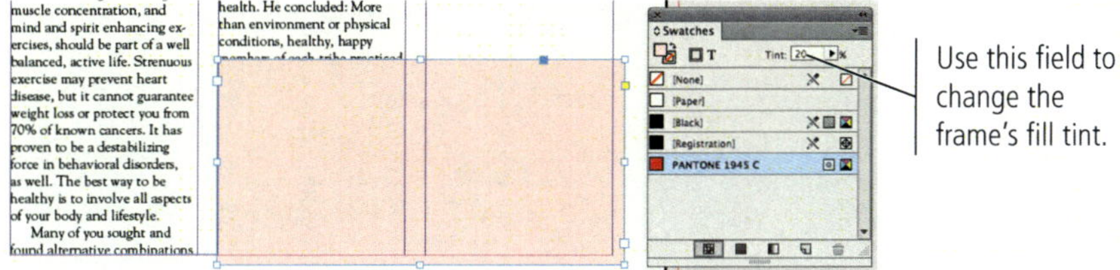

3. **Place the file `sidebar.doc` into the new frame, preserving the formatting in the imported file. Click OK if you see a Missing Font warning.**

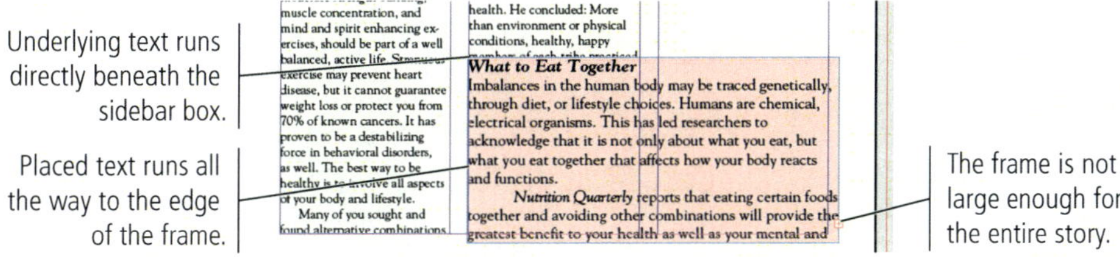

4. **With the sidebar box selected, press Command/Control-B to open the Text Frame Options dialog box.**

5. **Make sure the Preview option is checked, and click the Auto-Size button at the top of the dialog box to display those options.**

   Auto-size options allow a text frame to expand or shrink as necessary to fit the contained text. You are going to use these options to dynamically change the sidebar box to fit the entire story, regardless of formatting options.

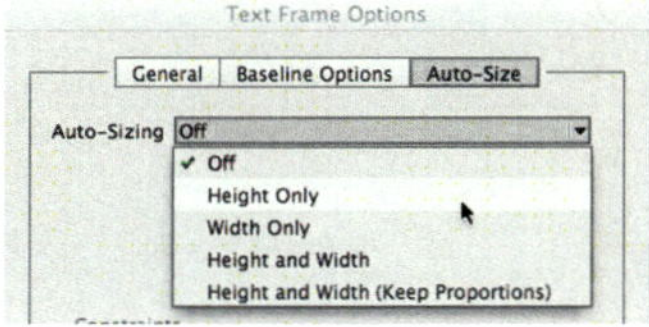

6. **Choose Height Only in the Auto-Sizing menu and choose the bottom-center reference point.**

   The reference points in this dialog box are very similar to the ones in the Control panel; they determine which point will remain fixed when the box changes size.

   In this case, you want the bottom edge to remain in place, so you are choosing the bottom reference point. Because you are only allowing the box's height to change, the left and right reference points are not available.

   You can also use the Constraints options to define a minimum height and width — in other words, the smallest possible size the frame can be.

   If you allow the frame to change width, you can check the No Line Breaks option to enlarge the frame as much as necessary to fit the entire text on one line.

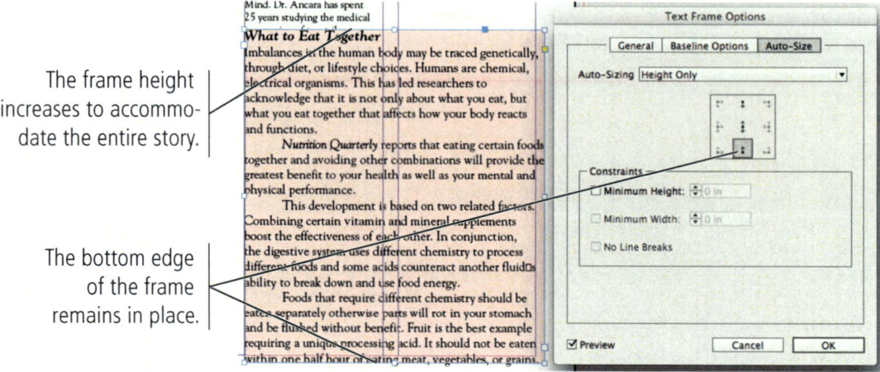

7. **Click OK to apply your changes.**

8. **Format the first line of the sidebar with the Sidebar Heading style.**

9. **Format the rest of the text in this frame using the Sidebar Text style.**

10. **If any applied style shows local overrides, clear overrides for the affected paragraphs.**

    The type sizes in the applied styles are considerably smaller, which requires less space for the sidebar. As you can see, the Auto-Size feature shrinks the height of the frame as necessary to exactly fit the contained text.

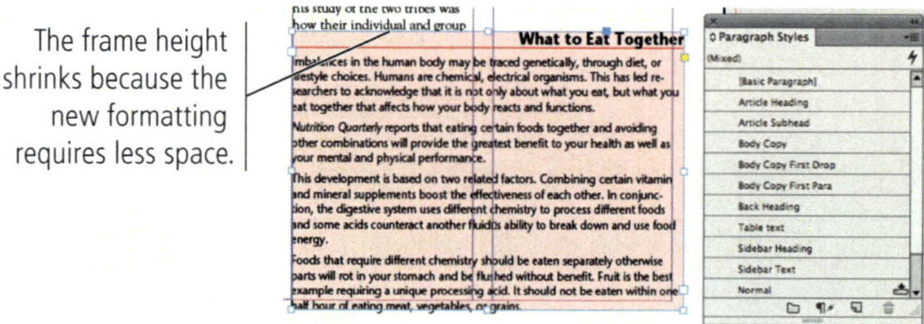

11. **Save the file and continue to the next exercise.**

Edit Text Inset and Wrap Settings

A number of frame attributes can affect the appearance of text both within and around a text frame. In this exercise, you adjust the text inset and text wrap to force text into the proper position.

1. **With `newsletter_dec.indd` open, select the sidebar box and open the Text Frame Options dialog box (Objects>Text Frame Options).**

2. **With the Preview option checked, make sure the chain icon for the Inset Spacing fields is active.**

   Like the same chain icon in other dialog boxes, this forces all four inset values to the same value.

3. **Change the Top Inset field to `0.1"`, and then press Tab to move the highlight and apply the new Inset Spacing value to all four fields.**

   Text inset spacing is the distance text is moved from the inside edge of its containing frame. You can define different values for each edge, or you can constrain all four edges to a single value.

Note:

If you check the Ignore Text Wrap option in the Text Frame Options dialog box, the frame is not affected by wrap attributes of overlapping objects.

The frame height enlarges to accommodate the new frame options and still contain the entire story.

Increasing the text inset moves the text away (in) from the frame edges.

When this button is active (an unbroken chain), all four inset fields have the same value.

4. **Click OK to close the dialog box and apply your choices.**

5. **Open the Text Wrap panel (Window>Text Wrap).**

   Text wrap is the distance around the edge of an object where surrounding text will flow.

6. **Click the sidebar frame with the Selection tool, and then click the second button from the left in the Text Wrap panel.**

7. **Make sure the chain icon is active so all four offset values are the same. Change the Top Offset field to `0.1"` and then press Tab to apply the value to all four fields.**

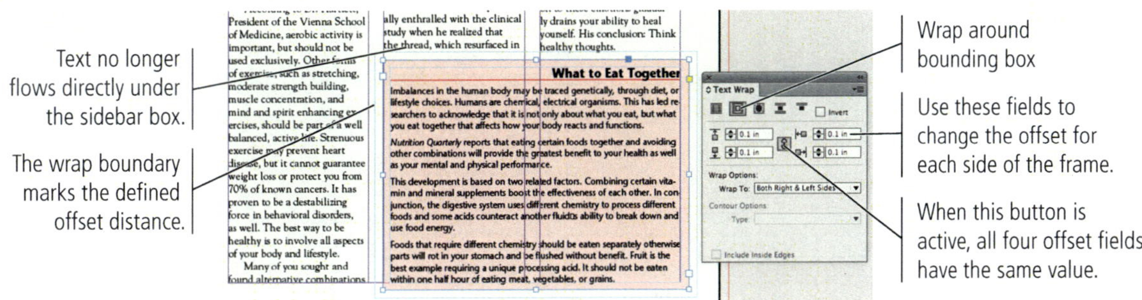

8. **Save the file and continue to the next stage of the project.**

Text Wrap Options

By default, text wrap attributes affect all overlapping objects, regardless of stacking order; you can turn this behavior off by checking the Text Wrap Only Affects Text Beneath option in the Composition pane of the Preferences dialog box. InDesign provides five options for wrapping text around an object; specific wrap attributes are controlled in the Text Wrap panel.

- **No Text Wrap** allows text to run directly under the object.
- **Wrap Around Bounding Box** creates a straight-edged wrap around all four sides of the object's bounding box.
- **Wrap Around Object Shape** creates a wrap in the shape of the object. In this case, you can also define which contour to use:
  - **Bounding Box** creates the boundary based on the object's bounding box.
  - **Detect Edges** creates the boundary using the same detection options you use to create a clipping path.
  - **Alpha Channel** creates the boundary from an Alpha channel saved in the placed image.
  - **Photoshop Path** creates the boundary from a path saved in the placed image.
  - **Graphic Frame** creates the boundary from the containing frame.
  - **Same as Clipping** creates the boundary from a clipping path saved in the placed image.
  - **User-Modified Path** appears by default if you drag the anchor points of the text wrap boundary.
- **Jump Object** keeps text from appearing to the right or left of the frame.
- **Jump to Next Column** forces surrounding text to the top of the next column or frame.

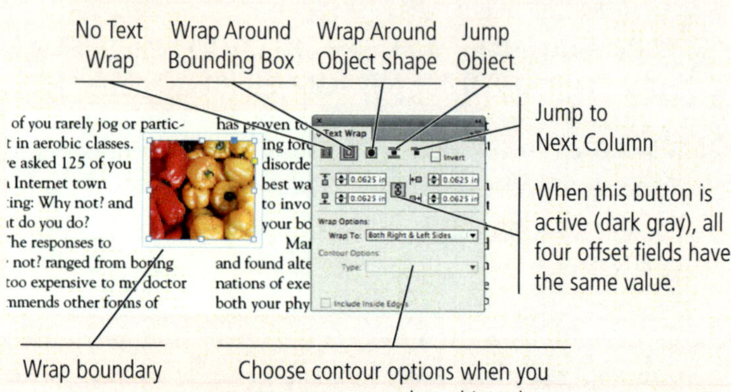

Regardless of which wrap you apply, you can define the offset value, the distance that any surrounding text will remain away from the object. (If you use the Object Shape wrap option, you can define only a single offset value; for the other types, you can define a different offset value for each edge.

If you use the Bounding Box or Object Shape wrap option, you can also define the Wrap To options — whether the wrap is applied to a specific side (right, left, right and left, or the largest side), or toward or away from the spine.

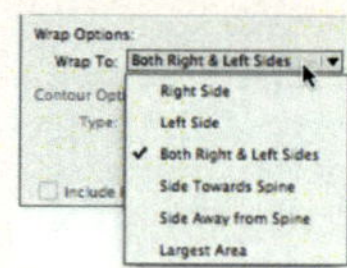

Stage 3 Working with Tables

Many page layouts incorporate tables of information, from basic tables with a few rows and columns to multi-page catalog spreadsheets with thousands of product numbers and prices. InDesign includes a number of options for building tables, each having advantages and disadvantages depending on what you need to accomplish. Regardless of which method you use to create a table, the same options are available for formatting the table, the cells in the table, and the content in the cells.

When you place an insertion point in an existing text frame, you can create a new table from scratch by choosing Table>Insert Table. This method allows you to define your own table parameters, including the number of rows and columns, the number of header and footer rows (top and bottom rows that appear in every instance of the table if the table breaks across multiple columns or frames), and even a defined style for the new table (table styles store formatting options such as gridline weight and color, cell inset, and other attributes that will you learn about in this stage of the project).

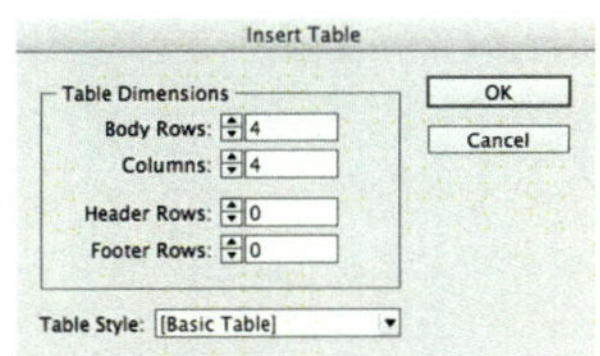

You can also create a table by selecting a series of tab-delimited text in the layout and choosing Table>Convert Text to Table. (Tab-delimited means that the content of each column is separated by a tab character.) Using this method, the new table becomes an inline object in the text frame that contained the original tabbed text.

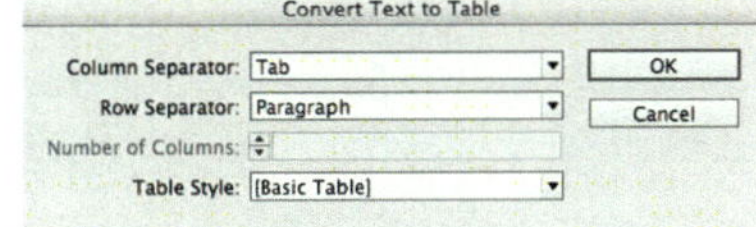

Finally, you can create a new table in InDesign by placing a file created in Microsoft Excel, the most common application for creating spreadsheets. You'll use this method to complete this stage of the HeartSmart newsletter project.

Place a Microsoft Excel Table

Microsoft Excel spreadsheets can be short tables of text or complex, multi-page spreadsheets of data. In either case, Microsoft Excel users tend to spend hours formatting their spreadsheets for business applications. Those formatting options are typically not appropriate for commercial printing applications, but they give you a better starting point in your InDesign file than working from plain tabbed text.

1. **With newsletter_dec.indd open, navigate to Page 2. Click the pasteboard area to make sure nothing is selected.**

2. **Choose File>Place and navigate to the file nutrition.xls in the WIP>HeartSmart>December folder.**

3. **Uncheck the Replace Selected Item option, make sure Show Import Options is checked, and click Open.**

4. **Review the options in the resulting dialog box. Make sure your options match what is shown in the following image, and then click OK.**

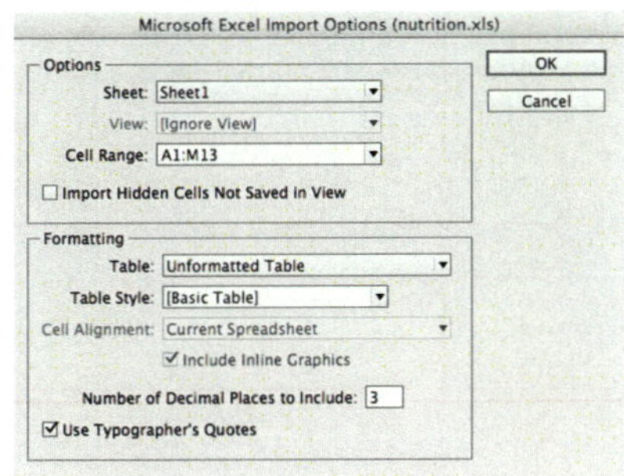

Note:

If you see a warning about missing fonts, click OK; you're going to reformat the table text in the next exercise, so missing fonts won't be a problem.

5. **With the table loaded into the cursor, click in the empty right column in the top half of the page.**

   The new table is placed into the layout; a text frame is automatically created to contain the table. Although your table might not exactly match what you see in our screen capture, several things will be consistent: the table currently extends beyond the right edge of the text frame, and the overset text icon in the frame's Out port indicates that the frame is not high enough to fit all the rows of the table.

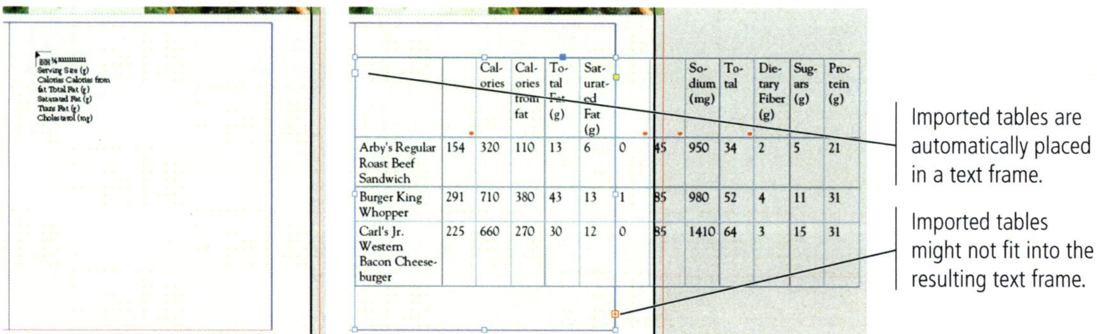

Imported tables are automatically placed in a text frame.

Imported tables might not fit into the resulting text frame.

   Obviously this table still needs some significant modification to make it a cohesive part of the newsletter layout. Some placed tables require more work than others, but be prepared to do at least some clean-up work whenever you place a spreadsheet or table.

6. **Drag the text frame with the table to the top edge of the right column.**

7. **Control/right-click the table and choose Fitting>Fit Frame to Content. If you still see an overset text icon, click the bottom-center handle of the text frame and drag to the bottom page edge.**

   This is the same command you can use to resize a graphics frame; in this case, you're making the text frame big enough to show the entire table width and height. You should now be able to see the bottom row of the table.

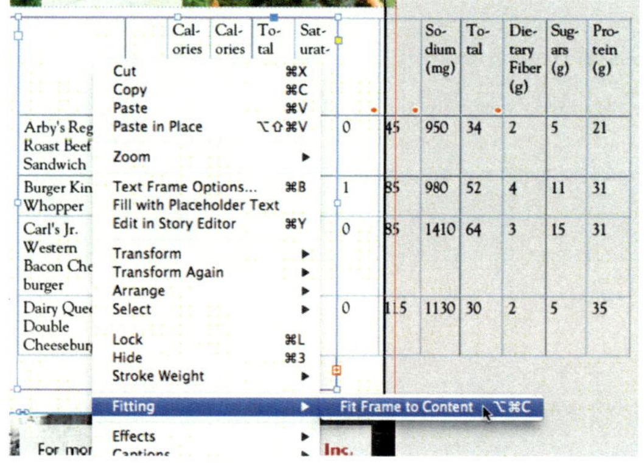

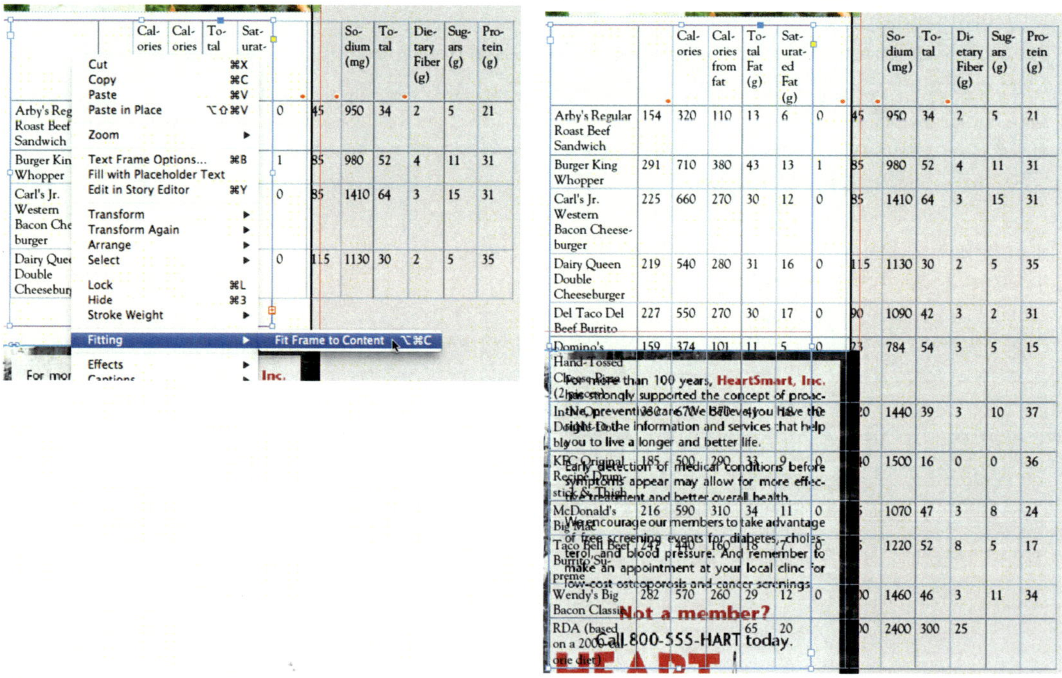

8. **Save the file and continue to the next exercise.**

Format Cell Contents

When you work with tables in InDesign, think of the table cells as a series of text frames. Text in a table cell is no different than text in any other text frame; it can be formatted using the same options you've already learned, including with paragraph and character styles.

> *Note:*
>
> *When working with tables in InDesign, pressing Tab moves the insertion point from one table cell to the next (from left to right, top to bottom). This means you can't press Tab to insert a tab character into text in an InDesign table; you have to choose Type>Insert Special Character>Other>Tab.*

1. **With `newsletter_dec.indd` open, select the Type tool and click in the top-left cell of the table.**

   You have to use the Type tool to select table cells, either individually, or as entire rows/ columns.

2. **Move the cursor over the top-left corner of the table. When you see a diagonal arrow pointing down and right, click to select all cells in the table.**

   At the time of this writing, there is a bug on the Macintosh operating system that might cause this method to fail. If the entire table does not appear to be selected after clicking near the top-left corner, you can click and drag to select all cells in the table.

3. **Click Table Text in the Paragraph Styles panel to format all the text in the selected table cells.**

4. **If a plus sign appears next to the Table Text style name (in the Paragraph Styles panel), click the Clear Overrides in Selection button at the bottom of the panel to apply only the base style definition to the text.**

   As with files from Microsoft Word, some options in Microsoft Excel spreadsheets might require this two-step process to apply your style definitions to the selected text.

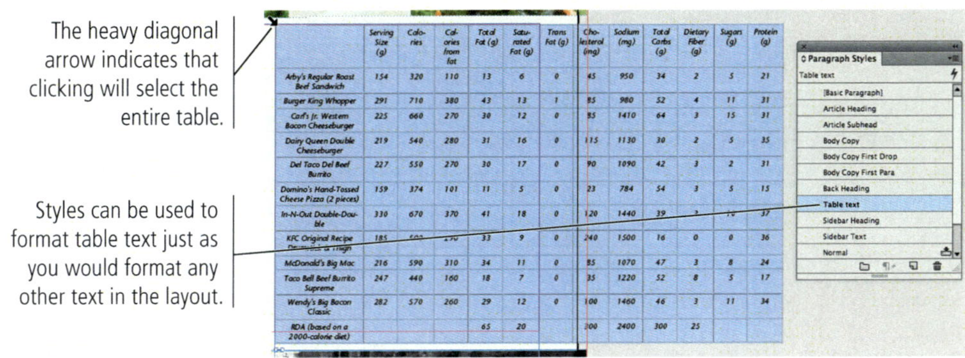

5. **Click in any cell to deselect all table cells.**

6. **Place the cursor over the top edge of the first column of the table. When you see a down-pointing arrow, click to select the entire column.**

   You can also select rows by placing the cursor immediately to the left of a row and clicking when the cursor changes to a right-facing arrow.

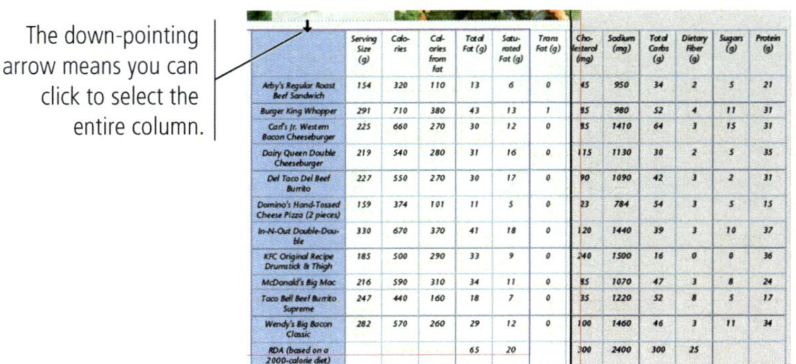

7. **Change the selected column to left paragraph alignment.**

   You can use the Control panel or Paragraph panel, or simply press Command/Control-L to change the alignment of the text within the table cell.

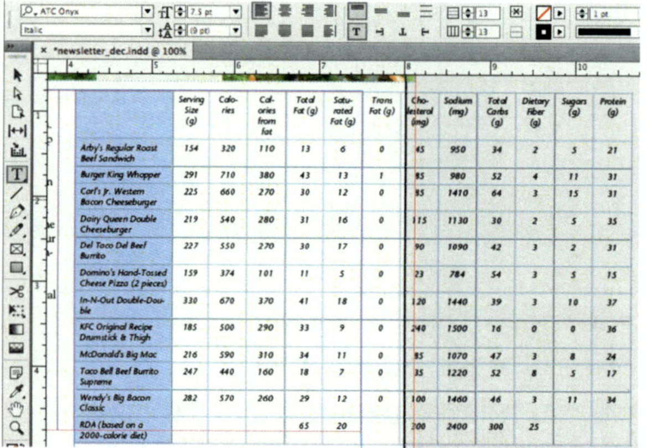

> ***Note:***
>
> *Text is still text, even though it's placed inside a table cell. You can apply all of the same text-formatting options to table text that you can apply to text in a regular text frame.*

8. **Save the file and continue to the next exercise.**

Format Cell Attributes

As we mentioned in the previous exercise, table cells are very similar to regular text frames. Individual cells can have different attributes such as height and width, text inset, vertical positioning, and text orientation. These options can be controlled in the Table panel, the Control panel, and the Cell Options dialog box.

1. **With newsletter_dec.indd open, click in the second cell of the first row and then drag right to select all cells in the row except the first cell.**

2. **In the Table panel (Window>Type & Tables>Table), choose Exactly in the Row Height menu, and then change the field to 0.875".**

3. **Change the Column Width field to 0.2785".**

4. **Click the Rotate Text 270° button so the left edge of the text aligns to the bottom edge of the cell.**

5. **Click the Align Center button so the text in each cell is centered vertically.**

   Because the text is rotated, this button actually aligns the text between the left and right cell edges. It's important to remember that the vertical align options are based on the orientation of the text.

6. **Apply left paragraph alignment to the selected text.**

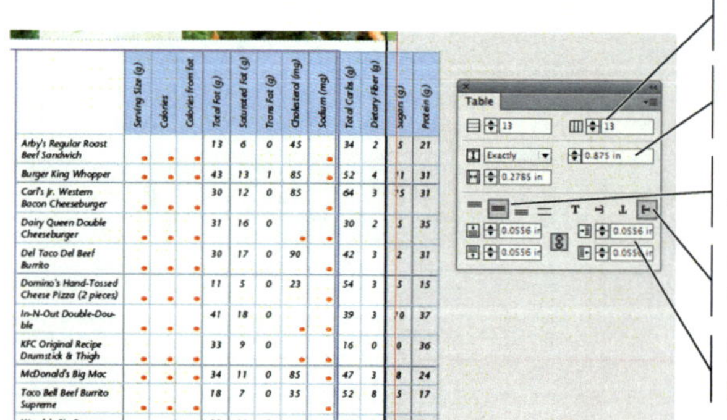

Use these fields to change the number of rows and columns.

Use these fields to control the height and width of cells.

Use these buttons to change the vertical alignment of text within cells.

Use these buttons to rotate text within the cells.

Use these fields to define inset values for cells.

7. **Click the second cell in the second row, then drag down and right to select all the cells that contain numeric data.**

8. **Apply centered vertical alignment to the selected cells.**

9. **Make sure the chain icon for the cell inset fields is active. Change the Top Cell Inset field to 0 and then press Tab to apply the same value to all four fields.**

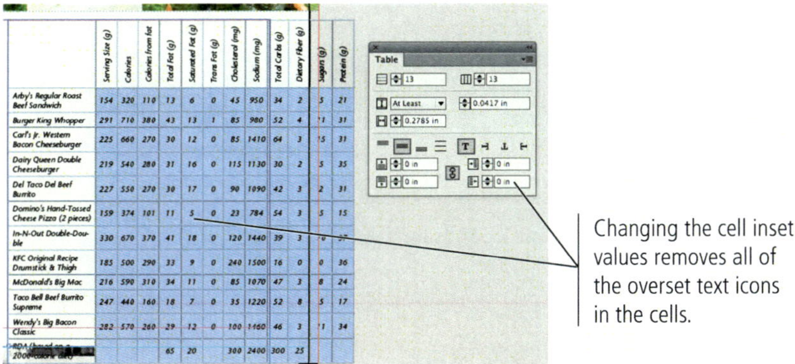

10. **Select the entire first column of the table and change only the Left Cell Inset value to `0.0625`″.**

    To change only one value, you have to make sure the chain icon is not active.

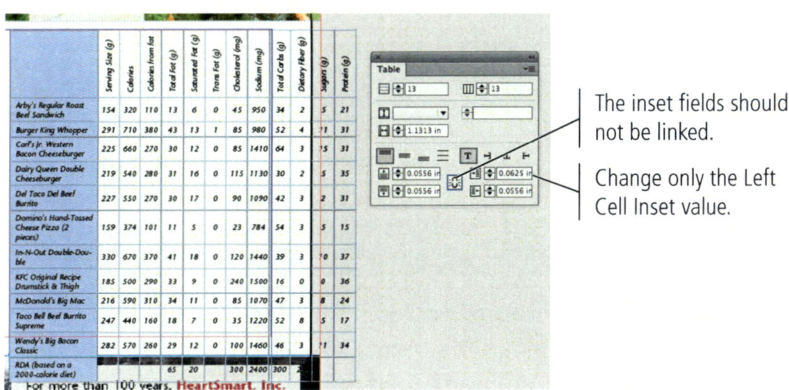

11. **Place the cursor over the right edge of the first column until the cursor becomes a two-headed arrow.**

    When you see this cursor, you can drag the gridline to resize a column or row.

12. **Click and drag right until the column is wide enough to allow the Wendy's Big Bacon Classic to fit on one line.**

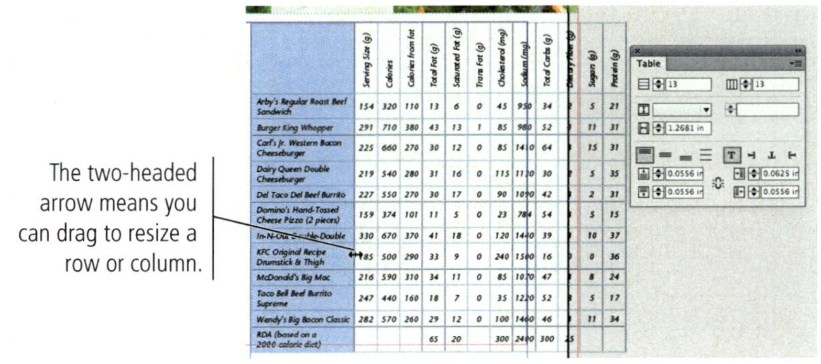

Note:

Resizing the width of a cell resizes the entire column; resizing the height of a cell resizes the entire row.

You can press the Shift key while dragging a gridline to resize a row or column without affecting the overall table size; only the rows or columns next to the gridline you drag are resized.

13. **Place the insertion point in the cell with the Wendy's product name.**

When you make the column wide enough to fit the text, the row automatically shrinks to one row. In the Table panel, you can see that the Row Height menu is set to At Least; this option allows cells to shrink to fit the height of cell contents, down to the defined minimum height.

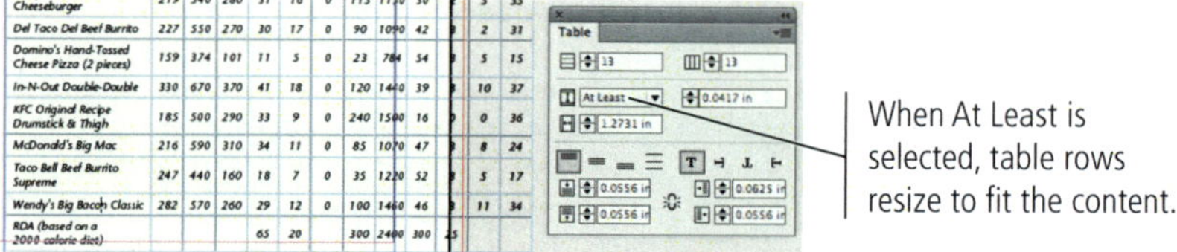

When At Least is selected, table rows resize to fit the content.

14. **Select the first four cells in the last row and choose Table>Merge Cells.**

This function extends the contents of a single cell across multiple cells. (You can also open the Table panel Options menu and choose Merge Cells.)

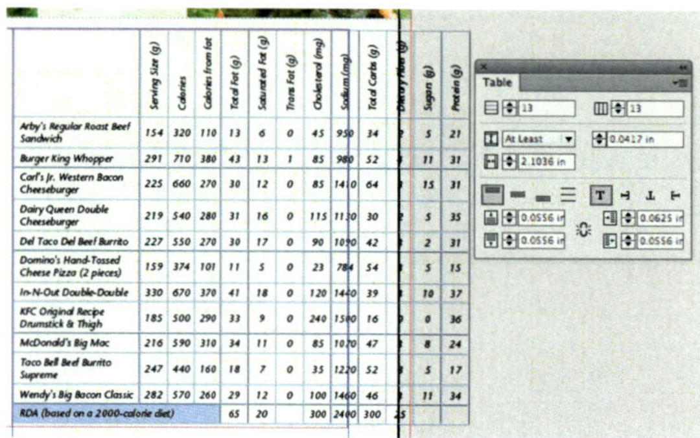

> *Note:*
>
> *When the insertion point is placed in a table cell, press the Escape key to select the active cell.*

15. **Save the file and continue to the next exercise.**

Define Table Fills and Strokes

Like text frames, table cells can also have fill and stroke attributes. InDesign includes a number of options for adding color to tables, from changing the stroke and fill of an individual cell to defining patterns that repeat every certain number of rows and/or columns.

1. **With newsletter_dec.indd open, make sure the insertion point is somewhere in the table on Page 2. Open the Table panel Options menu and choose Table Options>Table Setup.**

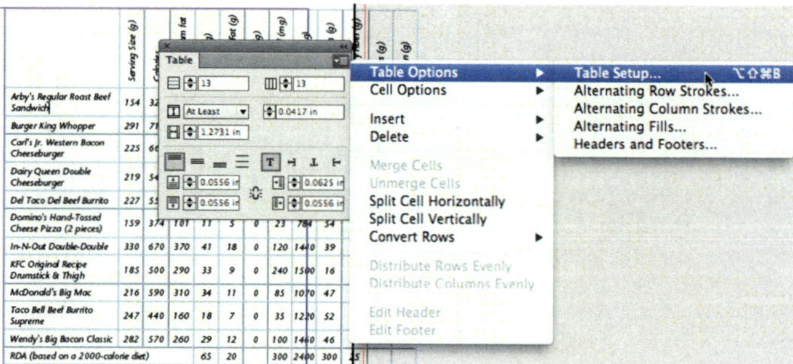

2. **In the Table Setup tab, apply a 0.5-pt solid border of 100% Pantone 1945 C.**

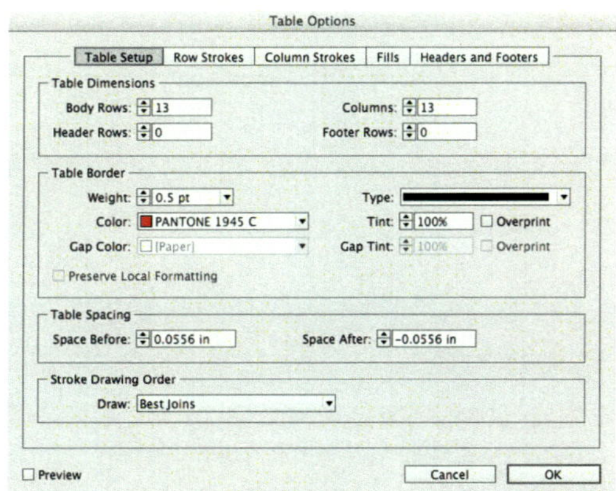

> *Note:*
>
> *You can also choose Table>Table Options>Table Setup to access this dialog box.*

> *Note:*
>
> *In the Table Options dialog box, you can use the Row Strokes and Column Strokes tabs to define patterns based on a sequence you choose in the Alternating Pattern menus.*

3. **In the Fills tab, choose Every Other Row in the Alternating Pattern menu.**
   Set the First field to 1 row and apply 20% Pantone 1945 C.
   Set the Next field to 1 row and apply None as the color.
   Change the Skip First field to 1 Row.

When frame edges are visible, it's difficult (if not impossible) to see the table border and cell strokes.

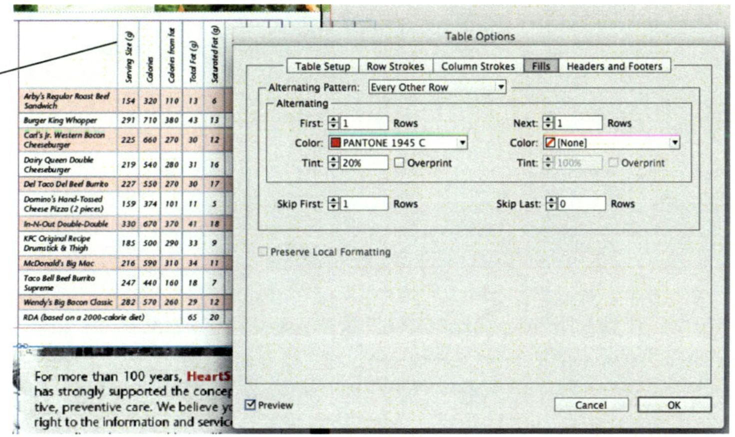

4. **Click OK to apply your choices.**

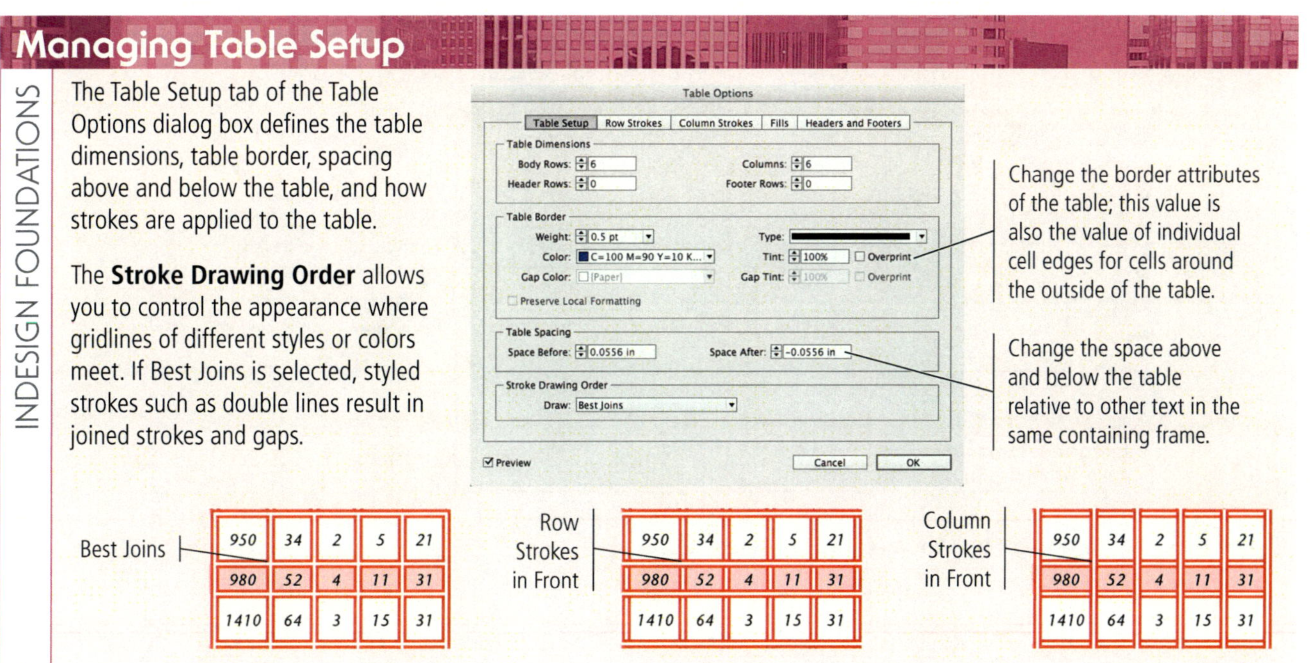

Managing Table Setup

INDESIGN FOUNDATIONS

The Table Setup tab of the Table Options dialog box defines the table dimensions, table border, spacing above and below the table, and how strokes are applied to the table.

The **Stroke Drawing Order** allows you to control the appearance where gridlines of different styles or colors meet. If Best Joins is selected, styled strokes such as double lines result in joined strokes and gaps.

5. **Select the last row in the table. Using the Swatches panel, change the cell fill tint to 50% of the Pantone 1945 C swatch.**

   Remember, table cells are very similar to individual text frames. You can change the color of cell fills and strokes using the Swatches panel, and you can change the cell stroke attributes using the Stroke panel.

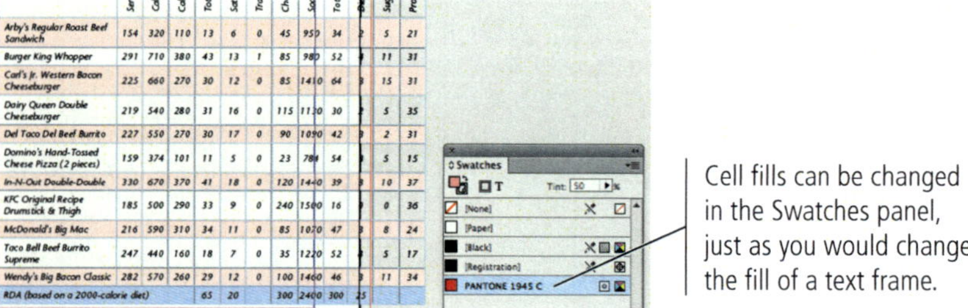

Cell fills can be changed in the Swatches panel, just as you would change the fill of a text frame.

6. **Select all cells in the table. Open the Table panel Options menu and choose Cell Options>Strokes and Fills.**

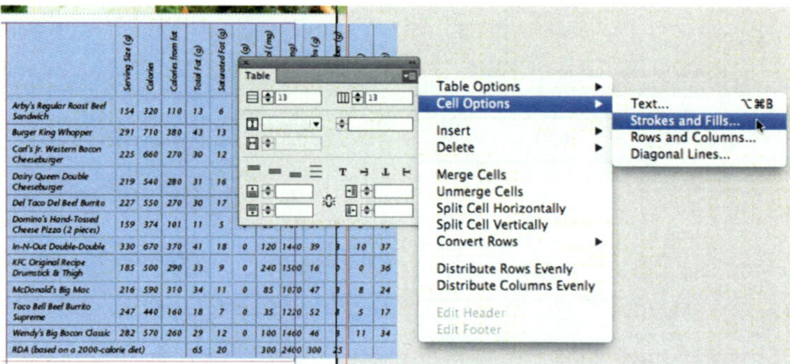

7. **In the preview area of the dialog box, click all three horizontal lines to remove the strokes from the active selection.**

   The preview area shows what strokes you are affecting in the dialog box. Because only the vertical lines are still visible in the preview, you are going to change only the attributes of the vertical gridlines in the table.

8. **Apply a 0.5-pt, 100% Pantone 1945 C stroke value, using the Solid stroke type.**

   These settings change the attributes of the vertical gridlines for all selected cells.

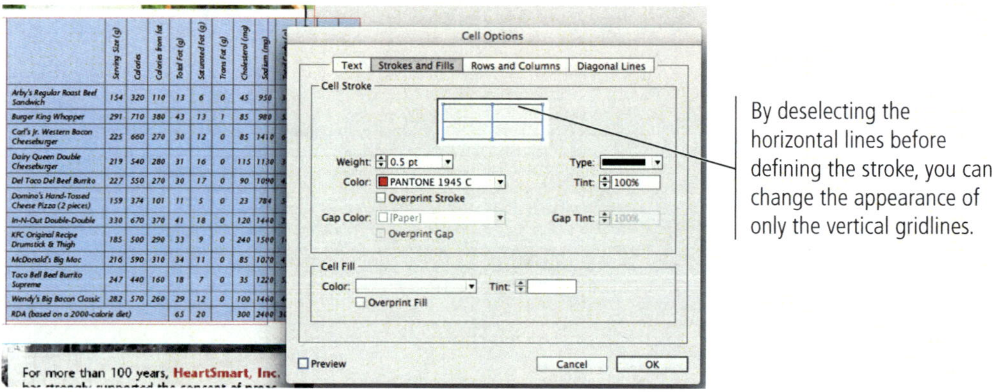

By deselecting the horizontal lines before defining the stroke, you can change the appearance of only the vertical gridlines.

9. **Click OK to apply the stroke values to your table.**

10. **Click away from the table to deselect it, and then choose View>Extras> Hide Frame Edges to review the table formatting.**

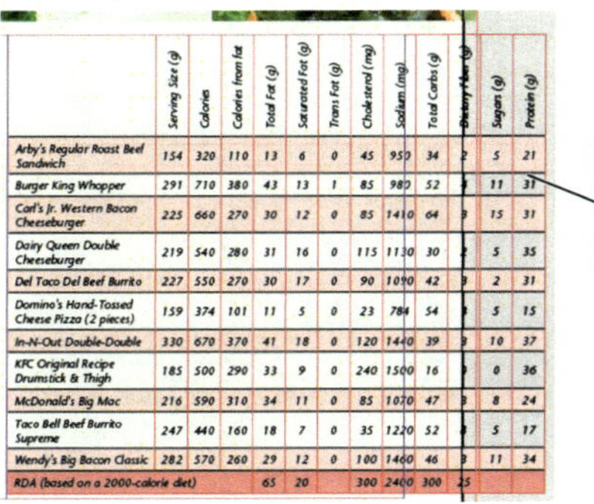

	Serving Size (g)	Calories	Calories from fat	Total Fat (g)	Saturated Fat (g)	Trans Fat (g)	Cholesterol (mg)	Sodium (mg)	Total Carbs (g)	Dietary Fiber (g)	Sugars (g)	Protein (g)
Arby's Regular Roast Beef Sandwich	154	320	110	13	6	0	45	950	34	[illegible]	5	21
Burger King Whopper	291	710	380	43	13	1	85	980	52	[illegible]	11	31
Carl's Jr. Western Bacon Cheeseburger	225	660	270	30	12	0	85	1410	64	[illegible]	15	31
Dairy Queen Double Cheeseburger	219	540	280	31	16	0	115	1130	30	[illegible]	5	35
Del Taco Del Beef Burrito	227	550	270	30	17	0	90	1090	42	[illegible]	2	31
Domino's Hand-Tossed Cheese Pizza (2 pieces)	159	374	101	11	5	0	23	784	54	[illegible]	5	15
In-N-Out Double-Double	330	670	370	41	18	0	120	1440	39	[illegible]	10	37
KFC Original Recipe Drumstick & Thigh	185	500	290	33	9	0	240	1500	16	[illegible]	0	36
McDonald's Big Mac	216	590	310	34	11	0	85	1070	47	[illegible]	8	24
Taco Bell Beef Burrito Supreme	247	440	160	18	7	0	35	1220	52	[illegible]	5	17
Wendy's Big Bacon Classic	282	570	260	29	12	0	100	1460	46	[illegible]	11	34
RDA (based on a 2000-calorie diet)				65	20		300	2400	300	25		

The table still has a black stroke on the horizontal gridlines.

Note:

If you can't see the borders and strokes, try hiding frame edges (View>Extras>Hide Frame Edges) while you experiment with these options.

11. **Select all but the first and last rows of the table, then open the Cell Options dialog box again.**

Controlling Cell Attributes

INDESIGN FOUNDATIONS

Basic attributes of table cells can be defined in the Text tab of the Cell Options dialog box (Table>Cell Options). Most table cell options are exactly the same as for regular text frames; the only choice unique to tables is **Clip Contents to Cell**. If you set a fixed row height that's too small for the cell content, an overset text icon appears in the lower-right corner of the cell. (You can't flow text from one table cell to another.) If you check the Clip Contents to Cell option, any content that doesn't fit in the cell will be clipped.

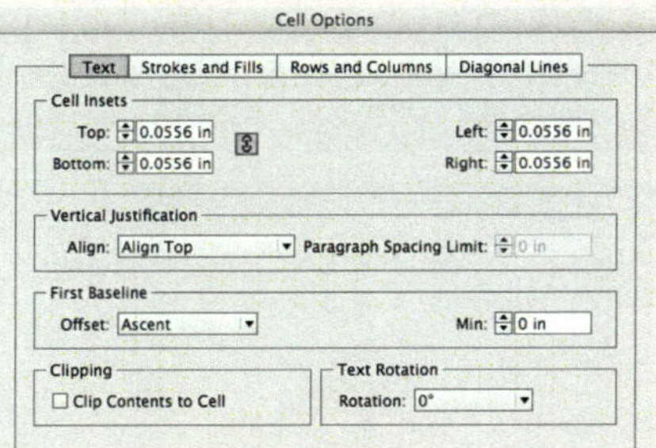

As with any text frame, a table cell can have its own fill and stroke attributes. These attributes can be defined in the Strokes and Fills tab (or using the Swatches and Stroke panels). You can turn individual cell edges (strokes) on or off by clicking specific lines in the preview.

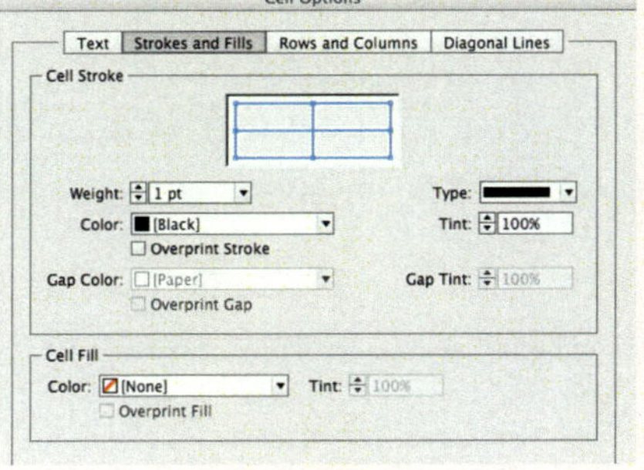

The Rows and Columns tab controls row height and column width. If **At Least** is selected in the Row Height menu, you can define the minimum and maximum possible row height; rows change height if you add or remove text, or if you change the text formatting in a way that requires more or less space. If **Exactly** is selected, you can define the exact height of the cell.

If you're working with an extremely long table, you can break the table across multiple frames by threading (as you would for any long block of text). The **Keep Options** can be used to keep specific (selected) rows together after a break, and they determine where those rows will go, based on your choice in the Start Row menu.

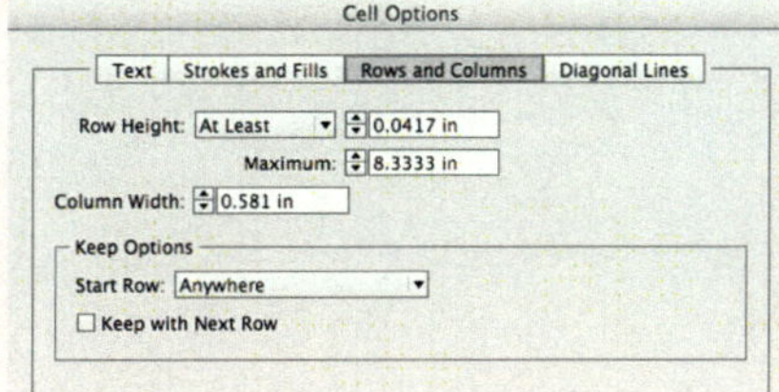

You can add diagonal lines to specific cells using the Diagonal Lines tab. You can apply lines in either direction (or both) and choose a specific stroke weight, color, style, and tint. The Draw menu determines whether the line is created in front of or behind the cell's contents.

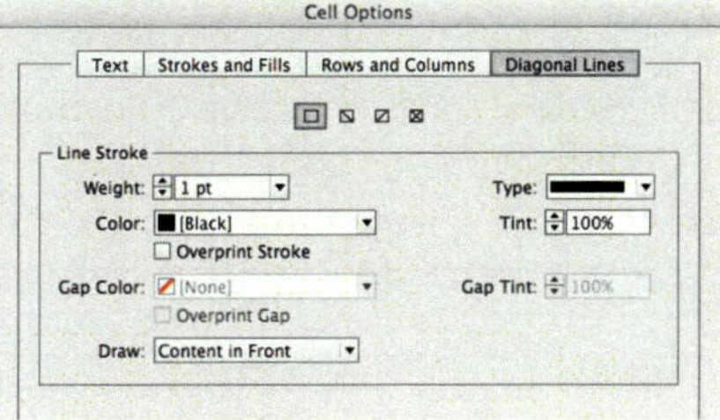

12. **In the Strokes and Fills pane, click the three vertical lines in the preview area to remove those strokes from the active selection. With the three horizontal lines selected, change the Weight field to 0 pt, then click OK.**

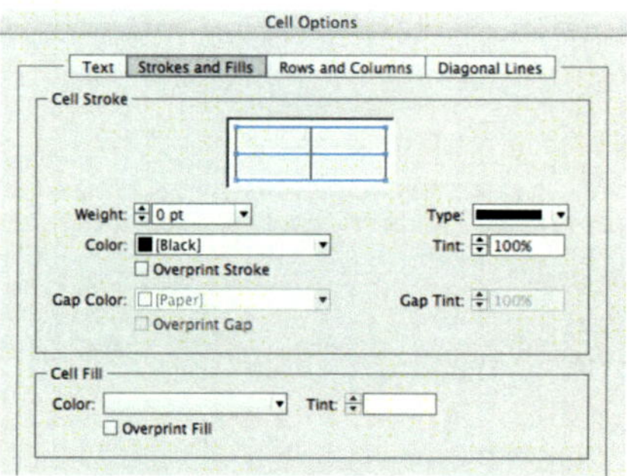

13. **Click away from the table and review the result.**

If you had selected the top and bottom rows, you would have removed the border from the top and bottom edges of the table.

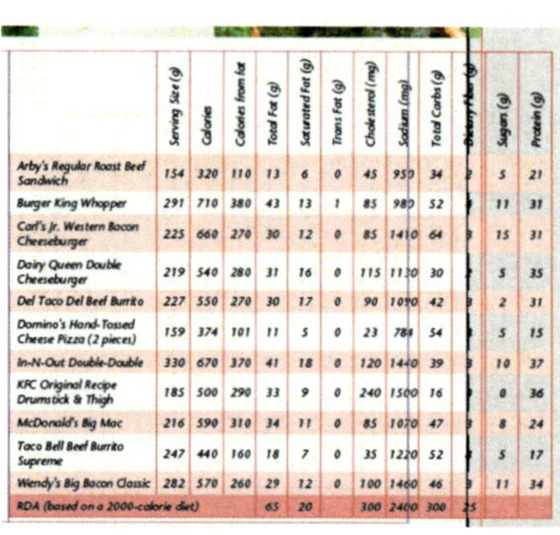

	Serving Size (g)	Calories	Calories from fat	Total Fat (g)	Saturated Fat (g)	Trans Fat (g)	Cholesterol (mg)	Sodium (mg)	Total Carbs (g)	Dietary Fiber (g)	Sugars (g)	Protein (g)
Arby's Regular Roast Beef Sandwich	154	320	110	13	6	0	45	950	34	[illegible]	5	21
Burger King Whopper	291	710	380	43	13	1	85	980	52	[illegible]	11	31
Carl's Jr. Western Bacon Cheeseburger	225	660	270	30	12	0	85	1410	64	[illegible]	15	31
Dairy Queen Double Cheeseburger	219	540	280	31	16	0	115	1130	30	[illegible]	5	35
Del Taco Del Beef Burrito	227	550	270	30	17	0	90	1090	42	[illegible]	2	31
Domino's Hand-Tossed Cheese Pizza (2 pieces)	159	374	101	11	5	0	23	784	54	[illegible]	5	15
In-N-Out Double-Double	330	670	370	41	18	0	120	1440	39	[illegible]	10	37
KFC Original Recipe Drumstick & Thigh	185	500	290	33	9	0	240	1500	16	[illegible]	0	36
McDonald's Big Mac	216	590	310	34	11	0	85	1070	47	[illegible]	8	24
Taco Bell Beef Burrito Supreme	247	440	160	18	7	0	35	1220	52	[illegible]	5	17
Wendy's Big Bacon Classic	282	570	260	29	12	0	100	1460	46	[illegible]	11	34
RDA (based on a 2000-calorie diet)				65	20		300	2400	300	25		

Understanding Table Styles

If you've spent any amount of time refining the appearance of a table, and you think you might want to use the same format again, you can save your formatting choices as a style. InDesign supports both table styles and cell styles, which are controlled in the Table Styles panel and Cell Styles panel.

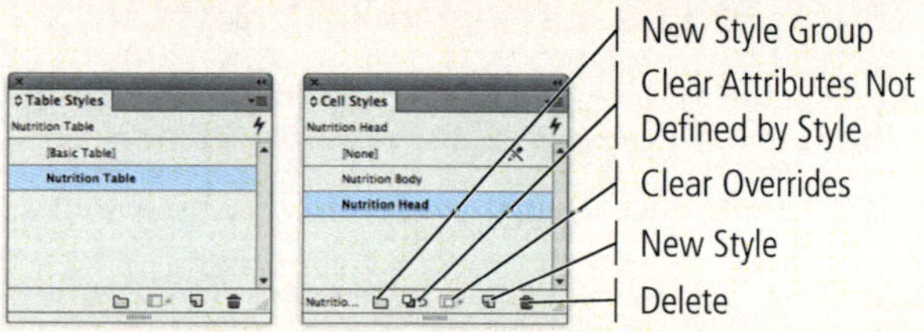

Table and cell styles use the same concept as text-formatting styles. You can apply a cell style by selecting the cells and clicking the style name in the Cell Styles panel. Clicking a style in the Table Styles panel applies the style to the entire selected table.

Table styles store all options that can be defined in the Table Setup dialog box (except the options for header and footer rows). You can also define cell styles (called **nesting styles**) for specific types of rows, as well as the left and right columns in the table.

Cell styles store all options that can be defined in the Cell Options dialog box, including the paragraph style that is applied to cells where that style is applied.

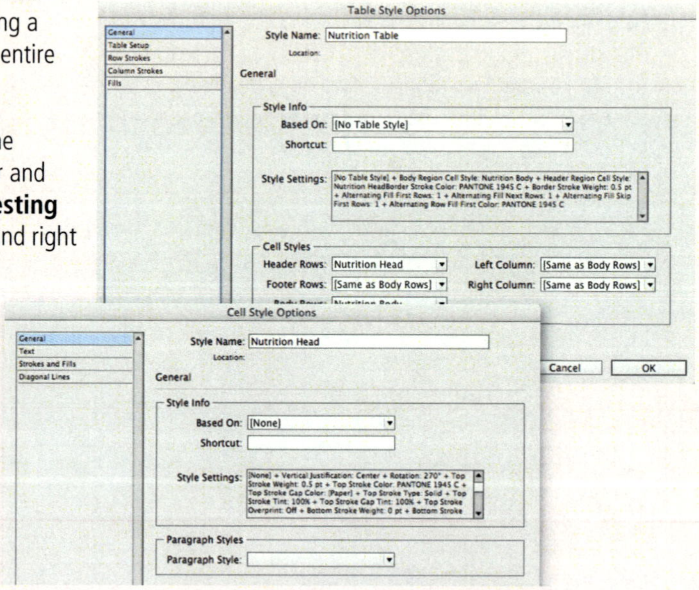

- New Style Group
- Clear Attributes Not Defined by Style
- Clear Overrides
- New Style
- Delete

INDESIGN FOUNDATIONS

Creating Table Headers and Footers

Long tables of data often require more than one text frame (or column, depending on the table). In this case, you can break a table across multiple frames and use repeating headers and footers for information that needs to be part of each instance of the table (for example, column headings). Repeating headers and footers eliminate the need to manually insert the repeating information in each instance of the table.

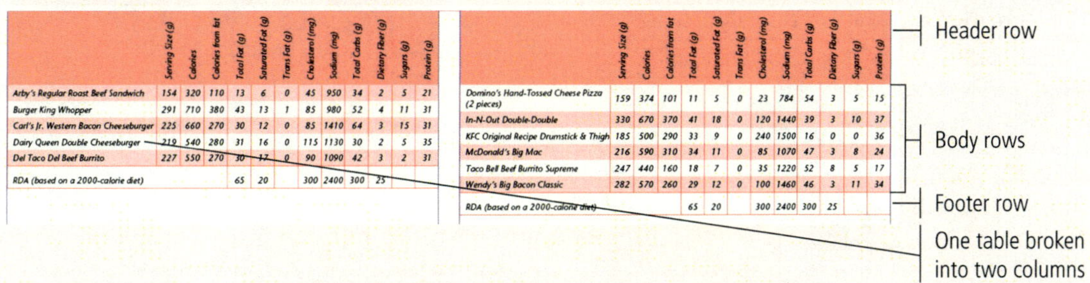

Repeating header and footer rows are dynamically linked; this means that changing one instance of a header or footer changes all instances of the same header or footer.

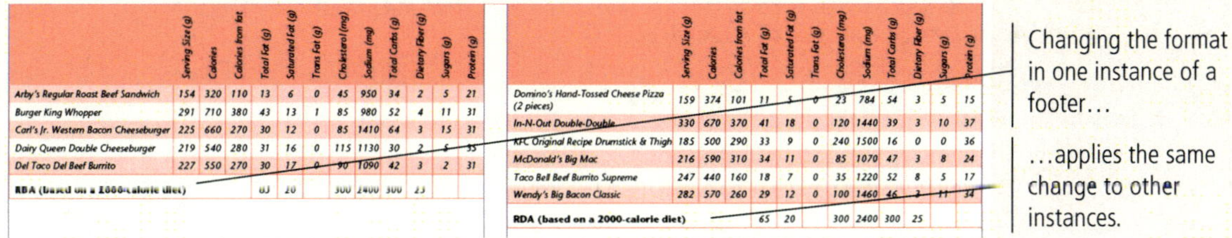

Finally, this capability also means the headers and footers remain at the top and bottom of each instance even if other body rows move to a different instance.

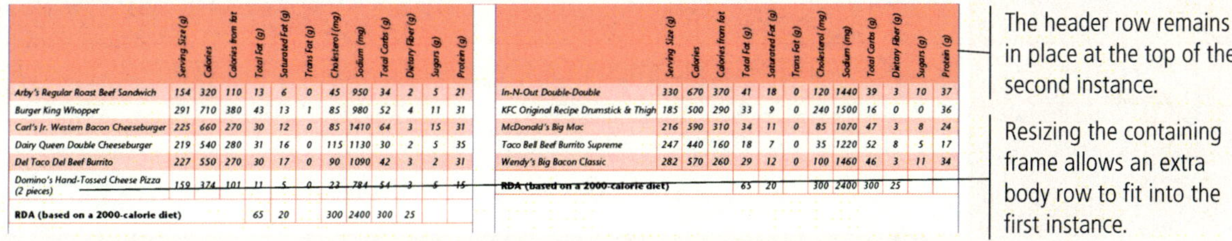

You can add new header and footer rows to a table when you create the table, or by changing the options in the Headers and Footers tab of the Table Options dialog box. You can also convert existing rows to headers or footers by selecting one or more rows and choosing Table>Convert Rows>To Header or To Footer. You can also control these elements in the Headers and Footers dialog box.

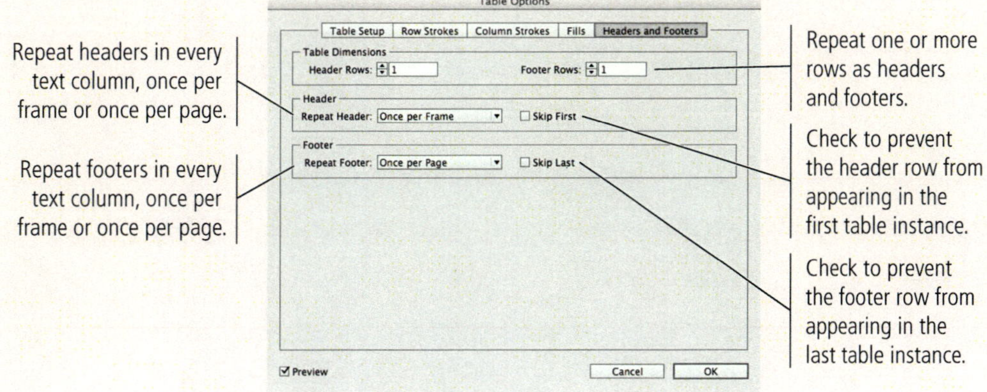

14. **Using the Selection tool, Control/right-click the table and choose Fitting>Fit Frame to Content from the contextual menu.**

15. **Drag the table until the top-right corner of the frame snaps to the top-right margin guide on Page 2.**

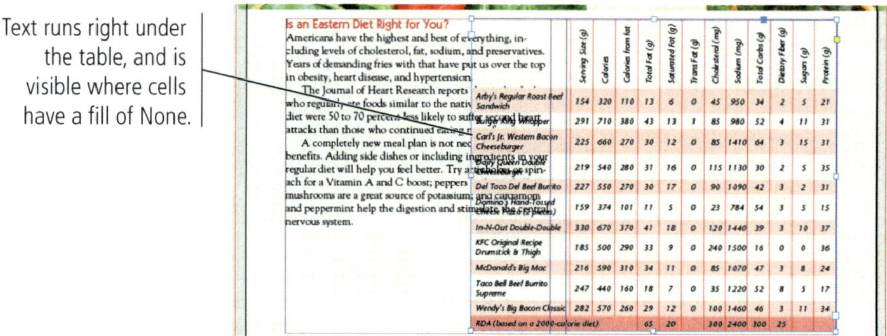

	Serving Size (g)	Calories	Calories from fat	Total Fat (g)	Saturated Fat (g)	Trans Fat (g)	Cholesterol (mg)	Sodium (mg)	Total Carbs (g)	Dietary Fiber (g)	Sugars (g)	Protein (g)
Arby's Regular Roast Beef Sandwich	154	320	110	13	6	0	45	950	34	2	5	21
Burger King Whopper	291	710	380	43	13	1	85	980	52	4	11	31
Carl's Jr. Western Bacon Cheeseburger	225	660	270	30	12	0	85	1410	64	3	15	31
Dairy Queen Double Cheeseburger	219	540	280	31	16	0	115	1130	30	2	5	35
Del Taco Del Beef Burrito	227	550	270	30	17	0	90	1090	42	3	2	31
Domino's Hand-Tossed Cheese Pizza (2 pieces)	159	374	101	11	5	0	23	784	54	3	5	15
In-N-Out Double-Double	330	670	370	41	18	0	120	1440	39	3	10	37
KFC Original Recipe Drumstick & Thigh	185	500	290	33	9	0	240	1500	16	0	0	36
McDonald's Big Mac	216	590	310	34	11	0	85	1070	47	3	8	24
Taco Bell Beef Burrito Supreme	247	440	160	18	7	0	35	1220	52	8	5	17
Wendy's Big Bacon Classic	282	570	260	29	12	0	100	1460	46	3	11	34
RDA (based on a 2000-calorie diet)				65	20		300	2400	300	25		

Text runs right under the table, and is visible where cells have a fill of None.

16. **With the frame still selected, click the second button in the Text Wrap panel (Window>Text Wrap) so the Eastern Diet story wraps around the frame that contains the table. Change the Left Offset field to 0.125″.**

A table is always contained inside a text frame. To control the wrap around a table, you have to actually apply the wrap attributes to the frame that contains the table.

The table's text wrap keeps the copy away from the table edge.

Note:

Remember, you can turn off the Link button in the Text Wrap panel to apply different wrap values to each side of the frame.

17. **Save the file and continue to the final stage of the project.**

Stage 4 Preflighting and Packaging the Job

When you submit an InDesign layout to a commercial output provider, you need to send all of the necessary pieces of the job — the layout file, any placed (linked) graphics or other files, and the fonts used in the layout. Before you copy everything to a disk and send it out, however, you should check your work to make sure the file is ready for commercial printing.

When you opened the original template at the beginning of this project, you replaced missing fonts and graphics — two of the most common problems with digital layout files. However, successful output on a commercial press has a number of other technical requirements that, if you ignore them, can cause a file to output incorrectly or not at all. InDesign includes a preflighting utility that makes it easy to check for potential errors, as well as a packaging utility that gathers all of the necessary bits for the printer.

Check Document Spelling

In this stage of the project, you will learn about preflighting and how to verify that required elements (graphics and fonts) are available. This simple process prevents potential output disasters such as font replacement or low-resolution preview images in the final print.

Many designers understand these issues and carefully monitor the technical aspects of a job. It is all too common, however, to skip another important check — for spelling errors. Misspellings and typos creep into virtually every job despite numerous rounds of content proofs. These errors can ruin an otherwise perfect print job.

Note:

You might not (and probably won't) create the text for most design jobs, and you aren't technically responsible for the words your client supplies. However, you can be a hero if you find and fix typographical errors before a job goes to press; if you don't, you will almost certainly hear about it after it's too late to fix. Remember the cardinal rule of business: the customer is always right. You simply can't brush off a problem by saying, "That's not my job" — at least, not if you want to work with that client in the future.

1. **With newsletter_dec.indd open, open the Dictionary pane of the Preferences dialog box.**

   InDesign checks spelling based on the defined language dictionary — by default, English: USA. You can choose a different language dictionary in the Language menu.

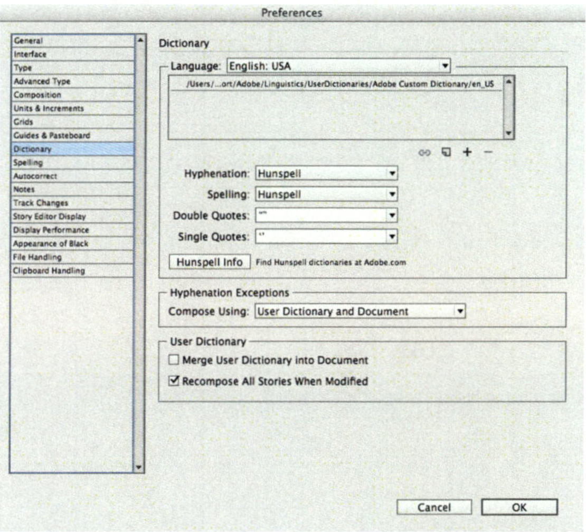

   The application also includes English: USA Legal and English: USA Medical dictionaries that will be of significant benefit to anyone working for either of those industries. If you work with foreign-language publishing, you can choose one of more than 40 different language dictionaries that are installed with InDesign.

2. **Make sure English: USA is selected in the Language menu and click OK.**

3. Choose Edit>Spelling>User Dictionary.

When you check spelling, you are likely to find words that, although spelled correctly, are not in the selected dictionary. Proper names, scientific terms, corporate trademarks, and other custom words are commonly flagged even though they are correct. Rather than flagging these terms every time you recheck spelling, you can add them to a custom user dictionary so InDesign will recognize them the next time you check spelling.

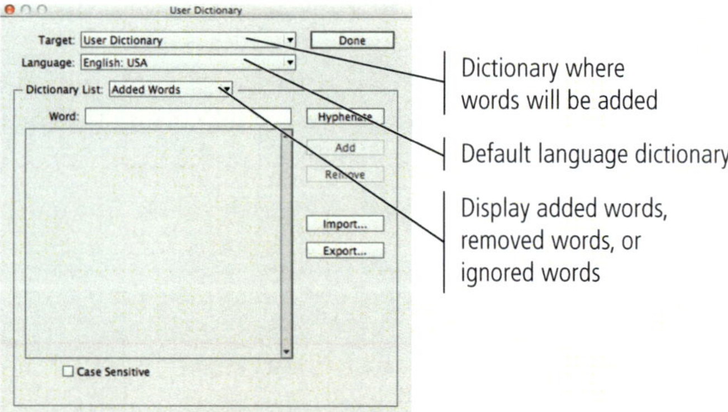

4. In the Target menu, choose newsletter_dec.indd.

By default, the user dictionary is associated with all documents. You can define custom words for a specific file using the Target menu; when you change the user dictionary for a specific file, words you add for that file will still be flagged in other files.

5. In the Word field, type HeartSmart.

Your client's newsletter name is not a real word (even though it is a combination of two real words). If you know that certain words will be flagged, you can manually add those words to the user dictionary at any time.

By adding this word to the file's dictionary (not the language dictionary), you prevent potential errors that might arise if you work on a project that uses the term in a more generic sense. For example, a magazine article about "Heart Smart Casual Dining Choices" should result in an error if the first two words are not separated by a space.

6. Check the Case Sensitive option at the bottom of the dialog box, and then click Add.

If Case Sensitive is not checked, InDesign will not distinguish between HeartSmart (which is correct) and heartsmart (which is incorrect).

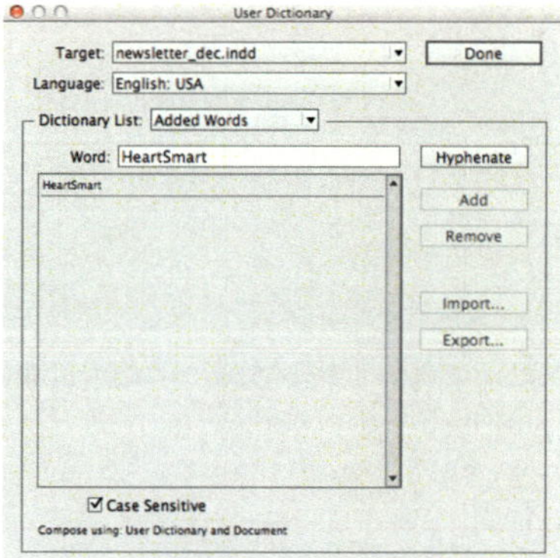

7. Click Done to close the User Dictionary dialog box.

8. **With nothing selected in the layout, choose Edit>Spelling>Check Spelling.**

As soon as you open the Check Spelling dialog box, the first flagged word is highlighted in the layout. The same word appears in the Not in Dictionary field of the Check Spelling dialog box.

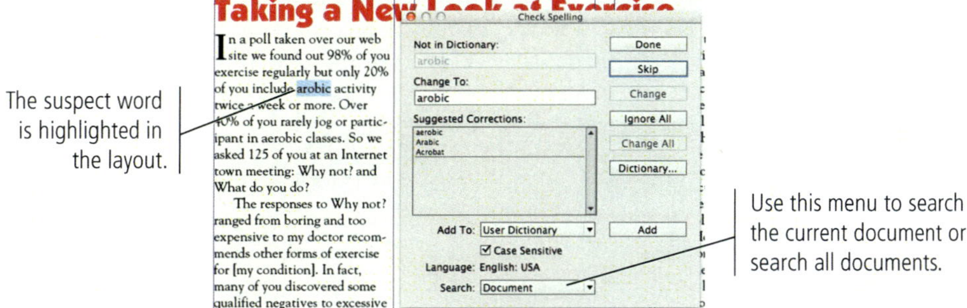

The flagged word (arobic) is misspelled. However, never simply click Change when checking spelling. Review each flagged word carefully and make the correct choices within the context of the layout.

Note:

If the insertion point is currently placed in a story, the Search menu also includes options to search the selected story or the selected story after the insertion point.

9. **Highlight the correct spelling (aerobic) in the Suggested Corrections list and click Change.**

As you can see in the layout, the misspelled word is replaced with the selected alternative; the next suspect word is automatically highlighted in the layout.

InDesign sees the word "and" as an uncapitalized sentence because of this question mark.

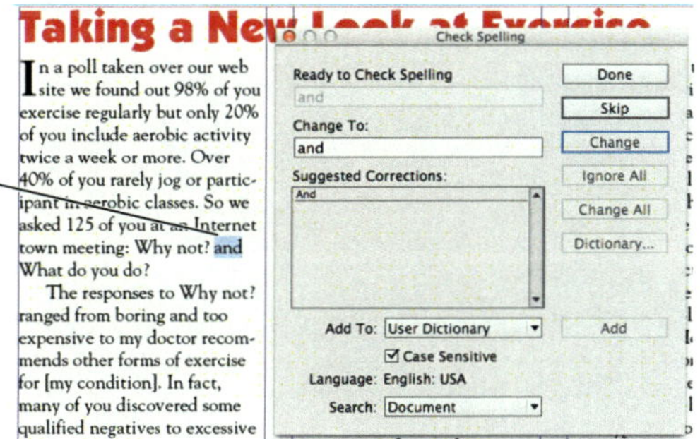

In this case, the suspect is an uncapitalized word following what the software perceives as the end of the previous sentence — as indicated by the question mark. (InDesign recognizes punctuation as the end of a sentence.) Based on the context of the suspect, this is an editorial choice and not an error.

Note:

In addition to misspellings, InDesign also identifies repeated words (such as "the the"), uncapitalized words, and uncapitalized sentences. These options can be turned off in the Spelling pane of the Preferences dialog box.

10. **Click Skip.**

The next suspect is another instance of a suspected uncapitalized sentence; but again, the context shows that this is not an error.

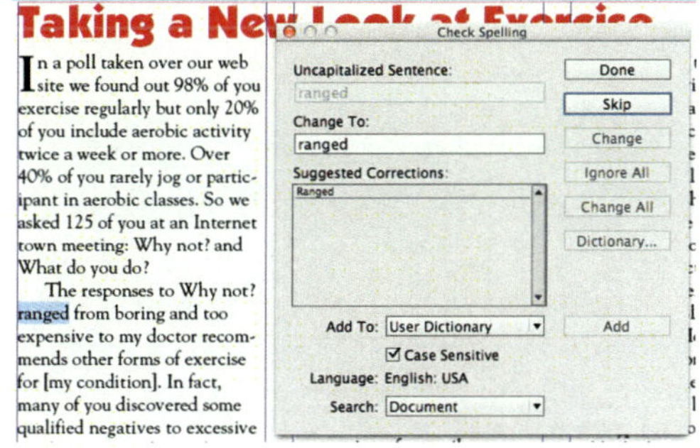

11. **Click Skip again, then review the next flagged word (Hartlett).**

This word is a proper name, and it is spelled correctly according to your client.

12. **Click the Dictionary button in the Check Spelling dialog box. Choose newsletter_dec.indd in the Target menu, make sure the Case Sensitive option is checked, and click Add.**

    If you click the Add button in the Check Spelling dialog box, the words are added to the default user dictionary — which applies to all InDesign files on your computer. When you open the User Dictionary dialog box from the Check Spelling dialog box, you can choose the file-specific dictionary in the Target menu and click Add to add the word to the dictionary for the selected file only.

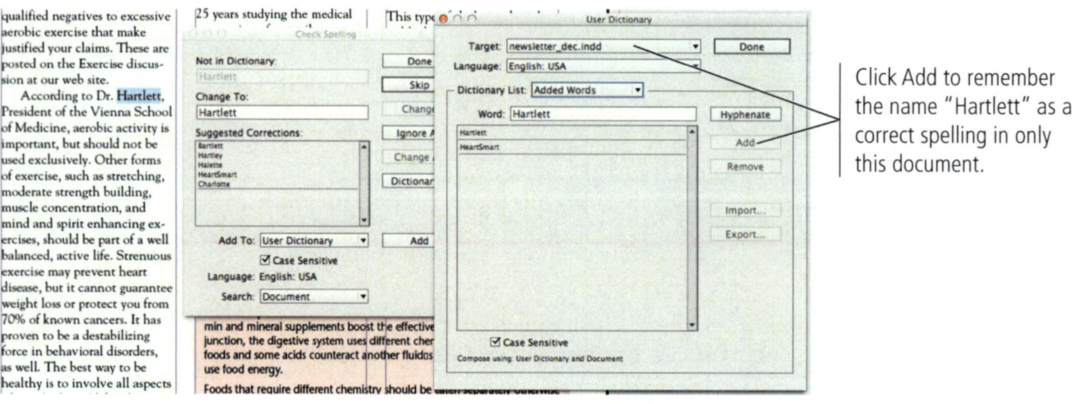

13. **Click Done to close the User Dictionary dialog box and return to the Check Spelling dialog box. Click Skip.**

    When you return to the Check Spelling dialog box, Hartlett still appears in the Word field. You have to click Skip to find the next suspect word.

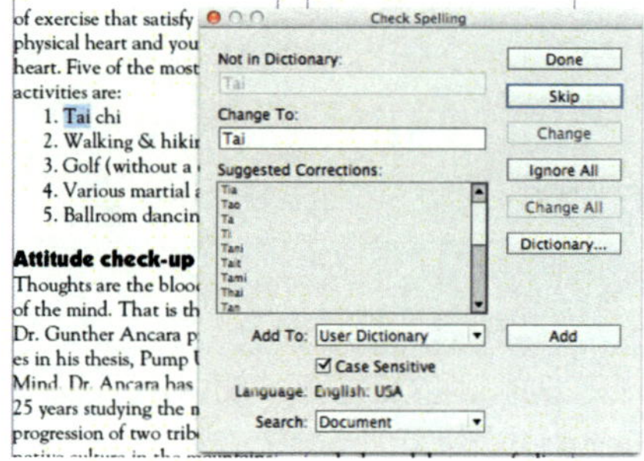

14. **With Tai highlighted, click Ignore All.**

    When you click Ignore All, the word is added to a special list in the user dictionary, so it will not be flagged again.

15. **Add the next incorrect spelling (Ancara) to the user dictionary for the newsletter_dec.indd file, then click Skip.**

16. **Review the next error.**

    This is an example of a very common typo. The word "studiest" is identified as an error, but if you look closely, you can see that the next word is "he" — which the software will not identify as an error. You have to correct this problem manually.

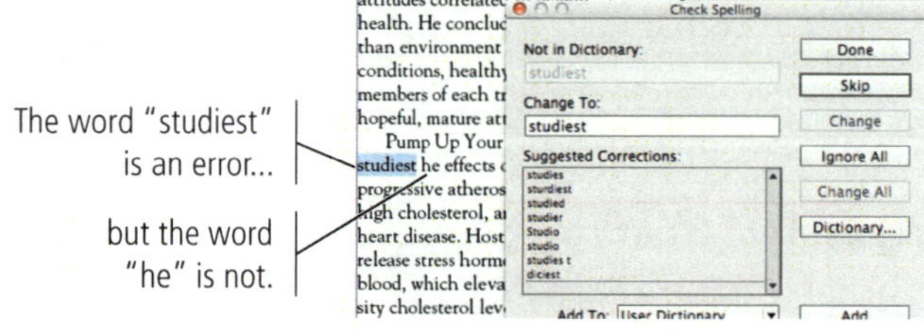

17. **Place the insertion point before the second "t" in "studiest", then press the Spacebar. Delete the space between the "t" and "he".**

As soon as you click to place the insertion point in the story, the Check Spelling dialog box reverts to show the Start button. By interacting directly with the document to manually correct an error that the software can't fix, you have to start the spell-check process over again.

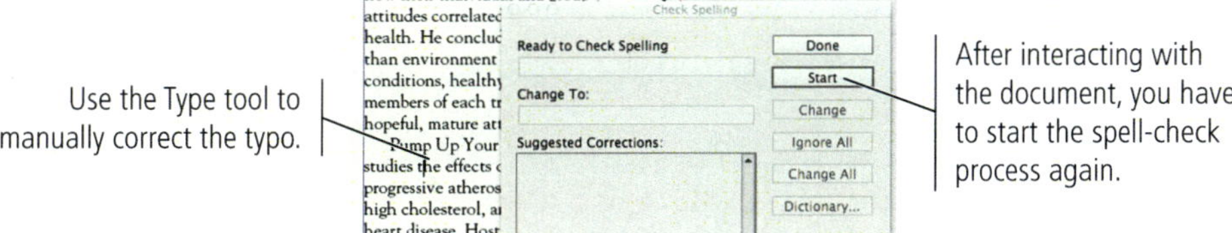

18. **Click the Start button in the Check Spelling dialog box.**

The process continues from the current insertion point to the end of the active story.

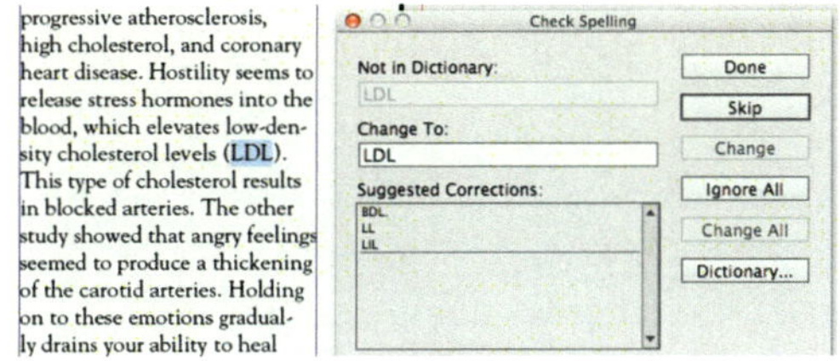

Note:

Be careful adding acronyms to the user dictionary; they often resemble words that are commonly misspelled. For example, adding TEH (without the case-sensitive option) could cause you to miss "teh" as a typo for "the".

19. **With LDL highlighted, click Ignore All.**

The next suspect is the same uncapitalized sentence that you already reviewed. When you use the Skip option, the same suspect will be flagged every time you check spelling in the document.

20. **Continue checking the spelling in the document. Make the following choices when prompted:**

and	**Skip**
ranged	**Skip**
portobello	**Click the Add button to add the word to the default user dictionary.**
Carbs	**Skip**
Arby's	**Ignore All**
KFC	**Ignore All**

21. **When you see the check mark at the top of the dialog box, click Done to close the Check Spelling dialog box.**

22. **Using the Edit Original function in the Links panel, open membership.indd and check spelling in the file. Correct any errors, then save and close the file.**

The Check Spelling function only interacts with nested files if those files are already open and the All Documents option is selected in the Search menu.

Review the suspects carefully before you decide to make a change. The word HeartSmart is flagged as an error because you added it to the user dictionary of only the newsletter file. There are two actual spelling errors in the file that you should fix ("clinc" and "screnings").

23. **Save newsletter_dec.indd and then continue to the next exercise.**

Using Dynamic Spelling

You can turn on dynamic spelling (Edit>Spelling>Dynamic Spelling) to underline potential spelling and capitalization errors in a document without opening the Check Spelling dialog box. You can use the Spelling pane of the Preferences dialog box to assign a different-color underline for each of the four potential problems.

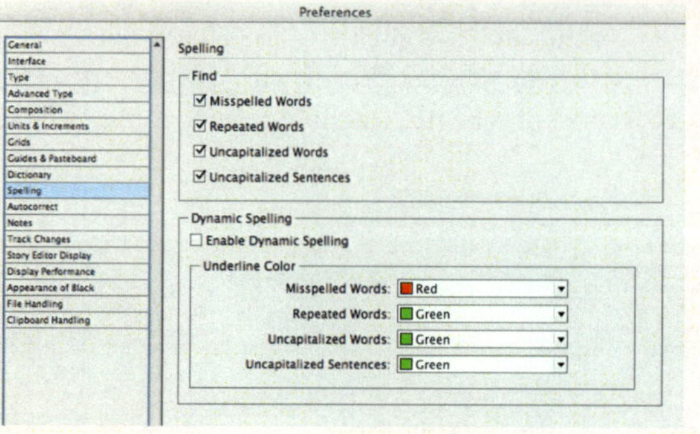

The repeated word is underlined in green.

Some of the earliest existing examples of writi pictographic writings (or hieroglyphics) of an tablets, written on papyrus scrolls, and and ir used for comunicating evolved over time — t to writing on animal skins, clay tablets, vellu high-quality papers (and low-quality newspri

The misspelled word is underlined in red.

If you type directly into InDesign, you can turn on the Autocorrect feature (Edit>Spelling>Autocorrect) to correct misspelled words as you type. Of course, automatic corrections are not always correct; software can't always select the correct word within the context of the layout, and it might produce some very strange results for words that aren't in the active dictionary (technical or corporate terms, for example). To avoid the potential for fixing "errors" that aren't really errors, you can define what misspellings to replace and what spelling should replace those specific errors.

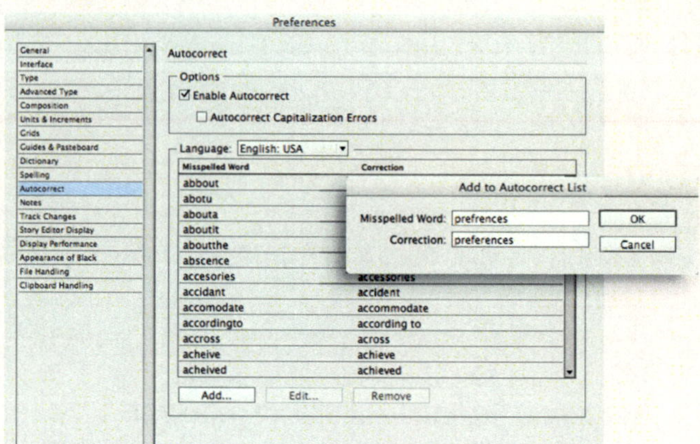

In the Autocorrect pane of the Preferences dialog box, you can click Add to define a specific misspelling, as well as the correct spelling to use. The Autocorrect List is maintained for the specified language dictionary.

Define a Preflight Profile

InDesign includes a dynamic, built-in preflighting utility that can check for common errors as you build a file. If you introduce a problem while building a file, the bottom-left corner of the document window shows a red light and the number of potential errors. In the following exercise, you define a profile to check for errors based on the information you have. This is certainly not an exhaustive check for all possible output problems. You should always work closely with your output provider to build responsible files that will cause no problems in the output workflow.

> ***Note:***
>
> *Ask your output provider if they have defined an InDesign preflight profile that you can load into your application to check for the problems that will interrupt their specific workflows.*

1. **With newsletter_dec.indd open, look at the bottom-left corner of the document window.**

2. **Click the arrow to the right of the No Errors message and choose Preflight Panel from the menu.**

   The message currently shows no errors, but at this point you don't know exactly what is being checked. The Preflight panel provides an interface for defining preflight profiles, as well as reviewing the specific issues identified as errors.

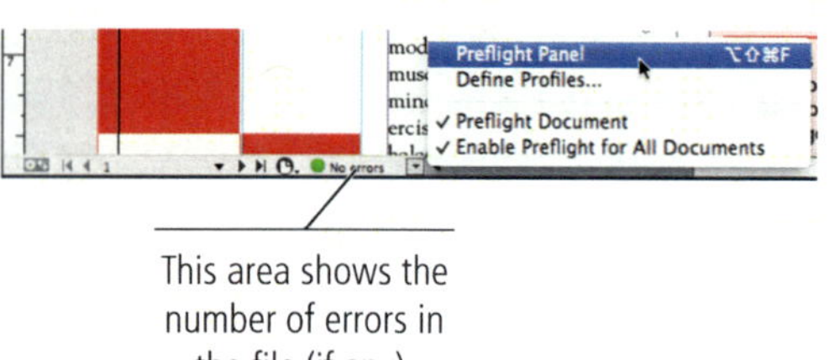

This area shows the number of errors in the file (if any).

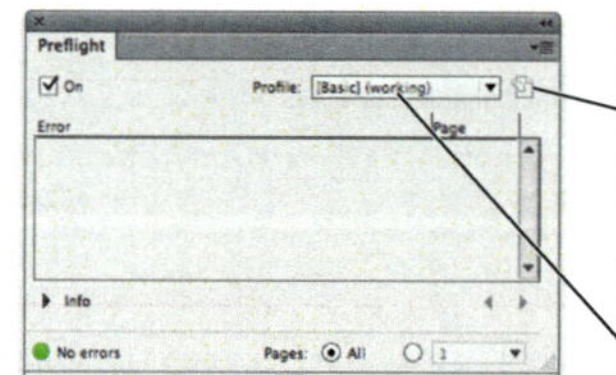

Click this button to embed the current profile into the active document.

The Preflight panel shows which profile is being used to check for errors.

3. **Open the Preflight panel Options menu and choose Define Profiles.**

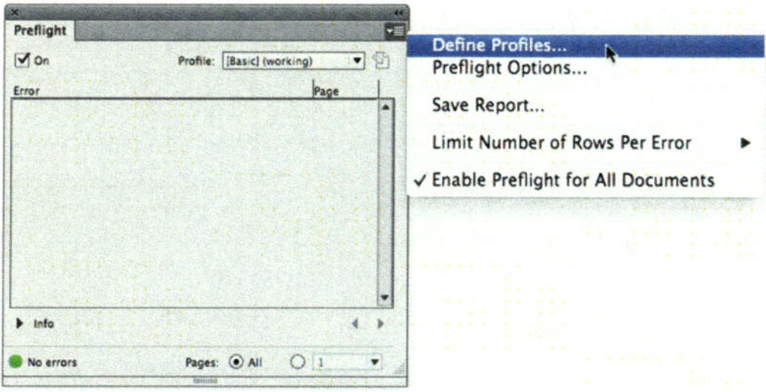

4. **In the Preflight Profiles dialog box, click the "+" button in the left side of the dialog box to create a new profile.**

   Rather than relying on generic built-in profiles, you should be aware of and able to control exactly what is (and is not) flagged as an error.

5. **Type HeartSmart Check in the Profile Name field, then click the empty area below the list of profiles to finalize the new name.**

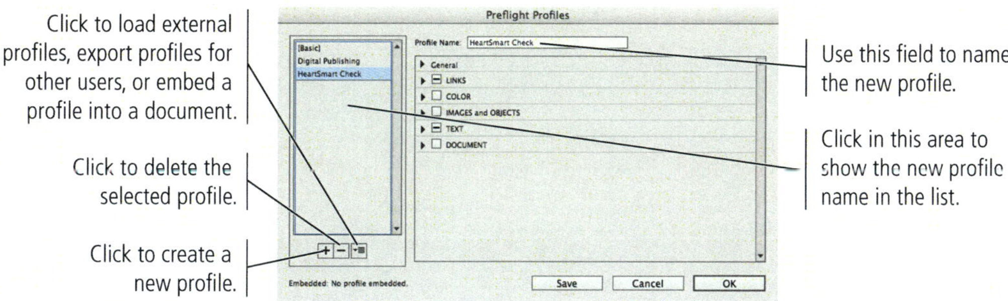

6. **With the HeartSmart Check profile selected on the left side of the dialog box, expand the General category on the right. Highlight the existing text in the Description field, and then type Verify newsletter for 4c press.**

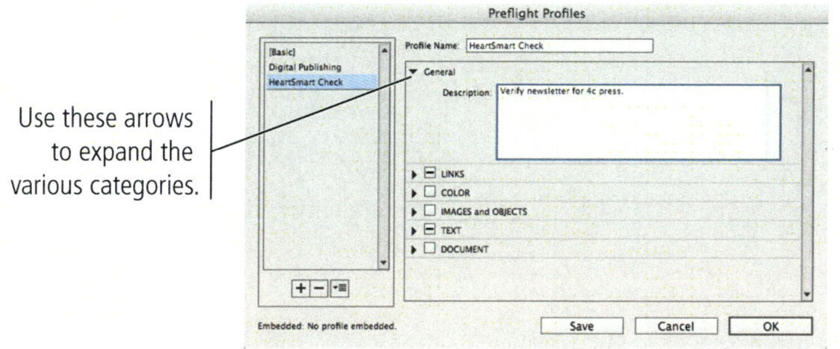

> ***Note:***
>
> *This description is simply a reminder of the profile's intent.*

7. **Collapse the General category and expand the Links category. Check the Links Missing or Modified option.**

   Image files placed in a layout need to be available when the job is output. By checking this option, you are warned if any placed image has been moved or modified since it was placed into the layout.

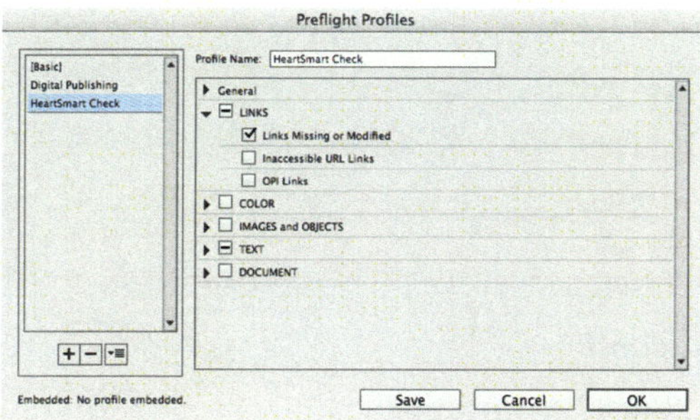

8. **Collapse the Links category and expand the Color category. Check and expand the Color Spaces and Modes Not Allowed option, and then check the RGB and Spot Color options.**

   You know this newsletter is going to be output as a 4-color job. Spot colors will create an extra separation, which can be a very costly error. By setting these options, you will receive a warning if you create a spot color in a job that should be output as 4-color.

   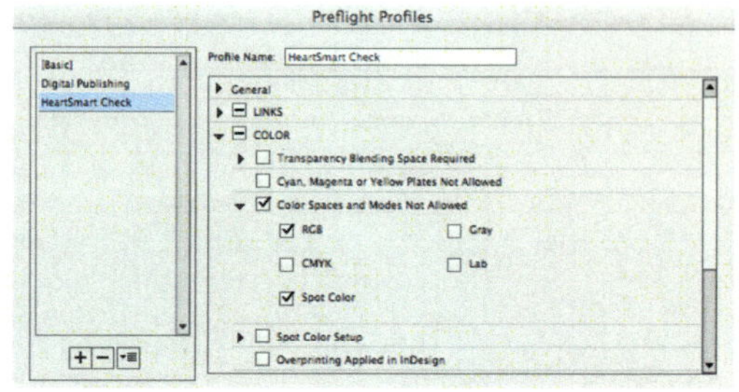

   To achieve the best-quality, predictable output, it's a good idea to check for RGB images and control the conversion process in an image-editing application (i.e., Photoshop).

Note:

Some output processes use a method called in-RIP separation to convert RGB images to CMYK during the output process. However, the conversion process can cause significant color shift if it is not controlled.

9. **Collapse the Color category and expand the Images and Objects category. Check and expand the Image Resolution option. Check the three Minimum Resolution options. Change the Color and Grayscale minimums to `300` and change the 1-bit option to `1200`.**

   As you learned in Project 1: Letterhead Design, commercial output devices typically require at least 300 ppi to output raster images at good quality. By setting these minimum restrictions, you will receive a warning if your (or your client's) images do not have enough resolution to output at good quality using most commercial printing processes.

   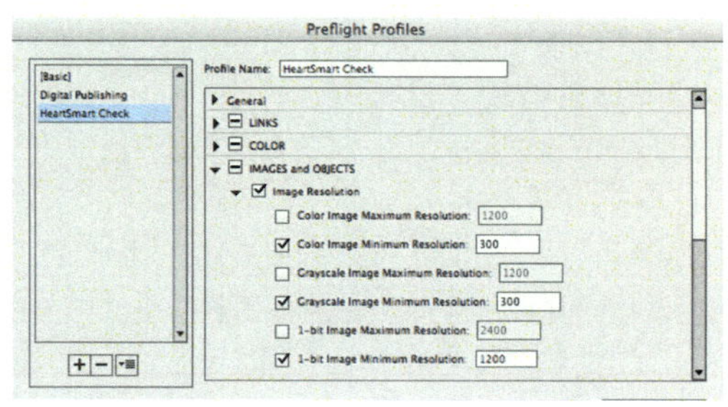

Note:

Remember: required resolution is actually two times the line screen (lpi) used for a specific job. If possible, always ask your service provider what resolution to use for your job. If you don't know the lpi (and can't find out in advance), 300 ppi resolution is a safe choice for most printing.

10. **Collapse the Images and Objects category and expand the Text category. Check the Overset Text and Font Missing options.**

    Overset text could simply be the result of extra paragraph returns at the end of a story. However, you should always check these issues to be sure that some of the client's text has not been accidentally overset.

    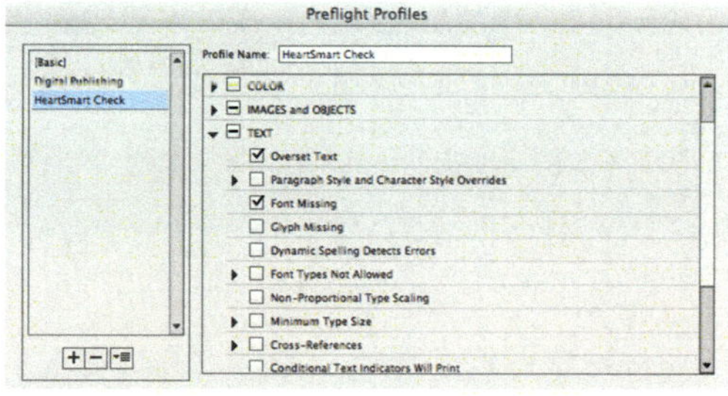

11. **Collapse the Text category and expand the Document category. Check the Number of Pages Required option. Expand that option, choose Exactly in the menu, and type `2` in the field.**

    You know that every issue of the newsletter should be exactly 2 pages. If your file has fewer or more than 2 pages, you will receive an error message.

    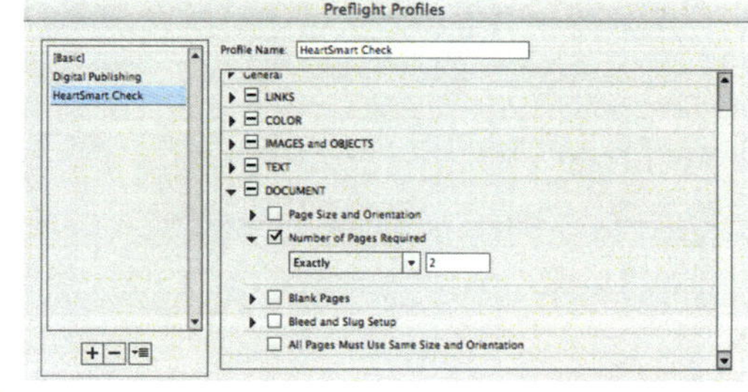

12. **Click OK to save the profile and close the dialog box.**

13. **Continue to the next exercise.**

Evaluate the Layout

Now that you have defined the issues that you know are errors, you can check your file for those issues and make the necessary corrections.

1. **With newsletter_dec.indd open, click the Profile menu in the Preflight panel and choose HeartSmart Check as the profile to use.**

2. **In the bottom of the panel, make sure the All radio button is checked.**

   When the All option is active, the entire document is checked. You can use the other radio button to define a specific page or range of pages to preflight.

   As soon as you call the HeartSmart Check profile, the panel reports 10 errors.

> *Note:*
>
> *Preflight profiles become part of the application, but are not linked to or saved in a specific document unless you intentionally embed the profile.*

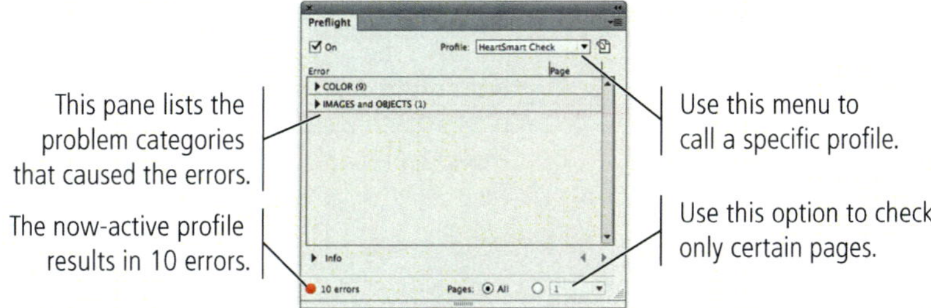

3. **Expand the Info section of the Preflight panel.**

   This area offers information about a specific error, and offers suggestions for fixing the problem.

4. **Click the arrow to expand the Color list, and then click the arrow to expand the Color Space Not Allowed list.**

5. **Click the rectangle listing to select it, and then click the hot-text page number for that item.**

   The hot-text link on the right side of the Preflight panel changes the document window to show the specific item that caused the error.

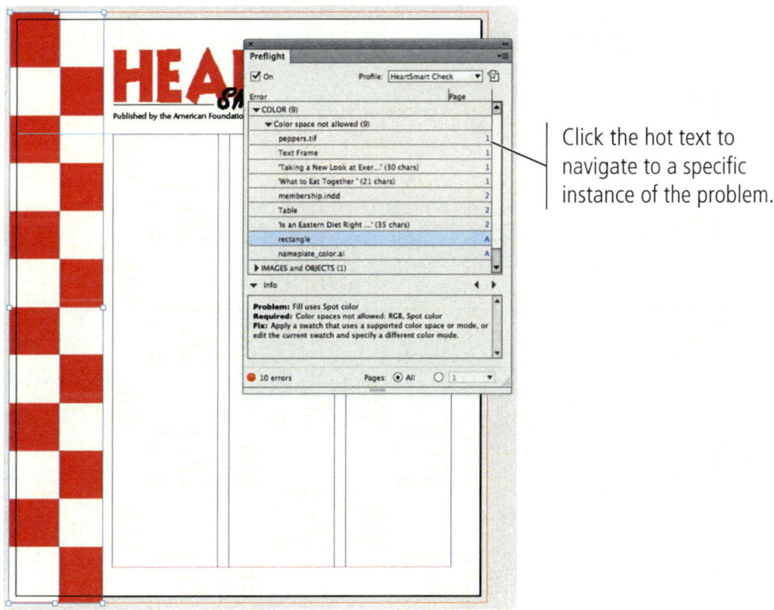

What's in a Preflight Profile?

The Preflight Profiles dialog box includes a number of options for identifying potential errors. If you are going to build responsible files, you should have a basic understanding of what these options mean.

This is by no means an exhaustive list of all potential problems in digital page-layout files; it's a list of the problems Adobe included in the Preflight Profile dialog box. Other problems are beyond the scope of most graphic designers and are better left to prepress professionals to correct, given the specific equipment conditions in their workflows.

It should also be noted that some of these issues are not necessarily errors, but nonetheless should be reviewed before a job is output. For example, blank pages might be intentionally placed into a document to force a chapter opener onto a right-facing page; in this case, the blank page is not an error. In other cases, a blank page might be left over after text is edited; in this case, the blank page would be an error. You can use the Preflight panel to find definite errors, but also use it to verify that what you have is exactly what you want.

Links

- **Links Missing or Modified.** Use this option to receive a warning if a placed file has been moved (missing) or changed (modified) since it was placed into a layout. If a placed file is missing, the output will use only the low-resolution preview that you see on screen. If a placed file has been modified, the output will reflect the most up-to-date version of the placed file — which could be drastically different than the original, potentially destroying your overall layout.
- **Inaccessible URL Links.** Use this option to find hyperlinks that might cause problems if you are creating an interactive PDF document.
- **OPI Links.** OPI is a workflow tool that allows designers to use low-resolution FPO (for placement only) files during the design stage. When the job is processed for output, the high-resolution versions are swapped out in place of the FPO images. Although not terribly common anymore, some larger agencies still use OPI workflows.

Document

- **Page Size and Orientation.** Use this option to cause an error if the document size is not a specific size; you can also cause an error if the current document is oriented other than the defined page size (i.e., portrait instead of landscape or vice versa).
- **Number of Pages Required.** Use this option to define a specific number of pages, the smallest number of pages that can be in the document, or whether the document must have pages in multiples of a specific number (for example, multiples of 16 for 16-page signature output).
- **Blank Pages.** Use this option to find blank pages in the document.
- **Bleed and Slug Setup.** Use this option to verify the document's bleed and slug sizes against values required by a specific output process.
- **All Pages Must Use Same Size and Orientation.** Because InDesign supports multiple page sizes in the same document, you can check this option to verify that all pages in the file have the same size.

Color

- **Transparency Blending Space Required.** Use this option to define whether CMYK or RGB should be used to flatten transparent objects for output. (Refer to Project 2: Festival Poster for more on transparency flattening.)
- **Cyan, Magenta, or Yellow Plates Not Allowed.** Use this option to verify layouts that will be output with only spot colors, or with black and spot colors.
- **Color Spaces and Modes Not Allowed.** Use this option to create errors if the layout uses RGB, CMYK, Spot Color, Gray, or LAB color models. (Different jobs have different defined color spaces. The option to flag CMYK as an error can be useful, for example, if you are building a layout that will be output in black only.)
- **Spot Color Setup.** Use this option to define the number of spot colors a job should include, as well as the specific color model that should be used (LAB or CMYK) when converting unwanted spot colors for process printing.
- **Overprinting Applied in InDesign.** Use this option to create an error if an element is set to overprint instead of trap.
- **Overprinting Applied to White or [Paper] Color.** By definition, White or [Paper] is technically the absence of other inks. Unless you are printing white toner or opaque spot ink, white cannot, by definition, overprint. Use this option to produce an error if White or [Paper] elements are set to overprint.
- **[Registration] Applied.** The [Registration] color swatch is a special swatch used for elements such as crop and registration marks. Any element that uses the [Registration] color will output on all separations in the job. Use this option to find elements that are incorrectly colored with the [Registration] color instead of (probably) black.

What's in a Preflight Profile? (continued)

Images and Objects

- **Image Resolution.** Use this option to identify placed files with too little or too much resolution. As you know, commercial output devices typically require 300 ppi to output properly. The maximum resolution options can be used to find objects that, typically through scaling, result in unnecessarily high resolutions that might take considerable time for the output device to process.
- **Non-Proportional Scaling of Placed Object.** Use this option to find placed files that have been scaled with different X and Y percentages.
- **Uses Transparency.** Use this option to find any element affected by transparency. As you learned in Project 2: Festival Poster, you should carefully preview transparency flattening before outputting the job.
- **Image ICC Profile.** Use this option to find placed images that have embedded ICC profiles. Typically used in color-managed workflows, placed images often store information — in the form of profiles — about the way a particular device captured or created the color in that image. You can cause errors if the image profile results in CMYK conversion, or if the embedded image profile has been overridden in the layout.
- **Layer Visibility Overrides.** Use this option to find layered Photoshop files in which the visibility of specific layers has been changed within InDesign.
- **Minimum Stroke Weight.** There is a limit to the smallest visible line that can be produced by any given output device. Use this option to find objects with a stroke weight smaller than a specific point size.
- **Interactive Elements.** Use this option to find elements with interactive properties (more on this in Project 6: Digital Layout Variations).
- **Bleed/Trim Hazard.** Use this option to find elements that fall within a defined distance of the page edge or spine for facing-page layouts (i.e., outside the live area).
- **Hidden Page Items.** Use this option to create an error if any objects on a page are not currently visible.

Text

- **Overset Text.** Use this option to find any frames with overset text.
- **Paragraph Style and Character Style Overrides.** Use this option to find instances where an applied style has been overridden with local formatting.
- **Font Missing.** Use this option to create an error if any required font is not available on the computer.
- **Glyph Missing.** Use this option to identify glyphs that aren't available (more on glyphs in Project 4: Realtor Collateral Booklet).
- **Dynamic Spelling Detects Errors.** Use this option to cause an error if InDesign's dynamic spelling utility identifies any errors in the document.
- **Font Types Not Allowed.** Use this option to prohibit specific font types that can cause problems in modern output workflows.
- **Non-Proportional Type Scaling.** Use this option to identify type that has been artificially stretched or compressed in one direction (i.e., where horizontal or vertical scaling has been applied).
- **Minimum Type Size.** Use this option to identify any type set smaller than a defined point size. You can also identify small type that requires more than one ink to reproduce (a potential registration problem on commercial output devices).
- **Cross-References.** Use this option to identify dynamic links from one location in a file to another. You can cause errors if a cross reference is out of date or unresolved.
- **Conditional Text Indicators Will Print.** Use this option to create an error if certain visual indicators will appear in the final output. (You explore conditional text in Project 5: Ireland Travel Brochure.)
- **Unresolved Caption Variable.** Use this option to find dynamic caption variables for which there is no defined metadata. (You will learn about creating captions in Project 5: Ireland Travel Brochure.)
- **Span Columns Setting Not Honored.** Use this option to find paragraphs with a defined column-span setting that is prevented by other objects on the page.
- **Tracked Change.** Use this option to find instances of text that have been changed but not accepted when Track Changes is enabled. (You will explore this utility in Project 6: Digital Layout Variations.)

6. **In the Swatches panel, Control/right-click the Pantone 1945 C swatch and choose Swatch Options from the contextual menu.**

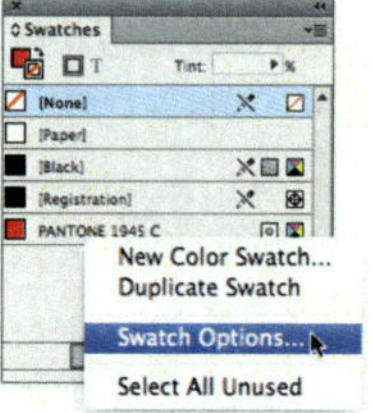

7. **In the Swatch Options dialog box, change the Color Type menu to Process.**

   Because this color swatch is used in the placed logo file, you can't change any of the other swatch options. If the swatch existed only in the layout file and not any of the placed images, you would be able to change the swatch component inks and name after converting it to process.

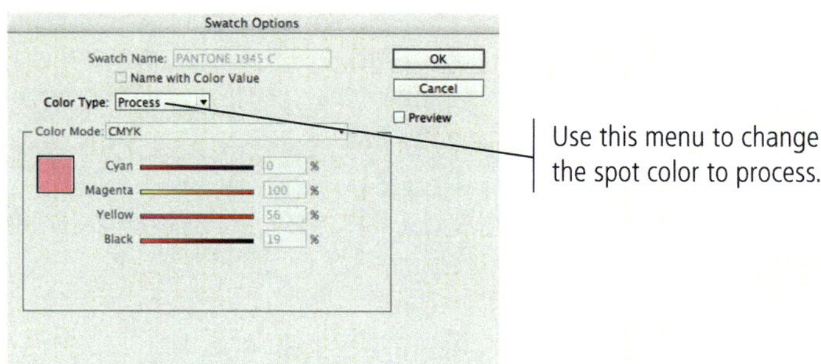

Use this menu to change the spot color to process.

Note:

Spot colors are not always errors. Check the project's specifications carefully before you convert spot colors to process. Also, be aware that spot colors are often outside the CMYK gamut; converting a spot color to process can result in drastic color shift.

8. **Click OK to apply the new swatch options.**

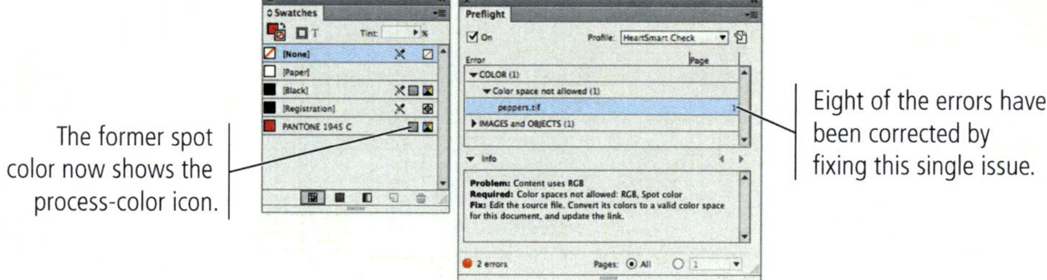

The former spot color now shows the process-color icon.

Eight of the errors have been corrected by fixing this single issue.

9. **Select the remaining color problem instance in the Preflight panel and click the hot-text link to show that element in the layout.**

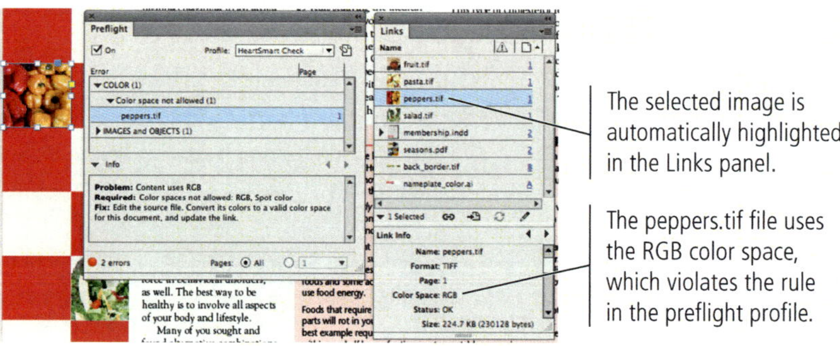

The selected image is automatically highlighted in the Links panel.

The peppers.tif file uses the RGB color space, which violates the rule in the preflight profile.

10. **In the Links panel, click the Relink button. Navigate to `peppers_cmyk.tif` in the WIP>HeartSmart>December Issue>CMYK folder and click Open. If you see the Image Import Options dialog box, click OK to accept the default options.**

    After the image has been relinked, all of the color problems have been corrected. That category no longer appears in the Preflight panel.

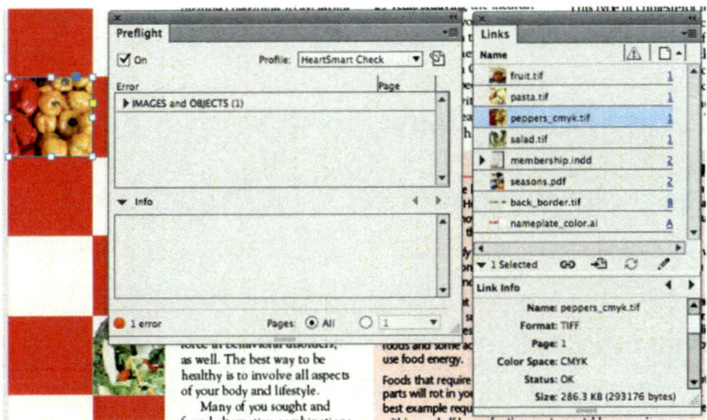

11. **Expand the Images and Objects category, then expand the Image Resolution listing. Click the page link to navigate to the problem file.**

    This image is a placed PDF file, supplied by your client. The Links panel shows that the image is 266 ppi, which is lower than the minimum 300 that you defined for this file.

    In this case, the 266 will probably be enough to satisfy the output process and still produce good quality. But in many instances, supplied-image resolution will be far below what you need for commercial printing. Low resolution is a common problem with client-supplied images. Because the placed image is a PDF file, you can't access the individual components and make changes; you would have to contact the client to resolve the problem.

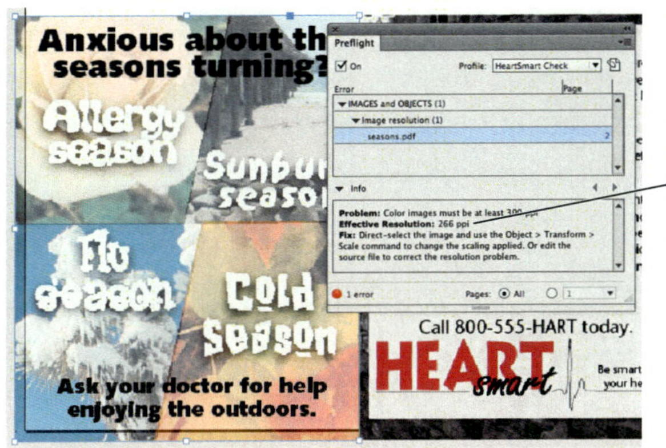

The placed PDF file does not meet the minimum resolution that you defined in the profile.

12. **Save the file and continue to the next exercise.**

Create the Job Package

Now that your file is error-free, you can package it for the output provider. As we have already stated, the images and fonts used in a layout must be available on the computer used to output the job. When you send the layout file to the printer, you must also send the necessary components. InDesign includes a Package utility that makes this process very easy.

1. **With newsletter_dec.indd open, choose File>Package.**

2. **Review the information in the Package dialog box and then click Package.**

   If you had not preflighted the file before opening the Package dialog box, you would see warning icons identifying problems with image color space or missing fonts. Because you completed the previous exercise, however, potential errors have been fixed, so this dialog box simply shows a summary list of information about the file you are packaging.

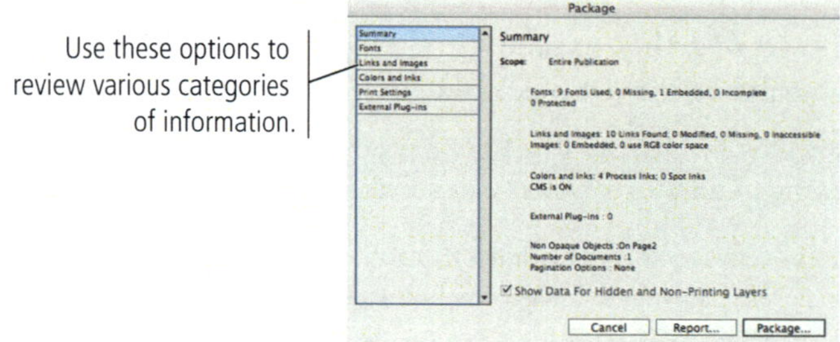

Use these options to review various categories of information.

3. **If you see a message asking you to save, click Save.**

4. **In the Printing Instructions dialog box, add your contact information, and then click Continue.**

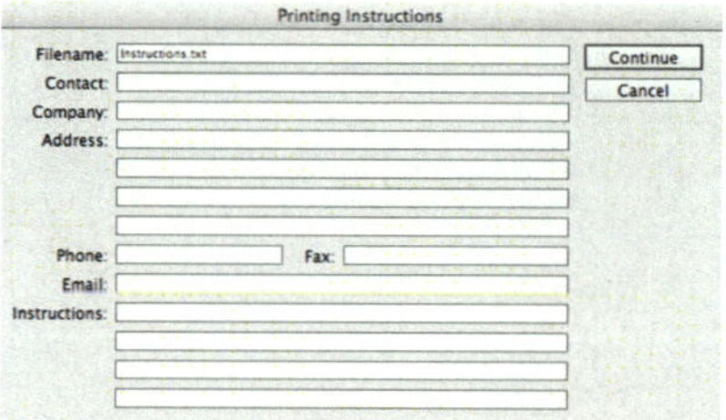

5. **Navigate to your WIP>HeartSmart folder as the target location. Make sure the Copy Fonts, Copy Linked Graphics, and Update Graphic Links options are checked and then click Package.**

   When you create a job package, InDesign automatically creates a new folder for the job.

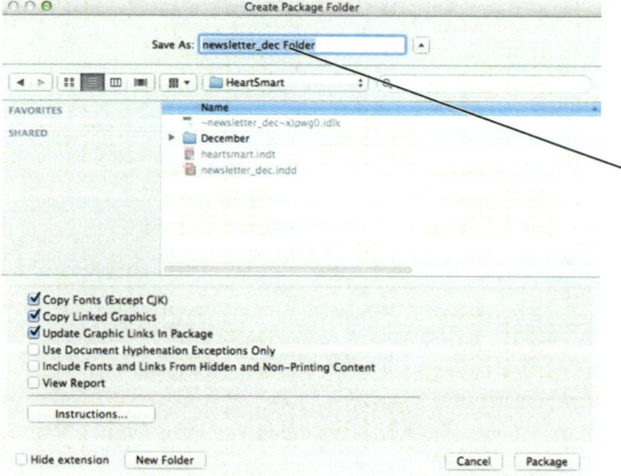

This field defines the name of the folder that will be created. All files for the job will be placed in this folder.

6. Read the resulting warning and click OK.

As with any software, you purchase a license to use a font — you do not own the actual font. It is illegal to distribute fonts freely, as it is illegal to distribute copies of your software. Most (but not all) font licenses allow you to send your copy of a font to a service provider, as long as the service provider also owns a copy of the font. Always verify that you are not violating font copyright before submitting a job.

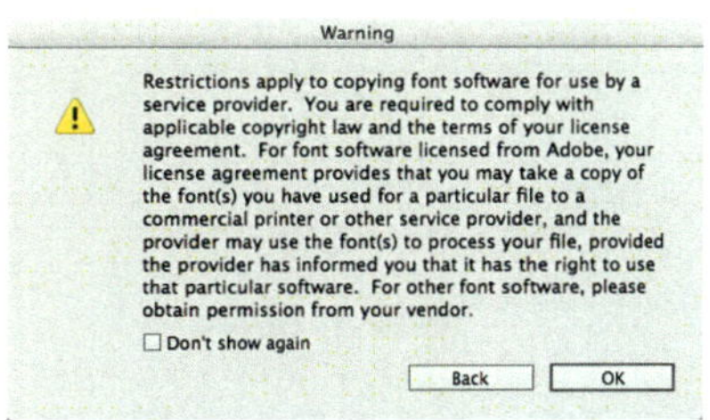

When the process is complete, the necessary job elements appear in the job folder (in your WIP>HeartSmart folder).

If you hand off the job package folder to another user (or if someone sends you a job package), the fonts in the collected Document Fonts folder will be available in InDesign when you open the packaged INDD file — even if those fonts are not installed at the computer's system level.

Document-installed fonts are installed when the related document is opened and uninstalled when you close that file. These fonts supersede any existing font of the same PostScript name within the document. Document-installed fonts are not available to other documents or in other applications.

7. Close the InDesign file.

Project Review

fill in the blank

1. An image file that has been renamed since it was placed into an InDesign layout shows the status of _______________.

2. The _______________ is used to monitor the status of images that are placed into a layout.

3. _______________ is the distance between the edge of a frame and the text contained within that frame.

4. _______________ is the distance between the edge of an object and text in other overlapping frames.

5. _______________ apply only to selected text characters; this is useful for setting off a few words in a paragraph without affecting the entire paragraph.

6. _______________ apply to the entire body of text between two ¶ symbols.

7. While working in a table, the _______________ key has a special function; pressing it does not insert the associated character.

8. When the _______________ row height method is selected, table rows change height if you add or remove text from the table cells, or if you change the text formatting in a way that requires more or less space.

9. A(n) _______________ is a special kind of table row that repeats at the top of every instance of the same table.

10. _______________ is the process of checking a layout for errors before it goes to print.

short answer

1. Briefly explain the significance of a Missing Font warning.

2. List three advantages of using templates.

3. Briefly define "styles" in relation to text formatting.

Portfolio Builder Project

Use what you learned in this project to complete the following freeform exercise.
Carefully read the art director and client comments, then create your own design to meet the needs of the project.
Use the space below to sketch ideas; when finished, write a brief explanation of your reasoning behind your final design.

art director comments

Your client is a local food market that sells gourmet and specialty products. To help promote the business, the owners have hired you to create a series of flyers that can be handed out at art festivals and farmers markets.

To complete this project, you should:

- ❑ Design an 8.5″ × 11″ template that can be reused to feature different sections of the store. The flyer can be printed on both sides of the paper, but should not include bleeds.
- ❑ Include some type of category identifier that will change for each flyer in the series.
- ❑ Use the content that has been provided in the **IDCC_PB_Project3.zip** archive on the Student Files Web page. You can use some or all of the images that were provided by the client.

client comments

Center Market includes an artisanal cheese market, an old-world bakery that offers hand-crafted breads and desserts, an in-house butcher shop that features a variety of wild game meats, and a large international section with hard-to-find ingredients for just about any type of cuisine.

Our target customers are the home-gourmet "foodie" types, so we want the flyers to speak to that higher-end market. We definitely prefer a classier approach than the "Sale! Sale! Sale!" flyers that you see in regular weekly grocery ads.

We already have text and images for the artisanal cheese, so start with that one. Once we've approved what you come up with, we'll gather up everything you will need for the other pieces.

Other than the text that we already provided you, be sure to include the store name, address, and phone number prominently on the flyer:

4127 West Alton Drive, Los Angeles, CA 90016
800-555-3663

project justification

Project Summary

This project introduced a number of concepts and tools that will be very important as you work on more complex page-layout jobs. Importing text content from other applications — specifically, Microsoft Word and Microsoft Excel — is a foundational skill that you will use in most projects; this newsletter showed you how to control that content on import, and then re-format it as appropriate in the InDesign layout.

Templates, master pages, and styles are all designed to let you do the majority of work once and then apply it as many times as necessary; virtually any InDesign project can benefit from these tools, and you will use them extensively in your career as a graphic designer. This project provided a basic introduction to these productivity tools; you will build on these foundations as you complete the remaining five projects of this book.

project 4

Realtor Collateral Booklet

Your client is the Southern California Realtors Association, which provides support materials for member realtors. They hired you to create a booklet with tips for sellers who want to make their homes more attractive to buyers. The booklet will be printed in very large quantities and distributed to realty offices, so the individual agents can use it as a tool when they are contacted about listing a home for sale. The ultimate consumer for this piece is the home seller (not the agent), so it needs to be visually inviting and easy to read.

This project incorporates the following skills:

- ❑ Understanding and controlling facing-page layouts
- ❑ Converting regular layout pages to master pages
- ❑ Using master pages to apply repetitive layout elements
- ❑ Using special characters and markers
- ❑ Automatically flowing text across multiple pages
- ❑ Basing style sheets on other style sheets to improve consistency
- ❑ Applying bulleted list formatting
- ❑ Controlling page breaks with paragraph Keep options
- ❑ Controlling automatic hyphenation
- ❑ Printing a booklet using built-in imposition options
- ❑ Exporting a PDF file with animated page transitions

Project Meeting

client comments

The idea behind this booklet is to give realtors something they can hand to potential sellers — kind of a tactful way to point out what homeowners need to do to prepare their house for sale. This way the agents don't have to blatantly say things like "scrub the mold off your bathtub before showing it." So really, the booklet is a tool for the agents to hand out, but ultimately it's for the sellers to use as a checklist of things to do before an open house.

The text was created in Microsoft Word, using a custom template with all the text formats we use in a number of similar collateral pieces. We're also sending you some images from our agents' files; we have permission to use them in marketing materials without paying a specific licensing fee. Our research shows that a 5.5 × 8.5″ booklet is well received by most consumers, so we want the finished booklet to be that size.

art director comments

This booklet was originally specified as 16 pages with a separate cover, but the client decided that a self-cover will work just as well. We had already designed the front and back covers for the initial pitch, so you can import the cover layouts into the main booklet file.

People don't like to read long blocks of body copy, and this project has a large amount of text. A lot of it will work well as lists, however, so you'll use bullets to break up most of the body text. Each spread will also have a large picture and a callout box to add visual interest.

This project — like most documents with a lot of text — will also require tighter control over the text flow than when you work with smaller bits of text. Long documents like this one require special attention to detail to prevent problems such as bad line and page breaks.

Consistency is important for any document with more than a few pages; the same basic grid should be used for most internal pages in the booklet. Completing this project will be much easier if you take the time to build the basic layout on master pages.

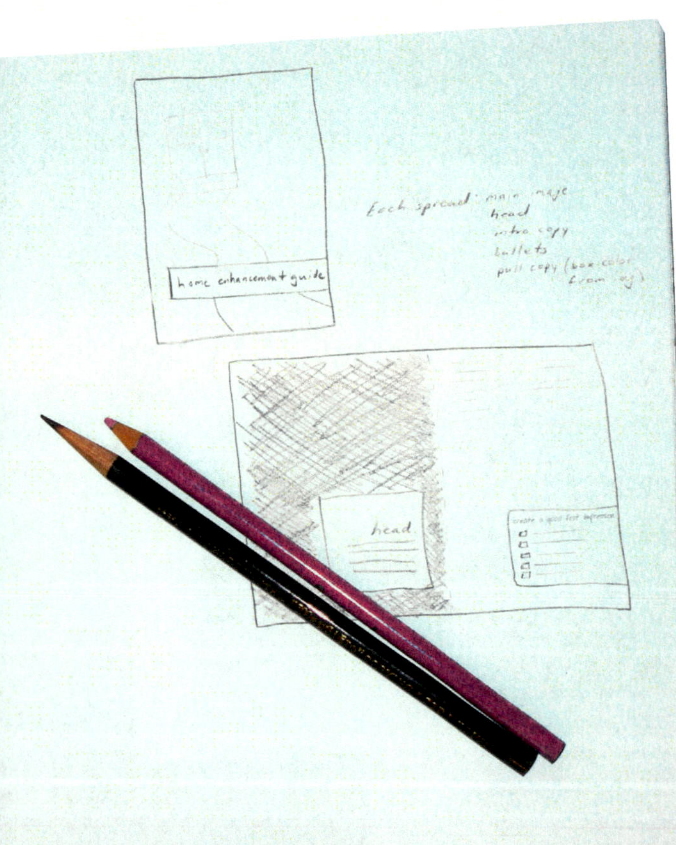

project objectives

To complete this project, you will:

- ❑ Convert layout pages to master pages and import them into the main booklet file
- ❑ Build master pages with placeholders for the different elements of the layout
- ❑ Define styles based on other styles to improve consistency and facilitate changing multiple styles at once
- ❑ Format paragraphs as bulleted lists to improve readability
- ❑ Control paragraph positioning using Keep options in applied styles
- ❑ Control automatic hyphenation to prevent bad line breaks
- ❑ Print a sample booklet for client approval
- ❑ Export a PDF version with page transitions

Stage 1 Working with Master Pages

In Project 3: HeartSmart Newsletter, you worked with the existing master pages in a newsletter template. To complete this booklet project, you will dig deeper into the capabilities and advantages of master pages. As a general rule, you should use facing pages any time a design will be read like a book — left to right, Page 2 printed on the back of Page 1 and facing Page 3, and so on. For facing-page layouts, the left page mirrors the right page of each **spread**. The side margins are referred to as "inside" (near the spine) and "outside" (away from the spine) instead of "left" and "right."

Create the Booklet File

Multi-page documents, such as the booklet you build in this project, typically require special layout considerations so that the pages will appear in the correct arrangement when the job is finished. You'll deal with output considerations in Stage 3. For now, however, you need to understand two issues related to setting up this type of file:

- Books and booklets usually have facing pages, which means opposing left and right pages of a spread mirror each other.
- Files with facing pages can have different margin values on the inside (near the spread center) and outside (away from the spread center) edges.

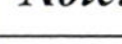

Note:

*Layout pages can be viewed as individual pages, or they can be viewed as two or more pages at a time, which is called a **spread**.*

1. **Download IDCC_RF_Project4.zip from the Student Files Web page.**

2. **Expand the ZIP archive in your WIP folder (Macintosh) or copy the archive contents into your WIP folder (Windows).**

   This creates a folder named **Realtors**, which contains the files you need for this project. You should also use this folder to save the files you create in this project.

3. **In InDesign, choose File>New>Document. In the New Document dialog box, set the document to have 1 page that starts with page number 1.**

4. **Choose Letter – Half in the Page Size menu, using portrait orientation.**

   The 5.5 × 8.5″ size is common enough to be included in the list of built-in page sizes.

5. **Make sure the Facing Pages and Primary Text Frame options are checked.**

   The Primary Text Frame option creates an automatic text frame that snaps to the defined margins, using the number of columns and gutter width defined in the Columns area of the dialog box. This frame is placed on the default master page layout, so it will also appear on every layout page that is associated with the default master page layout.

6. **In the Columns area, define 2 columns with a 0.2″ gutter.**

7. **In the Margins area, apply a 0.5″ margin to all four sides of the page.**

8. **Define a 0.125″ bleed on all four sides.**

   If you can't see the Bleed and Slug options, click the right-facing arrow button to show those options.

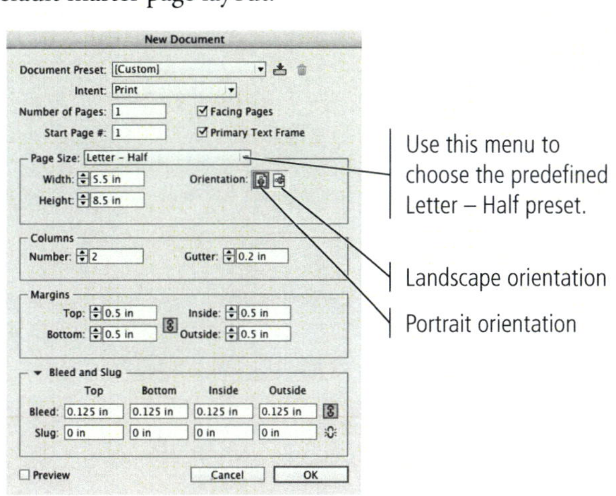

9. **Click OK to create the new document.**

10. **If rulers are not visible, choose View>Rulers.**

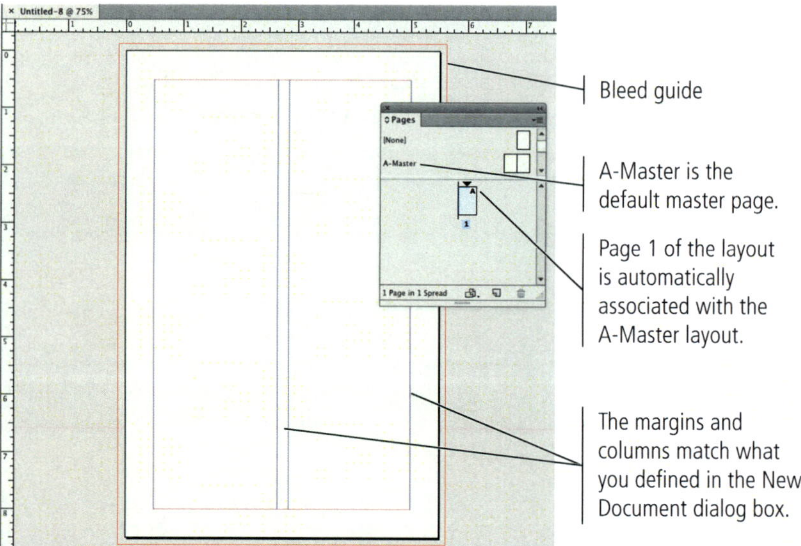

11. **Save the file as realty_booklet.indd in your WIP>Realtors folder and continue to the next exercise.**

Understanding Master Page Icons

INDESIGN FOUNDATIONS

When you work with facing pages, the default master page is actually a spread. In the Pages panel, the A-Master layout icon shows two pages, representing the two pages in the master page spread. Depending on your needs, you can also create master pages with a single page instead of a spread.

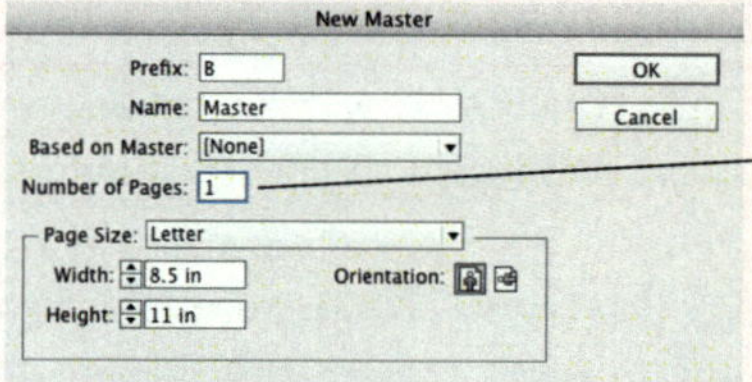

Change this field to "1" if you want a master layout with only a single page.

If you double-click the name of a master page in the Pages panel, you select the entire page or spread that makes up that master layout. You can select only one page of a master page spread by clicking the left or right page icon for that master.

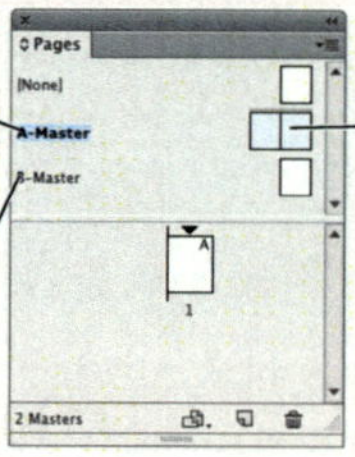

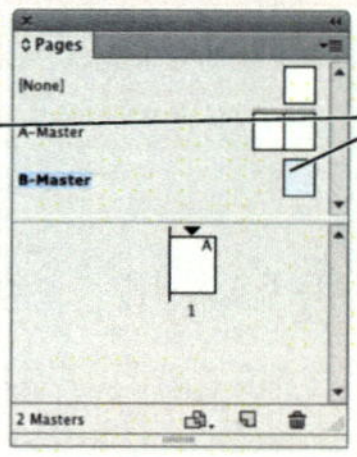

In a facing-page document, the default A-Master has two pages (a spread).

You can add a single-page master layout to a facing-page document.

Double-clicking the master page name selects all pages in the master layout.

If an entire master page spread is already selected (both page icons are highlighted), you have to first deselect the spread before you can select only one page of the spread. You can do this by simply clicking any other page icon — master page or regular page — in the panel.

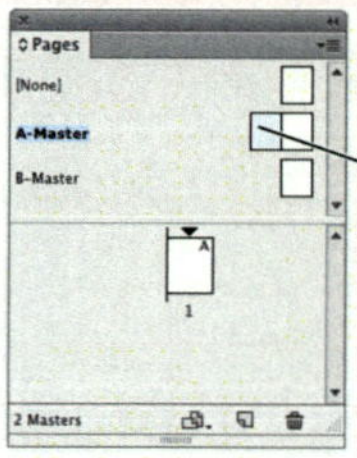

Single-click either page icon in a master page spread to select only that page, rather than the entire spread.

Create Master Pages from Layout Pages

This project was originally defined by the client as a 16-page booklet "plus cover." In other words, the main booklet file would have 16 pages, but the cover would be created and printed as a separate file. Once printed, the two pieces would be combined and bound together into a single finished piece.

Based on the amount of text they created, your clients have decided to create the booklet as 16 pages "including self cover," which means the first and last pages of the main booklet file will be the front and back covers (respectively). The first step in completing this project is to bring the cover pages into the main layout.

1. **Open the file `cover.indd` from the WIP>Realtors folder.**

   This layout includes two pages — the front cover and the back cover. Like many projects, however, these pages were not created using master pages.

   Although you could simply copy the page contents from this file into your main file, it is a better idea to work with master pages whenever possible. Doing so gives you the most flexibility and control over the various layouts. Once you develop master pages, you can easily import the layouts into other files and apply the layouts to specific layout pages as necessary.

   Fortunately, it is very easy to create a master page layout from a regular page layout.

Note:

You can create a new master page from scratch by choosing New Master in the Pages panel Options menu.

2. **In the Pages panel, click the Page 1 icon and drag it to the top section of the panel (where the A-Master appears).**

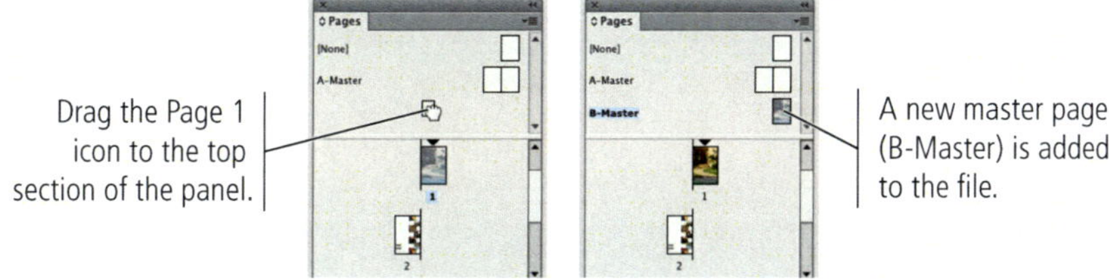

3. **Control/right-click the new B-Master icon (in the top section of the Pages panel) and choose Master Options for "B-Master" from the contextual menu.**

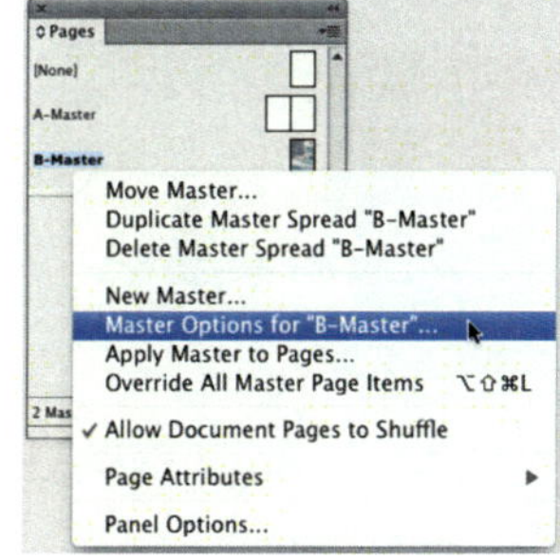

4. **In the resulting Master Options dialog box, change the name to `Front Cover` and click OK.**

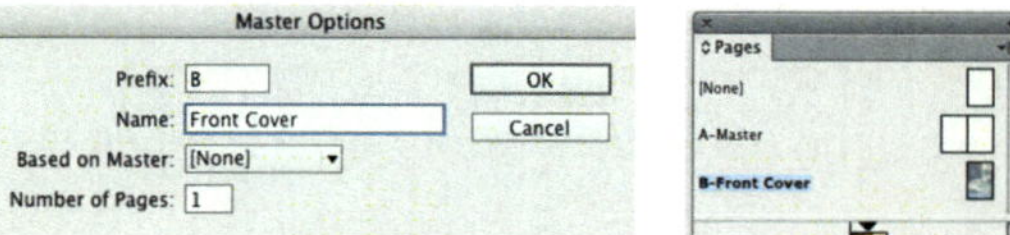

5. **Repeat this process to convert the Page 2 layout to a master page layout named `Back Cover`.**

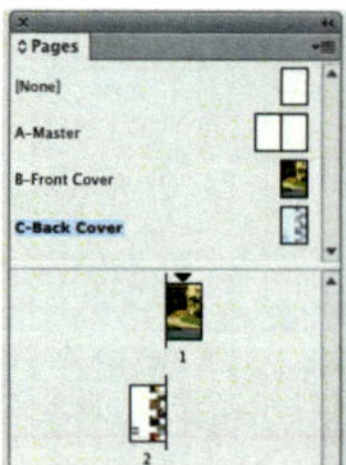

6. **In the top section of the Pages panel, Control/right-click the A-Master layout name and choose Delete Master Spread "A-Master" from the contextual menu.**

   The default master layout in this file was never used, so you can simply delete it.

7. **Save the file as `cover_masters.indd` in your WIP>Realtors folder, and then close the file.**

8. **Continue to the next exercise.**

Import Master Pages

Now that the front and back covers are saved as master pages, you can easily import and apply them in the booklet file.

1. **With `realty_booklet.indd` open, choose Master Pages>Load Master Pages from the Pages panel Options menu.**

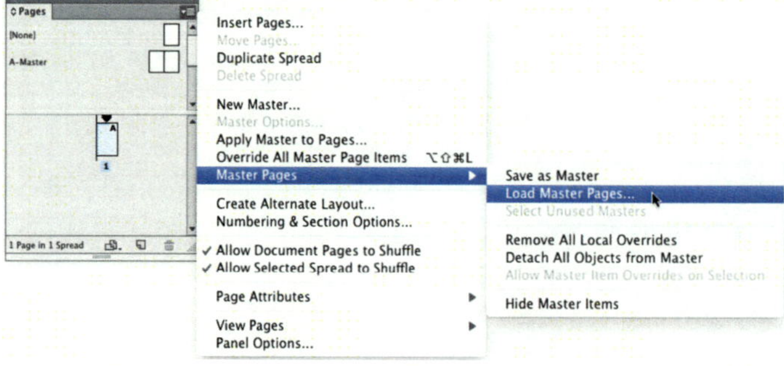

2. **In the resulting dialog box, navigate to the file cover_masters.indd in your WIP>Realtors folder and click Open.**

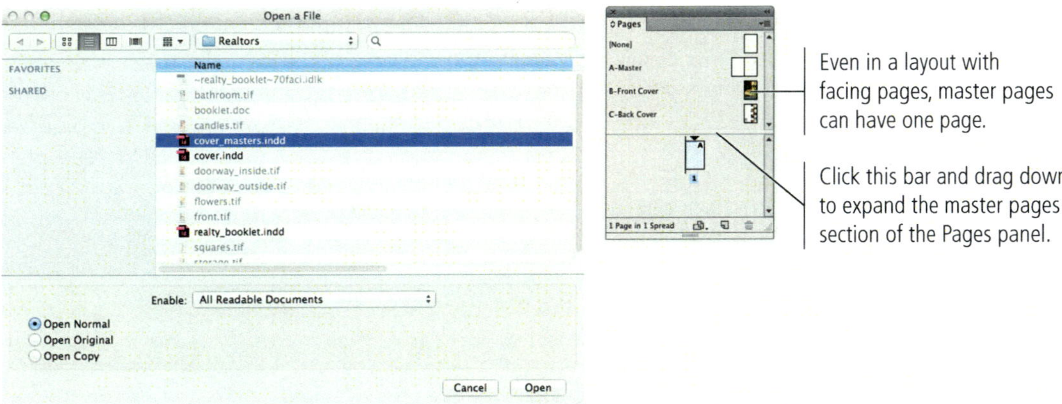

Even in a layout with facing pages, master pages can have one page.

Click this bar and drag down to expand the master pages section of the Pages panel.

3. **Open the Swatches and Paragraph Styles panels.**

Loading master pages from one file to another is an all-or-nothing process. Both master pages from the cover_masters.indd file are now part of the new file.

When you load a master page from one file to another, all required assets (styles, swatches, etc.) are also imported. One color swatch has been added to the Swatches panel (in addition to the default swatches); two paragraph styles have been added to the Paragraph Styles panel.

Note:

There is no dynamic link between the master pages now in the booklet file and the master pages in the original cover file. Changing one version of the front cover master (for example) will not affect the other version.

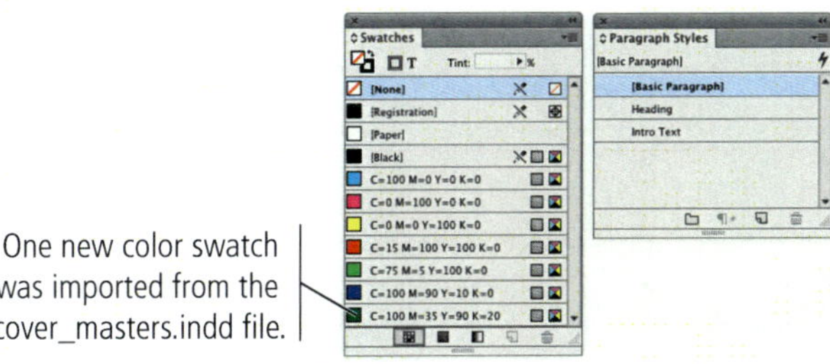

One new color swatch was imported from the cover_masters.indd file.

4. **In the Pages panel, drag the B-Front Cover icon onto the Page 1 icon.**

By default, Page 1 of any new file is associated with the A-Master layout. You can change this by simply dragging a different master onto the page icon.

A dark black outline indicates that you are dragging the B-Front Cover master onto the existing page icon.

After releasing the mouse button, Page 1 is associated with the B-Front Cover master.

5. **In the Pages panel, select only the left page of the A-Master spread and drag it below the Page 1 icon.**

   If both pages of the master spread are highlighted, dragging the selected icons into the lower half of the panel will add the entire master page spread. If only one page of the master spread is selected, you can add a single page to the layout.

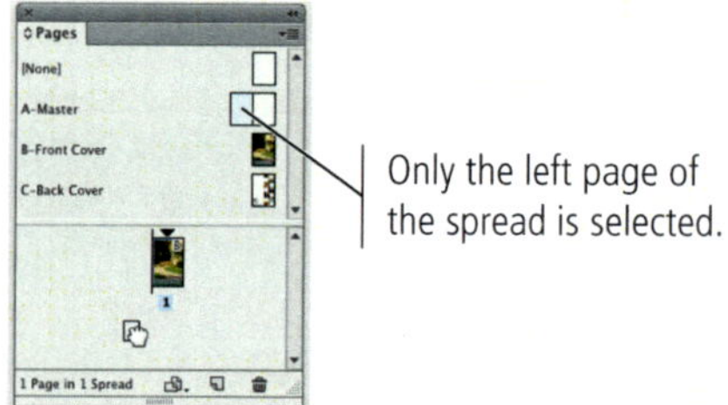

Only the left page of the spread is selected.

   Using facing pages, new pages are added to the left and right of the spread center. When you release the mouse button, the new Page 2 is automatically added on the left side of the spread center.

6. **Double-click the Page 2 icon in the Pages panel to show that page in the document window.**

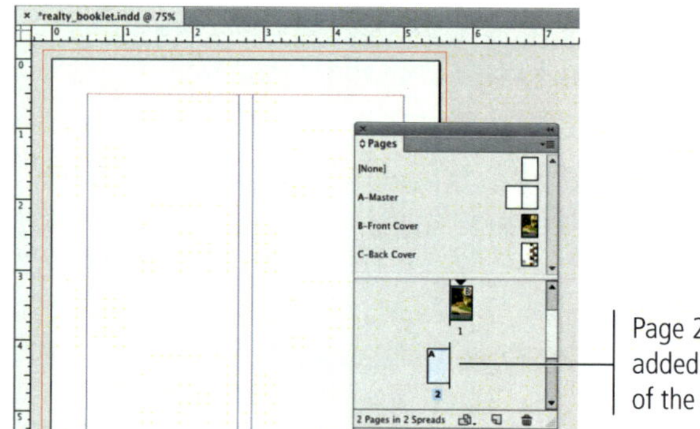

Page 2 is automatically added to the left side of the spread.

7. **Drag the C-Back Cover icon onto the Page 2 icon to change the associated master.**

8. **Make sure guides (View>Grids & Guides>Show Guides) and frame edges (View>Extras>Show Frame Edges) are visible.**

   Two objects now appear on Page 2 — a text frame and a graphics frame. The frame edges appear as dotted lines instead of solid lines. This indicates that the objects are from the associated master page; you can't select them on the layout page unless you override the master page items for that layout page.

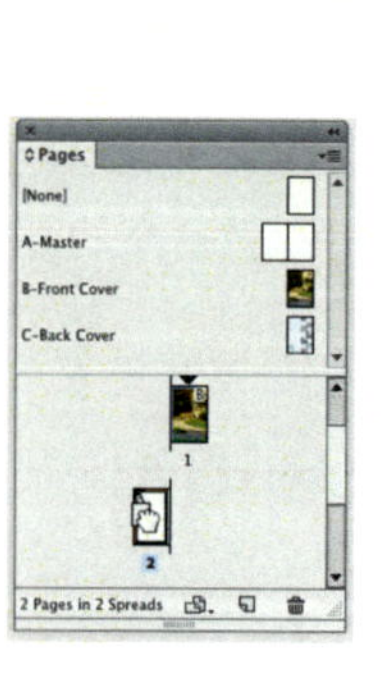

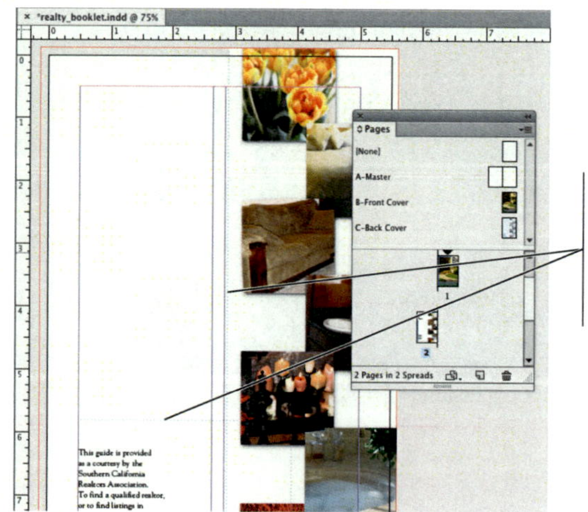

Dotted frame edges mean the object is placed on the master. You can't select these objects unless you override master items for the page.

Note:

You can also Control/right-click a page icon in the lower section of the Pages panel and choose Apply Master to Page from the contextual menu.

Note:

*Pages on the left side of the spread center are called **left-facing** or **verso** pages.*

*Pages on the right side of the spread center are called **right-facing** or **recto** pages.*

Note:

By convention, odd-numbered pages are right-facing and even-numbered pages are left-facing.

9. **In the Pages panel, drag the left page of the A-Master spread to the left of the Page 2 icon.**

   Before you release the mouse button, a vertical black bar indicates the potential position of the new page.

   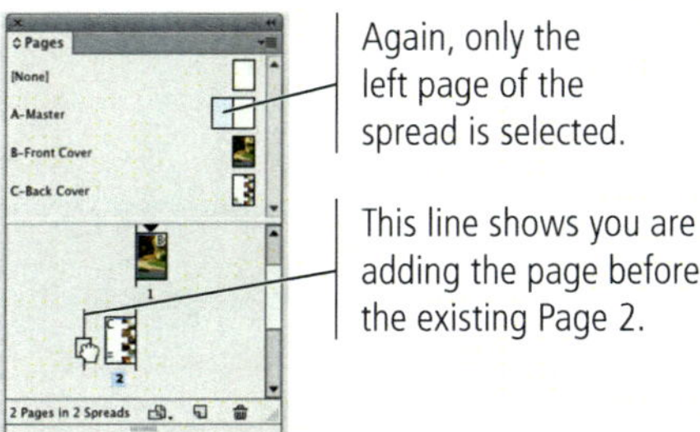

   After you release the mouse button, the new page is automatically added before Page 2. Because this is a facing-page layout, the new Page 2 becomes the left-facing page, and the old Page 2 — now Page 3 — moves to the right side of the spread.

   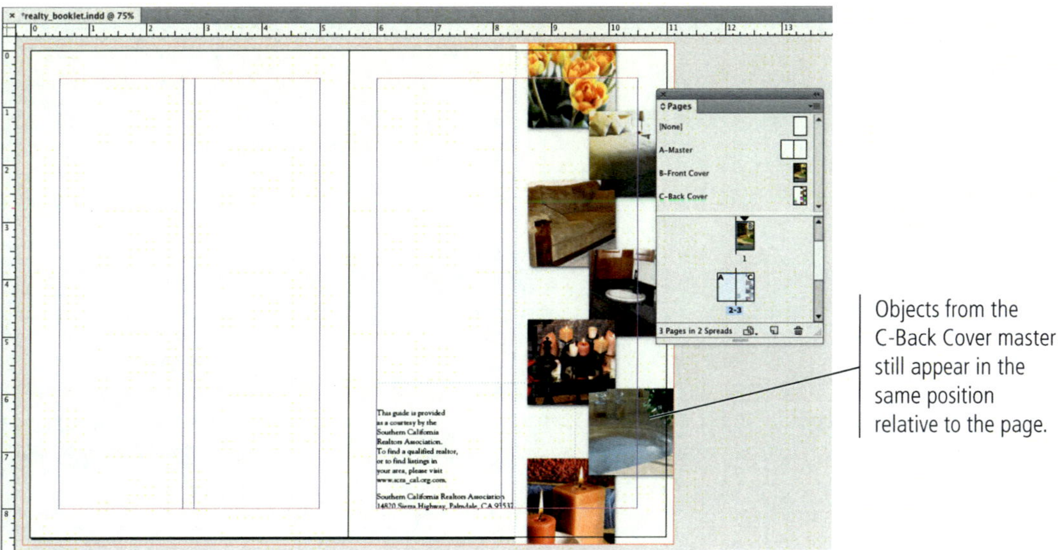

10. **Save the file and continue to the next exercise.**

Edit the Default Master Page

The main body of the booklet will be 14 pages in 7 spreads; each spread will have the same basic layout:

- A large image fills the background of each left-facing page.
- A heading and introductory paragraph sits at the bottom of each left-facing page.
- The right-facing page of each spread has two columns of body copy.
- Each right-facing page has a callout box of related checklist items.
- The right-facing page of each spread includes the page number and the words "Home Enhancement Guide."

Because these elements are common to most pages in the layout, it makes sense to create them on a master page layout. You could either create a new master page for the body spread or simply edit the existing default master page.

Understanding Relative Object Positioning

You need to understand the differences between spread master pages and single-page master pages, especially when working with facing pages. In the booklet file you're building now, you have both kinds of master pages — the covers are single-page masters and the A-Master layout is a spread of two facing pages.

When you work with a spread master page, the objects on the master page layout are positioned relative to the entire spread. Objects on regular layout pages, however, are positioned relative to the page on which they are created.

This concept is particularly important if you work with objects that bleed off the left or right side of a page, or if you override the master page items on a specific page.

When you move a page from one side of a spread to the other (e.g., from left to right), any bleed object will continue to bleed past the same edge of its new page position — possibly interfering with the other page of the spread.

A related problem occurs when you override and change master page items on regular layout pages. When you override master page items, they become regular layout page items. Adding pages to the middle of a layout moves those items relative to their new page position; the original master page objects are added directly behind the overridden objects. (If necessary, you can eliminate the overridden objects by choosing Remove All Local Overrides from the Pages panel Options menu, or you can select specific objects and choose Remove Selected Local Overrides.)

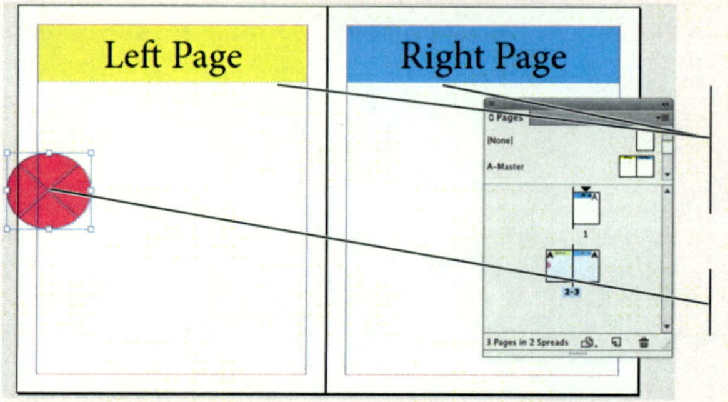

Dotted frame edges indicate that these objects are master page objects.

This shape was created on Page 2 of the layout.

After adding a new A-Master page in front of Page 2...

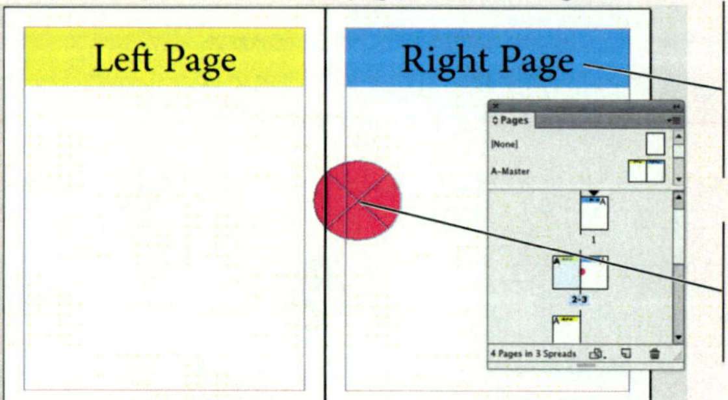

On the new Page 3, the object from the right side of the master spread replaces the object from the left side of the master spread.

The object from Page 2 is in the same position relative to the page where it was created, which is now Page 3.

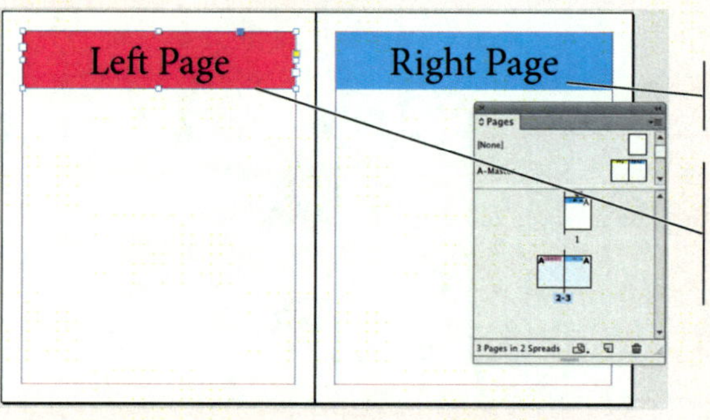

This frame is still a master page object.

We overrode master page items for Page 2, then changed the object fill color from yellow to magenta.

After adding a new A-Master page in front of Page 2...

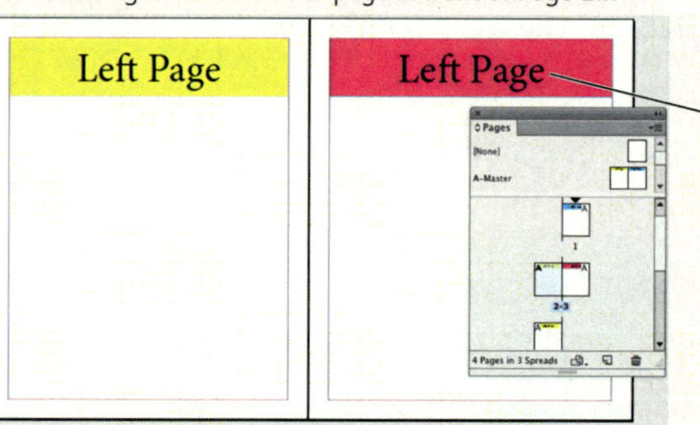

Because overriding master page items converts them into regular page items, the overridden object moves relative to the page on which it is placed (the moved Page 2).

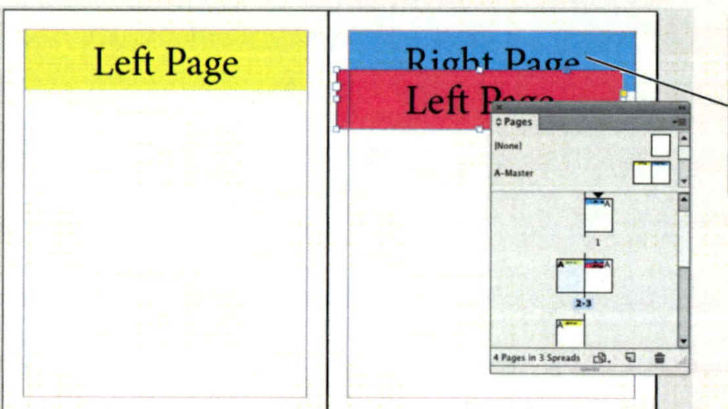

Moving the overridden object shows that the correct master page object has been added to the page, directly behind the overridden object.

1. **With realty_booklet.indd open, double-click the words "A-Master" in the top section of the Pages panel.**

   Double-clicking a master page navigates to that master layout in the document window. Each page of the A-Master spread has the margin and column settings you defined in the New Document dialog box.

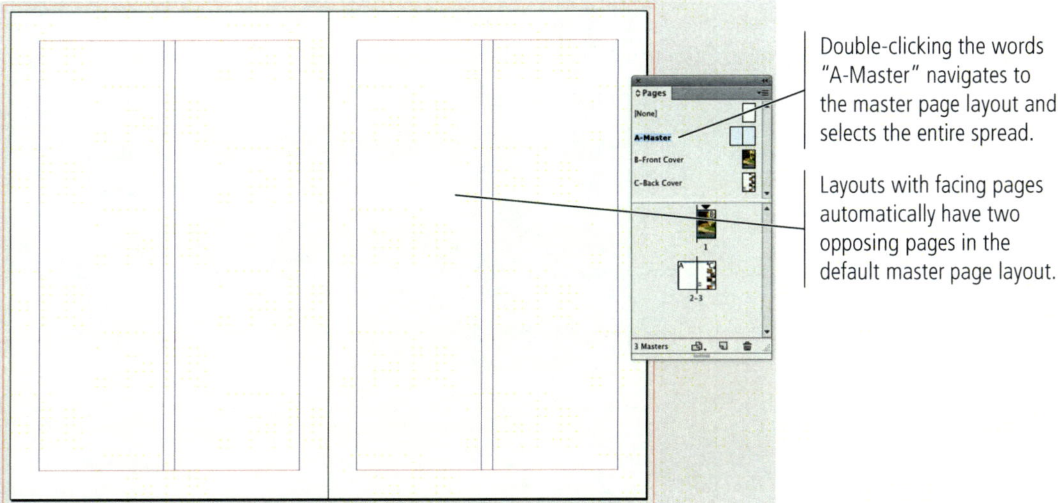

Double-clicking the words "A-Master" navigates to the master page layout and selects the entire spread.

Layouts with facing pages automatically have two opposing pages in the default master page layout.

   Based on the specified elements of the interior pages, each page in this spread has different margin and column requirements. Fortunately, InDesign allows you to modify those settings for individual pages in the spread.

2. **Click once on any page other than the A-Master spread in the Pages panel.**

   When you double-click the master page name in the Pages panel, the entire spread is selected (highlighted) in the panel. To change a setting for only one page of the spread, you first have to deselect the spread (by selecting some other page), and then select only the specific page you want to modify.

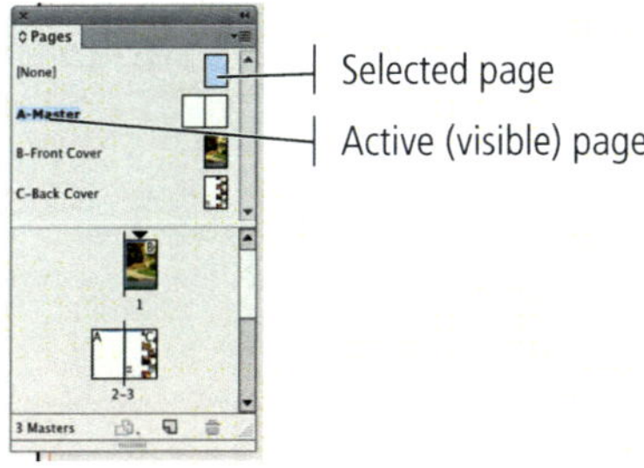

Selected page

Active (visible) page

> ***Note:***
>
> *You can click a regular page or a master page icon; the important point is to deselect the A-Master spread.*

3. **In the Pages panel, click once on the left page icon of the A-Master spread.**

   Clicking a page icon once selects that page without changing the visible (active) page in the document window.

4. **With the left page of the A-Master layout selected, choose Layout>Margins and Columns.**

5. **With the Preview option checked, make sure the four margin fields are not linked. Change the top margin to 5", change the outside margin to 2", and change the number of columns to 1.**

   Make sure you see the broken chain links between the margin fields; you do not want all four margins to be constrained to the same value.

   Unfortunately, changing the margins and columns does not automatically change the settings of the primary text frame. You have to change those separately.

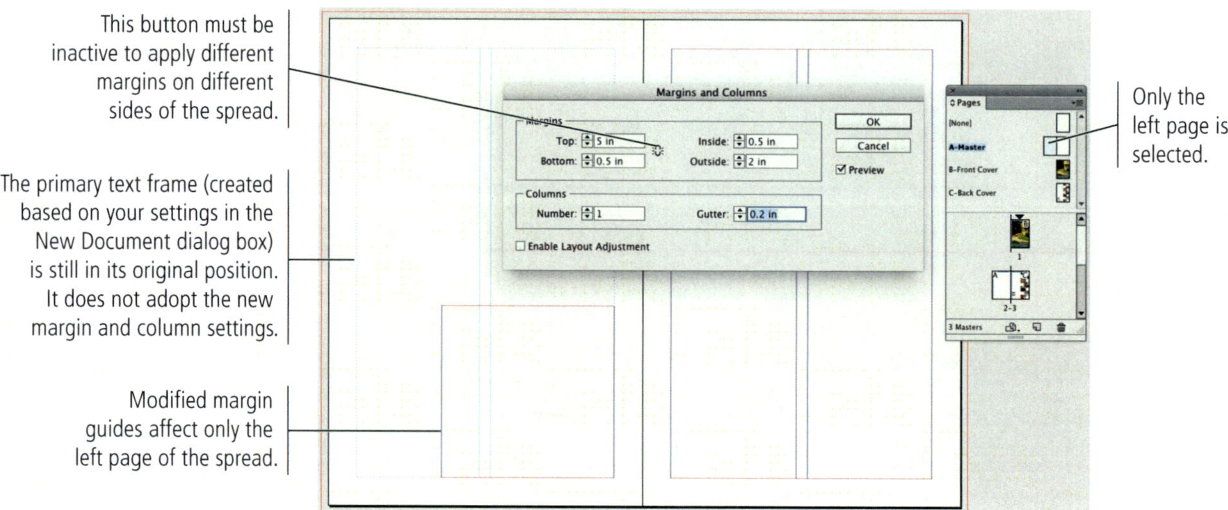

6. **Click OK to apply the changes.**

7. **In the document window, choose the Gap tool in the Tools panel. Place the cursor in the top margin area of the left-facing page.**

   The Gap tool allows you to actively manipulate white space on a page, rather than manipulating only specific objects. When you place the cursor between existing objects, or between an object and the page edge, the gray highlight shows which space you are editing; the arrow indicator behind the cursor icon shows what can be moved by clicking and dragging.

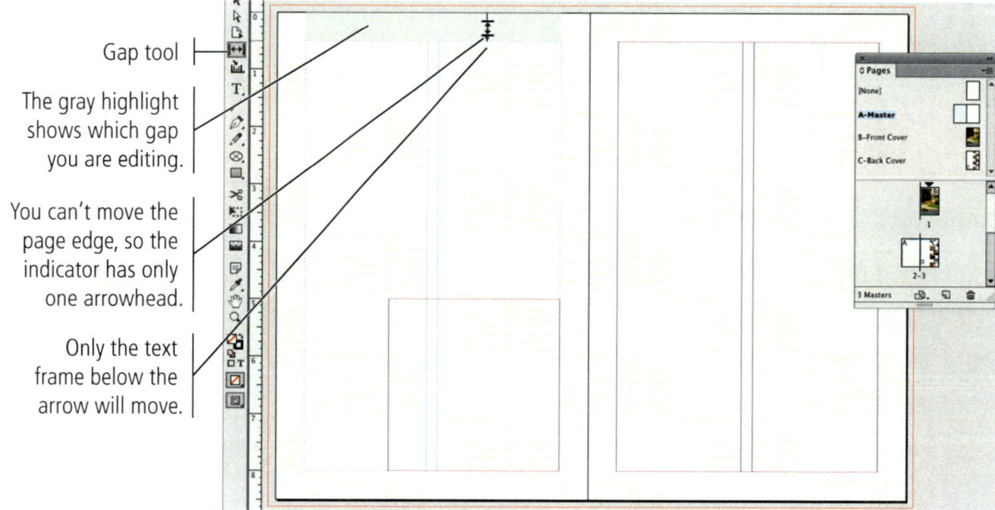

8. **Click in the margin area above the left page of the spread. Drag down until the cursor feedback shows a height of 5″.**

   When you edit the gap between a page edge and an object, you resize the object in the direction you drag. When you drag near the adjusted margin guide, the frame edge snaps to align with the guide.

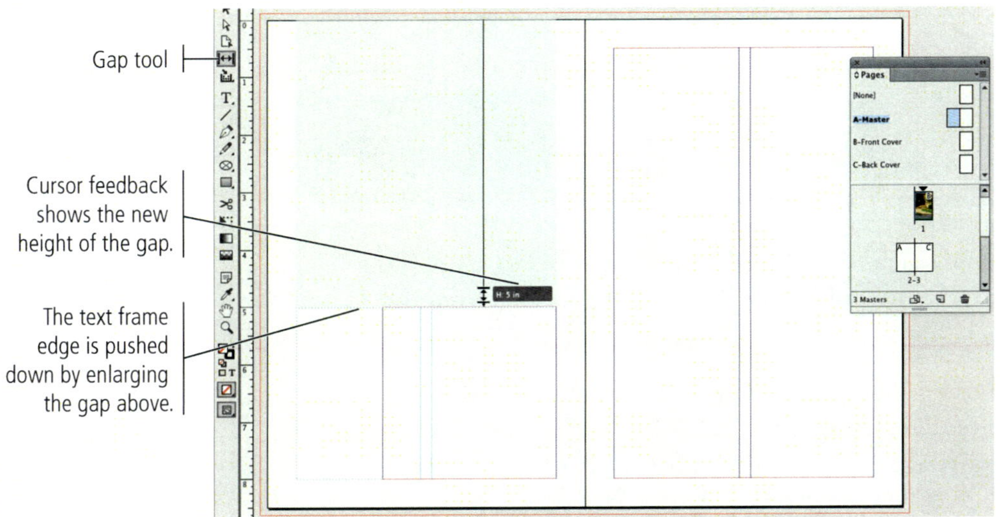

Note:

If you press Option/Alt while dragging the margin, you can increase the margin without affecting the object's size; the existing object edge simply moves based on the new margin gap.

Understanding the Gap Tool

INDESIGN FOUNDATIONS

The Gap tool is designed to let you actively manipulate the white space on a page. Using one or more modifier keys, the Gap tool can also resize or move objects that touch the gap you edit.

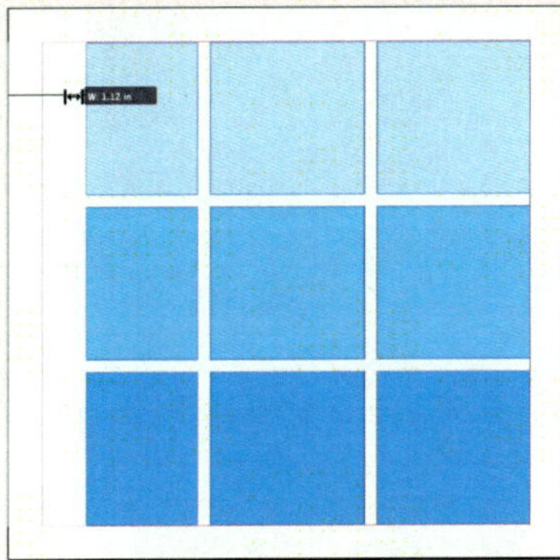

Click and drag a margin to change the space between the page edge and nearby objects, and affect the size of objects that touch the margin.

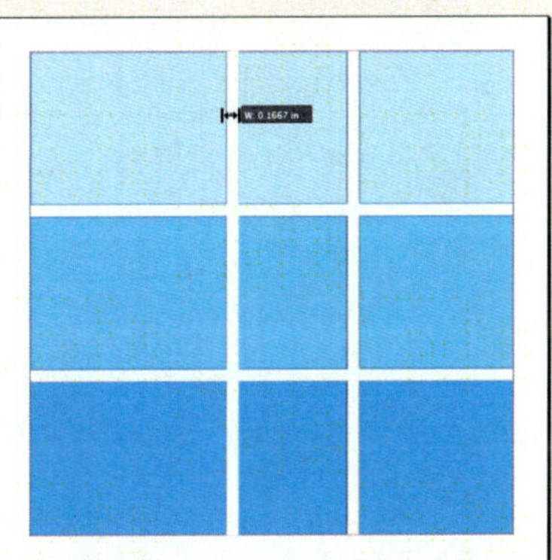

Click and drag a gap between objects to move the gap and affect the size of adjacent objects.

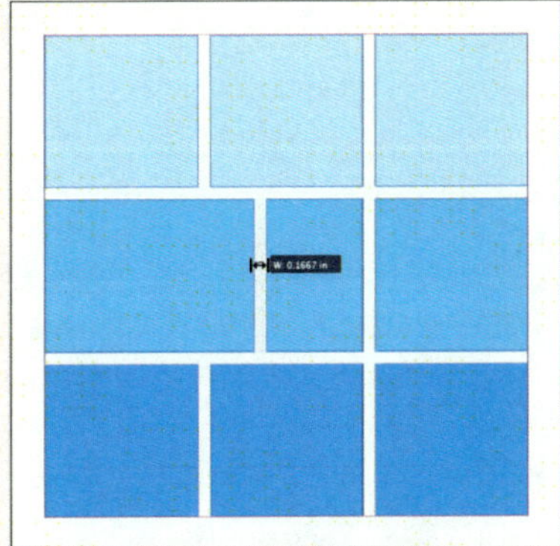

Shift-click and drag to move the gap only between immediately adjacent objects.

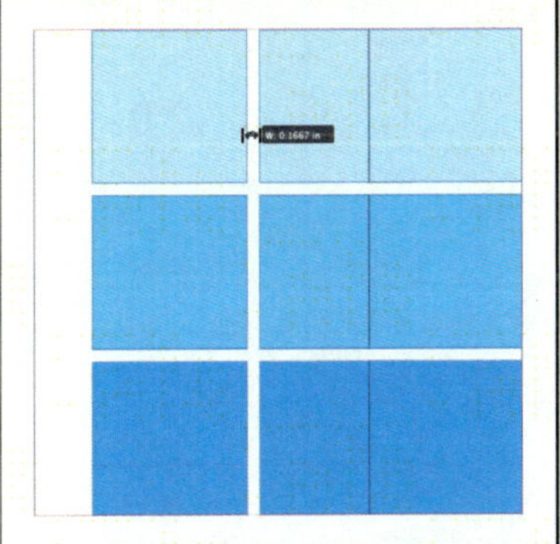

Option/Alt-click and drag to move the white space and adjacent objects, without affecting the objects' size.

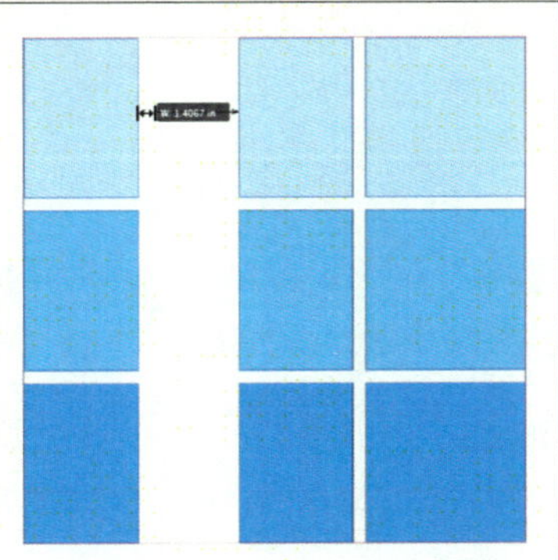

Command/Control-click and drag to resize the gap and change the size of adjacent objects.

9. **Click in the margin area on the left side of the page. Drag right until the cursor feedback shows a width of 2″.**

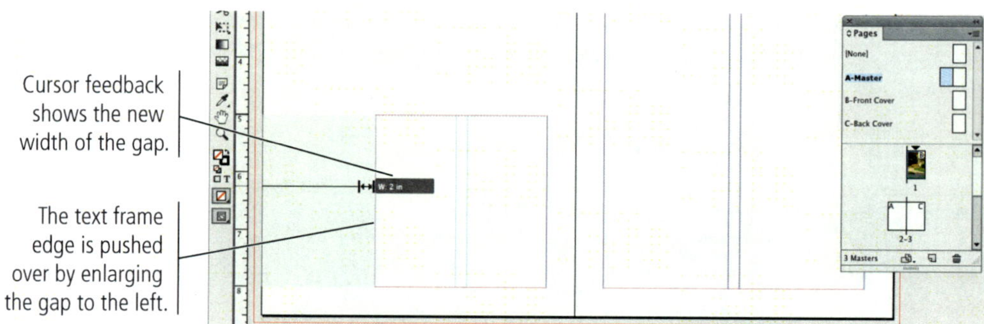

10. **Using the Selection tool, click the reduced text frame to select it. Control/right-click the frame and choose Text Frame Options from the contextual menu.**

11. **In the Text Frame Options dialog box, change the number of columns to 1, change all four Inset Spacing values to 0.125″, and choose Center in the Vertical Justification Align menu. Click OK to apply the changes.**

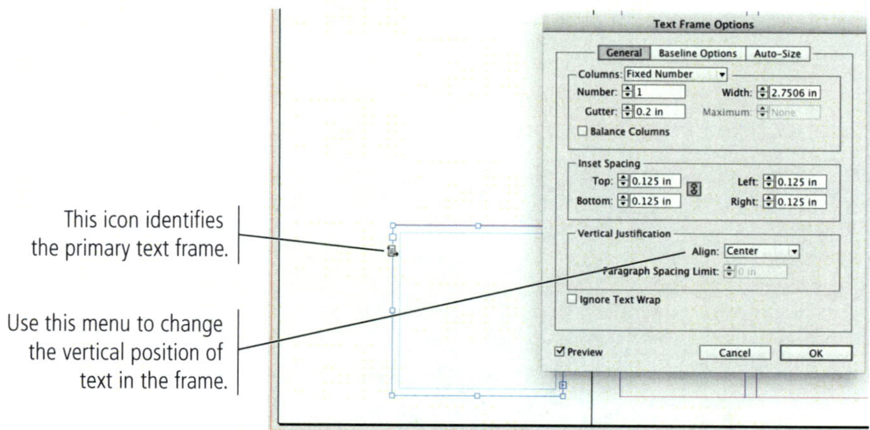

12. **In the Pages panel, select only the right page of the A-Master spread. Choose Layout>Margins and Columns and change the bottom margin to 3.25″. Click OK.**

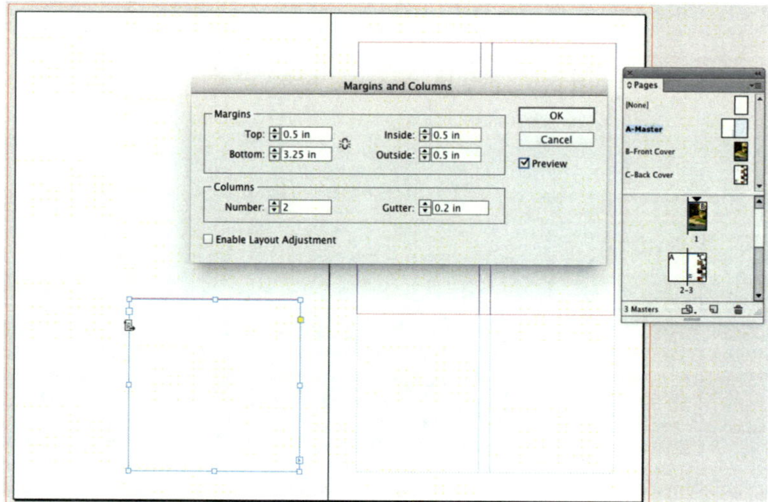

13. **Using the Gap tool, click and drag to change the white space at the bottom of the right-facing page to 3.25″.**

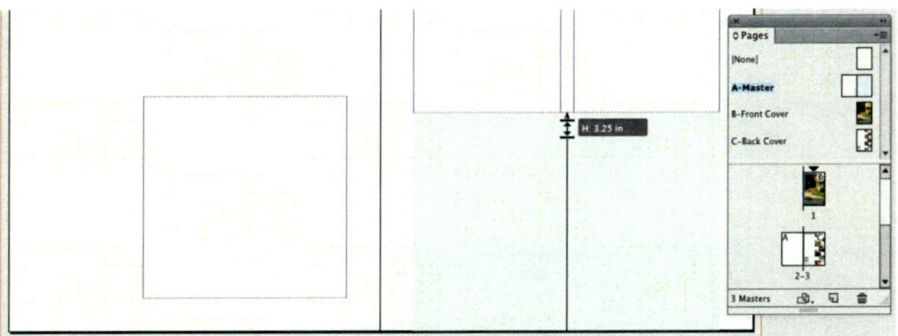

14. **Save the file and continue to the next exercise.**

Add Common Elements to a Master Page Layout

In addition to the primary text frame, you need several other elements to appear on every spread in the body of the document: the graphics frame on the left page of the spread, as well as the callout box and page footer on the right page of the spread. Again, it makes sense to create master page placeholders for these objects rather than recreating the objects on every individual layout page.

1. **With realty_booklet.indd open, make sure the A-Master layout is showing in the document window.**

2. **Create a new text frame with the following dimensions (based on the top-left reference point):**

   X: 7.375″ W: 3.75″
   Y: 5.65″ H: 2.35″

   By default, InDesign measurements reflect an object's position relative to the entire spread; the X: 7.375″ position is actually 1.875″ from the left edge of the right page. You can change this behavior by changing the Ruler Units origin in the Units & Increments pane of the Preferences dialog box.

3. **Fill the new text frame with the C=100 M=35 Y=90 K=20 swatch.**

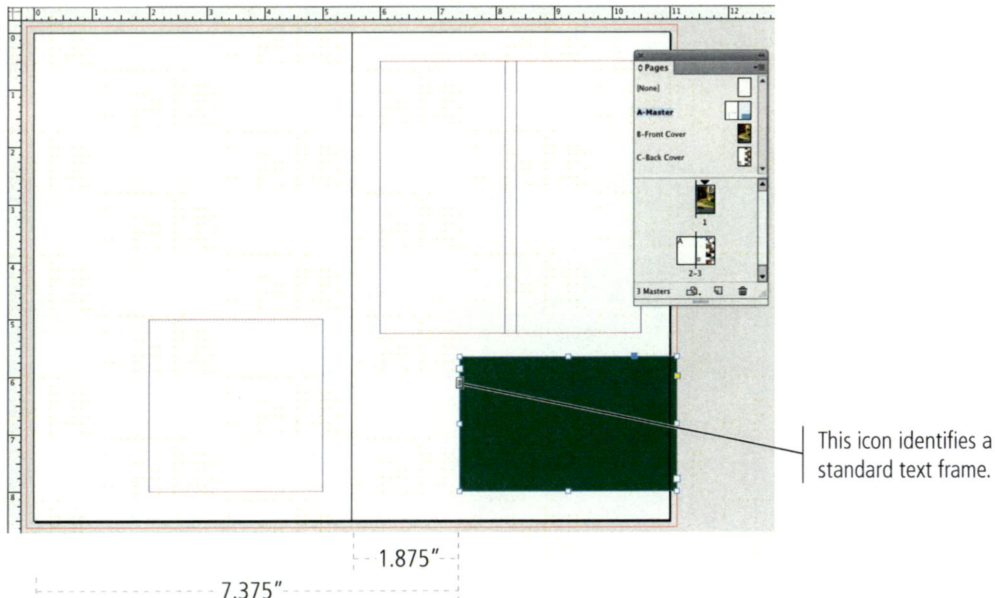

This icon identifies a standard text frame.

4. **Control/right-click the new frame and choose Text Frame Options from the contextual menu. Change the Top, Bottom, and Left Inset Spacing fields to 0.125″, and change the Right Inset Spacing field to 0.625″. Click OK.**

   Because the frame bleeds off the page edge, you need to adjust the frame inset on only the bleed side to match the rest of the layout. Instead of overlaying two frames — one with the green fill and one with the text frame — you can use uneven inset spacing to achieve the same goal.

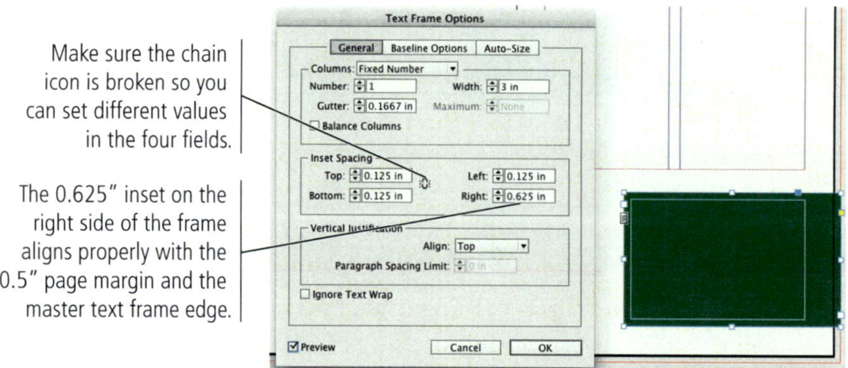

5. **Using the Selection tool, click the primary text frame on the right page of the spread. Click the Out port of the primary text frame, and then immediately click the green text frame to link the two frames.**

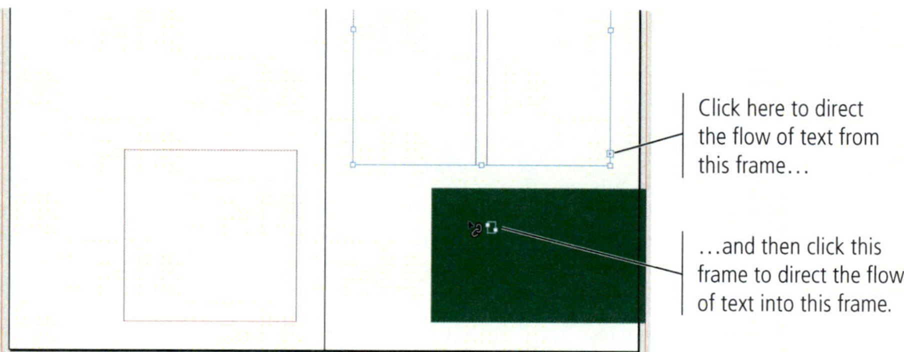

After adding the green frame to the text thread, it becomes part of the primary text frame. Keep in mind that you can only have one primary text thread on each master page, but that thread can have multiple linked frames.

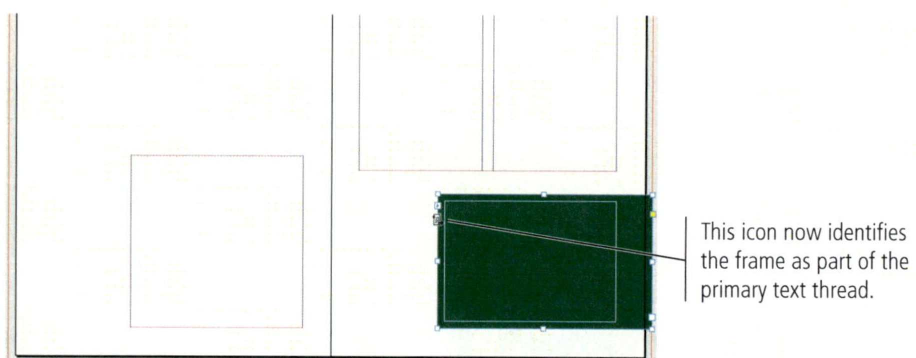

Note:

The client's content is supplied in a single file, and the callout text for each spread appears within the main body of the text. The text includes the heading "Through the Buyer's Eyes," so you can identify the appropriate text.

6. **Choose View>Extras>Show Text Threads.**

   The primary text frames on each side of the spread are automatically linked. The thread then moves to the green frame, as you defined in Step 5.

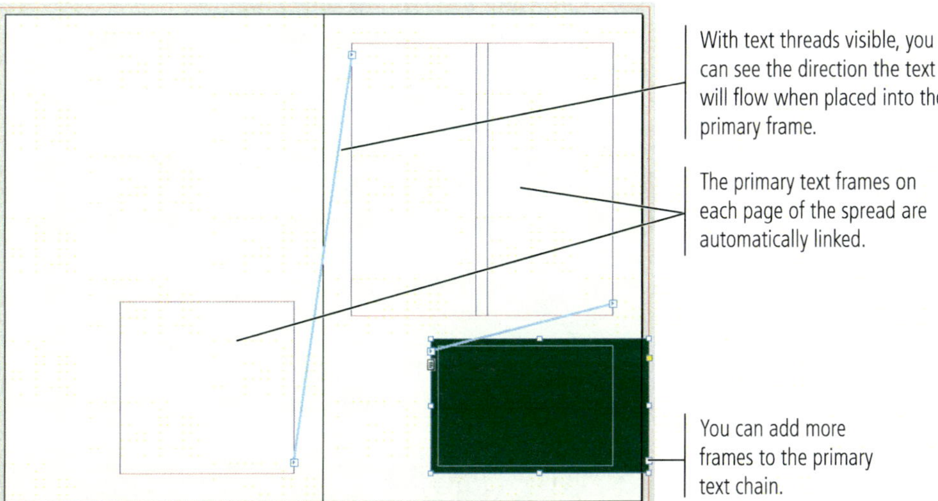

With text threads visible, you can see the direction the text will flow when placed into the primary frame.

The primary text frames on each page of the spread are automatically linked.

You can add more frames to the primary text chain.

7. **Turn off the text threads (View>Extras>Hide Text Threads).**

8. **Using the Rectangle Frame tool, create an empty graphics frame that fills the entire left page of the spread (including the bleed area). Fill the frame with a 20% tint of the dark green swatch.**

9. **Choose Object>Arrange>Send to Back to move the graphics frame behind the text frame.**

   Each spread in the booklet will include a large image on the left side of the spread. Placing it on the master layout eliminates the need to manually draw the frame on each spread. You added the fill color simply as a visual reference for placing the image.

10. **Select the primary text frame on the left page of the spread. Change its fill color to Paper and change its Opacity value to 85%.**

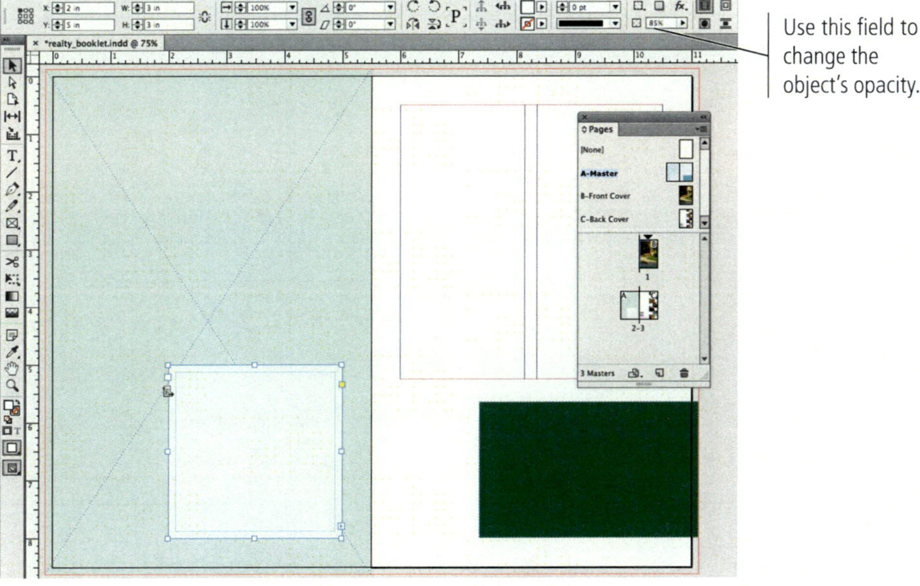

Use this field to change the object's opacity.

11. **Save the file and continue to the next exercise.**

Place Automatic Page Number Markers

The next item to add to the master page layout is the page footer information — the page number and the name of the booklet. Rather than manually numbering each page in the booklet, which can be time consuming and invites human error, you can use special characters to automatically number the pages in any layout.

1. **With realty_booklet.indd open, make sure the A-Master layout is showing.**

2. **Create a new text frame with the following dimensions (based on the top-left reference point):**

   X: 6″ W: 4.5″
   Y: 8.125″ H: 0.25″

3. **Inside the new frame, type Home Enhancement Guide, and then change the formatting to 12-pt ATC Agate Bold with right paragraph alignment.**

Special Characters and White Space

INDESIGN FOUNDATIONS

A number of special characters can be accessed in the Type submenus. Use the following chart as a how-and-why guide for accessing these characters.

Menu			What it's used for
Insert Special Character	Markers	Current Page Number	Places the current page number
		Next Page Number	Places the page number of the next frame in the same story
		Previous Page Number	Places the page number of the previous frame in the same story
		Section Marker	Places a user-defined text variable that is specific to the current layout section. (You'll work with section numbering in Project 8.)
		Footnote Number	Inserts a number character based on the options defined in the Footnote Options dialog box
	Hyphens and Dashes	Em Dash	Places a dash that has the same width as the applied type size
		En Dash	Places a dash equivalent to one-half of an em dash
		Discretionary Hyphen	Allows you to hyphenate a word in a location other than what is defined by the currect dictionary, or hyphenate a word when automatic hyphenation is turned off; the discretionary hyphen only appears if the word is hyphenated at the end of a line
		Nonbreaking Hyphen	Places a hyphen character that will not break at the end of a line; used to keep both parts of a phrase on the same line of the paragraph
	Quotation Marks	Double Left Quotation Marks	“
		Double Right Quotation Marks	”
		Single Left Quotation Mark	‘
		Single Right Quotation Mark	’
		Straight Double Quotation Marks	"
		Straight Single Quotation Mark	'
	Other	Tab	Forces following text to begin at the next defined or default tab stop
		Right Indent Tab	Forces following text to align at the right indent of the column or frame
		Indent to Here	Creates a hanging indent by forcing all following lines in the paragraph to indent to the location of the character
		End Nested Style Here	Interrupts nested style formatting before the defined character limit
		Non-joiner	Prevents adjacent characters from being joined in a ligature or other alternate character connection

4. **Place the insertion point immediately after the word "Guide" and press the Spacebar once.**

Because the text is right-aligned, the Space character is not visible; a space at the end of a line is not considered in the line length or type position when InDesign aligns paragraphs.

5. **With the insertion point flashing after the space character (which you can't see), choose Type>Insert Special Character>Markers>Current Page Number.**

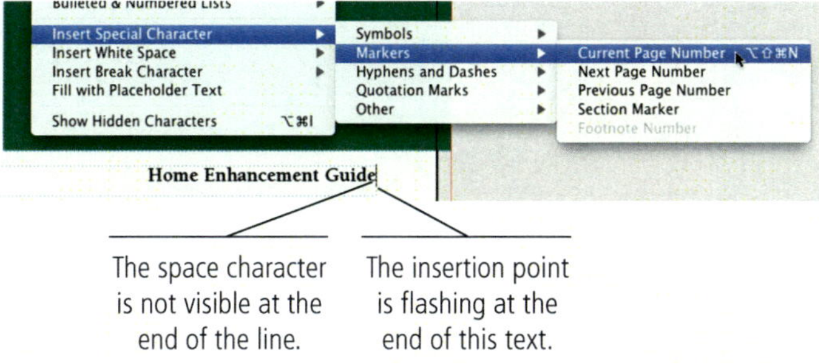

The space character is not visible at the end of the line.

The insertion point is flashing at the end of this text.

Special Characters and White Space (continued)

Menu		What it's used for
Insert White Space	Em Space	Space equivalent to a capital M in the applied font and type size
	En Space	One-half of an em space
	Nonbreaking Space	Places a space character the same width as pressing the Spacebar; this character prevents a line break from occurring, which allows you to keep related words together on the same line.
	Nonbreaking Space (Fixed Width)	Same as the regular nonbreaking space, but does not change size when a paragraph uses justified alignment.
	Hair Space	One-twenty-fourth of an em space
	Sixth Space	One-sixth of an em space
	Thin Space	One-eighth of an em space
	Quarter Space	One-fourth of an em space
	Third Space	One-third of an em space
	Punctuation Space	Same width as a period in the applied font
	Figure Space	Same width as a number in the applied font
	Flush Space	Variable space in a justified paragraph placed between the last character of the paragraph and a decorative character (a "bug") used to indicate the end of a story
Insert Break Character	Column Break	Forces text into the next available column (or frame, if used in a one-column frame or the last column of a multi-column frame)
	Frame Break	Forces text into the next available frame
	Page Break	Forces text into the first available frame on the next page, skipping any available frames or columns on the same page
	Odd Page Break	Forces text into the first available frame on the next odd-numbered page
	Even Page Break	Forces text into the first available frame on the next even-numbered page
	Paragraph Return	Creates a new paragraph (same as pressing Return/Enter)
	Forced Line Break	Creates a new line without starting a new paragraph (called a "soft return")
	Discretionary Line Break	Creates a new line if the character falls at the end of the line; if the character falls in the middle of the column, the line is not broken

6. **If the hidden characters are not visible, choose Type>Show Hidden Characters.**

The Current Page Number command inserts a special character that reflects the correct page number of any page where it appears. Because you placed this character on the A-Master page, the character shows as "A" in the text frame.

Now that the Space character is no longer the last character in the line, you can see it — as long as hidden characters are showing.

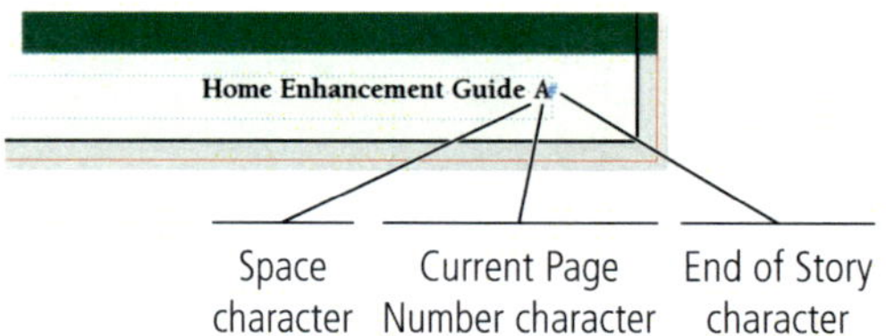

In this case, the single, regular Space character is not enough to separate the booklet name from the page number. InDesign provides a number of options for increasing (and decreasing) white space without simply pressing the Spacebar numerous times.

7. **Highlight the Space character before the Page Number character.**

Keyboard Shortcuts for Special Characters

INDESIGN FOUNDATIONS

Character	Keyboard Shortcut	
	Macintosh	**Windows**
Current page number	Command-Option-Shift-N	Control-Alt-Shift-N
Em dash	Option-Shift-Hyphen (-)	Alt-Shift-Hyphen (-)
En dash	Option-Hyphen	Alt-Hyphen
Discretionary hyphen	Command-Shift-Hyphen	Control-Shift-Hyphen
Nonbreaking hyphen	Command-Option-Hyphen	Control-Alt-Hyphen
Double left quotation marks	Option-[	Alt-[
Double right quotation marks	Option-Shift-[	Alt-Shift-[
Single left quotation mark	Option-]	Alt-]
Single right quotation mark	Option-Shift-]	Alt-Shift-]
Straight double quotation marks	Control-Shift-'	Alt-Shift-'
Straight single quotation mark	Control-'	Alt-'
Tab	Tab	Tab
Right indent tab	Shift-Tab	Shift-Tab
Indent to here	Command-\	Control-\
Em space	Command-Shift-M	Control-Shift-M
En space	Command-Shift-N	Control-Shift-N
Nonbreaking space	Command-Option-X	Control-Alt-X
Thin space	Command-Option-Shift-M	Control-Alt-Shift-M
Column break	Enter (numeric keypad)	Enter (numeric keypad)
Frame break	Shift-Enter (numeric keypad)	Shift-Enter (numeric keypad)
Page break	Command-Enter (numeric keypad)	Control-Enter (numeric keypad)
Paragraph return	Return	Enter
Forced line break	Shift-Return	Shift-Enter

8. **Choose Type>Insert White Space>Em Space.**

An **em** is a typographic measure equivalent to the applied type size. An em space is white space equal to one em.

9. **Add a second Em Space character immediately after the first.**

10. **Select all text in the footer and change the type size to 10 pt.**

Special and hidden characters are still characters; changing the type formatting affects these characters in the same way as regular characters.

11. **Save the file and continue to the next stage of the project.**

Stage 2 Controlling the Flow of Text

Because you imported the covers as master pages and built a spread layout to hold the various body elements, all the necessary pieces are now in place to import the client's provided text and graphics. The time you spent building effective master pages will enable you to quickly place the layout content and create a multi-page document; you significantly reduced overall development time because you don't have to manually create these elements on each page.

You are building a document with 16 facing pages. You could manually insert the necessary pages, and then manually link the text from one page to the next. But anytime you see the word "manually," you should look for ways to automate some or all of the process. The ability to automate work is one of the defining characteristics of professional page-layout software such as InDesign.

 Import and Auto-Flow Client Text

In Project 3: HeartSmart Newsletter, you used styles in an InDesign template to format the text imported from a Microsoft Word file. You learned that by applying styles, you can apply multiple formatting attributes — both character and paragraph — with a single click. InDesign is not the only software that supports text-formatting styles; Microsoft Word does as well.

Many clients will submit text with local formatting — they might have highlighted some text and changed the font, size, spacing, etc. — that you will strip out and replace with the proper InDesign translations. More sophisticated users, however, will send files that are formatted with Microsoft Word styles. In this case, you can import the styles from Microsoft Word directly into your InDesign layout to use as the basis for your work.

1. **With `realty_booklet.indd` open, open the Type pane of the Preferences dialog box.**

   Remember, preferences are accessed in the InDesign menu on Macintosh and the Edit menu on Windows.

2. **Make sure the Smart Text Reflow option is checked, choose End of Story in the Add Pages To menu, and check the Delete Empty Pages option. Click OK.**

   When Smart Text Reflow is active, InDesign automatically adds pages to accommodate an entire story that is placed in a primary text frame. This option applies to adding text within a story, and to changing formatting in a way that affects the number of required pages — which you will do in a later exercise.

   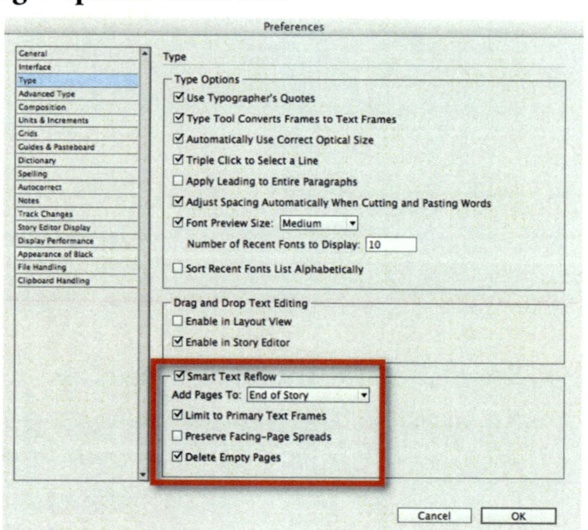

   - You can use the **Add Pages To** menu to determine where pages are added to the file (at the end of the current story, the current section, or the current document).
   - If **Limit To Primary Text Frames** is not checked, you can add or remove pages when editing text in frames other than a primary text frame. This option only applies if the existing frame is already part of a text thread with at least one other frame. (New pages added when the text frame is not a primary text frame have a single-column text frame that matches the default page margins for the file.)
   - If **Preserve Facing-Page Spreads** is active, pages added to the middle of a document are added as document spreads based on the applied master layout. When unchecked, only the necessary pages will be added; subsequent existing pages are reshuffled (left-facing to right-facing) if necessary.
   - If **Delete Empty Pages** is active, unnecessary pages are removed from the layout if you delete text (or format text to require less space).

> ***Note:***
>
> *If Smart Text Reflow is not active, you can press Shift and click the loaded text cursor in a primary text frame (on a layout page) to automatically flow the entire story; InDesign adds pages as necessary to accommodate the entire story. (In this case, new pages are always added at the end of the document, regardless of the position of the text box where you first click to place the text. The Smart Text Reflow preference is not activated.)*

3. **Navigate to Page 2 of the layout and then choose File>Place. Navigate to the file `booklet.doc` in the WIP>Realtors folder. Make sure the Show Import Options box is checked and click Open.**

   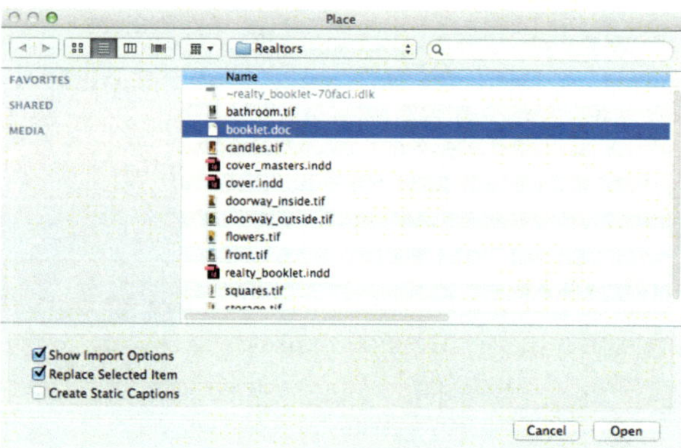

4. **In the Import Options dialog box, make sure the Preserve Styles and Formatting from Text and Tables option is selected.**

5. **In the Manual Page Breaks menu, choose No Breaks.**

   This command removes any page and section breaks that exist in the client's Microsoft Word file.

6. **Select the Import Styles Automatically option, choose Auto Rename in both conflict menus, then click OK.**

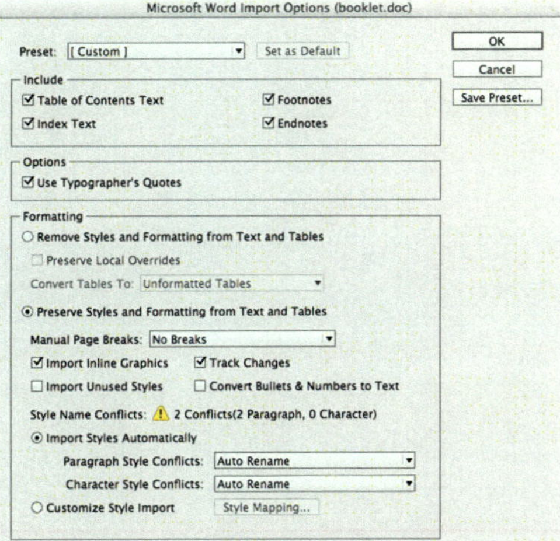

7. **Review the resulting warning, then click OK to import the text.**

When you import Microsoft Word files with their formatting, you frequently see the Missing Fonts warning.

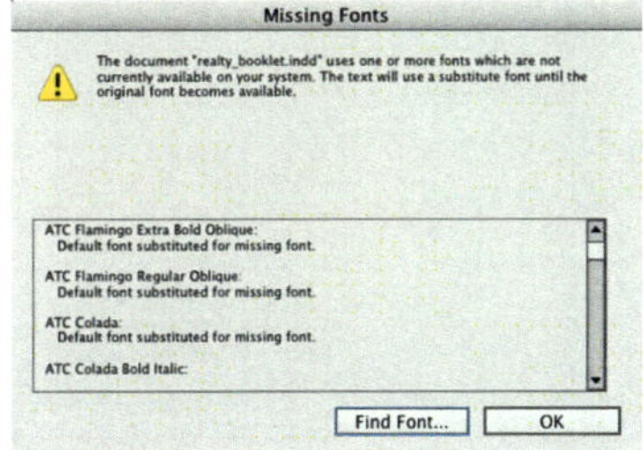

Many actions in Microsoft Word — such as using the B or I buttons to apply **faux bold** or **faux italic** type styles — can cause problems in InDesign because InDesign tries to translate those faux formatting options to the best-possible "real" font variants required for commercial printing applications.

The good news is that in many cases, you can replace the fonts used in the Microsoft Word file with something more appropriate for your overall design. It would be a waste of time to correct these font problems until you know that it's necessary. In this case, you're eventually going to replace the style that calls for the missing fonts, so there's no point in spending time resolving the missing-font problem.

This is a common workflow issue when you work with client-supplied files. Every situation is different, but we find it best to import client formatting so we can review the editorial priority, and then edit or define styles as necessary to complete the page layout.

8. **Click the loaded text cursor inside the margin guides on Page 2.**

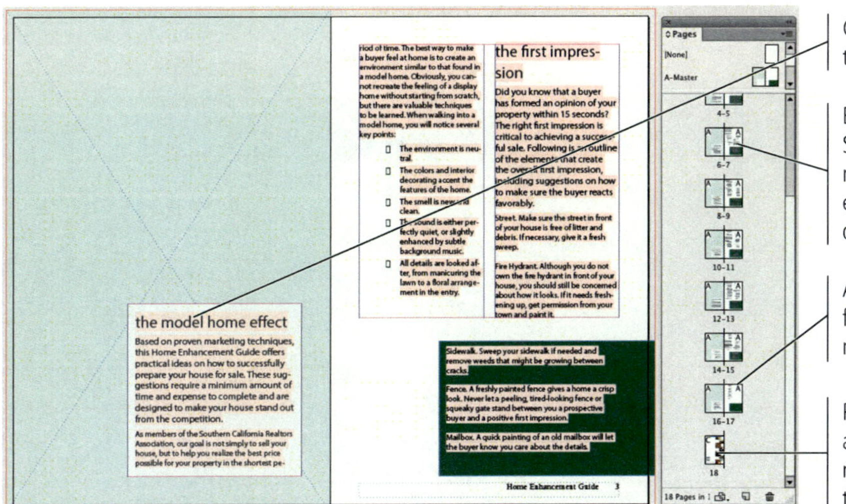

Click the loaded text cursor in this frame to place the story.

Because of your choices in the Smart Text Reflow preferences, new pages are added at the end of the story to accommodate the entire placed story.

As it is currently formatted, the placed text requires 16 pages (2–17).

Page 3 becomes Page 18, after the pages that are required to accommodate the placed story.

9. **Save the file and continue to the next exercise.**

Understanding the Primary Text Frame

It is important to understand how the primary text frame affects placed text. If you change the master-page layout that is associated with a specific page, text inside the primary text frame reflows based on the dimensions of the primary text frame on the newly applied master page.

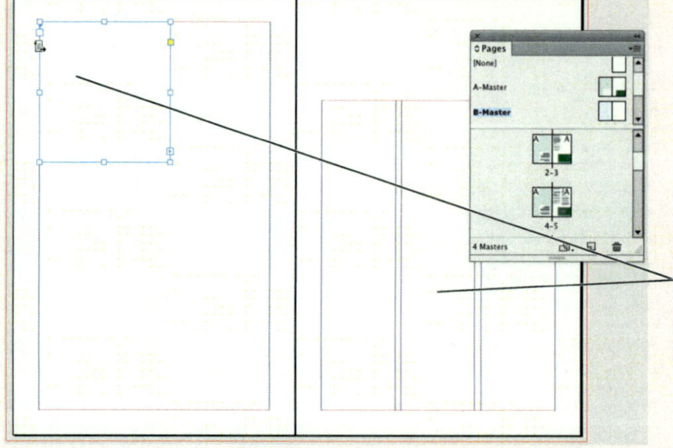

The primary text frames on the B-Master have different dimensions and parameters than the primary text frames on the A-Master layout.

To illustrate this point in the examples here, we added a new facing-page master page layout named B-Master, with text frames in different properties (position, size, and number of columns) than the frames on the A-Master in the realty booklet file.

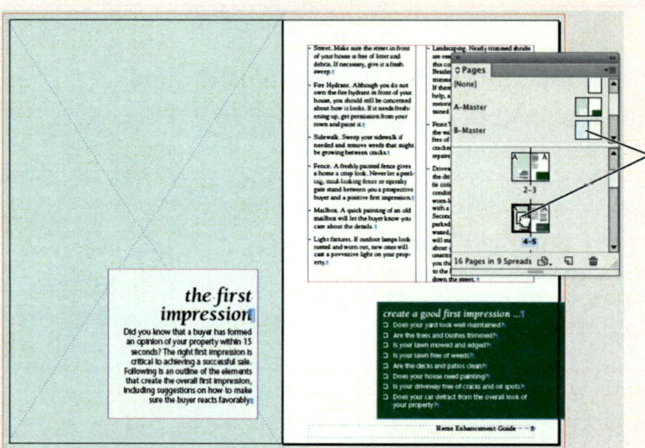

We dragged the left page of the B-Master onto the Page 4 icon to change the master that is applied to the page.

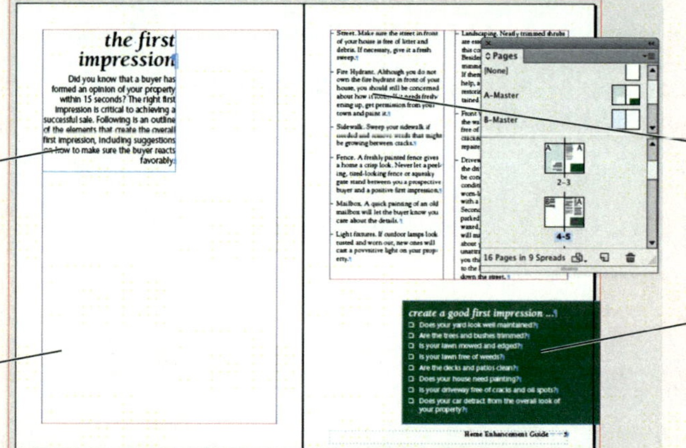

Text in the primary frame reflows into the primary text frame dimensions that are defined on the newly applied master page.

The background frame does not exist on the B-Master layout, so it is no longer on the regular page.

Text on the page reflows based on how much text can fit in the smaller frame on the left-facing page.

Frames on the right page of the spread are not affected because we did not change the master layout associated with that page.

Keep the following in mind when you work with primary text frames:

- When you work on the master-page layout, you can click the Primary Text Frame icon to convert a frame to a standard text frame, or click the Standard Text Frame icon to convert a frame to the primary text frame.

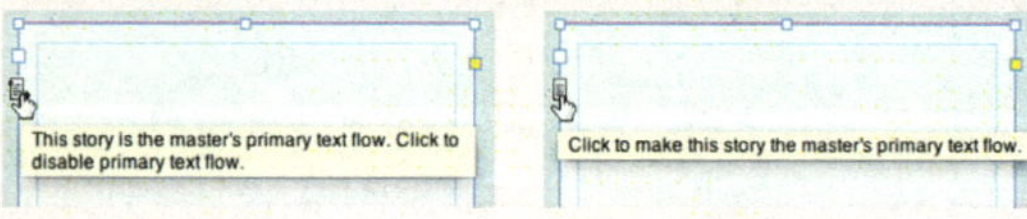

- You can only have one primary text frame (or series of threaded frames) per page.
- If you convert one frame in the primary text thread, all frames in the thread are converted to regular frames.
- If you convert a different frame to the primary text frame, the existing primary text frame is automatically converted to a standard text frame.

Review and Replace Imported Styles

As you can see in the current booklet file, the text is just a long block with little to identify the editorial priority (e.g., headings, subheadings, and so on). Fonts used in the client's file aren't available, as indicated by the pink "missing font" highlight.

This type of situation occurs frequently. When it does, you should begin by reviewing the text to see if applied styles can provide any clues about which elements belong where and at what editorial priority.

1. **With Page 2 of `realty_booklet.indd` showing, click the Type tool in the first paragraph ("the model home effect").**

2. **Look at the Paragraph Styles panel (Window>Styles>Paragraph Styles).**

   The first paragraph is formatted with the Section Head style. You can assume that other text with the same basic appearance is also a section head.

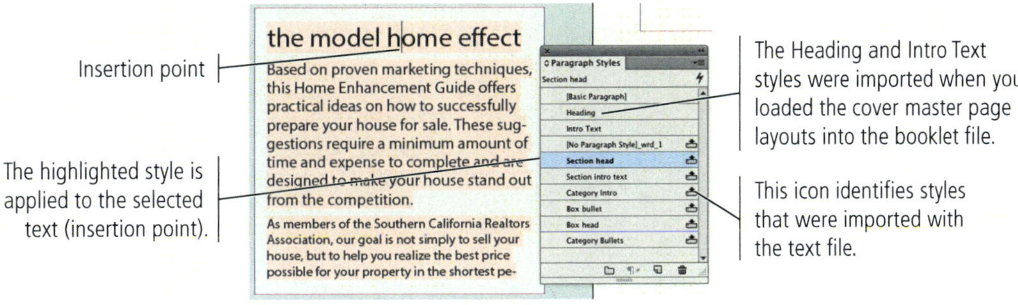

3. **In the Paragraph Styles panel, Control/right-click the Section head style and choose Delete Style from the contextual menu.**

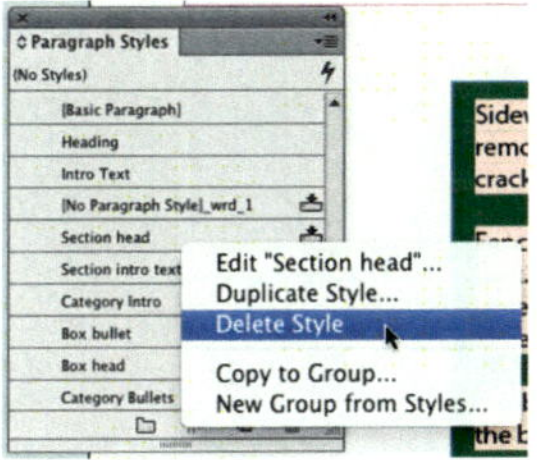

4. **In the Delete Paragraph Style dialog box, choose Heading in the Replace With menu and click OK.**

   If you delete a style that's being used, you have to determine what to do with text that uses the style you want to delete. If you want to maintain the formatting of that text without applying a different style, you can choose [No Paragraph Style].

   After the Section Head style has been replaced with the Heading style, the associated headings in the layout change in appearance to match the new style definition.

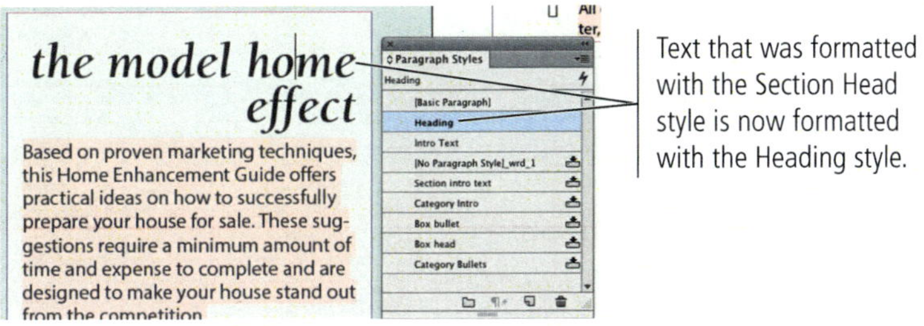

5. **Move the insertion point to the next paragraph.**

   The second paragraph is formatted with the Section Intro Text style. Again, you can assume that other text with the same appearance is also introductory text for a section.

6. **Using the same process as in Steps 3–4, replace the Section intro text style with the Intro Text style.**

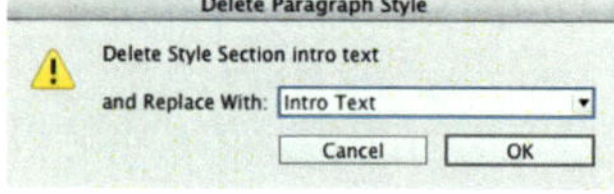

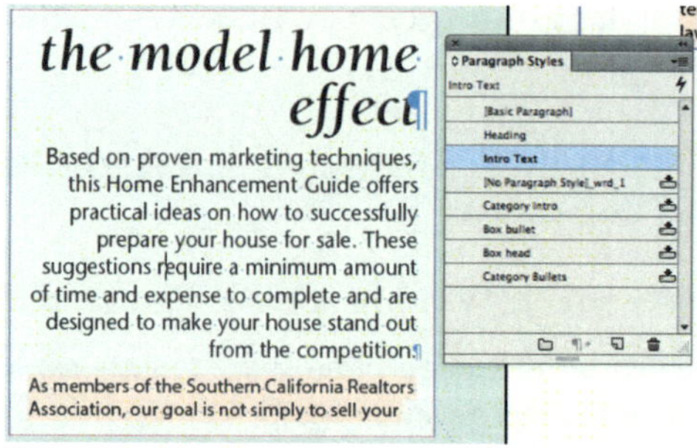

7. **In the Paragraph Styles panel, drag [No Paragraph Style]_wrd_1 to the panel's Delete button.**

   It's a good idea to remove unnecessary styles from the InDesign document.

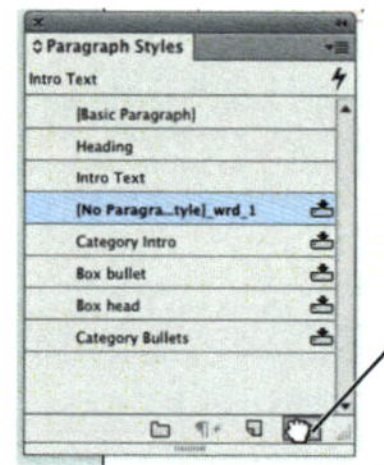

Dragging a style to the panel's Delete button is the same as choosing Delete from the style's contextual menu.

8. **In the resulting dialog box, choose [No Paragraph Style] in the Replace With menu. Make sure the Preserve Formatting option is selected, then click OK.**

   InDesign's default [No Paragraph Style] is not a style — in fact, it is the express lack of a defined style. The imported [No Paragraph Style]_wrd_1 is considered a style, so you have to decide what to do with the formatting that was applied to any text associated with that style.

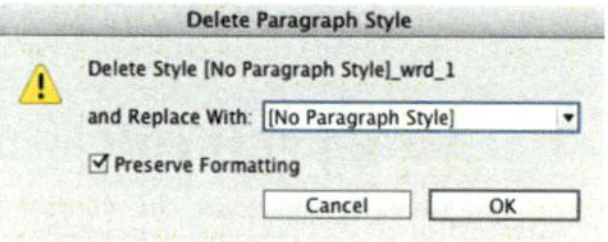

9. **Save the file and continue to the next exercise.**

Note:

Depending on the exact size of your text frames, only one line in the third paragraph might appear in the frame on Page 2. Don't worry if your text doesn't appear exactly like what you see in our screen captures. By the time you finish this stage of the project, you will exercise precise control over the position of every paragraph in the layout.

Note:

Any time you choose [No Paragraph Style] in the Replace With menu, the Preserve Formatting option becomes available in the Delete Paragraph Style dialog box.

Edit a Style Definition

In most cases, styles that are imported with a text file will need at least some modification — if for no other reason than InDesign has more sophisticated options that are relevant to commercial printing. In addition, your clients are not designers, so their formatting choices are most likely not up to par with professional-quality graphic design.

1. **With Page 2 of `realty_booklet.indd` visible in the document window, zoom out so you can see the entire spread.**

2. **Place the insertion point in the third paragraph of imported copy.**

   This paragraph is formatted with the Category Intro style.

Note:

You can edit the default type settings for a layout by editing the [Basic Paragraph] style. You can edit the default type settings for all new InDesign layouts by editing the [Basic Paragraph] style when no file is open.

3. **Control/right-click the Category Intro style and choose Edit "Category Intro" in the contextual menu.**

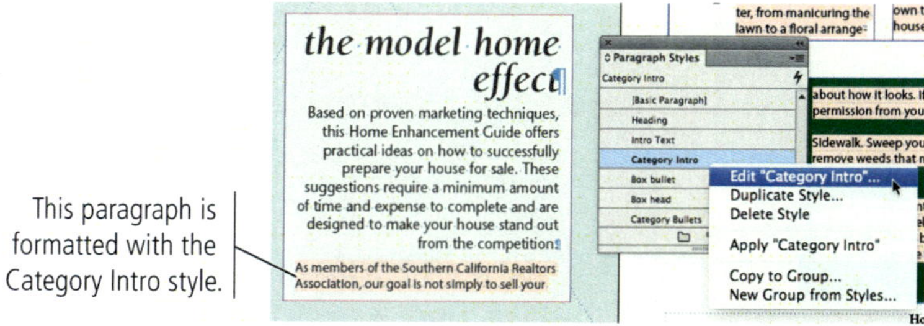

Editing styles is both easy and efficient. When you change the options in a style definition, any text formatted with that style reformats with the changed definition.

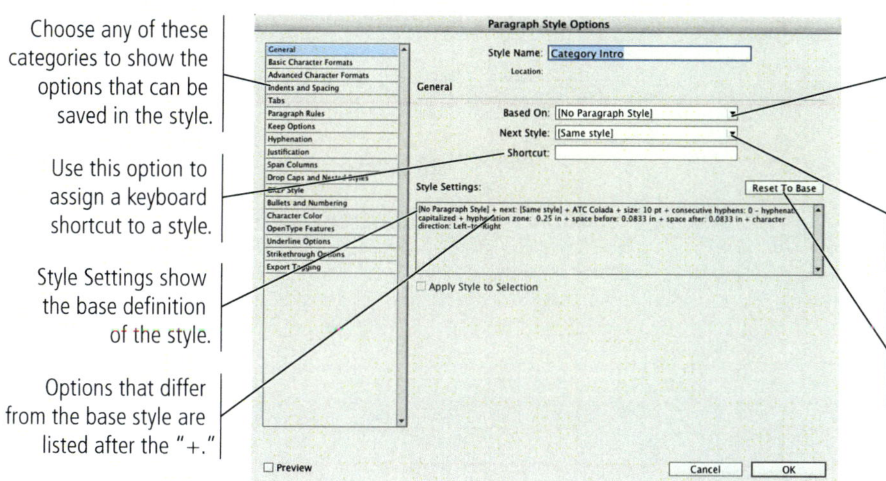

4. **In the Basic Character Formats options, change the formatting to 9.5-pt ATC Pyrite Normal.**

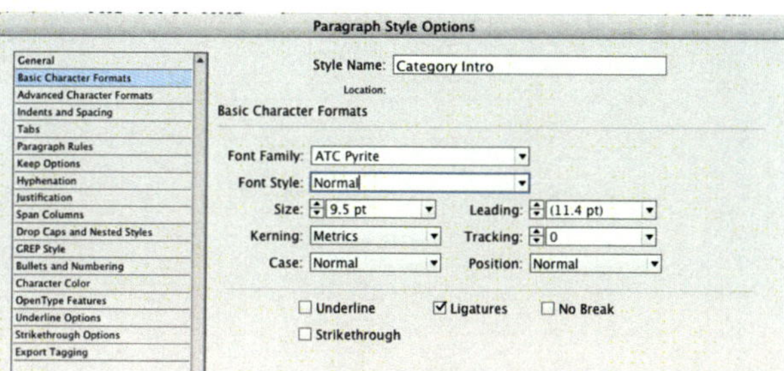

5. **In the Indents and Spacing options, change the Space Before field to 0.1" and change the Space After field to 0".**

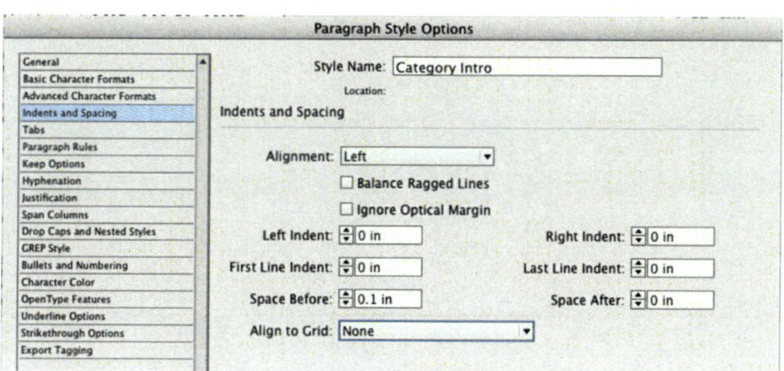

Note:

You can also edit a style by double-clicking the style in the panel. However, double-clicking a style in the panel applies the style to the current text, and then opens the Paragraph Style Options dialog box.

By Control/right-clicking the style in the panel, you can edit the style without applying it to the currently selected text.

Note:

If you check the Preview box in the Paragraph Style Options dialog box, you can see the effect of your changes before you click OK.

6. **Click OK to change the style definition.**

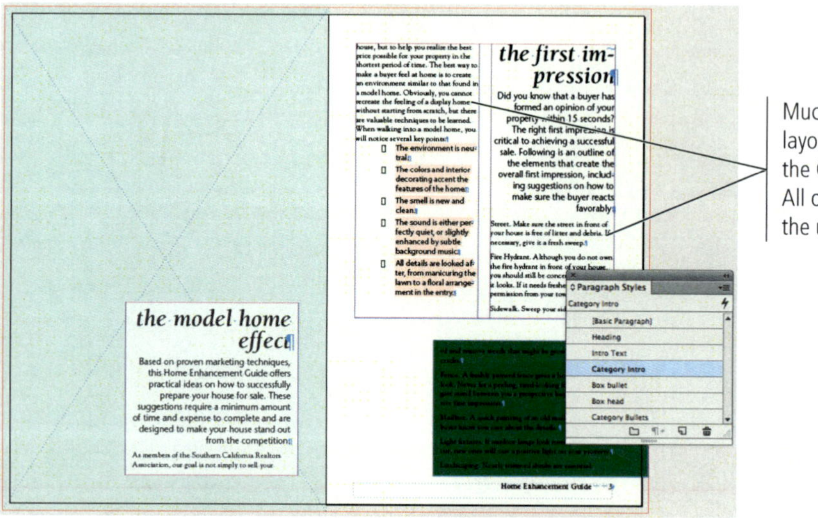

Much of the text in this layout is formatted with the Category Intro style. All of that text now reflects the updated definition.

> ***Note:***
>
> *Any Space Before value is ignored when a paragraph begins at the top of a frame or column.*

7. **Save the file and continue to the next exercise.**

 Define Parent-Child Style Relationships

There are two important points to remember about designing long documents. First, changing the definition of a style changes all text formatted with that style. Second, text should be consistently formatted from one page to the next; body copy (for example) should use the same basic font throughout the entire layout.

If you think of these two points together, consider what happens if you decide to change the font for the main body copy (for example, changing from Times New Roman to Adobe Garamond). Changing the main body font means you should also change any related styles that are variations of the main body text, such as bulleted or numbered lists.

The best way to manage this type of situation is to create secondary styles that are based on the main style. This way, changes to the main style (called the **parent style**) are reflected in styles that are based on that style (the **child styles**).

1. **With Pages 2–3 of realty_booklet.indd visible, place the insertion point in the first bulleted paragraph where the font is still missing.**

   This text is formatted with the Category Bullets style. The plus sign to the right of the style name indicates that some formatting other than the style definition has been applied to the selected paragraph — called a **local formatting override**.

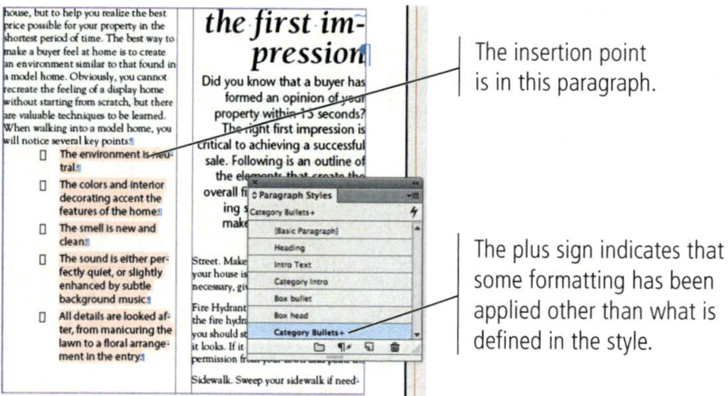

The insertion point is in this paragraph.

The plus sign indicates that some formatting has been applied other than what is defined in the style.

> ***Note:***
>
> *Local formatting overrides are common when you import text from a client-supplied Microsoft Word file.*

What's in a Paragraph Style?

By completing the first three projects, you've already learned about a considerable number of options for formatting text — both character and paragraph attributes — but there's still more to learn. Styles can store a very large number of settings, which you'll see as you complete the next exercise. Use the following chart as a reminder of exactly what can be stored in a paragraph style definition, as well as where to find the equivalent in the application interface for selected text. (Character styles include a subset of these same options: General, Basic Character Formats, Advanced Character Formats, Character Color, OpenType Features, Underline Options, and Strikethrough Options.)

Category	Options			Application Equivalent
General	Based On Style Settings	Next Style Reset to Base	Shortcut Apply Style to Selection	N/A
Basic Character Formats	Font Family Leading	Style Kerning	Size Tracking	Character panel
	Case	Position	Styles	Character panel Options menu
Advanced Character Formats	Horizontal Scale Skew	Vertical Scale Language	Baseline Shift	Character panel
Indents and Spacing	Alignment Left & Right Indent Space Before	Balance Ragged Lines First Line Indent Space After	Ignore Optical Margin Last Line Indent Align to Grid	Paragraph panel
Tabs	X position	Leader	Align On	Tabs panel
Paragraph Rules	Rule Above On Width Rule attributes (Weight, Type, Color, etc.)	Rule Below On Offset	 Left & Right Indents Gap attributes	Paragraph panel Options menu
Keep Options	Keep with Previous Keep Lines Together	Keep with Next [N] Lines Start Paragraph		Paragraph panel Options menu
Hyphenation	Hyphenate On/Off (and all related options)			Paragraph panel Options menu
Justification	Word Spacing Auto Leading	Letter Spacing Single Word Justification	Glyph Scaling Composer	Paragraph panel Options menu
Span Columns	Paragraph Layout Single Column	 Span Columns	 Split Column	Paragraph panel Options menu
Drop Caps and Nested Styles	Number of Lines	Number of Characters		Paragraph panel
	Character Style for Drop Characters Scale for Descenders	 Nested Styles	Align Left Edge Nested Line Styles	Paragraph panel Options menu
GREP Style	New GREP Style	Apply [Style]	To Text Pattern	Paragraph panel Options menu
Bullets and Numbering	List Type Text After Bullet	List Style Character Style	Bullet Character Bullet/Number Position	Paragraph panel Options menu
Character Color	Fill Color, Tint, Overprint attributes Stroke Color, Tint, Weight, Overprint attributes			Swatches panel/ Control panel
OpenType Features	Titling, Contextual, & Swash Alternates Ordinals, Fractions, Discretionary Ligatures, Slashed Zero, Figure Style, Positional Form Stylistic Sets			Character panel Options menu
Underline Options	Underline On	Stroke attributes	Gap attributes	Character panel Options menu
Strikethrough Options	Strikethrough On	Stroke attributes	Gap attributes	Character panel Options menu
Export Tagging	EPUB and HTML Tag, Class		PDF Tag	N/A

2. **Control/right-click the Category Bullets style in the Paragraph Styles panel and choose Edit "Category Bullets" from the contextual menu.**

3. **In the General options pane, choose Category Intro in the Based On menu.**

   When you redefine an existing style to be based on another style, InDesign tries to maintain the original formatting of the style that you are editing instead of the one it is being based on. In the Style Settings area, you can see the style will be Category Intro +. Everything after the plus sign is different than the style defined in the Based On menu.

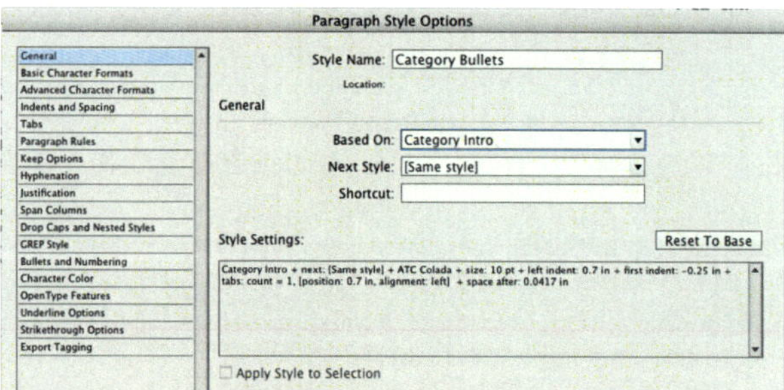

4. **Click the Reset To Base button above the Style Settings area.**

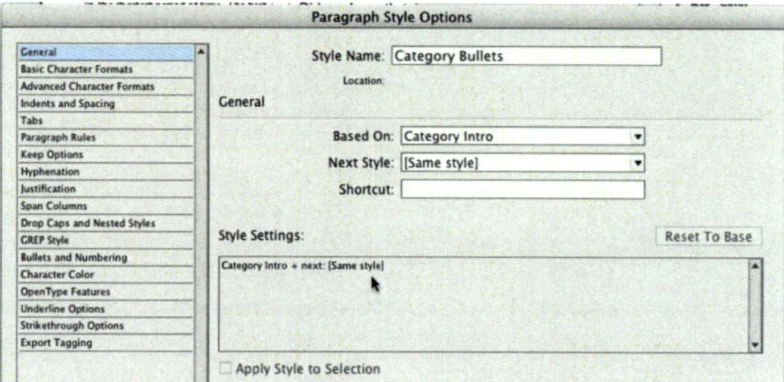

5. **In the Indents and Spacing options, change the Space Before field to 0.05" and click OK.**

   The missing-font problem is solved because the Category Bullet style now calls for the same font as its parent (ATC Pyrite Normal).

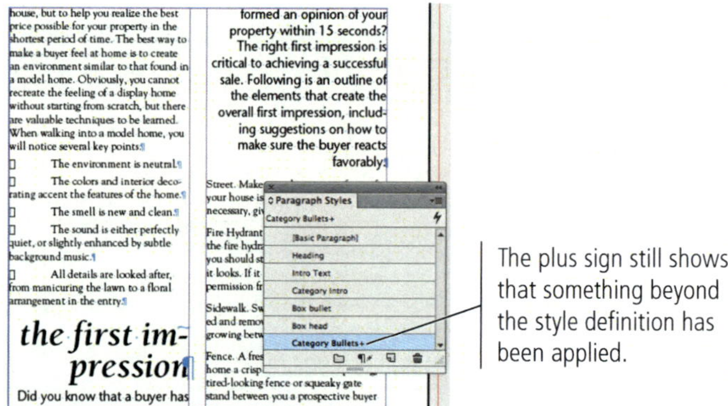

The plus sign still shows that something beyond the style definition has been applied.

6. **With the insertion point anywhere in the selected text, choose Edit>Select All to select the entire story.**

   You can clear overrides for any selected text, whether for a single character or an entire story. In this case, all overrides were created in the original Microsoft Word file; rather than manually clearing overrides in each paragraph, you can simply select the entire story and clear all overrides at once.

7. **At the bottom of the Paragraph Styles panel, click the Clear Overrides in Selection button.**

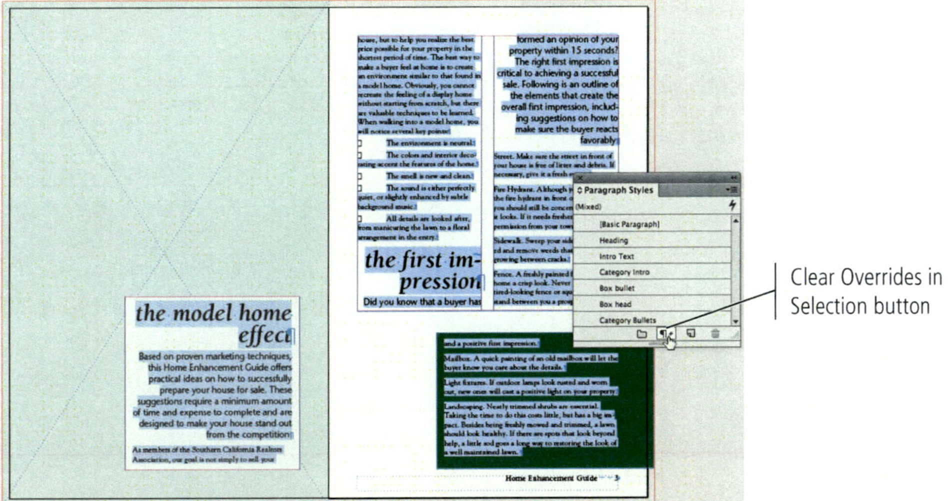

By clearing overrides, the bullet characters are removed from the Category Bullets style. You will add these back in later when you edit the style definition again.

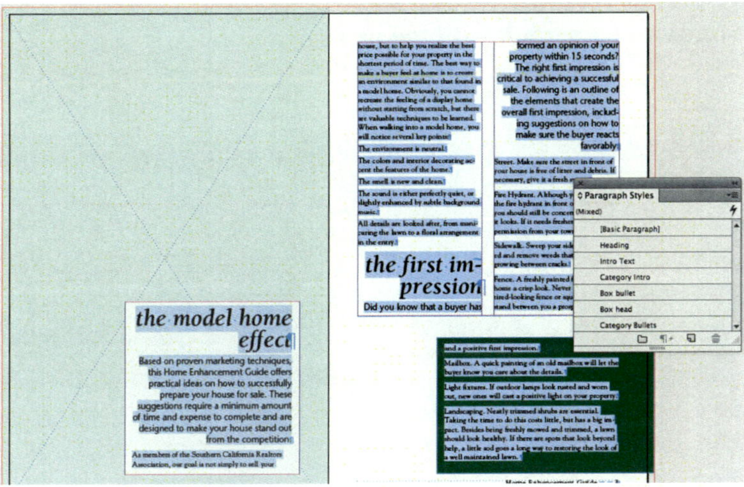

8. **Deselect all text, navigate to the Page 4-5 spread, and place the insertion point in the first paragraph with the missing font highlight ("create a good...").**

This text is formatted with the Box head style.

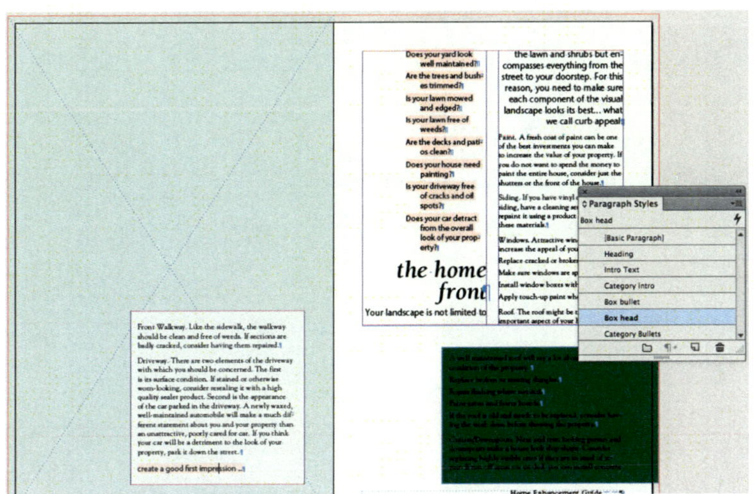

Note:

Depending on the exact size of the text frame you created on the left page of the A-Master layout, the relevant paragraph might appear at the end of the frame on Page 4, or at the beginning of the two-column frame on Page 5.

9. **Using the same method as in Steps 2–5, edit the Box head style to be based on the Heading style. Click the Reset to Base button, then define the following differences:**

Basic Character Formats	**Size: 15 pt** **Leading: Auto**
Indents and Spacing	**Paragraph Alignment: Left**

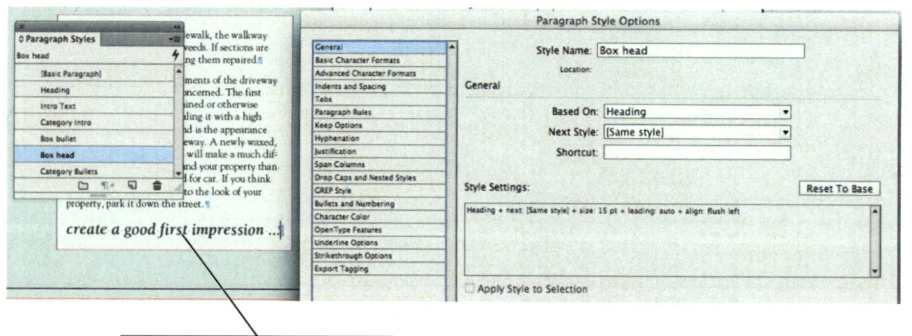

You can see that the Box head formatting is now very similar to the Heading text.

10. **Place the insertion point in the first bulleted paragraph with the missing font highlight.**

    This text is formatted with the Box bullet style.

11. **Using the same method from Steps 2–5, change the Box bullet style to be based on the Category Intro text style, with a 0.05″ Space Before value.**

    You could actually base this style on the Category Bullet style, but we try to avoid too many levels of nested styles. More levels of nesting means greater complexity when you need to make changes.

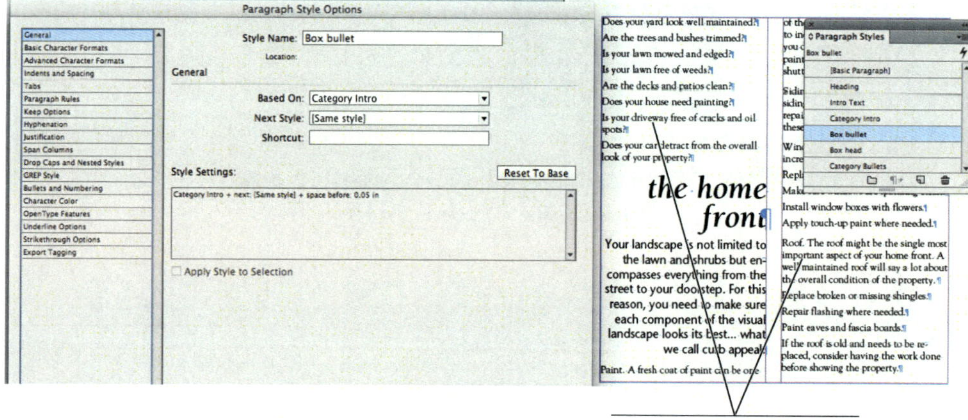

The Box bullet paragraphs are now very similar to the Category Intro paragraphs.

12. **Save the file and continue to the next exercise.**

Define Bullets and Numbering Options

By changing the style definitions in the previous exercise, you removed the bullets from two different types of lists (the category bulleted lists and the box bulleted lists); these bullets need to be replaced. You also need to convert the Category Intro text paragraphs to bullets to create improved visual separation.

You could manually type the bullet characters at the beginning of each line, but it's much easier and more efficient to use the Bullets and Numbering formatting options.

1. **With realty_booklet.indd open, make the Page 2–3 spread visible in the document window.**

2. **Control/right-click the Category Intro style in the Paragraph Styles panel and choose Edit "Category Intro" from the contextual menu.**

3. **In the Paragraph Style Options dialog box, display the Bullets and Numbering pane. In the List Type menu, choose Bullets.**

   By default, you can apply the Bullets or Numbers type of list.

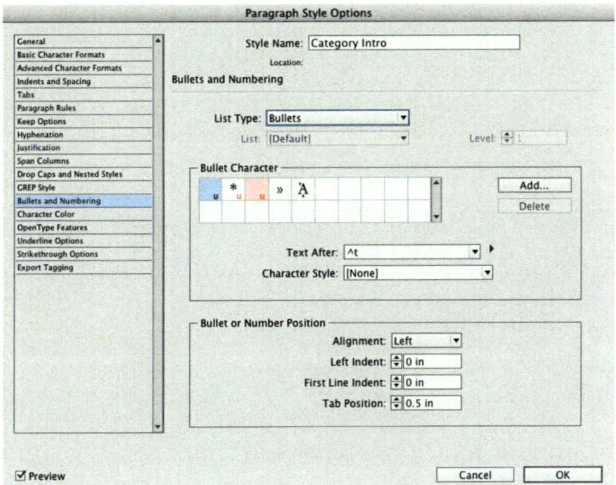

> *Note:*
>
> *You can also define custom lists by choosing Type>Bulleted & Numbered Lists>Define Lists. If you've defined a custom list type, it will be available in the List Type menu of the Paragraph Style Options dialog box.*

4. **Click the Add button to the right of the Bullet Character list.**

   The Add Bullets dialog box allows you to choose a character for the bullet. This character defaults to the same font used in the style, but you can choose any font and font style from the menus at the bottom of the dialog box.

5. **In the Add Bullets dialog box, find and select the tilde (~) character.**

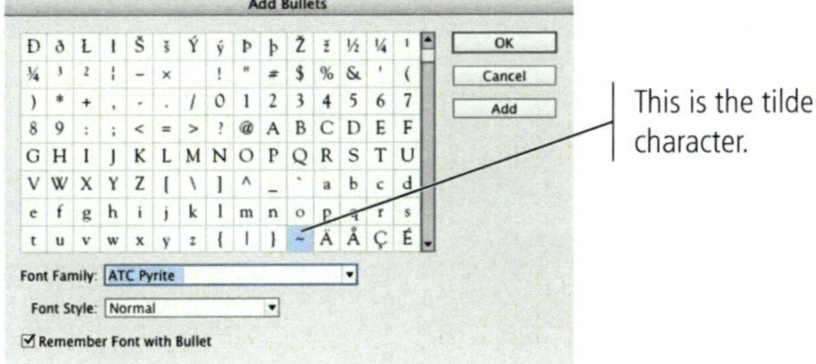

6. **Make sure the Remember Font with Bullet option is checked, and then click OK to return to the Paragraph Style Options dialog box.**

   The selected bullet character is added to the list of available bullet characters. If you don't check the Remember Font with Bullet option, the character will be applied in whatever font is used for the style.

7. **Click the tilde character in the grid of available characters to select it.**

8. **Leave the Text After field at the default (^t, which is the code for a Tab character).**

9. **In the Bullet or Number Position area, change the Left Indent value to 0.125", and change the First Line Indent value to –0.125". Leave the Tab Position value at its default.**

   This negative first-line indent is called a **hanging indent**.

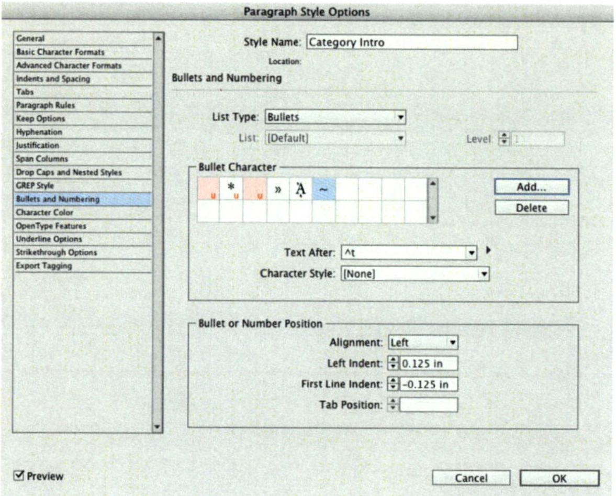

10. **Click OK to change the style definition and return to the layout.**

    Because the two bullet styles are based on the Category Intro style, virtually all text in the layout (except the heading and intro text) now has the initial tilde character and the hanging indent you just defined.

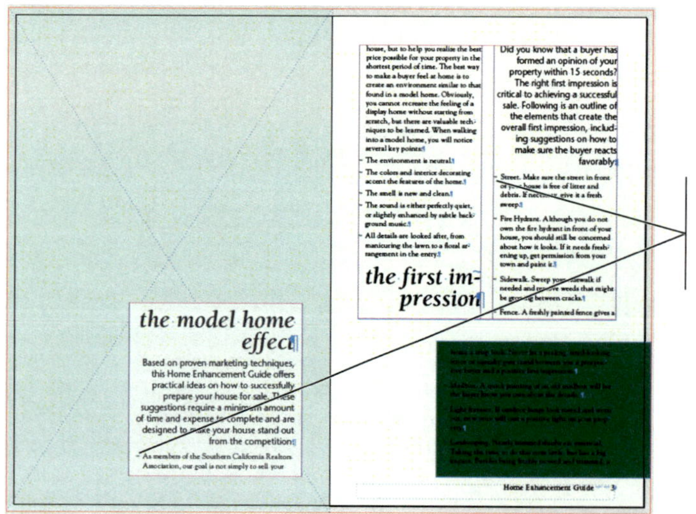

All Category Intro paragraphs now begin with the tilde character (~).

Note:

The Remember Font with Bullet option can be important if you use extended characters or decorative or dingbat fonts as bullet characters. If you select the solid square character (■) in the Zapf Dingbats font, for example, changing to a different font would show the letter "n" as the bullet character.

Note:

Changing these fields also changes the same fields in the Indents and Spacing options.

11. **Control/right-click the Category Bullets style and choose Edit "Category Bullets" in the contextual menu.**

12. **In the Bullets and Numbering options, click the Double-Chevron (») character from the default Bullet Character list.**

13. **Change the Left Indent field to 0.25″ and click OK.**

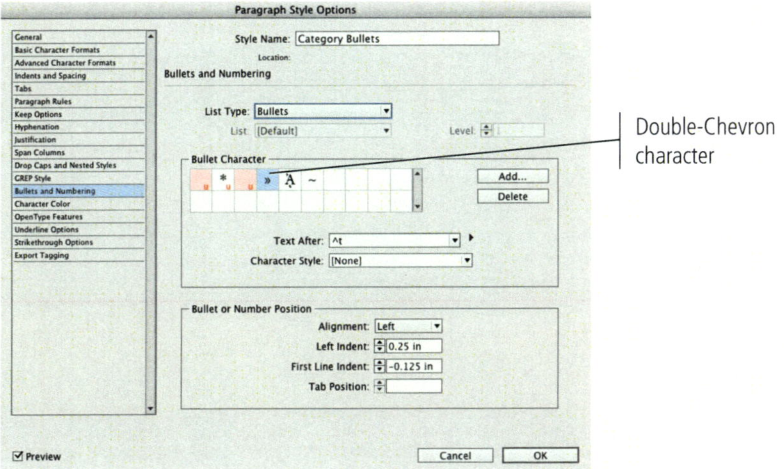

Double-Chevron character

14. **Navigate through the layout to review the effect of changing the character and indent options for the secondary bulleted list.**

The Category Bullets paragraphs are indented 0.125″ from the column edge because the negative first-line indent was less than the left indent value. In other words:

Left Indent + First-Line Indent = Indent location of the first line

0.25 + (–0.125) = 0.125

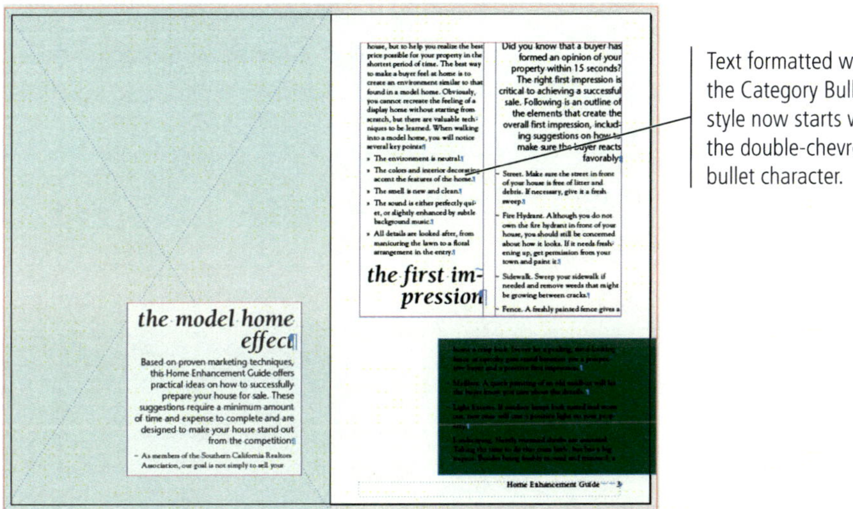

Text formatted with the Category Bullets style now starts with the double-chevron bullet character.

15. Edit the Box bullet style to use a check box-like character as the bullet character, with a 0.2″ left indent and –0.2″ first-line indent.

For the bullet character, try the Zapf Dingbats (Macintosh) or Wingdings (Windows) fonts. If you don't have one of these fonts, use any character from any font that you think works well as a bullet character.

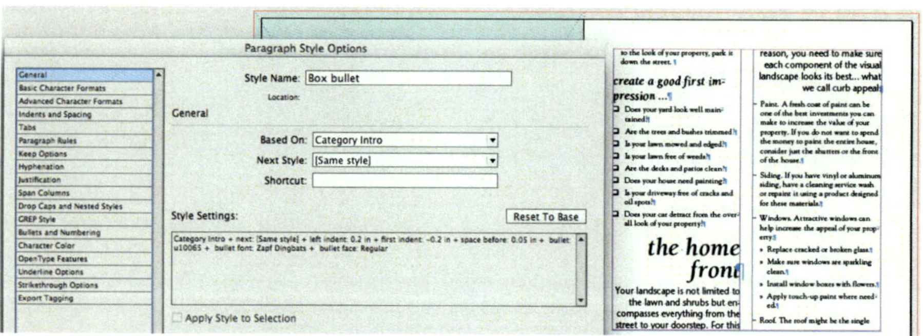

16. Save the file and continue to the next exercise.

The Glyphs Panel in Depth

INDESIGN FOUNDATIONS

ASCII is a text-based code that defines characters with a numeric value between 001 and 256. The standard alphabet and punctuation characters are mapped from 001 to 128. **Extended ASCII characters** are those with ASCII numbers higher than 128; these include symbols (bullets, copyright symbols, etc.) and some special characters (en dashes, accent marks, etc.). Some of the more common extended characters can be accessed in the Type>Insert submenus.

OpenType fonts can store more than 65,000 **glyphs** (characters) in a single font — far beyond what you could access with a keyboard (even including combinations of the different modifier keys). The large glyph storage capacity means that a single OpenType font can replace the multiple separate "Expert" fonts that contain variations of fonts (Minion Swash, for example, is no longer necessary when you can access the Swashes subset of the Minion Pro font).

Unicode fonts include two-bit characters that are common in some foreign language typesetting (e.g., Cyrillic, Japanese, and other non-Roman or pictographic fonts).

The Glyphs panel (Window>Type & Tables>Glyphs or Type>Glyphs) provides access to individual glyphs in a font, including basic characters in regular fonts, extended ASCII and OpenType character sets, and even pictographic characters in Unicode fonts.

Using the Glyphs panel is simple: make sure the insertion point is flashing where you want a character to appear, and then double-click the character you want to place. You can view the character set for any font by simply changing the menu at the bottom of the panel. By default, the panel shows the entire font, but you can show only specific character sets using the Show menu.

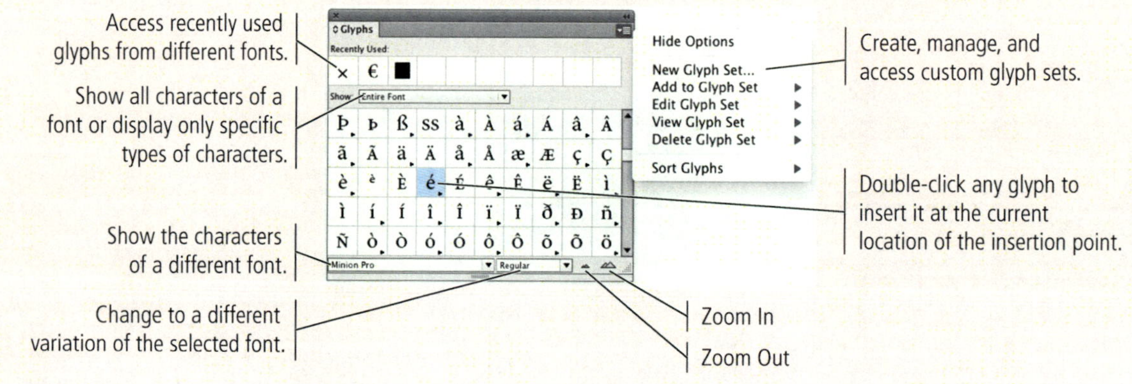

Using OpenType Attributes

The OpenType font format enables you to use the same font files on both Macintosh and Windows computers; it provides storage capacity for more than 65,000 glyphs in a single font. In many cases, these extra glyphs are alternative formatting for other characters (such as ligatures and fractions). You can also use these glyphs for special formatting needs.

OpenType features are treated as a character-formatting attribute. You can apply OpenType features to specific text using the OpenType menu in the Character panel Options menu.

It's important to understand that OpenType attributes can be applied even if they aren't available for the font you are currently using. For example, you can apply the Fractions attribute to a list of ingredients; as you experiment with different fonts, the Fractions attribute will be applied if it's available in the applied font.

It's also important to realize that OpenType attributes change the appearance of glyphs, but do not change the actual text in the layout. When the Fractions attribute replaces "1/2" with "½", the text still includes three characters; the OpenType Fractions attribute has simply altered the glyphs that represent those three characters to display a styled fraction. You can turn off OpenType attributes by toggling off the option in the Character panel Options menu. With OpenType attributes turned off, the styled characters return to their basic appearance.

Bodoni Roman is not an OpenType font.

OpenType attributes are bracketed if they are unavailable for the currently selected font.

When an OpenType font is used, the Fractions attribute is applied if the font includes the appropriate glyphs.

Warnock Pro is an OpenType font.

Exploring OpenType Fonts in the Glyphs Panel

You can also use the Glyphs panel to explore the different character sets available for a specific font. The Show menu allows you to access different character sets, including extended character sets such as symbols and OpenType alternative character sets. If you select a specific character in the panel, you can also review possible alternatives for the selected character only.

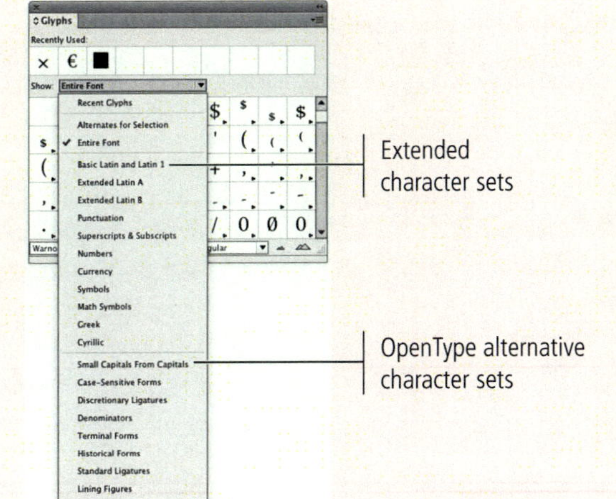

Extended character sets

OpenType alternative character sets

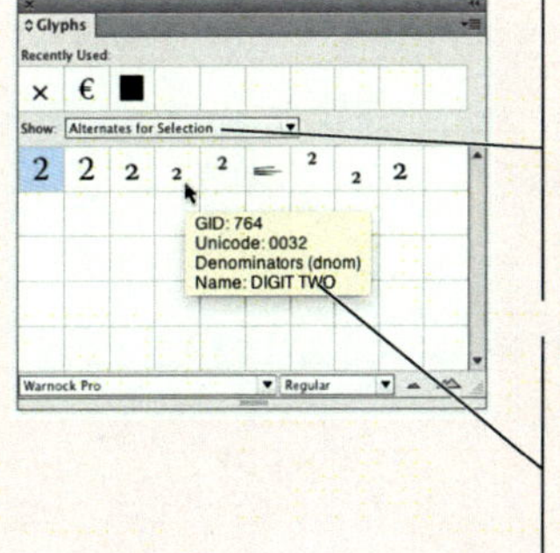

Selecting the "1" glyph and choosing Alternates for Selection in the Show menu shows the different characters that can be applied using OpenType formatting attributes.

Rolling the mouse over a specific glyph shows the alternative set that includes that glyph (in this case, the Numerators set).

Control Page and Frame Breaks

In the completed booklet, each spread will have a single section heading followed by a section intro on the left page. The main and secondary bullet points will all appear on the right side, and the "create a good first impression" bullets will appear in the colored frame. Rather than manually placing page and frame breaks, you can use styles and paragraph formatting options to automatically place text in the correct frames on the correct sides of the spread.

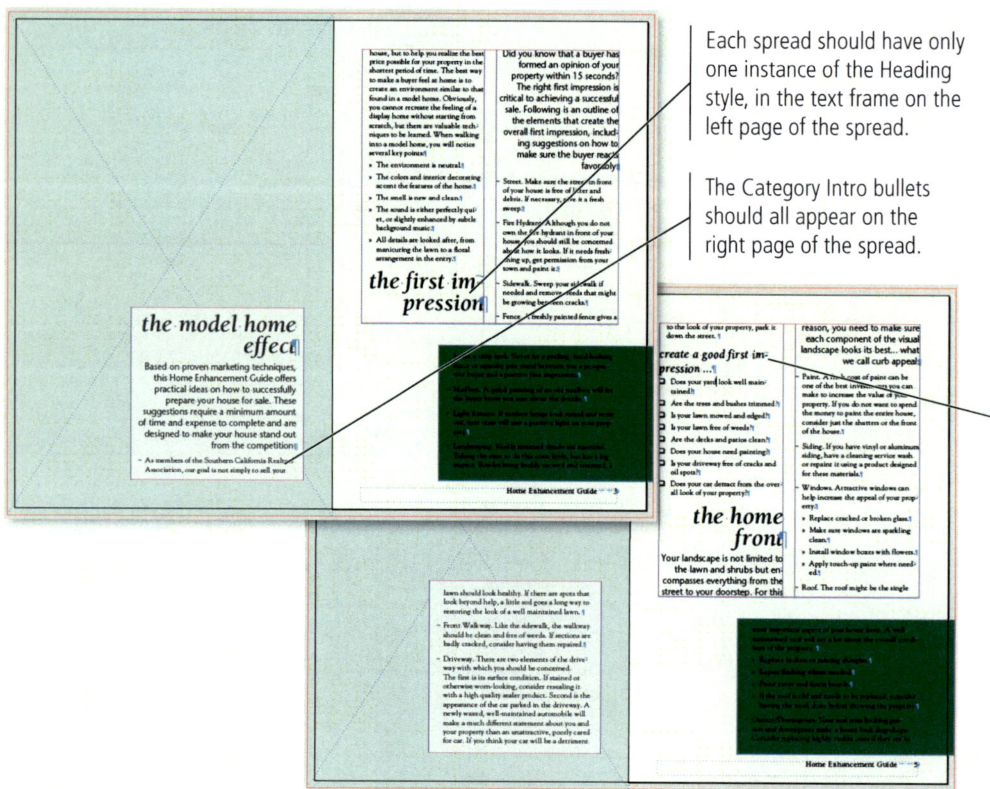

Each spread should have only one instance of the Heading style, in the text frame on the left page of the spread.

The Category Intro bullets should all appear on the right page of the spread.

The callout heading and bullets should appear in the colored frame on the right page of the spread.

1. **With the Page 2–3 spread of realty_booklet.indd visible, Control/right-click Heading in the Paragraph Styles panel and choose Edit "Heading" from the contextual menu.**

2. **Display the Keep Options pane. In the Start Paragraph menu, choose On Next Even Page. Click OK to change the style definition.**

   Each section heading should appear on the left page of a spread, and left-facing pages are even-numbered.

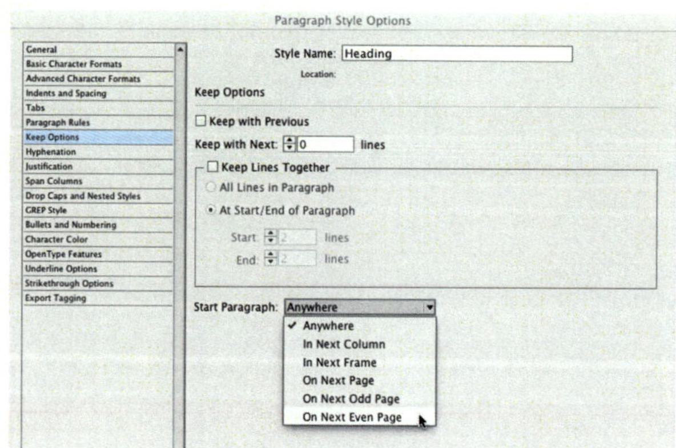

> ***Note:***
>
> *These same options can be applied to any specific paragraph by choosing Keep Options from the Paragraph panel Options menu.*

3. **Navigate through the layout and review the results.**

When you get to Page 5, you might notice a problem — the "create a good first impression" heading has moved to the wrong place. Because the Box head style is based on the Heading style, it adopts the Start Paragraph option that requires this heading to appear on the next even-numbered page. It should move to the green frame on the right side of the spread, which requires a different Start Paragraph option.

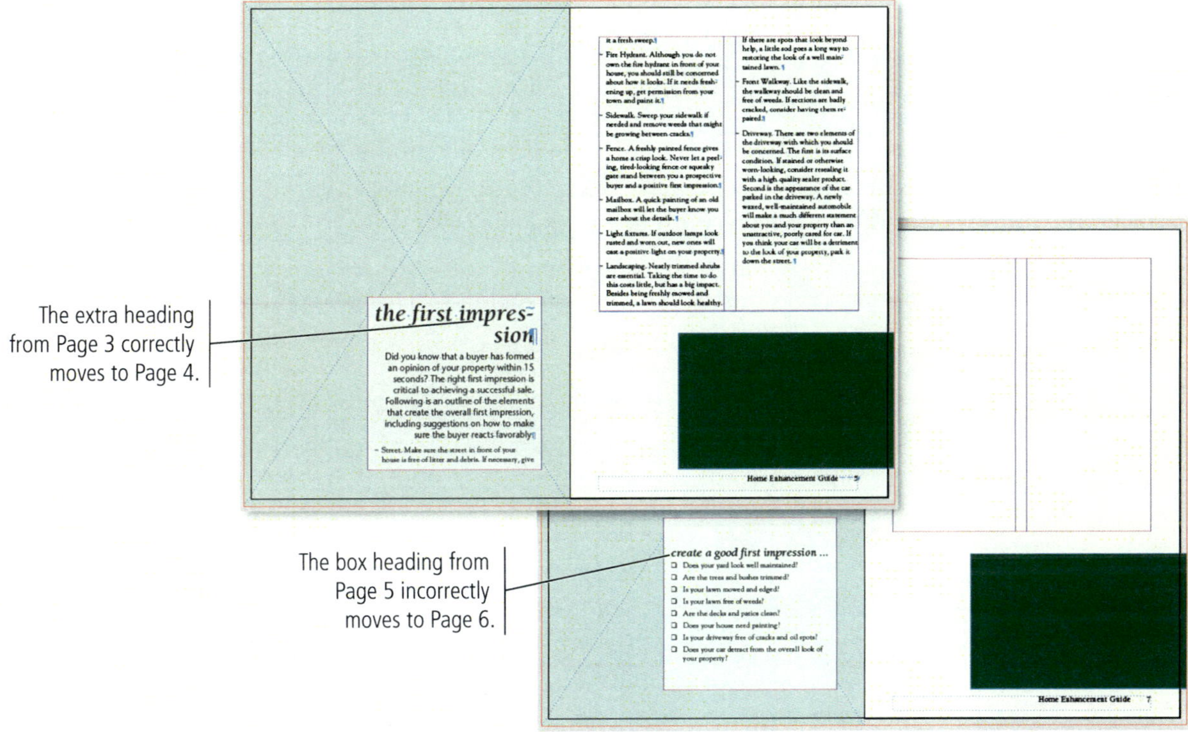

4. **Control/right-click the Box head style and choose Edit "Box head" from the contextual menu. In the Keep Options pane, choose In Next Frame in the Start Paragraph menu and click OK to redefine the style.**

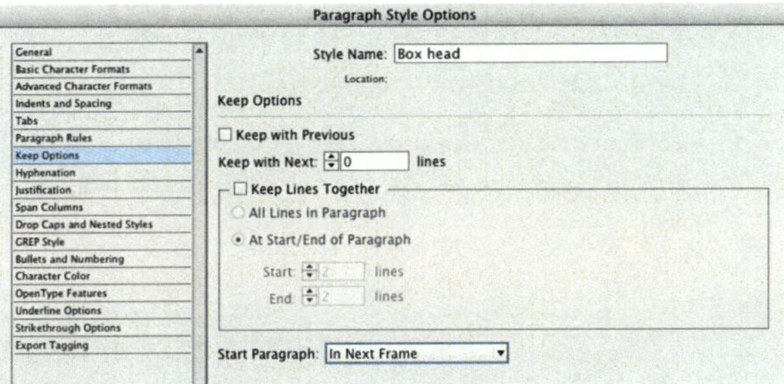

5. **Navigate through the layout and review the results.**

The even-numbered pages show another problem with the current formatting. The left page of the spread should contain only the heading and the intro text; you need to force all remaining text onto the right side of the spread. You could do this manually, but a new style can handle the formatting for you.

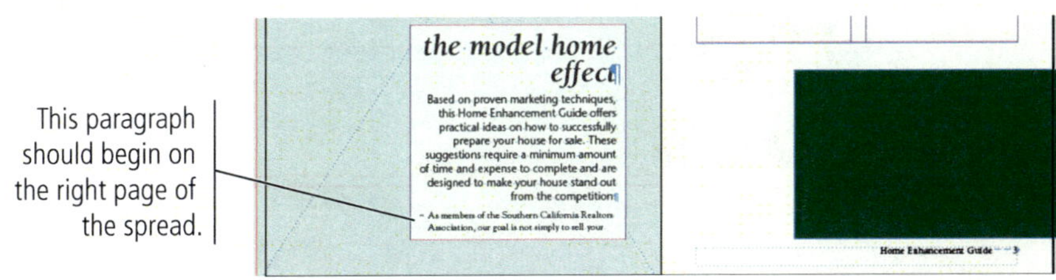

6. **Control/right-click the Category Intro style and choose Duplicate Style from the contextual menu.**

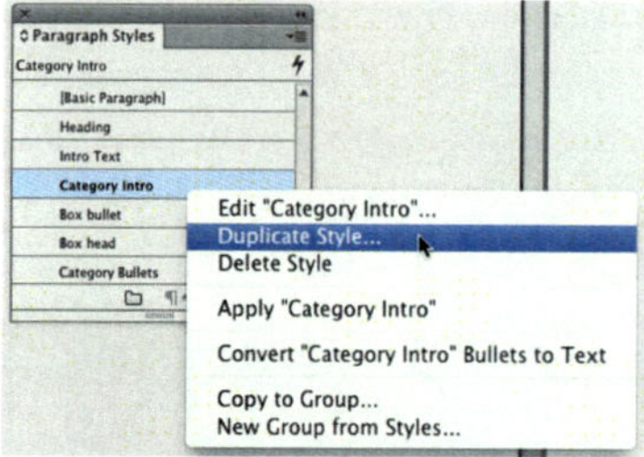

7. **Change the Style Name field to** Category Intro - First **and choose Category Intro in the Based On menu. In the Keep Options pane, choose In Next Column from the Start Paragraph menu and click OK.**

The In Next Column option moves a paragraph to the next column in the same frame or to the next frame if the text is already in the last (or only) column of a frame.

Note:

As with the bulleted lists, it's a good idea to base the new style on the existing style, so later changes will reflect in the duplicate style.

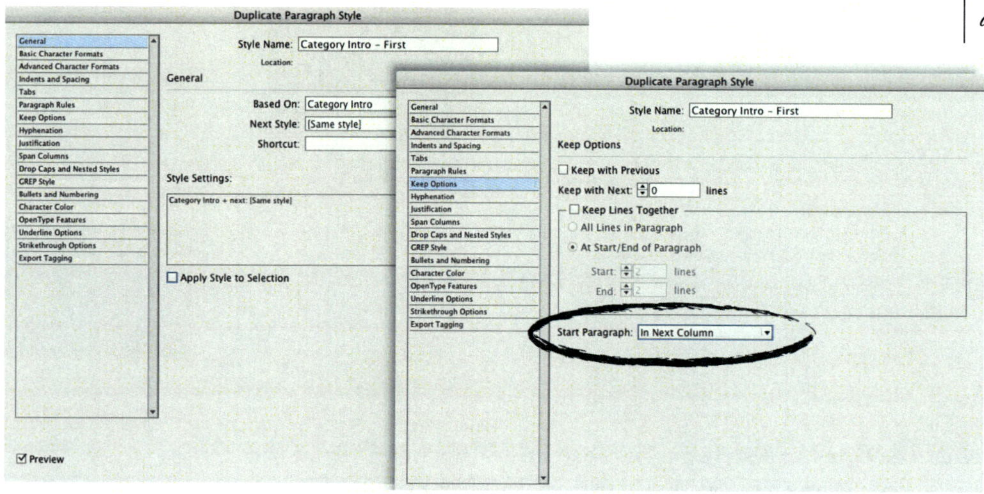

8. **Place the insertion point in the first Category Intro paragraph on Page 2 (the first paragraph with a tilde character as the bullet character), and then click the Category Intro – First style in the Paragraph Styles panel.**

As soon as you apply the style, the paragraph automatically moves to the next available frame in the text chain.

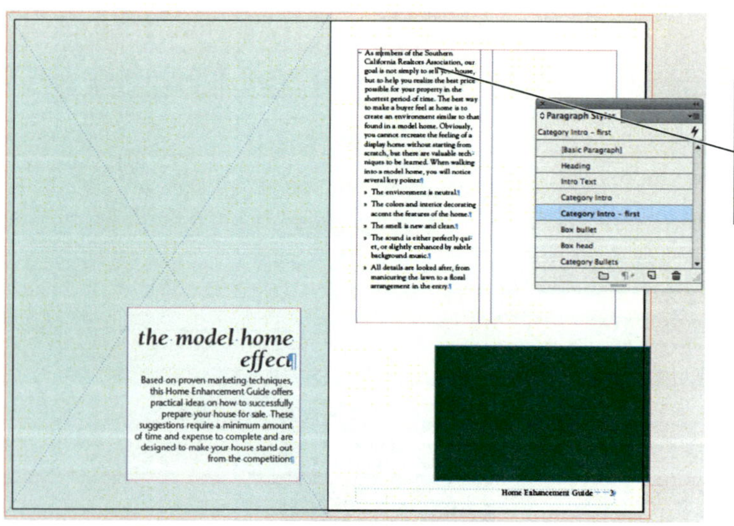

The In Next Column option forces the paragraph to begin in the correct location (the left column of the frame on the right page of the spread).

9. **Navigate through the layout and apply the Category Intro – First style to the third paragraph on each spread.**

10. **Navigate through the layout and review your work.**

    Page 7 highlights another potential issue with the position of text in the layout. Despite all the available automation and productivity options, some things simply must be resolved manually. There is no way to tell InDesign, for example, "If only one secondary bullet fits in the first column, move the preceding primary bullet to the next column." Resolutions to issues such as these, which add polish to a professional layout, must be determined and applied manually.

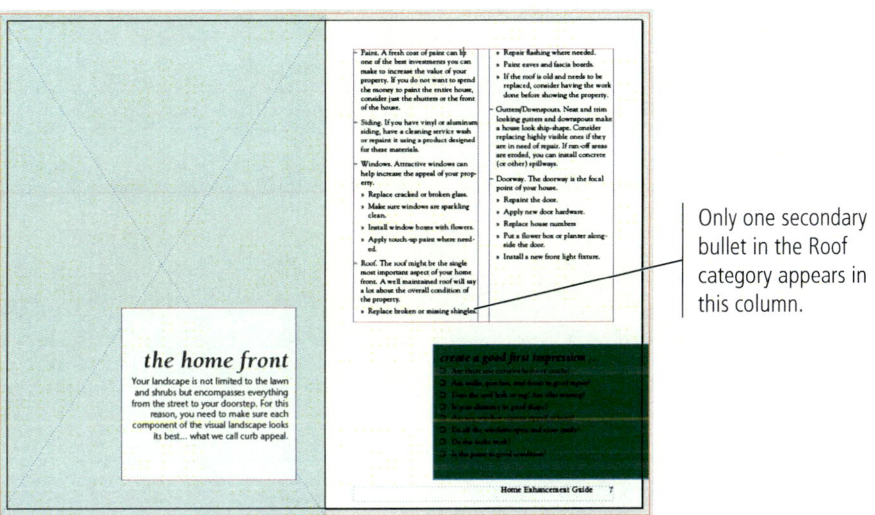

11. **On Page 7, place the insertion point in the intro paragraph of the Roof category, and then apply the Category Intro – First style.**

12. **Navigate through the layout and apply the same change as necessary.**

    We applied the formatting on Pages 9, 11, and 15.

13. **Navigate through the layout and review your work.**

    Page 5 shows a problem with unbalanced columns, in this case resulting from a few lines of one paragraph remaining at the bottom of the left column.

    In addition to determining where a paragraph can start, the Keep options are also used to control **orphans** (single lines of a paragraph at the end of a column) and **widows** (single lines of a paragraph at the top of a column, or a very short last line of a paragraph). Typography conventions suggest that at least two lines of a paragraph should be kept together at the beginning and end of a column or frame. (Headings at the end of a frame or column are also sometimes considered orphans.)

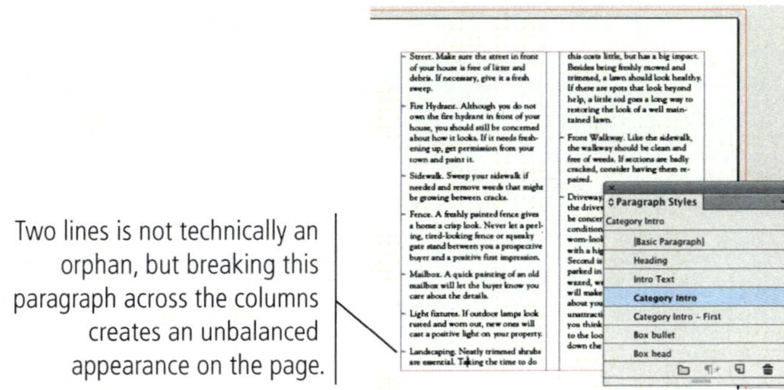

14. **Control/right click Category Intro in the Paragraph Styles panel and choose Edit "Category Intro" from the contextual menu. In the Keep Options pane, activate the Keep Lines Together check box and choose the All Lines in Paragraph option. Click OK to change the style definition.**

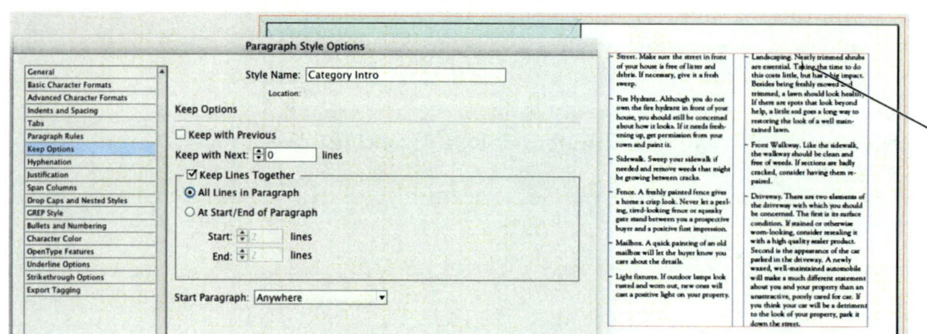

This entire paragraph moves to the next column because all lines in the paragraph must be kept together.

15. **Save the file and continue to the next exercise.**

Paragraph Composition Options

INDESIGN FOUNDATIONS

InDesign offers two options for controlling the overall flow of text (called **composition**) within a paragraph: **Adobe Paragraph Composer** (the default) and **Adobe Single-line Composer**. Both methods create breaks based on the applied hyphenation and justification options for a paragraph.

You can change the composition method for an individual paragraph in the Paragraph panel Options menu or the Justification dialog box; or you can change the composition method for a paragraph style in the Justification pane of the Paragraph Style Options dialog box.

Change the composer for a paragraph style in the Justification options for that style.

The Adobe Paragraph Composer evaluates the entire paragraph as a unit; changing one line of a paragraph might alter other lines in the paragraph (including earlier lines) to create what the software defines as the "best" overall paragraph composition. For example, adding a manual line break on Line 6 to eliminate a hyphen might also cause Lines 2 through 5 to reflow if InDesign determines the shift will create a better overall paragraph. (Although primarily a matter of personal preference, Adobe Paragraph Composer can be annoying for anyone who wants tight or exact control over the text in a layout.)

Change the composer for selected paragraphs in the Paragraph panel Options menu.

The Adobe Single-line Composer is a better choice if you prefer to control your own text flow. Using Single-line Composer, adding a manual line break on Line 6 (for example) will not affect preceding lines in the paragraph.

Control Automatic Hyphenation

Automatic hyphenation is another key to professional page layout. Typographic conventions recommend no hyphenation in headings, no more than three hyphens in a row, and at least three characters before or after a hyphen. Some designers follow stricter rules, such as not hyphenating proper nouns; others prefer no hyphenation at all. Whatever your requirements, you can control the hyphenation of any paragraph either locally or in a style definition.

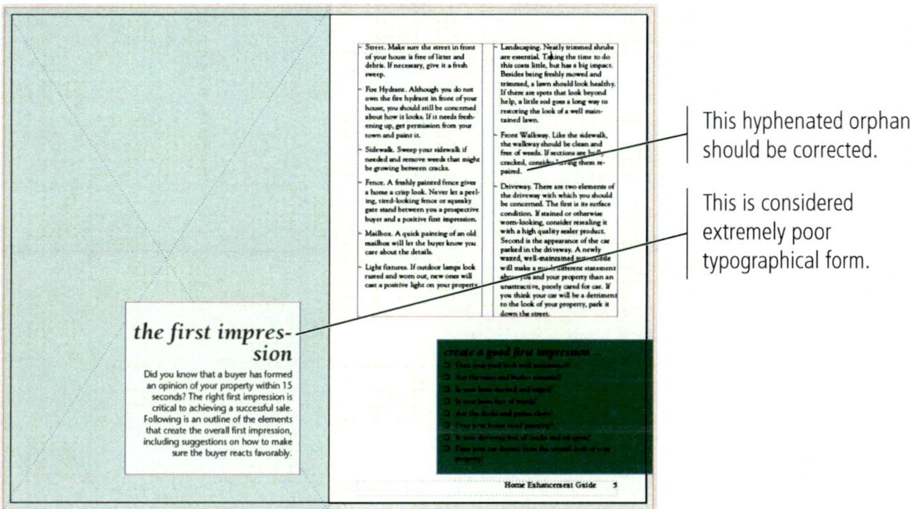

1. **With the Page 4–5 spread of `realty_booklet.indd` visible, Control/right-click the Heading style and choose Edit "Heading" from the contextual menu.**

2. **In the Paragraph Style Options dialog box, show the Hyphenation options.**

3. **Uncheck the Hyphenate option and click OK.**

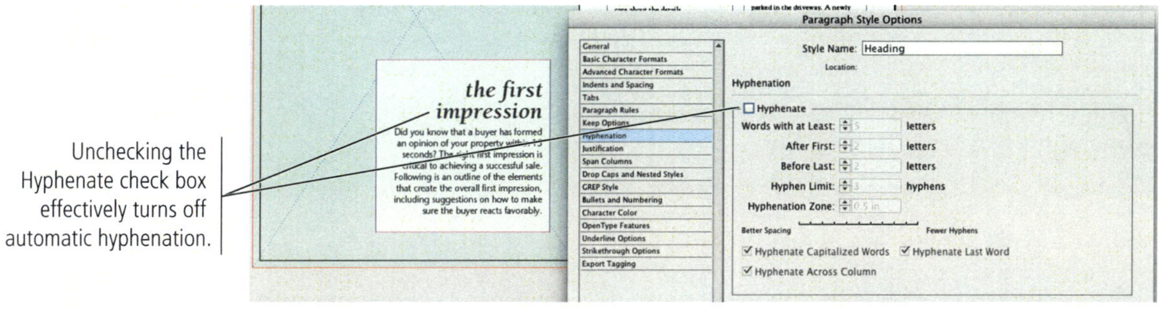

4. **Control/right-click the Category Intro style and choose Edit "Category Intro" from the contextual menu.**

   Remember, most of the other styles are based on the Category Intro style; by changing the hyphenation options for this style, you also change the options for all styles based on it.

5. **In the Hyphenation options, change the After First and Before Last fields to 3. Click OK to change the style definition.**

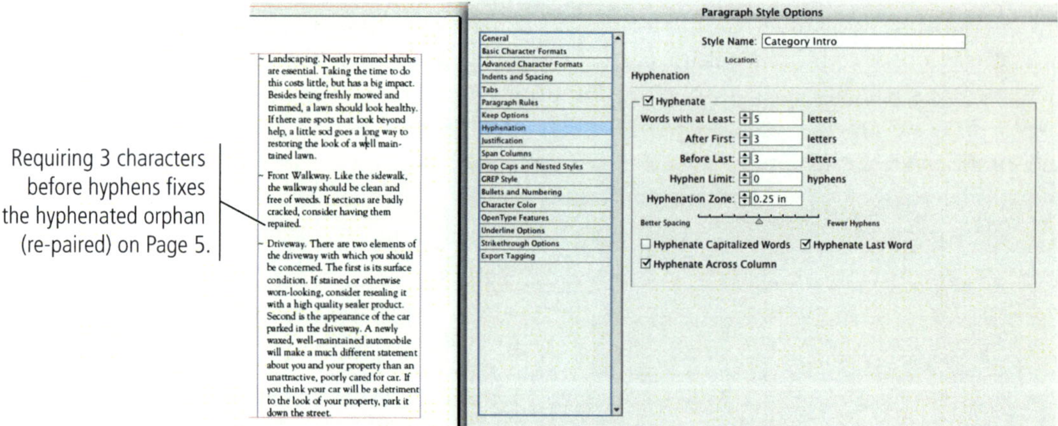

The Hyphenation options allow you to control the way InDesign hyphenates text. (If the Hyphenate box is unchecked, InDesign will not hyphenate text in the paragraph.)

- **Words With At Least _ Letters** defines the minimum number of characters that must exist in a hyphenated word.
- **After First _ Letters** and **Before Last _ Letters** define the minimum number of characters that must appear before and after a hyphen.
- **Hyphen Limit** defines the maximum number of hyphens that can appear on consecutive lines. (Remember, you are defining the limit here, so zero means there is no limit — allowing unlimited hyphens.)
- **Hyphenation Zone** defines the amount of white space allowed at the end of a line of unjustified text before hyphenation begins.
- If **Hyphenate Capitalized Words** is checked, capitalized words (proper nouns) can be hyphenated.
- If **Hyphenate Last Word** is checked, the last word in a paragraph can be hyphenated.
- If **Hyphenate Across Column** is checked, the last word in a column or frame can be hyphenated.

Note:

These options can be applied to any specific paragraph by choosing Hyphenation from the Paragraph panel Options menu.

6. **Navigate to Page 2. Place the insertion point before the word "home" in the heading and press Shift-Return/Enter.**

This character, called a **soft return**, forces a new line without starting a new paragraph.

As with balancing columns, there is some subjective element to balancing lines of copy — especially headlines.

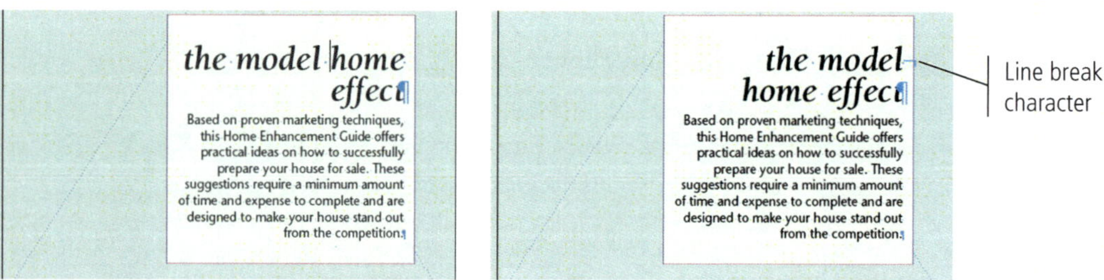

7. **Navigate through the layout and add soft returns as necessary to balance the two-line headings.**

We adjusted the headings on Pages 8, 10, and 14.

8. **Save the file and continue to the next exercise.**

Overriding Automatic Hyphenation

INDESIGN FOUNDATIONS

InDesign applies automatic hyphenation based on the defined language dictionary. You can override the hyphenation as defined in the dictionary by choosing Edit>Spelling>User Dictionary.

If you highlight a word before opening the dictionary, it automatically appears in the Word field. Clicking the Hyphenate button shows the possible hyphenation locations as defined in the dictionary. You can override the automatic hyphenation by adding or deleting the consecutive tilde characters in the Word field. When you change the hyphenation of a word, you have to click the Add button to add the new hyphenation scheme to the dictionary.

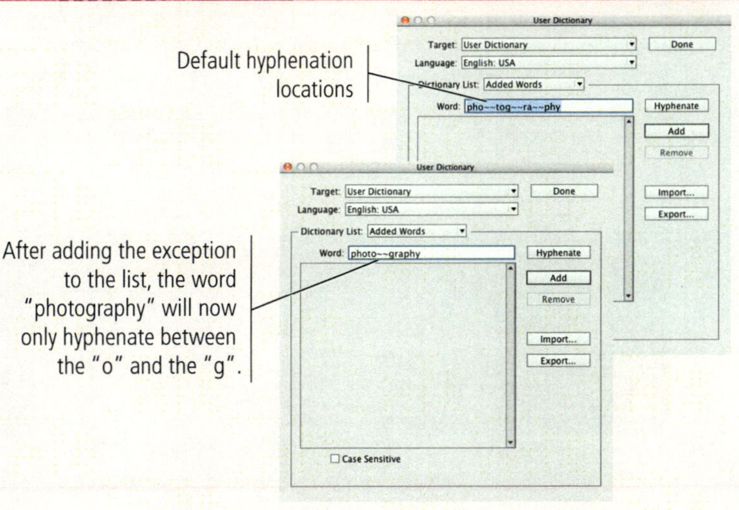

Default hyphenation locations

After adding the exception to the list, the word "photography" will now only hyphenate between the "o" and the "g".

Redefine Styles Based on Local Formatting Overrides

You might have noticed one final formatting problem when you reviewed the current layout: the black text in the callout boxes (on the right-facing pages) is very difficult to read because the boxes have a dark fill color. Although you are going to change the box color on each spread, you are going to use other dark colors that still make the black text difficult to read.

Rather than simply changing the style definitions for text in the colored boxes, you are going to experiment with different options within the layout. When you're satisfied with the results, you're going to use local formatting to redefine the applied styles.

1. **With realty_booklet.indd open, navigate to the green box on Page 5.**

2. **Select the entire first paragraph in the green box ("create a good ...").**

3. **Using the Swatches panel, change the text color to 10% of the dark green swatch.**

4. **Move the insertion point to the end of the paragraph and review the results.**

   The light tint of the green swatch makes the text far more readable. However, in the next exercise you're going to change the box colors to match the respective images on the left-facing page of each spread. Rather than using a light green tint — which won't match the end result on every spread — you can use the Paper swatch to knock out the text from any background color.

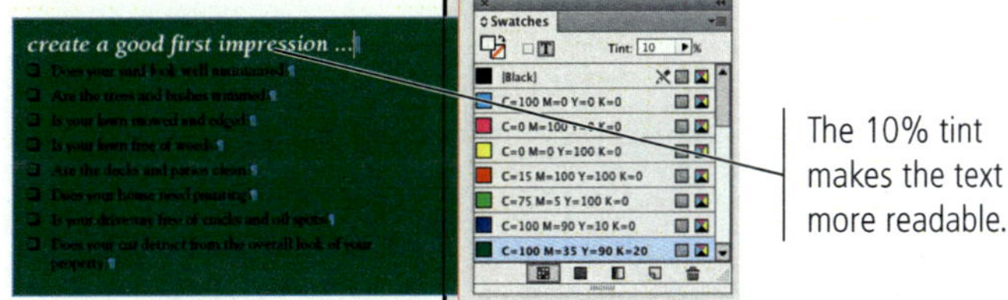

The 10% tint makes the text more readable.

5. **Select the paragraph again and change the text color to Paper, then move the insertion point to any location within the reformatted heading.**

6. **Open the Paragraph Styles panel Options menu and choose Redefine Style.**

   This option makes it easy to experiment with formatting within the context of the layout, and then change a style definition to match what you created with local formatting. In this case you are redefining the Box head style based on the changes you made in Step 5.

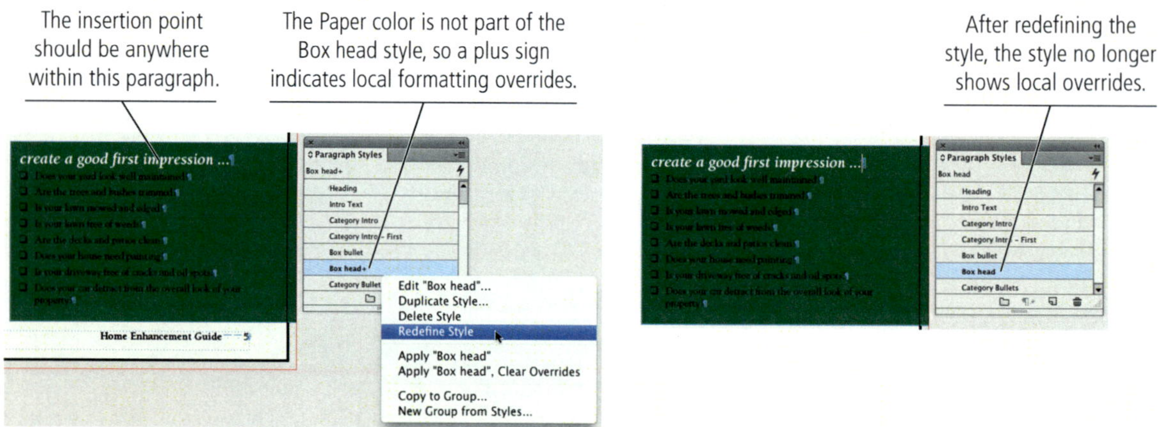

7. **Select one of the bulleted paragraphs (below the heading) and change the text color to Paper.**

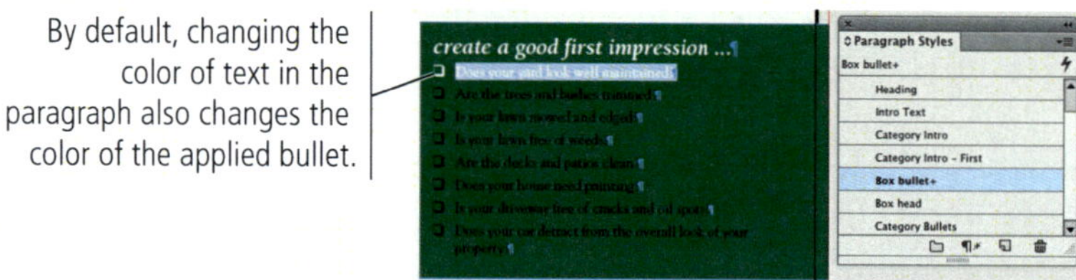

8. **With the same paragraph selected, open the Paragraph Styles panel Options menu and choose Redefine Style.**

   Because more than one Box bullet paragraph appears on this page, you can see how redefining the style based on local formatting affects all text where that style is applied.

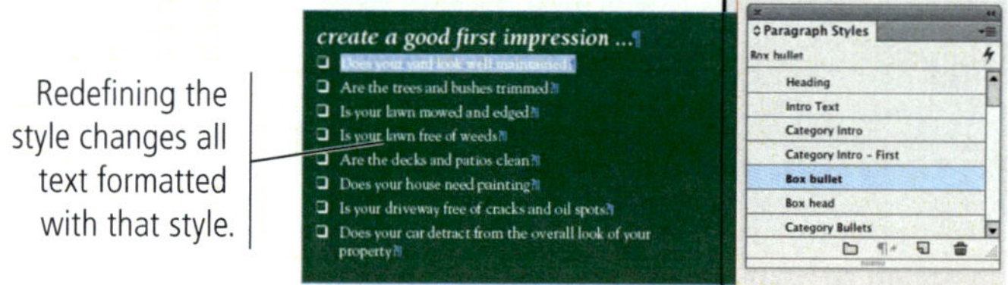

9. **With the same paragraph selected, change the font to ATC Onyx Normal, then redefine the Box bullet style to match the local formatting override.**

   White text on a colored background is called **knockout text**. Anything "white" is actually removed from the colored areas because you typically don't print white ink. Knocking out small text — especially a serif font, such as this 9.5-pt ATC Pyrite Normal text — can cause output problems. To help minimize potential problems on press, you are changing the formatting for the small knockout text to a sans-serif font.

10. **Save the file and continue to the next exercise.**

Place Images into Master Frames

For all intents and purposes the booklet text is finished. The next task is to place the images. Because you placed the graphics frame on the master page layout, you can simply place most of these images into the existing frames without any additional intervention.

1. **With `realty_booklet.indd` open, navigate to Page 2 of the layout and choose File>Place.**

2. **Navigate to the file `front.tif` (in your WIP>Realtors folder) and turn off the Show Import Options and Replace Selected Item options.**

3. **Click Open to load the image into the cursor, and then click inside the graphics frame on Page 2 to place the image.**

   As with placing text into the primary text frame, you don't have to override the master page to place the image into the graphics frame. InDesign assumes that clicking inside an existing frame — even one from the master page — means you want to place the image inside that frame. Once you place the image, the frame is automatically detached from the master page.

   If you look carefully at the text frames on the left side of each spread, you might notice that the underlying images are slightly visible behind the text. Because you defined the frame's opacity as 85% when you defined the page, all attributes of the frame are 85% opaque — including the text inside the frame.

4. **Navigate to the A-Master layout. Select the text frame on the left page of the spread, then open the Effects panel.**

   As you can see, the entire object is 85% opaque. The Stroke, Fill, and Text are listed spearately, however, which means you can change each of those values independently.

   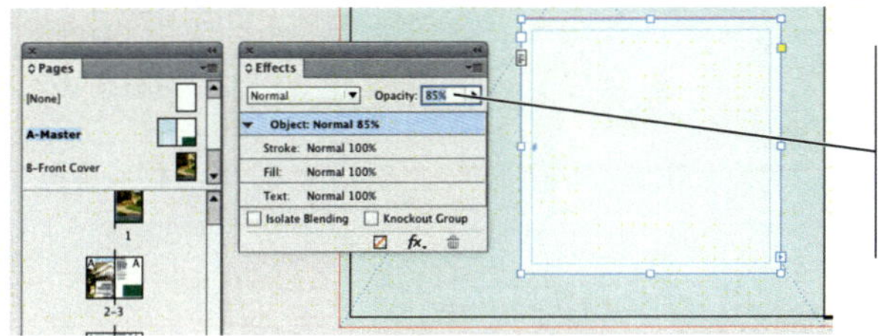

   When you use the Opacity field in the Control panel, you change the opacity of the entire object (including any contents).

5. **With Object selected in the panel, change the Opacity field to 100%.**

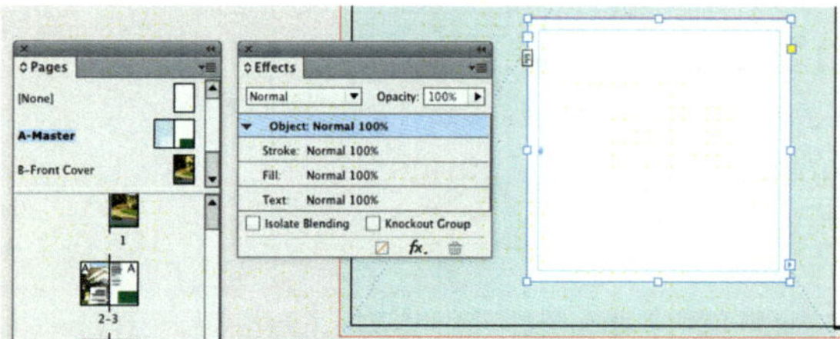

6. **Select Fill in the panel, then change the Opacity field to 85%.**

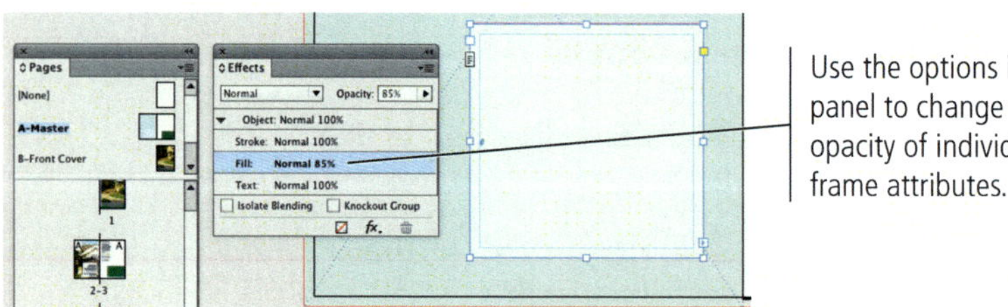

Use the options in this panel to change the opacity of individual frame attributes.

7. **Navigate to Page 2 of the layout and review the text frame on the left side of the spread.**

   You can still see the graphic behind the frame, but the text in the frame is now 100% opaque.

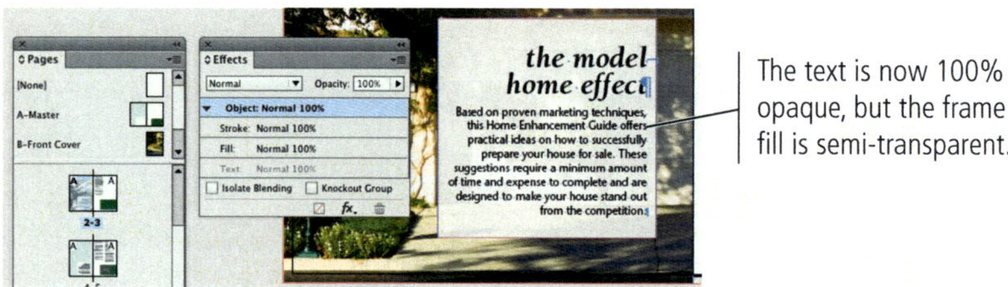

The text is now 100% opaque, but the frame fill is semi-transparent.

8. **Place the remaining images on the left page of each layout spread:**

Page 4	**doorway_outside.tif**
Page 6	**doorway_inside.tif**
Page 8	**candles.tif**
Page 10	**flowers.tif**
Page 12	**bathroom.tif**
Page 14	**storage.tif**

   Use whatever method you prefer to place these images. If you use the Mini Bridge panel, simply click and drag an image into the layout and then click the frame where you want to place the image. Because the frames are not technically on the layout pages until you place the images, you can't simply release the mouse button over the frame to place the images; you have to intentionally click to place the images and detach the frames from the master layout.

Note:

The Stroke, Fill, and Text opacity percentages are applied as a percentage of the object's opacity.

9. **Navigate to Page 3 of the layout. Using the Selection tool, select and delete the green-filled text frame.**

10. **Place the file `squares.tif` (in the WIP>Realtors folder) onto Page 3 and position the file as shown in the following image.**

11. **Deselect the squares.tif image.**

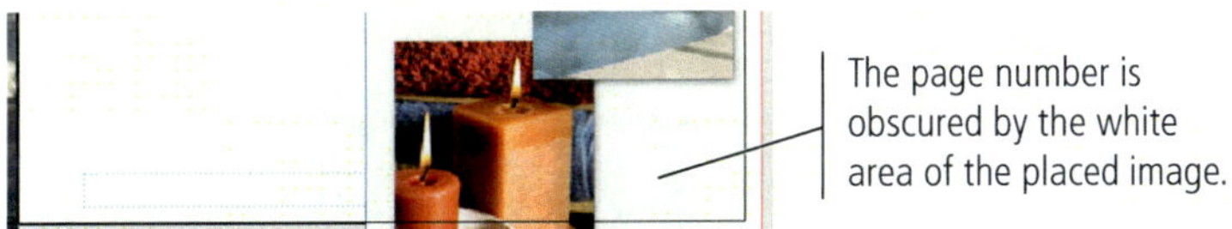

12. **Command/Control-Shift-click the text frame at the bottom of the page.**

    Command/Control-Shift-clicking a master page object allows you to detach a single master page item without detaching the entire page from the master page.

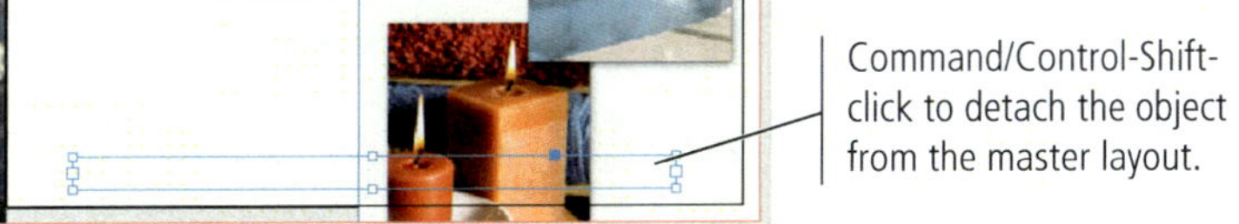

13. **With the text frame selected, choose Object>Arrange>Bring to Front. Delete the words "Home Enhancement Guide" from the text frame, leaving only the page number.**

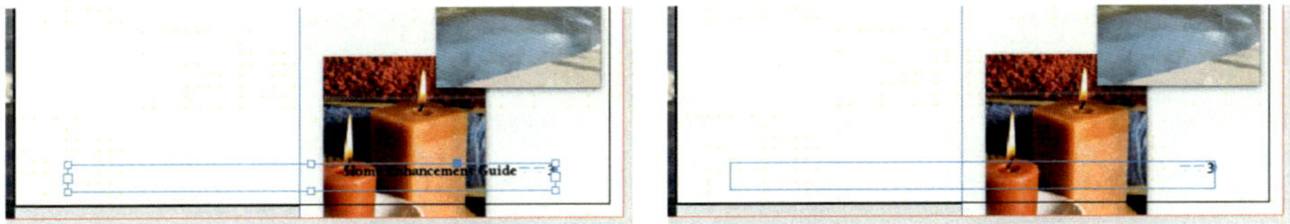

14. **Save the file and continue to the next exercise.**

Unify Spreads with Color

Using similar or complementary colors on each page of a spread is one way to help unify a design. When you created the master pages, you applied a dark green fill to the sidebar text box. Now that the images are in place, it would be better to use colors from each spread's image on the associated sidebar box. The Eyedropper tool, which you can use to pull or **sample** colors from existing objects, makes it easy to apply image colors to native object fills.

1. **With realty_booklet.indd open, navigate to the Page 4–5 spread.**

2. **Click the pasteboard area with the Selection tool to make sure nothing is selected in the file.**

3. **Choose the Eyedropper tool. Using whatever method you prefer, change the Stroke color to None and then make sure the Fill color is the active attribute.**

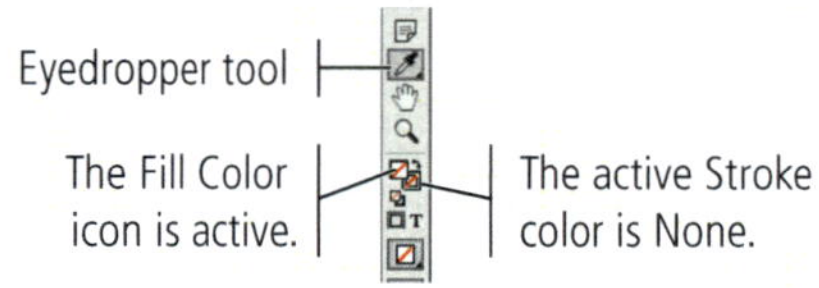

4. **Click a dark green area in the image on the left side of the spread.**

5. **Move the filled Eyedropper cursor over the green-filled text frame and click to change the frame's fill color to the sampled color from Step 4.**

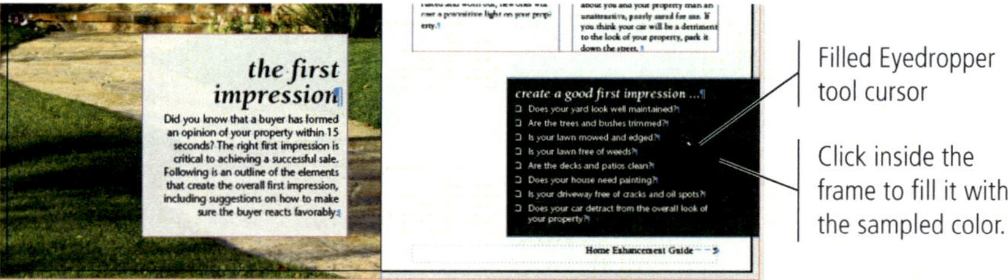

6. **Navigate to the Page 6–7 spread. Press Option/Alt to clear the Eyedropper tool, and then click a dark brown area in the image on the left side of the spread.**

   As long as the Eyedropper tool remains selected, it retains the last-sampled color, so you can continuously apply the sampled attributes to multiple objects. Pressing Option/Alt allows you to sample a new color.

7. **Click the green-filled text frame on Page 7 to fill it with the new sampled color.**

Click inside the frame to fill it with the new sampled color.

8. **Repeat the process from Steps 6–7 to change the box color on each spread.**

9. **Save the file, and then continue to the final stage of the project.**

Understanding Imposition

INDESIGN FOUNDATIONS

If you fold a piece of paper in half twice, number the pages, and then unfold the paper, you will see the basic imposition for an eight-page signature.

If you look at your folded piece of paper, you can see that the tops of all the pages are folded together. If elements bleed to the top of a page, given the inaccuracy of folding machines (±0.03125″), that ink would appear on the edge of the page it abutted on the signature (for example, see Pages 12 and 13 in the following illustration).

The pages of a signature must be cut apart at the top, which requires at least 1/8″ at the top of the page for the trim. The outside edge of half the pages also must be cut apart (this is called a **face trim**) so the pages of the finished piece can be turned. This face trim also requires 1/8″ around the page edge. That trim would shorten an 8.5 × 11″ book to 8.375 × 10.875″. This shorter size might be fine, but it could also ruin a design and layout. There's a better solution.

On the press-sheet layout, space is added between the tops of the printer's spreads to allow room for bleed and cutting apart the pages. This separation is probably all that's required for a 16-page saddle-stitched booklet printed on a 70# text-weight paper. If you use a heavier paper (for example, a 100# coated sheet for an annual report), or if

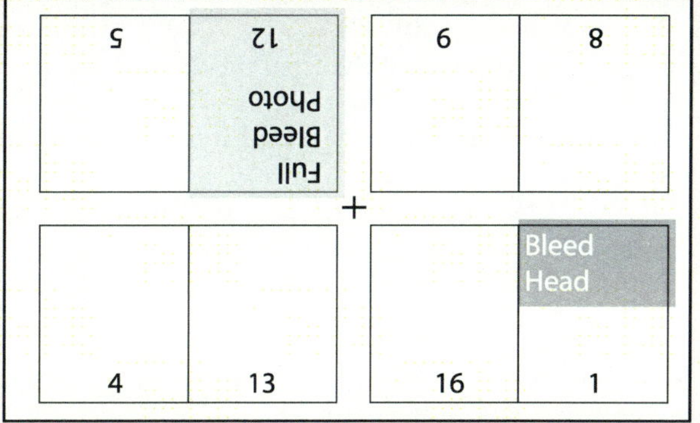

you have more than one 16-page signature, you need to allow room for **creep**, which is the progressive extension of interior pages of the folded signature beyond the trim edge of the outside pages.

If you have questions about folds or imposition, you should always call your service provider. Somebody there will be able to advise you on the best course to take. In most cases, these issues will be handled entirely by the service provider, often using software specifically designed for the prepress workflow. If you try to do too much, you might cause them extra work (and yourself extra expense).

Stage 3 Outputting Variations of Files

The final stage of this project requires creating two versions of final output:

- A desktop proof for your client, showing the spreads as they will appear in the final bound booklet
- A low-resolution PDF file that prospective clients can download from the organization's Web site

InDesign includes a number of tools that make it easy to create both versions without destroying the integrity of the original layout file.

Create a Folding Dummy

When a page is printed, it is typically output on a sheet larger than the job's trim size. Multiple pages are often **imposed** (arranged) on a single press sheet, and the printed pieces are later cut from the press sheet and trimmed to their final size. In some cases, entirely different jobs can be **ganged** (combined) together to make the best use of available space on the press sheet.

Multi-page documents that use facing pages have special output requirements; understanding these requirements means you will also be able to see how your design might be affected by output processes after the file leaves your desk. When multiple-page books and booklets are produced, they are not printed as individual pages. Instead, they are printed in signatures of eight, sixteen, or more pages at a time. A **signature** consists of multiple pages of a document, all printed on the same press sheet, which is later folded and cut to the final trim size. Each signature is composed of two flats. (The term **flat** is a relic of the days when film was manually stripped together on a light table; it is still sometimes used to describe one side of one signature.)

Layouts are designed in reader's spreads, but arranged into printer's spreads on the printing plate. (**Imposition** refers to the arrangement of a document's pages on a printing plate to produce the final product.)

1. Fold a piece of paper in half lengthwise, and then in half widthwise.

2. While the paper is still folded, write the sequential page numbers 1 through 8 on the folded sections.

3. Unfold it and you will see the printer's spreads for an eight-page document.

The dummy unfolds to show how an eight-page signature is laid out. Page 8 and Page 1 create a single printer's spread.

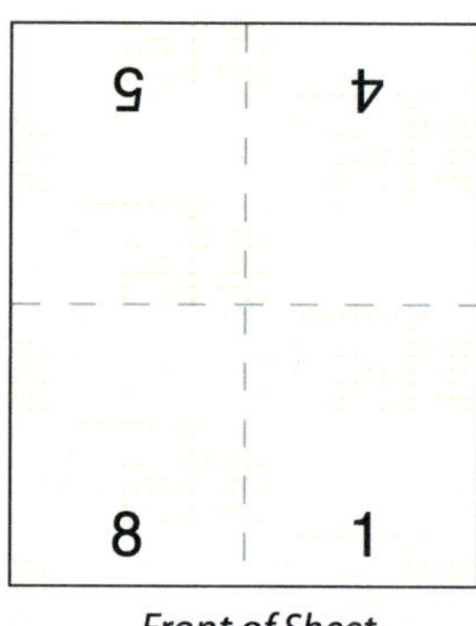

Front of Sheet

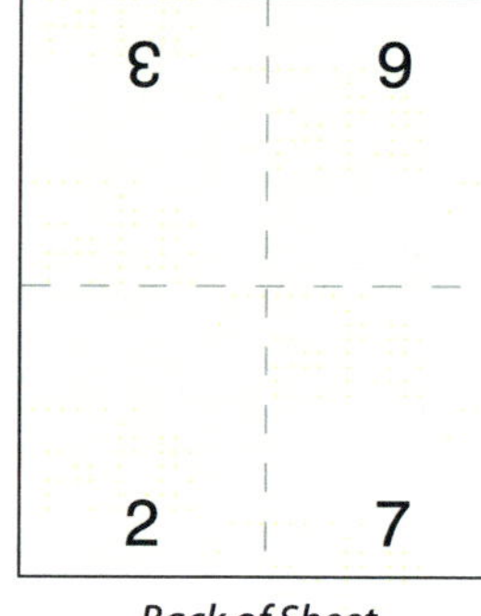

Back of Sheet

Note:

*A **reader's spread** is a set of two pages that appear next to each other in a printed document — Page 2 faces Page 3, and so on.*

*A **printer's spread** refers to the way pages align on a press sheet so, after a document is folded and cut, the reader's spreads will be in the correct locations.*

In printer's spreads, the sum of pairs of page numbers always totals the number of pages in the signature, plus 1. For example, in a 16-page signature, Page 4 faces Page 13, Page 16 faces Page 1, and so on.

If a saddle-stitched (stapled) book is made up of multiple signatures, the page numbers on printer's spreads equal the total number of pages in the publication, plus 1. For example, a saddle-stitched booklet is 32 pages, made up of two 16-page signatures. The page numbers on each printer's spread total 33: Page 16 faces Page 17, Page 22 faces Page 11, and so on.

Print a Booklet Proof

You probably don't want to (and really, you shouldn't have to) think about creating full impositions for a press. At times, however, you might want to print proofs in printer's spreads to show clients. You could work through a complicated manual process of rearranging pages, but the InDesign Print Booklet command is far easier — and it's non-destructive.

1. **With realty_booklet.indd open, choose File>Print Booklet.**

   This dialog box shows only the output options related to printing printer's spreads. These options are set; you can't directly change the printer that will be used for output.

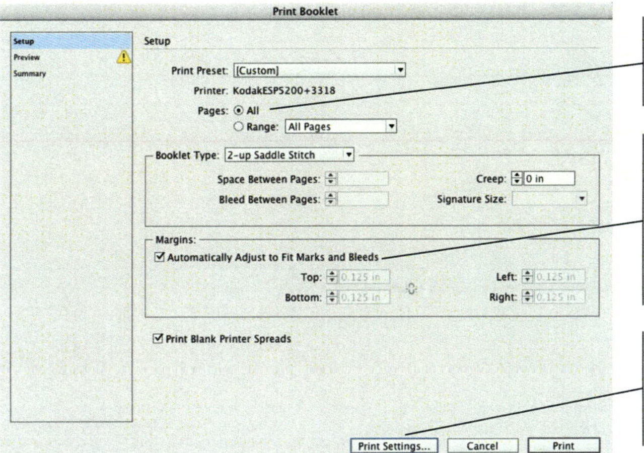

Use these options to output the entire file as a booklet, or output only a specific range of pages.

Check this box to allow InDesign to automatically calculate the margins to accommodate bleeds (as defined in the Document Setup dialog box) and printer's marks (as applied in the Print dialog box).

Click this button to access the Print dialog box, change the printer-specific settings, and define printer's marks.

2. **In the Setup pane of the dialog box, make sure 2-up Saddle Stitch is selected in the Booklet Type menu.**

   In the Booklet Type menu, you can choose what kind of imposition to create.

   - **2-up Saddle Stitch** creates two-page printer's spreads from the entire layout or selected page range. If the layout doesn't contain enough pages to create the necessary printer's spreads, InDesign automatically adds blank pages at the end of the layout.
   - **2-up Perfect Bound** creates two-page printer's spreads that fit within the specified signature size (4, 8, 12, 16, or 32 pages). If the number of layout pages to be imposed is not divisible by the selected signature size, InDesign adds blank pages as needed at the end of the finished document.
   - **Consecutive** creates a two-, three-, or four-page imposition appropriate for a foldout brochure.

   You can also define settings to adjust for imposition issues related to printer's spreads versus reader's spreads.

   - **Space Between Pages** defines the gap between pages in the printer's spread. This option is available for all but saddle-stitched booklet types.
   - **Bleed Between Pages** defines the amount that page elements can bleed into the space between pages in a printer's spread (from 0 to half the defined space between the pages) for perfect-bound impositions.
   - **Creep** defines the amount of space necessary to accommodate paper thickness and folding on each signature.
   - **Signature Size** defines the number of pages in each signature for perfect-bound impositions.
   - **Print Blank Printer Spreads** determines whether any blank pages added to a signature will be printed.

3. **Click the Print Settings button. In the resulting Print dialog box, choose the printer and PPD you will use to output the booklet.**
4. **In the Setup options, choose US Letter in the Paper Size menu and choose landscape orientation.**

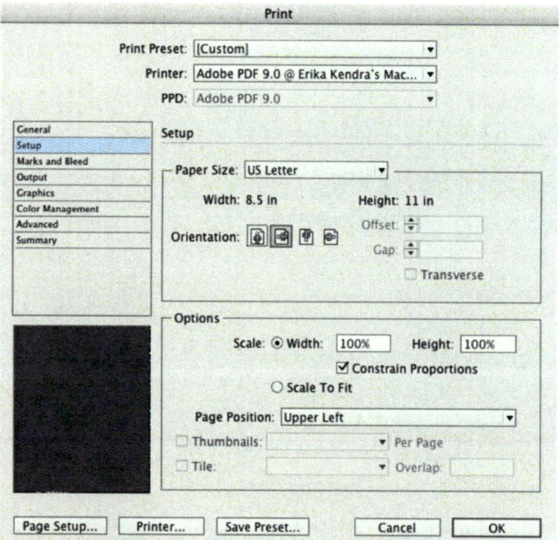

5. **In the Marks and Bleed options, uncheck the All Printer's Marks and Use Document Bleed Settings options, and change all four Bleed values to 0″.**

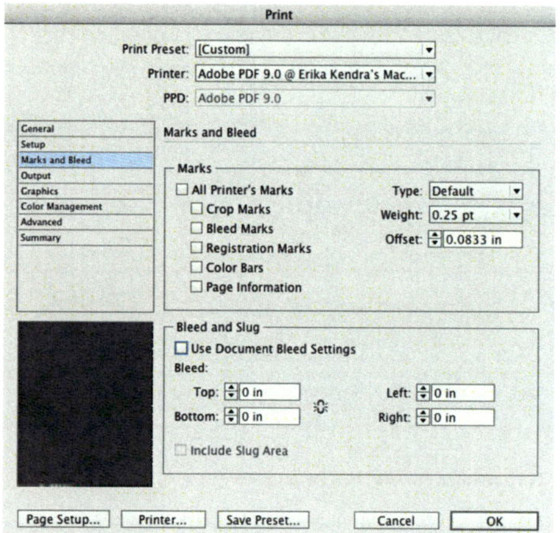

Note:

If you have a printer with tabloid-paper capability, you could output the file with marks and bleeds, and then trim the proof to size. Doing so would eliminate any issue with the margins required by some desktop printers, which would prevent the pages from printing the outer edges of the layout.

6. **Click OK to return to the Print Booklet dialog box.**
7. **In the Print Booklet dialog box, uncheck the Automatically Adjust to Fit Marks and Bleeds option. With the Chain icon active, change all four Margin fields to 0″.**

   You're only printing a client proof on letter-size paper, so you do not need bleeds or printer's marks.

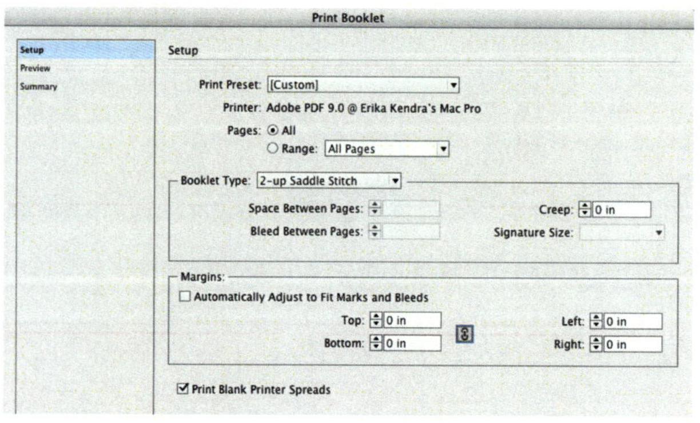

8. **Click Preview in the list of options.**

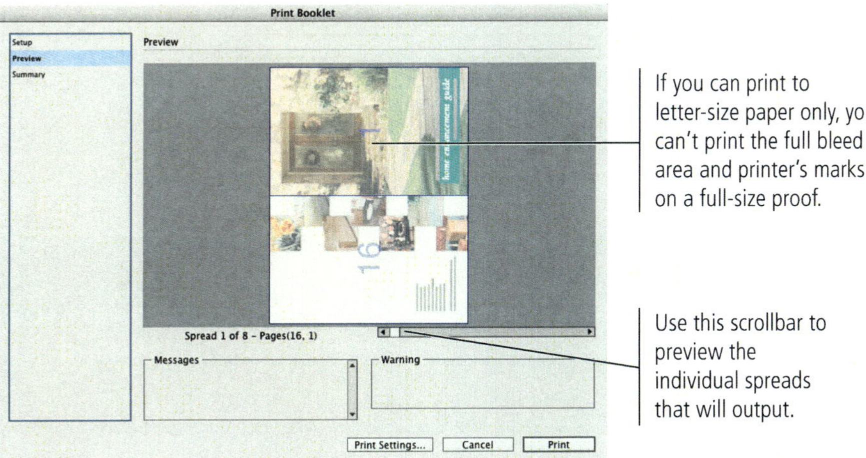

9. **Click Print.**

10. **When the file is finished spooling to the printer, continue to the next exercise.**

 Create a PDF with Page Transitions

In addition to the printed job, your client requested a low-resolution PDF file that can be posted on the organization's Web site. To add interest to the digital version, you are going to add interactive page transitions that affect the way new pages appear when users navigate through the PDF file.

1. **With realty_booklet.indd open, open the Page Transitions panel (Window>Interactive>Page Transitions).**

2. **In the Pages panel, double-click the Page 2-3 spread numbers (below the page icons) to select the entire spread.**

   Remember, there can be a difference between the active and selected pages. Double-clicking the targeted page or spread ensures that the spread you want is the one selected.

3. **Open the Page Transitions panel Options menu and select Choose.**

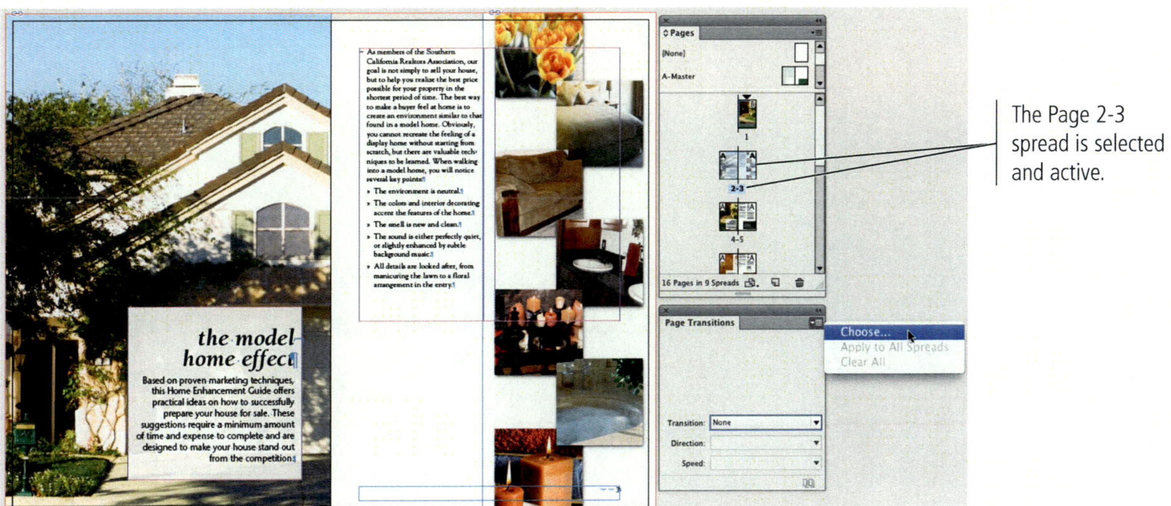

4. **In the resulting Page Transitions dialog box, roll your mouse cursor over the icons to preview the general effect of each.**

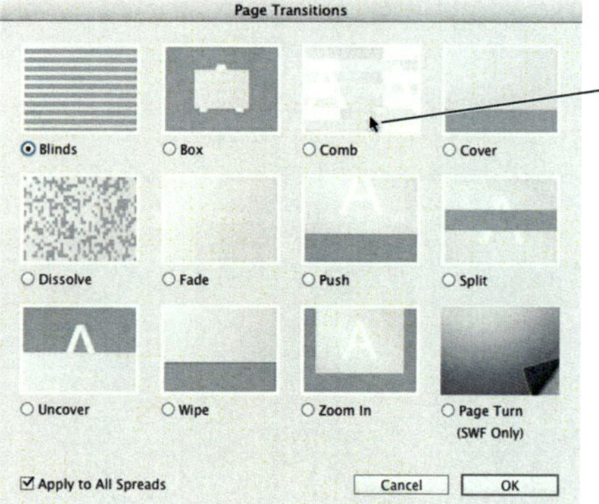

Rolling your mouse over an option shows a preview of that transition.

5. **Make sure the Apply to All Spreads option is unchecked, then activate the Comb radio button and click OK.**

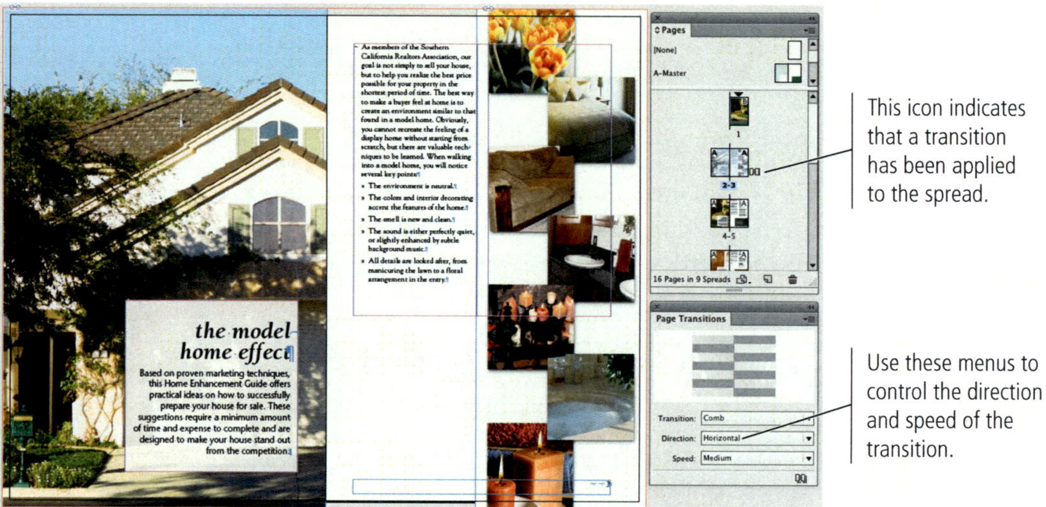

This icon indicates that a transition has been applied to the spread.

Use these menus to control the direction and speed of the transition.

6. **Double-click the Page 4-5 spread numbers in the Pages panel. In the Page Transitions panel, choose Wipe in the Transition menu.**

Different spreads can have different transitions (although this is not typically a good idea).

7. **With the Page 4-5 spread selected, click the Apply to All Spreads button at the bottom of the Page Transitions panel.**

Clicking this button applies the selected transition to all spreads in the layout.

8. **Choose File>Export. Choose Adobe PDF (Interactive) in the Format/Save As Type menu and then click Save.**

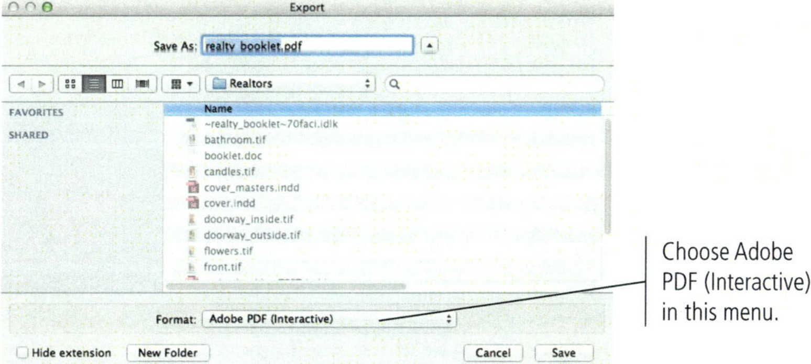

Choose Adobe PDF (Interactive) in this menu.

9. **Review the options in the resulting Export to Interactive PDF dialog box.**

The Adobe PDF (Interactive) option opens a simplified dialog box with only the settings that are relevant to PDF files intended for digital distribution.

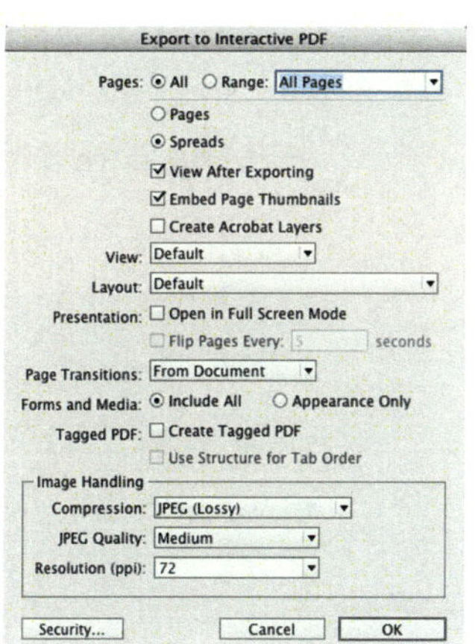

- **Pages** determines which pages will be included in the resulting PDF file. You can export All pages, or select the Range radio button and define a specific page range to include.
- The **Pages** and **Spreads** radio buttons determine how pages are treated in the resulting PDF file. When the Spread option is checked, facing-page spreads (as in this document) result in a single page in the PDF file.
- **View After Exporting**, when active, automatically opens the file in your system's default PDF application.
- **Embed Page Thumbnails** creates a thumbnail preview for every page that is exported.
- **Create Acrobat Layers** maintains any InDesign layers as Acrobat layers in the resulting PDF file. (If you have Acrobat 6.0 or later, you can access those layers to create multiple versions from the same PDF file.)
- **View** determines the default view percentage of the exported PDF file. You can cause the file to open at actual size, fit the page into the Acrobat window based on a number of dimensions, or choose a specific percentage (25, 50, 75, or 100).

- **Layout** determines how spreads appear in the resulting PDF file.
  - The **Single Page** options export each spread separately.
  - The **Continuous** options export files so that users can scroll through the document and view parts of successive pages at the same time. Using the non-continuous options, scrolling has the same effect as turning a page; you can't view successive spreads at once.
  - The **Two-Up Facing** options exports two spreads side-by-side.
  - The **Two-Up Cover Page** options export the first spread as a single page and then the remaining spreads two at a time side-by-side. This allows the pages to appear as they would in a book, with even-numbered pages on the left and odd-numbered pages on the right.

Note:

The default view and layout options open the file based on the reader application's default options.

- **Presentation Opens In Full Screen Mode** opens the resulting PDF without showing Acrobat's menus or panels. You can then use the Flip Pages Every field to automatically change pages after a defined interval.
- **Page Transitions** defaults to the From Document option, which maintains the settings that you define in the Transitions panel. You can choose None to export the PDF without page transitions, or choose one of the available methods in the attached menu to override any settings that exist in the document.
- **Forms and Media** options can be used to include movies, sounds, buttons, and form fields that are placed in the InDesign file. If you choose Appearance Only, the PDF will show only the static version of those interactive objects.
- **Create Tagged PDF** automatically tags elements in the story based on a subset of the Acrobat tags that InDesign supports (basic text formatting, lists, tables, etc.).
- **Compression** determines how images in the resulting PDF are managed to reduce file size for digital distribution. JPEG (Lossy) removes data, and can result in poor image quality. JPEG 2000 (Lossless) reduces file size without discarding image data, but can result in larger file size than JPEG (Lossy). Automatic allows the software to determine the best quality for images.
- **JPEG Quality** defines how much compression is applied if you choose JPEG (Lossy) or Automatic compression. Higher quality settings result in larger files.
- **Resolution** defines the resolution of raster images in the exported PDF. High resolution is important if you want users to be able to zoom in close to an image, but higher resolution settings mean larger file sizes.

10. **Define the following settings:**
    - **Make sure the All [Pages] radio button is selected.**
    - **Choose the Spreads radio button.**
    - **Check the View After Exporting option.**
    - **Check the Embed Page Thumbnails option.**
    - **Choose Fit Height in the View menu.**
    - **Choose Single Page in the Layout menu.**
    - **Check the Open in Full Screen Mode option.**
    - **Leave the Flip Pages Every option unchecked.**
    - **Choose From Document in the Page Transitions menu.**
    - **Choose JPEG 2000 (Lossless) in the Compression menu.**
    - **Define the target Resolution as 72 ppi.**

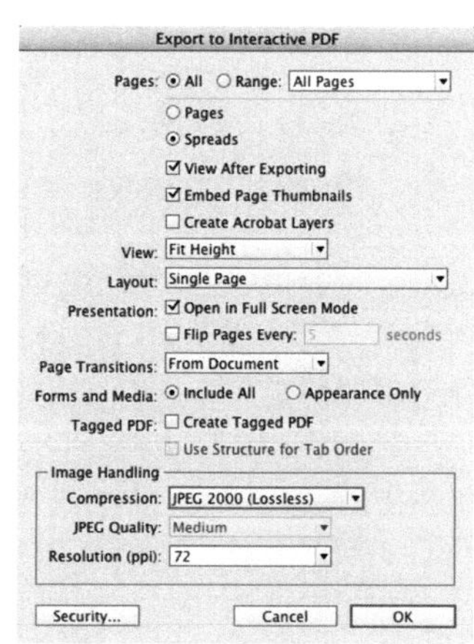

11. **Click OK to create the PDF file.**

12. **Read the resulting warning message, and then click OK.**

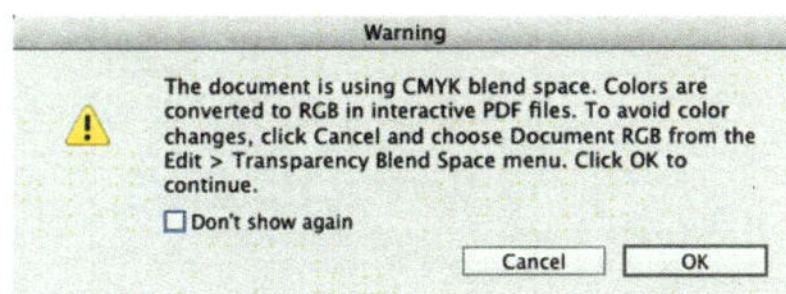

If you get a Full Screen warning message when Acrobat opens, click Yes to allow the file to switch to Full Screen mode.

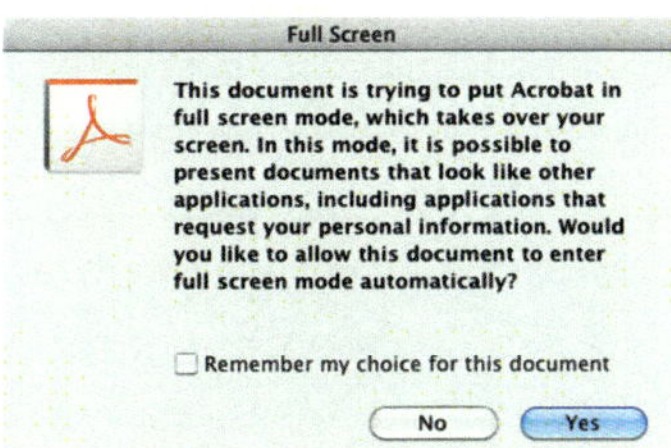

13. **When the PDF file opens, press the Down Arrow button to see the interactive page transitions.**

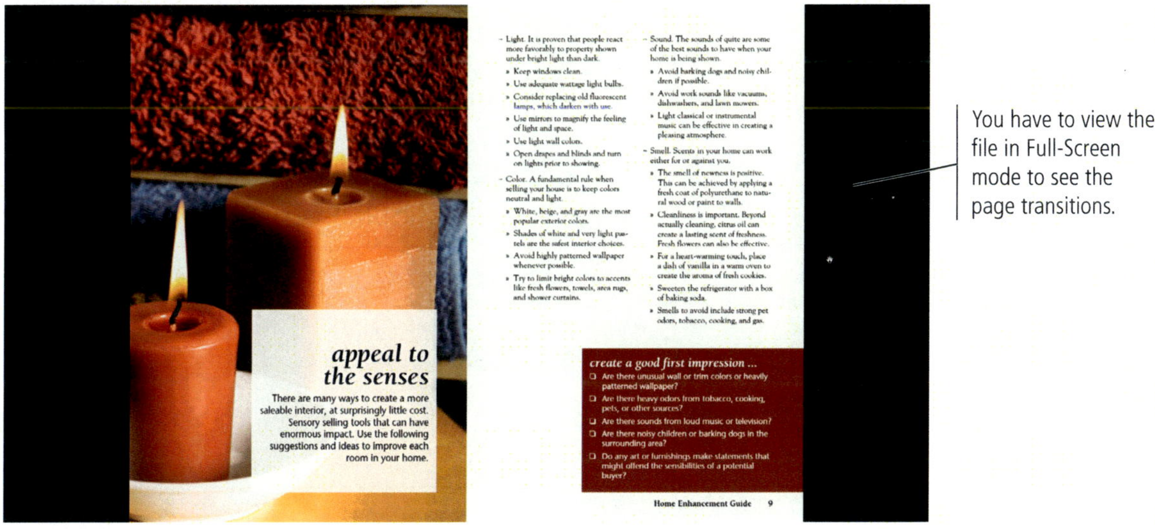

You have to view the file in Full-Screen mode to see the page transitions.

14. **Press the Escape key to exit Full-Screen mode, then close the PDF file. Return to InDesign, then save and close the InDesign file.**

Project Review

fill in the blank

1. _______________ have inside and outside margins instead of left and right margins.

2. When _______________ is active, InDesign automatically adds pages to accommodate an entire story that is placed in a primary text frame.

3. A local formatting override is indicated by _______________ next to the style name in the Paragraph Styles panel.

4. A negative first-line indent is called a(n) _______________.

5. A(n) _______________ is a single line of a paragraph at the end of a column.

6. A(n) _______________ is a single line of a paragraph at the top of a column, or a very short (one-word) last line of a paragraph.

7. _______________ in the Paragraph Style Options dialog box can be used to force a paragraph to begin in the next linked frame.

8. _______________ fonts can store more than 65,000 glyphs (characters) in a single font file; the same font file works on both Macintosh and Windows.

9. You can use the _______________ option to create a parent/child relationship between two styles, in which changes made to the parent style reflect in the child style as well.

10. _______________ is the process of arranging pages on a press sheet so, when folded and trimmed, the pages of a job appear in the correct order.

short answer

1. Briefly explain the difference between facing pages and non-facing pages.

2. Briefly explain the difference between reader's spreads and printer's spreads.

3. Briefly explain the advantages and disadvantages of nesting text-formatting styles.

Portfolio Builder Project

Use what you learned in this project to complete the following freeform exercise.
Carefully read the art director and client comments, then create your own design to meet the needs of the project.
Use the space below to sketch ideas; when finished, write a brief explanation of your reasoning behind your final design.

art director comments

Your clients are very happy with the finished Home Enhancement Guide. They would like you to create another collateral booklet that they can provide to prospective home buyers, providing contact information for agents in specific geographic areas.

To complete this project, you should:

- ❑ Download the **IDCC_PB_Project4.zip** archive from the Student Files Web page to access the client-supplied text.
- ❑ Create a 16-page booklet using the same document size as the Home Enhancement Guide.
- ❑ Design a facing-page layout that is aesthetically pleasing, which clearly presents the necessary information.
- ❑ Find or create supportive images for each spread that match the overall theme of the project.

client comments

This booklet will list each member agent by general location, including their name and photo, contact information, and their types of property specialties. We sent you a text file with a short blurb for the inside front page, as well as the realtor information from our database. We don't have the agents' photos yet; we'll forward them as soon as possible. Just make sure you leave space for them in the layout.

For the covers, use the same layout as the Home Enhancement Guide. On the front cover, use a different picture and change the title to "Buyer's Resource Guide". On the back, replace the checkerboard image with the same pictures that you use in the Buyer's Guide booklet.

We want the first spread to include only the introductory blurb and some kind of graphics — maybe a montage of different home styles.

One last thing: for now, leave the center spread open. We might want to add something different there, but we haven't figured out what yet.

project justification

Project Summary

Controlling the flow of text in a document — especially for documents with more than one or two pages — is just as important as controlling the appearance of the different type elements. InDesign provides powerful tools that let you control virtually every aspect of document design, from the exact position of individual paragraphs to entire blocks of text to automatic page numbers based on the location of special characters in the layout.

Changing the master page settings for this booklet allowed you to automatically flow a single story across multiple pages. Using the Keep options for the applied styles, you were able to position each element in the appropriate frame on the appropriate spread, which significantly reduced the amount of manual evaluation and adjustment that would have been required without these features.

Using effective master pages also allowed you to place repeating elements to appear on every spread in the layout. Combining that functionality with special characters, you also eliminated a number of unnecessarily repetitive tasks, such as manually numbering the pages.

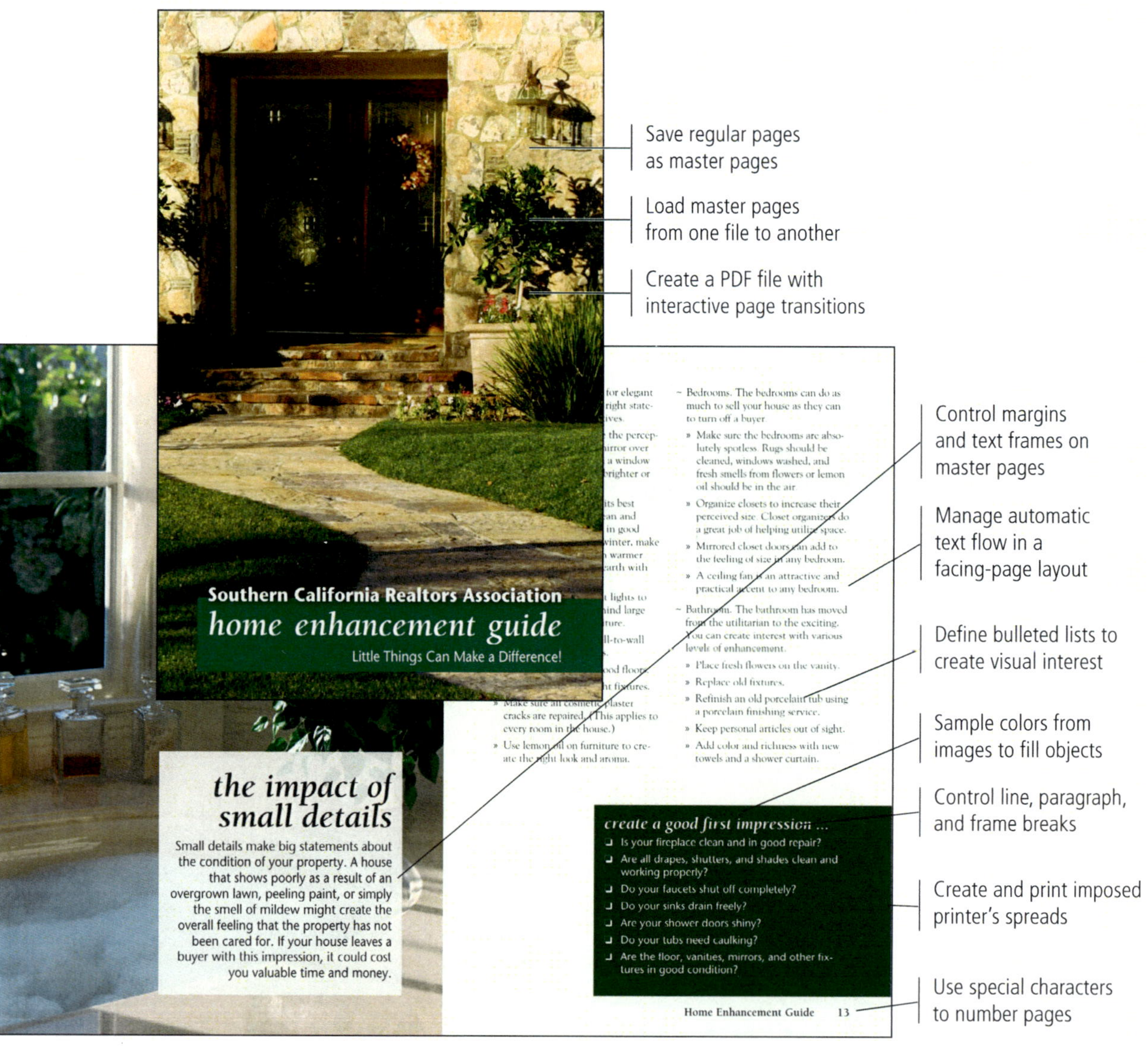

Project 5

Ireland Travel Brochure

Your client is a travel agency that is creating a set of brochures to promote a series of travel packages to various countries in Europe. The client wants to create a letterfold rack brochure for Ireland tourism. The job includes a relatively small amount of copy, a number of images, and a basic form that people can fill out and enter to win a free trip — a common technique for gathering potential clients' contact information.

This project incorporates the following skills:

- ❑ Building a template for specific folding requirements
- ❑ Defining slug information using static and variable text
- ❑ Converting text to complex frames
- ❑ Using a library to access frequently used objects
- ❑ Using object styles to reduce repetitive tasks
- ❑ Working with embedded clipping paths and Alpha channels
- ❑ Controlling irregular text wraps
- ❑ Importing text from a Microsoft Word file
- ❑ Importing styles from existing InDesign files
- ❑ Creating captions using stored image metadata
- ❑ Controlling tabs to format columns of text

Project Meeting

client comments

We are planning a new series of brochures to promote our European vacation packages. These need to fit into our standard rack holders, which means the finished size should be 4″ wide by 9″ high. A letterfold will give us three panels on each side, which should be plenty for the information we want to include.

The brochures will mostly be hand-outs for people who walk into our office or visit our booth at trade shows, but some will be mailed, so we want the brochure to be a self-mailer.

These brochures will be mostly visual, with a little bit of descriptive copy. We're sending you the text and images for the Ireland brochure first because that's the only one that's been finalized so far.

We went back and forth for weeks over the styles for our other collateral, and we were all finally happy with the results on other pieces your agency designed. We want to use the same formatting in these brochures that you used in all our other jobs.

art director comments

A lot of people design folding documents incorrectly. Some use a six-page layout with each page the size of the final folded job; others use two pages, each divided into three equal "columns." In both cases, all panels on the job are the exact same width — which is wrong.

For a letterfold, the job needs to have one panel narrower than the others. Plus, each side of the brochure has to mirror the other so the narrow panel is in the correct location when the job is printed, trimmed, and folded.

The last item to remember is that the brochure will be a self-mailer; the back panel needs to be left blank, with only the return address in the upper-left corner.

project objectives

To complete this project, you will:

- ❑ Create a folding layout template on master page spreads
- ❑ Use the slug area to mark folding panels
- ❑ Define a custom text variable to track file status
- ❑ Use InDesign library files to store and access frequently used objects and groups
- ❑ Use object styles to apply consistent formatting to multiple frames
- ❑ Apply an Alpha channel that is embedded in a Photoshop file
- ❑ Control text wraps around basic frames and irregular shapes
- ❑ Import text and styles from a Microsoft Word file
- ❑ Create new styles based on existing formatting in the layout
- ❑ Add dynamic captions based on image metadata

Stage 1 Building a Folding Template

There are several common types of folds:

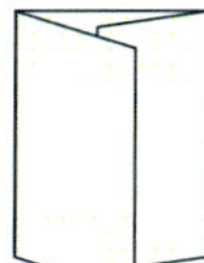

Letterfolds have two folds and three panels to a side. (These are often incorrectly called "trifold" because they result in three panels.) The panel that folds in should be 1/16″ to 1/8″ narrower than the two outside panels; ask your service provider how much allowance is required for the paper you're using.

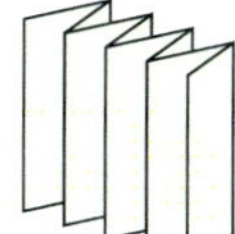

Accordion folds can have as many panels as you prefer. When it has six panels (three on each side), it's often referred to as a **Z-fold** because it looks like the letter Z. Because the panels don't fold into one another, an accordion-fold document has panels of consistent width.

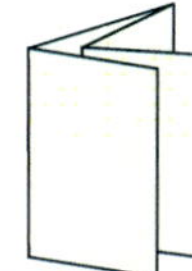

Double-parallel folds are commonly used for eight-panel rack brochures (such as those you often find in a hotel or travel agency). Again, the panels on the inside are narrower than the outside panels. This type of fold uses facing pages because the margins need to line up on the front and back sides of the sheet.

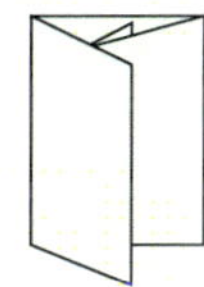

Barrel folds (also called **roll folds**) are perhaps the most common fold for 14 × 8.5″ brochures. The two outside panels are full size, and each successive panel is narrower than the previous one. You can theoretically have as many panels as you want, but at some point the number of fold-in panels will become unwieldy.

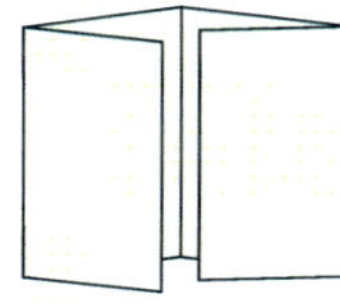

Gate folds result in a four-panel document; the paper is folded in half, and then each half is folded in half toward the center so the two ends of the paper meet at the center fold. The panels that fold in are narrower than the two outside panels. This type of brochure allows two different spreads: the first revealed when you open the outer panels, and the second revealed when you open the inner flaps.

It's important to consider the output process when planning a job with documents that are not just a single sheet of standard-size paper — documents with multiple pages folded one or more times, or other non-standard page sizes. The mechanics of commercial printing require specific allowances for cutting, folding, and other finishing processes. There are two basic principles to remember when designing documents that fold:

- Folding machines are mechanical devices, and paper sometimes shifts as it flows through the machine's paper path. Most are accurate to about 0.0125″.
- Paper has thickness; thicker paper requires more allowance for the fold.

Because of these two principles, any panel that folds into the other panels needs to be smaller than the other panels. You should note that the issues presented here have little to do with the subjective elements of design. Layout and page geometry are governed by specific variables, including mechanical limitations in the production process. These principles are rules, not suggestions. If you don't leave adequate margins, for example, design elements will be cut off or won't align properly from one page to the next.

Create the Outside Master Pages

When working with folding documents, the trim size of a folded document is actually the size of the flat sheet *before* it's folded. Once you know the flat trim size of a job, you have to calculate the size of individual panels before you set up the layout.

For example, imagine that you're printing a letterfold brochure on a laser printer that can only print to letter-sized paper. The flat trim size, then, is 11″ wide by 8.5″ high. The first required calculation is the base size of each panel:

11″ ÷ 3 = 3.6667″

But remember, the fold-in panel has to be narrower than the other two panels; you also have to factor the required folding variance (which your service provider can tell you) into the panel size. Half of the difference is removed from the fold-in panel, and one-fourth of the difference is added to each outer panel. Assuming a folding variance of 1/8″ (0.125):

Fold-in panel = 3.6667 – 1/16 = 3.6042″

Outer panel 1 = 3.6667 + 1/32 = 3.698″

Outer panel 2 = 3.6667 + 1/32 = 3.698″

You can safely round these values to 3.6″ and 3.7″, resulting in a panel variance of 0.1″, which is enough for most papers that can be run through a desktop laser printer. This seems like a complicated series of calculations, and it is only relevant when printing to a defined flat trim size.

In other cases, however, you might know the finished size of your folding brochure. For example, a rack card or brochure is commonly 4″ × 9″, which fits into standard display racks (hence the name). If you know the final target size, it is easy to calculate the size of individual panels used to build the folding document. Using the 4″ × 9″ rack card with a required 1/8″ panel variance as an example:

Outer Panel 1 = 4″

Outer Panel 2 = 4″

Fold-in Panel = 4″ – 0.125″ = 3.875″

Because the different panels in a folding document are different sizes, earlier versions of the software required you to define each side of a folding document as a separate page. You had to use page guides to define the folds and margins of individual panels. Fortunately, InDesign supports multiple page sizes in a single document — which makes it far easier to set up the basic document layout for items such as folding brochures.

1. **Download IDCC_RF_Project5.zip from the Student Files Web page.**

2. **Expand the ZIP archive in your WIP folder (Macintosh) or copy the archive contents into your WIP folder (Windows).**

   This results in a folder named **Ireland**, which contains the files you need for this project. You should also use this folder to save the files you create in this project.

3. **Choose File>New>Document. In the New Document dialog box, define the following parameters, then click OK to create the new file:**

Intent	**Print**
Number of Pages	**1**
Start Page #	**1**
Facing Pages	**Not Checked**
Primary Text Frame	**Checked**
Page Size	**Width: 4″**
	Height: 9″
Columns	**1**
Margins	**0.25″ on all four sides**
Bleed	**0.125″ on all four sides**
Slug	**0.5″ on the top and bottom**
	0″ on the left and right

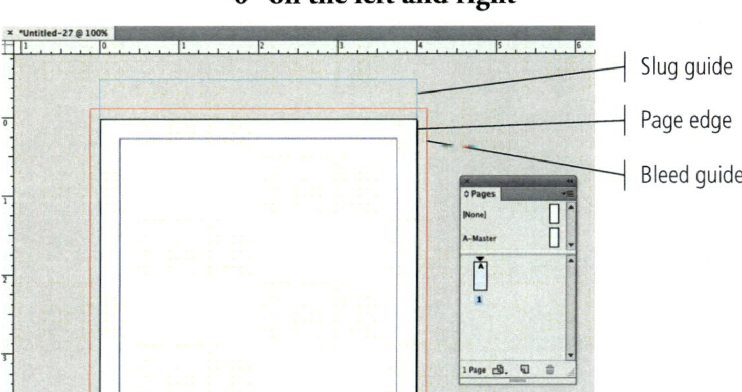

4. **In the Pages panel, Control/right-click the A-Master page name and choose Master Options for "A-Master" in the contextual menu.**

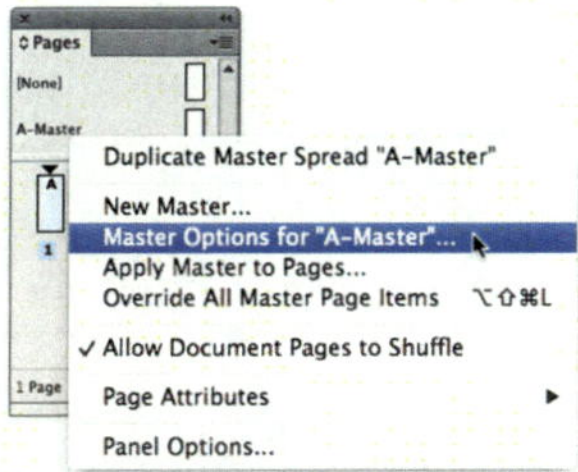

5. **In the resulting dialog box, type Outside in the Name field and type 3 in the Number of Pages field. Click OK to return to the layout.**

The outside of the brochure has three panels, so you are defining three pages in the master page spread — one page for each panel.

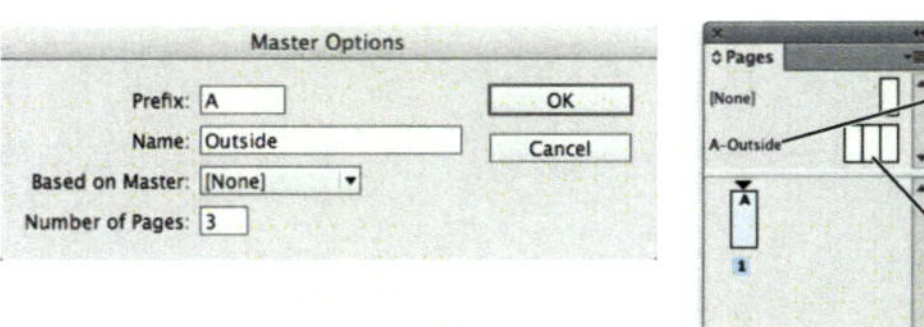

After you click OK, the new name appears in the Pages panel.

The master page icon now shows all three pages in the spread.

Note:

It's always a good idea to use a meaningful name for any element you define in InDesign, including a master page.

6. **Double-click the A-Outside layout to display the master page in the document window.**

   The master page spread now has three pages, as you defined in Step 5. All three pages have 0.25″ margins, as you defined when you created the file. The bleed area surrounds the entire spread because each page automatically abuts the other pages in the spread.

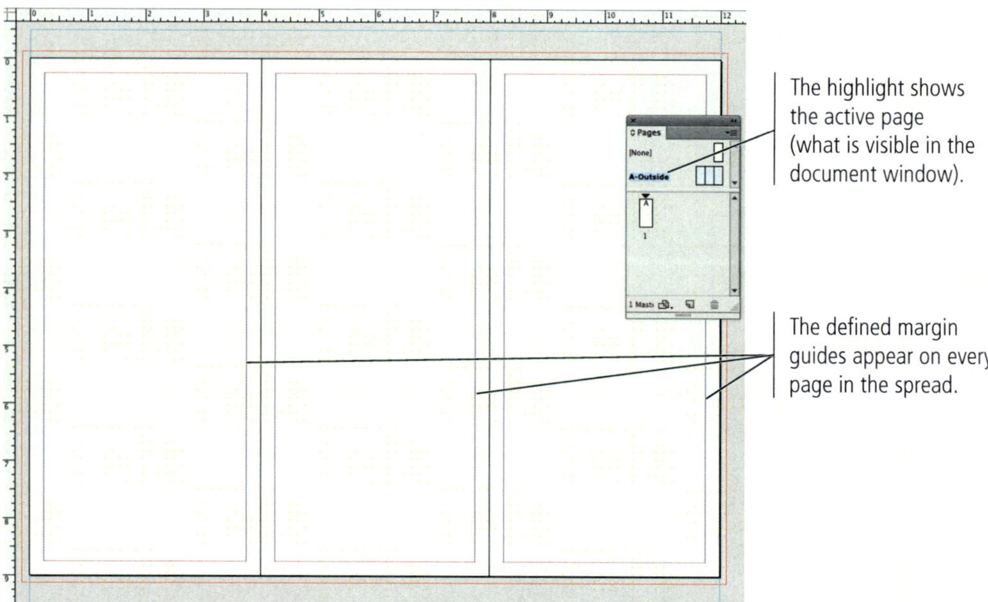

7. **Using the Selection tool, click inside the margin area on the left page of the spread to select the primary text frame.**

   Unfortunately, adding pages to a master page does not automatically place a primary frame on each new page. You have to manually create the frames on the two new pages.

8. **Option/Alt-click the primary text frame and drag right to clone it. Drag until the cloned frame snaps to the margins on the center page.**

   When you release the mouse button, the icon in the top-left corner of the frame identifies the cloned frame as a regular text frame. A master layout can have only one primary text frame (or thread). The text on each panel will not always be a single story, so you are not going to link these frames into a primary thread.

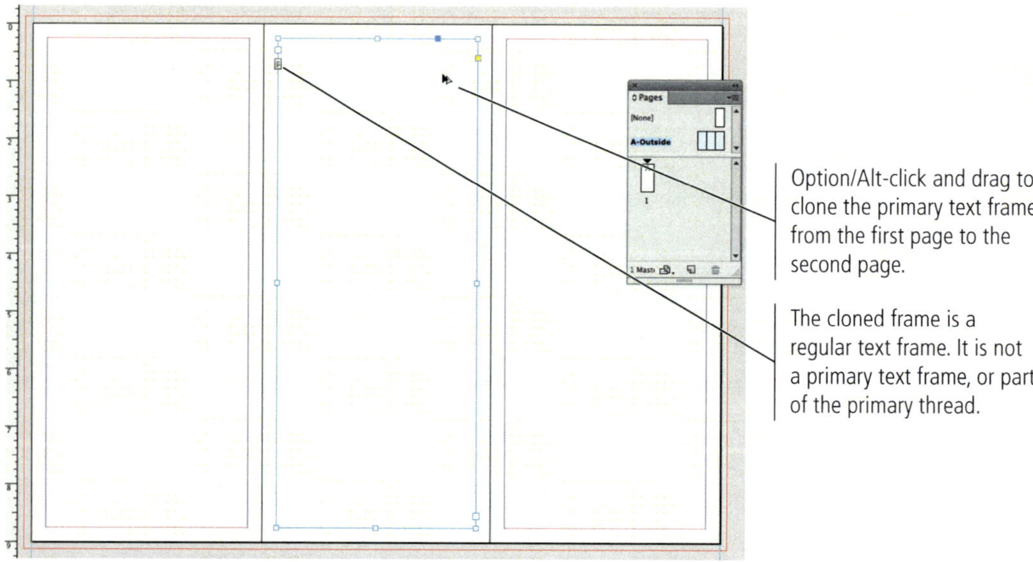

9. Repeat Step 8 to add a text frame to the right page in the spread.

10. Choose the Page tool in the Tools panel, and then click the left page in the spread to select it.

The Page tool makes it possible to change the dimensions of a single (selected) page in the document.

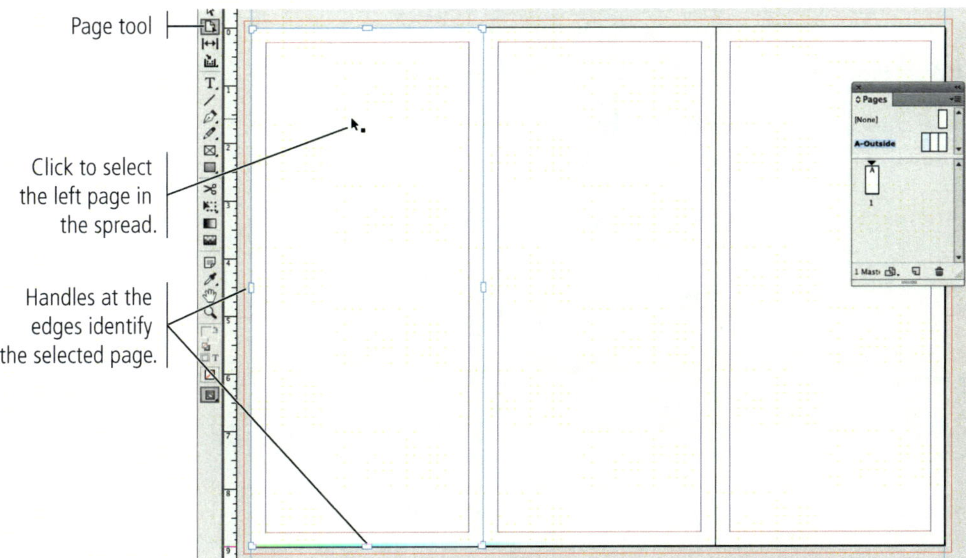

11. In the Control panel, choose Object-based in the Liquid Page Rule menu, and check the Objects Move with Page option.

12. Choose the right-center reference point. Click in the W field after the existing value, then type `-.125` and press Return/Enter to apply the change.

InDesign understands mathematical operators in most dialog box and panel fields. Because you know you need to remove 1/8″ from the fold-in panel width, it is very easy to simply subtract that amount from the existing value.

> *Note:*
>
> *You will work in depth with liquid page rules in Project 6: Digital Layout Variations.*

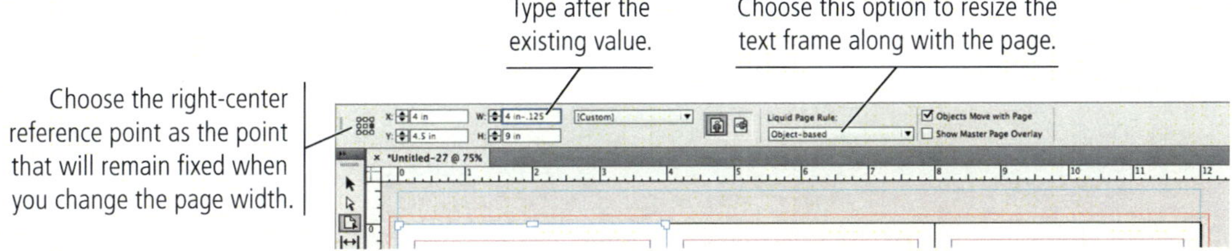

The margins on the selected page are still 0.25″ from the adjusted page edges. Because you activated the Object-based liquid page rule, the text frame on the page adjusted to remain snapped to the adjusted margins.

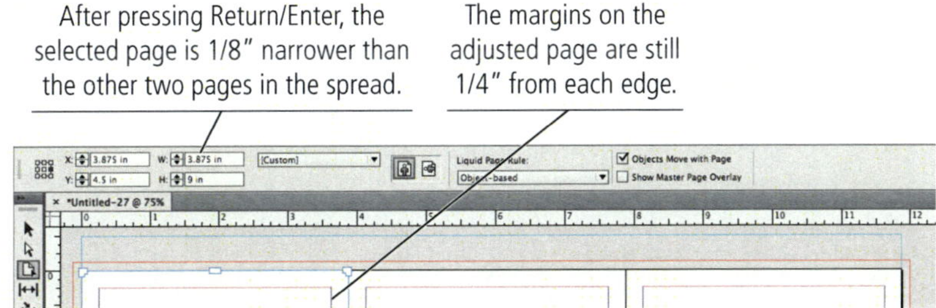

13. Save the file as `letterfold.indd` in your WIP>Ireland folder, and then continue to the next exercise.

Add Slug Information and Fold Marks

When you work with folding grids, it's easy to forget which panel goes where. You can use the layout slug area to add nonprinting elements as self-reminders, as well as to place folding marks that the output provider can use for reference. These elements should be placed on the master page layout.

1. **With letterfold.indd open, make sure the A-Outside master page layout is showing in the document window.**

2. **Select the Type tool and create a text frame above the left panel of the left-facing page, between the bleed and slug guides.**

3. **Type Outside Left Panel - Fold In in the frame, and then apply centered paragraph alignment.**

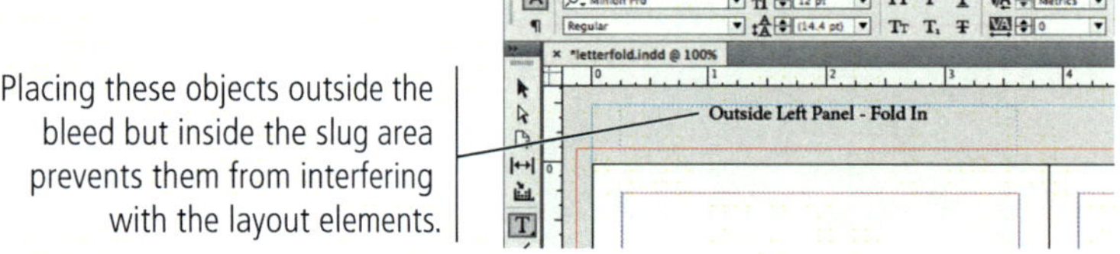

Placing these objects outside the bleed but inside the slug area prevents them from interfering with the layout elements.

4. **Choose Window>Output>Attributes to open the Attributes panel.**

5. **Select the text frame in the slug area with the Selection tool, and then check the Nonprinting box in the Attributes panel.**

   These objects are for your information only; they should not be included in the output.

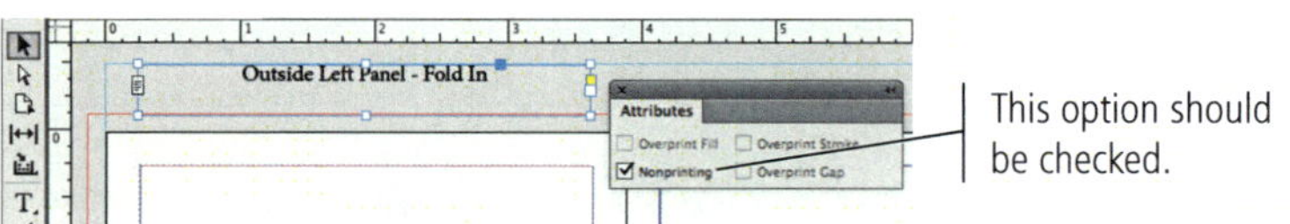

This option should be checked.

Note:

If you want to print these frames, you can override this setting using the Print Nonprinting Objects option in the General print settings.

6. **Control/right-click the text frame and choose Allow Master Item Overrides to deactivate the option and protect this object on associated layout pages.**

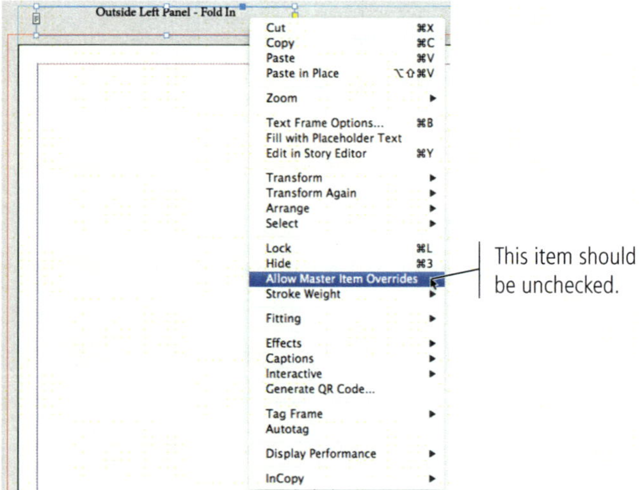

This item should be unchecked.

7. **Using the Selection tool, press Option/Alt, then click and drag to clone the text frame to the right.**

8. **Position the clone above the center page in the spread, and then change the text in the frame to Outside Center Panel - Mailing Area.**

9. **Repeat Steps 7–8 to place a text frame over the right page of the spread, with the text Outside Right Panel - Front.**

Note:

Like the original frame from which they are cloned, these text frames are also set as nonprinting objects.

10. **Using the Line tool, click the slug guide above the line that separates the left and center pages in the spread. Press Shift and drag down to the top page edge.**

    Pressing Shift constrains the line to a multiple of 45° angle (45, 90, 135, 180, etc.).

11. **In the Stroke panel (Window>Stroke), change the line Weight to 0.5-pt and choose Dashed in the Type menu. After applying the Dashed line type, type 3 pt in the first Dash field at the bottom of the panel.**

    If you don't see the Type menu in the Stroke panel, open the panel Options menu and choose Show Options.

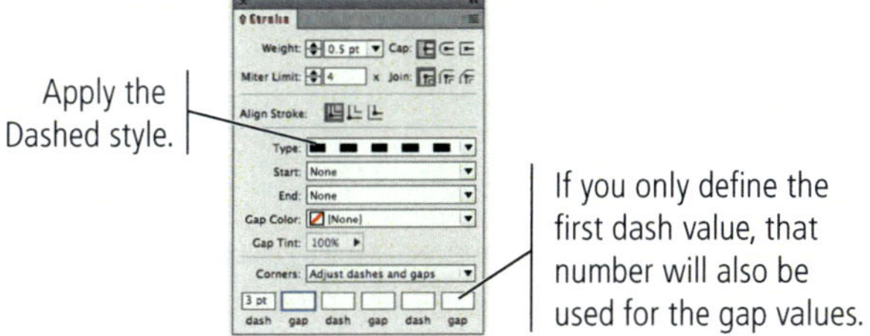

12. **Using the Control panel, select one of the horizontal-center reference points and then position the line at X=3.875″ (the same as the left page's width).**

    In general, lines have thickness; you have to first select one of the horizontal-center reference points for the line to be correctly centered over the panel edges.

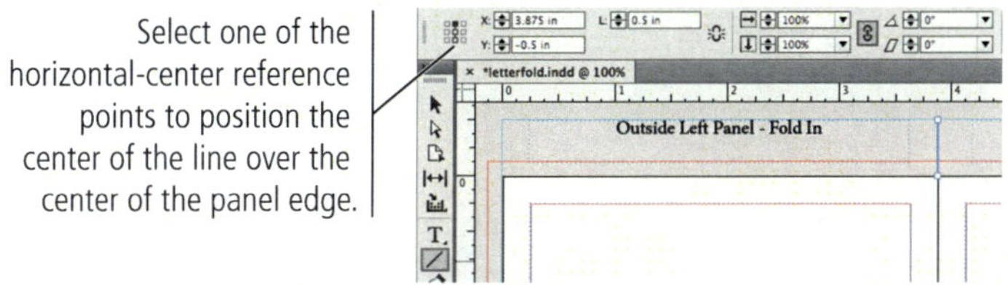

13. **Using the Selection tool, Control/right-click the dashed line and toggle off the Allow Master Item Overrides option.**

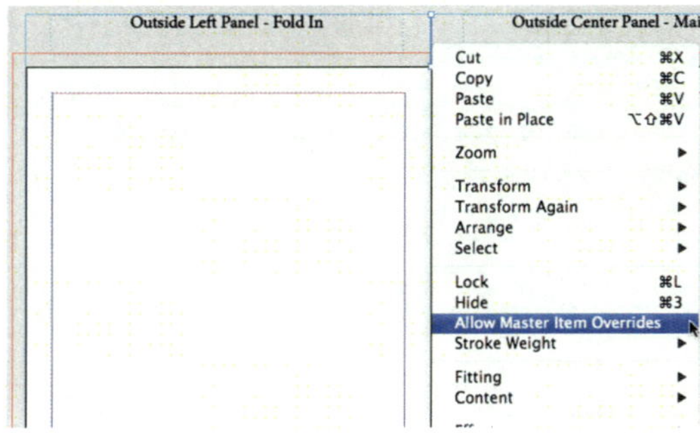

14. **Clone the line and place the copy centered above the line that separates the center and right pages in the spread (X: 7.875″).**

Select one of the horizontal-center reference points to position the center of the line over the center of the panel edge.

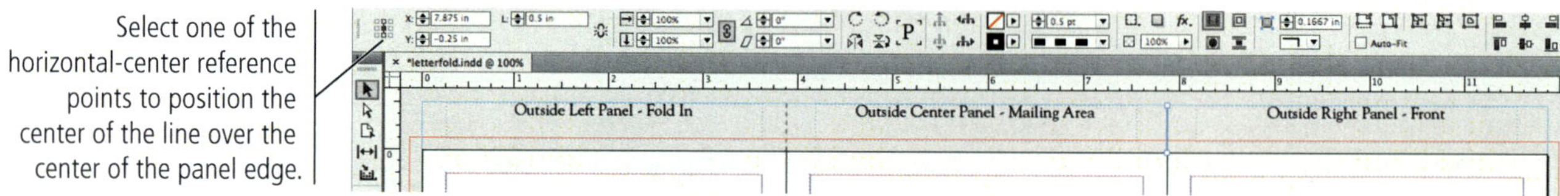

15. **Select the two lines and clone them down, placing the cloned lines in the bottom slug area.**

    Press Shift while cloning the lines to constrain them to be in the same X position as the original lines.

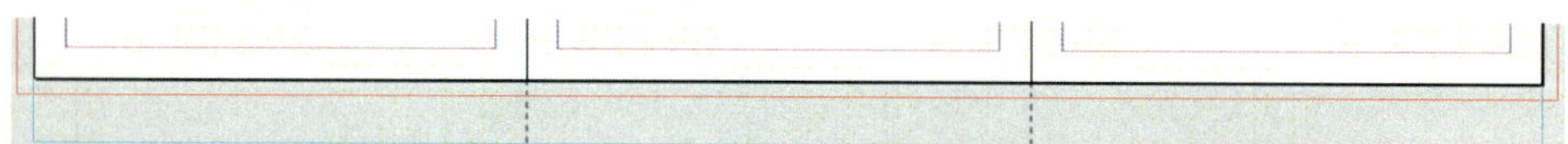

16. **Save the file and continue to the next exercise.**

Place Text Variables

The final item to add on the master page is a custom slug containing information about the file's development status. You can use text variables to place the same information on each of the three master pages in the layout.

1. **With letterfold.indd open, make sure the A-Outside layout is showing.**

2. **Create a new text frame in the slug area below the left page of the spread.**

3. **With the insertion point flashing in the new text frame, choose Type>Text Variables>Insert Variable>File Name.**

Insertion point

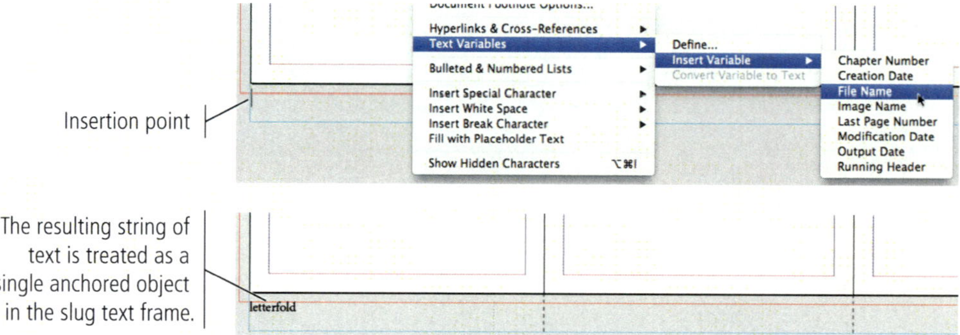

The resulting string of text is treated as a single anchored object in the slug text frame.

4. **With the insertion point after the File Name variable, press the Spacebar, type / Modified:, then press the Spacebar again.**

5. **Choose Type>Text Variables>Insert Variable>Modification Date.**

6. **If necessary, adjust the frame width so that the entire footer slug fits on one line, but remains only under the left page of the spread.**

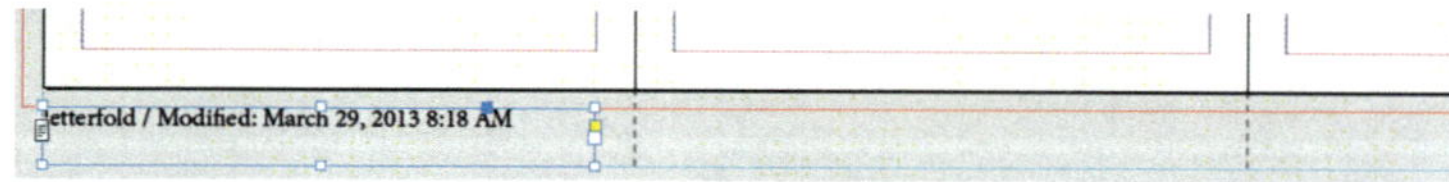

7. **Save the file and continue to the next exercise.**

> *Note:*
>
> *Even though you can't select the actual characters within the text variable instance, you can still change the formatting of variables by highlighting the instance in the layout and making whatever changes you want.*

Define a Custom Text Variable

In this exercise, you will add a custom variable to track the current status of the project as you build it. This information should appear on both spreads, which means it needs to be placed on both master page layouts. (You will create the second spread in the next exercise.) You could accomplish the same result by simply typing the status in the slug of each master page; however, you would have to make the same change on each of the master pages in each stage of the project.

By defining a text variable that you will place on both master pages, you can simply change the variable definition as you progress through each stage of the project, and then all instances of the placed variable will automatically reflect that change.

1. **With letterfold.indd open, choose Type>Text Variables>Define.**

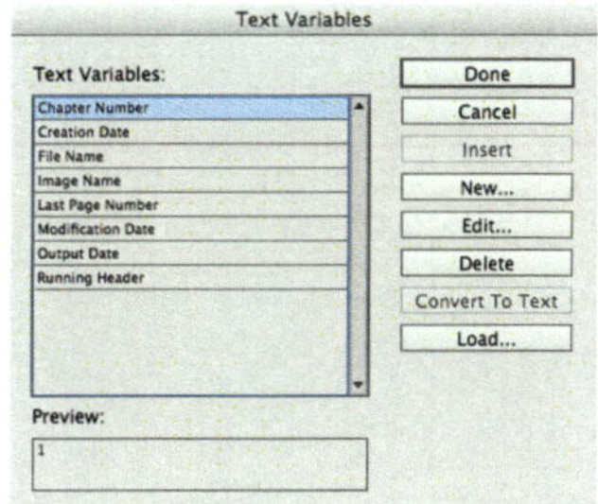

2. **In the Text Variables dialog box, click the New button.**

3. **In the Name field of the New Text Variable dialog box, type Project Status.**

4. **In the Type menu, choose Custom Text.**

   Eight of these options are the same as those that already appear in the Text Variables>Insert Variable submenu. You can, however, define more than one variable for a single type. For example, you can define two different modification date variables — one that shows the day, month, year, and time; and one that shows only the day and month.

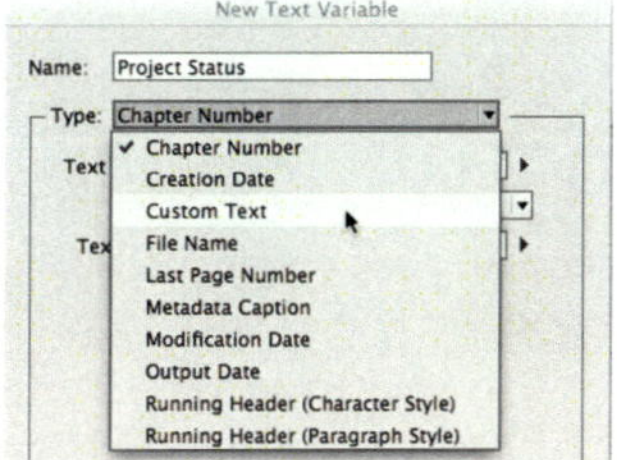

5. **Click the menu to the right of the Text field.**

   Using the Custom Text option, you can determine what text appears in the variable. The menu provides access to common special characters (these are the same characters you can access in the Type>Insert Special Character submenus).

6. **Choose Ellipsis from the menu.**

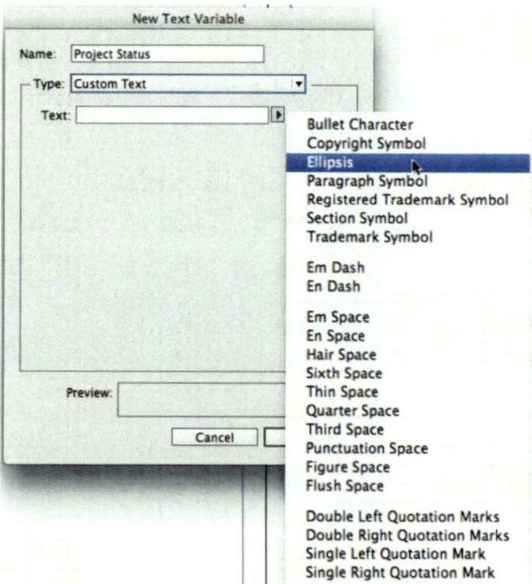

7. **With the insertion point after the code for the Ellipsis character, press the Spacebar and then type Work in Progress.**

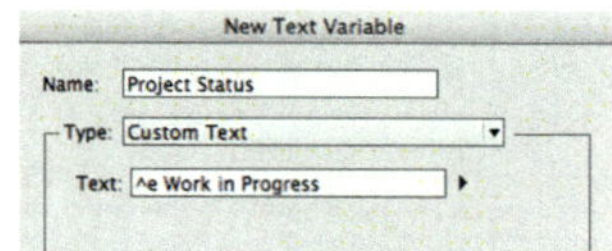

8. **Click OK to close the New Text Variable dialog box.**

The new Project Status variable now appears in the list.

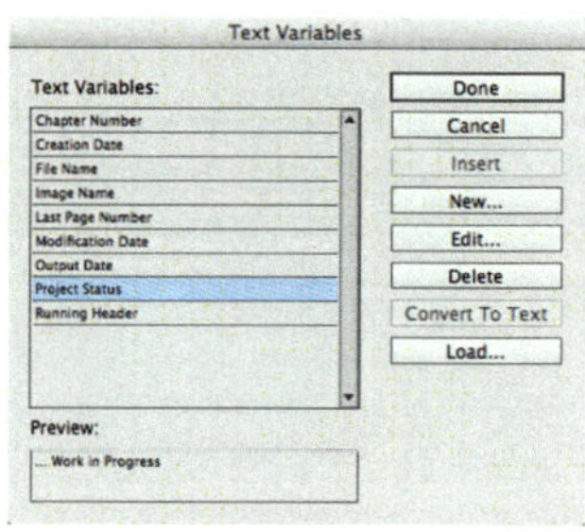

> ***Note:***
>
> *If you delete a variable that is used in the layout, you can choose to replace placed instances with a different variable, convert the instances to regular text, or simply remove the placed instances.*

Custom Text Variable Options

INDESIGN FOUNDATIONS

The built-in text variables are based on the types of variables you can define. When you choose Type>Text Variables>Define, the dialog box lists those default variables. You can select any of these variables and click Edit to change the options for the selected variable, or you can create a new variable by clicking the New button.

Your choice in the Type menu of the New/Edit Text Variable dialog box, whether creating a new variable or editing an existing one, determines what options are available.

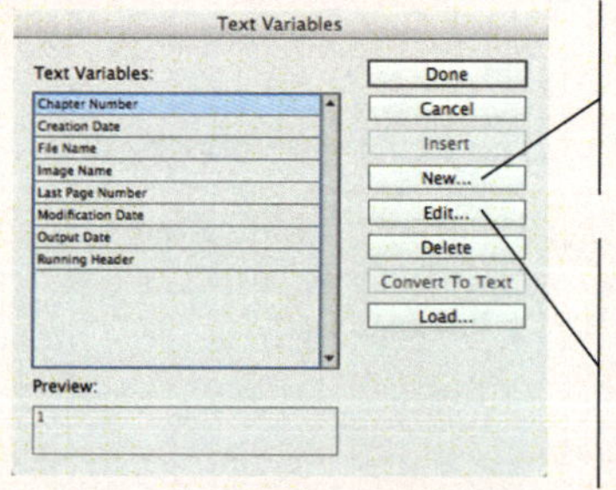

Click here to open the New Text Variable dialog box and define a new text variable.

Click here to open the Edit Text Variable dialog box and change the formatting options of the selected variable.

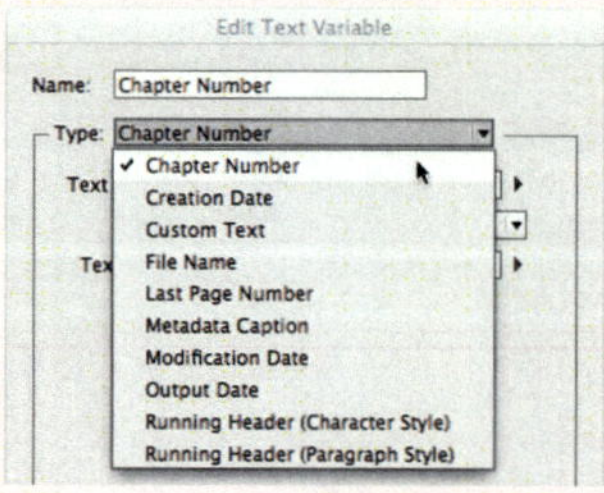

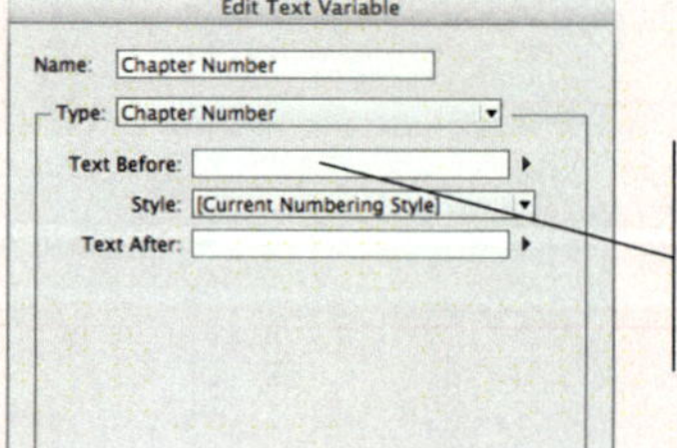

The type of variable determines what options can be defined in the lower half of the dialog box.

Custom Text Variable Options (continued)

For all but the Custom Text variable, you can define the characters that precede (Text Before field) or follow (Text After field) the variable information. You can type specific information in either of these fields, or you can use the associated menus to place symbols, em or en dashes, white-space characters, or typographer's quotation marks.

The **Chapter Number** variable inserts the chapter number based on the file's position in a book document (you will work with InDesign books in Project 8: Multi-Chapter Booklet). You can use the Style menu to format the chapter number as lowercase or uppercase letters, lowercase or uppercase Roman numerals, or Arabic numbers.

The **Creation Date** variable inserts the time the document is first saved. The **Modification Date** variable inserts the time the document was last saved. The **Output Date** variable inserts the date the document was last printed, exported to PDF, or packaged. You can use the **Date Format** menu to modify the date format for all three of these variables. You can either type a format directly into the field, or you can use the associated menu to choose the options you want to include. If you want to simply type the format into the field, you have to use the correct abbreviations.

The **File Name** variable inserts the name of the open file. You can use the check box options to include the entire folder path and the file extension. (The path and extension will not appear until you save the file at least once.)

Abbreviation	Description	Example
M	Month number	1
MM	Month number (two digits)*	01
MMM	Month name (abbreviated)	Jan
MMMM	Month name (full)	January
d	Day number	3
dd	Day number (two digits)*	03
E	Weekday name (abbreviated)	Wed
EEEE	Weekday name (full)	Wednesday
yy	Year number (last two digits)	13
yyyy	Year number (four digits)	2013
G	Era (abbreviated)	AD
GGGG	Era (full)	Anno Domini
h	Hour	1
hh	Hour (two digits)*	01
H	Hour (24-hour format)	16
HH	Hour (two digits, 24-hour format)*	16
m	Minute	9
mm	Minute (two digits)*	09
s	Second	2
ss	Second (two digits)*	02
a	AM or PM	AM
z	Time zone (abbreviated)	PST
zzzz	Time zone (full)	Pacific Standard Time

*The two-digit formats force a leading zero in front of numbers lower than 10 (for example, 9/25/13 would appear as 09/25/13 if you use the two-digit Month format).

The **Last Page Number** variable can be used to create a "Page x of y" notation. This variable can indicate the last page number of the entire document or the current section (in the Scope menu). You can also determine the numbering style (with the same options as in the Chapter Number variable).

The **Metadata Caption** option is the same as the Live Caption option in the Object>Captions submenu. (You will use this option later in this project.)

The **Running Header** variables can be used to find content on the page based on applied paragraph or character styles.

In the Style menu, you can choose the paragraph or character style to use as the variable content. The Use menu identifies which instance of the defined style (first or last on the page) to use as the variable content. For example, say you have a glossary page and all the terms are formatted with the Glossary Term character style. You could define two Running Header (Character Style) variables — one that identifies the first use of the Glossary Term style and one that identifies the last use of the Glossary Term style on the current page. You can then place the two variables in a text frame to create a running header that shows the first and last terms on the page — e.g., [First Term] – [Last Term].

The Delete End Punctuation option identifies the text without punctuation. For example, you can identify a Bold Run-In character style that is applied to text that always ends with a period. When the style is identified as the variable, the period will not be included in the variable text.

The Change Case options determine capitalization for the variable text:

- Upper Case capitalizes the entire variable.
- Lower Case removes all capitalization.
- Title Case capitalizes the first letter in every word.
- Sentence Case capitalizes only the first word.

The **Custom Text** variable inserts whatever text you define in the associated field.

9. **Click Done to close the Text Variables dialog box.**

10. **Create a new text frame in the slug area under the right page of the spread.**

11. **With the insertion point flashing in the new frame, type `Project Status`, press the Spacebar, and then choose Type>Text Variables>Insert Variable>Project Status.**

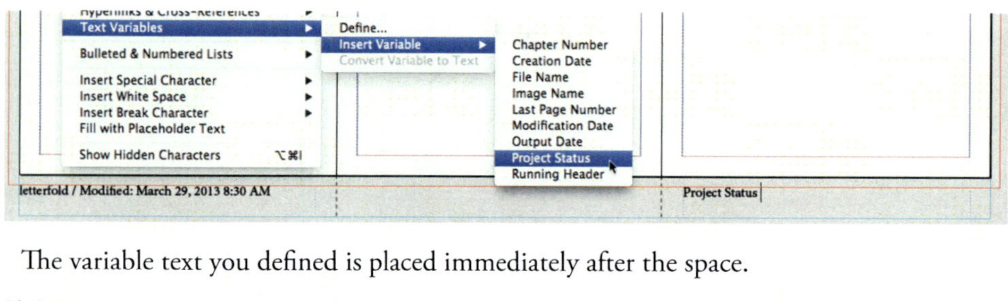

The variable text you defined is placed immediately after the space.

12. **Select both text frames in the bottom slug area. Control/right-click either frame and choose Allow Master Item Overrides to deactivate the option and protect both objects on associated layout pages.**

13. **Save the file and then continue to the next exercise.**

Note:

You can convert a particular instance of a text variable to regular text by selecting an instance in the layout and choosing Type>Text Variables>Convert Variable to Text. You can convert all instances of a specific variable to regular text by opening the Text Variables dialog box, selecting a specific variable, and clicking the Convert to Text button.

Create the Inside Master Pages

When you plan a folding document layout, it is also important to understand how the two sides of the document relate to one another. Fold marks on the front and back should line up; this means that if one panel is a different size than the others, the back side of the sheet must be laid out as a mirror image of the front side.

In the illustration to the right, a document has one fold — a smaller panel that folds over to cover half of the inside of the brochure. Fold marks on the outside layout must mirror the inside of the brochure so that, when folded, the two sides line up properly.

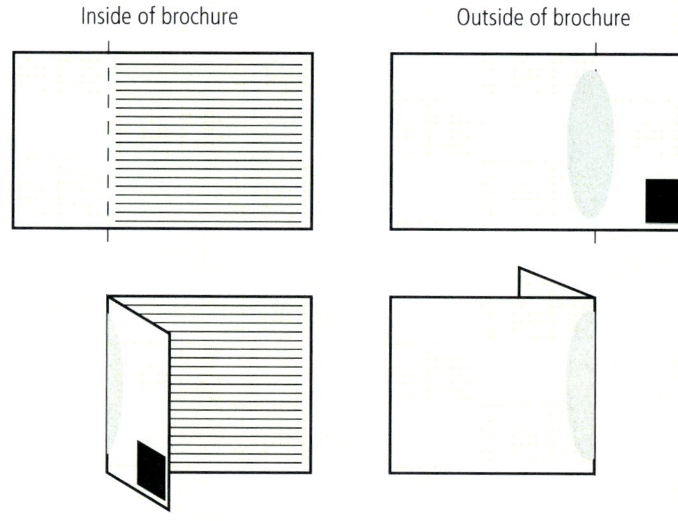

1. **With `letterfold.indd` open, Control/right-click the A-Outside master page name and choose Duplicate Master Spread "A-Outside" in the contextual menu.**

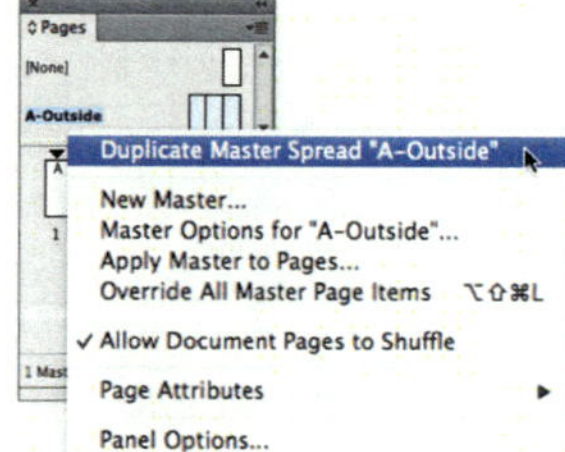

2. **Control/right-click the resulting B-Master layout name and choose Master Options for "B-Master" in the contextual menu.**

3. **Type Inside in the Name field and then click OK to apply the new name to the B master page layout.**

   The new B-Inside master page spread is automatically displayed in the document window. All of the elements that you created on the A-Inside master are in place because you duplicated the existing master page.

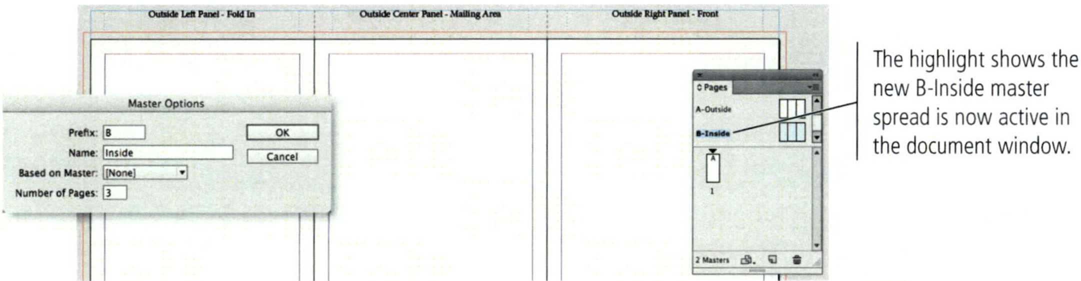

The highlight shows the new B-Inside master spread is now active in the document window.

4. **Zoom out so you can see the entire pasteboard area around the master page spread.**

5. **Choose the Page tool in the Tools panel. In the Control panel, make sure the Objects Move with Page option is checked.**

   Because the inside of the brochure needs to be a mirror image of the outside of the brochure, you need to move the shorter panel to the other side of the spread.

6. **Click the left page in the spread to select it, and then drag right until the reduced panel snaps to the right edge of the spread.**

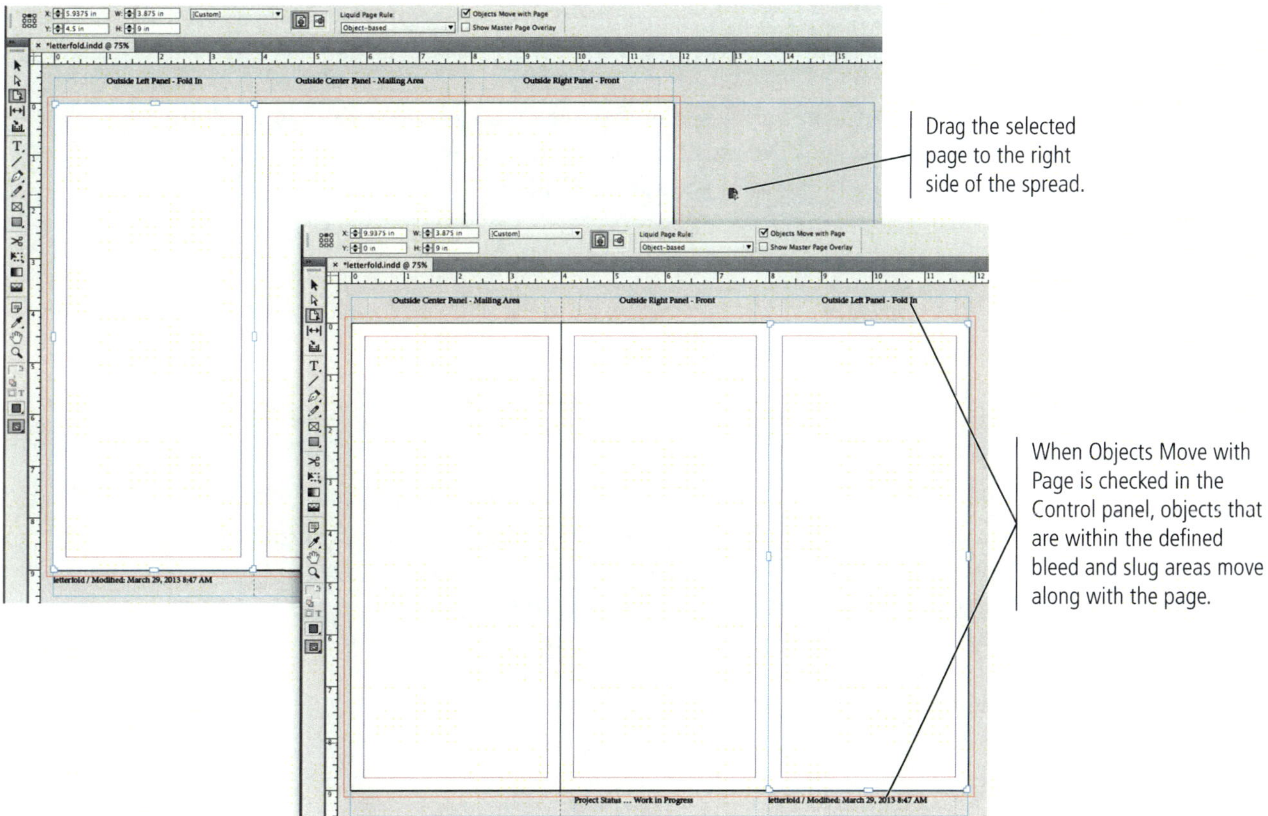

Drag the selected page to the right side of the spread.

When Objects Move with Page is checked in the Control panel, objects that are within the defined bleed and slug areas move along with the page.

7. **In the text frames in the top slug area, change the text to:**

Left page	**Inside Left Panel**
Center page:	**Inside Center Panel**
Right page:	**Inside Right Panel - Fold In**

8. **Click the slug guide over the right edge of the right page.**

   The folding guide that was over the right page edge is still over the right page edge — which is incorrect. You need to move this guide into place over the line between the center and right pages of the spread.

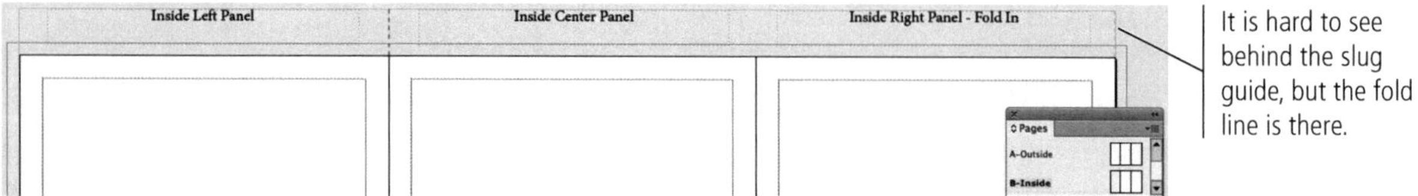

It is hard to see behind the slug guide, but the fold line is there.

9. **Drag the fold line left until it is centered over the line between the center and right pages of the spread (X: 8″).**

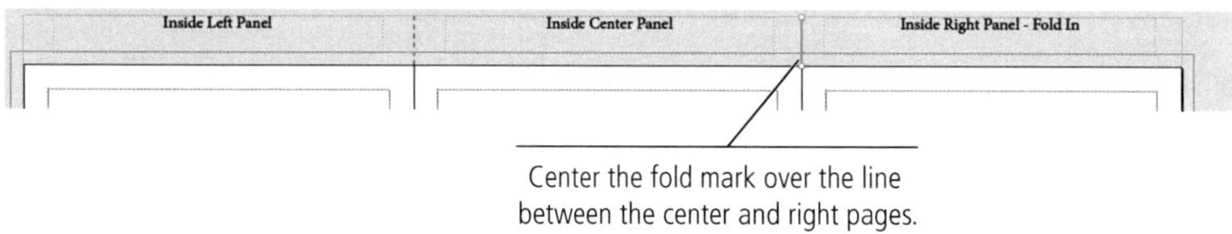

Center the fold mark over the line between the center and right pages.

10. **In the bottom slug area, drag the text frame with the file name and modification date to be below the left page of the spread.**

11. **Drag the frame with the project status (with the "Work in Progress" message) to be below the right page of the spread.**

12. **Click the slug guide below the right edge of the right page to select the folding line, then drag the fold line until it is centered below the line between the center and right pages of the spread (X: 8″).**

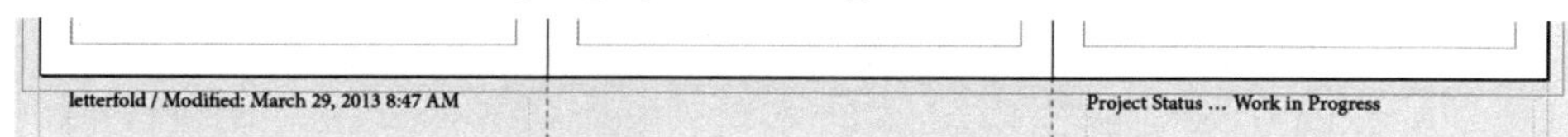

13. **Save the file and continue to the next exercise.**

 Save a Template

As the previous exercises demonstrated, setting up a brochure properly can be time-consuming. Once you have set up a folding layout, it's a good idea to save the layout as a template so that the same structure can be applied to any similar type of layout. Every time you want to create a rack card with the same folded size, you can open this template and begin with an empty file that contains the correct guides and marks.

1. **With letterfold.indd open, click the A-Outside master page layout name to select the entire spread.**

   Clicking a master page name selects all pages in that spread. If you wanted to select actual layout pages (instead of master pages), you could click the page number sequence below a spread (in the lower half of the panel) to select all pages in that spread.

2. **Click and drag the master page layout into the lower half of the Pages panel, below the existing Page 1.**

   Because all three pages in the master layout are selected, releasing the mouse button adds a three-page spread below the existing Page 1.

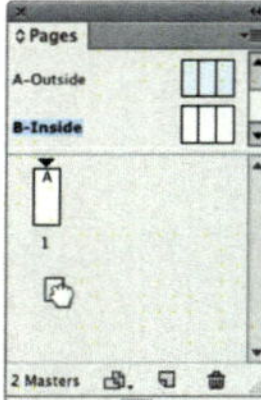

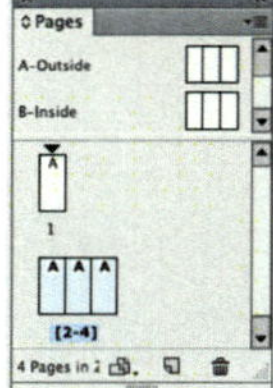

3. **Click the Page 1 icon in the Pages panel, and drag it to the panel's Delete button. When asked if you want to delete the page, click OK.**

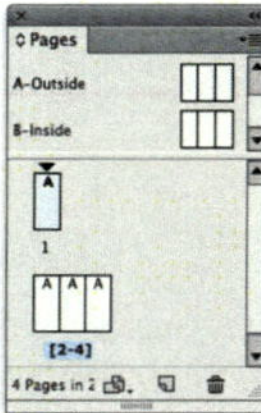

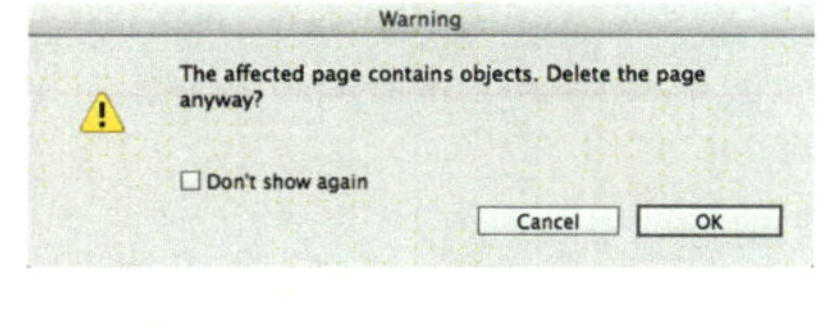

Pages Panel Options

INDESIGN FOUNDATIONS

In addition to features you have already used (in this and earlier projects), the Pages panel Options menu has a number of other choices for working with document pages. (Options related to alternate and liquid layouts are explained in Project 7: National Parks Info Pieces.)

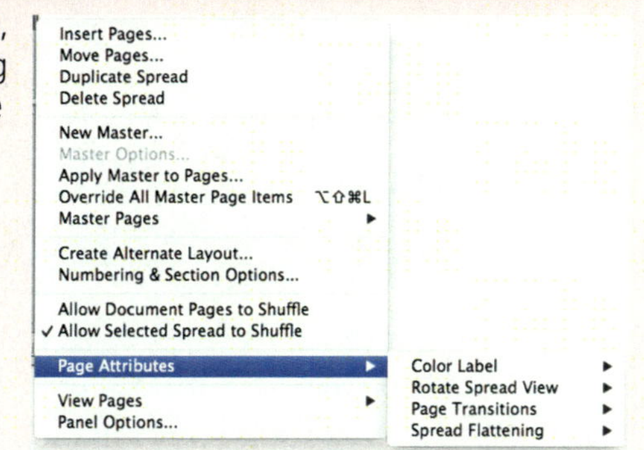

- **Insert Pages** allows you to insert from 1 to 9999 pages before or after a specific page, or at the start or end of the document. You can also determine which master page to base the new pages on.
- **Move Pages** allows you to reposition specific pages anywhere in the current document or in another open document.
- **Duplicate Page/Spread** allows you to replicate the selected page (or spread), including all elements on that page or spread.
- **Delete Page/Spread** removes the page (or spread) from the document.
- **Allow Document Pages to Shuffle** is checked by default. You can toggle off this option if you want to create spreads of more than two pages (called an **island spread**) in a facing-page layout.
- **Allow Selected Spread to Shuffle** is checked by default. If you toggle this option off, adding pages before an island spread maintains the island spread pages as you created them.

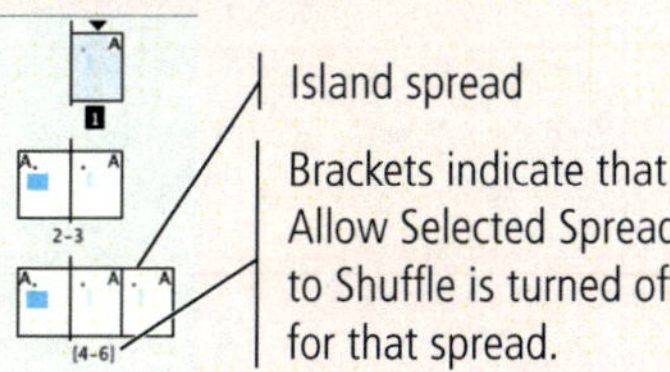

- **Color Label** applies a colored bar below the selected page icon(s), which provides an additional visual indicator of a specific, user-defined status.
- **Rotate Spread View** changes the appearance of the page within the document window. This option does not affect the physical dimensions of the page, but it is useful for working with a page that's oriented differently than the overall document.
- **Page Transitions** are visual effects that apply when a document is exported as a PDF or SWF file that will be distributed digitally.
- **Spread Flattening** allows you to apply flattener settings to individual spreads in a document, overriding the document flattener settings. Default uses the document settings. None (Ignore Transparency) eliminates any function that requires transparency. Custom opens the Custom Spread Flattener settings.
- The **View Pages** submenu can be used to view alternate layouts in a file.

4. **Click the B-Inside master page layout name to select the entire spread.**

5. **Click and drag the B-Inside layout into the lower half of the Pages panel, below the spread you added in Step 2.**

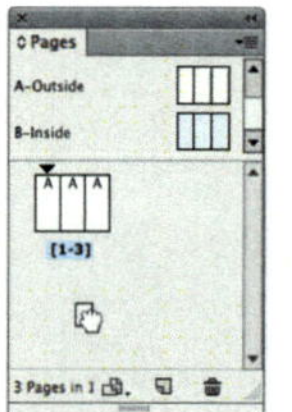

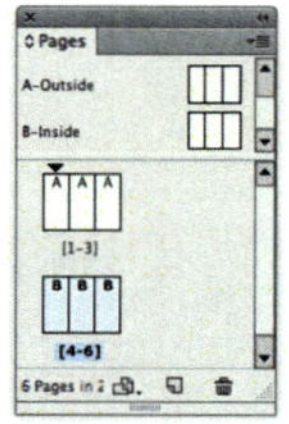

> ***Note:***
>
> *You can also use the Layout>Pages>Insert Pages option to add multiple pages to a layout.*

6. **In the lower half of the Pages panel, double-click the [1-3] page numbers below the first spread to navigate to that spread.**

7. **Choose View>Fit Spread in Window.**

   This command shows the entire spread of Pages 1–3, including the defined bleed areas. The slug areas, however, are not entirely visible.

8. **If necessary, reduce your view percentage so the slug areas are visible.**

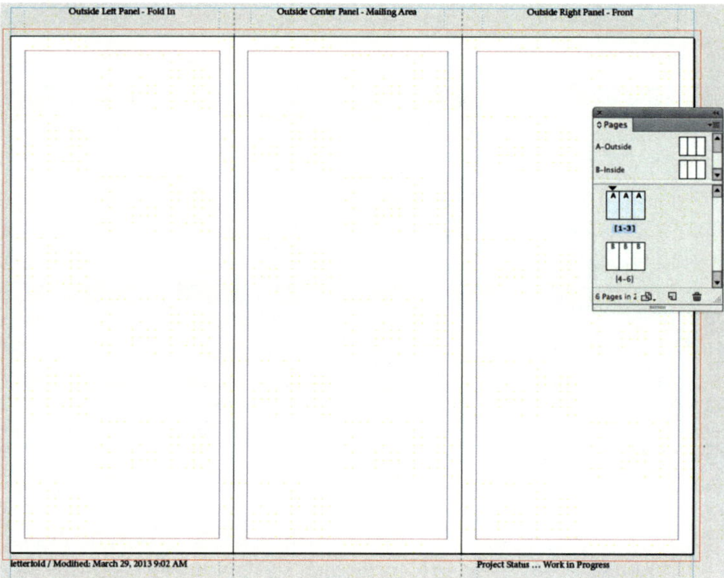

9. **Control/right-click the selected spread and choose Override All Master Page Items in the contextual menu.**

   This command allows you to access the text frames you created on the master layout. You won't be able to access the fold marks or nonprinting slug items, which you protected by toggling off the Allow Master Item Overrides option.

> ***Note:***
>
> *You can Shift-click to select multiple pages in the Pages panel and override master page items for all selected pages at one time.*

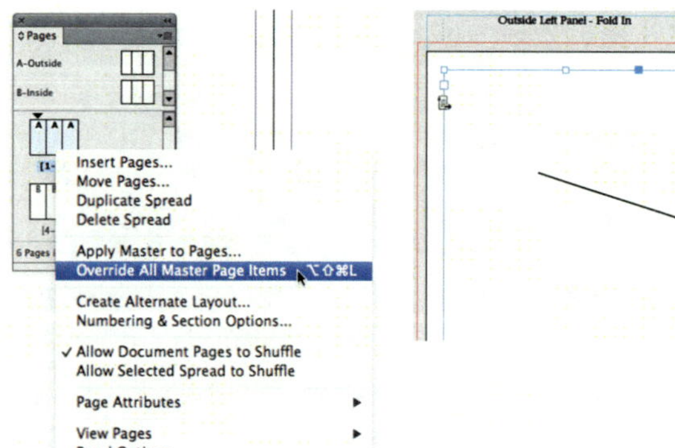

After overriding master page items on Page 1, you can select, modify, and add text to the text frames from the master layout.

10. **Repeat Control/right-click the page numbers under the 4–6 spread and choose Override All Master Page Items.**

By Control/right-clicking the page numbers under the spread thumbnails, you are applying this command to all three pages in the spread. If you want to affect only one page in a spread, you can Control/right-click a specific page thumbnail in the panel.

11. **Open the Type pane of the Preferences dialog box. Uncheck the Smart Text Reflow option and then click OK.**

Because you know this type of brochure will always have only the specific number of pages that you already defined, you don't want the software to automatically add pages to fit long blocks of text.

> *Note:*
>
> *If this option is already unchecked, simply click Cancel to close the Preferences dialog box.*

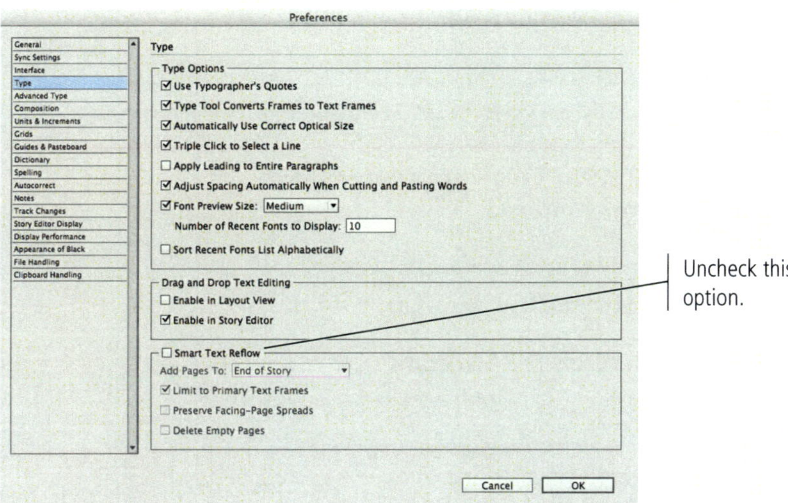

12. **Choose File>Save As and navigate to your WIP>Ireland folder. Choose InDesign CC Template in the Format/Save As Type menu and click Save.**

These pages and settings will be available whenever you implement the layout. Remember, every click you can save by adding template elements will save that much time later — every time you re-use the same template.

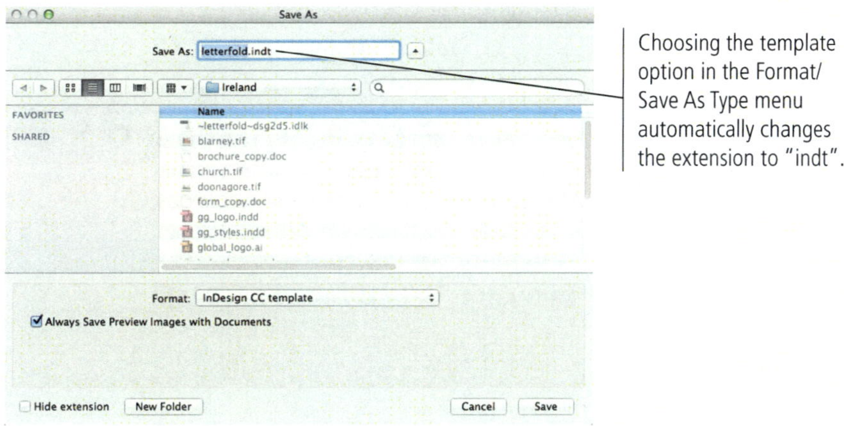

13. **Close the file and continue to the next stage of the project.**

Stage 2 Advanced Frame Options

You've already learned how to place graphics and control them within their frames. InDesign, of course, offers many more functions that provide control over graphics. Some of these (such as libraries and object styles) improve your productivity by automating repetitive tasks; other options (such as creating a custom frame from formatted text) enhance your creative capabilities when designing a page layout.

Convert Text to Outlines

1. **Create a new file by opening your letterfold.indt template (WIP>Ireland).**

   Remember, to create a new file from a template, you have to open the template file using the Open Normal option.

2. **Save the new file as letterfold_ireland.indd in your WIP>Ireland folder.**

3. **In the Pages panel, double-click the [1-3] page numbers below the page icons to show that spread in the document window.**

4. **Using the Type tool, click inside the empty text frame on Page 3. Type IRELAND in the frame, and format it as 120-pt ATC Onyx Bold.**

5. **Press Command/Control to temporarily access the Selection tool and reveal the frame's handles. Drag the frame handles until the frame is large enough to show the entire word you just typed.**

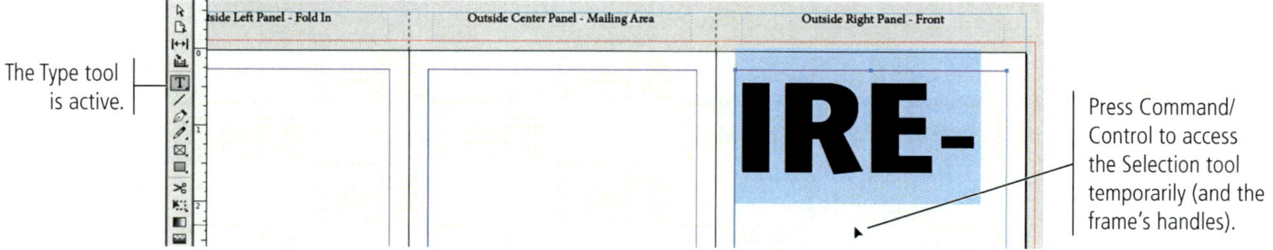

   When you release the Command/Control key, the Type tool is still active.

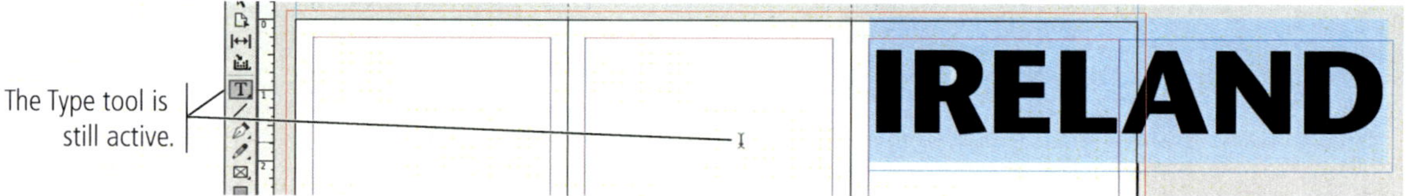

6. **Click with the Type tool between the I and the R to place the insertion point. Using the Character panel, change the kerning to -70 to reduce the space between these two letters.**

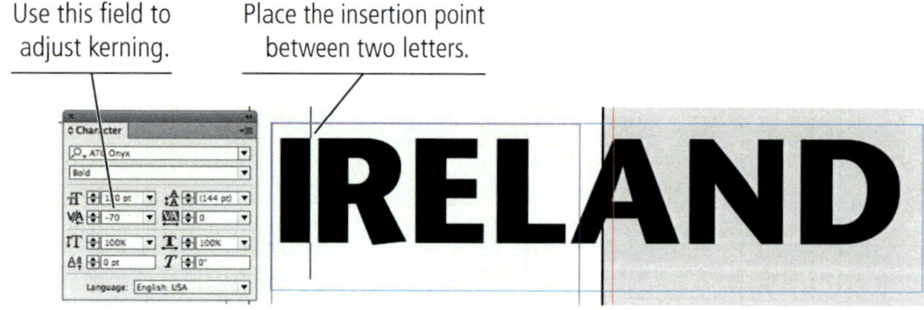

7. **Continue adjusting the kerning in this word as necessary.**

   Kerning is largely a matter of personal preference. Our choices are shown here.

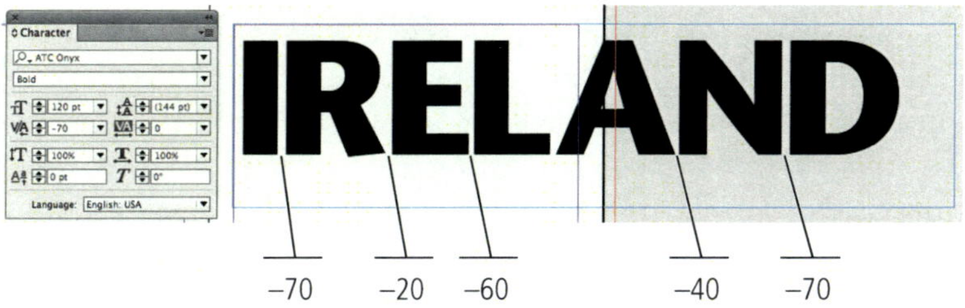

8. **Choose the Selection tool in the Tools panel.**

9. **Click the text frame to select it, and then choose Type>Create Outlines.**

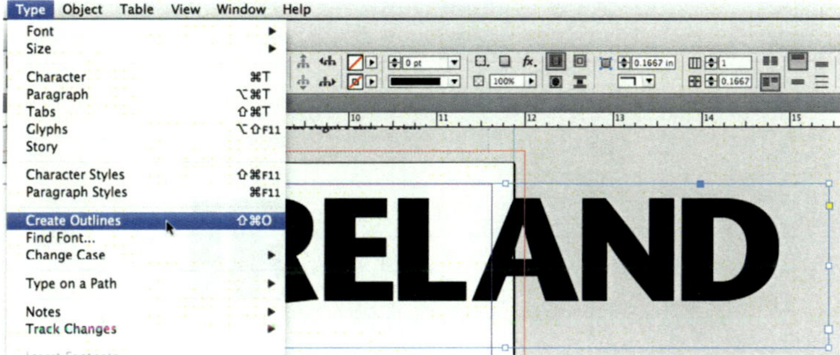

Note:

You can convert individual characters to inline objects by selecting specific characters before you choose Type>Create Outlines.

By converting the text to outlines, you eliminate the potential problem of a missing font file. You also create a group of letter-shaped objects that can contain other objects — such as a picture of Ireland's iconic shamrocks.

After converting the text to outlines, the text frame is gone; it is replaced by a bounding box for the group of letter shapes.

10. **With the new frame selected, choose File>Place. Navigate to `shamrocks.tif` in your WIP>Ireland folder, activate the Replace Selected Item option, and then click Open.**

    The image is placed directly into the shape of the letters.

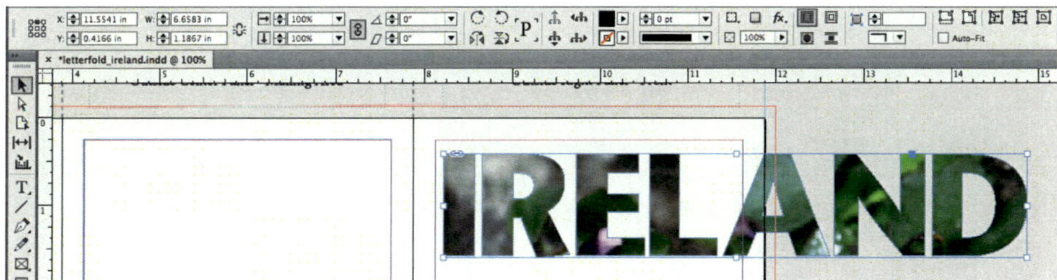

11. **Save the file and continue to the next exercise.**

Control Object Stacking Order

When you create a compound path out of multiple shapes, attributes and contents of the topmost selected shape are applied to the resulting combined shape. Even when objects do not technically overlap, the concept of stacking order still applies. Objects created later are higher in the stacking order than older objects unless you manually rearrange those objects. You can always use the Layers panel subitem listings to monitor and control the stacking order of objects.

1. **With letterfold_ireland.indd open, click any of the letter-shaped frames with the Selection tool to select the entire group.**

2. **Use the Control panel to rotate the group counterclockwise by 90°.**

3. **Drag the rotated group until the top-right corner snaps to the top-right bleed guide on Page 3.**

4. **Drag the bottom-center handle until the group's width is 7.625″.**

   Because the group is rotated, dragging the bottom handle actually changes the objects' *width* rather than its height.

5. **Drag the left-center handle until the group's height 1.875″.**

   Because the group is rotated, dragging the left handle changes the group's height.

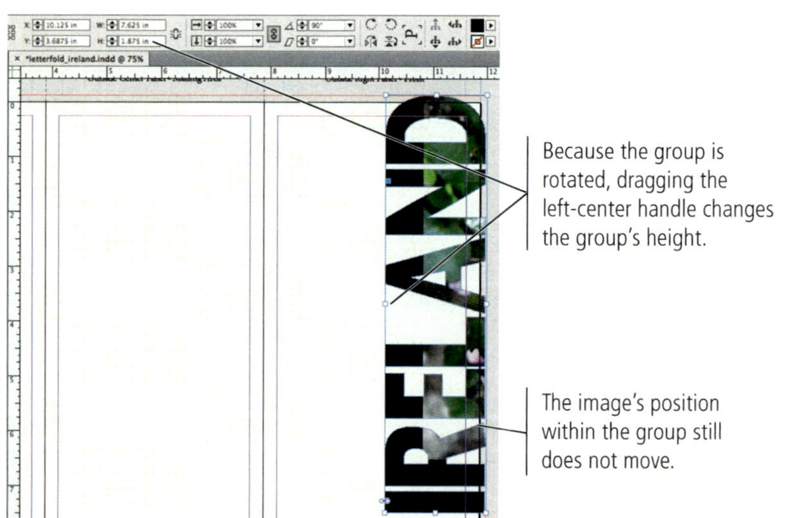

> ***Note:***
>
> *When you drag a specific handle, the X and Y fields in the Control panel show the position of the handle you drag. The selected reference point is not relevant.*

6. **Using the Rectangle tool, click and drag to create a frame on the left half of Page 3, aligning its bottom edge to the left edge of the rotated frame.**

   Use the image after Step 7 as a positioning guide.

7. **Open the Layers panel and expand the Layer 1 listing.**

   As you know, you created the rectangle after the IRELAND group; that means the rectangle is higher in the stacking order than the shamrocks.tif image.

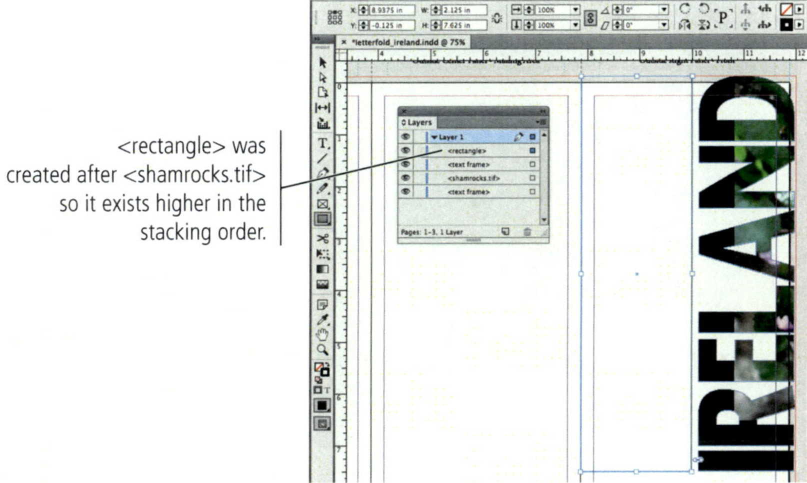

   You want to extend the shamrock image beyond the letter-shaped frames into the rectangle. You can easily combine the rectangle and letter-shaped frames using the Pathfinder functions. Most Pathfinder operations, however, apply attributes of the topmost object to the entire resulting shape. This means you have to rearrange object stacking order before you can combine the two shapes into a single compound path.

8. **In the Layers panel, click the <rectangle> item and drag it below the <shamrocks.tif> item.**

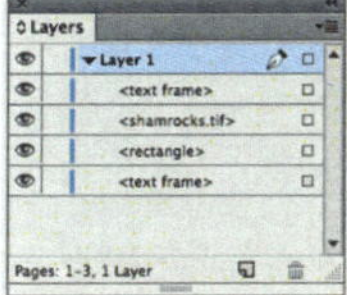

9. **Using the Selection tool, Shift-click the rectangle and the IRELAND frame to select both objects in the layout.**

10. **Choose Object>Pathfinder>Add.**

This command combines the selected objects into a single compound path. The black fill of the original IRELAND shapes now extends into the rectangle.

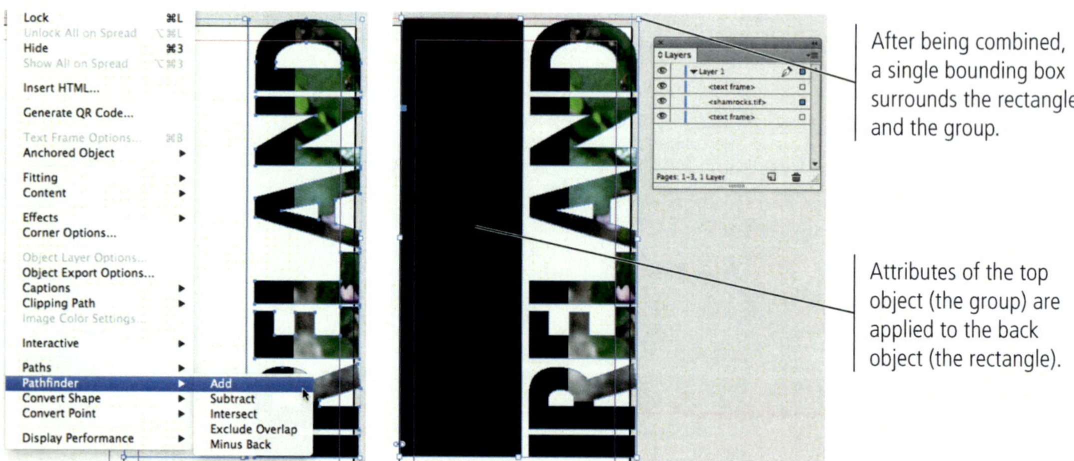

After being combined, a single bounding box surrounds the rectangle and the group.

Attributes of the top object (the group) are applied to the back object (the rectangle).

11. **Place the Selection tool cursor over any part of the combined shape to reveal the Content Grabber.**

12. **Click the Content Grabber to access the placed image.**

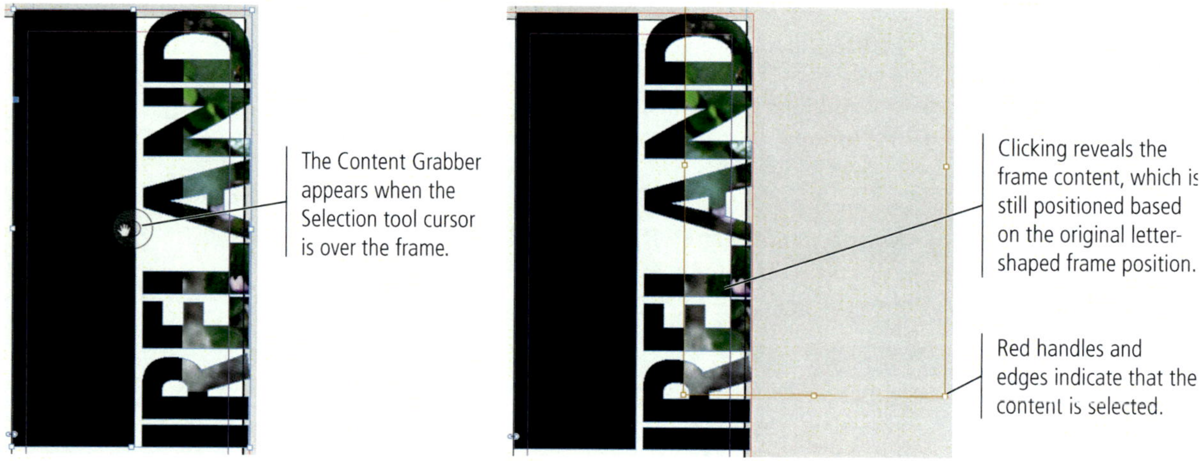

The Content Grabber appears when the Selection tool cursor is over the frame.

Clicking reveals the frame content, which is still positioned based on the original letter-shaped frame position.

Red handles and edges indicate that the content is selected.

13. **Drag the placed image to fill the entire combined frame.**

After holding down the mouse button for a moment, you can see the entire image, even beyond the frame edges.

14. **Save the file and continue to the next exercise.**

Work with an InDesign Library

In many cases, you might need to use the same content (such as a logo) or the same group of objects with different content (such as a logo with a grouped text frame containing contact information) on multiple pages throughout a single document, or even in multiple documents. In these situations, you can use an InDesign library to speed the process.

A library is a special type of file that stores objects (including the objects' content) for use in any InDesign file. Library files are not linked or specific to any individual layout (.indd) file, so you can open and use items from any existing library in any layout that you subsequently build.

1. **With letterfold_ireland.indd open, make the inside spread (Pages 4–6) visible in the document window.**

2. **Choose File>Open. Select the ireland.indl library file from your WIP>Ireland folder and click Open.**

   You can open a library file using the same File>Open command (Command/Control-O) that you use to open a regular InDesign file. This library contains two items that will be part of the Ireland tourism brochure.

> *Note:*
>
> *You can choose File>New>Library to create a new InDesign library file.*

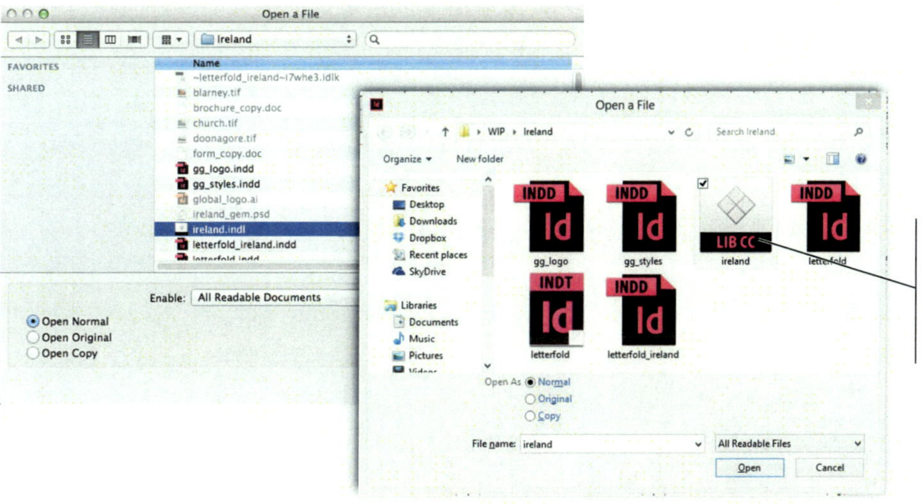

If extensions are not visible on Windows, use the icon to identify the library file.

3. **Move your mouse over the left item in the library panel and read the description.**

   If a library item includes descriptive text, that text appears in the tool tip when you move your mouse over that item. This description provides useful information about what you should do with the item.

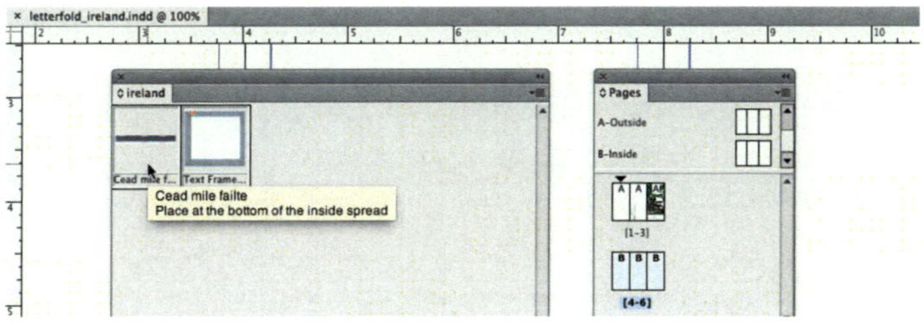

4. **Click the left item and drag it into the active layout. Position the object at the bottom of the spread (aligned to the bottom bleed guide).**

   Library items do not store fonts. If a library item uses a specific font, that font must be active on whatever system uses the library item. You probably don't have the MacLachlan Bold font that is used in this library item, so the text should appear highlighted in pink — the indication of a missing font.

5. **Open the Swatches and Paragraph Styles panels.**

   If a library item uses styles or other assets (including defined swatches), those required assets are placed in any file where you place the library item.

   Library items are subject to the same requirements as objects in a regular InDesign file. If a library item contains text, the fonts used to format that text must be available on any system that uses that library item.

Note:

If a library item uses a style (text or object) that conflicts with a style in the document where you're placing an instance, the style definition from the document overrides the style definition from the library item.

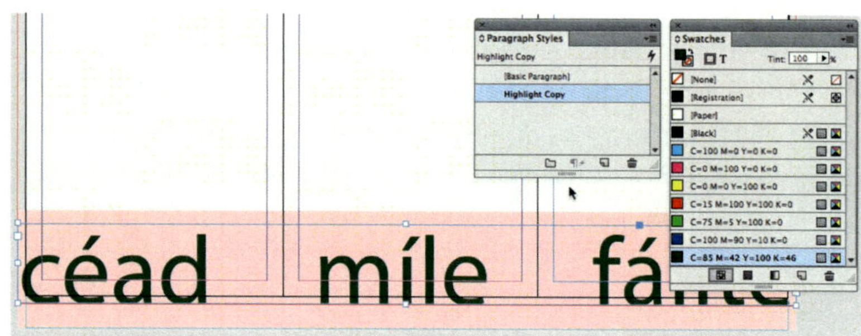

6. **Double-click the Highlight Copy paragraph style to open the Paragraph Style Options dialog box.**

7. **In the Basic Character Formats options, change the font to ATC Onyx Bold, then click OK to redefine the style.**

   When the missing-font highlight is gone, you can see the dark green fill color of the text frame that you placed from the library.

Note:

Céad míle fáilte is Gaelic for "a hundred thousand welcomes."

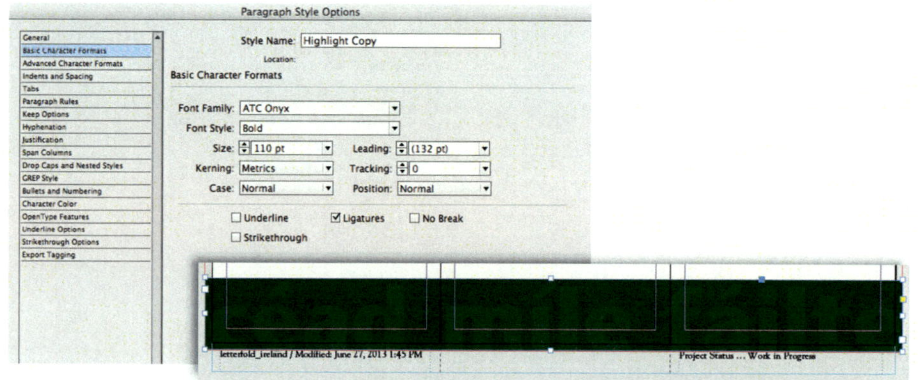

8. **Move your mouse over the Text Frame item in the Library panel and read the description.**

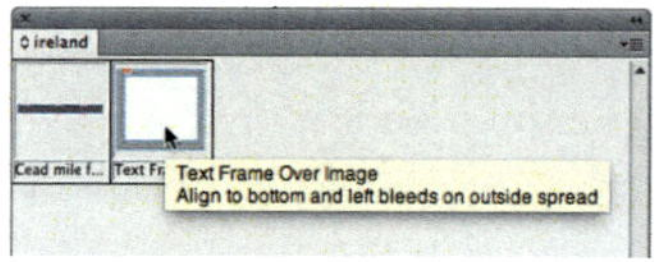

9. **Navigate to the outside spread (Pages 1–3).**

10. **Click the Text Frame item and drag into the open file. Position the placed instance aligned to the bottom-left bleed guide on the spread.**

Library items store the links to placed graphics files; if a library item contains a placed image or graphic, the placed file must be available in the same location as when it was added to the library.

Because the graphic is not embedded in the library item, you have to make sure the links are up to date before outputting the file.

11. **Click the Missing Image icon in the top-left corner of the image. Navigate to pastoral.tif in your WIP>Ireland folder and click Open.**

The title bar of the Locate dialog box identifies the file you want to find.

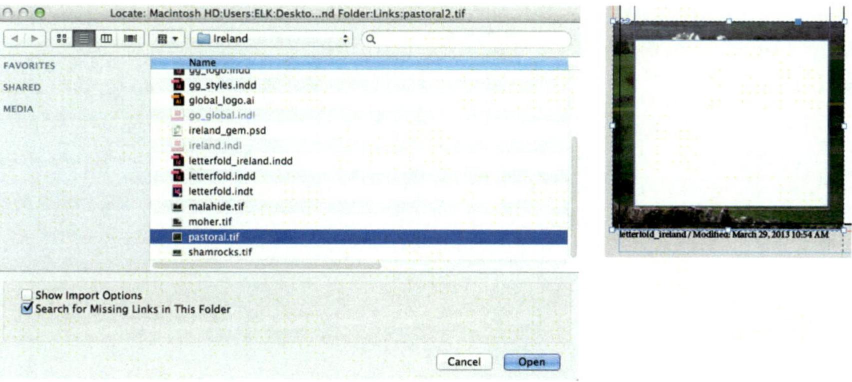

12. **Open the file gg_logo.indd from the WIP>Ireland folder.**

This file includes a single group, with your client's logo and address information. It has been used with this same alignment in many other projects, and the client wants to maintain consistency from document to document.

Rather than copying and pasting the group from one document to another, you can use an InDesign Library file to make the group easily accessible in any InDesign file.

13. **In the gg_logo layout, select the group on the page and drag it into the ireland library panel.**

The Library panel appears as soon as you click Save in the New Library dialog box.

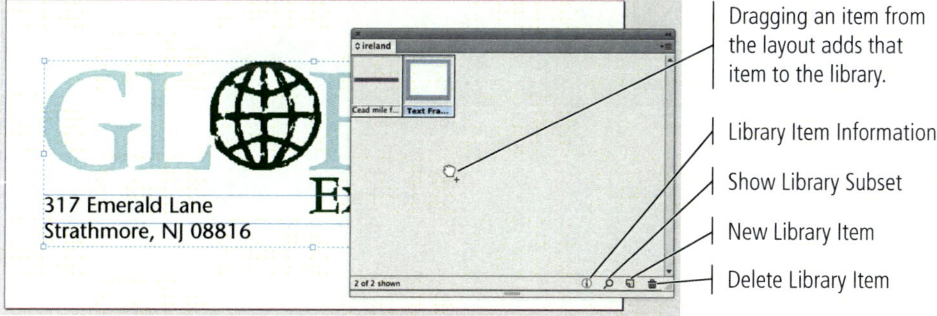

Dragging an object from the layout into the Library panel has no effect on the object that is already placed in the layout. When you release the mouse button, the new library item appears in the panel and the original item in the layout is exactly the same as it was before you dragged it into the library.

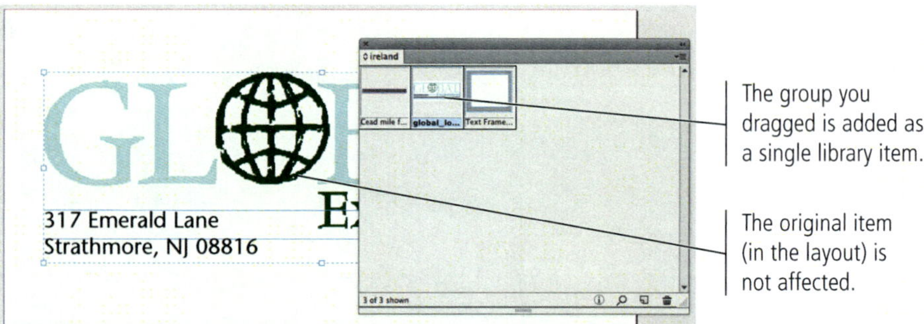

14. **With the new library item selected, click the Library Item Information button at the bottom of the panel.**

15. **In the resulting Item Information dialog box, change the Item Name field to Logo with Address.**

16. **In the Description field, type Use this group wherever the logo and address are required, then click OK.**

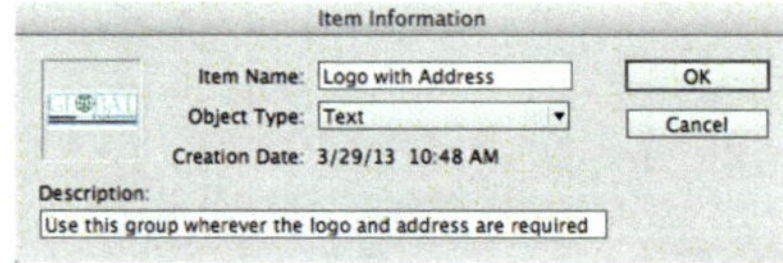

17. **Close the gg_logo.indd file without saving.**

    Library files are not linked to a specific InDesign file; you can use them to access common styled elements from any InDesign file.

18. **With the outside spread of letterfold_ireland.indd visible, drag the Logo With Address item from the Library panel into the layout.**

19. **Rotate the placed group 90° counterclockwise, and align it to the bottom-left margin guide on Page 2 (the center page in the spread).**

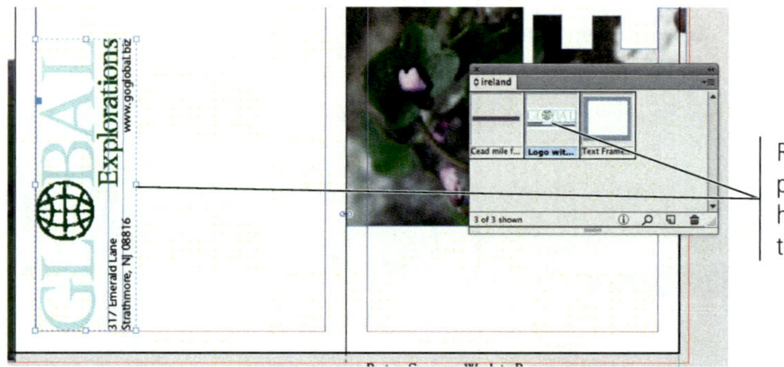

> ***Note:***
>
> *You can also click the New Library Item button at the bottom of the Library panel to add the selected object as a new library item.*

> ***Note:***
>
> *Choose Add Items On Page [N] As Separate Objects in the Library panel Options menu to add all objects on the page as separate library items.*
>
> *Choose Add Items On Page [N] in the panel Options menu to add all objects on the page as a single library item.*

20. **Drag a second copy of the library item into the layout, and position the new instance at the bottom of Page 3. Leave approximately 1/8″ between the bottom edge of the IRELAND image frame and the top edge of the logo. (Use the image after Step 21 as a guide.)**

21. **Using the Selection tool, double-click the text frame at the bottom of Page 3 to select only that frame in the group. Press Delete/Backspace to remove the selected frame.**

Double-click the frame to access only one piece of the group.

There is no dynamic link between items in the library and instances placed in a layout. Changing one placed instance has no effect on the original library item or on other placed instances of the same item.

> ***Note:***
>
> *Deleting an object from the library has no effect on placed instances in the layout. Deleting a placed instance has no effect on the item in the library.*

22. **Click the Close button on the Library panel to close the library file.**

This project is only a two-page brochure, and all instances of the library item appear on the same spread. But think of a layout with more than a few pages — a newsletter, a booklet, or even a multi-file multi-chapter book. You can use library items to easily access common graphics such as logos; to maintain consistency between sidebars on Page 1 and Page 42; and even to use the same graphic-and-text-frame structure for graphics with captions on every page of a 240-page book.

23. **Save the InDesign file and continue to the next exercise.**

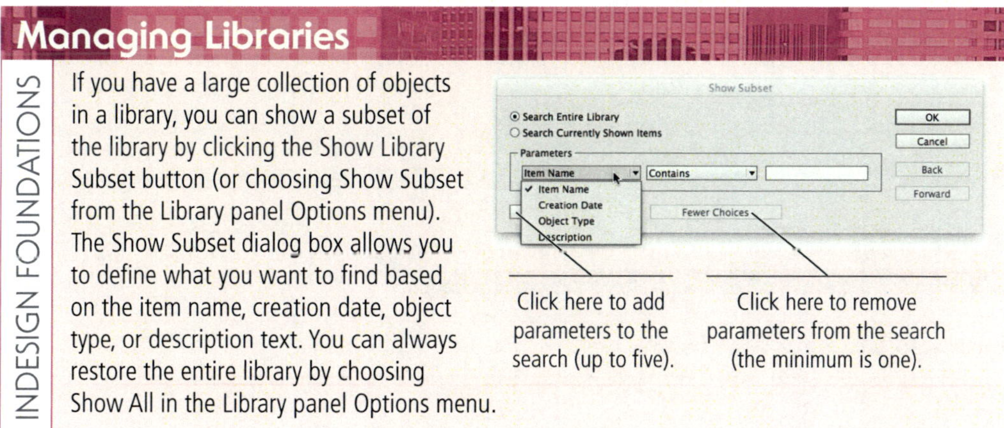

Managing Libraries

INDESIGN FOUNDATIONS

If you have a large collection of objects in a library, you can show a subset of the library by clicking the Show Library Subset button (or choosing Show Subset from the Library panel Options menu). The Show Subset dialog box allows you to define what you want to find based on the item name, creation date, object type, or description text. You can always restore the entire library by choosing Show All in the Library panel Options menu.

Click here to add parameters to the search (up to five).

Click here to remove parameters from the search (the minimum is one).

Edit the Basic Graphics Frame Style

An object style stores multiple frame formatting options in a single unit so that you can apply all settings with one click. Object styles can include virtually any attribute that can be applied to a frame in the layout. Like text-formatting styles, object styles are dynamic — which means that changing an object style automatically changes the appearance of any object that uses that style.

Object styles are accessed and managed in the Object Styles panel (Window> Styles>Object Styles). Every layout includes a default [Basic Graphics Frame] and a default [Basic Text Frame] style, which are applied to all frames you create in the layout.

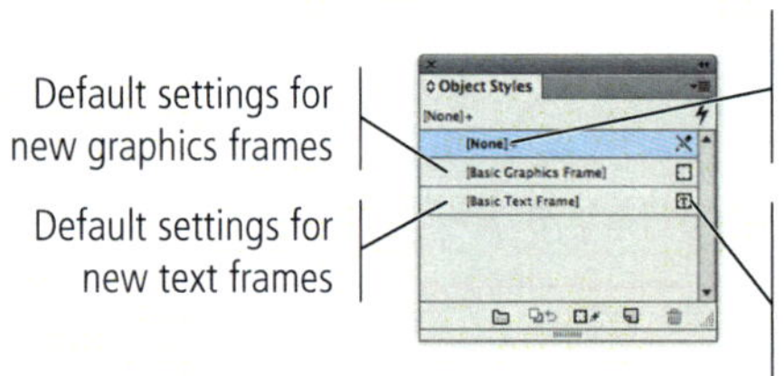

Note:

By default, the [Basic Graphics Frame] style has a 1-pt black stroke and no text wrap. You're going to change the default settings so you can apply the same settings to all three graphics on the page.

You can edit object styles just as you edit a text-formatting style; changes to the style automatically apply to objects that use the style. In this exercise, you apply and change the Basic Graphics Frame style — which exists by default in every layout — so a number of frames can have the same basic settings (i.e., no stroke value, and a defined text wrap attribute).

1. **With `letterfold_ireland.indd` open, make the inside spread visible in the document window.**

2. **Using the Rectangle Frame tool, click the left margin guide on Page 4 and drag to the right margin guide on Page 6.**

3. **While still holding down the mouse button, press the Right Arrow key three times to split the frame into four equal-sized, evenly spaced frames.**

   Remember, the frame tools are "gridified"; pressing the Arrow keys while dragging creates a grid of frames within the area you drag.

4. **Release the mouse button to create the four frames.**

5. **With the four frames still selected, use the Control panel to change the frames' height to 2.35″ and position the top edge at 5.8″.**

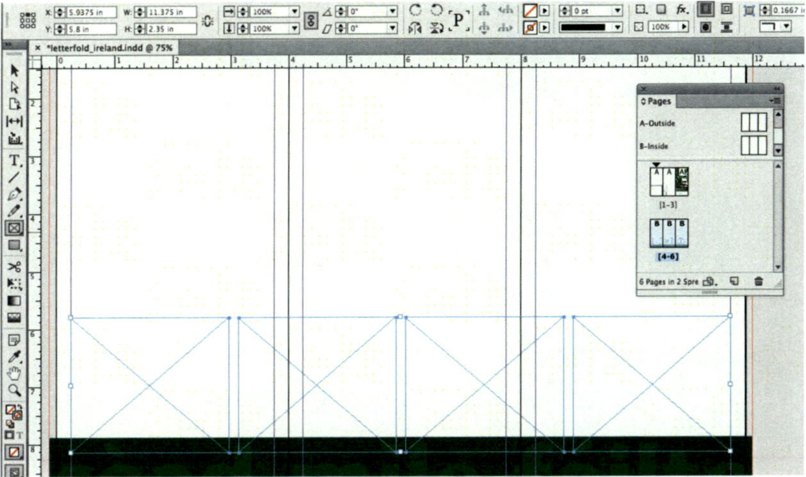

6. **With all four frames selected, Control/right click any of the frames and choose Fitting>Frame Fitting Options in the contextual menu.**

7. **In the resulting dialog box, check the Auto-Fit option and choose Fill Frame Proportionally in the Fitting menu. Click OK to apply the change.**

   By setting this option for the empty frames, you ensure the images you place later will entirely fill the frames without leaving white space inside any frame edge.

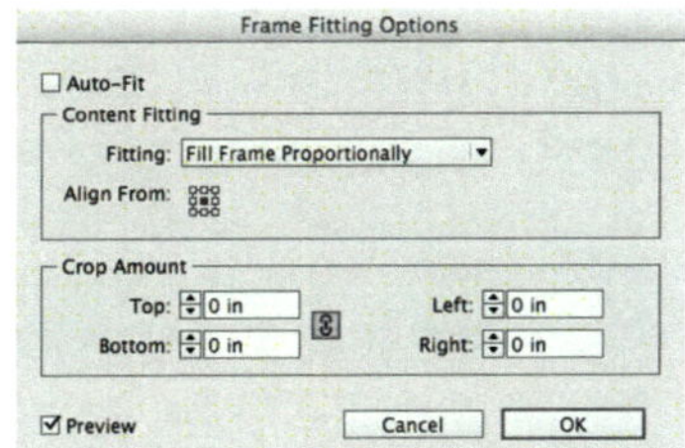

Note:

If it is available, you can also check the Auto-Fit option in the Control panel.

8. **Open the Object Styles panel (Window>Styles>Object Styles). With the four frames selected in the layout, click [Basic Graphics Frame] in the Object Styles panel.**

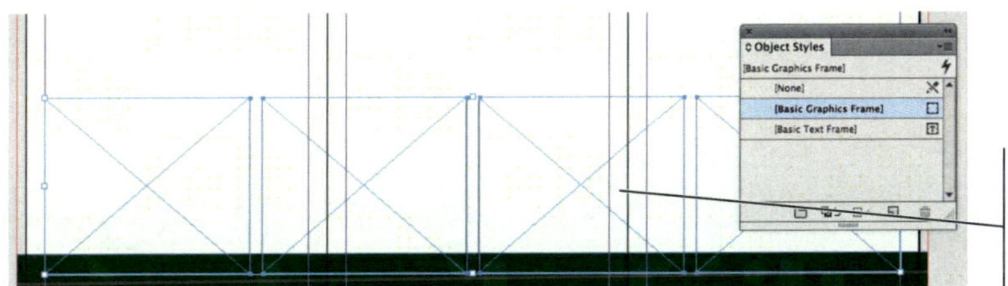

All four selected frames now use the [Basic Graphics Frame] style.

9. **In the Object Styles panel, Control/right-click [Basic Graphics Frame] and choose Edit "[Basic Graphics Frame]".**

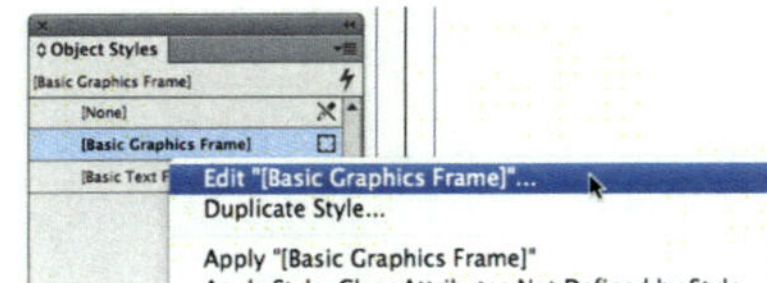

Note:

You can also double-click an object style in the panel to open the Object Style Options dialog box for that style. In this case, the first click would apply the selected style to any object that is selected in the layout.

10. **Click Fill in the Basic Attributes list and choose Paper as the Fill color.**

11. **Click Stroke in the Basic Attributes list and change the weight to 0.5 pt.**

12. **Click Text Wrap & Other in the Basic Attributes list and apply a text wrap based on the object bounding box with a 0.0625″ offset on all four sides.**

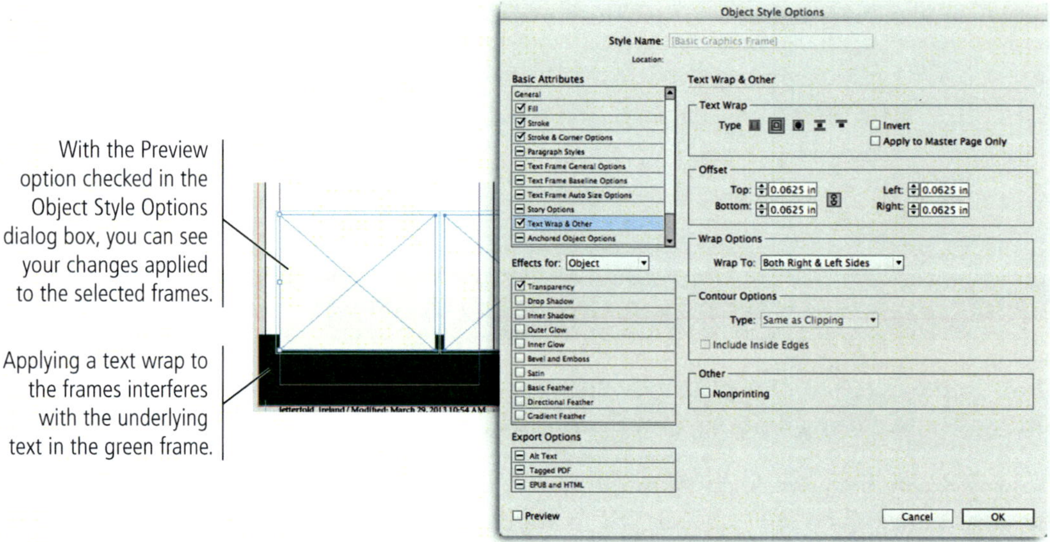

With the Preview option checked in the Object Style Options dialog box, you can see your changes applied to the selected frames.

Applying a text wrap to the frames interferes with the underlying text in the green frame.

13. **Click OK to return to the layout.**

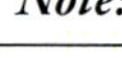

Note:

If you want to change the default attributes of new frames, you should edit the [Basic Graphics Frame] or [Basic Text Frame] object style.

14. **Using the Selection tool, click to select the green text frame under the empty frames. Control/right-click the green frame and choose Text Frame Options from the contextual menu.**

15. **In the Text Frame Options dialog box, check the Ignore Text Wrap option and then click OK.**

This option allows the text to reappear in the frame because the frame is no longer affected by the text wrap attributes of the four overlying empty graphics frames.

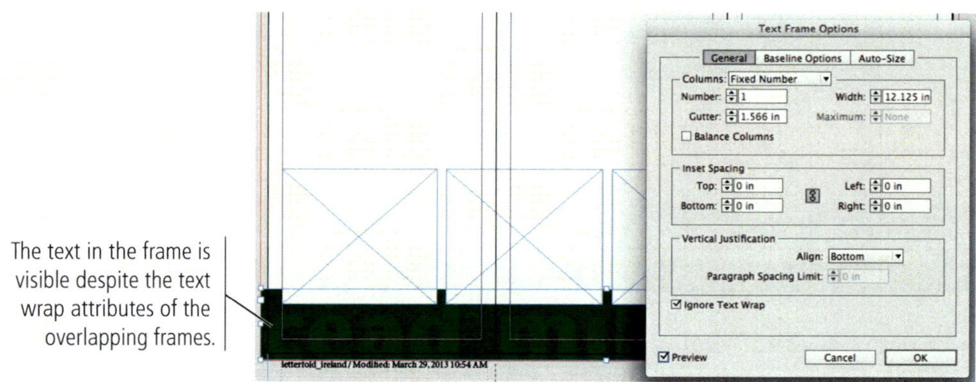

The text in the frame is visible despite the text wrap attributes of the overlapping frames.

16. **Save the file and continue to the next exercise.**

What's in an Object Style?

Use the following chart as a reminder of exactly what can be stored in an object style definition, as well as where to find the equivalent in the application interface for a selected object.

Category	Options		Application Equivalent
General	Based on Reset to base	Shortcut	N/A
Fill	Color	Tint	Swatches panel
Stroke	Color	Tint	Swatches panel
	Weight Gap attributes	Type	Stroke panel
Stroke & Corner Options	Stroke alignment End cap End treatment (arrowheads)	Join Miter limit Corner effects (bevel, etc.)	Stroke panel
Paragraph Styles	Default paragraph style for frame		Paragraph Styles panel
Text Frame General Options	Columns Vertical justification	Inset spacing Ignore text wrap	Text Frame Options dialog box (Object>Text Frame Options)
Text Frame Baseline Options	First baseline	Custom baseline grid options	Text Frame Options dialog box (Object>Text Frame Options)
Story Options	Optical margin alignment		Story panel
Text Wrap & Other	Text wrap type Wrap options	Offset Contour options	Text Wrap panel
	Nonprinting check box		Attributes panel
Anchored Object Options	Position (Inline, Above Line, Custom) Prevent manual positioning		Anchored Object Options dialog box (Object>Anchored Object>Options)
Frame Fitting Options	Crop amount Fitting on empty frame	Alignment reference point	Frame Fitting Options dialog box (Object>Fitting>Frame Fitting Options)
Effects	Effect (including Transparency) for object, fill, stroke, or text		Effects panel
Export Options	Alt Text EPUB and HTML	Tagged PDF	Object Export Options dialog box (Object>Object Export Options)

Create a New Object Style

As you saw in the previous exercise, you can edit the default styles for new text and graphics frames. When you need to define the same options for multiple frames, but you don't want to affect every new object that you create, you can create a new object style to minimize repetitive work.

1. **With letterfold_ireland.indd open, select the empty graphics frame on the left side of the inside spread.**

2. **Change the frame stroke weight to 2 pt and change the stroke color to the custom green swatch (C=85 M=42 Y=100 K=46).**

3. **Click the Drop Shadow button in the Control panel to apply a drop shadow to the frame. Click the *fx* button and choose Drop Shadow to open the Effects dialog box.**

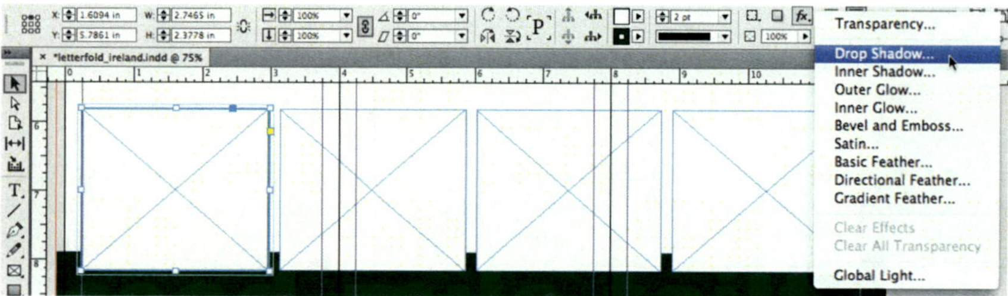

4. **Click the color swatch in the Blending area to open the Effect Color dialog box. Choose the custom green swatch and click OK.**

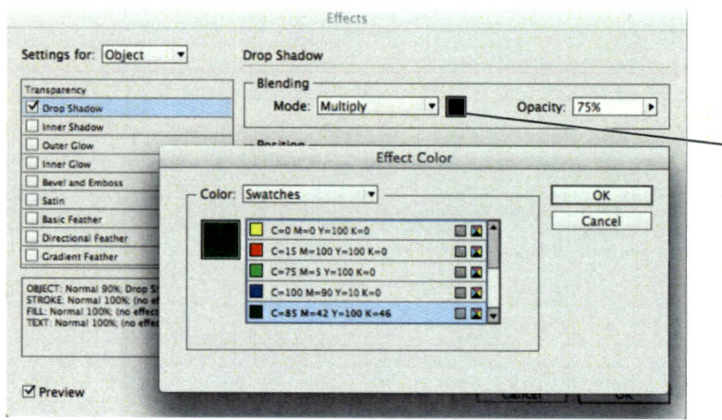

Click this swatch to change the color of the applied effect.

> ***Note:***
>
> *Object styles do not store the dimensions or position of a frame.*

5. **In the Effects dialog box, change the Opacity setting to 45%. Change the X Offset and Y Offset to 0.04″ to reduce the strength of the effect, and then click OK to return to the document.**

   When you define specific X and Y Offset values, the Distance is automatically calculated. In this case, the resulting Distance value is 0.0566″.

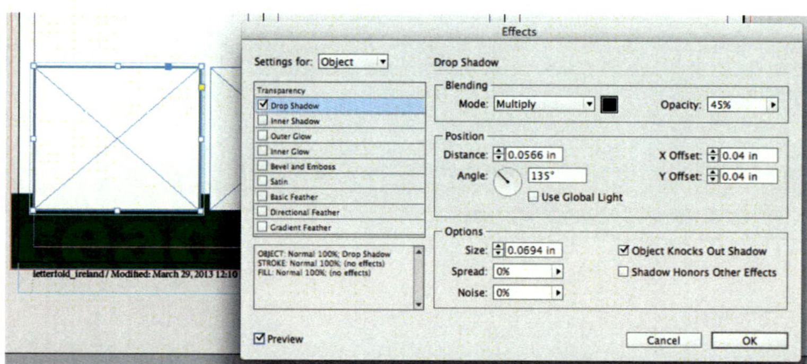

6. **With the frame selected, click the Create New Style button in the Object Styles panel.**

   Object styles follow the same basic principles as text-formatting styles. When you create a new style, it is added with the default name "Object Style [N]" (where "N" is a sequential number); the new style has the same settings as the currently selected object.

> ***Note:***
>
> *You can also open the Object Styles panel Options menu and choose New Object Style.*

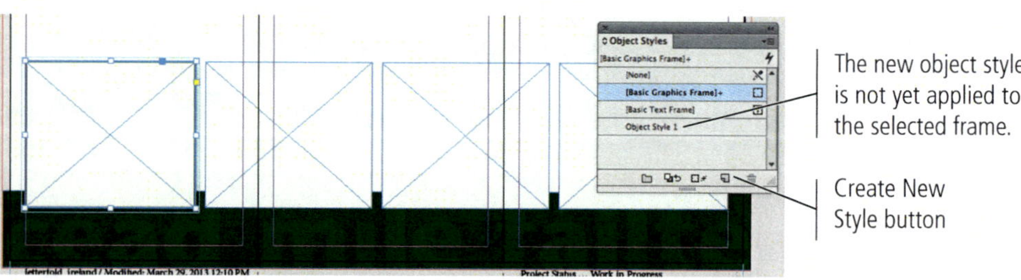

The new object style is not yet applied to the selected frame.

Create New Style button

7. **Control/right-click Object Style 1 in the panel and choose Edit "Object Style 1" in the contextual menu.**

8. **In the Object Style Options dialog box, change the style name to Image with Shadow.**

9. **Choose Stroke in the category list to review the related settings. Change the Weight field to 0 pt, and then click OK to rename the style and return to the document.**

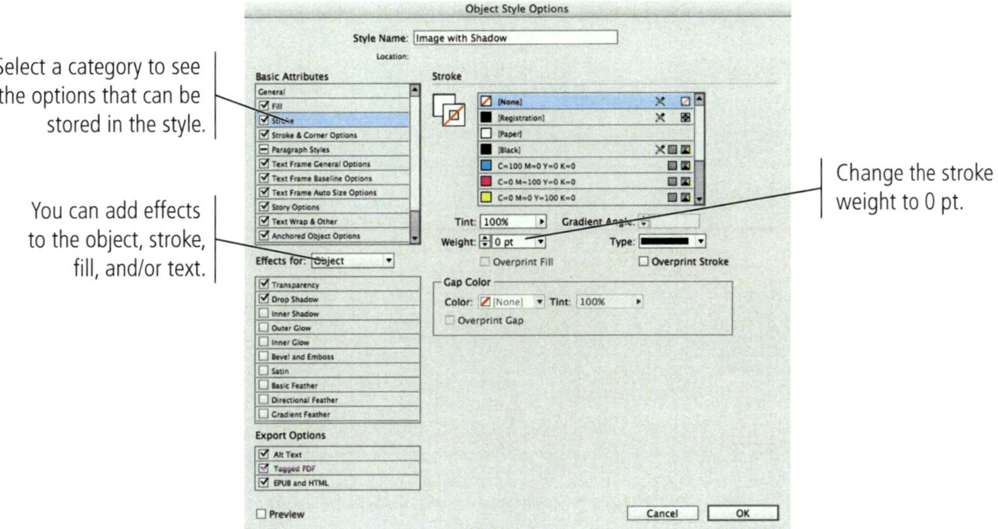

10. **With the original graphics frame still selected in the layout, click Image with Shadow in the Object Styles panel to apply the style to the frame.**

Even though the object style is based on the selected object, you still have to manually apply the new style to the object. It's easy to forget this step.

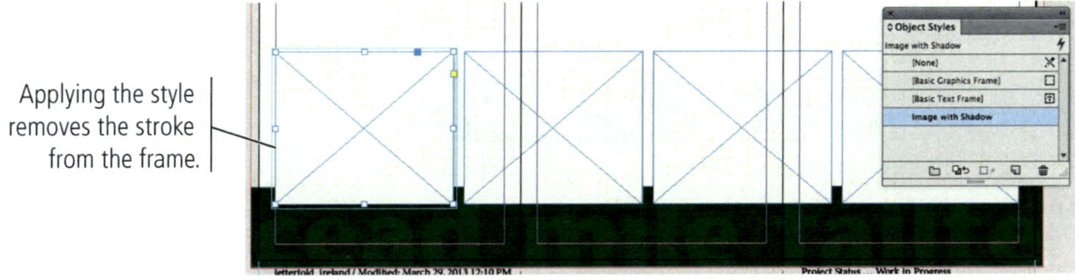

11. **Select the three remaining empty frames, and then apply the Image with Shadow style to those frames.**

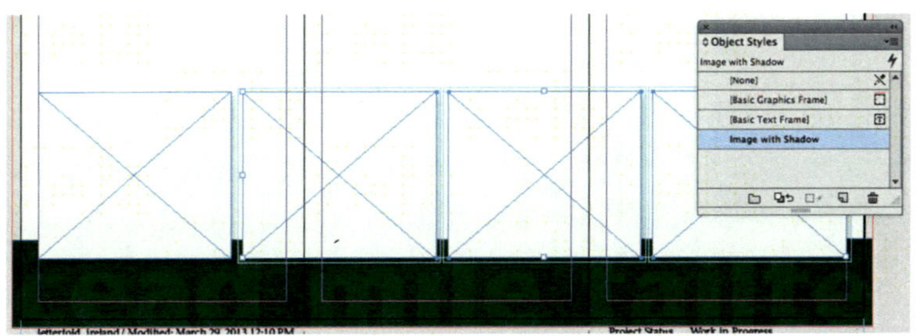

Note:

By defining an object style, you consolidated a number of formatting options into a single click.

12. **Control/right-click Image with Shadow in the Object Styles panel and choose Edit "Image with Shadow".**

13. **Click Text Wrap & Other in the list of Basic Attributes. Change the Top offset value to 0.1875″ and change the Bottom offset value to 0″.**

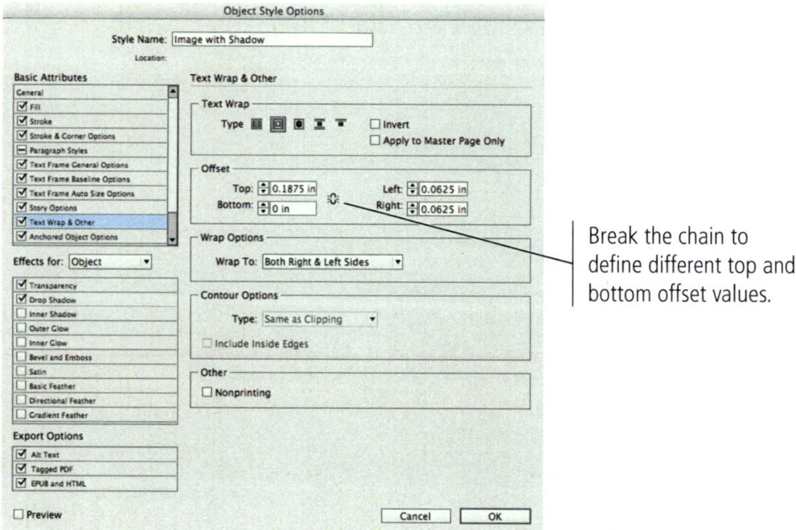

Break the chain to define different top and bottom offset values.

14. **Click OK to redefine the object style.**

    As with text styles, changing an object style definition applies the same changes to all objects where the style is applied. (You can only see the text wrap lines on the three selected frames, but it has been modified in all four frames.)

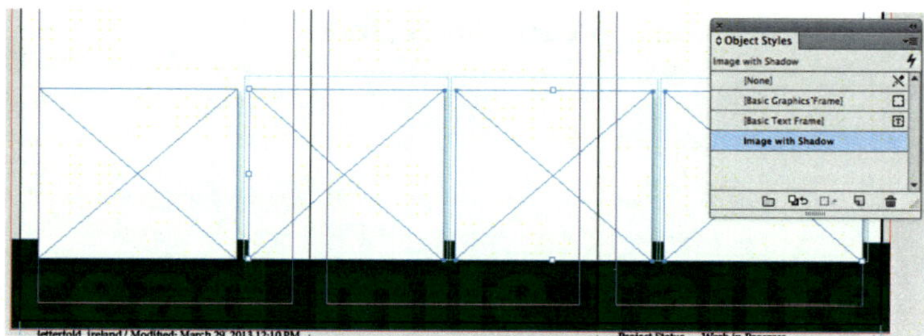

15. **Save the file and continue to the next exercise.**

Import an Object Style

If you have already taken the time to build an element once, why not save time and effort by reusing that same element? Object styles are not limited to the file in which you create them. You can easily import object styles from one InDesign file to another.

1. **With `letterfold_ireland.indd` open, make the outside spread visible in the document window.**

2. **Using the Type tool, click to place the insertion point in the white text frame at the bottom of Page 1.**

3. **Choose File>Place. Choose `form_copy.doc` in the WIP>Ireland folder. Check the Replace Selected Item option and click Open.**

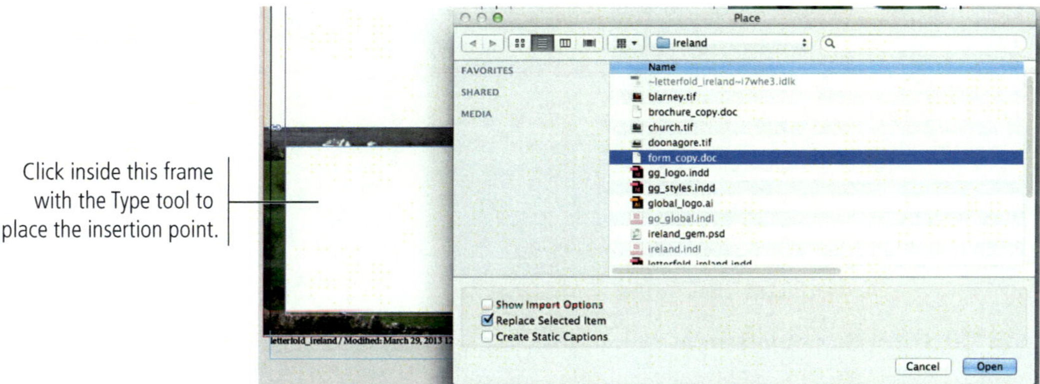

Click inside this frame with the Type tool to place the insertion point.

Text wrap attributes apply to all objects on the same layer, regardless of the stacking order of those objects. Because you edited the [Basic Graphics Frame] object style to include a text wrap, the graphics frame behind the white text frame now has a text wrap that interferes with the overlapping text frame.

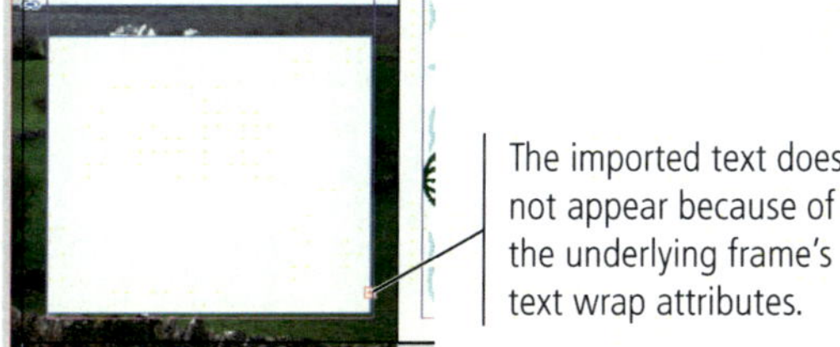

The imported text does not appear because of the underlying frame's text wrap attributes.

4. **Control/right-click the white text frame and choose Text Frame Options in the contextual menu. Check the Ignore Text Wrap option and then click OK.**

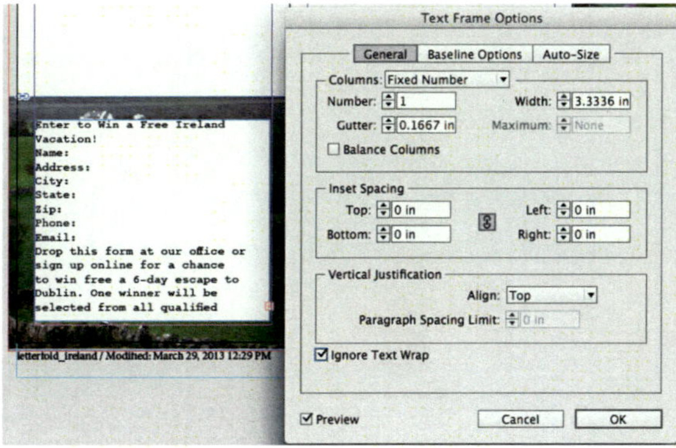

5. **Open the Object Styles panel (Window>Styles>Object Styles), and choose Load Object Styles in the Object Styles panel Options menu.**

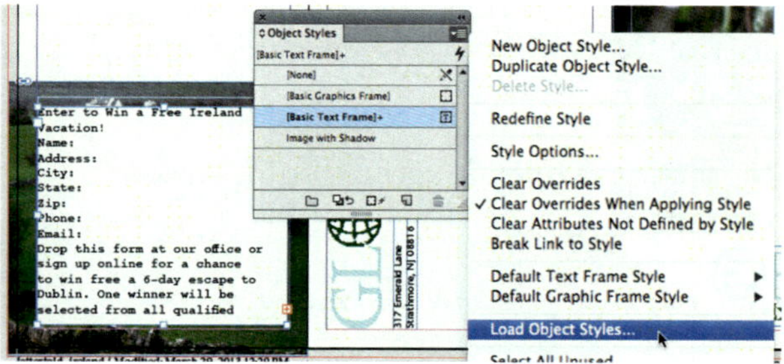

6. **Navigate to gg_styles.indd (in the WIP>Ireland folder) and click Open.**

7. **Uncheck the two basic frame styles, leaving only the Form Box option checked.**

If you change the [Basic Graphics Frame] style for a file (as you did in an earlier exercise), be careful when importing object styles from one InDesign file to another. You could inadvertently overwrite the changes you already made, meaning you would have to redo your earlier work.

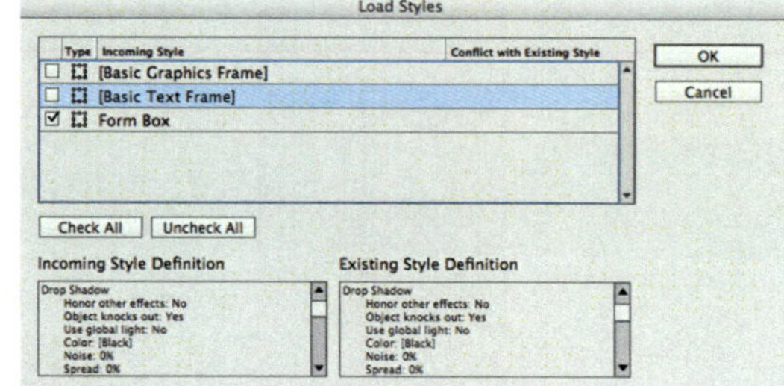

8. **Click OK to import the Form Box object style.**

9. **Click the text frame with the Selection tool, and then click Form Box in the Object Styles panel.**

The Form Box style automatically applies the Form Line paragraph style to text in the frame. The Form Line style uses tab settings and an underscore (_) as the leader character to create the line.

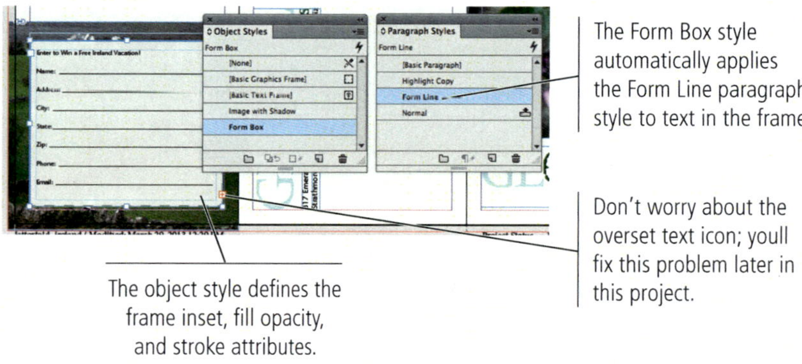

The Form Box style automatically applies the Form Line paragraph style to text in the frame.

Don't worry about the overset text icon; youll fix this problem later in this project.

The object style defines the frame inset, fill opacity, and stroke attributes.

10. **Save the file and continue to the next stage of the project.**

Stage 3 Advanced Text Formatting

If you completed the first four projects in this book, you have already learned about many options for formatting text, both locally and using styles. And yet, there are still more options, including more complex ones that meet very specific needs (such as formatting tabbed text), improving consistency from one document to another (such as importing styles from another InDesign document), and even automatically generating text from stored image data. As we mentioned very early in this book, InDesign gives you almost unlimited control over the text in your layout; this stage of the project introduces some of the more sophisticated options for doing just that.

Import and Flow Client-Supplied Text

In the previous project you learned the basics of importing user-defined styles from a Microsoft Word file. When your clients use more sophisticated styles in their layouts, you need to understand what to do with those styles when you import the files into your InDesign layout.

1. **With `letterfold_ireland.indd` open, make the Page 4–6 spread visible in the document window with nothing selected.**

   Remember: you can double-click the page numbers below the page icons to show the entire spread in the document window.

2. **Choose File>Place. Navigate to `brochure_copy.doc` in your WIP>Ireland folder. Make sure the Show Import Options box is checked and click Open.**

   The Formatting section of the resulting Import Options dialog box shows that three conflicts exist between the styles in the Microsoft Word file and the styles in the InDesign file.

3. **Under Preserve Styles and Formatting from Text and Tables, make sure the Import Styles Automatically option is selected, and then choose Auto Rename in the Paragraph Style Conflicts menu. Click OK.**

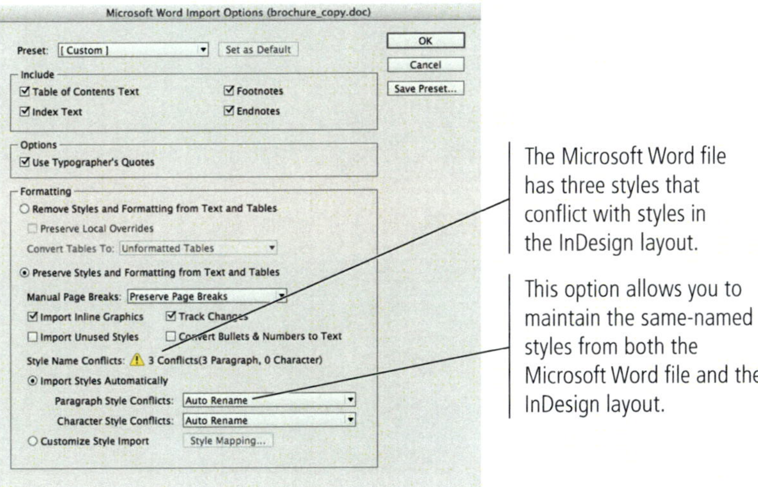

The Microsoft Word file has three styles that conflict with styles in the InDesign layout.

This option allows you to maintain the same-named styles from both the Microsoft Word file and the InDesign layout.

4. **If you see a Missing Font warning, review the information and then click OK.**

   You will replace the fonts from the Word file in the next exercise; you are including the formatting so that you can more clearly see the editorial priority of various text elements. This is a common problem with client-supplied text files.

5. **In the document window, press Option/Alt and move the cursor over the text frame on Page 4.**

Normally, clicking with the loaded text cursor fills the current frame and leaves overset text as overset text. By pressing Option/Alt before clicking, however, you can keep overset text loaded in the cursor so you can choose the next frame where the story will thread; this is called **semi-automatic text flow**.

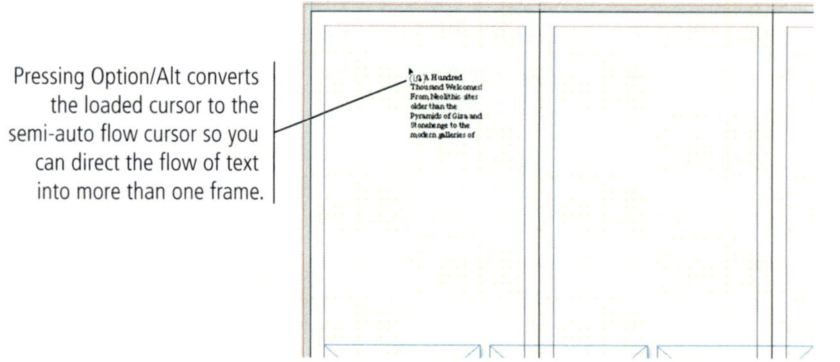

6. **While holding down the Option/Alt key, click once to place the loaded text into the frame on Page 4.**

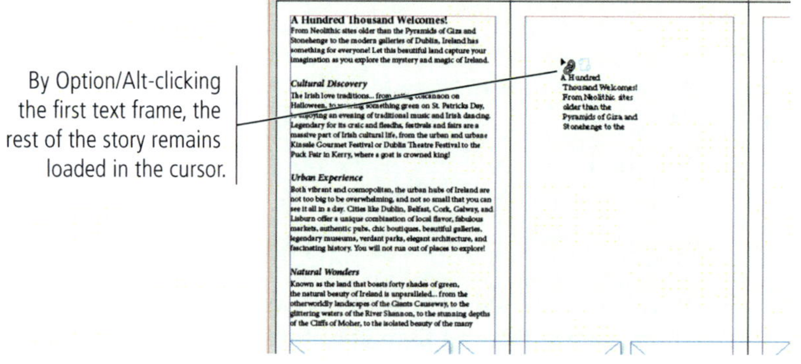

7. **While holding down the Option/Alt key, click in the text frame on the middle page of the spread to place more of the story.**

8. **Click the third frame to place the rest of the story.**

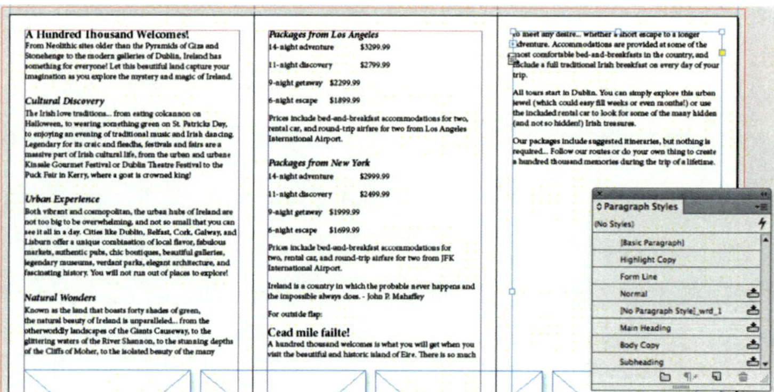

Note:

Semi-automatic text flow works on one frame at a time, so you have to Option/Alt-click each frame to keep overset text loaded in the cursor.

You can automatically flow an entire story by Shift-clicking with the loaded cursor. In this case, pages are added as necessary to accommodate the entire story. This method works even when the Smart Reflow option is turned off in the Type preferences.

Note:

Remember: the loaded place cursor always shows the first part of the story even when the first part has already been placed.

9. **Highlight all text including and after the paragraph "For outside flap:".**

   In some cases, you might want to thread text across multiple frames (as you just did for the inside of the brochure). In other cases, it is better to break a single story into multiple stories to prevent text from accidentally flowing into the wrong place.

   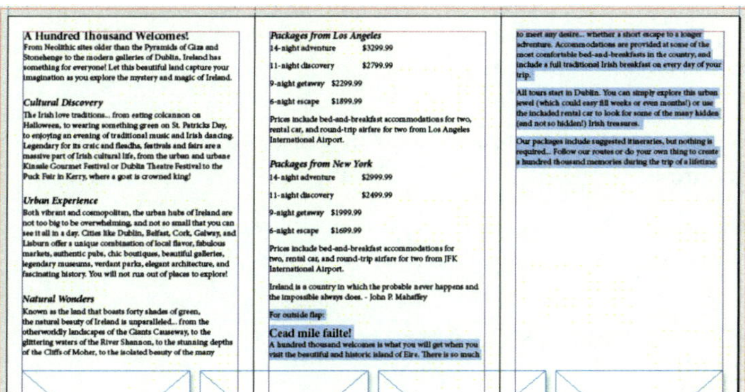

> ***Note:***
>
> *This kind of notation is common in client-supplied text.*

10. **Cut the text from the frame (Edit>Cut or Command/Control-X).**

    As in many applications, when you cut text from a story, the text is stored in the Clipboard so you can paste it somewhere else.

11. **Using the Type tool, click the empty text frame on Page 1 (on the outside spread) to place the insertion point and then paste the text you just cut (Edit>Paste or Command/Control-V).**

    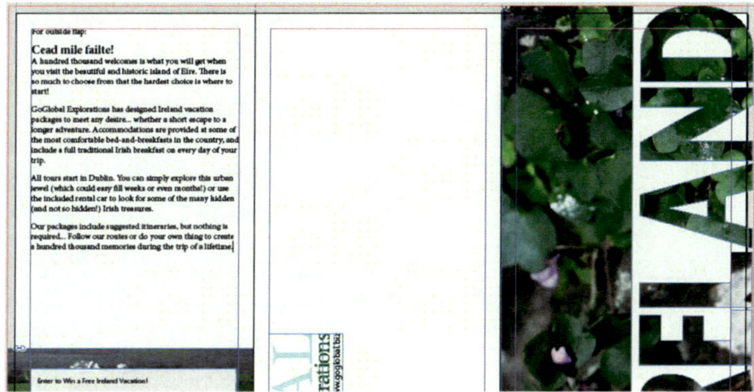

12. **Highlight the entire first paragraph in the frame ("For outside flap:", including the paragraph-return character) and press Delete/Backspace.**

    Pressing Delete/Backspace removes the selected text from the story; the deleted text is not stored in the Clipboard.

13. **Save the file and continue to the next exercise.**

Import InDesign Styles

In many instances, the styles you need for a particular job have already been created for another job. For example, a particular client likes to use 12-pt Garamond with 14-pt leading for the main body copy in every job. If you've already spent the time to create styles once, you can simply import them into your current file instead of repeatedly redefining the same styles.

1. **With letterfold_ireland.indd open, choose Load All Text Styles from the Paragraph Styles panel Options menu.**

   You could also choose Load Paragraph Styles, but the Load All Text Styles allows you to access both character and paragraph styles in a single pass, instead of requiring two steps to import the two different types of styles.

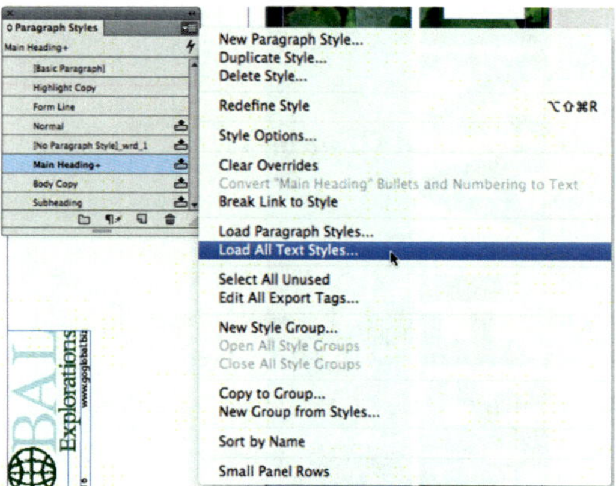

2. **Navigate to the file gg_styles.indd in the WIP>Ireland folder and click Open.**

   This file contains several styles that were used when your agency created other printed products for the client; for consistency, the client would like to use the same styles in this brochure.

   The Load Styles dialog box shows all styles available in the gg_styles.indd file. By default, the incoming style definitions will override the existing style definitions. You can choose Auto-Rename in the Conflict with Existing Style menu to maintain both versions of a same-named style.

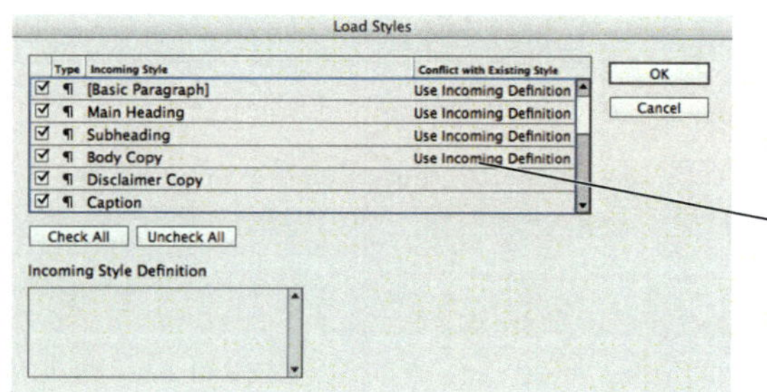

Anything with an option in this column conflicts with a style already in the InDesign file.

3. **Click the box to the left of [Basic Paragraph] to uncheck that style.**

   By unchecking the style, it will not be imported into the active InDesign file.

4. **Click OK to import the selected styles (eight paragraph and three character).**

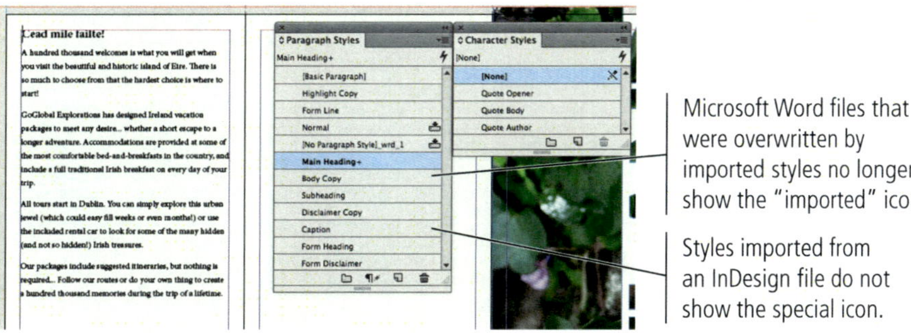

5. **Select all the text in the frame on Page 1 and then click the Clear Overrides in Selection button in the Paragraph Styles panel.**

   When you have conflicts between styles imported from Microsoft Word and styles in InDesign, it is fairly common to see the + indicator next to style names, indicating that something other than the style definition is applied. Clearing overrides solves this problem.

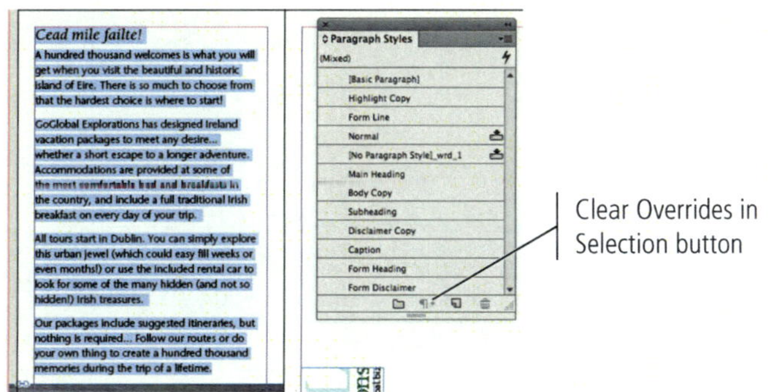

Note:

Clearing overrides could also remove intentional formatting such as a bold or italic word. Carefully review client-supplied text before making sweeping changes.

6. **On Page 4, place the insertion point in the first text frame and then choose Edit>Select All. Click the Clear Overrides in Selection button in the Paragraph Styles panel.**

   If you read the imported text, you might notice another problem: the text at the end of Frame 1 doesn't make sense with the text at the beginning of Frame 2.

   The text frames on each panel occupy the space within each panel's margin guides. Although the empty graphics frames have an applied text wrap attribute, the green text frame has no defined text wrap. Unfortunately, you can't see the hidden text because the text frames are below the green frame in the stacking order.

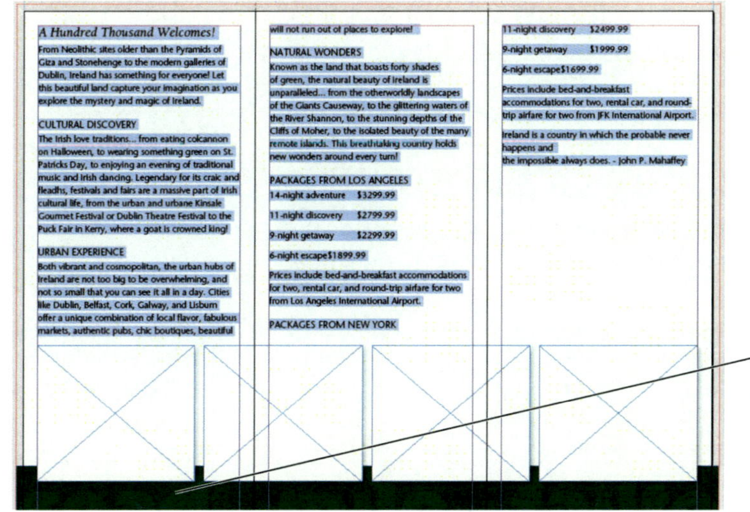

7. **Using the Selection tool, click the green text frame at the bottom of the spread. In the Text Wrap panel, click the Wrap Around Bounding Box option.**

   This forces the main copy to appear only above the four empty graphics frames.

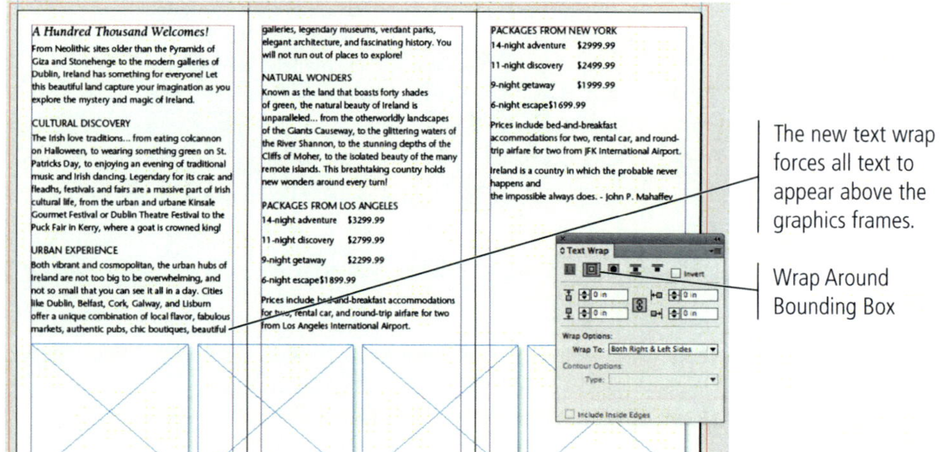

8. **Save the file and continue to the next exercise.**

Create a Custom Text Wrap

At times, you might want to show a specific part of an image instead of the entire image. You can accomplish this task in a number of ways, but the two most common methods involve using either Alpha channels or clipping paths stored in the image.

A **clipping path** is a vector-based path used to mask (cover) specific parts of an image; areas inside the path are visible, and areas outside the path are hidden. Because the clipping path is vector-based, is always results in hard edges on the clipped image.

An **Alpha channel** is a special type of image channel that masks specific parts of an image by determining the degree of transparency in each pixel. (In other words, a 50% value in the Alpha channel means that particular spot of the image will be 50% transparent). The soft edge created by a blended Alpha channel means you can blend one image into another, blend one layer into another, or blend an entire image into a background in a page-layout application.

1. **With letterfold_ireland.indd open, make the inside spread visible and make sure nothing is selected in the layout.**

2. **Choose File>Place. Select ireland_gem.psd in the WIP>Ireland folder. Make sure Show Import Options is checked and then click Open.**

3. **In the resulting Image Import Options dialog box, click the Image tab and review the options.**

   If the Photoshop file includes transparent areas, the Alpha Channel menu defaults to "Transparency", which refers to the actual transparent areas in the file. You can use this menu to choose another saved alpha channel, which will define the transparent areas in the file that is placed into the layout.

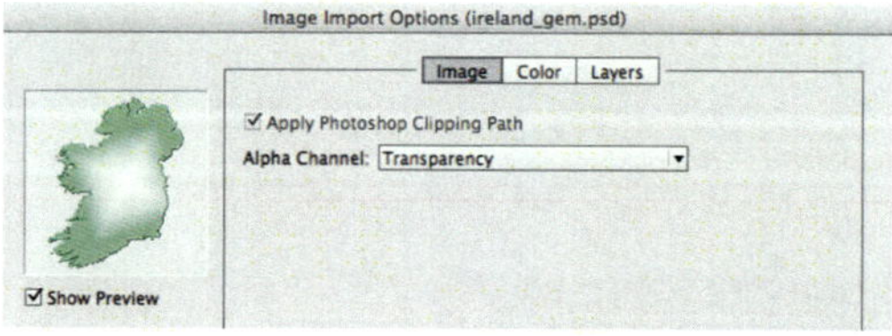

> ***Note:***
>
> *If the Photoshop file includes a saved clipping path, you can activate the Apply Photoshop Clipping Path option to make that clipping path active in the placed image.*

4. **Click the Layers tab and review the options, then click OK.**

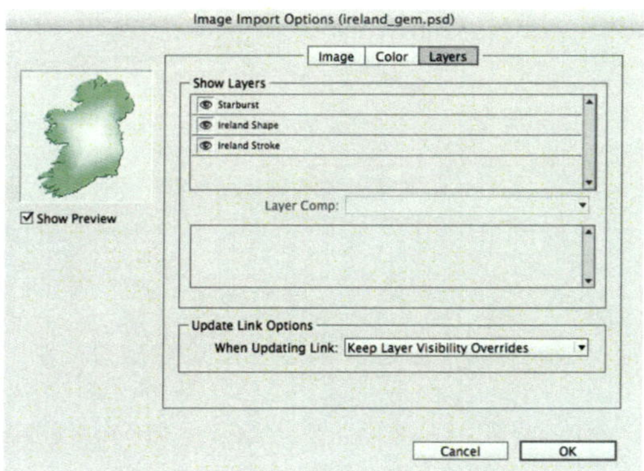

Note:

Unless you know what the different layers contain, it is difficult to decide what you want to place based on the very small preview image.

Note:

After you place a Photoshop file into the layout, you can change the visible layers by choosing Object>Object Layer Options.

Photoshop files can include multiple layers and layer comps (saved versions of specific layer position and visibility). You can turn off specific layers by clicking the eye (visibility) icon for that layer. If the file includes layer comps, you can use the Layer Comp menu to determine which comp to place.

If you change the layers that are visible in the file, you can use the Update Link Options to cause InDesign to determine what happens if you relink or update the link to the placed image file. Using the Keep Layer Visibility Overrides option, InDesign remembers which layers you defined as visible in the InDesign file. If you choose Use Photoshop's Layer Visibility, the file reverts to the actual saved state whenever you relink or update the link to the Photoshop file.

5. **Click to place the loaded image on the left page of the spread. Using the Control panel, place the image (based on the top-left reference point) at X: –1.45″, Y: –0.5″.**

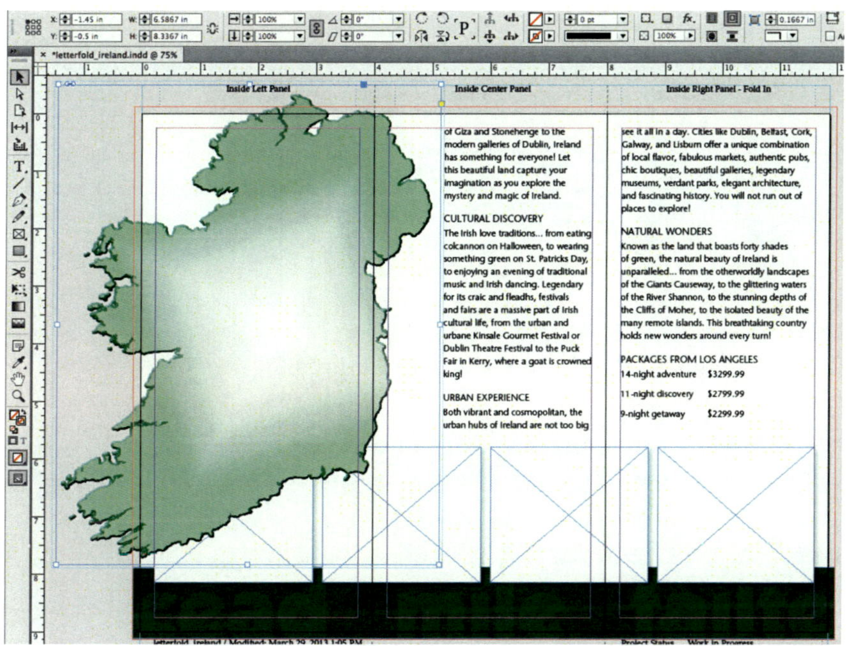

6. **Open the Text Wrap panel. Click the Wrap Around Object Shape option, and then choose Alpha Channel in the Contour Options Type menu.**

7. **Change the Top Offset field to 0.1875".**

There are no "sides" to the non-standard shape, so you can only define a single offset value (using the Top Offset field).

Note:

You can use the Direct Selection and Pen tool variants to manually edit the text wrap in the document window. If you manually edit the clipping path, the Contour Options Type menu changes to show "User-Modified Path" and the Offset field becomes unavailable.

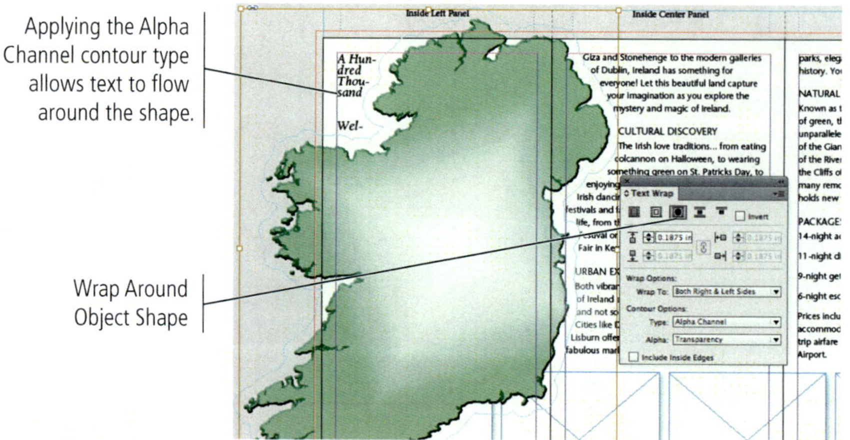

8. **Using the Layers panel, click the <ireland_gem.psd> item and drag it below the four <rectangle> items.**

The empty graphics frames are now entirely visible on top of the placed Ireland image. Always remember that the Layers panel makes it very easy to rearrange the stacking order of objects without worrying about manually selecting anything in the layout.

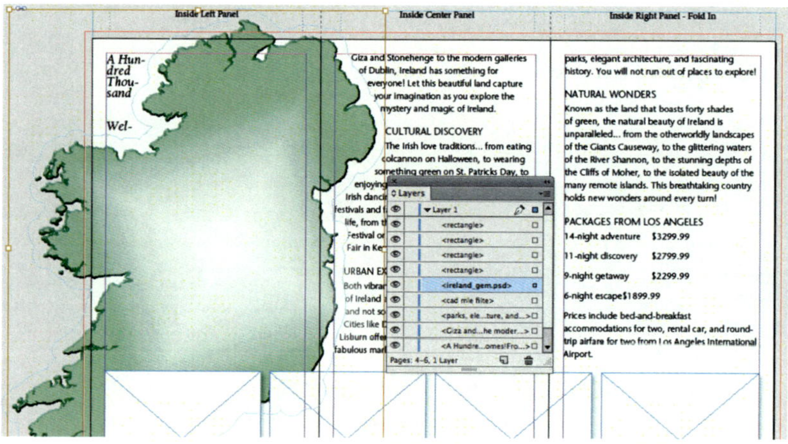

9. **In the Layers panel, click the rectangle to the right of the <A Hundred...> text frame to select that frame in the layout.**

The Layers panel also makes it easy to select objects that are entirely behind other objects, as is the case with the first main text frame and the frame that contains the Ireland graphic.

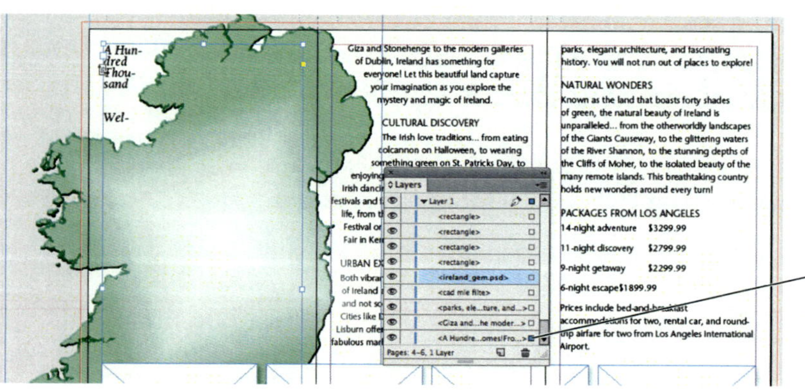

10. **Press Delete/Backspace to remove the selected frame.**

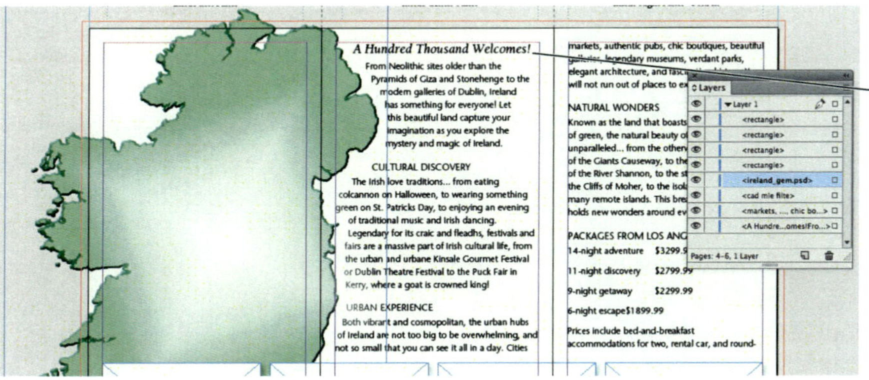

Deleting the first text frame forced the text into the next available frame in the thread.

11. **Save the file and continue to the next exercise.**

Create a Style for Pull Quotes

Your client asked you to include a **pull quote**, which is a special visual treatment for text that is either pulled from the story (hence the name) or somehow supports the surrounding text. For the pull quote in this layout, you have been asked to use the following structure:

- Format the first character in the pull quote as a quotation mark using the Quote Character character style.
- Format the text of the quote with the Quote Copy character style. All quotes have one or more paragraphs.
- Format the author's name (preceded by an en dash) with the Quote Author character style.

You could simply format these elements in the layout, but nested styles allow you to create the structure once and apply it anywhere.

1. **With `letterfold_ireland.indd` open, click the text frame on Page 6 to select it.**

2. **Using the Selection tool, click the overset text icon to load the rest of the story into the cursor.**

3. **Click the pasteboard area to the right of the spread to place the remaining text in a new text frame.**

   When you work with a defined (and limited) space, it's common to have overset text that you need to place in other locations. Using the pasteboard as a temporary workspace is an easy way to review and access the remaining text.

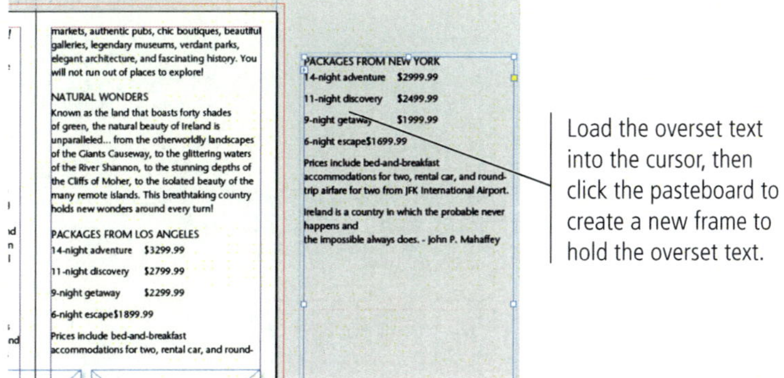

Load the overset text into the cursor, then click the pasteboard to create a new frame to hold the overset text.

4. **Highlight the last paragraph in the copy and cut it (Edit>Cut or Command/ Control-X).**

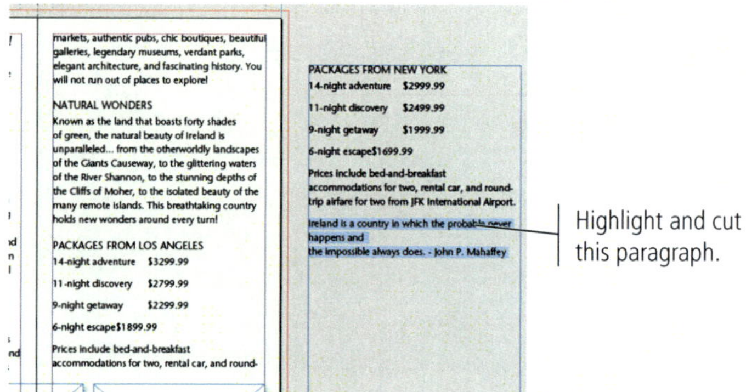

5. **Create a new text frame on the left page of the spread (over the Ireland picture), snapping to the top, left, and right margins. Paste the cut text into the new frame.**

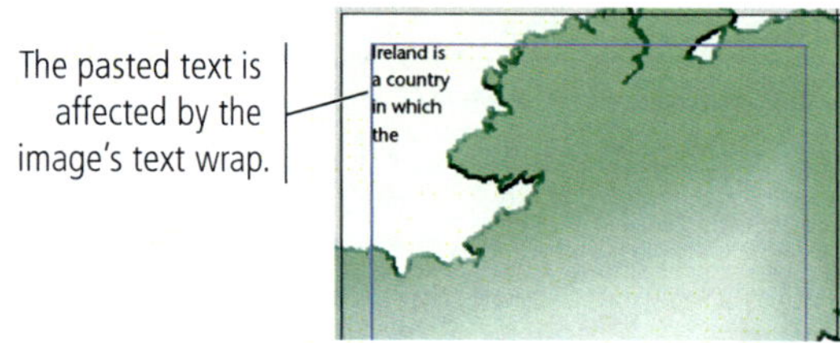

6. **Select the new frame with the Selection tool and open the Text Frame Options dialog box. Check the Ignore Text Wrap option and then click OK.**

7. **Place the insertion point anywhere in the pasted text, and apply right paragraph alignment to the paragraph.**

8. **With the insertion point anywhere in the quote paragraph, click the Create New Style button in the Paragraph Styles panel.**

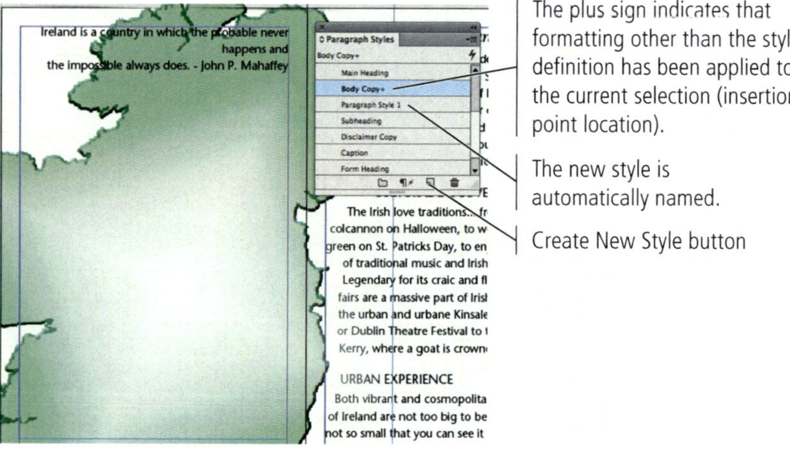

9. **Double-click Paragraph Style 1 in the panel to edit the style.**

   Because the insertion point is flashing in the quotation text, the first click in the double-click applies the new style to the paragraph. The new style defaults to the formatting of the current insertion point (or selection, if any characters are highlighted).

10. **Change the style name to Pull Quote and make sure the Preview check box is active.**

11. **Click Drop Caps and Nested Styles in the list of categories to display those options, then click the New Nested Style button.**

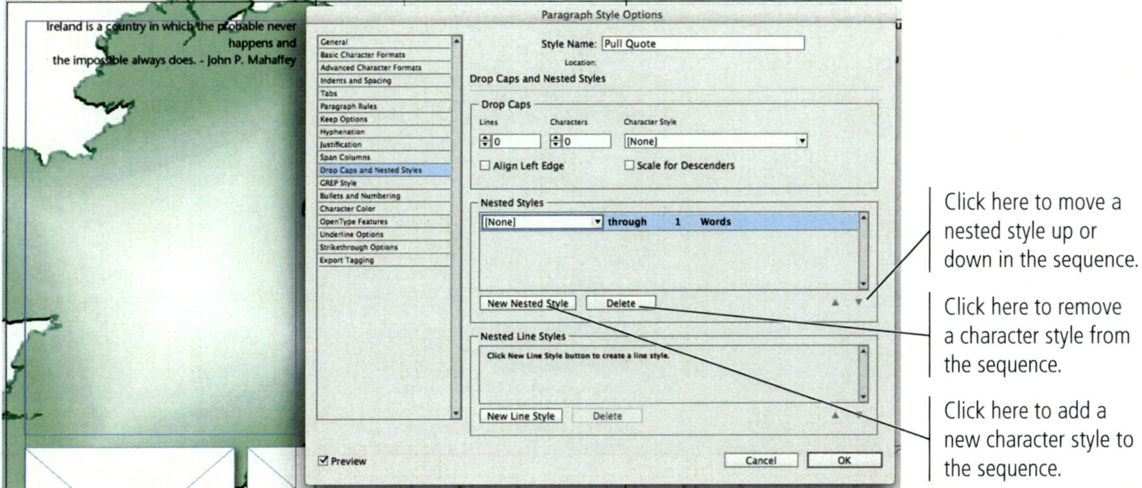

Click here to move a nested style up or down in the sequence.

Click here to remove a character style from the sequence.

Click here to add a new character style to the sequence.

12. **Click the first menu (the one that says "[None]") and choose Quote Opener in the list of available character styles.**

When you imported the styles from the gg_styles.indd file, you imported three character styles that should be used to format pull quotes. In the next few steps, you will create a nested style that automatically applies those styles to the appropriate parts of the quote.

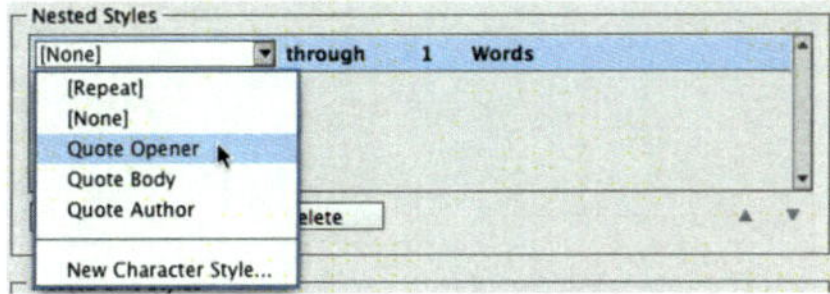

13. **Click the Words menu and choose Characters from the list.**

Nested styles can be applied up to or through a specific character sequence; if you choose the Through option, the character(s) you specify will be formatted with the character style you define. For this layout, the first character in any pull quote will be formatted with the Quote Opener style; you can leave the default Through 1 option.

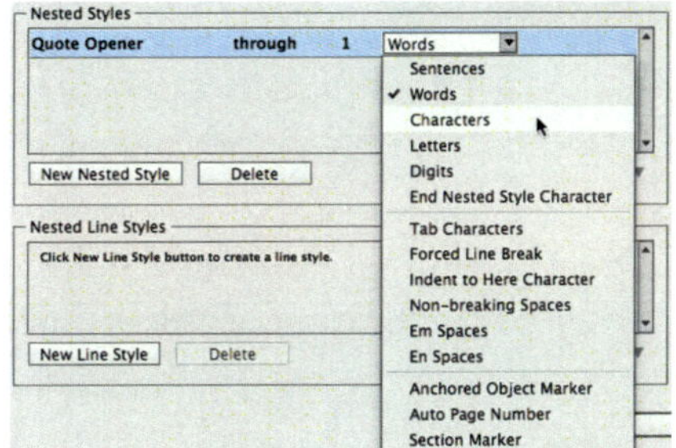

Because the Preview option is checked, the layout shows a dynamic preview of your choices. The nested styles apply the Quote Opener character style to the first character in the paragraph.

Note:

You might need to toggle the Preview option off and back on to see the results of your choices in the Drop Caps and Nested Styles options.

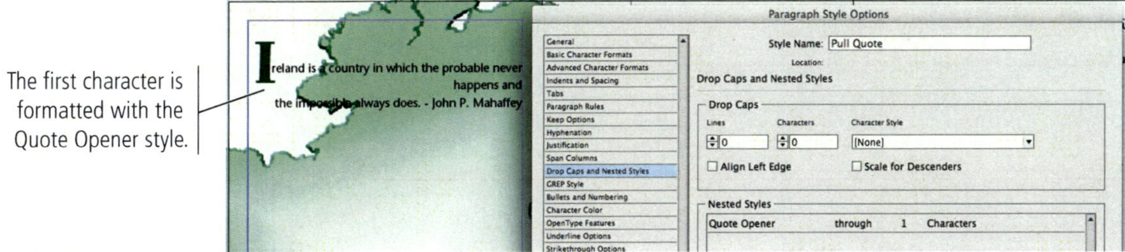

The first character is formatted with the Quote Opener style.

Understanding Nested Styles

InDesign supports three basic kinds of nested styles. The first is the basic parent/child relationship, in which one style is based on another. When you base one style on another, you change all related styles by changing the parent style.

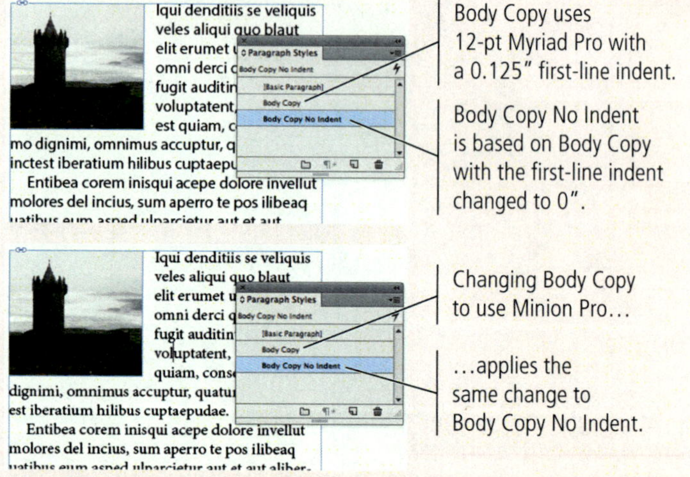

Body Copy uses 12-pt Myriad Pro with a 0.125" first-line indent.

Body Copy No Indent is based on Body Copy with the first-line indent changed to 0".

Changing Body Copy to use Minion Pro…

…applies the same change to Body Copy No Indent.

The second type of nested style incorporates different character styles for specific parts of a paragraph (as you do to create the Pull Quote style in this project). You can also use nested character styles to format drop caps, bulleted lists, and numbered lists.

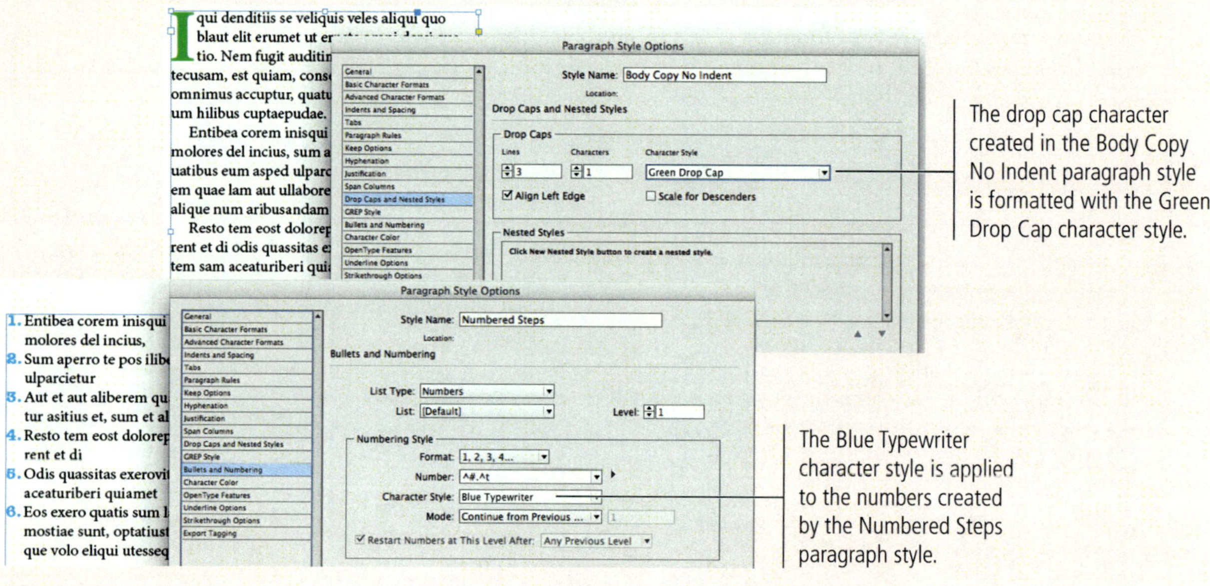

The drop cap character created in the Body Copy No Indent paragraph style is formatted with the Green Drop Cap character style.

The Blue Typewriter character style is applied to the numbers created by the Numbered Steps paragraph style.

Nested Line Styles (at the bottom of the dialog box) affect the appearance of entire lines of text. You can define specific character styles to apply to a specific number of lines; the Repeat option allows you to continue a sequence of defined styles for the remainder of the paragraph. In this example, the applied paragraph style defines two Nested Line Styles, which tell InDesign to apply the Red Text character style to the first line of the paragraph, and then apply the Green Text character style to the second line of the paragraph. The third item in the list — [Repeat] — determines what to do with the remaining lines of the paragraph; in this example, InDesign will <u>repeat</u> the <u>last</u> <u>10</u> <u>lines</u> of the Nested Line Styles list.

The applied paragraph style defines a sequence of two character styles that will be applied to every other line in the paragraph.

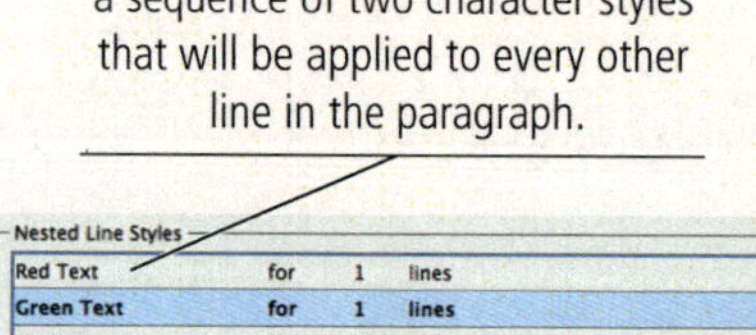

Entibea corem inisqui acepe dolore invellut molores del incius, Sum aperro te pos ilibeaq uatibus eum asped ulparcietur Aut et aut aliber-em quae lam aut ullabore ratur asitius et, sum et alique num aribusandam Resto tem eost dolore-pudi officium es simpor rent et di Odis quassitas exerovitas ium quidentem sam aceaturiberi quiamet Eos exero quatis sum latecto maximus toremostiae sunt, optatiust aped expedis et, cum que volo eliqui utesseque pore lis quiat.

Nested Style Character Options

- **Sentences** applies the style up to or through the defined number of sentences. InDesign recognizes the end of a sentence as the location of a period, question mark, or exclamation point. (Quotation marks following punctuation are included as part of the sentence.)
- **Words** applies the style up to or through the defined number of words. InDesign recognizes the division of individual words by space characters.
- **Characters** applies the style up to or through the defined number of characters. Nonprinting characters (tabs, spaces, etc.) are included in the character count.
- **Letters** applies the style up to or through the defined number of letters.
- **Digits** applies the style up to or through the defined number of Arabic numerals (0–9).
- **End Nested Style Character** applies the style up to or through a manually added End Nested Style Here character (Type>Insert Special Character>Other>End Nested Style Here).
- **Tab Characters** applies the style up to or through a nonprinting tab character. (Choose Type>Show Hidden Characters to see tab characters in the text.)

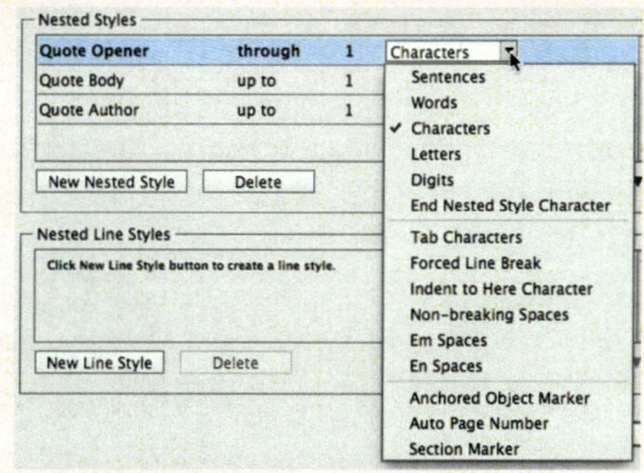

- **Forced Line Break** applies the style up to or through a nonprinting forced line break character.
- **Indent to Here Character** applies the style up to or through a nonprinting Indent to Here character.
- **Non-Breaking Spaces**, **Em Spaces**, and **En Spaces** apply the style up to or through these space characters.
- **Anchored Object Marker** applies the style up to or through an inline graphics frame (which exists by default wherever you have an inline object in the text).
- **Auto Page Number** and **Section Marker** apply the style up to or through page or section markers.

14. **Add another nested style to the list, applying the Quote Body character style and using the Up To option instead of the Through option. Highlight the contents of the fourth menu and type a hyphen (-).**

You can define a specific character by highlighting the field and typing the character. In this case, you're formatting all text up to the hyphen preceding the author's name.

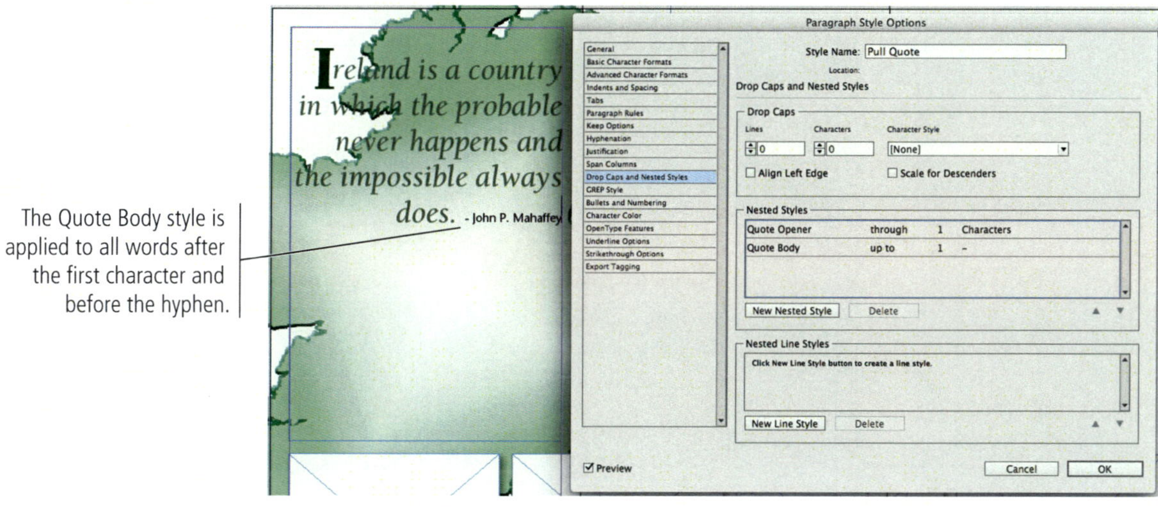

The Quote Body style is applied to all words after the first character and before the hyphen.

15. **Add a third nested style to the list, applying the Quote Author character style up to one Tab character.**

    In this case, you want the style to go through the end of the paragraph. The Up To 1 Tab Character option means the Quote Author style will apply until the application encounters a Tab character; because the author information is the end of the text frame, there will never be a Tab character to interrupt the style.

The Quote Author style is applied to the hyphen and all following text.

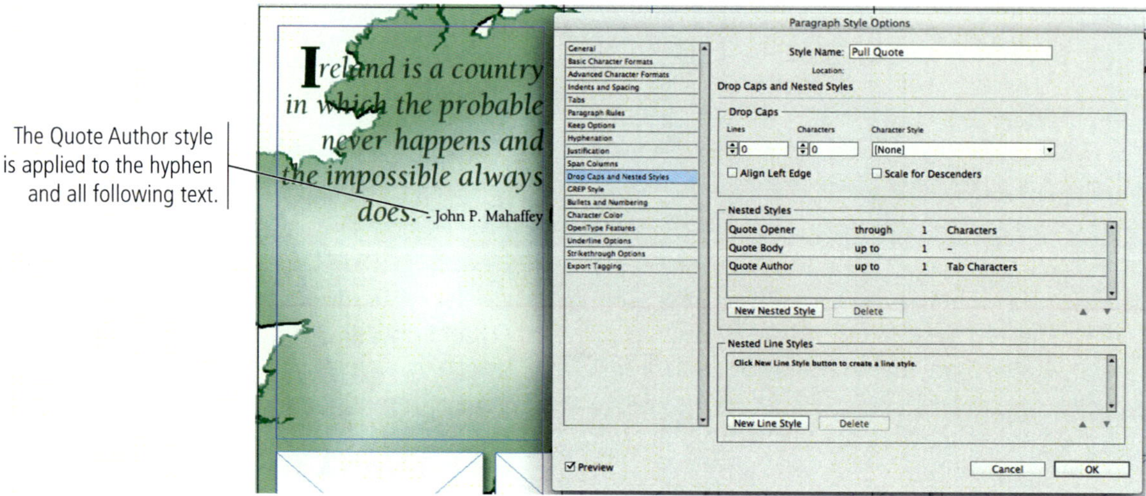

16. **Click OK to return to the document.**
17. **Place the insertion point before the hyphen and press Shift-Return/Enter to force the author information onto a new line without starting a new paragraph.**
18. **Add soft-returns before the words "country" and "always" in the quote.**
19. **Adjust the top edge of the frame until you are satisfied with the position of the quote over the Ireland image.**

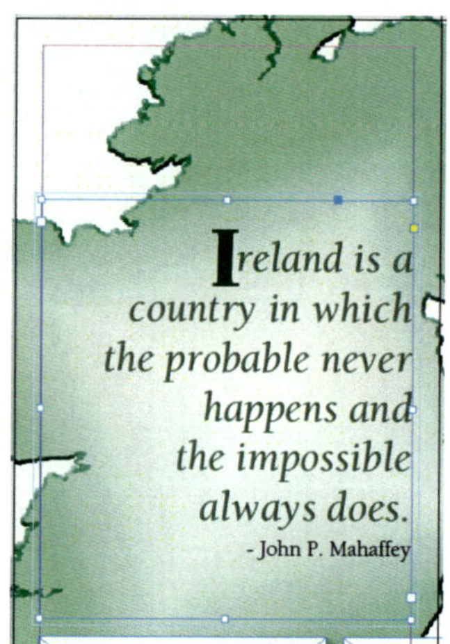

20. **Save the file and continue to the next exercise.**

Note:

Remember, Shift-Return/Enter is the key command for a forced line break or "soft return," which starts a new line without starting a new paragraph.

Control Tab Formatting

Some people incorrectly rely on the Spacebar for aligning columns of text, or they rely on the default tab stops (usually every half-inch in InDesign and Microsoft Word), adding multiple tab characters to align text. Both methods can be time consuming, and both are unnecessary to properly format tabbed text.

1. **With the inside spread of `letterfold_ireland.indd` visible, make sure hidden characters are showing (Type>Show Hidden Characters).**

2. **Click with the Type tool to place the insertion point in the first paragraph after the Packages from Los Angeles heading.**

3. **Using the Control or Paragraph panel, change the Space After value to 0".**

4. **If possible, make the top of the selected frame visible in the document window.**

5. **Choose Type>Tabs.**

   This is the only InDesign panel not accessed in the Window menu. If the top edge of the active text frame is visible, the Tabs panel will automatically appear at the top of the frame. If the top edge of the frame is not visible, the panel floats randomly on the screen.

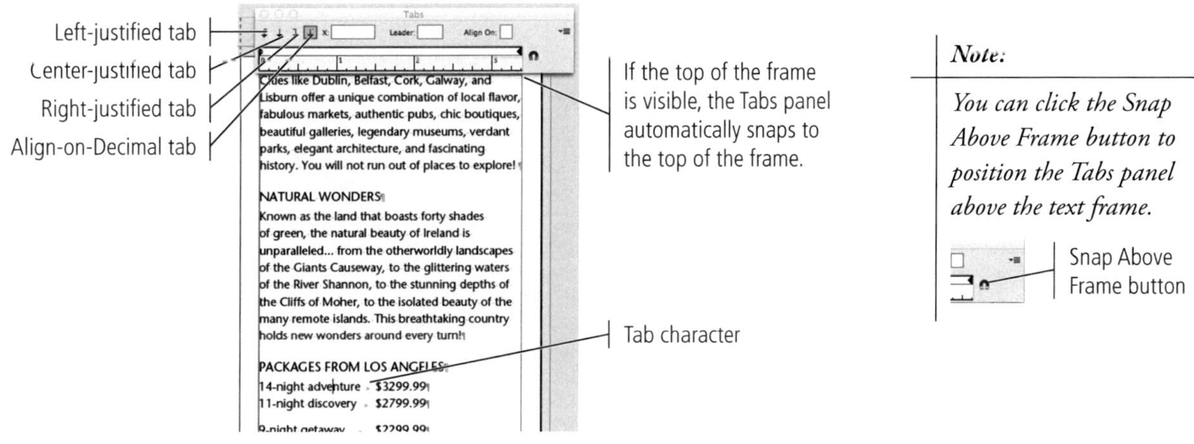

Note:

You can click the Snap Above Frame button to position the Tabs panel above the text frame.

6. **Click the Align to Decimal tab marker in the Tabs panel and then click the ruler to add a tab stop.**

   Remember that tab settings are a paragraph formatting option. Adding the tab stop affects only the selected paragraph(s).

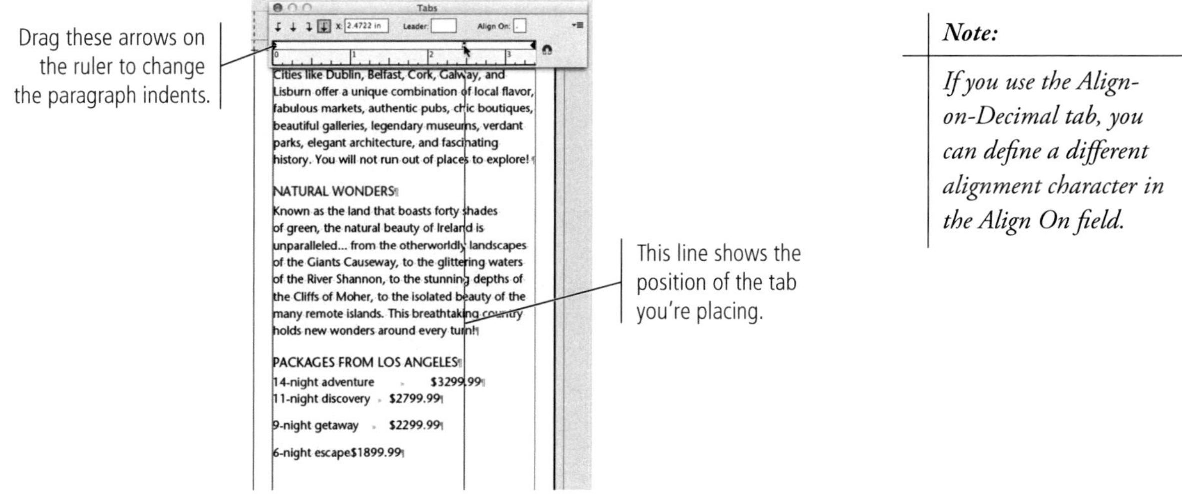

Note:

If you use the Align-on-Decimal tab, you can define a different alignment character in the Align On field.

7. **With the stop you added in Step 6 selected on the ruler, change the X field to 3.125″.**

You can either drag markers on the ruler to adjust tab-stop positions, or you can use the X field to define a precise location. If you drag an existing stop to a new position, make sure you drag straight across the tab ruler; if you drag too high or too low, you might delete the tab stop when you release the mouse button.

8. **Type ". " (period space) in the Leader field, then press Return/Enter to apply the change.**

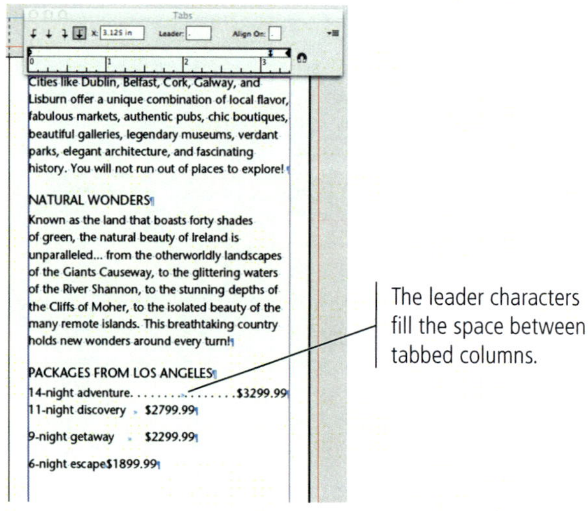

> ***Note:***
>
> *You can use the Tabs panel Options menu to clear all tabs in the existing paragraph or delete the selected tab. The Repeat Tab option creates a series of equally spaced tabs acros the ruler based on the position of the selected tab. The Reset Indents option restores the paragraph indent markers to 0.*

9. **With the insertion point still in the first price line, Option/Alt-click the Create New Style button at the bottom of the Paragraph Styles panel.**

Option/Alt-clicking the Create New Style button automatically opens the New Paragraph Style dialog box.

When you create a new style from scratch, the new style automatically adopts the settings of the current insertion point. In this case, the new style has all of the formatting that is defined in the paragraph you just edited — including the tab with its leader characters.

> ***Note:***
>
> *If you Option/Alt-click the Create New button in most panels, the options dialog box for the new style, layer, etc. automatically opens.*

10. **Type Price Line in the Style Name field. Check the Apply Style to Selection option, then click OK to return to the document window.**

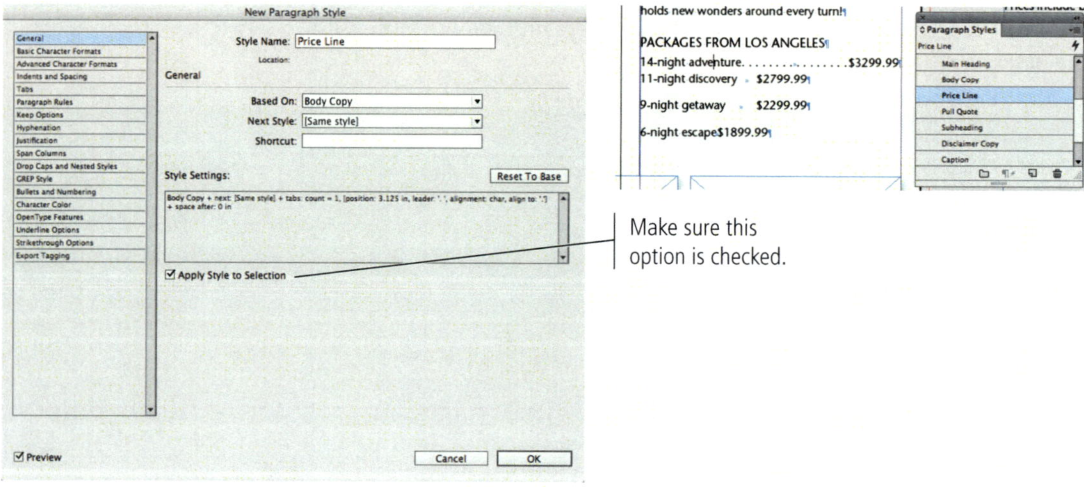

11. **Select the remaining three lines of prices, then click the new Price Line style to apply it to those paragraphs.**

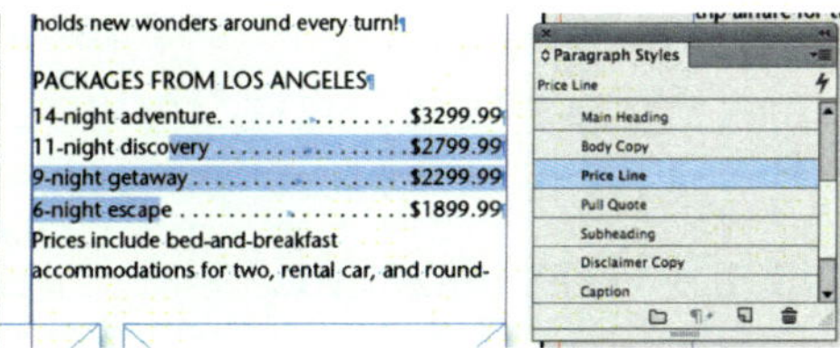

12. **Place the insertion point in the last paragraph of the story and then click the Disclaimer Copy style to apply it.**

13. **In the text frame on the pasteboard (to the right of Page 6), apply the Price Line style to the four paragraphs after the Packages from New York heading. Apply the Disclaimer Copy style to the last paragraph.**

Don't worry that the price lines don't fit onto one line in the overset frame. In a later exercise, you will use conditional text to move those lines into the Page 6 frame; because you know the lines currently on Page 6 fit into the frame width, the overset lines — which are formatted with the same styles — will also fit in that frame.

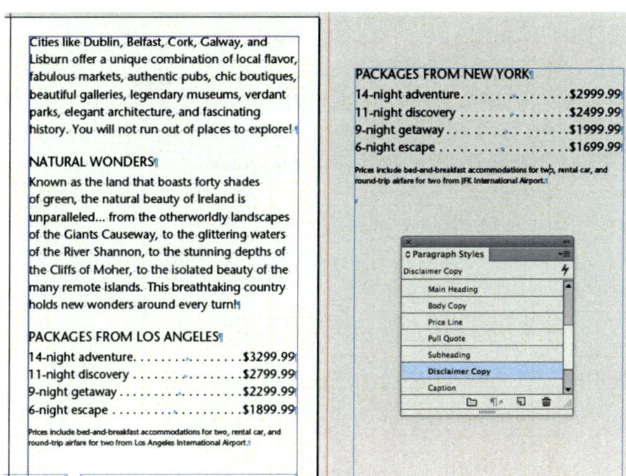

14. **Save the file and continue to the next exercise.**

Define Paragraph Rules

The brochure layout is almost complete with only a few remaining issues to address. In this exercise, you are going to use paragraph rules to add more visual weight to the subheadings in the body copy. You will then perform whatever clean-up tasks are required to finish the layout.

1. **With letterfold_ireland.indd open, make sure the inside spread is visible.**

2. **Control/right-click the Subheading style in the Paragraph Styles panel and choose Edit "Subheading".**

Note:

Many client files will have multiple tab characters separating one bit of text from another. You should almost always remove extra tab characters and use tab-formatting options to create the appropriate columns.

3. **Click Paragraph Rules in the list of formatting categories and make sure the Preview option is checked.**

   Paragraph rules are simply lines that are attached to a specific paragraph. Rules can be placed above or below any paragraph (or above *and* below a paragraph) to add visual interest and importance to specific text elements.

4. **Choose Rule Below in the first menu, and then check the Rule On box.**

   If Rule Above appears in the menu, click to open the menu and choose Rule Below.

5. **Change the rule weight to 6 pt. Change the rule color to the custom green swatch (C=85 M=42 Y=100 K=46) with a 15% tint.**

   This swatch is used by one of the styles you imported from another InDesign file in a previous exercise. When you import a style from one InDesign file to another, any other required assets — such as color swatches — are also imported into the current file.

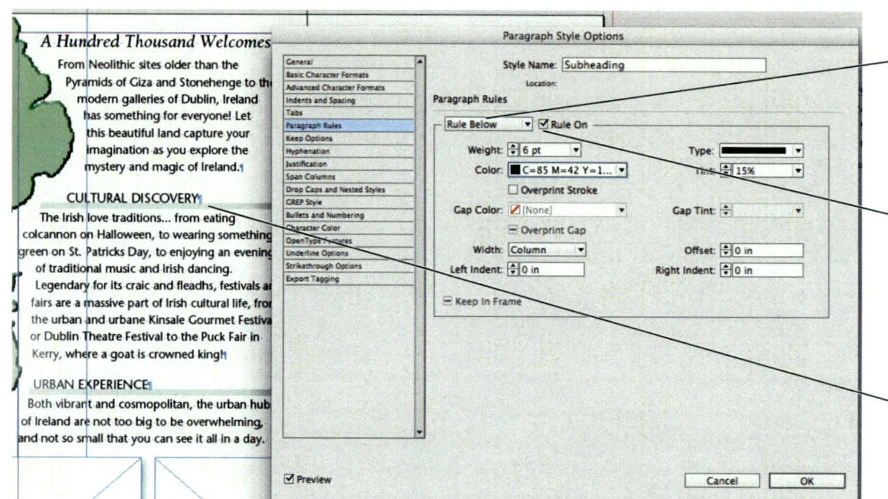

Choose Rule Above or Rule Below to change the settings for each rule.

Check this box to add the selected rule (above or below).

The active Preview option shows the result of adding the rule below the style.

6. **Change the Offset field to `-0.0625"`.**

   Before changing the Offset value:

   NATURAL WONDERS¶
   Known as the land that bo
   of green, the natural beaut

   After changing the Offset value:

   NATURAL WONDERS¶
   Known as the land that bo
   of green, the natural beaut

   By default, paragraph rules align to the baseline of the text. The Offset value moves the position of the rule relative to the baseline.

   - Using the Rule Below option, the top of the rule aligns to the baseline. Increasing the offset value moves the rule down away from the baseline; decreasing the baseline moves the rule up.
   - Using the Rule Above option, the bottom of the rule aligns to the baseline. Increasing the offset value moves the rule up away from the baseline; decreasing the baseline moves the rule down.

   The Width option defines whether the rule extends the length of the text in the paragraph or across the entire width of the column (or frame, if it's a one-column frame). You can also use the Left Indent and Right Indent fields to move the rule in from the column (or frame) edge by a specific distance.

Note:

Paragraph rules do not need to be applied as part of a style. You can apply paragraph rules to paragraphs in the layout by placing the insertion point and then choosing Paragraph Rules in the Paragraph panel Options menu.

7. **Click OK to close the dialog box and return to the layout.**

   By editing the style definition, you simultaneously changed the appearance of all four paragraphs formatted with the Subheading style.

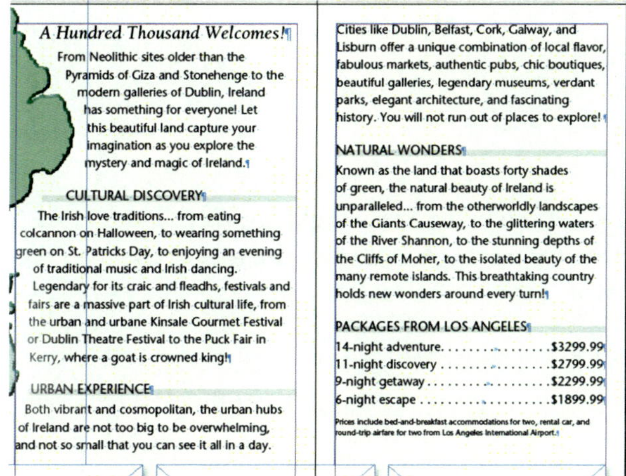

8. **Save the file and continue to the next exercise.**

Create Variations with Conditional Text

The concept of versioning is a growing segment of graphic design. Clients are using a single base document, adding varying content for different users based on specific demographics — geographic region, age, gender, or any other factor that differentiates one group from another. Other reasons for versioning include producing special editions of documents with content that does not appear on all copies; customization based on known information about past purchases or preferences; and even individual personalization using variable data to target individual users.

Rather than creating multiple versions of the same file, InDesign offers a number of options for creating variations within a single layout. To complete this project, you will use conditional text to create two variations of this brochure — one for East Coast clients and one for West Coast clients.

1. **With letterfold_ireland.indd open, make sure the inside spread is visible.**

2. **Open the Conditional Text panel (Window>Type & Tables>Conditional Text).**

3. **Click the New Condition button at the bottom of the panel. In the New Condition dialog box, type West Coast text in the Name field and then click OK.**

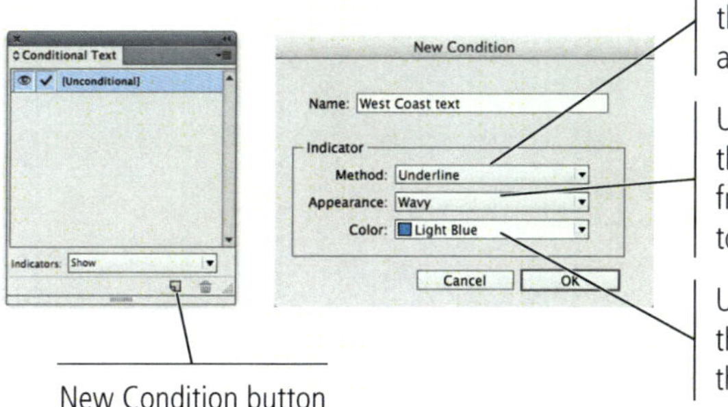

New Condition button

Use this menu to change the style of indicators from an underline to a highlight.

Use this menu to change the conditional indicator from the default Wavy style to the Solid or Dashed style.

Use this menu to change the color of indicators for the specific condition.

4. **Click the New Condition button again. In the New Condition dialog box, type East Coast text in the Name field and then click OK.**

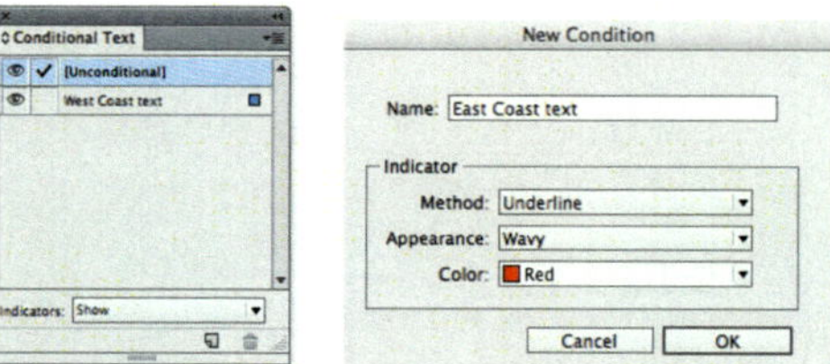

5. **In the text frame on Page 6, highlight all text related to packages from Los Angeles. Make sure you include the paragraph return at the end of the disclaimer copy as part of the selection.**

6. **Click West Coast text in the Conditional Text panel.**

   Applying a condition is as simple as selecting the targeted text and choosing the appropriate condition in the panel. The selected text is part of the condition, which you can turn off when you need to display the East Coast packages.

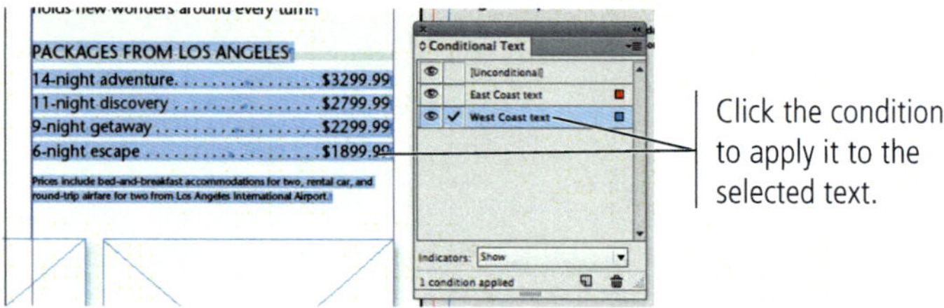

7. **Place the insertion point at the end of the active selection and review the text.**

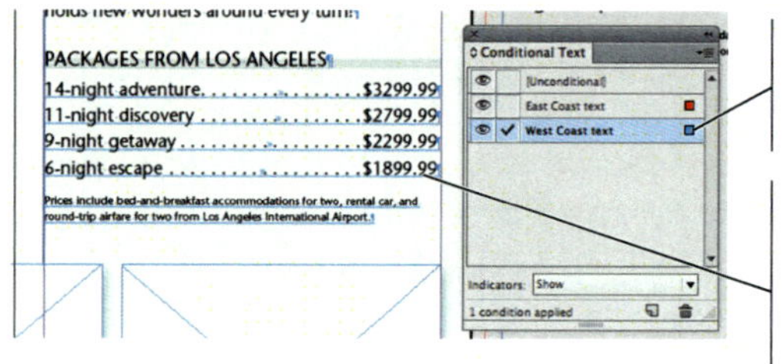

The color of conditional indicators matches the color of the item in the panel.

These lines are conditional-text indicators. They do not appear in the output unless you choose Show and Print in the Indicators menu of the Conditional Text panel.

Note:

You can print conditional indicators by choosing Show and Print in the Indicators menu of the Conditional Text panel.

8. **Click the Eye icon to the left of the West Coast text condition.**

   When you have multiple conditions in a file, only the visible conditions will be included in the output. By default, the conditional indicators do not appear on the output.

   When the West Coast conditional text is hidden, the "Packages from New York" list, which is part of the existing text thread, moves into place on Page 6.

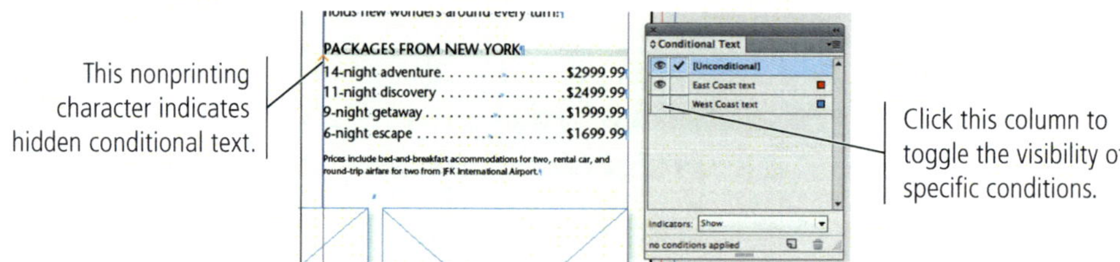

9. **Highlight all text related to the New York packages then click the East Coast text condition.**

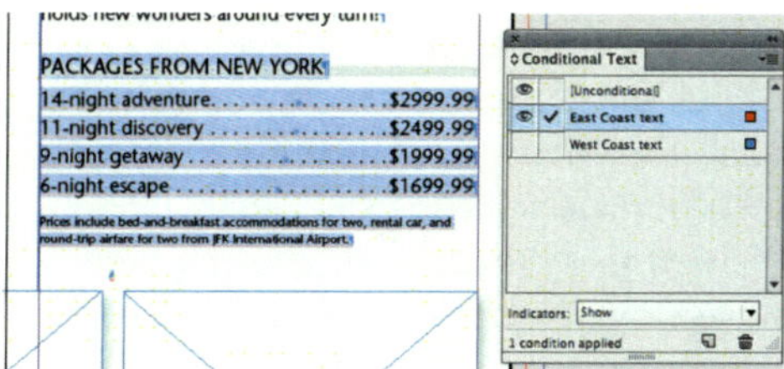

10. **Place the insertion point at the end of the active selection and review the text.**

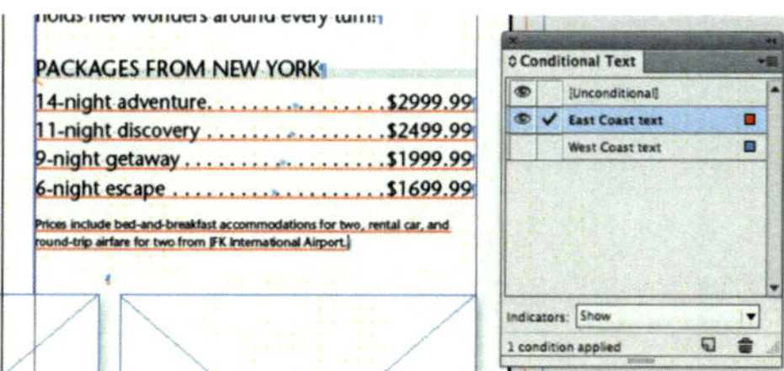

11. **Save the file and continue to the next exercise.**

Create Dynamic Captions

The final elements that need to be added to this layout are the four images at the bottom of the inside spread. The client wants to include captions to identify each location, but did not send any specific text for those captions; instead, they added titles to the various image files as metadata. In this exercise, you will generate captions directly in the layout based on the metadata that is defined for the placed images.

1. **With `letterfold_ireland.indd` open, make the inside spread visible in the document window.**

2. **With nothing selected in the document, choose File>Place. In the resulting dialog box, press Command/Control to select `blarney.tif`, `doonagore.tif`, `malahide.tif`, and `moher.tif`.**

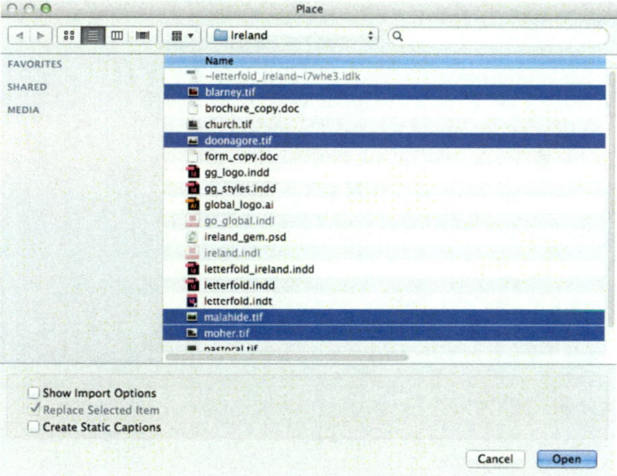

3. **Uncheck the Show Import Options box, then click Open to load the four selected images into the cursor.**

4. **Click in each of the four empty frames at the bottom of the spread to place the four loaded images.**

5. **Click the left image to select it, and then open the Links panel. Review the information in the lower half of the panel.**

   Files can include a wide range of metadata, including information about how and when the image was captured; file dimensions and resolution; color mode; and a number of other factors. You can also define custom metadata for a file, including a title, keywords, and descriptive text that make searching in a content management system easier. These images have all been assigned unique titles, which identifies the location shown in the image. You are going to use those titles to automatically generate captions in the layout.

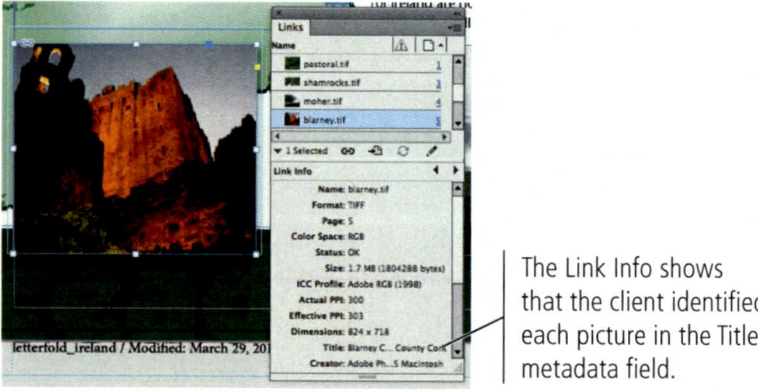

The Link Info shows that the client identified each picture in the Title metadata field.

6. **Choose Object>Captions>Caption Setup. In the resulting dialog box:**

   - **Choose Title in the Metadata menu.**

     You can use the empty text fields to define specific text before and after the selected metadata.

   - **Choose Below Image in the Alignment menu.**

     You can align the caption to the left, right, top, or bottom edge of the image frame.

   - **Change the Offset field to 0.0625″.**

     The offset determines how far the caption text appears from the image frame; it is applied as a text inset within the resulting caption frame.

   - **Choose Caption in the Paragraph Style menu.**

     You can use any existing paragraph style to automatically format the resulting caption.

   - **Check the Group Caption with Image option.**

     When this option is checked, the resulting caption frame is automatically grouped with the related image frame. When Group Caption with Image is *not* checked, you can use the Layer menu to choose a specific layer where the resulting caption frames will be placed; this is useful, for example, if you want to add captions for development purposes (file name, color mode, etc.) that you want to see but should not be included in client proofs or final output.

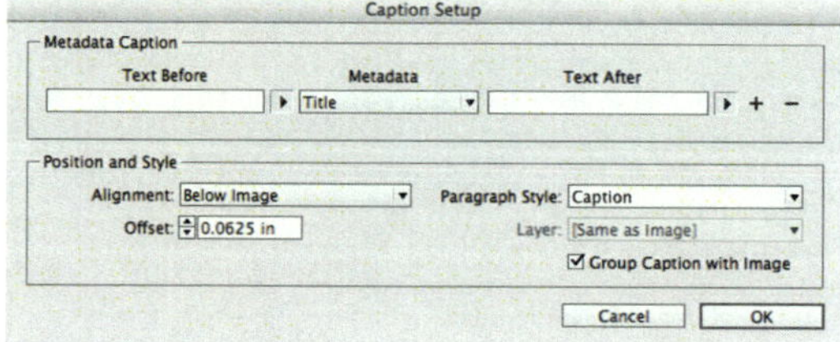

7. **Click OK to close the dialog box.**

   Nothing yet appears in the layout because you haven't yet created the captions.

Note:

Captions can be generated from a large number of available metadata fields:

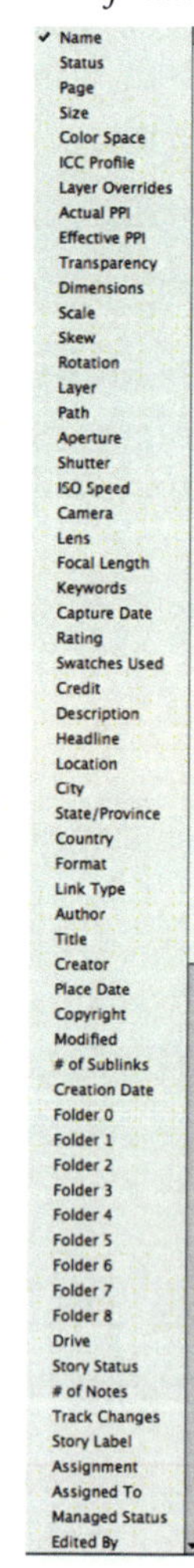

8. **With the left image selected, choose Object>Captions>Generate Live Caption.**

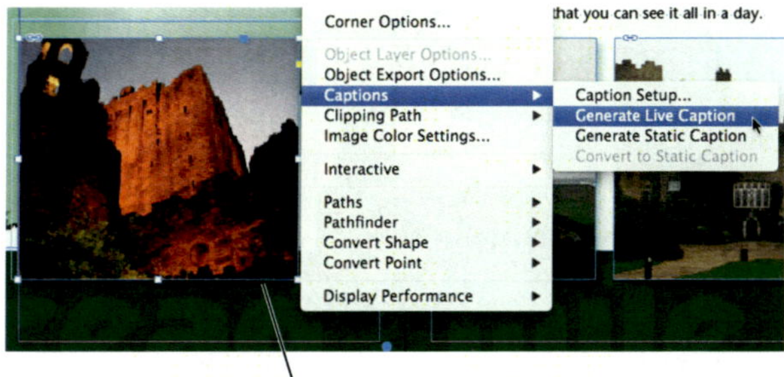

The caption does not appear until you generate it.

The caption, based on the Setup you just defined, is created in a new text frame.

9. **Select the other three image frames and choose Object>Captions>Generate Live Caption.**

   Once you have defined the caption setup in a file, you can apply the same setup to other images — including multiple selected images at once.

   The second image caption shows a placeholder that indicates the placed image has no defined Title metadata. This is referred to as an **unresolved caption variable**, and can be flagged as an error using the Preflight panel.

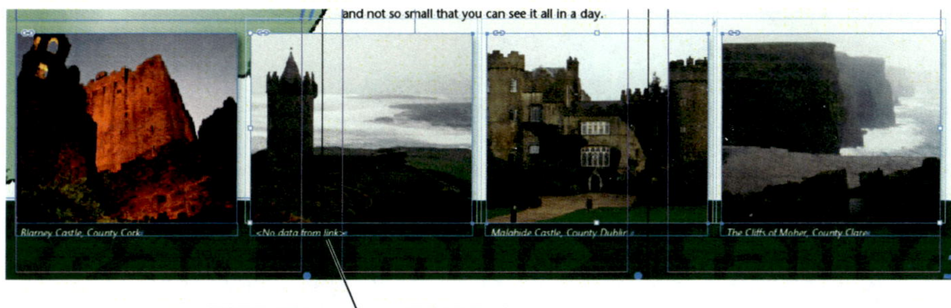

The caption shows that the file does not include the necessary metadata.

10. **Double-click the second image to select only the image frame within the group.**

11. **Choose File>Place. Select `church.tif` in the dialog box, check the Replace Selected Item option, and click Open.**

    Because you used the Live Caption option, the existing caption automatically changes to show the Title metadata for the replacement image.

Note:

If you used the Static Caption option, the caption would not change when you replace the image.

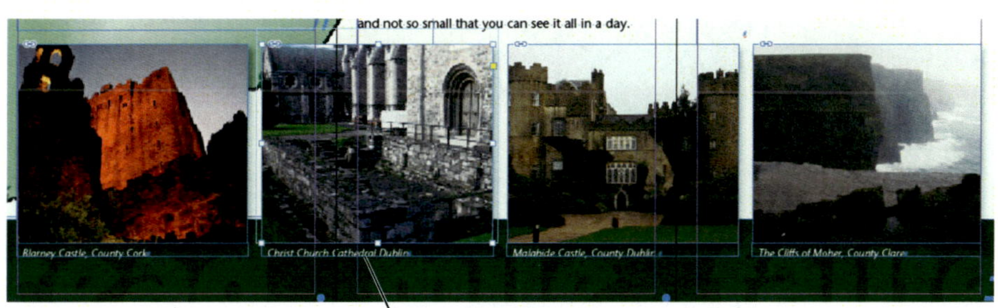

The Live Caption option allows the caption to automatically update when you replace the image.

12. **Save the file and continue to the next exercise.**

Clean and Finish the File

Almost every job requires some amount of clean-up work at the end, even if only to optimize your file. In this exercise, you perform this last check before creating a PDF file for the output provider.

1. **With `letterfold_ireland.indd` open, make the inside spread visible in the document window.**

2. **Choose View>Fit Spread in Window to review the entire spread at once.**

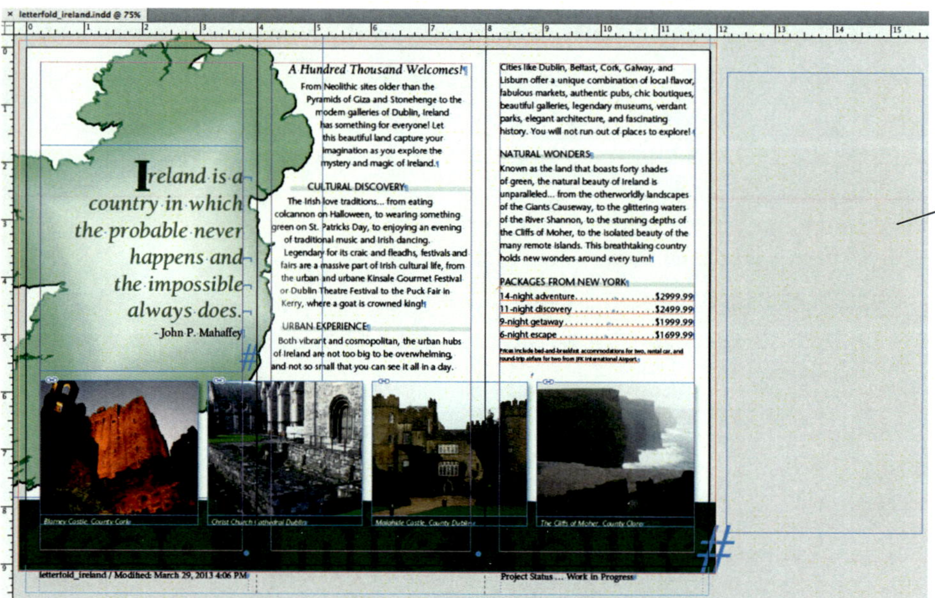

This text frame is no longer needed.

3. **Select the empty text frame on the right side of the pasteboard and press Delete/Backspace to remove it.**

   As a general rule, objects on the pasteboard should be removed before the file is considered "final." Since this frame is empty, you can simply delete it.

4. **Navigate to the outside spread.**

   Unlike the extraneous frame on the inside spread pasteboard, the outside spread has a very real problem — overset text in the form. You need to fix this problem before outputting the file.

This text frame has overset text.

> *Note:*
>
> *Leaving extraneous text and graphics on the pasteboard can trigger false alarms for missing fonts and graphics. It's a good idea to delete these objects to avoid unnecessary potential problems.*

5. **Zoom into the form at the bottom of Page 1.**

6. **Apply the style Form Heading to the first line in the form.**

7. **Place the insertion point at the beginning of the Zip paragraph. Press Delete/Backspace to make it part of the previous paragraph.**

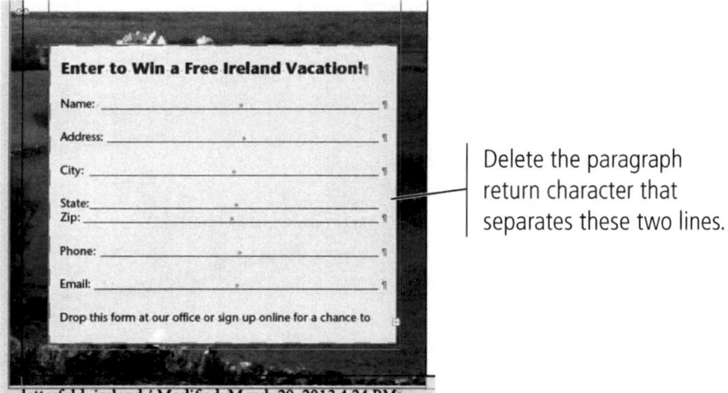

Delete the paragraph return character that separates these two lines.

8. **Choose Type>Tabs to open the Tabs panel.**

9. **Choose the Left-Justified Tab marker and then click to place a new tab stop at 2″. Type an underscore character (_) in the Leader field and press Return/Enter.**

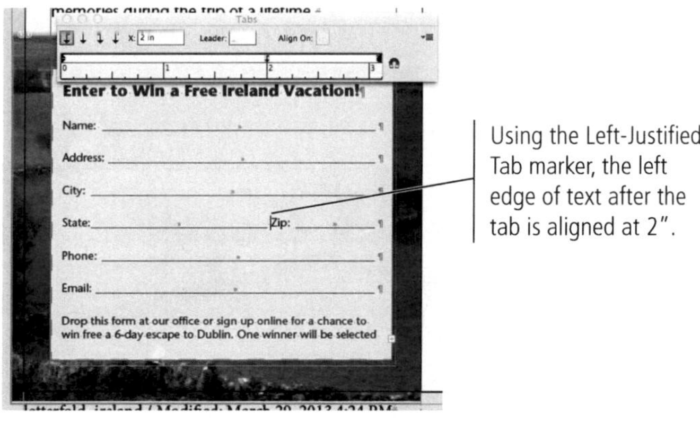

Using the Left-Justified Tab marker, the left edge of text after the tab is aligned at 2″.

10. **Apply the Form Disclaimer style to the last line in the frame.**

11. **Choose Type>Text Variables>Define.**

The Project Status variable that you defined in an earlier exercise allows you to monitor the status of the project while you work. As you finalize the project, you should change the variable to reflect the new status.

12. **Select Project Status in the list and click Edit. In the Text field, change "Work in Progress" to Finished.**

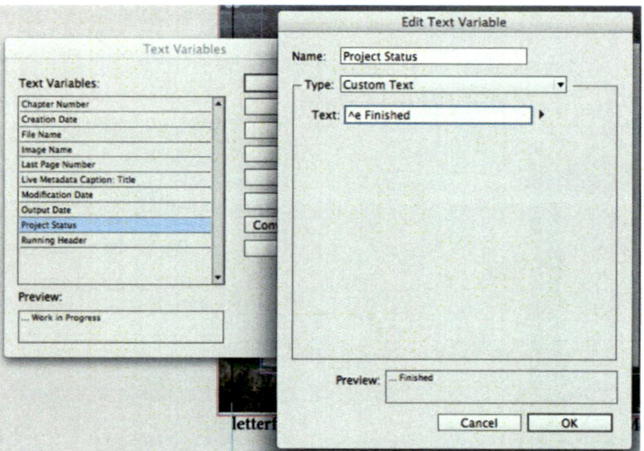

13. **Click OK, and then click Done to return to the layout.**

Because you placed the Project Status variable on each master page layout, changing the variable definition automatically changes all placed instances. Because you placed the variable instances on the master page layouts, the same change automatically reflects on the associated layout pages.

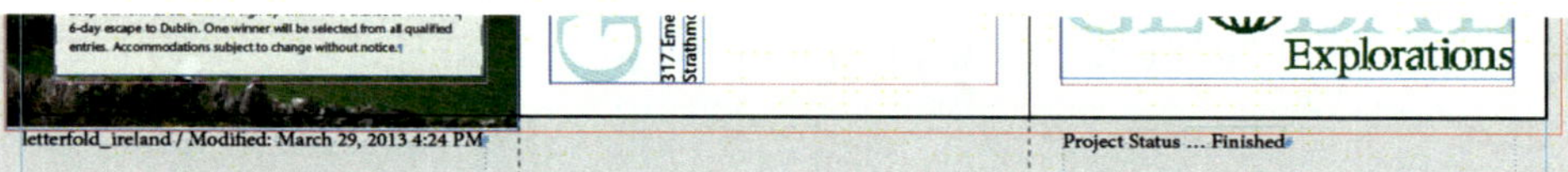

14. **Save the file and continue to the final exercise.**

Export Variations as PDF Files

The file is now complete and ready for output. To create the various versions of the file, you have to output the same file a number of times, selecting different conditions for each version.

1. **With letterfold_ireland.indd open, open the Conditional Text panel.**

2. **In the Conditional Text panel, show the West Coast text and hide the East Coast text condition.**

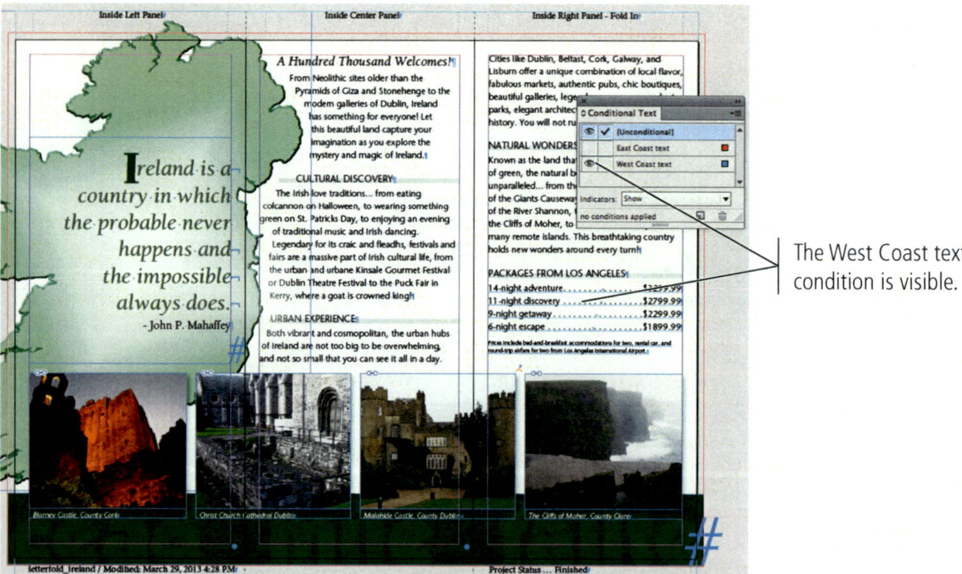

The West Coast text condition is visible.

3. **Choose File>Export. Change the file name to letterfold_ireland_west.pdf, and choose Adobe PDF (Print) in the Format/Save As Type menu. Click Save.**

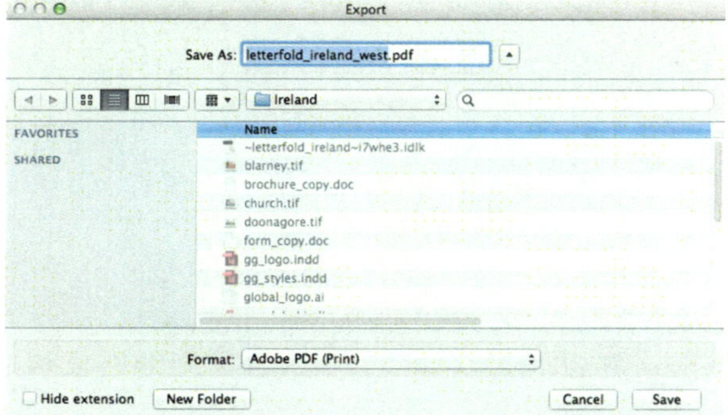

4. **In the resulting dialog box, choose Press Quality in the Preset menu.**

5. **In the General pane, make sure the All [pages] option is selected. Check the Spreads and View PDF After Exporting options.**

   Because you created each panel as a separate page, you need to export each entire spread as a single page in the resulting file.

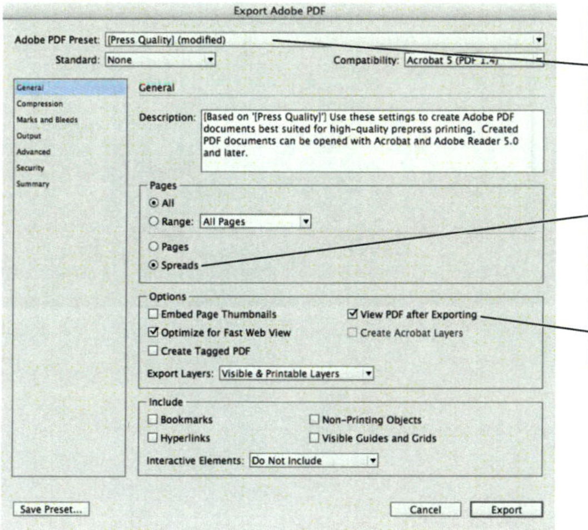

Start with the [Press Quality] preset; the [modified] indicator will appear when you change the Spreads option.

Check the Spreads option to output each side of the brochure as a single page in the PDF file.

Check this option to open the PDF when it is complete.

6. **In the Marks and Bleeds pane, turn on Crop Marks with a 0.125″ offset. Activate the Use Document Bleed Settings and Include Slug Area options.**

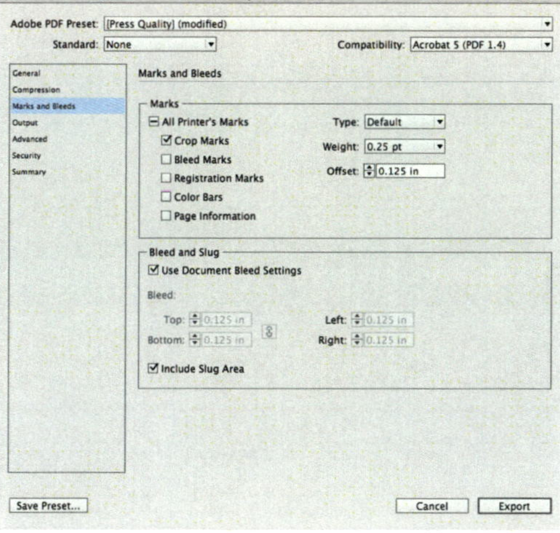

7. **Click the Save Preset button at the bottom of the Export Adobe PDF dialog box. In the resulting Save Preset dialog box, name the preset Ireland Brochure and click OK.**

You're going to export this file again; creating a preset means you need to make your export choices only once.

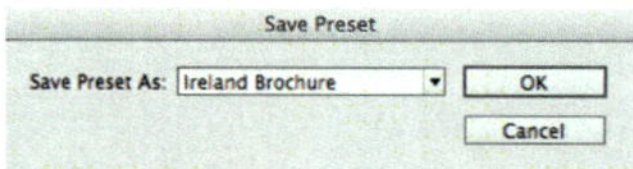

8. **Click Export to create the PDF file. Review the PDF file when it appears in Acrobat (or your default PDF reader application).**

Text frames in the upper slug areas are not included because you checked the Nonprinting option in the Attributes panel when you created them.

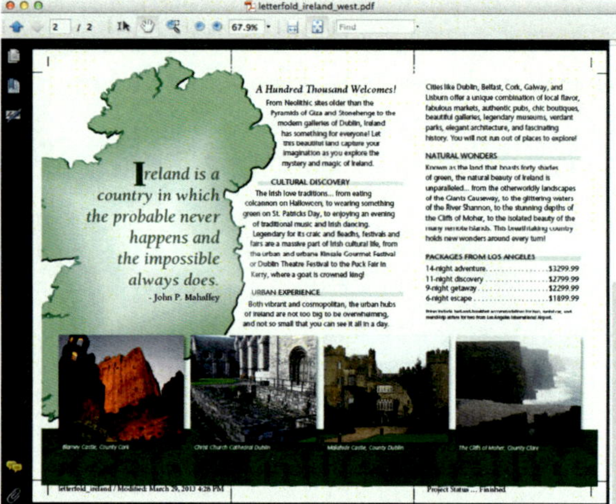

9. **Close the PDF file and return to InDesign.**

10. **In InDesign, hide the West Coast text condition and show the East Coast text condition.**

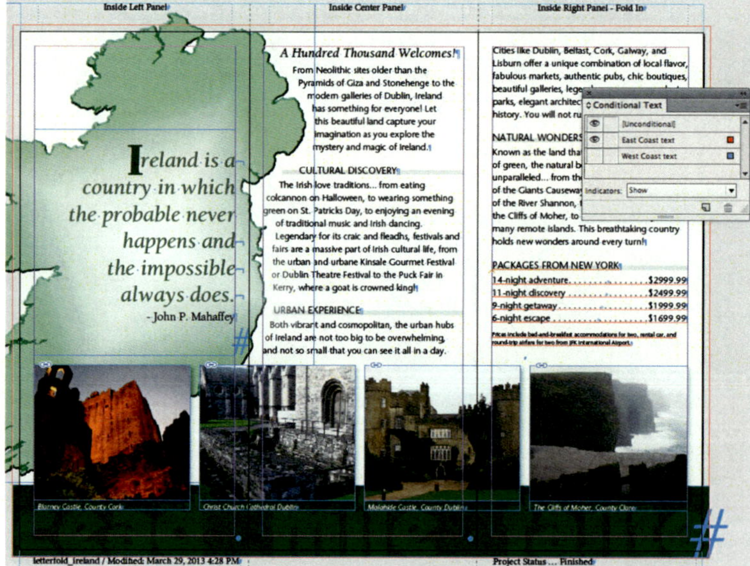

11. **Choose File>Export. Change the file name to letterfold_ireland_east.pdf and then click Save.**

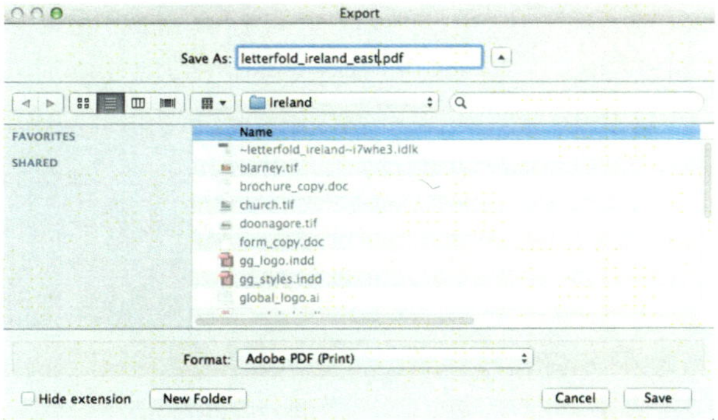

12. **Make sure Ireland Brochure is selected in the Adobe PDF Preset menu and click Export.**

When you reopen the Export Adobe PDF dialog box, the Ireland Brochure preset should be already selected; the menu remembers the last-used settings. The preset calls all the same options that you already defined.

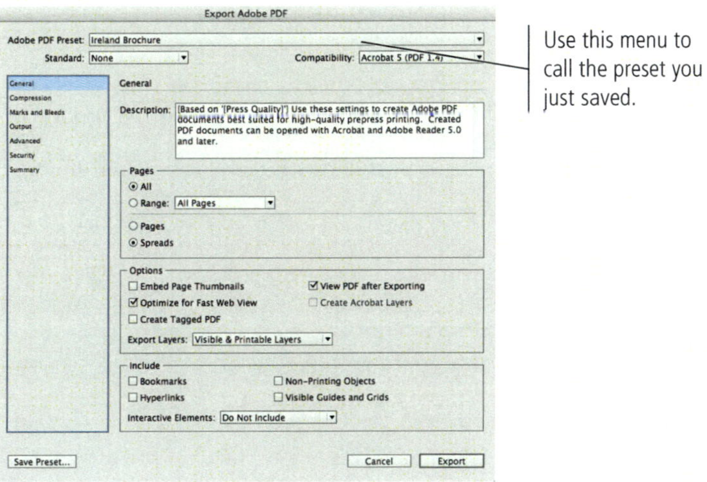

Use this menu to call the preset you just saved.

13. **Review the PDF file, then close it and return to InDesign.**

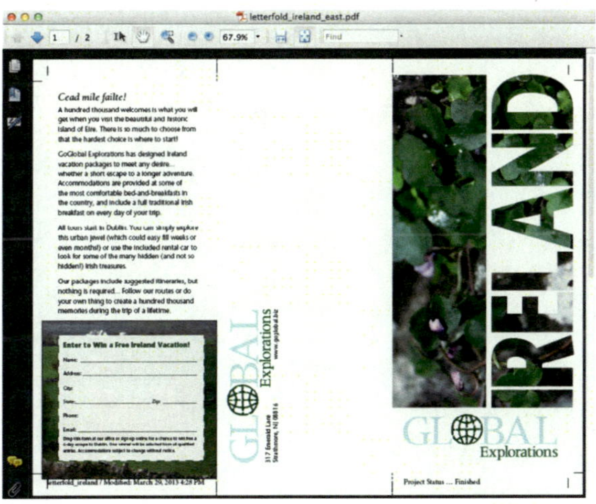

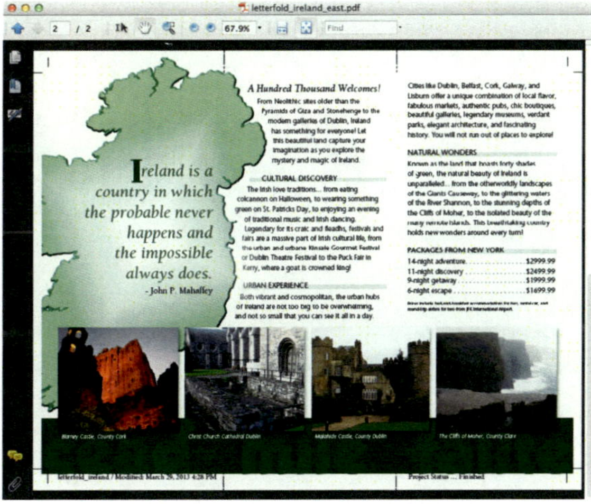

14. **Save and close the letterfold_ireland file.**

Project Review

fill in the blank

1. A(n) _______________ folds three times, resulting in four panels on each side of the sheet. The paper is folded in half, and then each half is folded in half toward the center so the two ends of the paper meet at the center fold.

2. A(n) _______________ can be used to place information such as creation/modification date, file name, or custom text.

3. A(n) _______________ is a spread with more than two pages.

4. You can use the _______________ panel to define whether certain objects are printed when the job is output.

5. The _______________ is used to modify the dimensions of a master page.

6. A(n) _______________ is a special visual treatment for text that is either pulled from the story or somehow supports surrounding text.

7. A(n) _______________ caption will not change if you replace one image with another in a layout.

8. A(n) _______________ can be used to define multiple styles that will be used for different portions of the same paragraph, based on specific sequences of characters or markers.

9. A(n) _______________ is used to format entire lines of text within a single paragraph.

10. A(n) _______________ can be used to apply the same attributes (such as text wrap and stroke weight) to multiple text frames.

short answer

1. Briefly explain the rules of page geometry regarding panels that fold into other panels in a folding document.

2. Explain three different ways that text formatting styles might appear in an InDesign file.

3. Describe two scenarios in which multiple page sizes in a document might be useful.

Portfolio Builder Project

Use what you learned in this project to complete the following freeform exercise.
Carefully read the art director and client comments, then create your own design to meet the needs of the project.
Use the space below to sketch ideas; when finished, write a brief explanation of your reasoning behind your final design.

art director comments

Your client, the owner of Blue Moon Café, has hired you to redesign the look of the café's menus. The new menu design should reflect the gourmet style of the ocean-front bistro.

- ❑ Determine the best size and shape to present the menu content. The menu should be contained on a single sheet, but it can be printed on both sides of the sheet.
- ❑ Design a template that you can reuse to create the bistro's new breakfast, lunch, and dinner menus once the layout is approved.
- ❑ Use the client's provided text (in the **IDCC_PB_Project5.zip** archive on the Student Files Web page) to design the catering menu and present the new layout.
- ❑ You must use the client's supplied logo. You can use some or all of the photos that were provided by the client, or you can find or create your own images to illustrate the menu.

client comments

We used to have a huge menu with more than 100 options listed on eight pages. The menu included all three meals at once, and it was a nightmare for our customers to decide what they wanted.

We've decided to simplify both the meals that we offer and the way the options are presented. We're going to separate out our menus for each meal — breakfast, lunch, and dinner — and we want each menu to be on a single sheet of paper.

We also need a fourth menu to present our breakfast catering options, which is a huge segment of our business. We actually want you to start with that one and then move on to the bistro offerings once we've settled on a basic design.

We would like to be able to print and reprint the menus at the local quick-print shop since they get messy very quickly. The owner advised using standard-size paper (letter- or tabloid-size) with no bleeds to keep down the printing cost. He also suggested that the paper not be cut, although it can be folded in halves or thirds at very little extra cost.

project justification

Project Summary

This project built on the skills you learned in previous projects. To begin the letterfold layout, you built a technically accurate folding guide by taking advantage of InDesign's ability to incorporate multiple page sizes into a single layout. You also incorporated dashed fold guides and nonprinting text frames into the slug area. To speed up the process for the next time you need to build one of these common jobs, you saved your initial work as a template.

You also learned about several more options for improving workflow. Object styles allow you to store and apply multiple frame-formatting options (including nested paragraph styles) with a single click. Libraries store entire objects or groups of objects (including their formatting and even contents) so you can place as many instances as necessary on any page of any file.

Finally, you learned about a number of advanced text-formatting options, including importing styles from another InDesign document, creating a complex text wrap, converting text to frames, building a nested paragraph style, formatting tabs and paragraph rules, and even adding dynamic image captions based on information that is stored in a placed image.

project 6

Digital Layout Variations

You have been hired to create four different versions of a brochure for the local city government to promote the redevelopment and rebranding of its downtown area. You need to create a color-managed print brochure with a metallic spot color; a digitally distributed PDF with an interactive slideshow and form; an e-book that can be used on popular e-reader devices; and an HTML file that can be fed into the client's Web site.

This project incorporates the following skills:

- ❑ Managing color in a print layout
- ❑ Searching for and replacing text and object attributes
- ❑ Defining hyperlinks for digital output
- ❑ Creating an interactive slideshow
- ❑ Creating PDF form fields
- ❑ Exporting an interactive PDF file
- ❑ Preparing files for e-book and Web publishing
- ❑ Exporting EPUB and HTML files

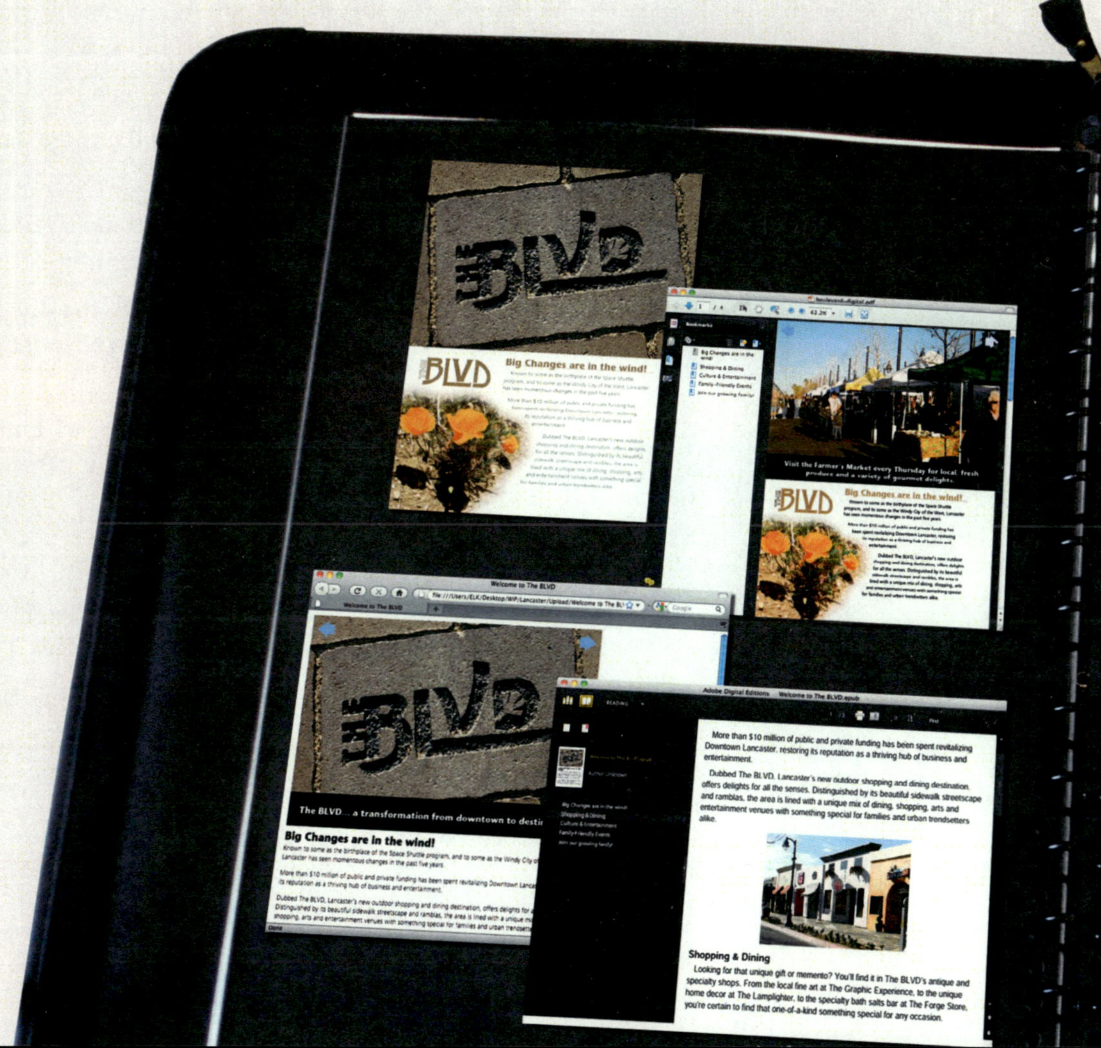

Project Meeting

client comments

We just heard from the printer that we can only use one spot color based on the quote he provided. The logo uses two different spot colors, and those are used throughout the layout as well. We decided to keep the metallic gold, but we need you to change the other one.

Now that it's official, we'd also like to use the actual name "The BLVD" rather than just saying "Downtown Lancaster" in most places.

Once you've finalized the print file, we need you to use the same content to create a PDF we can email to people, an e-book we can distribute, and an HTML file that we can add into the content area of our Web site.

We have a lot of great pictures from Charlie Essers, a local photographer. We weren't able to use them all in the print version, but we'd like to show as much as we can in the digital PDF and on the Web site.

We'd also like the form on the final page to actually function as a form in the file we email to people. There's no point making people print something out when they can just submit the form by email.

art director comments

You have a lot of work to do, but InDesign has the tools to make all of this possible in the same layout. Of course, so many different versions do require some careful planning and attention to detail.

The only thing you won't be able to establish in InDesign is the form distribution settings. We'll have to set that up in Acrobat, but you can still define the necessary form fields right in the layout.

Layers are a great choice for managing interactive content that won't work in the print layout. If you set everything up properly, you'll be able to accomplish all four versions without saving separate files for different output media.

project objectives

- ❑ Review the colors in the existing file
- ❑ Search for and change specific content and attributes
- ❑ Export a color-managed PDF file for commercial printing
- ❑ Prepare layers to manage static and interactive content in the same file
- ❑ Define hyperlinks and other interactive elements as necessary for digital document delivery
- ❑ Create PDF form fields
- ❑ Export an interactive PDF file
- ❑ Define a table of contents for EPUB navigation
- ❑ Link images to text for EPUB and HTML export
- ❑ Create an interactive slideshow
- ❑ Export an e-book in EPUB format
- ❑ Export the document to HTML for Web publishing

Stage 1 Controlling Color for Output

You can't accurately reproduce color without some understanding of color theory, so we present a very basic introduction in the following pages. We highly recommend that you read this information. Be aware that there are entire, weighty books written about color science; we're providing the condensed version of what you absolutely must know to work effectively with color.

While it's true that color management science can be extremely complex and beyond the needs of most graphic designers, applying color management in InDesign is more intimidating than difficult. We believe this foundational knowledge of color management will make you a more effective and practically grounded designer.

Additive vs. Subtractive Color Models

The most important thing to remember about color theory is that color is light, and light is color. You can easily demonstrate this by walking through your house at midnight; you will notice that what little you can see appears as dark shadows. Without light, you can't see — and without light, there is no color.

The **additive color** model (RGB) is based on the idea that all colors can be reproduced by combining pure red, green, and blue light in varying intensities. These three colors are considered the additive primaries. Combining any two additive primaries at full strength produces one of the additive secondaries — red and blue light combine to produce magenta, red and green combine to produce yellow, and blue and green combine to produce cyan. Although usually considered a "color," black is the absence of light (and, therefore, of color). White is the sum of all colors, produced when all three additive primaries are combined at full strength.

Note:

Additive color theory is practically applied when a reproduction method uses light to reproduce color. A television screen or computer monitor is black when turned off. When the power is turned on, light in the monitor illuminates at different intensities to create the range of colors that you see.

Printing pigmented inks on a substrate is a very different method of reproducing color. Reproducing color on paper requires **subtractive color** theory, which is essentially the inverse of additive color theory. Instead of adding red, green, and blue light to create the range of colors, subtractive color begins with a white surface that reflects red, green, and blue light at equal and full strength. To reflect (reproduce) a specific color, you add pigments that subtract or absorb only certain wavelengths from the white light. To reflect only red, for example, the surface must subtract (or absorb) the green and blue light.

Additive color model

Remember that the additive primaries (red, green, and blue) combine to create the additive secondaries (cyan, magenta, and yellow). Those additive secondaries are also called the subtractive primaries because each subtracts one-third of the light spectrum and reflects the other two-thirds:

- Cyan absorbs red light, reflecting only blue and green light.
- Magenta absorbs green light, reflecting only red and blue light.
- Yellow absorbs blue light, reflecting only red and green light.

A combination of two subtractive primaries, then, absorbs two-thirds of the light spectrum and reflects only one-third. As an example, a combination of yellow and magenta absorbs both blue and green light, reflecting only red.

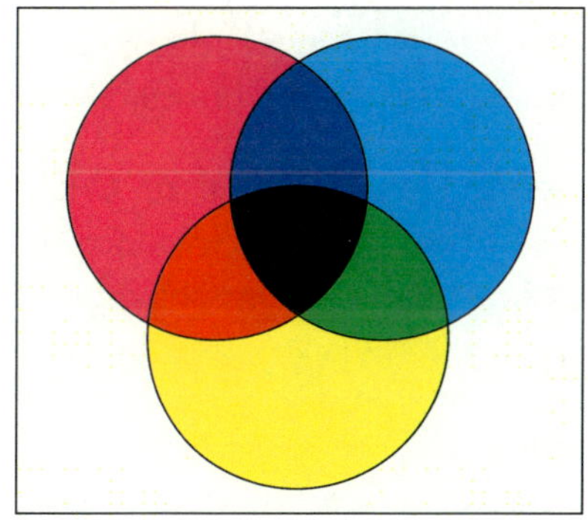

Subtractive color model

Color printing is a practical application of subtractive color theory. The pigments in the cyan, magenta, yellow, and black inks are combined to absorb different wavelengths of light. To create the appearance of red, the green and blue light must be subtracted or absorbed, thus reflecting only red. Magenta absorbs green light, and yellow absorbs blue light; combining magenta and yellow inks on white paper reflects only the red light. By combining different amounts of the subtractive primaries, it's possible to produce a large range (or gamut) of colors.

Because white is a combination of all colors, white paper should theoretically reflect equal percentages of all light wavelengths. However, different papers absorb or reflect varying percentages of some wavelengths, thus defining the paper's apparent color. The paper's color affects the appearance of ink colors printed on that paper.

Understanding Gamut

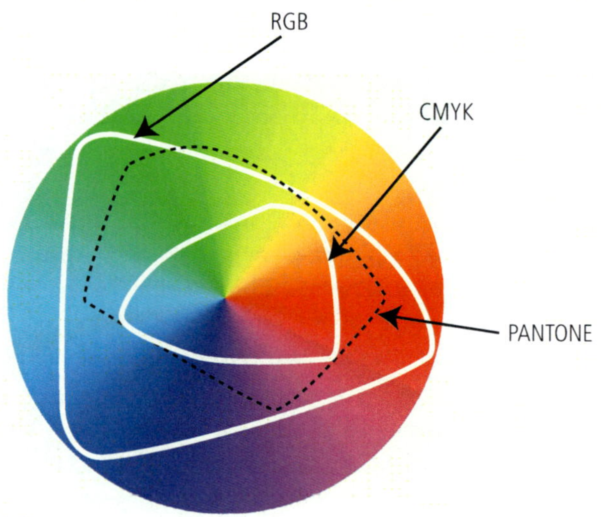

Different color models have different ranges or **gamuts** of possible colors. A normal human visual system is capable of distinguishing approximately 16.7 million different colors. Color reproduction systems, however, are far more limited. The RGB model has the largest gamut of the output models. The CMYK gamut is far more limited; many of the brightest and most saturated colors that can be reproduced using light cannot be reproduced using pigmented inks.

This difference in gamut is one of the biggest problems graphic designers face when working with color images. Digital image-capture devices (including scanners and digital cameras) work in the RGB space, which, with its larger gamut, can more closely mirror the range of colors in the original scene. Printing, however, requires images to be first converted or separated into the CMYK color space.

The usual goal in color reproduction is to achieve a color appearance equivalent to the original. Depending on the images, it is likely that at least some colors in the RGB model cannot be reproduced in the more limited gamut of the CMYK color model. These out-of-gamut colors pose a challenge to faithfully reproducing the original image. If the conversion from RGB to CMYK is not carefully controlled, color shift can result in drastic differences between the original and the printed images.

> ***Note:***
>
> *Color shift can also result when converting from one CMYK profile to another (e.g., a sheetfed press profile to a web press profile), or (though less likely) from one version of RGB to another. Whatever models are being used, color management gives you better control over the conversion process.*

Color Management in Brief

Color management is intended to preserve color predictability and consistency as a file is moved from one color mode to another throughout the reproduction process. Color management can also eliminate ambiguity when a color is specified by only some numbers. For example, you might create a royal purple in the Swatches panel; without color management, that same set of RGB numbers might look more lilac (or even gray) when converted to CMYK for printing. A well-tuned color management system can translate the numbers that define a color in one space to numbers that can better represent that same color in another space.

It's important to have realistic expectations of color management, and to realize that color management isn't a replacement for a thorough understanding of the color-reproduction process. Even at its best, color management can't fix bad scans or bad photos — all it can do is provide consistency and predictability to a process that otherwise rarely has either.

Color management relies on color profiles, which are data sets that define the reproduction characteristics of a specific device. A profile is essentially a recipe that contains the ingredients for reproducing a specific color in a given color space. The color recipes in profiles are known as look-up tables (LUTs), which are essentially cross-reference systems for finding matching color values in different color spaces.

Source profiles are the profiles of the devices (scanners, digital cameras, etc.) used to capture an image. **Destination profiles** are the profiles of output devices. LAB (or L*a*b*, or CIELAB) is a device-independent, theoretical color space that represents the entire visible spectrum. The color management engine uses LAB as an intermediate space to translate colors from one device-dependent space to another.

The mechanics of color-managed conversions are simple. Regardless of the specific input and output spaces in question, the same basic process is followed for every pixel in the image:

1. The color-management engine looks up the color values of a pixel in the source (input-space) profile to find a matching set of LAB values.
2. The color-management engine looks up the LAB values in the destination (output-space) profile to find the matching set of color values that will display the color of that pixel as accurately as possible in the output space.

Note:

Color profiles are sometimes called "ICC profiles," named after the International Color Consortium (ICC), which developed the standard for creating color profiles.

Note:

Most professional-level devices come with profiles you can install when you install the hardware; a number of generic and industry-specific destination profiles are also built into InDesign.

INDESIGN FOUNDATIONS

Color Management in Theory and Practice

RGB and CMYK are very different entities. The two color models have distinct capabilities, advantages, and limitations. There is no way to exactly reproduce RGB color using the CMYK gamut because many of the colors in the RGB gamut are simply too bright or too saturated. Rather than claiming to produce an exact (but impossible) match from your monitor to a printed page, the true goal of color management is to produce the best possible representation of the color using the gamut of the chosen output device.

A theoretically ideal color-managed workflow looks like this:

- Image-capture devices (scanners and digital cameras) are profiled to create a look-up table that defines the device's color-capturing characteristics.
- Images are acquired using a profiled device. The profile of the capturing device is tagged to every image captured.
- You define a destination (CMYK) profile for the calibrated output device that will be used for your final job.
- InDesign translates the document and embedded image profiles to the defined destination profiles.

This ideal workflow mentions the word "calibrate," which means to check and correct the device's characteristics. Calibration is an essential element in a color-managed workflow; it is fundamentally important to consistent and predictable output.

Taking this definition a step further, you cannot check or correct the color characteristics of a device without having something to compare the device against. To calibrate a device, a known target — usually a sequence of distinct and varying color patches — is reproduced using the device. The color values of the reproduction are measured and compared to the values of the known target. Precise calibration requires adjusting the device until the reproduction matches the original.

As long as your devices are accurately calibrated to the same target values, the color acquired by your RGB scanner will match the colors displayed on your RGB monitor and the colors printed by your CMYK desktop printer. Of course, most devices (especially consumer-level desktop devices, which are gaining a larger market share in the commercial graphics world) are not accurately calibrated, and very few are calibrated to the same set of known target values.

Keeping in mind these ideals and realities, the true goals of color management are to:

- Compensate for color variations in the different devices
- Accurately translate one color space to another
- Compensate for limitations in the output process
- Better predict the final outcome when a file is reproduced

One final note: It's important to realize that color perception is a function of the human visual system. Many people perceive color differently, and some have deficiencies in one or more ranges of the spectrum. Despite your best efforts at color management, your client might perceive color differently than what you see.

Define Application Color Settings

InDesign's color management options allow you to integrate InDesign into a color-managed workflow. This includes managing the color profiles of placed images, as well as previewing potential color problems on screen before the job is actually output.

There are two primary purposes for managing color in InDesign: previewing colors based on the intended output device and converting colors to the appropriate space when a file is output (whether to PDF or an output device for commercial printing).

1. **With no file open in InDesign, choose Edit>Color Settings.**

   The Color Settings dialog box defines default working spaces for RGB and CMYK colors, as well as general color management policies.

   The RGB working space defines the default profile for RGB colors and images that do not have embedded profiles. The CMYK working space defines the profile for the device or process that will be used to output the job.

2. **Choose North America Prepress 2 in the Settings menu.**

   InDesign includes a number of common option groups, which you can access in the Settings menu. You can also make your own choices and save those settings as a new preset by clicking Save, or you can import settings files created by another user by clicking Load.

   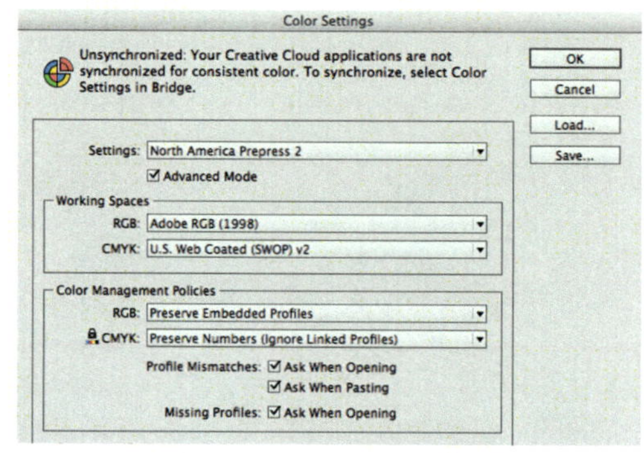

   A working space is a specific profile that defines color values in the associated mode. Using Adobe RGB (1998), for example, means new RGB colors in the InDesign file and imported RGB images without embedded profiles will be described by the values in the Adobe RGB (1998) space.

Note:

The Adobe RGB (1998) space is a neutral color space that isn't related to a specific monitor's display capabilities. Using this space assumes you are making color decisions on numeric values, not by what you see on your monitor.

3. **In the CMYK menu, choose U.S. Sheetfed Coated v2.**

   There are many CMYK profiles; each output device has a gamut unique to that individual device. U.S. Sheetfed Coated v2 is an industry-standard profile for a common type of printing (sheetfed printing on coated paper). In a truly color-managed workflow, you would actually use a profile for the specific press/paper combination being used for the job. (We're using one of the default profiles to show you how the process works.)

Note:

The Working Spaces menus identify exactly which version of each space defines color within that space.

4. **In the Color Management Policies, make sure Preserve Embedded Profiles is selected for RGB, and Preserve Numbers (Ignore Linked Profiles) is selected for CMYK.**

   These options tell InDesign what to do when you open existing files, or if you copy elements from one file to another.

   - When an option is turned off, color is not managed for objects or files in that color mode.
   - **Preserve Embedded Profiles** maintains the profile information saved in the file; files with no profile use the current working space.
   - If you choose **Convert to Working Space**, files automatically convert to the working space defined at the top of the Color Settings dialog box.
   - For CMYK colors, you can choose **Preserve Numbers (Ignore Linked Profiles)** to maintain raw CMYK numbers (ink percentages) rather than adjusting the colors based on an embedded profile.

5. **Check all three options under the Color Management Policies menus.**

The check boxes control InDesign's behavior when you open an existing file or paste an element from a document with a profile other than the defined working space (called a profile mismatch), or when you open a file that does not have an embedded profile (called a missing profile).

6. **If it is not already checked, activate the Advanced Mode check box (below the Settings menu).**

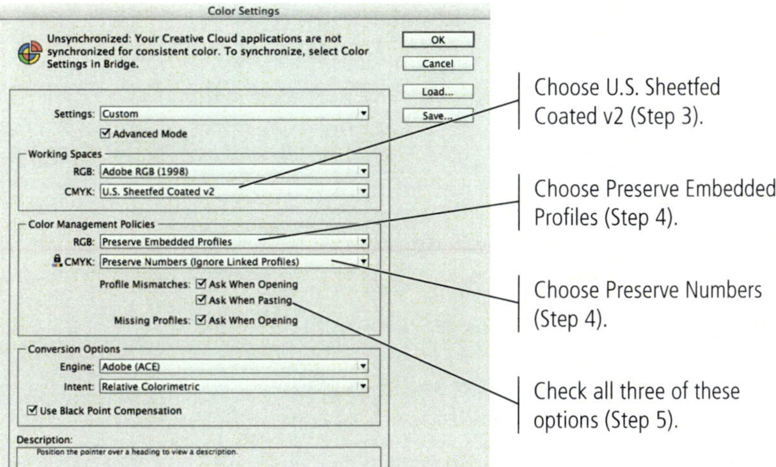

Choose U.S. Sheetfed Coated v2 (Step 3).

Choose Preserve Embedded Profiles (Step 4).

Choose Preserve Numbers (Step 4).

Check all three of these options (Step 5).

The Engine option determines the system and color-matching method for converting between color spaces:

- **Adobe (ACE)**, the default, stands for Adobe Color Engine.
- **Apple CMM** (Macintosh only) uses the Apple ColorSync engine.
- **Microsoft ICM** (Windows only) uses the Microsoft ICM engine.

The **Intent** menu defines how the engine translates source colors outside the gamut of the destination profile.

When the **Use Black Point Compensation** option is selected, the full range of the source space is mapped into the full-color range of the destination space. This method can result in blocked or grayed-out shadows, but it is most useful when the black point of the source is darker than that of the destination.

7. **Click OK to apply your settings, then continue to the next exercise.**

Understanding Rendering Intents

INDESIGN FOUNDATIONS

LAB color has the largest gamut, RGB the next largest, and CMYK the smallest. If you need to convert an image from an RGB space to a more limited CMYK space, you need to tell the CMS how to handle any colors that exist outside the CMYK space. You can do this by specifying the **rendering intent** that will be used when you convert colors.

- **Perceptual** presents a visually pleasing representation of the image, preserving visual relationships between colors. All colors in the image — including those available in the destination gamut — are shifted to maintain the proportional relationship within the image.
- **Saturation** compares the saturation of colors in the source profile and shifts them to the nearest-possible saturated color in the destination profile. The focus is on saturation instead of actual color value, which means this method can produce drastic color shift.
- **Relative Colorimetric** maintains any colors in both the source and destination profiles; source colors outside the destination gamut are shifted to fit. This method adjusts for the whiteness of the media and is a good choice when most source colors are in-gamut.
- **Absolute Colorimetric** maintains colors in both the source and destination profiles. Colors outside the destination gamut are shifted to a color within the destination gamut without considering the white point of the media.

Assign Color Settings to an Existing File

This project requires working on a file that has already been started, so some work has been completed before the file was handed off to you. To manage the process throughout the rest of this project, you need to make sure the existing file has the same color settings that you just defined.

1. **Download IDCC_RF_Project6.zip from the Student Files Web page.**

2. **Expand the ZIP archive in your WIP folder (Macintosh) or copy the archive contents into your WIP folder (Windows).**

   This results in a folder named **Lancaster**, which contains the files you need for this project. You should also use this folder to save the files you create in this project.

3. **Open the file boulevard.indd from the WIP>Lancaster folder.**

4. **If you get a warning about missing or modified images, update the links once the file opens.**

   All the required images are available in the WIP>Lancaster>Links folder.

5. **In the Profile or Policy Mismatch dialog box, select the second option (Adjust the document to match current color settings).**

   The existing file has neither a defined RGB nor a CMYK profile. Because you activated the Ask When Opening option in the Color Settings dialog box, InDesign asks how you want to handle RGB color in the file.

   This option assigns the existing RGB color settings (which you defined in the previous exercise) to the existing file.

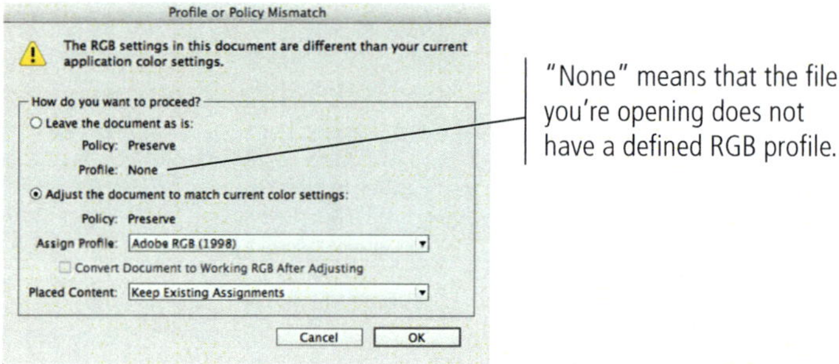

"None" means that the file you're opening does not have a defined RGB profile.

6. **Leave the remaining options at their default values and click OK.**

   Again, your choice in the Color Settings dialog box was to Ask When Opening if a file was missing a CMYK profile. Because the file does not have a defined CMYK profile, you see that warning now.

7. **In the second warning message, choose the second radio button (Adjust the document to match current color settings).**

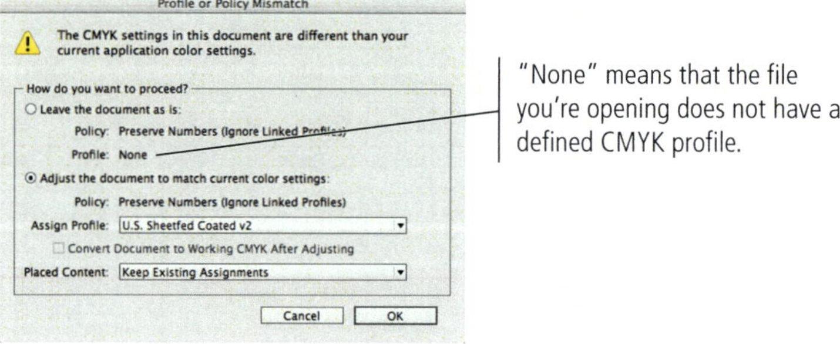

"None" means that the file you're opening does not have a defined CMYK profile.

8. **Click OK to open the file.**

This file contains the layout for a four-page brochure.

9. **Save the file and continue to the next exercise.**

Assigning and Converting Color Profiles

If you need to change the working RGB or CMYK space in a document, you can use either the Assign Profiles (Edit>Assign Profiles) or Convert to Profile (Edit>Convert to Profile) dialog box. Although these two dialog boxes have slightly different appearances, most of the functionality is exactly the same.

In the Assign Profiles dialog box:

- **Discard (Use Current Working Space)** removes the current profile from the document. This option is useful if you do not want to color manage the document. Colors will be defined by the current working space, but the profile is not embedded in the document.
- **Assign Current Working Space** embeds the working space profile in the document.
- **Assign Profile** allows you to define a specific profile other than the working space profile. However, colors are not converted to the new space, which can dramatically change the appearance of the colors as displayed on your monitor.

You can also define different rendering intents for solid colors, placed raster images, and transparent elements that result from blending modes, effects, or transparency settings. All three Intent menus default to use the intent defined in the Color Settings dialog box, but you can change any or all menus to a specific intent.

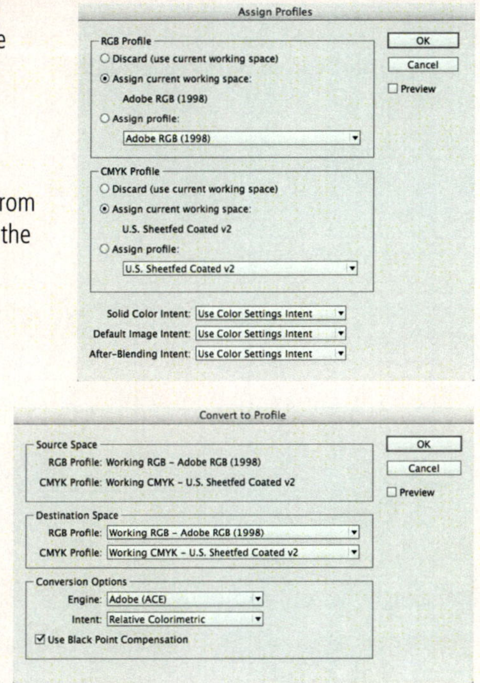

In the Convert to Profile dialog box, the menus can be used to change the RGB and CMYK destination spaces. This is basically the same as using the Assign Profile options in the Assign Profiles dialog box. You can also change the color management engine, rendering intent, and black point compensation options.

Preview Separations

To be entirely confident in color output, you should check the separations that will be created when your file is output to an imagesetter. InDesign's Separations Preview panel makes this easy to accomplish from directly within the application workspace.

1. **With boulevard.indd open, choose Window>Output>Separations Preview.**

2. **In the View menu of the Separations Preview panel, choose Separations.**

   When Separations is selected in the View menu, all separations in the current file are listed in the panel. You can turn individual separations on and off to preview the different ink separations that will be created:

   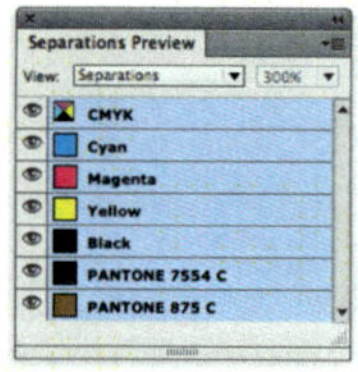

   - To view a single separation and hide all others, click the name of the separation you want to view. By default, areas of coverage appear in black; you can preview separations in color by toggling off the Show Single Plates in Black command in the panel Options menu.
   - To view more than one separation at the same time, click the empty space to the left of the separation name. When viewing multiple separations, each separation is shown in color.
   - To hide a separation, click the eye icon to the left of the separation name.
   - To view all process plates at once, click the CMYK option at the top of the panel.

3. **Click Pantone 875 C in the Separations Preview panel to see where that color is used.**

   As your client stated, the brochure should use a single spot color — the metallic gold in the main logo.

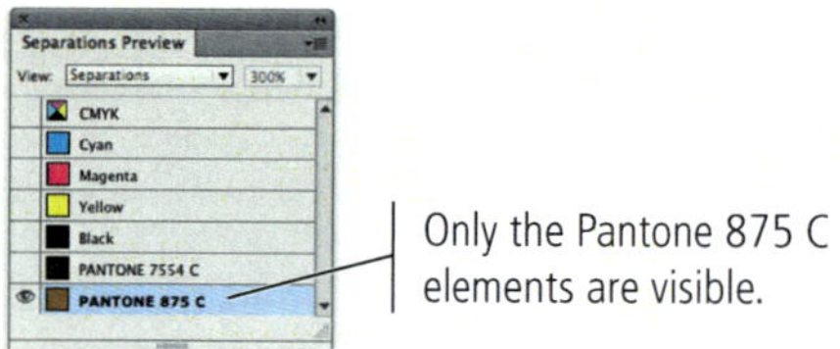

4. **Click Pantone 7554 C in the Separations Preview panel to review where that color is used in the layout.**

   By reviewing the separation, you can see that the dark brown from the logo is used for all the headings in the text, and for the frames on Page 4.

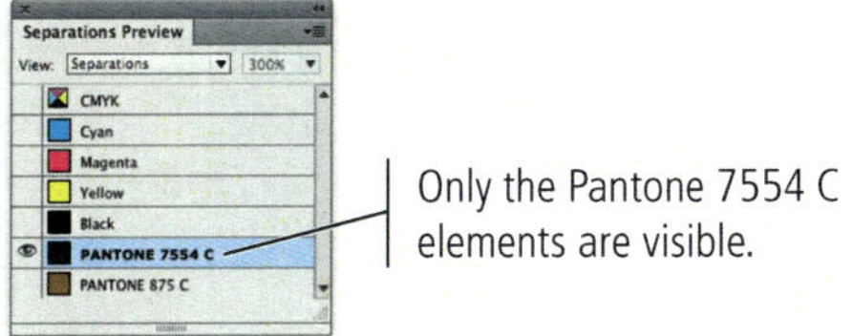

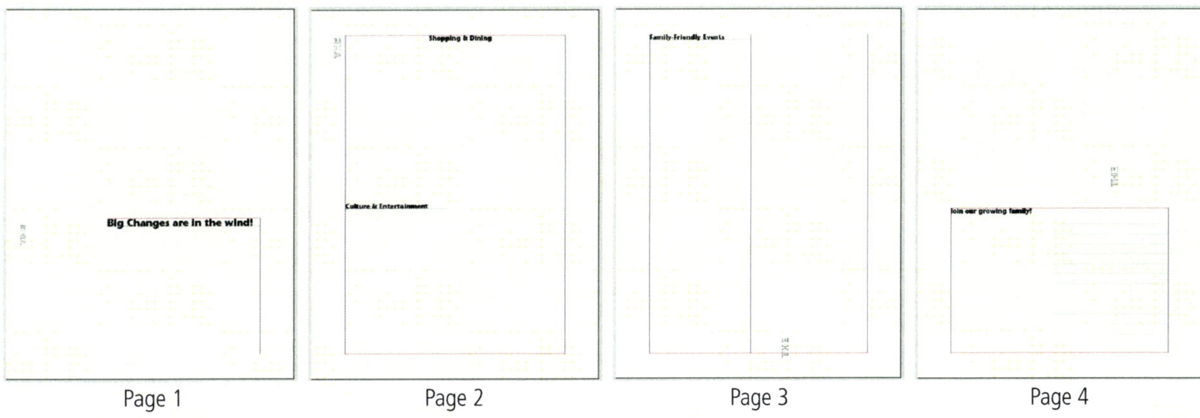

   You can't simply delete the extra spot color because it is used in the placed logo file. Since the job does allow for one spot color, you are going to replace the Pantone 7554 color with Pantone 875 for all layout elements.

5. **Click the empty space left of CMYK in the Separations Preview panel to view the CMYK separations in addition to the Pantone 7554 C separation.**

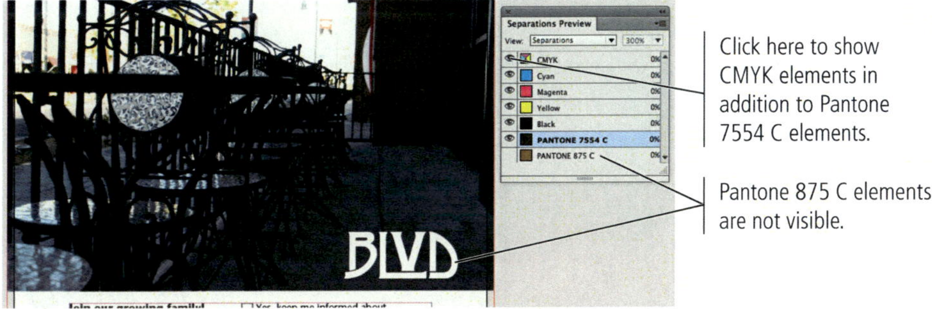

6. **Choose Off in the View menu at the top of the Separations Preview panel.**

   When you turn off the separations preview, you again see the frame edges.

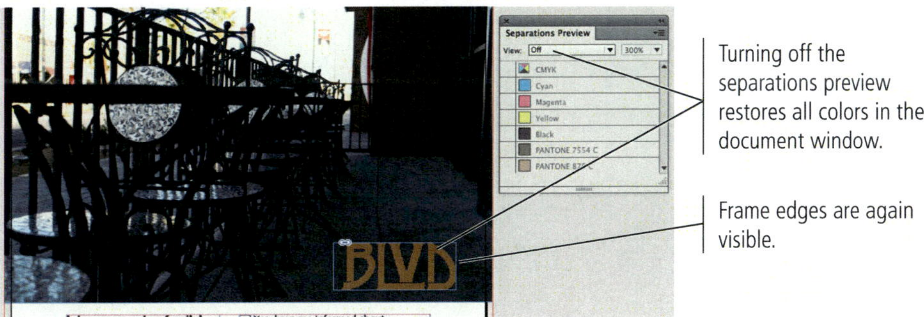

7. **Continue to the next exercise.**

Enable Track Changes

In many cases, multiple users collaborate on a single document — designers, editors, content providers, and clients all go back and forth throughout the design process. Each person in the process will request changes, from changing the highlight color in a document to rewriting the copy to fit in a defined space. Because the words in a design are a vital part of communicating the client's message, tracking text changes throughout the process can be useful to make sure that all changes are accurate and approved before the job is finalized.

1. **With boulevard.indd open, use the Type tool to place the insertion point in any story.**

2. **Choose Type>Track Changes>Enable Tracking in All Stories.**

   The Track Changes feature can be activated to monitor text editing during development. This allows multiple users to edit the text without permanently altering that text until the changes have been reviewed and approved or rejected. (After you have made all the changes in this stage of the project, you will review and finalize those changes.)

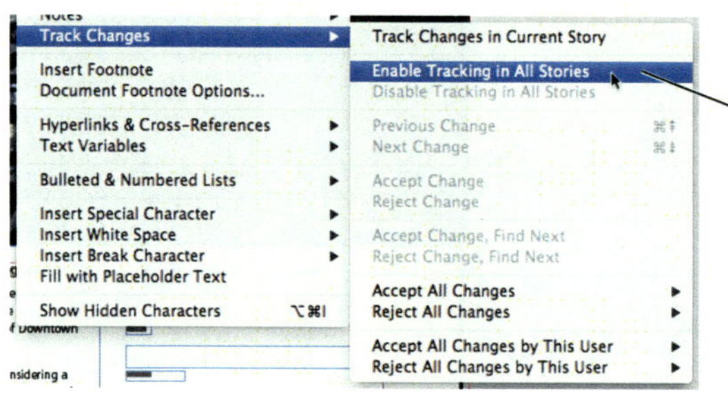

These options are not available unless the insertion point is currently placed.

3. **Open the Track Changes pane of the Preferences dialog box. Make sure the Added Text, Deleted Text, and Moved Text options are checked.**

4. **Choose Underline in the Added Text Marking menu.**

   The Marking options add a visual indicator (strikethrough, underlining, or outlining) so you can more easily identify text that is affected by the Track Changes function.

5. **Choose Red in the Deleted Text Background menu.**

   The Text Color options define the color of highlighting that will identify each type of change. All three options default to the same color; changing the color for Deleted Text will make it easier to identify this type of change when you review the corrections at the end of this stage of the project.

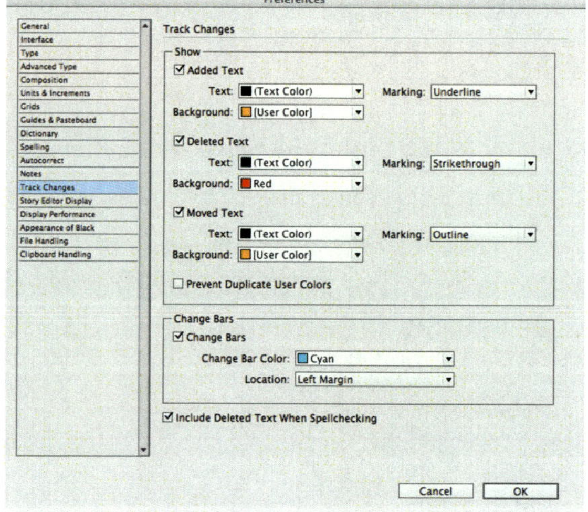

6. **Click OK to return to the document, then save the file and continue to the next exercise.**

Note:

Some text issues, however, have little to do with typography and more to do with "user malfunction" — common errors introduced by the people who created the text (most often, your clients). Regardless of how knowledgeable or careful you are, some problems will inevitably creep into the text elements of your layouts.

Note:

Remember, preferences are accessed in the InDesign menu on Macintosh or in the Edit menu on Windows.

Note:

It is very easy to make a mistake when spellchecking, so it's a good idea to check the Include Deleted Text When Spellchecking option at the bottom of the Preferences dialog box.

Find and Change Text

You will often need to search for and replace specific elements in a layout — a word, a phrase, a formatting attribute, or even a specific kind of object. InDesign's Find/Change dialog box allows you to easily locate exactly what you need whether your layout is two pages or two hundred. For this brochure, you can use the Find/Change dialog box to correct the name of the client's project.

> *Note:*
>
> *Two consecutive spaces after a period and two consecutive paragraph returns are common typing errors that are relics from the days before digital typesetting, when people were taught to type with manual typewriters. Although many people have never even seen an actual typewriter, these conventions still persist. When you import client-supplied text files into an InDesign document, you should immediately check for these issues, and use the Find/Change dialog box to fix them.*

1. **With boulevard.indd open, navigate to Page 1.**

2. **Using the Type tool, place the insertion point at the beginning of the story on that page.**

3. **Choose Edit>Find/Change.**

4. **Place the insertion point in the Find What field and type Downtown Lancaster.**

5. **Press Tab to highlight the Change To field, and type The BLVD.**

6. **In the Search menu, choose Document.**

   When the insertion point is placed, you can choose to search the entire Document, All [open] Documents, only the active Story, or only text following the insertion point in the selected story (To End of Story).

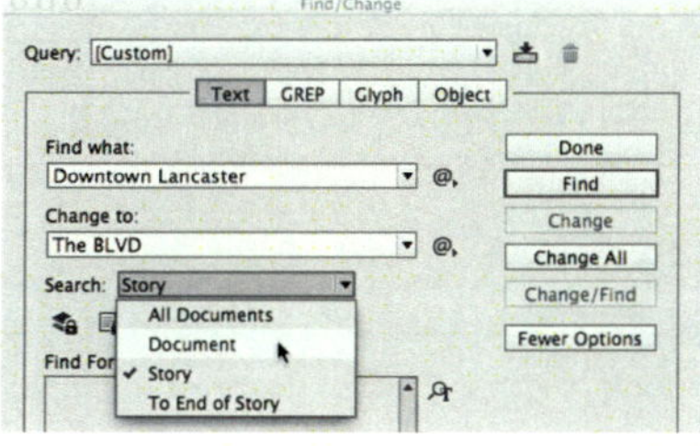

7. **Click Find.**

   The first instance of the Find What text is automatically highlighted in the document.

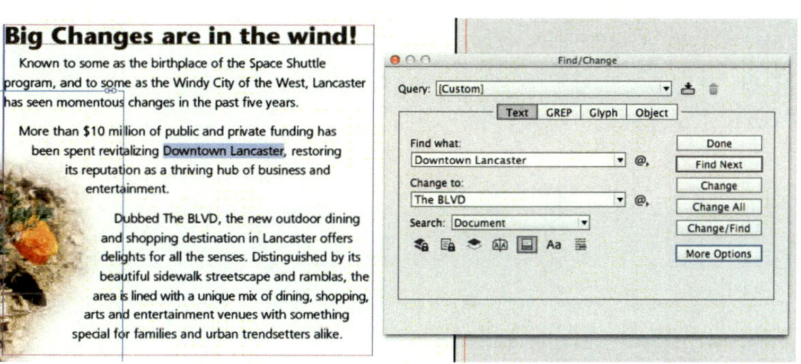

> *Note:*
>
> *If the insertion point is not currently placed, you can only choose to search the active Document or All Documents.*

> *Note:*
>
> *The Find/Change dialog box is one of the few dialog boxes that allow you to interact directly with the document even while the dialog box is still open.*

The Find/Change Dialog Box in Depth

As you have seen, the Text tab allows you to search for and change specific character strings, with or without specific formatting options. The Object tab identifies specific combinations of object formatting attributes, such as fill color or applied object effects. In addition to the tools you use in this project, the Find/Change dialog box has a number of options for narrowing or extending a search beyond the basic options. The buttons below the Search menu are toggles for specific types of searches (from left to right):

- When **Include Locked Layers and Locked Objects** is active, the search locates instances on locked layers or individual objects that have been locked; you can't replace locked objects unless you first unlock them.
- When **Include Locked Stories** is active, the search locates text that is locked; you can't replace locked text unless you first unlock it.
- When **Include Hidden Layers** is active, the search includes frames on layers that are not visible.
- When **Include Master Pages** is active, the search includes frames on master pages.
- When **Include Footnotes** is active, the search identifies instances within footnote text.
- When **Case Sensitive** is active, the search only finds text with the same capitalization as the text in the Find What field. For example, a search for "InDesign" will not identify instances of "Indesign," "indesign," or "INDESIGN."
- When **Whole Word** is active, the search only finds instances where the search text is an entire word (not part of another word). For example, if you search for "old" as a whole word, InDesign will not include the words "gold," "mold," or "embolden."

The GREP tab is used for pattern-based search techniques, such as finding phone numbers in one format (e.g., 800.555.1234) and changing them to the same phone number with a different format (e.g., 800/555-1234). Adobe's video-based help system (www.adobe.com) provides some assistance in setting up an advanced query.

The Glyph tab allows you to search for and change glyphs using Unicode or GID/CID values. This is useful for identifying foreign and pictographic characters, as well as characters from extended sets of OpenType fonts.

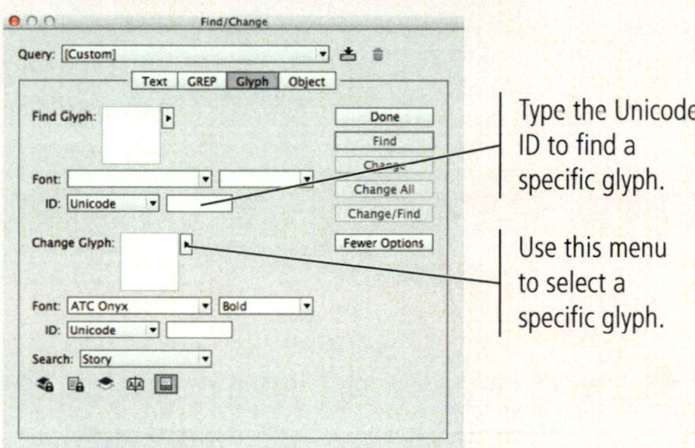

Type the Unicode ID to find a specific glyph.

Use this menu to select a specific glyph.

You can also save specific searches as queries, and you can call those queries again using the Query menu at the top of the Find/Change dialog box. This option is useful if you commonly make the same modifications, such as changing Multiple Return to Single Return (this particular search and replacement is so common that the query is built into the application).

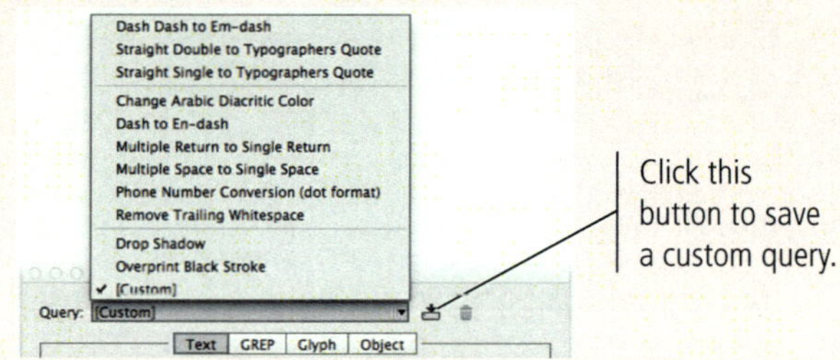

Click this button to save a custom query.

8. **Click the Change/Find button.**

   The next instance of the Find What text is highlighted in the document. Because you selected the option to search the entire document, the search finds the next instance in the second story.

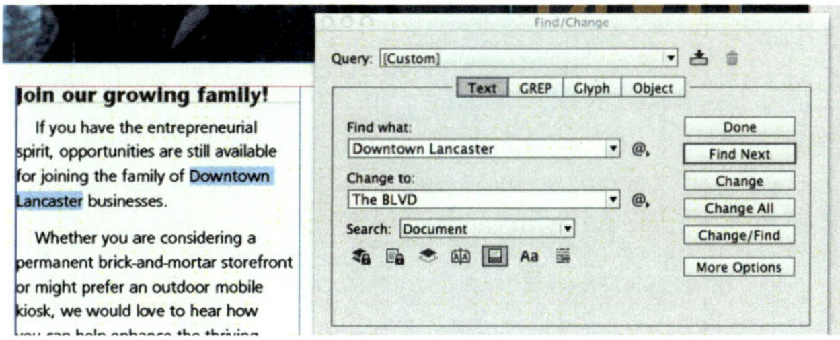

9. **Click Change All.**

10. **When you see the message that 6 replacements were made, click OK.**

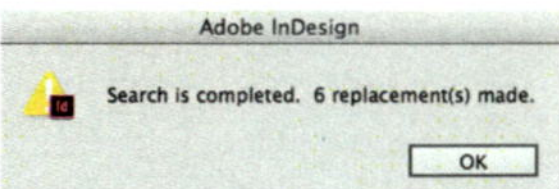

11. **Save the file and continue to the next exercise.**

Find and Change Text Formatting Attributes

In addition to finding and replacing specific text or characters, you can also find and replace formatting attributes for both text and objects. For this project, you need to use the gold spot color as the accent, replacing the brown spot color. You can't simply delete the brown spot color from the Swatches panel, however, because that color is used in the placed logo file. The Find/Change dialog box makes this kind of replacement a relatively simple process.

1. **With boulevard.indd open, choose Edit>Find/Change (if the dialog box is not already open).**

2. **Delete all text from the Find What and Change To fields.**

3. **Choose Wildcards>Any Character in the menu to the right of the Find What field.**

   Wildcards allow you to search for formatting attributes, regardless of the actual text. In addition to searching for Any Character, you can also narrow the search to Any Digit, Any Letter, or Any White Space characters.

Click here to access the menu of special characters.

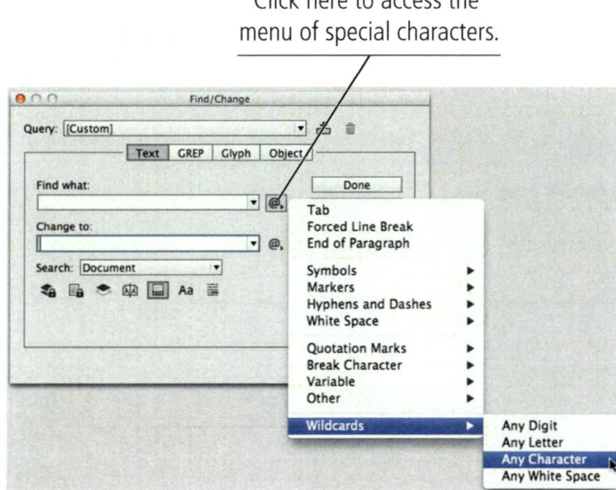

^? is the special code for a wildcard character.

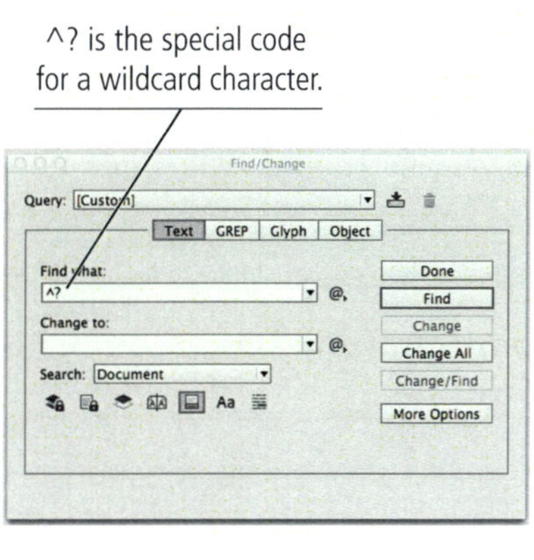

4. **Click the More Options button to show the expanded Find/Change dialog box.**

   When more options are visible, you can find and replace specific formatting attributes of the selected text.

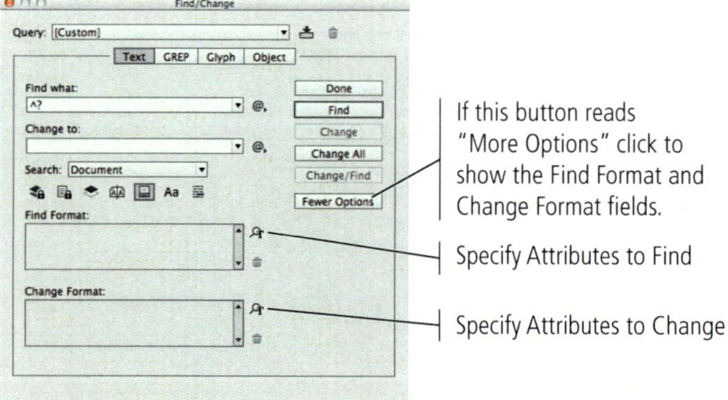

5. **Click the Specify Attributes to Find button to open the Find Format Settings dialog box.**

   You can search for and replace any character formatting option (or combination of options) that can be applied in the layout.

6. **Show the Character Color options and click the Pantone 7554 C swatch.**

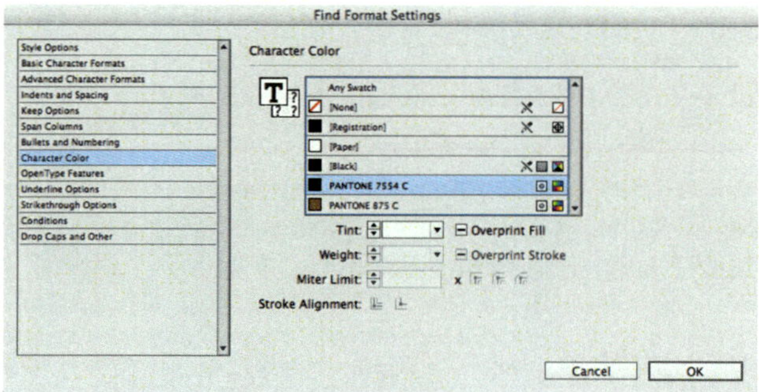

7. **Click OK to return to the Find/Change dialog box.**

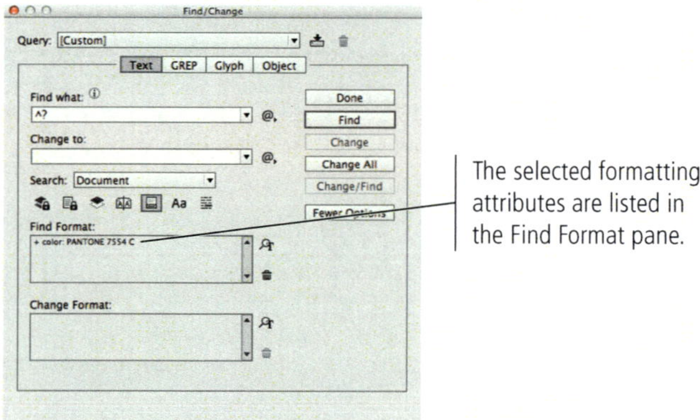

8. **Click the Specify Attributes to Change button to open the Change Format Settings dialog box.**

9. **Show the Character Color options and click the Pantone 875 C swatch.**

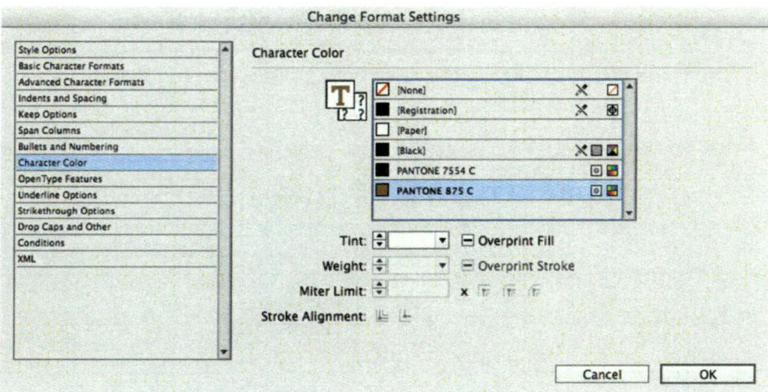

10. **Click OK to return to the Find/Change dialog box.**

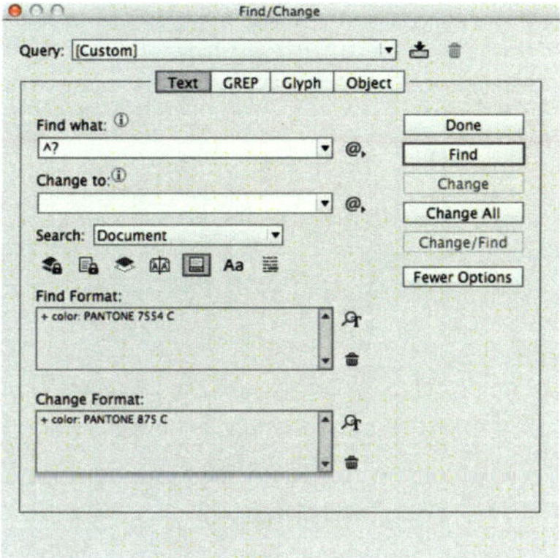

11. **Make sure Document is selected in the Search menu and click Change All. Click OK to close the message about the number of replacements.**

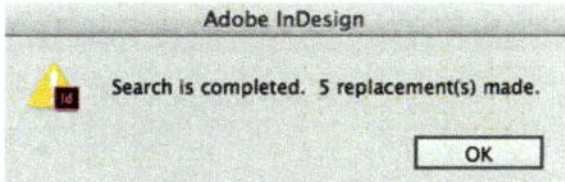

12. **In the Find/Change dialog box, click the Delete buttons to remove the formatting options from the Find Format and Change Format fields.**

    It can be easy to forget to remove these formatting choices. However, if you leave them in place, your next search will only find the Find What text with the selected formatting. It's a good idea to clear these formatting choices as soon as you're done with them.

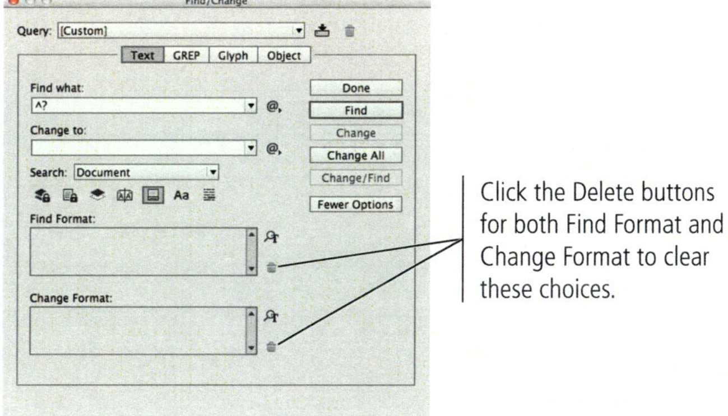

13. **Save the file and continue to the next exercise.**

Entering Special Characters in Dialog Boxes

You can enter special characters in InDesign dialog boxes using the following special codes, called metacharacters. (Note that these metacharacters are case specific; for example, "^n" and "^N" refer to different special characters.)

Character	Code (Metacharacters)
Symbols	
Bullet (•)	^8
Caret (^)	^^
Copyright (©)	^2
Ellipsis (…)	^e
Paragraph	^7
Registered Trademark (®)	^r
Section (§)	^6
Trademark (™)	^d
Dashes and Hyphens	
Em Dash (—)	^_
En Dash (–)	^=
Discretionary hyphen	^-
Nonbreaking hyphen	^~
White Space Characters	
Em space	^m
En space	^>
Third space	^3
Quarter space	^4
Sixth space	^%
Flush space	^f
Hair space	^| (pipe)
Nonbreaking space	^s
Thin space	^<
Figure space	^/
Punctuation space	^.
Quotation Marks	
Double left quotation mark	^{
Double right quotation mark	^}
Single left quotation mark	^[
Single right quotation mark	^]
Straight double quotation mark	^"
Straight single quotation mark	^'
Page Number Characters	
Any page number character	^#
Current page number character	^N
Next page number character	^X
Previous page number character	^V

Character	Code (Metacharacters)
Break Characters	
Paragraph return	^p
Forced line break (soft return)	^n
Column break	^M
Frame break	^R
Page break	^P
Odd page break	^L
Even page break	^E
Discretionary line break	^j
Formatting Options	
Tab character	^t
Right indent tab character	^y
Indent to here character	^i
End nested style here character	^h
Nonjoiner character	^k
Variables	
Running header (paragraph style)	^Y
Running header (character style)	^Z
Custom text	^u
Last page number	^T
Chapter number	^H
Creation date	^S
Modification date	^o
Output date	^D
File name	^l (lowercase L)
Markers	
Section marker	^x
Anchored object marker	^a
Footnote reference marker	^F
Index marker	^I
Wildcards	
Any digit	^9
Any letter	^$
Any character	^?
White space (any space or tab)	^w
Any variable	^v

Find and Change Object Attributes

In addition to searching for specific text formatting attributes, you can also find and replace specific object formatting attributes. In this exercise you will replace all brown-stroked frames with the gold spot color.

1. **With boulevard.indd open, open the Find/Change dialog box if it is not already open.**

2. **Click the Object tab to display those options.**

3. **In the Type menu, choose All Frames.**

   You can limit your search to specific kinds of frames, or you can search all frames.

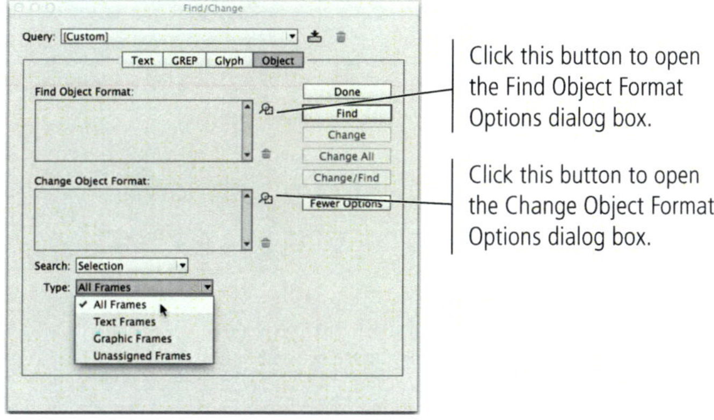

4. **Click the button to open the Find Object Format Options dialog box.**

   You can find and change any formatting attributes that can be applied to a frame.

5. **Display the Stroke options and click the Pantone 7554 C swatch.**

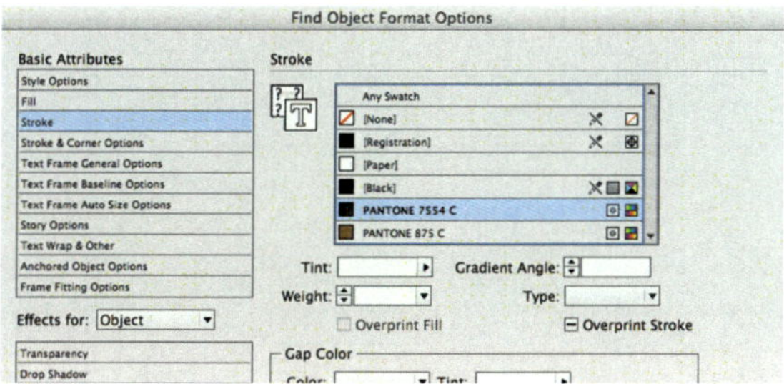

6. **Click OK to return to the Find/Change dialog box.**

7. **Open the Change Object Format Options dialog box and choose the Pantone 875 C swatch in the Stroke options.**

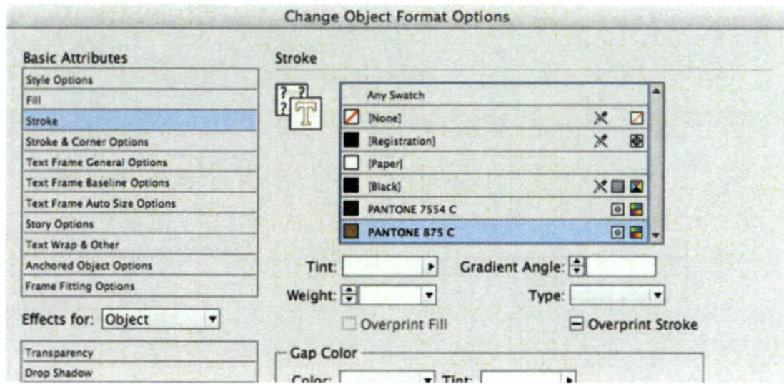

8. **Click OK to return to the Find/Change dialog box.**

9. **Make sure Document is selected in the Search menu.**

   When you search objects, you can search the current document, all documents, or the current selection.

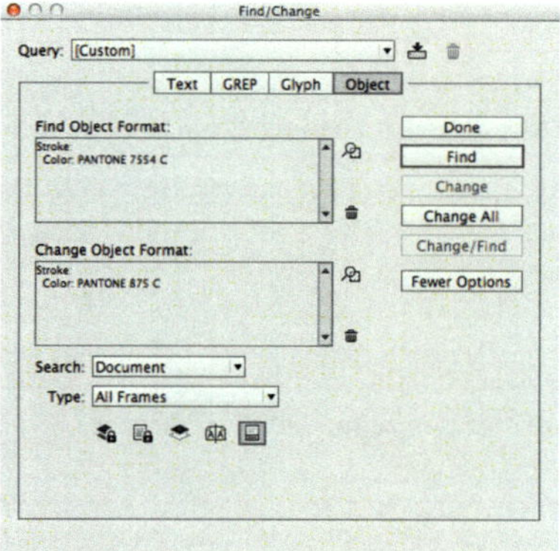

10. **Click Change All, then click OK to dismiss the message about the number of changes.**

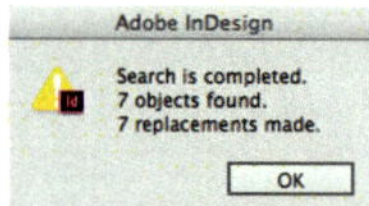

11. **Click the Delete buttons for both the Find Object Format and Change Object Format options to clear your choices.**

12. **Click Done to close the Find/Change dialog box.**

13. **Open the Separations Preview panel (Window>Output>Separations Preview). Choose Separations in the View menu at the top of the panel.**

14. **Click Pantone 875 C in the panel and review each page of the layout.**

15. **Click Pantone 7554 C in the panel and review each page of the layout.**

The only thing now set with the second spot color is the word "THE" in the placed logo file. Because you can't change the logo in InDesign, you will use other options to convert that spot color to process.

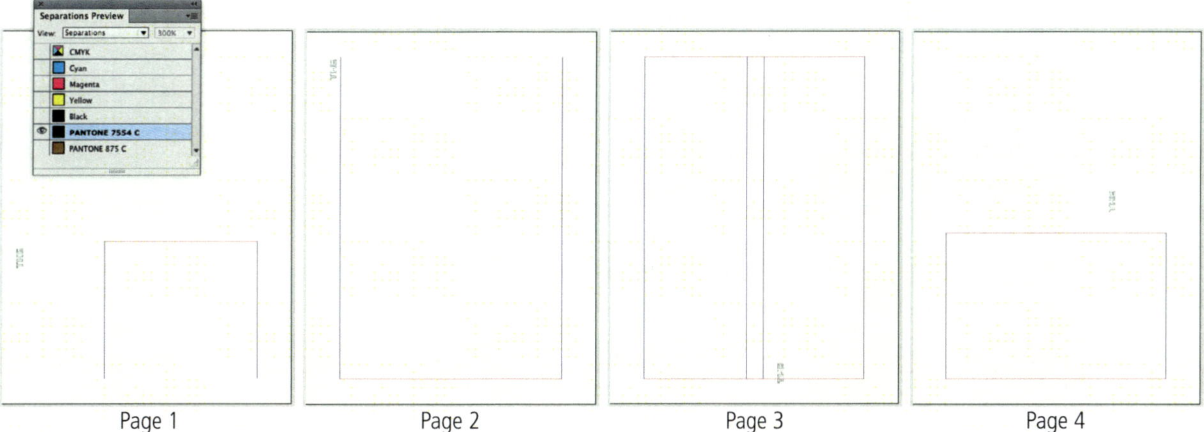

16. **Choose Off in the View menu of the Separations Preview panel, then close the panel.**

17. **Save the file and continue to the next exercise.**

Review Tracked Changes

Earlier in this project, you enabled the Track Changes feature for all stories in this document. You might have noticed, however, that there is no visual indication of those changes in the layout. Tracking editorial changes is useful for monitoring changes in the text, but displaying those changes in the layout would make it impossible to fit copy and accurately format the text in a layout. To avoid this confusion, changes are tracked in a special utility called the Story Editor, which more closely resembles a word-processor screen.

1. **With boulevard.indd open, place the insertion point at the beginning of the text frame on Page 1.**

2. **Choose Edit>Edit in Story Editor.**

The Story Editor opens in a separate window, showing only the current story. (A **story** in InDesign is the entire body of text in a single frame or string of linked frames.)

Note:

If your deleted text is not highlighted red, you missed a step in the earlier exercise where you enabled the Track Changes feature (see page 348). You can open the Track Changes pane of the Preferences dialog box and change the highlight options now.

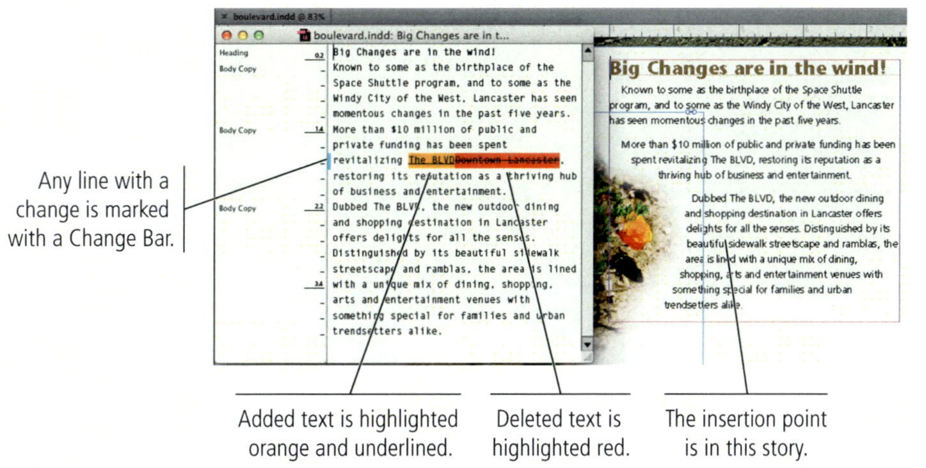

3. **Open the Track Changes panel (Window>Editorial>Track Changes).**

   When the Story Editor window is active, you can use the Track Changes panel to review the tracked changes.

   A. Enable/Disable Track Changes in Current Story toggles the track changes function on and off.

   B. Show/Hide Changes toggles the visibility of tracked changes in the Story Editor window.

   C. Previous Change highlights the first change before the current location of the insertion point.

   D. Next Change highlights the first change after the current location of the insertion point.

   E. Accept Change makes the highlighted change permanent.

   F. Reject Change restores the original text for deleted text or removes added text.

   G. Accept All Changes in Story applies the same result as the Accept Change button, but for all tracked changes in the active story; you do not get the opportunity to individually review each change.

   H. Reject All Changes in Story applies the same result as the Reject Change button, but for all tracked changes in the active story; again, you do not get the opportunity to individually review each change.

> **Note:**
>
> *You can also Option/Alt click the Accept or Reject Change button to apply the change and then automatically highlight (find) the next change.*

4. **Click the Next Change button in the Track Changes panel.**

   If you read the text, you can see that this instance refers to the area of Downtown Lancaster. The next paragraph goes on to explain that the area was rebranded as "The BLVD" — so it wouldn't make logical sense to use the term before it is defined.

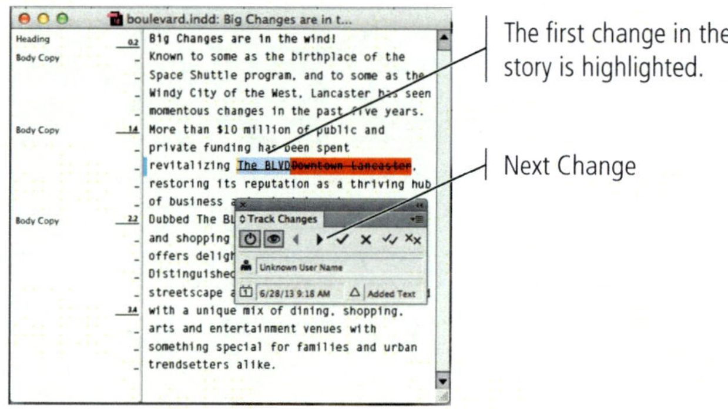

> **Note:**
>
> *This type of decision is usually the client's to make; in this exercise, we are assuming the client would agree.*

5. **Click the Reject Change button, then click the Next Change button.**

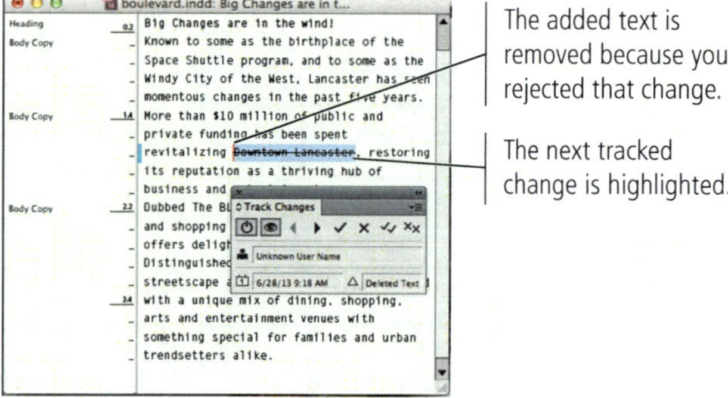

6. **Click the Reject Change button again.**

   Because you did not keep the replacement text, you need to keep the deleted text.

7. **Click the Next Change button in the Track Changes panel.**

   Because there were no more changes in the first story, clicking the Next Change button opens the next story where a change is located. Each story appears in a separate Story Editor window.

   As you can see, the only changes in this story are the replacement of "Downtown Lancaster" with "The BLVD." rather than reviewing each instance separately, you can simply accept all changes in the story at one time.

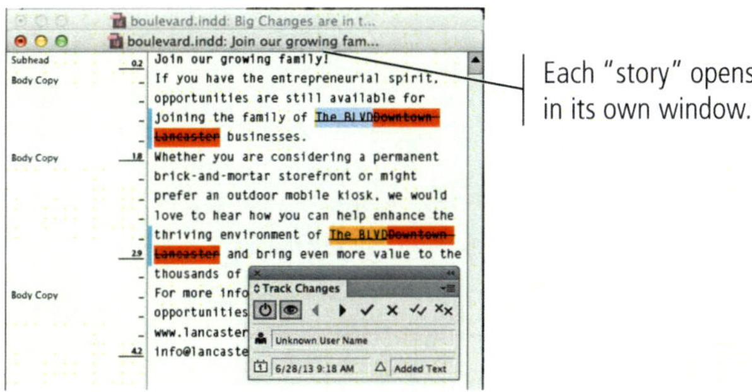

Each "story" opens in its own window.

8. **Click the Accept All Changes in Story button at the top of the Track Changes panel.**

9. **When asked to confirm the change, click OK.**

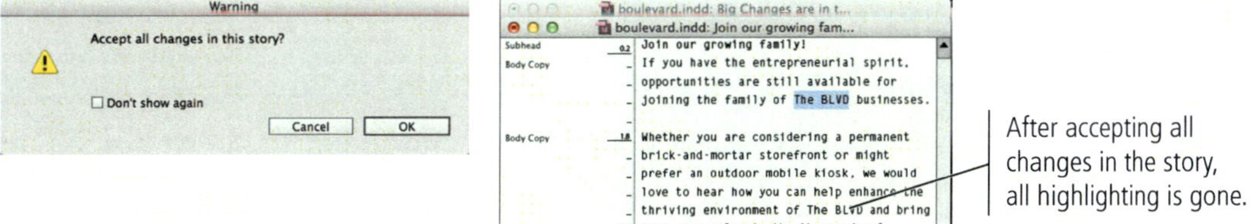

After accepting all changes in the story, all highlighting is gone.

10. **Click the Next Change button.**

    The third story has a number of changes, but they are all the same text replacement that you saw in the first two stories.

    In Step 8 you only accepted all changes in the active story; the third story in the layout still has tracked changes that should be reviewed.

11. **Open the Track Changes panel Options menu and choose Accept All Changes>In This Document.**

    The In This Document option affects all stories in a file, even if they are not currently open in a Story Editor window.

    Accepting all changes without reviewing them essentially defeats the purpose of tracking changes. We are telling you that, in this case, it is safe to simply accept all the changes.

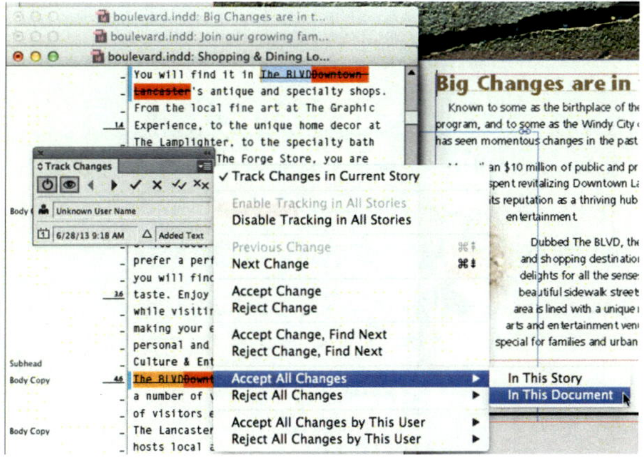

> ***Note:***
>
> *In a professional environment — and especially if more than one person has been working on the same document — you should be sure to carefully review all tracked changes before finalizing the job.*

12. **Click OK to dismiss the Warning dialog box and accept the changes.**

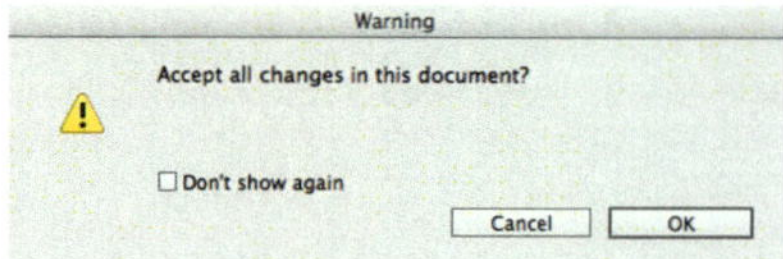

13. **Close all three Story Editor windows.**

14. **Save the file and continue to the next exercise.**

Export a Color-Managed PDF File

Because you're going to use the same file for several digitally delivered formats (PDF, EPUB, and HTML), all photographs in the layout use the RGB model to maintain the best possible color for the digital output.

InDesign allows you to convert the image data to the defined output profile when you create the PDF file for print while still maintaining the RGB images for the digitally distributed formats. However, because the RGB model allows a much greater gamut than CMYK, some color shift might occur when you export the PDF file for print. It's a good idea to review the potential color shift before you create the final print PDF.

Note:

RGB images in a layout are extremely common, especially when you work with files created by non-professionals. Be prepared to either correct the images in Photoshop and replace them, or convert them to CMYK when you export the PDF file for print.

1. **With boulevard.indd open, navigate to Page 1.**

2. **Choose View>Proof Setup>Working CMYK.**

   Remember from the beginning of this project, the working CMYK profile is what you defined as the color characteristics of the intended output device — in this case, a standardized sheetfed press.

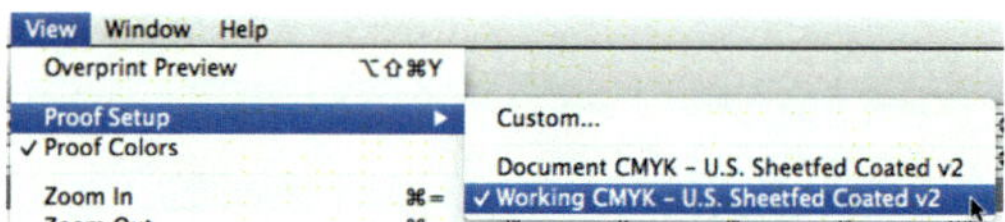

3. **Choose View>Proof Colors.**

   This toggle provides an on-screen preview of what will happen when the image is converted to the CMYK working-space profile without affecting the actual file data. (This option, called **soft proofing**, is more valuable with an accurately calibrated monitor; but even with an uncalibrated monitor, you should be able to see any significant trouble areas.)

When Proof Colors is active, the document tab shows the profile being used for soft proofing.

4. **Navigate through the layout and review the differences. Toggle the Proof Colors option on and off for each page to look for significant color shift.**

   In many instances, the color shift will be subtle; most obvious changes will be visible in the brightest colors, such as the blue tarp in the image on the lower half of Page 3.

   We do not include images of the differences here because they do not reproduce well in print. However, you should be able to see the differences on your screen when you toggle the Proof Colors option on and off.

5. **Turn off the Proof Colors option, then choose File>Export.**

6. **Change the file name to boulevard-print.pdf and choose Adobe PDF (Print) in the Format menu. Click Save.**

7. **In the Export Adobe PDF dialog box, choose Press Quality in the Adobe PDF Preset menu.**

8. **In the Marks and Bleeds options, check the Crop Marks option and change the Offset value to 0.125″. In the lower half of the dialog box, check the option to Use Document Bleed Settings.**

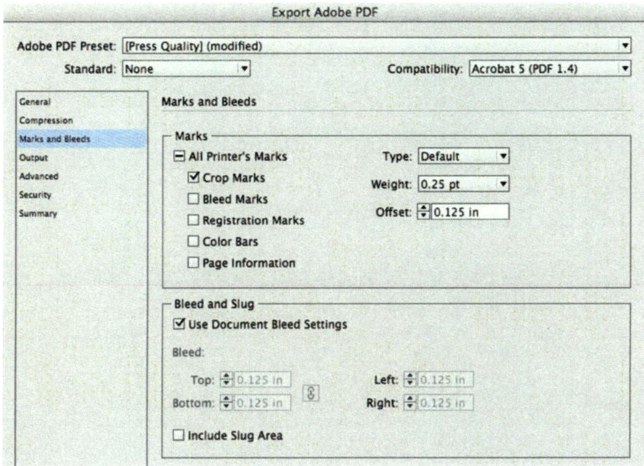

9. **In the Output options, choose Convert to Destination in the Color Conversion menu.**

You have several options for converting colors when you output a file:

- **No Color Conversion** maintains all color data (including placed images) in its current space.
- **Convert to Destination** converts colors to the profile selected in the Destination menu.
- **Convert to Destination (Preserve Numbers)** converts colors to the destination profile if the applied profile does not match the defined destination profile. Objects without color profiles are not converted.

The Destination menu defines the gamut for the output device that will be used. (This menu defaults to the active destination working space.) Color information in the file (and placed images) is converted to the selected Destination profile.

Note:

Spot-color information is preserved when colors are converted to the destination space.

10. **Choose Include Destination Profile in the Profile Inclusion Policy menu.**

The **Profile Inclusion Policy** menu determines whether color profiles are embedded in the resulting PDF file. (Different options are available, depending on what you selected in the Color Conversion menu.)

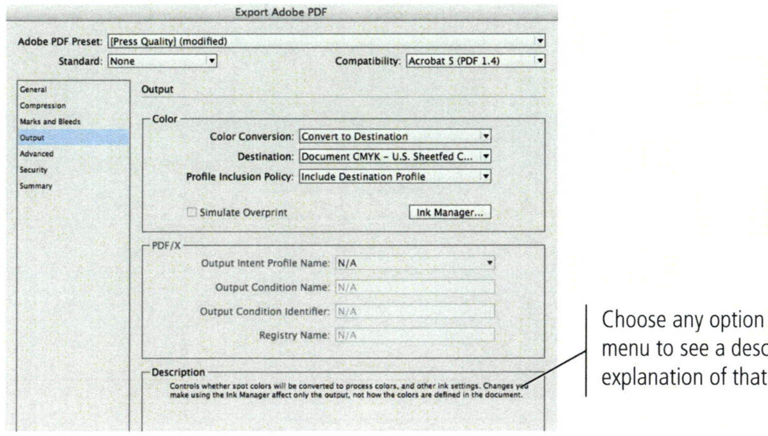

Choose any option in any menu to see a description or explanation of that option.

11. **Click the Ink Manager button.**

As you already know, this file is only allowed to use one spot color — Pantone 875 C (metallic gold) — when it is printed.

The Ink Manager offers control over specific ink separations at output time. Changes here affect the current output, not how the colors are defined in the document.

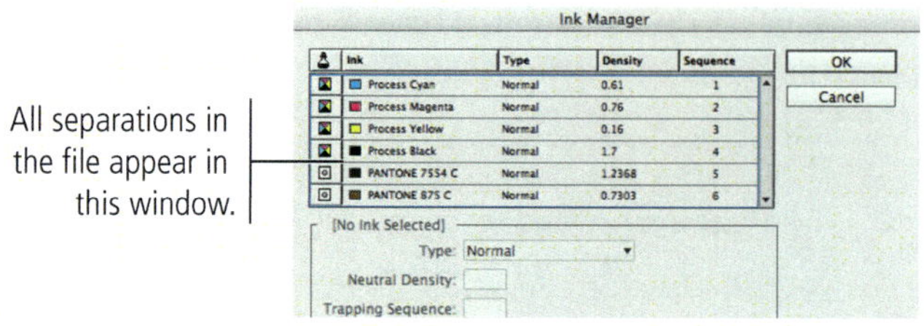

> ***Note:***
>
> *You can also access this dialog box by clicking the Ink Manager button in the Output pane of the Print dialog box.*

12. **Click the Spot Color icon to the left of the Pantone 7554 C ink.**

This converts the individual ink to a process color for the current output. (Keep in mind that spot colors are often outside the CMYK gamut; there will almost always be color shift in the resulting CMYK build.)

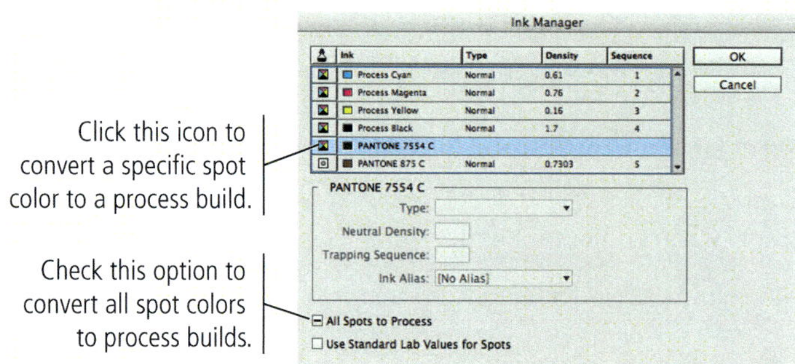

13. **Click OK to return to the Export Adobe PDF dialog box, then click Export.**

14. **If the PDF file opens, close it and then return to InDesign.**

15. **Save the InDesign file and then continue to the next stage of the project.**

Soft Proofing to Custom Profiles

INDESIGN FOUNDATIONS

You can soft proof to any profile — not just the defined working profile — by choosing View>Proof Setup>Custom. In the resulting dialog box, choose any profile in the Device to Simulate menu.

InDesign also allows soft proofing and export to grayscale profiles, which are included near the bottom of the various device profile menus. This is particularly useful if you are creating a file that might be placed in a newspaper or other document that only prints with black ink.

Stage 2 Creating Interactive Elements

The print file is now complete, but you still need to repurpose the content into several different versions for digital distribution — a common assignment in the professional market. To complete this type of repurposing, you need to understand the options and capabilities of each format.

You already know that the PDF format can contain all of the elements — fonts, images, etc. — required to create high-quality printing. Digitally distributed PDF files support interactive elements and multimedia, which are not possible in static print jobs.

If you completed Project 5: Ireland Travel Brochure, you also saw that you can create interactive page transitions for files that are delivered digitally. Those transitions are only one of the interactive and multmedia elements that are supported by the PDF format. In this stage of the project, you are going to create an interactive table of contents, hyperlinks, a slideshow of images, and a form that users can fill out directly in Adobe Acrobat. InDesign allows you to create all of these elements directly in the layout, without the need for additional software.

Create Versions with Layers

Rather than saving and editing multiple versions of the same basic file, you are going to use layers to identify elements that function properly for all output versions, as well as isolating objects that are only appropriate for certain formats.

When you use layers to create multiple versions of a document, the first step is to determine how many layers you need. Elements that will appear in all versions should exist on one layer. Each different version that you need to create requires its own layer to hold those elements that will change from one version to the next.

Note:

Layers are also useful for designing die-cut documents, which are cut in non-rectangular shapes or contain an area cut out within the page. The tab on a manila folder and a folded carton are two examples of die-cut jobs.

1. **With boulevard.indd open, navigate to Page 1 of the layout.**
2. **In the Layers panel (Window>Layers), double-click the Layer 1 name to open the Layer Options dialog box.**

   The default in every file is named "Layer 1", which is not terribly useful when you use multiple layers. Descriptive names are far better for any asset — including layers.

3. **Change the Name field to Common Elements and review the other options.**

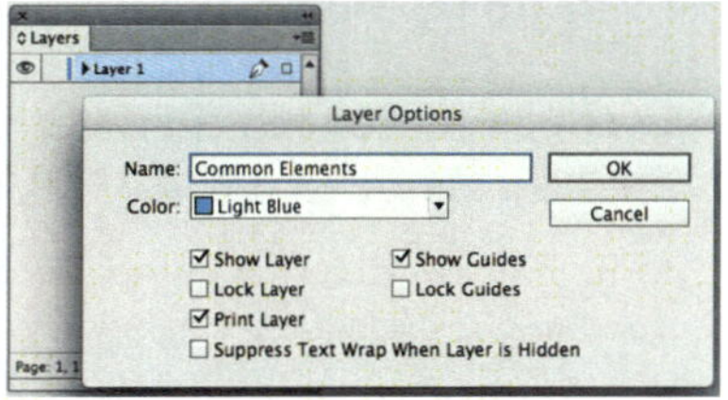

   - The **Color** menu determines the color of frame edges and bounding box handles for objects on that layer. You can choose a different color from the menu, or choose Custom and define your own color.
   - If **Show Layer** is checked, the layer contents are visible in the document. You can also change visibility by toggling the eye icon in the Layers panel.
   - If **Lock Layer** is checked, you can't select or change objects on that layer.
   - If **Print Layer** is checked, the layer will output when you print or export to PDF.
   - The **Show Guides** option allows you to create and display different sets of guides for different layers; this is a more versatile option than showing or hiding all guides (which occurs with the View>Grids & Guides>Show/Hide Guides toggle).
   - The **Lock Guides** option allows you to lock and unlock guides on specific layers.
   - If **Suppress Text Wrap When Layer is Hidden** is checked, text on underlying layers reflows when the layer is hidden.

4. **Click OK to close the Layer Options dialog box.**

5. **Click the Create New Layer button at the bottom of the Layers panel.**

6. **Double-click Layer 2 in the Layers panel. Change the layer name to** Static Print **and click OK.**

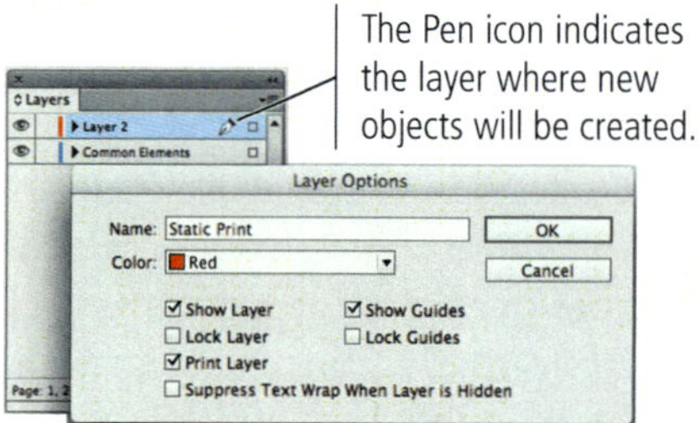

The Pen icon indicates the layer where new objects will be created.

7. **In the Layers panel, click the arrow to the left of the Common Elements layer to expand it.**

8. **Click the pavement.jpg item, and drag until a line appears between the Static Print and Common Elements layers.**

   Later in this project, you will create an interactive slideshow that will take the place of the main image on Page 1. Because you need to be able to output this file with interactive elements or with static print elements, you need to move the existing image frame to a layer that can be hidden when you export the interactive version.

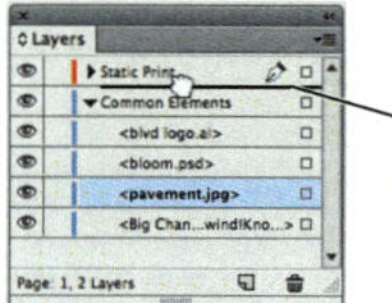

This line indicates that you are moving the selected item to the Static Print layer.

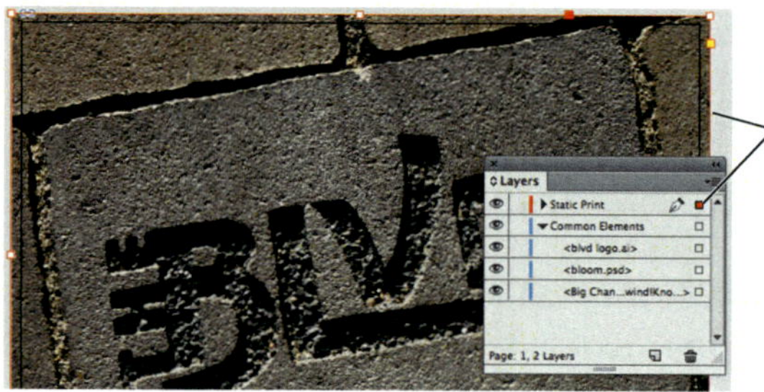

Frame borders are now red, matching the color of the Static Print layer.

9. **Navigate to Page 4 of the layout.**

10. **Using the Selection tool, draw a marquee that touches all of thc objects that make up the form.**

11. **In the Layers panel, drag the Selected Items icon from the Common Elements layer to the Static Print layer.**

    Although you want to include these objects in the printed version, you are also going to use them as the basis for creating actual form objects for the interactive PDF file. The interactive objects will be slightly different than the static print objects, but you can still use these as a good starting point.

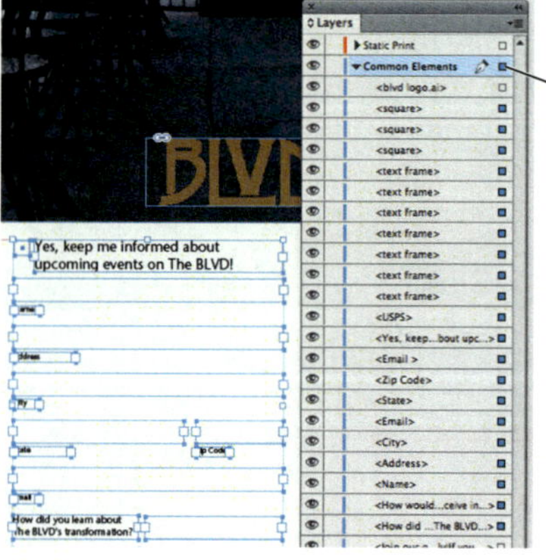

Drag the Selected Items icon for the layer to move all selected items to another layer.

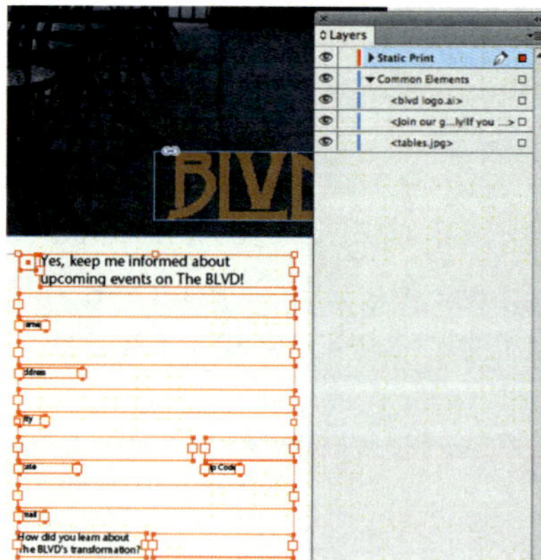

12. **Control/right-click the Static Print layer and choose Duplicate Layer in the contextual menu.**

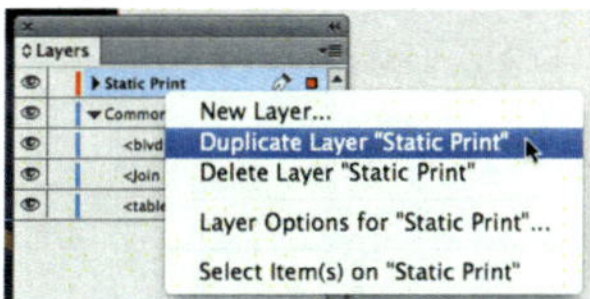

13. **Double-click the new Static Print Copy layer. Rename the layer Interactive, choose Green in the Color menu, then click OK.**

Duplicating a layer applies the same layer color to the duplicate. So you can better see where an object resides, you should change the layer to use a different color.

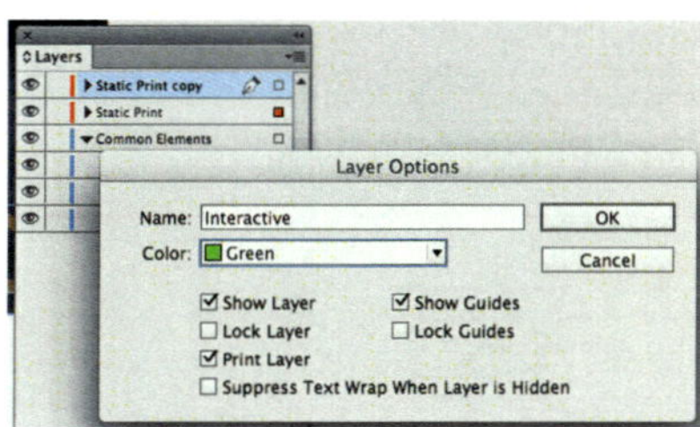

Note:

Having two layers use the same color defeats the purpose of unique layer identifiers. When you duplicate a layer, it's a good idea to change the layer color for the duplicate.

14. **Navigate to Page 1 of the layout.**

15. **In the Layers panel, expand the Interactive layer.**

The Layers panel only shows objects on the active layer or spread.

Only objects on the active page or spread appear in the Layers panel.

16. **Click the Selected Item icon to the right of pavement.jpg to select that item, then press Delete/Backspace to remove the selected item from the layer.**

For the interactive PDF and HTML files, you are going to place an interactive slideshow (which you will create in the next project) in this space.

After deleting the selected image from the Interactive layer, the red frame indicates that the remaining image exists on the Static Print layer.

17. **In the Layers panel, click the visibility icon for the Static Print layer to hide that layer.**

18. **Save the file and continue to the next exercise.**

Controlling Text Wrap on Different Layers

By default, an object's text wrap attributes affect all text frames that touch that wrap object; the wrap object's position in the stacking order, as well as a layer's position in the layer stack, are both irrelevant.

If you want text wrap to affect only objects on underlying layers, you can activate the Text Wrap Only Affects Text Beneath option in the Composition preferences.

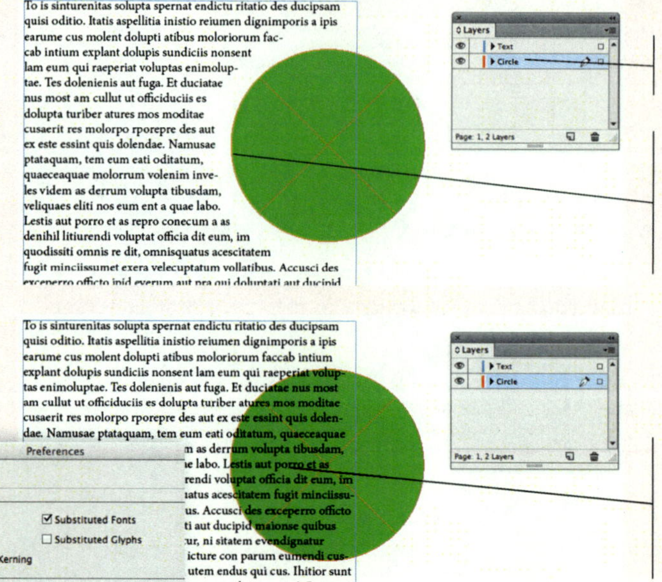

The Circle layer is below the Text layer.

By default, the circle's text wrap affects the text frame regardless of the Circle layer's position in the stacking order.

When **Text Wrap Only Affects Text Beneath** is active, the circle's text wrap does not affect text on the layer above.

If Suppress Text Wrap When Layer is Hidden is checked in the Layer Options dialog box, text on other layers reflows when the layer is hidden. The text wrap attributes of objects on the layer are only applied when the layer is visible.

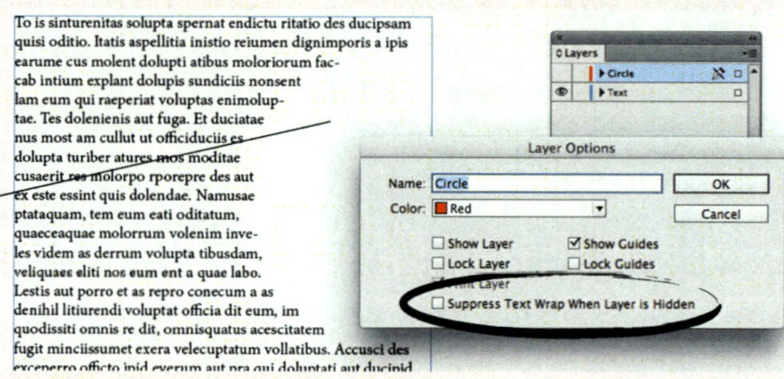

If **Suppress Text Wrap When Layer is Hidden** is not checked for the Circle layer, affected text does not reflow when the layer is hidden.

If **Suppress Text Wrap When Layer is Hidden** is checked for the Circle layer, affected text reflows when the layer is hidden.

Define a Table of Contents

The PDF format supports interactive tables of contents, which appear separate from the main document in the Acrobat document window. If you use styles to format the text in an InDesign layout, you can define a table of contents based on those styles. That table of contents can be automatically converted into the PDF table of contents.

1. **With boulevard.indd open, choose Layout>Table of Contents Styles.**

The Table of Contents Styles dialog box stores groups of settings that define different lists. If you choose Table of Contents in the Layout menu, you can define settings for a table of contents without saving it as a style, then generate the list and place it into the layout.

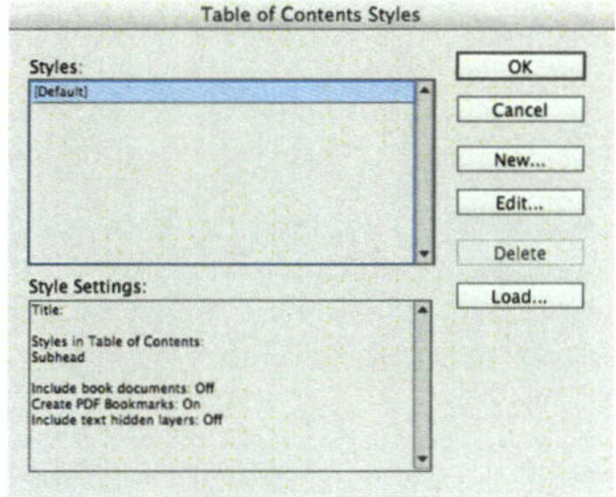

2. **Click New in the resulting dialog box.**

You can use this dialog box to define the styles that will appear in the resulting table of contents. All available styles appear in the Other Styles list by default.

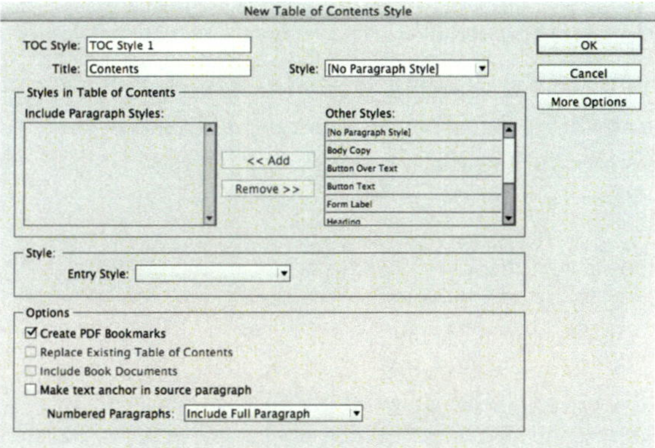

3. **In the Other Styles list, select the Heading style and click the Add button.**

4. **In the Other Styles list, select the Subhead style and click the Add button.**

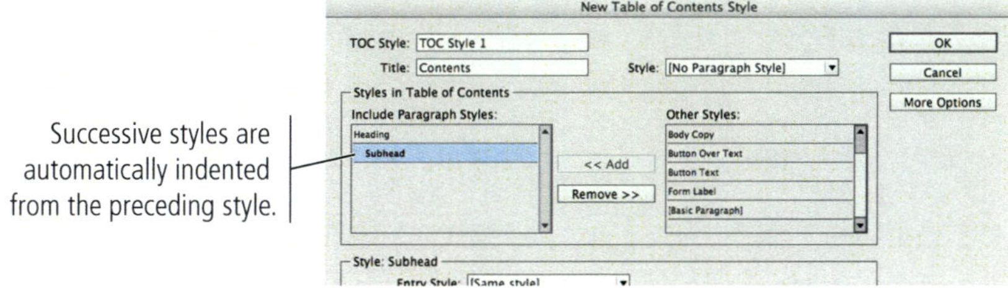

5. **Click the More Options button on the right side of the dialog box.**

6. **With Subhead selected in the list, change the Level field to 1.**

   The Level of a style automatically defaults to the next level after the previously selected style in the Include Paragraph Styles list.

   The designer correctly used a separate style for the larger heading on Page 1 of the layout, but in this case the nested levels of headings are not necessary. By changing the Level field for the Subhead style, all items in the PDF table of contents will appear at the same level of editorial priority.

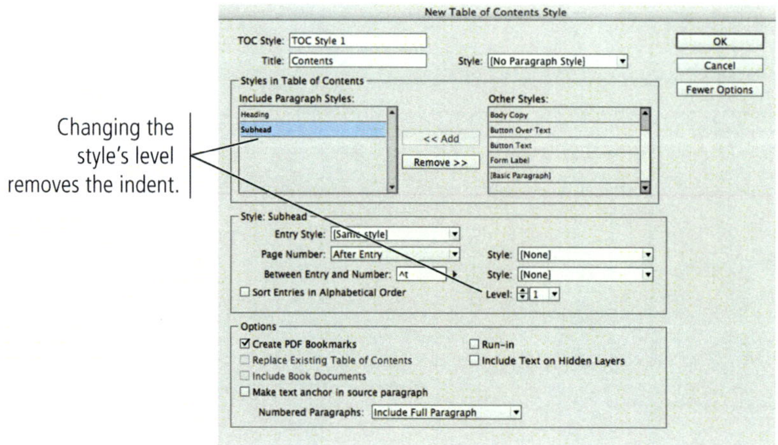

Changing the style's level removes the indent.

7. **At the bottom of the dialog box, make sure the Create PDF Bookmarks option is checked.**

8. **Click OK to return to the Table of Contents Styles dialog box, then click OK to return to the document window.**

9. **Add a new blank page at the end of the document.**

   Unfortunately, PDF bookmarks are not created unless the table of contents is actually placed somewhere in the file. To work around this problem, you are going to place the table of contents on a new page but not include that page in the exported PDF file.

10. **Choose Layout>Table of Contents.**

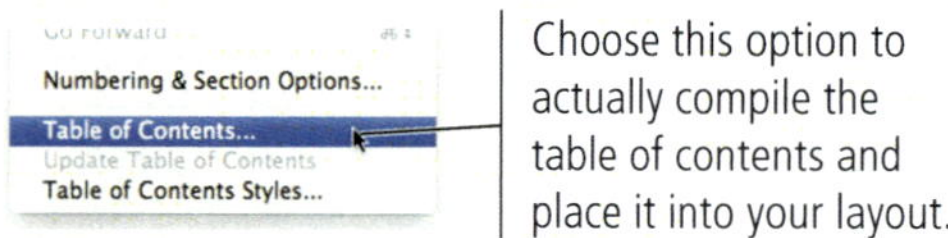

Choose this option to actually compile the table of contents and place it into your layout.

Note:

You are defining this table of contents style to create bookmarks in the interactive PDF file. Since you are not including the table of contents in the actual layout, most of the other options in this dialog box are not relevant. You will work with tables of contents in greater detail in Project 8: Multi-Chapter Booklet.

11. **Make sure TOC Style 1 is selected in the TOC Style menu, then click OK.**

Because you defined a table of contents style, you can call those same options by calling the defined style in the TOC Style menu.

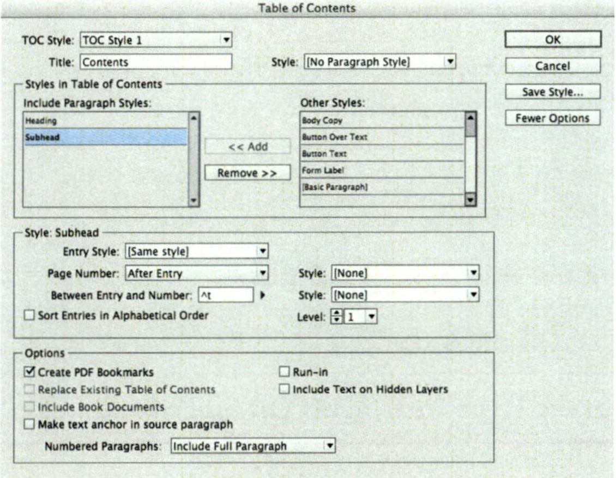

12. **Click the loaded text cursor in the empty page to compile the table of contents.**

Don't worry about the appearance of the list; you are not going to include this page in your final output.

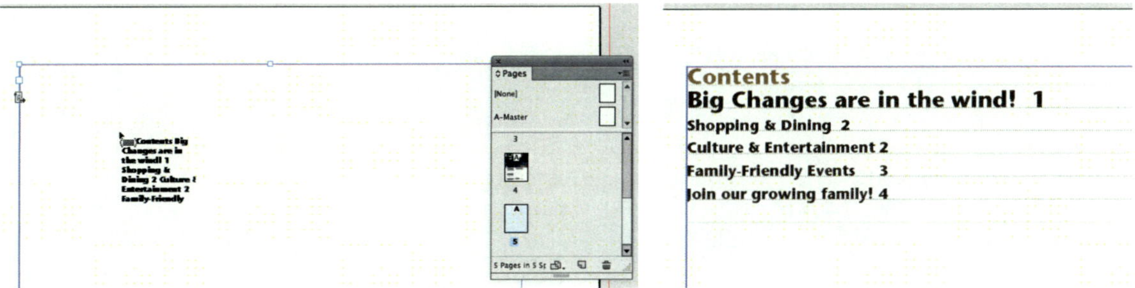

13. **Open the Bookmarks panel (Window>Interactive>Bookmarks).**

This panel lists all bookmarks that exist in the file. You can also use the panel to create a new bookmark — independent of the defined table of contents list — from any selected text or object.

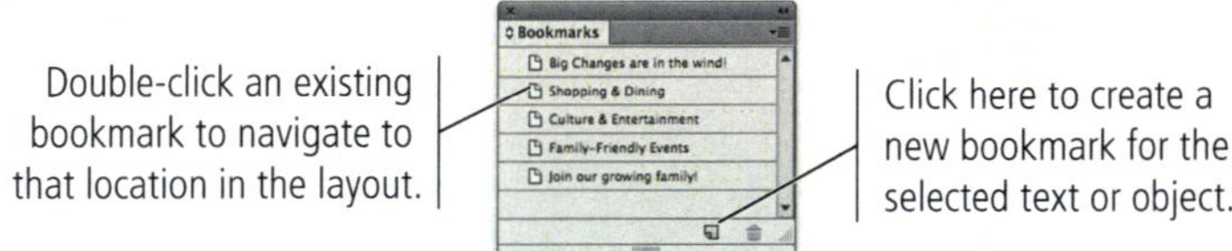

14. **Save the file and continue to the next exercise.**

Define Hyperlinks

Hyperlinks are the most basic — and the most common — interactive elements in digital documents. Every hyperlink has two parts — the hyperlink object (which can be text) and the destination. The destination is the document, a specific place in the file, or another location that is called by clicking the hyperlink. InDesign's Hyperlinks panel makes it very easy to create and apply hyperlinks to elements of a layout.

1. **With boulevard.indd open, navigate to Page 4 of the layout and zoom into the bottom of the text frame in the left column.**

2. **Open the Hyperlinks panel (Window>Interactive>Hyperlinks).**

3. **Highlight the Web address near the end of the text.**

4. **Choose New Hyperlink from URL in the Hyperlinks panel Options menu.**

   This option automatically creates a URL destination based on the selected text.

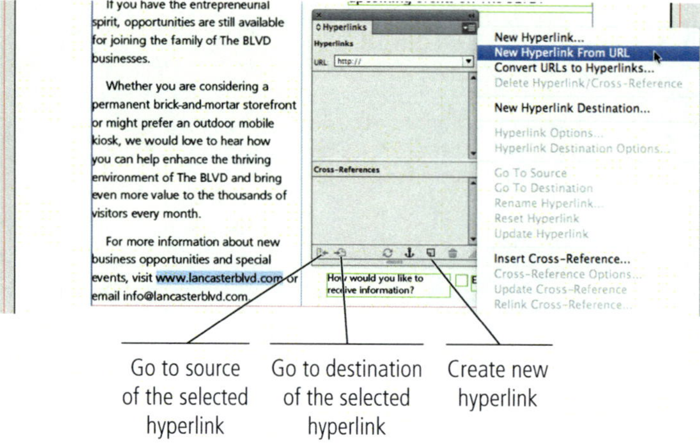

5. **With the new hyperlink selected in the panel, choose Hyperlink Options in the panel Options menu.**

   The New Hyperlink dialog box defines the type and destination of the link, as well as the default appearance of the link in the layout. The highlighted text, which you used to create the link, automatically appears in the Name menu.

   By default, hyperlinks in a print layout have no visual identification. You can use the Appearance section of this dialog box to change the invisible rectangle to a visible rectangle. (In this case, the layout will be exported for both print and Web, so you want the hyperlink to be invisible in the layout.)

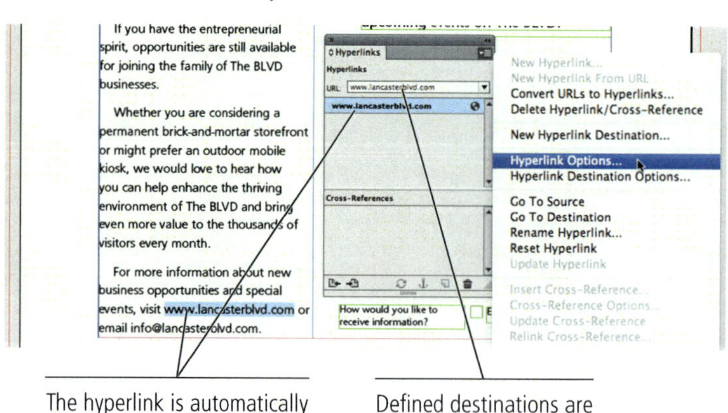

> ***Note:***
>
> *You can choose Convert URLs to Hyperlinks to find and convert all URLs in your document.*
>
> *You can apply this command to the entire document, the entire active story, or the current selection.*

6. **Check the Character Style option, then choose hyperlink in the attached menu.**

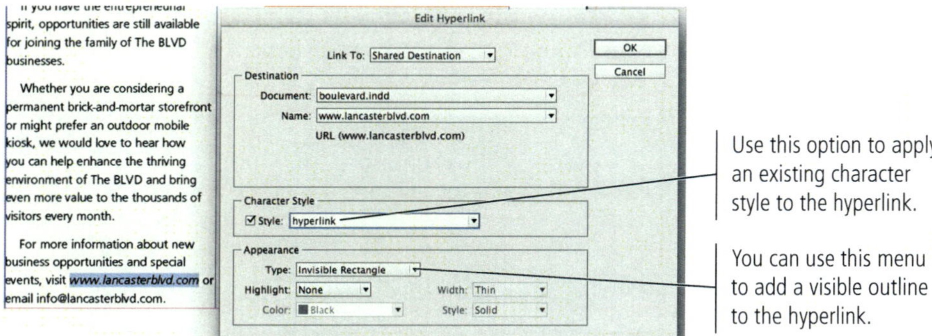

7. **Click OK to close the dialog box.**

8. **Highlight the email address in the last of line of text and copy it.**

9. **Click the Create New Hyperlink button at the bottom of the Hyperlink panel.**

10. **In the New Hyperlink dialog box, choose Email in the Link To menu, then paste the copied address in the Address field.**

    InDesign supports five different kinds of hyperlinks:

    - **URL** opens a Web page at the address you define.
    - **File** opens another file based on the location you define. (This file must be available on a computer or server that users of the file can access. If you define a file on your computer, users won't be able to access the file.)
    - **Email** links open a new mail message that is preaddressed using the address you define.
    - **Page** links navigate to a specific page in the layout.
    - **Text Anchor** opens a page to a specific, defined location.

11. **In the Subject Line field, type Re: The BLVD pdf brochure.**

    When a user clicks an email link, a new mail message opens in their default email client application. The text you enter in the Subject Line field automatically appears in the subject line of the new email message.

12. **Check the Character Style option and choose hyperlink in the Style menu.**

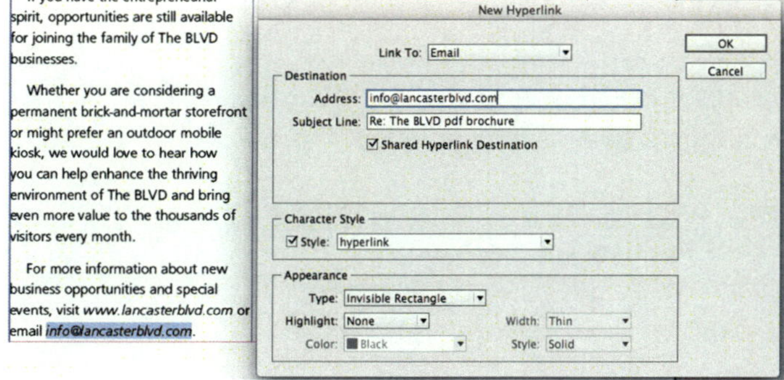

13. **Click OK to apply the change, then save the file and continue to the next exercise.**

Create a File for Web Intent

As you already know, a static print layout can only show a single picture in any given spot. Digitally distributed files are not restricted by this limitation. In the next several exercises, you are going to use a number of built-in tools to create an interactive slideshow that shows multiple images in a single position.

In this exercise, you are going to create a new file to contain the elements of an animated slideshow; when you ultimately finish the file, you will export an SWF file and then place that file into the brochure layout.

1. **Choose File>New>Document. In the New Document dialog box, choose Web in the Intent menu.**

   Because this slideshow will only be used for digital delivery, you are using the built-in Web intent. Measurements automatically default to pixels, and colors are created with the RGB model.

2. **Highlight the Width field and type 8.5". Press Tab, then type 6".**

   Although pixels are the default measurements for web documents, you know you need to fill a space that is 8.5″ wide by 6″ high in the brochure layout. By typing the width and height in inches, the software automatically makes the necessary conversion to pixels.

3. **Change all four Margin fields to 10 px.**

4. **Turn off the Facing Pages and Primary Text Frame options, then click OK to create the new file.**

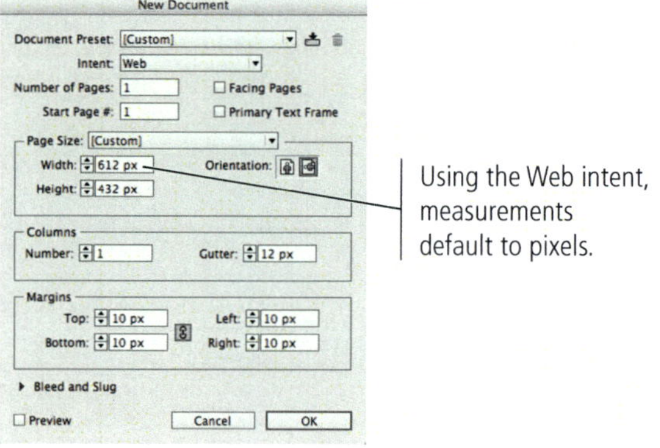

Using the Web intent, measurements default to pixels.

5. **Save the file immediately as `slideshow.indd` in your WIP>Lancaster folder.**

6. **Choose File>Place. Navigate to `1-pavement.jpg` in the WIP>Lancaster> Slides folder. Uncheck the Show Import Options box and click Open.**

7. **Click the loaded cursor on the page to place the image. Using the Control panel, position the top-left corner of the image at X: 0, Y: 0.**

8. **Using the Type tool, create a new type frame with the following parameters (based on the top-left reference point):**

X: 0 px	**W: 612 px**
Y: 365 px	**H: 67 px**

9. **Fill the text frame with black, then open the Text Frame Options dialog box (Object>Text Frame Options). Define a 20-px inset on the left and right edges of the frame, set the Vertical Justification Align option to Center, then click OK.**

   In InDesign, animation and interactivity work around the same basic objects (frames) that you use to create a print layout. This means you can apply the same settings that you are already familiar with to control the appearance of an object in a dynamic file.

> *Note:*
>
> *You might notice that the column width in the Text Frame Options dialog box changes to 572 px. This is the result of subtracting the left and right inset values (20 px each) from the frame size (612 px).*

Using the Web intent, default colors are created in the RGB color model.

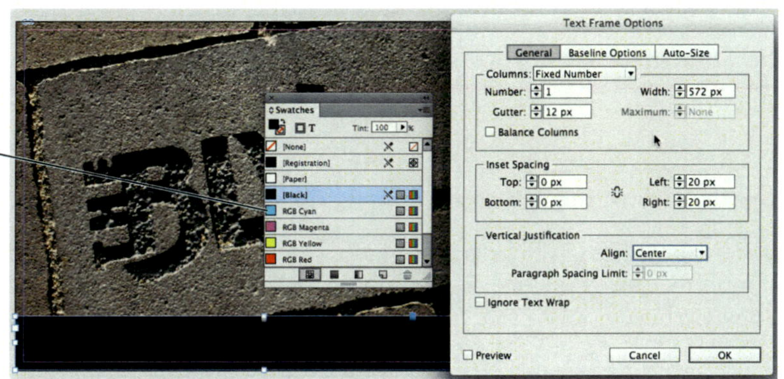

10. **Save the file and continue to the next exercise.**

Create a Basic Animation

Digital PDF and HTML files can include dynamic elements, including objects that move from one place to another. You can use InDesign to add basic animation without the need for a separate application. In this exercise you are going to add motion to the image frame that will contain the different slides in the slideshow.

1. **With slideshow.indd open, select the placed image frame on the page.**

2. **Open the Animation panel (Window>Interactive>Animation).**

3. **Open the Preset menu and choose Fly in From Top.**

   InDesign includes a number of predefined animation presets. You can use these as defined or use them as starting points and modify the settings to customize the animation.

The image frame is selected.

4. **Move your mouse cursor over the preview area in the Animation panel to review the effect of the active settings.**

   The green line is called a **motion path**; it defines the path over which an object will move throughout the animation. Each dot on the path represents a frame in the animation.

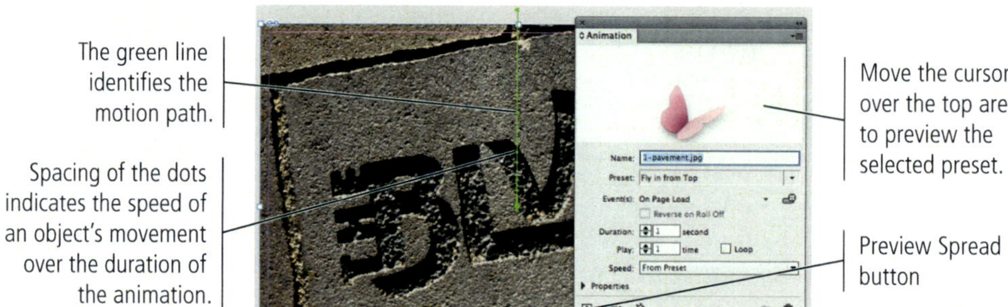

5. **At the bottom of the Animation panel, click the Preview Spread button.**

   This opens the SWF Preview panel, which you can use to preview the defined animation using the actual artwork in your file.

6. **Click the bottom-right corner of the panel and drag to enlarge it.**

7. **Click the Play button at the bottom of the panel.**

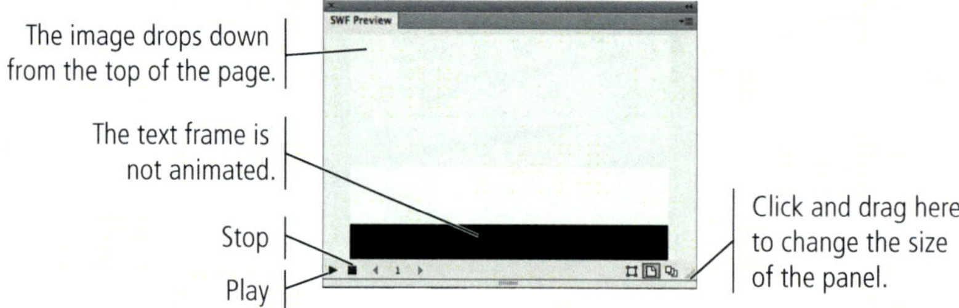

8. **In the Animation panel, change the Duration field to 1.5 seconds.**

   Animations function based on the concept of frames per second or the number of frames that flash to create the illusion of continuous movement. When you increase the duration of an animation, you add more dots (frames) to the motion path.

9. **Choose None in the Speed menu.**

   The spacing of dots on the motion path is a function of easing, or how quickly an object moves at various parts of an animation. Closer spacing between dots represents slower movement; wider spacing represents faster motion. By choosing None in the Speed menu, the dots on the motion path are equally spaced; this animation will have a uniform speed over the entire duration.

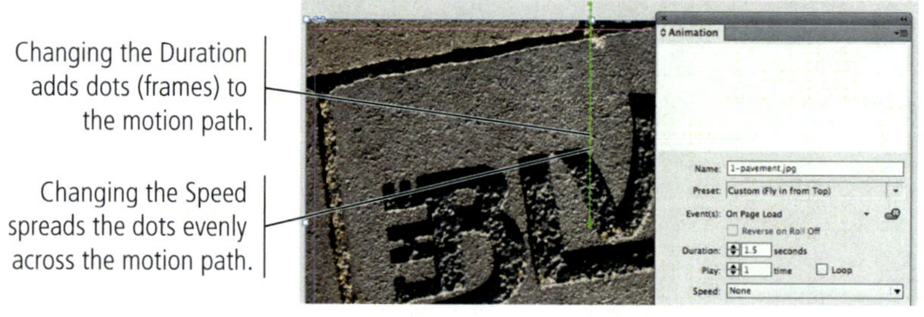

10. **Click the Play button at the bottom of the SWF Preview panel and review the difference.**

11. **Save the file and continue to the next exercise.**

Note:

If you click the motion path to select it, you can use the built-in tools (e.g., the Pen tool and its variants) to edit the motion path — effectively editing the direction of an object's movement throughout the animation.

Note:

You can change the frame rate, or number of frames that are generated per second when you export the final SWF file.

The Animation Panel in Depth

The Animation panel offers a variety of options for controlling the details of an animation.

Event(s) defines what event triggers the animation:

- On Page Load, the default, means the animation plays when the page is opened in the SWF file.
- On Page Click triggers when the page is clicked.
- On Click (Self) and On Roll Over (Self) trigger the animation when the object itself is clicked or moused over, respectively. If you choose On Roll Over (Self), you can also select Reverse On Roll Off, which reverses the animation when the mouse moves off the object.

Although you will learn about button events later in this project, you should understand that you can also create a button that triggers the animation. In this case, On Button Event is added to the Event(s) menu.

You can click **Create Button Trigger** to define an existing object that will trigger the animation. After you click Create Button Trigger, click the object that you want to trigger the animation. The clicked object is converted to a button and the Buttons and Forms panel opens.

This object is animated.

Click Create Button Trigger, then click the object you want to trigger the animation.

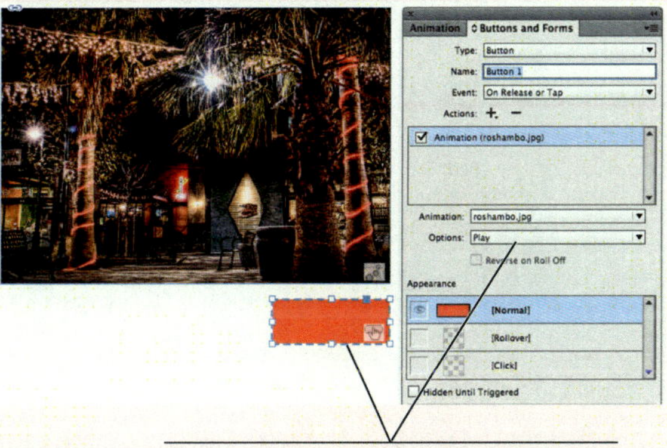

The Buttons and Forms panel automatically opens to control the new button's behavior.

Duration defines how much time it takes for the animation to play (start to finish).

Play defines the number of times the animation is played. Check the Loop option to play the animation repeatedly.

Speed controls the change in animation speed over time.

- Using None, the animation speed is a steady rate.
- Using Ease In, the animation speeds up over time.
- Using Ease Out, the animation slows down over time.

If you expand the **Properties** section of the Animation panel, you can define additional options.

If you look closely, one end of the motion path includes an arrow, indicating the direction the object will travel. You can change the direction using the **Animate menu**:

- From Current Appearance uses the object's current properties as the animation's starting point.
- To Current Appearance uses the object's properties as the animation's ending point.
- To Current Location uses the current object's properties as the starting point of the animation and the object's position as the ending point.

The effect of the Rotate, Scale, and Opacity properties depends on which option is selected in the Animate menu:

- If From Current Appearance or To Current Location is active, the properties define the ending appearance of the animated object.
- If To Current Appearance is active, the properties define the starting appearance of the animated object.

You can use the **animation proxy** to get a rough idea of how your properties affect the animation.

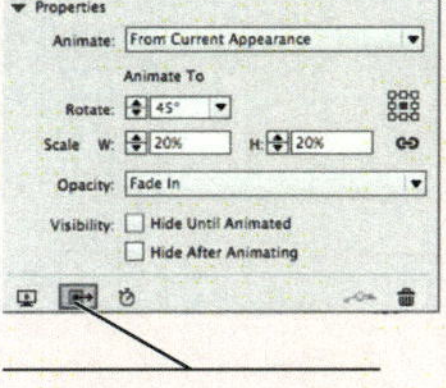

Click here to show the animation proxy on the motion path.

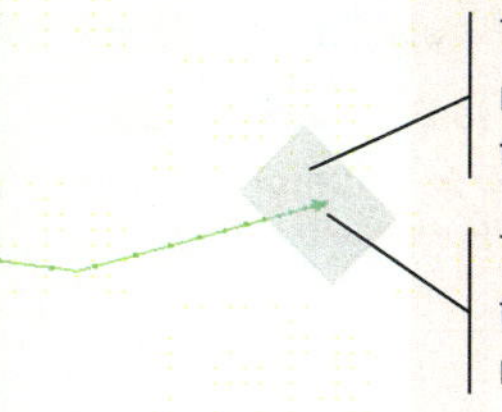

The proxy shows the ending rotation and scale defined in the Animation panel.

This arrow indicates that the object will move *to* this position.

Define Object States

As you know, you are going to display multiple images in the same space. The Object States panel makes this process not only possible, but relatively easy.

1. **With slideshow.indd open, open the Object States panel (Window>Interactive>Object States).**

2. **Using the Selection tool, select the image frame on the page. Click the Convert Selection to Multi-State Object button at the bottom of the Object States panel.**

   Object states are *object* specific, not *content* specific. You have to select the containing frame — not the frame's content — before converting to a multi-state object.

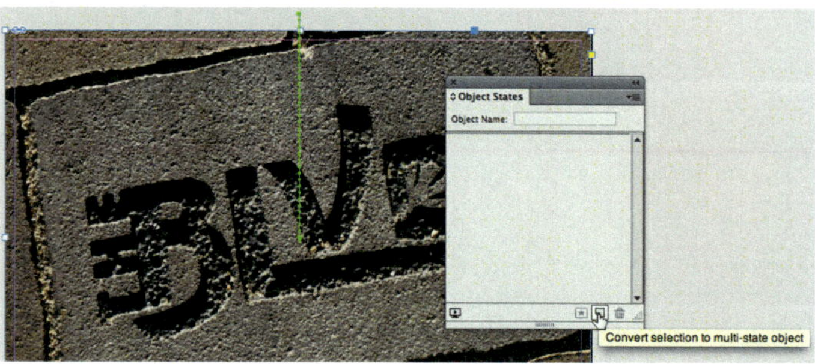

   When you convert the image to a multi-state object, a second state is automatically added to the panel.

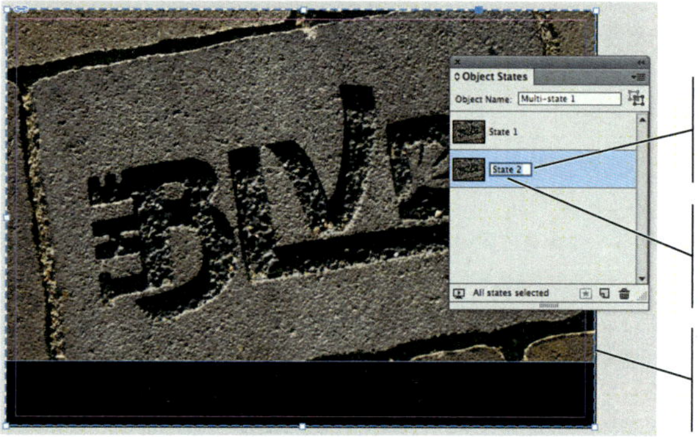

A second state is automatically added to the new multi-state object.

The name of the second state is automatically highlighted.

The multi-state object's frame edge is identified with a dashed border.

3. **Highlight the Object Name field at the top of the panel and type Images.**

4. **Click State 2 in the panel to select it.**

   When you work with multi-state objects, it is important to pay attention to exactly what is selected. The Object States panel includes different icons to help you identify the active selection.

   - When the entire object is selected, you can make transformations (move, resize, etc.) that affect the entire object (and all of its states).
   - When a specific state is selected, object transformations affect only the active state.
   - When the object inside the state is selected, you can change that object — image, text, or other content — in only that state.

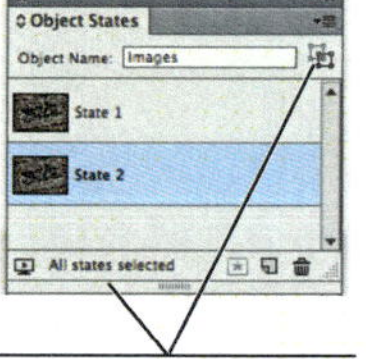

The object (all states) is selected.

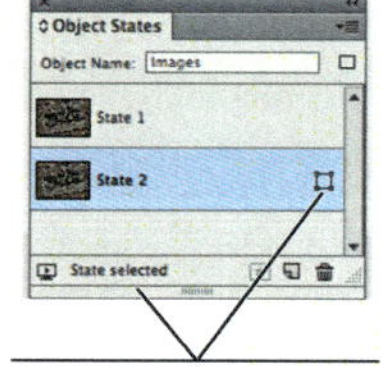

The state is selected.

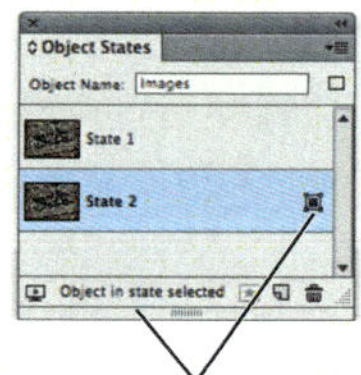

The object in the state is selected.

5. **Using the Direct Selection tool or Content Grabber, select the placed image inside the frame.**

   In this case, you are replacing the content of the object in each state. You have to select the actual content — not the frame — in order to replace it in each successive state.

6. **Choose File>Place. Select `2-cycle.jpg` (in the WIP>Lancaster>Slides folder). Make sure the Replace Selected Item option is checked, then click Open.**

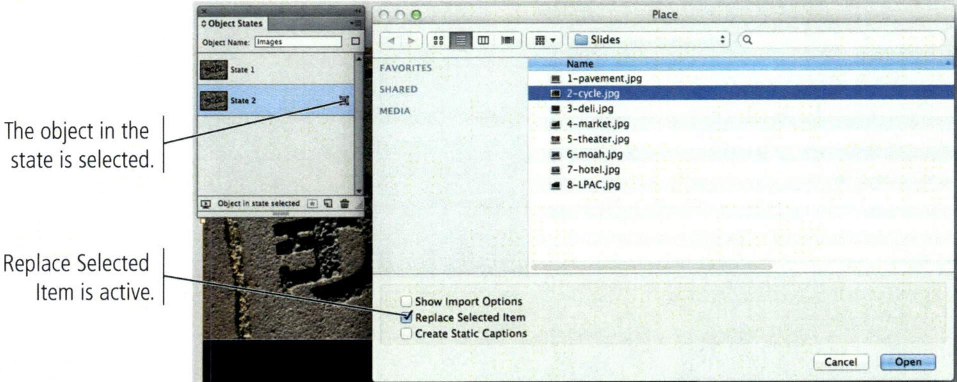

7. **Click the image frame to select it.**

   When the new image is placed, the States panel appears empty because nothing is actually selected in the layout. You have to click the object to again show the states in the panel.

8. **Click the Create New State button at the bottom of the Object States panel.**

9. **With the new state (State 2 Copy) highlighted, immediately type `State 3`, then press Return/Enter to finalize the new name.**

   All successive states are named "State X copy"; unfortunately, if you do not immediately rename them, there is no way to do so later.

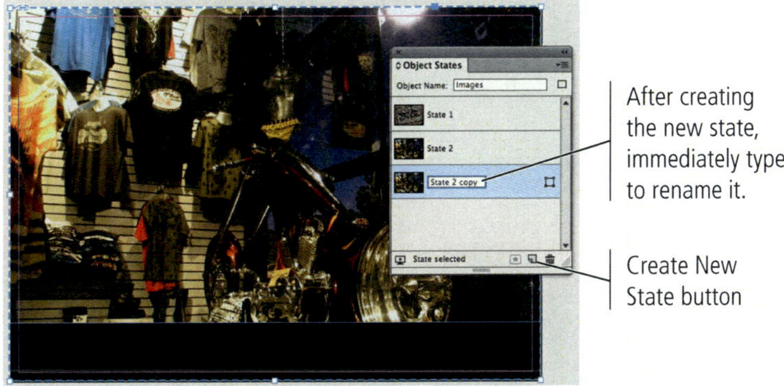

10. **With State 3 selected in the Object States panel, select the image inside the frame.**

11. **Choose File>Place. Select `3-deli.jpg`, make sure Replace Selected Item is active, and click Open.**

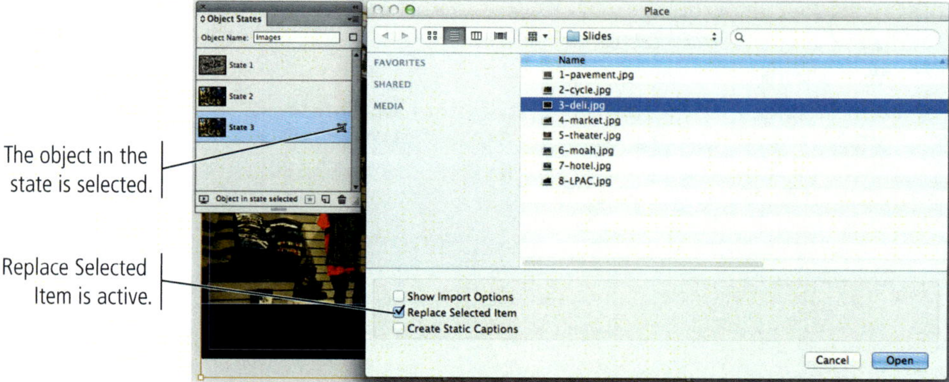

12. **Repeat the process from Steps 8–11 to add additional states for the remaining five images in the Slides folder.**

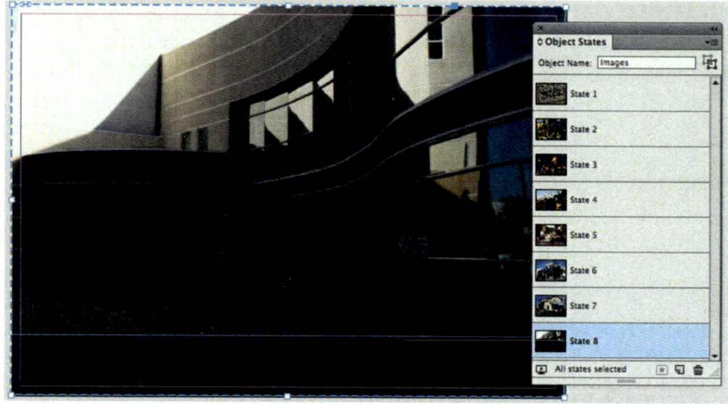

13. **Click away from the image frame to deselect it.**

14. **Choose File>Place. Select `captions.rtf` in the WIP>Lancaster folder, then click Open. Place the loaded file on the pasteboard to the right of the page.**

These captions need to be placed into the text frame below the animated image. You now need to convert the text frame into a second multi-state object to display the correct caption with the correct image.

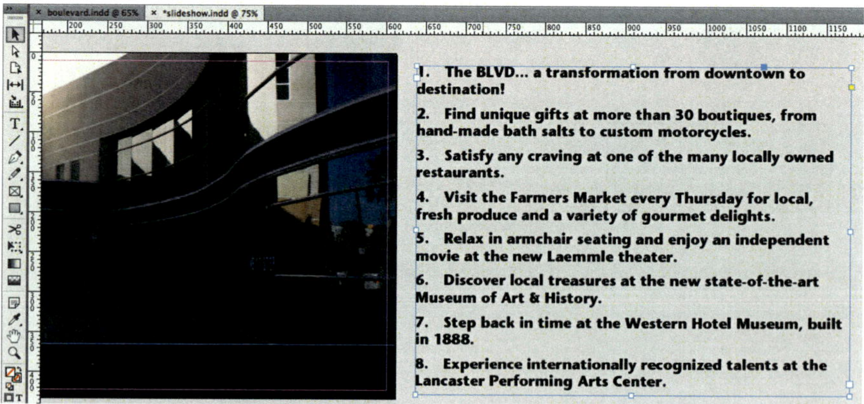

15. **Highlight the text of the first caption (excluding the number) and choose Edit>Cut. Place the insertion point in the black text frame at the bottom of the page, then choose Edit>Paste.**

16. **Select all text in the frame. Change the text color to Paper and apply centered paragraph alignment.**

17. **With the insertion point in the active text, create a new paragraph style named Caption based on the current formatting.**

    This step will make it easier to format the captions for each of the remaining states that you are going to create.

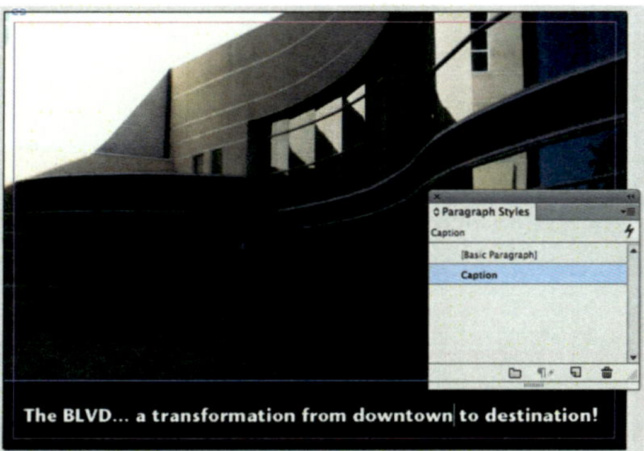

18. **Select the text frame with the Selection tool, then click the Convert Selection to Multi-State Object button at the bottom of the Object States panel.**

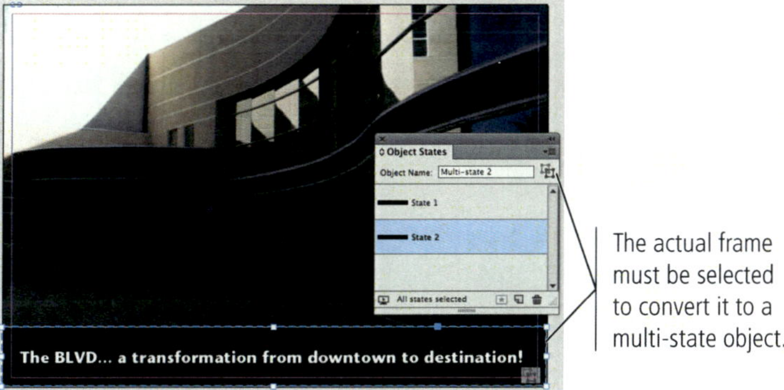

The actual frame must be selected to convert it to a multi-state object.

19. **At the top of the panel, change the Object Name field to Captions.**

20. **In the text frame on the pasteboard, use the Type tool to highlight and cut the text of the second caption.**

21. **Press Command/Control to temporarily access the Selection tool, then click the text frame on the page to select it.**

    Remember: pressing Command/Control temporarily activates the Selection tool, so you can select an object. When you release the modifier key, you automatically return to the last-used tool (in this case, the Type tool). Because the process of creating multiple object states requires a lot of switching from object to content to object again, this shortcut is invaluable to accomplishing your goal in this exercise.

The object in the state must be selected to change the text in the active state.

22. **With State 2 highlighted in the Object States panel, highlight the existing caption, then paste the one you cut in Step 20.**

    If you exactly followed the instructions in this exercise, the image frame currently shows the image from State 8 because we did not tell you to select a different state after completing Step 12. The caption frame shows the caption in State 2 because that state is active for that object.

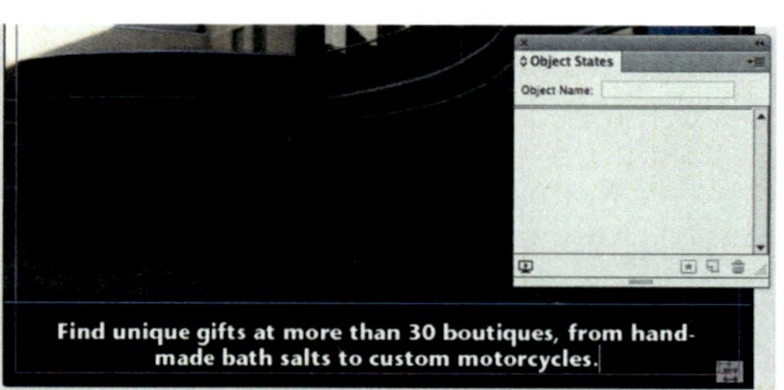

Note:

It is important to realize that these two objects are entirely separate; they are not yet dynamically linked.

23. **Apply the Caption style to the pasted text, then Command/Control-click to select the text frame.**

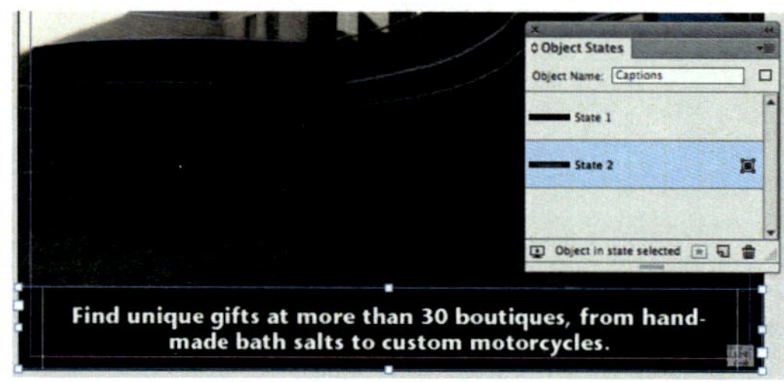

24. **Click the Create New State button at the bottom of the Object States panel. Rename the new state State 3.**

25. **Using the same basic process outlined above, create new states for each caption in the text file that you placed on the pasteboard.**

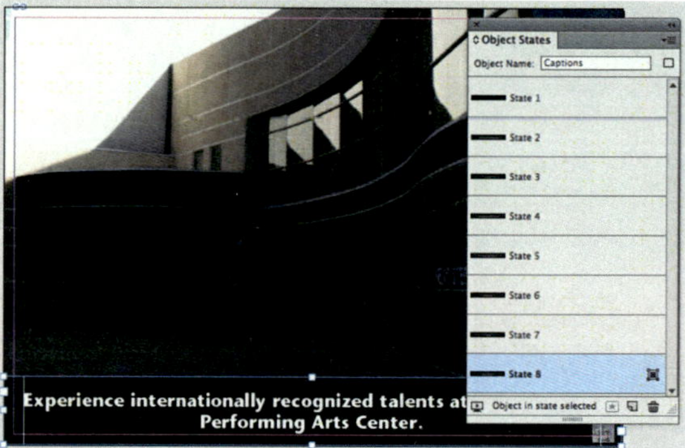

26. **When you're finished creating new states for the captions, delete the text frame from the pasteboard.**

27. **Save the file and continue to the next exercise.**

Create Buttons to Control the Animation

The final piece of this animated slideshow is a set of buttons that allows the user to navigate through the different pictures and captions. You can use built-in tools to create and program buttons to accomplish this task.

1. **With slideshow.indd open, choose Interactive for PDF in the Workspace Switcher.**

   This built-in workspace includes most of the panels you will need to create the animations and interactive elements that make up the slideshow. In addition to the interactive panels that are available in the Window menu, the workspace also opens a library of sample buttons and form objects that is installed with the application.

Note:

This library is not directly accessible in the InDesign interface, although you can open it from the Application>Presets> Button Library folder.

2. **Click the Library panel icon to expand it from the dock. Scroll through the library panel until you find the item labeled "144".**

3. **Click that library item and drag it onto the page. Use the Control panel to resize it to 200% proportionally, then drag it until it snaps to the top and right margin guides.**

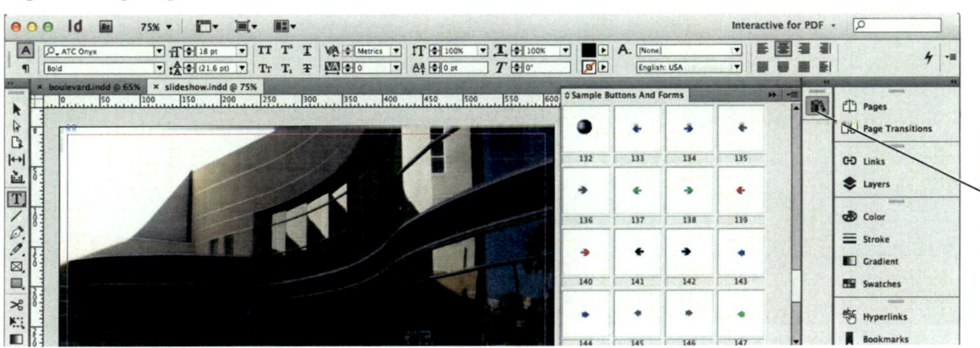

The Interactive for PDF workspace provides access to a library of buttons that is installed with the application.

4. **Zoom in to at least 100%, so you can clearly see the placed button object.**

5. **With the button object selected, open the Buttons and Forms panel (Window>Interactive>Buttons and Forms).**

   An InDesign button can have three states, which are based on the position of the user's mouse cursor. The default Normal state displays when the cursor is not touching the button; the Rollover and Click states are called by the position and action of the user's mouse.

   The buttons in the built-in library are created from objects created entirely in InDesign; the defined rollover states were created by simply modifying the objects in the Normal state. You can use the buttons as-is, or modify them to meet the needs of your project.

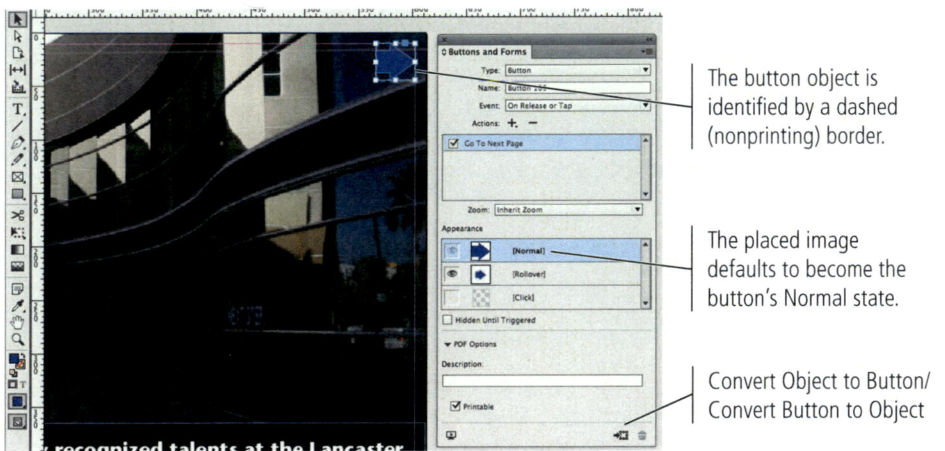

The button object is identified by a dashed (nonprinting) border.

The placed image defaults to become the button's Normal state.

Convert Object to Button/ Convert Button to Object

Note:

You can click the Convert Object to Button option at the bottom of the panel to create a new button from an existing object on the page.

When the selected object is already a button, the Convert Object to Button icon becomes the Convert Button to Object icon.

6. **At the top of the panel, change the Name field to Next Image.**

7. **With the Normal state selected in the Appearance section of the Buttons and Forms panel, change the object's fill-color tint to 50%.**

   This change will help make the buttons more visible over dark images.

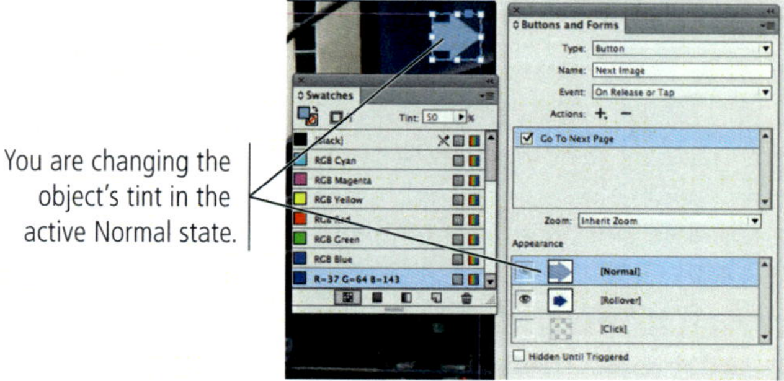

8. **Choose the Rollover state in the panel, then change the object's fill-color tint to 25%.**

   The rollover state will display when a user's mouse cursor moves over the button area. This is a very basic change from one state to another; you can make any number of changes — even add or remove objects — in the various states to create unique effects.

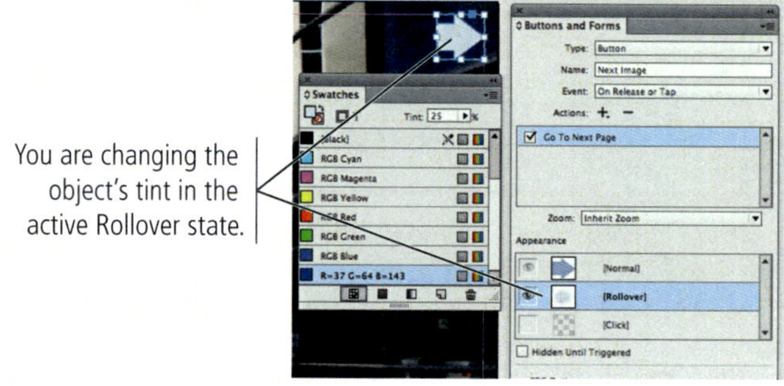

9. **With the button object still selected on the page, open the Event menu in the panel and review the options. Make sure On Release or Tap is selected.**

   InDesign supports six different types of events:

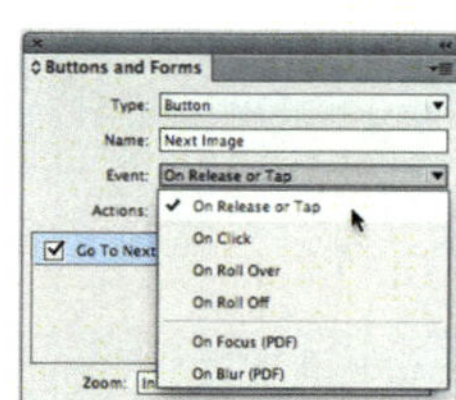

   - **On Release or Tap** triggers when the mouse button is released after clicking, or tapped on a touch-screen device.
   - **On Click** triggers as soon as the mouse button is clicked.
   - **On Roll Over** triggers when the cursor enters the button area.
   - **On Roll Off** triggers when the cursor leaves the button area.
   - **On Focus (PDF)** triggers when pressing the Tab key highlights the button (called "being in focus").
   - **On Blur (PDF)** triggers when the focus moves to another button.

10. **Select the existing action in the list, then click the Delete Selected Action button. Click OK when asked to confirm the deletion.**

The two buttons in your file will both cause something to happen when clicked; the "something" that happens is called an **action**. The default buttons include the Go to Next Page as a default; because you want to control states, not pages, you have to first delete the existing action.

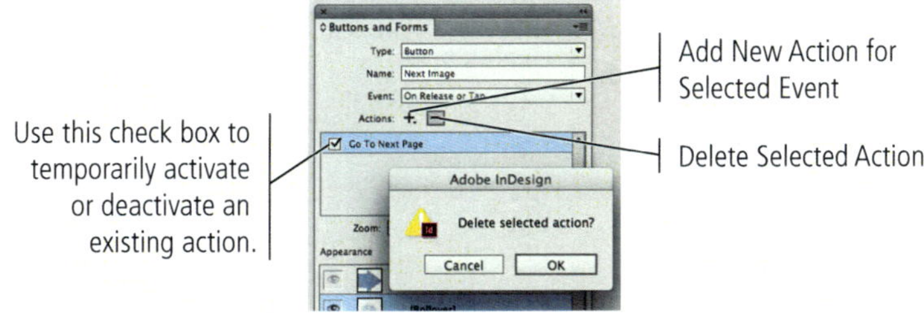

11. **Click the Add New Action button to open the menu of available options.**

The specific action that occurs is defined in this menu:

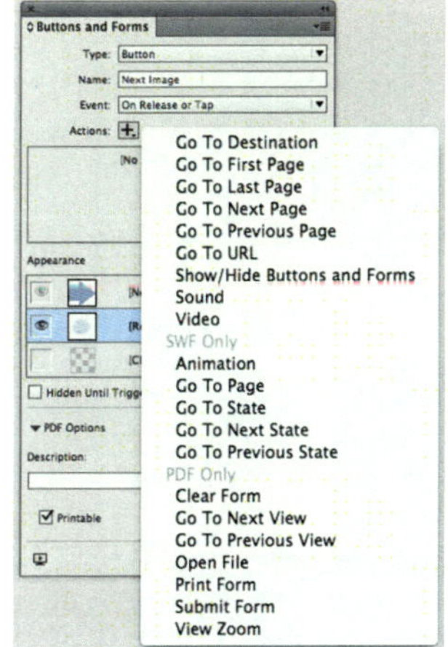

- **Go To Destination** navigates to a specific bookmark or anchor.
- **Go To [First/Last/Next/Previous] Page** navigates to the specified page in a file.
- **Go To URL** opens a Web page in the user's default browser.
- **Show/Hide Buttons and Forms** toggles between showing and hiding specified buttons and form fields in the exported file.
- **Sound** allows you to play, pause, stop, or resume a placed sound file.
- **Video** allows you to play, pause, stop, or resume a placed movie file.
- **Animation** lets you play, pause, stop, or resume a selected animation.
- **Go To Page** navigates to the page that you specify in a defined SWF file.
- **Go To State** navigates to a specific state in a multi-state object.
- **Go To Next/Previous State** navigates to the next or previous state in a multi-state object. These options are especially useful for clicking through a slideshow.
- **Clear Form** resets the defined form fields to their default states.
- **Go To Next View** navigates to a page after going to the previous view (similar to the Forward button in a browser).
- **Go To Previous View** navigates to the most recently viewed page in the PDF file, or returns to the last-used zoom size (similar to the Back button in a browser).
- **Open File** opens the specified file in the file's native application (if possible).
- **Print Form** prints the form on the active page.
- **Submit Form** submits the form on the active page.
- **View Zoom** displays the page according to the zoom option you specify.

12. **Choose Go to Next State.**

When you choose this option, an Object menu appears and automatically defaults to the first multi-state object in the file.

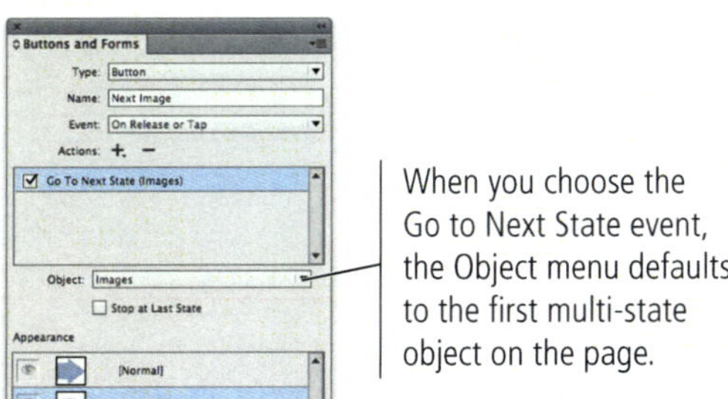

13. **Open the Add New Action button again and choose Go to Next State. In the Object menu, choose Captions.**

Because you want this button to control two objects, you need to add a second action that controls the Captions state.

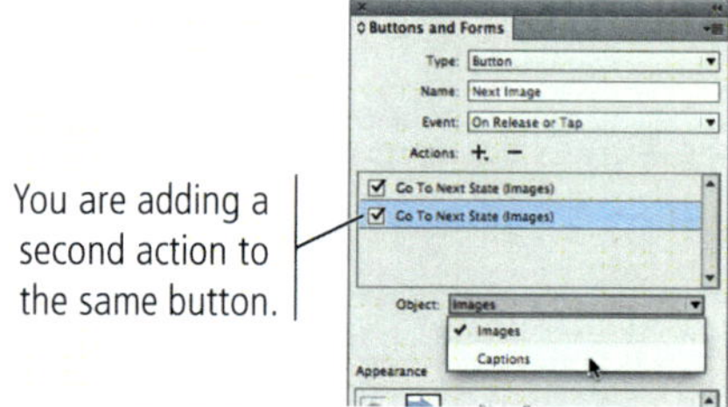

14. **Using the Selection tool, Option/Alt-click and drag to clone the button object. Rotate the clone 180°, then align it to the top and left margin guide.**

15. **In the Buttons and Forms panel, change the button name to Previous Image.**

Because you cloned the existing button, the two Go to Next State actions are already in place. Unfortunately, you can't edit an existing action; you have to delete the ones you don't want and then add what you do want.

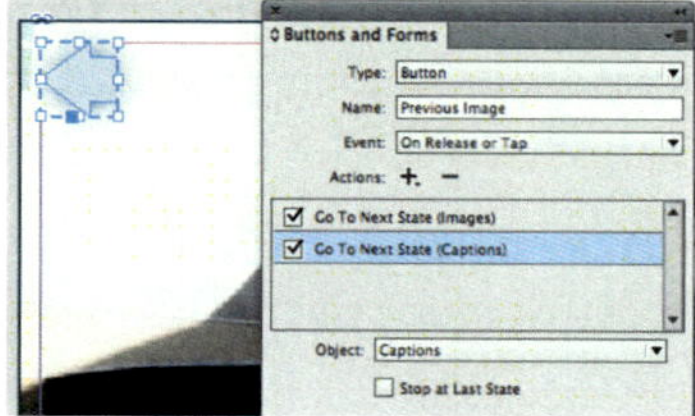

16. **Select and delete both existing actions from the button.**

17. **Using the same process from Steps 11–13, add two actions to the button, using the Go to Previous State action.**

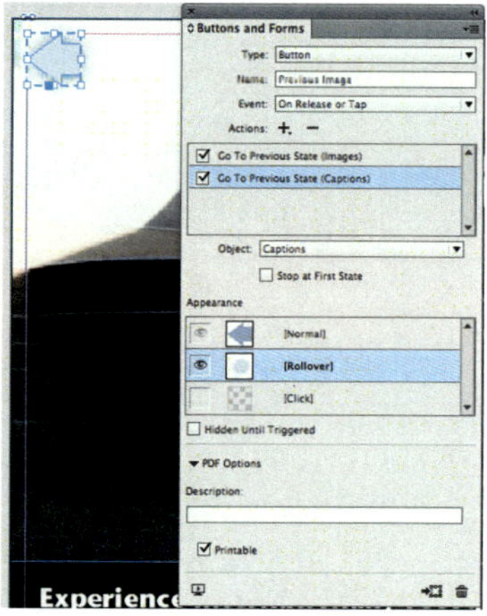

18. **Click the Preview Spread button at the bottom of the Buttons and Forms panel.**

19. **In the resulting SWF Preview panel, test the buttons' functionality.**

Click the buttons to test their functionality and review the various image- and-caption combinations.

20. **Save the file and continue to the next exercise.**

Create and Place an SWF File

You now have a file with several animated elements. The image "flies in" from the top of the page; when a user clicks a button, a different image and caption appear in the frames. You now need to export the file to a format that supports animation, then place the animated file into your brochure.

1. **With slideshow.indd open, choose File>Export.**

2. **Choose Flash Player (SWF) in the Format/Save as Type menu of the Export dialog box, then click Save.**

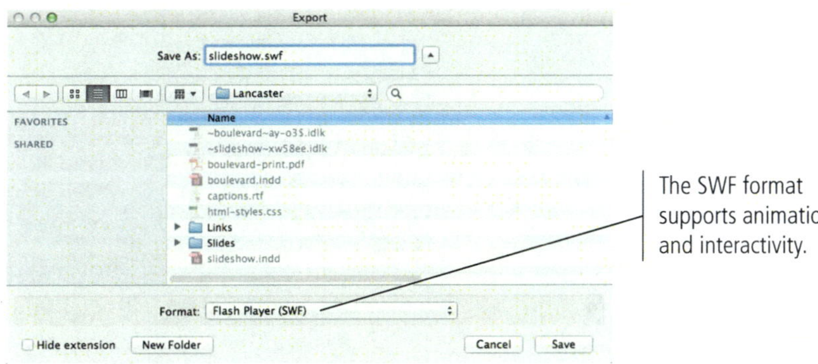

The SWF format supports animation and interactivity.

Note:

You can also export to an FLA file if you want to edit the file in Adobe Flash before exporting to SWF, or if you want to export to a different interactive format.

3. **Review the options in the General tab of the Export SWF dialog box.**

When you export to SWF, you create an interactive file that's ready for viewing in Adobe Flash Player or in a web browser with the Flash Player plug-in.

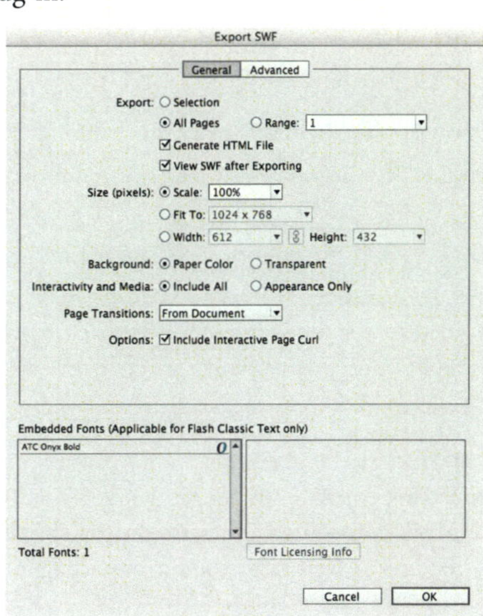

In the **Export** area, you can export the active selection, all pages, or a specific range of pages. If you export more than one page, each spread becomes a separate clip, on a separate frame in a timeline.

If **Generate HTML File** is active, the export process creates an HTML file that contains the SWF file.

View SWF After Exporting, available only when Generate HTML is active, opens the resulting SWF file in your default web browser when the export process is complete.

The **Size (pixels)** options can be used to output a file at a different size than what is defined in the layout. You can output to a specific scale percentage, fit to a specific monitor size, or to a defined size (in pixels).

The **Background** options determine whether transparent areas of the file remain transparent or use the Paper color from the current Swatches panel.

In the **Interactivity and Media** options, the default Include All allows movies, sounds, buttons, and animations to be interactive in the exported SWF file. If you select Appearance Only, the exported file includes the normal state of buttons and video posters as static objects.

(Appearance Only is selected if you choose Flatten Transparency in the Advanced panel.)

You can use the **Page Transitions** menu to define a page transition that applies to all pages. You can choose the From Document option to use the settings that are already defined in the layout.

If **Include Interactive Page Curl** is checked, users playing the SWF file can drag a page corner to turn it, creating the appearance of turning a page in a physical book.

Note:

Page transitions were explained in Project 4: Realtor Collateral Booklet.

4. Uncheck the Generate HTML File option.

Because you are going to place this file into another InDesign layout, you don't need the container HTML file.

5. Click the Advanced button and review those options.

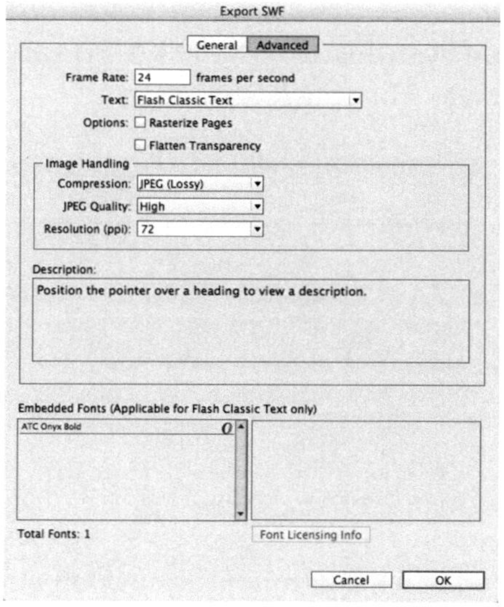

Frame Rate defines the number of frames in one second. Higher frame rates create smoother animations but also increase the file size.

The **Text** menu determines how InDesign text is output.

- Flash Classic Text outputs searchable text that results in the smallest file size.
- Convert to Outlines outputs the text as vector objects.
- Convert to Pixels outputs the text as bitmap images.

The **Embedded Fonts** area at the bottom of the dialog box lists all fonts used in the document. If you choose to export Flash Classic Text, the listed fonts will be embedded in the SWF file so that the text appears exactly as you defined in the layout. (Some fonts do not allow embedding; in that case, you will have to change to a different font if you want to be sure text appears as you intended.)

Rasterize Pages converts all page items to bitmaps.

Flatten Transparency removes live transparency from the SWF and preserves the transparency appearance; all interactivity is removed from the exported SWF file.

The **Compression** option defines how compression is applied in the resulting file.

- Automatic allows InDesign to determine the best quality for color and grayscale images.
- JPEG (lossy) compression removes image data, which might reduce image quality.
- PNG (Lossless) exports the file without lossy compression, but can result in larger file size.

JPEG Quality, available if you choose Automatic or JPEG (Lossy) compression, defines the amount of detail in the exported image. Higher quality means less compression and larger file size.

Resolution (ppi) defines the pixels per inch of bitmap images in the exported SWF. Lower resolution is appropriate for monitor display at 100%. Keep in mind, however, that some tablet devices support higher resolution. Higher resolutions also produce better results if the user zooms in to the bitmap images.

6. **Click OK to export the SWF file, then close slideshow.indd.**

7. **If necessary, open boulevard.indd (from your WIP>Lancaster folder) and navigate to Page 1.**

8. **In the Layers panel, click Interactive to make that layer active.**

   Remember, you are using one file to contain both print and interactive layouts. The Interactive layer, as the name suggests, will contain the interactive objects — including the slideshow.

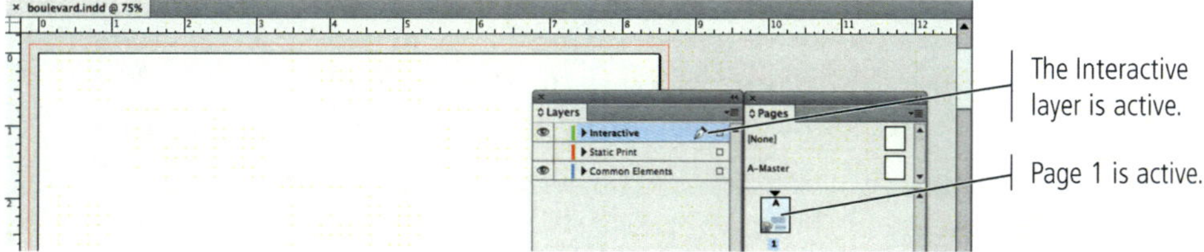

9. **Choose File>Place. Select the slideshow.swf file you just created and click Open. Position the placed object so the top-left corner is at X: 0, Y: 0.**

   When you place a SWF file, a media object appears in a frame. This object links to the media file. You can resize the media object to determine the size of the play area.

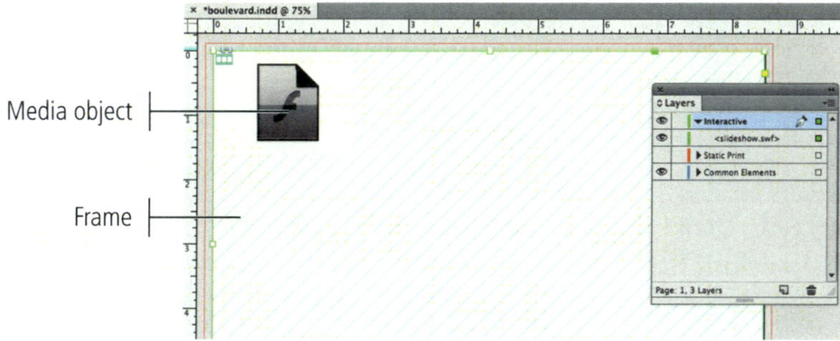

10. **Open the Media panel (Window>Interactive>Media).**

11. **Check the Play on Page Load option, then choose From Current Frame in the Poster menu.**

    The **poster image** is simply the image that appears in the frame when the multimedia file is not playing. From Current Frame displays a graphic preview of the active frame of the SWF file in the placed object frame. You can also use the Choose Image option to define a separate image that appears until the animation plays.

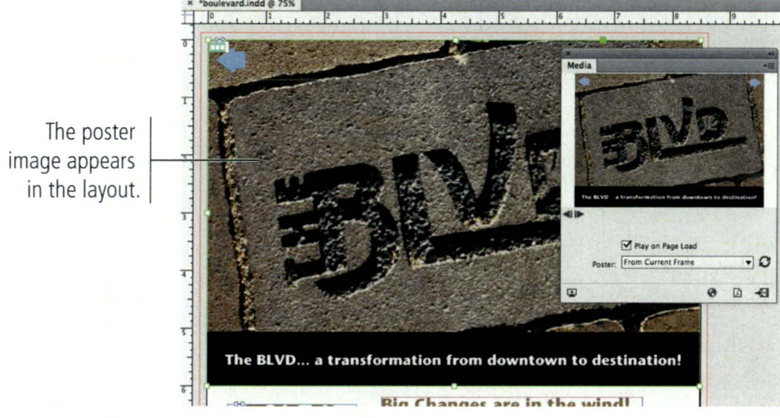

12. **Save the file and continue to the next exercise.**

Create Text Form Fields

The PDF format allows you to create forms that a user can fill out and submit directly in Acrobat without the need to print and mail the page. Until now, creating these forms has been a time-consuming and tedious process that could only be completed in Adobe Acrobat. If you changed the layout and regenerated the PDF file, you also needed to redo all the form-creation work in Acrobat. In InDesign, you can create form objects directly in InDesign.

1. **With boulevard.indd open, navigate to Page 4.**

2. **Click to select the empty frame above the "Name" label. In the Buttons and Forms panel, open the Type menu and choose Text Field.**

   As you can see, form objects can easily be created from standard InDesign objects, such as the empty frames in this layout.

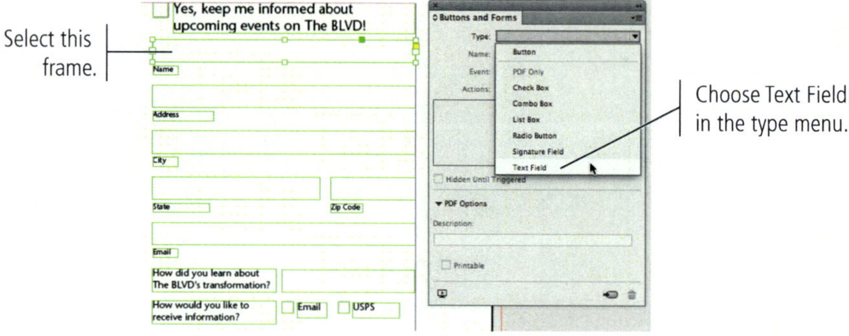

3. **At the top of the panel, change the Name field to Name. At the bottom of the panel, check the Required option.**

   Form objects, like button objects, can trigger actions. In this simple form, you do not need to assign actions to these basic text fields.

   You do, however, need to make sure people include at least the basic contact information. By checking the **Required** box, users won't be able to submit the form unless they fill out this field.

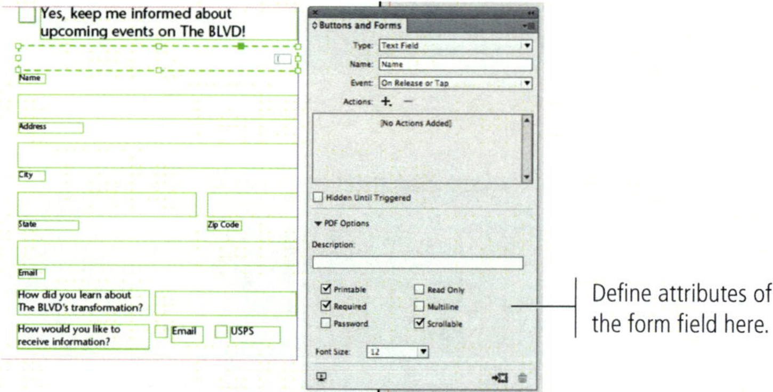

   If you check **Password**, content in the field will appear as asterisks.

   If you check **Read Only**, users will not be able to enter data into the field.

   If you check the **Multiline** option, the field can contain more than one line of entered text. If the **Scrollable** option is also checked, the field will display scrollbars as soon as more text is entered than will fit into the defined field height.

4. **Repeat this same process to convert the Address, City, State, Zip Code, and Email frames to required text fields.**

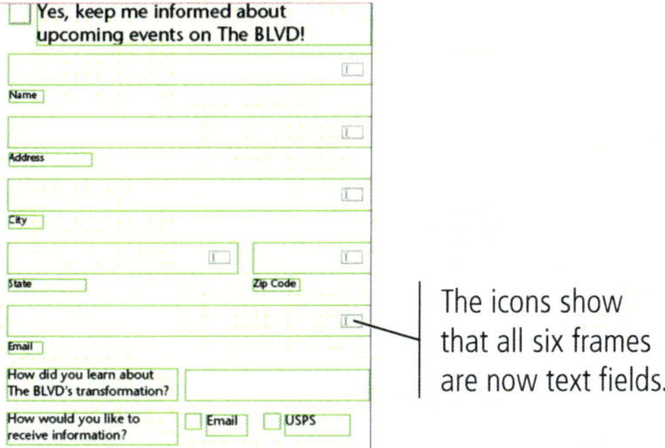

The icons show that all six frames are now text fields.

5. **Save the file and continue to the next exercise.**

Create a Radio Button Form Field

A radio button is a toggle that allows users to make a yes-or-no choice; the control is either on (selected) or off (not selected). You can also create a radio button group in which users can choose only one of a defined set of options.

1. **With boulevard.indd open, zoom in to the frame in front of the word "Yes" (at the top of the form area), then click to select it.**

2. **In the Buttons and Forms panel, choose Radio Button in the Type menu.**

3. **Change the Name field to Add to Mailing List.**

   When you convert a frame to a radio button, InDesign automatically creates a variety of states in the Appearance section of the Buttons and Forms panel. The selected state is what appears in the layout.

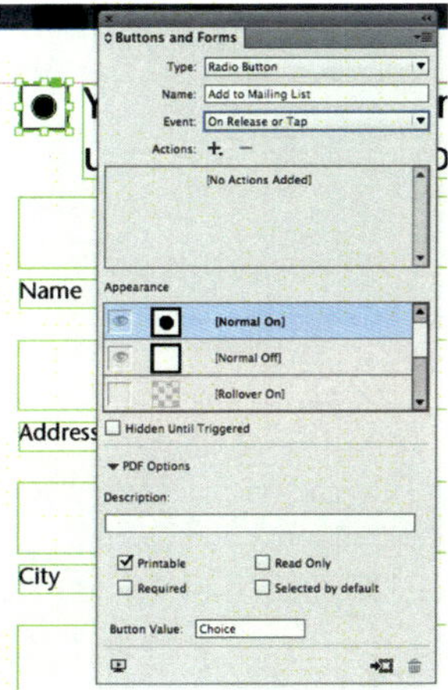

4. **Click away from the radio button object, then click to select it again.**

   If you don't deselect then reselect, the new object name does not register in the Layers panel. This is a small bug in the software but an important one.

Note:

To create a radio button group, in which a user can select only one of several options, define the same name to each radio button that you want to include in the group.

5. **Open the Layers panel, then expand the Add to Mailing List group on the Interactive layer, then expand the [Normal On] group.**

The various radio button states are simply groups of InDesign objects — in this case, a circle and a square.

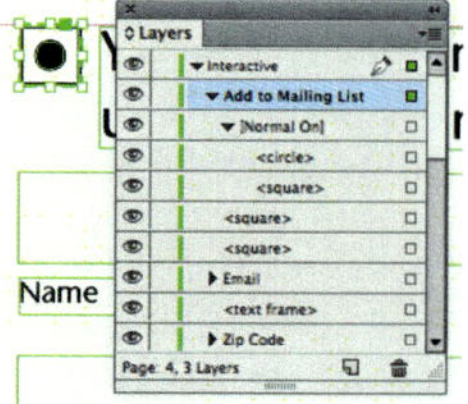

6. **Use the Selected Item icon in the Layers panel to select the circle. Change the Stroke and Fill colors of the circle to Pantone 875 C.**

You can edit the elements of a form object just as you would any other object in the layout. You simply need to select the correct object state in the Appearance area of the panel so you can access the pieces you want to change.

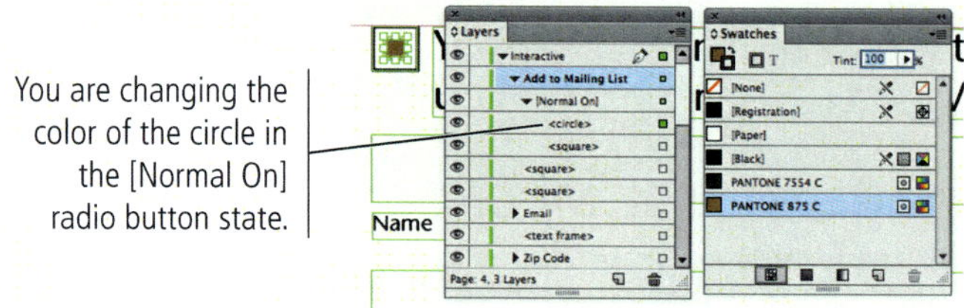

7. **Click the Normal Off option in the Buttons and Forms panel.**

Because it is selected, this will be the default object state in the resulting PDF file.

8. **At the bottom of the panel, activate the Required option, and change the Button Value field to `Yes`.**

The Button Value is the data that will be sent when a user chooses the radio button and submits the form.

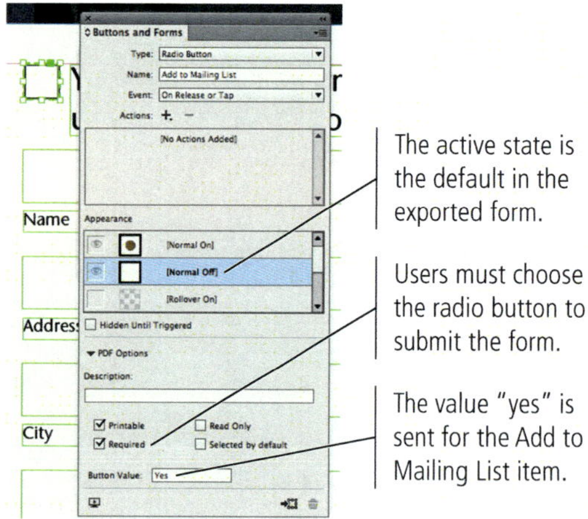

9. **Save the file and continue to the next exercise.**

Note:

If you want to allow users to select more than one option in a list, use the List Box field type.

Create a Combo Box Form Field

A combo box is a type of list in which users click to open the drop down menu of options. An example is the Type menu at the top of the Buttons and Forms panel. You can define a list of options that will appear in the menu; users will be able to make a single choice from the list.

1. **With `boulevard.indd` open, select the frame to the right of the question "How did you learn…".**

2. **In the Buttons and Forms panel, choose Combo Box in the Type menu and change the Name field to `Source`.**

   A combo box is a menu in which users can select only one from a defined list of options. You can use the options at the bottom of the Buttons and Forms panel to define the options that appear in the list.

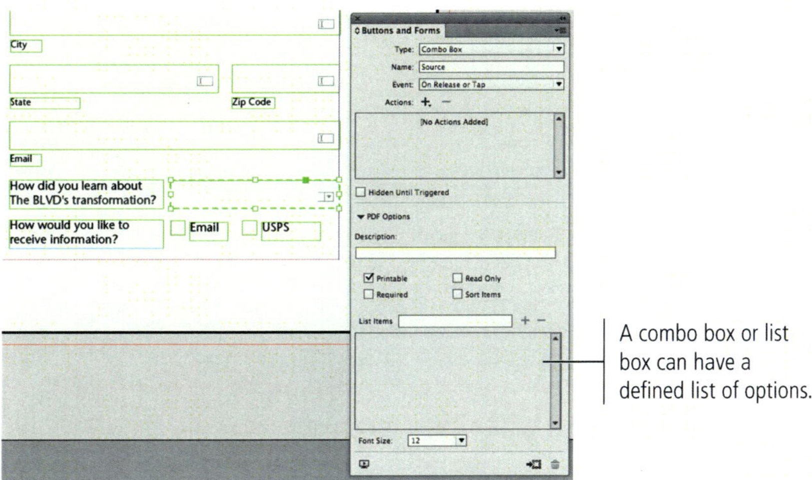

A combo box or list box can have a defined list of options.

3. **Type `Direct mail` in the List Items field and then click the + button.**

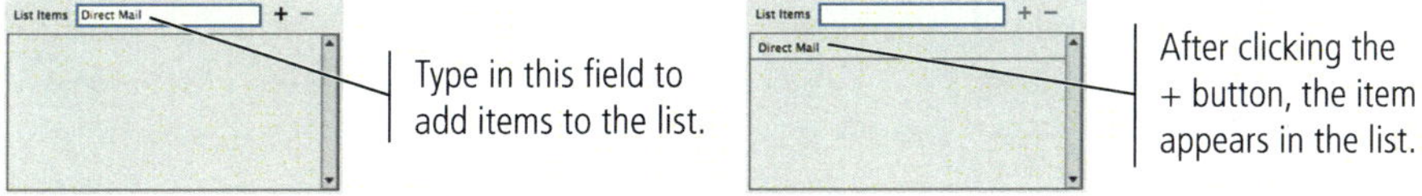

Type in this field to add items to the list.

After clicking the + button, the item appears in the list.

4. **Using the same method as in Step 3, add five more items to the list:**

   `City employee`
   `Email`
   `Newspaper`
   `Friend/Family`
   `Other`

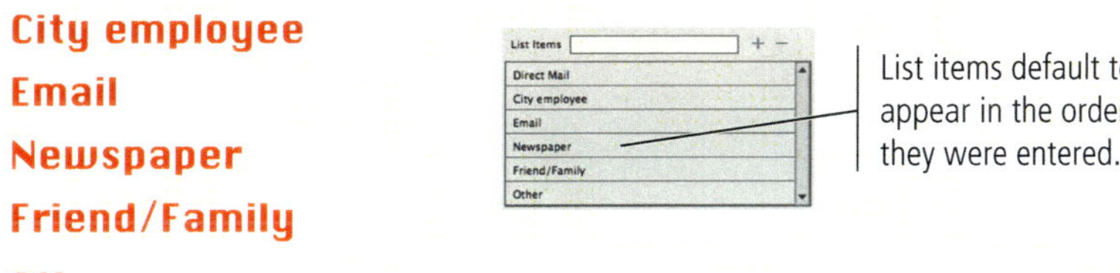

List items default to appear in the order they were entered.

5. **Check the Sort Items option.**

   This option organizes the defined list items alphabetically.

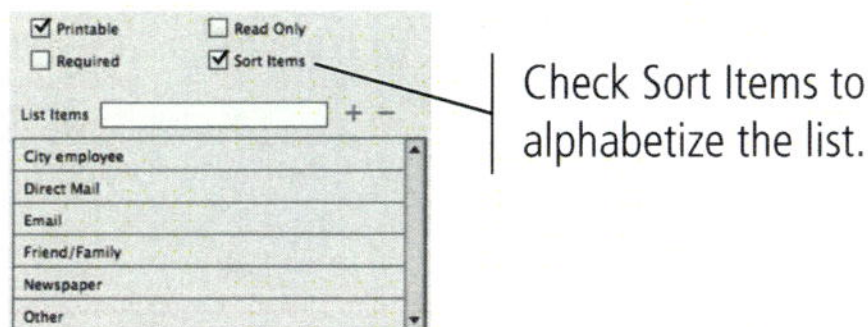

Check Sort Items to alphabetize the list.

6. **Add Select one... as another list item.**

   Because the list is being sorted alphabetically, this new item is added to the bottom of the list (S comes after O). However, the first item in the list appears in the menu in the exported PDF; because you want this item to appear at the top of the list, you need to manually rearrange the list items.

7. **Uncheck the Sort Items option. Click the Select one... item and drag in the list to move it to the top of the panel.**

   A black line identifies where the list item will appear when you release the mouse button.

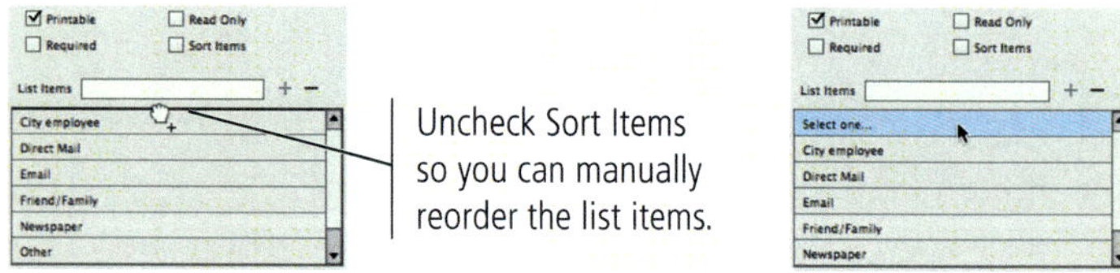

8. **Save the file and continue to the next exercise.**

Create Check Box Form Fields

A check box is similar to a radio button; users can turn it on or off to select an option or not. If a check box is part of a group, however, users can typically select more than one option — unlike radio button groups, which allow only one choice from the available options.

1. **With boulevard.indd open, select the empty frame to the left of the Email label.**

2. **In the Buttons and Forms panel, choose Check Box in the Type menu and change the Name field to Send Email.**

3. **At the bottom of the panel, select the Normal Off state as the default state.**

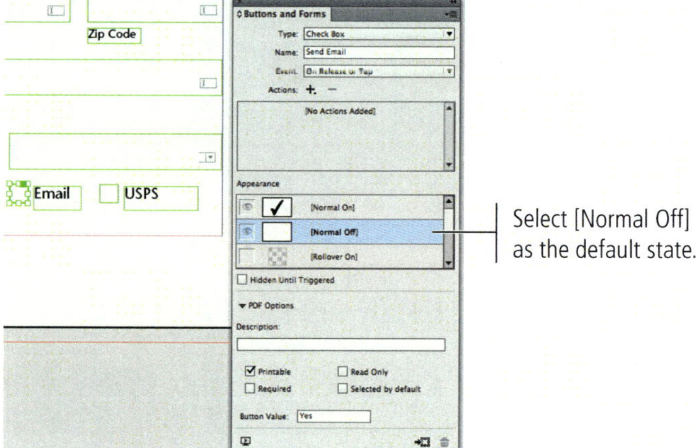

4. **Repeat this process to create a second check box named Send Mail for the frame to the left of the "USPS" label.**

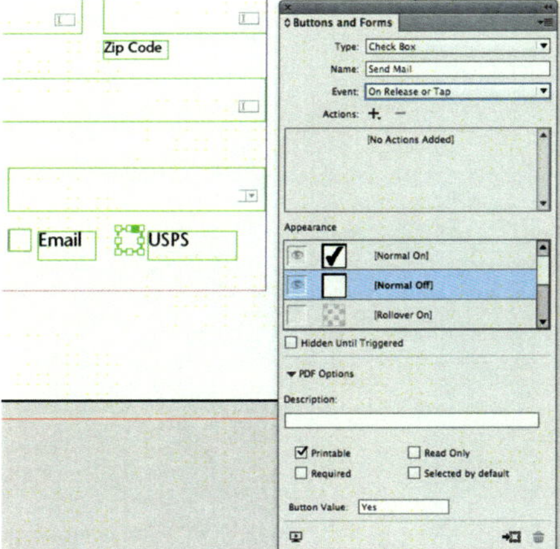

5. **Save the file and continue to the next exercise.**

Create Form Control Buttons

As you have already learned, buttons have multiple states based on the position of the user's mouse cursor. In this exercise, you are going to use built-in actions to create buttons that allow users to clear and submit the form.

1. **With boulevard.indd open, open the Sample Buttons and Forms library. Drag an instance of the button labeled "125" onto the layout and position it as shown in the folowing image.**

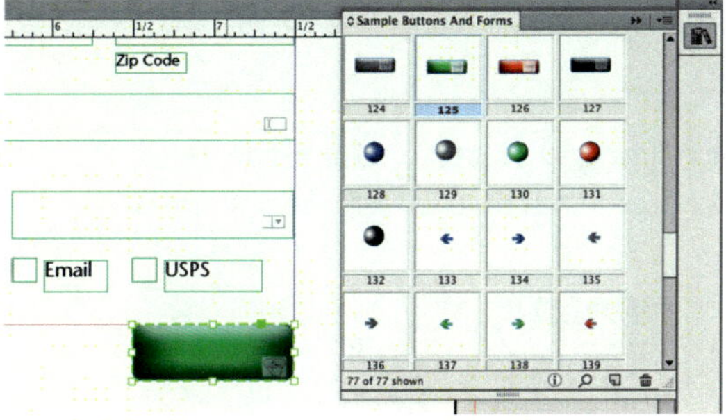

2. **In the Buttons and Forms panel, change the button's name to Submit.**

3. **Click the Delete Selected Action button, then click OK to confirm the deletion.**

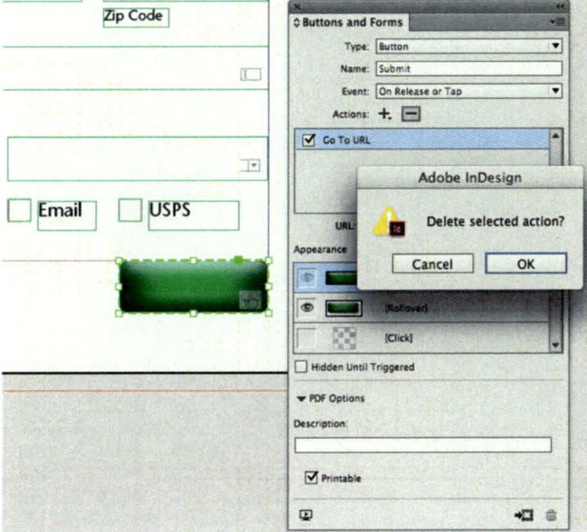

4. Open the Add a New Action menu and choose Submit Form.

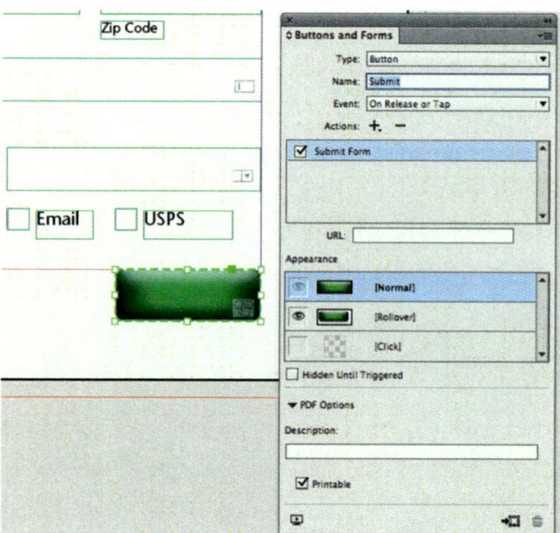

5. Deselect then reselect the button object. With the Normal state selected, use the Layers panel to expand the Submit group and the Normal group on the Interactive layer.

6. Click to select the top rectangle in the group. Change the object's fill color to Pantone 875 C.

7. Using the Type tool, click inside the selected object to convert it to a type frame.

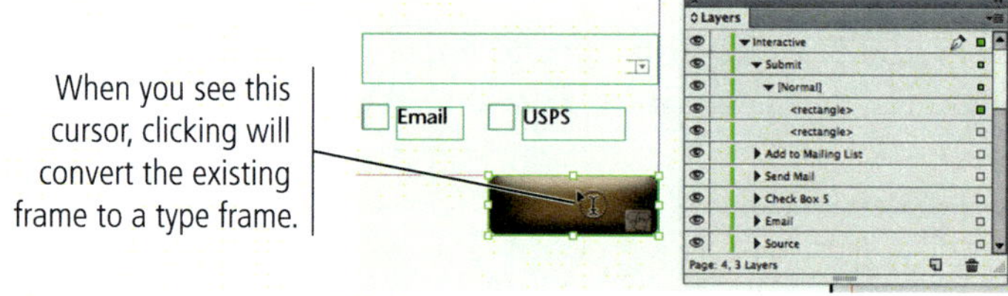

8. Type **Submit** and apply the Button Text paragraph style. Open the Text Frame Options dialog box and apply centered vertical alignment, then click OK to close the dialog box.

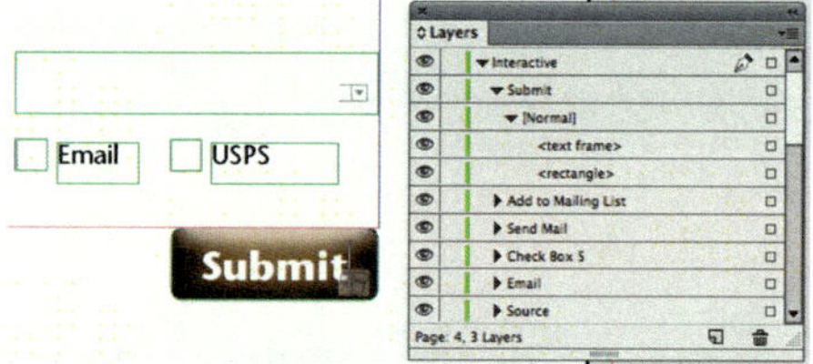

9. Command/Control-click to select the button object, then select the Rollover state in the Buttons and Forms panel.

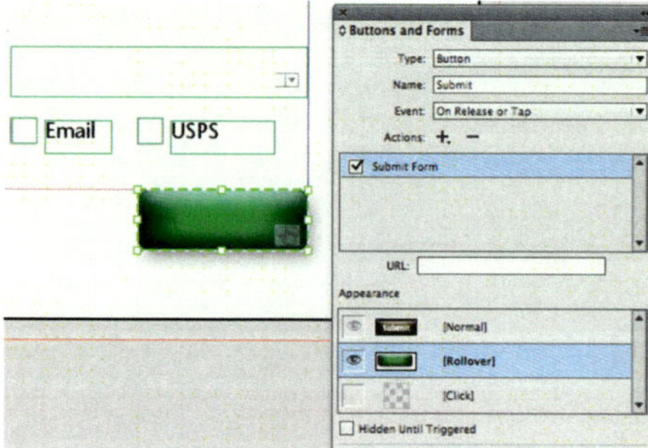

10. **Repeat Steps 5–8 to add the necessary text to the state, using the Button Over Text paragraph style.**

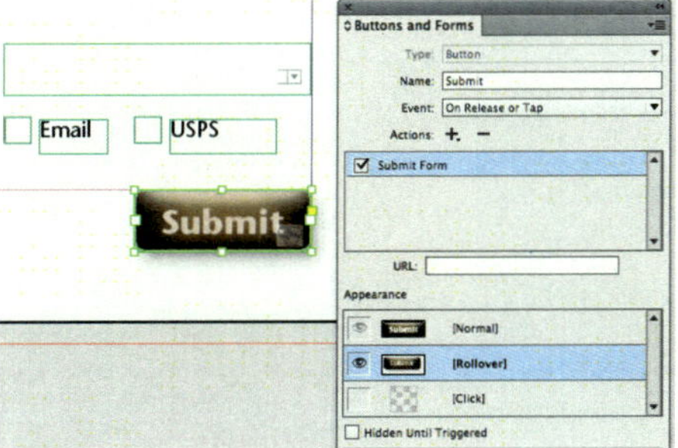

11. **Click away from the button to deselect it, then select the entire button object.**
12. **Option/Alt-drag the button to clone it. Place the clone immediately to the left of the existing button.**
13. **Using what you have already learned about buttons, change the cloned button to clear the form. Use Reset as the button text and Clear Form as the button action.**

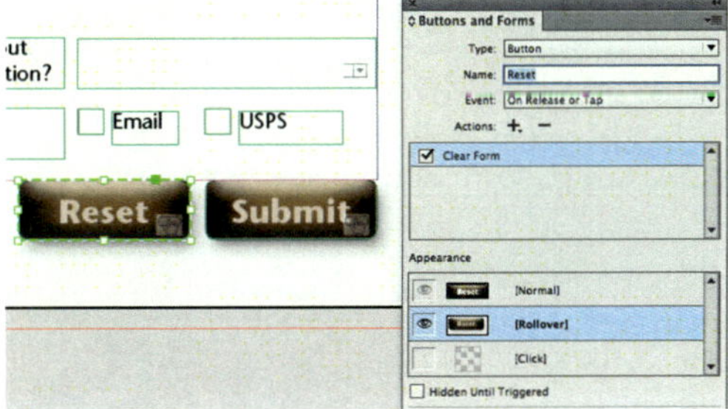

14. **Save the file and continue to the next exercise.**

Export an Interactive PDF

Now that you have defined a number of interactive elements, you need to export the PDF file with the appropriate settings. If you completed Project 5: Ireland Travel Brochure, you already used the Export to Interactive PDF option to create a file with dynamic page transitions. You will use the same options here to create a PDF file that includes your table of contents, hyperlinks, slideshow, and form.

1. **With boulevard.indd open, choose File>Export.**
2. **Choose Adobe PDF (Interactive) in the Format/Save as Type menu, then change the file name to boulevard-digital.pdf.**

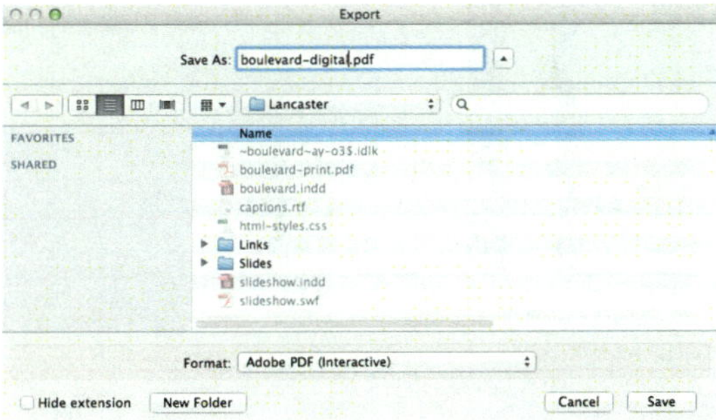

3. **Make the following choices in the Export to Interactive PDF dialog box, then click OK:**

Export to Interactive PDF
Pages: All / Range: 1-4
Pages
Spreads
View After Exporting
Embed Page Thumbnails
Create Acrobat Layers
View: Fit Page
Layout: Default
Presentation: Open in Full Screen Mode
Flip Pages Every: 5 seconds
Page Transitions: From Document
Forms and Media: Include All / Appearance Only
Tagged PDF: Create Tagged PDF
Use Structure for Tab Order
Image Handling
Compression: Automatic
JPEG Quality: Medium
Resolution (ppi): 72
Security... Cancel OK

- **Type 1-4 in the Range field.**

  Remember, you added a fifth page to contain the table of contents that you want to function as bookmarks in the resulting PDF file. By exporting the specific page range, you exclude the unwanted page from the final file.

- **Check the View After Exporting option.**
- **Choose Fit Page in the View menu.**
- **Make sure Include All is selected in the Forms and Media option.**
- **Choose Automatic in the Compression menu.**

4. **Read the resulting warning, then click OK.**

Remember, you are exporting from a file that was originally created for commercial print. As the message states, colors are converted to RGB in interactive PDF files.

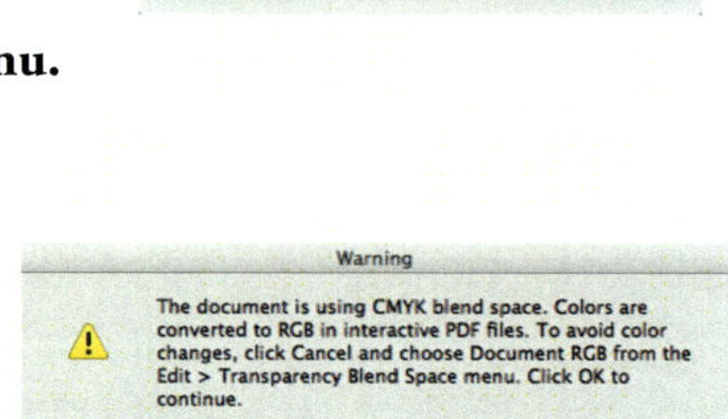

If you recall from the first stage of this project, the images placed in this layout use the RGB color model; you used the Export to PDF (Print) dialog box to convert the image colors only on output. Also, the main highlight color in the layout is a PANTONE spot color, which will be converted in any case for digitally delivered files (there is no spot ink on a monitor or tablet).

In this case you are safe to simply click OK and let the software make the necessary conversions.

Note:

Form distribution is relatively easy using Adobe Acrobat Pro; although not technically part of this project, we encourage you to explore the options in the Forms menu if you have Acrobat Pro.

5. **When the new PDF file opens, navigate through the pages and test your interactive elements.**

Although the form still needs to be officially distributed so that data can be easily gathered, you can still test the functionality of the form fields and buttons

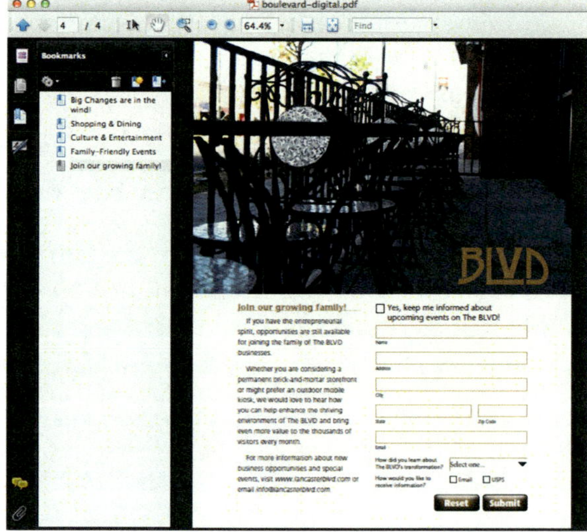

6. **Close the PDF file and return to InDesign.**

7. **Save the InDesign file and continue to the next stage of the project.**

Stage 3 Creating EPUB and HTML Files

Clients need to be able to distribute their information in as many ways as possible to reach the broadest audience; to meet that need, they are turning to a variety of digital media in addition to print communication. Consider the following data:

- As of June 2012, more than 78% of the U.S. population had access to the internet.[1]
- As of September 2012, 45% of American adults owned a smart phone. This number jumps to 66% for the 18-29 year old demographic.[2]
- In November 2012, 25% of American adults owned a tablet device and 19% owned a dedicated e-reader device — both up from only 10% in 2011. Together, 33% of American adults own at least one of these (tablet or e-reader).[3]

Digital media publishing is already one of the fastest-growing markets in the professional design community. The almost exponential growth in consumer interest is only going to expand that market.

In the final stage of this project, you are going to export two more versions of the file — a Web page using the HTML format, and an e-book using the EPUB format. The built-in tools make it relatively easy to export these formats from the same layout that you used to create the static print layout and interactive PDF file.

Anchor Graphics to Text

If you look through the layout, you might notice that the images simply float on the page — a perfectly appropriate approach for print design, where the position of objects is fixed wherever you place them. For HTML and EPUB output, however, objects are exported based on their left-to-right, top-to-bottom order on the page. If you simply export an HTML or EPUB file from the existing layout, the images will appear in odd places that are inappropriate at best and confusing at worst.

To solve this probem, you need to define exactly where the images should go before exporting the files. You will accomplish this by anchoring the images to the related text.

1. **With boulevard.indd open, navigate to Page 2.**

2. **Make sure frame edges are visible (View>Extras>Show Frame Edges).**

   Two images appear on the spread (not including the logo). The layout suggests (correctly) that each image is related to the nearby heading. As we already explained, however, you need to physically connect the images to the text so they will be in the correct position when you export the EPUB and HTML files.

3. **Using the Selection tool, click the image to the left of the Shopping and Dining heading.**

4. **Zoom in to at least 100% so you can clearly see the handles that surround the image.**

---

1 Internet World Stats, *http://www.internetworldstats.com/*

2 Rainie, Lee. Smartphone Ownership Update: September 2012. Pew Internet & American Life Project, Sep 11, 2012, *http://www.pewinternet.org/Reports/2012/Smartphone-Update-2012/Findings.aspx*, accessed on Apr 1, 2013.

3 Rainie, Lee and Maeve Duggan. E-book Reading Jumps; Print Book Reading Declines. Pew Internet & American Life Project, Dec 27, 2012, *http://libraries.pewinternet.org/2012/12/27/e-book-reading-jumps-print-book-reading-declines/*, accessed on Apr 1, 2013.

5. **Click the blue square near the top-right corner of the image frame and drag until the insertion point appears before the "S" in the heading text.**

When you create the EPUB and HTML files, anchored images will appear immediately above the text where they are anchored.

When the image frame is selected, click this icon and drag to anchor the image to the text.

Watch the insertion point to see where the image will be anchored.

Be careful when you drag to anchor an image; it is very easy to drop the anchor after a character instead of before it, especially if you are using a small view percentage. You can always drag again from the anchor icon to redirect the image to anchor in a different location.

When you release the mouse button, a dotted line connects the image to the text where it is anchored. If you don't see the dotted line connecting the anchored image to the text, choose View>Extras>Show Text Threads.

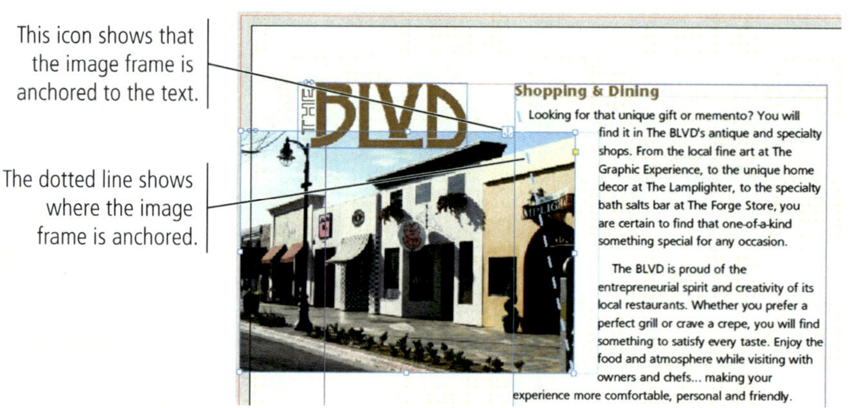

6. **Repeat this process to anchor the bottom image in front of the Culture & Entertainment heading.**

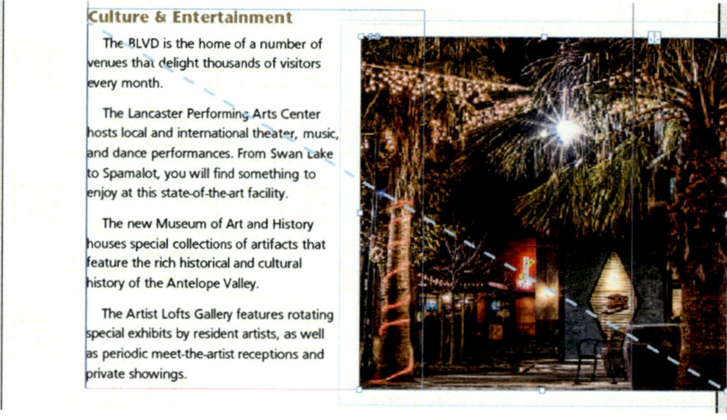

Note:

If you don't see the blue square, choose View>Extras>Show Anchored Object Control.

Note:

You can unanchor an image by choosing Object>Anchored Object>Release.

7. **Navigate to Page 3 of the layout.**

8. **Using the same method as for Page 2, anchor the top image in front of the second paragraph of body copy, and anchor the bottom image in front of the Celebrate America paragraph.**

9. **Save the file and continue to the next exercise.**

 Define Articles

You have three options when you export HTML or EPUB:

- Export the file based on the existing page layout. This option allows the software to make assumptions based on the top-to-bottom position of objects in the page layout. Every object in the layout is included.
- Export the file based on the content of the Structure panel, which allows you to define the order of tagged content. (You will use the Structure panel in Project 7: National Parks Info Pieces.)
- Export the file based on a user-defined set of articles. This option allows you to define the content that will be included in the exported file, as well as the order in which it will appear. You will use this approach to complete this exercise.

1. **With `boulevard.indd` open, open the Articles panel (Window>Articles).**

2. **Navigate to Page 1 and select the text frame at the bottom of the page. Click the Create New Article button at the bottom of the Articles panel.**

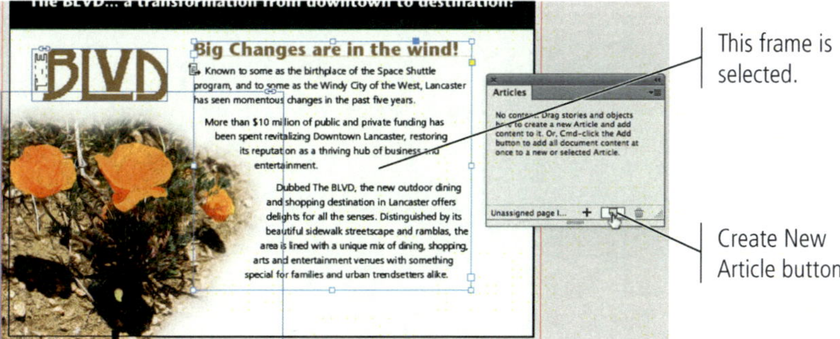

3. **In the resulting dialog box, change the article name to Intro. With the Include When Exporting option checked, click OK.**

   The articles you define will be used to create the EPUB and HTML files.

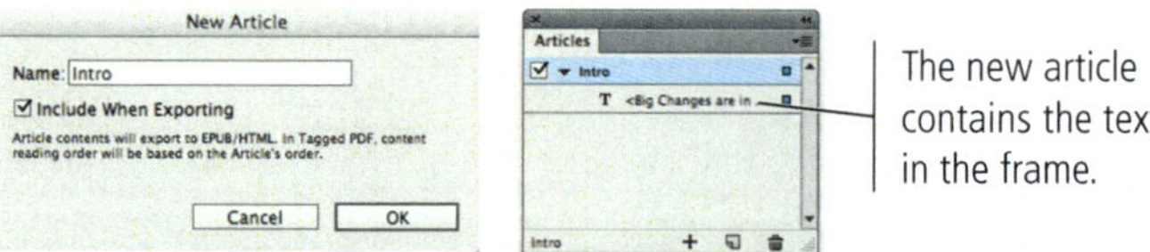

The new article contains the text in the frame.

4. **Select the placed slideshow at the top of the page, then click the Create New Article button at the bottom of the Articles panel. Name the new article Intro Movie and click OK.**

5. **In the Articles panel, drag the Intro Movie article above the Intro item.**

   The order in which items appear in the Articles panel determines the order in which they will appear in the exported HTML and EPUB files. New articles are always added at the bottom of the list. You can drag articles to reorder them, drag items within an article, and even drag items from one article to another.

The black line indicates where the article will be ordered when you release the mouse button.

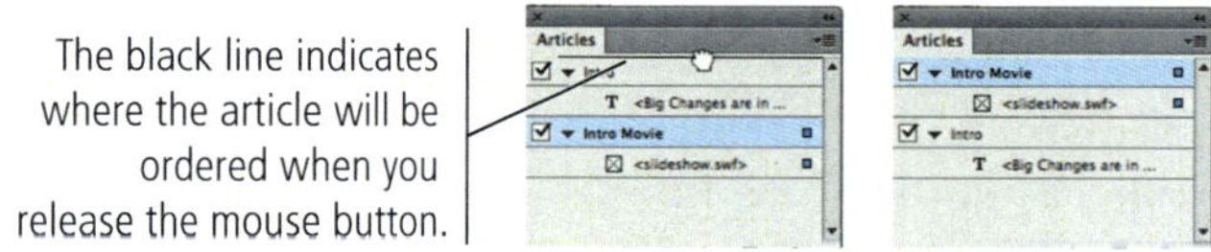

6. **Using the Layers panel, hide the Interactive layer and show the Static Print layer.**

7. **Select the image at the top of the page, then click the Create New Article button again. Name the new article Intro Picture and click OK.**

   The HTML format supports interactivity, but the EPUB format functions better with static images. Because you need to be able to turn off individual articles for each type of export, you are including the image and the movie as separate articles.

> *Note:*
>
> *Object visibility in the Layers panel has no effect on the exported HTML and EPUB files. You need to use the Articles panel to determine what will be included in the exported file.*

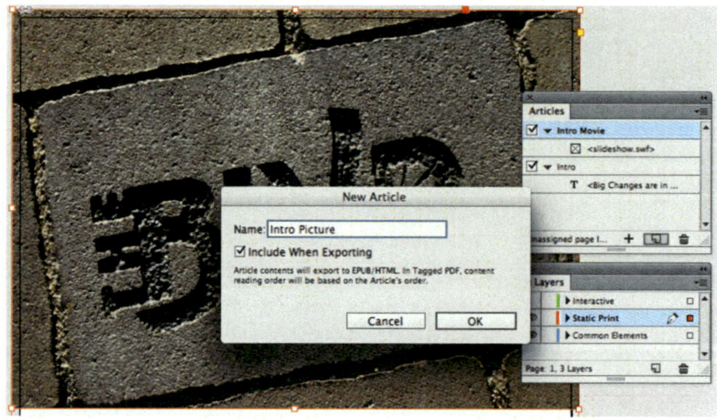

8. **Drag the Intro Picture article between the two existing articles.**

9. **Collapse the three existing articles, then navigate to Page 2.**

10. **Select the top text frame on the page, then click the Create New Article button. Name the new article Body Copy, then click OK.**

    If you look at the bottom of the layout, you can see that the second text frame is threaded to the frame on Page 3. When you add a story as an article, the entire story is part of that article; you don't need to add the frames on Page 3 independently.

    Also, remember that you anchored the images on Pages 2 and 3. As anchored images, they are technically part of the story; you do not need to add those images to the article.

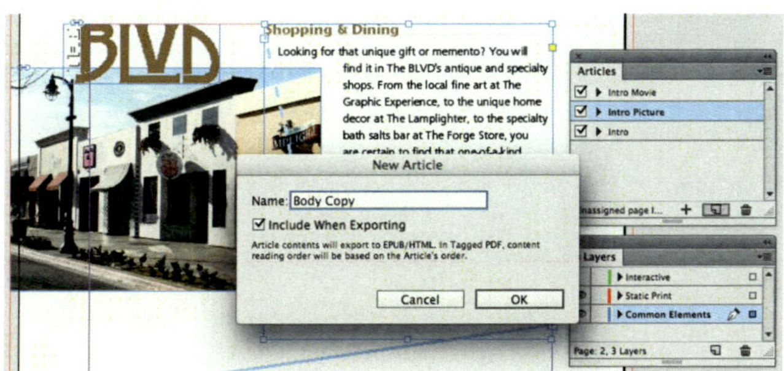

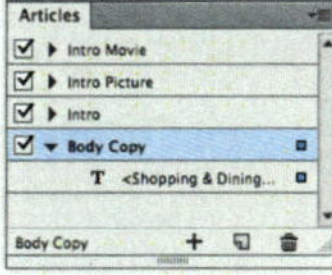

11. **Collapse the Body Copy article in the panel, then navigate to Page 4.**

    The text frame on this page is not linked to the previous story. If you want to include it, you need to create another article.

12. **Select the text frame on the page, then click the Create New Article button at the bottom of the panel. Name the new article Call to Action, then click OK.**

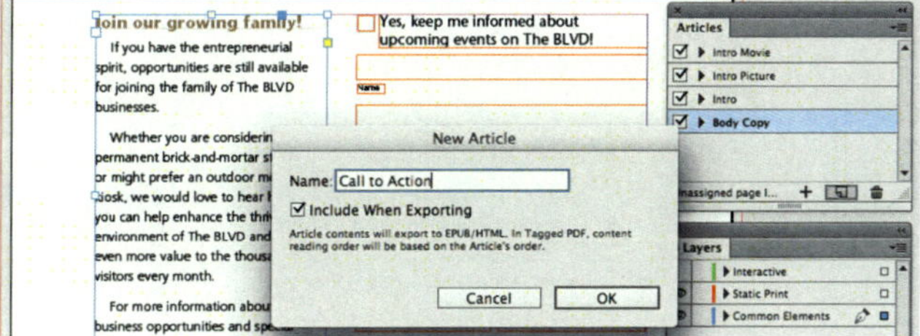

13. **Select the image frame at the top of the page. Drag the selected image into the Articles panel, above the text item in the Call to Action article.**

    Although this image is not anchored to the text, you can still add it to the article.

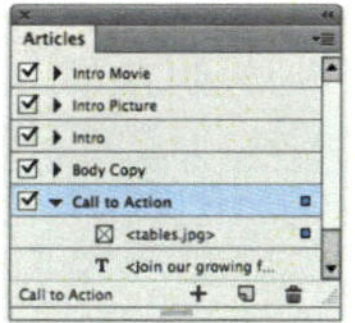

> ***Note:***
>
> *You can also click the Add Selection to Articles button at the bottom of the panel to add the selected item to the active article.*

Notice that you did not include the poppy image, the logos, or the form objects in the Articles panel. You do not need to include every element in a file when you export to EPUB or HTML; only items in the Articles panel will be included.

14. **Save the file and continue to the next exercise.**

Tag Styles for Exporting

The HTML and EPUB formats support a specific text structure, which is based on tags that identify different elements of text (headings, paragraphs, and so on). The layout you are working with was designed with several paragraph and character styles that control the appearance of the copy. You can use export tagging to map the existing styles to defined tags that are recognized by the digital formats.

1. **With boulevard.indd open, open the Paragraph Styles panel (Window>Styles>Paragraph Styles).**

2. **Control/right-click the Heading style and choose Edit "Heading".**

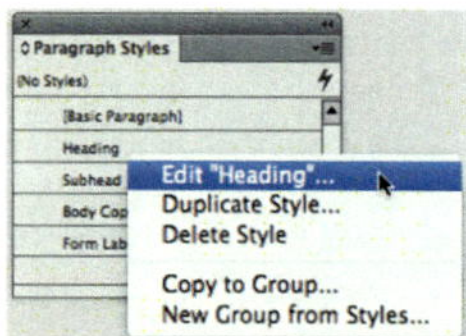

3. **In the resulting dialog box, display the Export Tagging options.**

   These options define how text formatted with the style is mapped to the tags that are supported by EPUB and HTML.

4. **Open the Tag menu in the EPUB and HTML menu and choose h1.**

   EPUB and HTML formats include tags for a number of levels of headings; the number in each tag indicates its level of editorial priority. As a general rule, each page should have only one paragraph tagged as h1.

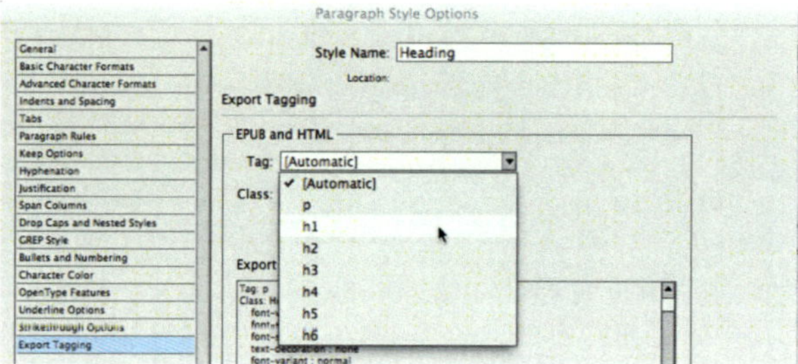

5. **Type heading in the class field, then press Tab.**

   If you don't press Tab (or click to select a different field), the class information does not appear in the Export Details pane.

   A class is an option for formatting content in an EPUB or HTML file. If you do not define a class name in the Export Tagging options, the exported file will use the browser's default setting for the applied tags.

   As you can see in the Export Details pane, the class information defines the same formatting attributes that are applied in the InDesign paragraph style (or at least, those attributes that are supported in the EPUB and HTML formats).

   Classes are important because you can define different formatting options for different styles. For example, say you have a Body Copy style and a Body Copy - No Indent format. Both styles would be tagged as paragraphs (with the p tag), but you can use classes to define different formatting options for each style.

Note:

The class name can be anything; it does not need to be the same as the style name.

6. **Check the Emit CSS and Split Document (EPUB only) options.**

   The Emit CSS option causes the class name you define here to take precendence in case there is a conflict with other classes.

   The Split Document option forces a new "page" every time the defined style is applied. This option is automatically checked for every heading tag.

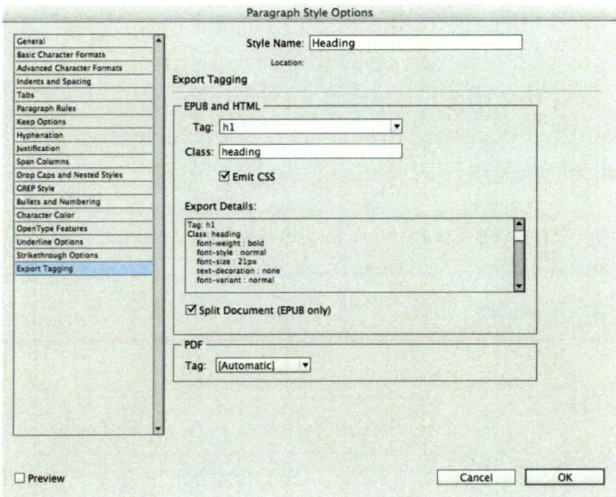

7. **Click OK to return to the layout.**

8. **Repeat this process for the Subhead and Body Copy paragraph styles, using the following information:**

   Subhead

   Tag: h2

   Class: subhead

   Emit CSS: Checked

   Split Document: Unchecked

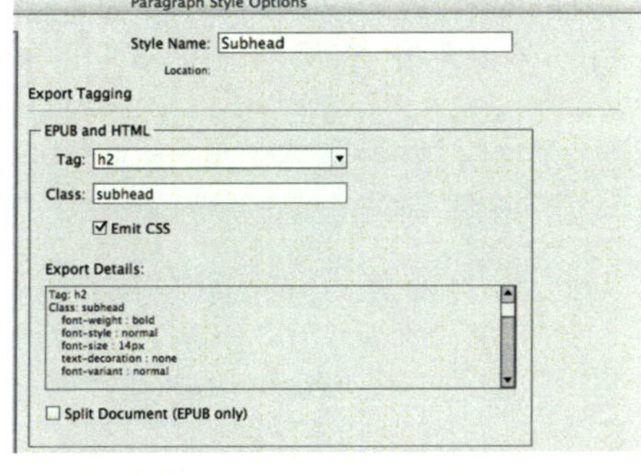

   Style: Body Copy

   Tag: p

   Class: body

   Emit CSS: Checked

   Split Document: Unchecked

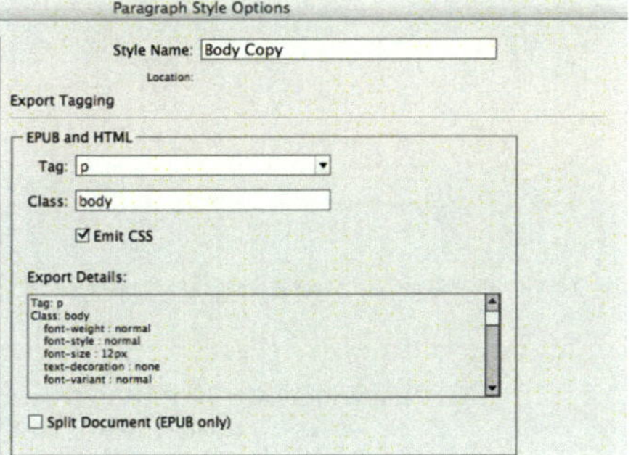

> ***Note:***
>
> *The p tag identifies a paragraph in the HTML and EPUB files.*

9. **Save the file and continue to the next exercise.**

Export HTML

As you probably know, HTML is the code that defines a Web page. Although InDesign is not a professional Web design application, you can export HTML code from an existing layout to make repurposing the content far easier than creating the HTML from scratch.

Your client has stated that the HTML file you create is going to be placed into the content area of the primary Web site; he is primarily concerned with the content — text and images — rather than duplicating the print brochure layout. By completing the previous exercises, you have laid the groundwork for exporting an HTML file that will be an excellent starting point to meet those needs.

Note:

The exercises in this project assume no working knowledge of XHTML, XML, CSS, or other technologies that drive the HTML and EPUB formats. Our goal is to show you the basics of the process.

We recommend studying applications such as Adobe Dreamweaver if you plan to work as a Web design professional.

1. **With `boulevard.indd` open, review the Articles panel. Uncheck the Intro Picture item and check the Intro Movie item.**

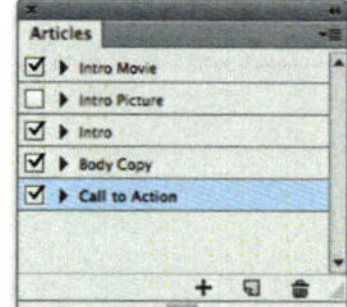

2. **Choose File>Export. Create a new folder named `Upload` in your WIP>Lancaster folder, and choose that folder as the target location.**

3. **Choose HTML in the Format/Save As Type menu and define the file name as `Welcome to The BLVD.html`.**

   The file name is essentially the page name, which appears in the browser window's title bar and in the page's document tab, so you are using a slightly more colloquial title than we normally use in InDesign.

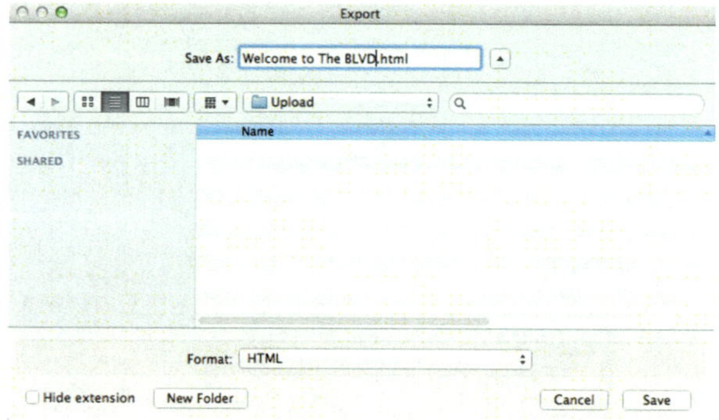

4. **Click Save.**

5. **In the resulting dialog box, review the General options.**

   Content Order. This menu defines how content is ordered in the exported file. You can allow InDesign to export the file based on the page layout; order content based on the defined XML structure (see Project 7: National Parks Info Pieces); or order content based on defined articles.

   Bullets and Numbers. You can use these menus to map text formatted with these options to the unordered list (ul) and ordered list (ol) tags that are supported by EPUB and HTML. If you don't want to use those tags, you can choose Convert to Text to treat bullet characters and numbers as regular text.

   View HTML after Exporting. When this option is checked, the resulting file automatically opens in a browser.

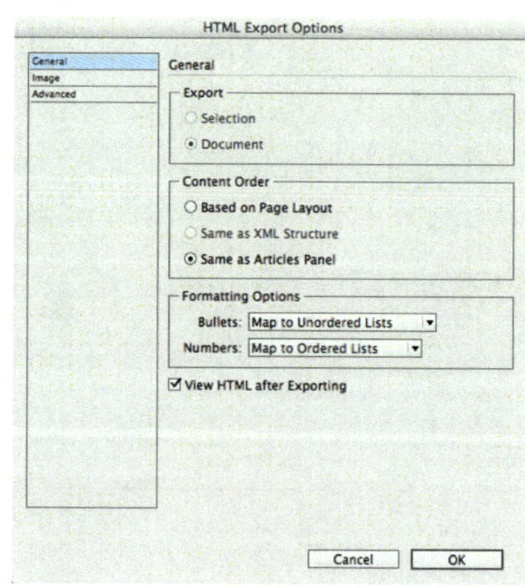

6. **Choose the Same as Articles Panel option.**

7. **Click Image in the left pane and review the options.**

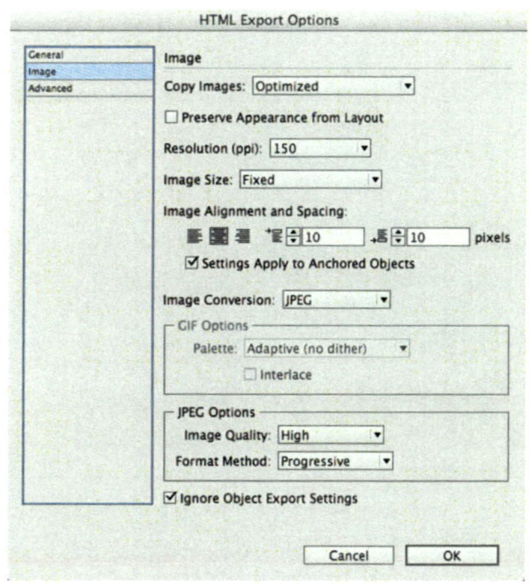

Copy Images. This option refers to the linking process that is required for HTML to properly display images. Like a print layout, an HTML file does not include actual image data. Rather, the HTML file links to the image files in a defined location. When InDesign exports the HTML file, it creates the optimized images and moves them into a folder inside the target location you defined when you chose to export the file.

Optimized, the default option in this menu, refers to the images that are generated by the export process based on the Image Conversion settings in the lower half of the dialog box. You can also choose Original to copy the originally placed images, ignoring the optimization options selected below. The Link to Server Path option can be used to define the location of image files that already exist on a server.

Preserve Appearance from Layout. If this option is checked, InDesign applies any transformations to the images before exporting. For example, consider an image with its opacity reduced to 50% in the layout; if Preserve Appearance from Layout is not checked, the exported image will have the appearance of regular 100% opacity.

Resolution. This menu defines the resolution of exported images. Although monitors only use 72 or 96 ppi, keep in mind that many tablet devices support higher image resolution. Higher resolutions are also important if you want to allow zooming.

Image Size. This menu determines whether images are Fixed (at the size they appear in the layout) or Relative to Page, which refers to the "page" size in the browser.

Image Alignment and Spacing. These options define the position of images, as well as spacing that is added above and below the images in the exported file.

Settings Apply to Anchored Objects. This option determines whether alignment and spacing settings apply to images that are anchored in the text. If you turn this option off, anchored images will appear in place in the same paragraph where they are anchored, rather than occupying a separate line.

Image Conversion. You can use this menu to define the image format(s) that should be used in the exported images. Automatic allows InDesign to make the best choice based on image content. You can also specify whether all images should export as GIF, JPEG, or PNG files.

GIF Options and **JPEG Options.** For GIF files, you can define a specific color palette to use. For JPEG files, you can determine how much compression should be applied.

Ignore Object Export Settings. You can define object export settings for specific images in the layout by choosing Object>Object Export Settings. The options in that dialog box are the same as the options listed here, except they apply only to the selected object. If this box is checked in the HTML Export Options dialog box, your settings here override any settings that you defined for specific images.

8. **In the Image options, change both Image Spacing fields to 10 pixels.**

9. **Click OK to export the HTML file.**

10. Review the resulting file in your browser.

The resulting file includes as much of your defined formatting as is supported by the HTML/CSS formats. As you can see, this is a very basic HTML file.

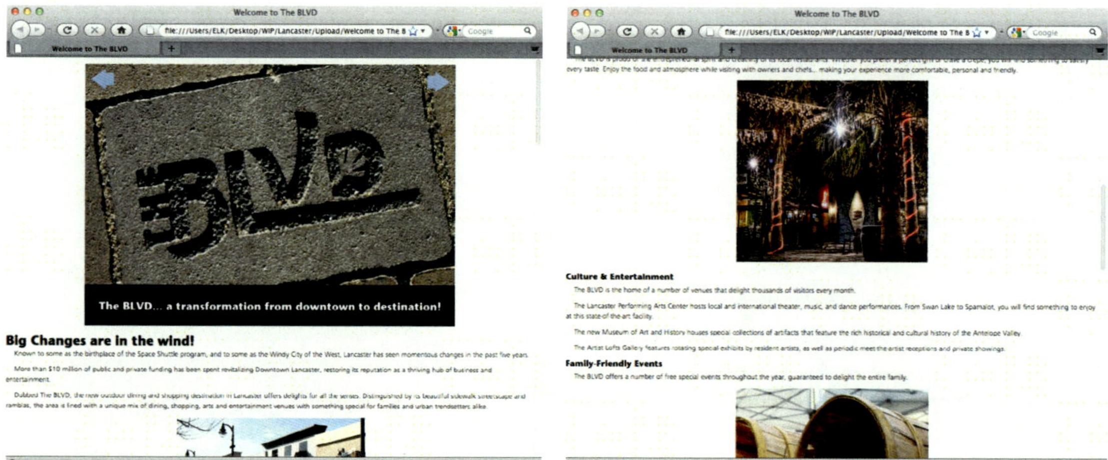

11. Close the browser window and return to InDesign.

12. Choose File>Export again. Without changing any options, click Save. When asked if you want to replace the existing file, click Replace/Yes.

As you can see, the export process generates a number of additional files that are required for the HTML file to work properly. When you complete the project, the entire Upload folder needs to be sent to the client.

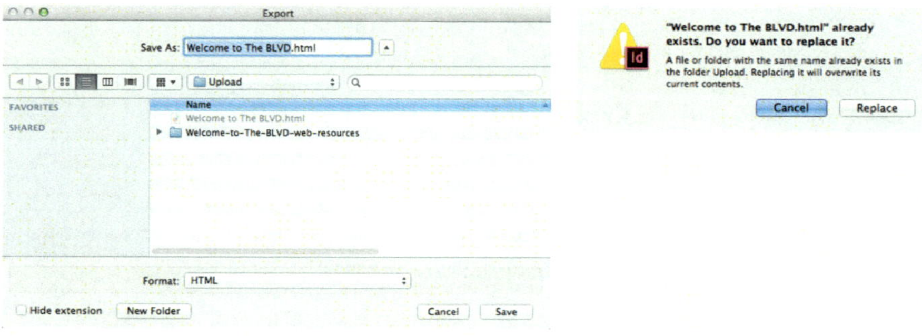

13. In the Advanced options, click the Add Style Sheet button. Navigate to `html-styles.css` in your WIP>Lancaster folder, then click Open.

A cascading style sheet (CSS) file includes instructions that define the appearance of various tags and classes in an HTML file. You can use these options to not include CSS rules, or to embed CSS into the resulting HTML file based on existing document formatting. You can click the Add Style Sheet button to define an existing CSS file that controls the appearance of tags and classes in the resulting EPUB file.

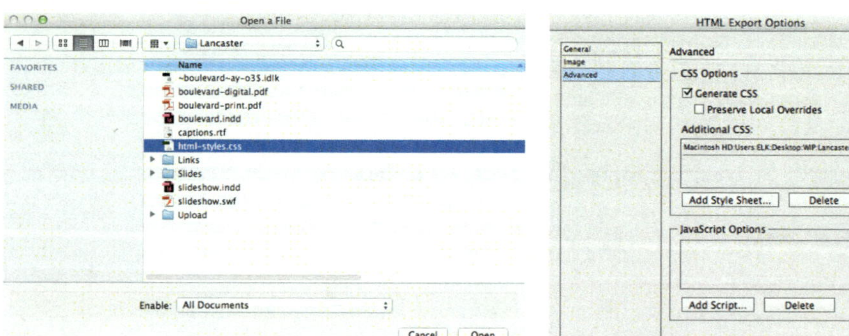

Note:

Unfortunately, InDesign does not include a CSS editor. We used Adobe Dreamweaver to create the external CSS file, although you can accomplish the same task in any text editor if you know how to write CSS code.

14. **Click OK to export the HTML file again.**

    The CSS file that you attached redefines the appearance of several tags. Most notably, we defined a specific width for the body tag, which contains the entire page. We also assigned fixed sizes and relative positions for the various images.

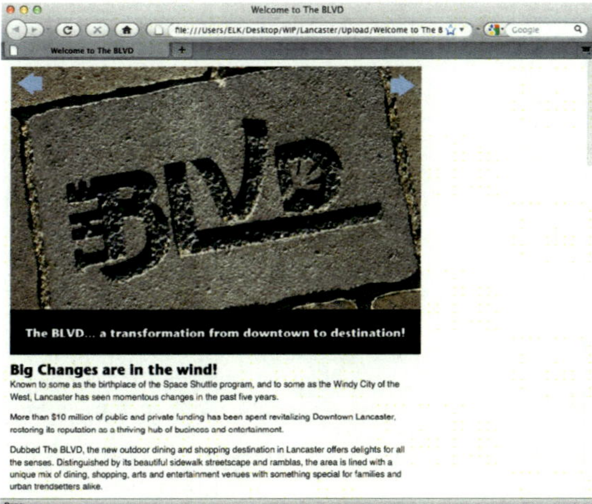

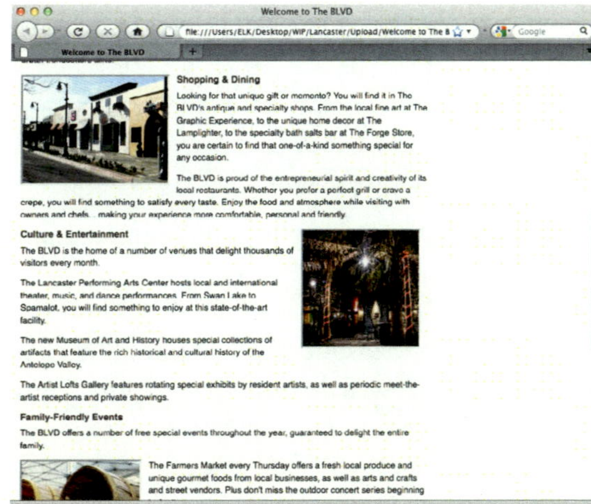

15. **Close the browser window and return to InDesign, then continue to the next exercise.**

Export EPUB

As of February 2012, 43% of Americans 16 and older have read long-form digital text such as e-books and magazines, using a variety of devices:

- 42% consume e-content on a computer
- 41% use a dedicated e-book reader like original Kindles or Nooks
- 29% use cell phones
- 23% use a digital tablet device[4]

Because e-books can be read on anything from a large-screen monitor to a handheld smartphone, the concept of a "page" is somewhat different than it is for a print document. Users can enlarge the text size in an e-book reader by adjusting hardware or software settings, which means the text reflows throughout the document. The content on Page 2 in one reader probably won't look the same as the content on Page 2 in a different user's reader. Although a designer can create page breaks in specific locations of an e-book, the user controls how much of that "page" appears at one time.

Generally speaking, the basic EPUB format was designed for reflowable content — essentially, text and (maybe) images. The format is now a de facto standard format for publishing e-content; virtually all devices support the format, except Amazon's Kindle devices.

> ***Note:***
>
> *There are a number of free tools available on the Internet for converting EPUB files to work on Kindle devices.*

4 Rainie, Lee, et al. The rise of e-reading. Pew Internet & American Life Project, April 4, 2012, *http://www.pewinternet.org/Press-Releases/2012/The-rise-of-ereading.aspx*, accessed on May 1, 2012.

EPUB is actually a container, which includes a number of pieces necessary to display the e-content:

- An XHTML file (a variant of HTML) that defines the document content and structure.
- A cascading style sheet (CSS) file that defines the specific appearance of various elements.
- Image files that are called by the XHTML file.
- Font files that are defined as embedded.
- An XML file that defines the links between documents in the package, as well as metadata for the EPUB.

EPUB 3 is the current revision of the standard; it includes support for rich media such as video and sound, as well as a number of other features that are not supported by the previous versions. (Keep in mind, however, that many people still have older devices, which do not support EPUB 3.)

It is important to note that there is much, much more to consider when publishing e-books than the basic concepts that we discuss here. Our goal is not to make you an expert on e-book publishing or even the EPUB format; rather, it is simply to show you how to use the tools that are available in InDesign.

Note:

If you plan to work in the publishing market, we encourage you to learn as much as possible about e-book publishing and, more specifically, the EPUB format (including EPUB 3).

1. **With boulevard.indd open, review the Articles panel.**
2. **Uncheck the Intro Movie article and check the Intro Picture article.**

   The EPUB format does not support SWF files without a number of workarounds. Instead, you are going to include the static image at the top of the document.

   Uncheck the Intro Movie item to exclude it from the export process.

   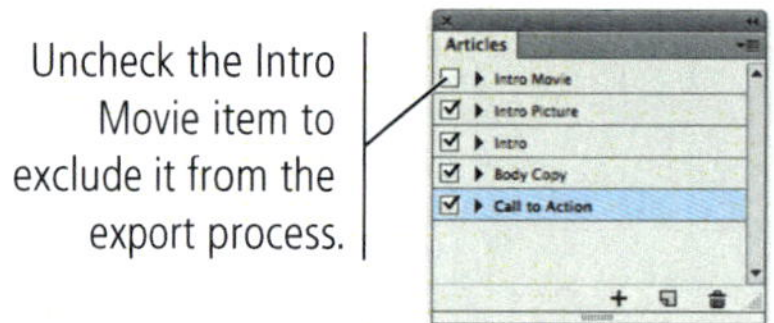

3. **Choose File>Export. Navigate to the WIP>Lancaster folder as the target location.**
4. **Choose EPUB in the Format/Save As Type menu, then click Save.**

   The Save As field defaults to the last-used file name. For an EPUB file, the file name is essentially the book title.

   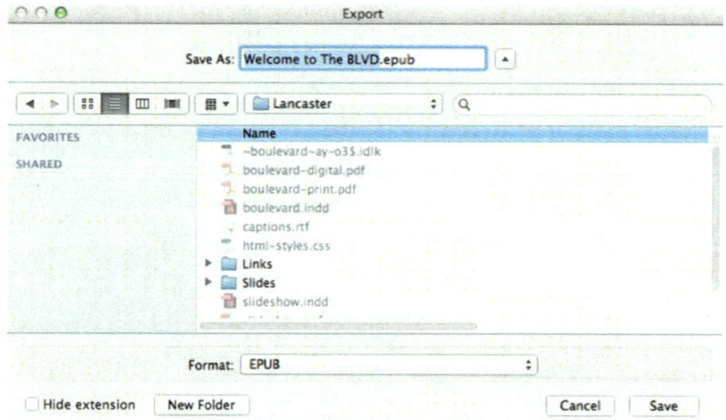

5. **Review the General options in the EPUB Export Options dialog box.**

Version. You can use this menu to export to EPUB 2.0.1 or EPUB 3.

Cover. This menu defines the "book cover" image that will appear on the digital book shelf of e-reader devices. You can rasterize the first page of the active file or choose another image to use as the cover.

Navigation. You can use this menu to determine how the table of contents will be generated in the resulting EPUB file. If you choose File Name, the InDesign filename will be used as the table of contents in the resulting EPUB file; clicking the filename link returns the reader to the beginning of the EPUB file. If you choose TOC Style, you can then define an existing TOC style that will be used as the EPUB table of contents.

TOC Style. This menu defines the existing style to use as the table of contents links in the exported EPUB file.

Margins. These options add padding around the page edges of the exported file.

Content Order. These are the same as for exporting an HTML file.

Place Footnote after Paragraph. If this option is checked, any existing footnotes will appear immediately after the paragraph in which they are placed, rather than at the bottom of the page or end of a section (as is conventional in print design).

Remove Forced Line Breaks. This option removes any soft-return characters that have been added to fine-tune the appearance of text in the print layout. (Remember, you have no real control over the position of line breaks in an e-book.)

Bullets and Numbers. These options are the same as for exporting an HTML file.

View EPUB after Exporting. When this option is checked, the resulting EPUB file automatically opens in Adobe Digital Editions.

6. **Make the following choices for the general settings (leave all other options at the default settings):**

   - **Choose TOC Style in the Navigation menu and choose TOC Style 1 in the secondary menu.**
   - **Change all four margin fields to 20 pixels.**
   - **Choose Same as Articles Panel in the Content Order menu.**

7. **Review the Image options.**

Most of the Image options are the same as for exporting an HTML file. For an EPUB file, you can also use the **Insert Page Break** menu to add page breaks before, after, or before and after images.

8. **Choose Relative to Page in the Image Size menu, and change both Image Spacing fields to 10 pixels. Leave all other options at the default settings.**

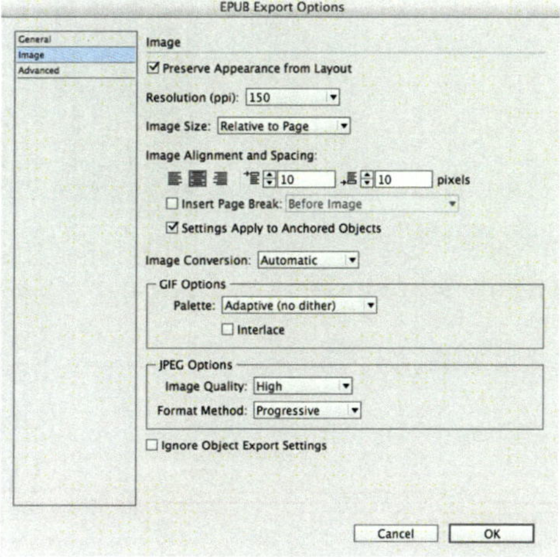

9. **Review the Advanced options.**

Split Document. This option can be used to add page breaks before specific paragraph styles.

EPUB Metadata. This is information that helps define a file for distribution systems.

CSS Options. These options determine how text formatting options are managed in the exported file. You can click the Add Style Sheet button to define an existing CSS file that controls the appearance of tags and classes in the resulting EPUB file.

JavaScript Options. These options are available if you choose the EPUB 3 format. You can attach external JavaScript files to add a variety of options to the exported file.

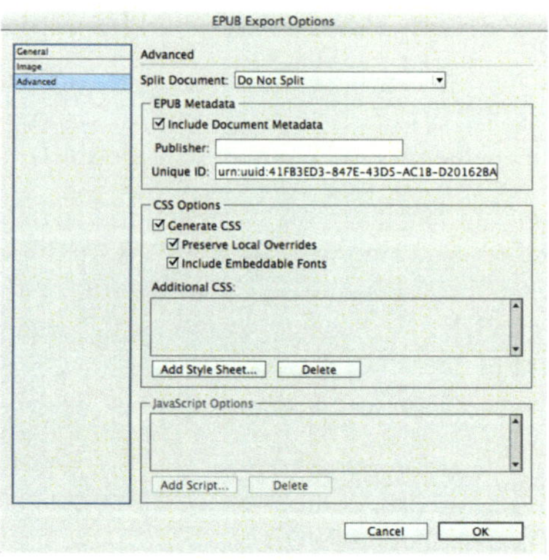

10. **Click OK to create the EPUB file.**

11. **If possible, review the resulting file in Adobe Digital Editions.**

If you have an e-reader device, you might consider side-loading the file and testing its appearance on that device.

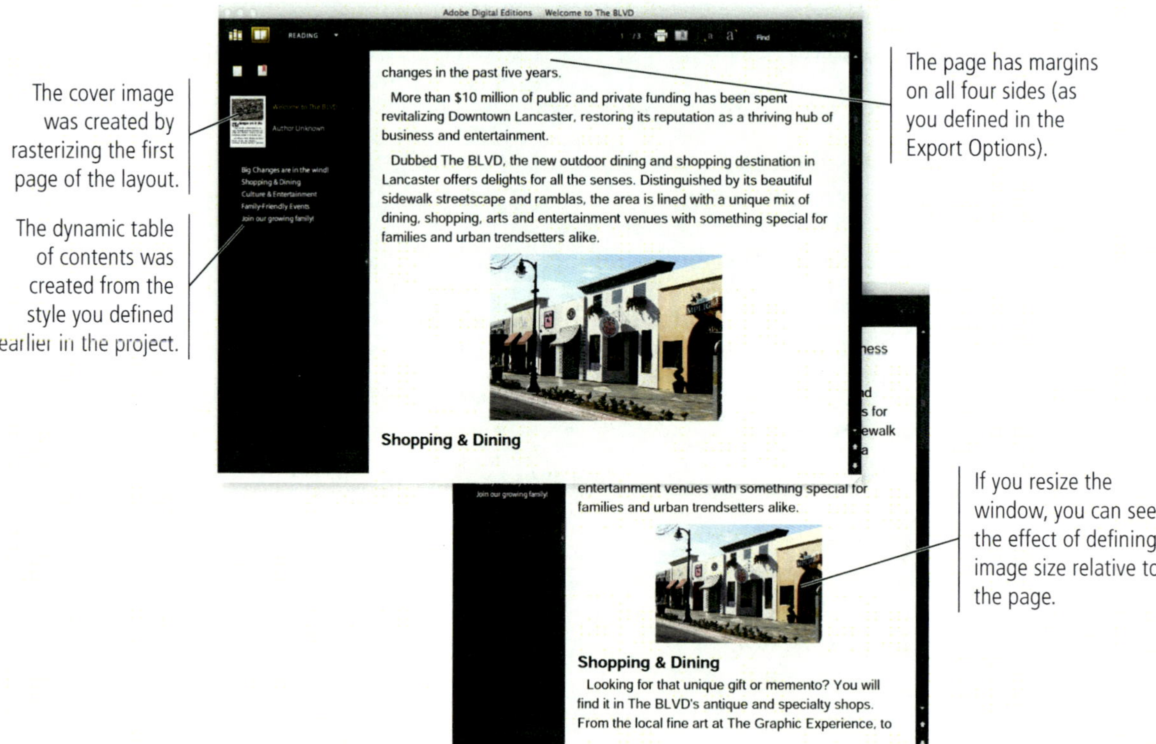

The cover image was created by rasterizing the first page of the layout.

The dynamic table of contents was created from the style you defined earlier in the project.

The page has margins on all four sides (as you defined in the Export Options).

If you resize the window, you can see the effect of defining image size relative to the page.

12. **Close the EPUB file and return to InDesign.**

13. **Save the InDesign file and close it.**

Project Review

fill in the blank

1. A(n) _______________ describes the color reproduction characteristics of a particular input or output device.

2. _______________ is the range of possible colors within a specific color model.

3. ____ are the four component colors in process-color output.

4. A _______________ hyperlink opens a Web page at the address you define.

5. A _______________ can be used to display more than one image in the same frame.

6. The _______________ format can be used to display dynamic, interactive content.

7. The _______________ button action can be used to remove the user's choices from the form fields.

8. The _______________ format is designed for scalable, reflowable text.

9. The _______________ options in a paragraph style can be used to map styles to HTML and EPUB tags.

10. A _______________ can be used to assign different formatting options to various text with the same tag.

short answer

1. Briefly explain the difference between additive and subtractive color.

2. Briefly explain the concept of color management as it relates to building a layout in InDesign.

3. Briefly explain at least two considerations when using a single layout to export content to multiple media.

Portfolio Builder Project

Use what you learned in this project to complete the following freeform exercise.
Carefully read the art director and client comments, then create your own design to meet the needs of the project.
Use the space below to sketch ideas; when finished, write a brief explanation of your reasoning behind your final design.

art director comments

The Lancaster city planners were very happy with your work on their rebranding project. Your local city government representatives saw the various pieces at a recent convention, and they would like to create a similar campaign to help promote local tourism.

To complete this project, you should:

- ❑ Find images (or create your own) that highlight different events and attractions in the local area.
- ❑ Write compelling copy to promote the area to visitors. Look at the local chamber of commerce and city government Web sites for ideas or for detailed information about specific events.
- ❑ Design the print layout first, then repurpose the same content for digital PDF, EPUB, and HTML files.

client comments

We've been trying to reach out to a larger audience to promote the local attractions and events that make our city special.

We'd like to plan and design a promotional brochure that we can hand out at various events, as well as create digital versions that can more easily reach beyond our local community.

We don't have any specific text or images in mind, so we're hoping you can find or create whatever you need to make the project successful.

project justification

Project Summary

This project highlighted a number of methods for repurposing content for multiple output media. Completing this work in a single InDesign file offers a distinct advantage if you need to make editorial changes — you can open the single file, make the necessary changes, then re-export the various formats.

You should realize, however, that this type of repurposing work requires a significant amount of planning and careful consideration. You need to determine what to include in each version, whether for aesthetic purposes or to meet the specific needs and capabilities of a given output medium. You also need to prepare elements to work in various output media, and create assets to take best advantage of different delivery methods.

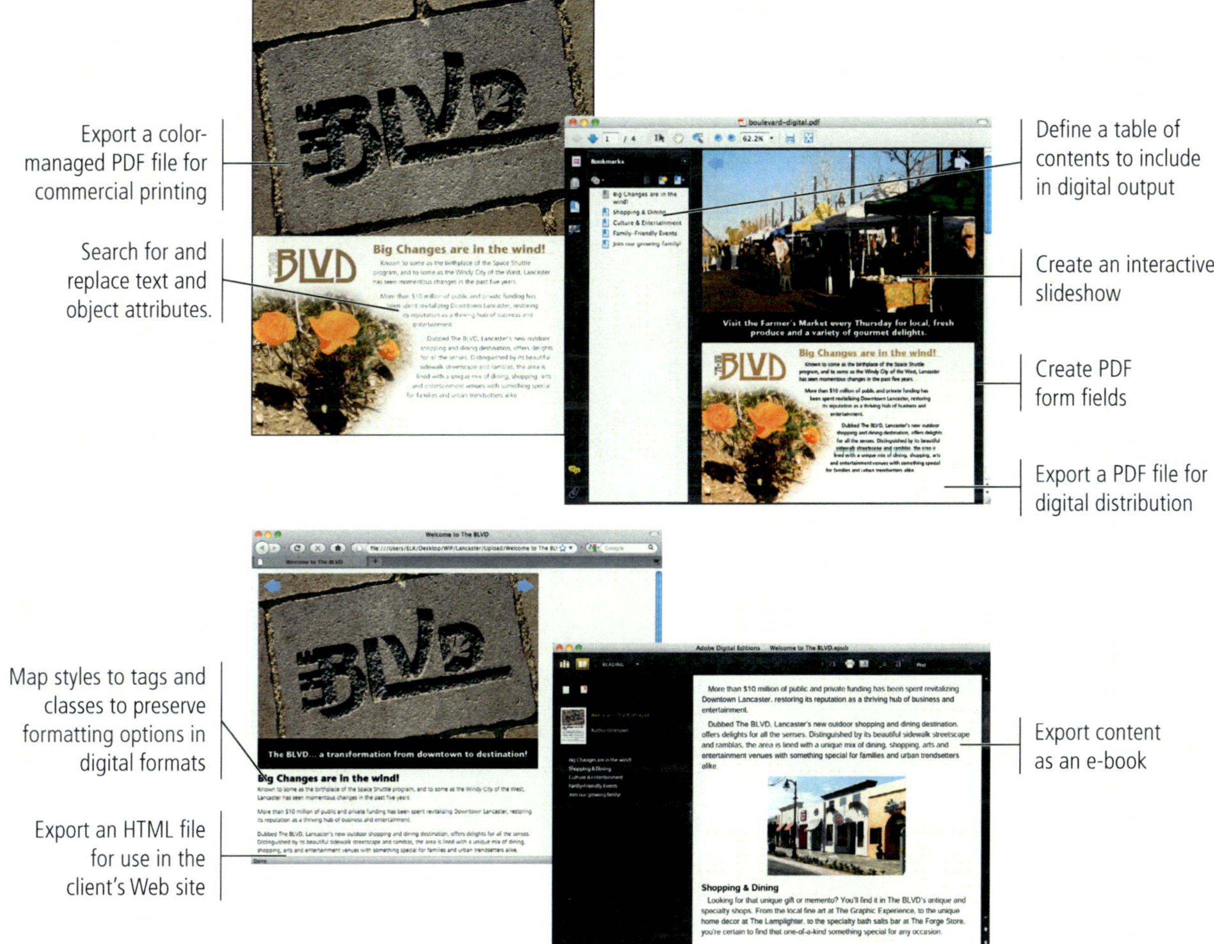

National Parks Info Pieces

Your client is the marketing manager for the National Parks Service (NPS). She wants to create a series of collateral pieces that will be used at tourism centers to lure potential visitors. She hired you to produce a one-sheet flyer that will be distributed in print and online, a rack card that can be placed in area hotels, a postcard that will be given away to park visitors, and a folio file that will work on digital tablet devices.

This project incorporates the following skills:

- ❑ Creating an XML file using tagged frames and content
- ❑ Building a layout from imported XML content
- ❑ Controlling the structure of a layout to merge XML content into tagged frames
- ❑ Placing linked content into alternate layouts
- ❑ Creating interactive overlays for digital folio files
- ❑ Creating alternate layouts for horizontal and vertical tablet orientations
- ❑ Creating a digital folio file for tablet devices

Project Meeting

client comments

We want to create several pieces to promote tourism in the national parks. We already have a flyer layout that we like, but we want you to create other versions for different purposes:

- The flyer will be sent to tourism boards and agencies as a handout.
- The rack card will be placed in hotels near the park for potential visitors.
- The postcard will be given away as a souvenir to park visitors.
- The folio file will be made available on the park's Web site for people who want to download it to their digital tablets.

art director comments

This could be a huge project for us since there are more than 350 national parks, monuments, and other protected areas in the national park system.

InDesign offers several methods for repurposing content into different layouts. I already created basic templates for the rack card and postcard; I want you to use XML to map the flyer content into those template layouts.

For the digital folios, you need to create two versions — horizontal and vertical. They don't need to be exact matches, but they should have all of the same content. Keep in mind that this is a digital file. You can use interactivity to take advantage of the medium.

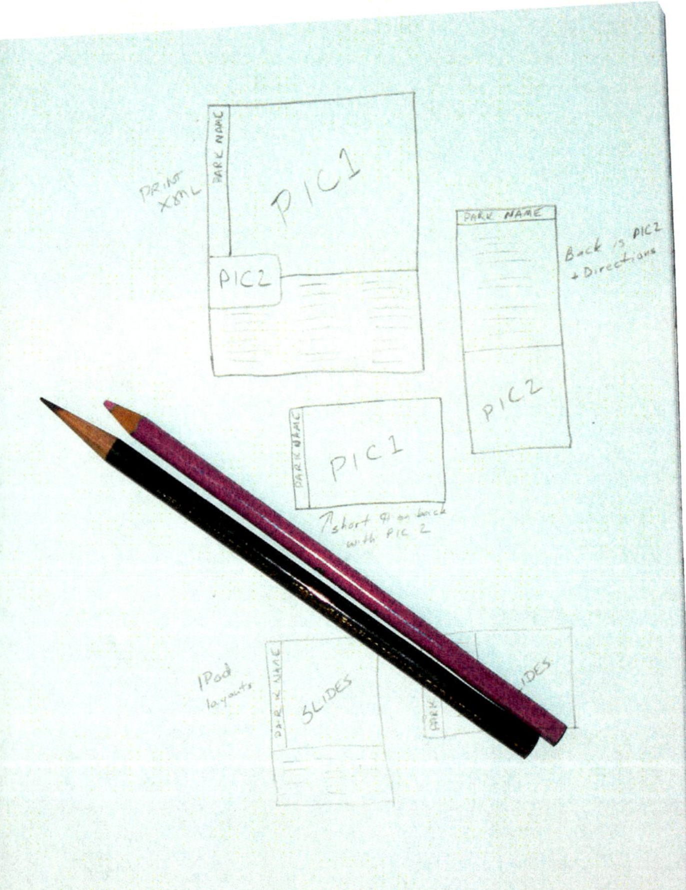

project objectives

To complete this project, you will:

- ❑ Tag Frames for XML
- ❑ Review Document Structure
- ❑ Review XML Structure and Attributes
- ❑ Place Unstructured XML Content
- ❑ Update Linked XML Data
- ❑ Import Structured XML
- ❑ Create a File for Digital Publishing
- ❑ Use the Content Collector
- ❑ Manage Linked Object Options
- ❑ Create an Interactive Overlay
- ❑ Define Liquid Page Rules
- ❑ Create an Alternate Layout
- ❑ Create a Digital Folio

Stage 1 Working with XML

Repurposing content — placing the same content into different-size layouts for one or more output media — is a common design task. InDesign includes a number of methods for accomplishing this task. In the first stage of this project, you will use XML (Extensible Markup Language) to use the same content in three different print layouts.

For many designers, XML is an intimidating concept among the alphabet soup of industry-related acronyms. Despite all the complexities that underlie this programming language, InDesign makes it very easy to implement XML in your layout documents.

As you know, styles define the appearance of content. All paragraphs formatted with the Subhead style display the characteristics defined for that style, regardless of the actual content in those headings. XML, on the other hand, describes the actual content marked with a specific tag; in other words, the heading is the actual text identified by the XML Heading tag, regardless of the applied formatting.

In the following exercises, you create an XML file from the flyer content, and then use that XML file to generate two additional layouts — a rack card and a postcard.

Tag Frames for XML

The first step in creating an XML file is to identify the elements that make up the document content, each of which will be enclosed within tags as shown below:

<Heading>Much Ado About Nothing</Heading>

The first tag, <Heading>, is the opening tag; it identifies the beginning of the content. The second tag, </Heading>, is the closing tag; it identifies the end of the content.

When the XML file is imported into a layout, InDesign places the content from the Heading tag into the appropriate location.

To create the XML file for this project, you first have to define and apply tags for the different elements of the layout.

> ***Note:***
> *When InDesign reads an XML file, it finds the content within tags and places that content into the appropriate locations in the layout.*

1. **Download IDCC_RF_Project7.zip from the Student Files Web page. Expand the ZIP archive in your WIP folder (Macintosh) or copy the archive contents into your WIP folder (Windows).**

   This results in a folder named **Parks**, which contains the files you need for this project. You should also use this folder to save the files you create in this project.

2. **Open flyer_bryce.indd from the WIP>Parks folder.**

   If you get a warning about missing or modified images, update those links in the open file. The two placed image files are in the WIP>Parks>Links folder.

3. **Choose Window>Utilities>Tags to open the Tags panel.**

   The Tags panel allows you to create and manage XML tags within an InDesign layout. One tag, "Root," exists by default in every file; it is the basic container tag that encloses all other tags in the document.

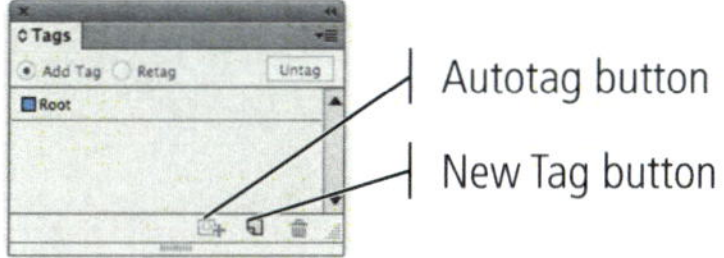

4. **Using the Selection tool, select the larger image in the layout.**

5. **In the Tags panel, click the Autotag button.**

   The Image tag is automatically created and applied to the selected frame.

6. **If your image is not bordered and overlaid with a purple color, choose View>Structure>Show Tagged Frames.**

   The border and overlay color are for identification purposes. They only appear while you are working in the file; they do not appear when the file is output.

7. **In the Tags panel, double-click the Image tag to open the Tag Options dialog box.**

8. **Change the Name field to Main_Img and click OK.**

   Because you want to identify two different images, you have to assign a unique name to each tag. If you use the basic Image tag for both images, it will be difficult to control image placement when the XML file is imported into a different InDesign layout.

Note:

Tag names cannot include spaces, so you must use the underscore character if you want to separate words in the tag name.

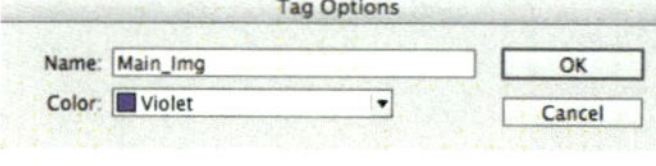

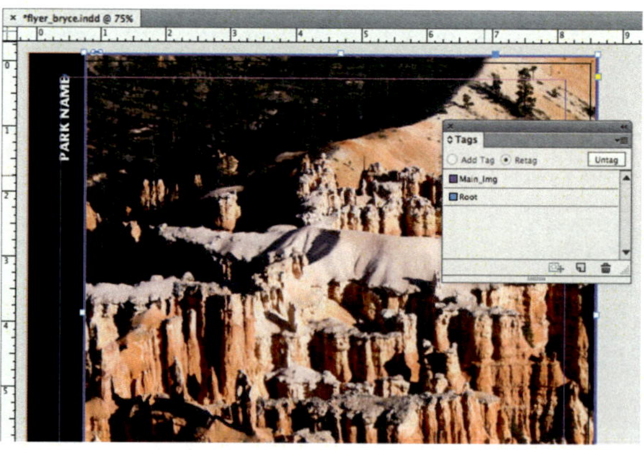

9. **Using the same method, tag the other image frame with a tag named Sub_Img.**

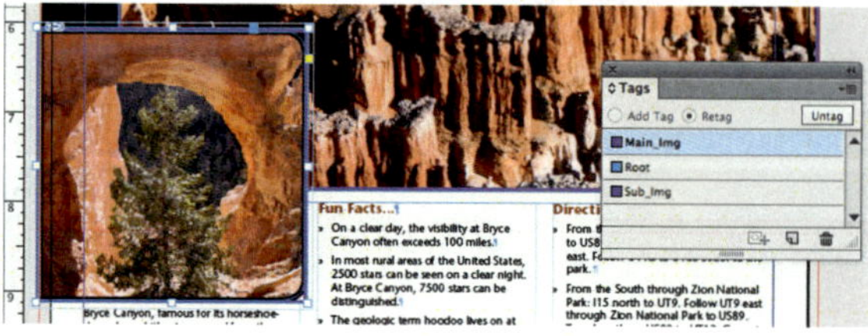

10. Select the text frame with the park name placeholder and click the Autotag button in the Tags panel.

Text frames are automatically tagged with the Story tag. You need to identify two different stories in this job, so you should use a unique tag for each.

Note:

You might notice that the park name is currently incorrect. You will fix this in a later exercise.

11. Double-click the Story tag and change the name to Park_Name. Click OK to close the Tag Options dialog box.

This is the same name as the paragraph style applied to the text; using the same name for both elements allows you to easily map the tagged content to styles of the same name (which you will do later).

After you change the tag name, the frame is tagged with the Root tag instead of the (newly renamed) Park_Name tag. This is a minor bug in the software; it is important to recognize, but is fortunately easy to fix.

After changing the tag name, it is no longer applied to the selected Park Name text frame.

The Root tag is applied to the selected frame.

12. With the same text frame still selected, click Park_Name in the Tags panel.

13. Repeat Steps 10–12 to create a new tag named Main_Text and apply it to the three-column text frame at the bottom of the page.

The file now has four tagged frames, each identified by a unique tag.

14. Save the file and continue to the next exercise.

Review Document Structure

In addition to tagging frames, you can also tag specific content within frames. Doing so enables you to automatically format XML content in other layouts, and allows you to access specific content when necessary.

> *Note:*
>
> *When you tag different kinds of text, make sure you don't select the final paragraph return character at the end of the selection.*

1. **With `flyer_bryce.indd` open, highlight the first paragraph in the three-column text frame (excluding the paragraph return character), and then click the New Tag button at the bottom of the Tags panel.**

   The new Tag1 is automatically added and highlighted.

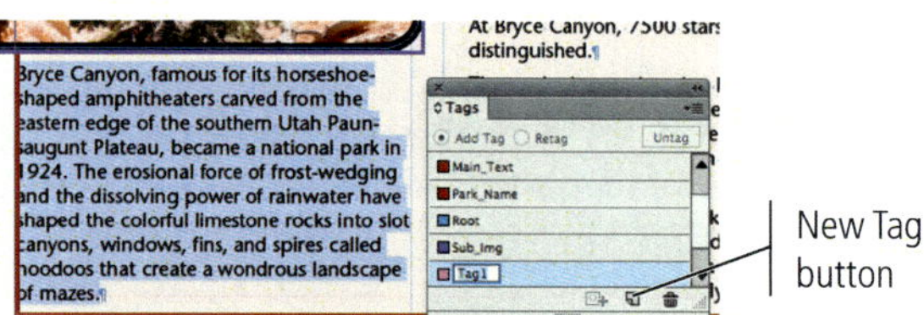

2. **With the tag name highlighted, type `Body_Copy` and press Return/Enter to finalize the name change.**

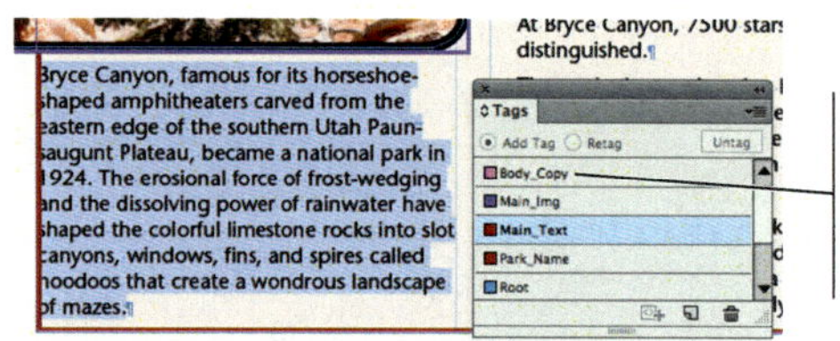

3. **With the paragraph still selected in the layout, click the new Body_Copy tag to apply it.**

> *Note:*
>
> *If you click the New Tag button to create a tag, that new tag is not automatically applied to the selected object.*

4. **In the Tags panel, double-click the Body_Copy tag to open the Tag Options dialog box. Choose Dark Green in the Color menu, then click OK.**

   The tag color refers to the color of the nonprinting markers that identify tagged elements. For tagged frames, this color refers to the color of the frame edge and overlay (when Show Tagged Frames is active). For tagged text, this color refers to the brackets surrounding the tagged text (when Show Tag Markers is active).

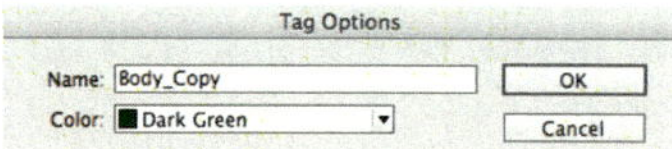

5. **Click in the paragraph to place the insertion point and remove the text highlighting.**

6. **If you don't see brackets around the paragraph, choose View>Structure>Show Tag Markers.**

   Like the overlay and border on tagged frames, these brackets will not appear in the printed piece.

7. **Using the Type tool, select the Fun Facts heading (excluding the paragraph return character). Create and apply a tag named Subhead.**

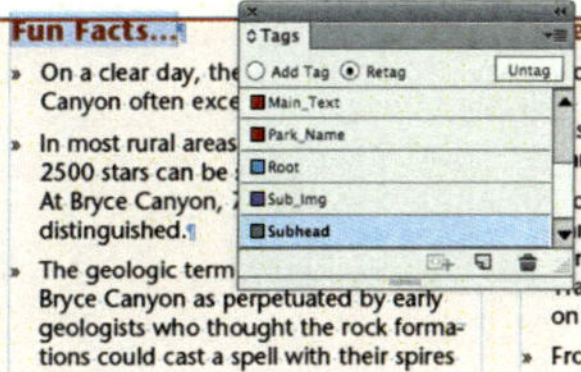

8. **Select the bulleted paragraphs below the subhead (excluding the final paragraph return character). Create and apply a tag named Fact_List.**

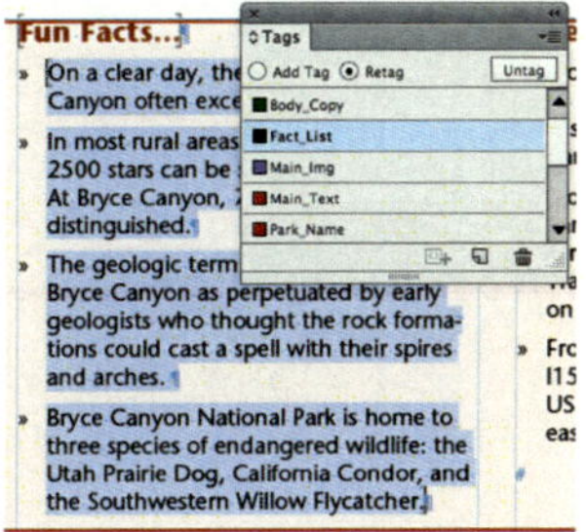

9. **Select the Directions heading (excluding the paragraph return character) and apply the Subhead tag.**

10. **Select the paragraphs after the Directions heading (excluding the final paragraph return character) and apply the Fact_List tag.**

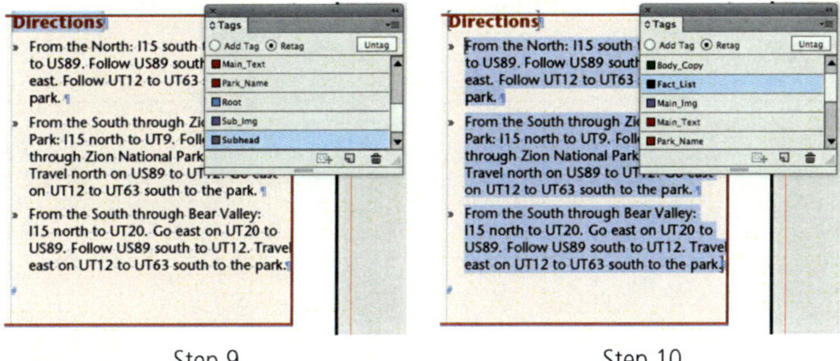

Step 9 Step 10

11. **Save the file and continue to the next exercise.**

 Review XML Structure and Attributes

XML files allow you to share content across multiple files, using either a structured or an unstructured method. Using the unstructured method (which you will utilize to create the postcard in a later exercise), you can simply import the XML into a document, and then drag elements into the layout. Structured repurposing requires more planning, but allows you to merge tagged XML content into tagged frames in another layout.

1. **With flyer_bryce.indd open, choose View>Structure>Show Structure. In the Structure pane, click the arrow to the left of Root to expand the structure.**

   The Structure pane appears in the left side of the document window, showing the hierarchical order of tagged elements in the file. Elements appear in the order in which they were created; any element with an arrow next to its name can be expanded to show nested elements and associated attributes (we explain those attributes shortly).

2. **If you don't see the words "Park Name" to the right of the Park_Name element, open the Structure pane Options menu and choose Show Text Snippets.**

When snippets are visible, the first 32 characters of text in that element display in the pane.

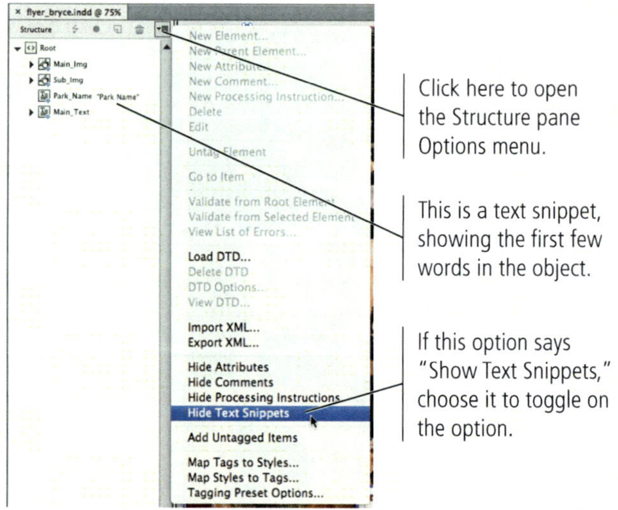

> ***Note:***
>
> *You can drag the bar on the right edge of the Structure pane to make the pane wider or narrower.*

Identifying Structure Pane Icons

Use the following as a guide to the different icons in the Structure pane.

Icon	Name	Use
	Root element	Every document includes one root element at the top, which can be renamed but not moved or deleted
	Story element	Tagged story (one or more linked frames)
	Text element	Tagged text within a frame
	Graphic element	Tagged frame that includes a placed image; includes an href attribute that defines the path or URL to the linked file
	Unplaced text element	Unplaced text element not yet associated with a page item
	Unplaced graphic element	Unplaced graphic element not yet associated with a page item
	Table element	Table
	Header cell element	Cell in the header row of a table
	Body cell element	Cell within the body of a table
	Footer cell element	Cell in the footer row of a table
	Empty element	An empty frame is associated with this element
•	Attribute	Metadata, such as keywords or location of a linked image (href attribute)
	Comment	Comments that appear in the XML file, but not the InDesign document
	Processing instruction	Instruction to trigger an action in applications that can read instructions
	DOCTYPE element	Tells InDesign which DTD file to use when validating the XML file

3. **In the Structure pane, click the Main_Img element and drag it to the bottom of the list.**

   XML follows a linear, top-down structure. Although the elements are listed in the order you create them, you should modify the structure to more accurately reflect the order they appear in the layout.

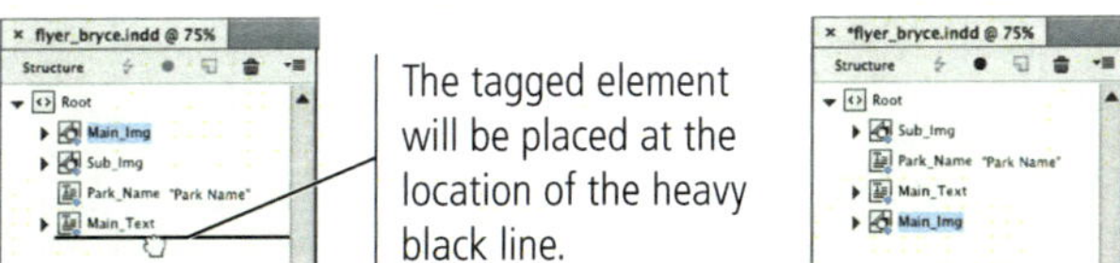

4. **Expand all elements by clicking the arrow to the left of each element.**

   The Main_Text element contains additional tagged elements.

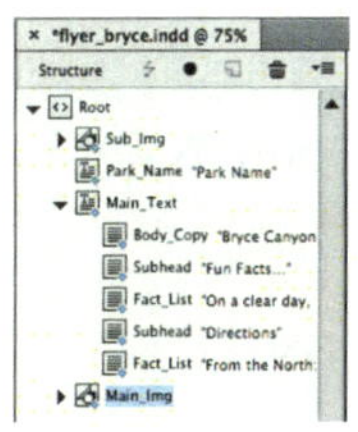

   When expanded, each of the two image elements shows the path to the placed image, with the "href" prefix. This path is an attribute of the image element, defining the location of the content placed within the element. This path information tells InDesign which image to use when the file is imported into another layout.

Note:

Attributes are identified in the Structure pane by a large bullet character

5. **Save the InDesign file.**

6. **Choose File>Export and navigate to your WIP>Parks folder as the target destination.**

7. **Choose XML in the Format/Save As Type menu. Change the file name to bryce.xml, then click Save.**

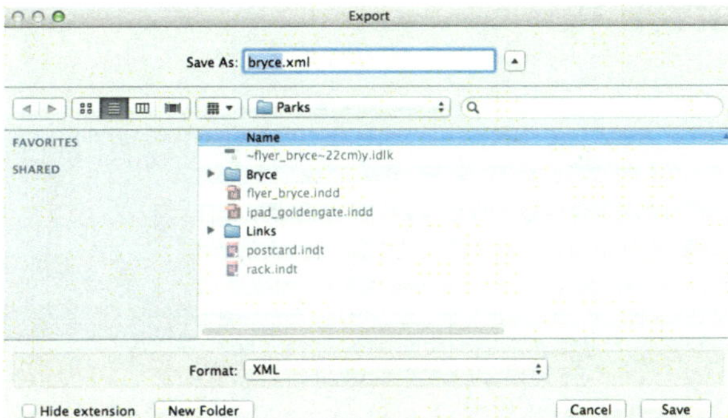

8. **Make sure no boxes are checked in either tab of the Export XML dialog box that appears, and then click Export.**

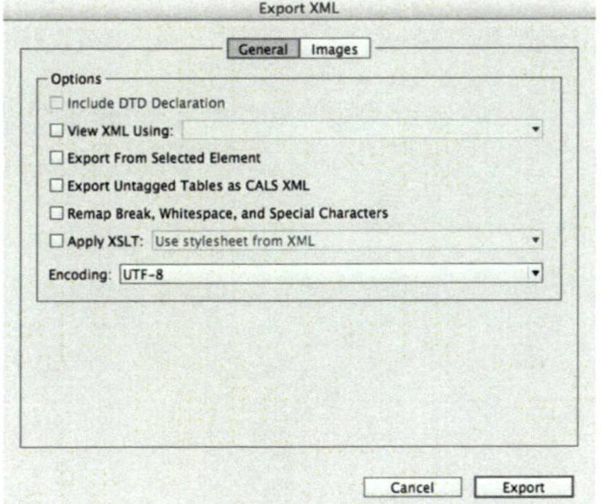

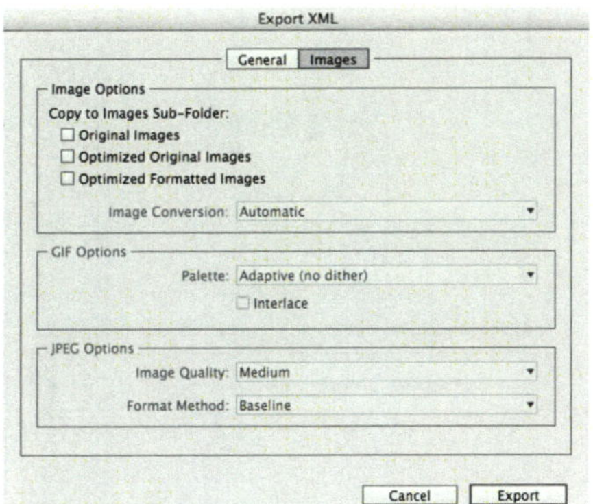

9. **Continue to the next exercise.**

Options for Exporting XML

INDESIGN FOUNDATIONS

You can control a number of options when you export an XML file from an InDesign layout. The following options are available in the General tab:

- **Include DTD Declaration** exports a reference to the defined DTD (if any) along with the XML file. This option is only available if a DOCTYPE element is showing in the Structure pane. (DTD stands for Document Type Definition.)
- **View XML Using** opens the exported file in the defined browser or editing application.
- **Export From Selected Element** starts exporting from the currently selected element in the Structure pane.
- **Export Untagged Tables As CALS XML** exports untagged tables in CALS XML format. (CALS is an extension of XML, designed by the U.S. Department of Defense Continuous Acquisition and Life-Cycle Support project.)
- **Remap Break, Whitespace, and Special Characters** converts special characters to their XML code equivalents (if equivalents exist).
- **Apply XSLT** applies a style sheet from the XML file or from an external file. (XSLT stands for Extensible Stylesheet Language Transformation.)
- **Encoding** defines the encoding mechanism for representing international characters in the XML file.

In the Images tab, you can move images identified in the XML code to a folder created during the export process. (This is similar to the Links folder created when you use the Package utility.)

- **Original Images** copies the original image file into an Images subfolder.
- **Optimized Original Images** optimizes and compresses the original image files, and places the optimized versions in an Images subfolder.
- **Optimized Formatted Images** permanently applies transformations (rotation, scaling, etc.) in the optimized images that are placed in the Images subfolder.

Using either Optimized option, you can choose the format (GIF or JPEG) to use in the Image Compression menu. You can also define the optimization options for each format. The Optimized options are more useful if you are repurposing the XML content into a Web layout; GIF and JPEG are not recommended for print layout design.

Place Unstructured XML Content

As we mentioned earlier, you can use either an unstructured or a structured method for applying tagged XML content into a new layout. The unstructured method is easiest because you can simply drag the content from the Structure pane and place it into your new document.

1. **Open the file `postcard.indt` from the WIP>Parks folder to create a new file. Save the new file as `postcard_bryce.indd` in your WIP>Parks folder.**

   We created this basic postcard template with placeholders for the same two images, park name, and body copy elements that you already used in designing the single-sheet flyer.

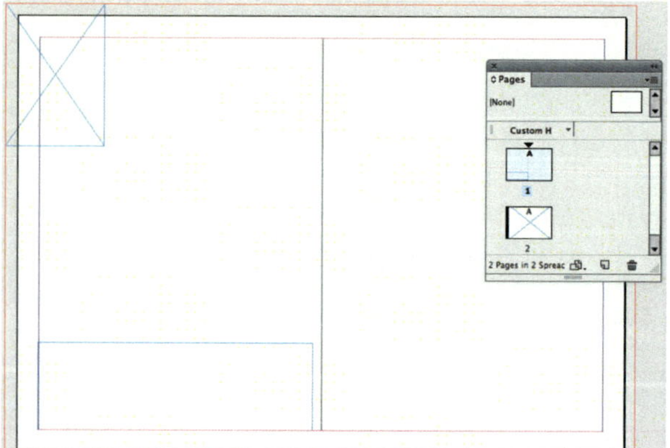

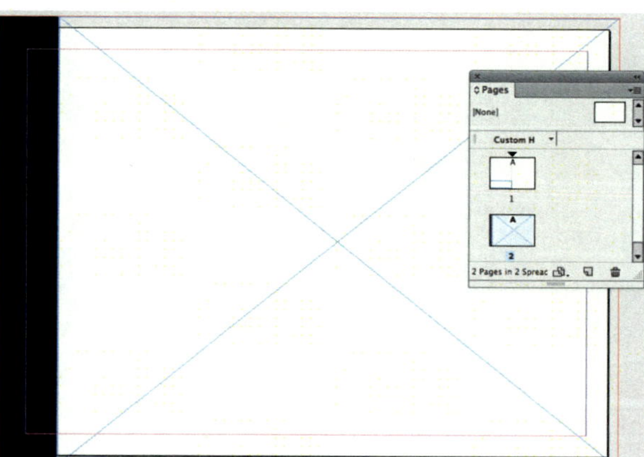

2. **Open the Structure pane for the postcard layout. In the Structure pane Options menu, choose Import XML.**

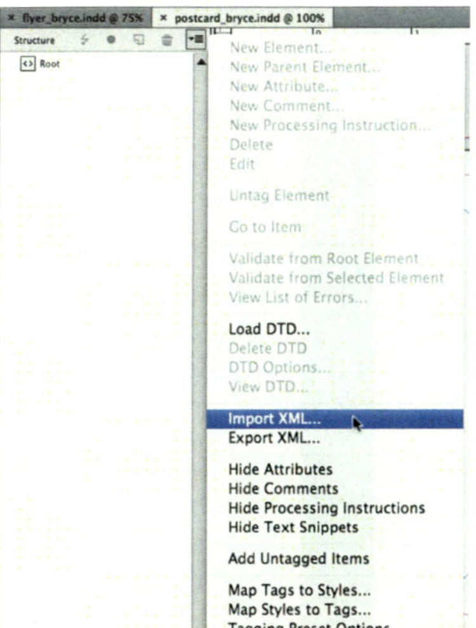

> *Note:*
>
> *You can also simply choose File>Import XML.*

3. **Navigate to the file `bryce.xml` in your WIP>Parks folder. Make sure the Show XML Import Options box is checked and click Open.**

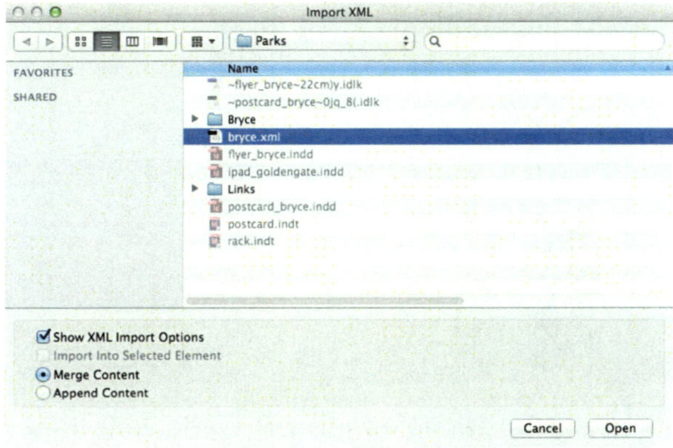

> *Note:*
>
> *The Merge Content and Append Content radio buttons are available in the Import XML dialog box because you need to make this choice even if you don't review the other import options.*

4. **Review the choices in the XML Import Options dialog box.**

The most important option is the Mode menu:

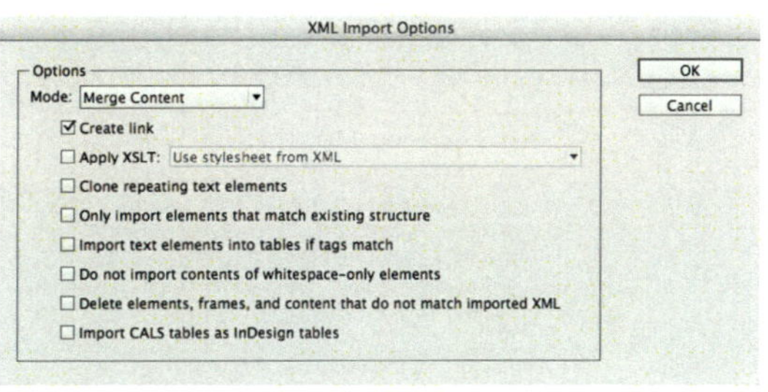

- If **Merge Content** is selected, the XML content will be placed into the Root element of the current file. Content in the XML file will be automatically placed into tagged frames in the current layout. If frames in the layout are not tagged, elements from the XML file will be added to the Structure pane.
- If **Append Content** is selected, the entire XML file will be placed into the Root element of the current document, *after* any elements that already exist.

5. **Make sure Merge Content is selected in the Mode menu and check the Create Link option.**

The **Create Link** option maintains a dynamic link to the XML file, just as a placed image is linked to the original image file. If content in the XML file changes, you can update the layout to automatically reflect the same changes.

Import XML Options

INDESIGN FOUNDATIONS

When importing and placing XML data using the Merge Content option, the XML Import Options dialog box offers the following options:

- **Create Link** links to the XML file, so if the XML file is changed, the XML data in the InDesign document is automatically updated.
- **Apply XSLT** defines a style sheet that transforms XML data from one structure to another.
- **Clone Repeating Text Elements** replicates the formatting applied to tagged placeholder text for repeating content (for example, formatting applied to different elements of an address placeholder).
- **Only Import Elements That Match Existing Structure** filters imported XML content so only elements from the imported XML file with matching elements in the document are imported. When this option is unchecked, all elements in the XML file are imported into the Structure pane.
- **Import Text Elements Into Tables If Tags Match** imports elements into a table if the tags match the tags applied to the placeholder table and its cells.
- **Do Not Import Contents Of Whitespace-only Elements** leaves existing content in place if the matching XML content contains only whitespace (such as a paragraph return character).
- **Delete Elements, Frames, and Content That Do Not Match Imported XML** removes elements from the Structure pane and the document layout if they don't match any elements in the imported XML file.
- **Import CALS Tables As InDesign Tables** imports any CALS tables in the XML file as InDesign tables.

6. Click OK to import the XML file into the postcard document. In the Structure pane, expand all items.

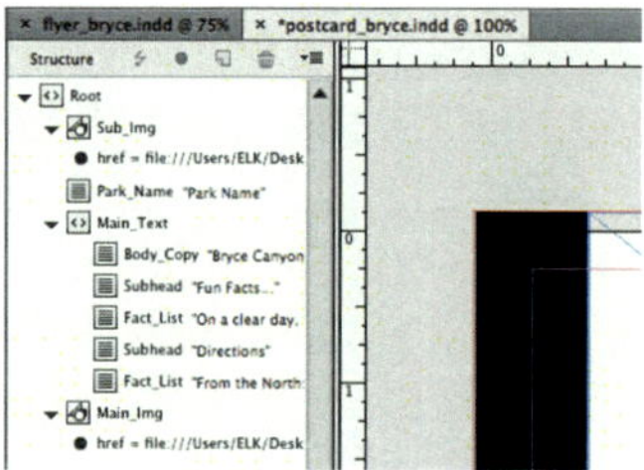

7. With Page 1 of the postcard showing in the document window, drag the Sub_Img element from the Structure pane onto the empty frame in the top-left corner.

Adding content is as easy as dragging it into the layout. If you drag an element into an empty area, a frame is automatically created.

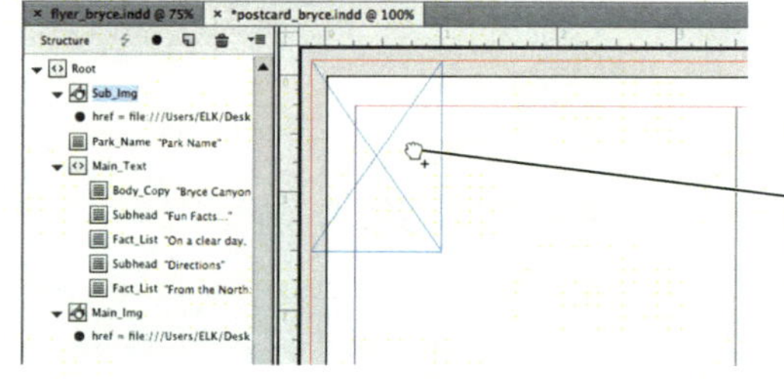

This cursor indicates that you are adding content from the Structure pane into this frame.

When you release the mouse button, the frame is automatically tagged with the Sub_Img tag.

This icon indicates a graphic element that has been placed in the document.

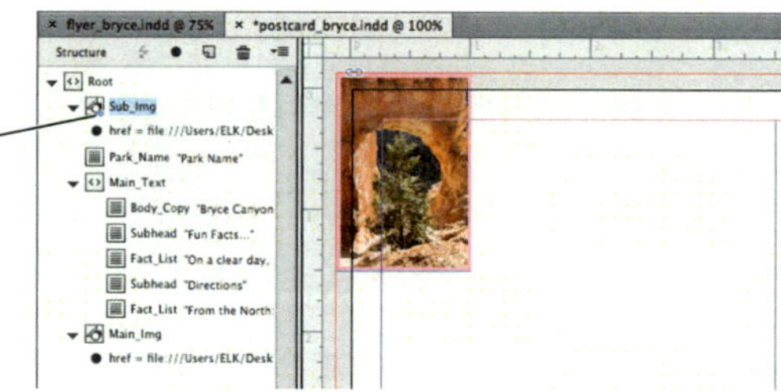

8. **Drag the Body_Copy element from the Main_Text element to the empty text frame at the bottom of Page 1.**

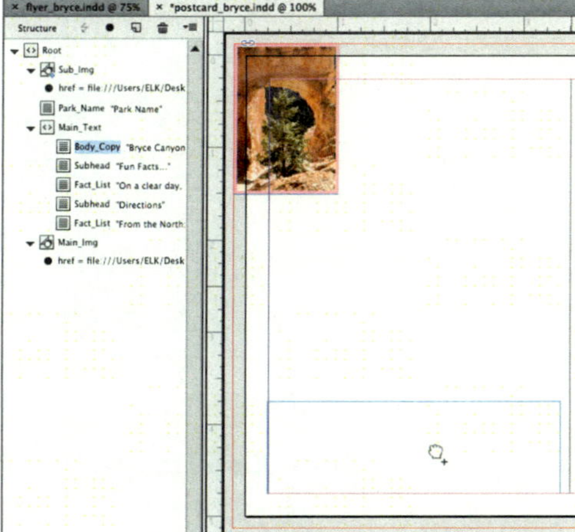

When you release the mouse button, the content of the selected Body_Copy element is placed into the frame. The paragraph doesn't fit in the assigned space.

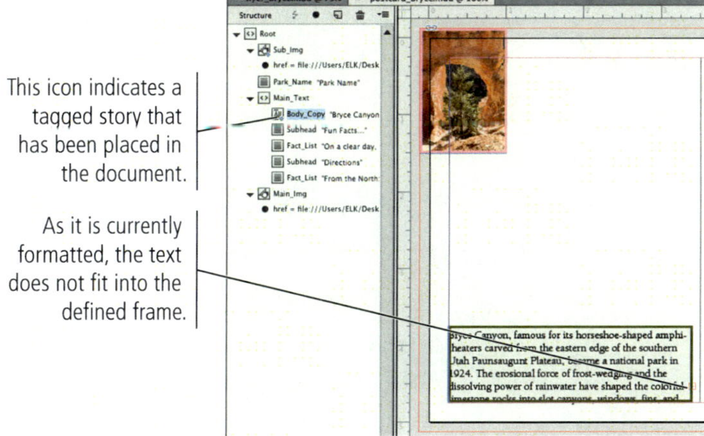

9. **In the Structure pane Options menu, choose Map Tags to Styles.**

This dialog box allows you to assign specific styles to specific elements.

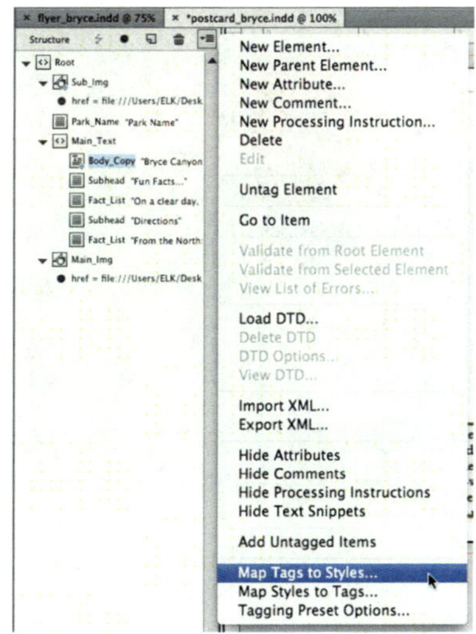

Note:

Make sure you choose Map Tags to Styles, not Map Styles to Tags.

10. Click the Map by Name button at the bottom of the dialog box.

Using the same names for tags and styles allows you to easily format different elements with the appropriate style. The Park_Name tag matches the style of the same name, so it is properly mapped to that style. Notice, however, that the Body_Copy tag is not mapped to a style.

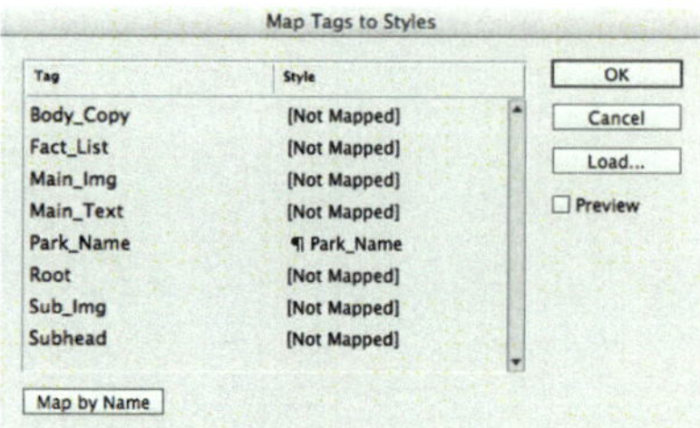

> *Note:*
>
> *Each of the template files for this project defines different formatting options (appropriate for each layout) for the same-named styles. There is no link between the styles in one file and the styles in another, other than the same style names.*

11. Click the words "[Not Mapped]" to the right of the Body_Copy tag and choose Body Copy from the menu.

This menu lists all styles defined in the layout. Paragraph, character, table, cell, and object styles are all listed because any of these five might apply to a specific type of tag.

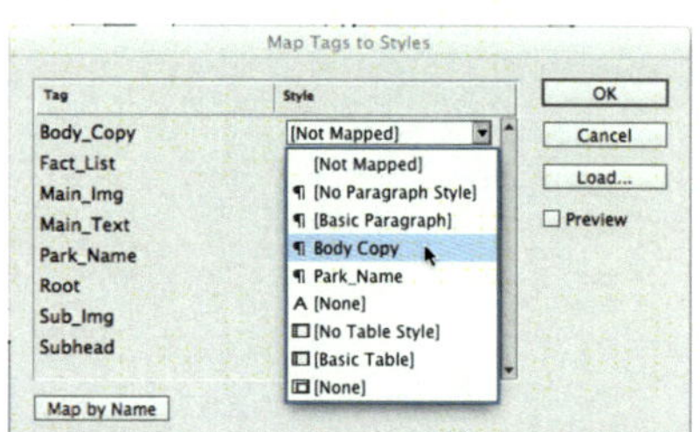

> *Note:*
>
> *The difference between the names of the XML tag and the style is the underscore character.*

12. Click OK to apply the defined formatting to the XML tags.

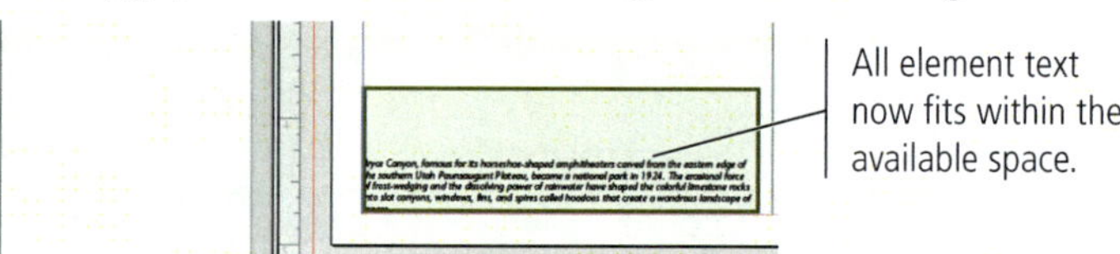

13. On Page 2 of the layout, drag the XML elements into the layout as shown in the following image.

The text element is automatically formatted because you already mapped that tag (Park_Name) to the existing document style (Park_Name).

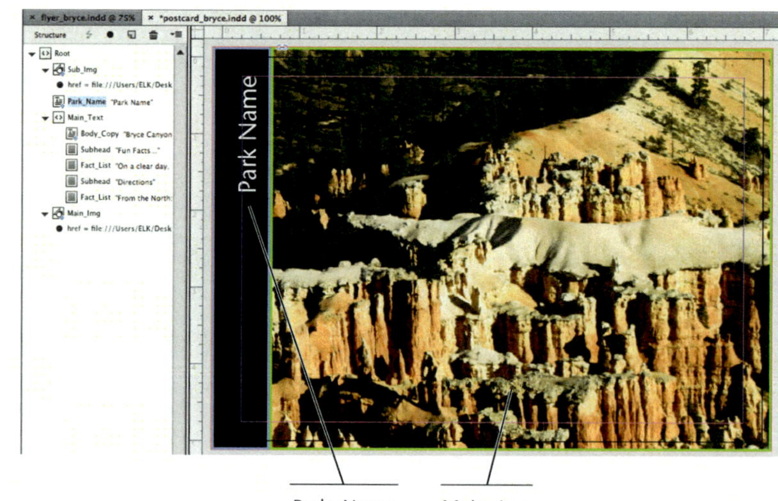

XML does not communicate the appearance of the different elements, just the content. After mapping the tags to the postcard styles (which we defined in the provided template file), the Park_Name text is placed with the ATC Onyx Normal font with no type styles — as defined by the Park_Name style in the postcard template — instead of ATC Onyx Bold with All Caps that is used in the flyer style.

14. Save the file, then continue to the next exercise.

Update Linked XML Data

When you placed the XML file into the postcard layout, you checked the Create Link option. This means that changes to the XML file can easily be updated in the postcard layout, just as you would update a placed image.

1. **Make sure flyer_bryce.indd is open and active.**

2. **In the page heading, change the words "Park Name" to Bryce Canyon National Park, then click away from the type object to deselect it.**

   After deselecting the text frame, the text snippet in the Structure pane changes to show the new text in that object.

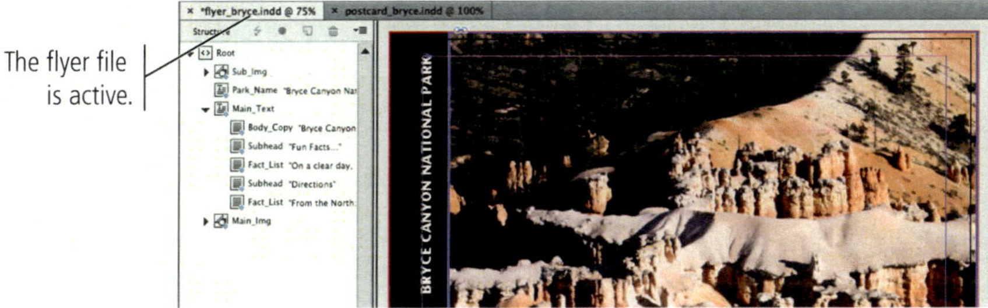

3. **Save the file.**

4. **Choose File>Export and navigate to the WIP>Parks folder as the target. Make sure XML is selected in the Format/Save As Type menu and the file name is bryce.xml, then click Save.**

5. **When asked if you want to overwrite the existing file, click Replace/Yes.**

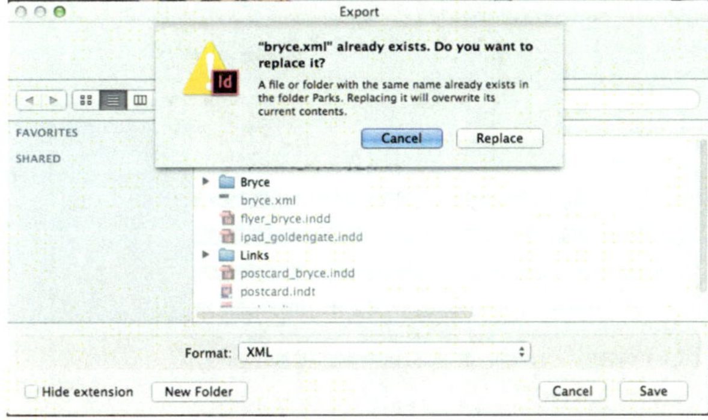

6. **Click Export in the resulting dialog box to rewrite the XML file.**

7. **Make postcard_bryce.indd the active file, and then display the Links panel.**

   The XML file is linked to the document, so it appears (appropriately) in the Links panel. The Warning icon indicates that the file was changed since being imported.

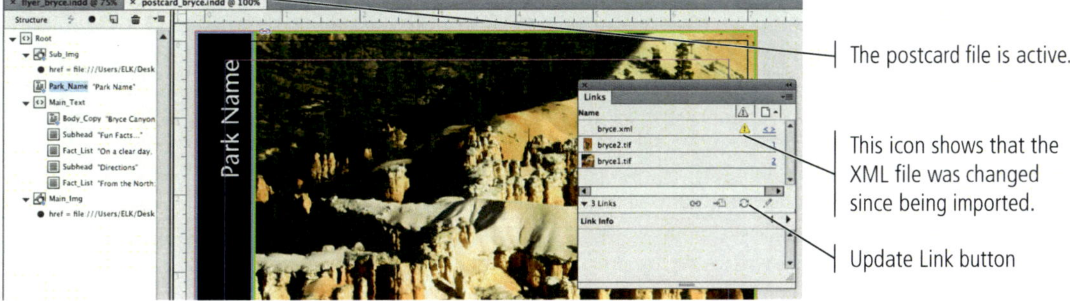

8. **Select bryce.xml in the Links panel and click the Update Link button.**

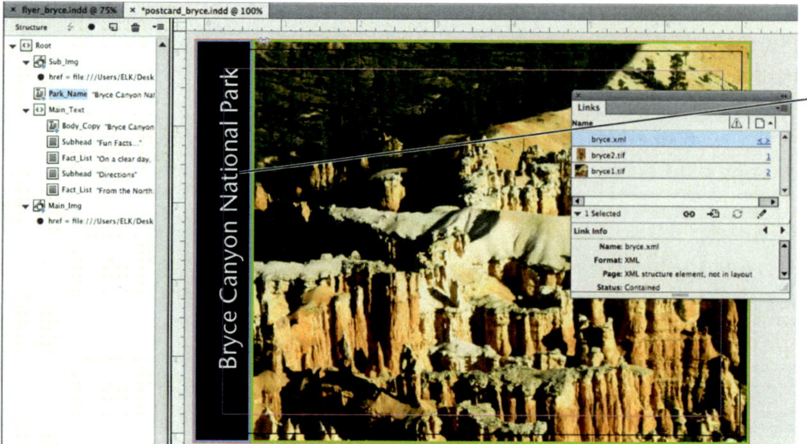

When the linked XML file is updated, the text change is automatically reflected in the postcard.

9. **Save the postcard file and close it.**

10. **Continue to the next exercise.**

Import Structured XML

With some advance planning, you can build a layout with tagged frames to automatically contain elements when the XML file is imported. For this process to work correctly, keep the following points in mind:

- The tag names must be exactly the same in the document file as in the XML data. (You can load tags from one InDesign file to another to be sure the names match.)
- You can automatically format imported XML content by mapping tag names to styles. (Style names need to exactly match the tag names.)
- The tagged layout should have the same structure as the data in the XML file. (Remember, the structure in the XML file is based on the order of elements in the Structure pane.)

Keep in mind, XML can be far more complex than what you applied in these short documents; in fact, entire books have been written on the subject. The point of this project is to introduce you to the concepts of XML and to show you how InDesign's XML capabilities make it relatively easy to work with XML data. With some careful planning, you can set up multiple files to read the same information and repurpose content into whatever physical format is necessary.

Note:

To learn more about the capabilities of XML, we encourage you to explore www.xml.org. This site offers a wealth of information about XML from experts and standards organizations in multiple industries.

1. **Create a new file by opening the rack.indt template in the WIP>Parks folder. Save the new file as rack_bryce.indd in your WIP>Parks folder.**

   This layout includes two pages with placeholder frames for all the same elements used in the flyer. To prepare these frames for XML import, you have to tag those frames with the same tag names used in the XML file you want to import.

2. **In the Tags panel Options menu, choose Load Tags.**

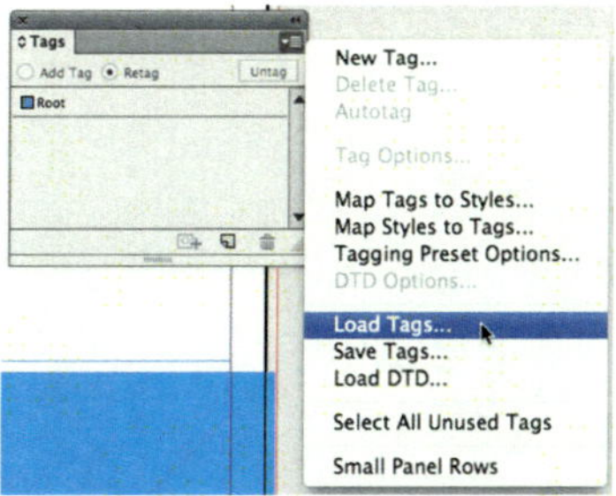

3. **Navigate to `flyer_bryce.indd` in your WIP>Parks folder and click Open.**

   You used this file to generate the XML file, so its tags match those in the XML file. This method of loading tags ensures that the tags you add in the rack card file exactly match the tags in the flyer (and thus, in the XML file).

4. **Open the Structure pane for the rack card file (View>Structure>Show Structure).**

   Adding tags to the file does not automatically add elements to the structure. Elements aren't added to the structure until you attach the loaded tags to frames in the layout.

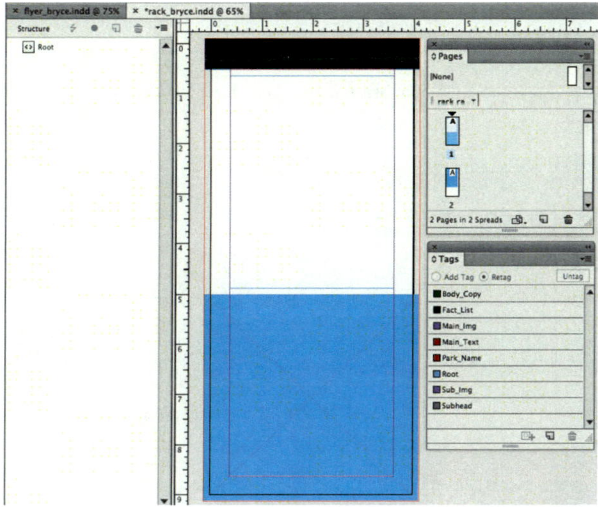

5. **Place the Tags panel next to the Paragraph Styles panel and compare the two lists.**

   Remember, for tags to correctly map to styles, the names of the styles must exactly match the names of the tags.

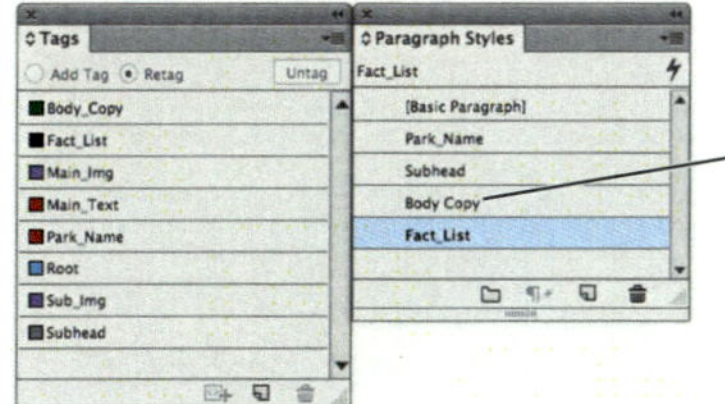

The space character in the Body Copy style means the style name does not exactly match the tag name (the underscore is missing).

> ***Note:***
>
> *Tag names can't have spaces but style names can, so this type of mismatch is not uncommon.*

6. **Control/right-click the Body Copy paragraph style and choose Edit "Body Copy" from the contextual menu.**

7. **In the Paragraph Style Options dialog box, change the style name to Body_Copy and click OK.**

The style name now matches the tag name.

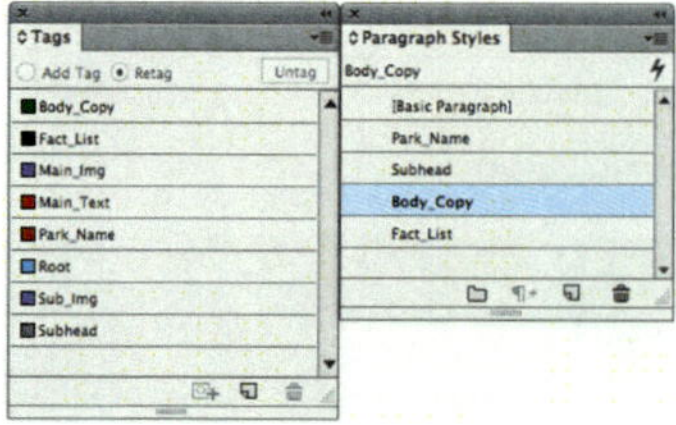

8. **Select the black frame at the top of Page 1 in the layout and then click the Park_Name tag in the Tags panel.**

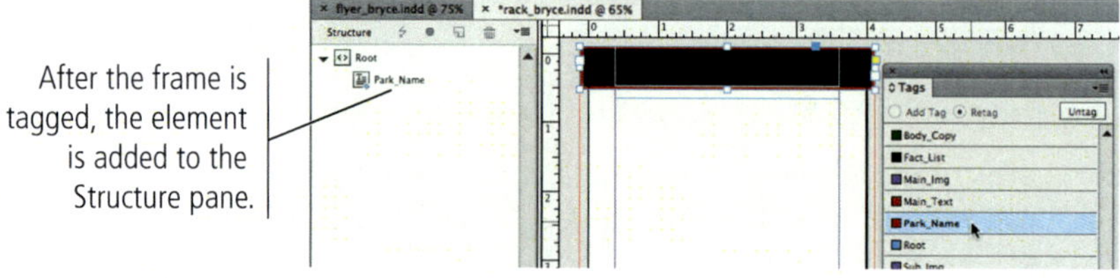

9. **Using the same method, assign the Main_Text tag to the large text frame and assign the Sub_Img tag to the cyan graphics frame on Page 1 of the layout.**

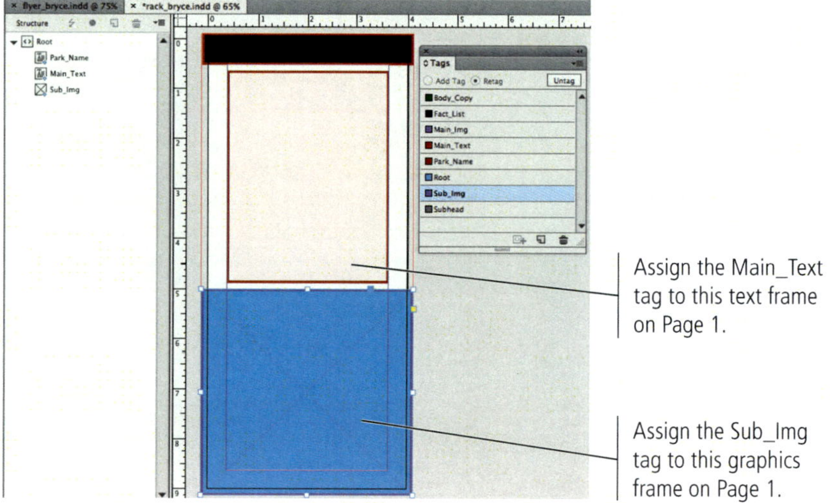

10. **On Page 2 of the layout, assign the Main_Img tag to the cyan graphics frame.**

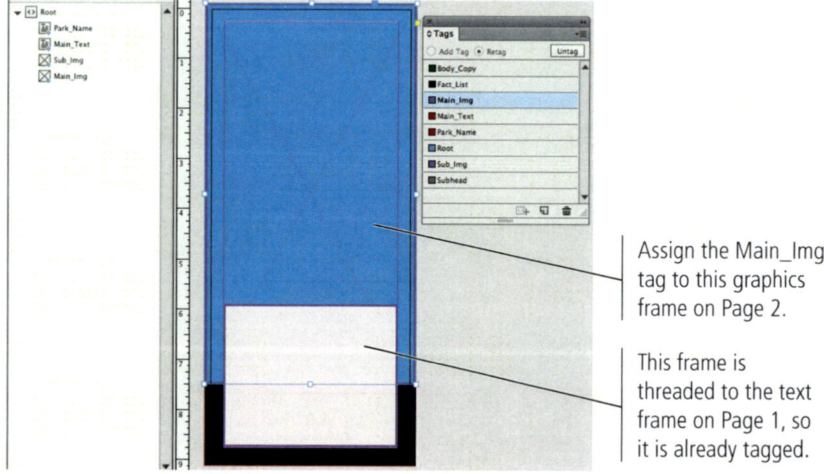

11. Make sure flyer_bryce.indd is open. Choose the 2-Up (side-by-side) document arrangement in the Application/Menu bar.

To be sure the XML will import properly, the tagged document structure should exactly match the structure in the XML file. The two Structure panes show that the Sub_Img element is not in the same order; you need to fix this before importing the XML file.

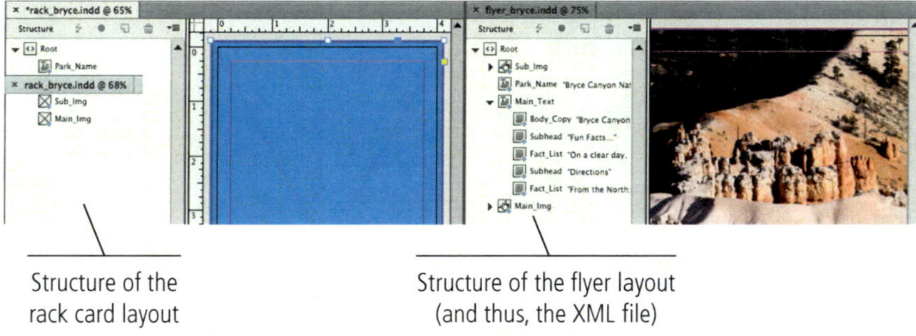

12. In the rack card Structure pane, drag the Sub_Img element to the top of the list.

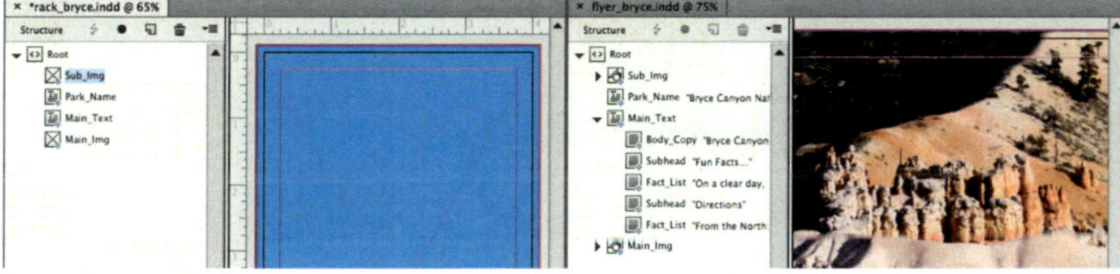

13. Return to the single-document arrangement and make the rack card file active.

14. With the rack card document active, choose File>Import XML.

This is the same as choosing the Import XML option in the Structure pane Options menu.

15. Navigate to the file bryce.xml in your WIP>Parks folder. Uncheck Show XML Import Options and Import Into Selected Element. Choose the Merge Content radio button.

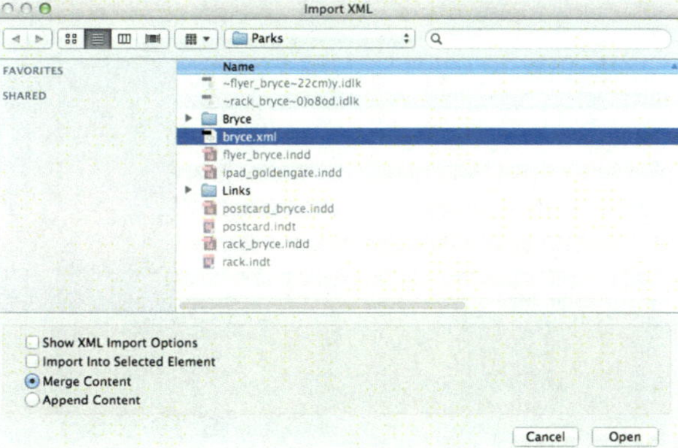

16. **Click Open to import the XML file into the rack card layout and merge the data into the tagged frames.**

    The tagged elements are all placed into the matching tagged frames, but they do not yet show the appropriate style settings.

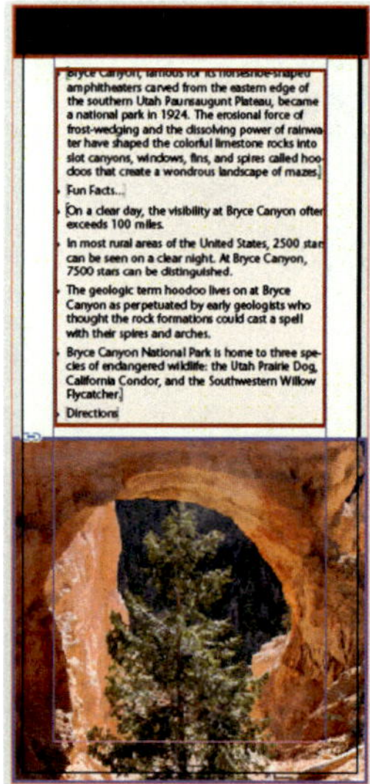

17. **In the Structure pane Options menu, choose Map Tags to Styles. In the resulting dialog box, click Map by Name, and then click OK.**

    Again, make sure you choose Map Tags to Styles, not Map Styles to Tags.

    Because you took the time to define style names that exactly matched the tag names, the mapping process requires no additional intervention.

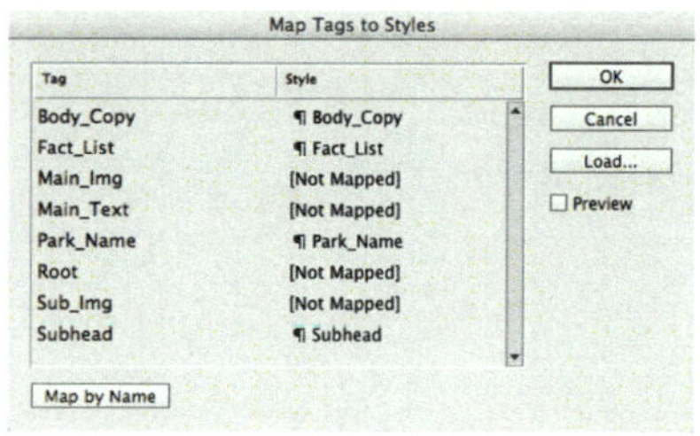

18. **Choose View>Structure>Hide Tagged Frames and View>Structure>Hide Tag Markers to turn off the nonprinting visual indicators.**

19. **Save the file and close it, then continue to the next stage of the project.**

Stage 2 Creating Alternate Layouts

As you have already seen throughout this book, there is almost always more than one way to accomplish a specific goal in InDesign. In the first stage, you used XML to feed content into several existing templates. In this second stage, you will use another method to create versions that are appropriate for digital tablet display.

When designing for mobile devices, one of the problems we face is the range of different hardware — most of which have different physical sizes, even if that difference is slight. For example:

Device	Physical size (diagonal)	Pixel dimensions	Pixels per inch (PPI)
Apple iPad with Retina display	9.7″	2048 × 1536	264
Apple Mini	7.9″	1024 × 768	163
Apple iPad2	9.7″	1024 × 768	132
Google Nexus 7	7″	1280 × 800	216
Samsung Galaxy 10.1; Motorola Zoom	10.1″	1280 × 800	150
Samsung Galaxy Tab 7; Kindle Fire	7″	1024 × 600	169

This list is hardly exhaustive; we only mention several of the most common devices. But as you can see, there is no single consistent size or resolution from one device to another. This issue is even further compounded when you consider the wide range of smart phones that are available, each (it seems) with a different physical size and resolution.

Ideally, when you design for mobile devices, you would create separate files for each device to take best advantage of the available screen capabilities. However, this would mean dozens of iterations for individual devices, which is not always possible given the immediate nature of some publishing projects.

At the very least, you should create different files for each of the common sizes — which is why the application includes those four basic presets in the New Document dialog box when you choose the Digital Publishing intent.

Note:

It's also important to realize that new devices are being introduced all the time, and each new phase of mobile-communication evolution will almost certainly introduce more variables into the picture (literally).

Update the InDesign Application Files

In this stage of the project, you will use a number of tools to create a folio file for a digital tablet device, which will contain two articles — one from the Bryce Canyon layout, and one from a similar layout that we provided for the Golden Gate National Recreation Area.

The Digital Publishing Suite (DPS), which drives folio creation and sharing, is part of the InDesign toolset. However, the DPS Desktop Tools are not included in the basic InDesign install process. If the update has not already been installed on your computer, you need to do so before you can complete the rest of this project.

1. **Make sure your computer is connected to a high-speed Internet connection.**

2. **In InDesign, open the Folio Builder panel (Window>Folio Builder).**

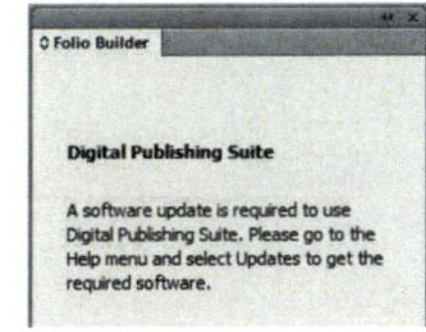

Note:

Software updates are relased periodically throughout the release cycle. The Adobe Creative Cloud application should automatically alert you to their availability, but it's a good idea to manually check every now and then.

3. **If the panel mentions a required update, choose Help>Updates.**

4. **Make sure anything related to InDesign CC and DPS is checked, then click Update.**

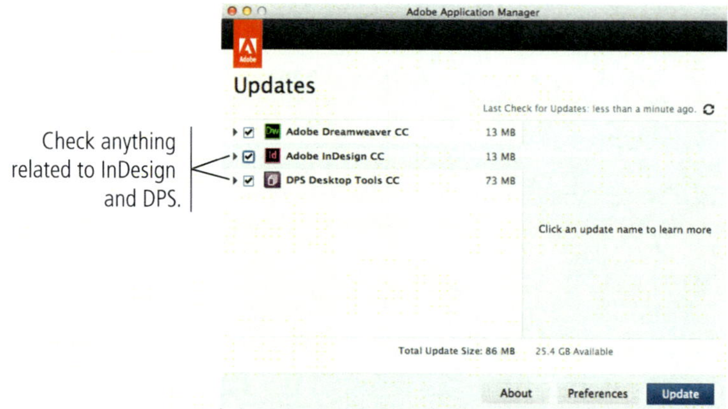

Note:

If you do not have administrative access to your computer's operating system (in other words, you aren't allowed to install software or otherwise affect the operating system), you won't be able to install the update. In that case, you must ask your IT administrator to install the update for you so that you can complete the rest of this project.

5. **Follow the on-screen prompts to install the update.**

You will be asked to quit InDesign so that the application files can be updated.

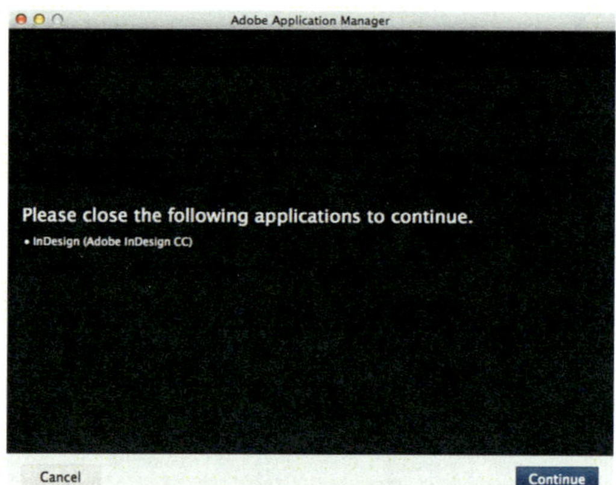

6. **When the update is complete, relaunch InDesign.**

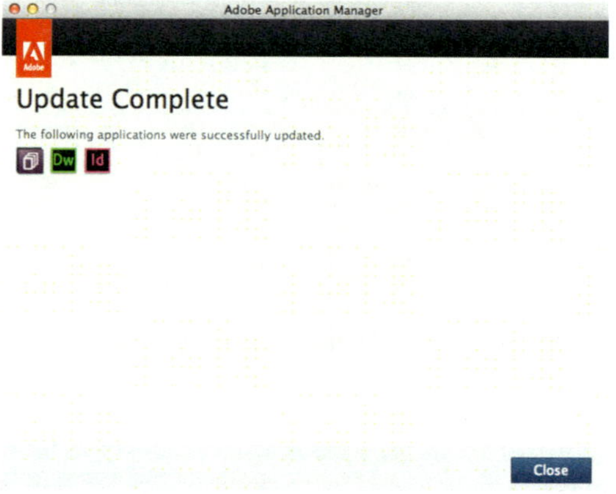

7. **Continue to the next exercise.**

Create a File for Digital Publishing

You can now use built-in options to easily create a new file for a number of standard digital media sizes — specifically, common tablets such as iPads and Android devices.

1. **With flyer_bryce.indd open, choose File>New>Document.**

2. **Choose Digital Publishing in the Intent menu.**

   When you choose the Digital Publishing intent, the Page Size menu includes presets for several common devices.

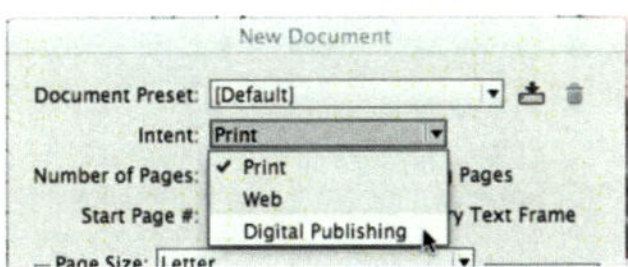

3. **Choose iPad in the Page Size menu, then choose the Portrait orientation.**

   The Digital Publishing intents default to landscape (horizontal) orientation. Although you eventually have to create both orientations for tablet devices, it is often easier to start with the version closer to the file you already have (the portrait-orientation flyer).

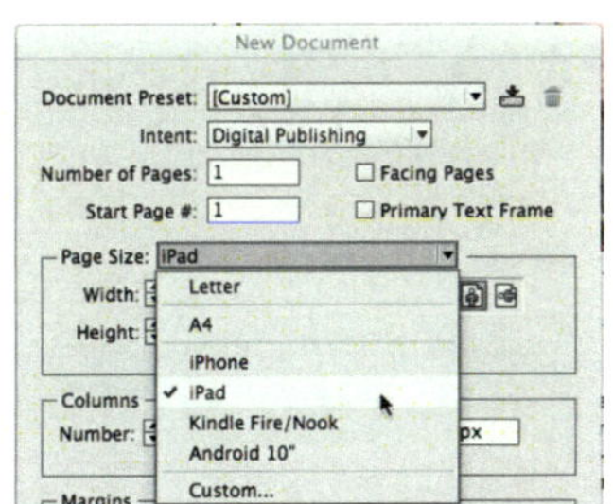

4. **Uncheck the Primary Text Frame option, then click OK to create the new file.**

   You do not need a primary text frame in this file because you will be copying the entire text frame from the flyer layout to the iPad layout.

5. **Save the file as ipad_bryce.indd in your WIP>Parks folder, then continue to the next exercise.**

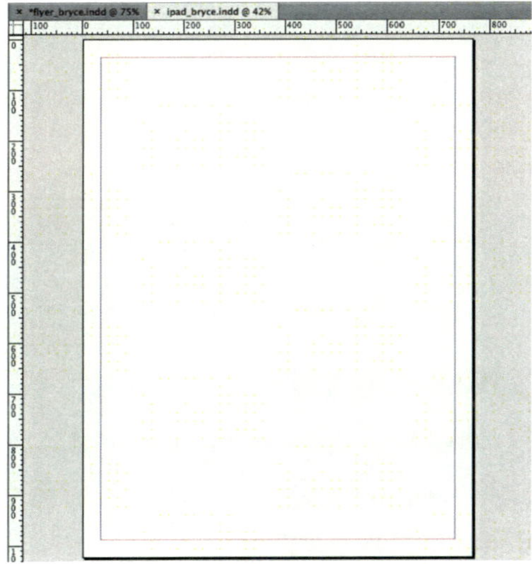

Note:

In this project you will use a number of InDesign features to create a file using the iPad dimensions; in a professional environment, you would likely have to also create files for other mobile devices.

Note:

The digital publishing intents use pixels as the units of measurement and RGB as the default color mode.

Use the Content Collector

The Content Collector/Content Placer toolset is a new option for sharing and linking content throughout a layout and across multiple layouts; you might think of it as copy-and-paste in hyperdrive. In this exercise, you are going to use these tools to repurpose the flyer content to a size suitable for an iPad.

> *Note:*
>
> *When the Tools panel is in two-column mode, the Content Placer tool appears to the right of the Content Collector tool (instead of nested under it).*

1. **Make flyer_bryce.indd the active file.**

2. **Choose the Content Collector tool.**

   Make sure you choose the *Collector* tool and not the *Placer*. The arrow in the Collector tool icon points down.

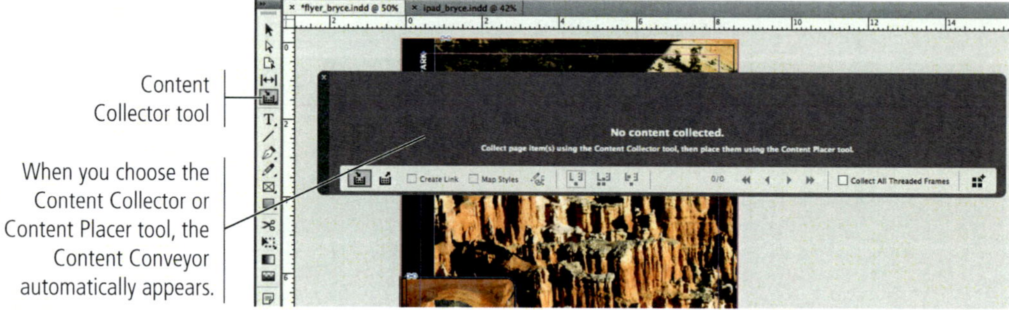

3. **Click the three-column text frame on the page to select it.**

   When you select an object with the Content Collector, it is added to the Content Conveyor. The cursor icon shows how many objects are currently stored in the conveyor.

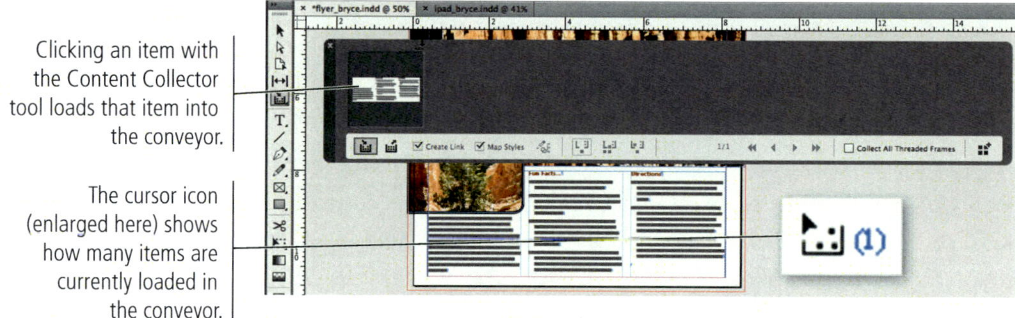

4. **Draw a selection marquee that touches both frames in the top half of the page (the large image frame and the black text frame with the park name).**

   When you select more than one object at a time, those objects are added to the conveyor as a **set**. The cursor icon shows that two objects are now stored in the conveyor (the text frame and the set that includes the park name frame and the image). In the conveyor, the set thumbnail shows that the set contains two items.

> *Note:*
>
> *If you click the Load Conveyor button on the right side of the panel, you can load the conveyor with all objects in the active selection, on a specific page, or on all pages. You can load these objects as individual items or as a single set.*

5. **Make the ipad_bryce file active, then press B to switch to the Content Placer tool.**

When the Content Placer tool is active, the cursor shows the number of items that are loaded in the conveyor, a thumbnail of the active item, and an icon indicating the type of active item (text frame, image, set, etc.).

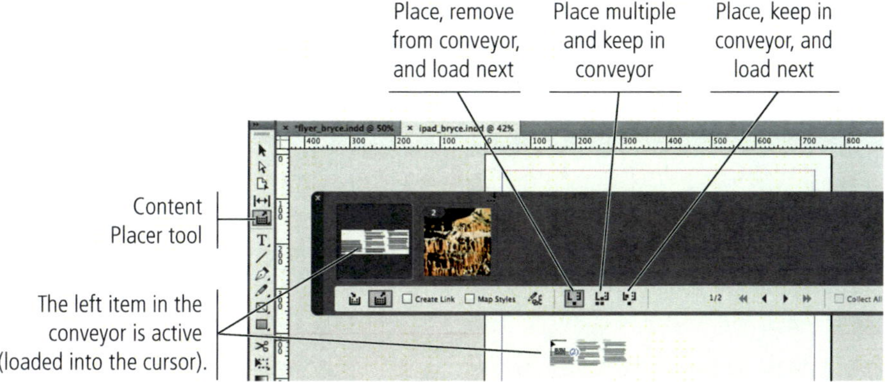

6. **Check the Create Link and Map Styles options at the bottom of the Content Conveyor.**

These options are explained in the next exercise. For now, simply make sure they are checked.

7. **Make sure the first placement option is selected at the bottom of the Content Conveyor.**

The buttons in the conveyor determine what will happen when you drop an item.

- **Place, remove from conveyor, and load next.** Clicking places the active item; that item is removed from the conveyor and the next is automatically loaded into the cursor.
- **Place multiple and keep in conveyor.** The active item in the conveyor remains active until you intentionally change to another item; this allows you to place multiple copies of the same item.
- **Place, keep in conveyor, and load next.** After placing the active item, the next item becomes active; all items remain in the conveyor.

8. **Click to place the active item (the text frame) near the bottom of the layout.**

The leftmost item in the conveyor is the active one (the one that will be placed when you click). You can use the navigation buttons at the bottom of the conveyor to change the active item, or use the Left and Right Arrow keys to move from one item to the next.

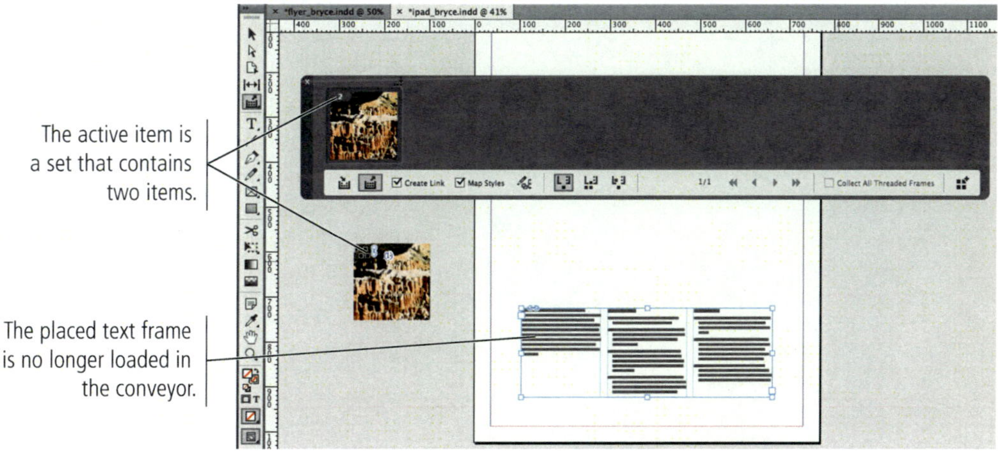

Note:

You can also use the buttons at the bottom of the conveyor to switch tools.

Note:

If the active item is a text object, you can click inside an existing text frame to place the loaded story into that frame.

Note:

Press ESC to remove the active item from the Content Conveyor.

Note:

You can hide the content conveyor by choosing View>Extras>Hide Conveyor. If you hide it, it remains hidden even after you select the Content Collector or Placer tool.

If you choose the Content Collector or Content Placer tool and do not see the Content Conveyor, choose View>Extras>Show Conveyor.

9. **With the Content Placer tool still active, press the Down Arrow key to display the set items in the Content Conveyor.**

   When the active item is a set, you can press the Down Arrow key to drill into that set — the conveyor shows only the individual items in the set.

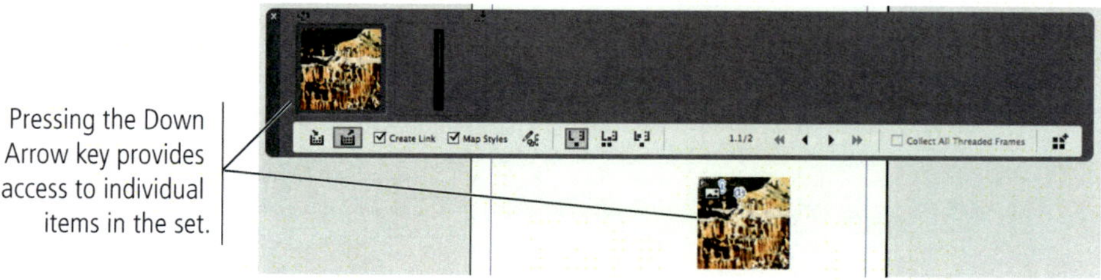

10. **Press the Up Arrow key to make the entire set active again.**

    When you are currently viewing the contents of a set, you can press the Up Arrow button to exit the set and show the previous level of conveyor items.

11. **Click anywhere on the page to place the active set.**

    If you click when a set is active, you place the entire set at one time.

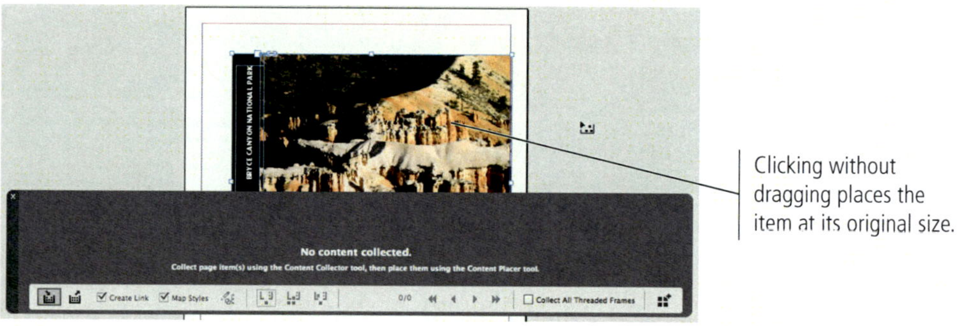

12. **Choose Edit>Undo Drop Item, then select the Content Placer tool again.**

    After you undo the placment from Step 11, the active tool automatically switches back to the Content Collector. The previously placed set is returned to the Content Conveyor.

13. **Click the top-left corner of the page and drag until the preview shows the new object filling the entire page width.**

You can simply click to place the active item with the same dimensions as the original.

Click and drag to place the item at a different size than the original; when you drag, the frame preview shows that the object's original aspect is maintained in the new frame. (To create the new frame without maintaining the aspect ratio, press Shift while you drag.)

Clicking and dragging draws the frame preview with the same aspect ratio as the original.

Cursor feedback shows the copy will be scaled to approximately 122% to fit the iPad dimensions.

Note:

If you want to place a copy without maintaining the original aspect ratio, press Shift while you drag the new object's shape.

This is the only time the Shift key does not constrain a transformation.

14. **Deselect everything in the layout, then save the file and continue to the next exercise.**

Manage Linked Object Options

When you use the Content Placer with the Create Links option checked, the content you place is linked to the original file instead of simply being a copy. If you need to make changes, you can edit the flyer content and the changes can be automatically updated in the iPad file's linked objects.

Because InDesign keeps track of link update status — just as it does for regular placed images — you don't need to worry about forgetting to make changes in any specific file. However, if you make a change to a linked object and then later update the links, you are warned that your edits in the linked copies will be lost.

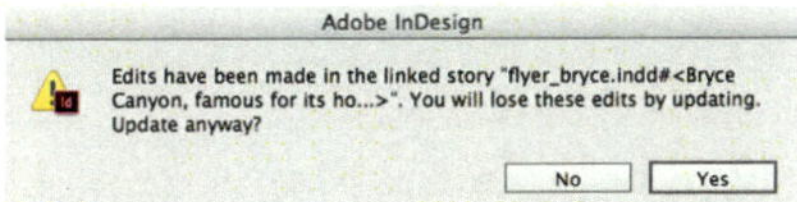

Compare this to the XML workflow in the first stage of this project. Using that process, you have to re-export the XML file if you make changes in the original flyer file, and then update the linked XML file in any secondary layouts. Using the Content Collector/Placer, you don't need to take that extra step.

In this project, you are going to modify the linked objects and define settings that will protect your changes.

1. **With ipad_bryce.indd open, open the Links panel and review the list.**

2. **Expand the Links panel as necessary so you can see most of the items' names.**

Although you only placed three items into the file, the Links panel lists six items. The software creates separate links for the objects and the objects' content. Icons identify the type of content; the containing frames do not display icons.

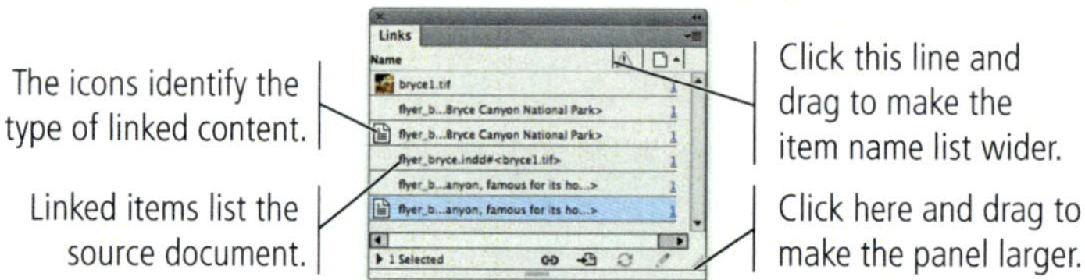

> *Note:*
>
> *Choosing the Edit>Place and Link command has the same general effect as selecting an item with the Content Collector tool.*

Because frames and contents are linked separately, you can update the linked content without affecting the object attributes, and vice versa:

- Update individual items or contents by selecting a specific listing in the Links panel and then clicking the Update Links button. This method allows you to update the item without affecting the content (and vice versa).
- Update individual copies by clicking the Modified icon on individual items in the layout (using the Selection tool). If you use this method, both the item and the item content will be updated.

> *Note:*
>
> *There is no dynamic link **from** the linked copies back to the original, or to other copies of the same object. If you want changes to reflect in all linked copies, you have to edit the original object. This is easily accomplished by Control/right-clicking any of the copies — in the layout or in the Links panel — and choosing **Go to Source** in the contextual menu.*

3. **Using the Selection tool, select the three-column text frame. Define its position as X: 36 px, Y: 720 px based on the top-left reference point.**

When you placed the text frame, you simply clicked to place it. You did not click and drag to define the placed text frame's size. You are making this change to better fit the available space in the iPad layout.

4. **Click the bottom-right corner of the text frame and drag to the bottom-right margin.**

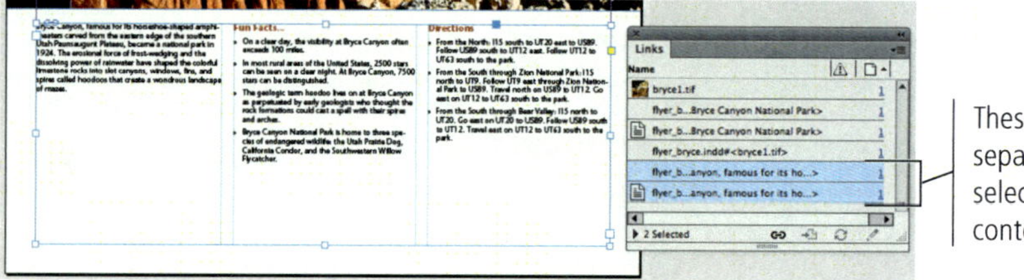

5. **Click away from the text frame to deselect it.**

6. **In the Links panel, click to select only the three-column text frame item, then expand the Link Info section of the panel.**

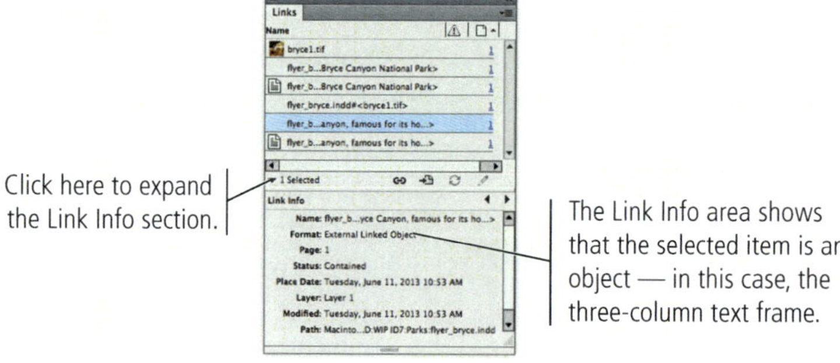

7. **Control/right-click the text frame item for the flyer copy. Choose Link Options in the contextual menu.**

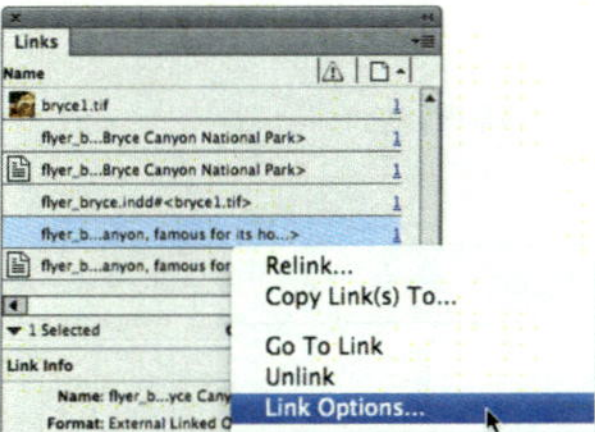

8. **In the Preserve Local Edits area, check the Size and Shape option. Click OK.**

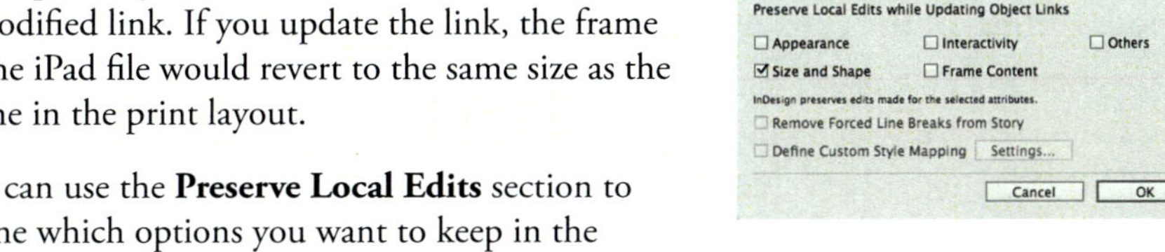

Because the object is linked to the object in the print flyer, any changes to the frame size or shape in the print layout would cause this item to show a Modified link. If you update the link, the frame in the iPad file would revert to the same size as the frame in the print layout.

You can use the **Preserve Local Edits** section to define which options you want to keep in the linked copies when you update the links. By checking the Size and Shape option, you are telling InDesign to keep the frame's size and shape that you defined in the iPad layout; you have essentially unlinked specific properties, while other attributes of the frame (appearance, etc.) are still linked to the print flyer frame.

Note:

It is important to realize that the Preserve Local Edits options relate to all objects in the file. You cannot define different settings for individual objects.

9. **Open the Paragraph Styles panel.**

When you resized the frame, you should have noticed that the text reflowed. The text formatting that was applied in the print layout left a lot of empty space at the bottom of the page. You should adjust the text size to best take advantage of the available space.

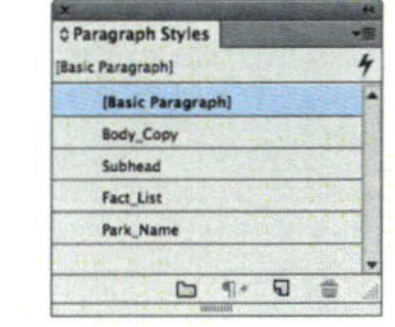

When you use the Content Placer tool to make copies, any assets (styles, color swatches, etc.) that are required by the linked object are added to the file where you place the copy.

10. **Make the following changes to the paragraph styles:**

Park_Name	**Change the type size to 24 pt**
Subhead	**Change the type size to 18 pt**
Body_Copy	**Change the type size to 12 pt** **Turn off automatic hyphenation**

There is no link between the styles in the original file (the flyer) and the styles in the file where copies are placed (the iPad layout). You can use styles to change the appearance of the type in either location without affecting the other.

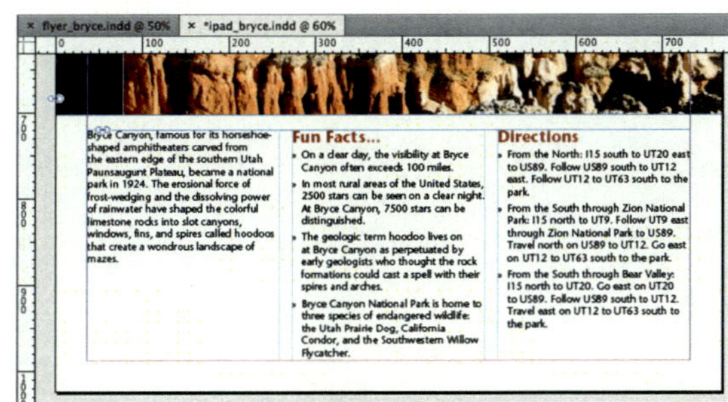

Note:

The Fact_List style is based on the Body_Copy style; both are changed when you edit the Body_Copy style.

11. **Using the Selection tool, select the image frame in the layout.**

When you select an object in the layout, the object and the object contents are both selected in the Links panel.

If you select the frame in the layout, both the object and the object contents are highlighted in the Links panel.

12. **Deselect everything in the layout.**

13. **In the Links panel, click to select only the image frame. Control/right-click the frame listing and choose Unlink in the contextual menu.**

You are going to use this frame to create an interactive slideshow that displays when someone opens the file on a tablet device. To avoid problems if you make changes to the image frame in the flyer file, you are breaking the link for only this frame.

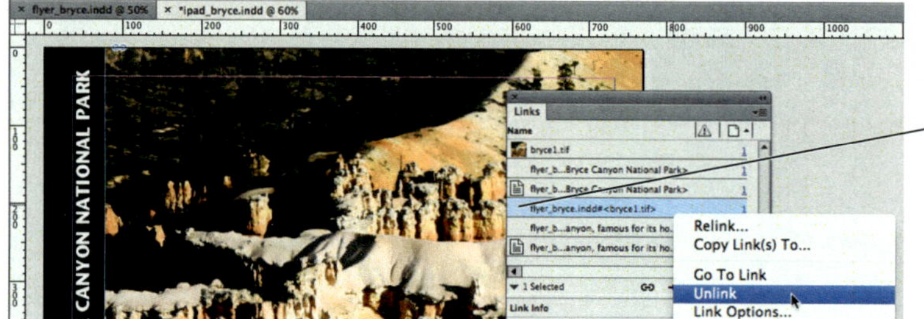

There is no icon to identify the image frame. The item name includes the name of the contained image.

The image frame remains in the layout, and it still shows the link icon because this is still a linked image — linked to the actual image source file. There is no longer any link to the original object in the flyer file.

The frame still shows the link icon because the placed image is linked to the image file.

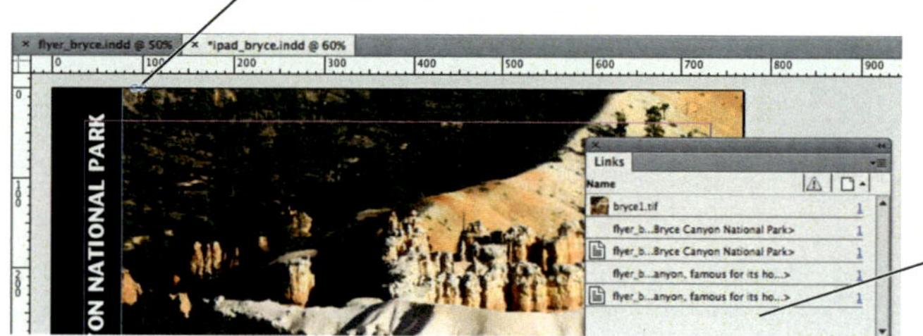

The frame is no longer linked; it has been removed from the Links panel.

14. **Save the file and continue to the next exercise.**

Defining Style Mapping Rules

In the previous exercise, you saw that styles applied in the placed content are automatically copied into the file where you place that content.

If the target file has existing styles of the same name as the styles in the source file, the target-file style definition is automatically applied in the placed content. In other words, the target file style definition overrides the same-named style in the source file.

If you are placing content into a file that has existing styles, but those styles don't have the same names as the styles in the source file, you can define style mapping rules to determine which styles in the target file will be used instead of styles in the source file.

When the Content Placer tool is active, you can click the Edit Custom Style Mapping button in the Content Conveyor to determine what styles you want to apply in the file where you place the content.

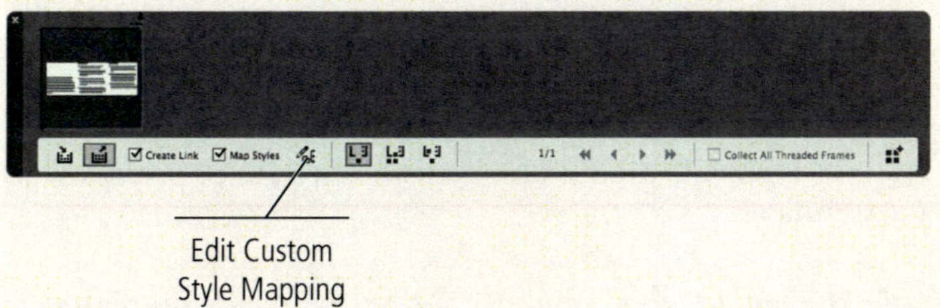

In the Custom Style Mapping dialog box, you first choose the source document that contains the styles you want to replace. You can create style mapping rules for paragraph, character, table, and cell styles.

Clicking the New Style Mapping button adds an item to the list. In the left side of the dialog box, you choose the style you want to replace (the source style); in the right side of the dialog box, you choose the style you want to apply (the mapped style).

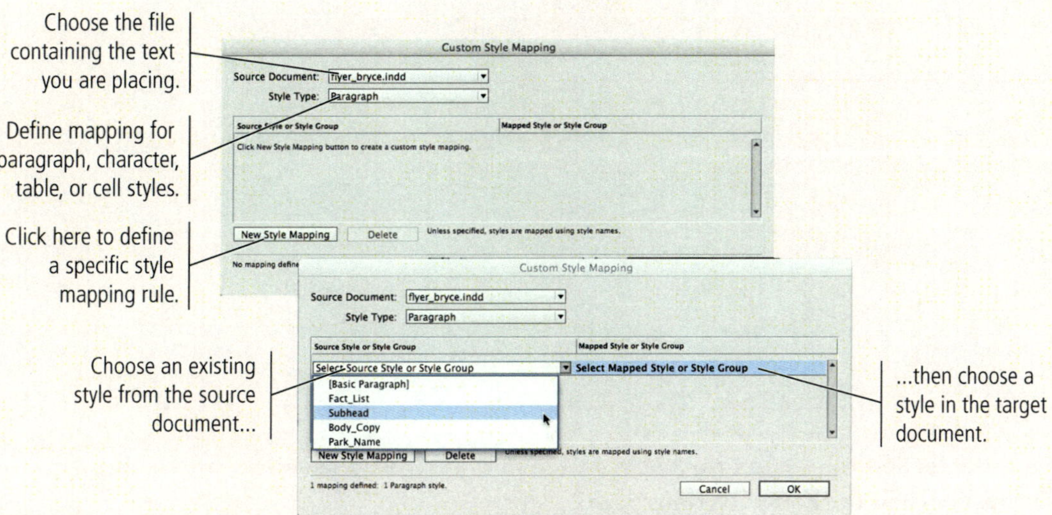

Once you define style mapping rules, those choices will be applied as long as the Map Styles option is checked in the Content Conveyor.

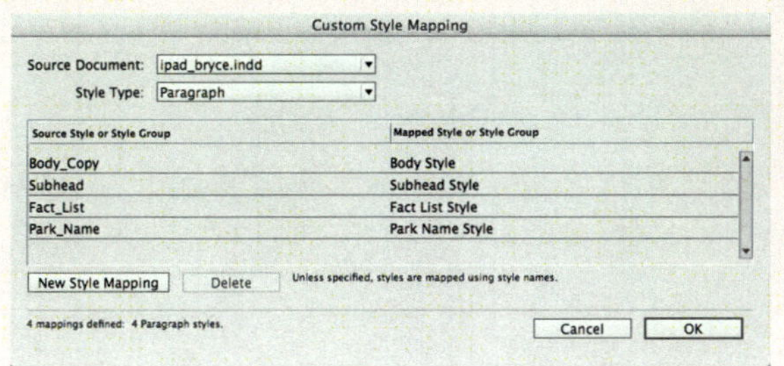

Check this option to apply your custom style-mapping rules when you place content.

Create an Interactive Overlay

You might have noticed that you did not include the second image from the print layout in the iPad layout. As you know, print is static — objects stay where you put them, and they do not change. If you want to show two pictures, you place two pictures into the layout.

If you completed Project 6: Digital Layout Variations, you have already seen that digital publishing is not subject to this restriction. You can use a single frame to show multiple images or even play a video. In this exercise, you will use an interactive overlay to display multiple images in the same frame in the published file (called a "folio").

1. **With ipad_bryce.indd open, open the Folio Overlays panel (Window>Folio Overlays).**

   This panel includes a number of common interactive elements that can be added to a digital publication using only tools in the InDesign interface. You don't need an external application to create these elements.

2. **Deselect everything in the layout, then click Image Sequence in the Folio Overlays panel.**

   If you select an overlay when nothing is selected in the layout, you automatically see more information about the selected overlay type.

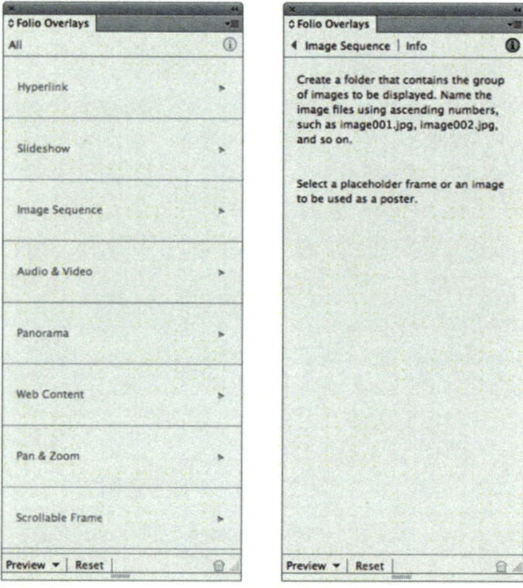

3. **Using the Selection tool, select the image frame in the layout, then click Image Sequence in the Folio Overlays panel.**

Click the Info button to find specific information about the selected type of overlay.

When the frame is selected in the layout, the panel shows options related to the specific type of overlay.

4. **Click the Folder icon to the right of the Load Images field.**

5. **Select the Bryce folder in the WIP>Parks folder, then click Open/OK.**

   This folder contains a number of images that will be used in the interactive slideshow.

   At this point, there is no visible indication that the frame in the layout has changed. By default, the image currently placed in the frame will appear when the file opens.

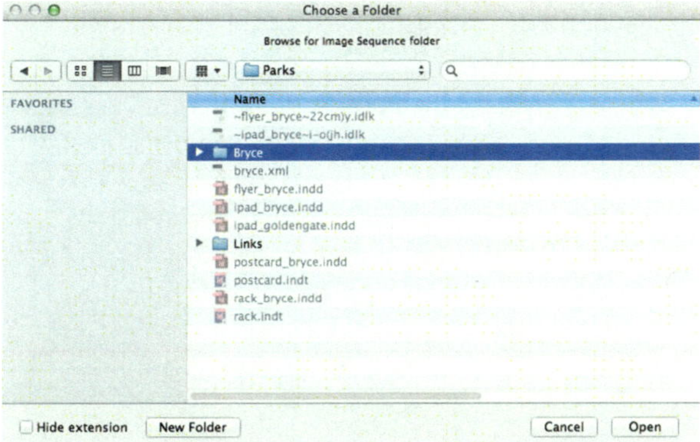

6. **In the panel, check the option to Show First Image Initially.**

   If you look carefully, a small amount of the frame's cyan fill color appears at the top and bottom of the image frame.

7. **Control/right-click the placed image and choose Fitting>Frame Fitting Options in the contextual menu.**

   Because the Auto-Fit option is checked, the loaded images will automatically scale to the frame based on the defined Fitting option. The center point is selected in the Align From proxy, which is why the frame fill color is visible at the top and bottom of the placed content.

   This image frame is currently set to Fit Content Proportionally, which means the image is made only large enough to fit the width or the height — whichever requires the least amount of scaling.

8. **Choose Fill Frame Proportionally in the Fitting menu, then click OK.**

   Using this option, the image will be scaled (proportionally) as necessary to fill the entire frame. The frame's fill color will no longer be visible, regardless of the source file's actual physical size.

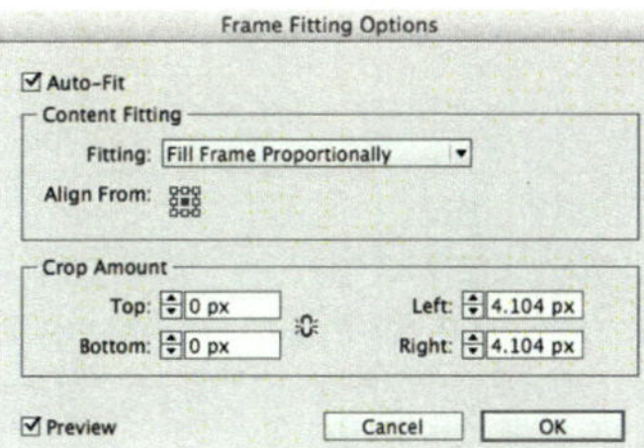

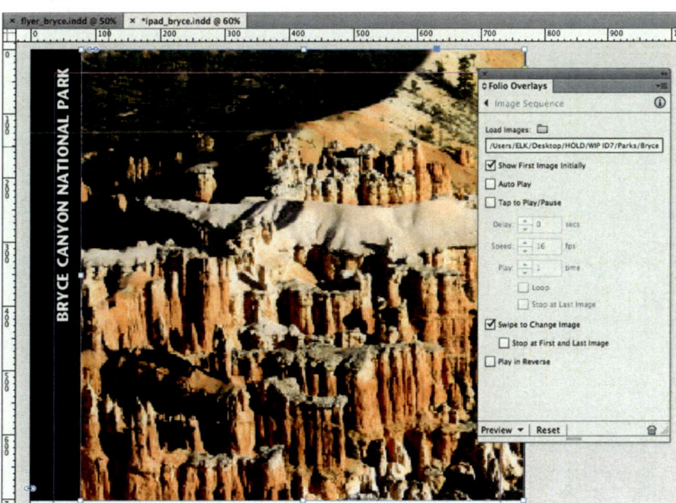

Folio Overlay Options

When you create a folio file to be viewed on a digital tablet, the visible content — including text — is rasterized into a single image. Interactivity is technically added on top of the image as a separate "layer" on top of the existing content (hence the term, "overlay").

The interactive layer is not a true InDesign layer that you can turn on and off; you can't directly access the layer containing the interactivity. Instead, you use the Folio Overlays panel to define interactive settings, which will be used to generate the necessary code in the final folio file. InDesign supports seven interactive elements that are common in digital publishing.

The **Hyperlink** overlay can be applied to any object that has been defined as a hyperlink (using the Hyperlinks panel), or to a button object that uses the Go to URL action.

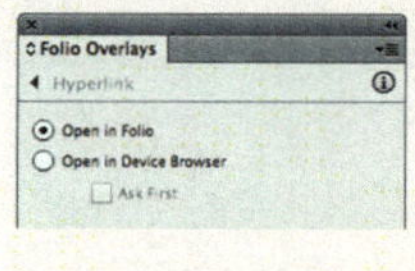

The **Slideshow** overlay can be applied to a multi-state object. It provides controls similar to those you created using buttons in Project 6: Digital Layout Variations.

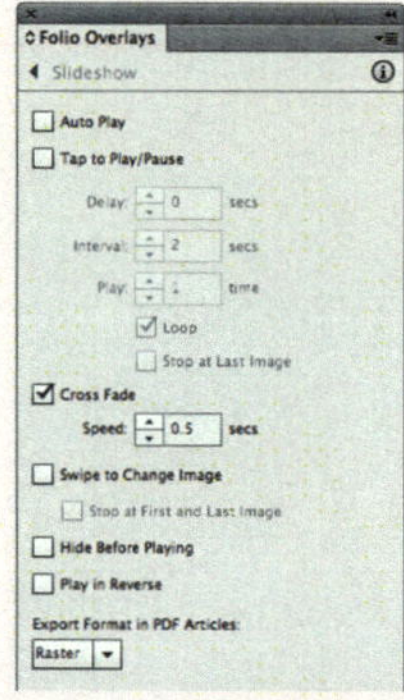

The **Image Sequence** overlay creates a slideshow from a folder of images. You can apply this overlay to any rectangle frame, whether or not it already contains an image.

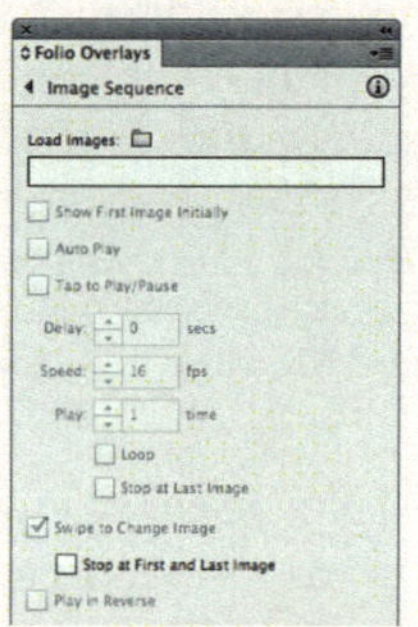

The **Audio & Video** overlay adds controls to audio and video files that are placed in the layout.

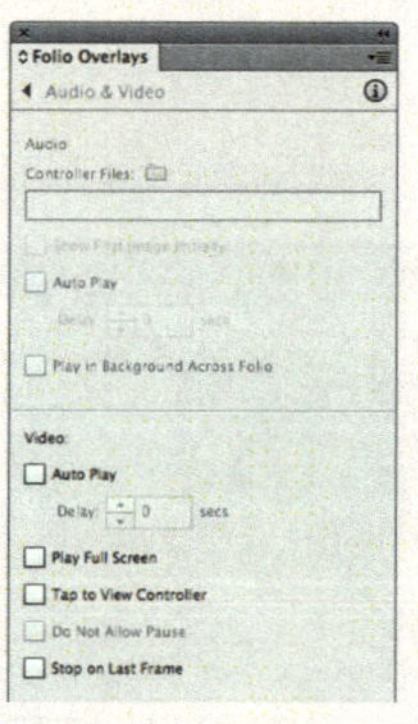

The **Panorama** overlay can be used to create a single panoramic image by stitching together a sequence of individual images. (The individual images should represent the six sides of a three-dimensional cube.) The user can drag around the image to view different areas of the scene.

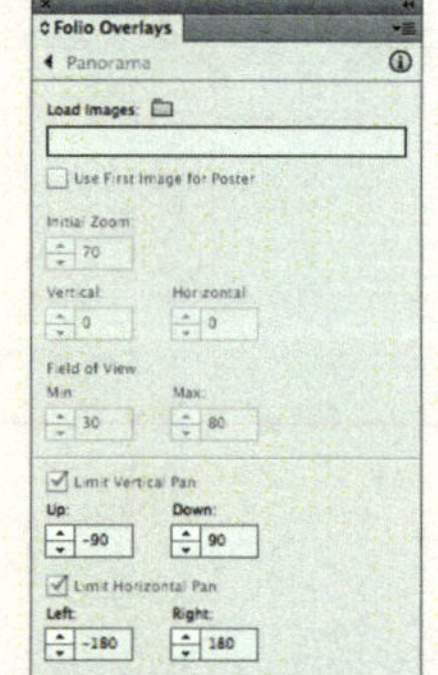

The **Web Content** overlay can be used to feed HTML content into a frame in the layout.

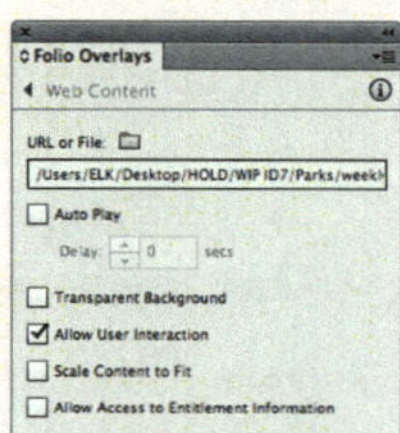

The **Pan & Zoom** overlay can be applied to any image frame in which the image has been cropped by the frame edges; the frame defines the scrollable area that is visible in the folio file. If you choose Pan & Zoom, users can use pinch gestures to zoom into a specific image area.

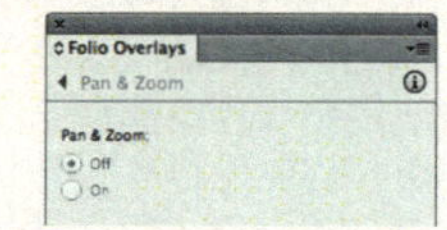

The **Scrollable Frame** option creates a frame in which the user can scroll to see more content.

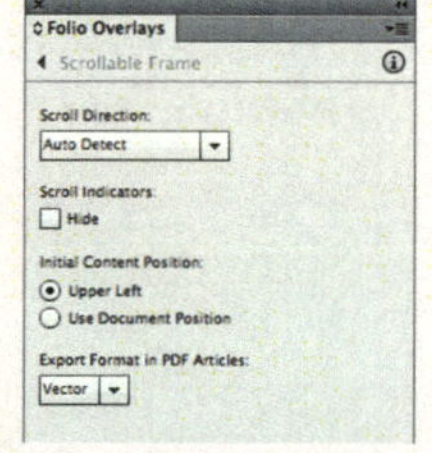

To create a scrollable frame, you have to first create the frame that will define the scrollable area, and the content objects that you want to be included in the frame. Next, select the content object(s) with the Selection tool and choose Edit>Cut, then select the frame object and choose Edit>Paste Into.

Finally, apply the Scrollable Frame overlay to the frame object and define the properties in the Folio Overlays panel.

9. **With the image frame still selected, make the following choices in the Folio Overlays panel:**
    - **Check the Auto Play option**
    - **Check the Tap to Play/Pause option**
    - **Change the Delay to 2 secs**
    - **Change the Speed to 1 fps**
    - **Check the Loop option**
    - **Uncheck the Swipe to Change Image option**

    These options should be self explanatory — testament to the ease with which you can create interactive elements directly in InDesign.

    In our testing, the Delay field accurately controlled the image sequence timing on Android devices, but not on the iPad. Changing the frames per second (fps) to 1 second did accurately control the image timing on the iPad.

10. **Save the file, then continue to the next exercise.**

Define Liquid Page Rules

If you have a tablet device, you already know that it can display content both horizontally and vertically depending on the device's physical position. When you publish files for digital tablets, you can create different layout versions to take best advantage of each orientation.

1. **With ipad_bryce.indd open, select the text frame at the bottom of the page.**

2. **Open the Text Frame Options dialog box.**

3. **Choose Flexible Width in the Columns menu, and change the Maximum field to 250 px.**

    When you assign a frame to have flexible column widths, you can define the maximum width that will be allowed when you resize the frame. (This will make more sense shortly when you resize the page.)

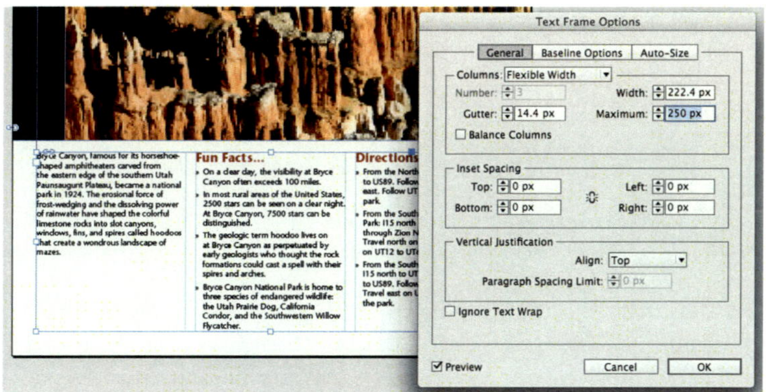

4. **Click OK to return to the layout.**

Note:

Flexible column widths are not only valuable when you resize an entire page. They are also useful if you need to resize the text frame in a layout — which you will do later in this project.

Understanding Column Options

Fixed Number means the frame has a defined number of columns. When you resize the frame, the columns resize to equally divide the frame width.

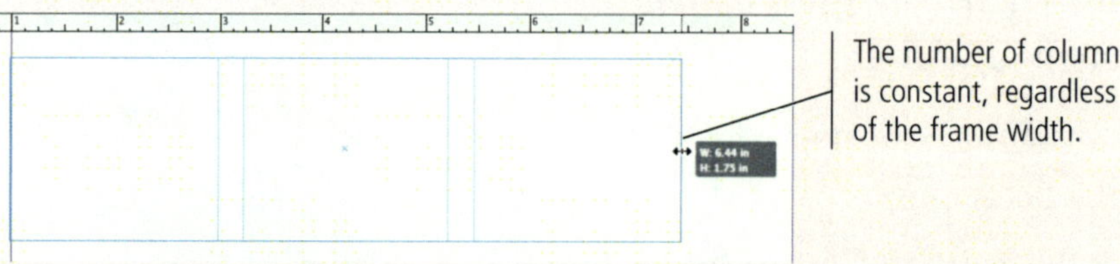

The number of columns is constant, regardless of the frame width.

Fixed Width means columns in the frame always have the exact width defined in this box. If you resize the frame, columns are added or removed based on the available space. Using this option, the frame will always be exactly wide enough to contain the number of columns (including gutters).

Say you define Fixed Width columns of 2″ with a gutter of 0.25″. With two columns, the frame will be 4.25″ wide. If you make the frame at all wider, it automatically snaps to the next size that accommodates the defined column width (6.5″, 8.75″, etc.).

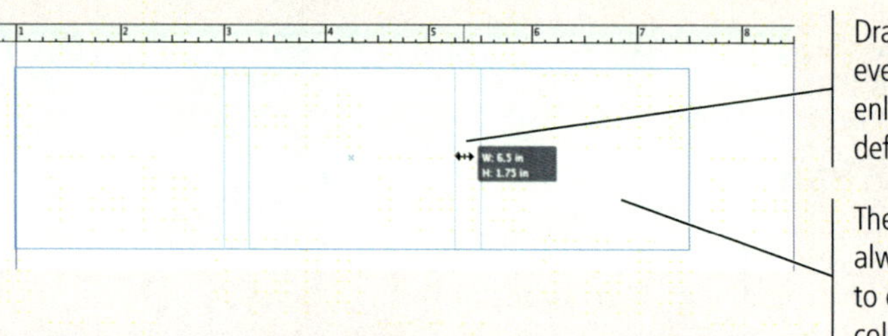

Dragging the handle even a small distance enlarges the frame by the defined column width.

The frame width is always exactly enough to contain the number of columns (plus gutters).

Flexible Width means the number of columns in a frame adjusts dynamically when the frame is resized. When you change frame's overall width, columns resize until the maximum width triggers adding or removing a column.

Say you define flexible-width columns with a maximum width of 2″ and a gutter of 0.25″. When the overall frame width is more than 4.25″ (2″ column + 0.25″ gutter + 2″ column), another column is added. Column width varies based on the overall frame width.

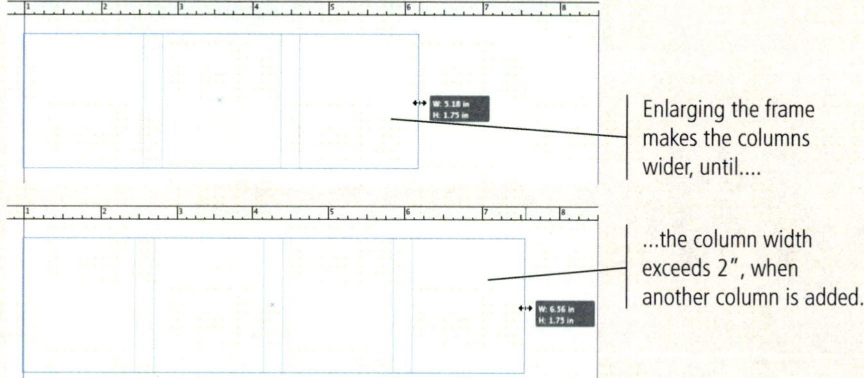

Enlarging the frame makes the columns wider, until....

...the column width exceeds 2″, when another column is added.

5. **Choose the Page tool in the Tools panel. In the Control panel, choose Object Based in the Liquid Page Rule menu.**

   When the Page tool is active, the Liquid Page Rule menu defines how existing objects react when you change the page size or create an alternate layout.

6. **Click the three-column text frame with the Page tool to make sure that object is selected.**

   When the Object Based rule is applied and you select a specific object with the Page tool, you can use on-screen controls to define how the image will behave when you resize the page. The hollow circles outside the frame edges mean the object is not locked ("pinned") to the page edges. The solid circles on the frame edges (and the lock icons inside the frame) mean the object's dimensions are pinned.

7. **Open the Liquid Layout panel (Window>Interactive>Liquid Layout).**

   The options in this panel correlate to the on-screen controls for the selected object.

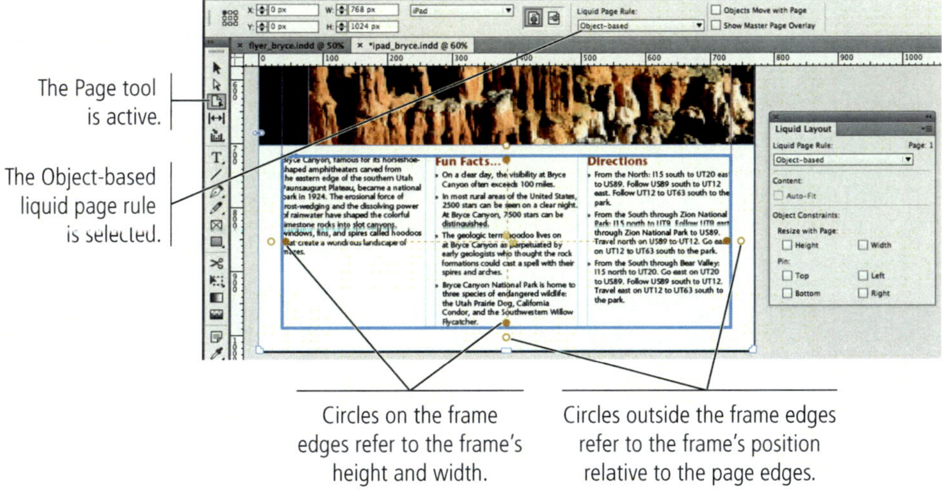

The Page tool is active.

The Object-based liquid page rule is selected.

Circles on the frame edges refer to the frame's height and width.

Circles outside the frame edges refer to the frame's position relative to the page edges.

8. **Click the bottom-right corner of the page and drag to approximate the size of a horizontal iPad.**

   Using the Page tool, you can drag a page handle to preview the effect of resizing the page. Remember that both the frame dimensions are pinned, and the frame is not pinned to any page edge. As you can see, the text frame retains the same size, centered horizontally in the resized page area when you resize the page.

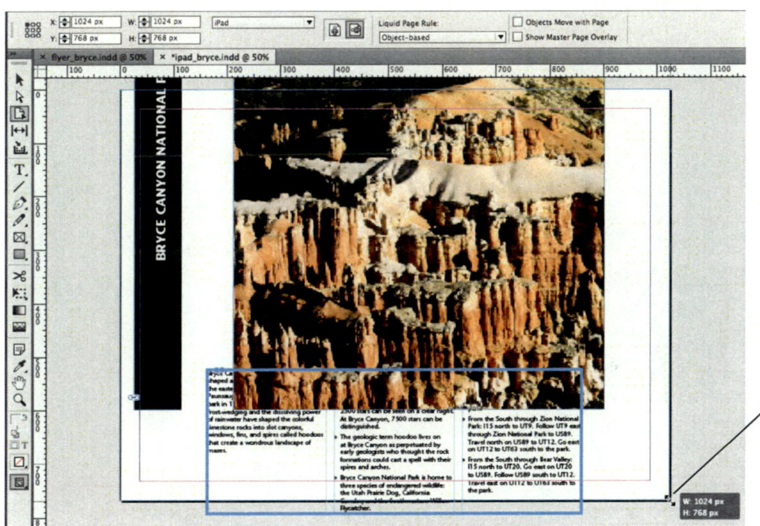

Using the Page tool, drag one of the handles to preview the page contents at a different page size.

> ***Note:***
>
> *You can press Option/Alt to retain the new page size when you release the mouse button.*

Understanding Liquid Page Rules

If the **Show Master Page Overlay** option is checked in the Control panel, the active master page appears in the bottom-left corner of the active page.

Using the **Off** liquid page rule, resizing the page has no effect on placed objects.

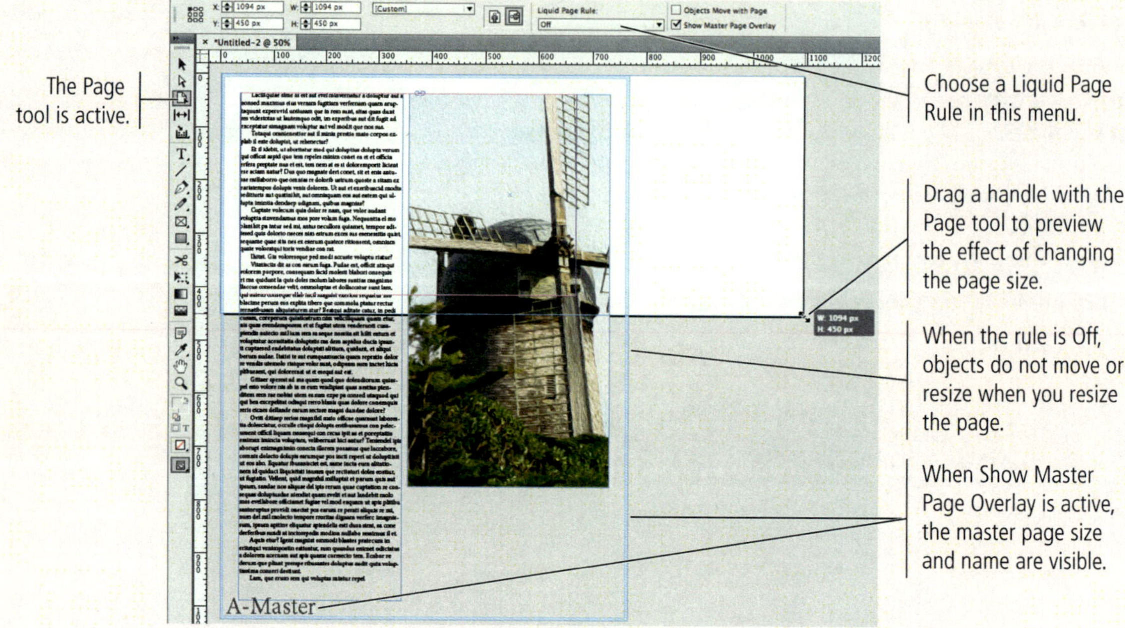

Using the **Scale** liquid page rule, content is scaled proportionally, adding or removing space around the page if the content can't be scaled in a specific direction.

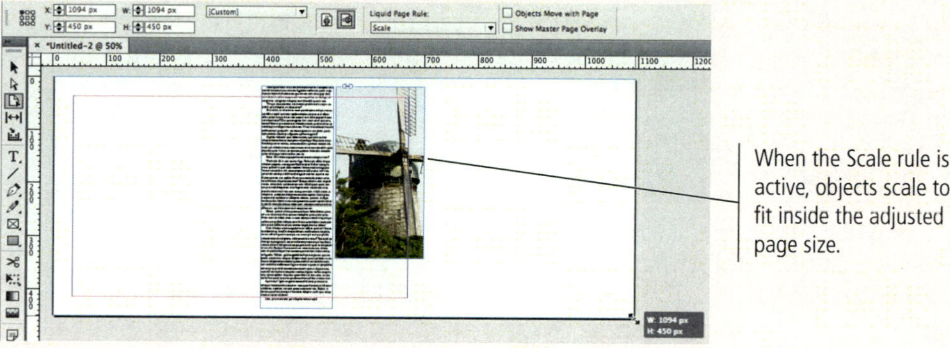

Using the **Re-center** liquid page rule, content is centered in the new page area; its size is not affected.

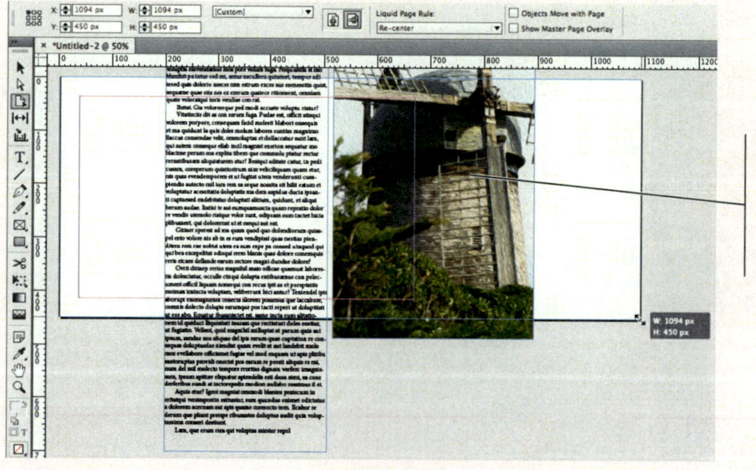

Understanding Liquid Page Rules (continued)

Using the **Guide-Based** liquid page rule, you can use the Page tool to drag "liquid" guides; any object touched by a liquid guide will resize when you change the layout size. Horizontal liquid guides allow objects to resize vertically, and vertical liquid guides allow an object to resize horizontally. You can select a guide with the Selection tool, then click the icon on the end of the guide to convert it from a page guide to a liquid guide (and vice versa).

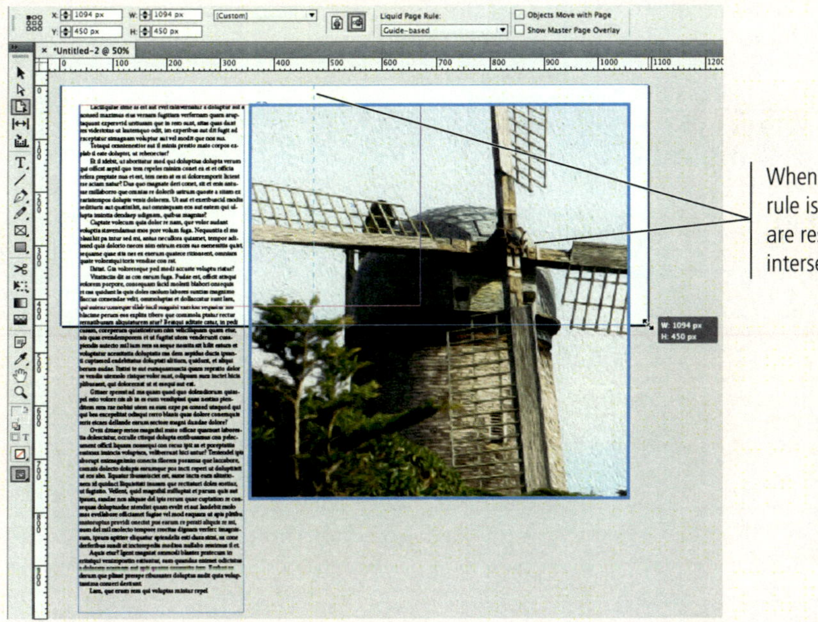

Using the **Object-Based** liquid page rule, you can use on-screen and panel-based controls to resize and reposition individual objects. This rule gives you the most control over the layout. (You will use this option in this project.)

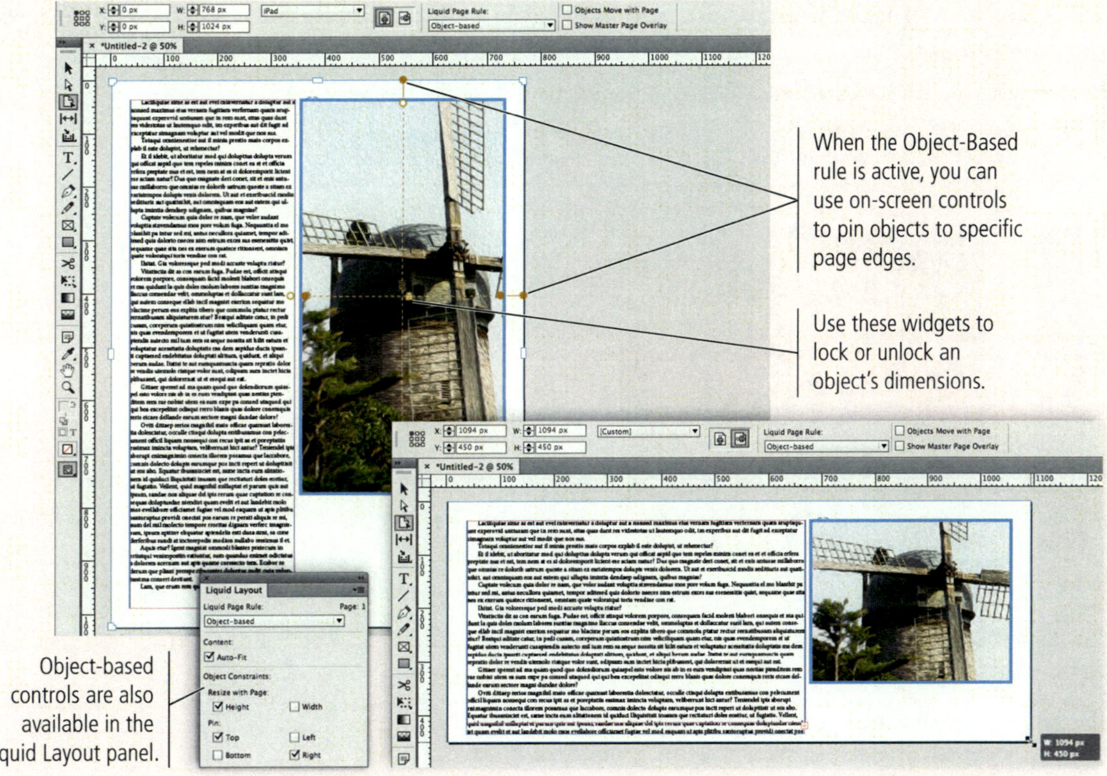

If the **Controlled by Master** option is selected, the rules that are applied to the active master page will be applied if you resize the layout page. (If you resize a layout page and the Controlled by Master rule is selected, the applied master page resizes as well.)

9. **Release the mouse button.**

When you release the mouse button, the page — and objects on the page — return to their original state.

10. **Click the bottom, left, and right hollow circles outside the frame edges.**

Because you pinned the object to both sides of the page (left and right), the frame's width is automatically unlocked — a frame can't be pinned on both sides and locked in the same orientation.

> ***Note:***
>
> *Zooming in can be helpful to see the on-screen controls.*

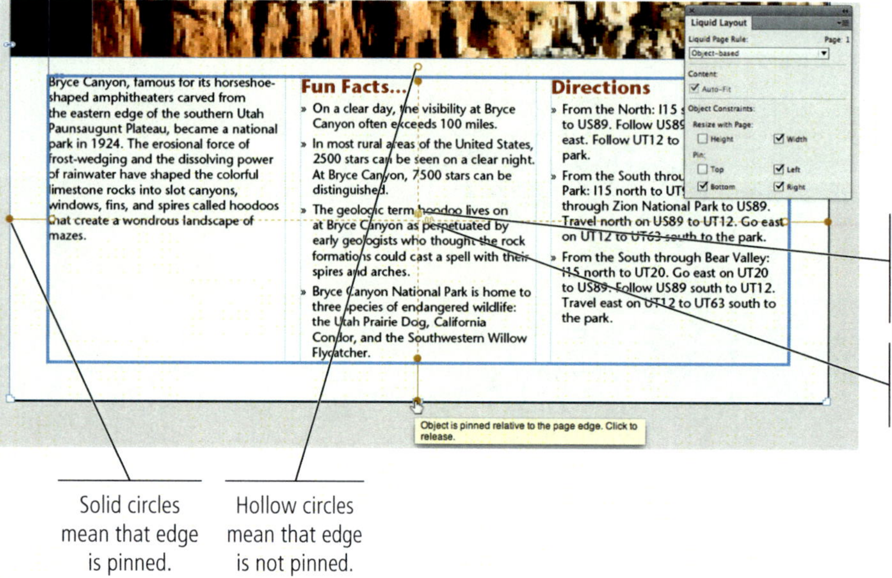

The lock icon means that dimension will not change when you resize the page.

The spring icon means that dimension can change.

Solid circles mean that edge is pinned.

Hollow circles mean that edge is not pinned.

> ***Note:***
>
> *When you move the mouse over the on-screen controls, tool tips tell you the function of each icon.*

11. **Click the bottom-right page handle, and drag again to approximate the size of a horizontal iPad.**

Remember, your object-based rules allow the text frame to become wider. You also allowed the frame to have flexible column width, up to 250 px. When the frame becomes wider than three columns of 250 px (plus the defined gutter width), the frame automatically changes to have four columns.

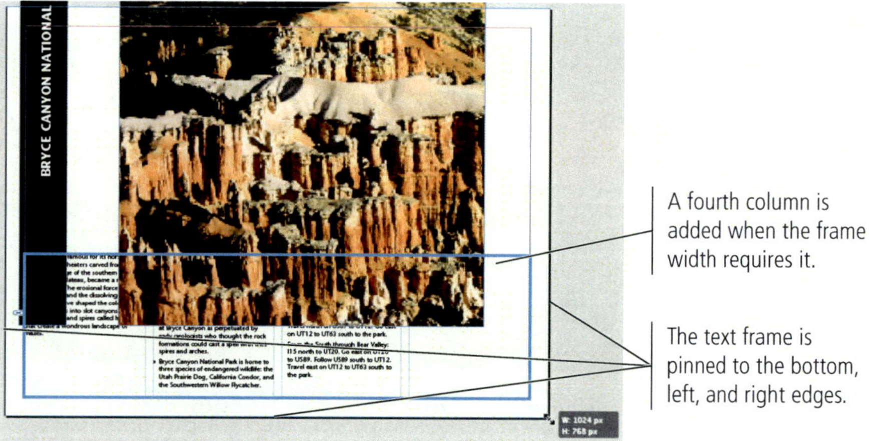

A fourth column is added when the frame width requires it.

The text frame is pinned to the bottom, left, and right edges.

12. **Release the mouse button to restore the original page size.**

13. **With the Page tool still active, click the image frame in the layout. In the Liquid Layout panel, check the Top and Right pin options.**

This means the image frame will remain attached to the top and right edges; the frame will not resize when the page is resized.

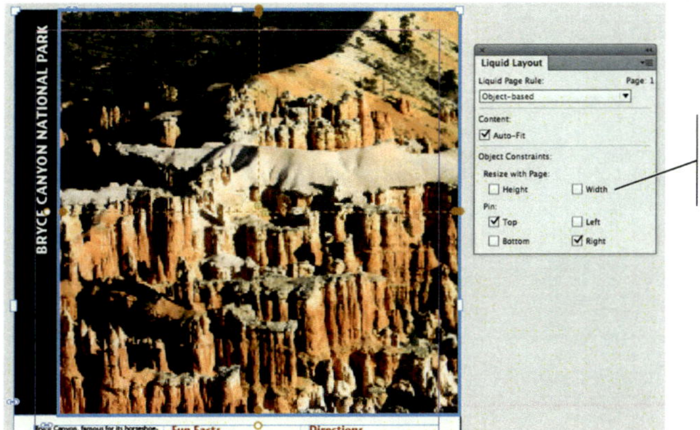

These options correlate to the on-screen controls.

Note:

You could also use the Layers panel to hide the placed image so that you can better see the on-screen controls.

14. **Using either method (the on-screen controls or the Liquid Layout panel), pin the top and left edges of the black text frame. Do not allow the object to resize.**

15. **Save the file and continue to the next exercise.**

 Create an Alternate Layout

Rather than creating multiple files for each possible variation, InDesign makes it very easy to create an alternate layout for the existing pages — all in the same file. Keep in mind, of course, that repurposing content for multiple layouts is almost never a one-click process. Even though InDesign makes the process much easier than ever before, some elements will still require choices and manual intervention to best take advantage of the available space.

1. **With ipad_bryce.indd open, open the Pages panel.**

When you use the built-in presets, InDesign recognizes the layout name and orientation you are creating. The Pages panel reflects both above the existing page icons.

2. Open the Pages panel Options menu and choose Create Alternate Layout.

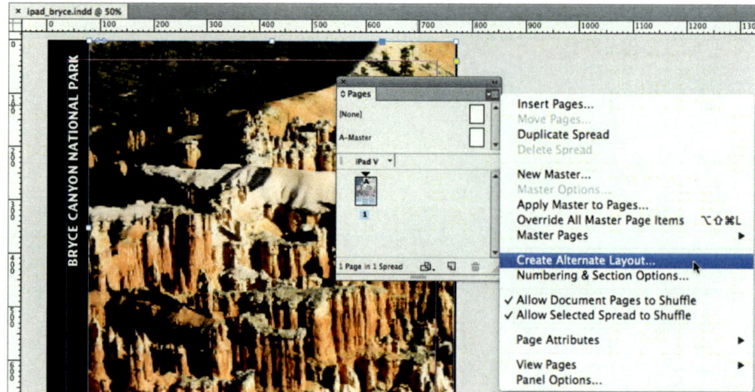

Because you already have the iPad V (vertical) layout created, the dialog box defaults to create the opposite orientation of the same layout — in this case, the iPad H (horizontal) layout.

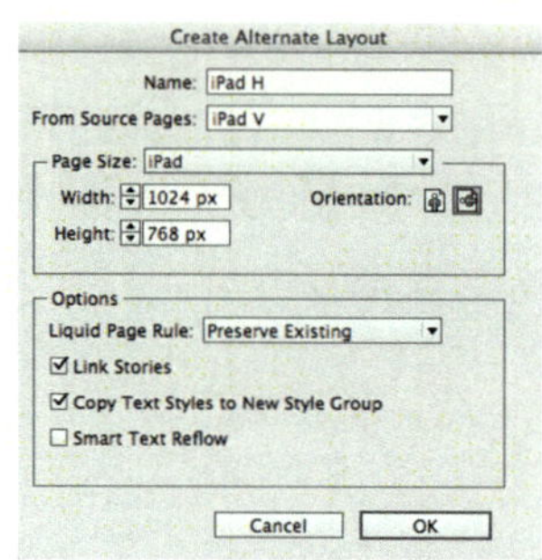

You can choose a different page size in the menu, or choose Custom to define a new preset with dimensions other than those already defined in a preset.

The Liquid Page Rule defaults to Preserve Existing, which applies the settings you manually defined while the Page tool was active. You can also use the menu to override the existing settings by calling one of the built-in rules (off, scale, re-center, guide-based, or object-based).

3. Make sure the Link Stories option is checked.

When this option is checked, the objects in the alternate layout are linked to the same objects in the original layout (which, if you remember, are linked to the objects in the print flyer layout).

4. Make sure the Copy Text Styles to New Style Group option is checked.

When this option is checked, the styles in your layout will be moved into a style group named according to the original layout (in this case "iPad V"). Another copy of those styles is placed in a second group (named "iPad H"), so you can change the style definition in one layout without affecting the same-named styles in the alternate layout.

5. Uncheck the Smart Text Reflow option.

If this option is checked, changing the size of the primary text frame will automatically result in extra pages being added to the layout. This layout does not use a primary text frame, so the option is irrelevant in this case.

> *Note:*
>
> *If you do use the primary text frame and want exactly the same number of pages in the alternate layout, make sure you turn off this option.*

6. Click OK to generate the alternate layout.

The Pages panel now shows both layouts. You can navigate to either layout just as you navigate pages — double-click a page icon to show that page in the document window, regardless of which layout it belongs to.

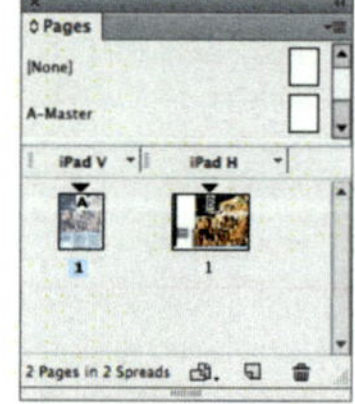

7. **Double-click the iPad H Page 1 icon.**

   As you can see, your defined liquid page rules defined the position and size of each object:

   - The black text frame did not resize; it is still attached to the top and left page edges.
   - The image frame did not resize; it is still attached to the top and right page edges.
   - The text frame resized horizontally, and a fourth column was added. It is still attached to the left, bottom, and right page edges; the same margin is maintained between the frame and page edges.

   You can also tell that some work still needs to be done. The two orientations do not have to have the same approximate layouts; in fact, they don't even need to have the same content (although they probably should, in most cases).

8. **Using the Selection tool, drag the bottom-center handle of the image frame until it snaps to the bottom page edge.**

   Because you set this frame to Auto-Fit using the Fill Frame Proportionally option, the image scales to fit the new frame size.

9. **Repeat Step 8 to extend the black text frame to the bottom page edge.**

10. **Select the four-column text frame. Change its parameters to:**

X: 100 px **W: 220 px**

Y: 36 px **H: 696 px**

Because you allowed a column width up to 250 px, the new frame width shows only a single column. The frame shows an overset text warning because the Subhead style is defined to start in the next column.

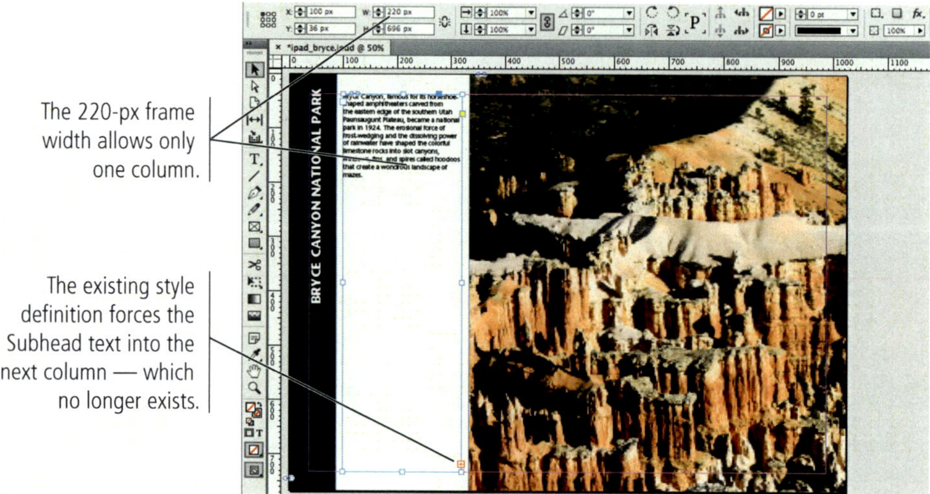

11. **Open the Paragraph Styles panel and expand both style groups.**

12. **Control/right-click the Subhead style in the iPad H group and choose Edit "Subhead".**

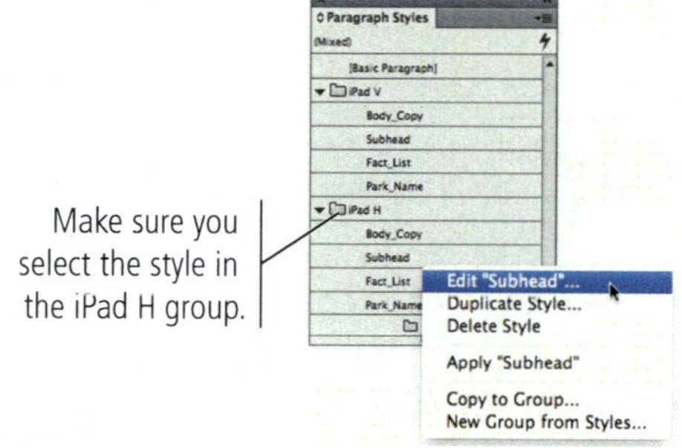

13. **Make sure the Preview option is checked. In the Keep Options, choose Anywhere in the Start Paragraph menu.**

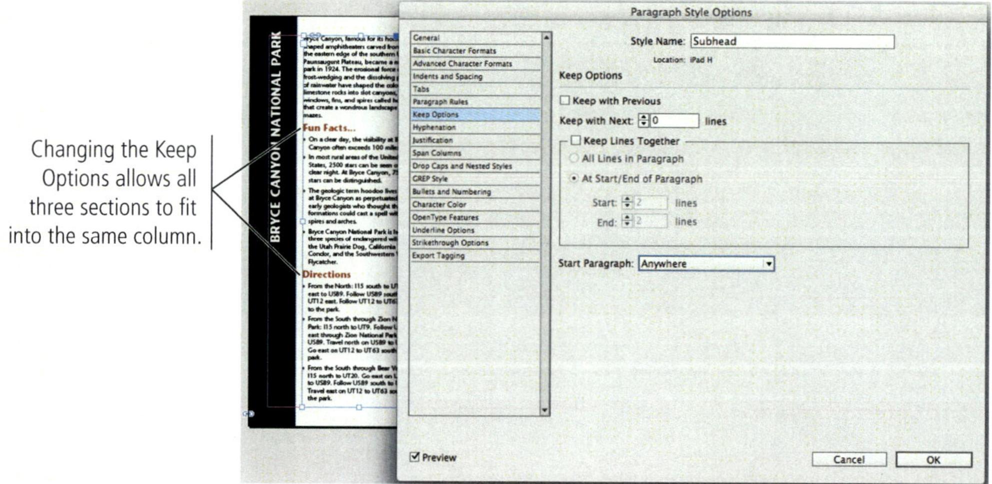

14. **In the Indents and Spacing options, change the Space Before field to 5 px.**

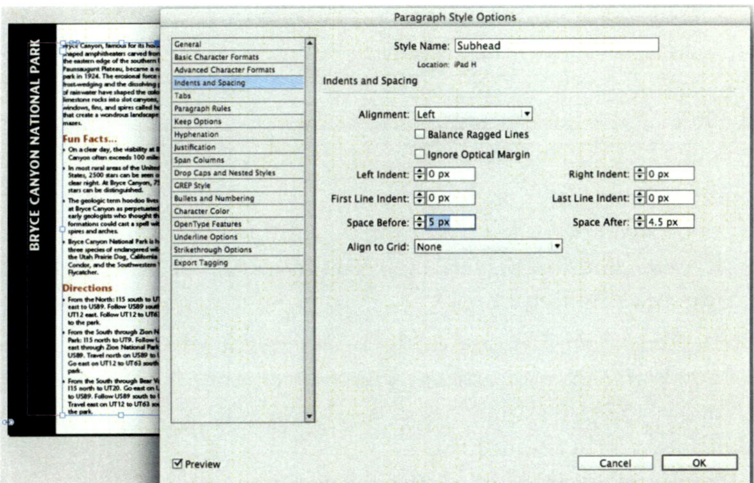

15. **Click OK to return to the layout.**

Because you created the style groups for each alternate layout, you can edit the styles in one layout without affecting the styles in the other.

16. **Click the Split Window button in the bottom-right corner of the document window.**

17. **With the left pane active, choose View>Fit Page in Window.**

18. **Click in the right pane to make it active. Double-click the iPad V layout in the Pages panel, then choose View>Fit Page in Window.**

The split window option allows you to view both alternate layouts at once. Each pane can have a separate view percentage.

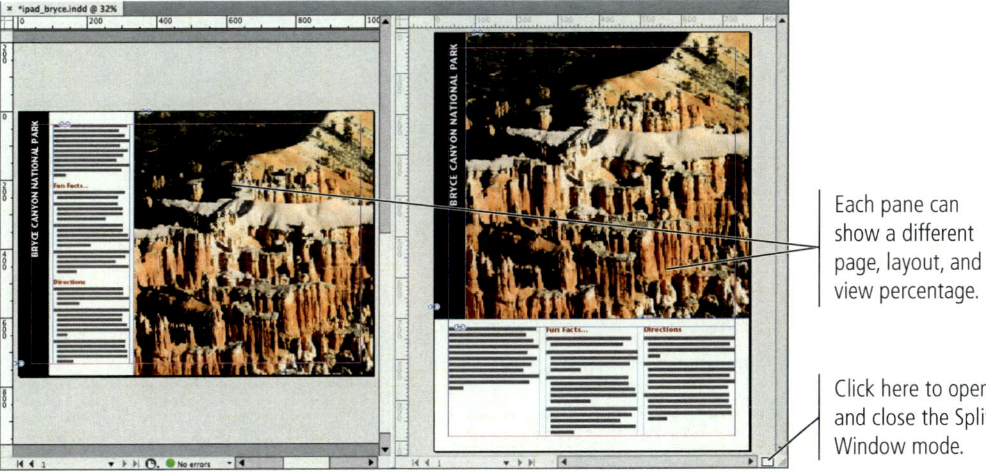

Each pane can show a different page, layout, and view percentage.

Click here to open and close the Split Window mode.

19. **Click the Split Window button again to close the split pane.**

20. **Save the file and continue to the next exercise.**

Create a Digital Folio

Anyone with InDesign can use DPS Desktop tools to create and review folios in the desktop Adobe Viewer app. When you build folios in InDesign, you can work locally (on your own computer) to define the folio and article settings. However, you can't share folios without going through Adobe's Digital Publishing Suite server in the Cloud.

Digital Publishing Suite, Single Edition, is included in your Creative Cloud membership; this version can be used to create apps for the iPad from your InDesign files. To create apps for other devices (iPhones, Android tablets, etc.), you have to subscribe to the DPS Professional or Enterprise Edition.

After you have installed the DPS Desktop tools, you can use the InDesign Folio Builder panel to define folios, which contain one or more articles, which contain one or more layouts. Think of the overall folio as the publication "issue" — the digital equivalent of the magazine that appears in retail check-out lines.

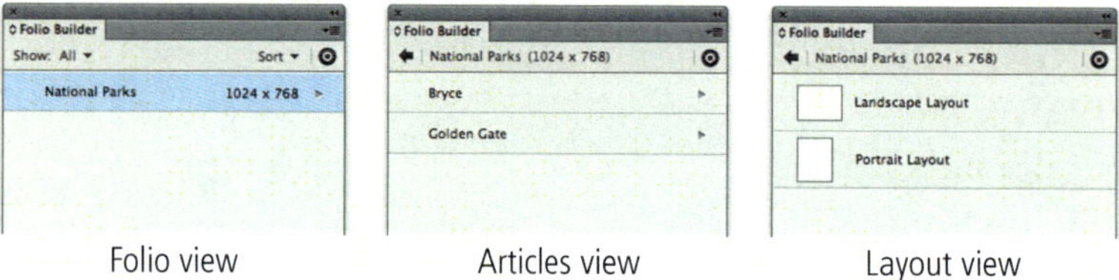

Folio view — Articles view — Layout view

1. **With InDesign running, open the Folio Builder panel.**

   When you are logged into your Creative Cloud account in InDesign, you are also automatically logged in to the Folio Builder panel.

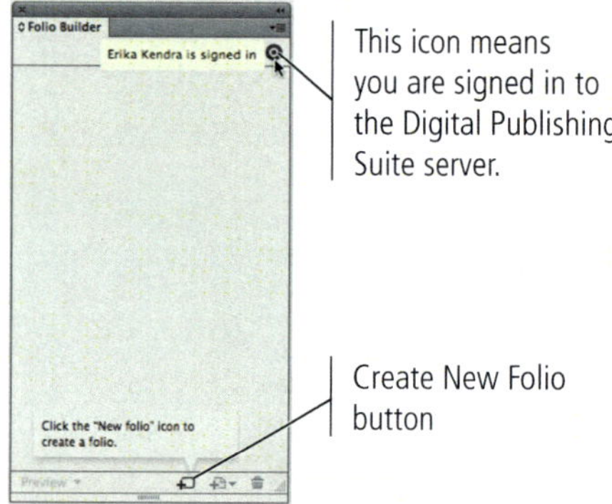

Note:

If you are not signed in, the panel includes a message that you must sign in.

You can choose Sign In in the panel's Options menu to sign in with your Adobe ID.

2. **Click the Create New Folio button at the bottom of the Folio Builder panel.**

3. **In the resulting New Folio dialog box, type National Parks in the Name field.**

   The **Folio Name** appears only in the Folio Builder panel. You will define the actual Publication Title, which appears in the viewer, later in this exercise.

4. **Leave the Size menu at its default value (Apple iPad).**

   The **Size** menu defines the physical size of the folio you are creating; this should match the size of the device you are targeting.

5. **Choose the Porttrait and Landscape Folio option.**

   The **Orientation** options determine whether the folio is portrait-only, landscape-only, or dual orientation. All articles in the folio need to match the defined folio orientation. In other words, you can't add an article with only a landscape orientation if the folio is defined as dual orientation.

   You can check the **Right Edge Binding** option to display articles from right to left in the viewer app, rather than left to right; this is especially important for Asian languages.

Note:

If you create articles with only one orientation, that orientation remains in place even when the user rotates the mobile device.

6. **Choose PDF in the Default Format menu.**

   The **Default Format** menu determines what format will be used for the images that are generated for the folio.

   You can choose to export all images as JPEG, PNG, or PDF images. Using the Automatic option, InDesign determines which format is best for each specific image.

   The PDF format results in smaller file sizes and enables pinch and zoom gestures.

   If you choose the Automatic or JPEG options, you can use the **Default JPEG Quality** menu to define the quality level of the resulting images. Keep in mind that higher quality means less compression, which results in larger files.

7. **Click the Folder icon to the right of the Vertical Cover Preview thumbnail. Navigate to the file `parks_cover_v.jpg` in the WIP>Parks>Links folder and click Open.**

   The **Cover Preview** images appear in the main library of the viewer app.

   Unlike the article thumbnail, InDesign does not automatically create a folio preview from a specific page of an article. This makes sense if you think about it — a magazine cover typically does not show the first page of any one of the articles inside the magazine; instead, you create a separate cover. The same is true of the folio cover; you should create cover preview images as 72-dpi JPEG or PNG files, using the same pixel dimensions as the target device (e.g., 1024 × 768 for iPad2).

Note:

You should get into the habit of using the _h and _v suffixes in file names that are intended for tablet publishing.

8. **Repeat Step 7 to define `cover_parks_h.jpg` as the Horizontal Cover Preview.**

9. **Check the Create Offline Folio option.**

   When you are connected to the DPS server, you can check this option to work only on your computer instead of automatically uploading the folio to the server.

   If you are not currently connected to the server, the Create Local Folio option is not available because the folio can only be local until you connect to the server.

10. **Click OK to create the folio.**

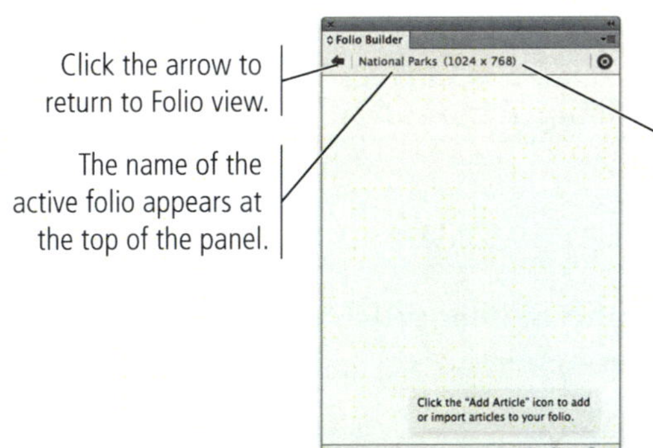

After creating the new folio, the panel automatically switches to Articles mode so you can add articles to the folio.

Note:

If you are not creating a local folio, the panel shows the upload status while the article is being added to the folio.

11. **Click the left-arrow button at the top of the Folio Builder panel to return to the Folios list.**

12. **With the National Parks folio selected, choose Folio Properties in the panel's Options menu.**

As with article properties, the folio properties define attributes that affect the way a folio appears in the viewer app.

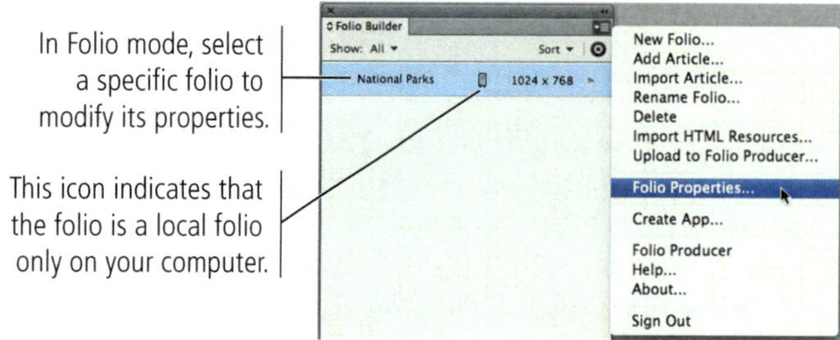

13. **In the Folio Properties dialog box, type `National Parks Quick Guides` in the Publication Name field.**

The **Publication Name** appears in the viewer app. This is not the same as the Folio Title, which appears only in the Folio Builder panel.

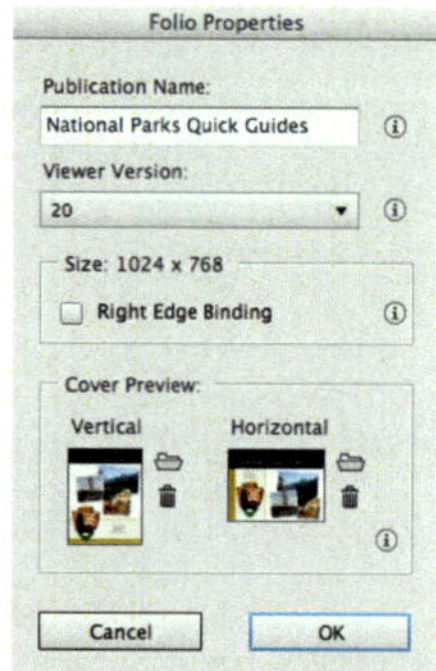

Note:

To avoid problems on Android devices, don't use punctuation or special characters in the publication name.

14. **Click OK to close the Folio Properties dialog box.**

15. **Continue to the next exercise.**

Add Articles to a Folio

As we already explained, folios contain articles — just as a printed magazine does. You can use the Folio Builder to easily add articles to an existing folio.

1. **Make sure the Folio Builder panel is open and the National Parks folio is selected in the panel.**

2. **If necessary, open `ipad_bryce.indd` from your WIP>Parks folder.**

3. **Click the Add Article button at the bottom of the Folio Builder panel, then choose Add Open InDesign Document from the pop-up menu.**

4. In the New Article dialog box, type **Bryce** in the Article Name field.

The **Article Name** appears only in the Folio Builder panel and is used for creating links between articles. This is not the same as the Publication Title, which you will define shortly.

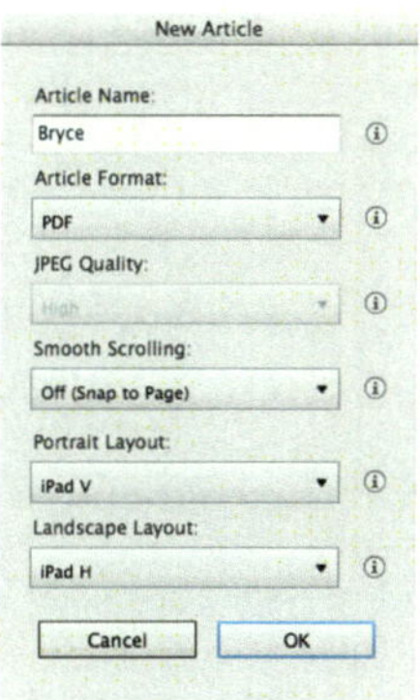

You can use the **Default Format** menu to define separate image formats for each article in the folio. The options here are the same as those in the New Folio dialog box.

The file you created has only two layouts, which you created specifically for the horizontal and vertical orientations on an iPad. Those layouts were automatically named based on the built-in presets and layout orientations. Using the default names, InDesign automatically recognizes which layout is intended for which orientation.

If you create additional layouts, or create layouts with custom names, you can use the **Portrait Layout** and **Vertical Layout** menus to define different layouts to use for each orientation.

The **Smooth Scrolling** option is turned off by default for new articles. When a user swipes to change the visible page, the new page automatically snaps into place and fills the screen. If you turn on smooth scrolling for a specific article, users can swipe horizontally, vertically, or both (depending on your choice in the Smooth Scrolling menu) to show more of the same page.

A smooth scrolling article can have only a single page; this is useful for long documents, such as a table of contents. In InDesign, you would create the single layout page large enough to accommodate the entire story. In the exported folio, the users would have to swipe to access parts of the page that do not fit into the first screen.

5. Leave all other options at their default values and click OK.

After clicking OK, InDesign processes the active file to create the article. When the process is complete, the article appears in the Folio Builder panel.

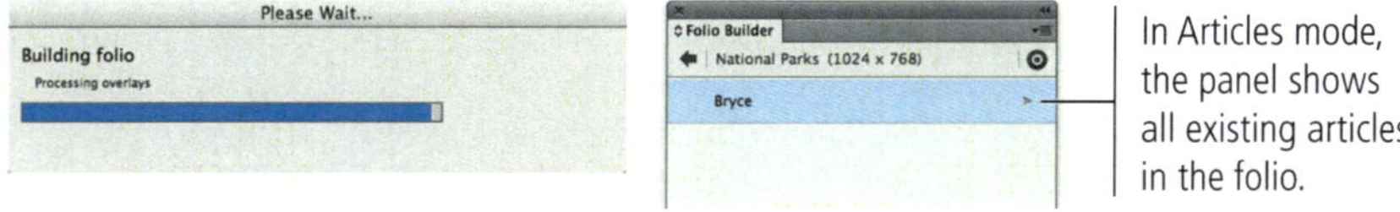

In Articles mode, the panel shows all existing articles in the folio.

6. With the new article selected in the panel, choose Article Properties in the panel Options menu.

Article properties control what appears in the viewer app for each article.

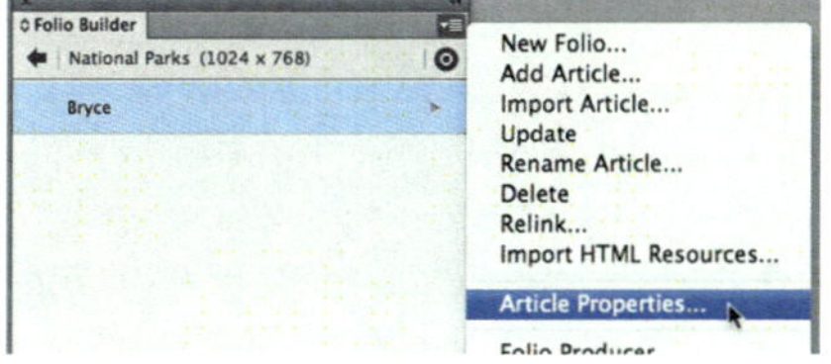

7. **Type Bryce Canyon National Park in the Title field, then click OK.**

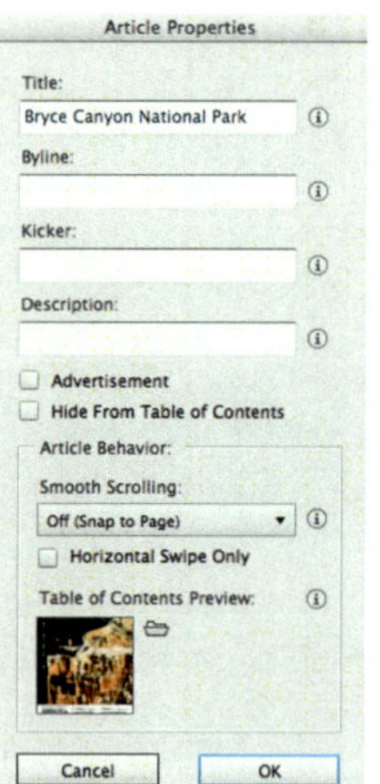

The article **Title** appears in the viewer. This is different from the Article Name, which you defined when you created the article.

The **Byline** defines the article author's name.

The **Kicker** can be used to define a section of a folio, such as "New England Area Parks."

The **Description** appears when the folio is viewed in browse mode.

You can check the **Advertisement** option to mark a specific article as an ad.

You can check the **Hide From Table of Contents** option to prevent an article from appearing in the table of contents in the viewer app.

You can use the **Smooth Scrolling** menu to enable that option for the selected article. If you select **Horizontal Swipe Only** for an article, users browse through the article by swiping left and right instead of up and down.

The **Table of Contents Preview** is a 70 × 70 pixel image that appears when a user views the folio's table of contents in the viewer app. This defaults to an image created from the first page of the article, but you can define a custom image (saved in the PNG format) that you have already created.

8. **In the Folio Builder panel, double-click the Bryce article.**

Double-clicking a specific article in the panel switches the panel to Layout mode; you can use this option to preview the individual layouts that are included in the article.

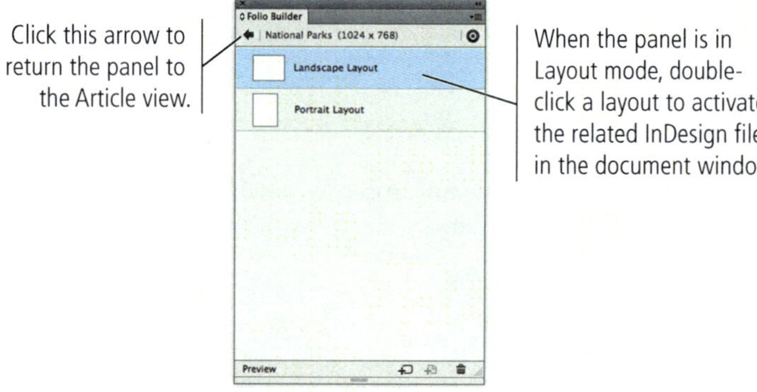

9. **Close the ipad_bryce.indd file.**

Folios are independent of specific InDesign files. The changes you made in this exercise did not affect the open INDD file, so there are no changes to save.

10. **Open the file ipad_goldengate.indd from your WIP>Parks folder.**

This layout includes a fact sheet for the Golden Gate National Recreation Area; we created this file using the same layouts as the Bryce Canyon iPad layout, but did not include the image sequence animation. You are simply going to use it to add a second article to the National Parks folio, so you can better understand the concept of working with multiple articles in a single folio.

11. **In the Folio Builder panel, click the Back-Arrow button at the top of the panel to switch the panel to Articles view.**

12. Click the Add Article button at the bottom of the panel and choose Add Open InDesign Document from the pop-up menu.

13. In the resulting dialog box, type **Golden Gate** in the Article Name field, then click OK.

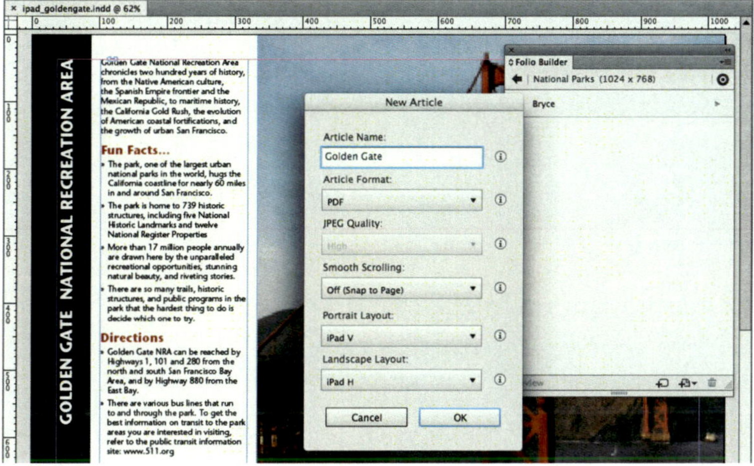

14. With the new article selected in the Folio Builder panel, choose Article Properties in the panel Options menu.

15. Type **Golden Gate National Recreation Area** in the Title field, then click OK.

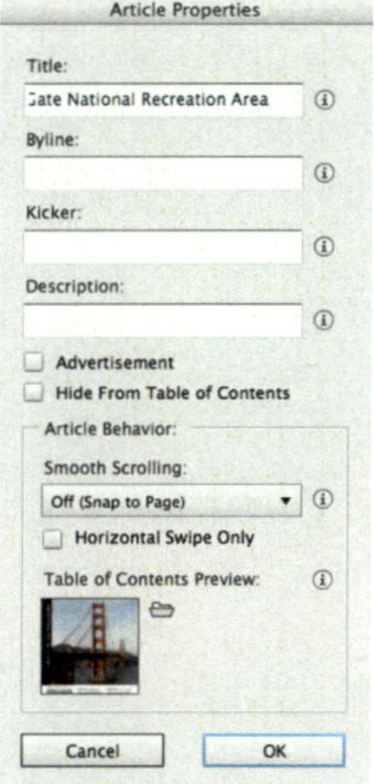

16. Close the **ipad_goldengate.indd** file, then continue to the next exercise.

Importing Articles into Folios

INDESIGN FOUNDATIONS

The ability to create multiple layouts in one InDesign file was added in CS6. You can import layouts created in previous versions — or CS6 or CC files with single layouts — as articles as long as they use the correct naming conventions.

(If an InDesign document includes multiple layouts, you can't import it as an article. Instead, you have to open the layout and use the Add button in the Folio Builder panel.)

In the Folio Builder panel, you can choose Import Article in the Add Article menu, or choose Import from the panel Options menu.

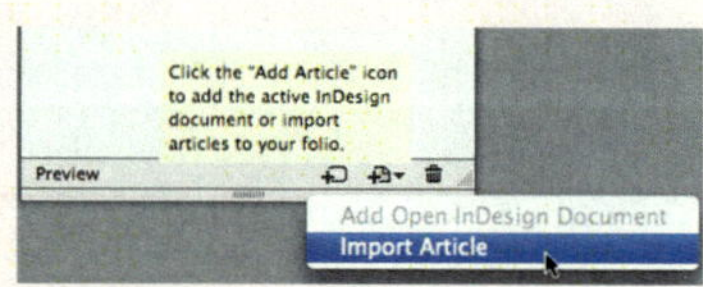

In the resulting dialog box, you can determine whether to import a single article or multiple articles at one time.

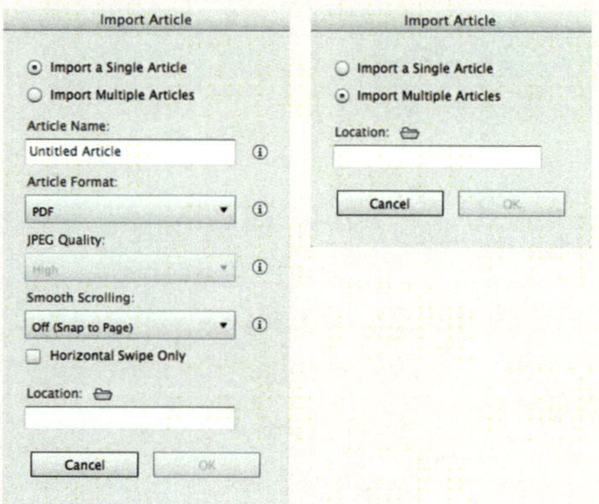

If you import a single article, you can define the same settings as you do when you add a new article based on the active layout. If you choose to import multiple articles, you can only choose the location of the files to import.

Clicking the folder icon for the Location field opens a navigation dialog box. As the title bar indicates, you are identifying an entire folder and not a specific file.

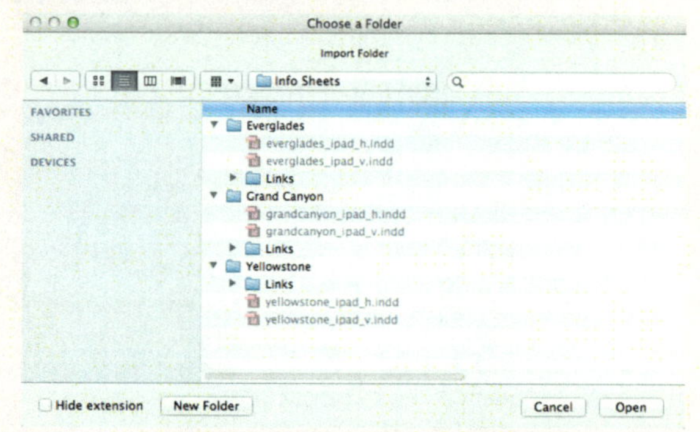

To import articles, they must be named with this convention:

Folder

filename_h.indd

filename_v.indd

After you select the containing folder, clicking OK in the Import Article dialog box initiates the import. When the files are processed, the new articles appear in the Articles mode of the Folio Builder panel.

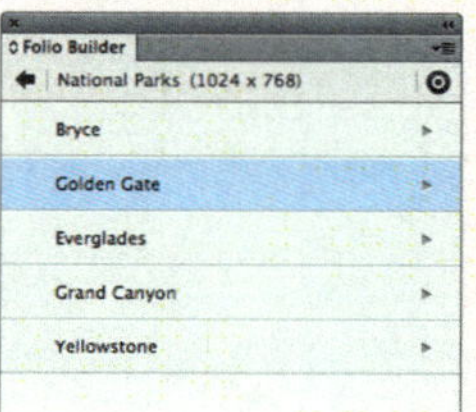

Preview the Folio on an iPad

Before you distribute a folio, you should test it to make sure everything works properly. A local folio, such a the one you created in this project, resides only on your computer. If you have an iPad connected to your computer via USB, you can test the file before you upload it to the DPS server ("to the Cloud").

> ***Note:***
>
> *Important: To complete this exercise, you must have an iPad connected to your computer.*

1. **If necessary, download the Adobe Content Viewer app for your iPad.**

   This free app is available in the Apple App Store.

2. **On your tablet, launch the Adobe Content Viewer app.**

   You do not need to be logged in to your user account to test a folio locally.

3. **Connect your iPad to your computer using the USB connection.**

4. **In InDesign, show the Folio Builder panel in Folio mode.**

5. **Click the Preview menu and choose Preview on [Your] iPad.**

It might take a few seconds for the folio to open, so be patient.

Remember, the image in this layout has an interactive overlay, which causes a number of images to appear sequentially in the frame. When you test the folio file, you can see the result of the applied overlay. The image frame changes to show each image in the Bryce folder (as you defined).

6. **Tap the image area to test the "Tap to Play/Pause" functionality.**

7. **Rotate your device to test the alternate layout.**

8. **Tap anywhere away from the image to access the navigation controls at the top of the screen.**

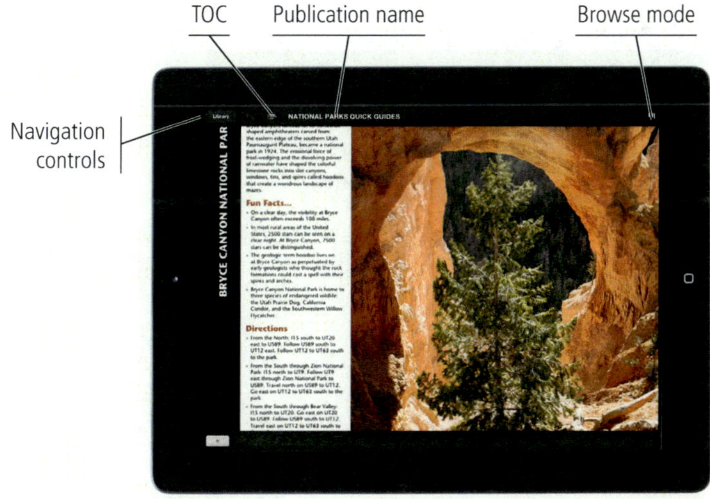

9. **Tap the TOC icon to access the Table of Contents for the open folio.**

10. **Tap Golden Gate National Recreation Area in the TOC to show that article.**

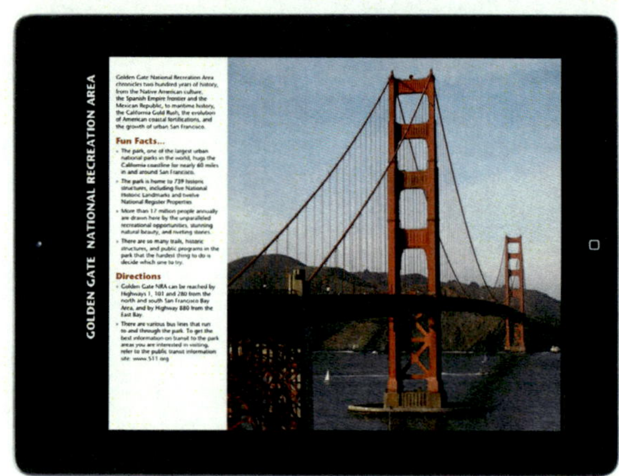

> ***Note:***
>
> *Adobe offers a free "Digital Publishing Suite Tips" app, which provides a number of articles with useful tips and examples for creating effective folio files. You can find this document by searching for the title in the Apple App store.*

11. **Tap anywhere on the screen to access the navigation controls, then tap the Library button.**

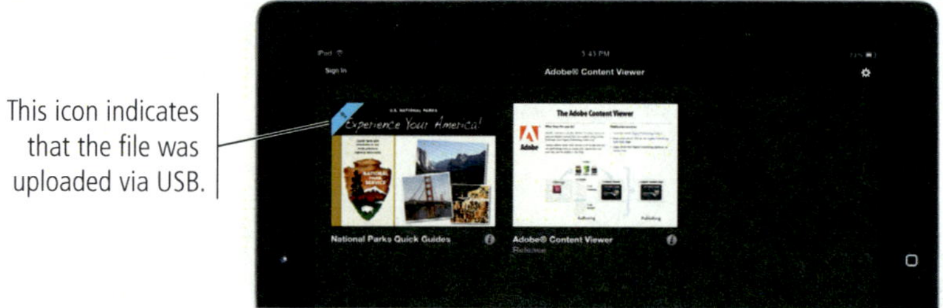

12. **With the National Parks folio selected in the InDesign Folio Builder panel, choose Upload to Folio Producer in the panel Options menu.**

As long as you have an Internet connection, you can easily upload a folio to the DPS server so that you can preview it on a tablet device or share it with other users.

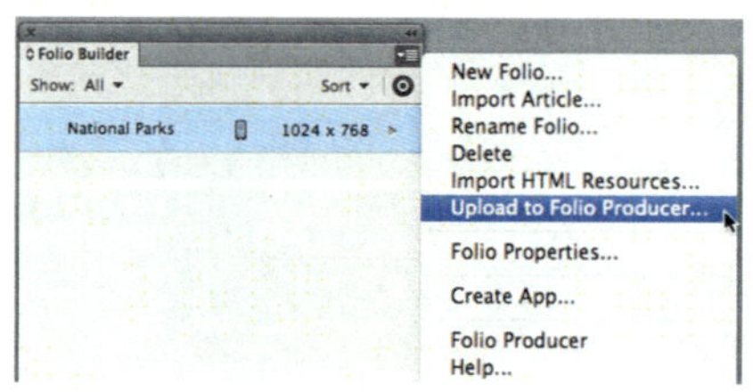

> ***Note:***
>
> *You can upload a local folio to the server, but you can't convert an uploaded folio to be only local.*

13. **When the upload process is complete, click OK to dismiss the message.**

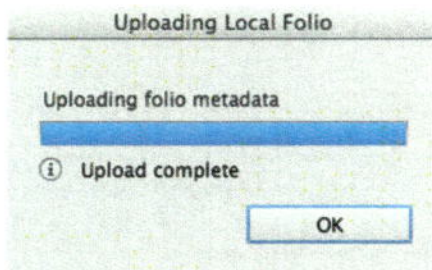

14. **On your iPad, launch the Adobe Content Viewer app (if necessary) and log in using your Adobe ID.**

15. **Tap the Free button for the National Parks Quick Guides file to download the folio to your device.**

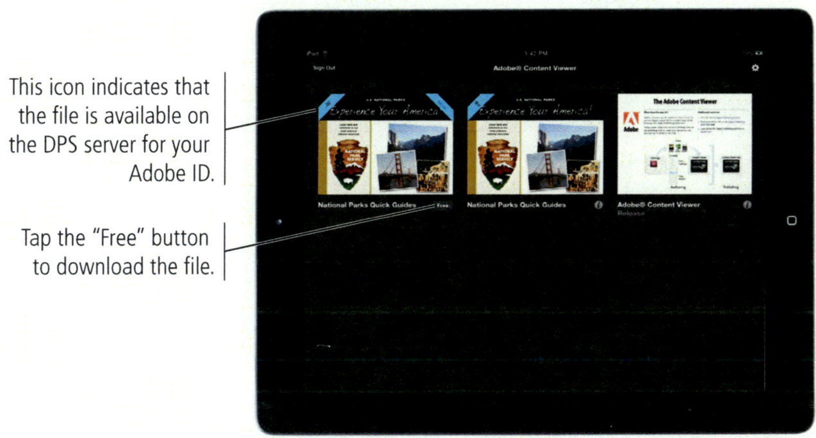

> ***Note:***
>
> *If you tap the image for the new folio, you will see an enlarged version with a download button.*

16. **In InDesign, open the Folio Builder panel Options menu and choose Sign Out.**

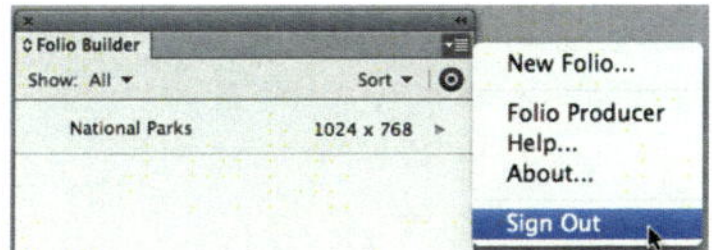

Sharing Folio Files

If you are signed in to the DPS server, you can use the Folio Builder panel to share a folio with other users.

When the Folio Builder is open in Folio mode and a specific folio is selected, choose Share from the panel Options menu. In the resulting dialog box, you can define one or more email addresses, and enter a custom subject line and message to your collaborators.

The email will include a link to the shared file on the DPS server; recipients will need to sign in with their own Adobe IDs to access the file.

Users can access the shared file in the Viewer app on a mobile device, or by logging into their accounts from the InDesign Folio Builder panel. Sharing users can add new articles to the shared folio, but they cannot edit the existing articles.

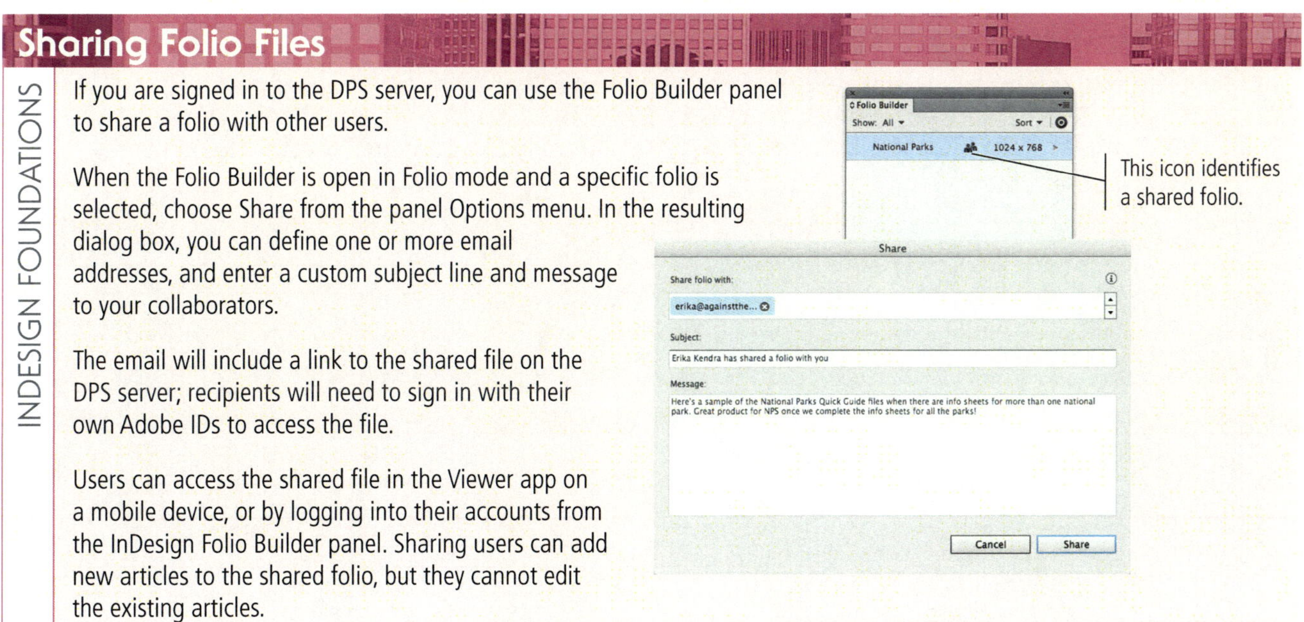

Project Review

fill in the blank

1. You can use the _______________ to review the content and hierarchy of tagged frames.

2. The _______________ tool is used to select objects that you want to share multiple times across one or more layouts.

3. When placing shared content, the _______________ displays items and sets that are ready for sharing.

4. When working with shared content, you can use the _______________ options to define which options you want to keep in the linked copies when you update the links.

5. Using the _______________ option, the number of columns in a text frame adjusts dynamically when the frame is resized; columns are limited to a maximum user-defined width.

6. Press _______________ while dragging a page handle with the Page tool to permanently change the page size.

7. Using the _______________ liquid page rule, you can pin the edges and/or dimensions of a frame, preventing that object from moving when you create an alternate layout.

8. The _______________ overlay creates a slideshow from all the images in a specific folder.

9. When creating a digital folio, the _______________ format enables the pinch and zoom gestures on a tablet device.

10. In a digital folio, the _______________ setting appears for each article in the TOC in the Content Viewer app.

short answer

1. Briefly explain the concept of using XML for repurposing content.

2. Briefly explain the differences between using XML and using the Content Collector/Placer to repurpose content.

3. Briefly explain the concept of an interactive overlay.

Portfolio Builder Project

Use what you learned in this project to complete the following freeform exercise.
Carefully read the art director and client comments, then create your own design to meet the needs of the project.
Use the space below to sketch ideas; when finished, write a brief explanation of your reasoning behind your final design.

art director comments

In order to increase marketing opportunities, your agency would like to create several more examples to showcase the ability to repurpose content for multiple media. Every designer in your agency has been asked to create a "How-To" piece that is available in both print and digital formats.

- ❑ Think of something you know how to do.
- ❑ Write clear instructions that detail how to create or accomplish the topic you are explaining.
- ❑ Find or create graphics or images to illustrate your topic.
- ❑ Design an 8.5″ × 11″ print document to present the content of your tutorial.
- ❑ Create digital versions of your tutorial, including HTML, EPUB, and a digital folio for iPad.

client comments

Cross-media publishing is not only the future — it's the present. The National Parks campaign is an excellent portfolio piece to showcase our capabilities, but I would like our salespeople to be able to show off more than one example when they meet with current and potential clients.

To increase our agency's portfolio, I've asked every staff designer to create a new example of cross-media publishing. I want this to be fun for you, and I want a range of different types of projects.

So, rather than give you a specific topic to work with, I want you to create a one-sheet tutorial on anything that interests you — how to rebuild a transmission, how to knit a sweater, how to sky dive, how to train a pet turtle... whatever you are good at or feel passionate about.

After you create the print version, repurpose it for digital media, taking advantage of interactive options for the digital presentations.

project justification

Project Summary

Repurposing the same content in multiple different layouts is becoming increasingly common in the design world. This project explored two different methods for repurposing content, both for multiple print formats and for digital media.

You used unstructured XML to drag specific types of content into a layout, and you used a more structured approach to automatically place content into tagged frames of a different layout. By maintaining a link to the XML file, you were able to automatically update the placed content to reflect changes in the text.

You also used the content sharing and alternate layout capabilities that are built into InDesign to create different layouts from existing content. You also added interactive overlays to take better advantage of the capabilities of digital media.

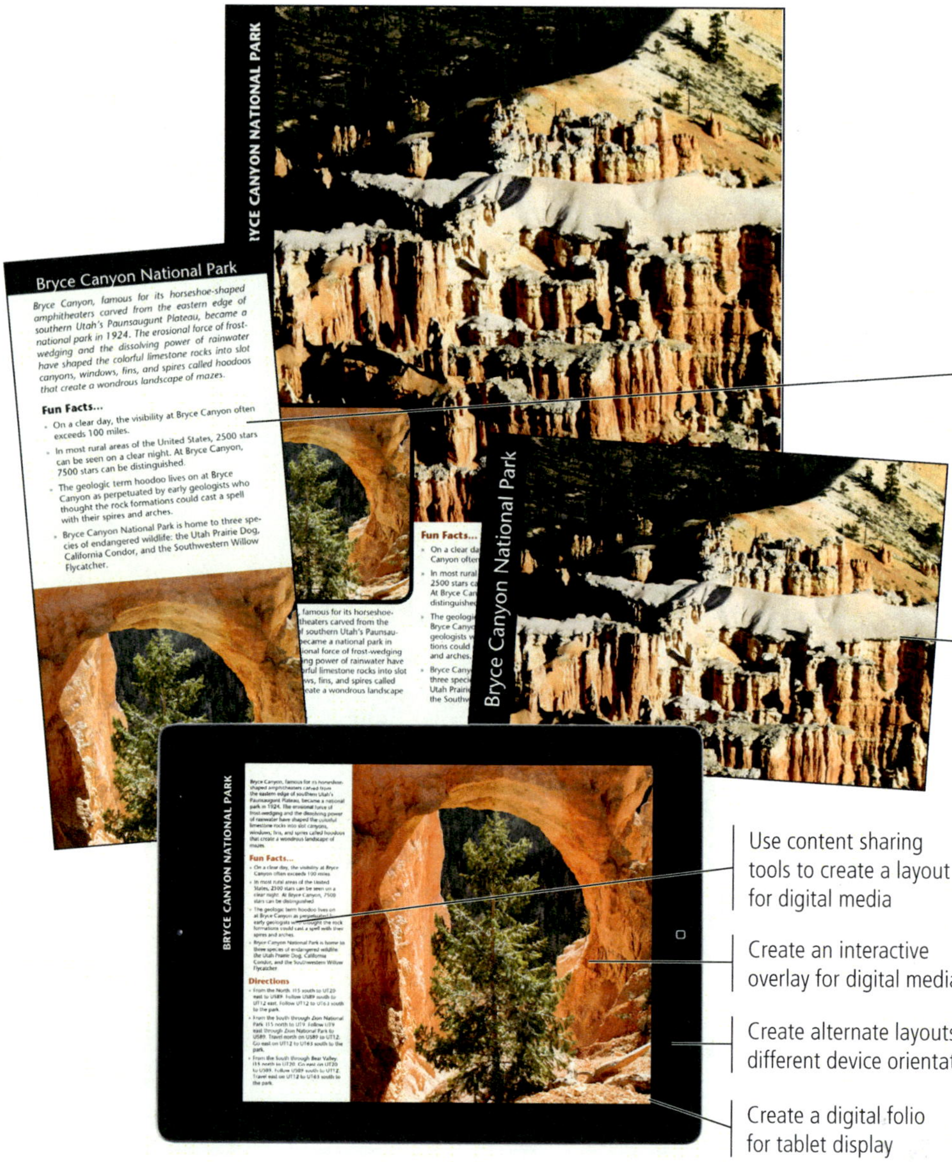

project 8

Multi-Chapter Booklet

Your client, Against The Clock (ATC), publishes books related to the computer graphics industry. In addition to application-specific books, it is also creating a series of "companion" titles that discuss the concepts underlying the use of digital software — basic design principles, type, color, and so on. You were hired to build an "excerpt" booklet of the companion titles, which ATC will use for marketing purposes.

This project incorporates the following skills:

- ❑ Combining multiple InDesign files into a single book
- ❑ Synchronizing the assets in multiple files to ensure consistency from one piece to the next
- ❑ Building a unified table of contents for the entire book
- ❑ Building an index that covers all chapters of the book
- ❑ Using variable data to build a personalized letter

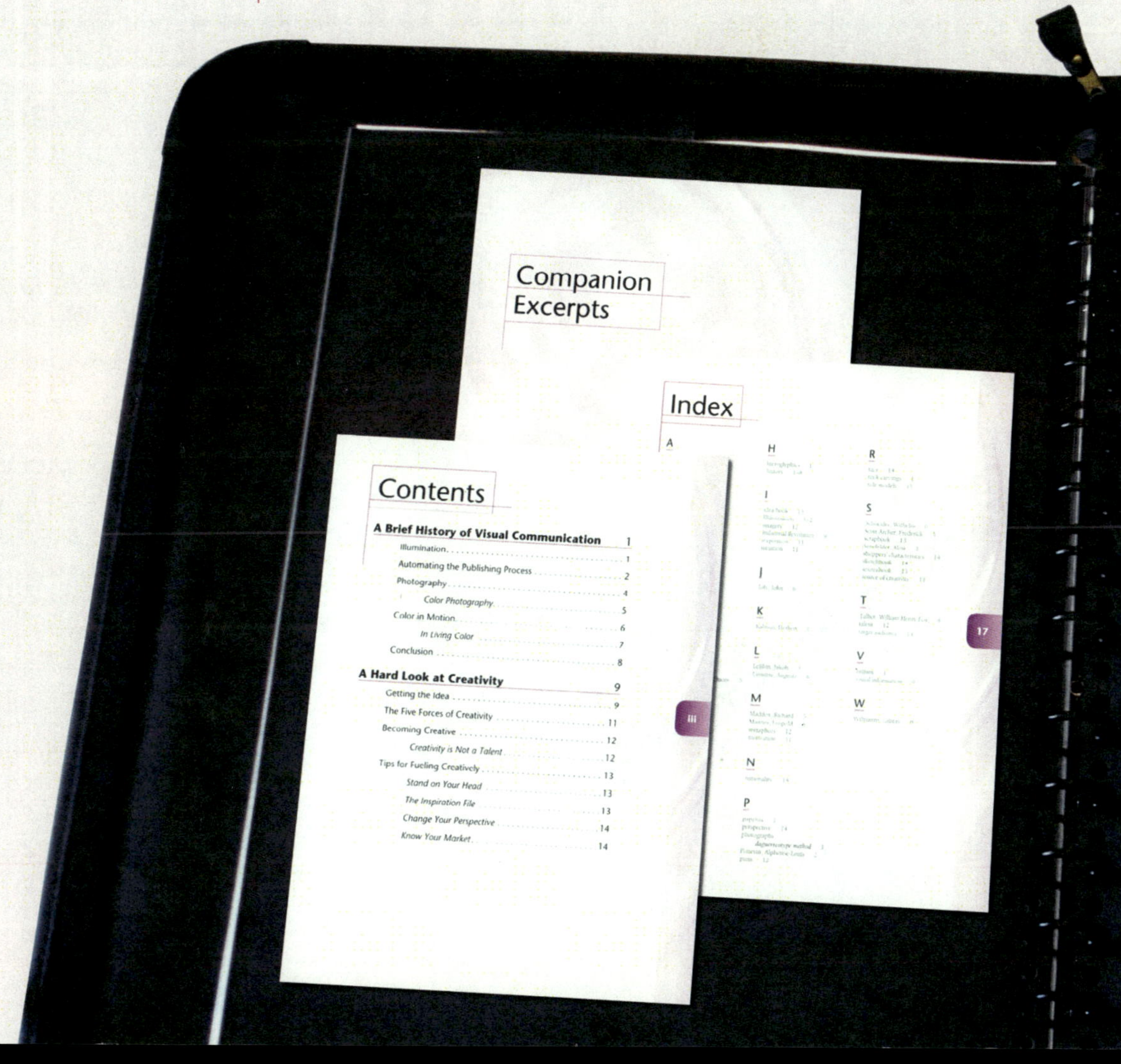

Project Meeting

client comments

We are launching a new series of books that will complement our application-specific books. We want to use the existing InDesign files to create a sample excerpt booklet that we can use in digital and print advertising.

We sent you the files for the first chapter from two of the books. Unfortunately, the file from the *Color Companion* seems to be one version behind — we can't find the version that was tagged for the book's index. We want the sample booklet to include a representative index, though, so we'd like you to tag a few entries in the *Color Companion* chapter and build a mini-index for the sample. The booklet should also have its own self-cover, title page, and table of contents.

The first set of these booklets will be printed and mailed to 50 clients that we selected from our database. We're asking these clients to review the sample chapters and provide quotes that we can use in marketing materials. We provided you with a comma-delimited data file that was exported from our database. We also sent you the text for a thank-you letter we want to include with the booklet.

art director comments

Long documents such as books (especially non-fiction) require several special elements, including a table of contents and an index. Many publishers spend countless hours manually composing these elements; they literally flip through pages and hand-write every entry in a spreadsheet. Fortunately, InDesign has built-in tools that make this process far easier.

If you use styles consistently, you can build a table of contents based on the styles in the files. An index is a bit more complicated — although the tools for tagging and compiling an index ease the process, identifying the content of an index remains a largely manual process. There is no software smart enough to decide exactly what to include in an index.

The advantage of using these tools is that you need to complete the process only once. Using the old methods, making changes late in the process — which happens almost every time — meant manually re-compiling the table of contents and index. Using InDesign's built-in tools, you can easily re-compile both elements as often as necessary, and you can format them automatically using other styles.

project objectives

To complete this project, you will:

- ❑ Create an InDesign book file
- ❑ Manage different files as chapters of a single book
- ❑ Control section and page numbering across multiple chapter files
- ❑ Synchronize assets in all files of the book
- ❑ Build a table of contents based on styles
- ❑ Tag index entries in each file of the book
- ❑ Compile the index for all book chapters at once
- ❑ Create a variable-data letter addressed to previous ATC clients

Stage 1 Combining Documents into Books

Publication design is a unique subset of graphic design. Attention to detail is critical. You must ensure that subhead formatting in early chapters matches the subhead formatting in later chapters, that captions are all set in the same font, that body copy is the same size throughout the document, and so on. Regardless of whether one or several designers work on the project, consistency is essential from the first page of the book to the last. To make long-document design easier, InDesign allows you to create a special type of book file for combining and managing multiple chapters as a single unit.

Long documents are frequently split into multiple files during the conception and design phases, then combined at the end of the process to create the final job. This workflow offers several advantages:

- Layouts with numerous images can become very large; dividing these layouts into pieces helps keep the file size smaller.
- If a long document is divided into multiple stand-alone files, several designers can work on different files of the same book without the risk of accidentally overwriting another designer's work.
- If a long document is split into several files, you won't lose the entire job if a single file becomes corrupt.

Before digital book-building utilities were introduced, working with multiple files required extreme care and attention to detail to maintain consistency from one file to the next. InDesign's book-building tools make the process much easier by automating many of the tasks that were previously done manually. (Of course, even though the InDesign book utilities automate much of the process, you must still — and always — pay close attention to the details of your work.)

> *Note:*
>
> *When a single design project is made up of several files, it is even more important to maintain consistency from one file to the next. If the font is slightly different from one issue of a newsletter to the next, few people are likely to spot the difference. That difference is far more noticeable, however, when two or more files are bound together in the same publication.*

Build an InDesign Book

An InDesign book is simply a container file into which multiple InDesign files are placed for easier organization and file management. The InDesign book utility offers several benefits, including:

- Synchronizing styles, colors, and other assets to the book's master file;
- Monitoring page and section numbering of each individual file in the book, and the book as a whole;
- Building a table of contents and index from all book files at once; and
- Printing or exporting the entire book, or outputting only selected chapters.

1. **Download IDCC_RF_Project8.zip from the Student Files Web page.**
2. **Expand the ZIP archive in your WIP folder (Macintosh) or copy the archive contents into your WIP folder (Windows).**

   This results in a folder named **Companions**, which contains the files you need for this project. You should also use this folder to save the files you create in this project.
3. **With nothing open in InDesign, choose File>New>Book. Navigate to your WIP>Companions folder as the target location.**

   Unlike creating a new file, creating a new book requires you to immediately name and save the book file.

> *Note:*
>
> *When you work with book files, you frequently open, save, and close the chapters of the book files; in fact, some operations happen without your direct intervention. Book chapter files need to be stored on a writable disk as long as you are still working on the book.*

4. **Change the book name to `excerpts.indb` and click Save.**

   The correct extension is automatically added for you, but if you accidentally remove it, add it to the file name.

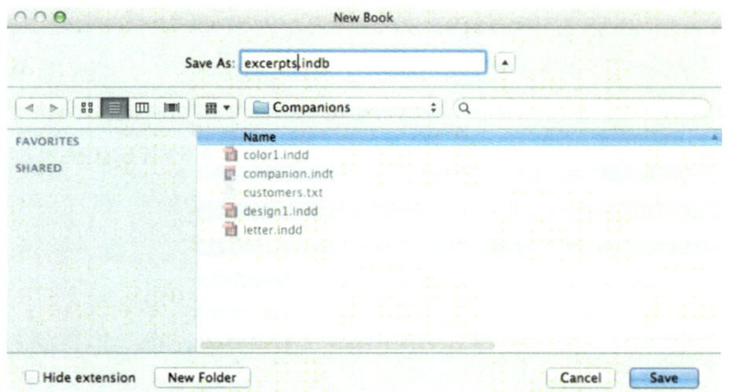

   Clicking Save opens the Book panel; the file name that you defined ("excerpts") appears in the panel tab. By default, the Book panel floats in the workspace; you can drag it anywhere you prefer (including into a specific panel group, whether docked or not).

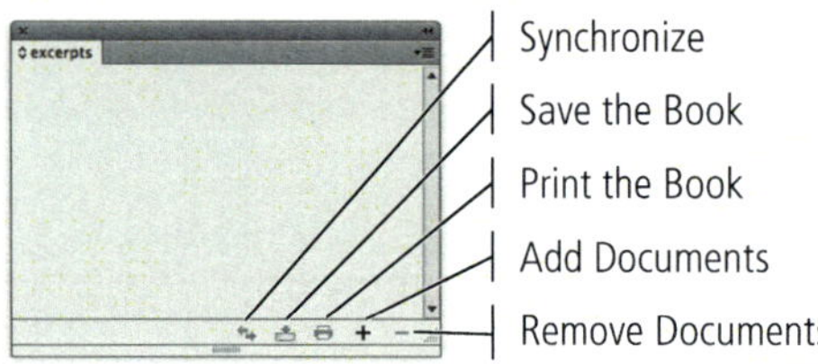

5. **Continue to the next exercise.**

> ***Note:***
>
> *You can open a book file the same way you open a regular document file (File>Open).*

> ***Note:***
>
> *You can save a book with a different name by choosing Save Book As from the panel Options menu.*

Add Book Chapters

Once the book file has been defined, adding chapters is easy. The first chapter you add becomes the style source chapter, to which other chapters can be synchronized. You can change the book's style source by clicking the empty space to the left of a chapter.

1. **With the `excerpts` book file open, click the Add Documents button at the bottom of the Book panel.**

2. **Navigate to `color1.indd` in your WIP>Companions folder and click Open.**

   Depending on the size of the chapter, it might take a few seconds to process the file.

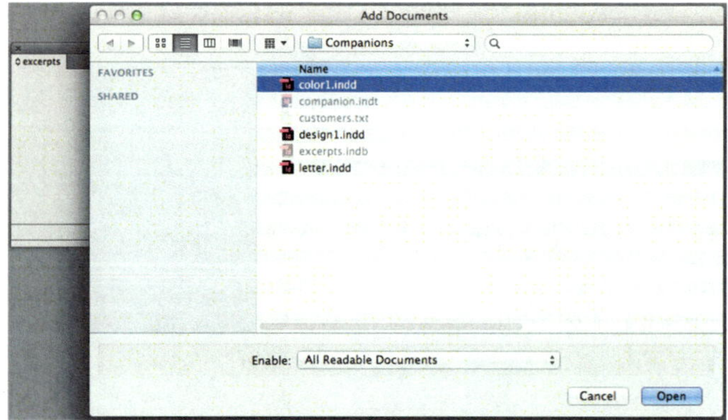

   When the process is complete, the file name appears in the Book panel.

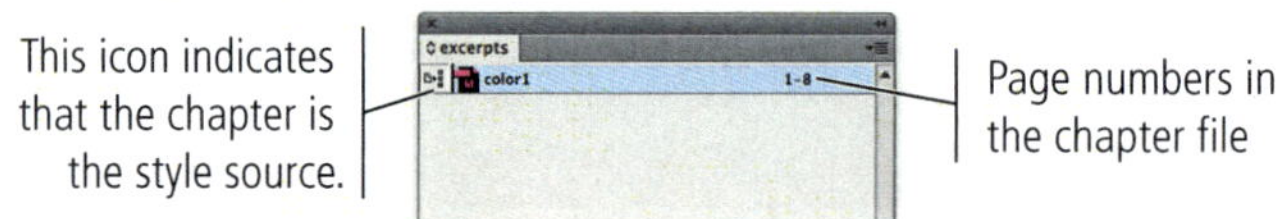

> ***Note:***
>
> *Don't worry about making these decisions early in the project. You can change the specific file to which the book is synchronized later; you will do this in a later exercise.*

3. **Click the Add Documents button again. Navigate to `design1.indd` in your WIP>Companions folder and click Open.**

   New files are automatically added below the previously selected chapter. If no chapter is selected in the panel, new files are added to the end of the book.

   If you haven't changed the section or page numbering options for the files you add, new book chapters are automatically numbered sequentially from one file to the next.

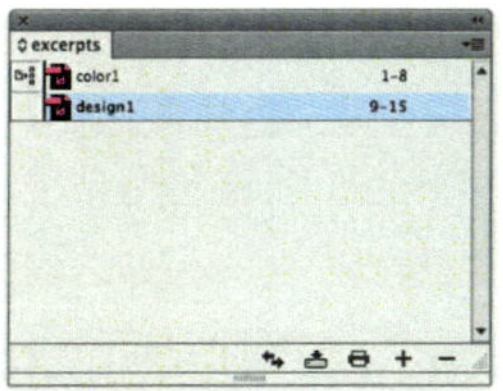

Note:

You can remove a file from a book by clicking the Remove Documents button at the bottom of the Book panel. Once you remove a chapter from a book, you can't undo the deletion. The file still exists in its original location, however, so you can simply add the file back into the book, if necessary.

4. **Create a new file by opening `companion.indt` from your WIP> Companions folder.**

   If you get a Profile or Policy Mismatch warning at any point in this project, select the option to leave the document as is and click OK.

   This is the template from which the companion chapters were created. Although the two excerpt chapters are already laid out, you need to create a front matter document that will hold a title page and the table of contents for the combined excerpts.

5. **In the Pages panel, drag the F-Title Page master page icon onto the Page 1 icon.**

   The front matter document will include the title page and table of contents — both conventional parts of book design, which have been planned for in the existing master page layouts. By dragging the F-Title Page master onto Page 1, you're applying the existing master page to the first page of the front matter file.

Scroll through the master page area (if necessary) to find the F-Title Page master at the bottom of the available layouts.

Drag the F-Title Page master onto the Page 1 icon in the lower section of the Pages panel.

Note:

***Front matter** typically refers to the information that precedes the main content of a book, including a title page, table of contents, copyright information, acknowledgements, and other important elements.*

6. **Press Command/Control-Shift and click the Book Title text frame to detach only that object from the master page.**

   The text frame for the book title is placed on the master page; to change the text and enter the actual book title, you either have to make the change on the master page or detach the master items on the regular layout page.

7. **Using the Type tool, highlight the text "Book Title" in the text frame and type `Companion Excerpts`.**

8. **Drag the right-center handle of the text frame until the word "Excerpts" moves to the second line and the right edge of the frame is approximately 1/8" from the edge of the text.**

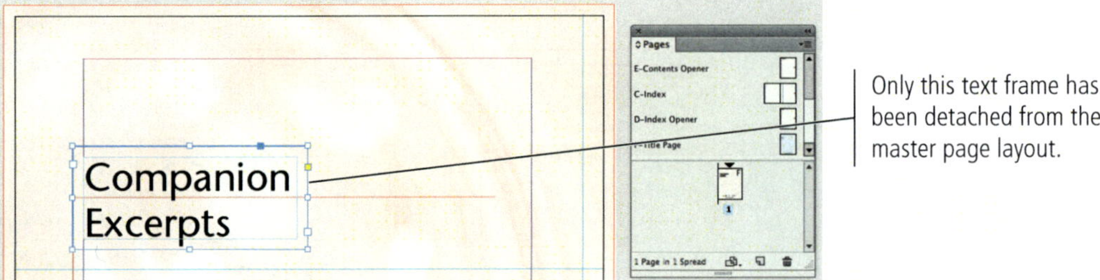

Only this text frame has been detached from the master page layout.

9. **Save the file as excerpts front.indd in your WIP>Companions folder, and then close the file.**

10. **In the excerpts Book panel, click the Add Documents button.**

11. **Navigate to the excerpts front.indd file that you just created and add it to the book file.**

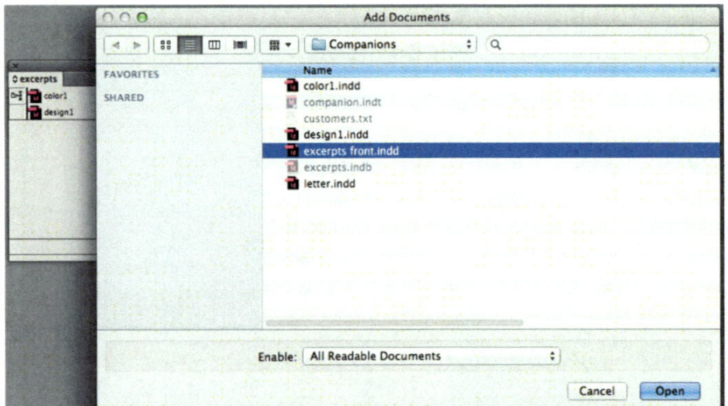

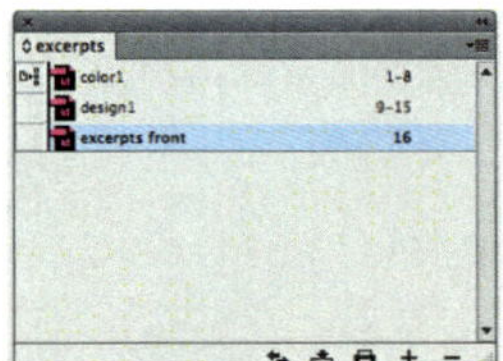

Managing Book Chapters

INDESIGN FOUNDATIONS

When you place a file into a book, the book file acts as a container; this process is very similar to placing an image into a layout. An InDesign layout stores the path to a placed image as a reference. Books use the same methodology, storing references to the files contained within the book; the book file does not contain the actual chapter files, only links to those chapters.

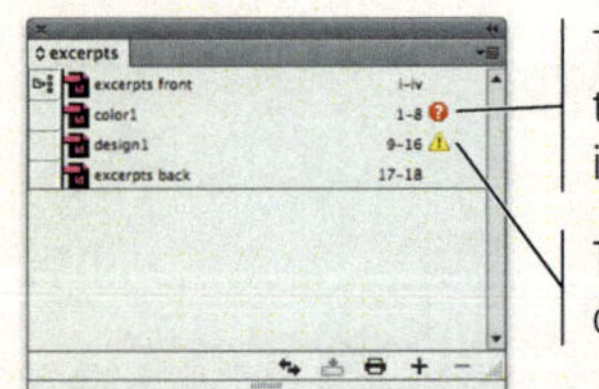

This chapter file is not in the same location as when it was placed in the book.

This chapter was modified outside the context of the book.

If the chapter files have been moved since being added to the book, the Book panel shows a missing-link warning icon. When you double-click a missing book chapter, InDesign asks if you want to replace the missing file; clicking Yes opens a navigation dialog box, so you can locate the missing file or identify a replacement file. (You can also select a missing file in the panel and choose Replace Document from the Book panel Options menu.)

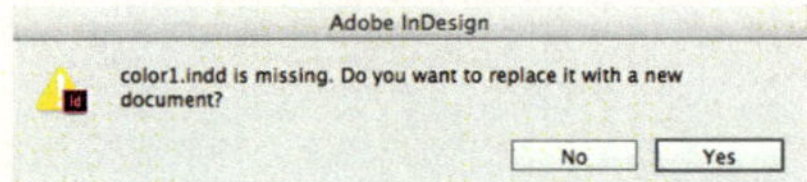

If you open a chapter using the Book panel, changes automatically reflect in the containing book. When you open a book chapter outside the context of the book, the Book panel displays a modified-link icon for that file.

You can update a modified book chapter by simply double-clicking the file in the panel to open it. When you save the chapter and close it, InDesign updates the book chapter link to reflect the most current version of the file. Once a chapter has been added to a book file, it is best to make changes only within the context of the book.

12. **Click excerpts front in the panel and drag up until a heavy line appears above color1 in the panel.**

When you release the mouse button, excerpts front becomes the first chapter in the book. However, color1 is still the style source; the style source does not need to be the first chapter in the book.

> *Note:*
>
> *When you drag a file within a book, align the thumb on the cursor icon with the location where you want to place the file.*

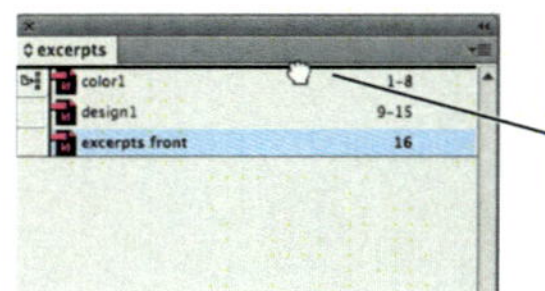

This line indicates the new position of the chapter (when you release the mouse button).

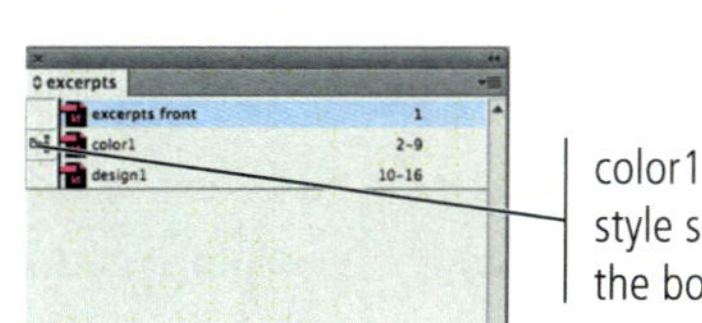

color1 is still the style source for the book file.

13. **Click the Save the Book button at the bottom of the panel.**

14. **Continue to the next exercise.**

 Control Section and Page Numbering

After moving the front matter chapter in front of the color chapter, the page numbers for each chapter automatically change to reflect their new position in the book. The problem, however, is that the second file (color1) begins on Page 2 and the third file (design1) begins on Page 10. Even-numbered pages are left-facing pages, but book design conventions dictate that book chapters begin on right-facing (odd-numbered) pages.

1. **With the excerpts book file open, choose Book Page Numbering Options from the Book panel Options menu.**

> *Note:*
>
> *Although some book designs intentionally break from convention and begin chapters on left-facing pages, this is not the norm. Right-facing chapter-starts are so common, in fact, that InDesign's long-document tools include the ability to force chapters to begin on the right side of the spread.*

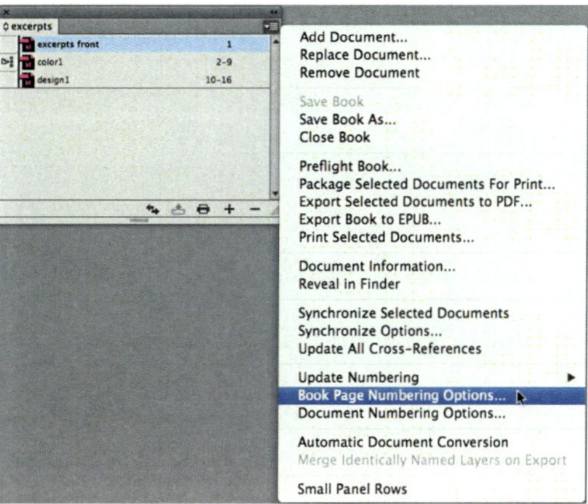

2. **In the Book Page Numbering Options dialog box, choose the Continue on Next Odd Page option.**

You can use this dialog box to control exactly where new chapter files begin:

Book Page Numbering Options
Options
Page Order: Continue from previous document
Continue on next odd page
Continue on next even page
Insert Blank Page
Automatically Update Page & Section Numbers
OK
Cancel

- **Continue from Previous Document**, the default option, allows new chapters to pick up numbering from the end of the previous file. This option allows new chapters to begin on odd- or even-numbered pages.
- **Continue on Next Odd Page** forces new chapter files to begin on odd-numbered pages. If your layouts use facing pages, this means new chapters will always begin on right-facing pages.
- **Continue on Next Even Page** forces new chapter files to begin on even-numbered pages. If your layouts use facing pages, this means new chapters will always begin on left-facing pages.

3. **Check the Insert Blank Page option and leave the Automatically Update option checked.**

   The Insert Blank Page option adds a blank page into any file where the defined page order leaves a blank space in the page numbering. When the Automatically Update option is checked (as it is by default), files in the book automatically adjust to reflect additional choices in this dialog box.

4. **Click OK to apply your changes.**

   The second and third files in the book now begin on odd-numbered (right-facing) pages. Blank pages have been added as necessary to fill empty spaces caused by moving the chapters to the appropriate side of the spread.

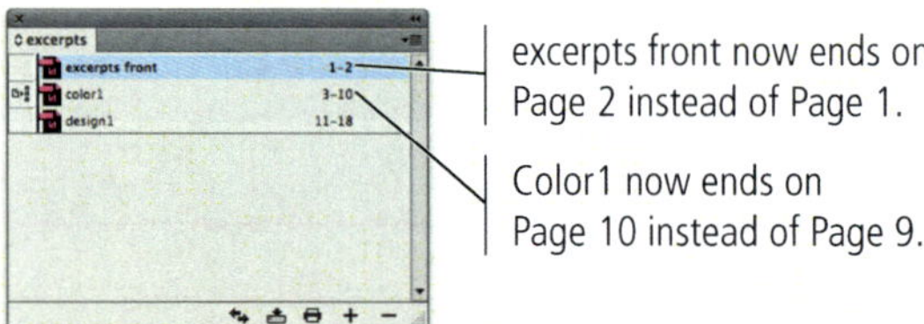

excerpts front now ends on Page 2 instead of Page 1.

Color1 now ends on Page 10 instead of Page 9.

5. **In the Book panel, click the `excerpts front` file to select it.**

6. **Open the Book panel Options menu, choose Document Numbering Options.**

   In addition to controlling the page numbering from one file to another, you can also control the page numbering for a specific file. This option is useful if, for example, you want the front matter of a book to be numbered separately from the main body of the document.

   To change document-specific settings such as page numbering and sections, the document must be open. When you choose Document Numbering Options in the Book panel Options menu, the selected file automatically opens so you can make changes.

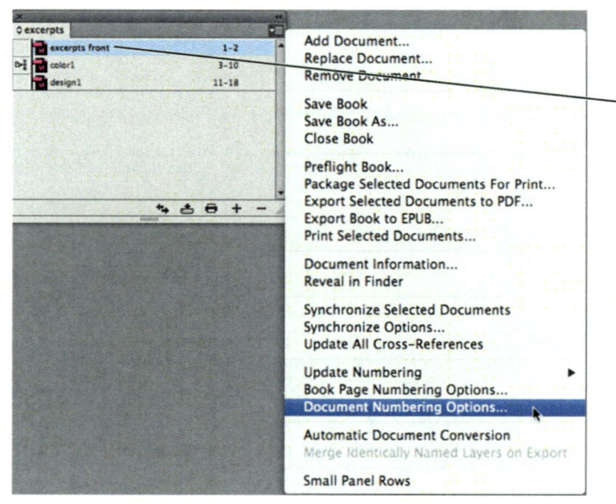

The excerpts front file is selected in the Book panel.

7. **In the Document Numbering Options dialog box, choose lowercase Roman numerals in the Page Numbering Style menu.**

   This is another convention in book design and layout — the front matter is numbered separately from the main part of the book, commonly in lowercase Roman numerals.

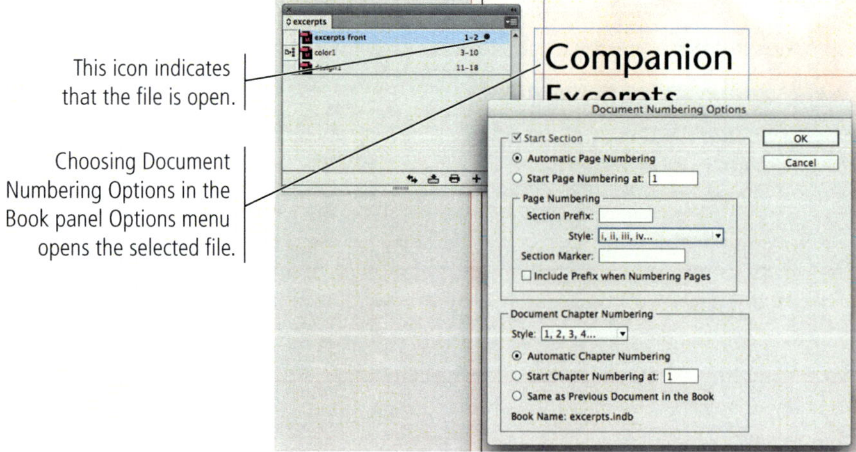

This icon indicates that the file is open.

Choosing Document Numbering Options in the Book panel Options menu opens the selected file.

8. **Click OK to apply the change, save the open layout, and then close the file.**

In the Book panel, the excerpts front file reflects the new numbering style. The problem, however, is that the first *content* chapter begins on Page 3; publishing convention typically specify that the main content of a book begins on Page 1. To accomplish this goal, you can use the Numbering & Section Options to start a new section with the color1 chapter.

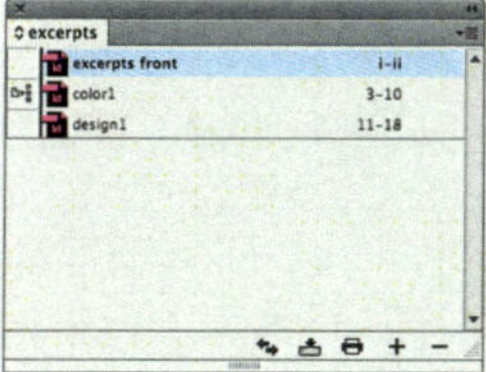

9. **Double-click `color1` in the Book panel.**

Double-clicking a file in the Book panel automatically opens that file.

10. **Control/right-click the Page 3 icon in the Pages panel and choose Numbering & Section Options.**

This command opens a dialog box similar to the Document Numbering Options dialog box. The primary difference is that this dialog box provides options for controlling a specific page (Page 3, which you Control/right-clicked to access the dialog box).

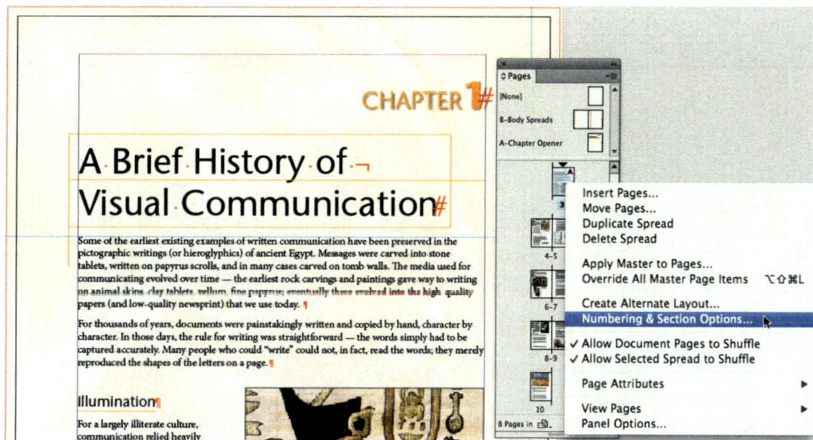

When you use the Document Numbering Options command, InDesign automatically applies your choices, beginning with the first page of the selected file. Using the Numbering & Section Options command, you can change the options for any page in the document.

Understanding Book Page Numbering

INDESIGN FOUNDATIONS

If you had not checked Insert Blank Pages in the Book Page Numbering Options dialog box, each chapter in your book would begin on a right-facing (odd-numbered) page. However, the last page in each file would remain unchanged. The image here shows the original pagination (on the left) in comparison to the renumbered pages; the first page of each file is highlighted in pink. In the middle version — the result of the steps you just took — blank pages are highlighted in yellow.

The third version (on the right) shows what would have happened if you had not selected the Insert Blank Pages option. Although the second and third files would have begun on odd-numbered (right-facing) pages, the blank pages would not have been added to fill the space. This could cause significant problems when the book is imposed into printer's spreads for commercial printing. (Refer to Project 4: Realtor Collateral Booklet for an explanation of printer's spreads.)

Original pagination

	1
2	3
4	5
6	7
8	9
10	11
12	13
14	15
16	

Pagination after modifying numbering (inserting blank pages)

	1
2	3
4	5
6	7
8	9
10	11
12	13
14	15
16	17
18	

Pagination without inserting blank pages

	1
	3
4	5
6	7
8	9
10	11
	13
14	15
16	17
18	

Section and Chapter Numbering in Depth

Section and Page Numbering in a Single File

Although there are distinct advantages to maintaining long documents in separate chapter files, there are times when you want to work with an entire booklet or other project in a single InDesign file. In this case, it is important to realize that you can change the page and section numbering options for any page in the layout; these options are not restricted to files placed in an InDesign book.

Sections allow you to create different page numbering sequences within a single file. For any section start page, you can restart page numbering at a specific page number, change the style of page numbers in the section, define a section marker for the section, and/or include the section prefix in the page number.

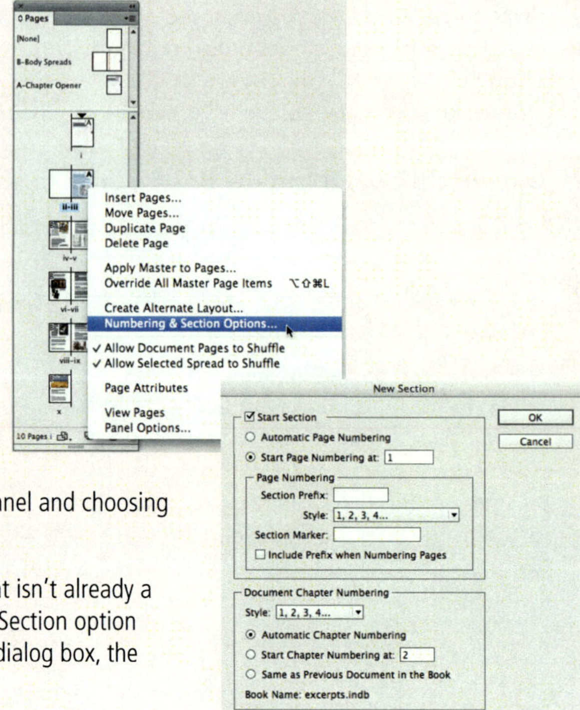

You can change the page and section options for any specific page by Control/right-clicking the page in the Pages panel and choosing Numbering & Section Options from the contextual menu.

When you choose Numbering & Section Options for a page that isn't already a section start, the New Section dialog box opens with the Start Section option automatically checked. When you click OK in the New Section dialog box, the selected page is designated as a section start.

If you choose Numbering & Section Options for an existing section start page, the Numbering & Section Options dialog box opens. The choices in this dialog box are exactly the same as those in the New Section dialog box; the only differences are the title bar and the choices already selected when you open the dialog box.

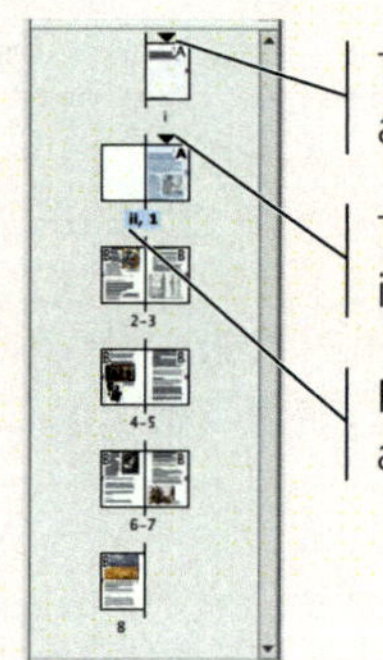

The first page in the file is a section start by default.

The triangle above the page icon indicates a section start.

Pages between two section starts are part of the preceding section.

Adding Section Prefixes

If you use the Page Number markers (Type> Insert Special Character>Markers>Current/Next/ Previous Page Number), you can add a section prefix to page numbers in the layout by checking the Include Prefix when Numbering Pages option. Whatever you type in the Section Prefix field is added in front of the page number.

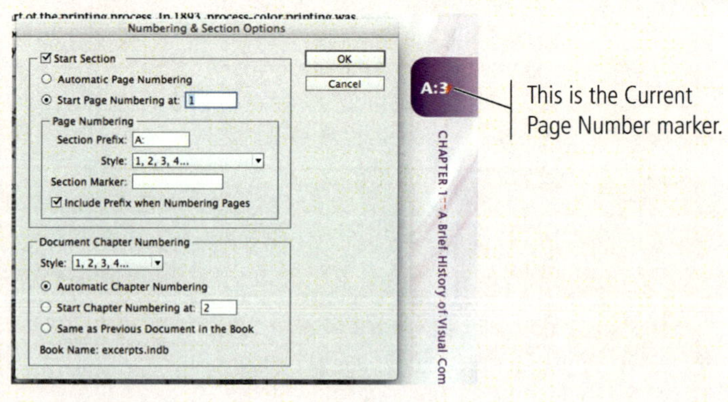

This is the Current Page Number marker.

11. In the Numbering & Section Options dialog box, choose the Start Page Numbering At option and change the number in the field to 1.

InDesign's default behavior — the Automatic Page Numbering option — causes pages to number sequentially from one file to the next in the book. By choosing the Start Page Numbering At option, you can override the default page numbering and determine the exact page number of any file in the book.

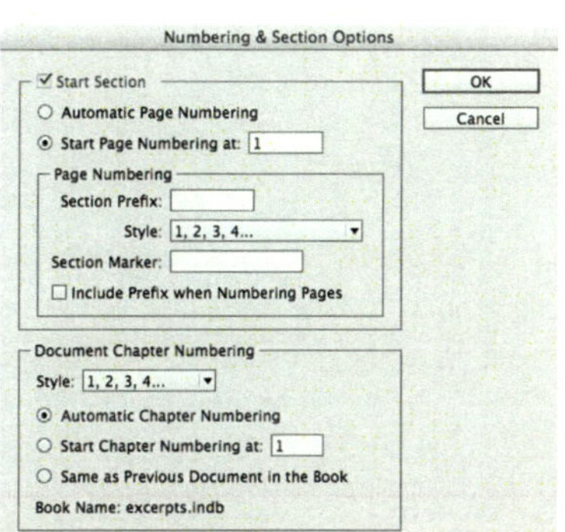

Note:

If you are using facing pages, changing an even-numbered page to an odd-numbered page moves the page to the other side of the spread. Remember from earlier chapters that this can cause objects to appear out of position in relation to the page's new location.

Section and Chapter Numbering in Depth (continued)

INDESIGN FOUNDATIONS

Adding Section Markers

Section markers are a type of variable. You can define the Section Marker text for a specific section, and then place the marker into the layout (Type>Insert Special Character>Markers>Section Marker).

The Section Marker special character displays the text in the Section Marker field of the Numbering & Section Options dialog box. If a section has no defined Section Marker text, the special character displays nothing. You can also change all instances of the section marker within a section by re-opening the dialog box for the section start page and changing the text in the Section Marker field.

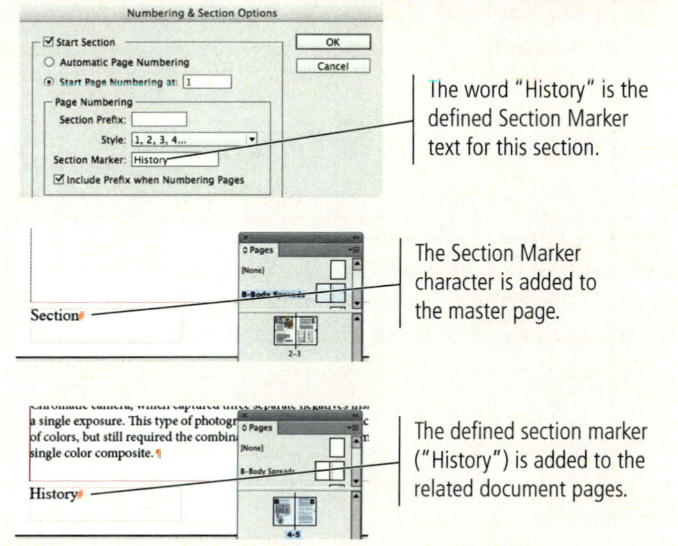

Chapter Numbering

When you work with book files, you can also define Document Chapter Numbering options, which is basically section numbering for files. If you define a specific chapter number in the Numbering & Section Options dialog box, you can place the built-in Chapter Number variable (Type>Text Variables>Insert Variable>Chapter Number) in the layout to reflect the current chapter number.

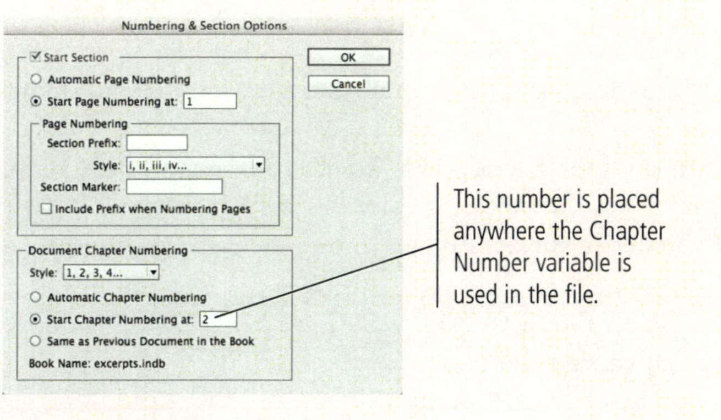

If nothing appears in the Insert Variable submenu, the document was probably created in an earlier version of InDesign. Several predefined variables — including Chapter Number — were added in InDesign CS3. In this case, you can either define your own Chapter Number variable (see Project 5: Ireland Travel Brochure) or load the variables from a file created in InDesign CS3 or later.

12. **Click OK to apply the new page number to the first page of the color1 file.**

Because you haven't changed the numbering options for the design1 file (or any specific page in that file), it is still automatically numbered in sequence with the color1 file.

> ***Note:***
>
> *The page numbering of a book relies on the Current Page Number marker (Type>Insert Special Character>Markers>Current Page Number).*

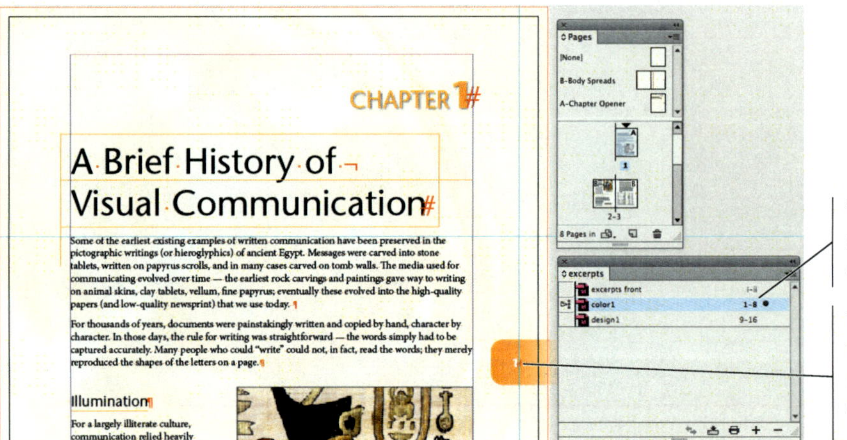

The page numbers for design1 change to reflect the new overall book page numbering.

This object is placed using the Current Page Number marker. It reflects the correct page number relative to the entire book.

13. **Save the open document (color1) and close it.**

14. **In the Book panel, click the Save the Book button, and then continue to the next exercise.**

Synchronize Book Files

Layout designers frequently manipulate, tweak, and even cheat to force-fit text into a desired amount of space, to make a runaround work correctly, or to achieve a specific effect. When the files are combined into the final book, these adjustments can cause problems if the variation is noticeable from one chapter to the next. A primary advantage of using the InDesign book-building functionality is the ability to easily synchronize various assets — swatches, styles, etc. — across multiple chapter files to ensure consistency thoughout a publication.

When a book is synchronized, assets in the style source file are applied to all other files in the book. (The synchronization process does not affect elements that are not in the style source file.)

- If an asset in the Style Source file does not exist in other book files, it is simply added to the other files.
- If an asset already exists in the other book files, the element definition from the Style Source file is applied to the same-named element in the other files.

In this exercise, you synchronize the assets in the Companion Excerpts files to make sure the highlight color has the same definition in all files, and to ensure consistency in the appearance of text styles throughout the document.

1. **With the `excerpts` book file open, double-click the `excerpts front` file to open that document.**

2. **Open the Swatches panel, and then open the Swatch Options dialog box for the Companion Color swatch.**

3. **Change the swatch definition to C=70 M=100 Y=0 K=0 and make sure the Name with Color Value option is not checked.**

Each book in the Companion series was printed with a different highlight color. When combining chapters from different books in the series, the highlight color needs to be unifed for consistency throughout the "combo" document. In this excerpt booklet, the client decided to use a purple shade as the highlight color.

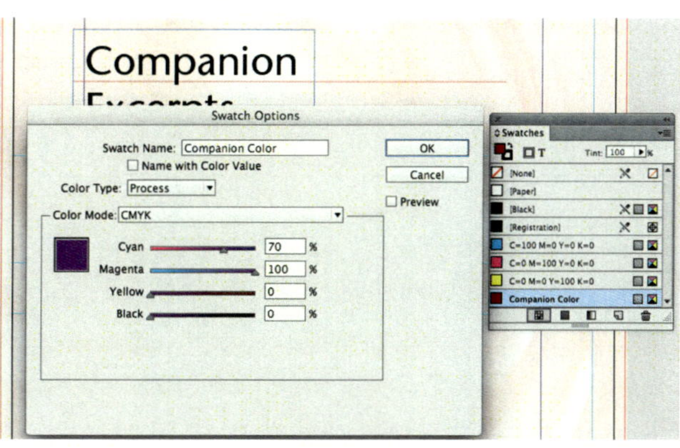

This is an instance where there is good reason to break from the color-naming convention based on color definition. The swatch is different in all companion books, but the swatch is named the same in all files of all books. By synchronizing the color in all book files to this new definition, you can change the Companion Color swatch in multiple files at one time.

Note:

The synchronization process does not create any type of report showing what has been done in which files. Some experts prefer to back up their book files before synchronization in case they need to go back to the pre-synchronized files for any reason.

4. **Click OK to close the Swatch Options dialog box, save the document and close it, but leave the book file open.**

5. **In the Book panel, click the empty space to the left of the `excerpts front` file to redefine the style source.**

Since the front matter file now has the Companion Color swatch definition that you want to use for the entire document, you need to synchronize other files in the book to the excerpt front file.

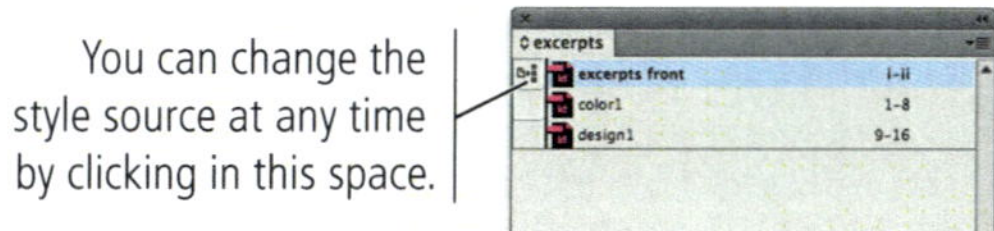

6. **Click in the empty area at the bottom of the Book panel to deselect all files.**

If nothing is selected in the Book panel, all chapter files will be synchronized to the style source file. You can also synchronize specific files by selecting them in the Book panel before clicking the Synchronize button. (Of course, synchronizing only certain files defeats the purpose of synchronizing, but the option is available nonetheless.)

7. **In the Book panel Options menu, choose Synchronize Options.**

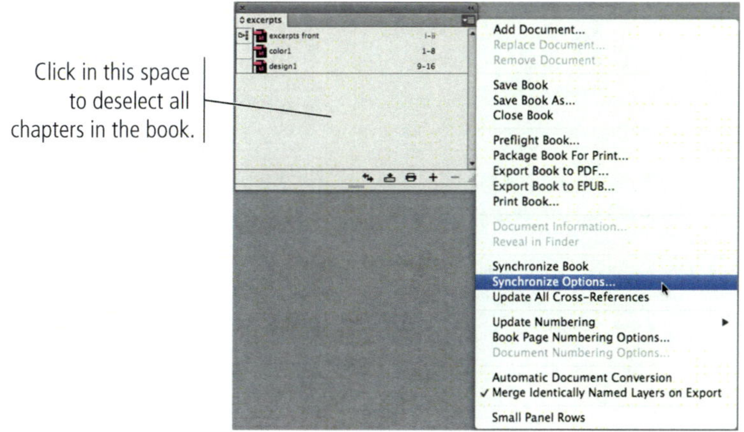

8. **In the Synchronize Options dialog box, uncheck all options except Character Styles, Paragraph Styles, and Swatches. At the bottom of the dialog box, leave the Smart Match Style Groups checked.**

   In this simple project, your primary concern is consistency of appearance between existing files from the same series of books. The three selected options are sufficient for this project. In other cases where you combine radically different files from a variety of designers, it might be useful — or, in fact, vital — to synchronize the other types of assets as well.

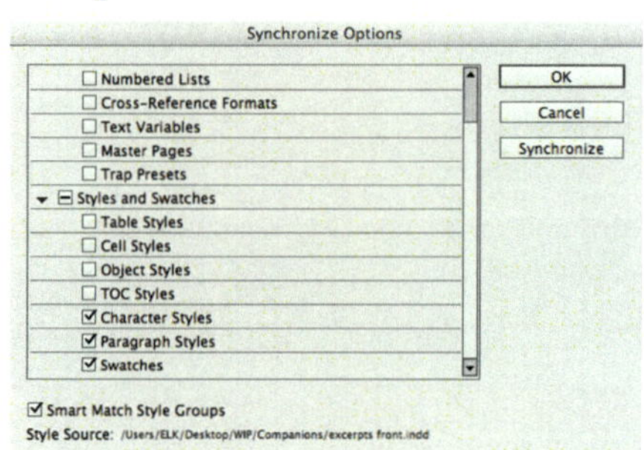

9. **Click OK to close the dialog box.**

10. **In the Book panel, click the Synchronize button.**

11. **Click OK in the resulting warning.**

    As we mentioned, synchronizing book files can cause problems. InDesign is smart enough to recognize and warn you about one of the most common and serious problems — overset text.

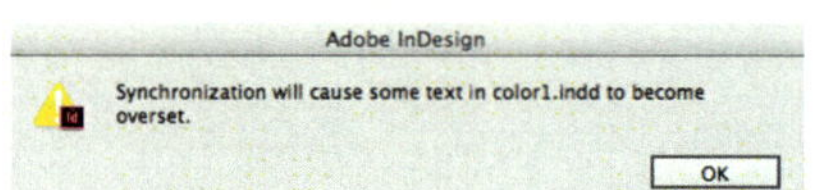

Note:

The tool tip name for the Synchronize button — Synchronize Styles and Swatches with the Style Source — is deceptively non-inclusive. Because you can synchronize far more than just these two elements, we refer to this button as simply "Synchronize."

Note:

Synchronizing a book does not delete any element from any file, but can override changes that you made to a particular file.

Smart Matching Style Groups

INDESIGN FOUNDATIONS

The Smart Match Style Groups option is useful if you use groups (folders) to organize styles in your layout files. The following images show the results of synchronizing styles that are stored in style groups.

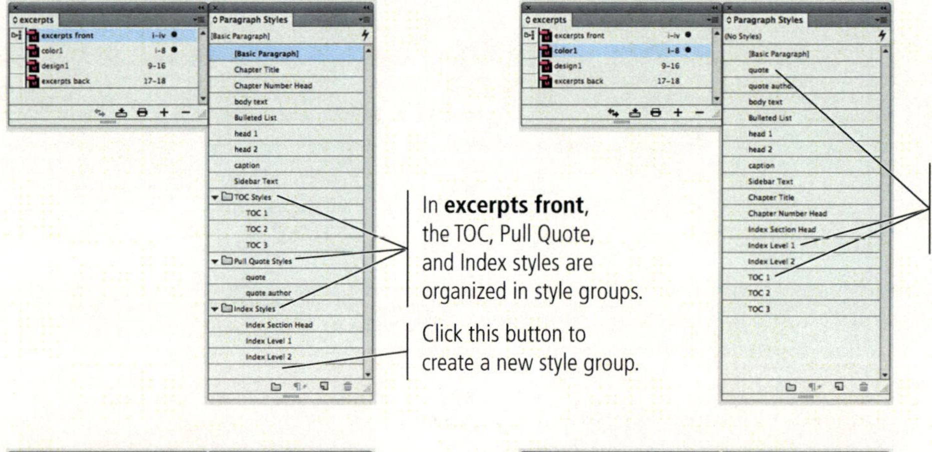

In **excerpts front**, the TOC, Pull Quote, and Index styles are organized in style groups.

Click this button to create a new style group.

The same styles exist in **color1**, but they are not grouped.

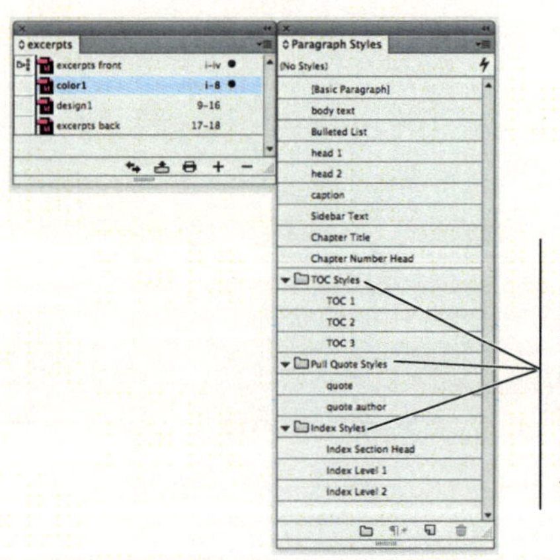

If you synchronize with Smart Match Style Groups checked, the groups from **excerpts front** are copied into **color1** and the same-named styles are moved into the appropriate groups.

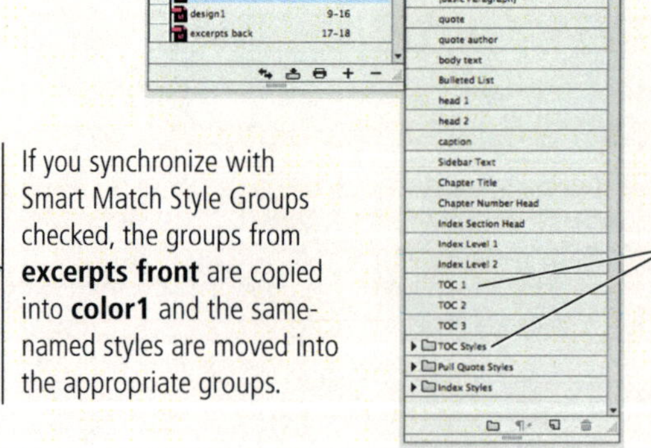

If you synchronize with Smart Match Style Groups unchecked, the grouped styles from **excerpts front** are copied into **color1** in addition to the same-named styles that are not grouped.

12. **When the process is complete, click OK to dismiss the resulting message.**

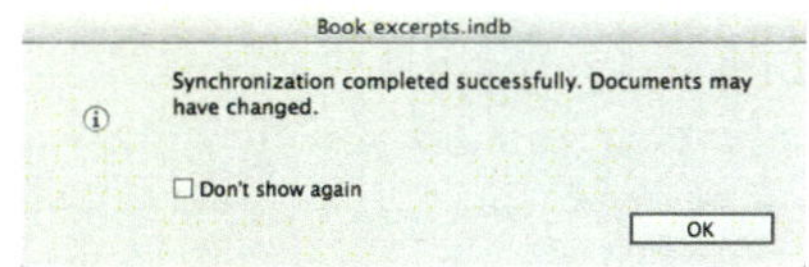

This message warns you of the potential problem we mentioned earlier — documents might have changed. When you synchronize book files — especially if you did not create the original files — you should carefully review the pages to be sure the content is still where it belongs.

13. **Double-click `color1` in the Book panel to open that file, and navigate to Page 8.**

When you synchronize files, you often have no idea what caused the problem — but you still need to fix it. You have several options:

- Edit the text to fit the overset line in the available space. Of course, this assumes you have permission to edit text, which you usually do not.
- Add text frames to the chain. This typically assumes you can add pages to a file, which you often can't.
- Change style definitions to fit text into the available space. If you synchronize again later, your changes will again be overwritten.
- Adjust local formatting of specific text to make the layout work properly.

> *Note:*
>
> *If you change a style — to fit text onto a page, for example — synchronizing the book to the master file overwrites the changes and the text no longer fits the same way.*

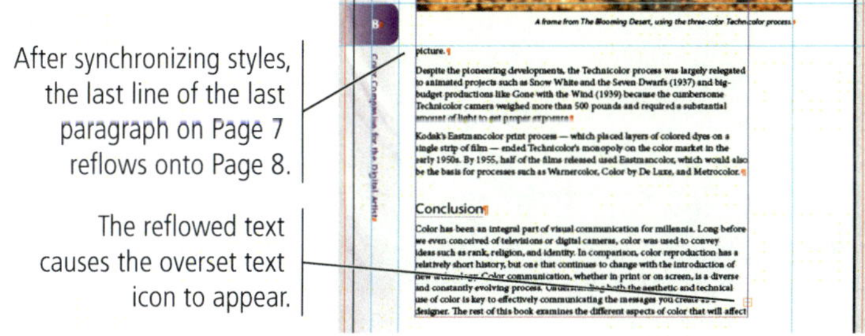

After synchronizing styles, the last line of the last paragraph on Page 7 reflows onto Page 8.

The reflowed text causes the overset text icon to appear.

> *Note:*
>
> *In case you were wondering, the Tracking setting for the body text style was reduced in the original color1 file to fit the text in eight pages, instead of placing only one line of text on Page 9 and inserting a blank Page 10.*

14. **On Page 7 of the file, click four times to select the entire last paragraph. Using the Control or Character panel, change the tracking of the selected paragraph to –10.**

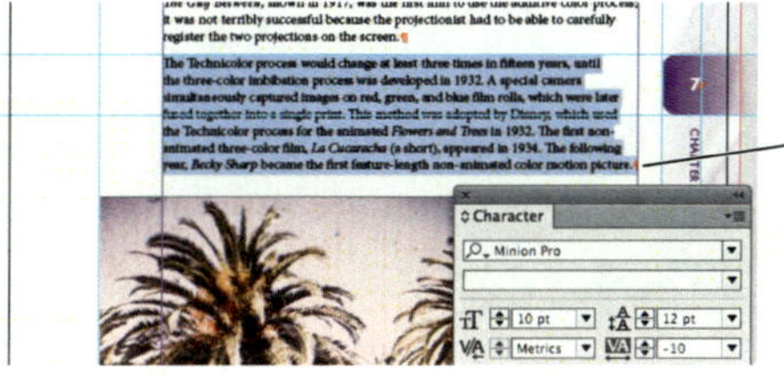

After changing the tracking for the selected paragraph, the last line again fits on Page 7.

> *Note:*
>
> *If you absolutely must adjust text in a particular file of a book, we recommend you manipulate the selected text and not the style.*

15. **Navigate to Page 8 and review the text.**

The end-of-story character now shows, and the overset text icon no longer appears in the frame's out port.

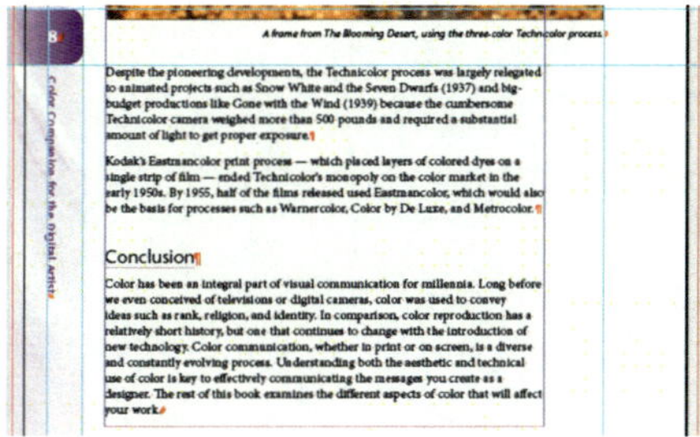

16. **Save the document and close it.**

17. **Save the book file and continue to the next stage of the project.**

Stage 2 Building a Table of Contents

Before desktop-publishing software automated the document-design process, tables of contents and other lists (figures, tables, etc.) were created manually from page proofs — by turning each page and writing down the appropriate text and page number, and then sorting and typesetting those hard-copy lists into the final document. The process was extremely time-consuming and required precise attention to detail. If the document changed after the lists were completed, the entire piece had to be rechecked, one page at a time.

Fortunately, InDesign includes a Table of Contents feature that automates this process, greatly improving production time and making it easier to maintain accuracy. InDesign tables of contents are based on the paragraph styles used in a layout. If you are conscientious about applying styles when you build a layout, you can easily create a thorough, accurate table of contents based on those styles.

You can define the styles that will be included in the compiled table of contents. For example, a table of contents might include Heading 1, Heading 2, and Heading 3 paragraph styles; any text set in those styles will appear in the list.

You can also determine the styles that will be used to format different elements in the compiled table of contents. Using the same example, TOC1 can be assigned to Heading 1 list items, TOC2 to Heading 2 items, and so on. When you compile the table of contents into the file, it is formatted automatically.

Define a Table of Contents Style

A table of contents can be defined and applied in a single process. You can also create and save table of contents styles, which you can apply as needed in the active file, as well as import into and apply in other files. Because of the versatility allowed by styles of all types (paragraph, table, object, etc.), we recommend creating table of contents styles rather than defining a single-case table of contents.

1. **With the excerpts book file open, double-click the excerpts front file in the panel to open that file.**

2. **Drag the E-Contents Opener master page to the right of the Page ii icon.**

   When the new page is added, another blank page is also added because of your choices (Insert Blank Page) in the Book Page Numbering Options dialog box.

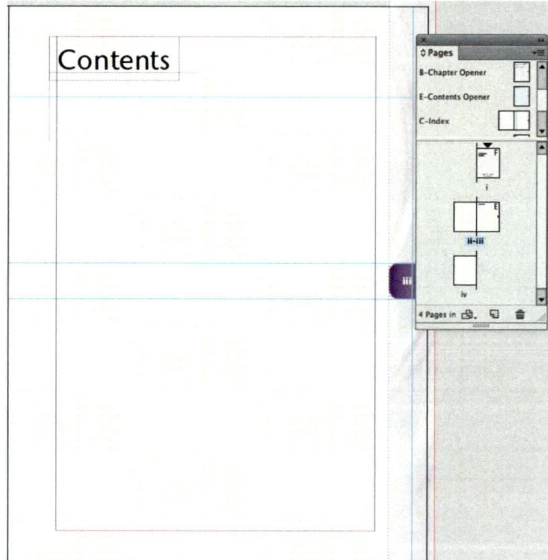

3. **Choose Layout>Table of Contents Styles.**

   You can create new styles, edit or delete existing styles, or load styles from other files.

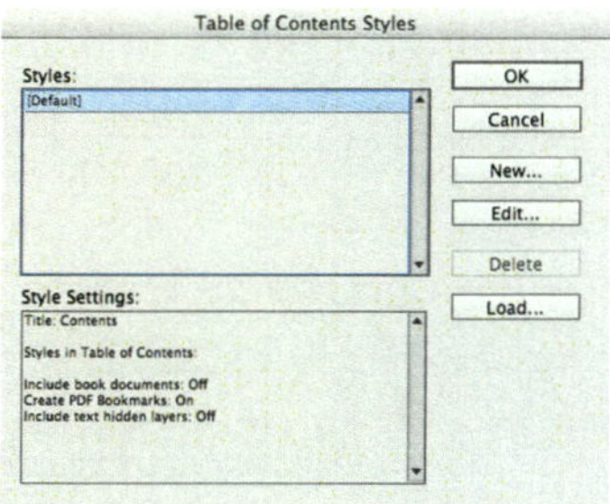

4. **Click New. In the resulting New Table of Contents Style dialog box, type `Companion Contents` in the TOC Style field.**

   The TOC Style field defines the style name. It is basically the same as a paragraph style name (an identifier).

5. **Delete the text from the Title field.**

   The Title field, on the other hand, is actual text that is included at the top of the compiled table of contents. Because the "Contents" title for this layout is built into the master page, you should not include a title in the compiled table of contents.

6. **If necessary, click the More Options button on the right side of the dialog box.**

   When More Options are showing, you can control the appearance of page numbers in the table of contents.

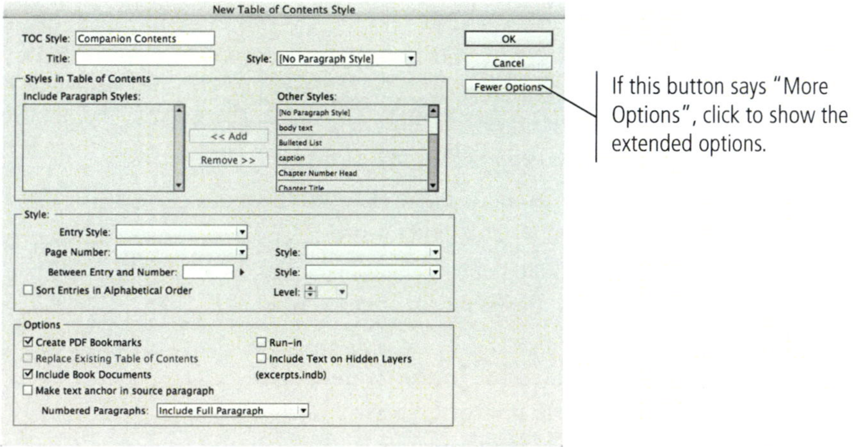

7. **Scroll though the Other Styles list, select Chapter Title, and click the Add button.**

8. **In the middle section of the dialog box, choose TOC 1 in the Entry Style menu.**

9. **Choose After Entry in the Page Number field, and choose TOC Page Number in the associated Style menu. Leave all other options at their default settings.**

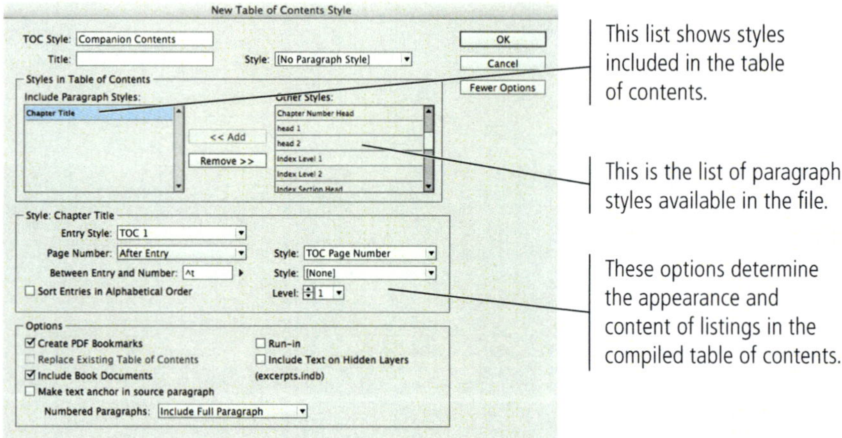

You can define a number of options for each style included in a table of contents:

- **Entry Style** defines the paragraph style that will be applied to those entries in the compiled list.
- **Page Number** determines where the page number will be included for each entry (After Entry or Before Entry). You can also choose No Page Number to add the list entry without the associated page number.
- **Between Entry and Number** defines the character(s) that are placed between the list entry and the associated page number. The default option (^t) is the code for a Tab character. The attached menu includes a number of common special characters, or you can type the code for a specific special character (see Project 6: Digital Layout Variations for details).
- You can use the Style menus in the right column to define separate character styles for the page number and the character between the entry and page number. If you don't choose a character style in one or both of these menus, that element will be formatted with the paragraph style settings defined for the list entry.
- If the **Sort Entries in Alphabetical Order** option is checked, the compiled list entries will appear in alphabetical order rather than page-number order.
- By default, each new style in the Include pane is added one level lower than the previous style. You can use the **Level** menu to change the hierarchy of styles in the list.

10. **In the Other Styles list, highlight head 1 and click Add. In the Style section of the dialog box, choose TOC 2 in the Entry Style menu. Choose After Entry in the Page Number field, and choose TOC Page Number in the associated Style menu.**

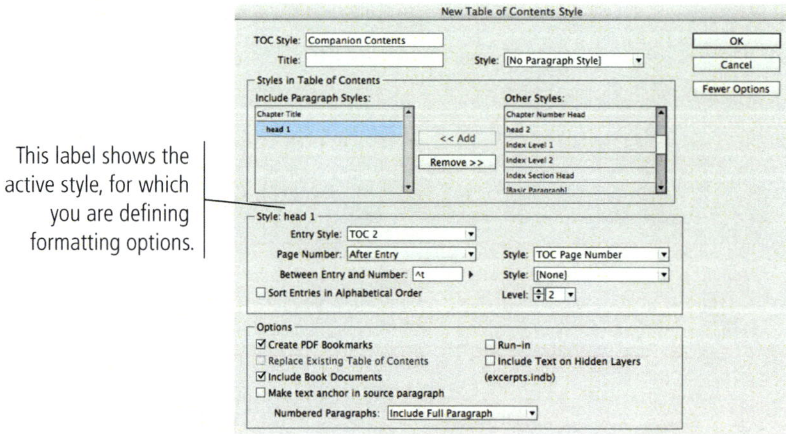

11. **In the Other Styles list, highlight head 2 and click Add. In the Style section of the dialog box, choose TOC 3 in the Entry Style menu. Choose After Entry in the Page Number field, and choose TOC Page Number in the associated Style menu.**

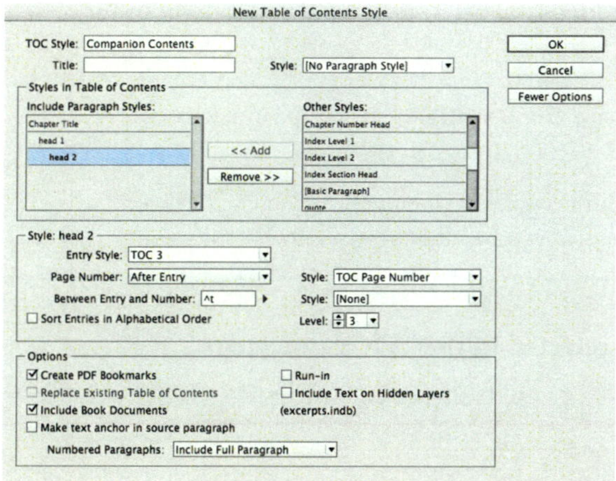

12. **In the Options area, check the Create PDF Bookmarks and Include Book Documents options.**

    - **Create PDF Bookmarks** tags the table of contents entries to appear in the Bookmarks panel of Adobe Acrobat or Adobe Reader (when the document is exported to PDF).
    - **Replace Existing Table of Contents** is only available if a table of contents has already been built in the open file. This option is more relevant when you build the table of contents than when you define a table of contents style.
    - **Include Book Documents** allows you to build a single table of contents for all files in an InDesign book file. This option is only available if the open file is part of an InDesign book.
    - **Run-in** builds a list in which all entries run into a single paragraph; individual entries are separated by a semicolon.
    - **Include Text on Hidden Layers** adds list entries even if the text is on a hidden layer. This option is unchecked by default, and it should almost always remain that way — unless you have a very specific reason for listing elements that do not actually appear in the document.
    - The **Numbered Paragraphs** menu determines whether the list entry includes the full numbered paragraph (number and text), only the numbers, or only the text.

13. **Click OK to return to the Table of Contents Styles dialog box.**

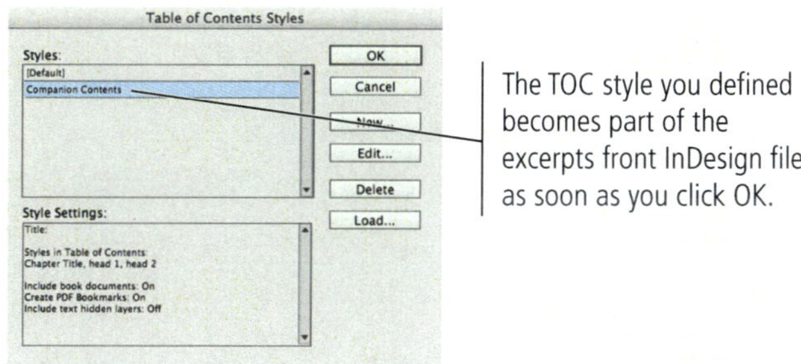

The TOC style you defined becomes part of the excerpts front InDesign file as soon as you click OK.

14. **Click OK to close the Table of Contents Styles dialog box and return to the document window.**

15. **Save the file and continue to the next exercise.**

Note:

Different types of projects call for different types of lists. Although called the Table of Contents utility, you can build a list of any editorial element formatted with a paragraph style. For example, some publications call for a separate table of contents for illustrations. If you define and apply a Figure Heading paragraph style, you can create a list of all entries formatted with that style.

Build and Update a Table of Contents

Once a list is defined, whether for a single file or a book, you can build it into the layout very easily. In fact, when you build a table of contents, the compiled list loads into the cursor; you can click to place the loaded list just as you would place any other text element.

1. **With `excerpts front.indd` open from the `excerpts` Book panel, choose Layout>Table of Contents.**

   This dialog box has the same options as those available when you defined a TOC style. The only difference is that here you define a one-time table of contents list (although you can click the Save Style button to create a style based on your choices).

2. **Make sure Companion Contents is selected in the TOC Style menu.**

   Because it is the only style in the open file, it should be selected by default.

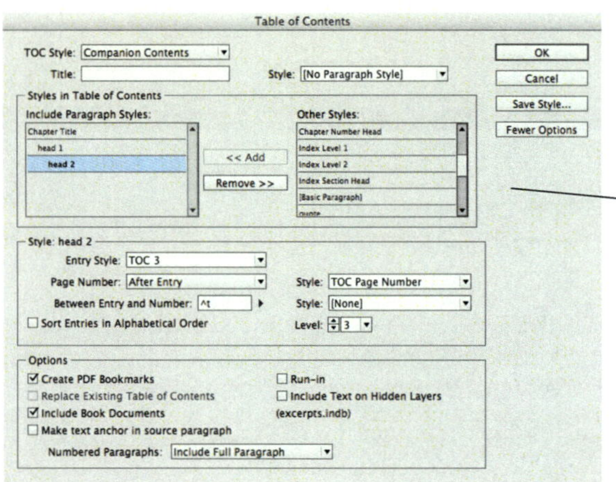

All options in this dialog box reflect your choices in the TOC style from the previous exercise.

3. **Click OK.**

   When the list is ready, it loads into the cursor. This process might take a little while to complete, depending on the size of your book, so don't panic or try to force-quit the application after a minute or two. If you're working on a very large book (such as this 500-plus-page Portfolio Series book), now is probably a good time for a coffee break.

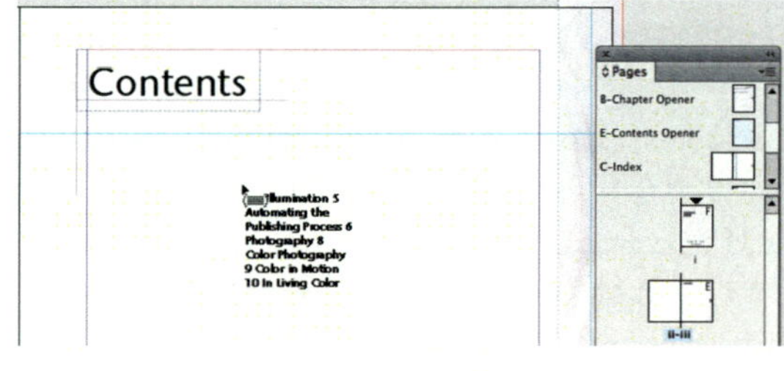

4. **Click the loaded cursor in the middle of Page iii to place the TOC into the text frame on the page.**

   That's all there is to building a table of contents — whether for a single file or for multiple documents combined in an InDesign book file. After a TOC is built into a document, it is a static block of text. The applied styles can be changed like any other styles, and you can change the text box in which a list is placed. You can change or delete items from the list without affecting the main layout.

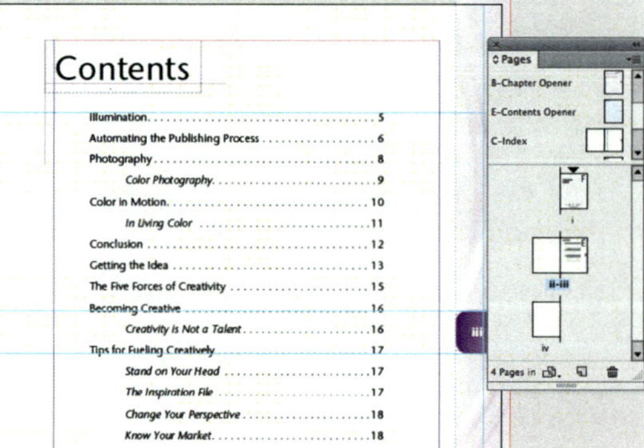

5. **Double-click `color1` in the Book panel to open the file, and navigate to Page 1. Command/Control-Shift-click the frame containing the document title to detach that frame from the master page.**

   The table of contents built for this file reveals one problem: text that exists on the master page only (i.e., where the layout page hasn't been detached from the master) is not included in the compiled lists. The text frames for each chapter title have not been detached from the master pages, so the chapter titles do not appear in the compiled list.

   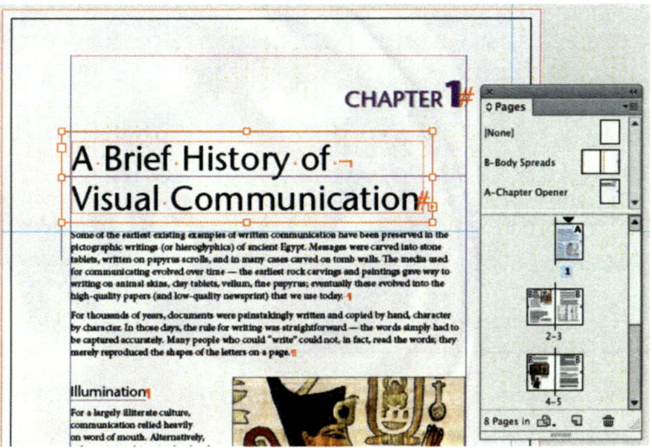

6. **Save the file and close it.**

7. **Repeat Steps 5–6 on the first page of the `design1` file (Page 9 in the book) to detach the title text frame from the master page.**

   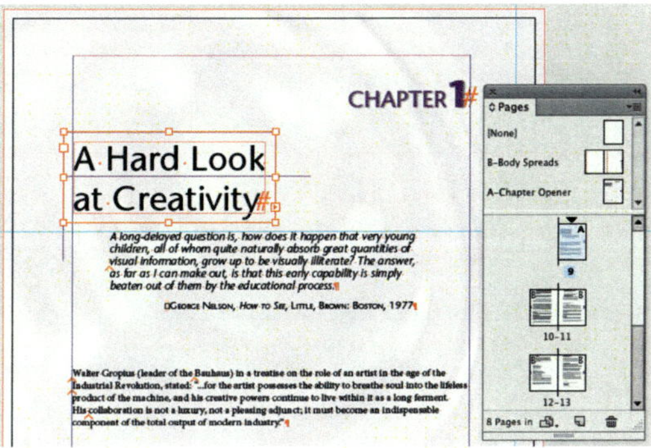

8. **With Page iii of the `excerpts front` file showing, place the insertion point anywhere within the current table of contents and then choose Layout>Update Table of Contents. Click OK in the resulting message.**

   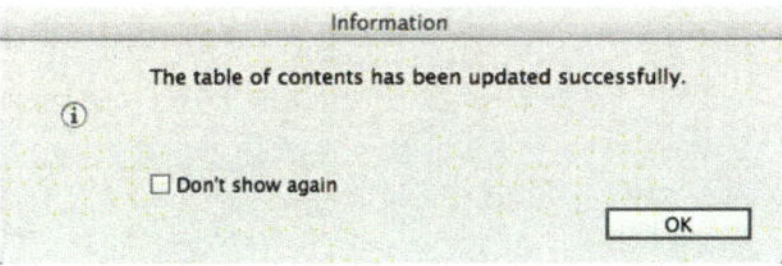

   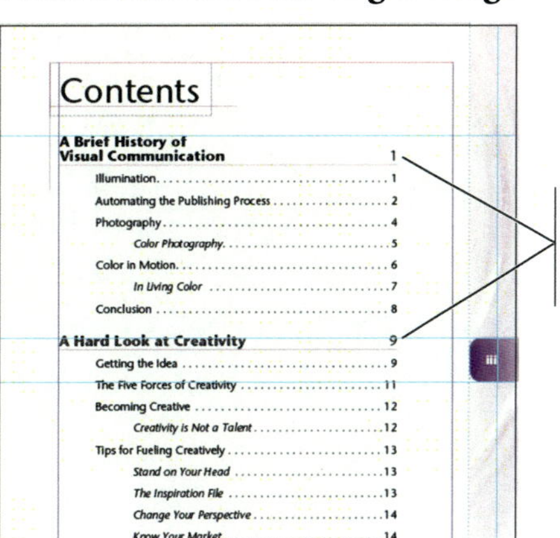

   Contents

   A Brief History of Visual Communication . . . 1
   Illumination . . . 1
   Automating the Publishing Process . . . 2
   Photography . . . 4
   Color Photography . . . 5
   Color in Motion . . . 6
   In Living Color . . . 7
   Conclusion . . . 8
   A Hard Look at Creativity . . . 9
   Getting the Idea . . . 9
   The Five Forces of Creativity . . . 11
   Becoming Creative . . . 12
   Creativity Is Not a Talent . . . 12
   Tips for Fueling Creatively . . . 13
   Stand on Your Head . . . 13
   The Inspiration File . . . 13
   Change Your Perspective . . . 14
   Know Your Market . . . 14

   When the update process is complete, the chapter titles appear in the compiled list.

9. **Save your changes and close the document.**

10. **Save the book file and continue to the next stage of the project.**

Note:

Be careful when building a table of contents for an InDesign book. For a book TOC to function properly, the styles must be consistent in every chapter file. In other words, you shouldn't format second-level headings with "Head 2" in one chapter, "H2" in another chapter, and "Heading 2" in other chapters. If you do, the TOC has to include all three of those styles as separate list items.

Capitalization counts, too; when building a table of contents, "Head 2" is not the same as "head 2."

Stage 3 Building an Index

An index is a map to a publication's contents, providing the reader with an easy reference to specific content. As with tables of contents and other lists, creating an index used to be an extremely time-consuming and labor-intensive process. A professional indexer was hired to read each hard-copy page of a document, write down index entries and page numbers, manually compile the final alphabetized list, and typeset that list into the document. Any changes after the index was finished meant the entire document had to be rechecked manually.

InDesign includes an Index tool that manages and automates part of the indexing process, improving the production workflow and saving considerable time when changes are inevitably made. Nonetheless, the process of identifying relevant terms and tagging them for inclusion in the index must still be done manually. Despite the manual nature of the process, some advance planning can make your indexing life easier. Indexing involves a number of styles, which you *should* plan in advance (although you can always change the style definitions later in the process):

- Paragraph styles for index headings (if you decide to use them).
- Paragraph styles for up to four levels of index entries. If you don't define these styles in advance, they will be automatically created for you when you generate the index.
- Character styles for the page numbers of each index entry (if you want them to be formatted differently than the paragraph style used for the index entry).
- Character styles for cross-references (if you want them to be formatted differently than the index entry).

Tag Basic and Reversed Index Topics

1. **Double-click color1 in the excerpts Book panel to open that document.**
2. **Choose Window>Type & Tables>Index to open the Index panel.**
3. **On Page 1 of the open document, highlight the word "hieroglyphics" in the middle of the second line of text.**

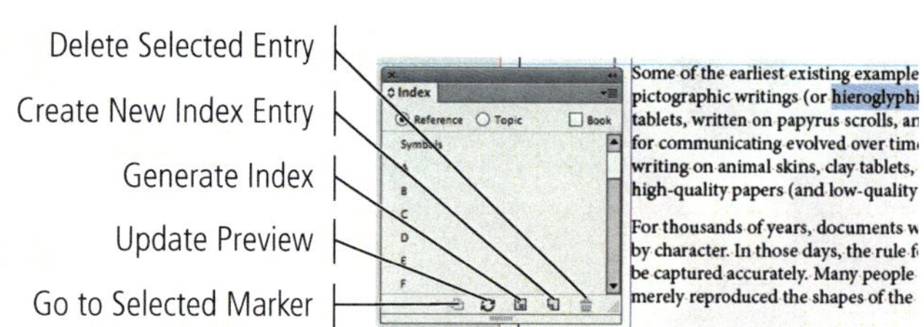

4. **Click the Create New Index Entry button at the bottom of the Index panel.**

   The New Page Reference dialog box shows the highlighted text in the first Topic Levels field.

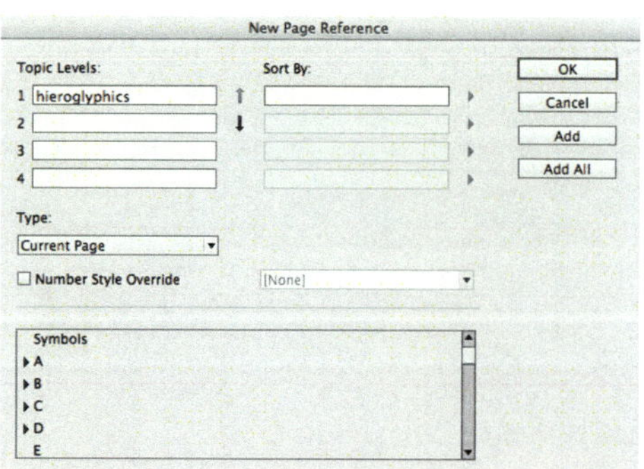

Note:

Reference mode (the default) is used to add index entries in a layout. Topic mode is used to define a list of topics and review the hierarchy of included topics before compiling the index.

5. **Make sure the Type menu is set to Current Page and click OK.**

   You can define a number of different types of index entries; the Current Page option adds a reference to the page number where the text is currently highlighted.

   When you close the New Page Reference dialog box, you see that the highlighted text is preceded by a large carat character. This nonprinting character is an **index marker** — it indicates the location of a tagged reference, but it will not appear in the output job.

6. **In the Index panel, click the arrow to the left of the "H", and then click the arrow to the left of the word "hieroglyphics".**

   You can see that the topic was added using the text in the Topic Levels field, and the reference was added with the Current Page number of the highlighted text.

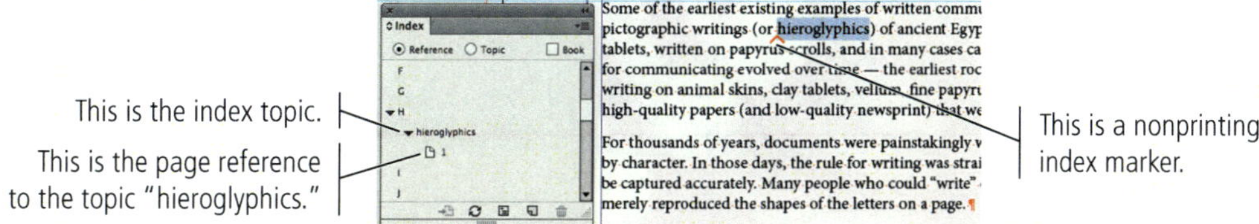

7. **Click the arrow to collapse the "H" section of the Index panel.**

8. **Highlight the word "papyrus" in the next line.**
   Macintosh: Press Command-Option-Shift-Left Bracket ([).
   Windows: Press Control-Alt-Shift-Left Bracket ([).

   Using this key command, you can add a new Current Page reference without opening the New Page Reference dialog box.

9. **In the Index panel, expand the "P" list and the "papyrus" topic.**

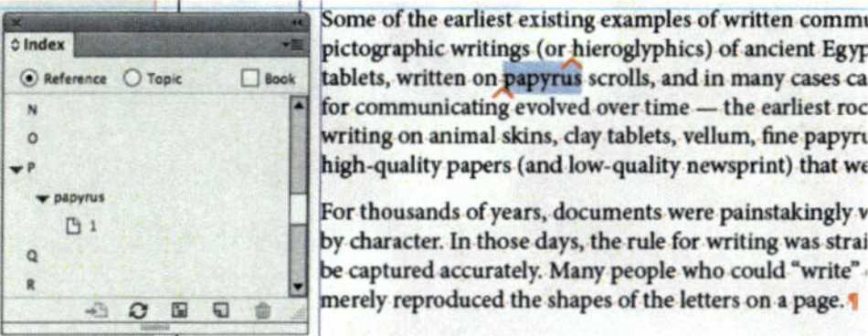

10. **Create new Current Page references to "rock carvings", "clay tablets", and "vellum" in the same paragraph.**

11. **On Page 2 of the document, highlight the words "Johannes Gutenberg" in the second line of the first paragraph after the "Automating…" heading.**

12. **Press Command-Option-Shift-] or Control-Alt-Shift-] to add a reversed topic reference to this name.**

13. **In the Index panel, expand the "G" list and the nested index topic.**

    The reference for index markers is always the current page unless you intentionally change the reference type in the New Page Reference dialog box.

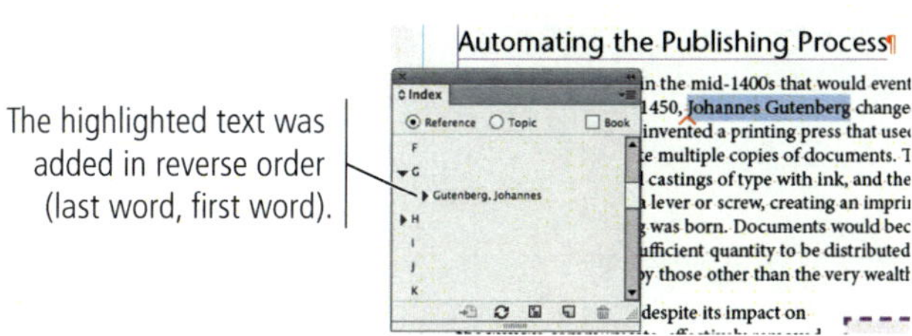

Note:

If text is highlighted, Command-Option-Shift-[(Macintosh) or Control-Alt-Shift-[(Windows) adds the highlighted text to the topic list and places an index marker for the selected text without opening the New Page Reference dialog box.

14. **On Page 4 of the layout, highlight the words "William Henry Fox Talbot" in the first line of the second paragraph.**

15. **Press Command-Option-Shift-] or Control-Alt-Shift-] to add a reversed topic reference to this name. Review the entry in the Index panel.**

    Only the last word of the highlighted text is placed before the comma in the index topic.

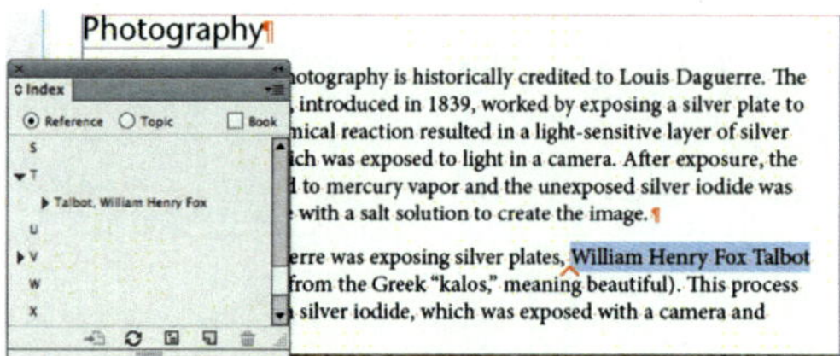

In this case, the index topic is technically correct because some people might look for the last name "Talbot" to find information about this person. Others, however, might look for his full last name ("Fox Talbot"), so you should add another index entry for the same text.

16. **In the text, highlight the space character between the words "Fox" and "Talbot". Choose Type>Insert White Space>Nonbreaking Space.**

> *Note:*
>
> *The key command for a nonbreaking space is Command-Option-X/ Control-Alt-X.*

17. **Highlight the entire name again and press Command-Option-Shift-] or Control-Alt-Shift-] to add a reversed topic reference to this name. Review the entry in the Index panel.**

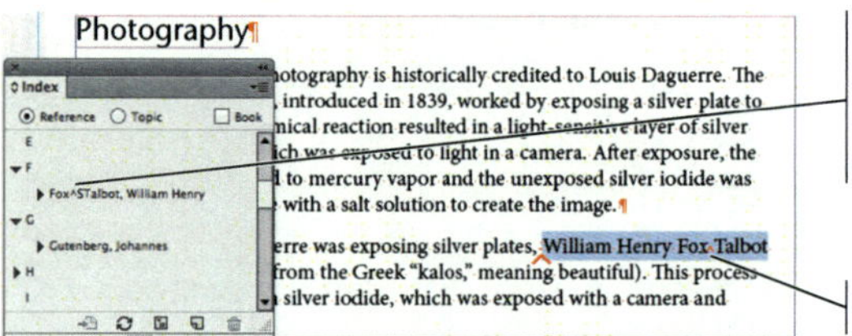

^S is the special code for a nonbreaking space. InDesign properly translates this code when it builds an index.

Nonbreaking space character

18. **Scan the text of the document and add Current Page index entries to all people mentioned in the chapter. Add all names in reverse order, using nonbreaking spaces as necessary to keep compound last names together.**

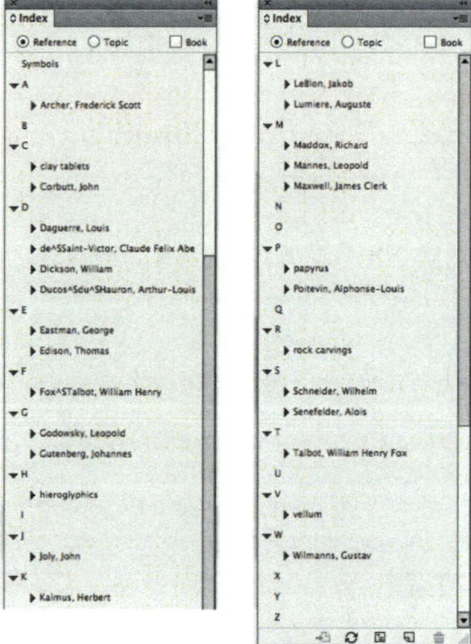

19. **Save the document and continue to the next exercise.**

Add Multiple Page References

In some cases, you need to add multiple references to a specific index topic. Rather than searching through the text to find every instance of the topic, you can use the Add All button in the New Page Reference dialog box.

1. **With the colorl file open from the excerpts Book panel, navigate to Page 3 of the layout.**

2. **Highlight the word "Printing" at the beginning of the first full paragraph, then click the Create New Index Entry button at the bottom of the Index panel.**

3. **In the New Page Reference dialog box, click the Add All button.**

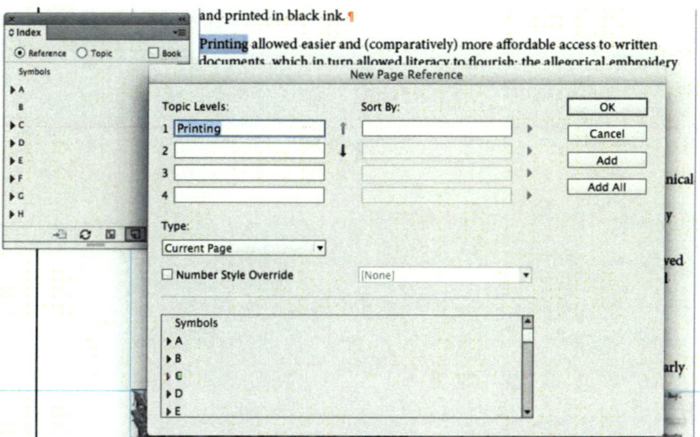

> ***Note:***
>
> *After you click Add or Add All in the New Page Reference dialog box, the OK button changes to Done.*

4. **Click Done to close the New Page Reference dialog box.**

5. **In the Index panel, expand the "Printing" topic in the "P" list.**

   When creating an index, topics are case-sensitive. "Printing" is not the same as "printing." The word "Printing" is capitalized only once in the layout, so the Add All function added only one reference to the topic "Printing".

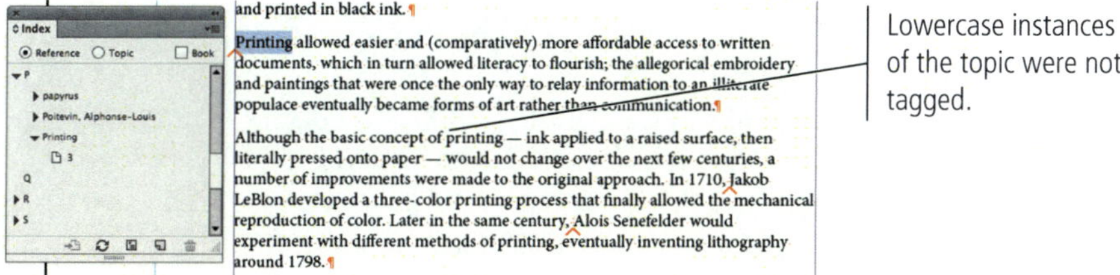

6. **Highlight the word "printing" in the first line of the second full paragraph and click the Create New Index Entry button.**

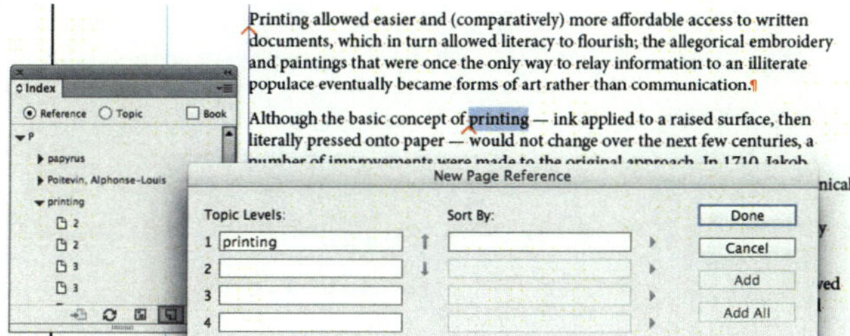

7. **In the New Page Reference dialog box, click the Add All button and then click Done.**

8. **Review the new topic and references in the Index panel.**

Your index now includes two references to the same term, one capitalized and one lowercase. This is not good practice, so you need to combine the two terms.

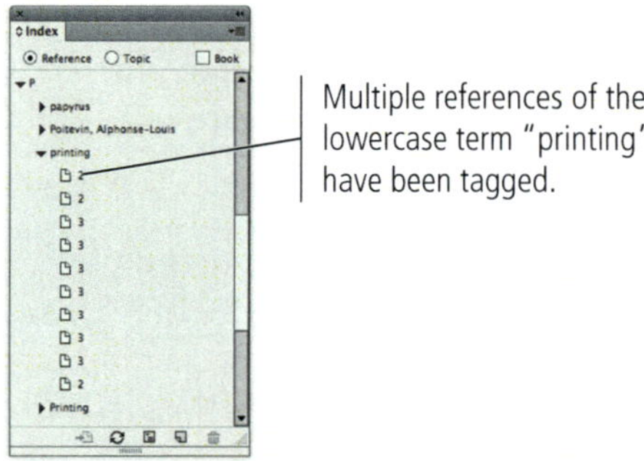

9. **In the Index panel, double-click the capitalized "Printing" topic.**

Double-clicking a term in the panel opens the Topic Options dialog box.

10. **In the pane at the bottom of the dialog box, expand the "P" list.**

This pane shows all topics currently used in the document or book. In this case, you are working with an InDesign book; topics defined in the other book files (such as "Perspective") are also included in the topic list.

11. **Double-click "printing" in the topic list.**

Double-clicking an existing topic changes the text in the Topic Levels field.

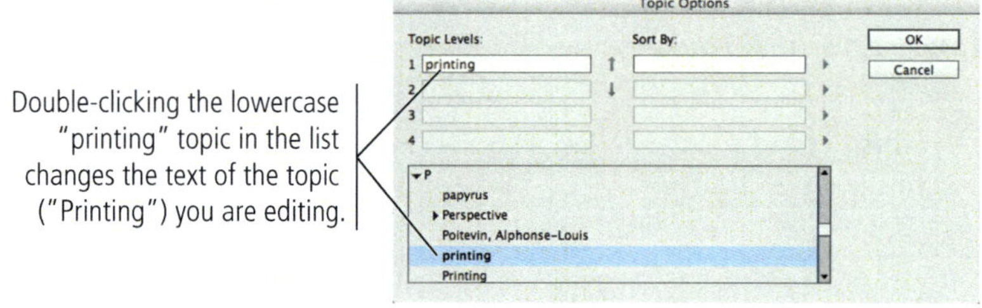

This method of choosing an existing topic also works in the New Page Reference dialog box. When you double-click a topic in the list at the bottom of the dialog box, text in the Topic Levels field changes to reflect the topic you double-click. The index marker will be placed at the location of the highlighted text, but the reference will be added for whatever was shown in the Topic Levels field.

12. **Click OK to close the dialog box, and then review the "P" list in the Index panel.**

Your index now includes a single reference to the term "printing." The page reference for the previously capitalized term has been merged into the references for the lowercase term.

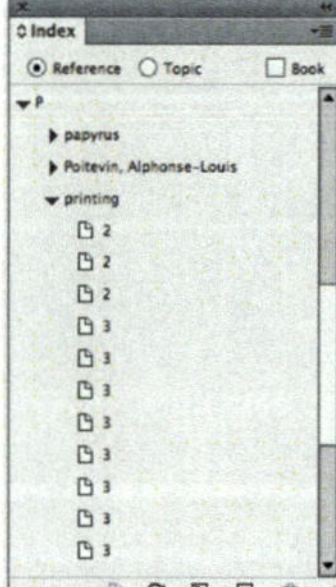

13. **Save the file and continue to the next exercise.**

Changing Index Topic Sort Order

The Sort By field allows you to change the alphabetical order of an index topic in the built index. When the index is built, the entries will appear in the list based on the Sort By text, but the entry text will still be the text defined in the Topic Levels field.

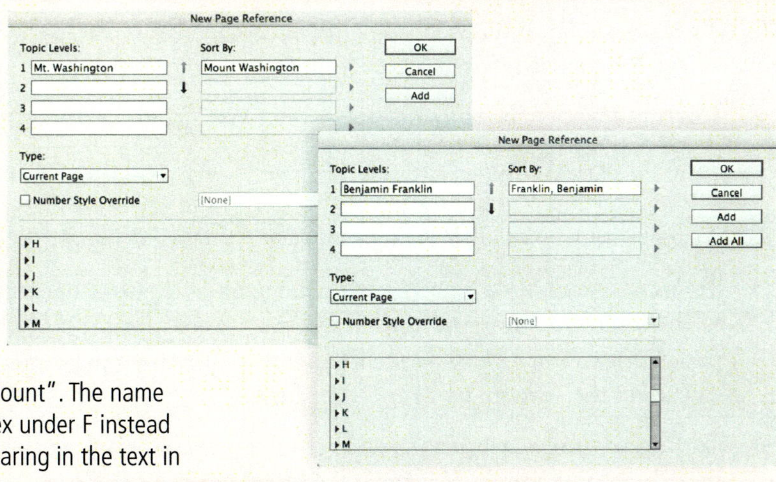

This option is particularly useful for indexing abbreviations and proper names. In the examples shown here, the abbreviated text "Mt." will be alphabetized according to the full word "Mount". The name "Benjamin Franklin" will appear in the index under F instead of B —alphabetized by last name but appearing in the text in standard first name/last name order.

Reversing Index Entries

In addition to changing the sort order of a name, you can also change the actual order of the highlighted words when you add an entry to the index. When text is selected, pressing Command-Option-Shift-] (Macintosh) or Control-Alt-Shift-] (Windows) adds a reversed index entry without opening the New Page Reference dialog box. Using this key command, the highlighted text is added as an entry with the format "last word, comma, all other words".

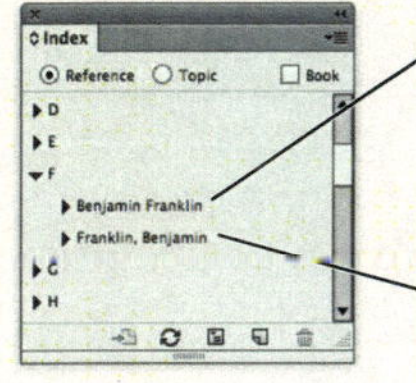

This entry was added with the text reversed in the Sort By field.

This entry was added by highlighting the text and pressing Command-Option-Shift-] (Macintosh) or Control-Alt-Shift-] (Windows).

If the text "Benjamin Franklin" is highlighted, for example, using this key command will add a reference to the term "Franklin, Benjamin." In this case, the added topic will appear in the built index with the reversed text instead of simply re-alphabetized based on the reversed Sort By text.

Compound nouns that are not hyphenated can cause problems. "Martin Luther King Jr.", for example, would be added as "Jr., Martin Luther King". Very few people would look for this reference in the "J" section of an index, and the point of an index is to be useable. To prevent this type of reference, you can change the text to a nonbreaking space between two words in the selection. With the nonbreaking space between "King" and "Jr.", the reversed index entry would be "King Jr., Martin Luther".

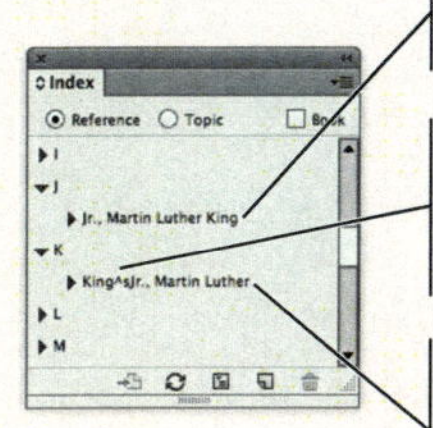

This entry was added in reverse without changing the highlighted text.

^S is the special code for a nonbreaking space. InDesign properly translates this code when it builds an index.

To create this entry, we replaced the standard space between "King" and "Jr." with a nonbreaking space.

Add Page-Range References

Index references are not limited to single page numbers. You can use the Type menu in the New Page Reference dialog box to define several other reference types:

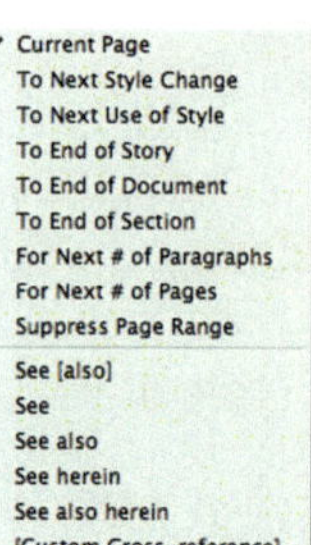

- **Current Page** includes a single-page reference for the index entry.
- **To Next Style Change** creates a page-range reference that starts at the location of the insertion point and ends at the first point where a different paragraph style has been applied in the text.
- **To Next Use of Style** creates a page-range reference that starts at the location of the insertion point and ends at the first instance in the story where a specific paragraph style has been applied in the text. When you choose this option, you can select the style that will end the range.
- **To End of Story** creates a page-range reference that starts at the location of the insertion point and ends at the last page of the current story.
- **To End of Document** creates a page-range reference that starts at the location of the insertion point and ends at the last page of the current document.
- **To End of Section** creates a page-range reference that starts at the location of the insertion point and ends at the last page of the current section.
- **For Next # of Paragraphs** creates a page-range reference that starts at the location of the insertion point and ends after the defined number of paragraphs.
- **For Next # of Pages** creates a page-range reference that starts at the location of the insertion point and ends after the defined number of pages.
- **Suppress Page Range** creates a topic reference with no associated page number.

1. **With the `color1` file open from the `excerpts` Book panel, navigate to Page 1 of the layout.**
2. **Highlight the word "History" in the chapter title and click the Create New Index Entry button in the Index panel.**
3. **In the New Page Reference dialog box, change the capital "H" in the first Topic Levels field to a lowercase "h".**
4. **Choose To End of Document in the Type menu and click the Add button.**

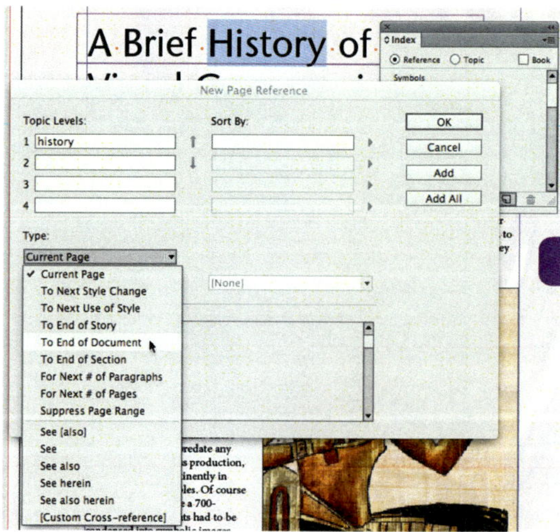

5. **Click Done to close the dialog box and then review the new topic and reference in the Index panel.**

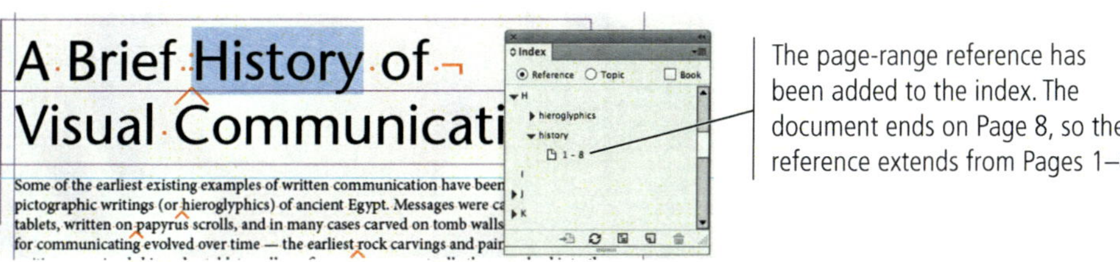

The page-range reference has been added to the index. The document ends on Page 8, so the reference extends from Pages 1–8.

6. **Highlight the word "Illumination" in the heading on Page 1 and click the Create New Index Entry button.**

7. **In the Type menu, choose To Next Use of Style. In the related Style menu, choose head 1.**

   This heading is formatted with the head 1 style. You are adding a reference that spans all text between this heading and the next instance of the head 1 style.

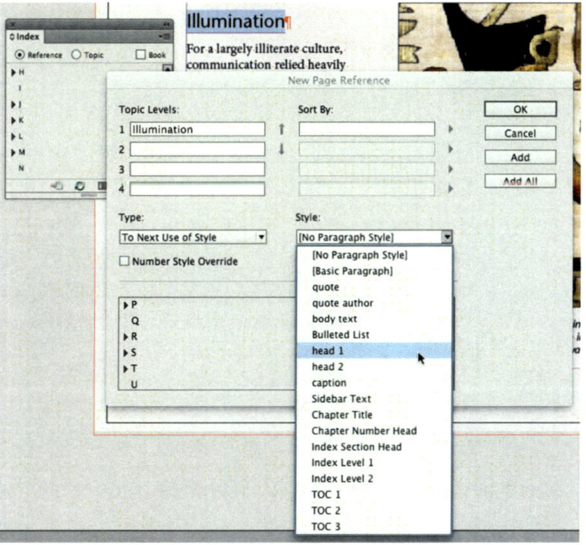

8. **Click Add, and then click Done to close the dialog box.**

9. **Review the new topic and reference in the Index panel.**

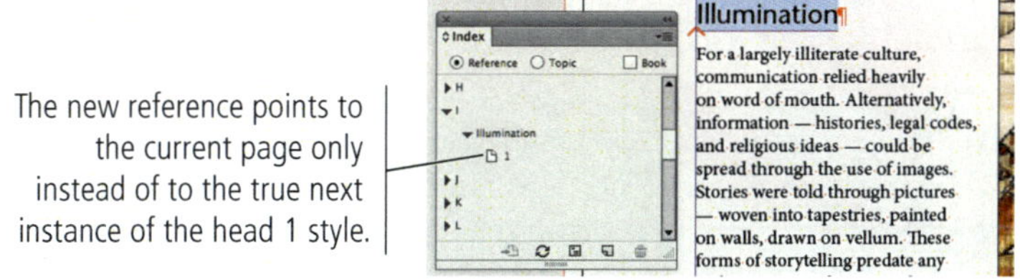

The new reference points to the current page only instead of to the true next instance of the head 1 style.

This problem highlights an apparent bug in the software or at least something that does not work intuitively. When you highlight text formatted with the same style defined in the To Next Use of Style menu, InDesign identifies the highlighted text as the next use of the style — the reference points to the location of the highlighted text only. Solving this problem requires a workaround.

10. **In the Index panel, click the "1" reference to the "Illumination" topic and click the panel's Delete button.**

11. **In the resulting message, click Yes to confirm the deletion.**

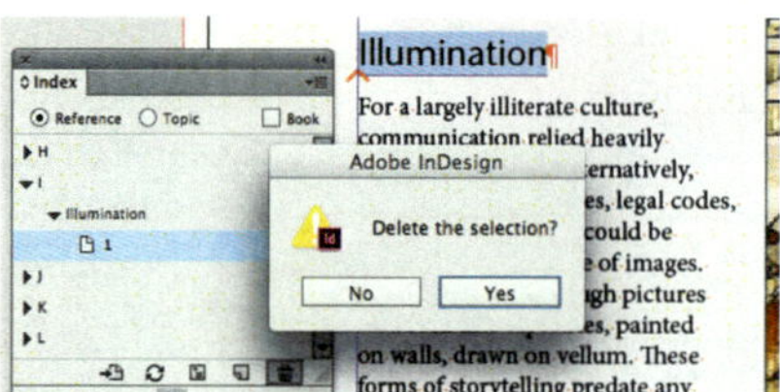

12. **In the document, highlight the word "For" at the beginning of the paragraph after the Illumination heading.**

13. **Click the Create New Index Entry button in the Index panel.**

14. **In the lower half of the dialog box, expand the "I" list of topics and double-click the word "Illumination" in the list of topics.**

    As in the Topic Options dialog box, this method changes the current text in the Topic Levels field to the topic you double-click in the list.

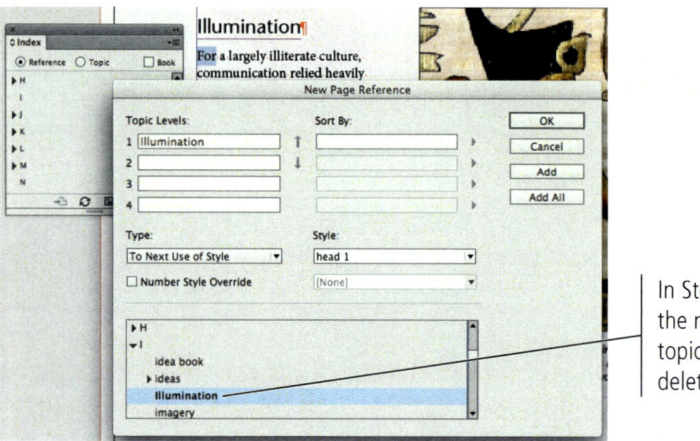

In Step 10 you deleted the reference to this topic, but you did not delete the topic itself.

15. **In the Type menu, choose To Next Use of Style. In the related Style menu, choose head 1.**

16. **Click Add, and then click Done to close the dialog box.**

17. **Review the new topic and reference in the Index panel.**

    The new reference shows the correct range between the selected text and the next instance of the head 1 paragraph style (on Page 2 of the document).

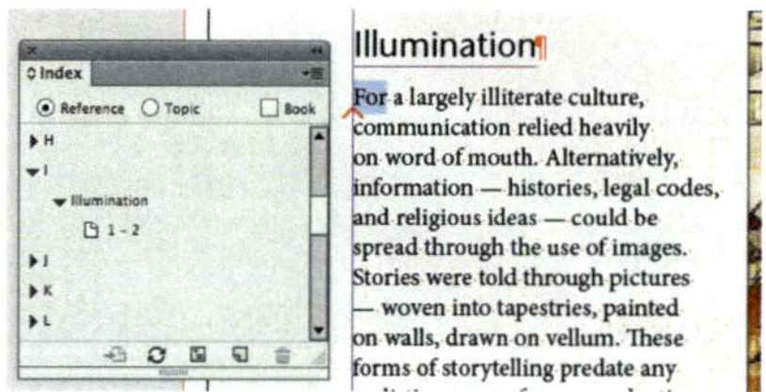

18. **Save the file and continue to the next exercise.**

Note:

If you use this workaround technique, you can simply type to replace the text in the Topic Levels field with the topic you want to reference. For this technique to work correctly, you can — but don't have to — select from the existing topics.

Note:

You can delete an entire topic from the index by selecting it in the panel and clicking the Delete button. If you delete a term from the index, all references to that term are also deleted.

Add Multiple-Level References

You might have noticed that the New Page Reference dialog box includes four fields in the Topic Levels area. These fields allow you to created multi-level or nested index entries. You can create up to four levels of nested index entries, depending on the complexity a particular project requires.

1. **With the color1 file open through the excerpts Book panel, navigate to Page 4 of the layout.**

2. **Highlight the words "daguerreotype method" in the second line of the first paragraph. Click the Create New Index Entry button in the Index panel.**

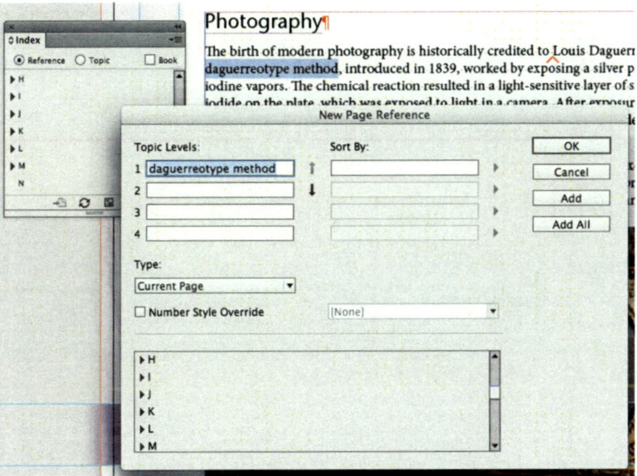

3. **In the New Page Reference dialog box, click the down-arrow button in the Topic Levels area.**

   This button moves the selected term down one level to become a second-level index term. Of course, when you add a second-level term, you also need to define the parent term for that nested entry.

Adding Cross-References in an Index

INDESIGN FOUNDATIONS

A cross-referenced item refers the reader to another index entry. For example, the index entry for "CIELAB" might say, "See LAB color." If you choose to create an entry as a cross-reference, you also need to define the type of notation. The Referenced field defines the topic to which a cross-reference will point; you can type in the field or drag an existing topic into the field from the list at the bottom of the dialog box.

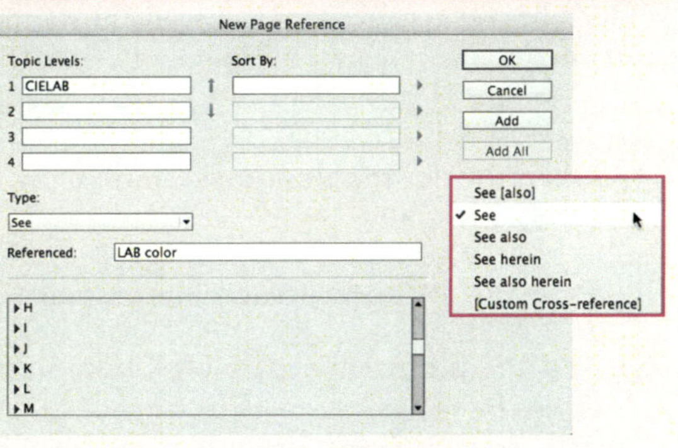

- **See [also]** allows InDesign to choose the appropriate cross-reference method — "See" if the topic has no page references of its own, or "See also" if the topic includes page numbers.
- **See** refers the reader to another topic or topics; the entry has no page number, only text listing the cross-referenced topic. For example, if the index entry is "Dogs", the cross-reference might be "See Canine".
- **See also** directs attention to the current topic, as well as other information elsewhere in the index. For example, an index item called "Dogs" may have its own list of page numbers, and then a cross-reference to "See also Pets".
- **See herein** and **See also herein** refer the reader to entries within the current index entry. For example, if the main (Level 1) index entry is "Dogs", you might want to direct the index to a subentry (Level 2 or Level 3 item) that might not be expected under this heading, such as "See herein Wolf".
- **[Custom Cross-Reference]** allows you to define the text that will be used as the cross-reference, such as "Go to" or some similar text.

4. **Click the first Topic Levels field and type photographs.**

   You can select an existing topic as the first level or type a new term in the field.

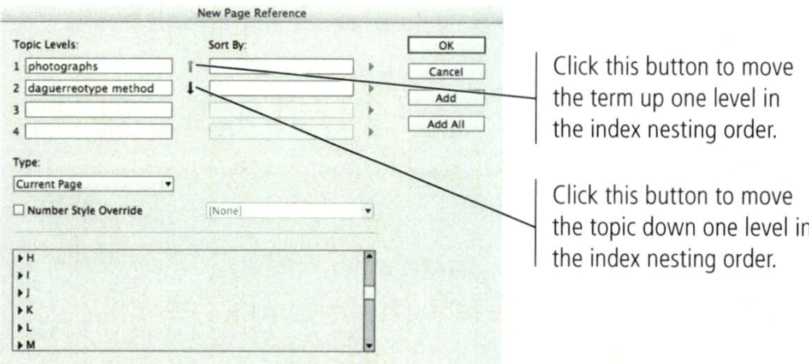

5. **Click OK to add the term and reference to the index.**
6. **In the Index panel, expand the "photographs" entry in the "P" list.**
7. **Within the "photographs" entry, expand the "daguerreotype method" entry.**

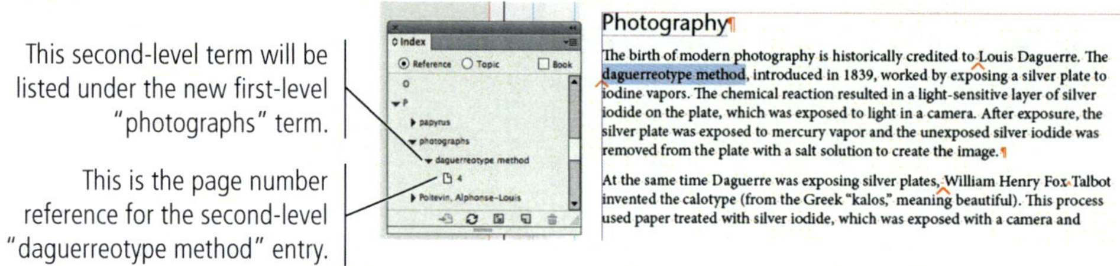

8. **Save the color1 file and close it.**
9. **Save the book file and continue to the next exercise.**

Build the Book's Index

Building an index into a document is very similar to building a table of contents. Once the index has been generated, it is loaded into the cursor so that you can place it in the layout. When you are working with a book file, you can build the index into an existing chapter file, or you can add a separate back matter file to hold the index.

> *Note:*
>
> ***Back matter*** *is anything that comes after the primary chapters of a document, such as appendices and an index.*

1. **Open the companion.indt template from the WIP>Companions folder to create a new file.**
2. **Drag the D-Index Opener master page onto the Page 1 icon.**
3. **Save the file as excerpts back.indd in your WIP>Companions folder and close the file.**
4. **In the excerpts Book panel, make sure nothing is selected in the panel and click the Add Documents button.**
5. **Navigate to the file excerpts back.indd file in your WIP>Companions folder and click Open.**

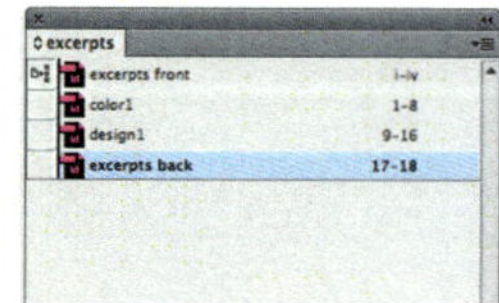

6. **Open the Synchronize Options dialog box from the Book panel Options menu.**

7. **Deselect all options but the Swatches check box. At the bottom of the dialog box, leave the Smart Match Style Groups checked. Click OK.**

   You can use the main check boxes (Other and Styles and Swatches) to deselect all items in the group, and then check only the Swatches check box.

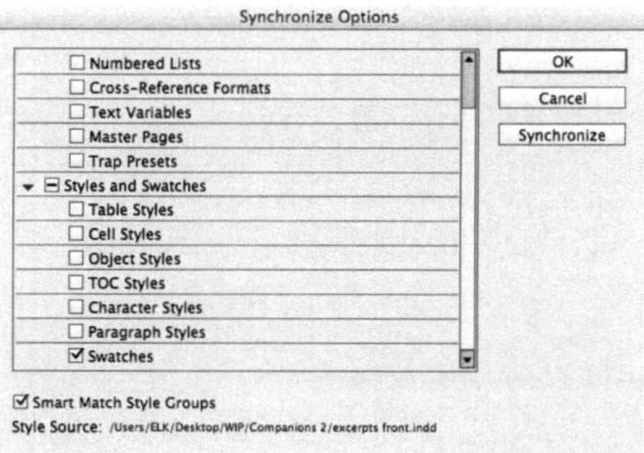

8. **Make sure no files are selected in the Book panel and click the Synchronize button at the bottom of the panel. Click OK to acknowledge that the synchronization is complete.**

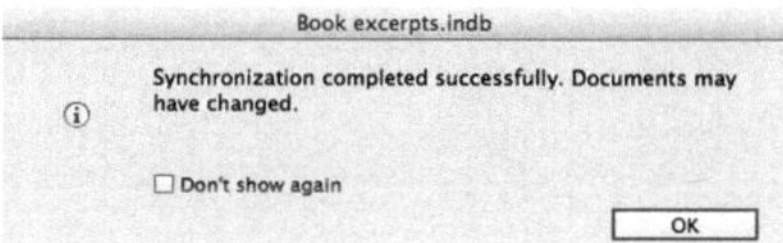

9. **Double-click the `excerpts back` file in the Book panel to open the file.**

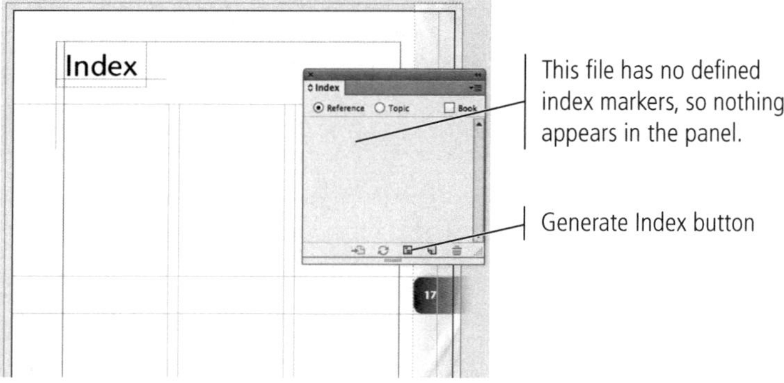

Note:

You can preview all index entries in a book file by opening the individual chapter files and checking the Book option at the top of the Index panel. (The panel only shows entries for files that are currently open.)

10. **At the bottom of the Index panel, click the Generate Index button.**

11. **In the Generate Index dialog box, delete the word "Index" from the Title field.**

    The Title and Title Style options are the same as the related options for building a table of contents. Because the master page you're using already includes the title "Index", you should not include a title in the built index.

12. **Select the Include Book Documents option.**

    Even though there are no index references in this back-matter file, it is part of the book with files that have index markers.

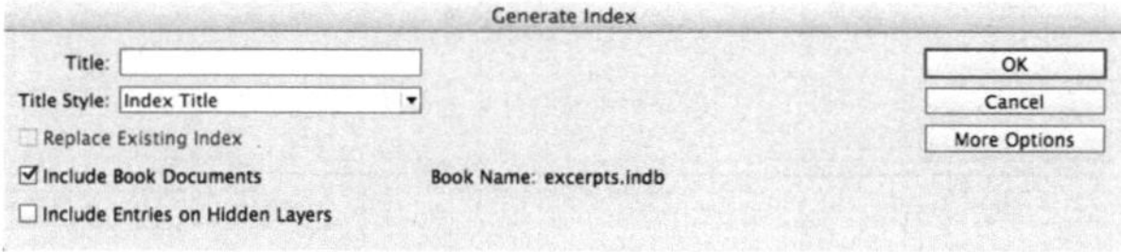

13. **If the third button on the right reads "More Options," click the button to expand the dialog box.**

14. **Review the available options. Click the Following Topic menu and choose Em Space as the character that will appear between the entry text and the associated references.**

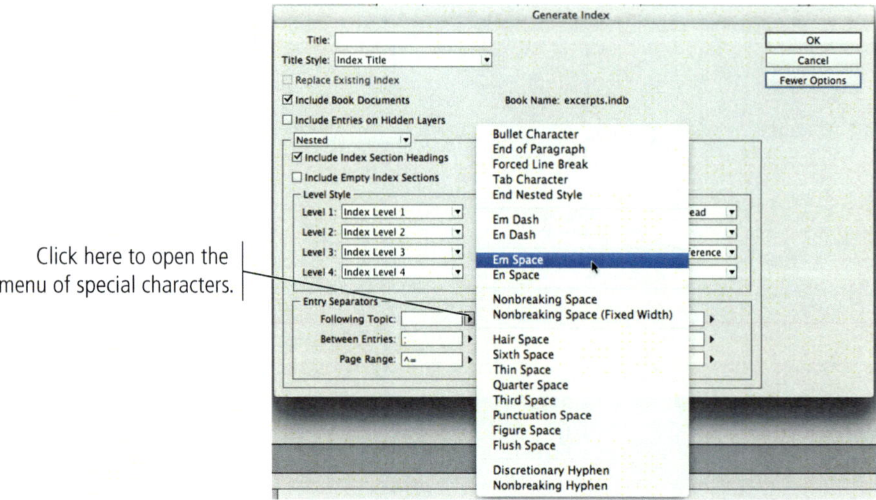

Options for Generating an Index

INDESIGN FOUNDATIONS

When you generate an index, you have a number of options for automatically formatting the compiled list. In many cases, the default settings will work perfectly well, but you can change any or all of the following options as necessary:

- The **Nested** or **Run-in** menu determines how individual entries in the index are placed. Nested creates each entry on its own line. Run-In forces all index entries to run together in the same paragraph.
- If **Include Index Section Headings** is checked, alpha-betical headings (A, B, C, etc.) are added to the index.
- If **Include Empty Index Sections** is checked, all letter headings are added to the built index, even if that letter has no associated terms.
- The **Level Style** menu defines paragraph styles used to format different levels of index entries. If you don't choose different styles in these menus, the default op-tions (Index Level 1, etc.) are created and applied to the headings. (If you define your own style named "Index Level 1," your settings are applied in the built index.)
- The **Section Heading** menu defines paragraph styles used to format the section headings in the index. If you don't choose a different style, the default Index Section Head is created and applied to the headings. (If you define your own style named "Index Section Head," your settings are applied in the built index.)
- The **Page Number** menu defines the character style applied to page numbers in the generated index.
- The **Cross-Reference** menu defines the character style applied to the cross-references in the index (for example, the "See also" part of "See also LAB color").

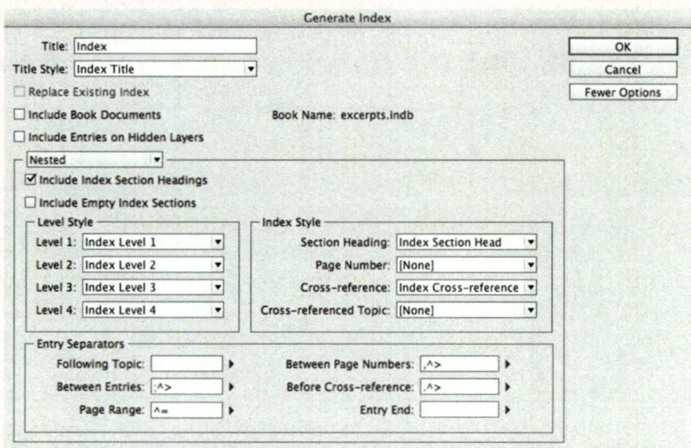

- The **Cross-Referenced Topic** menu defines the char-acter style applied to the text of a cross-reference (for example, the "LAB color" part of "See also LAB color").
- The **Entry Separators** area defines the characters used in specific parts of the index:
  - **Following Topic** is used between the entry text and the entry page references.
  - **Between Page Numbers** is used between individual page references.
  - **Between Entries** is used between entries in a run-in index.
  - **Before Cross-reference** is used before the text of a cross-reference.
  - **Page Range** separates numbers in a page range.
  - **Entry End** is added at the end of individual entries.

15. **Click OK to generate the index. Click the loaded cursor in the three-column text frame to place the index.**

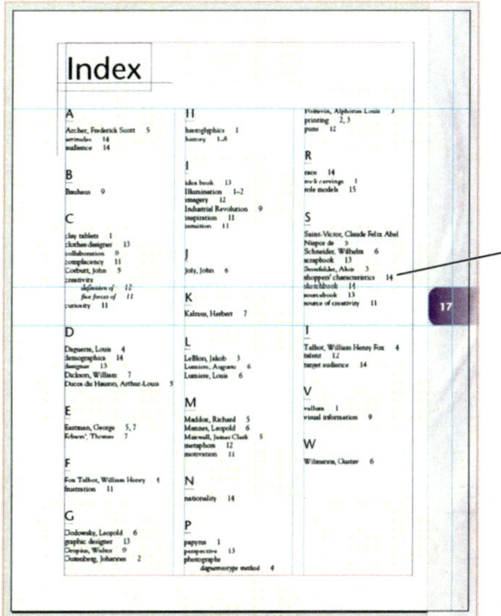

Some of these entries are from the second chapter (the file from the Design Companion); these tags were already created in the file provided by the publisher.

> *Note:*
>
> *Your index might be slightly different than our example depending on which names you added in the previous exercise.*

16. **Save the file and close it.**

17. **Save the book file and continue to the next stage of the project.**

Stage 4 Exporting Book Files

Another advantage of combining multiple files is the ability to output those files all at once — choosing print or export settings once, instead of opening each file and changing the print or export settings individually. Using the Book panel, you can output all chapter files simultaneously, or you can output specific selected chapters.

Export PDF Files for Print and Digital Distribution

Your client asked for two separate files — one that can be printed at high quality and one that can be posted on the company's Web site and sent via email. Because you're working with a single file for the entire book, you can easily create these two output files in a few steps.

1. **With the excerpts Book panel open, click the empty area at the bottom of the panel to deselect all files in the book.**

2. **Choose Export Book to PDF in the panel Options menu.**

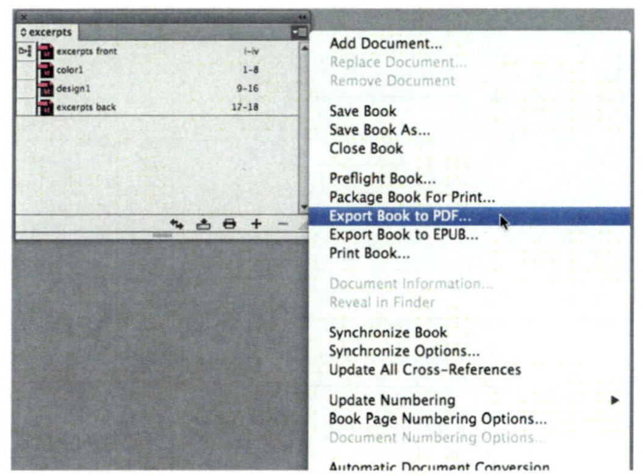

> *Note:*
>
> *If any files are selected, the menu option changes to Export Selected Documents to PDF.*

3. **Navigate to your WIP>Companions folder as the target and change the file name to `excerpts print.pdf`. Choose Adobe PDF (Print) in the Format/ Save As Type menu, and then click Save.**

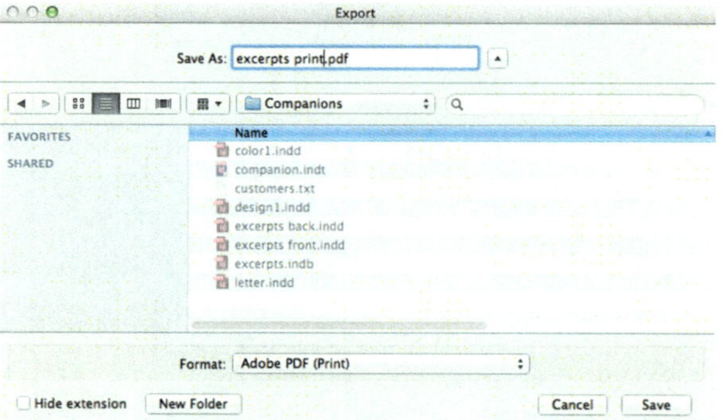

4. **In the Export Adobe PDF dialog box, choose [High Quality Print] in the Adobe PDF Preset menu.**

5. **In the Marks and Bleeds options, check the Crop Marks option. Change the Offset field to 0.125", and change all four Bleed fields to 0.125".**

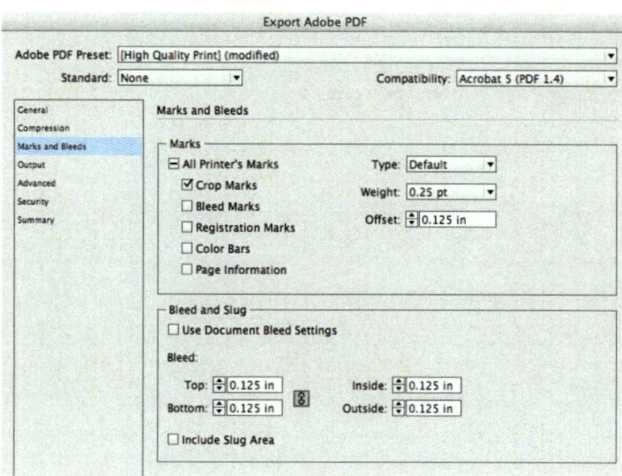

6. **Click Export.**

   Exporting a book does not occur in the background. You have to wait for the export process to finish.

7. **When the export process is complete, choose Export Book to PDF in the Book panel Options menu.**

8. **Choose Adobe PDF (Interactive) in the Format/Save As Type menu. Name the second file `excerpts digital.pdf` and click Save.**

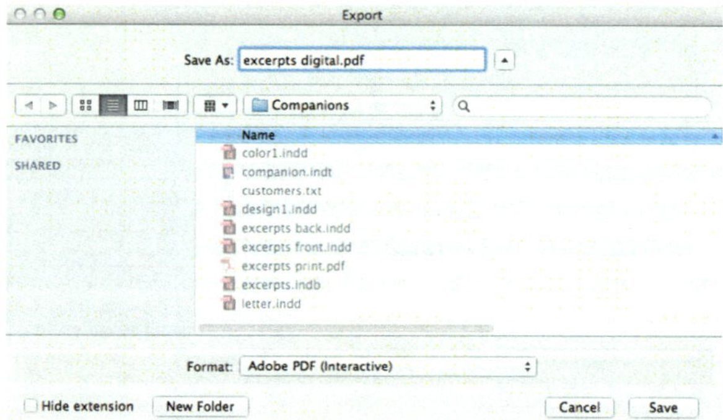

> *Note:*
>
> *In Project 4: Realtor Collateral Booklet, you used the Print Booklet command to output a booklet as printer's spreads for proofing purposes. In most commercial printing workflows, however, the output provider will create the necessary printer's spreads from the individual pages in your exported PDF file. Always consult with your output provider about what you need to supply to efficiently achieve the best possible result.*

9. **Choose the Pages radio button at the top of the dialog box and turn off the Open in Full Screen Mode option. Make sure the View After Exporting option is checked, then click OK.**

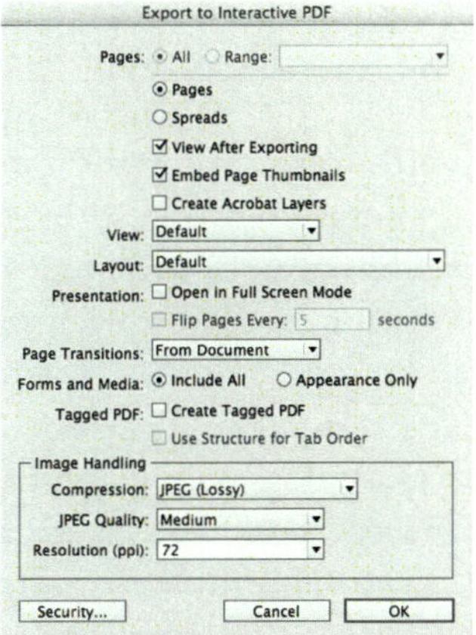

10. **When the PDF file opens, navigate to Page iii of the file. Move your cursor over any of the listings, then click to navigate to that section of the document.**

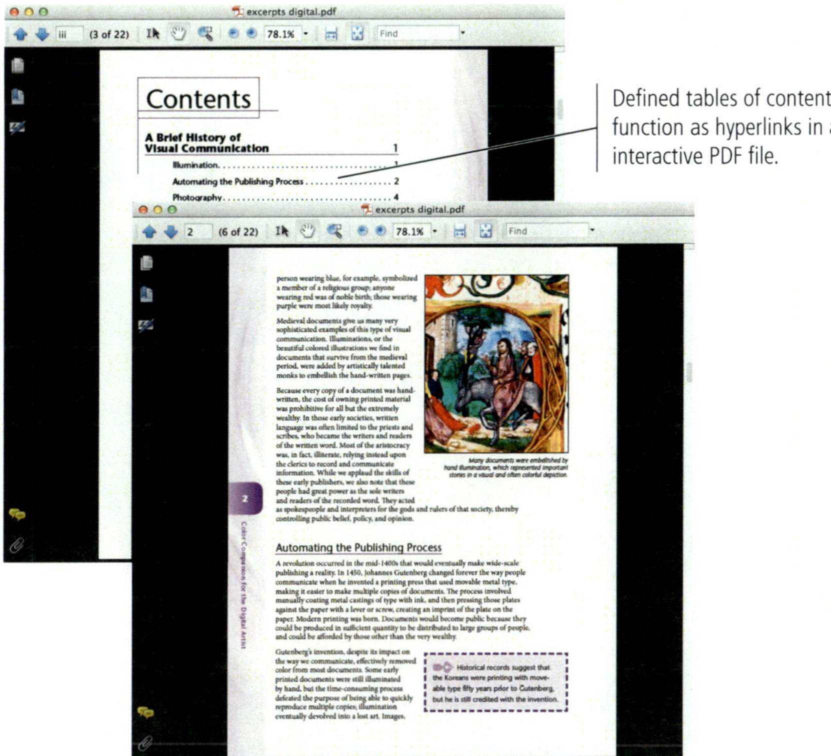

Defined tables of contents function as hyperlinks in an interactive PDF file.

11. **Save the book file and then close it.**

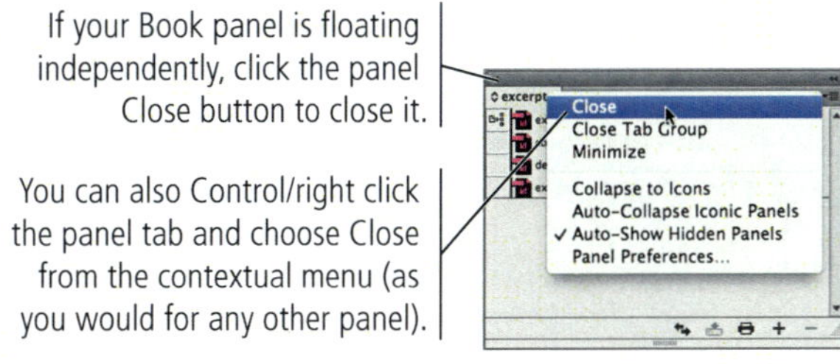

If your Book panel is floating independently, click the panel Close button to close it.

You can also Control/right click the panel tab and choose Close from the contextual menu (as you would for any other panel).

12. **Continue to the next stage of the project.**

Stage 5 Merging Data into an InDesign Layout

For the final stage of this project, you need to create a thank-you note from the publisher to previous clients. This note will be included with the printed copies of the Excerpts booklet when the sample is mailed to the clients. The publisher provided a comma-delimited file with the client mailing addresses; this file also identifies which book each client purchased.

Data merge is a fairly sophisticated utility in most word-processing applications; it allows you to combine text with information stored in a database or spreadsheet (such as a Microsoft Excel file). For example, data merge allows you to write one letter, click a few buttons, and print or export multiple copies of the letter, each with a different mailing address. InDesign's Data Merge capabilities can be used for this type of personal letter generation, but — with a bit of advance planning — it can also be used for more sophisticated database-driven layouts such as catalogs with graphics.

> ***Note:***
>
> *Variable database printing is currently one of the hottest topics in the graphic design and printing industries.*

Personalized printing uses data to produce items such as catalogs that specifically target your interests. Other applications for personalized printing include newspaper inserts for a specific region. A national company might create a single weekly sale advertisement with one page that varies according to the local distribution; why, for example, would a company want to advertise snow shovels in southern California?

InDesign's Data Merge feature makes it fairly simple to create a layout incorporating variable data. Once the data source file has been established, you can create any layout you want, add the data, and create multiple versions of a finished layout in one action.

The Data Source File

INDESIGN FOUNDATIONS

If you have a contact manager anywhere on your computer, you are familiar with the idea of a simple database. A database is made up of **fields** that contain information. Each field has a **field name**, which is usually descriptive text that defines the contents of the field. Each listing in a database is called a **record**; each record contains every field in the database (even if a particular field contains no information for a given record).

In the following example, Name, Address, and Telephone are all fields. The first line of the file contains the field names "Name," "Address," and "Telephone Number." Each record appears on a separate line.

Name	Address	Telephone Number
James Smith	123 Anywhere St., Someplace, MI 99999	800-555-0000
Susan Jones	3208 Street Ct., Small Town, ID 55555	800-555-8888

InDesign's Data Merge feature does not interact directly with a database application. Data must first be exported from a database into a tab- or comma-delimited ASCII text file.

In the text file, the information in each field (called a **text string**) is separated by the delimiter (comma or tab), which tells the software that the next text string belongs in the next field. Records are separated by a paragraph return, so each record begins on a new line.

If a particular text string requires one of the delimiter characters — for example, a comma within an address — that string is surrounded by double quotation marks in the text file.

A comma contained within quotation marks is treated as a text character, not as a delimiter.

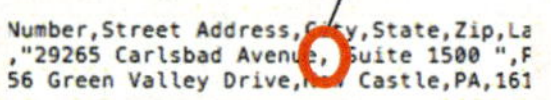

The first line of the text file should list the field names. If your database application does not export field names as the first line of the text-only file, you need to open the file in a text editor and add the field name line at the beginning.

Create the Merged Document and Load the Source Data

The target document for a data merge needs to include placeholders or locations where the data will appear after the data merge is complete. Once you have established the data source for the InDesign file, you can easily create these placeholders anywhere in the document.

1. **Open the file `letter.indd` from your WIP>Companions folder.**

   Your client wrote this letter using her InDesign letterhead template. She used all capital letters to indicate where she wants database information to be added in the letter text.

2. **Choose Window>Utilities>Data Merge to open the Data Merge panel.**

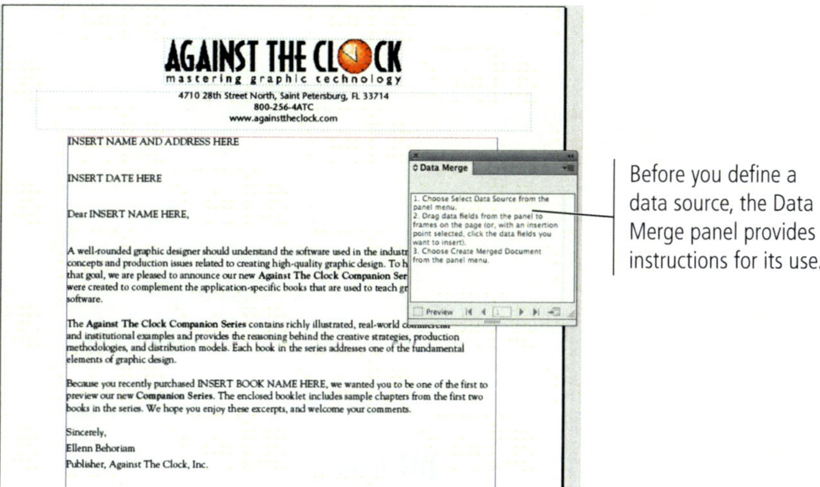

Before you define a data source, the Data Merge panel provides instructions for its use.

3. **Open the Data Merge panel Options menu and choose Select Data Source.**

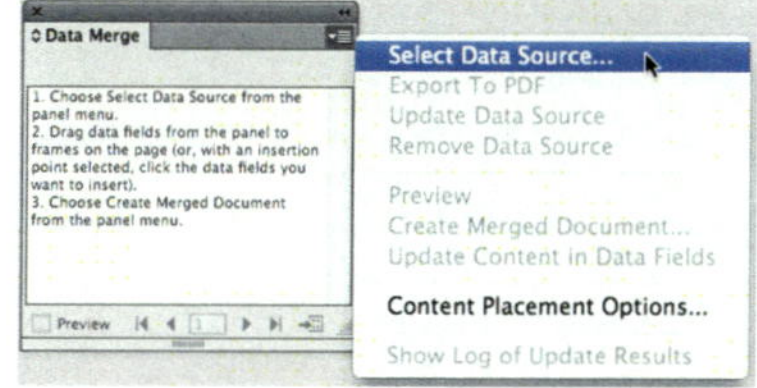

4. **Navigate to the file `customers.txt` in your WIP>Companions folder and click Open.**

   When the file is processed, the available fields (defined by the first line in the data file) are listed in the Data Merge panel.

The T icons indicate that these fields are text strings.

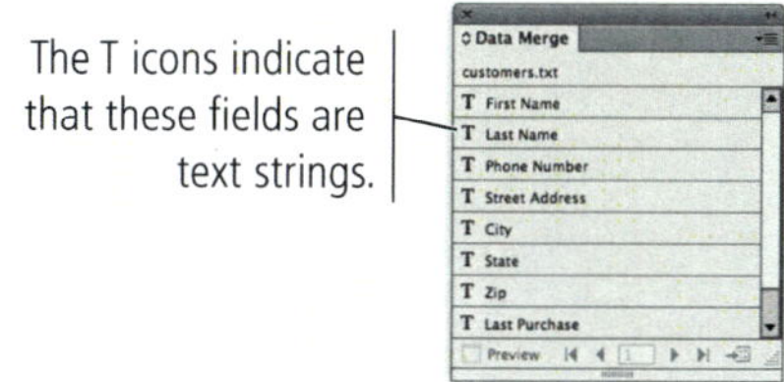

5. **In the document, turn on hidden characters (Type>Show Hidden Characters).**

6. **Highlight the first line in the letter (excluding the paragraph return character), and then double-click the First Name item in the Data Merge panel.**

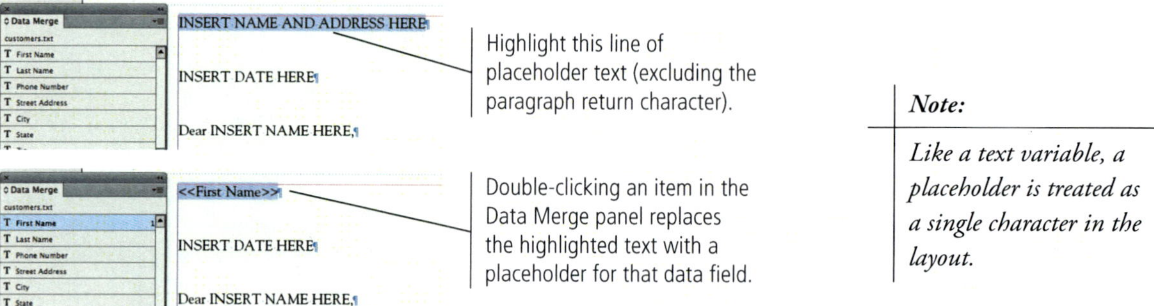

> ***Note:***
>
> *Like a text variable, a placeholder is treated as a single character in the layout.*

7. **Click to place the insertion point after the placeholder. Press the Spacebar, and then double-click the Last Name item in the Data Merge panel.**

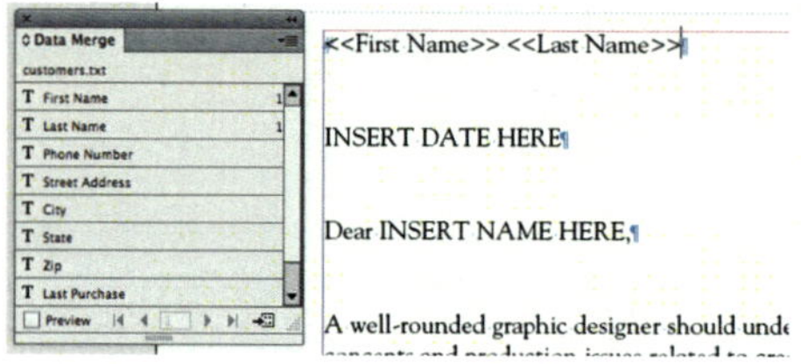

Cleaning up Data

Placeholders are made up of the field name enclosed within double brackets, such as <<Name>>, inserted anywhere in the target document.

<<Name>>
<<Address>>

Dear <<Name>>,

Congratulations! We are writing to inform you that your house at <<Address>> has been selected for a free facelift!

Once data from the source file has been merged into the document, it looks like this:

James Smith
123 Anywhere St., Someplace, MI 99999

Dear James Smith,

Congratulations! We are writing to inform you that your house at 123 Anywhere St., Someplace, MI 99999 has been selected for a free facelift!

The same document is reproduced for every record in the text file, personalizing each copy of the letter for the intended recipient.

Notice that the address is entirely on one line of text, and that the "Dear" line includes the person's whole name — not a tremendous improvement over "Dear Occupant."

You should make sure your data includes the exact information you need. The previous example would benefit greatly from a different arrangement:

First_Name,Last_Name,Street_Address,City,State,Zip

James,Smith,"123 Anywhere St.",Someplace,MI,99999

The target file can then appear much more personal. Placeholders can be positioned with text characters (including spaces) in between to make the document more personal:

<<First_Name>> <<Last_Name>>
<<Street Address>>
<<City>, <<State>> <<Zip>>

Dear <<First_Name>>,

Congratulations! We are writing to inform you that your house at <<Street_Address>> has been selected for a free facelift!

Once data from the source file has been merged into this version, it looks like this:

James Smith
123 Anywhere St.
Someplace, MI 99999

Dear James,

Congratulations! We are writing to inform you that your house at 123 Anywhere St. has been selected for a free facelift!

You could also include a title field, which would allow you to address the letter as "Dear <<title>> <<last name>>", which would result in "Dear Mr. Smith" instead of the less-formal "Dear James".

8. **Press Return/Enter to start a new paragraph in the document and then double-click the Street Address item in the Data Merge panel.**

9. **Press Return/Enter again. Add the City, State, and Zip fields on the third line, separated by the appropriate punctuation and spaces.**

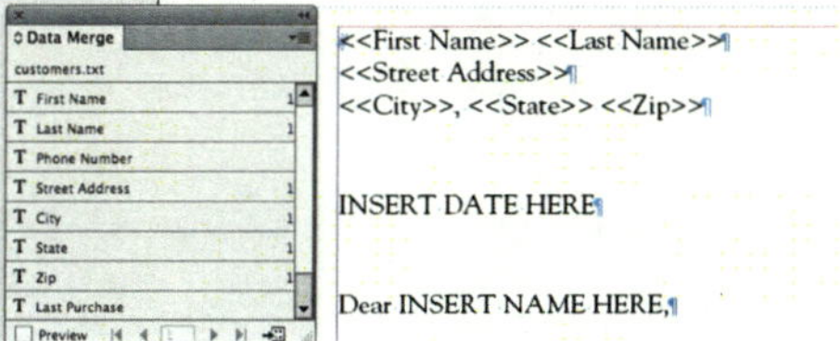

10. **Highlight the All Caps text in the salutation line, and then replace it with the First Name data field placeholder.**

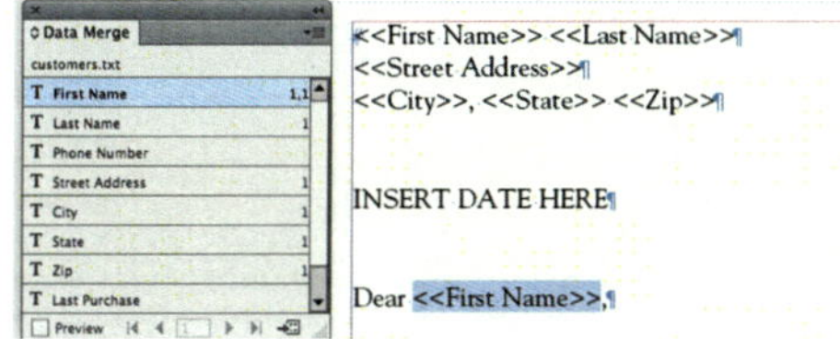

11. **In the third paragraph of the letter, replace the All Caps text with the Last Purchase data field placeholder.**

12. **With the Last Purchase placeholder selected, change the font to ATC Pyrite Italic.**

After placeholders have been entered in the document, you can apply text and paragraph formatting as you would for any other text element.

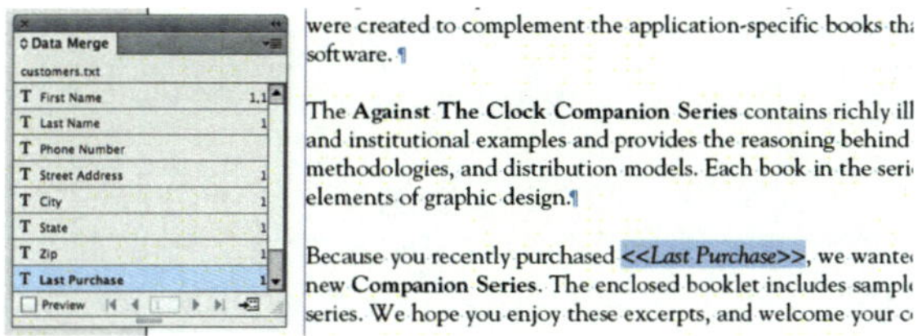

13. **Highlight the text "INSERT DATE HERE" and type today's date.**

14. **Save the file and continue to the next exercise.**

> ***Note:***
>
> *Highlighting a few letters in any field name (in the document) automatically highlights the entire field name, including the brackets.*

> ***Note:***
>
> *If you were going to re-use this letter, you might consider using a type variable for the date instead of typing an actual date.*

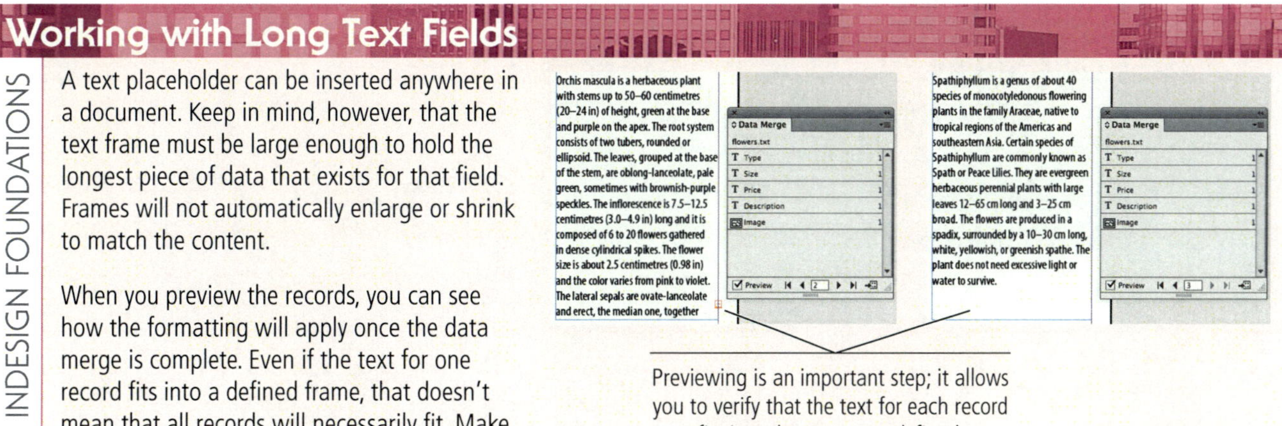

Working with Long Text Fields

INDESIGN FOUNDATIONS

A text placeholder can be inserted anywhere in a document. Keep in mind, however, that the text frame must be large enough to hold the longest piece of data that exists for that field. Frames will not automatically enlarge or shrink to match the content.

When you preview the records, you can see how the formatting will apply once the data merge is complete. Even if the text for one record fits into a defined frame, that doesn't mean that all records will necessarily fit. Make sure a text frame is large enough to fit the longest possible record field.

Previewing is an important step; it allows you to verify that the text for each record fits into the space you defined.

Incorporating Images in a Data Merge

A data source file is not limited to text; you can also incorporate images in the data source file to create variable images in a layout. If you want to incorporate graphics or images in your data merge, your data source file must include a field that contains the full path to the image, beginning with the drive name where the image resides (called an **absolute path**). In the field names, the name of the image field should start with the "@" symbol (for example, "@image").

The absolute path for an image tells the Data Merge processor where to find the necessary file. On a Macintosh, the components in the path name are separated by colons:

Hard Drive:Pictures:image.tif Mac:Catalog Files:Pictures:sweater.tif

On a Windows computer, the path name begins with the drive letter:

C:\My Documents\Pictures\image.tif D:\Vector files\graph.eps

The only spaces in the path name are those that exist in the name of a file or folder; no spaces should separate any of the backslash or colon characters.

Creating and Controlling Image Placeholders

When a data source includes an image field, the Data Merge panel shows a small picture icon for that field. You can attach an image placeholder to any graphics frame by selecting the frame in the layout and double-clicking the image item in the Data Merge panel.

When you use images from a data source file, you can choose Content Placement Options in the Data Merge panel Options menu to predetermine the appearance of the image in relation to the placeholder frame.

The image placeholder holds the images defined in the image data field.

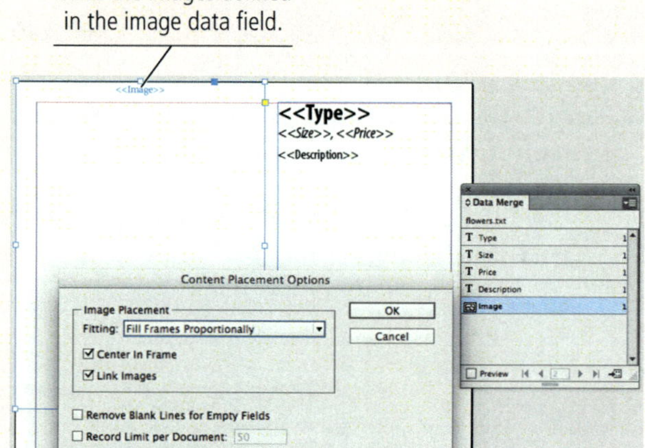

- The **Fitting** menu includes the same options that are available for fitting placed images in a graphics frame.
- If **Center in Frame** is checked, the image is centered within the placeholder frame after the Fitting option has been applied.
- The **Link Images** check box, active by default, links the data source images to the layout that's created when you generate the merged document. If this option is not checked, the images are embedded in the resulting file. (Embedding images drastically increases file size; as a general rule, you should leave the Link Images box checked.)

You can preview variable images just as you preview text. If an image path is incorrect or a file is not in the path defined in the data, you will see a warning when you try to preview that record.

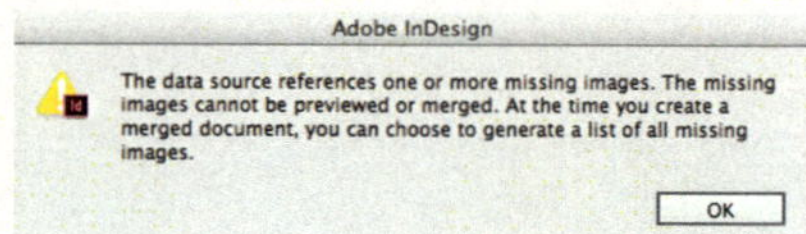

Complete the Merged Document

Once you have created your target document and formatted all the elements, you can preview the data and create the merged document. InDesign uses the data source file and the target layout to create a third document — the merged file. This third file is not linked to the data source; any changes you make to the data are not applied to the merged document. If you change the data file, you have to repeat the merge of the original layout file with the changed data.

1. **With letter.indd open from your WIP>Companions folder, activate the Preview check box at the bottom of the Data Merge panel.**

   You can preview your document at any time by activating the Preview check box in the Data Merge panel. The arrows to the left and right of the record number allow you to move through each record in the merged document.

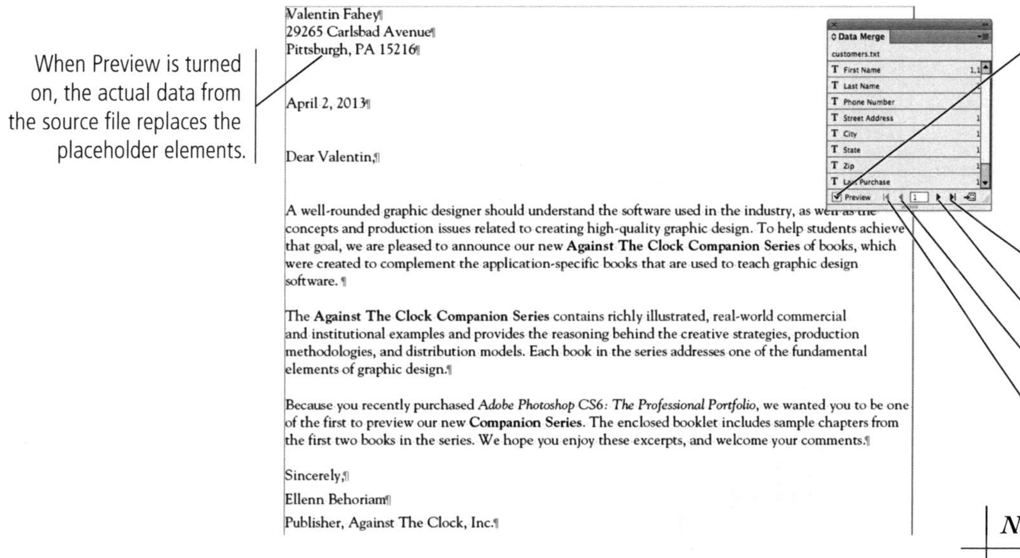

Check this box to preview the actual data in the layout.

Preview Last Record

Preview Next Record

Preview Previous Record

Preview First Record

> ***Note:***
>
> *If you choose Create Merged Document, the merge process results in an InDesign file with the necessary number of copies. The Export to PDF option skips this intermediary step.*

2. **Choose Export to PDF in the Data Merge panel Options menu.**

   In the Create Merged Document dialog box, you can define specific options for your merged document. The Records tab determines which records (all, one single record, or a specified range) will be included in the merged document.

   The two check boxes at the bottom of the dialog box provide feedback after you create the data merge. Checked by default, these important options allow you to make sure all your data is available and fits into the spaces you defined.

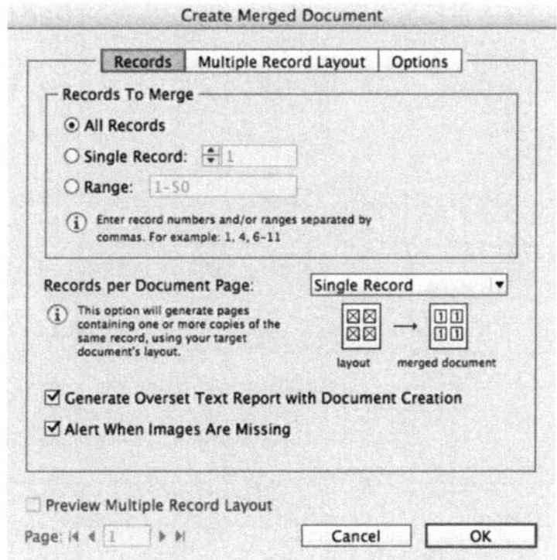

> ***Note:***
>
> *The Records per Document Page option allows you to place multiple records on a single page in the merged document. This option can be useful for creating catalog listings, multiple labels, or other projects with more than one database record on a single page.*

3. **Click OK in the Create Merged Document dialog box.**

4. **Choose the [High Quality Print] preset in the Export Adobe PDF dialog box. Check the View PDF after Exporting option, then click Export.**

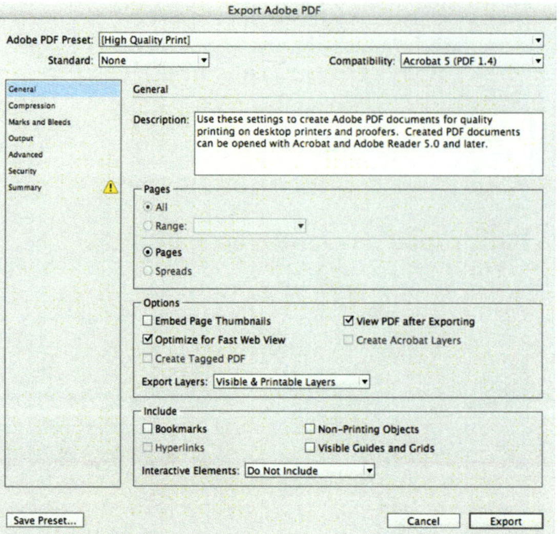

5. **In the resulting dialog box, navigate to your WIP>Companions folder as the target location, and then click Save.**

6. **When you see the message that the data merge resulted in no overset text, click OK.**

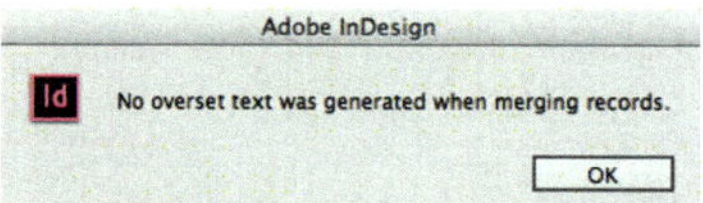

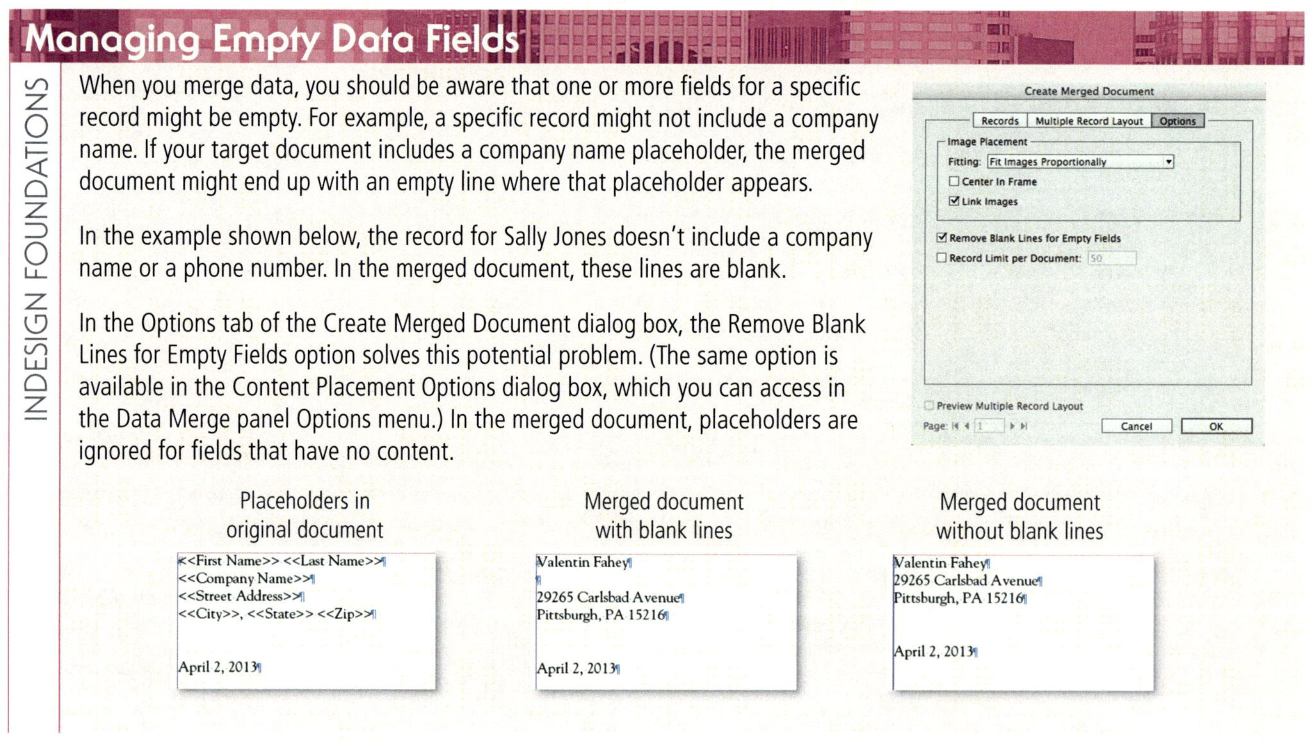

Managing Empty Data Fields

When you merge data, you should be aware that one or more fields for a specific record might be empty. For example, a specific record might not include a company name. If your target document includes a company name placeholder, the merged document might end up with an empty line where that placeholder appears.

In the example shown below, the record for Sally Jones doesn't include a company name or a phone number. In the merged document, these lines are blank.

In the Options tab of the Create Merged Document dialog box, the Remove Blank Lines for Empty Fields option solves this potential problem. (The same option is available in the Content Placement Options dialog box, which you can access in the Data Merge panel Options menu.) In the merged document, placeholders are ignored for fields that have no content.

7. **Review the resulting PDF file.**

Because there were 50 records in the data source file, the new document has 50 pages (one page for each record/letter).

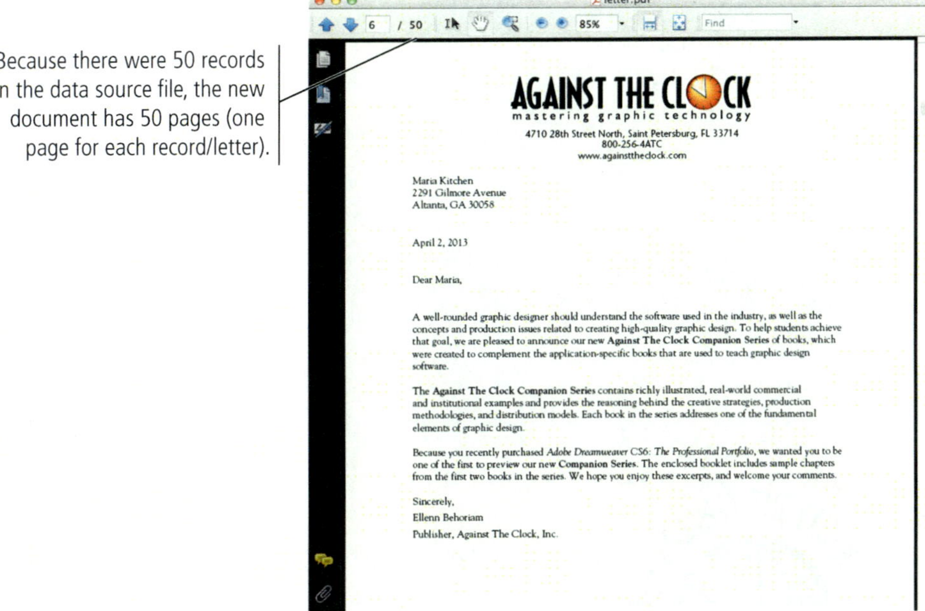

AGAINST THE CLOCK
mastering graphic technology
4710 28th Street North, Saint Petersburg, FL 33714
800-256-4ATC
www.againsttheclock.com

Maria Kitchen
2291 Gilmore Avenue
Atlanta, GA 30058

April 2, 2013

Dear Maria,

A well-rounded graphic designer should understand the software used in the industry, as well as the concepts and production issues related to creating high-quality graphic design. To help students achieve that goal, we are pleased to announce our new **Against The Clock Companion Series** of books, which were created to complement the application-specific books that are used to teach graphic design software.

The **Against The Clock Companion Series** contains richly illustrated, real-world commercial and institutional examples and provides the reasoning behind the creative strategies, production methodologies, and distribution models. Each book in the series addresses one of the fundamental elements of graphic design.

Because you recently purchased *Adobe Dreamweaver CS6: The Professional Portfolio*, we wanted you to be one of the first to preview our new **Companion Series**. The enclosed booklet includes sample chapters from the first two books in the series. We hope you enjoy these excerpts, and welcome your comments.

Sincerely,
Ellenn Behoriam
Publisher, Against The Clock, Inc.

8. **Close the PDF file, return to InDesign, and then save and close the letter.indd file.**

INDESIGN FOUNDATIONS

Merging Multiple Records on a Single Page

You can merge more than one record onto a single page by selecting Multiple Records in the Records per Document Page menu. When this option is selected, the Multiple Record Layout tab determines how records are placed and separated in the merged document.

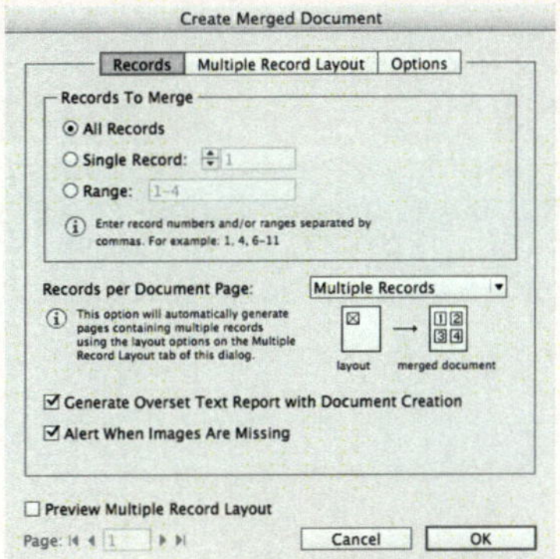

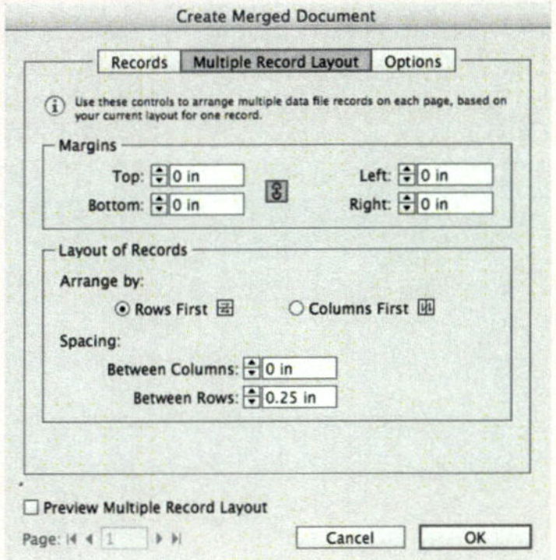

Two records fit onto each page in the merged document.

0.25" is added between each record in the merged document.

Project Review

fill in the blank

1. The _______________ is used to organize and manage multiple chapter files in a book.

2. If a chapter file shows a _______________ icon, it has been edited outside the context of the InDesign book.

3. Book chapters typically begin on _______________-numbered, _______________-facing pages.

4. _______________, typically including a title page and table of contents, is the content preceding the main body of a book.

5. _______________, typically containing indexes and appendices, appears after the primary content of a book.

6. The _______________ option can be used to renumber any specific page in a document.

7. You can change the _______________ of an index entry to rearrange its alphabetical position in the compiled index.

8. Clicking the _______________ button in the New Page Reference dialog box is case-sensitive. "Printing" will not be tagged if the topic is "printing".

9. A(n) _______________ is useful for tagging references to people based on their last names without changing the text in the document.

10. You can delete a(n) _______________ without deleting its parent topic from the Index panel. The reverse is not true; deleting a parent topic deletes all _______________ for that topic.

short answer

1. Describe three conventions that relate to and govern long-document design.

2. Briefly explain the concept of synchronization, including potential problems that might arise from it.

3. Briefly explain two advantages and two disadvantages of the InDesign indexing functionality.

Portfolio Builder Project

Use what you learned in this project to complete the following freeform exercise.
Carefully read the art director and client comments, then create your own design to meet the needs of the project.
Use the space below to sketch ideas; when finished, write a brief explanation of your reasoning behind your final design.

art director comments

Every professional designer needs a portfolio of their work. If you've completed the projects in this book, you should now have a number of different examples to show off your skills using InDesign CC.

The eight projects in this book were specifically designed to include a broad range of *types* of projects; your portfolio should use the same principle.

client comments

Using the following suggestions, gather your best work and create printed and digital versions of your portfolio:

- ❑ Include as many different types of work as possible — one-page layouts, folding brochures, multi-page booklets, etc.
- ❑ Print clean copies of each finished piece that you want to include.
- ❑ For each example in your portfolio, write a brief (one or two paragraph) synopsis of the project. Explain the purpose of the piece, as well as your role in the creative and production process.
- ❑ Design a personal promotion brochure — create a layout that highlights your technical skills and reflects your personal style.
- ❑ Create a digital version of your portfolio so you can send your portfolio via email, post it on job sites, and keep it with you on a flash drive at all times — you never know when you might meet a potential employer.

project justification

Project Summary

As you completed the exercises in this project, you learned to use InDesign tools to define special formatting, combine multiple files, build tables of contents and indexes, and merge variable data into a page layout.

Consistency is the key to effective long-document design. InDesign's book utility allows you to combine multiple chapter files into a single book, and to synchronize those files so related elements remain consistent from page to page and chapter to chapter. This book-building functionality works equally well for combining single-page documents or lengthy chapters with many pages.

By automating (as much as possible) the process of building tables of contents and indexes — which used to require days of manual checking and rechecking if even a single page in the layout changed — InDesign greatly improves the efficiency of your workflow. Effectively implementing styles throughout a long document makes it relatively easy to compile a thorough table of contents that includes every heading from Page 1 to the final page in the document.

Although no software is "smart" enough to identify which terms are important enough to appear in a document's index, the ability to store index markers in a document means compiling and recompiling the final index is far simpler than building and compiling the list by hand.

These skills are relatively rare in the graphics marketplace. Your ability to master them makes you much more marketable as a professional graphic designer.

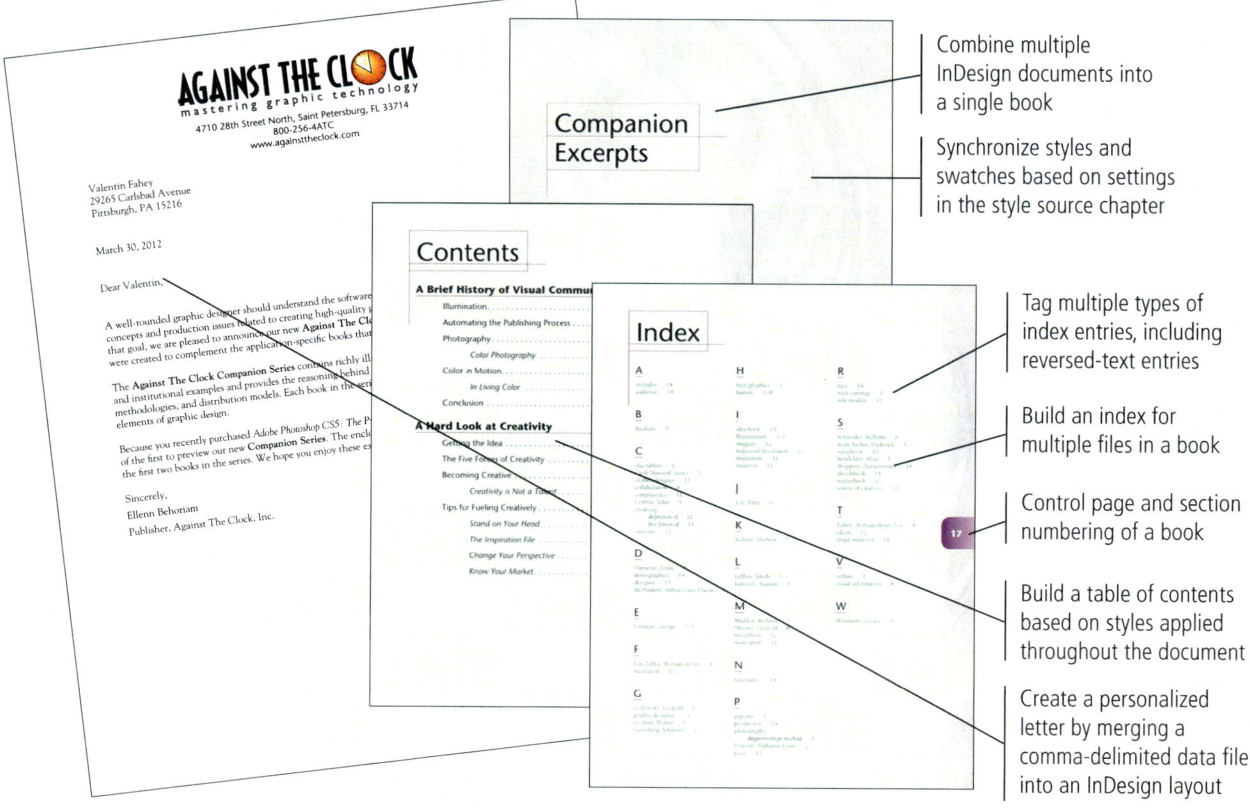

Index

D

E

Index

Index

Index

Q

R

S

T

U

V

W

X

Z